씨뮬 이제는 가르치는 효율적인 학습법!

온·오프 블렌디드 러닝 (on/off Blended Learning)

---

1 STEP ONE OFF-LINE

기출은 수능 대비의 기본!
기본에 가장 충실한 씨뮬로 실전연습하자

- 다양한 구성의 기출문제집으로 목표에 맞는 학습 가능
- 씨뮬 교재를 풀면 온라인에서 자동채점 & 성적분석 가능

---

2 STEP TWO ON-LINE

스터디센스 STUDY SENSE

QR 찍고 회원가입 → 씨뮬 문제 풀기 → 자동채점 → 성적분석

- 내 등급컷과 취약 유형까지 완벽 분석
- AI 문제 추천으로 취약 유형을 한 번 더 학습
- 오답노트로 복습 또 복습해서 틀린 문제 정복하기

---

3 STEP THREE OFF-LINE

모의고사 맞춤제작 OneUP

'원하는 문제만 골라서 맞춤 교재'를 만들고 싶다면? OneUP

- 원하는 제본 형태로 제작 가능
- 학평, 모평, 수능, 종로 사설 모의고사 맞춤 제작

CONTENTS

고 3 ▶ 영어 — 어법 · 어휘

구 성 + 특 징

01

내신 대비 서브 노트

고3을 총정리할 수 있는 영어 어법 사항 내신 요약입니다.

내신 및 수능 영이 시험에 지주 나오는 어법 사항을 정리한 학습 자료입니다. 서브
노트를 활용하여 중간 · 기말고사 직전에 빠르게 영어 어법을 익혀 봅시다.

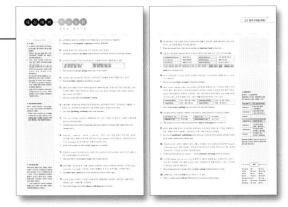

02

가장 효율적인 24일의 학습 체계

유형 학습이 처음이라 불안하다면? 수능 체계를 잘 모른다면?
더욱더 학습 효과가 큰 교재입니다.

❶ 수능, 모평, 학평, 사설 학원 기출 문제 중에서 최신 문제와 중요 빈출 문제를
24일 동안 학습합니다.

❷ 매일매일 12개 지문(어법 8개, 어휘 4개)으로 압축적, 효율적 학습이 가능하며
채점을 간단히 매일 할 수 있게 체크 박스를 붙였습니다.

❸ 어휘 문제를 매일 4개씩 배치해 꾸준히 어휘 실력을 늘릴 수 있도록
구성하였습니다.

❹ 수능과 모평 시험은 시험지 표기 명칭과 실시 연도가 다릅니다. 예를 들면,
2023학년도 6월 모평 시험은 2022년 6월에 실시되었습니다.

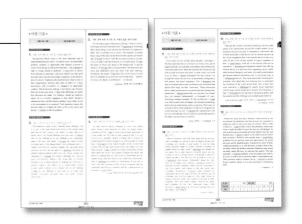

03

출제 트렌드와 1등급 꿀팁

기출 문제 분석을 통해 공부의 올바른 '방향'을 설정합니다.

❶ 최신 수능 출제 트렌드와 1등급 꿀팁을 제공합니다

❷ 1994학년도 수능부터 최신 수능까지 어법 출제 경향을 분석했습니다.

❸ 최신 수능 어법과 과거 수능 어법 문제의 차이점 중 하나는 최신 수능의 지문이
길어졌다는 것입니다. 그래서 과거 수능 어법 문제를 외면하기 쉽습니다.
그러나 과거 수능 어법 문제 중에도 보석처럼 좋은 문제가 있습니다. 온고지신의
정신으로 과거에서 배울 것은 배우고, 새 것을 연마하면 더 시험에 자신감을
갖게 될 것입니다.

❹ 교재의 주 대상은 고3학생이지만, 수능을 미리 대비하고자 하는 고1~2
학생들에게도 이 책을 권합니다.

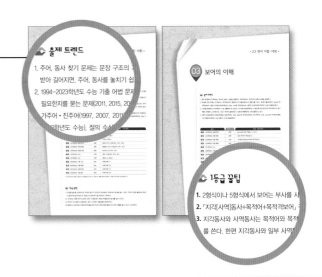

04

핵심 문법과 어휘·숙어 비밀 노트

❶ 핵심 문법 코너는 수능 문법을 총 20개로 분류하고, 각 문법 항목 중에서
매우 중요한 7개를 선별해 학습합니다. 문법을 학습한 것뿐만 아니라 체크
포인트 문제를 통해 점검하도록 하였습니다.

❷ 어휘·숙어 비밀 노트는 수능 영어의 비밀 병기가 될 것입니다. 독해의 기본
재료는 언어형식(문법)과 이휘입니다. 20일 동안, 매일 일정량의
어휘(40개)와 숙어(20개)를 공부하게 됩니다.

❸ 유형⁺ 씨뮬 어법·어휘 교재는 어법, 어휘 문제뿐만 아니라 매일 꾸준한
어휘력 확장을 통해 독해 실력 향상 및 영어 성적 향상도 꾀하고자 합니다.

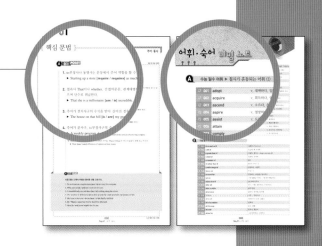

05

미니 고난도 Test

21~24일은 간단하게 미니 테스트를 할 수 있습니다.

❶ 미니테스트는 어법 4개, 어휘 4개 총 8 문제로 구성되어 있습니다.
❷ 20일 동안 공부한 내용을 어느 정도 소화했는지 점검합니다.

06

체계적이고 효율적인 해설

어려운 문항은 상세하게, 쉬운 문항은 명료하게~ 효율적인 똑똑한 해설입니다.

❶ 각 지문의 어려운 내용을 이해하기 쉽게 풀이하며 많이 틀린 문항에 대해서는
상세하게 문제 풀이를 제시합니다.

❷ 일부 문제는 직독직해를 통해 영어 문장의 기본 구조를 마스터하도록
하였습니다.

❸ 골드교육 홈피 학습 지원 자료 코너에서 지문에 나온 어휘를 한글 파일 형태로
다운받을 수 있습니다.

1. to부정사나 동명사는 문장에서 주어 역할을 할 수 있으며 단수로 취급한다.

》 Starting up a store **[require / requires]** as much as $200,000.

2. 주어가 길어진 경우 가주어 it을 쓰고 진주어는 뒤로 돌린다.

》 All things considered, **[it / that]** might be better to ask for the services of a moving company.

3. to부정사나 동명사, 의문사+to부정사는 문장에서 목적어 역할을 할 수 있다.

to부정사만을 목적어로 취하는 동사	동명사를 목적어로 취하는 동사
want, wish plan, agree, decide	finish, mind, enjoy, avoid, deny

》 They decided not **[to go / going]** out because of the weather.

4. that절, if절, whether절, 의문사절, 관계사절은 문장에서 목적어 역할을 할 수 있다.

》 Sam found **[that / what]** his smartphone was gone.

5. 2형식 동사 뒤에 주격보어 자리에 형용사가 나와야 하는데, 부사를 넣고 틀린 것을 찾는 문제가 종종 나왔다. 2형식 동사는 be, keep, stay, get, grow, become, look, seem, appear, feel, smell 등을 말한다.

》 The roses on the table smell **[sweetly / sweet]**.

6. 5형식에서 지각동사와 사역동사의 목적격보어는 동사원형이 나온다. 지각동사는 진행형도 가능하다. 단, 목적어와 목적격보어가 수동 관계인 경우는 과거분사가 나온다.

》 I see Sally **[drinking / to drink]** coffee with chocolate.

7. 주어, 동사 사이에 수식어구나 관계사절이 있는 경우, 주어를 잘 찾은 후, 주어의 수에 맞게 동사를 일치시켜야 한다.

》 Families that avoid conflict by ignoring unpleasant subjects or situations **[is / are]** weaker, not stronger for it.

8. most of ~, some of ~, all of ~, a lot of ~, 분수 + of~ 등이 주어로 쓰인 경우, 동사는 of 뒤에 나오는 명사(구)의 수에 일치시킨다. 「the number of+복수명사」는 뒤에 단수동사를 쓰고, 「A number of+복수명사」는 뒤에 복수동사를 쓴다.

》 Some of the people she walk with **[is / are]** not very friendly.

9. 부정어구나 only가 문두에 나오는 문장은 주어, 동사의 순서가 도치된다. 도치 구문은 뒤에 나오는 주어에 맞게 수를 일치시킨다.

》 Only after Mom's death **[were / was]** I able to appreciate her.

10. 과거시제는 과거의 동작, 상태, 습관을 표현하며, 과거를 뚜렷하게 나타내는 부사(구)(ago, yesterday, last week ~)가 있는 문장은 현재완료가 아닌, 과거시제로 나타내야 한다.

》 Sam **[have met / met]** her last week and they fell in love at first sight.

11. 시간과 조건을 나타내는 부사절은 미래 의미를 현재시제로 나타낸다. 명사절은 미래 의미를 나타내는 경우, 미래시제로 표현한다.

》 Sam will be happy when Sally **[shows / will show]** up to the party.

12. 과거완료형은 과거 이전에 일어난 일(대과거)에 대해서 말하거나, 대과거에 일어난 일이 과거의 어느 한 시점에 영향을 미칠 때 사용된다.

>> When she returned home, Sally discovered that she **[had lost / lost]** her door key.

13. 조동사는 완료형과 결합하여 과거의 추측이나 과거의 일에 대한 유감, 비난 등을 나타낸다.

should[ought to] have p.p.	~했어야 했는데	shouldn't have p.p.	~하지 않았어야 했는데
must have p.p.	~했음에 틀림없다	cannot have p.p.	~했을 리가 없다
may have p.p.	~했을지도 모른다	need not have p.p.	~할 필요가 없었는데

>> I regret having paid little attention to him. In other words, I **[must have paid / should have paid]** more attention to him.

14. 지각, 사역동사가 들어 있는 문장을 수동태로 바꿀 경우, 목적격보어인 원형부정사는 to부정사로 바뀌진다.

>> My son was heard **[sing / to sing]** by himself at midnight.

15. start, begin, continue, like, hate 동사는 to부정사와 동명사를 모두 목적어로 취한다. 의미 차이가 없다. 일부 동사는 to부정사와 동명사를 목적어로 가져올 수 있지만 의미 차이가 있다. stop은 뒤에 동명사를 목적어로 가져오면 '~하는 것을 멈추다'의 의미이며, stop 뒤에 to부정사가 오는 경우, 부사적 용법으로서 '~하기 위해 멈추다'의 의미를 가지고 있다.

| 「remember+동명사」 | (과거) ~했던 것을 기억하다 | 「remember+to부정사」 | (미래) ~할 것을 기억하다 |
| 「forget+동명사」 | (과거) ~했던 것을 잊다 | 「forget+to부정사」 | (미래) ~할 것을 잊다 |

>> Don't forget **[to get / getting]** your own food to the party this Saturday.

16. 전치사의 목적어는 동명사를 사용한다. 특히 전치사 to 뒤에 to부정사를 쓰지 않도록 유의한다.

| look forward to -ing | ~을 기대하다 | object to -ing | ~에 반대하다 |
| contribute to -ing | ~에 헌신하다 | devote oneself to -ing | ~에 헌신하다 |

>> This summer, my son is really looking forward to **[learn / learning]** how to scuba-dive.

17. 분사는 형용사처럼 명사를 수식하거나 주격보어나 목적격보어 역할을 할 수 있다. 현재분사는 능동, 진행의 의미를 나타내고, 과거분사는 수동, 완료의 의미를 나타낸다.

>> In a survey **[published / publishing]** earlier this year, seven out of ten parents said they would never let their children play with toy guns.

18. 완료분사구문은 주절의 시제보다 앞선 시제를 나타낸다. 또한 수동형 분사구문에서 being이나 having been은 생략 가능하다. 또한 분사구문의 주어가 주절의 주어와 다른 경우 명시해 주어야 한다. 부정어는 분사 바로 앞에 배치한다.

>> As the dog barked at him, he ran away. → The dog **[barked / barking]** at him, he ran away

19. 등위접속사(and, but, or, so, for)는 문법적으로 대등한 관계에 있는 단어와 단어, 구와 구, 절과 절을 연결한다. 이를 병렬 구조라고 한다. 등위접속사에 의해 연결되는 구조는 A가 동명사이면 B도 동명사로 해야 한다.

>> She is looking forward to going to Italy and **[eat / eating]** wonderful pasta every day.

20. 관계부사는 「전치사+관계대명사」로 바꾸어 쓸 수 있다.

>> That's a vending machine **[from / for]** which you can get prescription drugs.

★ 복합관계부사

관계부사 -ever를 붙이면 복합관계부사가 된다. 복합관계부사절은 주로 양보의 부사절로 사용될 수 있다.

복합관계부사	시간, 장소의 부사절
whenever	at any time when (~할 때마다)
wherever	at any place where (~하는 곳은 어디나)
however	

복합관계부사	양보의 부사절
whenever	no matter when (언제 ~할지라도)
wherever	no matter where (어디에서 ~할지라도)
however	no matter how (아무리 ~할지라도)

However humble it may be, there is no place like a home. (아무리 누추하더라도 집과 같은 곳은 없다.)

정답

01 requires	02 it	03 to go
04 that	05 sweet	06 drinking
07 are	08 are	09 was
10 met	11 shows	12 had lost
13 should have paid		14 to sing
15 to get	16 learning	17 published
18 barking	19 eating	20 from

DAY 01 》》》 주어·동사

1 ②	2 ④	3 ⑤	4 ⑤	5 ②
6 ③	7 ③	8 ④	9 ⑤	10 ④
11 ⑤	12 ④			

DAY 02 》》》 목적어의 이해

1 ②	2 ②	3 ⑤	4 ④	5 ⑤
6 ④	7 ②	8 ⑤	9 ②	10 ④
11 ③	12 ⑤			

DAY 03 》》》 보어의 이해

1 ②	2 ⑤	3 ②	4 ②	5 ③
6 ④	7 ③	8 ①	9 ④	10 ③
11 ④	12 ②			

DAY 04 》》》 수의 일치

1 ②	2 ⑤	3 ④	4 ⑤	5 ③
6 ④	7 ③	8 ③	9 ④	10 ⑤
11 ④	12 ⑤			

DAY 05 》》》 동사의 시제

1 ③	2 ②	3 ①	4 ⑤	5 ⑤
6 ③	7 ④	8 ④	9 ②	10 ②
11 ⑤	12 ⑤			

DAY 06 》》》 조동사

1 ③	2 ⑤	3 ②	4 ③	5 ①
6 ②	7 ③	8 ③	9 ③	10 ④
11 ④	12 ④			

DAY 07 》》》 수동태

1 ④	2 ④	3 ③	4 ①	5 ②
6 ①	7 ③	8 ④	9 ⑤	10 ⑤
11 ④	12 ④			

DAY 08 》》》 가정법

1 ④	2 ⑤	3 ③	4 ④	5 ⑤
6 ②	7 ③	8 ④	9 ④	10 ⑤
11 ⑤	12 ⑤			

DAY 09 》》》 부정사

1 ③	2 ③	3 ⑤	4 ②	5 ④
6 ③	7 ⑤	8 ④	9 ③	10 ②
11 ③	12 ④			

DAY 10 》》》 동명사

1 ⑤	2 ④	3 ①	4 ④	5 ①
6 ②	7 ⑤	8 ⑤	9 ⑤	10 ②
11 ⑤	12 ③			

DAY 11 》》》 분사, 분사구문

1 ③	2 ②	3 ④	4 ④	5 ④
6 ③	7 ②	8 ①	9 ①	10 ②
11 ③	12 ⑤			

DAY 12 》》》 준동사

1 ①	2 ⑤	3 ⑤	4 ①	5 ④
6 ③	7 ③	8 ④	9 ③	10 ④
11 ②	12 ②			

DAY 13 》》》 접속사, 전치사

1 ④	2 ③	3 ⑤	4 ⑤	5 ①
6 ④	7 ①	8 ③	9 ②	10 ⑤
11 ④	12 ④			

DAY 14 》》》 관계대명사

1 ③	2 ④	3 ③	4 ③	5 ②
6 ⑤	7 ⑤	8 ④	9 ⑤	10 ③
11 ②	12 ③			

DAY 15 》》》 관계부사

1 ①	2 ③	3 ②	4 ③	5 ④
6 ①	7 ②	8 ⑤	9 ④	10 ⑤
11 ②	12 ④			

DAY 16 》》》 병렬 구조

1 ⑤	2 ④	3 ③	4 ④	5 ②
6 ⑤	7 ③	8 ②	9 ②	10 ⑤
11 ④	12 ⑤			

DAY 17 》》》 대명사

1 ②	2 ②	3 ②	4 ②	5 ⑤
6 ③	7 ④	8 ③	9 ⑤	10 ④
11 ③	12 ④			

DAY 18 》》》 형용사, 부사

1 ⑤	2 ④	3 ④	4 ①	5 ④
6 ③	7 ①	8 ③	9 ④	10 ④
11 ②	12 ③			

DAY 19 》》》 비교 구문

1 ②	2 ④	3 ⑤	4 ①	5 ③
6 ③	7 ②	8 ⑤	9 ⑤	10 ④
11 ④	12 ④			

DAY 20 》》》 특수 구문

1 ②	2 ③	3 ⑤	4 ⑤	5 ①
6 ⑤	7 ⑤	8 ②	9 ⑤	10 ②
11 ③	12 ④			

DAY 21 》》》 미니 고난도 Test 1회

1 ③	2 ①	3 ②	4 ④	5 ④
6 ④	7 ②	8 ①		

DAY 22 》》》 미니 고난도 Test 2회

1 ⑤	2 ④	3 ③	4 ⑤	5 ③
6 ⑤	7 ②	8 ③		

DAY 23 》》》 미니 고난도 Test 3회

1 ③	2 ②	3 ⑤	4 ③	5 ④
6 ②	7 ①	8 ①		

DAY 24 》》》 미니 고난도 Test 4회

1 ④	2 ⑤	3 ④	4 ④	5 ④
6 ⑤	7 ④	8 ①		

주어·동사

출제 트렌드

1. 주어, 동사 찾기 문제는 문장 구조의 기본 골격인 주어, 동사를 알고 있는지 평가하는 문제이다. 주어가 구나 절의 수식을 받아 길어지면, 주어, 동사를 놓치기 쉽기 때문에 자주 출제되는 편이다.

2. 1994~2023학년도 수능 기출 어법 문제를 분석한 결과, 주어, 동사 찾기 문제 유형은 문장에서 정동사가 필요한지 준동사가 필요한지를 묻는 문제(2011, 2015, 2016, 2021학년도 수능)가 자주 출제되었다.

3. 가주어 • 진주어(1997, 2007, 2011학년도 수능), 동명사인 주어(1998, 2002학년도 수능), 과거분사구의 수식을 받는 주어(2012학년도 수능), 절의 수식을 받는 주어의 동사(2011, 2014 B, 2015학년도 수능), to부정사의 수식을 받는 주어의 동사(2016학년도 수능)가 출제되었다.

4. 또한 관계사절의 수식을 받는 주어의 동사(2004학년도 수능), It-to 가주어, 진주어(2011학년도 수능), 동명사구인 주어(2013학년도 수능), 주격 관계대명사 that절의 동사(2015학년도 수능), 전치사구의 수식을 받는 주어의 동사(2020학년도 수능) 구문이 선지로 출제되었다.

출처		문항 번호	어법 · 어휘 문제
1	2023학년도 09월 모평	29번	동명사구인 주어
2	2020학년도 07월 학평	29번	정동사 vs. 준동사
3	2020학년도 06월 학평	28번	가주어, 진주어
4	2017학년도 04월 학평	28번	전치사구의 수식을 받는 주어 · 동사
5	2015학년도 07월 학평	28번	현재분사구의 수식을 받는 주어 · 동사
6	2016학년도 06월 모평	28번	to부정사구인 주어 · 동사
7	2015학년도 수능	20번	절의 수식을 받는 주어 · 동사
8	2011학년도 수능	29번	정동사 vs. 준동사
9	2023학년도 11월 수능	30번	어휘 문제 01
10	2022학년도 10월 학평	30번	어휘 문제 02
11	2023학년도 09월 모평	30번	어휘 문제 03
12	2022학년도 11월 종로	30번	어휘 문제 04

※수능과 모평 시험은 시험지 표기 명칭과 실시 연도가 다릅니다. 예를 들면 2023학년도 시험은 2022년에 실시되었습니다.

1등급 꿀팁

1. 문장을 볼 때, 습관적으로 주어와 동사가 무엇인지 찾아본다. 준동사와 동사를 넣고 고르는 문제가 종종 출제되니 동사가 들어가야 할 자리인지, 준동사가 들어가야 할 자리인지 구분한다.

2. 수식어로 인해 주어가 길어진 경우 수식을 받는 핵심 주어를 찾아 동사를 일치 시킨다.

3. 주어가 구나 절의 수식을 받는 경우, 수식어는 양괄호를 치도록 한다.

4. 동명사나 to부정사가 뒤에 목적어를 길게 가지고 문장 제일 앞에 나와 주어 역할을 할 수 있으니 유의한다.

[핵심 문법]

A 출제 POINT

1. to부정사나 동명사는 문장에서 주어 역할을 할 수 있으며 단수로 취급한다.
  ▶ Starting up a store [**require** / **requires**] as much as $200,000.

2. 접속사 That이나 whether, 간접의문문, 관계대명사 what, 복합관계대명사가 이끄는 절은 주어 역할을 할 수 있으며 단수로 취급한다.
  ▶ That she is a millionaire [**are** / **is**] incredible.

3. 주어가 전치사구의 수식을 받아 길어진 경우, 주어, 동사를 잘 파악해야 한다.
  ▶ The house on that hill [**is** / **are**] my grandfathers's.

4. 주어가 분사구, to부정사구의 수식을 받아 길어진 경우, 문장의 주어, 동사를 잘 파악해야 한다.
  ▶ A weekly program dealing with social issues [**was** / **were**] loved by viewers.

5. 주어가 관계사절의 수식을 받아 길어진 경우, 문장의 동사가 무엇인지 유의해야 한다.
  ▶ The girl who lives besides us [**are** / **is**] ill.

6. 주어가 길어진 경우 가주어 it을 쓰고 진주어는 뒤로 돌린다.
  ▶ All things considered, [**it** / **that**] might be better to ask for the services of a moving company.

7. There is[are]~, Here is[are] ~ 문장에서 주어는 There나 Here가 아니라 be동사 뒤에 오는 어구다.
  ▶ There [**was** / **were**] differences of opinion on basic issues.

B 체크 POINT

다음 괄호 안에서 어법상 올바른 것을 고르시오.

1. To work out on a regular basis [**are** / **is**] not easy for everyone.
2. What you see [**is** / **are**] not a truth all the time.
3. A beautiful lady in a red dress [**are** / **is**] walking along the street.
4. The number of children taught by their parents [**is** / **are**] gradually increasing in USA.
5. Her hope to become a doctor [**was** / **to be**] finally fulfilled.
6. [**It** / **That**] is important that he should be informed.
7. Here [**is** / **are**] some helpful tips for you.

2023학년도 9월 모평 29번

1. 다음 글의 밑줄 친 부분 중, 어법상 틀린 것은?

Recognizing ethical issues is the most important step in understanding business ethics. An ethical issue is an identifiable problem, situation, or opportunity that requires a person to choose from among several actions that may ① be evaluated as right or wrong, ethical or unethical. ② Learn how to choose from alternatives and make a decision requires not only good personal values, but also knowledge competence in the business area of concern. Employees also need to know when to rely on their organizations' policies and codes of ethics or ③ have discussions with co-workers or managers on appropriate conduct. Ethical decision making is not always easy because there are always gray areas ④ that create dilemmas, no matter how decisions are made. For instance, should an employee report on a co-worker engaging in time theft? Should a salesperson leave out facts about a product's poor safety record in his presentation to a customer? Such questions require the decision maker to evaluate the ethics of his or her choice and decide ⑤ whether to ask for guidance.

2020학년도 7월 학평 29번

2. 다음 글의 밑줄 친 부분 중, 어법상 틀린 것은?

Metacognition simply means "thinking about thinking," and it is one of the main distinctions between the human brain and that of other species. Our ability to stand high on a ladder above our normal thinking processes and ① evaluate why we are thinking as we are thinking is an evolutionary marvel. We have this ability ② because the most recently developed part of the human brain—the prefrontal cortex—enables self-reflective, abstract thought. We can think about ourselves as if we are not part of ③ ourselves. Research on primate behavior indicates that even our closest cousins, the chimpanzees, ④ lacking this ability (although they possess some self-reflective abilities, like being able to identify themselves in a mirror instead of thinking the reflection is another chimp). The ability is a double-edged sword, because while it allows us to evaluate why we are thinking ⑤ what we are thinking, it also puts us in touch with difficult existential questions that can easily become obsessions.

2020학년도 6월 학평 29번

3. 다음 글의 밑줄 친 부분 중, 어법상 틀린 것은? [3점]

An interesting aspect of human psychology is that we tend to like things more and find them more ① appealing if everything about those things is not obvious the first time we experience them. This is certainly true in music. For example, we might hear a song on the radio for the first time that catches our interest and ② decide we like it. Then the next time we hear it, we hear a lyric we didn't catch the first time, or we might notice ③ what the piano or drums are doing in the background. A special harmony ④ emerges that we missed before. We hear more and more and understand more and more with each listening. Sometimes, the longer ⑤ that takes for a work of art to reveal all of its subtleties to us, the more fond of that thing — whether it's music, art, dance, or architecture — we become.

* subtleties: 중요한 세부 요소[사항]들

2017학년도 4월 학평 28번

4. 다음 글의 밑줄 친 부분 중, 어법상 틀린 것은? [3점]

In early modern Europe, transport by water was usually much cheaper than transport by land. An Italian printer calculated in 1550 ① that to send a load of books from Rome to Lyons would cost 18 *scudi* by land compared with 4 by sea. Letters were normally carried overland, but a system of transporting letters and newspapers, as well as people, by canal boat ② developed in the Dutch Republic in the seventeenth century. The average speed of the boats was a little over four miles an hour, ③ slow compared to a rider on horseback. On the other hand, the service was regular, frequent and cheap, and allowed communication not only between Amsterdam and the smaller towns, but also between one small town and another, thus ④ equalizing accessibility to information. It was only in 1837, with the invention of the electric telegraph, that the traditional link between transport and the communication of messages ⑤ were broken.

* scudi: 이탈리아의 옛 은화 단위(scudo)의 복수형

5. 다음 글의 밑줄 친 부분 중, 어법상 틀린 것은? [3점]

It has been proposed that sleep functions to conserve energy. This may be particularly relevant for warm-blooded animals (mammals and birds) that must expend a lot of energy to maintain a body temperature higher than ① that of their surroundings. Indeed, many small mammals living in cold climates, who lose heat easily by having an unfavorable surface area to body weight ratio, ② tending to sleep a lot, often in insulating burrows. Yet sleep does not appear ③ to have evolved only in warm-blooded animals. Some studies on reptiles and amphibians indicate that they also sleep, and there are now strong indications of a sleep -like state in some invertebrates, such as crayfish, fruit flies, and honey bees. Also, though it is true that the overall use of energy is reduced during sleep, as ④ compared with the active waking state, there is almost as much reduction in energy use from just resting quietly. The additional energy conservation in going from the resting state to sleep ⑤ is minimal.

* invertebrate: 무척추동물

6. 다음 글의 밑줄 친 부분 중, 어법상 틀린 것은? [3점]

An independent artist is probably the one ① who lives closest to an unbounded creative situation. Many artists have considerable freedom from external requirements about what to do, how to do it, when to do it, and why. At the same time, however, we know that artists usually limit themselves quite ② forcefully by choice of material and form of expression. To make the choice to express a feeling by carving a specific form from a rock, without the use of high technology or colors, ③ restricting the artist significantly. Such choices are not made to limit creativity, but rather to cultivate ④ it. When everything is possible, creativity has no tension. Creativity is strange in that it finds its way in any kind of situation, no matter how restricted, just as the same amount of water flows faster and stronger through a narrow strait ⑤ than across the open sea.

* strait: 해협

7. 다음 글의 밑줄 친 부분 중, 어법상 틀린 것은? [3점]

During the early stages when the aquaculture industry was rapidly expanding, mistakes were made and these were costly both in terms of direct losses and in respect of the industry's image. High-density rearing led to outbreaks of infectious diseases that in some cases ① devastated not just the caged fish, but local wild fish populations too. The negative impact on local wildlife inhabiting areas ② close to the fish farms continues to be an ongoing public relations problem for the industry. Furthermore, a general lack of knowledge and insufficient care being taken when fish pens were initially constructed ③ meaning that pollution from excess feed and fish waste created huge barren underwater deserts. These were costly lessons to learn, but now stricter regulations are in place to ensure that fish pens are placed in sites ④ where there is good water flow to remove fish waste. This, in addition to other methods that decrease the overall amount of uneaten food, ⑤ has helped aquaculture to clean up its act.

8. 다음 글의 밑줄 친 부분 중, 어법상 틀린 것은?

The word 'courage' takes on added meaning if you keep in mind that it is derived from the Latin word 'cor' ① meaning 'heart.' The dictionary defines courage as a 'quality which enables one to pursue a right course of action, through ② which one may provoke disapproval, hostility, or contempt.' Over 300 years ago La Rochefoucauld went a step further when he said: "Perfect courage is to do unwitnessed what we should be capable of doing before all men." It is not easy ③ to show moral courage in the face of either indifference or opposition. But persons who are daring in taking a wholehearted stand for truth often ④ achieving results that surpass their expectations. On the other hand, halfhearted individuals are seldom distinguished for courage even when it involves ⑤ their own welfare. To be courageous under all circumstances requires strong determination.

* provoke: 유발하다

제한 시간 : 7분　　　　정답 및 해설 005쪽

2023학년도 11월 수능 30번

9. 다음 글의 밑줄 친 부분 중, 문맥상 낱말의 쓰임이 적절하지 않은 것은? [3점]

Everywhere we turn we hear about almighty "cyberspace"! The hype promises that we will leave our boring lives, put on goggles and body suits, and enter some metallic, three-dimensional, multimedia otherworld. When the Industrial Revolution arrived with its great innovation, the motor, we didn't leave our world to go to some ① remote motorspace! On the contrary, we brought the motors into our lives, as automobiles, refrigerators, drill presses, and pencil sharpeners. This ② absorption has been so complete that we refer to all these tools with names that declare their usage, not their "motorness." These innovations led to a major socioeconomic movement precisely because they entered and ③ affected profoundly our everyday lives. People have not changed fundamentally in thousands of years. Technology changes constantly. It's the one that must ④ adapt to us. That's exactly what will happen with information technology and its devices under human-centric computing. The longer we continue to believe that computers will take us to a magical new world, the longer we will ⑤ maintain their natural fusion with our lives, the hallmark of every major movement that aspires to be called a socioeconomic revolution.

* hype: 과대광고　　** hallmark: 특징

2022학년도 10월 학평 30번

10. 다음 글의 밑줄 친 부분 중, 문맥상 낱말의 쓰임이 적절하지 않은 것은?

Musical performers and their labor union did not perceive early recordings as a threat to their livelihoods because the recordings were mostly of poor quality. It was not long before musicians began to wonder whether recordings of popular artists or songs would ① undermine the demand for live music. For a time, however, recorded music was too scratchy to pose a serious threat, even though it played in commercial places and offered a few performers a way to ② supplement their income. Additionally, during the early days of recording, radio stations ③ preferred using live musicians on their programs. Sound from live performances was better quality, and stations at this time rarely used recordings. Broadcasters ④ rejected union demands for employment and decent wages, because the alterative use of recordings was even less attractive. They made efforts to employ orchestras, bands, and vocalists to perform on radio programs. There was relative balance between live music and technology in the early innovation stages. With increased ⑤ improvements in electrical recording, however, this balance soon changed.

* alterative: 대체하는

2023학년도 9월 모평 30번

11. 다음 글의 밑줄 친 부분 중, 문맥상 낱말의 쓰임이 적절하지 않은 것은?

Although the wonders of modern technology have provided people with opportunities beyond the wildest dreams of our ancestors, the good, as usual, is weakened by a downside. One of those downsides is that anyone who so chooses can pick up the virtual megaphone that is the Internet and put in their two cents on any of an infinite number of topics, regardless of their ① qualifications. After all, on the Internet, there are no regulations ② preventing a kindergarten teacher from offering medical advice or a physician from suggesting ways to safely make structural changes to your home. As a result, misinformation gets disseminated as information, and it is not always easy to ③ differentiate the two. This can be particularly frustrating for scientists, who spend their lives learning how to understand the intricacies of the world around them, only to have their work summarily ④ challenged by people whose experience with the topic can be measured in minutes. This frustration is then ⑤ diminished by the fact that, to the general public, both the scientist and the challenger are awarded equal credibility.

* put in one's two cents: 의견을 말하다　** disseminate: 퍼뜨리다
*** intricacy: 복잡성

2022학년도 11월 종로 30번

12. 다음 글의 밑줄 친 부분 중, 문맥상 낱말의 쓰임이 적절하지 않은 것은?

Pedestrian areas provide a dramatic improvement in the environment for pedestrians, and have proved very successful in enhancing trade in many town and city centres. There is little evidence to ① support traders' claims that pedestrian streets cause a loss in trade, provided of course that they are well designed. As well as achieving environmental and safety benefits, they may well therefore have ② positive impacts on the urban economy and on land use policy. However, they present some ③ accessibility problems for car and bus users and, particularly, for goods deliveries and for disabled people. Exemptions for some of these, whether permanently or, as with deliveries, at certain times of day, inevitably reduce the benefits somewhat. Pedestrian areas almost inevitably reduce efficiency, by reducing road capacity. They also potentially ④ eliminate problems in the surrounding area, both by diversion of traffic and by attracting trade to the protected area. These potential negative impacts can be ⑤ reduced by careful design. Aesthetic design is of crucial importance in maintaining trade.

* exemption: 면제

총 문항					문항		맞은 문항				문항	
개별 문항	1	2	3	4	5	6	7	8	9	10	11	12
채점												

어휘·숙어 비밀 노트

A 수능 필수 어휘 ▶ 철자가 혼동되는 어휘 (1)

□ 001	adopt	v. 채택하다, 입양하다	adapt	v. 적응시키다, 적응하다, 각색하다
□ 002	acquire	v. 획득하다, 얻다	require	v. 요구하다, 필요로 하다
□ 003	ascend	v. 오르다, 올라가다	descend	v. 내려가다, 내려오다
□ 004	aspire	v. 열망하다	inspire	v. 격려하다, 고취하다
□ 005	assist	v. 도와주다	resist	v 저항하다, 참다
□ 006	attain	v. 획득하다	retain	v. 계속 유지하다
□ 007	comply	v. 따르다, 응하다	compile	v. 편집하다, 수집하다
□ 008	confine	v. 감금하다	define	v. 정의를 내리다, 명확히 하다
□ 009	contain	v. 포함하다	obtain	v. 획득하다
□ 010	cruel	a. 잔인한	crucial	a. 중대한, 결정적인
□ 011	describe	v. 묘사하다	subscribe	v. 정기구독하다
□ 012	evolve	v. 발전하다, 진화하다	revolve	v. 회전하다, 회전시키다
□ 013	guard	v. 지키다, 수호하다	guide	v. 안내하다, 지도하다
□ 014	impel	v. 억지로 시키다	expel	v. 내쫓다
□ 015	insert	v. 삽입하다, 끼워 넣다	desert	v. 버리다
□ 016	involve	v. 포함하다, 수반하다	revolve	v. 회전하다
□ 017	irrigate	v. 관개하다	irritate	v. 짜증나게 하다
□ 018	precede	v. 선행하다	proceed	v. 계속 진행되다
□ 019	rob	v. 강탈하다, 빼앗다	rub	v. 문지르다, 마찰하다
□ 020	soar	v. 높이 치솟다	roar	v. 으르렁거리다

B 수능 필수 숙어

□ 021	A as well as B	B뿐만 아니라 A도
□ 022	a bit of	조금의, 한 조각의
□ 023	a great deal of	다량의, 많은 (= a large amount of)
□ 024	a kind of	일종의, 유사한
□ 025	a number of	많은
□ 026	A rather than B	B라기 보다는 A
□ 027	a wide range of	광범위한, 다양한
□ 028	above all	무엇보다
□ 029	account for	설명하다, (비율을) 차지하다
□ 030	act on	~에 영향을 미치다, ~에 따라 행동하다
□ 031	adjust A to B	A를 B에 맞추다
□ 032	after all	결국, ~에도 불구하고, 무엇보다도
□ 033	after a while	잠시 후에
□ 034	all at once	갑자기, 불시에, 동시에
□ 035	all but	거의, ~외에 모두
□ 036	all in all	전반적으로 보아, 대체로
□ 037	all of a sudden	갑자기
□ 038	all the way	줄곧, 내내
□ 039	all told	합쳐서, 통틀어
□ 040	allow for	~을 참작하다, 고려하다

02 목적어의 이해

📌 출제 트렌드

1. 영어 문장에서 3형식부터 5형식에 사용되는 타동사는 목적어를 가져온다.

2. 1994~2023학년도 수능 기출 어법 문제를 분석한 결과, 목적어에 관련된 문제는 「stop+to부정사」와 「stop+동명사」의 의미 차이를 묻는 문제(2000, 2014학년도 수능 A형), 5형식 동사 make의 동명사형 목적어(2005학년도 수능), 간접의문문(2001학년도 수능), 가목적어·진목적어(2013학년도 수능), 전치사의 목적절(2018학년도 수능) 문제가 출제되었다.

3. 또한 「hope+to부정사」(1995학년도 수능), 과거분사의 수식을 받는 명사인 목적어(2021학년도 수능), 관계사 what이 이끄는 목적절(2017학년도 수능)이 선지로 출제되었다.

	출처	문항 번호	어법·어휘 문제
1	2018학년도 수능	28번	「전치사+ whether 목적절」
2	2016학년도 03월 학평	28번	find의 목적절
3	2015학년도 03월 학평	28번	타동사의 목적절(접속사 that절)
4	2014학년도 수능 A형	27번	「stop+목적어(동명사)」
5	2012학년도 10월 학평	21번	가목적어, 진목적어
6	2010학년도 06월 모평	20번	목적어(간접의문문)
7	2008학년도 06월 모평	21번	「전치사+why 목적절」
8	2019학년도 03월 종로	29번	타동사의 목적절(what ~ like)
9	2022학년도 07월 학평	30번	어휘 문제 01
10	2023학년도 06월 모평	30번	어휘 문제 02
11	2022학년도 04월 학평	30번	어휘 문제 03
12	2022학년도 10월 종로	30번	어휘 문제 04

📌 1등급 꿀팁

1. 가목적어, 진목적어 구조를 이해한다.

2. 목적어로 to부정사나 동명사를 가져오는 동사를 철저히 익히도록 한다.

3. 목적어로 뒤에 간접의문문을 가져오는 경우, 어순은 「의문사+주어+동사」 어순이다.

[핵심 문법]

정답 및 해설 · 008쪽

A 출제 POINT

1. to부정사나 동명사, 「의문사+to부정사」는 문장에서 목적어 역할을 할 수 있다.

to부정사만을 목적어로 취하는 동사	동명사를 목적어로 취하는 동사
want, wish plan, agree, decide	finish, mind, enjoy, avoid, deny

▶ Sally couldn't avoid [**to talk** / **talking**] about the situation

2. that절, if절, whether절, 의문사절, 관계사절은 문장에서 목적어 역할을 할 수 있다.

▶ Sam found [**that** / **what**] his smartphone was gone.

3. 4형식 문장은 간접목적어(사람)와 직접목적어(사물)를 갖는다.

▶ Peter asked a question [**of** / **for**] me.

4. 문장에서 목적어가 길어지면, 가목적어 it을 쓰고, (진)목적어를 문장 뒤로 보낸다.

▶ I took it for granted [**to** / **that**] Jack would come.

5. 직접의문문이 다른 문장의 주어, 목적어, 보어 부분에 들어간 간접의문문은 문장 구조가 「의문사+주어+동사」의 어순을 갖는다.

▶ She didn't know how old [**he was** / **was he**].

6. 동사 say, think, suggest 뒤에 오는 목적어를 이끄는 that은 흔히 생략한다. whether는 '예'나 '아니오'를 기대하는 의문문의 간접화법이나 대안 중에서 선택을 하는 내용일 때 쓸 수 있다.

▶ He said [**whether** / **that**] they were on the third floor.

cf. Sam asked <u>whether</u> I wanted a drink. ('예', '아니오'를 기대하는 의문문의 간접화법)

　　Sally didn't know <u>whether</u> she should email or phone. (대안 중에서 선택)

7. 전치사 다음에 오는 (대)명사, 명사구, 명사절을 전치사의 목적어라고 한다. 대명사의 경우에는 목적격이 와야 한다. 전치사 다음에 동사가 올 때는 동명사가 나온다. 단, but, except 뒤에는 to부정사가 올 수 있다. 또한 in, except는 that절을 목적어로 취할 수 있다.

▶ He stayed awake by [**drink** / **drinking**] coffee.

B 체크 POINT

다음 괄호 안에서 어법상 올바른 것을 고르시오.

1. After carefully thinking about it, I decided [**refusing** / **to refuse**] his suggestion.

2. I don't know [**that** / **whether**] she is glad or not.

3. I sent a storybook [**to** / **for**] my niece.

4. Many students find [**that** / **it**] difficult to build close relationship with others.

5. I don't know where [**they are** / **are they**] hiding.

6. She thought [**that** / **whether**] her friend was praising her.

7. You should be faithful with [**her** / **she**].

제한 시간 : 13분	정답 및 해설 008쪽

2018학년도 수능 28번

1. 다음 글의 밑줄 친 부분 중, 어법상 틀린 것은? [3점]

Psychologists who study giving behavior ① have noticed that some people give substantial amounts to one or two charities, while others give small amounts to many charities. Those who donate to one or two charities seek evidence about what the charity is doing and ② what it is really having a positive impact. If the evidence indicates that the charity is really helping others, they make a substantial donation. Those who give small amounts to many charities are not so interested in whether what they are ③ doing helps others — psychologists call them warm glow givers. Knowing that they are giving makes ④ them feel good, regardless of the impact of their donation. In many cases the donation is so small — $10 or less — that if they stopped ⑤ to think, they would realize that the cost of processing the donation is likely to exceed any benefit it brings to the charity.

2016학년도 3월 학평 28번

2. (A), (B), (C)의 각 네모 안에서 어법에 맞는 표현으로 가장 적절한 것은? [3점]

Water has no calories, but it takes up a space in your stomach, which creates a feeling of fullness. Recently, a study found (A) that / what people who drank two glasses of water before meals got full sooner, ate fewer calories, and lost more weight. You can put the same strategy to work by choosing foods that have a higher water content over those with less water. For example, the only difference between grapes and raisins (B) is / are that grapes have about 6 times as much water in them. That water makes a big difference in how much they fill you up. You'll feel much more satisfied after eating 100 calories' worth of grapes than you would after eating 100 calories' worth of raisins. Salad vegetables like lettuce, cucumbers, and tomatoes also have a very high water content, as (C) are / do broth-based soups.

* broth: 묽은 수프

	(A)		(B)		(C)
①	that	……	is	……	are
②	that	……	is	……	do
③	that	……	are	……	do
④	what	……	is	……	are
⑤	what	……	are	……	do

2015학년도 3월 학평 28번

3. 다음 글의 밑줄 친 부분 중, 어법상 틀린 것은? [3점]

Coming home from work the other day, I saw a woman trying to turn onto the main street and ① having very little luck because of the constant stream of traffic. I slowed and allowed her to turn in front of me. I was feeling pretty good until, a couple of blocks later, she stopped to let a few more cars into the line, causing us both to miss the next light. I found myself completely ② irritated with her. How dare she slow me down after I had so graciously let her into the traffic! As I was sitting there stewing, I realized ③ how ridiculous I was being. Suddenly, a phrase I once read ④ came floating into my mind: 'You must do him or her a kindness for inner reasons, not because someone is keeping score or because you will be punished if you don't.' I realized ⑤ what I had wanted a reward: If I do this nice thing for you, you (or someone else) will do an equally nice thing for me.

* stew: 안달하다

2014학년도 수능 A형 27번

4. 다음 글의 밑줄 친 부분 중, 어법상 틀린 것은?

I hope you remember our discussion last Monday about the servicing of the washing machine ① supplied to us three months ago. I regret to say the machine is no longer working. As we agreed during the meeting, please send a service engineer as soon as possible to repair it. The product warranty says ② that you provide spare parts and materials for free, but charge for the engineer's labor. This sounds ③ unfair. I believe the machine's failure is caused by a manufacturing defect. Initially, it made a lot of noise, and later, it stopped ④ to operate entirely. As it is wholly the company's responsibility to correct the defect, I hope you will not make us ⑤ pay for the labor component of its repair.

5. (A), (B), (C)의 각 네모 안에서 어법에 맞는 표현으로 가장 적절한 것은? [3점]

Albert Einstein talked about what influenced his life as a scientist. He remembered seeing a pocket compass when he was five years old and (A) marveling / marveled that the needle always pointed north. In that moment, Einstein recalled, he "felt something deeply hidden behind things." Around the age of six, Einstein began studying the violin. When after several years he recognized the mathematical structure of music, the violin became a lifelong friend of his. When Einstein was ten, his family enrolled him in the Luitpold Gymnasium, (B) there / where he developed a suspicion of authority. The trait served Einstein well later in life as a scientist. His habit of skepticism made (C) him / it easy to question many long-standing scientific assumptions.

	(A)		(B)		(C)
①	marveling	······	there	······	him
②	marveled	······	there	······	him
③	marveling	······	where	······	him
④	marveled	······	where	······	it
⑤	marveling	······	where	······	it

7. (A), (B), (C) 각 네모 안에서 어법에 맞는 표현으로 가장 적절한 것은?

Philosophy is, simply put, a way of thinking. More accurately, however, it is a set of mental tools. And that fact is directly related to the question of (A) what / why we study philosophy. It's not just to amaze our friends with our own profound thinking, or confuse them with (B) unexpected / unexpectedly questions, although some college students may value that possibility the most in taking philosophy courses. We study philosophy (C) because / because of the mental skills it helps us develop.

	(A)		(B)		(C)
①	what	······	unexpected	······	because
②	why	······	unexpected	······	because of
③	why	······	unexpected	······	because
④	why	······	unexpectedly	······	because
⑤	what	······	unexpectedly	······	because of

6. 다음 글의 밑줄 친 부분 중, 어법상 틀린 것은?

Mr. Brown wanted his students to learn math in the context of real life. He felt it was not enough for them just to work out problems from a book. To show his students how math could really help ① them, he held several contests during the year. The contests allowed his students ② to have fun while they practiced math and raised money. Once he filled a fishbowl with marbles, asked the students to guess how many marbles there were, and ③ awarded a free lunch to the winner. Another time they entered a contest to guess how many soda cans the back of a pickup truck ④ was held. To win, they had to practice their skills at estimating, multiplying, dividing, and measuring. They used ⑤ most of the prize money for an end-of-the-year field trip.

8. 다음 글의 밑줄 친 부분 중, 어법상 틀린 것은? [3점]

The development of the 'package' holiday in the 1960s and 1970s was actually one of the early drivers of food tourism. Prior to the advent of the overseas vacation, consumers were only exposed to foods made available in their daily life, which came from the local supermarket and grocery store and ① occasionally, if they were lucky, a local food market. Populations in many countries were also less cosmopolitan than they ② are today and hence exposed to a smaller variety of foods in their lives. The retailers needed to provide produce they could sell quickly as the shelf life of food, due to the lack of ③ developed refrigeration, was short. As a result, the food at the market was considered ④ safe. Exotic foods were rarely on offer as customers simply did not understand how to prepare or cook them and often feared ⑤ how they would taste like.

제한 시간 : 7분   정답 및 해설 011쪽

9. 다음 글의 밑줄 친 부분 중, 문맥상 낱말의 쓰임이 적절하지 않은 것은? [3점]

In poorer countries many years of fast growth may be necessary to bring living standards up to acceptable levels. But growth is the means to achieve desired goals, not the ① end in itself. In the richer world the whole idea of growth—at least as conventionally measured—may need to be ② maintained. In economies where services dominate, goods and services tailored to our ③ individual needs will be what determine the advance of our societies. These could be anything from genome-specific medicines to personalized care or tailored suits. That is different from more and more stuff, an arms race of growth. Instead, it means improvements in ④ quality, something that GDP is ill equipped to measure. Some fifty years ago one US economist contrasted what he called the "cowboy" economy, bent on production, exploitation of resources, and pollution, with the "spaceman" economy, in which quality and complexity replaced "throughput" as the measure of success. The ⑤ move from manufacturing to services and from analog to digital is the shift from cowboy to spaceman. But we are still measuring the size of the lasso.

* throughput: (일정 시간 내에 해야 할) 처리량
** lasso: (카우보이가 야생마를 잡는 데 사용하는) 올가미 밧줄

10. 다음 글의 밑줄 친 부분 중, 문맥상 낱말의 쓰임이 적절하지 않은 것은?

In recent years urban transport professionals globally have largely acquiesced to the view that automobile demand in cities needs to be managed rather than accommodated. Rising incomes inevitably lead to increases in motorization. Even without the imperative of climate change, the physical constraints of densely inhabited cities and the corresponding demands of accessibility, mobility, safety, air pollution, and urban livability all ① limit the option of expanding road networks purely to accommodate this rising demand. As a result, as cities develop and their residents become more prosperous, ② persuading people to choose *not* to use cars becomes an increasingly key focus of city managers and planners. Improving the quality of ③ alternative options, such as walking, cycling, and public transport, is a central element of this strategy. However, the most direct approach to ④ accommodating automobile demand is making motorized travel more expensive or restricting it with administrative rules. The contribution of motorized travel to climate change ⑤ reinforces this imperative.

* acquiesce: 따르다 ** imperative: 불가피한 것 *** constraint: 압박

11. 다음 글의 밑줄 친 부분 중, 문맥상 낱말의 쓰임이 적절하지 않은 것은?

One of the most productive strategies to build customer relationships is to increase the firm's share of customer rather than its market share. This strategy involves abandoning the old notions of ① acquiring new customers and increasing transactions to focus instead on more fully serving the needs of existing customers. Financial services are a great example of this. Most consumers purchase financial services from ② different firms. They bank at one institution, purchase insurance from another, and handle their investments elsewhere. To ③ solidify this purchasing pattern, many companies now offer all of these services under one roof. For example, Regions Financial Corporation offers retail and commercial banking, trust, mortgage, and insurance products to customers in a network of more than 1,500 offices. The company tries to more fully serve the financial needs of its ④ current customers, thereby acquiring a larger share of each customer's financial business. By creating these types of relationships, customers have ⑤ little incentive to seek out competitive firms to fulfill their financial services needs.

12. 다음 글의 밑줄 친 부분 중, 문맥상 낱말의 쓰임이 적절하지 않은 것은? [3점]

Archaeologists and historians have found quite a bit of evidence of group-on-group conflict during the last 10,000 years. The conflicts took many forms and occurred in many different places, but scholars have ① noted common features in the behavior of combatants, and we still observe them in people today. The observations gave ② support to the apemen competing in the savanna stories and the idea that it might be in the "nature" of humans to fight for territory and hate those who are different. They suggested that warlike behavior might be somehow programmed into our genes and generated ③ automatically by our human brain. If this were the case, the peaceful coexistence of different human groups would be ④ impossible. A deeper view of history gives peacekeepers and diplomats more reason to hope. Far from being part of our ancient biology, going to war seems to have begun rather recently in our evolutionary history. The archaeological evidence suggests that warfare was ⑤ common before about 8,000 years ago.

* combatant: 전투원 ** apeman: (사람과 고등 유인원 사이의) 원인(猿人)

총 문항					문항	맞은 문항					문항	
개별 문항	1	2	3	4	5	6	7	8	9	10	11	12
채점												

어휘·숙어 비밀 노트

idiom vocabulary

A 수능 필수 어휘 ▶ 철자가 혼동되는 어휘 (2)

□ 041	abroad	ad. 해외로, 해외에	aboard	ad. 승선하여, ~에 타고
□ 042	coverage	n. 보상 범위, 보도	covenant	n. 약속, 계약
□ 043	carrier	n. 운반인, 운반기	career	n. 직업, 경력
□ 044	commodity	a. 상품, 일용품	community	n. 지역사회, 공동체
□ 045	conception	n. 개념	exception	n. 제외, 예외
□ 046	confidence	n. 자신감	conference	n. 협의, 회의
□ 047	contract	n. 계약; v. 계약하다	contrast	n. 대조, 차이; v. 대조하다
□ 048	cooperation	n. 협동, 협력	corporation	n. 주식회사, 법인
□ 049	corruption	n. 타락, 부패	eruption	n. 폭발, 분화
□ 050	command	v. 명령하다	comment	n. 논평; v. 견해를 밝히다
□ 051	considerable	a. 상당히, 많은	considerate	a. 이해심이 있는, 사려 깊은
□ 052	employer	n. 고용주	employee	n. 종업원
□ 053	emergence	n. 출현, 발생	emergency	n. 비상사태
□ 054	fit	a. 적당한, 컨디션이 좋은	feat	n. 위업, 공적, 묘기
□ 055	generous	a. 관대한, 너그러운	general	a. 일반적인; n. 장군
□ 056	inventive	a. 창의적인, 발명의	incentive	a. 고무하는, 격려하는
□ 057	level	a. 수평의, 같은 수준의	label	n. 라벨; v. 라벨을 붙이다
□ 058	morality	n. 도덕, 덕행	mortality	n. 사망률, 사망자 수
□ 059	particle	n. (아주 작은) 입자	principle	n. 원리, 원칙
□ 060	thirsty	a. 목마른, 갈망하는	thrifty	a. 절약하는, 아끼는

B 수능 필수 숙어

□ 061	amount to	~이 되다, ~와 같다
□ 062	and so forth[on]	~등등
□ 063	and the like	기타 등등[따위]
□ 064	anything but	~이 결코 아닌
□ 065	apart from	~을 제외하고, ~뿐만 아니라
□ 066	apologize to A for B	B에 대해 A에게 사과하다
□ 067	appeal to	~에 호소하다, ~의 마음을 끌다
□ 068	approve of	~을 승인하다, ~을 찬성하다
□ 069	as a matter of fact	사실은(= in fact)
□ 070	as a (general) rule	대체로
□ 071	as a result of	~의 결과로서, ~때문에
□ 072	as far as	~까지, ~하는 한
□ 073	as for	~에 대해서 말하자면
□ 074	as it is	현재로서는
□ 075	as to	~에 관해서는
□ 076	ascribe A to B	A를 B의 탓으로 돌리다
□ 077	aside from	~을 제외하고, ~외에
□ 078	assent to	~에 동의하다, 찬성하다
□ 079	at (the) best	기껏해야
□ 080	at a time	한 번에

03 보어의 이해

🏷️ 출제 트렌드

1. 영어 문장에서 주격보어는 주어의 상태나 성질을 설명한다. 목적격보어는 목적어의 상태나 성질을 설명한다.

2. 보어에 관한 문제는 주격보어나 목적격보어로 형용사와 부사를 제시하고 형용사를 고르는 문제가 출제되었다. keep의 목적어보어로 사용된 과거분사(2004학년도 수능), find의 목적격보어로 사용된 과거분사(2011학년도 수능)가 출제되었다.

3. 사역동사(1995년, 2014학년도 수능 A형(9쪽 4번 참조))나 지각동사(2006학년도 수능(52쪽 6번 참조))의 목적격보어가 동사원형, 현재분사, 과거분사로 나오는 문제가 출제되었다. 모평과 학평에서도 자주 출제되고 있다.

4. 한편 to부정사형의 주격보어(1999, 2003학년도 수능), seem의 주격보어(2005, 2013학년도 수능), sound의 주격보어(형용사) 문제(2014학년도 수능 B형)가 선지로 출제되었다.

	출처	문항 번호	어법·어휘 문제
1	2022학년도 04월 학평	29번	become의 보어 (형용사 vs 부사)
2	2021학년도 07월 학평	29번	「with+목적어+목보(분사)」
3	2012학년도 07월 학평	21번	「지각동사(watch)+목적어+목적격보어」
4	2012학년도 03월 학평	20번	수동태의 주격보어(형용사)
5	2011학년도 수능	21번	「find+목적어+목보(과거분사)」
6	2009학년도 10월 학평	20번	「make+목적어+목보(형용사)」
7	2007학년도 04월 학평	23번	「make+목적어+목보(형용사)」
8	2004학년도 수능	30번	「keep+목적어+목보(형용사)」
9	2022학년도 03월 학평	30번	어휘 문제 01
10	2022학년도 수능	30번	어휘 문제 02
11	2021학년도 10월 학평	30번	어휘 문제 03
12	2022학년도 08월 종로	30번	어휘 문제 04

🏷️ 1등급 꿀팁

1. 2형식이나 5형식에서 보어는 부사를 사용하지 않고 형용사를 사용한다.

2. 「지각[사역]동사+목적어+목적격보어」 구조에서 목적격보어가 동사원형, 현재분사, 과거분사가 나올 때를 구분한다.

3. 지각동사와 사역동사는 목적어와 목적격보어가 능동 관계이면 목적격보어를 동사원형을 쓰고, 수동 관계이면 과거분사를 쓴다. 한편 지각동사와 일부 사역동사는 능동 관계인 경우 현재분사를 쓸 수도 있다.

[핵심 문법]

정답 및 해설 013쪽

A 출제 POINT

1. 주격보어는 명사, 형용사, 준동사, 명사절 등이 쓰일 수 있다.
▶ Bill was a very famous [**sing** / **singer**].

2. 2형식 동사 뒤 주격보어 자리에 형용사가 나와야 하는데, 부사를 넣고 틀린 것을 찾는 문제가 종종 나왔다.
2형식 동사는 be, keep, stay, get, grow, become, look, seem, appear, feel, smell 등을 말한다.
▶ The lilacs on the table smell [**sweetly** / **sweet**].

3. 목적격보어는 명사, 형용사, 현재분사, 과거분사, to부정사가 쓰일 수 있다.
▶ I'm sure she will keep the secret [**hiding** / **hidden**] forever.

4. 5형식에서 지각동사의 목적격보어는 동사원형이나 진행형이 나온다. 단, 목적어와 목적격보어가 수동 관계인 경우는 과거분사가 나온다.
▶ We see people [**drinking** / **to drink**] coffee with chocolate.

5. 5형식에서 사역동사의 목적격보어는 동사원형이 나온다. 단, get 동사는 목적어와 목적격 보어가 능동 관계인 경우 목적격 보어에 to부정사가 나오며, 수동 관계인 경우에는 과거분사가 나온다.
▶ He get the box [**to clean** / **cleaned**]

6. allow, cause enable, encourage, tell, urge, want 동사는 목적격보어로 to부정사가 나온다.
▶ Today many countries do not allow foreigners [**stay** / **to stay**] without visa.

7. 주격보어로 접속사 that, whether, 관계대명사 what으로 시작하는 절이 올 수 있다.
▶ The point is [**that** / **whether**] this is true or not.

B 체크 POINT

다음 괄호 안에서 어법상 올바른 것을 고르시오.

1. Sometimes many people don't feel [**connectedly** / **connected**] to their social security network.
2. This milk smells [**badly** / **bad**].
3. The can of coke made me even more [**thirstily** / **thirsty**]
4. I watched a beautiful smile [**flashed** / **flashing**] across her face.
5. The grammar book helps us [**improve** / **improved**] our understanding English grammar.
6. The latest technology allowed us [**get** / **to get**] access to the Internet all the time.
7. The worst part was [**what** / **that**] there was not enough food at the feast.

2022학년도 4월 학평 29번

1. 다음 글의 밑줄 친 부분 중, 어법상 틀린 것은?

The actual problems with monopolies are caused by statism, not capitalism. Under a statist social system, taxes, subsidies, tariffs, and regulations often serve to protect existing large players in the marketplace. Those players often use crony tactics to retain or expand the protections: a new tariff preventing foreign competition, a subsidy making it harder for new players ① to compete with them, or a regulatory measure that a large company has the resources to comply with. Under a capitalist social system, on the other hand, the government has no say in how ② dominantly a company may become in its industry or how companies take over and merge with one another. Furthermore, a capitalist society doesn't have rights−violating taxes, tariffs, subsidies, or regulations ③ favoring anybody nor does it have antitrust laws. Under capitalism, dominance can only be achieved by becoming really good at ④ what you're doing. And to maintain dominance, you have to continue to stay ahead of the competition, which sees your dominance and profits as a sign ⑤ that there is money to be made by others as well.

* statism: 국가 통제주의 ** crony: 정실(사사로운 정에 이끌리는 일)
*** antitrust law: 독점 금지법

2021학년도 7월 학평 29번

2. 다음 글의 밑줄 친 부분 중, 어법상 틀린 것은? [3점]

The idea that people ① selectively expose themselves to news content has been around for a long time, but it is even more important today with the fragmentation of audiences and the proliferation of choices. Selective exposure is a psychological concept that says people seek out information that conforms to their existing belief systems and ② avoid information that challenges those beliefs. In the past when there were few sources of news, people could either expose themselves to mainstream news — where they would likely see beliefs ③ expressed counter to their own — or they could avoid news altogether. Now with so many types of news constantly available to a full range of niche audiences, people can easily find a source of news ④ that consistently confirms their own personal set of beliefs. This leads to the possibility of creating many different small groups of people with each strongly ⑤ believes they are correct and everyone else is wrong about how the world works.

* fragmentation: 분열 ** proliferation: 급증 *** niche: 틈새

2012학년도 7월 학평 21번

3. (A), (B), (C)의 각 네모 안에서 어법에 맞는 표현으로 가장 적절한 것은?

Empathy is made possible by a special group of nerve cells called mirror neurons. These special cells enable us to "mirror" emotions. Mirror neurons were first discovered by Italian scientists who, while looking at the activity of individual nerve cells inside the brains of monkeys, (A) noticed / noticing that neurons in the same area of the brain were activated whether the animals were performing a particular movement or simply observing another monkey perform the same action. It appeared as though the cells in the observer's brain "mirrored" the activity in the performer's brain. A similar phenomenon takes place when we watch someone (B) experiencing / experienced an emotion and feel the same emotion in response. The same neural systems get activated in a part of the insula, (C) it / which is part of the mirror neuron system, and in the emotional brain areas associated with the observed emotion.

	(A)		(B)		(C)
①	noticed	......	experiencing	......	it
②	noticed	......	experiencing	......	which
③	noticed	......	experienced	......	which
④	noticing	......	experiencing	......	it
⑤	noticing	......	experienced	......	it

2012학년도 3월 학평 20번

4. 다음 글의 밑줄 친 부분 중, 어법상 틀린 것은?

We do not hear with our eyes, but sometimes it almost seems as if we do. An environment−agency official tells a surprising incident about some people ① who lived in an apartment building close to a busy state highway. The families were made ② miserably by the noise, and they complained to the city government. City officials went to the state capital again and again to ask that something ③ be done about quieting the highway noise. They were put off repeatedly. At last the city officials had an idea. They planted a single row of trees in front of the apartment house. The trees made hardly any difference in the amount of noise, but they ④ did block the view of the highway. After that, there were very ⑤ few complaints from the people in the building.

5. (A), (B), (C)의 각 네모 안에서 어법에 맞는 표현으로 가장 적절한 것은?

We anticipate the future as if we found it too slow in coming and we were trying to hurry it up. (A) So / Such imprudent are we that we wander about in times that are not ours and do not think of the one that belongs to us. We try to support the present with the future and (B) think / thinking of arranging things we cannot control, for a time we have no certainty of reaching. Examine your thoughts, and you will find them wholly (C) to occupy / occupied with the past or the future. We almost never think of the present, and if we do so, it is only to shed light on our plans for the future. The past and the present are our means; only the future is our end.

	(A)		(B)		(C)
①	So	⋯⋯	thinking	⋯⋯	occupied
②	So	⋯⋯	think	⋯⋯	to occupy
③	So	⋯⋯	think	⋯⋯	occupied
④	Such	⋯⋯	thinking	⋯⋯	occupied
⑤	Such	⋯⋯	thinking	⋯⋯	to occupy

6. 다음 글의 밑줄 친 부분 중, 어법상 틀린 것은?

Farmers plow more and more fields ①to produce more food for the increasing population. This increases pressure on our soil resources. Farmers plow soil to improve ②it for crops. They turn and loosen the soil, ③leaving it in the best condition for farming. However, this process removes the important plant cover that holds soil particles in place, making soil ④defenselessly to wind and water erosion. Sometimes, the wind blows soil from a plowed field. Soil erosion in many places occurs at a ⑤much faster rate than the natural processes of weathering can replace it.

7. 다음 글의 밑줄 친 부분 중, 어법상 틀린 것은?

The latest studies indicate that ①what people really want is a mate that has qualities like their parents. Women are ②after a man who is like their father and men want to be able to see their own mother in the woman of their dreams. Cognitive psychologist David Perrett studies what makes faces ③attractively. He has developed a computerized morphing system that can endlessly adjust faces to suit his needs. Perrett suggests that we ④find our own faces charming because they remind us ⑤of the faces we looked at constantly in our early childhood years — Mom and Dad.

8. (A), (B), (C)의 각 네모 안에서 어법에 맞는 표현을 골라 짝지은 것은?

Mom was an extraordinarily clean person. After feeding my brother and me breakfast, she would scrub, mop, and (A) dust / to dust everything. As we grew older, Mom made sure we did our part by keeping our rooms (B) neat / neatly. Outside, she would tend a small flower garden, which was the envy of the neighborhood. With Mom, everything she touched (C) turned / turning to gold. She didn't believe in doing anything halfway. She often told us that we always had to do our best in whatever we did.

	(A)		(B)		(C)
①	dust	⋯⋯	neat	⋯⋯	turned
②	dust	⋯⋯	neat	⋯⋯	turning
③	dust	⋯⋯	neatly	⋯⋯	turned
④	to dust	⋯⋯	neat	⋯⋯	turned
⑤	to dust	⋯⋯	neatly	⋯⋯	turning

제한 시간 : 7분	정답 및 해설 016쪽

9. 다음 글의 밑줄 친 부분 중, 문맥상 낱말의 쓰임이 적절하지 않은 것은?

Just as there's a tendency to glorify technological progress, there's a countertendency to expect the worst of every new tool or machine. In Plato's *Phaedrus*, Socrates bemoaned the ① development of writing. He feared that, as people came to rely on the written word as a ② substitute for the knowledge they used to carry inside their heads, they would, in the words of one of the dialogue's characters, "cease to exercise their memory and become forgetful." And because they would be able to "③ receive a quantity of information without proper instruction," they would "be thought very knowledgeable when they are for the most part quite ignorant." They would be "filled with the conceit of wisdom instead of real wisdom." Socrates wasn't ④ right — the new technology did often have the effects he feared — but he was shortsighted. He couldn't ⑤ foresee the many ways that writing and reading would serve to spread information, spark fresh ideas, and expand human knowledge (if not wisdom).

*bemoan: 한탄하다 **conceit: 자만심

10. 다음 글의 밑줄 친 부분 중, 문맥상 낱말의 쓰임이 적절하지 않은 것은?

It has been suggested that "organic" methods, defined as those in which only natural products can be used as inputs, would be less damaging to the biosphere. Large-scale adoption of "organic" farming methods, however, would ① reduce yields and increase production costs for many major crops. Inorganic nitrogen supplies are ② essential for maintaining moderate to high levels of productivity for many of the non-leguminous crop species, because organic supplies of nitrogenous materials often are either limited or more expensive than inorganic nitrogen fertilizers. In addition, there are ③ benefits to the extensive use of either manure or legumes as "green manure" crops. In many cases, weed control can be very difficult or require much hand labor if chemicals cannot be used, and ④ fewer people are willing to do this work as societies become wealthier. Some methods used in "organic" farming, however, such as the sensible use of crop rotations and specific combinations of cropping and livestock enterprises, can make important ⑤ contributions to the sustainability of rural ecosystems.

*nitrogen fertilizer: 질소 비료 **manure: 거름
***legume: 콩과(科) 식물

11. 다음 글의 밑줄 친 부분 중, 문맥상 낱말의 쓰임이 적절하지 않은 것은?

How people behave often depends on what others do. If other car drivers or subway users leave for work at 8 a.m., it may be to my ① advantage to leave at 6 a.m., even if that is really too early from my point of view. In equilibrium, flows ② stabilize so that each person makes the best trade-off between their ideal schedule and the congestion they will suffer on their commute. In making such choices, agents seek to ③ differentiate their behavior from that of others. On other occasions, agents have a problem with coordination. They would like to choose to behave the same way as others. For example, if most of my fellow citizens did not pay their parking tickets, there would be (unfortunately) strong pressure for an amnesty for such offenders, which would ④ increase my incentive to pay my parking tickets too. There may be multiple equilibria, so that two otherwise identical societies may ⑤ adopt different behavioral patterns.

*equilibrium: 균형(상태) **amnesty: 사면

12. 다음 글의 밑줄 친 부분 중, 문맥상 낱말의 쓰임이 적절하지 않은 것은?

It has become a commonplace that audiences are conceived of in terms of their lifestyles. Once more, it would be naive to argue that as members of society we simply have lifestyles which the market ① identifies and slots into. The market (as all our cultural assumptions about consumption) has been around for so long that we are born into lifestyles which it has already shaped. We grow up into a set of assumptions about what living is, what shopping is. And the market ② ceases to work on the idea of lifestyle through an apparently everlasting succession of campaigns. It is constructing and reconstructing lifestyles all the time. The main thing that lifestyle is about is the consumers' ③ conception of their place in society, their social relations, their persona — it has nothing to do with material needs as such. The ④ possession of SUVs or 4×4 vehicles is about how the owners wish to be seen by others. Few of these owners could support an argument that the vehicle was ⑤ necessary to their work or the material well-being of their family.

총 문항					문항	맞은 문항					문항
개별 문항	1	2	3	4	5	6	7	8	9	10	11	12
채점												

어휘·숙어 비밀 노트

A 수능 필수 어휘 ▶ 철자가 혼동되는 어휘 (3)

☐ 081	abject	a. 비참한, 비열한	object	n. 사물, 목표
☐ 082	abuse	v. 남용하다	amuse	v. 기쁘게 하다
☐ 083	accept	v. 허가하다	except	pre. ~을 제외하고
☐ 084	access	v. 접근하다, 이용하다	excess	n. 과다, 초과
☐ 085	accessible	a. 접근하기 쉬운	acceptable	a. 받아들일 수 있는
☐ 086	accompany	v. 동참하다	company	n. 회사, 일행
☐ 087	acquire	v. 획득하다	inquire	v. 묻다, 문의하다
☐ 088	active	a. 활동적인	actual	a. 현실의, 사실상의
☐ 089	addictive	a. 중독성의	additive	a. 부가적인; n. 첨가물
☐ 090	affect	v. 영향을 미치다	effect	n. 결과, 효과
☐ 091	affluent	a. 부유한, 풍족한	fluent	a. 유창한
☐ 092	altar	n. 제단	alter	v. 변경하다, 바꾸다
☐ 093	altitude	n. 고도, 높이	attitude	n. 태도
☐ 094	amuse	v. 즐겁게 하다	amaze	v. 놀라게 하다
☐ 095	angle	n. 각도	angel	n. 천사
☐ 096	anticipating	a. 기대하는	participating	a. 참여하는
☐ 097	appeal	v. 간청하다, 항의하다	appear	v. 나타나다
☐ 098	approve	v. 승인하다	improve	v. 개선하다
☐ 099	archive	v. 공문서, 기록	achieve	v. 성취하다
☐ 100	aspect	n. 외관, 모양, 관점	aspire	v. 열망하다

B 수능 필수 숙어

☐ 101	at ease	마음 편히
☐ 102	at hand	(거리가) 가까운, 가까운 미래에
☐ 103	at issue	논쟁 중인, 고려 중인
☐ 104	at last	마침내
☐ 105	at odds with	~와 의견이 일치하지 않는
☐ 106	at length	상세히, 한참 후에
☐ 107	at one time	예전에, 동시에
☐ 108	at other times	다른 때에는, 평소에는
☐ 109	at present	현재는, 지금은
☐ 110	at the cost of	~을 희생하고, ~의 비용을 지불하고
☐ 111	at the earliest	(아무리) 빨라도
☐ 112	at the moment	바로 지금
☐ 113	attach A to B	A를 B에 붙이다(첨부하다)
☐ 114	attribute A to B	A를 B의 탓으로 돌리다
☐ 115	avail oneself of	~을 이용하다
☐ 116	back and forth	앞뒤로
☐ 117	be all ears	주의 깊게 듣다
☐ 118	be apt to	~하는 경향이 있다, ~하기 쉽다
☐ 119	be bound to	반드시 ~하다, ~할 의무가 있다
☐ 120	be engaged in	~에 종사하다

04 수의 일치

📌 출제 트렌드

1. 주어의 수나 개념에 따라 동사 또는 대명사의 단·복수의 형태를 결정하는 것을 일치라고 한다. 수 일치 문제의 기본 개념은 단수주어에는 단수동사를 사용하고, 복수주어에는 복수동사를 사용한다는 것이다.

2. 1994-2023학년도 수능 기출 어법 문제를 분석한 결과, 수 일치 문제는 주어와 동사의 수 일치(1996, 2007, 2008학년도 수능), 「the+형용사」형의 주어와 동사의 수 일치(2017학년도 수능) 문제가 출제되었다. 이외에도 인칭대명사의 단·복수 형태를 결정하는 수 일치(2006학년도 수능) 문제가 출제되었다.

3. 또한 관계사절의 수식을 받는 주어와 동사의 수 일치(2004, 2006학년도 수능), 「부정부사(Rarely)+도치구문」의 수 일치(2010학년도 수능), 동명사 주어의 수 일치(2013학년도 수능)가 선지로 출제되었다.

4. 수 일치 문제는 모평과 학평에서도 자주 출제되고 있다.

출처	문항 번호	어법·어휘 문제
1 2021학년도 6월 모평	29번	동격절 that의 주어와 동사의 수 일치
2 2017학년도 수능	28번	「the+형용사」인 주어와 동사의 수일치
3 2014학년도 10월 학평	25번	전치사구 뒤에 나온 주어와 동사의 수 일치
4 2014학년도 03월 학평	25번 변형	most of ~인 주어와 동사의 수 일치
5 2010학년도 09월 모평	21번	의문사절과 동사의 수 일치
6 2009학년도 04월 학평	22번	관계사절과 동사의 수 일치
7 2020학년도 04월 종로	29번	정동사 vs. 준동사 / 긴 주어와 동사의 수 일치
8 2020학년도 11월 종로	29번	접속사 whether절과 동사의 수 일치 / 대명사의 수 일치
9 2022학년도 09월 모평	30번	어휘 문제 01
10 2021학년도 7월 학평	30번	어휘 문제 02
11 2022학년도 06월 모평	30번	어휘 문제 03
12 2022학년도 05월 종로	30번	어휘 문제 04

📌 1등급 꿀팁

1. 주어가 구나 절의 수식을 받아 길어진 경우, 동사의 수 일치에 유의해야 한다.

2. 관계대명사절의 수 일치는 선행사가 단수이면 관계대명사절의 동사를 단수동사를 사용하고, 선행사가 복수이면 관계대명사절의 동사를 복수동사를 사용한다.

3. 「the+형용사」는 복수보통명사, 추상명사로 사용될 수 있다.

4. 대명사의 단·복수의 형태를 결정하는 수 일치를 유의한다.

5. 상관접속사 either A or B, neither A nor B, not only A but also B(= B as well as A)는 B에 동사의 수를 일치시키고, Both A and B는 항상 복수 취급한다.

[핵심 문법]

정답 및 해설 019쪽

A 출제 POINT

1. 수 일치의 기본 원칙은 단수주어는 단수동사를, 복수주어는 복수동사를 사용한다.
   ▶ A famous professor and a musician **[is / are]** discussing the problem.

2. 주어, 동사 사이에 수식어구나 관계사절이 있는 경우, 주어를 잘 찾은 후, 주어의 수에 맞게 동사를 일치시켜야 한다.
   ▶ Families that avoid conflict by ignoring unpleasant subjects or situations **[is / are]** weaker, not stronger for it.

3. 관계대명사절 안의 동사는 선행사의 수에 일치시킨다. 선행사가 단수주어면 동사는 단수동사, 선행사가 복수 주어이면 복수동사를 사용한다.
   ▶ Kids shouldn't watch TV programs which **[contains / contain]** violence.

4. It … that ~ 강조 구문에서 주어가 강조되면, that 바로 뒤의 동사는 강조된 주어에 맞게 수를 일치시킨다. There is[are] 구문에서 be동사는 바로 뒤에 나오는 주어에 맞게 수를 일치시킨다.
   ▶ It is golf courses that **[has / have]** beautiful grass, plants and pretty ponds.

5. 도치 구문은 뒤에 나오는 주어에 맞게 수를 일치시킨다.
   ▶ Only after her death **[were / was]** I able to appreciate her.

6. most of ~, some of ~, all of ~, a lot of ~, 「분수+of ~」 등이 주어로 쓰인 경우, 동사는 of 뒤에 나오는 명사(구)의 수에 일치시킨다. 「the number of+복수명사」는 뒤에 단수동사를 쓰고, 「A number of+복수명사」는 뒤에 복수동사를 쓴다.
   ▶ Some of her friends **[thinks / think]** she is silly to work and save for a smartwatch, but I don't agree with them.

7. 명사를 대신하는 대명사는 그 명사의 수와 일치해야 한다.
   ▶ The tail of a rabbit is shorter than **[that / those]** of a cat.

B 체크 POINT

다음 괄호 안에서 어법상 올바른 것을 고르시오.

1. A famous professor and musician **[are / is]** talking on the phone.
2. The custom decorating the body with jewels **[is / are]** ancient.
3. Doctors are contacting patients with cancer, who **[has / have]** taken the drugs in the last three months.
4. There **[is / are]** no subway station near my house.
5. Seldom **[do / does]** Sam say anything bad about people.
6. Most of the shelves **[is / are]** empty.
7. An opening airing of disagreements is an excellent way to manage family conflict and keep **[them / it]** within acceptable bounds.

•어법 기출•

| 제한 시간 : 13분 | 정답 및 해설 019쪽 |

2021학년도 6월 모평 29번

1. 다음 글의 밑줄 친 부분 중, 어법상 틀린 것은?

People from more individualistic cultural contexts tend to be motivated to maintain self-focused agency or control ① as these serve as the basis of one's self-worth. With this form of agency comes the belief that individual successes ② depending primarily on one's own abilities and actions, and thus, whether by influencing the environment or trying to accept one's circumstances, the use of control ultimately centers on the individual. The independent self may be more ③ driven to cope by appealing to a sense of agency or control. However, people from more interdependent cultural contexts tend to be less focused on issues of individual success and agency and more motivated towards group goals and harmony. Research has shown ④ that East Asians prefer to receive, but not seek, more social support rather than seek personal control in certain cases. Therefore, people ⑤ who hold a more interdependent self-construal may prefer to cope in a way that promotes harmony in relationships.

2017학년도 수능 28번

2. 다음 글의 밑줄 친 부분 중, 어법상 틀린 것은? [3점]

When people face real adversity — disease, unemployment, or the disabilities of age — affection from a pet takes on new meaning. A pet's continuing affection becomes crucially important for ① those enduring hardship because it reassures them that their core essence has not been damaged. Thus pets are important in the treatment of ② depressed or chronically ill patients. In addition, pets are ③ used to great advantage with the institutionalized aged. In such institutions it is difficult for the staff to retain optimism when all the patients are declining in health. Children who visit cannot help but remember ④ what their parents or grandparents once were and be depressed by their incapacities. Animals, however, have no expectations about mental capacity. They do not worship youth. They have no memories about what the aged once ⑤ was and greet them as if they were children. An old man holding a puppy can relive a childhood moment with complete accuracy. His joy and the animal's response are the same.

2014학년도 10월 학평 25번

3. 다음 글의 밑줄 친 부분 중, 어법상 틀린 것은? [3점]

In most wilderness, the majority of groups ① visiting the area are small — usually between two and four people. But large groups do visit wilderness, and their potential to disturb campsites differs from ② that of small groups. Although the effect of party size on campsites has never been formally studied, it makes sense that a large group can cause impacts on an undisturbed site more ③ rapidly than a small group. For example, along the New River in West Virginia, the area of vegetation loss on sites used by large commercial rafting companies ④ were more than four times larger than the area on sites used by small groups of fishermen. At well-established campsites, however, a big group need not be a problem, as long as activities are ⑤ confined within the boundaries of the existing site.

2014학년도 3월 학평 25번 변형

4. 다음 글의 밑줄 친 부분 중, 어법상 틀린 것은? [3점]

I remember one of the smartest I.T. executives ① for whom I ever worked strongly resisting the movement to measure programmer productivity that was popular at the time. He was fond of saying that the biggest problem with managing computer programmers is that you can never tell ② whether they are working by looking at them. Picture two programmers working side by side. One is leaning back in his chair with his eyes ③ closed and his feet on the desk. The other is working hard, typing code into his computer. The one with his feet up could be thinking, and the other one may be too busy typing ④ to give it enough thought. In the end, the busy typist could well produce ten times as many lines of code as the thinker, which contain twice as many new problems as the thinker's. Unfortunately, most of the productivity measurement schemes I have encountered ⑤ measures effort or apparent activity. They would reward him and punish his thoughtful neighbor.

5. (A), (B), (C) 각 네모 안에서 어법에 맞는 표현으로 가장 적절한 것은?

No matter what we are shopping for, it is not primarily a brand we are choosing, but a culture, or rather the people associated with that culture. (A) Whatever / Whether you wear torn jeans or like to recite poetry, by doing so you make a statement of belonging to a group of people. Who we believe we are (B) is / are a result of the choices we make about who we want to be like, and we subsequently demonstrate this desired likeness to others in various and often subtle ways. Artificial as this process is, this is what becomes our 'identity,' an identity (C) grounded / grounding on all the superficial differences we distinguish between ourselves and others. This, after all, is what we are shopping for: self-identity, knowledge of who we are.

	(A)		(B)		(C)
①	Whatever	……	is	……	grounded
②	Whatever	……	are	……	grounding
③	Whether	……	is	……	grounded
④	Whether	……	are	……	grounding
⑤	Whether	……	are	……	grounded

6. 다음 글의 밑줄 친 부분 중, 어법상 틀린 것은?

Although life is different from nonlife, it is not ① completely different. Living things exist in a nonliving universe and depend on ② it in many ways. Plants absorb energy from sunlight, and bats find shelter in caves. Indeed, living things are made of the same tiny particles ③ that make up nonliving things. What makes organisms different from the materials that compose them ④ are their level of organization. Living things exhibit not just one but many layers of biological organization. This tendency toward order is sometimes ⑤ modeled in a pyramid of life.

7. 다음 글의 밑줄 친 부분 중 어법상 틀린 것은?

Most of us have been culturally conditioned to eat at least three meals a day, typically breakfast, lunch, and dinner. Thus, a day doesn't quite seem ① complete unless you've had all three of these, at a minimum. Our approach to eating is similar to a to-do list: you have got to have breakfast, you have got to have lunch, and you have got to have dinner. And you have got to do it more or less at the culturally ② prescribed times: Breakfasts are for morning, lunches are for midday, and dinners, or suppers, are to be saved until later in the day. This time-based three-meals-a-day paradigm ③ overlooking the basic fact that our energy demands vary on a day-to-day basis and that no two days are the same. As a result, we eat when we don't feel like eating and don't eat when we feel like eating — not ④ because of the chaotic ebb and flow of the food supply, but because our eating follows a mind schedule rather than a body schedule. It's no wonder ⑤ that this time-based eating results in mindless overeating.

8. 다음 글의 밑줄 친 부분 중, 어법상 틀린 것은? [3점]

When the natural communication systems of primates are examined, no straightforward increase in complexity from monkeys to apes to humans ① is observed. Many researchers characterize great ape communication systems as more limited in range than ② those of monkeys. For example, monkeys, but not other apes, have functionally referential alarm calls, although whether monkey calls are truly referential like human language ③ to remain contested. This particular ape-monkey difference makes biological sense. Great apes are larger and stronger than monkeys, and hence are less vulnerable to predation. Apes almost certainly didn't evolve referential alarm calls because they had comparatively little to be alarmed about. Indeed, there is little ④ that is learned at all in the vocal communication of nonhuman apes. Apes do possess gestures to initiate play, for instance, or when infants signal they wish to be carried — many of these gestures have learned elements. However, apes seemingly do not use their gestures referentially, nor ⑤ do their gestures exhibit any symbolic or conventionalized features.

•어휘 기출•

제한 시간 : 7분   정답 및 해설 022쪽

2022학년도 9월 모평 30번

9. 다음 글의 밑줄 친 부분 중, 문맥상 낱말의 쓰임이 적절하지 않은 것은? [3점]

In economic systems what takes place in one sector has impacts on another; demand for a good or service in one sector is derived from another. For instance, a consumer buying a good in a store will likely trigger the replacement of this product, which will generate ① demands for activities such as manufacturing, resource extraction and, of course, transport. What is different about transport is that it cannot exist alone and a movement cannot be ② stored. An unsold product can remain on the shelf of a store until bought (often with discount incentives), but an unsold seat on a flight or unused cargo capacity in the same flight remains unsold and cannot be brought back as additional capacity ③ later. In this case an opportunity has been ④ seized, since the amount of transport being offered has exceeded the demand for it. The derived demand of transportation is often very difficult to reconcile with an equivalent supply, and actually transport companies would prefer to have some additional capacity to accommodate ⑤ unforeseen demand (often at much higher prices).

* reconcile: 조화시키다

2021학년도 7월 학평 30번

10. 다음 글의 밑줄 친 부분 중, 문맥상 낱말의 쓰임이 적절하지 않은 것은?

Prior to the Industrial Revolution, the ① quantity of freight transported between nations was negligible by contemporary standards. For instance, during the Middle Ages, the totality of French imports via the Saint-Gothard Passage would not fill a freight train. The amount of freight transported by the Venetian fleet, which dominated Mediterranean trade, would not fill a ② modern container ship. The volume, but not the speed, of trade improved under mercantilism, notably for maritime transportation. In spite of all, distribution capacities were very limited and speeds ③ slow. For example, a stagecoach going through the English countryside in the sixteenth century had an average speed of 2 miles per hour; moving one ton of cargo 30 miles inland in the United States by the late eighteenth century was as costly as moving it across the Atlantic. The inland transportation system was thus very ④ limited. By the late eighteenth century, canal systems started to emerge in Europe. They permitted the large movements of bulk freight inland and expanded regional trade. Maritime and riverine transportation were consequently the ⑤ outdated modes of the pre-industrial era.

* fleet: 선단, 배의 무리 ** mercantilism: 중상주의

2022학년도 6월 모평 30번

11. 다음 글의 밑줄 친 부분 중, 문맥상 낱말의 쓰임이 적절하지 않은 것은?

Sport can trigger an emotional response in its consumers of the kind rarely brought forth by other products. Imagine bank customers buying memorabilia to show loyalty to their bank, or consumers ① identifying so strongly with their car insurance company that they get a tattoo with its logo. We know that some sport followers are so ② passionate about players, teams and the sport itself that their interest borders on obsession. This addiction provides the emotional glue that binds fans to teams, and maintains loyalty even in the face of on-field ③ failure. While most managers can only dream of having customers that are as passionate about their products as sport fans, the emotion triggered by sport can also have a negative impact. Sport's emotional intensity can mean that organisations have strong attachments to the past through nostalgia and club tradition. As a result, they may ④ increase efficiency, productivity and the need to respond quickly to changing market conditions. For example, a proposal to change club colours in order to project a more attractive image may be ⑤ defeated because it breaks a link with tradition.

* memorabilia: 기념품 ** obsession: 집착

2022학년도 5월 종로 30번

12. 다음 글의 밑줄 친 부분 중, 문맥상 낱말의 쓰임이 적절하지 않은 것은? [3점]

Traditionally, the state has developed competition policy, driven by the idea that monopolies are bad and competition is good. Today's top technology companies already find themselves clashing with the authorities tasked with putting this policy into practice — because all of them ① aspire to monopoly power. This ambition is not unique to the world of technology. Look through the literature on management and strategy, and you will find plenty of ideas for ② achieving economic supremacy, packaged in the disarmingly benign-sounding language of business writing. Take Michael Porter, the definitive business strategy guru of the last few decades, whose 1980s books *Competitive Strategy* and *Competitive Advantage* were on the shelves of all discerning corporate leaders. Those books guided readers toward nothing less than economic ③ domination: first, find markets ripe for monopolizing (or create new ones); second, dominate and exclude others from these chosen markets. Today, the same advice is given even more ④ forthrightly. "Competition is for losers," wrote Peter Thiel, the entrepreneur, in the *Wall Street Journal*. "If you want to create and capture lasting value, look to build a ⑤ cooperation."

* benign: 상냥한 ** guru: 권위자

총 문항				문항		맞은 문항					문항	
개별 문항	1	2	3	4	5	6	7	8	9	10	11	12
채점												

어휘·숙어 비밀 노트

A 수능 필수 어휘 ▶ 철자가 혼동되는 어휘 (4)

□ 121	asset	n. 자산	assert	v. 단언하다
□ 122	assume	v. 추정하다, ~인체하다	consume	v. 소비하다
□ 123	attention	n. 배려, 관심, 주의	intention	n. 의도, 의향
□ 124	attribute	v. ~의 탓으로 돌리다	contribute	v. 공헌하다, 기부하다
□ 125	bald	a. 대머리	bold	a. 대범한
□ 126	banish	v. 추방하다, 내쫓다	vanish	v. 사라지다
□ 127	blow	v. 바람에 날리다	glow	n. 백열, 달아 오름
□ 128	concentrate	v. 집중하다	contaminate	v. 오염시키다
□ 129	consistent	a. 일관된	conscious	a. 의식하고 있는, 지각 있는
□ 130	convenience	n. 편의, 편리	consequences	n. 결과, 중요성
□ 131	counsel	n. 상담, 조언	council	n. 위원회
□ 132	deliberate	a. 신중한	delicate	a. 섬세한
□ 133	economic	a. 경제의	economics	a. 경제학
□ 134	eliminate	v. 제거하다	illuminate	v. 비추다, 밝히다
□ 135	emerging	a. 최근 생겨난	encouraging	a. 힘을 북돋워 주는
□ 136	enclose	v. 에워싸다, 둘러싸다	enhance	v. 높이다, 강화하다
□ 137	evolved	v. 진화시키다	involved	a. 복잡한, 뒤얽힌
□ 138	fraction	n. 조각, 파편	friction	n. 마찰
□ 139	gem	n. 보석	germ	n. 세균
□ 140	high	a. 높은; ad. 높이	highly	ad. 매우, 대단히

B 수능 필수 숙어

□ 141	be fed up with	~에 진저리가 나다
□ 142	be free of	~에서 자유롭다, ~이 없다
□ 143	be in charge of	~을 떠맡다, 담당하다, 책임지다
□ 144	be in control of	~을 관리하다
□ 145	be in fashion	유행하고 있다
□ 146	be known for	~으로 유명하다
□ 147	be on board	승선하다
□ 148	be likely to	~할 것 같다
□ 149	be said that	~라고 말해지다
□ 150	be short of	~이 부족하다
□ 151	be through	끝내다, ~와 관계를 끊다
□ 152	be to blame for	~에 대해 책임이 있다
□ 153	be tired of	~에 싫증이 나다
□ 154	be used to	~에 익숙하다(= get used to)
□ 155	be worth –ing	~할 가치가 있다
□ 156	bear fruit	열매를 맺다
□ 157	before long	곧(= soon)
□ 158	beware of	주의하다, 조심하다
□ 159	beyond one's power	능력밖인
□ 160	beyond description	말로 표현할 수 없을 정도인

동사의 시제

🏷 출제 트렌드

1. 1994-2023학년도 수능 기출 어법 문제를 분석한 결과, 동사의 시제 문제는 과거시제(2002, 2014학년도 수능) 문제가 다른 시제에 비해 상대적으로 출제 비율이 높았다.

2. 현재완료[진행형]를 써야 할지, 현재완료 수동태를 써야 할지 고르는 문제(2010[2013]학년도 수능)가 출제되기도 했다.

3. insist 뒤에 「should+동사원형」를 써야 할지, 아니면 직설법 시제를 써야 할지 묻는 문제(1997학년도 수능)가 출제되었다.

4. 또한 현재완료 시제(2004학년도 수능), 현재완료 시제의 3인칭 단수동사(2015학년도 수능), 현재진행형(2018학년도 수능), 현재완료 시제의 3인칭 복수동사(2018학년도 수능)가 선지로 출제되었다.

	출처	문항 번호	어법 · 어휘 문제
1	2014학년도 07월 학평	24번	부사 ago와 과거시제
2	2013학년도 수능	20번	현재완료진행형
3	2009학년도 03월 학평	21번	시간, 조건 부사절의 미래 표현
4	2007학년도 03월 학평	23번	과거완료진행형
5	2007학년도 09월 모평	21번	현재완료
6	2002학년도 수능	31번	과거를 나타낸 부사구와 과거시제
7	1997학년도 수능	20번	insist+[(should+동사원형) vs. 직설법]
8	2018학년도 06월 종로	28번	역사적 사실은 과거시제로 표현
9	2021학년도 04월 학평	30번	어휘 문제 01
10	2021학년도 03월 학평	30번	어휘 문제 02
11	2021학년도 수능	30번	어휘 문제 03
12	2022학년도 04월 종로	30번	어휘 문제 04

🏷 1등급 꿀팁

1. 과거를 나타내는 부사(ago)나 시간 부사구가 있는 경우, 현재완료형을 쓰지 않고 현재시제를 쓰는 것을 유의해야 한다.

2. 시간, 조건 부사절에서 미래를 나타내고 싶을 경우, 미래시제 대신 현재시제를 쓰는 것을 유의해야 한다.

3. 과거시제를 나타낼 때 함께 쓰는 부사(구) 표현(yesterday, ago, last week)을 유의한다.

4. 과거 이전의 사실을 나타내려면 과거완료형을 사용한다는 것을 유의한다.

[핵심 문법]

A 출제 POINT

1. 현재시제는 현재의 습관, 일반적인 사실, 진리, 장기간 지속되는 동작을 표현한다. 과학적 사실과 진리는 주절의 동사에 상관없이 현재형으로 표현한다. 단순현재형은 장기간 지속되는 동작을, 현재진행형은 잠시 지속되는 동작을 나타낸다. 진행형은 원칙적으로 동작을 표시하는 동사이므로 지각동사(see, hear 등), 소유동사(have, belong), 인식동사(know, remember 등)와 같은 동사에는 진행형을 쓸 수 없다.

▶ Newton believed that gravity **[caused / causes]** objects to fall.

2. 시간과 조건을 나타내는 부사절은 미래 의미를 현재시제로 나타낸다. 명사절은 미래 의미를 나타내는 경우, 미래시제로 표현한다.

▶ Sam will be happy when Sally **[shows / will show]** up to the party.

3. 과거시제는 과거의 동작, 상태, 습관을 표현하며, 과거를 뚜렷하게 나타내는 부사(구)(ago, yesterday, last week ~)가 있는 문장은 현재완료가 아닌, 과거시제로 나타내야 한다.

▶ He **[have met / met]** her last week and they fell in love at first sight.

4. 현재완료형은 과거의 행위나 상태가 현재에 미치는 경우 사용한다.

▶ Sally has **[gone / been]** to London. She is not here now.

5. 과거완료형은 과거 이전에 일어난 일(대과거)에 대해서 말하거나, 대과거에 일어난 일이 과거의 어느 한 시점에 영향을 미칠 때 사용된다.

▶ When she returned home, Sally discovered that she **[had lost / lost]** her door key.

6. 미래를 표현하는 구문에는 단순미래형, 미래진행형, 미래완료형 등이 있다. 특히 미래의 특정 시점까지 계속을 나타내고 싶을 때는 미래완료형이 사용된다. 또한 일정상 확실한 미래는 현재형이나 현재진행형으로 미래를 나타낼 수 있다.

▶ By this Sunday Becky and I **[will have been / will be]** together for 100 days.

7. 시제 일치는 예외가 있다. 원칙상, 주절의 시제가 과거이면 시제일치의 원칙에 따라 종속절은 과거나 과거완료로만 쓸 수 있다. 그러나 시제일치에 상관없이 불변의 진리나 현재 습관, 상태는 현재시제로 나타내며, 역사적 사실은 과거시제로 나타낸다. 또한 주절에 주장(insist), 제안(suggest), 요구(demand), 명령(order) 등의 동사가 나오면 that이 이끄는 종속절은 「(should+)동사원형」으로 표현한다. 단, 실제로 발생한 단순한 사실을 전달할 때는 문장의 수와 시제에 맞춰 써야 한다.

▶ I was taught the French revolution **[had broken out / broke out]** in 1789.

B 체크 POINT

다음 괄호 안에서 어법상 올바른 것을 고르시오.

1. Water boils at 100°C and **[froze / freezes]** at 0°C.

2. By the time Sally **[will get / gets]** home, her father will have left for Paris.

3. The movie **[have started / started]** about 5 minutes ago.

4. He was supposed to be here half an hour ago, but he **[hadn't shown / hasn't shown]** up yet.

5. They **[hadn't / haven't]** made a reservation, so they didn't get a table.

6. The plane **[leaves / left]** for Paris at 9 0'clock tonight.

7. Galileo believed that the earth **[moves / moved]** around the sun.

•어법 기출•

제한 시간 : 13분   정답 및 해설 025쪽

2014학년도 7월 학평 24번

1. 다음 글의 밑줄 친 부분 중, 어법상 틀린 것은?

  Not many years ago, schoolchildren were taught that carbon dioxide is the ①<u>naturally</u> occurring lifeblood of plants, just as oxygen is ours. Today, children are more likely to think of carbon dioxide as a poison. That's because the amount of carbon dioxide in the atmosphere ②<u>has increased</u> substantially over the past one hundred years, from about 280 parts per million to 380. But what people don't know is that the carbon dioxide level some 80 million years ago—back when our mammalian ancestors were evolving—③<u>to be</u> at least 1,000 parts per million. In fact, that is the concentration of carbon dioxide you regularly breathe if you work in a new energy-efficient office building, for ④<u>that</u> is the level established by the engineering group that sets standards for heating and ventilation systems. So not only ⑤<u>is</u> carbon dioxide plainly not poisonous, but changes in carbon dioxide levels don't necessarily mirror human activity. Nor has atmospheric carbon dioxide necessarily been the trigger for global warming historically.

2013학년도 수능 20번

2. (A), (B), (C)의 각 네모 안에서 어법에 맞는 표현으로 가장 적절한 것은?

  In many countries, amongst younger people, the habit of reading newspapers has been on the decline and some of the dollars previously (A) spent / were spent on newspaper advertising have migrated to the Internet. Of course some of this decline in newspaper reading has been due to the fact that we are doing more of our newspaper reading online. We can read the news of the day, or the latest on business, entertainment or (B) however / whatever news on the websites of the *New York Times*, the *Guardian* or almost any other major newspaper in the world. Increasingly, we can access these stories wirelessly by mobile devices as well as our computers. Advertising dollars have simply been (C) followed / following the migration trail across to these new technologies.

	(A)		(B)		(C)
①	spent	……	however	……	followed
②	spent	……	whatever	……	following
③	were spent	……	however	……	following
④	were spent	……	whatever	……	followed
⑤	were spent	……	whatever	……	following

2009학년도 3월 학평 21번

3. (A), (B), (C)의 각 네모 안에서 어법에 맞는 표현으로 가장 적절한 것은?

  If properly stored, broccoli will stay fresh for up to four days. The best way to store fresh bunches (A) is / are to refrigerate them in an open plastic bag in the vegetable compartment, which will give them the right balance of humidity and air, and help preserve the vitamin C content. Don't wash the broccoli before storing it since moisture on its surface (B) encourages / to encourage the growth of mold. However, like most vegetables, it is at its best condition when used within a day or two after the purchase. Preparing broccoli is extremely easy, so all you have to do is boil it in water just until it (C) is / will be tender, three to five minutes.

	(A)		(B)		(C)
①	is	…	encourages	…	is
②	is	…	to encourage	…	will be
③	is	…	encourages	…	will be
④	are	…	to encourage	…	will be
⑤	are	…	encourages	…	is

2007학년도 3월 학평 23번

4. (A), (B), (C)의 각 네모 안에서 어법에 맞는 표현으로 가장 적절한 것은?

  One day last summer when I was in the bathroom, the lock on the door jammed. I couln't get it unlocked (A) how / however hard I tried. I thoughted about my predicament. I didn't think the neighbors could hear me if I shouted. Then I remembered the small window on the back wall. The basin (B) near / nearly the window provided an easy step up. After climbing out the window, I hung from the window sill for a few seconds and then easily dropped to the ground. Later my mother came home and asked me what I (C) have / had been doing. Laughing, I responded, "Oh, just hanging around."

*predicament: 곤경

	(A)		(B)		(C)
①	how	……	near	……	have
②	how	……	nearly	……	had
③	how	……	near	……	have
④	however	……	nearly	……	have
⑤	however	……	near	……	had

5. (A), (B), (C)의 각 네모 안에서 어법에 맞는 표현을 골라 짝지은 것으로 가장 적절한 것은?

Our basic nature is to act, and not to be acted upon. Not only does this enable us to choose our response to particular circumstances, but this encourages us to (A) create / creating circumstances. Taking the initiative means recognizing our responsibility to make things happen. Over the years, I (B) am / have frequently counseled people who wanted better jobs to show more initiative. The response is usually agreement. Most people can see (C) what / how powerfully such an approach would affect their opportunities for employment or advancement.

	(A)		(B)		(C)
①	create	----	have	----	what
②	create	----	am	----	how
③	create	----	have	----	how
④	creating	----	am	----	what
⑤	creating	----	have	----	what

6. 다음 글에서 밑줄 친 부분 중, 어법상 틀린 것은?

Former U.S. President Jimmy Carter, ① who promotes Habitat or Humanity, has toured various countries ② since 1994. In the summer of 2001, he ③ has visited Asan, Korea, to participate in a house-building project. It was part of Habitat for Humanity International's campaign ④ to build houses for homeless people. He worked along with volunteers for the program, which is ⑤ named after him—the Jimmy Carter Work Project 2001.

7. 다음 글의 흐름으로 보아, 어법상 적절하지 <u>않은</u> 문장은?

① One day a truck hit a pedestrian on the street. ② The driver argued that the careless pedestrian was to blame for the accident. ③ It was difficult to determine exactly where the accident had taken place. ④ Many witnesses insisted that the accident should take place on the crosswalk. ⑤ So, the driver was held responsible for the accident.

8. 다음 글의 밑줄 친 부분 중, 어법상 틀린 것은? [3점]

We should not be too surprised when we discover ① that self-help techniques and well-meaning advice don't necessarily deliver the changes they promise. The bottom line is that often the techniques don't work simply because there is no reason why ② they should. There is precious little quality control in the world of self-help, ③ where conviction is all too often a willing stand-in for reasonable proof. The biologist Thomas Huxley once stated that "The deepest sin against the human mind is to believe things without evidence." If he is right, the self-help section of the bookstore is truly sinful. We may roll our eyes at the medical practices of times gone by, when drilling holes in people's heads ④ to be seen as the best way of letting out the demons. But while contemporary remedies for the mental and emotional ills of our age may be less dramatic, many of our own psychological cures and theories boast ⑤ scarcely more scientific validity.

*stand-in: 대역
**boast: 자랑할 만한 ~을 갖고 있다

제한 시간 : 7분   정답 및 해설 028쪽

2021학년도 4월 학평 30번

9. 다음 글의 밑줄 친 부분 중, 문맥상 낱말의 쓰임이 적절하지 않은 것은?

It's likely that for a very long time people managed to survive with draped animal pelts and then began roughly sewing these together. Ultimately, though, the ① advantages of using woven fabric for clothing would have become obvious. A fur pelt offers ② inadequate thermal protection if someone is sitting still, but once on the move or in strong winds, this is less true, because pelts aren't shaped close to the body. The more air gets between the body and the clothing, the less effective it is at trapping an insulating layer of air close to the skin. In fact, the insulating properties of clothing ③ decrease very much when walking quickly. Clothing also needs to be breathable, because damp clothes are bad at keeping the wearer warm and become very heavy. Woven fabrics are more breathable than fur and, when specifically tailored to the body, make excellent internal layers, ④ preventing cold air from getting direct access to the skin's surface. Thus the ability to create woven clothing would have offered material advantages to our early ancestors once they had left Africa for ⑤ cooler areas.

* drape: 걸치다 ** thermal: 열의 *** insulate: 단열하다

2021학년도 3월 학평 30번

10. 다음 글의 밑줄 친 부분 중, 문맥상 낱말의 쓰임이 적절하지 않은 것은? [3점]

Those who limit themselves to Western scientific research have virtually ① ignored anything that cannot be perceived by the five senses and repeatedly measured or quantified. Research is dismissed as superstitious and invalid if it cannot be scientifically explained by cause and effect. Many continue to ② object with an almost religious passion to this cultural paradigm about the power of science — more specifically, the power that science gives them. By dismissing non-Western scientific paradigms as inferior at best and inaccurate at worst, the most rigid members of the conventional medical research community try to ③ counter the threat that alternative therapies and research pose to their work, their well-being, and their worldviews. And yet, biomedical research cannot explain many of the phenomena that ④ concern alternative practitioners regarding caring-healing processes. When therapies such as acupuncture or homeopathy are observed to result in a physiological or clinical response that cannot be explained by the biomedical model, many have tried to ⑤ deny the results rather than modify the scientific model.

* acupuncture: 침술 ** homeopathy: 동종 요법

2021학년도 수능 30번

11. 다음 글의 밑줄 친 부분 중, 문맥상 낱말의 쓰임이 적절하지 않은 것은?

How the bandwagon effect occurs is demonstrated by the history of measurements of the speed of light. Because this speed is the basis of the theory of relativity, it's one of the most frequently and carefully measured ① quantities in science. As far as we know, the speed hasn't changed over time. However, from 1870 to 1900, all the experiments found speeds that were too high. Then, from 1900 to 1950, the ② opposite happened — all the experiments found speeds that were too low! This kind of error, where results are always on one side of the real value, is called "bias." It probably happened because over time, experimenters subconsciously adjusted their results to ③ match what they expected to find. If a result fit what they expected, they kept it. If a result didn't fit, they threw it out. They weren't being intentionally dishonest, just ④ influenced by the conventional wisdom. The pattern only changed when someone ⑤ lacked the courage to report what was actually measured instead of what was expected.

* bandwagon effect: 편승 효과

2022학년도 4월 종로 30번

12. 다음 글의 밑줄 친 부분 중, 문맥상 낱말의 쓰임이 적절하지 않은 것은? [3점]

A potential explanation for negative spillover is single action bias. Single action bias shows that some people, in situations of uncertainty and risk, tend to ① simplify their decision-making and focus on a single action. Thus, consumers responding to a threat, such as potential environmental damage or negative social impact, are likely to focus on a single action, irrespective of whether the action taken is the most ② effective option — or would benefit from further actions being taken. The failure to engage in further or other actions is likely to occur as a result of the ③ success of the first action. As the first action is removing the cognitive dissonance or worry experienced, following actions are no longer needed to ④ restore cognitive balance. In other words, individuals following single action bias may feel as if they are doing enough, and are thus doing without other actions that would be beneficial. For example, individuals may switch to energy efficient light bulbs in their home, and feel that this single action is ⑤ insufficient.

* spillover: (어떤 일의) 여파 ** cognitive dissonance: 인지 부조화

총 문항					문항		맞은 문항				문항	
개별 문항	1	2	3	4	5	6	7	8	9	10	11	12
채점												

어휘·숙어 비밀 노트

A 수능 필수 어휘 ▶ 철자가 혼동되는 어휘 (5)

□	No.	단어	뜻	단어	뜻
□	161	alternation	n. 교체, 교대	alternative	n. 양자택일, 대안
□	162	infinite	a. 무한한, 끝없는	definite	a. 뚜렷한
□	163	inhibit	v. 억제, 제어하다	inhabit	v. 거주하다
□	164	jealous	a. 질투가 많은	zealous	a. 열심인, 열광적인
□	165	medication	n. 약물	meditation	n. 명상
□	166	momentary	a. 순간적인	momentous	a. 중요한
□	167	natural	a. 자연의	neutral	a. 중립의
□	168	objective	n. 목표, 목적	objection	n. 반대
□	169	preferred	a. 선취권이 있는	prepared	a. 준비되어 있는
□	170	principal	a. 주요한; n. 교장, 원금	principle	n. 원리, 원칙
□	171	quite	ad. 아주, 완전히	quiet	a. 고요한
□	172	shortage	n. 부족, 결핍	strength	n. 강점, 힘
□	173	sit	v. 앉다	seat	v. 앉히다
□	174	stain	n. 얼룩, 때, 반점	strain	n. 긴장
□	175	statue	n. 조상, 상	status	n. 지위
□	176	enclose	v. 둘러싸다	enhance	v. 높이다, 강화하다
□	177	stale	a. 신선하지 않은	stable	a. 안정된, 견실한
□	178	support	v. 유지하다, 받치다	manipulate	v. 교묘하게 다루다
□	179	thorough	a. 철저한, 완전한	through	prep. ~을 통하여
□	180	valuable	a. 귀중한	invaluable	a. 매우 귀중한(= priceless)

B 수능 필수 숙어

□	No.	숙어	뜻
□	181	boast of	~을 자랑하다, 뽐내다
□	182	break down	부수다, 고장나다
□	183	break into	침입하다, (대화) 방해하다
□	184	break off	갑자기 그만두다
□	185	break out	발생하다, 발발하다
□	186	break up	부수다, (관계를) 끝내다, 해산시키다
□	187	break (up) with	관계를 끊다, 절교하다
□	188	breathe in	숨을 들이마시다
□	189	bring about	초래하다, 야기하다(= cause)
□	190	bring back	돌려주다, 기억나게 하다
□	191	bring down	(짐을) 내리다, 낮추다, 줄이다
□	192	bring out	발휘되게 하다, 눈에 띄게 만들다
□	193	bring ~ to light	밝히다, 폭로하다
□	194	bring to an end	끝내다, 끝나다
□	195	bring up	~을 기르다, (의견, 문제 등을) 꺼내다
□	196	burst into	갑자기 ~하기 시작하다
□	197	but for	~을 제외하고, ~이 없다면(없었더라면)
□	198	by and large	전반적으로, 대체로
□	199	by degrees	서서히, 조금씩, 점차로
□	200	by far	단연코

조동사

출제 트렌드

1. 조동사는 본동사와 함께 쓰여, 본동사의 의미를 보충해 주는 역할을 한다.

2. 1994-2023학년도 수능 기출 어법 문제를 분석한 결과, 과거 이전의 일에 대한 유감을 나타낼 때 사용하는 「조동사 +have+p.p.」 표현(1994학년도 1차 수능, 1999학년도 수능)이 출제되었다.

3. 주장(insist)이나 제안(suggest), 요구(demand), 명령(order)을 나타내는 동사가 '아직 사실이 아닌 것 혹은 실현되지 않은 것'을 나타낼 때는 that절에서 「조동사 should+동사원형」을 쓰는데, 실제로 발생한 일을 나타낼 때는 직설법을 사용해야 한다는 것이 출제(1997학년도 수능(28쪽 7번 참조))되었다.

4. 또한 「had better+동사원형」 구문(2007학년도 수능(70쪽 7번 참조))이 선지로 출제되었다.

출처	문항 번호	어법·어휘 문제
1 2022학년도 06월 모평	21번 변형	「used to + 동사원형」
2 2021학년도 04월 학평	20번 변형	will be able to vs. will can
3 2021학년도 03월 학평	32번 변형	may have p.p.
4 2013학년도 04월 학평	26번 변형	「suggest +[should+동사원형]」
5 2011학년도 03월 학평	20번	may have p.p.
6 2008학년도 07월 학평	21번	「must + 동사원형」 vs. must have p.p.
7 1999학년도 수능	34번	should have p.p.
8 2017학년도 04월 종로	28번	「조동사+have+p.p.」의 병렬 구조
9 2020학년도 10월 학평	30번	어휘 문제 01
10 2021학년도 09월 모평	30번	어휘 문제 02
11 2020학년도 07월 학평	30번	어휘 문제 03
12 2021학년도 11월 종로	30번	어휘 문제 04

1등급 꿀팁

1. 조동사는 완료형과 결합하여 과거의 추측이나 과거의 일에 대한 유감, 비난을 나타내는 것을 유의한다.

2. 주장, 제안, 요구, 명령을 나타내는 동사는 that 절에서 주어 다음에 「should+동사원형」을 쓰거나, 조동사 없이 동사원형을 쓰지만, 단순한 사실을 전달할 때는 문장의 수와 시제에 맞춰 써야 한다.

[핵심 문법]

정답 및 해설 030쪽

A 출제 POINT

1. 조동사는 몇 가지 특성과 의미 차이가 있다. 조동사 뒤에는 동사원형을 써야 하며, 조동사는 두 개를 나란히 쓸 수 없다. must not은 '~해서는 안 된다'는 의미이며 'don't have to'는 '~할 필요가 없다'는 의미이다.

▶ You [**will can** / **will be able to**] do your homework.

2. 준동사와 같은 표현이 있다. 이것들은 조동사처럼 뒤에 동사원형을 쓰며 동사의 의미를 보충해 준다.

ought to	~해야 한다	used to	하곤 했다, 이전에는 ~했었다
had better	~하는 편이 낫다	be supposed to	~하기로 되어 있다
cf. be used+ to 부정사 : ~하기 위해 사용되다 cf. be used to + 동명사 : ~하는 데 익숙하다			

▶ You had better [**to tell** / **tell**] him that you won't be able to come to his party.

3. 조동사는 완료형과 결합하여 과거의 일에 대한 유감, 비난이나 과거의 추측 등을 나타낸다.

should[ought to] have p.p.	~했어야 했는데	shouldn't have p.p.	~하지 않았어야 했는데
must have p.p.	~했음에 틀림없다	cannot have p.p.	~했을 리가 없다
may have p.p.	~했을지도 모른다	need not have p.p.	~할 필요가 없었는데

▶ I regret having paid little attention to him. In other words, I [**should be paid** / **should have paid**] more attention to him.

4. 제안, 명령, 요구, 주장의 의미를 갖는 동사(suggest, order, demand, insist 등) 다음의 that절에서 주어 다음에 「(should+) 동사원형」이 쓰인다. 단, 실제로 발생한 단순한 사실을 전달할 때는 문장의 수와 시제에 맞춰 써야 한다.

▶ She suggested to me that I [**took** / **take**] some rest away from work.

5. 관용적으로 쓰이는 조동사 구문을 익힌다.

may well	~하는 것도 당연하다	may as well	~하는 것이 낫다
cannot but	~하지 않을 수 없다	would rather A than B	B보다 A 하고 싶다

▶ I cannot but [**point** / **pointed**] that we continue to face a reality.

6. had better를 부정할 때는 바로 뒤에 not을 쓴다.

▶ You'd better [**wake not** / **not wake**] Billy up when you come in.

7. 조동사 may와 can의 과거형 might와 could는 과거의 의미를 나타내기보다는 좀 더 불확실한 추측을 나타낸다. 하지만 주절이 과거인 경우, 시제 일치의 규칙에 따라 종속절에는 might와 could를 사용한다.

▶ He asked me if he [**may** / **might**] come to see me that evening.

B 체크 POINT

다음 괄호 안에서 어법상 올바른 것을 고르시오.

1. That will [**do** / **did**] beautifully.

2. He used to [**smoke** / **smoking**] a pipe; now he smokes e-cigarettes.

3. She [**needn't have cooked** / **don't need to cook**] so much food, but she cooked so much food.

4. He suggested that the conference [**should be** / **is**] put off.

5. I would rather walk the 5 miles to school than [**to ride** / **ride**] the bus again.

6. You don't look very well. You'd better [**not go** / **go not**] to work today.

7. Tom said that she [**may** / **might**] be twenty nine the following year.

2022학년도 6월 모평 21번 변형

1. 다음 글의 밑줄 친 부분 중, 어법상 틀린 것은?

The single most important change you can make in your working habits ① is to switch to creative work first, reactive work second. This means ② blocking off a large chunk of time every day for creative work on your own priorities, with the phone and e-mail off. I used to ③ being a frustrated writer. Making this switch turned me into a productive writer. Yet there wasn't a single day when I sat down to write an article, blog post, or book chapter without a string of people waiting for me to get back to them. It wasn't easy, and it still isn't, particularly when I get phone messages beginning "I sent you an e-mail two hours ago...!" By definition, this approach goes against the grain of others' expectations and the pressures they put on you. It takes willpower to switch off the world, even for an hour. It feels ④ uncomfortable, and sometimes people get upset. But it's better to disappoint a few people over small things, than ⑤ to abandon your dreams for an empty inbox. Otherwise, you're sacrificing your potential for the illusion of professionalism.

2021학년도 4월 학평 20번 변형

2. 다음 글의 밑줄 친 부분 중, 어법상 틀린 것은?

More often than not, modern parents are paralyzed by the fear that they will no longer be liked or even ① loved by their children if they scold them for any reason. They want their children's friendship above all, and are willing to sacrifice respect to get it. ② This is not good. A child will have many friends, but only two parents — if that — and parents are more, not less, than friends. Friends have very limited authority ③ to correct. Every parent therefore needs to learn to tolerate the momentary anger or even hatred ④ directed toward them by their children, after necessary corrective action has been taken, as the capacity of children to perceive or care about long-term consequences is very limited. Parents are the judges of society. They teach children how to behave so that other people ⑤ will can interact meaningfully and productively with them.

2021학년도 3월 학평 32번 변형

3. 다음 글의 밑줄 친 부분 중, 어법상 틀린 것은?

Jeffrey A. Rodgers, a vice president of a big company, was once taught the simple idea of pausing to refresh. It began when Jeff realized that as he drove home from work each evening his mind was ① still focused on work-related projects. We all know this feeling. We ② may had left the office physically, but we are very much still there mentally, as our minds get caught in the endless loop of replaying the events of today and ③ worrying about all the things we need to get done the following day. So now, as he gets to the door of his house, he applies what he calls "the pause that refreshes." He stops for just a moment. He closes his eyes. He breathes in and out once: deeply and slowly. As he exhales, he lets the work issues ④ fall away. This allows him ⑤ to walk through the front door to his family with more singleness of purpose. It supports the sentiment attributed to Lao Tzu: "In work, do what you enjoy. In family life, be completely present."

* loop: 루프(반복 실행되는 일련의 명령)

2013학년도 4월 학평 26번 변형

4. 다음 글의 밑줄 친 부분 중, 어법상 틀린 것은?

Sonya asked for my advice about her five-year-old child's separation anxiety. "Anna wants to be with me at all times," she said. In Anna's case, there was an early attempt ① to leave her at a nice, small preschool for half days. She seemed to enjoy the school, but was having a hard time ② departing from her mother in the morning. "She was fearful and ③ clingy and, over time, she started to be more whiny at home and less happy," her mother said. I suggested that she ④ stops taking her to preschool. The result was immediate and dramatic: "I got my child back," Sonya said. "She is happy again and self-engaged, but she is still unable to be away from me." Anna will regain her trust and confidence. She needs time ⑤ in which there is no reminder of her experience of separation from her mother.

5. 다음 글의 밑줄 친 부분 중, 어법상 틀린 것은?

Archaeologist Mark Aldenderfer set out last year to explore remote cliffside caves in Nepal's Mustang district, aiming to find human remains near an ancient settlement ① high in the Himalayas. Almost at once, he came face-to-face with ② what he was seeking: Sticking out from the rock, a skull was looking at him right ③ as he was looking at it. The skull, dating back perhaps 2,500 years, was among many human bones ④ piled inside several burial caves. Aldenderfer and his team hope that DNA analysis will pinpoint the origins of this isolated region's inhabitants, who may ⑤ migrate from the Tibetan Plateau or southern points.

6. (A), (B), (C)의 각 네모 안에서 어법에 맞는 표현으로 가장 적절한 것은?

There are several events that take place while jury selection is proceeding. First, everyone who has been summoned to appear at jury duty must (A) | arrive / have arrived | by nine o'clock in the morning and assemble in the jury room. A few minutes later, the court clerk usually shows a movie (B) | outlined / outlining | what is going to happen throughout the day as the jury is chosen for a particular trial. At around ten o'clock, twenty people are chosen from the jurors in attendance and are taken to a courtroom where a judge describes (C) | how / what | the process is going to work. About thirty minutes later, ten people are called to sit in the jury box to be questioned by the lawyers in the case.

	(A)	(B)	(C)
①	arrive	…… outlined	…… what
②	arrive	…… outlining	…… how
③	arrive	…… outlining	…… what
④	have arrived	…… outlining	…… how
⑤	have arrived	…… outlined	…… what

7. 다음 글의 흐름으로 보아, 밑줄 친 부분 중 어법상 자연스럽지 못한 것은?

It is often believed that the function of school is ① to produce knowledgeable people. If schools ② only provide knowledge, however, they may destroy creativity, ③ producing ordinary people. We often ④ hear stories of ordinary people who, if education had focused on creativity, could have become great artists or scientists. Those victims of education ⑤ should receive training to develop creative talents while in school. It really is a pity that they did not.

8. 다음 글의 밑줄 친 부분 중, 어법상 틀린 것은? [3점]

I was on vacation at the Disneyland Resort, ① which had a fantastic fitness center with some state-of-the-art strength-training equipment I'd never used before. I was ② fascinated by the hip-muscle weight machine; I just had to try it. But I started with weights that were too heavy, and I went too fast. I limped for two days after that. A safer approach would have been to start with a lower weight, do fewer repetitions, and do slower movements for a shorter time. I could have come back in two days and ③ increase the intensity of my workout. I had used (or abused) my hip muscles in ways I never had before and paid the painful price. If you are just beginning a strength program, words to keep in mind are *thoughtful*, *slow*, and *gradual*. Older muscles are more ④ easily injured if you do too much too fast. If you lift improperly and tear or injure a muscle, it usually takes at least six weeks ⑤ to heal, which is quite a setback. It's not worth the risk of injury.

제한 시간 : 7분　　　　　정답 및 해설 033쪽

9. 다음 글의 밑줄 친 부분 중, 문맥상 낱말의 쓰임이 적절하지 않은 것은?

In collectivist groups, there is considerable emphasis on relationships, the maintenance of harmony, and "sticking with" the group. Members of collectivist groups are socialized to avoid conflict, to ① empathize with others, and to avoid drawing attention to themselves. In contrast, members of individualist cultures tend to define themselves in terms of their independence from groups and autonomy and are socialized to ② value individual freedoms and individual expressions. In individualist cultures, standing out and being different is often seen as a sign of ③ weakness. Implicit in the characterization of collectivist and individualist groups is the assumption that deviance will be ④ downgraded more in groups that prescribe collectivism than in groups that prescribe individualism. Indeed, empirical research shows that individualist group norms broaden the latitude of ⑤ acceptable group member behavior and non-normative characteristics.

* deviance: 일탈, 표준에서 벗어남

10. 다음 글의 밑줄 친 부분 중, 문맥상 낱말의 쓰임이 적절하지 않은 것은?

If I say to you, 'Don't think of a white bear', you will find it difficult not to think of a white bear. In this way, 'thought suppression can actually increase the thoughts one wishes to suppress instead of calming them'. One common example of this is that people on a diet who try not to think about food often begin to think much ① more about food. This process is therefore also known as the *rebound effect*. The ② ironic effect seems to be caused by the interplay of two related cognitive processes. This dual-process system involves, first, an intentional operating process, which consciously attempts to locate thoughts ③ unrelated to the suppressed ones. Second, and simultaneously, an unconscious monitoring process tests whether the operating system is functioning effectively. If the monitoring system encounters thoughts inconsistent with the intended ones, it prompts the intentional operating process to ensure that these are replaced by ④ inappropriate thoughts. However, it is argued, the intentional operating system can fail due to increased cognitive load caused by fatigue, stress and emotional factors, and so the monitoring process filters the inappropriate thoughts into consciousness, making them highly ⑤ accessible.

11. 다음 글의 밑줄 친 부분 중, 문맥상 낱말의 쓰임이 적절하지 않은 것은?

At a time when concerns about overpopulation and famine were reaching their highest peak, Garrett Hardin did not blame these problems on human ① ignorance — a failure to take note of dwindling per capita food supplies, for example. Instead, his explanation focused on the discrepancy between the ② interests of individual households and those of society as a whole. To understand excessive reproduction as a tragedy of the commons, bear in mind that a typical household stands to gain from bringing another child into the world — in terms of the net contributions he or she makes to ③ household earnings, for example. But while parents can be counted on to assess how the well-being of their household is affected by additional offspring, they ④ overvalue other impacts of population growth, such as diminished per capita food supplies for other people. In other words, the costs of reproduction are largely ⑤ shared, rather than being shouldered entirely by individual households. As a result, reproduction is excessive.

* dwindling: 줄어드는

12. 다음 글의 밑줄 친 부분 중, 문맥상 낱말의 쓰임이 적절하지 않은 것은? [3점]

History suggests that change happens in much more dialectical ways than futurology usually recognizes. Changes bring out other changes. Trends generate countertrends. New concentrations of power prompt coalitions and campaigns to ① weaken them. As a result, simple linear forecasts in which technologies just wipe out jobs are ② misleading. This is partly a matter of economics. To the extent that robots or smart tools do replace existing jobs, relative price effects will kick in. Those sectors where productivity dramatically increases will see price reductions, and spending will shift over to other fields that are ③ harder to automate, such as personal coaches, tour guides, teachers, care workers, and craft workers. Their relative price will probably ④ fall. Labor markets have proven to be dynamic over the last two centuries, coping with massive destruction of jobs and equally massive creation, too. There is no obvious reason why a much more automated society would necessarily have ⑤ fewer jobs.

* dialectical: 변증법적인　　** futurology: 미래학
*** kick in: (효과가) 나타나기 시작하다

총 문항					문항	맞은 문항					문항	
개별 문항	1	2	3	4	5	6	7	8	9	10	11	12
채점												

어휘·숙어 비밀 노트

A 수능 필수 어휘 ▶ 반의어 (1)

☐ 201	ability	n. 능력	inability	n. 무능력
☐ 202	abnormal	a. 비정상적인	normal	a. 정상적인
☐ 203	absence	a. 결석	presence	n. 출석
☐ 204	absorb	v. 흡수하다	release	v. 방출하다
☐ 205	accelerate	v. 가속하다	decelerate	v. 감속하다
☐ 206	accept	v. 수락하다	refuse	v. 거절하다(= reject)
☐ 207	accurate	a. 정확한	inaccurate	a. 정확하지 않은
☐ 208	active	a. 활동적인	passive	a. 소극적인(= inactive)
☐ 209	adequate	a. 충분한	inadequate	a. 불충분한
☐ 210	aggressive	a. 공격적인	defensive	a. 방어적인
☐ 211	allow	v. 허용하다	prohibit	v. 금지하다
☐ 212	ally	n. 동맹국, 협력자	opponent	n. 적, 반대자
☐ 213	animate	a. 살아있는	inanimate	a. 죽은, 생기 없는
☐ 214	appropriate	a. 적절한	inappropriate	a. 부적당한
☐ 215	approve	v. 승인하다	disapprove	v. 불허하다
☐ 216	assemble	v. 조립하다	disassemble	v. 해체하다
☐ 217	attach	v. 붙이다	detach	v. 떼다
☐ 218	available	a. 이용할 수 있는	unavailable	a. 이용할 수 없는
☐ 219	backward	ad. 뒤로, 거꾸로	forward	ad. 앞으로
☐ 220	attraction	n. 끌림, 매력	distraction	n. 집중을 방해하는 것

B 수능 필수 숙어

☐ 221	by itself	저절로, 혼자
☐ 222	by nature	본래, 선천적으로
☐ 223	by no means	결코 ~이 아닌(= never)
☐ 224	call for	~을 요구하다, ~을 큰 소리로 부르다
☐ 225	call on	요청하다, 방문하다
☐ 226	call out	큰 소리로 외치다, (사람 등을) 부르다
☐ 227	can afford	~할 여유가 있다
☐ 228	cannot help but + 동사원형	~하지 않을 수 없다 (= cannot help - ing)
☐ 229	cannot wait to ~	~하기를 몹시 바라다
☐ 230	care about	~에 마음 쓰다 ~에 관심을 가지다
☐ 231	carry off	잘 해내다
☐ 232	carry out	이행하다, 완수하다
☐ 233	catch a cold	감기에 걸리다
☐ 234	catch one's yes	~의 눈길을 끌다
☐ 235	catch up with	따라가다, 따라잡다
☐ 236	clear A of B	A에게서 B를 제거하다
☐ 237	check in	투숙[탑승] 절차를 밟다
☐ 238	come about	(일, 사건 등이) 발생하다, 일어나다
☐ 239	come across	이해되다, 인상을 주다, ~을 우연히 만나다
☐ 240	come along	나타나다, 동행하다, 나아지다

 07 수동태

🏷️ 출제 트렌드

1. 수동태는 동작의 주체가 아니라 대상이 되며, 기본 형태가 「be+p.p.」임을 유의해야 한다.

2. 1994-2023학년도 수능 기출 어법 문제를 분석한 결과, 수동태가 될 수 없는 자동사 문제(1994학년도 수능 1차), 수동태와 능동태 구분 문제(1994년 2차, 1998학년도 수능), to부정사의 수동태(2005학년도 수능) 문제가 출제되었다.

3. 능동태 현재완료형과 수동태 현재완료형을 제시하고, 능동태 현재완료형을 고르는 문제(2009학년도 수능)도 출제되기도 했다.

4. 도치된 문장에서 수동태 be동사의 단·복수형을 고르는 문제(2012학년도 수능)도 출제되었다.

5. 또한 수동태 문제(2001, 2002, 2006, 2007, 2017학년도 수능)가 선지로 출제되었다.

	출처	문항 번호	어법·어휘 문제
1	2022학년도 10월 학평	29번	능동태 vs. 수동태
2	2017학년도 06월 모평	28번	관계사절 안의 수동태
3	2015학년도 10월 학평	20번	to부정사의 능동태 vs. 수동태
4	2012학년도 수능	21번	도치문장의 수동태 be동사
5	2008학년도 09월 모평	22번	조동사 및 지각동사의 수동태
6	2007학년도 04월 학평	22번	be laid vs. be lain
7	2006학년도 10월 학평	21번	현재진행형의 수동태
8	2022학년도 05월 종로	29번	능동태 vs. 수동태
9	2021학년도 06월 모평	30번	어휘 문제 01
10	2020학년도 04월 학평	30번	어휘 문제 02
11	2020학년도 03월 학평	29번	어휘 문제 03
12	2021학년도 10월 종로	30번	어휘 문제 04

🏷️ 1등급 꿀팁

1. 수동태의 기본 형태는 「be+p.p」인데, 진행형의 수동태는 「be+being+p.p.」이며, 완료형의 수동태는 「have/has+been+p.p.」가 된다.

2. 조동사의 수동태 형태와 준동사(부정사, 동명사, 분사)의 수동태 형태를 주의한다.

3. 분사는 수동의 의미를 갖는 경우, 과거분사로 나타낸다.

4. 5형식 문장을 이끄는 지각동사나 사역동사는 목적격보어로 동사원형을 가져오지만, 수동태로 전환되는 경우, 목적격보어가 to부정사 형태가 됨을 유의한다.

[핵심 문법]

정답 및 해설 036쪽

A 출제 POINT

1. 진행형, 완료형의 수동태 형태와 조동사와 함께 쓰일 경우 수동태 형태를 유의한다.

진행형 수동태 형태	be **being** p.p.	완료형 수동태 형태	have **been** p.p.
조동사 수동태 형태	「조동사+be p.p.」		

▶ The area [has cleared / **has been cleared**] of land mines.

2. 동사구는 하나의 동사로 취급해 수동태를 만든다.
▶ The pain [**was put up with** / was put up] by her.

3. 4형식 문장은 수동태를 만들 때 유의해야 한다. 동사에 따라서는 간접목적어만 또는 직접목적어만 수동태가 가능한 경우가 있다.
▶ He [is given / **was given**] a chance to speak yesterday.

4. to부정사, 동명사, 현재분사의 수동태 형태를 유의한다.

to부정사 수동태 형태	(단순형) to be p.p	동명사 수동태 형태	(단순형) being p.p.
	(완료형) to have been p.p		(완료형) having been p.p
* Would you help me if you saw me **being mugged** in the street? (현재분사 수동태)			

▶ The girl was afraid [to be left / **being left**] alone at night.

5. 지각, 사역동사가 들어 있는 문장을 수동태로 바꿀 경우, 목적격보어인 원형부정사는 to부정사로 바뀌진다.
▶ My son was heard [sing / **to sing**] by himself at midnight.

6. 「It+be+p.p.+that절」은 사람들의 말과 생각과 같은 일반적인 정보를 전달한다. say, think, believe 등의 동사가 that절을 목적어로 가지는 경우 (1) 「It+be+p.p.+that절」 형태의 수동태와 (2) that절 속의 주어를 문장 전체의 주어로 한 수동태가 가능하다.
▶ People say that she is a trustworthy person. → (1) It [says / **is said**] that she is a trustworthy person.
　　　　　　　　　　　　　　　　　　　　　　　　 (2) She is said to be a trustworthy person.

7. 자동사(appear, disappear)와 상태 동사(have, resemble, lack, fit 등)는 수동태로 쓸 수 없다. 태에 유의해야 할 동사구가 있다. consist of(~로 구성되다)는 능동태로 쓴다. 수동태로 나타내려면 be composed of, be made up of로 표현한다.
▶ Sally [was suddenly disappeared / **suddenly disappeared**] into the darkness.

B 체크 POINT

다음 괄호 안에서 어법상 올바른 것을 고르시오.

1. Data can be useful only after it [has collected / **has been collected**] and processed.

2. The baseball game [called off / **was called off**] because of heavy rain.

3. The baseball bat was bought [to / **for**] me by my dad.

4. Sam doesn't know how to get over [**being dumped** / to be dumped].

5. Unlike a stream, a glacer cannot be seen [**to move** / move].

6. It [thinks / **is thought**] that the launch of the euro brought about an increase in the cost of living.

7. You [are resembled / **resemble**] your mom very much.

| 제한 시간 : 13분 | 정답 및 해설 036쪽 |

2022학년도 10월 학평 29번

1. 다음 글의 밑줄 친 부분 중, 어법상 **틀린** 것은? [3점]

The idea that leaders *inherently* possess certain physical, intellectual, or personality traits that distinguish them from nonleaders ① was the foundational belief of the trait-based approach to leadership. This approach dominated leadership research from the late 1800s until the mid-1940s and has experienced a resurgence of interest in the last couple of decades. Early trait theorists believed that some individuals are born with the traits that allow ② them to become great leaders. Thus, early research in this area often presented the widely stated argument ③ that "leaders are born, not made." Also, some of the earliest leadership studies were grounded in what ④ referred to as the "great man" theory because researchers at the time focused on identifying traits of highly visible leaders in history who were typically male and associated with the aristocracy or political or military leadership. In more recent history, numerous authors have acknowledged that there are many enduring qualities, ⑤ whether innate or learned, that contribute to leadership potential. These traits include such things as *drive, self-confidence, cognitive ability, conscientiousness, determination, intelligence,* and *integrity.*

* resurgence: 되살아남 ** aristocracy: 귀족

2017학년도 6월 모평 28번

2. 다음 글의 밑줄 친 부분 중, 어법상 **틀린** 것은?

If an animal is innately programmed for some type of behaviour, then there ① are likely to be biological clues. It is no accident that fish have bodies which are streamlined and ② smooth, with fins and a powerful tail. Their bodies are structurally adapted for moving fast through the water. Similarly, if you found a dead bird or mosquito, you could guess by looking at ③ its wings that flying was its normal mode of transport. However, we must not be over-optimistic. Biological clues are not essential. The extent to which they are ④ finding varies from animal to animal and from activity to activity. For example, it is impossible to guess from their bodies that birds make nests, and, sometimes, animals behave in a way quite contrary to ⑤ what might be expected from their physical form: ghost spiders have tremendously long legs, yet they weave webs out of very short threads. To a human observer, their legs seem a great hindrance as they spin and move about the web.

2015학년도 10월 학평 20번

3. 다음 글의 밑줄 친 부분 중, 어법상 **틀린** 것은? [3점]

In professional sports these days, it is not unusual ① to hear players and coaches talking about process. They talk about focusing on the process and following the process. Rarely ② do they talk about scoring a goal, a touchdown, a home run, a point, or achieving a good shot. It's all about process. So, what do they mean by this? What they mean by focusing on the process is that they focus on the actions they need to ③ be taken in order to achieve their desired result. They don't focus on the result itself. The reasoning here is ④ that if you follow the steps required, then the result will look after itself. This is one of the big differences between professional and amateur sportspeople. Amateurs often focus on the result and forget about ⑤ doing all the things that would almost automatically lead to the result.

2012학년도 수능 21번

4. 다음 글의 밑줄 친 부분 중, 어법상 **틀린** 것은?

Researchers studied two mobile phone companies trying to solve a technological problem. One company developed what it called a 'technology shelf,' created by a small group of engineers, on which ① was placed possible technical solutions that other teams might use in the future. It also created an open-ended conversation among ② its engineers in which salespeople and designers were often included. The boundaries among business units were deliberately ambiguous because more than technical information was needed ③ to get a feeling for the problem. However, the other company proceeded with more seeming clarity and discipline, ④ dividing the problem into its parts. Different departments protected their territory. Individuals and teams, competing with each other, stopped sharing information. The two companies did eventually ⑤ solve the technological problem, but the latter company had more difficulty than the former.

5. 다음 글의 밑줄 친 부분 중, 어법상 틀린 것은?

The bodies of flowing ice we call glaciers ① <u>are</u> the most spectacular of natural features. They result from densely packed snow. Unlike a stream, a glacier cannot be seen ② <u>move</u>. Accurate measurements, however, show that it is flowing. Erosion of bedrock by glaciers and deposits of the eroded materials are characteristic and ③ <u>easily</u> recognizable. Their distribution enables us to infer that in the recent past glaciers have been far more extensive ④ <u>than</u> they are today. At the same time, this evidence has ⑤ <u>raised</u> the problem of the cause of the 'ice ages.'

* erode: 침식하다

6. (A) ~ (C)의 각 네모 안에서 어법에 맞는 낱말을 골라 바르게 짝 지은 것은?

Cats were at their highest position of domesticated life in ancient Egypt. There were more cats (A) living / lived in Egypt during the time of the pharaohs than in any other place in the world. This high concentration of cats (B) was / were probably due to the laws protecting the animal. Cats were associated with the moon goddess, Bast, so the Egyptians worshiped them as holy animals. If anyone was caught killing a cat, the person could be put to death. Families in Egypt also mourned the death of a cat and had the body of the dead cat wrapped in cloth before it was finally (C) laid / lain to rest.

	(A)	(B)	(C)
①	living	was	laid
②	living	were	lain
③	living	was	lain
④	lived	were	laid
⑤	lived	was	lain

7. (A), (B), (C) 각 네모 안에서 어법에 맞는 표현을 골라 짝지은 것으로 가장 적절한 것은?

People act strangely when a television camera comes their way. Some people engage in an activity known as the coverup. They will be calmly watching a sports game or a televised event (A) when / which they realize the camera is focused on them. Then there are those who practice their funny faces on the public. They take advantage of the television time to show off their talents, hoping to get that big chance that will carry (B) it / them to stardom. Finally, there are those who pretend they are not reacting for the camera. They wipe an expression from their faces and appear to be interested in something else. Yet if the camera stays on them long enough, they will slyly check to see if they are still (C) wathcing / being wathched .

	(A)	(B)	(C)
①	when	it	watching
②	when	them	being watched
③	when	it	being watched
④	which	them	watching
⑤	which	it	being watched

8. 다음 글의 밑줄 친 부분 중, 어법상 틀린 것은?

Accurate and honest reportage with the camera has always been problematic. The saying ① <u>that</u> "a photograph never lies" has been proven false many times. Photographers and picture editors have used lots of techniques to mislead the viewer of a photograph. ② <u>Taking</u> a subject out of context by careful framing or cropping, for example, is a simple way of giving the wrong impression of a person or event. Choice of lighting or camera angle, or the capture of a fleeting expression are other ways of influencing viewers' responses away from a truthful description of the situation. Photographers have posed their subjects ③ <u>to give</u> misleading impressions. Even from the early days of photography, some enterprising propagandists have found that outright manipulation of the photographs by cutting and pasting, rephotographing, retouching, or multiple printing techniques could ④ <u>be presented</u> a completely false view of reality. Digital image editing makes this manipulation process not only easier but virtually ⑤ <u>undetectable</u> in published photographs.

* cropping: (불필요한 부분) 다듬기   ** propagandist: 선전가

| 제한 시간 : 7분 | 정답 및 해설 039쪽 |

9. 다음 글의 밑줄 친 부분 중, 문맥상 낱말의 쓰임이 적절하지 않은 것은?

Chunking is vital for cognition of music. If we had to encode it in our brains note by note, we'd ① struggle to make sense of anything more complex than the simplest children's songs. Of course, most accomplished musicians can play compositions containing many thousands of notes entirely from ② memory, without a note out of place. But this seemingly awesome accomplishment of recall is made ③ improbable by remembering the musical *process*, not the individual notes as such. If you ask a pianist to start a Mozart sonata from bar forty-one, she'll probably have to ④ mentally replay the music from the start until reaching that bar — the score is not simply laid out in her mind, to be read from any random point. It's rather like describing how you drive to work: you don't simply recite the names of roads as an abstract list, but have to construct your route by mentally retracing it. When musicians make a mistake during rehearsal, they wind back to the ⑤ start of a musical phrase ('let's take it from the second verse') before restarting.

* chunking: 덩어리로 나누기   ** bar: (악보의) 마디

10. (A), (B), (C)의 각 네모 안에서 문맥에 맞는 낱말로 가장 적절한 것은?

Play can be costly because it takes energy and time which could be spent foraging. While playing, the young animal may be at great (A) comfort / risk. For example, 86 percent of young Southern fur seals eaten by sea lions were play−swimming with others when they were caught. Against these costs many functions have been proposed for play, including practice for adult behaviours such as hunting or fighting, and for developing motor and social interaction skills. However, for these theories, there is (B) much / little experimental evidence in animals. For example, detailed studies which tracked juvenile play and adult behaviour of meerkats couldn't prove that play−fighting influenced fighting ability as an adult. Therefore, the persistence of play across so many animal species (C) remains / resolves a mystery. The answers are likely to involve diverse and multiple factors, which may be quite different in different species, as might what we call *play* itself.

	(A)	(B)	(C)
①	comfort	little	remains
②	comfort	much	resolves
③	risk	little	remains
④	risk	much	remains
⑤	risk	little	resolves

11. 다음 글의 밑줄 친 부분 중, 문맥상 낱말의 쓰임이 적절하지 않은 것은? [3점]

Random errors may be detected by ① repeating the measurements. Furthermore, by taking more and more readings, we obtain from the arithmetic mean a value which approaches more and more closely to the true value. Neither of these points is true for a systematic error. Repeated measurements with the same apparatus neither ② reveal nor do they eliminate a systematic error. For this reason systematic errors are potentially more ③ dangerous than random errors. If large random errors are present in an experiment, they will manifest themselves in a large value of the final quoted error. Thus everyone is ④ unaware of the imprecision of the result, and no harm is done — except possibly to the ego of the experimenter when no one takes notice of his or her results. However, the concealed presence of a systematic error may lead to an apparently ⑤ reliable result, given with a small estimated error, which is in fact seriously wrong.

* arithmetic mean: 산술 평균   ** apparatus: 도구

12. 다음 글의 밑줄 친 부분 중, 문맥상 낱말의 쓰임이 적절하지 않은 것은?

Why should obesity cause our brains to shrink even more quickly with age than they would otherwise? Damage to blood vessels in the brain associated with diabetes and pre-diabetic conditions could ① play a role. Reduced blood flow can directly cause tissue damage to the brain, and it also slows down the clearance of neurotoxic substances that are produced during the development of Alzheimer's disease. In addition, obese individuals are likely to be less physically ② active than non-obese individuals. Physical activity, which ③ enhances cardiovascular health, is well known to decrease the risk for developing dementia. So, elderly obese individuals ④ reduce their risk for developing dementia via the combined effects of vascular damage from diabetes-related conditions and the poor maintenance of cerebrovascular health due to inactivity. This all sounds pretty depressing; what's worse, there is ultimately no way to avoid the cumulative effects of brain aging. However, at least diet and exercise provide a fairly straightforward path toward ⑤ maintaining the health of not only the body but the brain over the life span.

* dementia: 치매   ** vascular: 혈관의
*** cerebrovascular: 뇌혈관의

총 문항				문항	맞은 문항						문항	
개별 문항	1	2	3	4	5	6	7	8	9	10	11	12
채점												

어휘·숙어 비밀 노트

idiom vocabulary

A 수능 필수 어휘 ▶ 반의어 (2)

□					
241	cause	v. ~의 원인이 되다	result	v. 결과를 낳다
242	compatible	a. 양립할 수 있는	incompatible	a. 양립할 수 없는
243	competent	a. 유능한, 능숙한	incompetent	a. 무능한
244	complete	a. 완전한, 완료된	incomplete	a. 불완전한, 미완성의
245	compulsory	a. 강제적인	voluntary	a. 자발적인
246	conceal	v. 감추다, 숨기다	reveal	v. 드러내다 (= disclose)
247	concrete	a. 구체적인	abstract	a. 추상적인
248	deficient	a. 결핍된	sufficient	a. 충분한
249	demand	n. 수요	supply	n. 공급
250	deny	v. 부정하다	admit	v. 인정하다
251	descend	v. 하강하다	ascend	v. 상승하다
252	desirable	a. 바람직한	undesirable	a. 바람직하지 않은
253	diminish	v. 축소하다	increase	v. 증가하다
254	direct	a. 직접적인	indirect	a. 간접적인
255	discourage	v. 낙담시키다	encourage	v. 용기를 북돋다
256	disprove	v. 틀렸음을 입증하다	prove	v. 입증하다
257	domestic	a. 국내의	international	a. 국제적인
258	drought	n. 가뭄	flood	n. 홍수
259	encourage	v. 격려하다	discourage	v. 용기를 꺾다
260	exclude	v. 제외하다, 배제하다	include	v. 포함하다, ~을 포함시키다

B 수능 필수 숙어

□		
261	come around	~에 들르다, 다시 의식을 차리다
262	come by	얻다, 구하다, 잠깐 들르다
263	come down with	병에 걸리다
264	come of	~의 결과로 일어나다
265	come over	우연히 들르다
266	come through	통과하다, 견뎌내다, 해내다
267	come true	실현되다
268	come up to	~까지 오다, 미치다, 이르다
269	confess A to B	A를 B에게 자백하다
270	confine A to B	A를 B로 제한하다
271	contribute A to B	A를 B에 기부하다
272	convince A of B	A에게 B를 확신시키다
273	cool off	시원해지다, 진정하다
274	cope with	대처하다
275	count on	~에 의지하다
276	cover up	감추다, 은폐하다
277	cure A of B	A에게서 B를 낫게 하다
278	cut off	잘라내다, 중단하다
279	cut out	제거(삭제)하다, 그만두다
280	dare to	감히 ~하다

08 가정법

➡️ 출제 트렌드

1. 1994–2023학년도 수능 기출 어법 문제를 분석한 결과, 가정법 문제는 수능에서 정답으로 고르는 문제로는 거의 출제 되지 않았다. 그러나 고등학교 교육 과정상 가정법 과거, 가정법 과거완료의 기본 형태와 의미는 알고 있어야 한다.

	출처	문항 번호	어법·어휘 문제
1	2022학년도 06월 모평	19번 변형	「as if+가정법 과거」
2	2021학년도 03월 학평	20번 변형	「as if+가정법 과거」
3	2021학년도 03월 학평	24번 변형	가정법 과거
4	2012학년도 06월 모평	20번 변형	「as if+가정법 과거완료」
5	2009학년도 06월 모평	44번 변형	가정법 과거완료
6	2008학년도 04월 학평	22번 변형	가정법 과거
7	2006학년도 04월 학평	20번	가정법 과거완료
8	2016학년도 07월 종로	28번	가정법 과거 (선택지)
9	2020학년도 수능	30번	어휘 문제 01
10	2019학년도 10월 학평	30번	어휘 문제 02
11	2020학년도 09월 모평	30번	어휘 문제 03
12	2021학년도 08월 종로	30번	어휘 문제 04

➡️ 1등급 꿀팁

1. 가정법 과거, 과거완료, 가정법 미래, 혼합가정법의 기본 형태를 익힌다.

2. I wish 가정법이나 as if 가정법의 의미를 숙지한다.

3. It's time that 뒤에는 가정법 과거 표현이 사용된다.

4. 주장(insist), 제안(suggest), 요구(demand), 명령(order)을 나타내는 동사에 이어지는 that절에서는 「주어+(should)+동사 원형」을 쓴다. 단, 단순한 사실을 전달할 때는 문장의 수와 시제에 맞추어 써야 한다.

[핵심 문법]

Ⓐ 출제 POINT

1. 가정법 과거는 현재 사실과 반대되는 것을 가정한다.

「If+주어+과거동사 ~, 주어+조동사 과거형+동사원형~」	만일 ~하면 ~할 것이다

▶ If it were not for you, I would be lonely. (네가 아니었다면, 나는 외로웠을 거야.)

▶ If I **[have / had]** some money, I would lend it to him.

2. 가정법 과거완료는 과거의 사실과 반대되는 것을 가정한다.

「If+주어+had+과거분사 ~, 주어+조동사 과거형+have+과거분사~」	만일 ~했다면 ~했을 것이다

▶ Without (= But for) your advice, I would have failed. (너의 충고가 없었다면 나는 실패했을 텐데.)

▶ If he **[had / had had]** a basketball, he could have started a game.

3. 가정법 미래는 미래에 일어날 가능성이 거의 없는 상황에 쓰인다. 혼합가정법은 과거의 일이 현재에 영향을 미칠 때 사용한다.

가정법 미래: 「If+주어+should[were to]+동사원형~, 주어+조동사 과거형+동사원형~」	혹시라도 ~한다면 ~할 텐데
혼합가정법: 「If+주어+had+과거분사 ~, 주어+조동사 과거형+동사원형~」	(과거에) 만일 ~했다면, (지금) ~할 것이다

▶ If she **[took / had taken]** my advice then, she might still be alive.

4. 「I wish+가정법 과거[과거완료]」는 이루기 어려운 소망을 나타내며,「I wish+가정법 과거」는 주절과 종속절이 나타내는 시제가 동일할 때 쓰인다. 「I wish+가정법 과거완료」는 주절보다 종속절의 시제가 앞선 경우에 사용한다.

▶ I wish he **[weren't / hadn't been]** here now.

5. 「as if+가정법과거[과거완료]」는 '마치 ~인(이었던)것처럼'이라는 의미이다. 「as if+가정법 과거」는 주절과 종속절이 나타내는 시제가 동일할 때 쓰인다. 「as if+가정법 과거완료」는 주절보다 종속절의 시제가 앞선 경우에 사용한다. 「as if+직설법」은 as if 다음의 내용이 사실인지 아닌지 모르는 상태에서 사용한다.

▶ He looked as if he **[had had / have]** some bad news.

6. 가정법 「If+주어+동사~」에서 If가 생략되면,「동사+주어」로 문장이 도치된다.

▶ **[Had she known / She had known]** it was dangerous, she wouldn't have gone climbing the mountain.

7. It's time that 뒤에는 가정법 과거 표현이 사용된다. '~할 때이다'는 의미이다. 또한 주장(insist), 제안(suggest), 요구(demand), 명령(order)을 나타내는 동사에 이어지는 that절에서는 「주어+(should)+동사원형」을 쓴다. 하지만 실제로 발생한 단순한 사실을 전달할 때는 문장의 수와 시제에 맞추어 써야 한다.

▶ He demanded that she **[returns / return]** the books she had borrowed from him.

Ⓑ 체크 POINT

다음 괄호 안에서 어법상 올바른 것을 고르시오.

1. What would you do if it **[snowed / snows]** on your wedding day?

2. If I had known you were coming, I would **[prepare / have prepared]** dinner.

3. If you had followed my advice then, you would **[have had / be]** happier now.

4. I really wish I **[hadn't quit / quit]** school last year.

5. Sally behaves as if she **[were / is]** queen. In fact, she is not queen.

6. **[Had / Did]** Sam not told her to wear a seatbelt, she might have been more seriously injured.

7. It's time you **[settled / had settled]** your differences with your wife.

•어법 기출•

| 제한 시간 : 13분 | 정답 및 해설 042쪽 |

1. 다음 글의 밑줄 친 부분 중, 어법상 틀린 것은?

As Natalie was logging in to her first online counseling session, she wondered, "How can I open my heart to the counselor through a computer screen?" Since the counseling center was a long drive away, she knew ① that this would save her a lot of time. Natalie just wasn't sure ② if it would be as helpful as meeting her counselor in person. ③ Once the session began, however, her concerns went away. She actually started thinking that it was much more convenient than expected. She felt as if the counselor ④ is in the room with her. ⑤ As the session closed, she told him with a smile, "I'll definitely see you online again!"

2. 다음 글의 밑줄 친 부분 중, 어법상 틀린 것은?

I was waiting outside when the exam grades ① were posted on the bulletin board. I was perspiring. My heart started beating fast. What if I failed? A ② swarm of students rushed forward to see the exam results. Fortunately, I was ③ tall enough to see over their heads. The minute I saw the results, all my anxiety disappeared. I walked quickly back to my dormitory and ④ phoned my father. "Dad," I mumbled in a haze. "You won't believe this, but I passed the exams." My father was speechless. Finally he said, "Son, that is good news. I frankly never thought you'd do it." I was overjoyed as if I ⑤ had been walking on the cloud.

3. 다음 글의 밑줄 친 부분 중, 어법상 틀린 것은?

There is a story about F. Yates, a prominent UK statistician. During his student years at St. John's College, Cambridge, Yates had been keen on a form of sport. It consisted of ① climbing about the roofs and towers of the college buildings at night. In particular, the chapel of St. John's College ② has a massive neo-Gothic tower adorned with statues of saints, and to Yates it appeared obvious that it ③ will be more decorous if these saints were properly attired in surplices. One night he climbed up and did the job; next morning the result was generally much admired. But the College authorities were unappreciative and began to consider means of divesting the saints of their newly acquired garments. This was not easy, since they were well out of reach of any ordinary ladder. An attempt to lift the surplices off from above, using ropes with hooks ④ attached, was unsuccessful. No progress ⑤ was being made and eventually Yates came forward and volunteered to climb up in the daylight and bring them down. This he did to the admiration of the crowd that assembled.

4. 다음 글의 밑줄 친 부분 중, 어법상 틀린 것은?

Sir Arthur Conan Doyle, the creator of Sherlock Holmes, had a great sense of delicacy ① where other persons' feelings were concerned. He once paid a visit to George Meredith, the novelist, when Meredith was old and weak. Meredith suffered from an unusual disease that caused him ② to fall occasionally. The two men were walking up a path toward Meredith's summerhouse, Conan Doyle in the lead, when Conan Doyle heard the old novelist fall behind him. He judged by the sound ③ that the fall was a mere slip and could not have hurt Meredith. Therefore, he did not turn and he strode on as if he ④ heard nothing. "He was a fiercely proud old man," Conan Doyle later explained, "and my instincts told me that his humiliation in being helped up would be ⑤ far greater than any relief I could give him."

5. 다음 글의 밑줄 친 부분 중, 어법상 틀린 것은?

One of the most painful signs of the lack of readiness for the tsunami in the Indian Ocean in 2004 ① was the enthusiasm of children, who rushed excitedly down to the beach to gather fish during the initial retreat of water. Those ill-fated children had no idea ② what the sea's strange retreat meant. No one knew because nothing like that ③ had happened in living memory except for the 1883 tsunami disaster in the Indian Ocean. After the 19th century disaster, experts called for a tsunami warning system in the Indian Ocean similar to the successful one now ④ operating in the Pacific. If such a system ⑤ were up and running in the Indian Ocean, many of the thousands of lives lost in places relatively distant from the center of the earthquake might have been saved.

6. 다음 글의 밑줄 친 부분 중, 어법상 틀린 것은?

Is quicksand for real? Yes, but it's not as deadly as it is in the movies. Quicksand forms when sand gets mixed with too much water and ① becomes loosened and soupy. It may look like normal sand, but if you were to step on it, the pressure from your foot ② would have caused the sand to act more like a liquid, and you'd sink right in. Pressure from underground sources of water would separate and suspend the granular particles, ③ reducing the friction between them. In quicksand, the more you struggle, the ④ deeper you'll sink. But if you remain still, you'll start to float. So if you ever do fall into quicksand, remember to stay calm, and don't move until you've stopped ⑤ sinking.

7. (A), (B), (C)의 각 네모 안에서 어법에 맞는 표현으로 가장 적절한 것은?

After two hours surfing, Clauss was taking off his wet suit when a boy ran up, pointing to water. "Two kids are in trouble," he said. Clauss saw a pair of swimmers splashing and waving their arms. (A) Grabbing / Grabbed his board, he ran into the waves. As he paddled furiously, Clauss managed to reach one of the two and pick him up on his surfboard. He dived into the chilly water seven times, looking for (B) the other / another boy but had no luck. A policeman, who was on the beach, said that if Clauss (C) haven't / hadn't reacted so quickly and decisively, there would have been two drownings instead of one.

	(A)	(B)	(C)
①	Grabbing	the other	haven't
②	Grabbing	another	haven't
③	Grabbing	the other	hadn't
④	Grabbed	another	hadn't
⑤	Grabbed	the other	hadn't

8. 다음 글의 밑줄 친 부분 중, 어법상 틀린 것은? [3점]

Wealth and fame are thought of as guarantees for happiness. "If I only ① had a million dollars, I'd really be happy for the rest of my life." "If I could be famous, I'd never want anything else." To any person who tells you this, you need only reply with one name: Elvis Presley. He had more money ② than he could spend in a lifetime, and his fame continues years after his death. Yet he died miserably and prematurely, and by his own hand. This is not to say there is anything wrong with fame and wealth. I would prefer ③ to have wealth than to be poor. And I would rather be famous than unknown. What is wrong is to believe that these things ④ being guarantees to happiness. It is not wrong to set a goal or to work toward something, but it is wrong to let your happiness depend on ⑤ whether you can acquire it.

제한 시간 : 7분	정답 및 해설 045쪽

2020학년도 수능 30번

9. 다음 글의 밑줄 친 부분 중, 문맥상 낱말의 쓰임이 적절하지 않은 것은? [3점]

Suppose we know that Paula suffers from a severe phobia. If we reason that Paula is afraid either of snakes or spiders, and then ① establish that she is not afraid of snakes, we will conclude that Paula is afraid of spiders. However, our conclusion is reasonable only if Paula's fear really does concern either snakes or spiders. If we know only that Paula has a phobia, then the fact that she's not afraid of snakes is entirely ② consistent with her being afraid of heights, water, dogs or the number thirteen. More generally, when we are presented with a list of alternative explanations for some phenomenon, and are then persuaded that all but one of those explanations are ③ unsatisfactory, we should pause to reflect. Before ④ denying that the remaining explanation is the correct one, consider whether other plausible options are being ignored or overlooked. The fallacy of false choice misleads when we're insufficiently attentive to an important hidden assumption, that the choices which have been made explicit exhaust the ⑤ sensible alternatives.

* plausible: 그럴듯한 ** fallacy: 오류

2019학년도 10월 학평 30번

10. 다음 글의 밑줄 친 부분 중, 문맥상 낱말의 쓰임이 적절하지 않은 것은? [3점]

Discovering how people are affected by jokes is often difficult. People ① mask their reactions because of politeness or peer pressure. Moreover, people are sometimes ② unaware of how they, themselves, are affected. Denial, for example, may conceal from people how deeply wounded they are by certain jokes. Jokes can also be termites or time bombs, lingering unnoticed in a person's subconscious, gnawing on his or her self-esteem or ③ exploding it at a later time. But even if one could accurately determine how people are affected, this would not be an ④ accurate measure of hatefulness. People are often simply wrong about whether a joke is acceptable or hateful. For example, people notoriously find terribly hateful jokes about themselves or their sex, nationalities, professions, etc. ⑤ problematic until their consciousness becomes raised. And the raising of consciousness is often followed by a period of hypersensitivity where people are hurt or offended even by tasteful, tactful jokes.

* termite: 흰개미 ** gnaw: 갉아먹다

2020학년도 9월 모평 30번

11. 다음 글의 밑줄 친 부분 중, 문맥상 낱말의 쓰임이 적절하지 않은 것은?

One misconception that often appears in the writings of physical scientists who are looking at biology from the outside is that the environment appears to them to be a static entity, which cannot contribute new bits of information as evolution progresses. This, however, is by no means the case. Far from being static, the environment is constantly changing and offering new ① challenges to evolving populations. For higher organisms, the most significant changes in the environment are those produced by the contemporaneous evolution of other organisms. The evolution of a horse's hoof from a five-toed foot has ② enabled the horse to gallop rapidly over open plains. But such galloping is of no ③ advantage to a horse unless it is being chased by a predator. The horse's efficient mechanism for running would never have evolved except for the fact that meat-eating predators were at the same time evolving more efficient methods of ④ attack. Consequently, laws based upon ecological relationships among different kinds of organisms are ⑤ optional for understanding evolution and the diversity of life to which it has given rise.

* hoof: 발굽 ** gallop: 질주하다 *** predator: 포식자

2021학년도 8월 종로 30번

12. 다음 글의 밑줄 친 부분 중, 문맥상 낱말의 쓰임이 적절하지 않은 것은?

Many people believe that journalists should be impartial. At its most extreme, this view proposes that journalists should not have any personal political views, that they should be aloof from society and act as pure ① observers. However, journalists do need to be concerned about the society on which they are reporting and commenting. If they are not concerned about it and not involved in it, then they will probably be very ② poor journalists. Journalism is about people. Journalists should be gregarious and interested in the people and the issues on which they are reporting. This means that many reporters have political ideals and are politically ③ active. Furthermore, although some journalists find their hours of work militate against joining various clubs and societies, most journalists are involved in such groups and have other ④ outside interests. Because of this, journalists, more than many professional groups, ⑤ dislike each other's company.

* aloof: 떨어져서 ** gregarious: 사교적인
*** militate against: ~을 방해하다

총 문항		문항	맞은 문항		문항
개별 문항	1	2	3	4	5	6	7	8	9	10	11	12
채점												

어휘·숙어 비밀 노트

Ⓐ 수능 필수 어휘 ▶ 반의어 (3)

☐ 281	explicit	a. 명백한, 명시적인	implicit	a. 암묵적인, 묵시적인
☐ 282	extraordinary	a. 비범한	ordinary	a. 보통의, 평범한
☐ 283	fertile	a. 비옥한	barren	a. 불모지의
☐ 284	flexible	a. 융통성 있는, 유연한	inflexible	a. 융통성 없는
☐ 285	float	v. (물위, 공중에) 뜨다	sink	v. 가라앉다
☐ 286	fold	v. 접다, 포개다	unfold	v. 펼치다
☐ 287	frequently	ad. 자주	rarely	ad. 드물게
☐ 288	gradual	a. 점진적인	sudden	a. 갑작스러운
☐ 289	guilty	a. 유죄의	innocent	a. 순결한, 무죄의
☐ 290	hire	v. 고용하다	fire	v. 해고하다
☐ 291	horizontal	a. 수평의	vertical	a. 수직의
☐ 292	immigration	n. (국내로 오는) 이민	emigration	n. (타국으로 가는) 이민
☐ 293	immoral	a. 부도덕한	moral	a. 도덕적인
☐ 294	import	v. 수입하다; n. 수입	export	v. 수출하다; n. 수출
☐ 295	increase	v. 증가시키다	decrease	v. 감소시키다
☐ 296	inferior	a. 열등한, 하위의	superior	a. 보다 위의, 상위의
☐ 297	innate	a. 타고난, 선천적인	acquired	a. 습득한, 후천적인
☐ 298	interior	a. 내부의, 실내의	exterior	a. 외부의
☐ 299	intolerable	a. 참을 수 없는	tolerable	a. 참을 수 있는
☐ 300	intrinsic	a. 내재된, 본질적인	extrinsic	a. 외적인, 외부의

Ⓑ 수능 필수 숙어

☐ 301	dawn on(upon)	생각나다
☐ 302	day and night	밤낮으로
☐ 303	deal in	취급하다, 거래하다
☐ 304	decide on	~으로 결정되다
☐ 305	depart from	~에서 출발하다, ~에서 벗어나다
☐ 306	deprive A of B	A에게서 B를 빼앗다
☐ 307	devote oneself to -ing	~에 전념하다, 헌신하다
☐ 308	die from	~으로 죽다
☐ 309	die of	~으로 죽다(더 일상적으로 쓰임)
☐ 310	dig up	땅을 파내다, (비밀 등을) 알아내다
☐ 311	do a favor	부탁을 들어주다
☐ 312	do away with	~을 그만두다, ~을 제거하다
☐ 313	do harm	해를 입히다
☐ 314	dress up	잘 차려입다
☐ 315	drop by	잠깐 들르다
☐ 316	drop off	잠깐 졸다, 줄어들다, (차로) 내려주다
☐ 317	drop out	빠지다, 중퇴하다
☐ 318	due to	~ 때문에(= because of, owing to)
☐ 319	engage in	~에 종사하다
☐ 320	ever since	~이후로 줄곧

부정사

📑 출제 트렌드

1. to부정사는 일시적 미래 의미를 가지며 동명사는 반복적 과거 의미를 가진다.

2. 1994~2023학년도 수능 기출 어법 문항 분석 결과, 부정사 문제는 to 부정사의 수동태(2005학년도 수능), 「wait for+의미상의 주어+to부정사」(2006학년도 수능), It-to 가주어, 진주어(2007학년도 수능) 문제가 출제되었다.

3. 지각동사 watch의 목적격보어로 동사원형(2006학년도 수능), 사역동사 make의 목적격보어로 동사원형(1994학년도 2차 수능, 2014학년도 수능 A형)을 묻는 문제가 출제되었다.

4. 또한 hope 동사 뒤에 목적어로 나온 to부정사 문제(1995학년도 수능), to부정사의 부정어(1995학년도 수능(70쪽 8번 참조)), be about to부정사(2006학년도 수능) 선택지로 출제되었다. 또한 to부정사의 부사적 용법(2001, 2002, 2008, 2012, 2014학년도 수능 B형), 「stop+to부정사」(2018학년도 수능) 문제가 선지로 출제되었다.

	출처	문항 번호	어법·어휘 문제
1	2021학년도 07월 학평	33번 변형	to부정사의 능동태 vs. 수동태
2	2009학년도 03월 학평	22번 변형	「forget+to부정사」, to부정사의 능동태 vs. 수동태
3	2008학년도 03월 학평	23번	「forget+to부정사」, 지각동사의 목적격보어
4	2007학년도 10월 학평	21번	to부정사의 주어와 수일치
5	2008학년도 06월 모평	22번	가목적어, 진목적어
6	2006학년도 수능	20번	지각동사의 목적격보어
7	2022학년도 10월 종로	29번	to부정사의 형용사적 용법
8	2017학년도 06월 종로	28번	정동사 vs. 준동사
9	2019학년도 07 학평	29번	어휘 문제 01
10	2020학년도 06월 모평	30번	어휘 문제 02
11	2019학년도 04월 학평	30번	어휘 문제 03
12	2021학년도 05월 종로	30번	어휘 문제 04

📑 1등급 꿀팁

1. 가목적어, 진목적어 문장에서 to부정사 대신 that절을 선택하지 않도록 유의한다.

2. 지각동사나 사역동사의 목적어와 목적격보어가 능동 관계인 경우 to부정사를 취하지 않고, 동사원형을 취한다.

3. remember, forget, stop 동사 뒤에 to부정사를 취한 경우와 동명사를 취한 경우 의미 차이를 주의한다.

[핵심 문법]

A 출제 POINT

1. to부정사는 문장 속에서 명사 역할을 한다. 즉 주어, 목적어, 보어로 사용될 수 있다. to부정사구가 주어 역할을 할 때, 단수동사를 취한다.

▶ His great ambition is [**emigrated / to emigrate**] to USA.

2. plan, agree, refuse, decide 등의 동사는 to부정사를 목적어로 취한다.

▶ People will refuse [**paying / to pay**] the new tax.

3. start, begin, continue, like, hate 동사는 to부정사와 동명사를 모두 목적어로 취한다. 의미 차이가 없다. 일부 동사는 to부정사와 동명사를 목적어로 가져올 수 있지만 의미 차이가 있다. stop은 뒤에 동명사를 목적어로 가져오면 '~하는 것을 멈추다'의 의미이며, stop 뒤에 to부정사가 오는 경우, 부사적 용법으로서 '~하기 위해 멈추다'의 의미를 가지고 있다.

「remember+동명사」	(과거) ~했던 것을 기억하다	「remember+to부정사」	(미래) ~할 것을 기억하다
「forget+동명사」	(과거) ~했던 것을 잊다	「forget+to부정사」	(미래) ~할 것을 잊다

▶ Don't forget [to get / getting] your own food to the party this Saturday.

4. to부정사는 형용사처럼 문장 속에서 명사를 수식하거나 「be동사+to부정사」 구문의 형태로 사용될 수 있다.

▶ Her refusal [**to cooperate / cooperate**] was embarrassing.

5. to부정사는 부사 역할을 할 수 있으며 목적, 원인, 결과, 조건 등을 나타낸다.

▶ Peter came home [**finding / to find**] his house on fire.

6. to부정사의 관용 표현을 익힌다.

needless to say	말할 필요도 없이	A enough to B	B할 만큼 충분히 A하다
to say nothing of	~은 말할 것도 없이	too... to ~	너무 … 해서 ~할 수 없다

▶ The case is light enough for me [to carry / to carry it].

7. to부정사는 의미상의 주어를 쓸 수 있다. 의미상의 주어는 「for+목적격」으로 쓰며, kind, brave 등의 형용사 뒤에는 「of+목적격」을 의미상의 주어로 쓴다. 또한 to부정사의 부정은 not을 to부정사 앞에 쓴다.

▶ To make their dream come true, they decided [**not to waste / to waste not**] money.

B 체크 POINT

다음 괄호 안에서 어법상 올바른 것을 고르시오.

1. My Job is [**to report / reported**], not comment or judge.

2. They decided [**to take / taking**] a 15 minutes' break after CEO's speech.

3. I remember [**to swim / swimming**] in the river when I was a kid.

4. The company's failure [**to modernize / modernize**] caused its decline.

5. [**See / To see**] her walk, you'd never know she is blind.

6. The tiger is [**fat too / too fat**] to climb up the tree.

7. It was very kind [**of / for**] you to help such poor children.

•어법 기출•

제한 시간 : 13분 　　정답 및 해설 047쪽

1. 다음 글의 밑줄 친 부분 중, 어법상 틀린 것은?

The conventional view of what the state should do to foster innovation ① is simple: it just needs to get out of the way. At best, governments merely facilitate the economic dynamism of the private sector; at worst, their lumbering, heavy-handed, and bureaucratic institutions actively inhibit it. The fast moving, risk-loving, and pioneering private sector, by contrast, is ② what really drives the type of innovation that creates economic growth. According to this view, the secret behind Silicon Valley lies in its entrepreneurs and venture capitalists. The state can intervene in the economy—but only ③ to be fixed market failures or level the playing field. It can regulate the private sector in order to account for the external costs companies may impose on the public, such as pollution, and ④ it can invest in public goods, such as basic scientific research or the development of drugs with little market potential. It should not, however, directly attempt ⑤ to create and shape markets.

2. 다음 글의 밑줄 친 부분 중, 어법상 틀린 것은?

In business settings, it's really easy to forget ① to take the time to say Thank-You, and yet, it's an essential part of interaction with others. It's important to people that they feel valid, important, and ② respected. Just as saying sorry matters, so does remembering to thank those who help you move forward. And I think it's much nicer ③ to be sent along a physical card than an email. A personal note written by your own hand matters ④ far more than a few lines of typing into a window that's so easily available at your fingertips. One more thing: if you're going to go this route, put in the extra few minutes to purchase a nice card and ⑤ use a pen that gives you a decent flow.

3. (A), (B), (C)의 각 네모 안에서 어법에 맞는 표현으로 가장 적절한 것은?

Emma was very fond of singing. She had a very good voice, except that some of her high notes tended to sound like a gate which someone had forgotten (A) oiling / to oil . Emma was very conscious of this weakness and took every opportunity she could find to practice these high notes. As she lived in a small house, (B) where / which she could not practice without disturbing the rest of the family, she usually practiced her high notes outside. One afternoon, a car passed her while she was singing some of her highest and most difficult notes. She saw an anxious expression suddenly (C) come / to come over the driver's face. He put his brakes on violently, jumped out, and began to examine all his tires carefully.

	(A)	(B)	(C)
①	oiling	where	come
②	oiling	which	to come
③	oiling	where	to come
④	to oil	which	come
⑤	to oil	where	come

4. (A), (B), (C)의 각 네모 안에서 어법에 맞는 표현으로 가장 적절한 것은?

I was shocked by the news that people with mental disorders can be kept (A) from voting / to vote . Our constitutional right to vote does not require that any one of us should make a rational choice. We can vote for a candidate because he or she seems most qualified, or simply because we like his or her appearance. In addition, the mentally ill are faced with a unique set of challenges, and (B) its / their interests will not be adequately represented if they cannot vote. To exclude those from voting who are already socially isolated (C) destroy / destroys our democracy, as it creates a caste system.

	(A)	(B)	(C)
①	from voting	its	destroys
②	from voting	their	destroys
③	from voting	their	destroy
④	to vote	their	destroy
⑤	to vote	its	destroys

5. 다음 글의 밑줄 친 부분 중, 어법상 틀린 것은?

College life is busy. There are too many demands on your schedule. Activities, friends, and pastimes may cause some difficulties in your ① performing the real job at hand. When you are feeling ② overwhelmed by presentations, paper deadlines, or tests, you will probably spend all your time studying ③ to deal with these pressures. However, this lack of time for relaxation makes it more difficult ④ get the most out of your studies. Promise ⑤ yourself that no matter how much work you have, you will always relax during one full evening. You will work better if you take time off for relaxation.

6. (A), (B), (C) 각 네모 안에서 어법에 맞는 표현을 골라 짝 지은 것으로 가장 적절한 것은?

On most subway trains, the doors open automatically at each station. But when you are on the Métro, the subway in Paris, things are different. I watched a man on the Métro (A) try/tried to get off the train and fail. When the train came to his station, he got up and stood patiently in front of the door, waiting for it (B) opened/to open . It never opened. The train simply started up again and went on to the next station. In the Métro, you have to open the doors yourself by pushing a button, depressing a lever or (C) slide/sliding them.

```
     (A)           (B)           (C)
① try     ----- opened  ----- sliding
② try     ----- opened  ----- slide
③ try     ----- to open ----- sliding
④ tried   ----- to open ----- slide
⑤ tried   ----- opened  ----- sliding
```

7. 다음 글의 밑줄 친 부분 중, 어법상 틀린 것은?

The primary goal of Gordon's Music Learning Theory is to treat music education in a manner ① similar to language learning right from birth. Through consistent exposure to and reinforcement of musical concepts, the teacher assists the child through stages of musical development ② that will provide him with the basic knowledge to study music at school. Gordon believes that as the child matures he or she will learn to appreciate and participate in the making of music, thus ③ bringing more meaning to life. Once the educator has an understanding of early childhood characteristics and development, the next step is to observe the child and ④ develop lesson plans based upon the learning style and personal interests of the child. The most important tool in teaching this age group is engagement through play, and with the child's own enthusiasm, motivation, and willingness ⑤ participate, the role of the educator is simply to free the potential for self-development.

8. 다음 글의 밑줄 친 부분 중, 어법상 틀린 것은? [3점]

A switch to low-energy bulbs across the European Union ① has the potential to cut carbon emissions by 20 million tons a year. It is therefore not surprising ② that in 2009 the European Union banned the manufacture and import of 100-watt frosted incandescent bulbs. With many other kinds of electrical appliances ③ capable of becoming far more energy efficient, similar future initiatives are inevitable. Today, I am typing these words on a low-energy PC and monitor that together consume only 41 watts. In contrast, a year ago I would have been typing them on very typical desktop hardware that consumed around 220 watts. Very significant opportunities for all of us ④ reduce our energy usage really do exist. ⑤ Given the cost savings that they also deliver, many of us are therefore likely to be purchasing low-energy electrical devices.

*frosted incandescent bulb: 반투명 백열전구

•어휘 기출•

| 제한 시간 : 7분 | 정답 및 해설 050쪽 |

9. (A), (B), (C)의 각 네모 안에서 문맥에 맞는 낱말로 가장 적절한 것은? [3점]

One factor contributing to students' difficulty in making accurate judgments of their own knowledge is hindsight bias: the tendency to assume once something happens that one knew all along that it was going to happen. When students receive feedback suggesting that their knowledge is incomplete, such as getting an exam item (A) incorrect / right, they may respond by telling themselves that they actually did know the information. Although they do not have a strong grasp of the material, they feel as if they do because they recognize something about the item content. Looking back, once they know the answer, the solution seems obvious. This feeling of (B) familiarity / novelty can lead students to have an exaggerated sense of what they know. Hindsight bias therefore (C) diminishes / reinforces the feeling that their failure was due to the nature of the assessment rather than the nature of their knowledge—which makes it more difficult for them to learn from feedback.

	(A)	(B)	(C)
①	incorrect	familiarity	diminishes
②	incorrect	novelty	diminishes
③	incorrect	familiarity	reinforces
④	right	novelty	reinforces
⑤	right	familiarity	diminishes

10. 다음 글의 밑줄 친 부분 중, 문맥상 낱말의 쓰임이 적절하지 않은 것은?

Sometimes the awareness that one is distrusted can provide the necessary incentive for self-reflection. An employee who ① realizes she isn't being trusted by her co-workers with shared responsibilities at work might, upon reflection, identify areas where she has consistently let others down or failed to follow through on previous commitments. Others' distrust of her might then ② forbid her to perform her share of the duties in a way that makes her more worthy of their trust. But distrust of one who is ③ sincere in her efforts to be a trustworthy and dependable person can be disorienting and might cause her to doubt her own perceptions and to distrust herself. Consider, for instance, a teenager whose parents are ④ suspicious and distrustful when she goes out at night; even if she has been forthright about her plans and is not ⑤ breaking any agreed-upon rules, her identity as a respectable moral subject is undermined by a pervasive parental attitude that expects deceit and betrayal.

* forthright: 솔직한, 거리낌 없는 ** pervasive: 널리 스며 있는

11. (A), (B), (C)의 각 네모 안에서 문맥에 맞는 낱말로 가장 적절한 것은? [3점]

The conscious preference for apparent simplicity in the early-twentieth-century modernist movement in prose and poetry was echoed in what is known as the International Style of architecture. The new literature (A) avoided / embraced old-fashioned words, elaborate images, grammatical inversions, and sometimes even meter and rhyme. In the same way, one of the basic principles of early modernist architecture was that every part of a building must be (B) decorative / functional, without any unnecessary or fancy additions. Most International Style architecture aggressively banned moldings and sometimes even window and door frames. Like the prose of Hemingway or Samuel Beckett, it proclaimed, and sometimes proved, that less was more. But some modern architects, unfortunately, designed buildings that looked simple and elegant but didn't in fact function very well: their flat roofs leaked in wet climates and their metal railings and window frames rusted. Absolute (C) complexity / simplicity, in most cases, remained an ideal rather than a reality, and in the early twentieth century complex architectural decorations continued to be used in many private and public buildings.

* inversion: 도치

	(A)	(B)	(C)
①	avoided	decorative	complexity
②	avoided	functional	complexity
③	avoided	functional	simplicity
④	embraced	functional	simplicity
⑤	embraced	decorative	simplicity

12. 다음 글의 밑줄 친 부분 중, 문맥상 낱말의 쓰임이 적절하지 않은 것은? [3점]

A joint team of researchers from Tokyo University and Oxford University conducted a study on how well people can ① simultaneously perform two tasks. They found that doing two things at once often led to dual-task interference, with the result that both the tasks were ② poorly performed. Researchers looked at single-neuron activity in monkeys' lateral prefrontal cortexes while the animals performed tasks that required both spatial attention and memory. The monkeys were ③ stimulated visually, and then were distracted with another task while processing the visual information. The study showed that the strain of doing multiple tasks ④ enhanced the brain's ability to hold on to information related to the tasks. Due to dual-task interference, researchers said, it is virtually ⑤ impossible to carry out two tasks at once with any proficiency.

* prefrontal cortex: 전전두엽 피질

총 문항					문항		맞은 문항					문항
개별 문항	1	2	3	4	5	6	7	8	9	10	11	12
채점												

어휘·숙어 비밀 노트

A 수능 필수 어휘 ▶ 반의어 (4)

□						
□ 321	introvert	n. 내향적인 사람	extrovert	n. 외향적인 사람
□ 322	justice	n. 정의, 공정함	injustice	n. 불평등, 부당함
□ 323	latter	a. 나중의, 후자의	former	a. 전자의
□ 324	legal	a. 법률의, 합법적인	illegal	a. 불법적인; ad. illegally
□ 325	literacy	n. 읽고 쓸 줄 아는 능력	illiteracy	n. 문맹, 무식
□ 326	major	a. 주요한, 대다수의	minor	a. 소수의
□ 327	maximize	v. 극대화하다	minimize	v. 최소화하다
□ 328	meaningful	a. 의미 있는	meaningless	a. 의미 없는
□ 329	mental	a. 정신의, 마음의	physical	a. 신체의
□ 330	merge	v. 합치다	separate	v. 분리하다
□ 331	merit	n. 장점	demerit	n. 단점
□ 332	odd	a. 홀수의, 특이한	even	a. 짝수의, 빈번한
□ 333	optimistic	a. 낙관적인	pessimistic	a. 비관적인
□ 334	overestimate	v. 과대평가하다	underestimate	v. 과소평가하다
□ 335	patient	a. 참을성이 있는	impatient	a. 참을성이 없는
□ 336	permanent	a. 영구적인, 불변의	temporary	a. 임시의, 일시적인
□ 337	permit	v. 허락하다	forbid	v. 금하다
□ 338	pessimism	n. 비관주의	optimism	n. 낙관주의
□ 339	positive	a. 긍정적인	negative	a. 부정적인
□ 340	poverty	n. 가난	wealth	n. 부, 재산

B 수능 필수 숙어

□ 341	face to face	마주보고
□ 342	fade away	(소리, 기억이) 서서히 사라지다
□ 343	fall asleep	잠들다
□ 344	fall in love	사랑에 빠지다
□ 345	fall off	(아래로) 떨어지다, (수량 등이) 줄어들다
□ 346	fall on	~에 덤벼 들다, ~의 책임이다
□ 347	fall over	~에 걸려 넘어지다
□ 348	fill out	(서류, 빈칸) 채우다, 작성하다
□ 349	fit in	시간을 내다, 잘 어울리다
□ 350	for nothing	무료로, 헛되이
□ 351	for one thing	우선, 첫째로
□ 352	for sure	확실히, 틀림없이
□ 353	for the most part	대개, 보통
□ 354	free of charge	무료로
□ 355	from time to time	가끔, 이따금
□ 356	get along	~와 잘 지내다
□ 357	get lost	길을 잃다
□ 358	get off	손을 떼라, (버스, 지하철) 내리다
□ 359	get on with	(중단된 일을) 계속하다
□ 360	get over	극복하다, (병) 회복되다, (슬픔) 잊다

10 동명사

출제 트렌드

1. to부정사가 일시적, 미래 의미를 가진다면, 동명사는 반복적, 과거적 의미를 가진다.

2. 1994−2023학년도 수능 기출 어법 문제를 분석한 결과, 동명사 문제는 「stop+동명사」(2000학년도 수능, 2014학년도 수능 A형), 문장의 주어 역할을 하는 동명사(1998, 2002학년도 수능(100쪽 7번 참조)), 「전치사+동명사」(2009학년도 수능) 문제가 출제되었다.

3. 또한 문장의 주어 역할을 하는 동명사의 수 일치(2013, 2021학년도 수능), 「stop+동명사」(2018학년도 수능), 「전치사+동명사」(2019학년도 수능)가 선지로 출제되었다.

출처	문항 번호	어법 · 어휘 문제
1 2019학년도 03월 학평	28번	동명사 주어와 수 일치
2 2016학년도 10월 학평	28번	주어 역할을 하는 동명사
3 2015학년도 04월 학평	28번	정동사 vs. 동명사
4 2009학년도 수능	22번	「전치사+동명사」
5 2008학년도 09월 모평	21번	「get used to+ 동명사」
6 2000학년도 수능	44번	「stop+동명사」
7 2018학년도 10월 종로	28번	동명사 주어와 수 일치
8 2021학년도 10월 종로	29번	동명사 주어
9 2019학년도 03월 학평	29번	어휘 문제 01
10 2019학년도 수능	30번	어휘 문제 02
11 2018학년도 11월 종로	29번	어휘 문제 03
12 2021학년도 04월 종로	30번	어휘 문제 04

1등급 꿀팁

1. 동명사는 명사적 성질이 있으므로 문장 속에서 주어, 목적어, 보어 역할을 한다. 주어인 동명사는 단수동사를 취한다.

2. 동명사는 동사적 성질이 있으므로 타동사처럼 동명사 뒤에 목적어를 가져올 수 있다.

3. 전치사 뒤에는 동명사가 나온다.

4. 「stop+동명사」는 '~을 멈추다'의 의미이며 「stop+to부정사」는 '~하기 위해 멈추다'의 의미이다.

[핵심 문법]

A 출제 POINT

1. 동명사는 문장 속에서 명사 역할을 한다. 즉 주어, (동사나 전치사의) 목적어, 보어로 사용될 수 있다.
한편, 동명사가 주어일 경우, 동사는 단수동사를 사용한다.

▶ **[Set / Setting]** goals and not giving up helps you achieve a lot of things in your life.

2. finish, enjoy, mind, give up 등의 동사(구)는 동명사를 목적어로 취한다. 일부 동사는 to부정사와 동명사를 목적어로 가져올 수 있지만 의미 차이가 있다.

「regret+동명사」	~한 것을 후회하다	「regret+to부정사」	~해야 해서 유감이다
「try+동명사」	시험 삼아 ~해보다	「try+to부정사」	~하려고 노력하다

▶ Sam regrets **[having done / have done]** such a silly thing.

3. 전치사의 목적어는 동명사를 사용한다. 특히 전치사 to 뒤에 to부정사를 쓰지 않도록 유의한다.

look forward to -ing	~을 기대하다	object to -ing	~에 반대하다
contribute to -ing	~에 헌신하다	devote oneself to -ing	~에 헌신하다

▶ This summer, my son is really looking forward to **[learn / learning]** how to scuba-dive.

4. 동명사는 −ing형(단순형)과 「having+p.p형」(완료형)으로 시제를 나타낸다. 단순형은 술어 동사와 시제가 같다.

▶ Sam is sure that she was a singer. = Sam is sure of her **[being / having been]** a singer.

5. 동명사의 의미상의 주어는 동명사 앞에 배치한다. 의미상 주어가 사람일 때는 소유격, 목적격을 모두 사용할 수 있으며, 사물일 때는 그대로 쓴다. 또한 동명사를 부정할 때는 부정어를 동명사 바로 앞에 둔다.

▶ He insists on **[her / hers]** being innocent.

6. 수동형동명사 「being+p.p.」와 「having been+p.p.」는 의미상의 주어와 수동의 의미 관계를 갖는다.

▶ The boy doesn't like **[being / having been]** treated like a child.
= The boy doesn't like that he is treated like a child.

7. 동명사의 관용 표현을 익힌다.

cannot help –ing	~하지 않을 수 없다	feel like –ing	~하고 싶다
It's no use[good] –ing	~해도 소용없다	There is no –ing	~할 수 없다 (~하는 것이 불가능하다)
be used to –ing	~에 익숙하다	be accustomed to –ing	~에 익숙하다

▶ I feel like **[dancing / to dance]** with Sally now.

B 체크 POINT

다음 괄호 안에서 어법상 올바른 것을 고르시오.

1. **[Understand / Understanding]** why historic events took place is important.

2. My boss enjoyed **[to fish / fishing]** in the river during the weekend.

3. One of the keys to **[succeed / succeeding]** in life is to live it with some sense of balance.

4. She is sorry for **[being / having been]** late. = She is sorry that she is late.

5. The man objected to **[cars / cars']** being parked here.

6. Sally can't stand **[treating / being treated]** unequally.

7. It's no use **[to cry / crying]** over spilt milk.

2019학년도 3월 학평 28번

1. 다음 글의 밑줄 친 부분 중, 어법상 틀린 것은?

Baylor University researchers investigated ① whether different types of writing could ease people into sleep. To find out, they had 57 young adults spend five minutes before bed ② writing either a to-do list for the days ahead or a list of tasks they'd finished over the past few days. The results confirm that not all pre-sleep writing is created equally. Those who made to-do lists before bed ③ were able to fall asleep nine minutes faster than those who wrote about past events. The quality of the lists mattered, too; the more tasks and the more ④ specific the to-do lists were, the faster the writers fell asleep. The study authors figure that writing down future tasks ⑤ unloading the thoughts so you can stop turning them over in your mind. You're telling your brain that the task will get done — just not right now.

2016학년도 10월 학평 28번

2. (A), (B), (C)의 각 네모 안에서 어법에 맞는 표현으로 가장 적절한 것은? [3점]

Sometimes perfectionists find that they are troubled because (A) what / whatever they do it never seems good enough. If I ask, "For whom is it not good enough?" they do not always know the answer. After giving it some thought they usually conclude that it is not good enough for them and not good enough for other important people in their lives. This is a key point, because it suggests that the standard you may be struggling to (B) meet / be met may not actually be your own. Instead, the standard you have set for yourself may be the standard of some important person in your life, such as a parent or a boss or a spouse. (C) Live / Living your life in pursuit of someone else's expectations is a difficult way to live. If the standards you set were not yours, it may be time to define your personal expectations for yourself and make self-fulfillment your goal.

	(A)	(B)	(C)
①	what	…… meet	…… Live
②	what	…… be met	…… Living
③	whatever	…… meet	…… Live
④	whatever	…… meet	…… Living
⑤	whatever	…… be met	…… Live

2015학년도 4월 학평 28번

3. (A), (B), (C)의 각 네모 안에서 어법에 맞는 표현으로 가장 적절한 것은? [3점]

Leonardo da Vinci was one of the most learned and well-rounded persons ever to live. The entire universe from the wing of a dragonfly to the birth of the earth (A) was / were the playground of his curious intelligence. But did Leonardo have some mystical or innate gift of insight and invention, or was his brilliance learned and earned? Certainly he had an unusual mind and an uncanny ability to see (B) that / what others didn't see. But the six thousand pages of detailed notes and drawings present clear evidence of a diligent, curious student — a perpetual learner in laborious pursuit of wisdom who was constantly exploring, questioning, and testing. Expanding your mind is vital to being creative. Therefore, (C) invest / investing regularly in learning opportunities is one of the greatest gifts you can give yourself.

	(A)	(B)	(C)
①	was	…… what	…… investing
②	was	…… that	…… invest
③	was	…… what	…… invest
④	were	…… what	…… invest
⑤	were	…… that	…… investing

2009학년도 수능 22번

4. 다음 글의 밑줄 친 부분 중, 어법상 틀린 것은?

You may think that moving a short distance is so easy that you can do it in no time with ① little effort. You may decide to use your own car because you think that you don't need the services of a moving company. Well, you might be wrong. You are under the false impression that you do not have as many items to pack as you really ② do. You find out ③ too late that your car cannot carry as much as you thought it could. So, it takes you far more trips to your new home than you thought it would. There is also the possibility of ④ damage your stuff, some of it valuable. All these things ⑤ considered, it might be better to ask for the services of a moving company.

5. (A), (B), (C)의 각 네모 안에서 어법에 맞는 표현으로 가장 적절한 것은?

I had twenty village girls to teach, some of them with such a strong country accent (A) $\boxed{\text{that / what}}$ I could hardly communicate with them. Only three could read, and none could write, so at the end of my first day I felt quite (B) $\boxed{\text{depressing / depressed}}$ at the thought of the hard work ahead of me. But I reminded myself that I was fortunate to have any sort of job, and that I would certainly get used to (C) $\boxed{\text{teaching / being taught}}$ these girls, who, although they were very poor, might be as good and as intelligent as children from the greatest families in England.

	(A)		(B)		(C)
①	that	……	depressed	……	teaching
②	that	……	depressing	……	being taught
③	that	……	depressed	……	being taught
④	what	……	depressing	……	being taught
⑤	what	……	depressed	……	teaching

6. 다음 글의 흐름으로 보아, 밑줄 친 부분 중 어법상 자연스럽지 못한 것은? [1점]

As the zoo. Simaba the lion was very sick. The animal doctor came and tried giving him some red meat ① full of medicine. Poor Simba did not even raise his head. Finally, Simba ② stopped to breathe. The doctor said, ③ with tears in his eyes, "I regret to tell you that Simba is dead." The little children ④ were very shocked to hear it. "I feel like I've lost an old friend. I can remember ⑤ reporting Simba's birth," said a reporter.

7. 다음 글의 밑줄 친 부분 중, 어법상 틀린 것은? [3점]

What exactly are the conscious experiences that constitute the flow of the mind? Every subjective experience has two fundamental characteristics: sensation and desire. Robots and computers have no consciousness because ① despite their countless abilities they feel nothing and crave nothing. A robot may have an energy sensor that signals to its central processing unit when the battery is about ② to run out. The robot may then move toward an electrical socket, plug ③ itself in and recharge its battery. However, throughout this process the robot doesn't experience anything. In contrast, a human being ④ depleted of energy feels hunger and craves to stop this unpleasant sensation. That's why we say that humans are conscious beings and robots aren't, and why it is a crime to make people work until they collapse from hunger and exhaustion, whereas making robots work until their batteries run out ⑤ carrying no moral opprobrium.

*opprobrium: 맹비난

8. 다음 글의 밑줄 친 부분 중, 어법상 틀린 것은? [3점]

Although technology can't be blamed for the passion for growth, it is a great enabler. We are only just beginning to realize the potential of big data: its capacity to deliver highly ① customized content and products and to predict human behavior. The vast accumulation of personal data by Google, Amazon, Apple, and national governments ② promises everything from automated, personalized health care to preventative law enforcement. But with these tantalizing powers ③ come, necessarily, big risks. Just as Apple computers used to be safer from viruses because there were relatively fewer of them — which made them not worth ④ attacking — so the vast accumulation of personal data makes it an irresistible target for hackers and malware. Governments and regulators worry about the personal information stored and exploited by Google, but ⑤ what is precisely the scale of the accumulation of this information that makes Google's servers such tempting targets.

* tantalizing: 흥미를 부추기는   ** malware: 악성 소프트웨어

•어휘 기출•

9. 다음 글의 밑줄 친 부분 중, 문맥상 낱말의 쓰임이 적절하지 않은 것은? [3점]

Most people are confident that creativity is an individual possession, not a collective phenomenon. Despite some notable ① collaborations in the arts and sciences, the most impressive acts of creative thought—from Archimedes to Jane Austen—appear to have been the products of individuals (and often isolated and eccentric individuals who reject commonly held beliefs). I think that this perception is something of an ② illusion, however. It cannot be denied that the primary source of ③ novelty lies in the recombination of information within the individual brain. But I suspect that as individuals, we would and could accomplish little in the way of creative thinking ④ outside the context of the super-brain, the integration of individual brains. The heads of Archimedes, Jane Austen, and all the other original thinkers who stretch back into the Middle Stone Age in Africa were ⑤ disconnected with the thoughts of others from early childhood onward, including the ideas of those long dead or unknown. How could they have created without the collective constructions of mathematics, language, and art?

*eccentric: 기이한

10. 다음 글의 밑줄 친 부분 중, 문맥상 낱말의 쓰임이 적절하지 않은 것은?

Europe's first *Homo sapiens* lived primarily on large game, particularly reindeer. Even under ideal circumstances, hunting these fast animals with spear or bow and arrow is an ① uncertain task. The reindeer, however, had a ② weakness that mankind would mercilessly exploit: it swam poorly. While afloat, it is uniquely ③ vulnerable, moving slowly with its antlers held high as it struggles to keep its nose above water. At some point, a Stone Age genius realized the enormous hunting ④ advantage he would gain by being able to glide over the water's surface, and built the first boat. Once the ⑤ laboriously overtaken and killed prey had been hauled aboard, getting its body back to the tribal camp would have been far easier by boat than on land. It would not have taken long for mankind to apply this advantage to other goods.

*exploit: 이용하다 **haul: 끌어당기다

11. 다음 글의 밑줄 친 부분 중, 문맥상 낱말의 쓰임이 적절하지 않은 것은? [3점]

Sometimes it is argued that tariffs are a means of preventing a nation from becoming too dependent on foreign suppliers of goods vital to national security. That is, by making foreign goods more ① expensive, we can protect domestic suppliers. However, if oil is vital to operating planes and tanks, losing foreign supplies of oil during wartime could cripple a nation's defenses. The national security argument is usually not valid. If a nation's own resources are depletable, tariff-imposed reliance on domestic supplies will ② hasten depletion of domestic reserves, making the country even more dependent on imports in the future. If we impose a high tariff on foreign oil to protect domestic producers, we will ③ increase domestic output of oil in the short run. In the process, however, we will deplete the stockpile of available reserves. Thus, the defense argument is of ④ questionable validity. From a defense standpoint, it makes more sense to use foreign oil in peacetime and perhaps stockpile "insurance" supplies so that larger domestic supplies would be ⑤ unavailable during wartime.

12. 다음 글의 밑줄 친 부분 중, 문맥상 낱말의 쓰임이 적절하지 않은 것은?

At the root of environmental writing is a desire to change current thinking so that people see themselves as a part of the environment and not as masters who have a right to ① exploit resources. This is not a romantic ideal but a practical idea that stems from the politics of ② equitable distribution. In fact, such ideas have a traditional base in India. Here are a few examples. This anecdote comes from someone who was researching traditional agricultural practices. During a conversation with a farmer in which they were discussing the ownership of land and produce, the farmer said something that can only be described as greatly ③ greedy. He said that owning land did not mean he had a sole right to everything on it. Of his right over his crops, he said, "50 percent is for me, 25 percent is for you (that is, whoever in the community needed it) and 25 percent is for the birds." This belief and practice of ④ mutual benefit and survival stemmed from man's dependence on the natural world. His acknowledgement of it made him ⑤ assimilate with, rather than try and dominate, the environment.

총 문항					문항		맞은 문항					문항
개별 문항	1	2	3	4	5	6	7	8	9	10	11	12
채점												

어휘·숙어 비밀 노트

A 수능 필수 어휘 ▶ 반의어 (5)

□					
361	pure	a. 순수한, 깨끗한	impure	a. 순수하지 못한, 불결한
362	qualify	v. 자격을 얻다	disqualify	v. 자격을 잃게 하다
363	receive	받아들이다	reject	v. 거절하다
364	refuse	v. 거절하다, 거부하다	accept	v. 받아들이다, 수락하다
365	retail	a. 소매의	wholesale	a. 도매의
366	rigid	a. 뻣뻣한	flexible	a. 유연성이 있는
367	significant	a. 중요한	insignificant	a. 중요하지 않은
368	specific	a. 구체적인	vague	a. 애매모호한, 추상적인
369	static	a. 정적인, 고정된	dynamic	a. 동적인
370	subjective	a. 주관적인	objective	a. 객관적인
371	suitable	a. 적합한	unsuitable	a. 적합하지 않은
372	surplus	n. 흑자, 나머지	deficit	n. 적자, 부족분
373	tangible	a. 만질 수 있는	intangible	a. 무형의, 만질 수 없는
374	tragic	a. 비극의	comic	a. 희극의
375	understand	v. 이해하다	misunderstand	v. 오해하다
376	unpredictable	a. 예측할 수 없는	predictable	a. 예측할 수 있는
377	usual	a. 보통의, 평소의	unusual	a. 평소 같지 않은, 이상한
378	verbal	a. 언어의, 구두의	nonverbal	a. 비언어의
379	visible	a. 눈에 보이는	invisible	a. 눈에 보이지 않는
380	vulnerable	a. 취약한, 연약한	invulnerable	a. 해칠 수 없는, 안전한

B 수능 필수 숙어

□		
381	get rid of	~을 제거하다
382	get through	통과하다, 견뎌내다
383	give away	기부하다, 수여하다
384	give it a try	시도하다
385	give off	(빛, 가스, 냄새 등을) 발산하다
386	give out	나눠주다, 발산하다
387	give rise to	~이 생기게 하다
388	go ahead	앞서가다, (일 등이) 진행되다
389	go along	계속하다, 진행되다
390	go by	(시간) 흐르다, (장소) 지나가다
391	go off	떠나다, 발사되다, (경보기 등이) 울리다
392	go through	(절차) 거치다, (어려움) 겪다
393	hand in hand	손에 손을 맞잡고
394	hand in	제출하다
395	hand out	나눠주다
396	hang up	(옷, 그림 등을) 걸다, 전화를 끊다
397	have a look at	~을 한 번 보다
398	have an influence on	~에 영향을 미치다
399	have difficulty (in) –ing	~하는 데 어려움을 겪다
400	have in common	공통점을 지니다

분사, 분사구문

🔖 출제 트렌드

1. 동명사와 현재분사는 모두 「동사원형+-ing」의 형태를 가지고 있지만 동명사는 명사적 성질을 가지고 있으며, 현재분사는 형용사적 성질을 가지고 있다. 즉 분사는 명사(구)를 앞이나 뒤에서 수식하거나 보어로 사용되어 주어나 목적어를 서술한다.

2. 1994~2023학년도 수능 기출 어법 문제를 분석한 결과, 분사 문제는 수동분사구문(2005학년도 수능), 분사구문(2009학년도 수능), 「with+목적어+과거분사(2013학년도 수능)」, 명사를 수식하는 과거분사(2007, 2013, 2021학년도 수능), 명사를 수식하는 현재분사(2012, 2020학년도 수능)가 출제되었다.

3. 또한 분사구문(1999, 2004, 2009, 2022, 2023학년도 수능), 분사구문이 주절의 주어와 다른 경우(2009학년도 수능), 명사를 수식하는 현재분사(2011학년도 수능), 명사를 수식하는 과거분사(2014 B형, 2016, 2023학년도 수능), 생략된 「관계대명사+be동사」 뒤에 나온 과거분사구(2014 B형, 2023학년도 수능), 분사구문에서 being이 생략된 구문이 선지로 출제되었다.

4. 분사(구문) 문제는 수능에서 가장 많이 나오는 문제 중 하나이므로 유의해야 한다.

	출처	문항 번호	어법 · 어휘 문제
1	2022학년도 07월 학평	29번	명사를 수식하는 과거분사
2	2021학년도 10월 학평	29번	대명사를 수식하는 현재분사
3	2021학년도 03월 학평	29번	현재분사 vs. 과거분사
4	2020학년도 수능	29번	명사를 수식하는 현재분사
5	2018학년도 10월 학평	28번	주격보어로 쓰인 현재분사
6	2014학년도 09월 모평 B형	27번	「without+목적어+분사구」
7	2013학년도 수능	20번	「with+목적어+분사구」
8	2005학년도 수능	20번	수동형 분사구문
9	2019학년도 09월 모평	30번	어휘 문제 01
10	2018학년도 07월 학평	30번	어휘 문제 02
11	2019학년도 06월 종로	30번	어휘 문제 03
12	2020학년도 11월 종로	30번	어휘 문제 04

🔖 1등급 꿀팁

1. 분사는 형용사적 성질이 있으므로 명사를 수식하거나, 주어나 목적어를 설명하는 보어로 사용된다.

2. 「with+목적어+목적격보어」 구문에서 목적어와 목적격보어가 능동관계이면 현재분사를 쓰고, 수동관계이면 과거분사를 쓴다.

3. 주어[목적어]와 주격보어[목적격보어]의 관계가 능동 관계이면 현재분사를, 수동 관계이면 과거분사를 사용한다.

4. 분사구문에서 부사절의 주어와 주절의 주어가 다른 경우, 분사구문 앞에 주어를 밝혀야 한다.

[핵심 문법]

정답 및 해설 058쪽

A 출제 POINT

1. 분사는 형용사처럼 명사를 수식하거나 주격보어나 목적격보어 역할을 할 수 있다. 현재분사는 능동, 진행의 의미를 나타내고, 과거분사는 수동, 완료의 의미를 나타낸다.
▶ In a survey **[published / publishing]** earlier this year, seven out of ten parents said they would never let their children play with toy guns.

2. 주어와 주격보어의 관계가 능동 관계이면 현재분사를, 수동 관계이면 과거분사를 사용한다.
▶ He is a interesting writer, and I'm very **[interesting / interested]** in the subjects that he writes about.

3. 목적어와 목적격보어의 관계가 능동 관계이면 현재분사를, 수동 관계이면 과거분사를 사용한다.
▶ Sam felt something **[clawing / clawed]** up his back.

4. 분사구문은 「접속사+주어+동사」로 된 부사절을 대신하며, 시간, 이유, 조건, 양보, 동시동작, 연속동작의 의미를 나타낸다.
▶ **[Having / Had]** nothing to do, I went to bed earlier.

5. 완료분사구문은 주절의 시제보다 앞선 시제를 나타낸다. 또한 수동형 분사구문에서 being이나 having been은 생략 가능하다.
▶ **[Having found / Finding]** a hotel(= After they had found), they looked for somewhere to have dinner.

6. 「with+목적어+분사」 표현은 목적어와 분사의 관계가 능동이면 현재분사를, 수동이면 과거분사를 사용한다. 분사 자리에 형용사, 부사, 전치사구가 와서 목적어의 상태를 설명할 수도 있다.
▶ I can do that with my eyes **[closing / closed]**.

7. 분사구문의 주어가 주절의 주어와 다른 경우 분사구문의 주어를 분사 앞에 명시해 주어야 한다. 부정어는 분사 바로 앞에 배치한다.
▶ As the dog barked at him, he ran away. → The dog **[barked / barking]** at him, he ran away.

B 체크 POINT

다음 괄호 안에서 어법상 올바른 것을 고르시오.

1. I love the noise of **[fallen / falling]** rain.

2. Sam's job is boring, so he is **[boring / bored]**.

3. I'm sorry to have kept you **[waited / waiting]**.

4. **[Situated / Situating]** at an elevation of 1,300 meters, the city enjoys a warm climate year-round.

5. **[Having seen / Seen]** an accident, she stopped her car.

6. He jogs everyday with his dog **[following / followed]** him.

7. **[Not knowing / Knowing not]** the way, they soon got lost.

| 제한 시간 : 13분 | 정답 및 해설 058쪽 |

1. 다음 글의 밑줄 친 부분 중, 어법상 틀린 것은? [3점]

The spider chart, also called a radar chart, is a form of line graph. It helps the researcher to represent their data in a chart ① that shows the relative size of a response on one scale for interrelated variables. Like the bar chart, the data needs to have one scale which is common to all variables. The spider chart is drawn with the variables spanning the chart, ② creating a spider web. An example of this is seen in a research study looking at self-reported confidence in year 7 students across a range of subjects ③ have taught in their first term in secondary school. The researcher takes the responses from a sample group and ④ calculates the mean to plot on the spider chart. The spider chart allows the researcher to easily compare and contrast the confidence level in different subjects for the sample group. The chart, like the pie chart, can then be broken down for different groups of students within the study ⑤ to elicit further analysis of findings.

2. 다음 글의 밑줄 친 부분 중, 어법상 틀린 것은? [3점]

According to its dictionary definition, an anthem is both a song of loyalty, often to a country, and a piece of 'sacred music', definitions that are both applicable in sporting contexts. This genre is dominated, although not exclusively, by football and has produced a number of examples ① where popular songs become synonymous with the club and are enthusiastically adopted by the fans. More than this they are often spontaneous expressions of loyalty and identity and, according to Desmond Morris, have 'reached the level of something ② approached a local art form'. A strong element of the appeal of such sports songs ③ is that they feature 'memorable and easily sung choruses in which fans can participate'. This is a vital part of the team's performance ④ as it makes the fans' presence more tangible. This form of popular culture can be said ⑤ to display pleasure and emotional excess in contrast to the dominant culture which tends to maintain 'respectable aesthetic distance and control'.

* synonymous: 밀접한 연관을 갖는 ** tangible: 확실한

3. 다음 글의 밑줄 친 부분 중, 어법상 틀린 것은? [3점]

The formats and frequencies of traditional trade encompass a spectrum. At the simplest level ① are the occasional trips made by individual !Kung and Dani to visit their individual trading partners in other bands or villages. ② Suggestive of our open-air markets and flea markets were the occasional markets at which Sio villagers living on the coast of northeast New Guinea met New Guineans from inland villages. Up to a few dozen people from each side ③ sat down in rows facing each other. An inlander pushed forward a net bag containing between 10 and 35 pounds of taro and sweet potatoes, and the Sio villager sitting opposite responded by offering a number of pots and coconuts ④ judging equivalent in value to the bag of food. Trobriand Island canoe traders conducted similar markets on the islands ⑤ that they visited, exchanging utilitarian goods (food, pots, and bowls) by barter, at the same time as they and their individual trade partners gave each other reciprocated gifts of luxury items (shell necklaces and armbands).

* taro: (식물) 타로토란 ** reciprocate: 답례하다

4. 다음 글의 밑줄 친 부분 중, 어법상 틀린 것은?

Speculations about the meaning and purpose of prehistoric art ① rely heavily on analogies drawn with modern-day hunter-gatherer societies. Such primitive societies, ② as Steven Mithen emphasizes in *The Prehistory of the Modern Mind*, tend to view man and beast, animal and plant, organic and inorganic spheres, as participants in an integrated, animated totality. The dual expressions of this tendency are *anthropomorphism* (the practice of regarding animals as humans) and *totemism* (the practice of regarding humans as animals), both of ③ which spread through the visual art and the mythology of primitive cultures. Thus the natural world is conceptualized in terms of human social relations. When considered in this light, the visual preoccupation of early humans with the nonhuman creatures ④ inhabited their world becomes profoundly meaningful. Among hunter-gatherers, animals are not only good to eat, they are also *good to think about*, as Claude Lévi-Strauss has observed. In the practice of totemism, he has suggested, an unlettered humanity "broods upon ⑤ itself and its place in nature."

* speculation: 고찰 ** analogy: 유사점

*** brood: 곰곰이 생각하다

5. 다음 글의 밑줄 친 부분 중, 어법상 틀린 것은?

The Internet allows information to flow more ① freely than ever before. We can communicate and share ideas in unprecedented ways. These developments are revolutionizing our self-expression and enhancing our freedom. But there's a problem. We're heading toward a world ② where an extensive trail of information fragments about us will be forever preserved on the Internet, displayed instantly in a search result. We will be forced to live with a detailed record ③ beginning with childhood that will stay with us for life wherever we go, searchable and accessible from anywhere in the world. This data can often be of dubious reliability; it can be false; or it can be true but deeply ④ humiliated. It may be increasingly difficult to have a fresh start or a second chance. We might find ⑤ it harder to engage in self-exploration if every false step and foolish act is preserved forever in a permanent record.

* dubious: 의심스러운

7. 다음 글의 밑줄 친 부분 중, 어법상 틀린 것은?

Dropping your cell phone in water means you have to replace it, but sometimes if you're fast enough, you might be able to save the phone! If you want to suck the liquid out of the inner parts of the phone, try ① using a vacuum cleaner. Remove all residual moisture by drawing it away, with a vacuum cleaner ② holding over the affected areas for up to twenty minutes. This way you can completely dry out your phone and get it ③ working in thirty minutes. However, unless the exposure to water was extremely short, it's not recommended to attempt to turn your phone on ④ this soon. Be careful not to hold the vacuum too close to the phone, as a vacuum can create static electricity. It is even worse for the phone. The best way, of course, is ⑤ to bring your phone to the customer service center as soon as possible.

6. (A), (B), (C)의 각 네모 안에서 어법에 맞는 표현으로 가장 적절한 것은? [3점]

It had long been something of a mystery where, and on what, the northern fur seals of the eastern Pacific feed during the winter, (A) when / which they spend off the coast of North America from California to Alaska. There is no evidence that they are feeding to any great extent on sardines, mackerel, or other commercially important fishes. Presumably four million seals could not compete with commercial fishermen for the same species without the fact (B) being / is known. But there is some evidence on the diet of the fur seals, and it is highly significant. Their stomachs have yielded the bones of a species of fish that has never been seen alive. Indeed, not even its remains (C) has / have been found anywhere except in the stomachs of seals. Ichthyologists say that this 'seal fish' belongs to a group that typically inhabits very deep water, off the edge of the continental shelf.

* ichthyologist: 어류학자

(A)	(B)	(C)
① when	is	have
② when	being	have
③ which	being	have
④ which	being	has
⑤ which	is	has

8. (A), (B), (C)의 각 네모 안에서 어법에 맞는 표현으로 가장 적절한 것은?

(A) Situating / Situated at an elevation of 1,350m, the city of Kathmandu, which looks out on the sparkling Himalayas, enjoys a warm climate year-round that makes (B) living / to live here pleasant. Kathmandu sits almost in the middle of a basin, forming a square about 5km north-south and 5km east-west. It was the site of the ancient kingdom of Nepal. It is now the capital of Nepal and, as such, the center of (C) its / it's government, economy, and culture.

(A)	(B)	(C)
① Situated	living	its
② Situated	to live	its
③ Situated	living	it's
④ Situating	to live	it's
⑤ Situating	living	it's

| 제한 시간 : 7분 | 정답 및 해설 061쪽 |

9. (A), (B), (C)의 각 네모 안에서 문맥에 맞는 낱말로 가장 적절한 것은?

For every toxic substance, process, or product in use today, there is a safer alternative — either already in existence, or waiting to be discovered through the application of human intellect, ingenuity, and effort. In almost every case, the safer alternative is (A) available / unavailable at a comparable cost. Industry may reject these facts and complain about the high cost of acting, but history sets the record straight. The chemical industry denied that there were practical alternatives to ozone-depleting chemicals, (B) predicting / preventing not only economic disaster but numerous deaths because food and vaccines would spoil without refrigeration. They were wrong. The motor vehicle industry initially denied that cars caused air pollution, then claimed that no technology existed to reduce pollution from vehicles, and later argued that installing devices to reduce air pollution would make cars extremely expensive. They were wrong every time. The pesticide industry argues that synthetic pesticides are absolutely (C) necessary / unnecessary to grow food. Thousands of organic farmers are proving them wrong.

	(A)		(B)		(C)
①	available	······	predicting	······	necessary
②	available	······	preventing	······	necessary
③	available	······	predicting	······	unnecessary
④	unavailable	······	preventing	······	unnecessary
⑤	unavailable	······	predicting	······	necessary

10. (A), (B), (C)의 각 네모 안에서 문맥에 맞는 낱말로 가장 적절한 것은? [3점]

According to Derek Bickerton, human ancestors and relatives such as the Neanderthals may have had a relatively large lexicon of words, each of which related to a mental concept such as 'meat', 'fire', 'hunt' and so forth. They were able to string such words together but could do so only in a nearly (A) arbitrary / consistent fashion. Bickerton recognizes that this could result in some ambiguity. For instance, would 'man killed bear' have meant that a man has killed a bear or that a bear has killed a man? Ray Jackendoff, a cognitive scientist, suggests that simple rules such as 'agent-first' (that is, the man killed the bear) might have (B) increased / reduced the potential ambiguity. Nevertheless, the number and complexity of potential utterances would have been severely limited. The transformation of such proto-language into language required the (C) destruction / evolution of grammar — rules that define the order in which a finite number of words can be strung together to create an infinite number of utterances, each with a specific meaning.

	(A)		(B)		(C)
①	arbitrary	······	increased	······	destruction
②	arbitrary	······	reduced	······	evolution
③	arbitrary	······	reduced	······	destruction
④	consistent	······	reduced	······	evolution
⑤	consistent	······	increased	······	destruction

11. 다음 글의 밑줄 친 부분 중, 문맥상 낱말의 쓰임이 적절하지 <u>않은</u> 것은?

Cooperation and trust are important in every sphere of society. We often ① underestimate the role of trust in making our economy work or the importance of the social contract that binds us together. If every business contract had to be ② enforced by one party's taking the other to court, our economy, and not just our politics, would be in gridlock. The legal system enforces certain aspects of "good behavior," but most good behavior is ③ mandatory. Our system couldn't function otherwise. If we littered every time we could get away with it, our streets would be dirty, or we would have to spend an excessive amount on ④ policing to keep them clean. If individuals ⑤ cheated on every contract — so long as they could get away with it — life would be unpleasant and economic dealings would be unmanageable.

*gridlock: 정체 상태

12. 다음 글의 밑줄 친 부분 중, 문맥상 낱말의 쓰임이 적절하지 <u>않은</u> 것은?

Wherever we find creativity, we almost always find it was the result of a person who willingly went to work on a real problem. Thomas Edison once remarked that "Everything comes to him who hustles." Work. Don't worry. That was Edison's advice. And he proved its ① usefulness by his own example. But despite Edison's experience and that of countless others who continue to make breakthroughs, there remains considerable ② mystery about how creative ideas actually come to people. When we read the words of people like Giacomo Puccini, that great operatic composer, who once remarked, "The music of this opera *Madame Butterfly* was ③ dictated to me by God; I was merely instrumental in putting it on paper and communicating it to the public," what are we to think? Obviously, he and others feel as though they are merely the ④ instrument through which creative energies are flowing. While it might have felt this way to Puccini, it is also evident that Puccini ⑤ overestimated his own abilities.

* hustle: 힘차게 해내다

총 문항				문항	맞은 문항						문항		
개별 문항	1	2	3	4	5	6	7	8	9	10	11	12
채점												

A 수능 필수 어휘 ▶ 유의어 (1)

☐ 401	abundant, plentiful	a. 풍부한
☐ 402	accomplish, achieve	v. 성취하다
☐ 403	accumulate, collect	v. 축적하다
☐ 404	accurate, precise	a. 정확한
☐ 405	achieve, accomplish	v. 성취하다
☐ 406	acknowledge, admit	v. 인정하다
☐ 407	acquire, obtain	v. 획득하다
☐ 408	adjust, adapt	v. 적응하다
☐ 409	admire, respect	v. 존경하다
☐ 410	advance, progress	v. 진보하다
☐ 411	allow, permit	v. 허용하다
☐ 412	alter, change	v. 변경하다
☐ 413	amaze, astonish	v. 놀라게 하다
☐ 414	announce, declare	v. 알리다
☐ 415	anticipate, expect	v. 기대하다
☐ 416	anxiety, concern	n. 걱정, 불안
☐ 417	apparent, evident	a. 명백한
☐ 418	approach, access	v. 다가가다
☐ 419	appropriate, suitable	a. 적절한
☐ 420	argue, dispute	v. 논쟁하다

B 수능 필수 숙어

☐ 421	have in mind	~을 염두하다
☐ 422	have no choice but to + 동사원형	~할 수 밖에 없다
☐ 423	have nothing to do with	~와 관련이 없다
☐ 424	head for	~로 향하다
☐ 425	hear from	~에게서 연락을 받다
☐ 426	hear out	~의 말을 끝까지 듣다
☐ 427	help oneself	자기 스스로 하다
☐ 428	hold down	억제하다
☐ 429	hold on to	~을 붙잡다, 고수하다, ~을 맡아주다
☐ 430	hold out	내밀다, 지속하다
☐ 431	hold to	고수하다, (약속)을 지키게 하다
☐ 432	hold up	손들다, 견디다, 지체시키다
☐ 433	in a minute	곧, 즉시
☐ 434	in a sense	어떤 의미에서는
☐ 435	in a way	어느 정도는, 어느 면에서는
☐ 436	in brief	간략히 하면, 요약하면
☐ 437	in charge of	~을 담당하고 있는
☐ 438	in conclusion	결론적으로
☐ 439	in danger	위험에 처해 있는
☐ 440	in detail	상세하게

12 준동사

🔖 출제 트렌드

1. 부정사, 동명사, 분사를 준동사라고 한다. 준동사는 몇 가지 공통점을 가지고 있다. 예를 들면 준동사는 완료형과 수동태를 나타낼 수 있으며, 의미상의 주어를 나타낼 수도 있다. 또한 준동사를 부정하고 싶은 경우, 준동사 바로 앞에 부정어를 쓰면 된다.

2. 1994-2023학년도 수능 기출 어법 문제를 분석한 결과, 준동사의 공통 특징에 관한 문제는 to부정사의 부정어(1994년 2차 수능), to부정사의 수동태(2005학년도 수능(112쪽 8번 참조))가 출제되었다. 모평이나 학평 문제 중에는 to부정사의 완료형 (2009학년도 7월 학평)이 출제되었다.

출처	문항 번호	어법 · 어휘 문제
1 2019학년도 06월 종로	29번 변형	완료 분사구문
2 2012학년도 04월 학평	20번	「동명사의 의미상 주어+동명사」
3 2012학년도 09월 모평	21번	「현재분사+목적어」
4 2012학년도 06월 모평	20번	수동 분사구문
5 2009학년도 07월 학평	21번	to부정사의 완료형
6 2009학년도 04월 학평	21번	분사구문(시간)
7 2007학년도 수능	23번	과거분사의 후치 수식
8 1995학년도 수능	11번	「부정어(not)+to부정사」
9 2018학년도 04월 학평	29번	어휘 문제 01
10 2018학년도 03월 학평	28번	어휘 문제 02
11 2018학년도 수능	30번	어휘 문제 03
12 2020학년도 09월 종로	30번	어휘 문제 04

🔖 1등급 꿀팁

1. 준동사의 완료형은 동사의 시제보다 앞선 시제를 나타낸다.

2. 명사와 분사의 관계가 능동이면 현재분사를 쓰고 수동이면 과거분사로 쓴다.

3. 준동사의 의미상의 주어는 준동사 행위를 하는 주체가 의미상의 주어임을 나타낸다.

4. 준동사를 부정하고 싶은 경우, 준동사 바로 앞에 not을 쓴다.

[핵심 문법]

정답 및 해설 064쪽

A 출제 POINT

1. 완료형 부정사, 완료형 동명사는 동사의 시제보다 앞선 시제를 의미한다.

부정사 단순형 : to+동사원형	부정사 완료형 : to have p.p.
동명사 단순형 : 동사원형 -ing	동명사 완료형 : having p.p.

▶ He is believed **[to leave / to have left]** the country. = It is believed that he left the country.

2. 완료 분사구문은 주절의 시제보다 앞선 시제를 의미한다.

분사 단순형 : 동사원형 -ing	분사 완료형 : having p.p.

▶ Because she had seen the film twice, she didn't want to go to the cinema.

=**[Seeing already / Having already seen]** the film twice, she didn't want to go to the cinema.

3. 준동사도 수동태를 나타낼 수 있다. 주어와 준동사의 관계가 수동이면 to부정사는 「to be+p.p.」로 표현하고, 동명사와 분사는 「being+p.p.」로 표현한다.

수동형	부정사 : to be p.p.	동명사 : being p.p.	분사 : (being) p.p.

▶ Sally disconnected the phone so as not to **[be / being]** disturbed.

4. 명사와 분사의 관계가 능동이면 현재분사를 쓰고 수동이면 과거분사로 쓴다.

▶ I found her **[lied / lying]** on the floor.

5. 분사구문이 주절의 주어와 능동 관계이면 현재분사로, 수동 관계이면 과거분사로 쓴다.

▶ After **[spent / spending]** some time with people in the city, he found one of the problems was the performance of the city planning department.

6. 준동사는 의미상의 주어를 나타낼 수 있다.

의미상 주어	동명사 : 소유격 / 목적격	동명사가 문장의 주어로 문두에 나오는 경우 소유격을 쓴다.
	부정사 : 「for+목적격」	성품 형용사(kind, nice 등)는 「of+목적격」을 쓴다.
	분사 : 분사구문의 주어가 주절의 주어와 다른 경우에는 분사구문의 주어를 명시해 준다.	

▶ **[His / Him]** knowing I returned home unexpectedly is strange.

7. 준동사 부정은 바로 앞에 not을 둔다.

▶ I'm surprised at **[not his / his not]** having noticed.

B 체크 POINT

다음 괄호 안에서 어법상 올바른 것을 고르시오.

1. I'm sorry for **[wasting / having wasted]** your time. (= I'm sorry that I wasted your time.)

2. After she had completed the work, she took a vacation.

= **[Completing / Having completed]** the work, she took a vacation.

3. Sam says nothing without **[being spoken to / speaking to]**.

4. I saw Mark **[taking / taken]** away by the police.

5. His drama director, **[frustrating / frustrated]** with his acting, shouted at him.

6. It was careless **[for / of]** him to leave his smart phone in the bus.

7. **[Not wanting / Wanting not]** to interrupt the conversation, he stood quietly.

•어법 기출•

제한 시간 : 13분   정답 및 해설 064쪽

1. 다음 글의 밑줄 친 부분 중, 어법상 <u>틀린</u> 것은?

It is difficult to exaggerate the importance of trade in our modern world. The Founders, ①being read Adam Smith's *Wealth of Nations*, recognized this early on. By including the commerce clause in the U.S. Constitution (Article 1, Section 8), they helped set the stage for the development of a highly prosperous free trade zone within the United States. Trade makes it ②possible for most of us to consume a bundle of goods far beyond what we would be able to produce for ourselves. Can you imagine the difficulty ③involved in producing your own housing, clothing, and food, to say nothing of computers, television sets, dishwashers, automobiles, and cell phones? People who have these things do so largely because their economics are organized in such a way ④that individuals can cooperate, specialize, and trade. Countries that impose obstacles to exchange — either domestic or international — ⑤reduce the ability of their citizens to achieve more prosperous lives.

2. (A)~(C)에서 어법에 맞는 표현을 바르게 짝지은 것은?

Double Dutch is a style of jumping rope in which there are two participants turning two ropes while either one or two participants jump through the ropes. Double Dutch is a dynamic form of jumping rope that kids really love. In addition to its (A) is / being a beneficial cardiovascular exercise, Double Dutch also improves coordination and quickness. Furthermore, because it requires three to four participants working closely together, it is also great for (B) development / developing cooperative skills among children. At the most advanced levels, Double Dutch is also being done as an extreme competition sport (C) where / which groups of kids are doing high-energy dancing routines that are truly amazing.

* cardiovascular: 심장 혈관의

	(A)		(B)		(C)
①	is	······	development	······	where
②	is	······	developing	······	which
③	being	······	development	······	which
④	being	······	developing	······	which
⑤	being	······	developing	······	where

3. 다음 글의 밑줄 친 부분 중, 어법상 <u>틀린</u> 것은?

Fieldwork is the hallmark of cultural anthropology. It is the way we explore and learn about the vast ① detailed intricacy of human culture and individual behavior. And it is, importantly, the way ② in which most cultural anthropologists earn and maintain their professional standing. Some of the early personal accounts of anthropologists in the field make fieldwork ③ sound exciting, adventuresome, certainly exotic, sometimes easy. Malinowski, the classic anthropological fieldworker, describes the early stages of fieldwork as 'a strange, sometimes unpleasant, sometimes intensely interesting adventure which soon ④ adopts quite a natural course.' He goes on to describe his daily routine of strolling through the village ⑤ observed the intimate details of family life, and as he tells it, such observations seem possible and accessible.

4. (A), (B), (C)의 각 네모 안에서 어법에 맞는 표현으로 가장 적절한 것은?

When induced to give spoken or written witness to something they doubt, people will often feel bad about their deceit. Nevertheless, they begin to believe (A) what / that they are saying. When there is no compelling external explanation for one's words, saying becomes believing. Tory Higgins and his colleagues had university students read a personality description of someone and then (B) summarize / summarized it for someone else who was believed either to like or to dislike this person. The students wrote a more positive description when the recipient liked the person. Having said positive things, they also then liked the person more themselves. (C) Asked / Asking to recall what they had read, they remembered the description as being more positive than it was. In short, it seems that we are prone to adjust our messages to our listeners, and, having done so, to believe the altered message.

	(A)		(B)		(C)
①	what	······	summarize	······	Asked
②	what	······	summarize	······	Asking
③	what	······	summarized	······	Asked
④	that	······	summarized	······	Asking
⑤	that	······	summarized	······	Asked

5. (A), (B), (C)의 각 네모 안에서 어법에 맞는 표현으로 가장 적절한 것은?

In China it has never been rare for emperors to paint, but Huizong took it so seriously that the entire Northern Song Dynasty is thought (A) to fall / to have fallen because of it. He was from a long line of artistic emperors, who added to the Imperial collections and held discussions about painting, calligraphy, and art collecting. Collecting was easy for Huizong—if he wanted a painting, the owner would have to hand it over. When he inherited the throne, at age nineteen, (B) it / which was expected that he would continue his ancestors' royal patronage. This he did, but spent so much of the next twenty-five years (C) involving / involved in art that he ignored his official duties.

	(A)		(B)		(C)
①	to fall	-----	it	-----	involved
②	to fall	-----	which	-----	involving
③	to have fallen	-----	it	-----	involving
④	to have fallen	-----	it	-----	involved
⑤	to have fallen	-----	which	-----	involved

6. (A), (B), (C)의 각 네모 안에서 어법에 맞는 표현으로 가장 적절한 것은?

When we enter a room, we immediately recognize the floor, chairs, furniture, tables, and so forth. But when a robot scans a room, it sees nothing but a vast collection of straight and curved lines, (A) which / what it converts to pixels. It takes an enormous amount of computing time to make sense out of this jumble of lines. A computer sees only a collection of circles, ovals, spirals, straight lines, curly lines, corners, and so on. (B) Spending / Spent an enormous amount of computing time, a robot might finally recognize the object as a table. But if you rotate the image, the computer has to start all over again. In other words, robots can see, and in fact they can see (C) much / very better than humans, but they don't understand what they are seeing.

*jumble: 혼잡, 뒤범벅

	(A)		(B)		(C)
①	what	......	Spent	......	very
②	what	......	Spending	......	much
③	which	......	Spending	......	much
④	which	......	Spent	......	very
⑤	which	......	Spending	......	very

7. 다음 글의 밑줄 친 부분 중, 어법상 틀린 것은?

To be a mathematician you don't need an expensive laboratory. The typical equipment of a mathematician ① is a blackboard and chalk. It is better to do mathematics on a blackboard ② than on a piece of paper because chalk is easier to erase, and mathematical research is often filled with mistakes. One more thing you need to do is to join a club ③ devotes to mathematics. Not many mathematicians can work alone; they need to talk about what they are doing. If you want to be a mathematician, you had better ④ expose your new ideas to the criticism of others. It is so easy to include hidden assumptions ⑤ that you do not see but that are obvious to others.

8. 밑줄 친 부분 중 어색한 부분이 있는지를 찾아보고, 만약 있다면 그 부분은? [0.6점]

In order to make their dream <u>come true</u>, Mike and
　　　　　　　　　　　　　　　　　　　　　(A)
Amy decided <u>not to waste money</u>. By living temporarily
　　　　　　　　(B)
with Mike's parents and <u>drastically cut</u> their leisure
　　　　　　　　　　　　　　(C)
expenses, they hoped <u>to save enough money</u> to buy a
　　　　　　　　　　　(D)
modest house in two years.

① 어색한 부분 없음
② (A)
③ (B)
④ (C)
⑤ (D)

| 제한 시간 : 7분 | 정답 및 해설 067쪽 |

9. (A), (B), (C)의 각 네모 안에서 문맥에 맞는 낱말로 가장 적절한 것은? [3점]

Hypothesis is a tool which can cause trouble if not used properly. We must be ready to abandon or modify our hypothesis as soon as it is shown to be (A) consistent / inconsistent with the facts. This is not as easy as it sounds. When delighted by the way one's beautiful idea offers promise of further advances, it is tempting to overlook an observation that does not fit into the pattern woven, or to try to explain it away. It is not at all rare for investigators to adhere to their broken hypotheses, turning a blind eye to contrary evidence, and not altogether unknown for them to (B) deliberately / unintentionally suppress contrary results. If the experimental results or observations are definitely opposed to the hypothesis or if they necessitate overly complicated or improbable subsidiary hypotheses to accommodate them, one has to (C) defend / discard the idea with as few regrets as possible. It is easier to drop the old hypothesis if one can find a new one to replace it. The feeling of disappointment too will then vanish.
* subsidiary: 부차적인

	(A)		(B)		(C)
①	consistent	……	deliberately	……	defend
②	consistent	……	unintentionally	……	discard
③	inconsistent	……	deliberately	……	discard
④	inconsistent	……	unintentionally	……	discard
⑤	inconsistent	……	deliberately	……	defend

10. 다음 밑줄 친 부분 중, 문맥상 낱말의 쓰임이 적절하지 <u>않은</u> 것은? [3점]

The repairman is called in when the ① <u>smooth</u> operation of our world has been disrupted, and at such moments our dependence on things normally taken for granted (for example, a toilet that flushes) is brought to vivid awareness. For this very reason, the repairman's ② <u>presence</u> may make the narcissist uncomfortable. The problem isn't so much that he is dirty or the job is messy. Rather, he seems to pose a ③ <u>challenge</u> to our self-understanding that is somehow fundamental. We're not as free and independent as we thought. Street-level work that disrupts the infrastructure (the sewer system below or the electrical grid above) brings our *shared* ④ <u>isolation</u> into view. People may inhabit very different worlds even in the same city, according to their wealth or poverty. Yet we all live in the same physical reality, ultimately, and owe a ⑤ <u>common</u> debt to the world.
* narcissist: 자아도취자 ** electrical grid: 전력망

11. 다음 글의 밑줄 친 부분 중, 문맥상 낱말의 쓰임이 적절하지 <u>않은</u> 것은?

Some prominent journalists say that archaeologists should work with treasure hunters because treasure hunters have accumulated valuable historical artifacts that can reveal much about the past. But archaeologists are not asked to cooperate with tomb robbers, who also have valuable historical artifacts. The quest for profit and the search for knowledge cannot coexist in archaeology because of the ① <u>time</u> factor. Rather incredibly, one archaeologist employed by a treasure hunting firm said that as long as archaeologists are given six months to study shipwrecked artifacts before they are sold, no historical knowledge is ② <u>found</u>! On the contrary, archaeologists and assistants from the INA (Institute of Nautical Archaeology) needed more than a decade of year-round conservation before they could even ③ <u>catalog</u> all the finds from an eleventh-century AD wreck they had excavated. Then, to interpret those finds, they had to ④ <u>learn</u> Russian, Bulgarian, and Romanian, without which they would never have learned the true nature of the site. Could a "commercial archaeologist" have ⑤ <u>waited</u> more than a decade or so before selling the finds?
* prominent: 저명한 ** excavate: 발굴하다

12. 다음 글의 밑줄 친 부분 중, 문맥상 낱말의 쓰임이 적절하지 <u>않은</u> 것은? [3점]

Community supported agriculture (CSA) projects are developing direct links between groups of member-consumers (often urban) and their CSA farms. Restaurant agriculture describes a system of production and marketing in which farmers target their products ① <u>directly</u> to restaurants. New grower-controlled marketing cooperatives are emerging to more effectively tap regional markets. Marketing and trading clubs are groups of farmers who share marketing information and may ② <u>withdraw</u> in commodity futures contracts. Agricultural districts organized around particular commodities (such as wine) have served to ③ <u>stabilize</u> farms and farmland in many areas of the United States. Community kitchens provide the infrastructure and technical expertise ④ <u>necessary</u> to launch new food-based enterprises. What all of these efforts have in common is their potential to nurture local economic development and maintain diversity and quality in products as well as to provide forums in which producers and consumers can come together to ⑤ <u>solidify</u> bonds of community.
* future contract: 선물 계약(물건을 미래에 지정된 시간에 미리 정해진 가격으로 사고 파는 계약)

총 문항					문항	맞은 문항				문항	
개별 문항	1	2	3	4	5	6	7	8	9	10	11	12
채점												

A 수능 필수 어휘 ▶ 유의어 (2)

☐ 441	arise, occur	v. 발생하다
☐ 442	assessment, evaluation	n. 평가
☐ 443	assist, aid	v. 원조하다
☐ 444	associate, relate	v. 연관 짓다
☐ 445	attribute, ascribe	v. ~의 탓으로 돌리다
☐ 446	aware, conscious	a. 의식하고 있는
☐ 447	bare, naked	a. 벌거벗은
☐ 448	behave, conduct	v. 행동하다
☐ 449	bias, prejudice	n. 편견
☐ 450	blame, accuse	v. 비난하다
☐ 451	broad, wide	a. 광범위한
☐ 452	calculate, estimate	v. 추산하다
☐ 453	capacity, ability	n. 용량, 능력
☐ 454	circumstance, situation	n. 상황
☐ 455	colleague, coworker	n. 동료
☐ 456	combine, unite	v. 결합하다
☐ 457	comment, remark	n. 논평; v. 논평하다
☐ 458	commerce, trade	n. 무역
☐ 459	complex, complicated	a. 복잡한
☐ 460	compose, constitute	v. 구성하다

B 수능 필수 숙어

☐ 461	in effect	사실상, (법, 규정 등이) 시행 중인
☐ 462	in favor of	~에 찬성하여, ~을 위하여
☐ 463	in full	전부, 빠짐없이
☐ 464	in itself	그 자체로, 본질적으로
☐ 465	in need of	~이 필요한
☐ 466	in need	어려움에 처한
☐ 467	in no time	즉시, 당장
☐ 468	in order	순서대로, 알맞은, 적절한
☐ 469	in person	몸소, 직접
☐ 470	in place	제자리에 있는, 가동 중인
☐ 471	in place of	~대신에
☐ 472	in shape	건강 상태가 좋은
☐ 473	in terms of	~에 관하여, ~면에서
☐ 474	in that	~라는 점에서
☐ 475	in the distance	먼 곳에
☐ 476	in the end	마침내, 결국 (= after all)
☐ 477	in the first place	우선, 먼저, 첫째로
☐ 478	in the long run	결국에는, 긴 안목으로 보면
☐ 479	in the meantime	그 사이에(= meanwhile)
☐ 480	keep ~ in mind	~을 명심하다(= bear ~ in mind)

접속사, 전치사

📌 출제 트렌드

1. 두 단어 이상이 모여 주어와 동사의 기능을 갖추고 있는 것을 절이라고 하며, 절과 절을 연결하기 위해 사용하는 것을 접속 사라고 한다. 접속사 종류에는 등위, 종속, 상관접속사가 있다.

2. 접속사 뒤에는 「주어+동사」가 나오고, 전치사 뒤에는 구가 나오는지를 아는지 묻는 문제가 나왔다. 대표적인 문제가 접속사 because와 전치사구 because of를 비교하는 문제와 접속사 while과 전치사 during을 비교하는 문제이다.

3. 1994~2023학년도 수능 기출 어법 문제를 분석한 결과, 전치사, 접속사 문제 유형은 접속사구 as though(2005학년도 수능 (106쪽 7번 참조)), 접속사 that(2009, 2014학년도 수능 A형, 2022학년도 수능)이 출제되었고, whether(if)절이 전치사의 목 적어(2018학년도 수능(9쪽 1번 참조)), whether절이 타동사의 목적어(2021학년도 수능)로 사용되는 것이 출제되었다.

4. 또한 전치사 since(2002학년도 수능), 접속사 as(2008, 2010, 2020학년도 수능), 접속사 because(2008학년도 수능), 접속 사 that(2014 A형, 2023학년도 수능), 동격접속사 that(2016학년도 수능)이 선지로 출제되었다.

출처	문항 번호	어법·어휘 문제
1 2022학년도 수능	29번	접속사 that
2 2022학년도 09월 모평	29번	동격의 접속사 that
3 2021학년도 수능	29번	명사절 접속사 whether
4 2019학년도 09월 모평	29번	명사절 접속사 that(주어)
5 2017학년도 10월 학평	28번	명사절 접속사 that(목적어)
6 2010학년도 07월 학평	22번	전치사 during
7 2010학년도 04월 학평	21번	부사절 접속사 while
8 2009학년도 10월 학평	21번	전치사구 because of
9 2017학년도 10월 학평	29번	어휘 문제 01
10 2018학년도 09월 모평	30번	어휘 문제 02
11 2017학년도 07월 학평	28번	어휘 문제 03
12 2020학년도 08월 종로	30번	어휘 문제 04

📌 1등급 꿀팁

1. 전치사 뒤에는 명사(구)가 나오지만, 접속사 뒤에는 「주어+동사」로 이루어진 문장이 나온다.

   대표적으로 「because of+(구)」, 「because+주어+동사~」 구문이다.

2. 상관접속사는 병렬 구조나 시제일치와 연계되어 문제가 출제되고 있다.

3. 시간을 나타내는 접속사 while과 전치사 during을 구분해야 한다.

4. 접속사 whether[if]가 전치사의 목적절이나 타동사의 목적절로 나오거나, 접속사 that이 the fact 뒤에 동격절로 나올 수 있음을 유의한다.

[핵심 문법]

정답 및 해설 069쪽

A 출제 POINT

1. 전치사 뒤에는 명사(구)가 나오고, 접속사 뒤에는 절(「주어+동사」)이 나온다. 그런데 두 개 이상의 단어가 하나의 전치사나 접속사의 역할을 하기도 한다.

의미	전치사	접속사
~때문에	because of, due to, owing to	because, now that, in that
~할 경우	in case of	in case(= if)
~에도 불구하고	in spite of(= despite)	even though, even if
~에 따라(기준)	according to	according as
~하자마자	on	the moment, as soon as
~에 관해	with regard to, as to	–
~하는 동안	during	while

▶ According **[as / to]** the demand increases, the price goes up.

2. 등위접속사(and, but, or, so, for)는 문법적으로 대등한 관계에 있는 단어와 단어, 구와 구, 절과 절을 연결한다. 이를 병렬 구조라고 한다.

▶ I hope to go to that university and **[study / studying]** under Dr. Kim.

3. 상관접속사는 짝으로 이루어진 접속사를 말한다. not A but B(A가 아니라 B), not only A but also B(A뿐만 아니라 B도= B as well as A), either A or B(A 또는 B), neither A nor B(A도 B도 아닌), both A and B(A, B 둘 다) 등이 있다.

▶ How come neither you **[nor / or]** Sam came to my party?

4. 명사절을 이끄는 접속사는 that, if, whether 등이 있고, 의문사가 명사절을 이끌기도 한다.

▶ She didn't know **[whether / that]** she should bring her passport or not.

5. 종속접속사는 시간, 조건, 이유, 양보 등의 의미를 나타내는 부사절을 이끌 수 있다.

▶ The post office will not accept your mail, **[if / unless]** you seal it.

6. 「no sooner A than B」는 'A하자마자 B하다(= Hardly(Scarcely) A when(before) B)'의 의미이다. 이 경우, A에는 과거완료형이 나오고, B에는 과거시제가 나온다.

▶ Hardly had he come home **[when / than]** he started complaining.

7. 「의문사+ever」는 양보의 부사절을 이끌 수 있다(= 「no matter+의문사」).

▶ I will stand by you **[whatever / whoever]** happens.

B 체크 POINT

다음 괄호 안에서 어법상 올바른 것을 고르시오.

1. All the outdoor activities were canceled **[due to / because]** heavy snow.

2. He concentrated on improving his language ability and **[make / making]** friends in his school.

3. Their glory lies not in their achievements **[nor / but]** in their sacrifices.

4. **[That / Whether]** she will come is uncertain.

5. **[Because / Because of]** everything is interconnected, a change in one area may affect the other area.

6. No sooner had he finished a car washing **[when / than]** the rain began to fall.

7. **[Wherever, Whatever]** she goes, I will be right here waiting for her.

제한 시간 : 13분 　|　 정답 및 해설 069쪽

2022학년도 수능 29번

1. 다음 글의 밑줄 친 부분 중, 어법상 틀린 것은? [3점]

Like whole individuals, cells have a life span. During their life cycle (cell cycle), cell size, shape, and metabolic activities can change dramatically. A cell is "born" as a twin when its mother cell divides, ① producing two daughter cells. Each daughter cell is smaller than the mother cell, and except for unusual cases, each grows until it becomes as large as the mother cell ② was. During this time, the cell absorbs water, sugars, amino acids, and other nutrients and assembles them into new, living protoplasm. After the cell has grown to the proper size, its metabolism shifts as it either prepares to divide or matures and ③ differentiates into a specialized cell. Both growth and development require a complex and dynamic set of interactions involving all cell parts. ④ What cell metabolism and structure should be complex would not be surprising, but actually, they are rather simple and logical. Even the most complex cell has only a small number of parts, each ⑤ responsible for a distinct, well-defined aspect of cell life.

* metabolic: 물질대사의 　** protoplasm: 원형질

2022학년도 9월 모평 29번

2. 다음 글의 밑줄 친 부분 중, 어법상 틀린 것은?

Accepting whatever others are communicating only pays off if their interests correspond to ours—think cells in a body, bees in a beehive. As far as communication between humans is concerned, such commonality of interests ① is rarely achieved; even a pregnant mother has reasons to mistrust the chemical signals sent by her fetus. Fortunately, there are ways of making communication work even in the most adversarial of relationships. A prey can convince a predator not to chase ② it. But for such communication to occur, there must be strong guarantees ③ which those who receive the signal will be better off believing it. The messages have to be kept, on the whole, ④ honest. In the case of humans, honesty is maintained by a set of cognitive mechanisms that evaluate ⑤ communicated information. These mechanisms allow us to accept most beneficial messages—to be open—while rejecting most harmful messages—to be vigilant.

* fetus: 태아 　** adversarial: 반대자의 　*** vigilant: 경계하는

2021학년도 수능 29번

3. 다음 글의 밑줄 친 부분 중, 어법상 틀린 것은? [3점]

Regulations covering scientific experiments on human subjects are strict. Subjects must give their informed, written consent, and experimenters must submit their proposed experiments to thorough examination by overseeing bodies. Scientists who experiment on themselves can, functionally if not legally, avoid the restrictions ① associated with experimenting on other people. They can also sidestep most of the ethical issues involved: nobody, presumably, is more aware of an experiment's potential hazards than the scientist who devised ② it. Nonetheless, experimenting on oneself remains ③ deeply problematic. One obvious drawback is the danger involved; knowing that it exists ④ does nothing to reduce it. A less obvious drawback is the limited range of data that the experiment can generate. Human anatomy and physiology vary, in small but significant ways, according to gender, age, lifestyle, and other factors. Experimental results derived from a single subject are, therefore, of limited value; there is no way to know ⑤ what the subject's responses are typical or atypical of the response of humans as a group.

* consent: 동의 　** anatomy: (해부학적) 구조
*** physiology: 생리적 현상

2019학년도 9월 모평 29번

4. 다음 글의 밑줄 친 부분 중, 어법상 틀린 것은?

Not all organisms are able to find sufficient food to survive, so starvation is a kind of disvalue often found in nature. It also is part of the process of selection ① by which biological evolution functions. Starvation helps filter out those less fit to survive, those less resourceful in finding food for ② themselves and their young. In some circumstances, it may pave the way for genetic variants ③ to take hold in the population of a species and eventually allow the emergence of a new species in place of the old one. Thus starvation is a disvalue that can help make ④ possible the good of greater diversity. Starvation can be of practical or instrumental value, even as it is an intrinsic disvalue. ⑤ What some organisms must starve in nature is deeply regrettable and sad. The statement remains implacably true, even though starvation also may sometimes subserve ends that are good.

* implacably: 확고히 　** subserve: 공헌하다

5. 다음 글의 밑줄 친 부분 중, 어법상 틀린 것은?

People seeking legal advice should be assured, when discussing their rights or obligations with a lawyer, ① which the latter will not disclose to third parties the information provided. Only if this duty of confidentiality is respected ② will people feel free to consult lawyers and provide the information required for the lawyer to prepare the client's defense. Regardless of the type of information ③ disclosed, clients must be certain that it will not be used against them in a court of law, by the authorities or by any other party. It is generally considered to be a condition of the good functioning of the legal system and, thus, in the general interest. Legal professional privilege is ④ much more than an ordinary rule of evidence, limited in its application to the facts of a particular case. It is a fundamental condition on which the administration of justice as a whole ⑤ rests.

* confidentiality: 비밀 유지

6. 다음 글의 밑줄 친 부분 중, 어법상 틀린 것은? [3점]

Do you think the new or used vehicle you are purchasing is safe? Since the introduction of automotive crash-testing, the number of people killed and injured by motor vehicles ① has decreased in many countries. Obviously, it would be ideal ② to have no car crashes. However, car crashes are a reality and you want the best possible chance of survival. How are cars becoming safer? One of the reasons cars have been getting safer ③ is that we can conduct a well-established crash test with test dummies. The dummy's job is to simulate a human being ④ while a crash, collecting data that would not be possible to collect from a human occupant. So far, they have provided invaluable data on how human bodies react in crashes and have contributed greatly to ⑤ improved vehicle design.

7. (A)~(C)에서 어법에 맞는 표현을 바르게 짝지은 것은?

It is difficult to determine the shape of fire. There is a simplified design, (A) adopted / adopting for use in posters and signs. It resembles three upright tongues or a lotus flower. The design is a typical symbol of fire. However, the shape of fire is hard to define. In reality, fire comes in many forms (B) alike / like candle flame, charcoal fire, and torch light. The various nature of the shape of fire is evident in many words Koreans use to describe fire and its shape and movements. For instance, *iggle-iggle* is an adverb that describes a fire burning, but it focuses on the heat rather than the shape of the flame, (C) while / which *hwal-hwal* or *hweol-hweol* brings to mind flames that soar, as if to rise to the heavens.

	(A)	(B)	(C)
①	adopted	like	while
②	adopted	alike	which
③	adopted	like	which
④	adopting	like	while
⑤	adopting	alike	which

8. (A), (B), (C)의 각 네모 안에서 어법에 맞는 표현으로 가장 적절한 것은?

Unquestionably, the arts play a significant role in any society. They can be used to commemorate events or individuals. Or they often teach moral lessons or values (A) considered / considering important in a society and are also used to send political messages or draw attention to social issues. Yet the question is posed (B) which / whether the arts should reflect society's standards or question them. Art and artists are also severely criticized for being elitist, for not making art that would appeal to ordinary people. It is (C) because / because of their communicative properties that intense debates continue over the true role of the arts in today's world.

	(A)	(B)	(C)
①	considered	whether	because
②	considered	which	because
③	considered	whether	because of
④	considering	which	because of
⑤	considering	whether	because

• 어휘 기출 •

제한 시간 : 7분　　　　　정답 및 해설 073쪽

9. (A), (B), (C)의 각 네모 안에서 문맥에 맞는 낱말로 가장 적절한 것은? [3점]

In literature as distinct from journalism, the ablest writers will never assume that the bare bones of a story can be (A) enough / insufficient to win over their audience. They will not suppose that an attack or a flood or a theft must in and of itself carry some intrinsic degree of interest which will cause the reader to be appropriately moved or outraged. These writers know that no event, however shocking, can ever guarantee (B) detachment / involvement ; for this latter prize, they must work harder, practicing their distinctive craft, which means paying attention to language and keeping a tight rein on pace and structure. In certain situations, creative writers may even choose to (C) emphasize / sacrifice strict accuracy, and rather than feel that they are thereby carrying out a criminal act, they will instead understand that falsifications may occasionally need to be committed in the service of a goal higher still than accuracy.

	(A)	(B)	(C)
①	enough	…… detachment	…… emphasize
②	enough	…… involvement	…… sacrifice
③	enough	…… involvement	…… emphasize
④	insufficient	…… detachment	…… emphasize
⑤	insufficient	…… involvement	…… sacrifice

10. (A), (B), (C)의 각 네모 안에서 문맥에 맞는 낱말로 가장 적절한 것은? [3점]

Why does the "pure" acting of the movies not seem unnatural to the audience, who, after all, are accustomed in real life to people whose expression is more or less indistinct? Most people's perception in these matters is not very sharp. They are not in the habit of observing closely the play of features of their fellow men—either in real life or at the movies. They are (A) disappointed / satisfied with grasping the meaning of what they see. Thus, they often take in the overemphasized expression of film actors more easily than any that is too naturalistic. And as far as lovers of art are concerned, they do not look at the movies for imitations of nature but for art. They know that (B) artistic / real representation is always explaining, refining, and making clear the object depicted. Things that in real life are imperfectly realized, merely hinted at, and entangled with other things appear in a work of art complete, entire, and (C) free / inseparable from irrelevant matters. This is also true of acting in film. * entangle: 얽히게 하다

	(A)	(B)	(C)
①	disappointed	…… artistic	…… free
②	disappointed	…… real	…… free
③	satisfied	…… artistic	…… inseparable
④	satisfied	…… real	…… inseparable
⑤	satisfied	…… artistic	…… free

11. 다음 글의 밑줄 친 부분 중, 문맥상 낱말의 쓰임이 적절하지 <u>않은</u> 것은?

There is a reason that prey animals form foraging groups, and that is increased vigilance. An individual redshank is faced with a choice when feeding. It could spend all of its time being vigilant, looking out for approaching ① predators. If it did so, it would certainly significantly reduce the chance that it would be taken by surprise, but it would also ② starve. A bird with its head in the air scanning for predators cannot at the same time have its head down searching for food. In reality of course an individual balances the two behaviors in accordance with the situation in which it finds itself, and as a member of a group it can shift the balance towards ③ feeding. The bigger the flock of birds, the less time an individual bird devotes to ④ relaxation. This is possible because the ⑤ presence of many sets of eyes in the flock effectively means that there is always somebody on the look out.

* vigilance: 경계

12. 다음 글의 밑줄 친 부분 중, 문맥상 낱말의 쓰임이 적절하지 않은 것은?

The finding that as a general rule global attitudes are poor predictors of specific behaviors should come as no surprise. For global attitudes to ① predict a particular behavior, the behavior in question must exhibit the latent attitudinal disposition — it must reflect the global attitude of interest. However, it is unreasonable to expect any single behavior to be ② representative of a broad attitudinal domain. Consider, for example, the ③ relation between global attitudes toward African Americans and willingness to have one's picture taken with a black individual of the opposite sex for a variety of purposes. Although refusal to pose for a picture with a black person may well be an indication of prejudice, this behavior can also be influenced by a variety of other factors that have ④ something to do with prejudice. In fact, any single behavior in relation to African Americans is likely to be multiply determined and hence be a ⑤ poor indicator of the underlying disposition; that is, the tendency to discriminate.

* latent: 잠재하는

총 문항					문항	맞은 문항					문항	
개별 문항	1	2	3	4	5	6	7	8	9	10	11	12
채점												

어휘·숙어 비밀 노트

A 수능 필수 어휘 ▶ 유의어(3)

□ 481	comprehend, understand	v. 이해하다
□ 482	confirm, prove	v. 검증하다
□ 483	conflict, collide	v. 충돌하다
□ 484	consequence, result	n. 결과
□ 485	considerable, substantial	a. 상당한
□ 486	contain, include	v. 포함하다
□ 487	contrary, opposite	a. 반대의
□ 488	contribute, donate	v. 기부하다
□ 489	cooperate, collaborate	v. 협동하다
□ 490	correct, accurate	a. 정확한
□ 491	crop, yield	n. 수확(량)
□ 492	decide, determine	v. 결심하다
□ 493	decrease, reduce	v. 줄이다
□ 494	defend, protect	v. 방어하다
□ 495	deficient, lacking	a. 결핍한
□ 496	deliberate, intentional	a. 의도적인
□ 497	demand, request	v. 요구하다
□ 498	deny, refuse	v. 거절하다
□ 499	describe, relate	v. 기술하다
□ 500	desire, aspire	v. 바라다

B 수능 필수 숙어

□ 501	keep away from	멀리하다, 가까이 하지 않다
□ 502	keep in touch	연락하며 지내다
□ 503	keep on	계속 ~하다
□ 504	keep one's word	약속을 지키다
□ 505	keep track of	~을 기록하다, ~에 대해 계속 파악하다
□ 506	keep up with	~와 연락하고 지내다, 뒤떨어지지 않다
□ 507	kind of	약간, 어느 정도
□ 508	lay out	~을 펼치다, ~을 배치하다
□ 509	leave ~ behind	~을 훨씬 앞서다, ~을 두고 가다
□ 510	leave alone	그대로 두다, 내버려 두다
□ 511	leave for	~을 향해 떠나다
□ 512	leave out	생략하다(= omit)
□ 513	let alone	~은 말할 것도 없이
□ 514	line up	줄을 서다
□ 515	live up to	(기대, 요구 등에) 부응하다
□ 516	long for	~을 간절히 바라다
□ 517	look after	돌보다, 보살피다
□ 518	look back	회상하다, 되돌아보다
□ 519	look in	잠깐 들르다
□ 520	look into	들여다보다, 조사하다(= investigate)

14 관계대명사

🏷 출제 트렌드

1. 관계대명사는 접속사와 대명사의 역할을 한다. 두 개의 절을 하나의 문장으로 만들며, 관계대명사가 선행사를 수식하거나 서술한다.

2. 1994–2023학년도 수능 기출 어법 문제를 분석한 결과, 관계대명사 문제 유형은 관계사 what(2003학년도 수능)의 용법, 관계사 which의 한정적 용법(2008학년도 수능), 주격 관계대명사 who(2010학년도 수능), 「전치사(on)+관계대명사(which)」(2013학년도 수능), 복합관계형용사 whatever(2013학년도 수능, 27쪽 2번 문항 참조) 문제가 출제되었다.

3. 또한 관계사 who의 계속적 용법(2002학년도 수능), 목적격 관계대명사 that(2007학년도 수능), 「전치사(through)+관계사(which)」(2011학년도 수능), 주격 관계대명사 that(2014 B형, 2018학년도 수능), 「both of+관계사(which)」(2020학년도 수능)가 선지로 출제되었다.

출처	문항 번호	어법·어휘 문제
1	2023학년도 06월 모평	29번	관계대명사 whose
2	2020학년도 09월 모평	29번	관계사절의 동사, 관계사 whose
3	2018학년도 07월 학평	28번	「전치사(from)+관계대명사」
4	2009학년도 06월 모평	21번	whatever vs. however
5	2009학년도 06월 모평	21번	which의 한정적 용법
6	2008학년도 수능	22번	which의 한정적 용법
7	2003학년도 수능	29번	관계대명사 what
8	2020학년도 03월 종로	29번	목적격 관계사 that
9	2018학년도 06월 모평	29번	어휘 문제 01
10	2017학년도 04월 학평	29번	어휘 문제 02
11	2017학년도 03월 학평	29번	어휘 문제 03
12	2020학년도 07월 종로	30번	어휘 문제 04

🏷 1등급 꿀팁

1. 관계사 which의 제한적 용법과 계속적 용법이 있다. 계속적 용법 앞에는 콤마를 쓰고, 선행사를 설명한다. that은 계속적 용법이 없으며, which는 계속적 용법으로 사용될 때 선행사가 사물 이외에도 문장의 일부나 전체를 가리킬 수 있다.

2. 「전치사+관계대명사」는 선행사와 관계대명사가 이끄는 절을 자연스럽게 연결하기 위해서는 전치사가 필요하다.

3. 관계대명사 what(= the thing(s) that)은 자체에 선행사를 포함하고 있다.

[핵심 문법]

정답 및 해설 075쪽

A 출제 POINT

1. 관계대명사는 문장 내에서 「접속사+대명사」의 역할을 하며, 주격, 소유격, 목적격이 있다. 선행사 앞에 최상급, all, every, 서수, the only 등이 오면 that을 쓴다. 관계대명사는 관계사절 안에서 대명사 역할을 하기 때문에 뒤에 불완전 문장이 온다.

선행사	주격	목적격	소유격
사람	who	who(m)	whose
사물/동물	which	which	of which 또는 whose
사람/사물/동물	that	that	–

▶ He is the only man **[that / which]** I can trust.

2. 관계대명사 what(= the thing(s) which[that])은 선행사를 포함하고 있으므로, 따로 선행사가 앞에 나와 있지 않는다.

▶ **[What / Which]** is most important in life is love.

3. 관계대명사 계속적 용법은 관계대명사 앞에 콤마(,)를 쓴다. that은 계속적 용법으로 쓰지 않는다. 또한 which의 계속적 용법은 앞의 구나 절 등을 받을 수 있다.

▶ She discussed it with her friend, **[that / who]** is a lawyer.

4. 관계대명사가 타동사나 전치사의 목적어로 쓰인 경우에는 생략할 수 있다. 단, 관계대명사가 전치사의 목적어일 때는 전치사를 문장 가장 뒤로 보낸 후, 관계대명사를 생략할 수 있다. 전치사가 앞에 있을 때는 생략할 수 없다. 또한 「주격관계대명사+be동사」도 생략할 수 있다.

▶ The lady **[that / which]** I talked with is my aunt.

5. 접속사인 as, but than이 관계대명사처럼 쓰이는 경우 '유사관계대명사'라고 한다. 선행사 앞에 as, such, the same 등이 올 때 as를 쓴다. 부정어가 있을 때 유사관계대명사 but을 쓴다.

▶ This is the same watch **[but / as]** the one I lost.

6. 선행사 앞에 비교급이 올 때 유사관계대명사 than을 쓴다.

▶ He has more money **[as / than]** is needed.

7. 관계대명사에 –ever를 붙이면 복합관계대명사가 된다. 복합관계대명사는 명사절이나 양보의 부사절로 사용할 수 있다.

▶ **[Whoever / Whatever]** breaks this law will be punished.

B 체크 POINT

다음 괄호 안에서 어법상 올바른 것을 고르시오.

1. Sodas **[who / that]** have caffeine in them actually take water from the body.

2. Do you believe in **[that / what]** you cannot see?

3. Sally slid on the ice, **[who / which]** made everyone laugh.

4. The man who **[was / were]** working as an usher was looking for a new job.

5. Choose such friends **[but / as]** will help you.

6. She has **[more / but]** books than I have.

7. You can take **[which / whichever]** you like.

제한 시간 : 13분   정답 및 해설 075쪽

1. 다음 글의 밑줄 친 부분 중, 어법상 **틀린** 것은? [3점]

Ecosystems differ in composition and extent. They can be defined as ranging from the communities and interactions of organisms in your mouth or ① those in the canopy of a rain forest to all those in Earth's oceans. The processes ② governing them differ in complexity and speed. There are systems that turn over in minutes, and there are others ③ which rhythmic time extends to hundreds of years. Some ecosystems are extensive ('biomes', such as the African savanna); some cover regions (river basins); many involve clusters of villages (micro-watersheds); others are confined to the level of a single village (the village pond). In each example there is an element of indivisibility. Divide an ecosystem into parts by creating barriers, and the sum of the productivity of the parts will typically be found to be lower than the productivity of the whole, other things ④ being equal. The mobility of biological populations is a reason. Safe passages, for example, enable migratory species ⑤ to survive.

＊canopy: 덮개 ＊＊basin: 유역

2. 다음 글의 밑줄 친 부분 중, 어법상 **틀린** 것은? [3점]

To begin with a psychological reason, the knowledge of another's personal affairs can tempt the possessor of this information ① to repeat it as gossip because as unrevealed information it remains socially inactive. Only when the information is repeated can its possessor ② turn the fact that he knows something into something socially valuable like social recognition, prestige, and notoriety. As long as he keeps his information to ③ himself, he may feel superior to those who do not know it. But knowing and not telling does not give him that feeling of "superiority that, so to say, latently contained in the secret, fully ④ actualizing itself only at the moment of disclosure." This is the main motive for gossiping about well-known figures and superiors. The gossip producer assumes that some of the "fame" of the subject of gossip, as ⑤ whose "friend" he presents himself, will rub off on him.

＊prestige: 명성 ＊＊notoriety: 악명 ＊＊＊latently: 잠재적으로

3. 다음 글의 밑줄 친 부분 중, 어법상 **틀린** 것은? [3점]

When it comes to medical treatment, patients see choice as both a blessing and a burden. And the burden falls primarily on women, who are ① typically the guardians not only of their own health, but that of their husbands and children. "It is an overwhelming task for women, and consumers in general, ② to be able to sort through the information they find and make decisions," says Amy Allina, program director of the National Women's Health Network. And what makes it overwhelming is not only that the decision is ours, but that the number of sources of information ③ which we are to make the decisions has exploded. It's not just a matter of listening to your doctor lay out the options and ④ making a choice. We now have encyclopedic lay-people's guides to health, "better health" magazines, and the Internet. So now the prospect of medical decisions ⑤ has become everyone's worst nightmare of a term paper assignment, with stakes infinitely higher than a grade in a course.

＊lay-people: 비전문가

4. 다음 글의 밑줄 친 부분 중, 어법상 **틀린** 것은?

Though most bees fill their days visiting flowers and collecting pollen, some bees take advantage of the hard work of others. These thieving bees sneak into the nest of an ① unsuspecting "normal" bee (known as the host), lay an egg near the pollen mass being gathered by the host bee for her own offspring, and then sneak back out. When the egg of the thief hatches, it kills the host's offspring and then eats the pollen meant for ② its victim. Sometimes called brood parasites, these bees are also referred to as cuckoo bees, because they are similar to cuckoo birds, which lay an egg in the nest of another bird and ③ leaves it for that bird to raise. They are more ④ technically called cleptoparasites. *Clepto* means "thief" in Greek, and the term *cleptoparasite* refers specifically to an organism ⑤ that lives off another by stealing its food. In this case the cleptoparasite feeds on the host's hard-earned pollen stores.

＊brood parasite: (알을 대신 기르도록 하는) 탁란 동물

5. (A), (B), (C)의 각 네모 안에서 어법에 맞는 표현으로 가장 적절한 것은?

The most useful thing I brought out of my childhood was confidence in reading. Not long ago, I went on a weekend self-exploratory workshop, in the hope of getting a clue about how to live. One of the exercises we were given (A) was / were to make a list of the ten most important events of our lives. Number one was: "I was born," and you could put (B) however / whatever you liked after that. Without even thinking about it, my hand wrote at number two: "I learned to read." "I was born and learned to read" wouldn't be a sequence that occurs to many people, I imagine. But I knew what I meant to say. Being born was something (C) done / doing to me, but my own life began when I first made out the meaning of a sentence.

	(A)		(B)		(C)
①	was	⋯⋯	however	⋯⋯	done
②	was	⋯⋯	whatever	⋯⋯	done
③	was	⋯⋯	whatever	⋯⋯	doing
④	were	⋯⋯	however	⋯⋯	doing
⑤	were	⋯⋯	however	⋯⋯	done

6. 다음 글의 밑줄 친 부분 중, 어법상 틀린 것은?

In general, one's memories of any period necessarily weaken ① as one moves away from it. One is constantly learning new facts, and old ones have to drop out to ② make way for them. At twenty, I could have written the history of my school days with an accuracy which would be quite impossible now. But it can also happen that one's memories grow ③ much sharper even after a long passage of time. This is ④ because one is looking at the past with fresh eyes and can isolate and, as it were, notice facts which previously existed undifferentiated among a mass of others. There are things ⑤ what in a sense I remembered, but which did not strike me as strange or interesting until quite recently.

7. 다음 글에서 밑줄 친 부분 중, 어법상 틀린 것은? [2점]

Schubert spent his whole life ① in poverty. But he had one noble purpose in life. That was ② to write down the beautiful musical thoughts which seemed to flow from his brain in an endless rush of melody. As ③ one of the most productive composers, Schubert wrote music ④ as freely as one would write a friendly letter. He just produced ⑤ which was in him, and brought us a rich treasure of music.

8. 다음 밑줄 친 부분 중 어법상 틀린 것은?

No good can ever come from deviating from the path that you were destined to follow. Most often you deviate ① because of the temptation of money, of more immediate prospects of prosperity. Because this does not comply with something ② deep within you, your interest will lag and eventually the money will not come so easily. You will search for other easy sources of money, ③ moving further and further away from your path. Not seeing clearly ahead of you, you will end up in a dead-end career. Even if your material needs are met, you will feel an emptiness inside ④ where you will need to fill with any kind of belief system or diversions. There is no compromise here, no way of escaping the dynamic. You will recognize how far you have deviated by the depth of your pain and frustration. You must listen to the message of this frustration and pain, and let ⑤ it guide you as clearly as Fuller's voice guided him.

2018학년도 6월 모평 29번

9. (A), (B), (C)의 각 네모 안에서 문맥에 맞는 낱말로 가장 적절한 것은? [3점]

Some coaches erroneously believe that mental skills training (MST) can only help perfect the performance of highly skilled competitors. As a result, they shy away from MST, (A) denying / rationalizing that because they are not coaching elite athletes, mental skills training is less important. It is true that mental skills become increasingly important at high levels of competition. As athletes move up the competitive ladder, they become more homogeneous in terms of physical skills. In fact, at high levels of competition, all athletes have the physical skills to be successful. Consequently, any small difference in (B) physical / mental factors can play a huge role in determining performance outcomes. However, we can anticipate that personal growth and performance will progress faster in young, developing athletes who are given mental skills training than in athletes not exposed to MST. In fact, the optimal time for introducing MST may be when athletes are first beginning their sport. Introducing MST (C) early / later in athletes' careers may lay the foundation that will help them develop to their full potential.

	(A)	(B)	(C)
①	denying	physical	later
②	denying	mental	early
③	rationalizing	physical	early
④	rationalizing	physical	later
⑤	rationalizing	mental	early

20117학년도 4월 학평 29번

10. (A), (B), (C)의 각 네모 안에서 문맥에 맞는 낱말로 가장 적절한 것은? [3점]

You can use a third party to compliment a person you want to befriend and still get the "credit" for making the target of your compliment feel good about themselves and, by extension, feel good about you. When you (A) directly / indirectly compliment other people, particularly anybody who suspects you might want something from them, they tend to discount your efforts because they suspect you are intentionally trying to influence them through flattery. A third-party compliment (B) eliminates / encourages this skepticism. To construct a third-party compliment you will need to find a mutual friend or acquaintance who knows both you and your person of interest. Further, you should be relatively certain that the third-party individual you choose will be likely to pass along your compliment to the person for whom it was intended. If this (C) clarification / transmission of information is successful, the next time you meet your person of interest, he or she will see you from a positive perspective.

	(A)	(B)	(C)
①	directly	eliminates	clarification
②	directly	encourages	clarification
③	directly	eliminates	transmission
④	indirectly	encourages	transmission
⑤	indirectly	eliminates	clarification

2017학년도 3월 학평 29번

11. (A), (B), (C)의 각 네모 안에서 문맥에 맞는 낱말로 가장 적절한 것은? [3점]

Until the twentieth century, when composers began experimenting freely with form and design, classical music continued to follow basic rules relating to structure, not to mention harmony. There still was room for (A) conformity / individuality —the great composers didn't follow the rules, but made the rules follow them—yet there was always a fundamental proportion and logic behind the design. Even after many of the rules were (B) maintained / overturned by radical concepts in more recent times, composers, more often than not, still organized their thoughts in ways that produced an overall, unifying structure. That's one reason the atonal, incredibly complex works by Arnold Schönberg or Karlheinz Stockhausen, to name two twentieth-century Modernists, are nonetheless (C) approachable / inaccessible. The sounds might be very strange, but the results are still decidedly classical in terms of organization.

* atonal: 무조의, 장조나 단조 등의 조를 따르지 않는

	(A)	(B)	(C)
①	conformity	maintained	approachable
②	individuality	overturned	approachable
③	individuality	maintained	approachable
④	individuality	maintained	inaccessible
⑤	conformity	overturned	inaccessible

2020학년도 7월 종로 30번

12. 다음 글의 밑줄 친 부분 중, 문맥상 낱말의 쓰임이 적절하지 <u>않은</u> 것은? [3점]

When a bat is scanning its environment, it emits about ten to twenty clicks every second. But when it picks up an echo returned from a target, it ① <u>increases</u> that rate to as many as two hundred clicks a second in order to aim at the position and identity of its prey. Some species of moth, upon hearing a bat's clicks, will instantly fold their wings and drop straight down to ② <u>avoid</u> getting caught. Bats, in turn, have evolved ways of ③ <u>reducing</u> their clicks to take in a wide area in which even a plummeting bug will be tracked. Some moths have counter-adapted and evolved long extensions to the backs of their wings that twirl in flight to attract bats' attention. The extensions are ④ <u>disposable</u> to the moth, so if a bat targets and succeeds at biting them, the moth will simply break away and escape. It is a never ending battle between predator and prey — one in which bats will surely adapt once again to ⑤ <u>refine</u> their already outstanding ability to echolocate.

* plummet: 곤두박질치다
** echolocate: 초음파를 통해 위치를 탐지하다

총 문항					문항		맞은 문항					문항
개별 문항	1	2	3	4	5	6	7	8	9	10	11	12
채점												

어휘·숙어 비밀 노트

idiom vocabulary

A 수능 필수 어휘 ▶ 유의어 (4)

☐			
☐	521	differ, disagree	v. 일치하지 않다
☐	522	diminish, reduce	v. 축소하다
☐	523	disappoint, dismay	v. 실망시키다
☐	524	disaster, catastrophe	n 재해
☐	525	discover, detect	v. 발견하다
☐	526	discuss, debate	v. 논의하다
☐	527	distinguish, differentiate	v. 구별하다
☐	528	disturb, interrupt	v. 방해하다
☐	529	diverse, various	a. 다양한
☐	530	donate, contribute	v. 기증하다
☐	531	ease, comfort	v. 편하게 하다
☐	532	effect, impact	n. 영향
☐	533	effort, endeavor	n. 수고
☐	534	eliminate, remove	v. 제거하다
☐	535	emit, release	v. 내뿜다
☐	536	emphasize, stress	v. 강조하다
☐	537	endure, withstand	v. 견디다
☐	538	enhance, improve	v. 증진시키다
☐	539	enormous, tremendous	a. 거대한
☐	540	ensure, guarantee	v. 보장하다

B 수능 필수 숙어

☐			
☐	541	look over	~을 살펴보다
☐	542	look through	~을 빠르게 훑어보다
☐	543	look up	(정보를) 찾다
☐	544	lose weight	살이 빠지다(↔ gain weight)
☐	545	make a difference	차이를 가져오다, 차별을 두다
☐	546	make friends	~와 친구가 되다
☐	547	make it	해내다, 성공하다, 늦지 않게 도착하다
☐	548	make out	(문서를) 작성하다, ~을 이해하다, 지내다
☐	549	make sure	확실하게 하다
☐	550	make up	(이야기를) 꾸며 내다, ~을 형성하다
☐	551	make up for	(손해 등을) 보상하다, 만회하다
☐	552	make use of	~을 이용하다
☐	553	may well	~하는 것도 당연하다(= have good reason to)
☐	554	mean to do	~할 작정이다
☐	555	might as well	~하는 편이 낫다
☐	556	more or less	거의, 대략
☐	557	move on	(다음 주제로) 넘어가다
☐	558	much less	더구나 ~은 아니다
☐	559	name after	~의 이름을 따서 이름 짓다
☐	560	needless to say	말할 필요도 없이(= not to mention)

15 관계부사

🏷 출제 트렌드

1. 관계부사는 접속사와 부사의 역할을 한다. 두 개의 절을 하나의 문장으로 만들며, 관계부사가 선행사를 수식하거나 서술한다.

2. 1994~2023학년도 수능 기출 어법 문제를 분석한 결과, 관계부사 문제는 where의 한정적 용법(2012학년도 수능)과 「전치사+관계대명사」(2013학년도 수능)가 출제되었다.

3. 또한 관계부사 where(2015학년도 수능)가 선지로 출제되었다.

4. 관계사 문제는 관계대명사 문제가 관계부사 문제보다 더 비중 있게 출제되고 있다. 관계부사 중에는 where가 when, why, how보다 출제 비율이 높았다. where의 한정적 용법과 계속적 용법은 학평과 모평 시험에서도 자주 나오는 문제이므로 유의해야 한다.

	출처	문항 번호	어법·어휘 문제
1	2021학년도 09월 모평	29번	관계부사 where의 한정적 용법
2	2020학년도 09월 학평(경북)	29번	관계대명사 vs. 관계부사
3	2014학년도 06월 모평	27번	관계부사 where의 한정적 용법
4	2013학년도 수능	21번	「전치사(on)+관계대명사」
5	2012학년도 수능	20번	관계부사 where
6	2009학년도 07월 학평	22번	「전치사(for)+관계대명사」
7	2019학년도 09월 종로	29번	관계부사 when
8	2020학년도 09월 종로	29번	관계부사 where
9	2017학년도 수능	20번	어휘 문제 01
10	2016학년도 10월 학평	29번	어휘 문제 02
11	2017학년도 09월 모평	29번	어휘 문제 03
12	2020학년도 06월 종로	30번	어휘 문제 04

🏷 1등급 꿀팁

1. 관계부사는 「전치사+관계대명사」로 바꾸어 쓸 수 있다.

2. 관계부사 how는 선행사(the way)를 쓰든지, 관계부사를 쓰든지 하나만 써야 한다.

3. 복합관계부사 however 다음에는 형용사가 나온다.

정답 및 해설 081쪽

[핵심 문법]

A 출제 POINT

1. 관계부사는 문장 내에서 「접속사+부사」의 역할을 한다.
▶ After getting married we bought a flat, where we lived for the next 10 years.
= After getting married we bought a flat, and we lived for the next 10 years **[there / then]**.

2. 관계부사는 선행사가 시간이면 when, 장소이면 where, 이유이면 why, 방법이면 how를 사용한다. 관계부사 이하는 완전한 문장이 나온다.

때	장소	이유, 원인	방법
when / that	where / that	why / that	how / that
= in[at/on] which	= in[at/on] which	= for which	= in which

▶ There will be a time **[when / where]** you'll find true love.

3. 관계부사 how는 선행사(the way)를 쓰든지, 관계부사를 쓰든지 하나만 써야 한다. 단, how를 in which로 바꾼 경우 the way in which처럼 써도 된다.
▶ I don't like **[the way / the way how]** he looks at me.

4. 관계부사 when과 where는 계속적 용법으로 사용될 수 있으며, 이 경우 생략할 수 없다.
▶ They finally reached the mountaintop, **[when / where]** they could see nothing but clouds all around.

5. 관계부사는 「전치사+관계대명사」로 바꾸어 쓸 수 있다.
▶ That's a vending machine **[from / for]** which you can get prescription drugs.

6. 관계부사 when, where, why, how 대신 관계부사 that을 사용할 수 있으며, 생략할 수도 있다.
▶ They've come to the time **[that / where]** they have to make a decision.

7. 관계부사 –ever를 붙이면 복합관계부사가 된다. 복합관계부사절은 주로 양보의 부사절로 사용될 수 있다.

복합관계부사	시간, 장소의 부사절	양보의 부사절
whenever	at any time when(~할 때는 언제나)	no matter when(언제 ~할지라도)
wherever	at any place where(~하는 곳은 어디나)	no matter where(어디에서 ~할지라도)
however	–	no matter how(아무리 ~할지라도)

▶ **[Wherever / However]** you need me, just call me.

B 체크 POINT

다음 괄호 안에서 어법상 올바른 것을 고르시오.

1. We finally reached the top of Mt. Jiri, but **[then / there]** we could see nothing but clouds.
2. I don't know the reason **[when / why]** Sally refused my invitation.
3. I like **[the way / the place]** in which she looks at me.
4. My favorite month is February, **[where / when]** we celebrate Valentine's Day.
5. This is the place **[at / for]** which she lost her smartphone.
6. This is the way **[when / that]** migratory birds find their way.
7. **[Whenever / However]** you are, I'll be there with you.

•어법 기출•

2021학년도 9월 모평 29번

1. 다음 글의 밑줄 친 부분 중, 어법상 틀린 것은? [3점]

Competitive activities can be more than just performance showcases ① which the best is recognized and the rest are overlooked. The provision of timely, constructive feedback to participants on performance ② is an asset that some competitions and contests offer. In a sense, all competitions give feedback. For many, this is restricted to information about whether the participant is an award- or prizewinner. The provision of that type of feedback can be interpreted as shifting the emphasis to demonstrating superior performance but not ③ necessarily excellence. The best competitions promote excellence, not just winning or "beating" others. The emphasis on superiority is what we typically see as ④ fostering a detrimental effect of competition. Performance feedback requires that the program go beyond the "win, place, or show" level of feedback. Information about performance can be very helpful, not only to the participant who does not win or place but also to those who ⑤ do.

* foster: 조장하다　** detrimental: 유해한

2020학년도 9월 학평(경북) 29번

2. 다음 글의 밑줄 친 부분 중, 어법상 틀린 것은?

When asked, "What was one of your best days at work?" very few of us recount the time everything went smoothly and the big project we were working on came in on time and under budget. ① Considering how we work so hard to make things go well, that example should count as a pretty good day at work. But strangely, the days everything goes smoothly and as planned ② are not the ones we remember with fondness. For most of us, we have warmer feelings for the projects we worked on ③ which everything seemed to go wrong. We remember how the group stayed at work until 3 a.m., ate cold pizza and barely ④ made the deadline. Those are the experiences we remember as some of our best days at work. It was not because of the hardship, per se, but because the hardship was shared. It is not the work we remember with fondness, but the fellowship, how the group came together ⑤ to get things done.

* per se: 그 자체(로)

2014학년도 6월 모평 27번

3. 다음 글의 밑줄 친 부분 중, 어법상 틀린 것은? [3점]

Given that music appears to enhance physical and mental skills, are there circumstances where music is ① damaging to performance? One domain ② which this is of considerable significance is music's potentially damaging effects on the ability to drive safely. Evidence suggests an association between loud, fast music and reckless driving, but how might music's ability to influence driving in this way ③ be explained? One possibility is that drivers adjust to temporal regularities in music, and ④ that their speed is influenced accordingly. In other words, just as faster music causes people to eat faster, ⑤ so it causes people to drive at faster speeds, as they engage mentally and physically with ongoing repeated structures in the music.

2013학년도 수능 21번

4. 다음 글의 밑줄 친 부분 중, 어법상 틀린 것은?

We take it for granted that film directors are in the game of recycling. Adapting novels ① is one of the most respectable of movie projects, while a book that calls itself the novelization of a film is considered barbarous. Being a hybrid art as well as a late one, film has always been in a dialogue with ② other narrative genres. Movies were first seen as an exceptionally potent kind of illusionist theatre, the rectangle of the screen corresponding to the proscenium of a stage, ③ which appear actors. Starting in the early silent period, plays were regularly "turned into" films. But ④ filming plays did not encourage the evolution of what truly was distinctive about a movie: the intervention of the camera — its mobility of vision. As a source of plot, character, and dialogue, the novel seemed more ⑤ suitable. Many early successes of cinema were adaptations of popular novels.

*proscenium : 앞 무대

5. (A), (B), (C)의 각 네모 안에서 어법에 맞는 표현으로 가장 적절한 것은?

On January 10, 1992, a ship (A) traveled / traveling through rough seas lost 12 cargo containers, one of which held 28,800 floating bath toys. Brightly colored ducks, frogs, and turtles were set adrift in the middle of the Pacific Ocean. After seven months, the first toys made landfall on beaches near Sitka, Alaska, 3,540 kilometers from (B) what / where they were lost. Other toys floated north and west along the Alaskan coast and across the Bering Sea. Some toy animals stayed at sea (C) even / very longer. They floated completely along the North Pacific currents, ending up back in Sitka.

	(A)		(B)		(C)
①	traveled	·····	what	·····	even
②	traveled	·····	what	·····	very
③	traveling	·····	what	·····	even
④	traveling	·····	where	·····	even
⑤	traveling	·····	where	·····	very

6. 다음 글의 밑줄 친 부분 중, 어법상 틀린 것은? [3점]

Energize your life by starting each day with gratitude. When you wake up, before you do anything else, stop and count your blessings. Then find something special about each day ① that you can be thankful. It's a great way to get each day ② started on a positive note, and it can make a major difference throughout the day. ③ Actively practicing gratitude on a regular basis will keep you in touch with the very best of your possibilities. It will enable you to see opportunities and utilize resources which may otherwise have remained ④ hidden. So in a very real sense it will add value to each moment of the day. There are many good things in your life, waiting for you to fully appreciate and enjoy. When you do this, those positive things will grow ⑤ even stronger.

7. 다음 글의 밑줄 친 부분 중, 어법상 틀린 것은? [3점]

In the South Pacific Ocean, five hundred miles off the coast of central Chile, ① is a forbiddingly vertical volcanic island, seven miles long and four miles wide. It is populated by millions of seabirds and thousands of fur seals but is devoid of people, except in the warmer months, ② then a handful of fishermen come out to catch lobsters. To reach the island, which is officially called Alejandro Selkirk, you fly from Santiago in an eight-seater that ③ makes twice-weekly flights to an island a hundred miles to the east. Then you have to travel in a small boat from the airstrip to the island's only village, wait for a ride on another boat that occasionally makes the twelve-hour voyage, and then, often, wait further, sometimes for days, for weather conducive to ④ landing on the rocky shore. In the 1960s, Chilean tourism officials renamed the island after Alexander Selkirk, the Scottish adventurer ⑤ whose tale of solitary life on the island was probably the basis for Daniel Defoe's novel *Robinson Crusoe*, but the locals still use its original name, Masafuera.

*conducive: 도움이 되는, 좋은

8. 다음 글의 밑줄 친 부분 중, 어법상 틀린 것은?

Researchers of the Earth's system have been focused, appropriately, on developing a better understanding of the vast and interconnected processes that create our environment, and they ① have made a great deal of progress since the publication of *A Sand County Almanac*, a 1949 non-fiction book by Aldo Leopold. Although there are many problems left to solve, knowledge about planetary life-support systems has progressed far more ② rapidly than society's willingness to use this knowledge. The biggest challenge facing humanity is that our political, social, and economic systems are shortsighted. Long-term planning typically considers years or decades, but the global environmental processes we are now ③ influencing play out over centuries, millennia, or more. We need to instill a sense of geologic time into our culture and our planning, ④ to incorporate truly long-term thinking into social and political decision making. This is what "thinking like a mountain" should come to mean in the Anthropocene. If we succeed in transforming our culture, residents of the later Anthropocene will look back on the early twenty-first century as a time of human enlightenment, ⑤ which people learned to truly think like mountains by anticipating their long-lasting and complex effects on the world.

* instill: 서서히 불어넣다   ** the Anthropocene: 인류세(지구에 대한 인류의 영향을 특정으로 하는 지질학적 시기)

•어휘 기출•

제한 시간 : 7분 | 정답 및 해설 085쪽

9. (A), (B), (C)의 각 네모 안에서 문맥에 맞는 낱말로 가장 적절한 것은?

When teachers work in isolation, they tend to see the world through one set of eyes — their own. The fact that there might be someone somewhere *in the same building or district* who may be more successful at teaching this or that subject or lesson is (A) based / lost on teachers who close the door and work their way through the school calendar virtually alone. In the absence of a process that (B) allows / forbids them to benchmark those who do things better or at least differently, teachers are left with that one perspective — their own. I taught various subjects under the social studies umbrella and had very little idea of how my peers who taught the same subject did what they did. The idea of meeting regularly to compare notes, plan common assessments, and share what we did well (C) mostly / never occurred to us. Rather, we spent much time in the social studies office complaining about a lack of time and playing the blame game.

(A)	(B)	(C)
① based	……… allows	……… never
② based	……… forbids	……… mostly
③ lost	……… allows	……… mostly
④ lost	……… allows	……… never
⑤ lost	……… forbids	……… never

10. 다음 글의 밑줄 친 부분 중, 문맥상 낱말의 쓰임이 적절하지 않은 것은? [3점]

One reason conversational life can lack depth and excitement is that we easily fall into using ① formulaic questions to open a dialogue — How are you? What was the weather like? What do you do? How was your weekend? Although such questions can be important social lubricants, in themselves they generally fail to ② spark an engaging and enriching empathic exchange. We answer "Fine" or "OK," then move on down the corridor. The way a conversation ③ begins can be a major determinant of where it goes. So it is worth experimenting with adventurous openings. Instead of greeting a workmate with "How are things?" try taking your conversation in a different direction with something mildly ④ unusual like, "What have you been thinking about this morning?" or "What was the most surprising thing that happened to you over the weekend?" You need to come up with the kinds of questions that suit your own personality. The point is to ⑤ follow conventions so your conversations become energizing, memorable, and vehicles for empathic discovery.

* lubricant: 윤활유

11. (A), (B), (C)의 각 네모 안에서 문맥에 맞는 낱말로 가장 적절한 것은?

You can't have a democracy if you can't talk with your neighbors about matters of mutual interest or concern. Thomas Jefferson, who had an enduring interest in democracy, came to a similar conclusion. He was prescient in understanding the dangers of (A) concentrated / limited power, whether in corporations or in political leaders or exclusionary political institutions. Direct involvement of citizens was what had made the American Revolution possible and given the new republic vitality and hope for the future. Without that involvement, the republic would die. Eventually, he saw a need for the nation to be (B) blended / subdivided into "wards" — political units so small that everyone living there could participate directly in the political process. The representatives for each ward in the capital would have to be (C) resistant / responsive to citizens organized in this way. A vibrant democracy conducted locally would then provide the active basic unit for the democratic life of the republic. With that kind of involvement, the republic might survive and prosper.

* prescient: 선견지명이 있는 ** vibrant: 활력이 넘치는

(A)	(B)	(C)
① concentrated	…… blended	…… resistant
② concentrated	…… subdivided	…… responsive
③ concentrated	…… subdivided	…… resistant
④ limited	…… subdivided	…… resistant
⑤ limited	…… blended	…… responsive

12. 다음 글의 밑줄 친 부분 중, 문맥상 낱말의 쓰임이 적절하지 않은 것은?

Research published in 2017 on what's called "open-label placebos" is especially fascinating, since it ① supports the power of the subconscious and suggestibility. Unlike the traditional placebo study — where the patient doesn't know if he's getting the sugar pill or the drug — open-label placebo studies are those in which patients are actually ② told, "Yes, you are definitely getting the sugar pill." The doctor delivers this with a positive suggestion, telling the patient that although it is indeed a placebo, it has been shown to produce improvement through ③ healing that originates in the mind. We know that's how placebos work, don't we? A review of five studies showed that open-label placebos — where patients knew they weren't getting any real drug — had a ④ negative effect on depression, back pain, ADHD, and hay fever. The placebo effect extends even to the pill color because our brains associate certain colors with certain effects, thus making a pill more or less ⑤ effective.

* suggestibility: 암시 감응성(感應性), 암시할 수 있음

총 문항		문항	맞은 문항							문항		
개별 문항	1	2	3	4	5	6	7	8	9	10	11	12
채점												

어휘·숙어 비밀 노트

A 수능 필수 어휘 ▶ 유의어 (5)

□			
□ 561	entrance, admission		n. 입학, 입장
□ 562	enroll, regiser		v. 등록하다
□ 563	establish, found		v. 설립하다
□ 564	ethical, moral		a. 도덕상의
□ 565	evaluate, assess		v. 평가하다
□ 566	evident, obvious		a. 명백한
□ 567	evolve, progress		v. 발전하다
□ 568	exceed, surpass		v. 초과하다
□ 569	exchange, trade		v. 교환하다
□ 570	exhibit, display		v. 진열하다
□ 571	expect, anticipate		v. 기대하다
□ 572	expert, professional		n. 전문가
□ 573	expose, disclose		v. 폭로하다
□ 574	face, confront		v. 직면하다
□ 575	fascinate, attract		v. 매혹하다
□ 576	firm, company		n. 회사
□ 577	focus, concentrate		v. 집중하다
□ 578	follow, observe		v. 따르다
□ 579	frighten, terrify		v. 겁먹게 만들다
□ 580	fundamental, essential		a. 필수적인

B 수능 필수 숙어

□ 581	no more than		단지 ~에 지나지 않는(= only)
□ 582	not entirely		전적으로 ~인 것은 아닌
□ 583	not to mention		~은 말할 것도 없고
□ 584	now and then		때때로, 가끔
□ 585	of all ages		모든 연령의, 모든 시대의
□ 586	of itself		저절로
□ 587	of use		유용한(= useful)
□ 588	on (the) air		방송 중인
□ 589	on behalf of		~을 대표하여
□ 590	on earth		도대체
□ 591	on foot		도보로
□ 592	on one's own		혼자 힘으로, 혼자서
□ 593	on the contrary		~와는 반대로
□ 594	on the other hand		한편으로는, 반면에
□ 595	on the way		~가는 중인, ~하는 도중에
□ 596	once upon a time		옛날에
□ 597	one another		서로
□ 598	one by one		하나씩
□ 599	only a few		소수의
□ 600	or more		그 이상

16 병렬 구조

🏷 출제 트렌드

1. 단어나 단어, 구와 구, 절과 절이 연결될 때, 서로 동일한 구조와 형태를 가지는 것을 병렬 또는 병치라고 한다.

2. 병렬 구조 문제는 수능에서 매우 자주 출제되는 문제 중 하나이다. 대비가 필요하다.

3. 1994-2023학년도 수능 기출 어법 문제를 분석한 결과, 병렬 구조 문제는 등위접속사(or)가 현재분사를 병렬구조로 가져온 경우(1994학년도 수능 2차), 등위접속사(and)가 to부정사를 병렬 구조를 가져온 경우(2003, 2011학년도 수능(16쪽 5번 문제 참조)), 전치사(구) 뒤에 동명사를 병렬 구조로 가져온 경우(1995, 2006, 2010학년도 수능)의 문제가 출제되었다.

4. 또한 「조동사+A, B, and C(2004학년도 수능)」, 상관접속사 「either A or B」의 구조에서 A와 B가 병렬구조를 이루는 문제(2022학년도 수능)가 선지로 출제되었다.

	출처	문항 번호	어법·어휘 문제
1	2022학년도 06월 모평	29번	both A and B의 병렬 구조
2	2019학년도 06월 모평	28번	「can+동사원형 ~ or 동사원형」
3	2010학년도 수능	22번	be capable of [동명사 and 동명사]
4	2007학년도 03월 학평	22번	from 동명사 to 동명사의 병렬 구조
5	2019학년도 11월 종로	29번	등위접속사 뒤에 병렬 구조를 이루는 명사구
6	2022학년도 11월 종로	29번	동사 and 동사 구조를 이루는 병렬 구문
7	2016학년도 05월 종로	28번	병렬 구조를 이루는 동명사
8	2016학년도 03월 종로	28번	병렬 구조를 이루는 부정사
9	2016학년도 07월 학평	30번	어휘 문제 01
10	2017학년도 06월 수능	29번	어휘 문제 02
11	2016학년도 04월 학평	29번	어휘 문제 03
12	2020학년도 05월 종로	30번	어휘 문제 04

🏷 1등급 꿀팁

1. 등위접속사나 상관접속사가 병렬 구조를 이루는 경우가 많다.

2. 부정사, 동명사, 분사 등 준동사도 나열될 때 병렬 구조의 원리를 따른다.

3. A, B and C구조에서 C에 어떤 표현을 넣어야 할지 묻는 경우, A, B와 같은 문법 형태를 취하면 된다.

Day 16　　　　　　　　　　　　　　　　　　　　　　　　　　　　병렬 구조

[핵심 문법]

정답 및 해설 087쪽

A 출제 POINT

1. 등위접속사(and, or, but 등)에 의해 연결되는 내용은 비슷한 구조로 병렬되어야 한다.
　▶ It seizes the unsuspecting prey with a lightning-fast snap of the jaws, and **[swallows / to swallow]** the prey down head first.

2. 등위접속사에 의해 연결되는 구조는 A가 동명사이면 B도 동명사로 해야 한다.
　▶ She is looking forward to going to Italy and **[eat / eating]** wonderful pasta every day.

3. 등위접속사에 의해 연결되는 구조는 A가 부정사이면 B도 부정사로로 해야 한다.
　▶ But now the tools of the digital age give us a way to easily get, share, and **[acting / act]** on information in new ways.

4. 상관접속사에 의해 연결되는 내용도 비슷한 구조로 병렬되어야 한다.

not A but B	A가 아니라 B	either A or B	A 또는 B
not only A but also B	A뿐만 아니라 B도	neither A nor B	A도 B도 아닌
B as well as A	A뿐만 아니라 B도	both A and B	A, B 둘 다

　▶ The Mongol Empire was not a unified state **[but / nor]** a vast collection of territories held together by military force.

5. 상관접속사 not A but B, not only A but also B, B as well as A, either A or B, neither A nor B에서 동사의 시제 일치는 B에 일치시킨다. 단, both A and B는 복수 취급한다.
　▶ Mary as well as Jack **[is / are]** my close friends.

6. 비교 구문에서도 병렬 구조를 지켜야 한다.
　▶ His idea is better than **[me / mine]**.

7. 비교 구문이 병렬 구조를 이루는 경우, 명사의 반복을 피하기 위해 「the+명사」 대신에 that을 쓴다. 명사가 복수일 때는 those를 써야 한다.
　▶ The population of Tokyo is larger than **[that / those]** of Seoul.

B 체크 POINT

다음 괄호 안에서 어법상 올바른 것을 고르시오.

1. Sally is smart, beautiful and **[humorously / humorous]**.
2. The adults busied themselves preparing the food, supervising the children, and **[playing / played]** volleyball.
3. He hopes to go to London university and **[studying / study]** under Dr. Lee.
4. Neither Peter **[nor / or]** his wife mentions anything about moving house.
5. Either you or your sister **[have / has]** to stay here.
6. My Smartphone is similar to **[her / hers]** in color and shape.
7. Japan made an increase in electronic products, but the increase of Japan was smaller than **[that / those]** of South Korea.

092
Day 16 ・ 병렬 구조　　　　　　　　　　　　　　　　　　　　[고3 영어 어법・어휘]

제한 시간 : 13분 | 정답 및 해설 087쪽

2022학년도 6월 모평 29번

1. 다음 글의 밑줄 친 부분 중, 어법상 틀린 것은?

Most historians of science point to the need for a reliable calendar to regulate agricultural activity as the motivation for learning about what we now call astronomy, the study of stars and planets. Early astronomy provided information about when to plant crops and gave humans ① their first formal method of recording the passage of time. Stonehenge, the 4,000-year-old ring of stones in southern Britain, ② is perhaps the best-known monument to the discovery of regularity and predictability in the world we inhabit. The great markers of Stonehenge point to the spots on the horizon ③ where the sun rises at the solstices and equinoxes — the dates we still use to mark the beginnings of the seasons. The stones may even have ④ been used to predict eclipses. The existence of Stonehenge, built by people without writing, bears silent testimony both to the regularity of nature and to the ability of the human mind to see behind immediate appearances and ⑤ discovers deeper meanings in events.

* monument: 기념비 ** eclipse: (해·달의) 식(蝕)
*** testimony: 증언

2019학년도 6월 모평 28번

2. 다음 글의 밑줄 친 부분 중, 어법상 틀린 것은?

Humans are so averse to feeling that they're being cheated ① that they often respond in ways that seemingly make little sense. Behavioral economists — the economists who actually study ② what people do as opposed to the kind who simply assume the human mind works like a calculator — have shown again and again that people reject unfair offers even if ③ it costs them money to do so. The typical experiment uses a task called the ultimatum game. It's pretty straightforward. One person in a pair is given some money — say $10. She then has the opportunity to offer some amount of it to her partner. The partner only has two options. He can take what's offered or ④ refused to take anything. There's no room for negotiation; that's why it's called the ultimatum game. What typically happens? Many people offer an equal split to the partner, ⑤ leaving both individuals happy and willing to trust each other in the future.

* averse to: ~을 싫어하는 ** ultimatum: 최후통첩

2010학년도 수능 22번

3. 다음 글의 밑줄 친 부분 중, 어법상 틀린 것은?

While manned space missions are more costly than unmanned ① ones, they are more successful. Robots and astronauts use ② much of the same equipment in space. But a human is much more capable of operating those instruments correctly and ③ to place them in appropriate and useful positions. Rarely ④ is a computer more sensitive and accurate than a human in managing the same geographical or environmental factors. Robots are also not equipped with capabilities like humans to solve problems ⑤ as they arise, and they often collect data that are unhelpful or irrelevant.

2007학년도 3월 학평 22번

4. 다음 글의 밑줄 친 부분 중, 어법상 틀린 것은?

If you ever feel ill when ① traveling in remote foreign parts, just drop some gunpowder into a glass of warm, soapy water, and swallow it. That was the advice of Francis Galton in a book ② called The Art of Travel. Bee stings? Well, the tar scraped out of tobacco pipe and ③ applied on the skin relieves the pain. Galton's book proved a bestseller. It covered every situation, from constructing boats, huts, and tents in a hurry ④ to catch fish without a line. It told readers how to find firewood in a rainstorm (under the roots of a tree) and where ⑤ to put your clothes when it's raining so that they don't get wet (just take them off and sit on them).

5. 다음 글의 밑줄 친 부분 중, 어법상 틀린 것은? [3점]

Jerome Singer, a legendary cognitive psychologist, was the first scientist to suggest that the mental state in which the mind is allowed to wander ① freely is, in fact, our "default" state. Singer further argued in his 1966 book, *Daydreaming*, that daydreaming, imagination, and fantasy are essential elements of a healthy mental life. These elements include self-awareness, creative incubation, autobiographical planning, consideration of the meaning of events and interactions, ② take another person's perspective, reflecting on your own and others' emotions, and moral reasoning. All of this leads to ③ what we think of as "aha!" moments. The musician, bestselling writer, and neuroscientist Daniel J. Levitin ④ emphasizes that insights are far more likely to come when you are in the mind-wandering mode than in the task-focused mode. It is only when we let our minds wander that we make unexpected connections between things that we did not realize were ⑤ connected. This can help you solve problems that previously seemed to be unsolvable.

*default state: 기본 상태
**incubation: 숙고

6. 다음 글의 밑줄 친 부분 중, 어법상 틀린 것은?

Literary fiction provides much insight into social relations in novels or short stories. But it does not usually claim to offer systematic interpretation of social phenomena. Its great power is in the rich presentation of particularity in a way that ① evokes general interest. The telling of stories, the evocation of mood, character and circumstances can present human individuality as ② simultaneously a matter of unique and universal experiences. Fiction can offer to the reader a means of reflecting on the nature of the social world. It does this when it inspires the conviction ③ that its ideas extend social experience — the experience or observation of the reader. Fiction contributes to sociological ideas when it creates in the reader the sense that its stories, characterizations and evocations, or certain elements in them, can be used to ④ interpret aspects of social experience. The reader may empathize with characters or imagine situations as if they were presented as factual reports of experience. Empathy and imagination supply empirical reference for fiction, and ⑤ giving it its power to supply insight into 'the human condition' in some sense.

* empirical: 경험적인

7. 다음 글의 밑줄 친 부분 중, 어법상 틀린 것은? [3점]

In his youth Albert Einstein spent a year loafing aimlessly. You don't get anywhere by not "wasting" time — something, unfortunately, ① that the parents of teenagers tend frequently to forget. He was in Pavia. He had joined his family, having abandoned his studies in Germany, ② unable to endure the rigors of his high school there. It was the beginning of the twentieth century, and in Italy the beginning of its industrial revolution. Albert was reading Kant and attending occasional lectures at the University of Pavia: for pleasure, without being registered there or ③ had to think about exams. It is thus that serious scientists are made. After this he registered at the University of Zurich and immersed ④ himself in the study of physics. A few years later, in 1905, he sent three articles to the most prestigious scientific journal of the period, the *Annalen der Physik*. Each of these ⑤ is worthy of a Nobel Prize.

* loaf: 빈둥거리다

8. (A), (B), (C)의 각 네모 안에서 어법에 맞는 표현으로 가장 적절한 것은? [3점]

A good movie always starts with a clear presentation of the major elements of the story. The director knows (A) that / what if the dramatic conflict is not clear, the story will appear meaningless and boring to the audience. Clarity is one of the most important principles in film making. The screen-writer must have a clear-cut idea of what the story is about, otherwise the resulting movie will be (B) confused / confusing. A clear presentation of the subject matter is just as important in a multimedia system as in a movie. If the user does not understand right from the start what is going on, he or she can lose interest. Even though many multimedia systems are not centered around a dramatic story line, there is a need to state the purpose of the system clearly and (C) making / to make it clear which information the user can expect to find, where it can be found, and how it can be found.

	(A)		(B)		(C)
①	that	……	confused	……	making
②	that	……	confusing	……	to make
③	that	……	confused	……	to make
④	what	……	confusing	……	making
⑤	what	……	confused	……	making

제한 시간 : 7분	정답 및 해설 090쪽

9. (A), (B), (C)의 각 네모 안에서 문맥에 맞는 낱말로 가장 적절한 것은? [3점]

The theory of E-prime argues that if you wrote and spoke English without the verb *to be*, you'd describe events more accurately. For example, when you say, "Johnny is a failure," the verb *is* implies that "failure" is in Johnny rather than in your observation of Johnny. The verb *to be* (in forms such as *is*, *are*, and *am*) also implies (A) permanence / variation; the implication is that because failure is in Johnny, it will always be there; Johnny will always be a failure. A more (B) erroneous / precise statement might be "Johnny failed his last two math exams." Consider this theory as applied to your thinking about yourself. When you say, for example, "I'm not good at public speaking" or "I'm unpopular" or "I'm lazy," you imply that these qualities are in you. But these are simply (C) evaluations / solutions that may be incorrect or, if at least partly accurate, may change over time.

	(A)	(B)	(C)
①	permanence	erroneous	evaluations
②	permanence	precise	evaluations
③	permanence	precise	solutions
④	variation	erroneous	solutions
⑤	variation	precise	solutions

10. (A), (B), (C)의 각 네모 안에서 문맥에 맞는 낱말로 가장 적절한 것은? [3점]

In 2001, researchers at Wayne State University asked a group of college volunteers to exercise for twenty minutes at a (A) preset / self-selected pace on each of three machines: a treadmill, a stationary bike, and a stair climber. Measurements of heart rate, oxygen consumption, and perceived effort were taken throughout all three workouts. The researchers expected to find that the subjects unconsciously targeted the same relative physiological intensity in each activity. Perhaps they would (B) automatically / intentionally exercise at 65 percent of their maximum heart rate regardless of which machine they were using. Or maybe they would instinctively settle into rhythm at 70 percent of their maximum rate of oxygen consumption in all three workouts. But that's not what happened. There was, in fact, no (C) consistency / variation in measurements of heart rate and oxygen consumption across the three disciplines. Instead, the subjects were found to have chosen the same level of perceived effort on the treadmill, the bike, and the stair climber.

* treadmill: 러닝머신
** physiological: 생리학적인

	(A)	(B)	(C)
①	preset	intentionally	consistency
②	preset	automatically	variation
③	self-selected	intentionally	variation
④	self-selected	intentionally	consistency
⑤	self-selected	automatically	consistency

11. (A), (B), (C)의 각 네모 안에서 문맥에 맞는 낱말로 가장 적절한 것은?

With a power gap, the more hierarchical your culture or background, the greater the power gap is apt to be. This is because hierarchical cultures (A) decrease / reinforce the differences between managers and employees. If you tend to be more hierarchical in your orientation, you tend to put those in positions of authority at a higher level, and there is more respect for that status or position, divorced even from the person who occupies it. (B) Distance / Friendliness is seen as good if you have a hierarchical preference. It wouldn't be proper for a manager to be too familiar with his employees. The effect is that any power gap that exists is magnified through the lens of this dimension. A greater power gap can result in decreased communication as well as increased misunderstandings and conflict, potentially leading to (C) missed / unlimited opportunities for building significant business and career relationships.

	(A)	(B)	(C)
①	decrease	Distance	missed
②	decrease	Friendliness	unlimited
③	reinforce	Distance	missed
④	reinforce	Friendliness	unlimited
⑤	reinforce	Distance	unlimited

12. 다음 글의 밑줄 친 부분 중, 문맥상 낱말의 쓰임이 적절하지 않은 것은? [3점]

Today's ageing adults will be more advantaged in the employment domain as they age. Attitudes about older employees are becoming more ① favorable. In addition, because of the post-baby boom declines in birth rates, the number of employable adults will ② decrease relative to the number of new jobs. Consequently, older workers will become more valued and sought after, and those who do not feel ready to retire will be ③ less likely to be compelled to do so. The standard retirement age is ④ rising, based on observations that, in terms of health and life expectancy, age 70 today is roughly the equivalent of age 65 in the 1930s when Social Security was established in the USA. Although most individuals who have adequate (or better) financial resources will retire at the usual time or ⑤ reverse the trend toward early retirement, physically healthy elders will be able to choose whether or not they will continue to work.

총 문항				문항	맞은 문항						문항	
개별 문항	1	2	3	4	5	6	7	8	9	10	11	12
채점												

A 수능 필수 어휘 ▶ 유의어 (6)

□ 601	gather, assemble	v. 모으다
□ 602	generate, produce	v. 생성하다
□ 603	genuine, authentic	a. 진짜의
□ 604	ignore, disregard	v. 무시하다
□ 605	immediate, prompt	a. 즉각적인
□ 606	imitate, mimic	v. 모방하다
□ 607	impress, move	v. 감동시키다
□ 608	incredible, unbelievable	a. 믿어지지 않는
□ 609	indifferent, unconcerned	a. 무관심한
□ 610	induce, cause	v. 야기하다
□ 611	inevitable, unavoidable	a. 불가피한
□ 612	influence, affect	v. 영향을 미치다
□ 613	inherent, innate	a. 타고난
□ 614	integrate, combine	v. 통합하다
□ 615	interpret, translate	v. 통역하다
□ 616	invent, devise	v. 고안하다
□ 617	investigate, exam	v. 조사하다
□ 618	isolate, separate	v. 고립시키다
□ 619	jealous, envious	a. 시기하는
□ 620	measure, gauge	v. 측정하다

B 수능 필수 숙어

□ 621	or something[somebody]	~인가 무엇[누구]인가
□ 622	ought to	~해야 한다
□ 623	out of order	고장 난, 정리가 안 된, ~에 어긋나는
□ 624	out of place	제자리에 있지 않은, 부적절한
□ 625	over and over	반복해서
□ 626	pass away	사망하다
□ 627	pass by	(장소를) 지나가다, (시간이) 흘러가다
□ 628	pass down	(후대에) ~을 물려주다
□ 629	pass through	~을 통과하다
□ 630	pay back	(돈을) 갚다, 복수하다
□ 631	pay off	(빚을) 갚다, 성과를 올리다
□ 632	place an order	~을 주문하다
□ 633	play a role	역할을 맡다
□ 634	prevent A from B	A가 B하는 것을 막다
□ 635	provide A with B	A에게 B를 제공하다(= supply A with B)
□ 636	pull over	(차를) 길가에 대다
□ 637	put aside	따로 떼어 놓다, 무시하다
□ 638	put away	(물건을 제자리로) 치우다
□ 639	put off	~을 연기하다(= postpone), 미루다
□ 640	put together	조립하다

대명사

🏷️ 출제 트렌드

1. 명사를 대신하여 사용하는 품사를 대명사라고 한다. 대명사는 인칭대명사, 지시대명사, 소유대명사, 재귀대명사, 부정대명사 등이 있다.

2. 1994-2023학년도 수능 기출 어법 문제를 분석한 결과, 대명사 문제는 재귀대명사(1995, 2002, 2023학년도 수능), 국가의 지리를 나타낼 때 사용하는 소유격 its(2004학년도 수능), 인칭대명사의 소유격(2005, 2006학년도 수능), 지시대명사(2008학년도 수능) 문제가 출제되었다.

3. 또한 부정대명사 ones(2019학년도 수능), 인칭대명사의 소유격(2011, 2012, 2016학년도 수능), 대명사 those(사람들)(2017학년도 수능(21쪽 2번 참조)), 인칭대명사의 목적격(2018학년도 수능(9쪽 1번 참조)), 지시대명사 those(2019학년도 수능(117쪽 1번 참조)), 재귀대명사의 재귀용법(2020학년도 수능(63쪽 4번 참조)), 명사(구)를 대신하는 대명사 it (2021학년도 수능(75쪽 3번 참조))이 선지로 출제되었다.

	출처	문항 번호	어법·어휘 문제
1	2023학년도 수능	29번	재귀대명사
2	2018학년도 03월 학평	29번	재귀대명사(themselves)
3	2008학년도 04월 학평	21번	some... others~, 「동사+대명사+부사」
4	2008학년도 수능	21번	지시대명사 that
5	2006학년도 수능	21번	인칭대명사의 소유격 its vs. their
6	2004학년도 수능	29번	국가의 지리를 나타내는 소유격 its
7	2002학년도 수능	30번	재귀대명사(yourself), 지시대명사(it)
8	2015학년도 07월 종로	28번	지시대명사 that vs. those
9	2016학년도 03월 학평	30번	어휘 문제 01
10	2016학년도 11월 수능	29번	어휘 문제 02
11	2015학년도 10월 학평	30번	어휘 문제 03
12	2020학년도 04월 종로	30번	어휘 문제 04

🏷️ 1등급 꿀팁

1. 지시대명사는 가리키는 대상이 가까운 것은 this, 멀 때는 that을 사용한다. 또한 가리키는 대상이 단수일 때는 this /that을 사용하고, 복수일 때는 these/those를 사용한다.

2. 인칭대명사의 소유격은 단수는 its, 복수는 their를 사용한다. 국가의 지리적인 면을 나타내는 경우 소유격은 its를 사용하고, 국가의 정치적인 면을 나타내는 경우 her를 사용한다.

3. 문장의 주어가 문장의 목적어와 같을 때는 재귀대명사를 쓴다.

4. 부정대명사 (1) one... the other ~ (2) some... others~ (3) some... the others와 같은 기본 표현과 의미의 차이를 익힌다.

5. all이 대명사로 사용된 경우, 수를 셀 수 있는 대상을 나타낼 때는 복수로, 수를 셀 수 없는 대상을 나타낼 때는 단수로 나타낸다. all of~, none of~, much of~, most of~, each of~ 등이 명사 앞에 올 때는 all of my friends와 같이 한정어(my)를 명사 앞에 써야 한다.

[핵심 문법]

정답 및 해설 092쪽

A 출제 POINT

1. 인칭대명사는 주격, 소유격, 목적격과 단수형, 복수형이 있다. 대명사가 목적어일 때, 「타동사+대명사+부사」의 어순으로 써야 한다.

▶ A powerful flashlight will easily light your way, revealing marine life in [**its** / **their**] true colors.

2. 재귀대명사는 주어와 동일한 대상을 지칭하는 목적어에 사용한다. '~자신'이라는 의미를 나타낸다. 재귀대명사 강조 용법은 명사를 강조하기 위해 사용하고 생략 가능하다. 재귀대명사 관용 표현도 익혀 둔다.

for oneself	자기를 위하여	by oneself	혼자서
in itself	본질적으로	between ourselves	우리끼리 얘긴데

▶ We enjoyed [**us** / **ourselves**] very much last night.

3. 소유대명사는 「소유격+명사」를 대신하는 말이고 '~의 것'이라는 의미를 나타낸다.

▶ Are those his books? - No, they are [**her** / **hers**].

4. 지시대명사 this/that은 앞에 언급된 어구나 내용을 받는다. this[these]는 가까운 것, that[those]은 먼 것을 가리킨다. 명사의 반복을 피하기 위해 that이나 those를 쓸 수 있다.

▶ It is said that China's economy could be 2.5 times [**those** / **that**] of US by 2030.

5. 부정대명사 either, neither, someone, anyone, no one, everyone 등은 단수로 취급한다. both는 복수로 취급한다. 막연한 것을 지칭할 때는 부정대명사 one[some], 구체적인 것을 지칭할 때는 it을 쓴다.

one..., the other ~	(둘 중에서) 하나는 …, 다른 하나는 ~
one..., another ~, the other~	(셋 중에서) 하나는 …, 다른 하나는 ~, 또 다른 하나는 ~
some... others~	(막연한 다수 중) 일부는 …, 다른 일부는 ~
some... the others~	(한정된 다수 중) 일부는 …, 나머지 일부는 ~

▶ We have two puppies; one is white, and [**the other** / **another**] is black.

6. 의문대명사는 who, whose, whom, which, what이 있다. 직접의문문이 다른 문장의 일부로 들어가는 경우, 의문사가 있는 경우, 「의문사+주어+동사」의 간접의문문 형식을 갖는다. 의문사가 없는 경우에는 「whether[if]+주어+동사」의 형태를 취한다.

▶ Can you tell me [**what you like** / **what do you like**] most about your job?

7. 구체적인 지칭은 it/ they를 사용하고, 막연한 지칭은 one / some을 사용한다.

▶ In a sense, the fine art object is valued because [**it** / **one**] can be reproduced for popular consumption.

B 체크 POINT

다음 괄호 안에서 어법상 올바른 것을 고르시오.

1. Possibly the most effect way to focus on your goals is to [**write them down** / **write down them**].

2. I want to speak to the director [**him** / **himself**], not his secretary.

3. I have my pencil; have you got [**you** / **yours**]?

4. The picture I am referring to is [**this** / **these**] here.

5. Some tourists went to the beach; [**the others** / **others**] explored the town.

6. There are six books. One is mine, and [**others** / **the others**] are my brother's.

7. Did any letters come for me? Yes, [**they** / **some**] came.

•어법 기출•

제한 시간 : 13분	정답 및 해설 092쪽

1. 다음 글의 밑줄 친 부분 중, 어법상 **틀린** 것은?

Trends constantly suggest new opportunities for individuals to restage themselves, representing occasions for change. To understand how trends can ultimately give individuals power and freedom, one must first discuss fashion's importance as a basis for change. The most common explanation offered by my informants as to why fashion is so appealing is ① that it constitutes a kind of theatrical costumery. Clothes are part of how people present ② them to the world, and fashion locates them in the present, relative to what is happening in society and to fashion's own history. As a form of expression, fashion contains a host of ambiguities, enabling individuals to recreate the meanings ③ associated with specific pieces of clothing. Fashion is among the simplest and cheapest methods of self-expression: clothes can be ④ inexpensively purchased while making it easy to convey notions of wealth, intellectual stature, relaxation or environmental consciousness, even if none of these is true. Fashion can also strengthen agency in various ways, ⑤ opening up space for action.

2. (A), (B), (C)의 각 네모 안에서 어법에 맞는 표현으로 가장 적절한 것은?

The old maxim "I'll sleep when I'm dead" is unfortunate. (A) Adopt / Adopting this mind-set, and you will be dead sooner and the quality of that life will be worse. The elastic band of sleep deprivation can stretch only so far before it snaps. Sadly, human beings are in fact the only species that will deliberately deprive (B) them / themselves of sleep without legitimate gain. Every component of wellness, and countless seams of societal fabric, are being eroded by our costly state of sleep neglect: human and financial alike. So much so that the World Health Organization (WHO) has now declared a sleep loss epidemic throughout industrialized nations. It is no coincidence that countries (C) where / which sleep time has declined most dramatically over the past century, such as the US, the UK, Japan, and South Korea, and several in Western Europe, are also those suffering the greatest increase in rates of physical diseases and mental disorders.

	(A)		(B)		(C)
①	Adopt	······	them	······	where
②	Adopt	······	themselves	······	where
③	Adopt	······	themselves	······	which
④	Adopting	······	themselves	······	which
⑤	Adopting	······	them	······	which

3. (A), (B), (C)의 각 네모 안에서 어법에 맞는 표현으로 가장 적절한 것은?

Note taking is one of the activities by which students attempt to stay attentive, but it is also an aid to memory. "Working memory," or "short-term memory" is a term (A) used / using to describe the fact that one can hold only a given amount of material in mind at one time. When a lecturer presents a succession of new concepts, students' faces begin to show signs of anguish and frustration; some write furiously in their notebooks, while (B) other / others give up writing in complete discouragement. Note taking thus is dependent on one's ability to maintain attention, understand what is being said, and hold it in working memory long enough to (C) write down it / write it down .

	(A)		(B)		(C)
①	used	······	other	······	write down it
②	used	······	others	······	write it down
③	used	······	others	······	write down it
④	using	······	others	······	write it down
⑤	using	······	other	······	write down it

4. (A), (B), (C)의 각 네모 안에서 어법에 맞는 표현으로 가장 적절한 것은?

The first thing I notice upon entering this garden is that the ankle-high grass is greener than (A) that / those on the other side of the fence. Dozens of wildflowers of countless varieties cover the ground to (B) both / either sides of the path. Creeping plants cover the polished silver gate and the sound of bubbling water comes from somewhere. The perfume of wildflowers (C) fill / fills the air as the grass dances upon a gentle breeze. A large basket of herbs rests against the fence to the west. Every time I walk in this garden, I think, "Now I know what it is like to live in paradise."

	(A)		(B)		(C)
①	that	----	both	----	fill
②	that	----	both	----	fills
③	that	----	either	----	fills
④	those	----	either	----	fill
⑤	those	----	either	----	fills

5. 다음 글의 밑줄 친 부분 중, 어법상 틀린 것은?

I wonder how many people give up just when success is almost within reach. They endure day after day, and just when they're about ① to make it, decide they can't take any more. The difference between success and failure is not ② that great. Successful people have simply learned the value of staying in the game until it ③ is won. Those who never make it ④ are the ones who quit too soon. When things are darkest, successful people refuse to give up because they know they're almost there. Things often seem at ⑤ its worst just before they get better. The mountain is steepest at the summit, but that's no reason to turn back.

6. 다음 글의 밑줄 친 부분 중, 어법상 틀린 것은?

Recently, a severe disease hit Asian nations hard, ① causing several hundred deaths. Many people who live in this part of the world ② are likely to be worried again with the beginning of the cold weather. In spite of ③ their close location to these countries, however, Korea ④ has remained free of the deadly disease. Many people think the secret is kimchi, a traditional Korean dish served with ⑤ almost every meal.

7. (A), (B), (C)의 각 네모 안에서 어법에 맞는 표현으로 가장 적절한 것은?

When you attempt to do something and fail, you have to ask (A) you / yourself why you have failed to do what you intended. (B) Answer/ Answering this question in a new, unexpected way is the essential creative act. (C) It / They will improve your chances of succeeding next time.

	(A)		(B)		(C)
①	you	……	Answer	……	It
②	you	……	Answering	……	They
③	yourself	……	Answer	……	They
④	yourself	……	Answering	……	It
⑤	yourself	……	Answering	……	They

8. 다음 글의 밑줄 친 부분 중, 어법상 틀린 것은? [3점]

Leisure has more recently been conceptualized either as a form of activity engaged in by people in their free time or, preferably, as time ① free from any sense of obligation or compulsion. As such, the term leisure is now broadly used to characterize time not spent at work (where there is an obligation to perform). Naturally, in so defining leisure by ② what it is not, metaphysical issues remain largely unresolved. There is, for example, a question of how to categorize work-related time such as ③ those consumed in preparation for, and in transit to and from, the workplace. And sometimes the distinctions between one person's vocation and another's avocation are difficult ④ to draw: People have been known to "work" pretty hard at their hobbies. Although such problems of definition appear quite often, they fortunately do not affect analysis of the ⑤ underlying concepts.

*metaphysical: 극히 추상적인
**avocation: 취미, 여가 활동

•어휘 기출•

제한 시간 : 7분	정답 및 해설 095쪽

9. 다음 글의 밑줄 친 부분 중, 문맥상 낱말의 쓰임이 적절하지 않은 것은? [3점]

The basic task of the preschool years is to establish a sense of competence and initiative. The core struggle is between initiative and guilt. Preschool children begin to initiate many of their own activities as they become physically and psychologically ready to engage in pursuits of their own ① choosing. If they are allowed realistic freedom to make some of their own decisions, they tend to develop a ② positive orientation characterized by confidence in their ability to initiate and follow through. If their choices are ridiculed, however, they tend to experience a sense of guilt and ultimately to withdraw from taking an ③ active stance. One middle-aged woman we talked with still finds herself extremely vulnerable to being seen as ④ foolish. She recalls that during her childhood family members laughed at her attempts to perform certain tasks. She took in certain messages she received from her family, and these messages greatly influenced her attitudes and actions. Even now she vividly carries these pictures in her head, and these messages ⑤ cease to control her life.

10. (A), (B), (C)의 각 네모 안에서 문맥에 맞는 낱말로 가장 적절한 것은?

The Atitlán Giant Grebe was a large, flightless bird that had evolved from the much more widespread and smaller Pied-billed Grebe. By 1965 there were only around 80 birds left on Lake Atitlán. One immediate reason was easy enough to spot: the local human population was cutting down the reed beds at a furious rate. This (A) accommodation / destruction was driven by the needs of a fast growing mat-making industry. But there were other problems. An American airline was intent on developing the lake as a tourist destination for fishermen. However, there was a major problem with this idea: the lake (B) lacked / supported any suitable sporting fish! To compensate for this rather obvious defect, a specially selected species of fish called the Large-mouthed Bass was introduced. The introduced individuals immediately turned their attentions to the crabs and small fish that lived in the lake, thus (C) competing / cooperating with the few remaining grebes for food. There is also little doubt that they sometimes gobbled up the zebra-striped Atitlán Giant Grebe's chicks.

	(A)	(B)	(C)
①	accommodation	lacked	competing
②	accommodation	supported	cooperating
③	destruction	lacked	competing
④	destruction	supported	cooperating
⑤	destruction	lacked	cooperating

11. (A), (B), (C)의 각 네모 안에서 문맥에 맞는 낱말로 가장 적절한 것은? [3점]

Until the mid-20th century, only a few immigrants paid a visit to their homeland once or twice before they died, but most never returned to the land of their birth. This pattern has completely changed with the advent of globalization, coupled with the digital revolution that has (A) enhanced / hindered communication. As a result, immigration is a very different experience from what it was in the past. The ability of immigrant families to (B) object / reconnect to their old culture via phone, television, and the Internet has changed their approach to integration into mainstream American society. This has also greatly influenced immigrant practices of socialization with children. Contacts with the country of origin are now more frequent, and result in more immigrant families being influenced to (C) abandon / maintain cultural patterns from the homeland, and to attempt to influence their children to keep them.

	(A)	(B)	(C)
①	enhanced	object	abandon
②	hindered	object	abandon
③	enhanced	reconnect	maintain
④	hindered	reconnect	maintain
⑤	enhanced	reconnect	abandon

12. 다음 글의 밑줄 친 부분 중, 문맥상 낱말의 쓰임이 적절하지 않은 것은?

In the past several decades, China achieved rapid economic growth with monetary, mercantile, and military policies. It ① continued to push massive food and water development projects. On the other hand, in 2014, the desert area of China was nearly ten times the size of Japan. In particular, for the last several decades, China's desert area ② expanded every year by more than two thousand square kilometers on average. As a result, the ecological system is also collapsing in the wide area. The problem has ③ prompted China to develop vast farming areas in Africa and lease vast agricultural lands from Ukraine and other Eastern European countries to secure its growing domestic food needs. However, China's agricultural investment concentrates in a few kinds of cereals and animals. It is ④ helpful to the ecological diversity of the developed or leased areas. If a serious drought or flood takes place in those areas, it will bring about social chaos, not only there, but in China itself because of the sudden food ⑤ shortage.

* mercantile: 상업의, 무역의

총 문항			문항	맞은 문항		문항						
개별 문항	1	2	3	4	5	6	7	8	9	10	11	12
채점												

어휘·숙어 비밀 노트

A 수능 필수 어휘 ▶ 유의어 (7)

□ 641	necessity, requirement	n. 필요성
□ 642	observe, watch	v. 관찰하다
□ 643	obtain, acquire	v. 획득하다
□ 644	occur, happen	v. 일어나다
□ 645	opportunity, chance	n. 기회
□ 646	outcome, consequence	n. 성과
□ 647	overall, general	a. 전체의
□ 648	overcome, overwhelm	v. 압도[극복]하다
□ 649	particular, specific	a. 특정한
□ 650	passion, enthusiasm	n. 열정
□ 651	patient, tolerant	a. 참을성이 있는
□ 652	peer, gaze	v. 응시하다
□ 653	perceive, notice	v. 알아차리다
□ 654	permanent, eternal	a. 불변의
□ 655	persuade, convince	v. 설득시키다
□ 656	pollute, contaminate	v. 오염시키다
□ 657	populate, reside	v. 거주시키다
□ 658	portray, describe	v. 표현하다
□ 659	potential, possibility	n. 가능성
□ 660	predict, foretell	v. 예견하다

B 수능 필수 숙어

□ 661	regardless of	~에 상관없이
□ 662	rich in	~이 풍부한
□ 663	rule out	~을 배제하다
□ 664	run away	달아나다, 도망가다
□ 665	run down	(자동차 등이) ~을 치다
□ 666	run for	~을 출마하다
□ 667	run into	~에 충돌하다, 우연히 만나다
□ 668	run out	다 써버리다
□ 669	run the risk	위험을 무릅쓰다
□ 670	see off	배웅하다
□ 671	send out	발송하다
□ 672	set aside	따로 떼어두다, ~을 한 쪽으로 치워놓다
□ 673	set off	(경보 등을) 울리다, 폭발시키다
□ 674	settle down	진정되다, 정착하다
□ 675	shake hands with	~와 악수하다
□ 676	show off	과시하다
□ 677	shut down	문을 닫다, (기계가) 멈추다
□ 678	side by side	나란히
□ 679	slip out	(비밀이 입에서) 무심코 튀어 나오다
□ 680	sort out	정리하다, 선별하다

18 형용사, 부사

출제 트렌드

1. 형용사는 명사를 수식하거나, 서술한다. 부사는 형용사, 동사, 다른 부사를 수식한다.

2. 1994-2023학년도 수능 기출 어법 문제를 분석한 결과, 형용사, 부사 문제는 ① 형용사 most와 부사 almost의 어법 구분 문제(2003학년도 수능), ② 「동사+대명사+부사」의 어법 문제(2005학년도 수능(112쪽 8번 참조)), ③ 전치사 like와 형용사 alike의 어법 구분 문제(2005학년도 수능), ④ 「both, either」의 어법 구분 문제(2008학년도 수능(99쪽 4번 참조)), ⑤ 「so, such」의 어법 구분 문제(2011학년도 수능(16쪽 5번 참조)), ⑥ 「the+형용사」의 어법 문제(2017학년도 수능(21쪽 2번 참조))가 출제되었다.

3. 또한 ① 부사 only(1999학년도 수능), ② 「전치사(in)+명사(poverty)」로 이루어진 부사구(2003학년도 수능), ③ 「almost every+명사」(2004학년도 수능), ④ 지시부사 that(2006학년도 수능(99쪽 5번 참조)), ⑤ 「형용사(little), 부사(too)」(2009학년도 수능), ⑥ much of~(2010학년도 수능), ⑦ 형용사 other(2013학년도 수능), ⑧ 동사를 수식하는 부사(2014 수능 B형, 2023학년도 수능), ⑨ 「명사+(관계대명사+be동사)+close 이하 형용사구」(2015학년도 수능), ⑩ 전치사구를 수식하는 부사(2016학년도 수능), ⑪ 명사를 수식하는 과거분사(2017학년도 수능), ⑫ 「remain+부사(deeply)+형용사(problematic)」(2021학년도 수능) 구문이 선지로 출제되었다.

	출처	문항 번호	어법 · 어휘 문제
1	2021학년도 04월 학평	29번	도치 문장(형용사 vs. 부사 선택)
2	2020학년도 04월 학평	29번	보어로 쓰이는 형용사
3	2019학년도 04월 학평	29번	be동사의 보어(as+형용사 원급+as)
4	2011학년도 04월 학평	21번	보어로 쓰이는 형용사
5	2010학년도 09월 모평	22번	every vs. all
6	2009학년도 09월 모평	20번	a few vs. a little
7	2005학년도 수능	22번	alike vs. like
8	2003학년도 수능	30번	most vs. almost
9	2016학년도 09월 모평	29번	어휘 문제 01
10	2015학년도 07월 학평	30번	어휘 문제 02
11	2016학년도 06월 모평	29번	어휘 문제 03
12	2020학년도 03월 종로	30번	어휘 문제 04

1등급 꿀팁

1. 형용사 alike는 서술적 용법으로 사용되며 전치사 like는 뒤에 목적어를 가져올 수 있다.

2. most(대부분)는 「most(형용사)+명사의 복수형」, 「most(대명사) of the+명사의 복수형」, 「most(대명사) of+소유격+명사의 복수형」으로 사용된다. 한편, almost(거의 대부분)는 부사로서 뒤에 every, any 등이 종종 뒤따라온다.

3. many, few는 뒤에 셀 수 있는 명사가, much, little은 셀 수 없는 명사가 뒤에 나온다.

[핵심 문법]

A 출제 POINT

1. 정관사 the가 형용사 앞에 붙으면 형용사가 명사처럼 사용되기도 한다. 「the+형용사」는 일반적으로 복수 보통 명사의 의미를 나타내고, 단수 보통명사, 추상명사의 의미를 나타내기도 한다.

▶ Why [do / does] the elderly live alone?

2. 형용사는 명사를 수식하거나 주어나 목적어의 보어로서 서술적 용법으로 사용된다. 형용사 alike, alive, awake, asleep, ashamed, afraid 등은 서술적 용법으로 사용된다. 형용사 drunken, main, live, mere 등은 한정 적 용법으로 사용된다.

▶ They are not family, but they look [like, alike].

3. 부사는 형용사, 동사, 다른 부사를 수식한다. 빈도부사는 대개 일반동사 앞에, 조동사와 be동사 사이에 위치한다.

▶ He is [completely / complete] dependant on the prejudices of his times.

4. ① 형용사와 형태가 같은 부사와 ② -ly가 붙은 부사의 의미 차이에 유의한다.

deep(깊게)	deeply(매우)	high(높이)	highly(매우)
dear(비싸게)	dearly(마음으로부터)	late(늦게)	lately(최근에)
free (공짜로)	freely(자유롭게)	near(가까이)	nearly(거의)
hard(열심히)	hardly(좀처럼 ~하지 않는)	pretty(대단히)	prettily(예쁘게)

▶ I was [high / highly] pleased and full of expectations about being in a new place.

5. most(대부분의)가 형용사일 때는 '대부분의' 의미이다. most가 대명사로 쓰일 때는 「most of+한정어(the, these, those, 소유격)+복수명사」의 형태로 쓴다. '~의 대부분'의 의미이다. almost(거의)는 부사로 쓰인다. almost 뒤에는 종종 all, every, any 등이 온다.

▶ [Most / Almost] people like apples.

6. 동사와 부사가 결합된 동사구에서 목적어가 대명사일 경우에는 「동사+대명사+부사」의 어순이 되어야 한다.

▶ I told her to turn down the volume, not to [turn it up / tun up it].

7. 「enough+to부정사」 구문에서 enough가 형용사[부사]를 수식하는 경우, 「형용사[부사]+enough+to부정사」 순서 로 나온다.

▶ He is not [old enough / enough old] to watch that program.

B 체크 POINT

다음 괄호 안에서 어법상 올바른 것을 고르시오.

1. The English [talks / talk] about the weather a lot.

2. My uncle enjoys eating [live / alive] octopus.

3. We [usually go / go usually] out for dinner.

4. The brother's kite rose [high / highly] in the sky.

5. She's [most / almost] always punctual for appointments.

6. Do your science homework now. Don't [put off it / put it off] until tomorrow.

7. Those tomatoes aren't [ripe enough / enough ripe] to eat.

•어법 기출•

제한 시간 : 13분 | 정답 및 해설 097쪽

1. 다음 글의 밑줄 친 부분 중, 어법상 <u>틀린</u> 것은? [3점]

The world's first complex writing form, Sumerian cuneiform, followed an evolutionary path, moving around 3500 BCE from pictographic to ideographic representations, from the depiction of objects to ① that of abstract notions. Sumerian cuneiform was a linear writing system, its symbols usually ② set in columns, read from top to bottom and from left to right. This regimentation was a form of abstraction: the world is not a linear place, and objects do not organize ③ themselves horizontally or vertically in real life. Early rock paintings, thought to have been created for ritual purposes, were possibly shaped and organized ④ to follow the walls of the cave, or the desires of the painters, who may have organized them symbolically, or artistically, or even randomly. Yet after cuneiform, virtually every form of script that has emerged has been set out in rows with a clear beginning and endpoint. So ⑤ uniformly is this expectation, indeed, that the odd exception is noteworthy, and generally established for a specific purpose.

* cuneiform: 쐐기 문자 ** regimentation: 조직화

2. 다음 글의 밑줄 친 부분 중, 어법상 <u>틀린</u> 것은? [3점]

Mental representation is the mental imagery of things that are not actually present to the senses. In general, mental representations can help us learn. Some of the best evidence for this ① comes from the field of musical performance. Several researchers have examined ② what differentiates the best musicians from lesser ones, and one of the major differences lies in the quality of the mental representations the best ones create. When ③ practicing a new piece, advanced musicians have a very detailed mental representation of the music they use to guide their practice and, ultimately, their performance of a piece. In particular, they use their mental representations to provide their own feedback so that they know how ④ closely they are to getting the piece right and what they need to do differently to improve. The beginners and intermediate students may have crude representations of the music ⑤ that allow them to tell, for instance, when they hit a wrong note, but they must rely on feedback from their teachers to identify the more subtle mistakes and weaknesses.

* crude: 투박한

3. 다음 글의 밑줄 친 부분 중, 어법상 <u>틀린</u> 것은? [3점]

The present moment feels special. It is real. However much you may remember the past or anticipate the future, you live in the present. Of course, the moment ① during which you read that sentence is no longer happening. This one is. In other words, it feels as though time flows, in the sense that the present is constantly updating ② itself. We have a deep intuition that the future is open until it becomes present and ③ that the past is fixed. As time flows, this structure of fixed past, immediate present and open future gets carried forward in time. Yet as ④ naturally as this way of thinking is, you will not find it reflected in science. The equations of physics do not tell us which events are occurring right now—they are like a map without the "you are here" symbol. The present moment does not exist in them, and therefore neither ⑤ does the flow of time.

4. (A)~(C)에서 어법에 맞는 표현을 바르게 짝지은 것은?

People avoid feedback because they hate being criticized. Psychologists have a lot of theories about why people are so (A) sensitive / sensitively to hearing about their own imperfections. One is that they associate feedback with the critical comments received in their younger years from parents and teachers. (B) What / Whatever the cause of our discomfort is, most of us have to train ourselves to seek feedback and listen carefully when we hear it. Without that training, the very threat of critical feedback often leads us to (C) practice / be practiced destructive, maladaptive behaviors that negatively affect not only our work but the overall health of our organizations.

	(A)	(B)	(C)
①	sensitive	Whatever	practice
②	sensitive	Whatever	be practiced
③	sensitive	What	practice
④	sensitively	Whatever	practice
⑤	sensitively	What	be practiced

5. 다음 글의 밑줄 친 부분 중, 어법상 틀린 것은?

Almost every day I play a game with myself ① that I call 'time machine.' I made it up in response to my erroneous belief that what I was all worked up about was really important. ② To play 'time machine' all you have to do is to imagine that whatever circumstance you are dealing with is not happening right now but a year from now. It might be an argument with your spouse, a mistake, or a lost opportunity, but it is highly ③ likely that a year from now you are not going to care. It will be one more irrelevant detail in your life. While this simple game will not solve ④ every your problems, it can give you an enormous amount of needed perspective. I find myself laughing at things that I used to ⑤ take far too seriously.

6. (A), (B), (C)의 각 네모 안에서 어법에 맞는 표현으로 가장 적절한 것은?

If you need to buy food, there is probably a shop or a department store close to your home that sells just (A) which / what you want. But shopping has not always been so easy. Shops started only with the introduction of money. In earlier times, people traded crops or objects they had made in exchange for the goods they needed. The first shops sold just (B) a few / a little products such as meat and bread. In 1850, the first department store, a shop which sells many different items under one roof, opened in Paris. Self-service stores developed in the United States in the 1930s. They replaced the old methods of serving customers individually by (C) selling / being sold prepackaged goods straight from the shelves.

	(A)		(B)		(C)
①	which	⋯⋯	a little	⋯⋯	being sold
②	what	⋯⋯	a few	⋯⋯	being sold
③	what	⋯⋯	a few	⋯⋯	selling
④	what	⋯⋯	a little	⋯⋯	selling
⑤	which	⋯⋯	a little	⋯⋯	selling

7. 다음 글의 밑줄 친 부분 중, 어법상 틀린 것은?

Falling in love is ① alike being wrapped in a magical cloud. The air feels fresher, the flowers smell sweeter, food tastes more delicious, and the stars shine more ② brilliantly in the night sky. You feel light and happy ③ as though you are sailing through life. Your problems and challenges suddenly seem ④ insignificant. Your body feels alive, and you jump out of bed each morning ⑤ with a smile on your face. You are in a state of supreme delight.

8. (A), (B), (C)의 각 네모 안에서 어법에 맞는 표현으로 가장 적절한 것은?

The jobs that (A) most / almost companies are doing with information today would have been impossible several years ago. At that time, getting rich information was very expensive, and the tools for (B) analysis / analyzing it weren't even available until the early 1990s. But now the tools of the digital age give us a way to easily get, share, and (C) act / acting on information in new ways.

	(A)		(B)		(C)
①	most	⋯⋯	analysis	⋯⋯	acting
②	almost	⋯⋯	analyzing	⋯⋯	act
③	most	⋯⋯	analyzing	⋯⋯	act
④	almost	⋯⋯	analysis	⋯⋯	acting
⑤	most	⋯⋯	analysis	⋯⋯	act

제한 시간 : 7분	정답 및 해설 100쪽

9. 다음 글의 밑줄 친 부분 중, 문맥상 낱말의 쓰임이 적절하지 않은 것은?

An Egyptian executive, after entertaining his Canadian guest, offered him joint partnership in a new business venture. The Canadian, delighted with the offer, suggested that they meet again the next morning with their ① respective lawyers to finalize the details. The Egyptian never showed up. The surprised and disappointed Canadian tried to understand what had gone wrong: Did Egyptians ② lack punctuality? Was the Egyptian expecting a counter-offer? Were lawyers unavailable in Cairo? None of these explanations proved to be correct; rather, the problem was ③ caused by the different meaning Canadians and Egyptians attach to inviting lawyers. The Canadian regarded the lawyers' ④ absence as facilitating the successful completion of the negotiation; the Egyptian interpreted it as signaling the Canadian's mistrust of his verbal commitment. Canadians often use the impersonal formality of a lawyer's services to finalize ⑤ agreements. Egyptians, by contrast, more frequently depend on the personal relationship between bargaining partners to accomplish the same purpose.

10. 다음 글의 밑줄 친 부분 중 문맥상 낱말의 쓰임이 적절하지 않은 것은? [3점]

The dominance of conclusions over arguments is most pronounced where emotions are involved. The psychologist Paul Slovic has proposed a theory in which people let their likes and dislikes determine their beliefs about the world. Your political ① preference determines the arguments that you find compelling. If you like the current health policy, you believe its benefits are substantial and its costs ② more manageable than the costs of alternatives. If you are a hawk in your attitude toward other nations, you probably think they are relatively weak and likely to ③ submit to your country's will. If you are a dove, you probably think they are strong and will not be easily persuaded. Your emotional attitude to such things as red meat, nuclear power, tattoos, or motorcycles ④ follows your beliefs about their benefits and their risks. If you ⑤ dislike any of these things, you probably believe that its risks are high and its benefits negligible.

11. (A), (B), (C)의 각 네모 안에서 문맥에 맞는 낱말로 가장 적절한 것은? [3점]

The desert locust lives in two remarkably different styles depending on the availability of food sources and the density of the local locust population. When food is scarce, as it usually is in their native desert habitat, locusts are born with coloring designed for camouflage and lead (A) solitary / social lives. But when rare periods of significant rain produce major vegetation growth, everything changes. At first, the locusts continue to be loners, just feasting off the (B) insufficient / abundant food supply. But as the extra vegetation starts to die off, the locusts find themselves crowded together. Suddenly, baby locusts are born with bright colors and a preference for company. Instead of avoiding one another and hiding from predators through camouflage and inactivity, these locusts gather in vast groups, feed together, and (C) overwhelm / overestimate their predators simply through numbers. * camouflage: 위장

	(A)		(B)		(C)
①	solitary	⋯⋯	insufficient	⋯⋯	overwhelm
②	solitary	⋯⋯	abundant	⋯⋯	overwhelm
③	solitary	⋯⋯	insufficient	⋯⋯	overestimate
④	social	⋯⋯	abundant	⋯⋯	overwhelm
⑤	social	⋯⋯	insufficient	⋯⋯	overestimate

12. 다음 글의 밑줄 친 부분 중, 문맥상 낱말의 쓰임이 적절하지 않은 것은?

Psychologists used to assume that infant minds were ① blank slates. But when developmental psychologists invented ways to look into infant minds, they found a great deal of writing already on that slate. The trick was to see what surprises babies. Infants as young as two months old will look ② longer at an event that surprises them than at an event they were expecting. If everything is a buzzing confusion, then everything should be equally surprising. But if the infant's mind comes already wired to interpret events in certain ways, then infants can be surprised when the world ③ meets their expectations. Psychologists discovered that infants are born with some knowledge of physics and mechanics, and they get ④ startled when shown scenes that should be physically impossible such as a toy car seeming to pass through a solid object. Psychologists know this because infants stare longer at impossible scenes than at similar but less magical scenes. Babies seem to have the ⑤ innate ability to process events in their physical world.

총 문항				문항		맞은 문항				문항		
개별 문항	1	2	3	4	5	6	7	8	9	10	11	12
채점												

A 수능 필수 어휘 ▶ 유의어(8)

□ 681	prey, victim	n. 희생자
□ 682	proceed, continue	v. 진행하다
□ 683	produce, manufacture	v. 제조하다
□ 684	progress, advance	v. 발전하다
□ 685	promote, encourage	v. 촉진하다
□ 686	property, possessions	n. 소유물
□ 687	propose, suggest	v. 제안하다
□ 688	protect, preserve	v. 지키다
□ 689	prove, verify	v. 입증하다
□ 690	provide, supply	v. 공급하다
□ 691	purpose, intention	n. 의도
□ 692	pursue, chase	v. 추적하다
□ 693	rapid, swift	a. 신속한
□ 694	rational, reasonable	a. 합리적인
□ 695	realize, recognize	v. 알아차리다
□ 696	receive, accept	v. 받아들이다
□ 697	recognize, admit	v. 인정하다
□ 698	refuse, reject	v. 거절하다
□ 699	regard, consider	v. 간주하다
□ 700	region, district	n. 지방, 지역

B 수능 필수 숙어

□ 701	specialize in	~을 전공하다, ~을 전문으로 하다
□ 702	spend (money) on ~	~에 돈을 쓰다
□ 703	spread out	퍼지다, (접힌 것을) 펴다
□ 704	stand for	나타내다, 지지하다, 용납하다
□ 705	stand out	두드러지다
□ 706	stand up for	지지하다, 옹호하다, 지키다
□ 707	stay up	(늦게까지) 깨어 있다
□ 708	step in	(문제, 사건 등에) 개입하다
□ 709	step up	앞으로 나가다, ~을 증가시키다
□ 710	stick out	튀어나오다, 눈에 띄다, ~을 내밀다
□ 711	stop by	잠깐 들르다
□ 712	subject to	~을 조건으로 하여
□ 713	succeed in	~에 성공하다
□ 714	take ~ into account	~을 고려하다
□ 715	take a break	휴식을 취하다
□ 716	take action	조치를 취하다
□ 717	take away	제거하다
□ 718	take in	이해하다, 섭취하다, 받아들이다
□ 719	take off	~을 벗다, (비행기가) 이륙하다
□ 720	take out	~을 꺼내다, ~을 데리고 나가다

19 비교 구문

🏷 출제 트렌드

1. 비교 구문은 크게 원급 비교, 비교급 비교, 최상급 비교가 있다. 일반적으로 원급 비교는 「as+형용사/부사의 원급+as」, 비교급 비교는 「형용사/부사의 비교급+than」, 최상급 비교는 「the+형용사/부사의 최상급」 형태를 취한다.

2. 1994~2023학년도 수능 기출 어법 문제를 분석한 결과, 비교급 문제는 수능에서 「as+원급(형용사)+as possible」, 구문 (2005학년도 수능), 「less+형용사/부사 than」 구문(2009학년도 수능), 비교급 강조 표현(2012학년도 수능(88쪽 5번 참조)) 이 출제되었다.

3. 또한 「one of the+최상급」(2003학년도 수능(82쪽 7번 참조)), 「as+부사+as」(2003학년도 수능(82쪽 7번 참조)), 「동사를 수 식하는 부사의 비교급」(2005학년도 수능(106쪽 7번 참조)), 비교급 비교(2007학년도 수능), 비교급 강조 표현(2008학년도 수능)이 선지로 출제되었다.

4. 비교급 강조 문제가 모평과 학평 시험에서도 상대적으로 빈번하게 출제되었다.

	출처	문항 번호	어법·어휘 문제
1	2022학년도 03월 학평	29번	비교 구문 more~than
2	2021학년도 07월 학평	38번 변형	비교급 형용사 vs. 부사
3	2021학년도 07월 학평	20번 변형	비교급의 강조어 much
4	2012학년도 09월 모평	20번	「as+원급+as」
5	2011학년도 03월 학평	21번	the 비교급, the 비교급(형용사)
6	2010학년도 03월 학평	22번	「as+원급+as」
7	2009학년도 수능	21번	「less+형용사/부사 than」
8	2005학년도 수능	21번	as ~ as possible
9	2015학년도 04월 학평	30번	어휘 문제 01
10	2015학년도 03월 학평	30번	어휘 문제 02
11	2014학년도 수능 B형	28번	어휘 문제 03
12	2019학년도 11월 종로	30번	어휘 문제 04

🏷 1등급 꿀팁

1. be동사 뒤에 나오는 as 원급(형용사/부사) as 표현에서 원급은 be 동사의 보어가 될 수 있는 형용사가 나와야 한다.

2. 비교급을 강조할 때는 even, still, far, a lot 등이 사용되고, 원급을 강조할 때는 very가 사용된다.

3. 「the 비교급..., the 비교급~」 표현은 '…하면 할수록 더 ~하다'의 의미이다.

[핵심 문법]

정답 및 해설 · 102쪽

A 출제 POINT

1. 원급 비교는 「as+형용사/부사+as」의 형태로, 둘 사이에 비교의 정도가 같음을 나타낸다. 부정은 not as ~as로 표현하고 몇 가지 관용 표현을 익히는 것이 좋다.

not so much A as B	A라기 보다는 B다	as ~ as possible	가능한 한 ~하게

▶ Sam is as **[diligent / diligently]** as his brother.

2. 비교급 비교는 「비교급+than」의 형태로, 비교되는 대상의 우열을 나타낸다. 비교급을 강조하는 경우 비교급 앞에 much, even, still, far, a lot 등을 쓴다. 몇 가지 관용 표현을 익혀야 한다.

비교급 and 비교급	점점 더 ~한	the 비교급... the 비교급 ~	...하면 할수록 더 ~하다

▶ Sally is **[very / much]** wiser than her friends.

3. 비교급은 정관사 the를 붙이지 않지만, of the two가 나오면 비교급에 정관사 the를 붙인다.

▶ Peter is **[taller / the taller]** of the two.

4. 최상급은 「the+최상급」 형태로 셋 이상 중에서 하나가 최고인 것을 나타낸다. 몇 가지 주의할 표현이 있다.

「one of the 최상급+ 복수명사」	가장 ~중의 하나
「the+서수+최상급」	...번째로 ~한
비교급 than any other 단수명사	다른 어떤 ~보다도 더 ...하게
비교급 than all the other 복수명사	다른 모든 ~보다도 더 ...하게
「the 최상급+주어+have[has] ever p.p.」	지금껏 ~한 것들 중 가장 ~하게
「as ~ as any+단수명사」	다른 어떤 ...못지 않게 ~한

▶ He is one of the best **[novelist / novelists]** in Korea.

5. 최상급은 정관사 the를 붙이지만, 동일 대상 내에서나 부사의 최상급은 정관사 the를 붙이지 않는다.

▶ Since you know her **[the best / best]**, you should ask her.

6. 「부정주어+원급 / 비교급」으로 최상급의 의미를 나타낼 수 있다.

부정주어 ~ as 원급 as	어떤 ~도 ...만큼 ~하지 않다
부정주어 ~ 비교급 than	어떤 ~도 ...보다 ~하지 않다

▶ Nothing is more precious **[as / than]** health.

7. 기타 주의해야 할 비교 구문 관용 표현이 있다.

no more than	단지(= only)	not more than	기껏해야(= at most)
no less than	~만큼(= as much as)	not less than	적어도(= at least)
▶ A is no more than B C is D A가 B가 아닌 것은 C가 D가 아닌 것과 같다			

▶ A child must sleep not **[more / less]** than eight hours.

B 체크 POINT

다음 괄호 안에서 어법상 올바른 것을 고르시오.

1. Sally is not **[more / as]** beautiful as her sister.

2. Sarah is **[prettier / pretty]** than Jane.

3. Of the two pens this one is **[longer / the longer]**.

4. Jack is as brave as any **[boy / boys]** in his class.

5. This lake is **[the deepest / deepest]** here.

6. To me, nothing in the world is funnier **[than / as]** fishing.

7. Tom is not **[more / less]** than(= at most) an average salesman.

제한 시간 : 13분	정답 및 해설 103쪽

2022학년도 3월 학평 29번

1. 다음 글의 밑줄 친 부분 중, 어법상 틀린 것은? [3점]

We don't know what ancient Greek music sounded like, because there are no examples of it in written or notated form, nor ① has it survived in oral tradition. Much of it was probably improvised anyway, within certain rules and conventions. So we are forced largely to guess at its basis from the accounts of writers such as Plato and Aristotle, who were generally more concerned with writing about music as a philosophical and ethical exercise ② as with providing a technical primer on its practice. It seems Greek music was predominantly a vocal form, ③ consisting of sung verse accompanied by instruments such as the lyre or the plucked kithara (the root of 'guitar'). In fact, Plato considered music in which the lyre and flute played alone and not as the accompaniment of dance or song ④ to be 'exceedingly coarse and tasteless'. The melodies seem to have had a very limited pitch range, since the instruments ⑤ generally span only an octave, from one E (as we'd now define it) to the next.

* primer: 입문서 ** lyre: 수금(竪琴) *** coarse: 조잡한

2021학년도 7월 학평 38번 변형

2. 다음 글의 밑줄 친 부분 중, 어법상 틀린 것은?

Why does the skin on the extremities wrinkle after a bath? And why only the extremities? ① Despite its appearance, your skin isn't shrinking after your bath. Actually, it is expanding. The skin on the fingers, palms, toes, and soles ② wrinkles only after it is soaked with water. The stratum corneum —the thick, dead, rough layer of the skin that protects us from the environment and that makes the skin on our hands and feet ③ tougher and thicker than that on our stomachs or faces — expands when it soaks up water. This expansion causes the wrinkling effect. So why doesn't the skin on other parts of the body also wrinkle when soaked? Actually, it does, but there is more room for the moisture to be absorbed in these ④ less dense packed areas before it shows. One doctor we contacted said that soldiers ⑤ whose feet are submerged in wet boots for a long period will exhibit wrinkling all over the covered area.

* extremities: 손발 ** submerge: (물에) 잠그다

2021학년도 7월 학평 20번 변형

3. 다음 글의 밑줄 친 부분 중, 어법상 틀린 것은?

The immense improvement in the yield of farming during the twentieth century, as a result of innovations in mechanization, fertilizer, new varieties, pesticides and genetic engineering, ① has banished famine from the face of the planet ② almost entirely, and drastically reduced malnutrition, even while the human population has continued to expand. Few predicted this, yet ③ many are concerned that this improvement has come at the expense of nature. In fact the evidence is strong that the opposite is the case. Innovation in food production has spared land and forest from the plough, the cow and the axe on a grand scale by ④ increasing the productivity of the land we do farm. It turns out that this 'land sparing' has been ⑤ very better for biodiversity than land sharing would have been—by which is meant growing crops at low yields in the hope that abundant wildlife lives in fields alongside crops.

2012학년도 9월 모평 20번

4. (A), (B), (C)의 각 네모 안에서 어법에 맞는 표현으로 가장 적절한 것은?

You have to pay close attention to someone's normal pattern in order to notice a deviation from it when he or she lies. Sometimes the variation is as (A) subtle / subtly as a pause. Other times it is obvious and abrupt. I recently saw a news interview with an acquaintance (B) who / whom I was certain was going to lie about a few particularly sensitive issues, and lie she did. During most of her interview she was calm and direct, but when she started lying, her manner changed dramatically: she threw her head back, laughed in 'disbelief,' and shook her head back and forth. It is true that the questions (C) dealt / dealing with very personal issues, but I have found that in general, no matter how touchy the question, if a person is telling the truth his or her manner will not change significantly or abruptly.

	(A)		(B)		(C)
①	subtle	……	who	……	dealt
②	subtle	……	who	……	dealing
③	subtle	……	whom	……	dealt
④	subtly	……	who	……	dealt
⑤	subtly	……	whom	……	dealing

5. (A), (B), (C)의 각 네모 안에서 어법에 맞는 표현으로 가장 적절한 것은?

Ultrasound, an imaging technique, produces an image by (A) [bounce / bouncing] sound waves off an object inside the body. A picture is then made using the reflected sound waves. The frequency of sound waves used in ultrasound imaging (B) [range / ranges] above human hearing. The choice of frequency depends on how deep into the body the sound waves are needed to penetrate. Lower frequencies allow doctors to see structures deeper inside the body. The lower the frequency, however, the less (C) [clear / clearly] the image will become. Doctors use ultrasound to visualize the size and structure of internal organs.

	(A)		(B)		(C)
①	bounce	……	range	……	clear
②	bounce	……	ranges	……	clearly
③	bouncing	……	ranges	……	clear
④	bouncing	……	ranges	……	clearly
⑤	bouncing	……	range	……	clearly

6. (A), (B), (C)의 각 네모 안에서 어법에 맞는 표현으로 가장 적절한 것은?

Sleep deprivation has a great influence on the immune system. Consider what happens in public schools in December just before the winter break. Kids get sick. Teachers get sick. Parents get sick. We tend to think there are just a lot of viruses (A) [go / going] around. In reality, the main reason for these minor but unpleasant illnesses (B) [are / is] that we are exhausted. Students and teachers are all sleep-deprived from the constant stress of the first semester, and it begins to catch up with us. Our immune systems are not functioning as (C) [effective / effectively] as they do when we are well rested, and we get sick. What do most of us do when the winter break comes? We try to get caught up on sleep.

	(A)		(B)		(C)
①	go	……	are	……	effective
②	go	……	are	……	effectively
③	going	……	is	……	effectively
④	go	……	is	……	effectively
⑤	going	……	is	……	effective

7. (A), (B), (C)의 각 네모 안에서 어법에 맞는 표현으로 가장 적절한 것은?

Many social scientists have believed for some time (A) [that / what] birth order directly affects both personality and achievement in adult life. In fact, people have been using birth order to account for personality factors such as an aggressive behavior or a passive temperament. One might say, "Oh, I'm the eldest of three sisters, so I can't help that I'm so overbearing," or "I'm not very successful in business, because I'm the youngest child and thus less (B) [aggressively / aggressive] than my older brothers and sisters." Recent studies, however, have proved this belief to be false. In other words, birth order may define your role within a family, but as you mature into adulthood, (C) [accepted / accepting] other social roles, birth order becomes insignificant.

	(A)		(B)		(C)
①	that	……	aggressively	……	accepting
②	that	……	aggressive	……	accepting
③	that	……	aggressive	……	accepted
④	what	……	aggressive	……	accepted
⑤	what	……	aggressively	……	accepted

8. (A), (B), (C)의 각 네모 안에서 어법에 맞는 표현을 골라 짝지은 것은?

Possibly the most effective way to focus on your goals is to (A) [write them down / write down them]. Although this may sound like an obvious first step, it is a step that many people ignore. As a result, their goals often remain unfocused, and therefore unrealized. Go to a fairly quiet place where you are not likely to (B) [disturb / be disturbed]. Make a list of every goal you have. Include goals about finances, relationships, and your career. Be as (C) [specifically / specific] as possible.

	(A)		(B)		(C)
①	write them down	……	disturb	……	specifically
②	write them down	……	be disturbed	……	specifically
③	write them down	……	be disturbed	……	specific
④	write down them	……	disturb	……	specifically
⑤	write down them	……	be disturbed	……	specific

제한 시간 : 7분	정답 및 해설 106쪽

9. 밑줄 친 부분 중, 문맥상 낱말의 쓰임이 적절하지 <u>않은</u> 것은? [3점]

We're all told at school that white reflects sunlight and black absorbs it, so the ① <u>paler</u> your clothes are, the cooler you'll be. But it's not quite that simple. In many hot countries, locals often wear ② <u>dark</u> colors. Peasants in China and old ladies in southern Europe, for instance, traditionally wear black, and the Tuareg, the nomadic people of the Sahara, favor indigo blue. These clothes are ③ <u>effective</u> because there are two thermal processes happening at once. Heat is coming downwards from the sun but it is also going outwards from the body. Though light clothes are better at ④ <u>reflecting</u> the sun's heat, dark clothes are better at radiating the body's heat. Given that no one born in a hot climate willingly stands in direct sunlight, the dark clothing has the ⑤ <u>defect</u> because it keeps you cooler when you're in the shade.

*thermal: 열의, 온도의

10. (A), (B), (C)의 각 네모 안에서 문맥에 맞는 낱말로 가장 적절한 것은? [3점]

It is often believed that an active person can make friends more easily than a shy person, and that a conscientious person may meet more deadlines than a person who is not conscientious. Walter Mischel found, however, that the typical correlation between personality traits and behavior was quite (A) apparent / modest . This news was really shocking, because it essentially said that the traits personality psychologists were measuring were just slightly better at predicting behavior than astrological signs. Mischel did not simply point out the problem; he diagnosed the reasons for it. He argued that personality psychologists had (B) overestimated / underestimated the extent to which the social situation shapes people's behavior, independently of their personality. To predict whether a person will meet a deadline, for example, knowing something about the situation may be more useful than knowing the person's score on a measure of conscientiousness. Situational influences can be very powerful, sometimes (C) emphasizing / overwhelming individual differences in personality.

*conscientious: 성실한 **astrological sign: 점성술의 별자리

	(A)		(B)		(C)
①	apparent	……	overestimated	……	emphasizing
②	apparent	……	underestimated	……	emphasizing
③	modest	……	overestimated	……	emphasizing
④	modest	……	overestimated	……	overwhelming
⑤	modest	……	underestimated	……	overwhelming

11. 다음 글의 밑줄 친 부분 중, 문맥상 낱말의 쓰임이 적절하지 <u>않은</u> 것은? [3점]

When people started to plant stored seed stock deliberately, they also began protecting their plants. This changed the evolutionary ① <u>pressure</u> that these food plants experienced, as they no longer had to survive in a natural environment. Instead, people created a new environment for them, and selected for other characteristics than nature previously had. Seeds recovered at archaeological sites clearly show that farmers selected for larger seeds and ② <u>thinner</u> seed coats. Thick seed coats are often ③ <u>essential</u> for seeds to survive in a natural environment because the seeds of many wild plants remain dormant for months until winter is over and rain sets in. But under human management thick seed coats are unnecessary, as farmers ④ <u>evade</u> responsibility for storing seeds away from moisture and predators. In fact, seeds with thinner coats were ⑤ <u>preferred</u> as they are easier to eat or process into flour, and they allow seedlings to sprout more quickly when sown.

12. 다음 글의 밑줄 친 부분 중, 문맥상 낱말의 쓰임이 적절하지 <u>않은</u> 것은? [3점]

A general and seemingly applicable assumption is that consumers and producers maximize the benefit related to the opportunity ① <u>accessible</u> in their particular circumstance. The desire to reach an optimal outcome for a given point in time is subjective and specific to how these ② <u>economic</u> agents view the concept of maximization, which in turn is likely to be highly correlated with cultural values. For example, in indigenous societies there is evidence that a balance between present and future periods along with that of the environmental system, as a whole, was ③ <u>included</u> in decision-making and optimization. In present consumerism-fostered economies, the cultural values are less likely or unlikely to ④ <u>disregard</u> environmental and social justice parameters proactively. The focus of observable and marketed consumption is immediate gratification. However, as consumer awareness of both the impact of consumption and the power of consumption to modify and catalyze economic outcomes ⑤ <u>increases</u> there is growing evidence of a shifting cultural paradigm to one of sustainability.

*parameter: (주로 복수로) 변수, 매개 변수
**catalyze: 촉진시키다

총 문항			문항		맞은 문항					문항		
개별 문항	1	2	3	4	5	6	7	8	9	10	11	12
채점												

A 수능 필수 어휘 ▶ 파생어 (1)

☐ 721	adherent	n. 지지자; a. 달라붙는	adherence	n. 고수, 집착
☐ 722	beneficial	a. 유익한, 이로운	beneficent	a. 도움을 주는
☐ 723	childish	a. 유치한, 어른답지 못한	childlike	a. 어린애 같은, 귀여운
☐ 724	comparable	a. 비교될 만한, 필적하는	comparative	a. 비교의, 상대적인
☐ 725	comprehensible	a. 이해하기 쉬운	comprehensive	a. 종합적인
☐ 726	confident	a. 자신감이 있는	confidential	a. 기밀의, 은밀한
☐ 727	considerable	a. 상당한	considerate	a. 사려 깊은
☐ 728	credible	a. 믿을 수 있는	credulous	a. 쉽게 속는
☐ 729	continual	a. 반복되는	continuous	a. 계속되는, 지속적인
☐ 730	different	a. 다른	indifferent	a. 무관심한
☐ 731	distinguishable	a. 구별할 수 있는	distinguished	a. 두드러진
☐ 732	economic	a. 경제의, 경제학의	economical	a. 절약하는, 실속 있는
☐ 733	famous	a. 유명한	infamous	a. 악명 높은
☐ 734	favorable	a. 호의적인, 유리한	favorite	a. 가장 좋아하는
☐ 735	forgetful	a. 잘 잊어버리는	forgettable	a. 쉽게 잊혀질
☐ 736	healthy	a. 건강한	healthful	a. 건강에 좋은
☐ 737	imaginable	a. 상상할 수 있는	imaginative	a. 상상력이 풍부한
☐ 738	industrious	a. 근면한	industrial	a. 산업의
☐ 739	ingenious	a. 독창적인	ingenuous	a. 솔직한, 정직한
☐ 740	literal	a. 문자 그대로의	literate	a. 읽고 쓸 수 있는, 교양이 있는

B 수능 필수 숙어

☐ 741	take part in	~에 참여하다(= participate in)
☐ 742	take place	개최되다, 일어나다
☐ 743	take turns	번갈아 하다, ~을 교대로 하다
☐ 744	tear down	파괴하다, 해체하다
☐ 745	tell from	~과 구별되다
☐ 746	that is	즉
☐ 747	the former..., while the latter	전자는 …, 후자는 ~
☐ 748	the number of	~의 수
☐ 749	the other day	일전에
☐ 750	the ratio of 100 to 1	100대 1의 비율로
☐ 751	think over	~을 숙고하다
☐ 752	to be sure	틀림없이
☐ 753	to one's surprise	놀랍게도
☐ 754	to some extent	어느 정도까지
☐ 755	to the point	간단명료한, 핵심적인
☐ 756	try on	(옷을) 입어보다, (신을) 신어보다
☐ 757	try one's best	최선을 다하다(= do one's best)
☐ 758	turn around	방향을 바꾸다, 뒤돌아보다, (상황이) 호전되다
☐ 759	turn down	(제안, 요구 등을) 거절하다
☐ 760	turn in	~을 반납하다, ~을 제출하다(= hand in)

20 특수 구문

출제 트렌드

1. 특수 구문은 도치, 강조, 부정, 동격과 생략과 같은 구문을 말한다. 도치란 (조)동사가 여러 가지 이유로 주어 앞에 위치하는 것을 말한다. 강조란 특정한 어휘나 구를 사용하여 문장의 특정 부분을 강조하는 것을 말한다.

2. 1994~2023학년도 수능 기출 어법 문제를 분석한 결과 특수 구문은 간접의문문의 어순(1996학년도 수능), 「부정부사 little+도치 구문」(2007학년도 수능), 「보어+도치 구문」(2011학년도 수능(15쪽 5번 참조)), do의 동사 강조(2012학년도 수능(39쪽 3번 참조)), 대동사로 쓰인 be동사(2022학년도 수능)이 출제되었다.

3. 또한 대동사 do(2009학년도 수능(57쪽 4번 참조)), 수동태의 공통 부분 생략(2019학년도 수능)이 선지로 출제되었다.

4. 「부정부사+도치 구문」도 학평, 모평에서 출제 빈도가 높다.

	출처	문항 번호	어법 · 어휘 문제
1	2019학년도 수능	29번	생략 및 대동사 was
2	2013학년도 10월 학평	27번	[only+전명구]+도치 구문
3	2011학년도 10월 학평	22번	대동사 선택 am vs. do
4	2011학년도 09월 모평	20번	so+does+주어
5	2007학년도 수능	22번	[부정부사 Little] +도치 구문
6	2021학년도 08월 종로	29번	It ~ that 강조 구문
7	2018학년도 04월 종로	28번	that절의 대동사
8	2017학년도 08월 종로	28번	It ~ that 강조 구문
9	2015학년도 11월 수능	30번	어휘 문제 01
10	2014학년도 10월 학평	28번	어휘 문제 02
11	2013학년도 수능	30번	어휘 문제 03
12	2019학년도 10월 종로	30번	어휘 문제 04

1등급 꿀팁

1. 부정부사, 장소 부사구, only가 문장의 문두에 나오는 경우 「(조)동사+주어」 어순으로 도치된다.

2. 대동사는 동사 대신 사용할 때 쓰는 표현이다. be동사를 써야 할지, 일반동사를 써야할지 구분해야 하고, 본동사에 맞춰 시제도 일치시켜야 한다.

3. 직접의문문이 다른 문장의 일부로 들어가는 경우 간접의문문 「의문사+주어+동사」의 어순을 갖는다.

[핵심 문법]

정답 및 해설·107쪽

A 출제 POINT

1. 부정어(구)가 문장 앞에 오면 「주어+(조)동사」가 도치된다.

► Not only [**could they** / **they could**] see nothing in front of them, but they were tired and ill and could not walk any more.

2. Only가 포함된 어구가 문장 앞에 와도 「주어+(조)동사」가 도치된다.

► Only for the love of his family [**Sam does** / **does Sam**] do such hard work.

3. 장소와 방향을 나타내는 부사(구)가 문장 앞에 오면 주어와 동사가 도치된다. 단, 주어가 대명사인 경우에는 도치되지 않는다. 또한 be동사가 쓰인 문장에서 보어를 문장의 앞에 두면, 주어와 be동사가 도치된다.

► Here [**comes the writer** / **the writer comes**]!

4. It is[was] ~ that 강조 구문은 주어, 목적어, 보어, 부사구를 It is[was] ~ that 사이에 넣어 강조한다. 강조되는 어구가 사람이면 who를, 사물이면 which를 that 대신에 쓸 수 있다.

► It is those explorers, through their unceasing trial and error, [**which** / **who**] have paved the way for us to follow.

5. 특정한 어휘나 구를 사용하여 문장의 특정 부분을 강조할 수 있다. 조동사 do를 사용하여 동사를 강조할 수 있고, 재귀대명사나 the very를 사용하여 명사를 강조할 수 있다. 소유격을 강조할 때는 「소유격+own+명사」를 사용한다.

► Rowling's books [**do** / **does**] contain supernatural creatures.

6. 전체를 나타내는 어구가 not과 함께 쓰이면 부분 부정의 의미를 나타낸다.

► [**Not every** / **Every not**] news on the Internet is true.

7. 동격 관계를 나타내는 어구는 앞의 표현을 부가적으로 설명하는 기능을 한다. 문장에서 일정어구가 반복되거나 의미적으로 추론이 가능할 때 생략한다. 특히, 일반동사로 시작하는 어구가 반복되면 대동사 do를 사용하여 생략한다. 앞에 나온 동사가 be동사이며 반복을 피하기 위해 be동사를 대동사로 쓸 수 있다.

► Sally, my best friend, plays the piano better than I [**do** / **does**].

cf. These experts **are** still with us, as a result so **is** the phrase.
　　(이 전문가들은 여전히 우리와 함께 하고 있으며, 결과적으로 이 문구도 그렇다.)

B 체크 POINT

다음 괄호 안에서 어법상 올바른 것을 고르시오.

1. Hardly [**had she** / **she had**] gone when he began to speak ill of her.

2. Only after hard work [**can rest** / **rest can**] be truly enjoyed.

3. Blessed [**are the poor** / **the poor are**] in spirit.

4. It was not her remarks [**which** / **who**] we found very unpleasant.

5. She is [**does** / **the very**] woman who helped me the other day.

6. It's okay if you don't like me. [**Everyone not** / **Not everyone**] has a good taste.

7. She wasn't expecting to have a good time at the party, but she actually [**did** / **does**].

•어법 기출•

제한 시간 : 13분	정답 및 해설 107쪽

1. 다음 글의 밑줄 친 부분 중, 어법상 **틀린** 것은? [3점]

"Monumental" is a word that comes very close to ① expressing the basic characteristic of Egyptian art. Never before and never since has the quality of monumentality been achieved as fully as it ② did in Egypt. The reason for this is not the external size and massiveness of their works, although the Egyptians admittedly achieved some amazing things in this respect. Many modern structures exceed ③ those of Egypt in terms of purely physical size. But massiveness has nothing to do with monumentality. An Egyptian sculpture no bigger than a person's hand is more monumental than that gigantic pile of stones ④ that constitutes the war memorial in Leipzig, for instance. Monumentality is not a matter of external weight, but of "inner weight." This inner weight is the quality which Egyptian art possesses to such a degree that everything in it seems to be made of primeval stone, like a mountain range, even if it is only a few inches across or ⑤ carved in wood.

* gigantic: 거대한 ** primeval: 원시 시대의

2. 다음 글의 밑줄 친 부분 중, 어법상 **틀린** 것은? [3점]

With all the passion for being slim, it is no wonder ① that many people view any amount of visible fat on the body as something to get rid of. However, the human body has evolved over time in environments of food scarcity; hence, the ability to store fat ② efficiently is a valuable physiological function that served our ancestors well for thousands of years. Only in the last few decades, in the primarily industrially developed economies, ③ have food become so plentiful and easy to obtain as to cause fat-related health problems. People no longer have to spend most of their time and energy ④ gathering berries and seeds and hoping that a hunting party will return with meat. All we have to do nowadays is drive to the supermarket or the fast-food restaurant, ⑤ where for very low cost we can obtain nearly all of our daily calories.

3. (A), (B), (C)의 각 네모 안에서 어법에 맞는 표현으로 가장 적절한 것은?

Most amateur speakers do not understand that when they are on stage they are actors and actresses. Most do have some idea that they should speak with more power on stage than they (A) are / do on a one-to-one basis, but they do not realize that their verbal eloquence must be matched with a nonverbal eloquence. If you move your hand two inches to emphasize a point when (B) speaking / to speak to one person, you may have to move it as much as two feet in front of a large audience. The general rule is, the bigger the audience, the bigger the motion. This is so difficult for people, especially businesspeople whose general style is that of understatement, (C) which / that they should take an acting course before they take a speech course.

	(A)		(B)		(C)
①	are	·····	speaking	·····	which
②	are	·····	to speak	·····	which
③	do	·····	to speak	·····	that
④	do	·····	to speak	·····	which
⑤	do	·····	speaking	·····	that

4. 다음 글의 밑줄 친 부분 중, 어법상 **틀린** 것은?

The phrase, 'jack-of-all-trades' is a ① shortened version of 'jack of all trades and master of none.' It refers to those who ② claim to be proficient at countless tasks, but cannot perform a single one of them well. The phrase was first used in England at the start of the Industrial Revolution. A large number of efficiency experts set up shop in London, ③ advertising themselves as knowledgeable about every type of new manufacturing process, trade, and business. For a substantial fee, they would impart their knowledge to their clients. But it soon became ④ evident that their knowledge was limited and of no practical value. Doubtful industrialists started calling these self-appointed experts 'jacks of all trades and masters of none.' These experts are still with us, and as a result so ⑤ does the phrase.

Day 20

5. (A), (B), (C)의 각 네모 안에서 어법에 맞는 표현을 골라 짝지은 것으로 가장 적절한 것은?

I was five years old when my father introduced me to motor sports. Dad thought (A) it / which was a normal family outing to go to a car racing event. It was his way of spending some quality time with his wife and kids. (B) Few / Little did he know that he was fueling his son with a passion that would last for a lifetime. I still remember the awesome feeling I had on that day in May when my little feet (C) carried / were carried me up the stairs into the grandstands at the car racing stadium.

	(A)		(B)		(C)
①	it	----	Little	----	carried
②	it	----	Few	----	were carried
③	it	----	Little	----	were carried
④	which	----	Few	----	carried
⑤	which	----	Little	----	were carried

6. 다음 글의 밑줄 친 부분 중, 어법상 틀린 것은? [3점]

Although technology can't be blamed for the passion for growth, it is a great enabler. We are only just beginning to realize the potential of big data: its capacity to deliver highly ① customized content and products and to predict human behavior. The vast accumulation of personal data by Google, Amazon, Apple, and national governments ② promises everything from automated, personalized health care to preventative law enforcement. But with these tantalizing powers ③ come, necessarily, big risks. Just as Apple computers used to be safer from viruses because there were relatively fewer of them — which made them not worth ④ attacking — so the vast accumulation of personal data makes it an irresistible target for hackers and malware. Governments and regulators worry about the personal information stored and exploited by Google, but ⑤ what is precisely the scale of the accumulation of this information that makes Google's servers such tempting targets.

* tantalizing: 흥미를 부추기는   ** malware: 악성 소프트웨어

7. 다음 글의 밑줄 친 부분 중, 어법상 틀린 것은? [3점]

Charles Darwin, the 19th century naturalist and father of evolutionary biology, was one of the first ① to try to explain why humans became musical. In his 1871 book on evolutionary theory, *The Descent of Man, and Selection in Relation to Sex*, he proposed it was analogous to bird song, in ② that it helped males attract mates and warn off rivals. The idea has now largely fallen out of fashion, though, because singing is not an ③ exclusively male pastime: in almost three-quarters of songbirds, for instance, females sing, too. More recently Thomas Geissmann at the University of Zurich in Switzerland, came up with ④ another interesting theory. In a book published in the year 2000, he pointed out that the four other singing primates (some lemurs, tarsiers, titi monkeys and gibbons) all form monogamous breeding pairs — as ⑤ are many humans, and amongst birds duetting mainly occurs in monogamous species. Perhaps, Geissmann suggested, singing is somehow related to the evolution of monogamy — although exactly how or why is still unclear.

*monogamous: 일부일처의

8. 다음 글의 밑줄 친 부분 중, 어법상 틀린 것은? [3점]

Neuroscience has shown that the more experiences we have of being in control, ① the better our higher brains function. It is when we are affected by things outside of our control — and cannot regain a sense of being in control of anything that will make a difference — ② what we hit a real brain slowdown. You can see why people who feel like they have little choice in life are more apt to give up and go into negative spirals. But if they can regain a sense of control, great things happen. This is ③ why leaders must turn into "control freaks" — just not in the way we usually think of. The popular meaning of control freak is someone who tries to control everything, and ④ drives everyone around him crazy. What I mean here is a leader who obsessively focuses on helping his or her people get back in control of ⑤ themselves, to drive their own activities that directly affect outcomes.

2015학년도 11월 수능 30번

9. (A), (B), (C)의 각 네모 안에서 문맥에 맞는 낱말로 가장 적절한 것은? [3점]

While the eye sees at the surface, the ear tends to penetrate below the surface. Joachim-Ernst Berendt points out that the ear is the only sense that (A) fuses / replaces an ability to measure with an ability to judge. We can discern different colors, but we can give a precise *number* to different sounds. Our eyes do not let us perceive with this kind of (B) diversity / precision . An unmusical person can recognize an octave and, perhaps once instructed, a quality of tone, that is, a C or an F-sharp. Berendt points out that there are few 'acoustical illusions' — something sounding like something that in fact it is not — while there are many optical illusions. The ears do not lie. The sense of hearing gives us a remarkable connection with the invisible, underlying order of things. Through our ears we gain access to vibration, which (C) underlies / undermines everything around us. The sense of tone and music in another's voice gives us an enormous amount of information about that person, about her stance toward life, about her intentions.

* acoustical: 청각의

	(A)	(B)	(C)
①	fuses	precision	undermines
②	replaces	diversity	underlies
③	fuses	diversity	undermines
④	replaces	precision	underlies
⑤	fuses	precision	underlies

2014학년도 10월 학평 28번

10. (A), (B), (C)의 각 네모 안에서 문맥에 맞는 낱말로 가장 적절한 것은?

In "The Frog Prince" story, a princess loses her favorite ball in a pond. However, a frog appears and promises to retrieve her ball if she lets him eat at her table, drink from her cup, and sleep in her bed. (A) Desperate / Unwilling to have her ball back, the princess agrees, but when the frog appears at her door the next day she is disgusted by the prospect of being truthful and fulfilling her promise. But her father, the king, gives her no choice and she is (B) compelled / forbidden to carry out her promise. When the promise has been fulfilled the frog disappears, its place being taken by a handsome prince with whom she falls in love. Grateful that she has been truthful and kept her promise, even if it was at her father's (C) indifference / insistence , the prince marries the princess and they live happily ever after.

	(A)	(B)	(C)
①	Desperate	compelled	indifference
②	Desperate	compelled	insistence
③	Desperate	forbidden	indifference
④	Unwilling	compelled	indifference
⑤	Unwilling	forbidden	insistence

2013학년도 수능 30번

11. 다음 글의 밑줄 친 부분 중, 문맥상 낱말의 쓰임이 적절하지 않은 것은?

Researchers have suggested that maintaining good social relations depends on two ① complementary processes: being sensitive to the needs of others and being motivated to make amends or pay compensation when a violation does occur. In short, maintaining good social relations depends on the ② capacity for guilt. Martin L. Hoffman, who has focused on the guilt that comes from harming others, suggests that the motivational basis for this guilt is empathetic distress. Empathetic distress occurs when people ③ deny that their actions have caused harm or pain to another person. Motivated by feelings of guilt, they are ④ inclined to make amends for their actions. Making amends serves to repair damaged social relations and ⑤ restore group harmony.

2019학년도 10월 종로 30번

12. 다음 글의 밑줄 친 부분 중, 문맥상 낱말의 쓰임이 적절하지 않은 것은? [3점]

The rise of diversity means that, although our political systems are theoretically founded on majority rule, it may be impossible to form a majority even on issues crucial to survival. In turn, this ① collapse of consensus means that more and more governments are minority governments, based on shifting and uncertain coalitions. The ② missing majority makes a mockery of standard democratic rhetoric. It forces us to question whether, under the convergence of speed and diversity, any constituency can ever be "represented." In a mass industrial society, when people and their needs were fairly uniform and basic, consensus was an ③ attainable goal. In a demassified society, we not only lack national purpose, we also lack regional, statewide, or city-wide purpose. The diversity in any congressional district or parliamentary constituency, whether in France, Japan or Sweden, is so ④ rare that its "representative" cannot legitimately claim to speak for a consensus. He or she cannot represent the ⑤ general will for the simple reason that there is none. What, then, happens to the very notion of "representative democracy"?

*coalition: 연합
**make a mockery of: ~을 조롱하다
***constituency: 유권자, 선거구(민)

총 문항				문항	맞은 문항					문항		
개별 문항	1	2	3	4	5	6	7	8	9	10	11	12
채점												

어휘 · 숙어 비밀 노트

A 수능 필수 어휘 ▶ 파생어(2)

☐ 761	medical	a. 의학의, 의술의	medicinal	a. 약용의, 약효 있는
☐ 762	memorable	a. 기억할 만한	memorial	a. 기념의, 추도의; n. 기념비
☐ 763	momentary	a. 순간적인	momentous	a. 중요한
☐ 764	nomination	n. 지명, 임명	nominee	n. 지명된 사람, 후보
☐ 765	nutritious	a. 영양분이 많은	nutritional	a. 영양(상)의
☐ 766	object	n. 목표, 물체; v. 반대하다	objection	n. 반대
☐ 767	observation	n. 관찰	observance	n. 준수
☐ 768	organic	a. 유기체의	organized	a. 조직적인
☐ 769	practical	a. 실용적인	practicable	a. 실천할 수 있는
☐ 770	precedence	n. 우선함	precedent	n. 선례; a. 앞서는
☐ 771	produce	v. 생산하다; n. 농산물	product	n. 제품
☐ 772	respectful	a. 예의바른	respective	a. 각각의
☐ 773	sensory	a. 감각의	sensuous	a. 감각적인, 육감적인
☐ 774	sensitive	a. 민감한	sensible	a. 지각 있는, 분별력 있는
☐ 775	sensation	n. (설명하기 힘든) 느낌(기분)	sensational	a. 선풍적인
☐ 776	successful	a. 성공적인	successive	a. 잇따른, 연속적인
☐ 777	tolerant	a. 관대한, 잘 견디는	tolerable	a. 참을 수 있는
☐ 778	variable	a. 변하기 쉬운	various	a. 다양한
☐ 779	valuable	a. 소중한, 값비싼	valueless	a. 무가치한
☐ 780	visible	a. 알아볼 수 있는	visual	a. 시각의, 눈으로 보는

B 수능 필수 숙어

☐ 781	turn into	~으로 변하다
☐ 782	turn off	(전기, 가스, 수도) 끄다, 잠그다
☐ 783	turn on	(전기, 가스, 수도) 켜다
☐ 784	turn to	의지하다, (성질이 ~로) 변하다
☐ 785	turn up	(사람이) 도착하다, (기회가) 생기다
☐ 786	under pressure	압박을 받는, 강요당하는
☐ 787	up and down	위아래로, 왔다 갔다
☐ 788	up to date	최신의
☐ 789	upside down	거꾸로
☐ 790	use up	다 써버리다
☐ 791	used to+동사원형	~하곤 했다, (과거에) ~이었다
☐ 792	vote for	~에 찬성 투표하다
☐ 793	warm up	준비 운동을 하다
☐ 794	warn ~ about	~에게 (위험 등)을 경고하다
☐ 795	what is called	소위, 이른바(= so called)
☐ 796	wipe out	~을 완전히 파괴하다
☐ 797	with respect to	~에 관하여
☐ 798	work out	운동하다, 일이 잘 풀리다
☐ 799	would rather	차라리 ~하고 싶다
☐ 800	wrap up	(회의 등을) 마무리 짓다, 포장하다

제한 시간 : 13분 　　　　 정답 및 해설 112쪽

2020학년도 10월 학평 29번

1. 다음 글의 밑줄 친 부분 중, 어법상 틀린 것은? [3점]

Mathematical practices and discourses should be situated within cultural contexts, student interests, and real-life situations ① where all students develop positive identities as mathematics learners. Instruction in mathematics skills in isolation and devoid of student understandings and identities renders them ② helpless to benefit from explicit instruction. Thus, we agree that explicit instruction benefits students but propose that incorporating culturally relevant pedagogy and consideration of nonacademic factors that ③ promoting learning and mastery must enhance explicit instruction in mathematics instruction. Furthermore, teachers play a critical role in developing environments ④ that encourage student identities, agency, and independence through discourses and practices in the classroom. Students who are actively engaged in a contextualized learning process are in control of the learning process and are able to make connections with past learning experiences ⑤ to foster deeper and more meaningful learning.

* render: (어떤 상태가 되게) 만들다 　** pedagogy: 교수법

2017학년도 9월 모평 28번

2. (A), (B), (C)의 각 네모 안에서 어법에 맞는 표현으로 가장 적절한 것은? [3점]

Like life in traditional society, but unlike other team sports, baseball is not governed by the clock. A football game is comprised of exactly sixty minutes of play, a basketball game forty or forty-eight minutes, but baseball has no set length of time within which the game must be completed. The pace of the game is therefore leisurely and (A) unhurried / unhurriedly , like the world before the discipline of measured time, deadlines, schedules, and wages paid by the hour. Baseball belongs to the kind of world (B) which / in which people did not say, "I haven't got all day." Baseball games *do* have all day to be played. But that does not mean that they can go on forever. Baseball, like traditional life, proceeds according to the rhythm of nature, specifically the rotation of the Earth. During its first half century, games were not played at night, which meant that baseball games, like the traditional work day, (C) ending / ended when the sun set.

	(A)	(B)	(C)
①	unhurried	in which	ended
②	unhurried	which	ending
③	unhurriedly	which	ended
④	unhurriedly	which	ending
⑤	unhurriedly	in which	ended

2022학년도 4월 종로 29번

3. 다음 글의 밑줄 친 부분 중, 어법상 틀린 것은?

Food insecurity can be generated by dynamics that may appear overall positive. In many cities, *gentrification*, the process ① through which whole neighborhoods are revitalized through the influx of higher-income inhabitants, has undesirable collateral effects. The arrival of new dwellers in previously low-income neighborhoods often ② push real estate, rent, services, and food costs up. Small farm-to-table restaurants, gourmet cafes, and natural food stores open to meet the needs and preferences of the newcomers. The markets that cities had built in previous decades to provide food for local dwellers of all walks of life are ③ turned into glamorous food halls, leisure places for affluent consumers and tourists. Abandoned factories and whole neighborhoods previously dedicated to industrial activities become hubs for food innovation, creative manufacturing, and intriguing new restaurants. However, prices inevitably increase, making ④ finding affordable food difficult. The changes often end up forcing the poorest segments of the preexisting communities ⑤ to move to more affordable destinations.

* gentrification: (주택가의) 고급 주택화
** collateral: 부차[이차]적인 　*** gourmet: 미식가

2016학년도 수능 28번

4. 다음 글의 밑줄 친 부분 중, 어법상 틀린 것은? [3점]

The Greeks' focus on the salient object and its attributes led to ① their failure to understand the fundamental nature of causality. Aristotle explained that a stone falling through the air is due to the stone having the property of "gravity." But of course a piece of wood ② tossed into water floats instead of sinking. This phenomenon Aristotle explained as being due to the wood having the property of "levity"! In both cases the focus is ③ exclusively on the object, with no attention paid to the possibility that some force outside the object might be relevant. But the Chinese saw the world as consisting of continuously interacting substances, so their attempts to understand it ④ causing them to be oriented toward the complexities of the entire "field," that is, the context or environment as a whole. The notion ⑤ that events always occur in a field of forces would have been completely intuitive to the Chinese.

* salient: 현저한, 두드러진
** levity: 가벼움

5. 밑줄 친 (a)~(e) 중에서 문맥상 낱말의 쓰임이 적절하지 <u>않은</u> 것은?

There is evidence that even very simple algorithms can outperform expert judgement on simple prediction problems. For example, algorithms have proved more (a) <u>accurate</u> than humans in predicting whether a prisoner released on parole will go on to commit another crime, or in predicting whether a potential candidate will perform well in a job in future. In over 100 studies across many different domains, half of all cases show simple formulas make (b) <u>better</u> significant predictions than human experts, and the remainder (except a very small handful), show a tie between the two. When there are a lot of different factors involved and a situation is very uncertain, simple formulas can win out by focusing on the most important factors and being consistent, while human judgement is too easily influenced by particularly salient and perhaps (c) <u>irrelevant</u> considerations. A similar idea is supported by further evidence that 'checklists' can improve the quality of expert decisions in a range of domains by ensuring that important steps or considerations aren't missed when people are feeling (d) <u>relaxed</u>. For example, treating patients in intensive care can require hundreds of small actions per day, and one small error could cost a life. Using checklists to ensure that no crucial steps are missed has proved to be remarkably (e) <u>effective</u> in a range of medical contexts, from preventing live infections to reducing pneumonia.

* parole: 가석방 ** salient: 두드러진 *** pneumonia: 폐렴

① (a) ② (b) ③ (c) ④ (d) ⑤ (e)

6. 다음 글의 밑줄 친 부분 중, 문맥상 낱말의 쓰임이 적절하지 <u>않은</u> 것은?

Until the 1920's, there were only three competitive swimming strokes — freestyle, backstroke, and breaststroke — and each had specific rules that described how it was to be performed. The rules of breaststroke ① <u>stated</u> that both arms must be pulled together underwater and then recovered simultaneously back to the start of the pulling position to begin the next stroke. Most people interpreted this arm recovery to mean an ② <u>underwater</u> recovery. In the 1920's, however, someone ③ <u>challenged</u> the rules and reinterpreted this arm recovery to be an out-of-the-water recovery. Since this new breaststroke was about 15% ④ <u>slower</u>, people using the conventional version couldn't effectively compete. Something had to be done to solve the problem. Finally, this new stroke — now known as the 'butterfly' — won ⑤ <u>recognition</u> as the fourth swimming stroke, and became an Olympic event in 1956.

7. (A), (B), (C)의 각 네모 안에서 문맥에 맞는 낱말로 가장 적절한 것은?

Anxiety has a damaging effect on mental performance of all kinds. It is in one sense a useful response gone awry — an overly zealous mental preparation for an anticipated threat. But such mental rehearsal is (A) | disastrous / constructive | cognitive static when it becomes trapped in a stale routine that captures attention, intruding on all other attempts to focus elsewhere. Anxiety undermines the intellect. In a complex, intellectually demanding and high-pressure task such as that of air traffic controllers, for example, having chronically high anxiety is an almost sure predictor that a person will eventually fail in training or in the field. The anxious are more likely to fail even given (B) | inferior / superior | scores on intelligence tests, as a study of 1,790 students in training for air traffic control posts discovered. Anxiety also sabotages academic performance of all kinds: 126 different studies of more than 36,000 people found that the more (C) | prone / resistant | to anxieties a person is, the poorer his or her academic performance is.

* go awry: 빗나가다

	(A)	(B)	(C)
①	disastrous	inferior	prone
②	disastrous	superior	prone
③	disastrous	superior	resistant
④	constructive	inferior	resistant
⑤	constructive	superior	resistant

8. (A), (B), (C)의 각 네모 안에서 문맥에 맞는 낱말로 가장 적절한 것은?

Even those of us who claim not to be materialistic can't help but form attachments to certain clothes. Like fragments from old songs, clothes can (A) | evoke / erase | both cherished and painful memories. A worn-thin dress may hang in the back of a closet even though it hasn't been worn in years because the faint scent of pine that lingers on it is all that remains of someone's sixteenth summer. A(n) (B) | impractical / brand-new | white scarf might be pulled out of a donation bag at the last minute because of the promise of elegance it once held for its owner. And a ripped T-shirt might be (C) | rescued / forgotten | from the dust rag bin long after the name of the rock band once written across it has faded. Clothes document personal history for us the same way that fossils chart time for archaeologists.

	(A)	(B)	(C)
①	evoke	impractical	rescued
②	evoke	impractical	forgotten
③	evoke	brand-new	forgotten
④	erase	impractical	rescued
⑤	erase	brand-new	forgotten

총 문항			문항	맞은 문항						문항	
개별 문항	1	2	3	4	5	6	7	8	9	10	11	12
채점												

Day 22

미니 고난도 Test 2회

제한 시간 : 13분   정답 및 해설 115쪽

2020학년도 3월 학평 29번

1. 다음 글의 밑줄 친 부분 중, 어법상 틀린 것은?

When children are young, much of the work is demonstrating to them that they ① do have control. One wise friend of ours who was a parent educator for twenty years ② advises giving calendars to preschool-age children and writing down all the important events in their life, in part because it helps children understand the passage of time better, and how their days will unfold. We can't overstate the importance of the calendar tool in helping kids feel in control of their day. Have them ③ cross off days of the week as you come to them. Spend time going over the schedule for the day, giving them choice in that schedule wherever ④ possible. This communication expresses respect — they see that they are not just a tagalong to your day and your plans, and they understand what is going to happen, when, and why. As they get older, children will then start to write in important things for themselves, ⑤ it further helps them develop their sense of control.

2017학년도 7월 학평 29번

2. 다음 글의 밑줄 친 부분 중, 어법상 틀린 것은? [3점]

The most dramatic and significant contacts between civilizations were ① when people from one civilization conquered and eliminated the people of another. These contacts normally were not only violent but brief, and ② they occurred only occasionally. Beginning in the seventh century A.D., relatively ③ sustained and at times intense intercivilizational contacts did develop between Islam and the West and Islam and India. Most commercial, cultural, and military interactions, however, were within civilizations. While India and China, for instance, were on occasion invaded and subjected by other peoples (Moguls, Mongols), both civilizations ④ having extensive times of "warring states" within their own civilization as well. Similarly, the Greeks fought each other and traded with each other far more often than they ⑤ did with Persians or other non-Greeks.

2020학년도 5월 종로 29번

3. 다음 글의 밑줄 친 부분 중, 어법상 틀린 것은?

If there is one problem in medicine that confounds doctors, insurers, and pharmaceutical companies alike, it's noncompliance — the unfriendly term for patients' not following doctors' orders. Most vexing ① are patients who don't take their medications as prescribed, which, it turns out, is pretty much most of us. Studies have shown that about half of patients who ② are prescribed medication take their pills as directed. For drugs like statin, which must be used for years, the rate is even worse, ③ drops to around 30 percent after a year. Since the effects of these drugs can be invisible, the thinking goes, patients don't detect any benefit from them. Research has found that noncompliance adds $100 billion annually to US healthcare costs and ④ leads to 125,000 unnecessary deaths from cardiovascular diseases alone every year. And it can be blamed almost entirely on human error — people failing to do ⑤ what they know they should.

* statin: 스타틴(혈관 내 콜레스테롤 억제제)
** cardiovascular: 심혈관의

2016학년도 11월 종로 28번

4. 다음 글의 밑줄 친 부분 중, 어법상 틀린 것은?

During the late 1800s, the department store emerged as a "one-stop shopping" destination, offering apparel and household goods to a diverse clientele. In 1848, A. T. Stewart's idea of a "department store" ① was put into operation in New York City. This shop employed 2,000 people and sold a wide assortment of ② manufactured articles. However, then, as today, the city was ③ much different from the rest of America. Thus, while it was possible to buy "imported luxuries" there, this luxury merchandise could not reach ④ outlying areas until the railway system was built and marketing strategies were developed. Some of the earliest department stores implemented new business tactics. These tactics included the encouragement of leisurely browsing, and the "one-price policy," ⑤ it eliminated the need to negotiate price, allowing merchandise to be exchanged or refunded.

5. 밑줄 친 (a)~(e) 중에서 문맥상 낱말의 쓰임이 적절하지 않은 것은?

Classifying things together into groups is something we do all the time, and it isn't hard to see why. Imagine trying to shop in a supermarket where the food was arranged in random order on the shelves: tomato soup next to the white bread in one aisle, chicken soup in the back next to the 60-watt light bulbs, one brand of cream cheese in front and another in aisle 8 near the cookies. The task of finding what you want would be (a) time-consuming and extremely difficult, if not impossible.

In the case of a supermarket, someone had to (b) design the system of classification. But there is also a ready-made system of classification embodied in our language. The word "dog," for example, groups together a certain class of animals and distinguishes them from other animals. Such a grouping may seem too (c) abstract to be called a classification, but this is only because you have already mastered the word. As a child learning to speak, you had to work hard to (d) learn the system of classification your parents were trying to teach you. Before you got the hang of it, you probably made mistakes, like calling the cat a dog. If you hadn't learned to speak, the whole world would seem like the (e) unorganized supermarket; you would be in the position of an infant, for whom every object is new and unfamiliar. In learning the principles of classification, therefore, we'll be learning about the structure that lies at the core of our language.

① (a)　② (b)　③ (c)　④ (d)　⑤ (e)

6. 다음 글의 밑줄 친 부분 중, 문맥상 낱말의 쓰임이 적절하지 않은 것은?

Many people take numerous photos while traveling or on vacation or during significant life celebrations to ① preserve the experience for the future. But the role of photographer may actually detract from their ② delight in the present moment. I know a father who devoted himself earnestly to photographing the birth of his first and only child. The photos were beautiful but, he ③ lamented afterward he felt that he had missed out on the most important first moment of his son's life. Looking through the camera lens made him ④ detached from the scene. He was just an observer, not an experiencer. Teach yourself to use your camera in a way that ⑤ neglects your ongoing experiences, by truly looking at things and noticing what is beautiful and meaningful.

7. (A), (B), (C)의 각 네모 안에서 문맥에 맞는 낱말로 가장 적절한 것은?

Contrary to what we usually believe, the best moments in our lives are not the passive, receptive, relaxing times — although such experiences can also be enjoyable, if we have worked hard to (A) attain / avoid them. The best moments usually occur when a person's body or mind is stretched to its limits in a voluntary effort to accomplish something difficult and worthwhile. (B) Optimal / Minimal experience is thus something that we make happen. For a child, it could be placing with trembling fingers the last block on a tower she has built, higher than any she has built so far; for a sprinter, it could be trying to beat his own record; for a violinist, mastering an (C) uncomplicated / intricate musical passage. For each person there are thousands of opportunities, challenges to expand ourselves.

	(A)	(B)	(C)
①	attain	Minimal	uncomplicated
②	attain	Optimal	intricate
③	attain	Optimal	uncomplicated
④	avoid	Optimal	intricate
⑤	avoid	Minimal	uncomplicated

8. (A), (B), (C)의 각 네모 안에서 문맥에 맞는 낱말로 가장 적절한 것은?

Responses to survey questions are influenced by events, and we should consider this when reviewing the results of a survey. The reputation of an airline, for example, will be (A) damaged / recovered if a survey is conducted just after a plane crash. A computer company lost its reputation in company surveys just after major news coverage about a defect in its products. On the positive side, surveys by a beverage company about its image showed very (B) hostile / favorable public attitudes just after its massive investment in the Olympics. Consequently, surveys should be conducted when the organization is not in the news or connected to a significant event that may influence public opinion. In neutral context, a more (C) valid / biased survey can be conducted about an organization's reputation, products, or services.

	(A)	(B)	(C)
①	damaged	hostile	biased
②	damaged	hostile	valid
③	damaged	favorable	valid
④	recovered	hostile	biased
⑤	recovered	favorable	valid

총 문항				문항		맞은 문항					문항
개별 문항	1	2	3	4	5	6	7	8	9	10	11	12
채점											

Day 23

 제한 시간 : 13분　　　　정답 및 해설 118쪽

2019학년도 10월 학평 29번

1. 다음 글의 밑줄 친 부분 중, 어법상 틀린 것은?

The modern adult human brain weighs only 1/50 of the total body weight but uses up to 1/5 of the total energy needs. The brain's running costs are about eight to ten times as high, per unit mass, as ① those of the body's muscles. And around 3/4 of that energy is expended on neurons, the ② specialized brain cells that communicate in vast networks to generate our thoughts and behaviours. An individual neuron ③ sends a signal in the brain uses as much energy as a leg muscle cell running a marathon. Of course, we use more energy overall when we are running, but we are not always on the move, whereas our brains never switch off. Even though the brain is metabolically greedy, it still outclasses any desktop computer both in terms of the calculations it can perform and the efficiency ④ at which it does this. We may have built computers that can beat our top Grand Master chess players, but we are still far away from designing one that is capable of recognizing and picking up one of the chess pieces as ⑤ easily as a typical three-year-old child can.

2015학년도 9월 종로 28번

2. 다음 글의 밑줄 친 부분 중, 어법상 틀린 것은? [3점]

Oxygen is what it is all about. Ironically, the stuff that gives us life eventually kills it. The ultimate life force lies in tiny cellular factories of energy, called mitochondria, ① that burn nearly all the oxygen we breathe in. But breathing has a price. The combustion of oxygen that keeps us alive and active ② sending out by-products called oxygen free radicals. They have Dr. Jekyll and Mr. Hyde characteristics. On the one hand, they help guarantee our survival. For example, when the body mobilizes ③ to fight off infectious agents, it generates a burst of free radicals to destroy the invaders very efficiently. On the other hand, free radicals move ④ uncontrollably through the body, attacking cells, rusting their proteins, piercing their membranes and corrupting their genetic code until the cells become dysfunctional and sometimes give up and die. These fierce radicals, ⑤ built into life as both protectors and avengers, are potent agents of aging.

* oxygen free radical: 활성 산소
** membrane: (해부학) 얇은 막

2022학년도 8월 종로 28번

3. 다음 글의 밑줄 친 부분 중, 어법상 틀린 것은?

There is one effective way of balancing the popular demand for greater regulation against the compliance costs that regulation imposes, and governments are likely to follow this. It is to subcontract regulation to independent, single-function bodies ① which specialize in regulating a particular area. All the evidence is that good regulation is an extremely subtle, flexible business. It involves deals between the regulator and the ② regulated, where cost and thoroughness are traded-off against each other. It involves regulatory bodies in different countries co-operating with each other, for the greater the freedom of businesses ③ to migrate, the greater the need for worldwide regulation. International banking provides perhaps the best example of ④ how a worldwide regulatory system can be built, for the central banks of the main industrial countries operate a series of mutual agreements on bank capital requirements which, in theory, should prevent any one country securing an unfair comparative advantage or any bank escaping the net of international regulation. However, the fact that BCCI did slip through ⑤ showing just how difficult it is to regulate a wholly international industry.

* subcontract: 하청을 주다　** BCCI: 1991년 도산한 다국적 은행
(Bank of Credit and Commerce International)

2015학년도 8월 종로 28번

4. (A), (B), (C)의 각 네모 안에서 어법에 맞는 표현으로 가장 적절한 것은? [3점]

Do you suffer from FoMO? If so, you're not alone. FoMO stands for "fear of missing out," which is a term coined to describe anxiety about not knowing (A) that / what is going on in others' lives. The desire to keep up with others' activities is not new, but social media have kicked it into overdrive. People who have a high fear of missing out are more likely than others (B) check / to check and send messages when driving and to check emails and text messages during class. But that's just part of the problem. FoMO is also interfering with people's effectiveness on the job. Effective communicators make eye contact 60% to 70% of the time, but many people today make eye contact less than that — sometimes as little as 30% of the time. A big part of the reason for the decreased eye contact (C) is / to be all the attention being paid to digital devices.

	(A)		(B)		(C)
①	that	.....	check	.....	to be
②	that	.....	to check	.....	to be
③	what	.....	to check	.....	is
④	what	.....	to check	.....	to be
⑤	what	.....	check	.....	is

5. 밑줄 친 (a)~(e) 중에서 문맥상 낱말의 쓰임이 적절하지 않은 것은? [3점]

Our irresistible tendency to see things in human terms — that we are often mistaken in attributing complex human motives and processing abilities to other species — does not mean that an animal's behavior is not, in fact, complex. Rather, it means that the complexity of the animal's behavior is not purely a (a) product of its internal complexity. Herbert Simon's "parable of the ant" makes this point very clearly. Imagine an ant walking along a beach, and (b) visualize tracking the trajectory of the ant as it moves. The trajectory would show a lot of twists and turns, and would be very irregular and complicated. One could then suppose that the ant had equally complicated (c) internal navigational abilities, and work out what these were likely to be by analyzing the trajectory to infer the rules and mechanisms that could produce such a complex navigational path. The complexity of the trajectory, however, "is really a complexity in the surface of the beach, not a complexity in the ant." In reality, the ant may be using a set of very (d) complex rules: it is the interaction of these rules with the environment that actually produces the complex trajectory, not the ant alone. Put more generally, the parable of the ant illustrates that there is no necessary correlation between the complexity of an (e) observed behavior and the complexity of the mechanism that produces it.

* parable: 우화 ** trajectory: 이동 경로

① (a)   ② (b)   ③ (c)   ④ (d)   ⑤ (e)

6. (A), (B), (C)의 각 네모 안에서 문맥에 맞는 낱말로 가장 적절한 것은?

The first experiments in television broadcasting began in France in the 1930s, but the French were slow to employ the new technology. There were several reasons for this (A) hesitancy / consistency . Radio absorbed the majority of state resources, and the French government was reluctant to shoulder the financial burden of developing national networks for television broadcasting. Television programming costs were too high, and program output correspondingly low. Poor (B) distribution / description combined with minimal offerings provided little incentive to purchase the new product. Further, television sets were priced beyond the means of a general public whose modest living standards, especially in the 1930s and 1940s, did not allow the acquisition of luxury goods. Ideological influences also factored in; elites in particular were (C) optimistic / skeptical of television, perceiving it as a messenger of mass culture and Americanization.

	(A)	(B)	(C)
①	hesitancy	distribution	optimistic
②	hesitancy	distribution	skeptical
③	hesitancy	description	optimistic
④	consistency	description	optimistic
⑤	consistency	distribution	skeptical

7. (A), (B), (C)의 각 네모 안에서 문맥에 맞는 낱말로 가장 적절한 것은?

There are few people who do not react to music to some degree. The power of music is diverse and people respond in different ways. To some it is mainly an (A) instinctive / inactive , exciting sound to which they dance or move their bodies. Other people listen for its message, or take an intellectual approach to its form and construction, (B) appreciating / confusing its formal patterns or originality. Above all, however, there can be hardly anyone who is not moved by some kind of music. Music (C) covers / removes the whole range of emotions: It can make us feel happy or sad, helpless or energetic, and some music is capable of overtaking the mind until it forgets all else. It works on the subconscious, creating or enhancing mood and unlocking deep memories.

	(A)	(B)	(C)
①	instinctive	appreciating	covers
②	instinctive	confusing	removes
③	instinctive	appreciating	removes
④	inactive	appreciating	covers
⑤	inactive	confusing	removes

8. (A), (B), (C)의 각 네모 안에서 문맥에 맞는 낱말을 골라 짝지은 것으로 가장 적절한 것은?

Although most people recognize it as a jewel, the diamond most directly affects our daily lives as a tool. Industrial diamonds are so important that a (A) shortage / strength would cause a breakdown in the metal-working industry and would destroy mass production. Industrial diamonds are crushed and powdered, and then used in many grinding and polishing operations. Their use (B) changes / ranges from the drill in a dentist's office to saws for cutting rocks, and to glass cutters. The great (C) hardness / hardship of a diamond makes it one of the most important industrial materials known.

	(A)	(B)	(C)
①	shortage	ranges	hardness
②	shortage	changes	hardship
③	strength	changes	hardness
④	strength	ranges	hardship
⑤	strength	ranges	hardness

총 문항				문항	맞은 문항						문항		
개별 문항	1	2	3	4	5	6	7	8	9	10	11	12
채점												

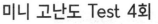

Day 24

제한 시간 : 13분   정답 및 해설 121쪽

2018학년도 4월 학평 28번

1. 다음 글의 밑줄 친 부분 중, 어법상 틀린 것은? [3점]

According to Pierre Pica, understanding quantities approximately in terms of estimating ratios is a universal human intuition. In fact, humans who do not have numbers have no choice but ①to see the world in this way. By contrast, understanding quantities in terms of exact numbers is not a universal intuition; it is a product of culture. The precedence of approximations and ratios over exact numbers, Pica suggests, ②is due to the fact that ratios are much more important for survival in the wild than the ability to count. ③Faced with a group of spear−wielding adversaries, we needed to know instantly whether there were more of them than us. When we saw two trees we needed to know instantly ④that had more fruit hanging from it. In neither case was it ⑤necessary to enumerate every enemy or every fruit individually. The crucial thing was to be able to make quick estimates of the relative amounts.

* enumerate: 일일이 세다

2017학년도 5월 종로 28번

2. 다음 글의 밑줄 친 부분 중, 어법상 틀린 것은?   [3점]

In the ideal news service of the future, every celebrity story would at heart be a piece of education: an invitation to learn from an admirable person about how to become a ①slightly better version of oneself. We are used to ②thinking that anyone who 'copies' a celebrity is sad, but in its highest form, imitation founded on admiration is integral to a good life. To refuse to admire, to take no interest in ③what distinguished others are up to, is to shut ourselves off from important knowledge. The job of the news is to make the celebrity section no less exciting than it ④is now, while ensuring that it provides us with psychologically rich, educational portraits of certain noble-minded individuals who will spark our imaginations because they properly help us to address the flaws in our personalities. Celebrity news should, in its mature form, be a serious and respectable medium ⑤which we learn to become more than we currently are.

2015학년도 6월 종로 28번

3. 다음 글의 밑줄 친 부분 중, 어법상 틀린 것은?   [3점]

After years of following our mother's advice to hold our cups up straight, we find that in the Incan culture, it's perfectly ①acceptable to spill your drink. In fact, it's expected. In reverence to Pachamama, the Incan fertility goddess, drinkers of chicha, a drink originally made from the berries of the pepper plant, now made with corn, purposely ②spill the first sip on the ground. It's a toast they call *challa*, and many people perform the toast every day. And there's a special celebration each year called Martes de Challa, when people not only dump their drink, but they bury food, and, if they're a *yatiri* (a traditional priest), ③sacrificing guinea pigs. It's an apology of sorts to Pachamama (Mother Earth) for all we've done ④to disturb her. Yatiris regularly create offerings for those who ask by wrapping up herbs, and small tablets of sugar with symbols (houses, hearts, condors, etc.), ⑤which are then burnt after pouring chicha on top.

* reverence: 숭배, 존경

2021학년도 11월 종로 29번

4. 다음 글의 밑줄 친 부분 중, 어법상 틀린 것은?

To the extent that cues to emotion in music are based on cues to emotion in speech, we should expect children to recognize emotion in music early. And they ①do. By age five, children use tempo as a cue to emotion, with faster tempos conveying positive emotions, and slower ones sounding more ②negative. Tempo conveys emotion in the same way in both speech and music. So do pitch and loudness; when ③asked to sing songs showing basic emotions, children use the cues of tempo, pitch, and loudness by the age of five. Mode (major and minor), however, has no counterpart in speech, and though one small study in 1990 showed that even three-year-olds heard major-minor as happy-sad, a more recent study ④to find no sensitivity to mode until age six. Sensitivity to the difference in emotional tone between major and minor modes may thus emerge only once children have been exposed to this contrast, ⑤suggesting that this is a learned association rather than a natural one.

* mode: 음계

5. 밑줄 친 (a)~(e) 중에서 문맥상 낱말의 쓰임이 적절하지 <u>않은</u> 것은? [3점]

For quite some time, science educators believed that "hands-on" activities were the answer to children's understanding through their participation in science-related activities. Many teachers believed that students merely engaging in activities and (a) <u>manipulating</u> objects would organize the information to be gained and the knowledge to be understood into concept comprehension. Educators began to notice that the pendulum had swung too far to the "hands-on" component of inquiry as they realized that the knowledge was not (b) <u>inherent</u> in the materials themselves, but in the thought and metacognition about what students had done in the activity. We now know that "hands-on" is a dangerous phrase when speaking about learning science. The (c) <u>missing</u> ingredient is the "minds-on" part of the instructional experience. (d) <u>Uncertainty</u> about the knowledge intended in any activity comes from each student's re-creation of concepts — and discussing, thinking, arguing, listening, and evaluating one's own preconceptions after the activities, under the leadership of a thoughtful teacher, can bring this about. After all, a food fight is a hands-on activity, but about all you would learn was something about the aerodynamics of flying mashed potatoes! Our view of what students need to build their knowledge and theories about the natural world (e) <u>extends</u> far beyond a "hands-on activity." While it is important for students to use and interact with materials in science class, the learning comes from the sense-making of students' "hands-on" experiences.

* pendulum: 추(錘) ** metacognition: 초(超)인지
*** aerodynamics: 공기 역학

① (a) ② (b) ③ (c) ④ (d) ⑤ (e)

6. (A), (B), (C) 각 네모 안에서 문맥에 맞는 낱말을 골라 짝지은 것으로 가장 적절한 것은?

The shapes of Korean kites are based on scientific (A) particles / principles which enable them to make good use of the wind. One particular Korean kite is the rectangular "shield kite," which has a unique hole at its center. This hole helps the kite fly fast regardless of the wind speed by (B) concentrating / contaminating the wind on days when the wind is light, and letting it pass through when the wind is blowing hard. The center hole also allows the kite to respond quickly to the flyer's (C) commands / comments For these reasons, Korean kites such as the shield kite are good at "kite fighting."

	(A)		(B)		(C)
①	particles	......	concentrating	......	commands
②	particles	......	contaminating	......	comments
③	particles	......	concentrating	......	comments
④	principles	......	contaminating	......	comments
⑤	principles	......	concentrating	......	commands

7. (A), (B), (C) 각 네모 안에서 문맥에 맞는 어휘를 골라, 짝지은 것으로 가장 적절한 것을 고르시오.

Like all other industries, the rose business must (A) adopt / adapt to changing conditions in the marketplace. In the past, a florist shop was most likely a local, independently owned business that bought roses from a wholesaler who purchased them from a farmer. On special days like Valentine's Day, the cost of a dozen roses rose twofold or more as a result of high (B) supply / demand. Today, suppliers of roses include large supermarket chains, wholesalers who sell directly at many locations, and direct telephone marketers. The romance of roses has been replaced by (C) economic / economics realities.

	(A)		(B)		(C)
①	adopt	....	supply	....	economic
②	adopt	....	demand	....	economics
③	adopt	....	supply	....	economics
④	adapt	....	demand	....	economic
⑤	adapt	....	supply	....	economic

8. (A), (B), (C) 각 네모 안에서 문맥에 맞는 어휘를 골라, 짝지은 것으로 가장 적절한 것을 고르시오.

I have been asked to (A) assist / resist in creating a committee to improve the Sunshine Charity. We are trying to form a strong committee, and I have been asked to request you to join it. I know you will be interested in the (B) objective / objection of our committee. We all know how invaluable your advice and help will be. The first meeting will be held here at 11 a.m. next Thursday. I hope you will be able to come, and that you will agree to (C) sit / seat on the committee.

	(A)		(B)		(C)
①	assist	......	objective	......	sit
②	assist	......	objection	......	sit
③	assist	......	objective	......	seat
④	resist	......	objection	......	seat
⑤	resist	......	objective	......	seat

총 문항		문항			맞은 문항				문항		
개별 문항	1	2	3	4	5	6	7	8	9	10	11	12
채점												

"Big Event 1+3" 한국사 · 사회탐구 · 과학탐구 교재 목록

1. 2022년 시행 모의고사 : 신청하시면 확인 후 바로 보내드리고 있습니다.

학년	과목(영역)	횟수	PDF 제공 교재
고1	한국사	4회	11-1 한국사
고2	한국사	4회	11-2 한국사
	사회탐구	4회	11-3 생활과 윤리, 11-4 윤리와 사상, 11-5 한국지리, 11-6 세계지리, 11-7 동아시아사, 11-8 세계사, 11-9 정치와 법, 11-10 경제, 11-11 사회·문화
	과학탐구	4회	11-12 물리학 I , 11-13 화학 I , 11-14 생명과학 I , 11-15 지구과학 I
고3	한국사	12회	11-16 한국사
	사회탐구	12회	11-17 생활과 윤리, 11-18 윤리와 사상, 11-19 한국지리, 11-20 세계지리, 11-21 동아시아사, 11-22 세계사, 11-23 법과 정치, 11-24 경제, 11-25 사회·문화
	과학탐구	12회	11-26 물리학 I , 11-27 화학 I , 11-28 생명과학 I , 11-29 지구과학 I
		11회	11-30 물리학 II , 11-31 화학 II , 11-32 생명과학 II , 11-33 지구과학 II

2. 2023년 시행 모의고사 : 2024년 2월부터 보내드릴 예정입니다.

학년	과목(영역)	횟수	PDF 제공 교재
고1	한국사	4회	12-1 한국사
고2	한국사	4회	12-2 한국사
	사회탐구	4회	12-3 생활과 윤리, 12-4 윤리와 사상, 12-5 한국지리, 12-6 세계지리, 12-7 동아시아사, 12-8 세계사, 12-9 정치와 법, 12-10 경제, 12-11 사회·문화
	과학탐구	4회	12-12 물리학 I , 12-13 화학 I , 12-14 생명과학 I , 12-15 지구과학 I
고3	한국사	11회	12-16 한국사
	사회탐구	11회	12-17 생활과윤리, 12-18 윤리와 사상, 12-19 한국지리, 12-20 세계지리, 12-21 동아시아사, 12-22 세계사, 12-23 법과 정치, 12-24 경제, 12-25 사회·문화
	과학탐구	11회	12-26 물리학 I , 12-27 화학 I , 12-28 생명과학 I , 12-29 지구과학 I
		10회	12-30 물리학 II , 12-31 화학 II , 12-32 생명과학 II , 12-33 지구과학 II

※ 과목별 수록 회차는 사정상 변경될 수 있습니다.

B I G
E V E N T
1 + 3

씨뮬 교재를 구매하신 모든 분들께
고1, 2, 3 한국사 · 사회탐구 · 과학탐구 과목
중에서 학년에 상관없이 원하는 3과목의
최신 모의고사(과목별 4~12회 구성)
PDF 파일을 메일로 보내 드립니다.

참 여 방 법

❶ 설문지를 작성하고, "Big Event 1+3"
한국사 · 사회탐구 · 과학탐구 교재 목록에서
교재번호와 과목명을 확인한 후
'Big Event 1+3 교재 신청란'에 정확히 기입합니다.

❷ 설문지 부분을 핸드폰(또는 디지털 카메라)으로 찍어서
골드교육 홈페이지(www.goldedu.co.kr)
커뮤니티 → "1+3 이벤트" 게시판에 올리시면 됩니다.

❸ "Big Event 1+3"은 3과목까지 신청할 수 있으며,
여러 과목을 신청하면 임의대로 3과목을 선정하여
보내 드립니다.

★ 2023년 시행 모의고사를
신청하면 출간 일정상 2024년
2월부터 보내 드리오니 이용에
착오 없으시기 바랍니다.
그리고 이 책의 1+3 이벤트 유효
기간은 발행일로부터 3년입니다.

★ 개인 정보는 이벤트 목적
외에는 사용하지 않으며 이벤트
마감 이후 폐기함을 알려드립니다.

(주)골드교육 씨뮬 교재를 이용해 주셔서 감사합니다.
더 좋은 교재를 만들기 위해 독자 여러분의 의견을 귀담아 듣고자 합니다.

1. 이 책을 구입하게 된 동기는 무엇입니까?

① 학교/학원 교재　　　② 선생님이 추천해 주셔서　　　③ 선배나 친구들이 추천해서
④ 직접 서점에서 보고　　⑤ 광고나 입소문을 들어서　　⑥ 기타(　　　　　　　)

2. 이 책의 전반적인 부분에 대한 질문입니다.

• 문제의 분량 : 많다□ 알맞다□ 적다□　　• 해설의 분량 : 많다□ 적당하다□ 부족하다□
• 책의 크기 : 크다□ 적당하다□ 작다□　　• 이용 편의성 : 편하다□ 보통이다□ 불편하다□
• 책의 가격 : 비싸다□ 적당하다□ 싸다□　　• 책의 만족도 : 만족□ 보통□ 불만족□

3. 이 책에서 좋았던 점은 무엇입니까? (복수 응답 가능)

① 24일 학습 체계　　　② 출제 트렌드 & 1등급 꿀팁　　　③ 핵심 문법
④ 어법 기출 문제　　　⑤ 어휘 기출 문제　　　　　　　⑥ 정답 및 해설
⑦ 내신 대비 서브노트　⑧ 어휘·숙어 비밀 노트　　　　　⑨ 기타(　　　　　　　)

4. 내가 구매한 씨뮬 교재에 대한 독자서평을 작성해 주세요.
베스트 독자서평으로 채택되면 다음 씨뮬 교재에 수록해 드립니다.

Big Event 1+3 교재 신청란　　　　　　　　　　　　(유형⁺ 씨뮬 고3 영어 어법·어휘)

이름			
		교재번호	과목명
신청 과목 1			
신청 과목 2			
신청 과목 3			

이벤트 신청은 위의 표를 보고 교재번호와 과목명을 빈칸에 정확히 적어 주시기 바랍니다. (교재번호 11-5, 과목명 한국지리)

믿을 수 있는 기출문제로 실전 연습하여 출제 경향과 유형을 파악하라!

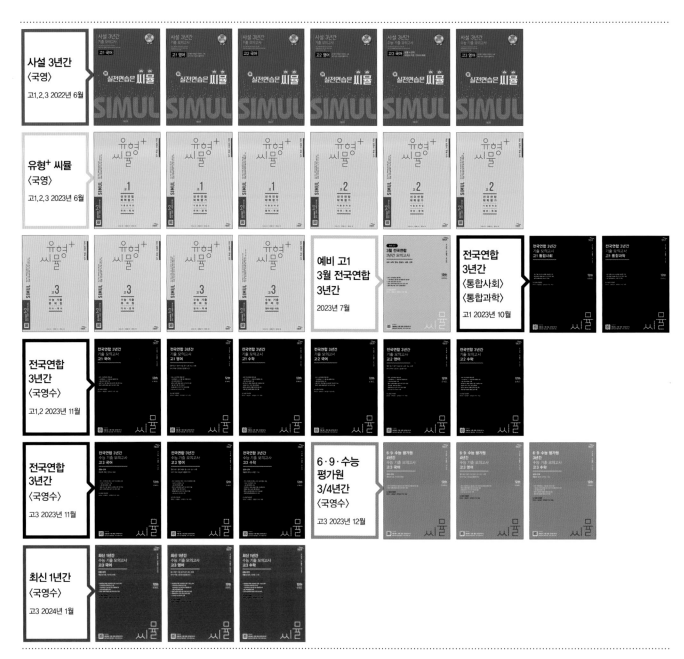

사설 3년간
〈국영〉
고1,2,3 2022년 6월

유형⁺ 씨뮬
〈국영〉
고1,2,3 2023년 6월

예비 고1
3월 전국연합
3년간
2023년 7월

전국연합
3년간
〈통합사회〉
〈통합과학〉
고1 2023년 10월

전국연합
3년간
〈국영수〉
고1,2 2023년 11월

전국연합
3년간
〈국영수〉
고3 2023년 11월

6·9·수능
평가원
3/4년간
〈국영수〉
고3 2023년 12월

최신 1년간
〈국영수〉
고3 2024년 1월

2024 씨뮬 시리즈
대한민국 No 1. 내신 / 학평, 수능 대비 문제집

국어	영어	수학	전과목 / 통합사회·과학
• 유형⁺ 씨뮬 고1 국어 독서	• 유형⁺ 씨뮬 고1 영어 독해	• 전국연합 3년간 고1 수학	• 예비고1 3월 학력평가
• 유형⁺ 씨뮬 고1 국어 문학	• 유형⁺ 씨뮬 고2 영어 독해	• 전국연합 3년간 고2 수학	• 전국연합 3년간 고1 통합사회
• 유형⁺ 씨뮬 고2 국어 독서	• 유형⁺ 씨뮬 고3 영어 독해	• 전국연합 3년간 고3 수학	• 전국연합 3년간 고1 통합과학
• 유형⁺ 씨뮬 고2 국어 문학	• 유형⁺ 씨뮬 고3 영어 어법·어휘	• 6·9·수능 3년간 고3 수학	
• 유형⁺ 씨뮬 고3 국어 독서	• 전국연합 3년간 고1 영어	• 최신 1년간 고3 수학	
• 유형⁺ 씨뮬 고3 국어 문학	• 전국연합 3년간 고2 영어		
• 전국연합 3년간 고1 국어	• 전국연합 3년간 고3 영어		
• 전국연합 3년간 고2 국어	• 사설 3년간 고1 영어		
• 전국연합 3년간 고3 국어	• 사설 3년간 고2 영어		
• 사설 3년간 고1 국어	• 사설 3년간 고3 영어		
• 사설 3년간 고2 국어	• 6·9·수능 4년간 고3 영어	**씨뮬 풀고 자동 채점 성적분석까지**	
• 사설 3년간 고3 국어	• 최신 1년간 고3 영어	⑤STUDY SENSE 온라인 성적분석 서비스	
• 6·9·수능 4년간 고3 국어			
• 최신 1년간 고3 국어			

유형+씨물

단기 특강, 24일의 기적!

고3

수 능 기 출
문 제 집

영어 어법·어휘

정답 및 해설

씨뮬 = 실전 연습

내신, 학평, 수능까지 실전 대비 최고의 연습, 씨뮬
씨뮬과 함께 1등급, SKY, 의치한까지

01

예비 고1 3월 전국연합
3년간 모의고사

고등학교 첫 시험을 발 빠르게 준비하여
단 한 권으로 학습 주도권을 잡는 교재

※ 국어, 수학, 영어, 한국사, 사회, 과학 수록

예비
고1

02

유형⁺ 씨뮬

학평, 수능의 문제 유형을 연습하고
출제 경향을 파악할 수 있는 교재

※ 고1~3 국어 독서/문학
※ 고1~3 영어 독해, 고3 영어 어법 · 어휘

고1~3

03

전국연합 3년간

최근 3년간 시행된 학평, 모평, 수능 문제들로
완벽한 수능 대비를 할 수 있는 기본 중의 기본서

※ 고1 통합사회, 통합과학
※ 고1~3 국어, 수학, 영어

고1~3

04

사설 3년간

종로, 이투스에서 출제된 고난도 모의고사
문제들을 연습할 수 있는 교재

※ 고1~3 국어, 영어

고1~3

05

6 · 9 · 수능 평가원 3/4년간

평가원에서 최근 3/4년간 출제한 6월,
9월 모평 및 수능 문제들이 수록된
수능 출제 경향 파악에 가장 적합한 교재

※ 고3 국어, 수학, 영어

고3

06

최신 1년간

최근 1년간 시행된 학평, 모평, 수능 문제 뿐
아니라 종로 모의고사까지 수록되어 최신 출제
경향을 한 권으로 파악할 수 있는 교재

※ 고3 국어, 수학, 영어

고3

독자 여러분의 애정 어린 충고로

씨뮬은 해마다
새롭게 완성되어 갑니다!

실제 크기의 시험지와 OMR 카드를 제공해 주어서 실제 시험을 보는 것 같아 실제 시험에서 떨리지 않았고 문제에 대한 해설이 친절히 서술되어 있어 어려운 문제도 혼자만의 노력으로 이해할 수 있었어요. 역시 씨뮬!
>>> 황*현

모의고사가 모아져 있는 책 중 씨뮬이 정말 최고예요. 특히 영어는 듣기 연습용 받아쓰기도 있어서 많은 도움이 되었습니다. 감사합니다.
>>> 조*빈

회차별 영단어 핸드북뿐 아니라 책 마지막 부분에 있는 수능 필수 영숙어 파트가 도움이 많이 되었다. 수능에서뿐만 아니라 내신 시험에도 나오는 표현들이 많아 유용했다.
>>> 김*희

모의고사를 대비하기 위해 구매하였습니다. 다른 문제집들은 실제 모의고사 시험지처럼 되어 있지 않아서 긴장감이 많이 떨어지는데, 씨뮬은 실제 시험지처럼 되어 있고 OMR 카드도 있어서 모의고사 대비하기 아주 좋아요!
>>> 김*연

씨뮬 교재가 실제 모의고사 종이 크기이다 보니 실제 시험을 치는 듯한 느낌이 들어 더 집중이 잘 되는 것 같다. 해설도 꼼꼼하게 되어 있어 내가 어디서 해석이 안 되는지 바로 찾을 수 있어서 좋았다.
>>> 김*진

국어에 자신감이 없어서 시작했는데 해설이 꼼꼼하고 추가적인 작품이나 문법이 수록돼 있어서 더 깊이 있게 공부할 수 있었어요.
>>> 배*진

이 책을 구매했던 이유들 중 하나인, 실전과 비슷한 종이 재질 덕분에 더욱 실감나게 학습할 수 있었습니다. 그리고 맨 뒤에 부착되어 있는 OMR 카드로 체킹 실수를 줄이는 연습도 되었습니다. 꼼꼼한 해설지와 문제 풀이로 공부하면서 그 외에 실전 감각 또한 함양할 수 있는 씨뮬 모의고사입니다!
>>> 권*희

백분위 95~96을 왔다갔다했어요. 수학 실력을 늘리기 위해 책을 구매해 풀어 본 후 높은 점수를 받게 되었습니다.
>>> 정*헌

모의고사 볼 때처럼 큰 종이로 되어 있어 더 몰입감 있게 집중할 수 있었던 것 같습니다. 또 해설도 자세하고 고난도 문제와 등급컷도 알려 주어 좋았습니다!
>>> 서*준

어느 정도 실력이 쌓이고 나면 모의고사로 실전 대비 훈련을 하며 실력을 굳혀 나가야 되죠. 그리고 그 연습 방법으로는 '씨뮬'이라는 교재가 정말 완벽한 것 같아요. 여러분들에게 '씨뮬' 적극 추천합니다.
>>> 백*민

내신에서 학평까지 실전 연습은
씨뮬 기출 하나로 충분하다

전국연합학력평가 3년간 모의고사　　**11th 국영수 고1~3**

01 실제 시험 그대로 실전 감각 익히기

02 핵심을 짚어주는 명쾌한 해설

03 오답 노트 & OMR 카드

04 같은 작가 다른 작품(국어), 기출문법[구문] 모아보기(영어),
　　 준 킬러 문항 연습(수학)

05 [12th] 전국연합 3년간 수학 교재의 중요 문항에 동영상 강의 제공 예정

DAY 01 >>>> 주어·동사

1 ②	2 ④	3 ⑤	4 ⑤	5 ②
6 ③	7 ③	8 ④	9 ⑤	10 ④
11 ⑤	12 ④			

DAY 02 >>>> 목적어의 이해

1 ②	2 ②	3 ⑤	4 ④	5 ⑤
6 ④	7 ②	8 ⑤	9 ②	10 ④
11 ③	12 ⑤			

DAY 03 >>>> 보어의 이해

1 ②	2 ⑤	3 ②	4 ②	5 ③
6 ④	7 ③	8 ①	9 ④	10 ③
11 ④	12 ②			

DAY 04 >>>> 수의 일치

1 ②	2 ⑤	3 ④	4 ⑤	5 ③
6 ④	7 ⑤	8 ③	9 ④	10 ⑤
11 ④	12 ⑤			

DAY 05 >>>> 동사의 시제

1 ③	2 ②	3 ①	4 ⑤	5 ③
6 ③	7 ④	8 ④	9 ②	10 ②
11 ⑤	12 ⑤			

DAY 06 >>>> 조동사

1 ③	2 ⑤	3 ②	4 ④	5 ⑤
6 ②	7 ⑤	8 ③	9 ③	10 ④
11 ④	12 ④			

DAY 07 >>>> 수동태

1 ④	2 ④	3 ③	4 ①	5 ②
6 ①	7 ②	8 ④	9 ④	10 ③
11 ④	12 ④			

DAY 08 >>>> 가정법

1 ④	2 ⑤	3 ③	4 ④	5 ⑤
6 ②	7 ③	8 ④	9 ④	10 ⑤
11 ⑤	12 ⑤			

DAY 09 >>>> 부정사

1 ③	2 ③	3 ⑤	4 ②	5 ④
6 ③	7 ⑤	8 ④	9 ③	10 ②
11 ③	12 ④			

DAY 10 >>>> 동명사

1 ⑤	2 ④	3 ①	4 ④	5 ①
6 ②	7 ⑤	8 ⑤	9 ⑤	10 ⑤
11 ⑤	12 ③			

DAY 11 >>>> 분사, 분사구문

1 ③	2 ②	3 ④	4 ④	5 ④
6 ③	7 ②	8 ①	9 ①	10 ②
11 ③	12 ⑤			

DAY 12 >>>> 준동사

1 ②	2 ⑤	3 ⑤	4 ①	5 ④
6 ③	7 ③	8 ④	9 ③	10 ④
11 ②	12 ②			

DAY 13 >>>> 접속사, 전치사

1 ④	2 ③	3 ⑤	4 ⑤	5 ①
6 ④	7 ①	8 ③	9 ②	10 ⑤
11 ④	12 ④			

DAY 14 >>>> 관계대명사

1 ③	2 ④	3 ③	4 ③	5 ②
6 ⑤	7 ⑤	8 ④	9 ⑤	10 ③
11 ③	12 ③			

DAY 15 >>>> 관계부사

1 ①	2 ③	3 ②	4 ③	5 ④
6 ①	7 ②	8 ⑤	9 ④	10 ⑤
11 ②	12 ④			

DAY 16 >>>> 병렬 구조

1 ⑤	2 ④	3 ③	4 ④	5 ②
6 ⑤	7 ③	8 ②	9 ②	10 ⑤
11 ③	12 ⑤			

DAY 17 >>>> 대명사

1 ②	2 ②	3 ②	4 ②	5 ⑤
6 ③	7 ④	8 ③	9 ⑤	10 ③
11 ③	12 ④			

DAY 18 >>>> 형용사, 부사

1 ⑤	2 ④	3 ④	4 ①	5 ④
6 ③	7 ①	8 ③	9 ④	10 ④
11 ②	12 ③			

DAY 19 >>>> 비교 구문

1 ②	2 ④	3 ⑤	4 ①	5 ③
6 ③	7 ②	8 ⑤	9 ⑤	10 ⑤
11 ④	12 ④			

DAY 20 >>>> 특수 구문

1 ②	2 ③	3 ⑤	4 ⑤	5 ①
6 ⑤	7 ⑤	8 ②	9 ⑤	10 ②
11 ③	12 ④			

DAY 21 >>>> 미니 고난도 Test 1회

| 1 ③ | 2 ① | 3 ② | 4 ④ | 5 ④ |
| 6 ④ | 7 ② | 8 ① | | |

DAY 22 >>>> 미니 고난도 Test 2회

| 1 ⑤ | 2 ④ | 3 ③ | 4 ⑤ | 5 ③ |
| 6 ⑤ | 7 ② | 8 ③ | | |

DAY 23 >>>> 미니 고난도 Test 3회

| 1 ③ | 2 ② | 3 ⑤ | 4 ③ | 5 ④ |
| 6 ② | 7 ① | 8 ① | | |

DAY 24 >>>> 미니 고난도 Test 4회

| 1 ④ | 2 ⑤ | 3 ③ | 4 ④ | 5 ④ |
| 6 ⑤ | 7 ④ | 8 ① | | |

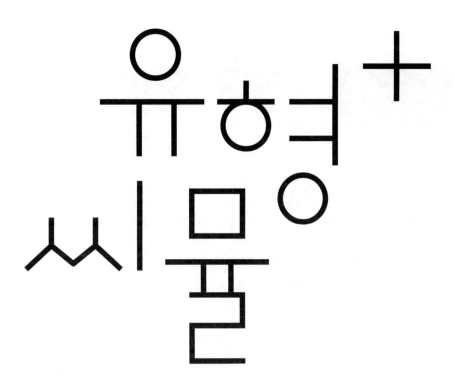

단기 특강, 24일의 기적!

정답 및 해설

고3 영어 어법·어휘

CONTENTS

01. 주어 · 동사

A 출제 POINT
본문 002쪽

1. requires 2. is 3. is
4. was 5. is 6. it
7. were

1 [해석]▶ 점포를 시작하는 것은 20만 달러나 하는 거액을 필요로 한다.
[해설]▶ 동명사는 문장에서 주어 역할을 할 수 있으며 단수로 취급한다.

2 [해석]▶ 그녀가 백만장자라는 것이 믿어지지 않는다.
[해설]▶ 접속사 That이 이끄는 절은 주어 역할을 할 수 있으며 단수로 취급한다.

3 [해석]▶ 저 언덕 위의 집은 나의 할아버지의 집이다.
[해설]▶ 주어가 전치사구의 수식을 받아 길어진 경우 주어, 동사를 잘 찾아야 한다. 주어는 단수주어 A movie이므로 단수동사가 나와야 한다.

4 [해석]▶ 시사적 문제를 다루는 주간 프로그램이 시청자들에 의해 사랑을 받았다.
[해설]▶ 주어가 분사구(현재분사)의 수식을 받아 길어진 경우로 주어는 단수주어 A weekly program이므로 단수동사가 와야 한다.

5 [해석]▶ 우리 옆집에 사는 그 소녀는 아프다.
[해설]▶ 주어가 관계사절의 수식을 받아 길어진 경우로, 주어는 The girl이므로 동사는 단수동사 is를 써야 한다.

6 [해석]▶ 모든 것을 고려했을 때, 이사짐 회사의 서비스를 받는 것이 더 좋을 것 같다.
[해설]▶ 주어가 길어진 경우 가주어 it을 쓰고 진주어(to ask for the services of a moving company)는 뒤로 돌린다.

7 [해석]▶ 기본 쟁점에 대한 의견 차이가 있었다.
[해설]▶ There was/were ~ 문장에서 주어는 be동사 다음에 나온 어구(differences)가 복수이면 복수동사를 쓰고, 단수주어이면 단수동사를 쓰므로 복수동사가 맞다.

B 체크 POINT
본문 002쪽

1. is 2. is 3. is
4. is 5. was 6. It
7. are

1 [해석]▶ 정기적으로 운동하는 것은 누구에게나 쉽지 않다.
[해설]▶ to부정사는 문장에서 주어 역할을 할 수 있으며 단수로 취급한다.

2 [해석]▶ 당신이 보는 것이 항상 진실인 것은 아닙니다.
[해설]▶ 관계사가 이끄는 절은 주어 역할을 할 수 있으며 단수로 취급한다.

3 [해석]▶ 빨간색 드레스를 입은 아름다운 여인이 거리를 걷고 있다.

[해설]▶ 주어가 전치사구의 수식을 받아 길어진 경우 주어, 동사를 잘 구분해야 한다. 주어는 단수주어 A beautiful lady이므로 단수동사가 나와야 한다.

4 [해설]▶ 미국에서 자기 부모에 의해서 교육을 받는 아이들의 수가 점진적으로 늘어나고 있다.
[해설]▶ 주어가 분사구(과거분사)의 수식을 받아 길어진 경우로 「The number of +복수명사」는 단수동사를 사용한다.

5 [해설]▶ 의사가 되고자 하는 그녀의 꿈이 마침내 이루어졌다.
[해설]▶ 주어가 to부정사구의 수식을 받아 길어진 경우로 하나의 문장에는 주어와 동사가 필요하므로 단수주어 Her hope에 해당하는 단수동사가 나와야 한다.

6 [해설]▶ 그에게 알리는 것이 중요하다.
[해설]▶ 문두에 주어가 길어진 경우 가주어 it을 쓰고 진주어(that he should be informed)는 뒤로 돌린다.

7 [해설]▶ 당신을 위해 유용한 조언이 몇 개 있다.
[해설]▶ Here is / are ~ 문장에서 주어는 be동사 다음에 나온 어구(some useful tips)이다. 어구가 복수이면 복수동사를 쓴다.

Day 01
본문 003쪽

1 ②	2 ④	3 ⑤	4 ⑤	5 ②
6 ③	7 ③	8 ④	9 ⑤	10 ④
11 ⑤	12 ④			

1. ②
기업 윤리의 이해

직독 직해

Recognizing ethical issues / is the most important step /
윤리적 문제를 인식하는 것은 / 가장 중요한 단계이다 /
in understanding business ethics.
기업 윤리를 이해하는 데
An ethical issue is an identifiable problem, situation, or opportunity /
윤리적 문제는 식별 가능한 문제, 상황 혹은 기회이다 /
that requires a person to choose from among several actions /
여러 행동 가운데에서 한 사람이 선택하기를 요구하는 /
that may be evaluated / as right or wrong, ethical or unethical.
평가받을 수 있는 / 옳거나 틀렸다고, 윤리적 혹은 비윤리적이라고
Learning how to choose from alternatives and make a decision / requires /
대안 중에서 선택하고 결정하는 방법을 배우는 것은 / 요구한다 /
not only good personal values, /
훌륭한 개인적 가치관뿐만 아니라 /
but also knowledge competence in the business area of concern.
관계가 있는 비즈니스 분야에 대한 지식 역량도
Employees also need to know /
또한 직원들은 알아야 한다 /
when to rely on their organizations' policies and codes of ethics /
언제 자신이 속한 조직의 정책과 윤리 강령에 의존할지 /
or have discussions with co-workers or managers / on appropriate conduct.
또는 언제 동료나 관리자와 논의해야 할지를 / 적절한 행동에 대해
Ethical decision making is not always easy /
윤리적 의사결정이 언제나 쉬운 것은 아닌데 /
because there are always gray areas /
왜냐하면 회색 영역이 항상 있기 때문이다 /

that create dilemmas, / no matter how decisions are made.
딜레마를 만드는 / 결정이 어떻게 내려지든
For instance, / should an employee report / on a co-worker engaging in time theft?
예를 들면 / 직원은 보고해야 할까 / 시간 훔치기를 하는 동료에 관해
Should a salesperson leave out facts / about a product's poor safety record /
판매원은 사실을 생략해야 할까 / 어떤 제품의 안전 상태가 좋지 않다는 기록에 관한 /
in his presentation to a customer?
고객에게 프레젠테이션할 때
Such questions require the decision maker /
그런 질문은 의사결정자에게 요구한다 /
to evaluate the ethics of his or her choice /
자신이 선택한 윤리를 평가할 것을 /
and decide whether to ask for guidance.
그리고 지침을 요청할 것인지 아닐지의 여부를 결정할 것을

윤리적 문제를 인식하는 것은 기업 윤리를 이해하는 데 가장 중요한 단계이다. 윤리적 문제는 옳거나 틀렸다고, 윤리적 혹은 비윤리적이라고 평가받을 수 있는 여러 행동 가운데에서 한 사람이 선택하기를 요구하는 식별 가능한 문제, 상황 혹은 기회이다. 대안 중에서 선택하고 결정하는 방법을 배우는 것은 훌륭한 개인적 가치관뿐만 아니라 관계가 있는 비즈니스 분야에 대한 지식 역량도 요구한다. 또한 직원들은 언제 자신이 속한 조직의 정책과 윤리 강령에 의존할지 또는 언제 동료나 관리자와 적절한 행동에 대해 논의해야 할지를 알아야 한다. 윤리적 의사결정이 언제나 쉬운 것은 아닌데, 왜냐하면 결정이 어떻게 내려지든 딜레마를 만드는 회색 영역이 항상 있기 때문이다. 예를 들면, 직원은 시간 훔치기를 하는 동료에 관해 보고해야 할까? 판매원은 고객에게 프레젠테이션할 때 어떤 제품의 안전 상태가 좋지 않다는 기록에 관한 사실을 생략해야 할까? 그런 질문은 의사결정자가 자신이 선택한 윤리를 평가하여 지침을 요청할 것인지 아닐지의 여부를 결정할 것을 요구한다.

문제풀이

① [수동태]
several actions는 '평가받는' 수동적 대상이므로, 수동태가 되어야 한다. 따라서 be evaluated가 온 것은 적절하다.
② [동명사]
문장의 동사는 requires로 앞에는 주어가 와야 한다. 따라서 Learn을 주어가 될 수 있는 동명사구를 이끄는 동명사 Learning으로 고쳐야 한다.
③ [병렬구조]
when to에 이어지는 rely on과 등위접속사 or로 연결되어 마찬가지로 to에 이어지는 동사원형이 와야 하므로 have가 온 것은 적절하다.
④ [관계대명사]
뒤에 이어지는 절에서 주어 역할을 하며 선행사 gray areas를 수식하고 있으므로, 주격 관계대명사 that이 온 것은 적절하다.
⑤ [whether+to부정사]
decide의 목적어 역할을 하는 명사구가 와야 하는데, to부정사 앞의 의문사가 '~할 것인지 (아닌지)'라는 의미가 되어야 하므로, whether가 온 것은 적절하다.

❖ 이렇게 풀자 어법상 틀린 부분을 찾는 문제는 밑줄이 있는 부분의 형태와 문맥을 보고 어법에 맞게 쓰였는지 확인해야 한다.
① 「be동사+p.p.」에 밑줄이 있는 경우, 주어와의 관계를 파악하여 수동태로 쓰이는 것이 적절한지 살펴야 한다.
② 밑줄이 그어진 부분이 문장에서 어떤 역할을 하는지 파악해야 한다.
③ 컴마(,)나 등위접속사 다음에 밑줄이 있는 경우는 병렬구조가 아닌지 살펴본다.
④ 문장에서 관계대명사가 필요한 경우인지를 확인한 후, 선행사의 종류 및 격에 따라 적절하게 쓰였는지 살펴봐야 한다.
⑤ 의문사에 밑줄이 있는 경우 의미상 적절한 의문사가 쓰였는지 확인해야 한다.

【 어휘 · 어구 】
ethical 윤리적인

identifiable 식별 가능한
evaluate 평가하다
alternative 대안, 선택 가능한 것
competence 능력, 역량
rely on ~에 의존하다
appropriate 적절한
conduct 행동
dilemma 딜레마, 진퇴양난
engage in ~에 관여하다
leave out ~을 빼다

2.④ 　　　　　　　　　　메타인지

직독/직해

Metacognition simply means / "thinking about thinking," /
메타인지는 단순히 의미한다 / '생각에 대해 생각하는 것'을 /

and it is one of the main distinctions /
그리고 그것은 주요 차이점 중 하나이다 /

between the human brain and that of other species.
인간의 두뇌와 다른 종의 두뇌 간의

Our ability to stand high on a ladder /
사다리에 높이 서 있는 능력은 /

above our normal thinking processes /
우리의 일반적인 사고 과정 위에 있는 /

and evaluate why we are thinking /
그리고 왜 우리가 생각하고 있는지를 평가할 수 있는 /

as we are thinking / is an evolutionary marvel.
지금 생각하고 있는 것처럼 / (우리의 능력은) 진화의 경이로운 결과이다

We have this ability / 우리는 이 능력을 가지고 있는데 /

because the most recently developed part of the human brain / 인간 두뇌의 가장 최근에 발달한 부분인 /

— the prefrontal cortex — / 전두엽 피질이 /

enables self-reflective, abstract thought.
자기 성찰적이고 추상적인 사고를 가능하게 하기 때문이다

We can think about ourselves /
우리는 우리 자신에 관해 생각할 수 있다 /

as if we are not part of ourselves.
우리가 우리 자신의 일부가 아닌 것처럼

Research on primate behavior indicates /
영장류의 행동에 관한 연구는 보여 준다 /

that even our closest cousins, the chimpanzees, /
우리의 가장 가까운 사촌인 침팬지조차도 /

lack this ability / 이 능력이 결여되어 있음을 /

(although they possess some self-reflective abilities, /
그들이 약간의 자기 성찰적인 능력을 갖추고 있기는 하지만 /

like being able to identify themselves in a mirror /
거울 속의 자신을 알아볼 수 있는 것과 같이 /

instead of thinking / the reflection is another chimp).
생각하는 대신 / 거울에 비친 모습을 다른 침팬지라고

The ability is a double-edged sword, /
그 능력은 양날의 칼이다 /

because while it allows us to evaluate /
왜냐하면 그것은 우리로 하여금 평가할 수 있게 해주기 때문이다 /

why we are thinking / what we are thinking, /
우리가 왜 생각하고 있는지 / 우리가 생각하고 있는 것을 /

it also puts us in touch with difficult existential questions /
그것은 또한 우리로 하여금 어려운 실존적인 질문들과 접촉하게 하기 (때문이다) /

that can easily become obsessions.
쉽게 강박 관념이 될 수 있는

메타인지는 단순히 '생각에 대해 생각하는 것'을 의미하며, 그것은 인간의 두뇌와 다른 종의 두뇌 간의 주요 차이점 중 하나이다. 우리의 일반적인 사고 과정 위에 있는 사다리에 높이 서서 왜 우리가 지금 생각하고 있는 것처럼 생각하고 있는지를 평가할 수 있는 우리의 능력은 진화의 경이로운 결과이다. 우리는 이 능력을 가지고 있는데, 인간 두뇌의 가장 최근에 발달한 부분인 전두엽 피질이 자기 성찰적이고 추상적인 사고를 가능하게 하기 때문이다. 우리는 우리가 우리 자신의 일부가 아닌 것처럼 우리 자신에 관해 생각할 수 있다. 영장류의 행동에 관한 연구는 우리의 가장 가까운 사촌인 침팬지조차도 (거울에 비친 모습을 다른 침팬지라고 생각하는 대신 거울 속의 자신을 알아볼 수 있는 것과 같이, 그들이 약간의 자기 성찰적인 능력을 갖추고 있기는 하지만) 이 능력이 결여되어 있음을 보여 준다. 그 능력은 양날의 칼인데, 왜냐하면 그것은 우리로 하여금 우리가 생각하고 있는 것을 왜 생각하고 있는지를 평가할 수 있게 해주는 한

편, 또한 우리로 하여금 쉽게 강박 관념이 될 수 있는 어려운 실존적인 질문들과 접촉하게 하기 때문이다.

문제풀이

① [to부정사의 형용사적 용법]
to stand와 (to) evaluate가 접속사 and로 병렬 연결되어 Our ability를 수식하는 to부정사의 형용사적 용법으로 쓰였다.

② [이유 접속사 because]
문맥상 이유를 나타내는 말이 나와야 하고, 뒤에 주어(the most recently developed part of the human brain)와 동사(enables)로 이루어진 절이 나오므로, 이유를 나타내는 접속사 because는 적절하게 쓰였다.

③ [재귀대명사 ourselves]
as if가 이끄는 절의 주어인 we와 동일한 대상을 나타내므로, 재귀대명사 ourselves는 적절하게 쓰였다.

④ [정동사 vs 준동사]
접속사 **that**이 이끄는 절에서 주어는 '**our closest cousins**'이고 동사가 없으므로, **lacking**은 **lack**으로 바꿔야 한다.

⑤ [관계대명사 what]
what 뒤에 불완전한 문장이 왔고 앞에 선행사가 없으므로, 선행사를 포함하는 관계대명사 what은 적절하게 쓰였다.

《 어휘·어구 》

metacognition 메타인지(사고 과정 자체에 대해 고찰하는 능력)
distinction 차이, 뛰어남
evaluate 평가하다
evolutionary 진화의
marvel 경이, 경이로운 결과
prefrontal 전두엽의
cortex 피질
enable 가능하게 하다
reflective 사색적인
abstract 추상적인
primate 영장류
indicate 나타내다, 보여 주다
possess 지니다, 소유하다
identify 확인하다, 알아보다
reflection (거울 등에 비친) 모습
double-edged 양날인
existential 실존적인
obsession 강박 관념, 강박 상태

3.⑤ 　　　　발견에서 즐거움을 느끼는 인간

직독/직해

An interesting aspect of human psychology is /
인간 심리의 흥미로운 측면은 ~이다 /

that we tend to like things more /
우리는 어떤 것들을 더 좋아하는 경향이 있다는 것 /

and find them more appealing /
그리고 그것들을 더 매력적으로 느끼는 경향이 있다는 것 /

if everything about those things is not obvious /
만약 그것들에 대한 모든 것이 명백하지 않다면 /

the first time we experience them.
우리가 처음 그것들을 경험할 때

This is certainly true in music.
이것은 음악에서 분명히 사실이다

For example, we might hear a song on the radio /
예를 들어, 우리는 라디오에서 노래를 들을 수도 있다 /

for the first time / that catches our interest /
처음으로 / 우리의 관심을 사로잡는 /

and decide we like it.
그리고 우리는 그것이 마음에 든다고 결정을 내릴 수도 있다

Then the next time we hear it, /
그리고 나서 다음에 우리가 그것을 들을 때 /

we hear a lyric / we didn't catch the first time, /
우리는 가사를 듣는다 / 우리가 처음에는 듣지 못한 /

or we might notice /
또는 우리는 알아차릴 수도 있다 /

what the piano or drums are doing in the background.
배경에서 피아노나 드럼이 무엇을 하는지

A special harmony emerges / that we missed before.
특별한 화음이 나타나기도 한다 / 우리가 전에 놓친

We hear more and more and understand more and
우리는 점점 더 많이 듣고 점점 더 잘 이해한다

more / with each listening.
/ 매번 들을 때마다

Sometimes, the longer it takes for a work of art /
때때로, 예술 작품이 걸리는 시간이 길수록 /

to reveal all of its subtleties to us, /
우리에게 모든 중요한 세부 요소를 드러내는 데 /

the more fond of that thing— / 그것을 더 좋아하게 /

whether it's music, art, dance, or architecture— /
그것이 음악이든, 미술이든, 춤이든, 혹은 건축이든 간에 /

we become. 우리는 된다

인간 심리의 흥미로운 측면은 우리가 처음 어떤 것들을 경험할 때 그것들에 대한 모든 것이 명백하지 않다면 우리는 그것들을 더 좋아하고 더 매력적으로 느끼는 경향이 있다는 것이다. 이것은 음악에서 분명히 사실이다. 예를 들어, 우리는 처음으로 라디오에서 우리의 관심을 사로잡는 노래를 듣고, 그 곡이 마음에 든다고 결정을 내릴 수도 있다. 그리고 나서 다음에 우리가 그것을 들을 때, 우리가 처음에는 듣지 못한 가사를 듣거나, 배경에서 피아노나 드럼이 무엇을 하는지 알아차릴 수도 있다. 우리가 전에 놓친 특별한 화음이 나타나기도 한다. 우리는 점점 더 많이 듣고 매번 들을 때마다 점점 더 잘 이해한다. 때때로, 예술 작품이 우리에게 모든 중요한 세부 요소들을 드러내는 데 걸리는 시간이 길수록, 그것이 음악이든, 미술이든, 춤이든, 혹은 건축이든 간에 우리는 그것을 더 좋아하게 된다.

문제풀이

① 동사 found의 목적격보어로는 형용사나 분사가 와야 하는데, '그것들을 더 매력적이라고 느끼다'라는 능동의 의미로 현재분사 appealing이 온 것은 적절하다.

② 등위접속사 and에 의해 조동사 might 뒤의 동사 hear와 연결되어 병렬구조를 이루고 있으므로, 마찬가지로 동사원형인 decide가 온 것은 적절하다.

③ 동사 noticed의 목적어절에서 동사 doing의 목적어가 없으므로, what이 온 것은 적절하다.

④ 주어인 A special harmony 뒤에 동사가 와야 하므로, emerges가 온 것은 적절하다. that we missed before는 주어를 수식하는 관계대명사절이다.

⑤ **to reveal all of its subtleties to us**가 진주어이기 때문에 가주어가 와야 한다. 따라서 **that**은 **it**으로 바꿔 써야 한다.

○ 이렇게 풀자 _ 어법상 틀린 부분을 찾는 문제는 밑줄이 있는 부분의 형태와 문맥을 보고 어법에 맞게 쓰였는지 확인해야 한다. ① find의 목적격보어 형태를, ② 병렬구조를, ③ what의 쓰임을, ④ 문장 구조를, ⑤ 가주어-진주어의 쓰임을 알아야 한다.

《 어휘·어구 》

aspect 측면
psychology 심리
appealing 매력적인
lyric 가사
harmony 화음
reveal 드러나다
fond of ~을 좋아하는
architecture 건축

4.⑤ 　　　　수로를 이용한 운송의 발달

근대 초 유럽에서 수로를 이용한 운송은 대개 육로를 이용한 운송보다 훨씬 더 저렴했다. 이탈리아의 한 인쇄업자는 1550년에 로마에서 리옹까지 한 짐의 책을 보내는 데 뱃길로는 4스쿠도인데 비해 육로로는 18스쿠도가 들 것이라고 추산했다. 편지는 보통 육로로 운반되었지만 사람뿐만 아니라 편지와 신문을 운하용 배를 이용해 운송하는 시스템이 17세기에 네덜란드 공화국에서 발달했다. 그 배의 평균 속력은 시속 4마일이 조금 넘었는데 말을 타고 다니는 사람에 비해 느렸다. 반면에 그 서비스는 규칙적이고 횟수가 잦고, 저렴해서 Amsterdam과 더 작은 마을들 사이뿐만 아니라 작은 마을과 또 다른 마을 간에도 연락할 수 있었고, 따라서 정보에 대한 접근을 동등하게 했다. 운송과 메시지 연락 사이의 전통적인 관계가 끊어진 것은 바로 1837년 전신의 발명 때문이었다.

문제풀이

① that 뒤에 완전한 문장이 왔으므로 calculated의 목적어 역할을 하는 명사절을 이끄는 접속사 that이 온 것은 적절하다.
② 주어인 a system의 동사가 와야 하므로 developed가 온 것은 적절하다. of ~ boat는 a system을 수식하는 전치사구이다.
③ slow ~ horseback은 분사구문으로 slow 앞에 being이 생략되어 있다. 따라서 slow가 온 것은 적절하다.
④ thus equalizing ~ information은 접속사가 생략되지 않은 분사구문이다. equalizing의 주어는 the service이고 '서비스가 동등하게 한다'는 능동의 의미이다. 따라서 현재분사인 equalizing이 온 것은 적절하다.
⑤ **that절의 주어는 the traditional link로 단수이므로 were를 단수 동사 was로 고쳐야 한다. between ~ of messages는 the traditional link를 수식하는 전치사구이다.** 따라서 정답은 ⑤이다.

《구문 및 어휘》

*9행 On the other hand, the service was regular, frequent and cheap, and allowed communication **not only** between Amsterdam and the smaller towns, **but also** between one small town and another, thus equalizing accessibility to information.
⑴「주절(the service ~)+분사구문(thus equalizing ~)」구조의 문장이다.
⑵ was와 allowed는 주절의 주어인 the service에 이어지는 동사로 and에 의해 병렬 연결되어 있다.
⑶「not only A but also B」는 'A뿐만 아니라 B도'라는 의미이다.
*13행 **It was only in 1837, with the invention of the electric telegraph, that the traditional link between transport and the communication of messages was broken.**
⑴「It-that」강조 구문으로 부사인 only in 1837, with the invention of the electric telegraph,를 강조하고 있다.

calculate 추정하다, 추산하다
a load of 한 짐의, 많은
compared with ~에 비해, ~와 비교하여
normally 보통
overland 육로의
canal 운하, 수로
regular 규칙적인, 정기적인
equalize 동등하게 하다
accessibility 접근

---

electric telegraph 전신

5.②	에너지 보존 기능을 하는 수면

수면은 에너지를 보존하는 기능을 한다고 주장되어 왔다. 이는 특히 그들 주변 온도보다 체온을 더 높게 유지하기 위해 많은 에너지를 소비해야 하는 온혈동물(포유류와 조류)과 관련이 있을 수 있다. 실제로, 추운 기후에서 살며 체중 대비 불리한 표면적 비율을 가지고 있어서 쉽게 열을 손실하는 많은 작은 포유동물은 흔히 단열이 되는 은신처에서 수면을 많이 취하는 경향이 있다. 하지만 수면은 온혈동물들에게서만 진화해 온 것 같지 않다. 파충류나 양서류에 관한 몇몇 연구들은 그것들 또한 잠을 자며 가재, 초파리, 꿀벌과 같은 몇몇 무척추동물들에게서 가수면 상태의 강한 징후가 있음을 보여준다. 또한 활발하게 깨어 있는 상태와 비교하여 잠을 자는 동안 에너지의 전반적인 사용이 감소되는 것이 사실이지만 단지 조용히 휴식을 취할 때에도 거의 그만큼의 에너지 사용의 감소가 있다. 휴식 상태에서 수면으로 옮겨갈 때 추가되는 에너지 보존은 최소이다.

문제풀이

②가 있는 문장에서 주어는 many small mammals이고 living in ~ weight ratio는 모두 주어를 수식하는 수식어구이다. 이때 문장의 동사가 필요하므로 tending이 아니라 tend로 쓰는 것이 올바르다.

《구문 및 어휘》

*2행 This may be particularly relevant for warm-blooded animals [**that** must expend a lot of energy **to maintain** a body temperature higher than that of their surroundings].
⑴ [that must expend ~ surroundings] 모두 warm-blooded animals를 수식하는 관계대명사절이며 이때 that은 which와 바꿔 쓸 수 있는 주격 관계대명사이다. to maintain은 '~하기 위해서'라는 의미의 부사적 용법의 to부정사이다.
⑵ a body temperature higher than that of their surroundings는 비교구문으로 앞에 나온 명사의 중복을 피하기 위해 that을 사용했으며 복수일 경우 those를 사용한다. 여기서 that은 a body temperature를 가리킨다.
*13행 Also, though **it** is true **that** the overall use of energy is reduced during sleep, as compared with the active waking state, ~
⑴ though 양보 접속사절에는 가주어 it과 진주어 that절이 사용되었으며 원래의 문장은 (The fact) that the overall ~ sleep is true이다.
⑵ as compared ~는 '(활발하게 깨어 있는 상태와) 비교하여'라는 의미로 의미상 주어는 the overall use of energy이다.

conserve 보존[보호]하다; 아끼다
insulate 단열 처리를 하다
burrow 굴, 은신처
reptile 파충류
amphibian 양서류
crayfish 가재

6.③	독립 예술가의 창의성

독립 예술가는 아마도 무한한 창조적 상황과 가장 가까이에서 살아가는 사람일 것이다. 많은 예술가는 무엇을, 어떻게, 언제, 왜 해야 하는지에 관한 외적인 요구로부터 상당한 자유를 갖는다. 그러나 그와 동시에 우리는 예술가들이 일반적으로 재료와 표현 형식에 대한 선택에 의해 스스로를 상당히 강력하게 제약한다는 사실을 알고 있다. 고도의 기술이나 색깔을 사용하지 않고 암석에서 특정한 형상을 깎아냄으로써 감정을 표현하는 선택을 하는 것은 예술가를 상당히 제약한다. 그러한 선택은 창의성을 제한하기 위해서가 아니라 오히려 창의성을 기르기 위해서 이루어진다. 모든 것이 가능할 때 창의성은 아무런 긴장도 없게 된다. 똑같은 양의 물이 탁 트인 바다를 가로지를 때보다 좁은 해협을 통과할 때 더 빠르고 더 세게 흐르는 것처럼 창의성은 아무리 제약을 받을지라도 어떤 종류의 상황에서도 그것이 갈 길을 찾아내기 때문에 이상한 것이다.

문제풀이

③ restricting은 부정사구 주어에 이어지는 서술어가 위치할 자리이므로, 현재분사 형태인 restricting은 문장의 동사가 될 수 있는 restricts로 바꿔야 한다.

《구문 및 어휘》

*7행 To make the choice to express a feeling by carving a specific form from a rock, [without the use of high technology or colors], restricts the artist significantly.
⑴ To make ~ rock의 to부정사구가 주어이며 [without the use ~ colors]의 삽입구가 문장 가운데에 위치하는 문장 구조이다.
⑵ To make the choice to express ~에서 To make는 to부정사의 명사적 용법으로 쓰였으며, 두 번째 부정사인 to express는 the choice를 수식하는 형용사적 용법으로 쓰였다.
*12행 Creativity is strange **in that** it finds its way in any kind of situation, [**no matter how** restricted].
⑴ in that은 '~란 점에서'라는 의미로 앞에 나온 내용에 대한 이유를 제시할 때 사용한다.
⑵ it은 모두 creativity를 가리킨다.
⑶ [no matter how restricted]는 삽입구로 이때 no matter how는 '아무리 ~할지라도'라고 해석되며, 복합관계부사 however로 바꾸어 표현할 수 있다.

independent 독립된
unbounded 무한한, 한정되지 않은
considerable 상당한
carve 깎아내다, 조각하다
cultivate 기르다, 함양하다

7.③	초기 수산 양식업의 폐해와 그에 따른 대책

직독 직해

During the early stages / 초기 단계 동안. /
when the aquaculture industry was rapidly expanding, /
양식업이 급속하게 팽창하고 있던 /
mistakes were made / and these were costly /
실수들이 발생하였으며 / 이것들은 대가가 상당했다 /
both in terms of direct losses
직접적인 손실 면에서
and in respect of the industry image.
그리고 산업의 이미지 측면에서
High-density rearing / 고밀도의 사육은 /
led to outbreaks of infectious diseases /

Column 1

전염병의 발생을 초래했다 /

that in some cases 몇몇 경우에

devastated / not just the caged fish, /
황폐화시키는 / 가두리에 있는 어류뿐만 아니라 /

but local wild fish populations too.
지역의 야생어류 개체군 또한

The negative impact / 부정적인 영향이 /

on local wildlife inhabiting areas /
서식하는 지역의 야생 생물에 /

close to the fish farms / continues /
양식장에서 가까운 지역에 / 계속해서 /

to be an ongoing public relations problem /

for the industry.
대민 관계의 문제가 되고 있다. / 그 산업에 대한

Furthermore, / a general lack of knowledge /
게다가 / 일반적인 지식의 부족과 /

and insufficient care being taken /
불충분하게 행해지던 관리는 /

when fish pens were initially constructed / meant /
어류양식용 가두리가 초기에 만들어졌을 때 / 의미했다 /

that pollution from excess feed and fish waste /
초과양의 사료와 어류 폐기물로부터 발생한 오염이 /

created huge barren underwater deserts. /
거대하고도 황폐해 해져 사막을 만들어 냈다는 것을 /

These were costly lessons to learn, /
이것들은 값비싼 대가를 치르고 배운 교훈이었으나 /

but now stricter regulations are in place to ensure/
지금은 더 엄격한 규제들이 시행되고 있다 /

that fish pens are placed in sites /
양식 가두리를 설치하도록 하는 /

where there is good water flow /
물의 흐름이 좋은 장소에 /

to remove fish waste. 어류 폐기물을 제거할 수 있는

This, in addition to other methods /
이것은 다른 방법들과 함께 /

that decrease the overall amount of uneaten food, /
섭취되지 않은 먹이의 전반적인 양을 줄이는 /

has helped aquaculture to clean up its act.
수산 양식이 자신의 행위를 깨끗이 청소하도록 도움을 주었다.

양식업이 급속하게 팽창하고 있던 초기 단계 동안, 실수들이 발생하였으며 이것들은 직접적인 손실 면에서 그리고 그 산업의이미지 측면 모두에 있어 대가가 상당했다. 고밀도의 사육은 몇몇 경우에 가두리에 있는 어류뿐만 아니라 지역의 야생어류 개체군 또한 황폐화시키는 전염병의 발발을 초래했다. 양식장에서 가까운 지역에 서식하는 지역 야생생물에 끼치는 부정적 영향이 계속해서 그 산업에 대한 지속적인 대민 관계의 문제가 되고 있다. 게다가, 어류양식용 가두리가 초기에 만들어졌을 때 일반적인 지식의 부족과 불충분하게 행해지던 관리는 초과량의 사료와 어류 폐기물로부터 발생한 오염이 거대하고도 황폐해 해져 사막을 만들어 냈다는 것을 의미했다. 이것들은 값비싼 대가를 치르고 배운 교훈이었으나, 지금은 어류 폐기물을 제거할 수 있는 물의 흐름이 좋은 장소에 양식 가두리를 설치하도록 하는 더 엄격한 규제들이 시행되고 있다. 섭취되지 않은 먹이의 전반적인 양을 줄이는 다른 방법들과 함께 이것은 수산 양식이 자신의 행위를 깨끗이 청소하도록 도움을 주었다.

문제풀이

③의 문장에서 a general lack of knowledge and insufficient <u>care</u> (which was) being taken when fish pens were initially constructed가 문장의 주어에 해당하므로 meaning을 동사 meant로 고쳐 써야 한다.

어휘 · 어구

aquaculture industry (수산) 양식업
in terms of ~면에서
in respect of ~의 측면에있어
high-density 고밀도의
rearing 사육, 양육
outbreak 발발, 발생
infectious 전염성의
devastate 황폐화하다
pen 우리, 작은 우리
barren 황폐한
in place 시행되고있는
ensure 반드시~하게하다

Column 2

overall 전반적인, 일반적인

왜 많이 틀렸을까?

①에서 devastated의 주어는 관계대명사 that 앞의 선행사 infectious diseases야. 따라서 주어와 동사가 능동의 관계이므로 적절해. ②에서 close 앞에는 주격관계대명사와 be동사가 생략된 것으로, local wildlife inhabiting areas (which are) close to the fish farms에서 close to the fish farms가 local wildlife inhabiting areas를 수식하고 있으므로 적절해. ④에서 where는 관계부사로 선행사인 sites를 수식하므로 적절해. ⑤에서 주어가 This이므로 단수 취급하여 has가 온 것은 적절해.

8. ④
용기의 의미와 결단력

직독 / 직해

The word 'courage' / takes on added meaning/
'용기'라는 말은 / 추가되는 의미를 지닌다 /

if you keep in mind / 만약 당신이 ~을 기억한다면 /

that it is derived from the Latin word 'cor' /
라틴어의 'cor'에서 파생되었다는 것을 /

meaning 'heart.' / '심장'을 뜻하는

The dictionary defines courage as a 'quality /
사전은 정의한다 용기를 '특질로 /

which enables one / 누군가 가능하게 하는/

to pursue a right course of action, /
올바른 행동의 과정을 추구하도록 /

through which one may provoke /
그 과정을 통해 누군가 유발할 수 있다 /

disapproval, hostility, or contempt.'
불찬성이나, 적의 또는 경멸을'

Over 300 years ago / 300년보다 이전에 /

La Rochefoucauld went a step further /
La Rochefoucauld는 한 걸음 더 나갔다. /

when he said: / 그가 ~라고 말했을 때 / **"Perfect courage is /**
"완전한 용기는 아무도 보지 않는데서 하는 것이다 /

to do unwitnessed /

what we should be capable of doing / before all men."
당신이 할 수 있는 것을 / 모든 사람 앞에서"

It is not easy to show moral courage /
도덕적 용기를 보여주기는 쉽지 않다. /

in the face of either indifference or opposition.
무관심이나 반대에 직면하여

But persons / who are daring /
그러나 사람들은 / 대담한 /

in taking a wholehearted stand for truth /
진실을 위한 진심어린 입장을 취하는 것에

often achieve results / that surpass their expectations.
종종 결과를 성취한다. / 그들의 기대를 능가하는

On the other hand, / halfhearted individuals /
반면에, / 마지못해 하는 개인들은 /

are seldom distinguished for courage /
용기가 두드러지지 않는다 /

even when it involves their own welfare.
심지어 그것이 그들 자신의 이익과 연관이 있을 때조차도

To be courageous / under all circumstances /
용감하게 되는 것은 / 모든 상황에서 /

requires strong determination.
강한 결단력을 필요로 한다.

'용기'라는 말이 '심장'을 뜻하는 라틴어의 'cor'에서 파생되었다는 것을 기억한다면, 그 말은 추가되는 의미를 지닌다. 사전은 용기를 '불찬성이나, 적의, 또는 경멸을 유발할 수도 있는 올바른 행동의 과정을 추구하게 되는 특질'로 정의한다. 300년보다 이전에 La Rochefoucauld는 그가 '완전한 용기는 모든 사람 앞에서 당신이 할 수 있는 것을 아무도 보지 않는데서 하는 것이다'라고 말했을 때 한 걸음 더 나갔다. 무관심이나 반대에 직면하여 도덕적 용기를 보여주기는 쉽지 않다. 그러나 진리를 위한 진심어린 입장을 취하는 것에 대담한 사람들은 종종 그들의 기대를 능가하는 결과를 성취한다. 반면에, 마지못해 하는 개인들은 그것이 그들 자신의 이익과 연관이 있을 때조차도 용기가 두드러지지 않는다. 모든 상황에서 용감하게 되는 것은 강한 결단력을 필요로 한다.

Column 3

문제풀이

① ~ 'cor' (which is) meaning 'heart.'에서 「관계대명사+be동사」가 생략된 문장이다.
② The dictionary defines courage as a 'quality which enables one to pursue [a right course of action].'이라는 문장과 One may provoke ~ contempt through [a right course of action].이라는 문장을 관계대명사를 사용하여 한 문장으로 만든 문장이다. 두 문장의 공통된 부분(a right course of action)을 선행사로 하고 뒷부분을 관계대명사 which로 만들었다.
③ it-to 가주어, 진주어 구문이다.
④가 포함된 문장에서 주어인 persons에 연결되는 동사가 없으므로 ④는 achieve로 바꾸어야 한다.
⑤ halfhearted individuals를 가리키므로 복수명사를 대신하는 인칭대명사 they의 소유격 their를 사용하였다.

어휘 · 어구

disapproval 불찬성
unwitnessed 목격되지 않은
indifference 무관심, 냉담
wholehearted 성심성의의
take a stand 입장을 취하다
half-hearted 마음이 내키지 않는
distinguished 눈에 띄는

9. ⑤
새로운 기술의 적응

직독 / 직해

Everywhere we turn / we hear about almighty "cyberspace"!
우리가 고개를 돌리는 모든 곳에서 / 우리는 전능하신 '사이버 공간'에 대해 듣는다

The hype promises /
과대광고는 약속한다 /

that we will leave our boring lives, put on goggles and body suits, /
우리가 지루한 삶을 떠나서 고글과 바디 수트를 착용할 것이라고 /

and enter some metallic, three-dimensional, multimedia otherworld.
그리고 어떤 금속성의, 3차원의, 멀티미디어로 만들어진 다른 세상으로 들어갈 (것이라고)

When the Industrial Revolution arrived / with its great innovation, the motor,
산업 혁명이 도래했을 때 / 위대한 혁신인 모터와 함께 /

we didn't leave our world / to go to some remote motorspace!
우리는 우리의 세상을 떠나지 않았다 / 어떤 멀리 떨어진 모터 공간으로 가기 위해

On the contrary, / we brought the motors into our lives, /
그와는 반대로 / 우리는 모터를 우리 삶에 가져왔다 /

as automobiles, refrigerators, drill presses, and pencil sharpeners.
자동차, 냉장고, 드릴 프레스, 연필깎이와 같은 것들로

This absorption has been so complete /
이런 흡수는 너무 완전해서 /

that we refer to all these tools /
우리는 이 모든 도구를 지칭한다 /

with names that declare their usage, / not their "motorness."
그것들의 사용을 분명하게 밝히는 이름으로 / 그것들의 '모터성'이 아니라

These innovations led to a major socioeconomic movement /
이 혁신품들은 주요한 사회경제적 운동으로 이어졌다 /

precisely because they entered and affected profoundly our everyday lives.

그것들은 정확히 우리의 일상생활에 들어와 깊은 영향을 주었기 때문에

People have not changed fundamentally in thousands of years.
사람들은 수천 년간 근본적으로 변하지 않았다

Technology changes constantly.
기술은 계속해서 변화한다

It's the one / that must adapt to us.
바로 그것이다 / 우리에게 적응해야 하는 것은

That's exactly what will happen / with information technology and its devices /
그것이 바로 일어날 일이다 / 정보 기술과 그 장치들이 /

under human-centric computing.
인간 중심의 컴퓨터 사용 하에서

The longer we continue to believe /
우리가 계속해서 더 오래 믿게 될수록 /

that computers will take us to a magical new world, /
컴퓨터가 우리를 마법 같은 새로운 세상으로 데려다줄 것이라고 /

the longer we will delay / their natural fusion with our lives, /
우리는 더 오래 늦출 것인데 / 컴퓨터와 우리 삶의 자연스러운 융합을 /

the hallmark of every major movement /
이는 모든 주요 운동의 특징이다 /

that aspires to be called a socioeconomic revolution.
사회경제적 혁명이라고 불리기를 열망하는

우리가 고개를 돌리는 모든 곳에서 우리는 전능하신 '사이버공간'에 대해 듣는다. 과대광고는 우리의 지루한 삶을 떠나서 고글과 바디 수트를 착용하고, 어떤 금속의, 3차원의, 멀티미디어로 만들어진 다른 세상으로 들어갈 것이라고 약속한다. 위대한 혁신인 모터와 함께 산업 혁명이 도래했을 때 우리는 어떤 ① 멀리 떨어진 모터 공간으로 가기 위해 우리의 세상을 떠나지 않았다! 그와는 반대로, 우리는 모터를 자동차, 냉장고, 드릴 프레스, 연필깎이와 같은 것들로 우리 삶에 가져왔다. 이런 ② 흡수는 너무 완전해서 우리는 그것들의 '모터성'이 아니라 그것들의 사용을 분명하게 밝히는 이름으로 이 모든 도구를 지칭한다. 이 혁신들은 정확히 우리의 일상생활에 들어와 깊은 ③ 영향을 주었기 때문에 주요한 사회경제적 운동으로 이어졌다. 사람들은 수천 년간 근본적으로 변하지 않았다. 기술은 계속해서 변화한다. 우리에게 ④ 적응해야 하는 것은 바로 그것이다. 그것이 바로 정보 기술과 그 장치들이 인간 중심의 컴퓨터 사용 하에서 일어날 일이다. 컴퓨터가 우리를 마법 같은 새로운 세상으로 데려다줄 것이라고 계속해서 더 오래 믿게 될수록, 우리는 컴퓨터와 우리 삶의 자연스러운 융합을 더 오래 ⑤ 유지할(→ 늦출) 것인데, 이는 사회경제적 혁명이라고 불리기를 열망하는 모든 주요 운동의 특징이다.

문제풀이

새로운 기술이 나타날 때 우리가 그 기술로 가는 것이 아니라, 그 기술이 우리에게 적응해야 한다고 했으므로, 컴퓨터가 우리를 마법 같은 새로운 세상으로 데려다줄 것이라고 계속해서 더 오래 믿게 되면 우리는 컴퓨터와 우리 삶의 자연스러운 융합을 더 오래 늦출 것이라고 해야 한다. 따라서 ⑤ 'maintain(유지하다)'을 'delay(늦추다)'와 같은 낱말로 고쳐야 한다.

○ 이렇게 풀자 'Technology changes constantly. It's the one that must adapt to us.(기술은 계속해서 변화한다. 우리에게 적응해야 하는 것은 바로 그것(기술)이다.)'에 '기술이 우리에게 적응해야 한다.'는 이 글의 중심 내용이 잘 드러나 있다. 'The longer we continue to believe that computers will take us to a magical new world(컴퓨터가 우리를 마법 같은 새로운 세상으로 데려다줄 것이라고 계속해서 더 오래 믿게 될수록)'은 주제와 반대되는 내용으로, 컴퓨터가 우리를 새로운 세상으로 데려다 줄 것이라고 오래 믿으면, 우리는 컴퓨터와 우리 삶의 융합을 더 오래 늦출 것이라고 추론할 수 있다.

《 어휘 · 어구 》

almighty 전능한
metallic 금속으로 된
three-dimensional 3차원의
remote 멀리 떨어진
absorption 흡수
refer to ~을 지칭하다

---

declare 선언하다, 분명하게 밝히다
precisely 정확히
profoundly 깊이
fundamentally 근본적으로
fusion 융합
aspire 열망하다

---

10. ④ 음반에 대한 음악 공연자와 방송사들의 인식

직독/직해

Musical performers and their labor union did not perceive early recordings /
음악 공연자들과 그들의 노동조합은 초기 음반들을 인식하지 않았다 /

as a threat to their livelihoods /
자신들의 생계에 대한 위협으로 /

because the recordings were mostly of poor quality.
그 음반들이 대체로 음질이 좋지 않기 때문에

It was not long before musicians began to wonder /
얼마 지나지 않아 음악가들은 궁금해하기 시작했다 /

whether recordings of popular artists or songs would undermine the demand for live music.
인기 있는 아티스트나 노래의 음반이 실황 음악에 대한 수요의 토대를 침식할까

For a time, / however, / recorded music was too scratchy /
한동안 / 그러나 / 녹음된 음악은 긁히는 소리가 매우 심했다 /

to pose a serious threat, /
심각한 위협을 제기하기에는 /

even though it played in commercial places and offered a few performers a way /
비록 그것이 상업적인 장소에서 재생되고 몇몇 연주자들에게 수단을 제공했음에도 불구하고 /

to supplement their income.
자신들의 수입을 보충할

Additionally, / during the early days of recording, /
게다가 / 녹음 초기에는 /

radio stations preferred using live musicians on their programs.
라디오 방송국들이 실황 공연을 하는 음악가를 자신들의 프로그램에 활용하기를 선호했다

Sound from live performances was better quality, /
실황 공연의 소리가 음질이 더 좋았다 /

and stations at this time rarely used recordings.
그리고 이 시기 방송국들은 음반을 거의 사용하지 않았다

Broadcasters respected union demands for employment and decent wages, /
방송사들은 고용과 적절한 임금에 대한 노조의 요구를 존중했다 /

because the alterative use of recordings was even less attractive.
(실황 공연을) 대체하여 음반을 사용하는 것이 훨씬 덜 매력적이기 때문에

They made efforts to employ orchestras, bands, and vocalists /
그들은 오케스트라, 악단, 그리고 가수를 고용하기 위해 애썼다 /

to perform on radio programs.
라디오 프로그램에서 공연할

There was relative balance between live music and technology /
실황 음악과 기술 사이에 상대적 균형이 있었다 /

in the early innovation stages.
초기의 혁신 단계에서는

With increased improvements in electrical recording, / however, /
전기 녹음이 점차 개선되면서 / 하지만 /

this balance soon changed.
이 균형은 곧 바뀌었다

음악 공연자들과 그들의 노동조합은 초기 음반들을 자신들의 생계에 대한 위협으로 인식하지 않았는데, 그 음반들이 대체로 음질이 좋지 않았기 때문이다. 얼마 지나지 않아 음악가들은 인기 있는 아티스트나 노래의 음반이 실황 음악에 대한 수요의 토대를 ① 침식할까 궁금해하기 시작했다. 그러나 한동안, 녹음된 음악은 상업적인 장소에서 재생되고 몇몇 연주자들에게 자신들의 수입을 ② 보충할 수단을 제공했음에도 불구하고, 심각한 위협을 제기하기에는 긁히는 소리가 매우 심했다. 게다가 녹음 초기

는 라디오 방송국들이 실황 공연을 하는 음악가를 자신들의 프로그램에 활용하기를 ③ 선호했다. 실황 공연의 소리가 음질이 더 좋았고, 이 시기 방송국들은 음반을 거의 사용하지 않았다. 방송사들은 고용과 적절한 임금에 대한 노조의 요구를 ④ 거부했는데(→ 존중했는데), 이는 (실황 공연을) 대체하여 음반을 사용하는 것이 훨씬 덜 매력적이었기 때문이다. 그들은 라디오 프로그램에서 공연할 오케스트라, 악단, 그리고 가수를 고용하기 위해 애썼다. 초기의 혁신 단계에서는 실황 음악과 기술 사이에 상대적 균형이 있었다. 하지만 전기 녹음이 점차 ⑤ 개선되면서 이 균형은 곧 바뀌었다.

문제풀이

초기 음반들은 실황 공연의 소리보다 음질이 좋지 않기 때문에 음악 공연자들과 노동조합은 녹음된 음반에 대해서 위협을 느끼지 않았고, 라디오 방송국들도 녹음된 음반을 사용하기보다는 그들의 프로그램에서 실황 공연할 오케스트라, 악단, 그리고 가수를 고용하기 위해 애썼기 때문에 고용과 적절한 임금에 대한 음악 공연자 조합의 요구를 수용했다는 내용의 글이다. 따라서 ④ 'rejected(거부했다)'를 'respected(존중했다)'나 'accepted(수용했다)' 등의 어휘로 바꿔야 한다.

○ 이렇게 풀자 문맥상 낱말의 쓰임을 묻는 문제에서는 밑줄 어휘의 주변 문맥을 보고 그 적절성을 점검할 필요가 있다. ① 'undermine (침식하다, 훼손하다)'는 그 뒤의 'however' 이하에서 녹음된 음반의 긁히는 소리가 매우 심했다는 내용으로 보아 '녹음 음악이 실황 음악의 수요를 감소시키기에는 음질이 좋지 않았다는 의미이므로 적절하고, ② 'supplement(보충하다)'는 'even though'로 보아 녹음 음질이 좋지 않지만 어느 정도의 수입은 될 수 있었다는 내용이므로 적절하다.

《 어휘 · 어구 》

labor union 노동조합
perceive 인식하다
threat 위협
livelihood 생계
undermine 약화시키다
scratchy 긁히는
supplement 보충하다
additionally 게다가
performance 공연
rarely 거의
decent 적당한
wages 임금
attractive 매력적인
improvement 개선

---

11. ⑤ 인터넷의 부정적인 면

직독/직해

Although the wonders of modern technology have provided people /
비록 현대 기술의 경이로운 것이 사람들에게 제공했지만 /

with opportunities beyond the wildest dreams of our ancestors, /
우리 선조들은 꿈에도 생각지 못한 기회를 /

the good, as usual, is weakened / by a downside.
항상 그렇듯이 좋은 점은 약해진다 / 부정적인 면에 의해

One of those downsides is /
그 부정적인 면 중 하나는 ~이다 /

that anyone who so chooses / can pick up the virtual megaphone /
그렇게 하기로 선택한 사람은 누구나 / 가상의 확성기를 집어 들 수 있다 /

that is the Internet / and put in their two cents /
인터넷이라는 / 그리고 의견을 말할 수 있는 /

on any of an infinite number of topics, /
무한히 많은 주제 중 어느 것에 대해서라도 /

regardless of their qualifications.

자신의 자격과 관계없이

After all, /on the Internet, / there are no regulations /
결국 / 인터넷에는 / 규제가 없다 /

preventing a kindergarten teacher from offering medical advice /
유치원 선생님이 의학적인 조언을 제공하는 것을 막는 /

or a physician from suggesting ways /
의사가 방법을 제안하는 것을 (막는) /

to safely make structural changes to your home.
여러분의 집에 안전하게 구조적인 변경을 할 수 있는

As a result, / misinformation gets disseminated as information, /
그 결과 / 잘못된 정보가 정보로 퍼져나가게 된다 /

and it is not always easy / to differentiate the two.
그리고 항상 쉽지만은 않다 / 그 둘을 구별하는 것이

This can be particularly frustrating for scientists, /
이것은 과학자에게 특히 좌절감을 줄 수 있는데 /

who spend their lives learning /
그들은 배우느라 인생을 보내지만 /

how to understand the intricacies of the world around them, /
자기 주변 세상의 복잡성을 이해하는 방법을 /

only to have their work summarily challenged by people /
결국 그들의 연구는 사람들에게 즉각 이의제기를 받게 된다 /

whose experience with the topic / can be measured in minutes.
그 주제에 대한 경험이 / 분 단위로 측정될 수 있는

This frustration is then amplified / by the fact /
그렇다면 이 좌절감은 증폭된다 / 사실에 의해 /

that, to the general public, / both the scientist and the challenger /
일반 대중에게는 / 과학자와 도전자 둘 다 /

are awarded equal credibility.
똑같은 신뢰성을 부여받는다는

비록 현대 기술의 경이로운 것이 사람들에게 우리 선조들은 꿈에도 생각지 못한 기회를 제공했지만, 항상 그렇듯이 좋은 점은 부정적인 면에 의해 약해진다. 그 부정적인 면 중 하나는 그렇게 하기로 선택한 사람은 누구나 자신의 ① 자격과 관계없이 인터넷이라는 가상의 확성기를 집어 들고 무한히 많은 주제 중 어느 것에 대해서라도 의견을 말할 수 있다는 것이다. 결국, 인터넷에는 유치원 선생님이 의학적인 조언을 제공하거나 의사가 여러분의 집에 안전하게 구조적인 변경을 할 수 있는 방법을 제안하는 것을 ② 막는 규제가 없다. 그 결과, 잘못된 정보가 정보로 퍼져나가게 되고, 그 둘을 ③ 구별하는 것이 항상 쉽지만은 않다. 이것은 과학자에게 특히 좌절감을 줄 수 있는데, 그들은 자기 주변 세상의 복잡성을 이해하는 방법을 배우느라 인생을 보내지만 결국 그들의 연구는 그 주제에 대한 경험이 분 단위로 측정될 수 있는 사람들에게 즉각 ④ 이의제기를 받게 된다. 그렇다면 일반 대중들에게는 과학자와 도전자 둘 다 똑같은 신뢰성을 부여받는다는 사실에 의해 이 좌절감은 ⑤ 줄어든다(→ 증폭된다).

문제풀이

자격과 관계없이 누구나 어떤 주제에 관해서든 의견을 말할 수 있는 인터넷상에서, 주변 세상의 복잡성을 이해하는 법을 배우느라 인생을 보내는 과학자는 그 주제에 경험이 극히 적은 사람에게 즉석에서 이의제기를 받고 과학자와 도전자 둘 다에 대한 신뢰가 동등하게 부여받게 되었을 때 좌절감이 증폭될 것이다. 따라서 ⑤ 'diminished(줄어들다)'를 'amplified(증폭되다)'와 같은 낱말로 고쳐야 한다.

〈어휘·어구〉

wonder 경이로운 것
beyond the wildest dreams 꿈에도 생각지 못한
ancestor 조상, 선조
downside 부정적인 면
virtual 가상의
megaphone 확성기
infinite 무한한
regardless of ~에 관계없이
qualification 자격
regulation 규정, 규제

---

kindergarten 유치원
physician 의사, 내과 의사
differentiate 구별하다
frustrating 좌절감을 주는
summarily 즉석으로, 즉결로
diminish 줄어들다
credibility 신뢰성

---

12. ④　　　　　　　　보행 구역의 장단점

직독/직해

Pedestrian areas provide a dramatic improvement /
보행 구역은 극적인 개선을 제공한다 /

in the environment for pedestrians, / and have proved very successful /
보행자들을 위한 환경에 / 그리고 매우 성공적인 것으로 입증되어 왔다 /

in enhancing trade / in many town and city centres.
상업을 증진시키는 데 있어 / 많은 마을과 도시 중심부에서

There is little evidence / to support traders' claims /
증거는 거의 없다 / 상인들의 주장을 뒷받침할 /

that pedestrian streets cause a loss in trade, /
보행 거리가 상업의 손실을 유발한다는 /

provided of course that they are well designed.
만약 물론 보행 거리가 잘 설계되었다면

As well as achieving environmental and safety benefits, /
환경과 안전상의 이득을 달성할 뿐만 아니라 /

they may well therefore have positive impacts /
그로 인해 그것은 아마도 긍정적인 영향을 미칠 것이다 /

on the urban economy and on land use policy.
도시 경제와 토지 사용 정책에

However, / they present some accessibility problems /
하지만 / 그것은 약간의 접근성 문제를 야기한다 /

for car and bus users / and, particularly, for goods deliveries /
자동차와 버스 이용자들에게는 / 그리고 특히 상품 배달자들에게는 /

and for disabled people.
그리고 장애를 가진 사람들에게는

Exemptions for some of these, / whether permanently or, /
이것 중 일부에 대한 면제는 / 영구적이든 아니면 /

as with deliveries, / at certain times of day, / inevitably reduce the benefits somewhat.
배달의 경우와 같이 / 하루 중 특정 시간대이든 / 어느 정도 그 이득을 불가피하게 감소시킨다

Pedestrian areas almost inevitably reduce efficiency, /
보행 구역은 효율성을 거의 불가피하게 감소시킨다 /

by reducing road capacity.　도로 수용력을 줄임으로써

They also potentially cause problems / in the surrounding area, /
그것은 또한 잠재적으로 문제를 야기한다 / 인접 지역에 /

both by diversion of traffic / and by attracting trade to the protected area.
교통량을 다른 곳으로 돌릴 뿐만 아니라 / 보호 구역으로 상업을 끌어들임으로써

These potential negative impacts / can be reduced by careful design.
이런 잠재적인 부정적 영향은 / 세심한 설계에 의해 감소될 수 있다

Aesthetic design is of crucial importance / in maintaining trade.
미적인 설계는 매우 중요하다 / 상업을 유지하는 데 있어

보행 구역은 보행자들을 위한 환경에 극적인 개선을 제공하고, 많은 마을과 도시 중심부에서 상업을 증진시키는 데 있어 매우 성공적인 것으로 입증되어 왔다. 만약 물론 보행 거리가 잘 설계되었다면, 보행 거리가 상업의 손실을 유발한다는 상인들의 주장을 ① 뒷받침할 증거는 거의 없다. 환경과 안전상의 이득을 달성할 뿐만 아니라, 그로 인해 그것은 아마도 도시 경제와 토지 사용 정책에 ② 긍정적인 영향을 미칠 것이다. 하지만, 그것은 자동차와 버스 이용자, 그리고 특히 상품 배달과 장애를 가진 사람들에게는 약간의 ③ 접근성 문제를 야기한다. 영구적이든, 아니면 배달의 경우와 같이, 하루 중 특정 시간대이든, 이것 중 일부에 대한 면제는, 어느 정도 그 이득을 불가피하게 감소시킨다. 도로 수용력을 줄임으로써, 보행 구역은 효율성을 거의 불가피하게 감소시킨다. 그것은 또한 교통량

을 다른 곳으로 돌릴 뿐만 아니라 보호 구역으로 상업을 끌어들임으로써, 잠재적으로 인접 지역에 문제를 ④ 제거한다(→ 야기한다). 이런 잠재적인 부정적 영향은 세심한 설계에 의해 ⑤ 감소될 수 있다. 미적인 설계는 상업을 유지하는 데 있어 매우 중요하다.

문제풀이

보행 구역은 도로 수용력을 줄임으로써 효율성을 감소시키며, 교통량을 다른 곳으로 돌리고 보호 구역으로 상업을 끌어들이기 때문에 잠재적으로 인접 지역에 문제를 야기한다는 흐름이 되어야 문맥상 자연스럽다. 따라서 ④ 'eliminate(제거하다)'를 'cause(야기한다)'로 고쳐야 한다.

구조 다시보기

도입	보행 구역은 보행자를 위한 환경과 상업 증진에 있어 성공적임
부연	보행 거리가 잘 설계되어 있으면 긍정적인 영향을 미침
반전	특정 사람들에게 접근성 문제를 야기함
부연	보호 구역은 잠재적인 부정적 문제를 야기함 • 도로 수용력을 줄임으로써 효율성을 감소시킴 • 교통량을 다른 곳으로 돌리고 보호 구역에 상업을 끌어들임
결론	세심한 설계를 통해 잠재적인 부정적인 영향은 감소될 수 있음

〈어휘·어구〉

pedestrian 보행자의; 보행자
dramatic 극적인
improvement 개선
enhance 높이다, 증진시키다
evidence 증거
achieve 달성하다
policy 정책
accessibility 접근성
permanently 영구적으로
inevitably 불가피하게
somewhat 어느 정도
efficiency 효율성
capacity 수용력
potentially 잠재적으로
eliminate 제거하다
surrounding 인근의, 주위의
diversion 다른 데로 돌리기
aesthetic 미적인
crucial 중대한
maintain 유지하다

02. 목적어의 이해

A 출제 POINT
본문 008쪽

1. talking 2. that 3. of
4. that 5. he was 6. that
7. drinking

1 [해석]▶ Sally는 그 상황에 대해 말하지 않을 수 없었다.
[해설]▶ 동사 avoid는 동명사를 목적어로 취한다. 동명사를 목적어로 취하는 동사 중에는 finish, mind, enjoy, postpone, deny 등이 있다. can't avoid ‑ing 또는 can't help ‑ing는 '～하지 않을 수 없다'는 의미이다.

2 [해석]▶ Sam은 자신의 스마트폰이 사라진 것을 알게 되었다.
[해설]▶ found 이하의 절이 완전한 문장이 나왔으므로 접속사가 필요하다. 접속사 that절 이하는 문장에서 목적어에 해당한다.

3 [해석]▶ Peter가 내게 질문을 했다.
[해설]▶ ask동사가 이끄는 4형식 문장은 3형식으로 바꿀 때, 전치사 of를 써야 한다. 즉 4형식 「ask +간접목적어(사람)+직접목적어(사물)」 문장을 3형식으로 바꾸면 「ask+직접목적어(사물)+of+간접목적어(사람)」 형식을 취한다.

4 [해석]▶ 나는 책이 당연히 올 거라고 생각했다.
[해설]▶ 문장에서 목적어(that Jack would come)가 길어지면, 가목적어 it을 쓰고, (진)목적어를 문장 뒤로 보낸다.

5 [해석]▶ 그녀는 그가 몇 살인지 모른다.
[해설]▶ 직접의문문이 다른 문장의 일부로 들어가는 간접의문문은 「의문사+주어+동사」의 형태를 취한다.

6 [해석]▶ 그는 그들이 3층에 있다고 말했다.
[해설]▶ 동사 say 뒤에 완전한 문장이 왔으므로 that이 와야 한다. say 뒤에 오는 목적어를 이끄는 that은 생략될 수 있다. whether는 '예', '아니오'를 기대하는 의문문의 간접화법이나 대안 중에서 선택을 하는 내용이 나올 때 쓸 수 있다.

7 [해석]▶ 그는 커피를 마심으로써 잠들지 않고 있다.
[해설]▶ 전치사 다음에 동사가 올 때는 동명사가 나온다.

B 체크 POINT
본문 008쪽

1. to refuse 2. whether 3. to
4. it 5. they are 6. that
7. her

1 [해석]▶ 그것에 대해 신중하게 생각한 후, 나는 그의 제안을 거절하기로 결심했다.
[해설]▶ decide는 to부정사를 목적어로 가져온다. 이와 같은 동사 중에는 plan, agree, want, wish, fail 등이 있다.

2 [해석]▶ 나는 그녀가 기쁜지 그렇지 않은지 모르겠다.
[해설]▶ that절과 whether[if]절은 목적어로 나올 수 있지만, don't know, doubt와 같이 불확실한 의미를 나타내는 동사가 나오는 경우, 뒤의 목적절은 whether[if]절을 사용하고, 확실한 내용은 that절을 사용한다.

3 [해석]▶ 나는 조카에게 동화책을 보냈다.
[해설]▶ send 동사가 이끄는 4형식 문장은 3형식으로 바꿀 때, 전치사 to를 써야 한다. 즉 4형식 「send +간접목적어(사람)+직접목적어(사물)」 문장을 3형식으로 바꾸면 「send+직접목적어(사물)+to+간접목적어(사람)」 형식을 취한다.

4 [해석]▶ 많은 학생들이 다른 이들과 가까운 관계를 형성하는 것을 어렵다고 생각한다.
[해설]▶ 문장에서 목적어가 길어지면, 가목적어 it을 쓰고, (진)목적어를 문장 뒤로 보낸다.

5 [해석]▶ 나는 그들이 어디에 숨어 있는지 모른다.
[해설]▶ 직접의문문의 다른 문장의 일부로 들어가는 경우, 간접의문문(의문사+주어+동사) 형태를 취한다.

6 [해석]▶ 그녀는 그녀의 친구들이 자신을 칭찬한다고 생각했다.
[해설]▶ thought 동사 뒤에 완전한 문장이 오는 경우 접속사 that을 쓴다. 동사 think 뒤에 목적어를 가져오는 경우, that은 흔히 생략한다.

7 [해석]▶ 너는 그녀에게 진실해야 한다.
[해설]▶ 전치사 다음에 대명사가 나오는 경우 목적격이 와야 한다.

Day 02
본문 009쪽

1	②	2	②	3	⑤	4	④	5	⑤
6	④	7	②	8	⑤	9	②	10	④
11	③	12	⑤						

1. ② 기부자의 두 가지 유형

기부하는 행위를 연구하는 심리학자들은 어떤 사람들은 한두 자선단체에 상당한 액수를 기부하는 반면에, 어떤 사람들은 많은 자선단체에 적은 액수를 기부한다는 것을 알게 되었다. 한두 자선단체에 기부하는 사람들은 그 자선단체가 무슨 일을 하고 있는지와 그것이 실제로 긍정적인 영향을 끼치고 있는지에 관한 증거를 찾는다. 자선단체가 정말로 다른 사람들을 도와주고 있다는 것을 증거가 보여줄 경우 그들은 상당한 기부금을 낸다. 많은 자선단체에 적은 액수를 내는 사람들은 그들이 하는 일이 다른 사람들을 돕는지에는 그다지 많은 관심을 두지 않는데, 심리학자들은 그들을 따뜻한 불빛 기부자라고 부른다. 그들이 내는 기부가 끼치는 영향과 관계없이 자신들이 기부하고 있다는 것을 아는 것은 그들을 기분 좋게 해 준다. 많은 경우 기부금은 10달러 이하의 아주 적은 금액이어서, 곰곰이 생각해 본다면, 그들은 기부금을 처리하는 비용이 그것(기부금)이 자선단체에 가져다주는 모든 이점을 넘어서기 쉽다는 것을 알게 될 것이다.

문제풀이

① 주어가 Psychologists이므로 복수취급하여 have가 온 것은 적절하다. who study giving behavior는 선행사 Psychologists를 수식하는 관계대명사절이다.
② 뒤에 완전한 절이 이어지고 있으므로 **what**은 올 수 없고, 문맥상 '～인지'의 의미가 되어야 하므로 **what**이 아니라 명사절을 이끄는 접속사 **whether**가 와야한다.
③ 주어 they와 동사가 능동의 관계이므로 be동사 are와 함께 현재진행형으로 쓰인 doing이 온 것은 적절하다.
④ Knowing that they are giving의 they를 가리키

며 makes의 목적어로 쓰인 대명사 them이 온 것은 적절하다.
⑤ 문맥상 '생각하기 위해 멈춘다'라는 의미가 되어야 하므로 목적의 의미를 지닌 부사적 용법의 to부정사 to think가 온 것은 적절하다.
따라서 정답은 ②이다.

《구문 및 어휘》

*12행 In many cases the donation is **so** small — $10 or less — [**that** **if** they **stopped** to think, they **would realize** {that the cost of processing the donation is likely to exceed any benefit it brings to the charity}].
(1) 「so+형용사/부사+that+주어+동사」는 '너무 ～해서 …하다'라는 의미이다.
(2) that절의 if they ~ the charity는 「if+주어+동사의 과거형, 주어+would+동사원형」의 가정법 과거 구문으로 '만약 ～한다면 …할 텐데'라는 의미이다.
(3) that the cost ~ the charity는 would realize의 목적어로 쓰인 명사절이다.

psychologist 심리학자
substantial 상당한
amount 양
donate 기부하다, 기증하다
evidence 증거
indicate 보여주다
glow (은은한) 불빛
regardless of ～에 관계없이
process 처리하다
exceed 넘어서다
benefit 이점

2. ② 수분 함량이 높은 음식과 포만감

물은 열량이 없지만, 위장 내에서 공간을 차지하며 그것이 포만감을 형성한다. 최근의 한 연구는 식사 전에 두 잔의 물을 마시는 사람이 더 빨리 배가 부르고, 더 적은 열량을 섭취하며, 더 많은 살이 빠진다는 것을 알아냈다. 더 적은 수분이 있는 음식보다 수분 함량이 더 높은 음식을 선택함으로써 같은 전략이 작동하게 할 수 있다. 예를 들어, 포도와 건포도의 유일한 차이는 포도가 그 속에 약 여섯 배 더 많은 수분을 가지고 있다는 것이다. 그 수분이 그것들이 얼마만큼 배가 부른지에 있어 큰 차이를 만든다. 100칼로리 상당의 건포도를 먹고 난 후에 느끼는 것보다 100칼로리 상당의 포도를 먹고 난 후에 훨씬 더 큰 만족감을 느끼게 된다. 상추, 오이, 그리고 토마토와 같은 샐러드 채소 또한 묽은 수프가 그런 것처럼 매우 높은 수분 함량을 가지고 있다.

문제풀이

(A) 네모 뒤에 완전한 문장이 왔으므로, found의 목적어 역할을 하는 명사절을 이끄는 접속사 that이 적절하다. (B) 문장의 주어는 the only difference이므로 동사는 3인칭 단수인 is가 적절하다. (C) 앞에 있는 일반동사 have를 대신하는 대동사로 do가 적절하다. 따라서 정답은 ②이다.

《구문 및 어휘》

*2행 Recently, a study found [that people (**who** drank two glasses of water before meals) **got** full sooner, **ate** fewer calories, and **lost** more weight.
(1) that 이하는 found의 목적어로 쓰인 명사절로 that

절의 주어는 people이고 got, ate, lost는 동사로 병렬 관계이다.

②who ~ meals는 선행사 people을 수식하는 관계대명사절이다.

*5행 You can put the same strategy to work by choosing foods [that have a higher water content] over those [with less water].

①「put+목적어+to부정사」는 '~가 …하도록 하다'라는 의미이고, 「by+-ing」는 '~함으로써'의 의미이다.

②that 이하는 foods를 수식하는 관계대명사절이다.

③ those는 앞에 나온 foods를 대신하는 대명사이다. with 이하는 those를 수식한다.

take up (공간을) 차지하다
strategy 전략
water content 수분 함량
raisin 건포도
content 내용물

---

3. ⑤ 보상을 원해서가 아니라 내적 동기로 친절을 베풀어야 한다.

며칠 전 퇴근하면서 나는 어떤 여자가 큰 길로 들어오려고 애쓰는데 계속되는 차량 흐름 때문에 운이 별로 없는 것을 봤다. 나는 속도를 줄이고 그녀가 내 앞에 들어오게 해주었다. 나는 기분이 꽤 좋았는데, 그 후 두어 블록 간 후에 그녀가 몇 대의 차를 끼워주려고 차를 멈추는 바람에 우리 둘 다 다음 신호를 놓치게 되었다. 나는 그녀에게 완전히 짜증이 나있는 나 자신을 발견했다. 내가 그렇게 친절하게 그녀가 들어오게 해주었는데 어떻게 감히 그녀가 나를 느리게 가게 한단 말인가! 내가 안달하면서 (자동차에) 앉아 있을 때 나는 내 자신이 참으로 어리석게 굴고 있다는 사실을 깨달았다. 불현듯 언젠가 읽었던 문구 하나가 마음속에 떠올랐다. '누군가 점수를 매기고 있기 때문이거나, 하지 않으면 처벌을 받기 때문이 아니라 내적 동기로 사람들에게 친절을 베풀어야 한다.' 나는 내가 보상을 원하고 있다는 사실을 깨달았다. 내가 당신에게 이런 친절을 베푼다면 당신(또는 어떤 다른 사람)이 나에게 그만한 친절을 베풀 것이라는 생각이었다.

문제풀이

① having은 접속사 and에 의해서 문장의 목적보어 trying과 병렬로 연결된 구조이므로, 마찬가지로 현재분사형태로 온 것은 적절하다.

② irritated는 「found+목적어+목적보어」 구조의 문장에서 목적보어로 쓰인 것으로, 목적어 myself와 의미상 관계가 수동이므로 과거분사 형태로 온 것은 적절하다.

③ 「how+형용사+주어+동사」구조의 감탄문이 realized의 목적어로 쓰인 구조로, how가 온 것은 적절하다.

④ came은 문장의 동사로, 주어는 a phrase이고 과거 시제이므로 적절히 사용되었다.

⑤ 「주어+동사+목적어」 형태의 완전한 문장인 'I had wanted a reward'가 동사 realized의 목적절로 사용된 구조이므로 절을 이끄는 접속사 that이 오는 것이 적절하다. what은 관계사로 뒤에 주어나 목적어가 없는 불완전한 문장이 와야 한다.

constant 지속적인
stream 흐름
traffic 차량, 교통(량)
irritated 짜증난
graciously 친절하게
ridiculous 어리석은
phrase 구절

---

float 떠오르다
punish 처벌하다
equally 똑같이, 동등하게

---

4. ④ 생산 결함의 세탁기 고장에 대해 무료 수리 기사 파견 요청

직독/직해

I hope you remember our discussion last Monday /
나는 당신이 지난 월요일에 있었던 우리의 논의를 기억하고 있기를 바랍니다.

about the servicing of the washing machine /
세탁기의 서비스에 대해 /

supplied to us three months ago.
3개월 전에 우리에게 공급된

I regret to say / that the machine is no longer working.
나는 ~을 말하게 되어 유감입니다 / 그 기계가 더 이상 작동하지 않는다는 사실을

As we agreed during the meeting, /
만났을 때 합의한 바와 같이 /

please send a service engineer
서비스 기사를 보내 주시기 바랍니다.

as soon as possible / to repair it.
가능한 한 빨리 / 그것을 수리할

The product warranty says /
제품 보증서에는 ~라고 되어 있습니다. /

that you provide spare parts and materials for free, /
귀사에서 여분의 부품과 재료들은 무료로 제공하지만, /

but charge for the engineer's labor. /
기사의 노동에 대해서는 비용을 부과한다고 /

This sounds unfair.
이것은 부당한 것 같습니다.

I believe / the machine's failure /
저는 믿습니다. / 기계의 고장이 /

is caused by a manufacturing defect.
생산 결함에 의해 발생한 것이라고

Initially, / it made a lot of noise, / and later, /
처음부터 / 그것은 많은 소음을 냈으며, / 나중에 /

it stopped operating entirely.
그것은 완전히 작동을 멈추었습니다.

As it is wholly the company's responsibility /
전적으로 회사의 책임이므로, /

to correct the defect, 결함을 고쳐 주는 것은

I hope / you will not make us pay /
나는 바랍니다. / 그 비용을 우리에게 지불하게 하지 마시기기를 /

for the labor component of its repair.
수리의 노동력 부분에 대해서도

- -

3개월 전에 우리에게 공급된 세탁기의 서비스에 대해 지난 월요일에 있었던 우리의 논의를 기억하고 있기를 바랍니다. 그 기계가 더 이상 작동하지 않는다는 사실을 말하게 되어 유감입니다. 만났을 때 합의한 바와 같이 가능한 한 빨리 그것을 수리할 서비스 기사를 보내 주시기 바랍니다. 제품 보증서에는 귀사에서 여분의 부품과 재료들은 무료로 제공하지만, 기사의 노동에 대해서는 비용을 부과한다고 되어 있습니다. 이것은 부당한 것 같습니다. 저는 기계의 고장이 생산 결함에 의해 발생한 것이라고 믿습니다. 처음부터 그것은 많은 소음을 냈으며, 나중에 그것은 완전히 작동을 멈추었습니다. 결함을 고쳐 주는 것은 전적으로 회사의 책임이므로, 수리의 노동력 부분에 대해서도 그 비용을 우리에게 지불하게 하지 마시기를 바랍니다.

문제풀이

① 수식을 받는 명사(the washing machine)가 분사가 나타내는 동작의 행위자로 해석되므로 과거분사 supplied는 적절하다.

② that은 동사 says의 목적어인 명사절을 이끄는 접속사이므로 적절하다.

③ sounds는 주어의 보충어를 필요로 하는 동사인데, 주어의 보충어는 형용사가 사용되므로 unfair는 적절하다.

④ 문맥상 '작동을 멈추다'의 의미가 되어야 하므로 to operate를 operating으로 바꾸어야 한다. stopped to operate는 '작동하기 위해 멈추다'로 해석된다.

⑤ make는 사역동사로 목적어의 보충어를 필요로

하는 동사이다. us가 pay의 행위자로 해석되므로 원형부정사를 목적어의 보충어로 사용한 것은 적절하다.

〔어휘·어구〕

servicing 수리, 정비
warranty 보증서, 담보
spare 여분의
manufacture 제조하다
defect 결함, 결점
entirely 완전히, 아주
wholly 전적으로, 완전히
component 부분, 구성 요소

---

5. ⑤ Albert Einstein의 과학자로서의 삶에 영향을 준 요인

직독/직해

Albert Einstein talked about /
Albert Einstein은 ~에 관한 이야기를 했다. /

what influenced his life / as a scientist.
무엇이 자신의 삶에 영향을 끼쳤는지 / 과학자로서의

He remembered / seeing a pocket compass /
그는 기억해 냈다 / 작은 나침반을 보고 /

when he was five years old / 다섯 살 때

and marveling / 놀랐던 일을

that the needle always pointed north.
나침반의 바늘이 항상 북쪽을 가리키는 것에

In that moment, / Einstein recalled, /
그 당시, / Einstein은 회상했다 /

he "felt something deeply hidden / behind things."
"깊이 숨겨진 무언가 대단한 것을 느꼈다"고 / 사물의 뒤에

Around the age of six, / 여섯 살 무렵. /

Einstein began studying the violin.
Einstein은 바이올린을 배우기 시작했다.

When after several years / 몇 년 후 /

he recognized the mathematical structure of music,/
음악의 수학적 구조를 인식했을 때, /

the violin became a lifelong friend of his.
바이올린은 그의 평생의 친구가 되었다.

When Einstein was ten, / Einstein이 열 살이 되었을 때/

his family enrolled him in the Luitpold Gymnasium, /
그의 가족은 그를 Luitpold 김나지움에 등록시켰고, /

where he developed a suspicion of authority.
그 곳에서 그는 권위에 대해 의심을 품는 법을 연마하였다.

The trait served Einstein well later /
그러한 특성은 Einstein에게 큰 도움이 되었다 /

in life as a scientist.
훗날 과학자로서의 삶을 사는데

His habit of skepticism / made it easy to question
그의 회의론적 인습관은 / 쉽게 의문을 제시할 수 있게 해주었다.

many long-standing scientific assumptions.
오랫동안 지속되어 온 여러 가지 과학적 가설에 대해

- -

Albert Einstein은 과학자로서의 자신의 삶에 영향을 끼친 것들에 관한 이야기를 했다. 그는 다섯 살 때 작은 나침반을 보고 나침반의 바늘이 항상 북쪽을 가리키는 것에 놀랐던 일을 기억해 냈다. Einstein은 그 당시, "사물의 뒤에 깊이 숨겨진 무언가 대단한 것을 느꼈다"고 회상했다. 여섯 살 무렵, Einstein은 바이올린을 배우기 시작했다. 몇년 후 음악의 수학적 구조를 인식했을 때, 바이올린은 그의 평생의 친구가 되었다. Einstein이 열 살이 되었을 때, 그의 가족은 그를 Luitpold 김나지움에 등록시켰고, 그 곳에서 그는 권위에 대해 의심을 품는 법을 연마하였다. 그러한 특성은 Einstein이 훗날 과학자로서의 삶을 사는데 큰 도움이 되었다. 그의 회의론적 인습관은 오랫동안 지속되어온 여러 가지 과학적 가설에 대해 쉽게 의문을 제시할 수 있게 해주었다.

문제풀이

(A)에는 seeing과 병렬 구조를 이루어야 하므로 marveling이 옳다.

(B)에는 앞의 Luitpold Gymnasium을 이어받는 관계부사가 와야 하므로 where가 옳다.

(C)는 가목적어, 진목적어 구문이므로 it이 옳다.

《어휘·어구》

influence 영향을 주다
needle 나침반
marvel 경탄하다
enroll 등록하다
assumption 가설

---

6. ④ 실생활의 맥락에서 수학을 가르치고자 하신 Brown 선생님

직독 직해

Mr. Brown wanted / his students to learn math /
Brown 선생님은 원했다 / 그의 학생들이 수학을 배우기를 /

in the context of real life.
실생활의 맥락에서

He felt / it was not enough for them /
그는 느꼈다 / 학생들에게 충분하지 않다고 느꼈다. /

just to work out problems from a book.
단지 책에서 나온 문제만 해결하는 것은

To show / his students /
보여주기 위해 / 그의 학생들에게 /

how math could really help them,
수학이 실제로 얼마나 그들을 도울 수 있는지를

he held several contests during the year.
그는 연중 몇 번의 대회를 개최했다.

The contests allowed his students to have fun /
그 대회는 학생들이 재미를 가지는 것을 가능하게 해 주었다. /

while they practiced math and raised money.
수학을 연습하고 돈을 마련하면서

Once he filled a fishbowl with marbles, /
한번은 그가 어항에 공깃돌을 채운 후에 /

asked the students to guess /
학생들에게 ~을 추측해 보라고 했다 /

how many marbles there were, /
얼마나 많은 공깃돌이 거기에 있는지를 /

and awarded a free lunch to the winner.
그리고 우승자에게는 공짜 점심을 상으로 주었다.

Another time / they entered a contest to guess /
또 언젠가는 / 추측해 보는 대회에 학생들은 참가했다. /

how many soda cans / 얼마나 많은 탄산음료 캔을 /

the back of a pickup truck held.
픽업트럭의 뒤 칸이 담을 수 있는지

To win, / they had to practice their skills /
이기기 위해서, / 그들은 그들의 기술을 연습해야만 했다. /

at estimating, multiplying, dividing, and measuring.
어림짐작하고, 곱하고, 나누고, 그리고 측정하는

They used most of the prize money /
그들은 상금으로 받은 돈의 대부분을 사용했다. /

for an end-of-the-year field trip.
연말의 현장 학습을 위해서

Brown 선생님은 그의 학생들이 실생활의 맥락에서 수학을 배우기를 원했다. 그는 학생들이 단지 책에서 나온 문제만 해결하는 것이 충분하지 않다고 느꼈다. 그의 학생들에게 수학이 실제로 얼마나 그들을 도울 수 있는지 보여주기 위해, 그는 연중 몇 번의 대회를 개최했다. 그 대회는 학생들이 수학을 연습하고 돈을 마련하면서 재미를 가지는 것을 가능하게 해 주었다. 한번은 어항에 공깃돌을 채운 후에 학생들에게 얼마나 많은 공깃돌이 거기에 있는 지 추측해 보라고 했고, 우승자에게는 공짜 점심을 상으로 주었다. 또 언젠가는 픽업트럭의 뒤 칸이 얼마나 많은 탄산음료 캔을 담을 수 있는지 추측해 보는 대회에 학생들은 참가했다. 이기기 위해서, 그들은 어림짐작하고, 곱하고, 나누고, 그리고 측정하는 그들의 기술을 연습해야만 했다. 그들은 상금으로 받은 돈의 대부분을 연말의 현장 학습을 위해서 사용했다.

문제풀이

① them은 앞부분의 to show his students에서 his students를 나타낸다.
② 「allow+목적어+목적격보어」 구문으로서 allow동사는 목적격보어에 to부정사를 가져온다.
③ Once he filled 〜, asked 〜 and awarded가 병렬 구조를 이루고 있다. once는 부사로 사용되면 '과거의 한 때(한번은)'의 의미가 있다. once가 접속사로 사용되면 'after(일단 〜하면)', 'as soon

---

as(〜하자마자)'를 의미를 가진다.
④가 포함된 문장에서 guess의 목적어로 사용된 간접의문문은 「의문사구+주어+동사」의 어순을 취하고 있는데, 주어인 the back of a pickup truck이 hold의 동작을 하는 주체이므로 was held는 능동형인 held로 바꿔야 한다.
⑤ most of 〜는 '대부분의 〜'의 의미를 가지고 있다.

《어휘·어구》

context 문맥, 맥락
work out 해결하다
fishbowl 어항
marble 공깃돌, 대리석
award 상을 주다
estimate 어림짐작하다, 산정하다
multiply 곱하다

---

7. ② 철학은 사고의 방법이며 정신적인 기술을 개발하는 데 도움을 준다.

직독 직해

Philosophy is, / simply put, / a way of thinking.
철학은 / 간단히 말하면 / 사고의 방법이다.

More accurately, / however, / it is a set of mental tools.
좀 더 정확하게 / 하지만, / 그것은 일련의 정신적인 도구들이다.

And that fact / is directly related to the question of /
그리고 그러한 사실은 / 〜의 문제와도 직접적으로 연결되어 있다. /

why we study philosophy.
왜 우리가 철학을 공부하는가

It's not / just to amaze our friends /
그것은 〜이 아닌데 / 단지 친구들을 놀라게 하거나 /

with our own profound thinking, /
우리들 자신의 심오한 생각으로 /

or confuse them with unexpected questions, /
또는 예기치 못한 질문으로 그들을 혼란하게 하는 것은

although some college students /
하지만 일부 대학생들은 /

may value that possibility the most /
그런 가능성을 중요하게 여길 수도 있다. /

in taking philosophy courses.
철학 과목을 수강할 때

We study philosophy / 우리는 철학을 공부한다. /

because of the mental skills it helps us develop.
철학이 정신적인 기술을 개발하는 데 도움을 주기 때문에

간단히 말하면 철학이란 사고의 방법이다. 하지만, 좀 더 정확하게 그것은 일련의 정신적인 도구들이다. 그리고 그러한 사실은 왜 우리가 철학을 공부하는가의 문제와도 직접적으로 연결되어 있다. 그것은 단지 우리들 자신의 심오한 생각으로 친구들을 놀라게 하거나 예기치 못한 질문으로 그들을 혼란하게 하는 것은 아닌데, 하지만 일부 대학생들은 철학 과목을 수강할 때 그런 가능성을 중요하게 여길 수도 있다. 우리는 철학이 정신적인 기술을 개발하는 데 도움을 주기 때문에 철학을 공부한다.

문제풀이

(A) 다음에 주어와 목적어가 있는 완전한 절이 이어지므로 의문대명사 what이 아니라 의문부사 why가 필요하다.
(B) 명사 questions의 앞이므로 형용사형인 unexpected가 알맞다.
(C) 접속사 because 뒤에는 「주어+동사」의 절이 오고, 전치사구 because of 뒤에는 명사(구)가 온다. 또한 because of the mental skills (which) it helps us develop 문장에서 타동사 develop의 목적어인 관계대명사 which가 생략되었다.

《어휘·어구》

philosophy 철학
simply put 간단히 표현하면

---

accurately 정확하게
mental 정신적인
tool 도구
amaze 〜을 놀라게 하다
profound 심오한
confuse 혼란시키다
possibility 가능성

---

8. ⑤ 다양함이 더 적은 음식에의 노출

직독 직해

The development of the 'package' holiday / in the
'패키지' 휴가의 발전은 / 1960년대와 1970년대의

1960s and 1970s / was actually one of the early drivers
/ 사실 음식 여행의 초기 동인이었다

of food tourism.

Prior to the advent of the overseas vacation, /
해외 휴가가 등장하기 전에 /

consumers were only exposed / to foods made
소비자들은 오직 노출되었다 / 일상에서 구할 수 있는 음식들에만

available in their daily life, / which came from the
/ 지역 슈퍼마켓과 식료품점에서 나온 것들

local supermarket and grocery store /

and occasionally, if they were lucky, / a local food
그리고 이따금 그들이 운이 좋다면 / 지역 식품 시장(에서 나온 것들인)

market.

Populations in many countries / were also less
많은 나라에서 주민들은 / 또한 덜 세계적이었고

cosmopolitan / than they are today /
/ 오늘날보다 /

and hence exposed to a smaller variety of foods /
그래서 다양함이 더 적은 음식에 노출되었다 /

in their lives. 그들의 삶에서

The retailers needed to provide produce / they could
소매업자들은 농산물을 공급해야 했다 / 그들이 빨리 팔 수 있는

sell quickly / as the shelf life of food, /
/ 식품의 유통 기한이 /

due to the lack of developed refrigeration, / was short.
발전된 냉동 보존 기술 부족으로 / 짧았기 때문에

As a result, / the food at the market / was considered
결과적으로 / 시장에 있는 음식은 / 안전한 것으로 여겨졌다

safe.

Exotic foods were rarely on offer /
외국 식품은 거의 제공되지 않았는데 /

as customers simply did not understand /
왜냐하면 고객들이 단지 이해하지 못했기 때문에 /

how to prepare or cook them / and often feared /
그것들을 준비하거나 요리하는 방법을 / 그리고 종종 두려워했기 때문에

what they would taste like. 그것들이 어떤 맛이 날지를

1960년대와 1970년대의 '패키지' 휴가의 발전은 사실 음식 여행의 초기 동인이었다. 해외 휴가가 등장하기 전에, 소비자들은 지역 슈퍼마켓과 식료품점에서 나온 것들, 이따금 운이 좋다면 지역 식품 시장에서 나온 것들인, 일상에서 구할 수 있는 음식에만 노출되었다. 많은 나라에서 주민들은 또한 오늘날보다 덜 세계적이었고, 그래서 그들의 삶에서 다양함이 더 적은 음식에 노출되었다. 소매업자들은 발전된 냉동 보존 기술 부족으로 식품의 유통 기한이 짧았기 때문에 그들이 빨리 팔 수 있는 농산물을 공급해야 했다. 결과적으로, 시장에 있는 음식은 안전한 것으로 여겨졌다. 외국 식품은 거의 제공되지 않았는데, 왜냐하면 고객들이 단지 그것들을 준비하거나 요리하는 방법을 이해하지 못했으며 종종 그것들이 어떤 맛이 날지를 두려워했기 때문이었다.

문제풀이

① which가 이끄는 절에서 동사인 came을 수식하는 부사로 쓰였으므로, occasionally는 적절하다.
② 대동사로서 주절의 be동사인 were에 상응해야 하고, today라는 말이 왔으므로 are는 적절하다. 뒤에 cosmopolitan이 생략되었다.
③ 뒤에 있는 명사 refrigeration을 수식해야 하고, 냉동 보존 기술은 '발전되는' 대상이므로 과거분사인 developed는 적절하다.

---

④ was considered의 보어가 필요하므로, 형용사 safe는 적절하다.
⑤ feared의 목적어로 쓰인 절에서 전치사 like의 목적어가 필요하므로, how는 what으로 고쳐야 한다.

구조 다시보기

도입	'패키지' 휴가의 발전은 음식 여행의 초기 동인임
전개	오늘날보다 덜 세계적이어서 다양함이 더 적은 음식에 노출됨
부연	냉동 보존 기술 부족으로 농산물을 빨리 공급해야 했음
결과	시장에 있는 음식은 안전한 것으로 여겨짐

어휘·어구

driver 동인, 추진 요인
advent 도래
cosmopolitan 세계적인
retailer 소매업자, 소매상인
produce 농산물
shelf life 유통 기한
refrigeration 냉동 보존
exotic 외국의, 이국적인

9. ② 전통적 양적 성장 개념의 변경 필요성

직독/직해

In poorer countries / many years of fast growth may be necessary /
가난한 나라에서는 / 수년 간의 빠른 성장이 필요할 수도 있다 /
to bring living standards up to acceptable levels.
생활 수준을 허용 가능한 수준으로 끌어올리기 위해
But growth is the means / to achieve desired goals, / not the end in itself.
그러나 성장은 수단이다 / 원하는 목표를 달성하기 위한 / 그 자체로 목적은 아니다
In the richer world / the whole idea of growth /
부유한 세계에서는 / 성장에 대한 개념 전체가
— at least as conventionally measured — / may need to be revised.
적어도 관습적으로 측정되는 것으로서의 / 개정될 필요가 있을지 모른다
In economies where services dominate, /
서비스가 지배하는 경제에서 /
goods and services / tailored to our individual needs /
재화와 서비스는 / 우리 개개인의 필요에 맞춘 /
will be what determine the advance of our societies.
우리 사회의 진보를 결정하는 것이 될 것이다
These could be anything / from genome-specific medicines /
이것들은 어느 것이든 될 수 있다 / 게놈 맞춤형 약에서부터 /
to personalized care or tailored suits.
개별화된 관리 또는 맞춤 정장에 이르기까지
That is different / from more and more stuff, / an arms race of growth.
그것은 다르다 / 점점 더 많은 물건과는 / 즉 무기의 확대 경쟁과는
Instead, / it means improvements in quality, /
그 대신에 / 그것은 질적인 향상을 의미한다 /
something that GDP is ill equipped to measure.
즉 GDP가 잘 측정하지 못하는 것을 (의미한다)
Some fifty years ago /
약 50년 전 /
one US economist contrasted / what he called the "cowboy" economy, /
미국의 한 경제학자는 대조했다 / 그가 '카우보이' 경제라고 칭한 것을 /
bent on production, exploitation of resources, and pollution, /
생산, 자원의 착취, 오염에 집중하는 /
with the "spaceman" economy, /
'우주인' 경제와 /
in which quality and complexity replaced "throughput" /
그곳에서는 품질과 복합성이 '처리량'을 대체하였다 /
as the measure of success.
성공의 척도로
The move from manufacturing to services and from analog to digital /
제조업에서 서비스업으로 그리고 아날로그에서 디지털로의 이동은 /
is the shift from cowboy to spaceman.
카우보이에서 우주인으로의 전환이다
But we are still measuring the size of the lasso.
하지만 우리는 여전히 올가미 밧줄의 크기를 측정하고 있다

가난한 나라에서는 생활 수준을 허용 가능한 수준으로 끌어올리기 위해 수년간의 빠른 성장이 필요할 수도 있다. 그러나 성장은 원하는 목표를 달성하기 위한 수단이지, 그 자체로 ① 목적은 아니다. 부유한 세계에서는 적어도 관습적으로 측정되는 것으로서의 성장에 대한 개념 전체가 ② 유지될(→ 개정될) 필요가 있을지 모른다. 서비스가 지배하는 경제에서 우리 ③ 개개인의 필요에 맞춘 재화와 서비스는 우리 사회의 진보를 결정하는 것이 될 것이다. 이것들은 게놈 맞춤형 약에서부터 개별화된 관리 또는 맞춤 정장에 이르기까지 어느 것이든 될 수 있다. 그것은 점점 더 많은 물건, 즉 무기의 확대 경쟁과는 다르다. 그 대신에, 그것은 ④ 질적인 향상, 즉 GDP가 잘 측정하지 못하는 것을 의미한다. 약 50년 전 미국의 한 경제학자는 생산, 자원의 착취, 오염에 집중하는, 그가 '카우보이' 경제라고 칭한 것과 성공의 척도로 품질과 복합성이 '처리량'을 대체하는 '우주인' 경제를 대조했다. 제조업에서 서비스업으로 그리고 아날로그에서 디지털로의 ⑤ 이동은 카우보이에서 우주인으로의 전환이다. 하지만 우리는 여전히 올가미 밧줄의 크기를 측정하고 있다.

문제풀이

성장은 목적이 아니라 수단에 불과하고, 서비스가 지배적인 경제에서 개인의 필요에 맞춰진 재화와 서비스가 우리 사회의 발전을 결정하게 되므로, 양적인 성장이 아니라 질적인 성장에 초점을 맞춰야 한다는 내용의 글이다. 따라서 전통적인 양적 측정을 중시하는 성장의 개념을 '유지할 필요가 있을 것이다'가 아니라 '변경할 필요가 있다'라고 하는 것이 문맥상 자연스러우므로 ②의 'maintained(유지하다)'를 'revised(개정하다)'등의 어휘로 고쳐야 한다.

이렇게 풀자 난이도 1위의 문제로 각각의 낱말의 쓰임이 적절한지 한 문장, 한 문장 살펴볼 필요가 있다. ①의 'end'는 앞에 'means(수단)'라는 대조적인 단어가 언급되어 있고, 'in itself(그 자체로)'라는 표현과 결합되어 '성장은 수단이지 그 자체로 목적은 아니다'라는 의미로 올바르게 사용되었다. ②의 'maintained(유지하다)'는 뒷부분을 마저 읽어봐야 문맥상 적절성 여부를 판단할 수 있다. ③의 'individual(개개인의)'은 'tailored(맞춘)'로 보아 문맥상 적절하게 쓰였다. ④의 'quality(질)'는 'GDP is ill equipped to measure(GDP가 잘 측정하지 못한다)'로 보아 양과 대조적인 개념으로 올바르게 사용되었다. ⑤의 'move(이동)'는 'the shift(전환)'로 보아 올바르게 사용되었다. 글 전체의 내용으로 보아 양보다는 질을 추구하는 것이 옳다는 내용이므로 양적 측정을 중시하는 성장 개념을 바꿀 필요가 있다가 되어야 한다는 것을 알 수 있다.

어휘·어구

acceptable 받아들일 만한
achieve 달성하다
in oneself 그 자체로
revise 개정하다
dominate 지배하다
goods 상품, 재화
tailor 맞추다, 조정하다
determine 결정하다
personalized 개별화된
suit 정장
stuff 물건
exploitation 착취
replace 대체하다
manufacture 제조업
shift 전환

10. ④ 자동차 수요 관리

직독/직해

In recent years / 최근 몇 년간 /
urban transport professionals globally have largely acquiesced to the view /
전 세계적으로 도시 교통 전문가들은 견해를 대체로 따랐다 /
that automobile demand in cities needs to be managed / rather than accommodated.
도시의 자동차 수요가 관리될 필요가 있다는 / 부응하기보다는
Rising incomes inevitably lead / to increases in motorization.
소득의 증가는 필연적으로 이어진다 / 자동차 보급의 증가로
Even without the imperative of climate change, /
기후 변화로 인한 불가피성이 없더라도 /
the physical constraints of densely inhabited cities /
인구 밀도가 높은 도시의 물리적 제약 /
and the corresponding demands of accessibility, mobility, safety, air pollution, and urban livability all /
그리고 그에 상응하는 접근성, 이동성, 안전, 대기 오염, 그리고 도시 거주 적합성에 대한 요구 모두가 /
limit the option of expanding road networks /
도로망을 확장하는 선택권을 제한한다 /
purely to accommodate this rising demand.
단지 이러한 증가하는 수요에 부응하기 위해
As a result, / as cities develop and their residents become more prosperous, /
그 결과 / 도시가 발전하고 도시의 거주자들이 더 부유해짐에 따라 /
persuading people to choose *not* to use cars /
사람들이 자동차를 사용하지 '않기로' 결정하도록 설득하는 것이 /
becomes an increasingly key focus of city managers and planners.
도시 관리자와 계획 설계자들의 핵심 중점 사항이 된다
Improving the quality of alternative options, /
대안적인 선택의 질을 향상하는 것이 /
such as walking, cycling, and public transport, /
걷기, 자전거 타기, 대중교통과 같은 /
is a central element of this strategy.
이 전략의 핵심 요소이다
However, / the most direct approach to managing automobile demand /
그러나 / 자동차 수요를 관리하는 가장 직접적인 접근 방법은 /
is making motorized travel more expensive /
자동차 여행을 더 비싸게 만드는 것이다 /
or restricting it with administrative rules.
또는 행정 규칙으로 그것을 제한하는 것이다
The contribution of motorized travel to climate change / reinforces this imperative.
자동차 여행이 기후 변화의 원인을 제공하는 것이 / 이런 불가피한 것을 강화한다

최근 몇 년간 전 세계적으로 도시 교통 전문가들은 도시의 자동차 수요에 부응하기보다는 관리될 필요가 있다는 견해를 대체로 따랐다. 소득의 증가는 필연적으로 자동차 보급의 증가로 이어진다. 기후 변화로 인한 불가피성이 없더라도, 인구 밀도가 높은 도시의 물리적 제약과 그에 상응하는 접근성, 이동성, 안전, 대기 오염, 그리고 도시 거주 적합성에 대한 요구 모두가 단지 이러한 증가하는 수요에 부응하기 위해 도로망을 확장하는 선택권을 ① 제한한다. 그 결과, 도시가 발전하고 도시의 거주자들이 더 부유해짐에 따라, 사람들이 자동차를 사용하지 '않기로' 결정하도록 ② 설득하는 것이 도시 관리자와 계획 설계자들의 핵심 중점 사항이 된다. 걷기, 자전거 타기, 대중교통과 같은 ③ 대안적인 선택의 질을 향상하는 것이 이 전략의 핵심 요소이다. 그러나 자동차 수요에 ④ 부응하는(→ (를) 관리하는) 가장 직접적인 접근 방법은 자동차 여행을 더 비싸게 만들거나 행정 규칙으로 그것을 제한하는 것이다. 자동차 여행이 기후 변화의 원인을 제공하는 것이 이런 불가피한 것을 ⑤ 강화한다.

문제풀이

최근 도시 교통 전문가들이 도시의 자동차 수요에 부응하기보다는 관리해야 한다는 견해를 따랐고, 사람들이 자동차를 사용하지 않도록 설득하는 것

이 도시 관리자들과 도시 계획 설계자들의 핵심 중점 사항이 되었다고 했으므로, 자동차 여행을 더 비싸게 만들거나 행정 규칙으로 제한하는 것은 자동차 수요를 관리하는 방법이라고 하는 것이 자연스럽다. 따라서 ④ 'accommodating(부응하는)'은 'managing(관리하는)'과 같은 단어로 고쳐 써야 한다.

《 어휘·어구 》

urban 도시의
globally 전세계적으로
demand 수요, 요구
accommodate (요구 등에) 부응하다, 맞추다
income 수입
inevitably 불가피하게
motorization 자동차 보급, 전동화
densely inhabited 인구 밀도가 높은
corresponding 상응하는
accessibility 접근성, 접근
mobility 이동성
livability 거주 적합성, 살기 좋음
expand 확장하다
purely 단지, 다만
prosperous 번영하는
alternative 대안적인, 대체의
restrict 제한하다
administrative 행정의
reinforce 강화하다

---

11. ③   고객 점유율을 높이기

직독/직해

One of the most productive strategies / to build customer relationships /
가장 생산적인 전략들 중 하나는 / 고객과의 관계를 구축하기 위한 /

is to increase the firm's share of customer / rather than its market share.
회사의 고객 점유율을 높이는 것이다 / 그것의 시장 점유율보다 /

This strategy involves / abandoning the old notions of /
이러한 전략은 포함한다 / 오래된 인식을 버리는 것을 /

acquiring new customers and increasing transactions /
신규 고객들을 확보해서 거래를 늘린다는 /

to focus instead on / more fully serving the needs of existing customers.
대신에 ~것에 집중하기 위해서 / 기존 고객들의 요구를 더 완벽히 충족시키는 /

Financial services are a great example of this.
금융 서비스들이 이것의 좋은 예시이다 /

Most consumers purchase financial services / from different firms.
대부분의 소비자들은 금융 서비스를 구입한다 / 다른 회사들로부터 /

They bank at one institution, / purchase insurance from another, /
그들은 한 기관과 은행 거래를 하고 / 또 다른 기관으로부터 보험을 구매하며 /

and handle their investments elsewhere.
그리고 다른 곳에서 자신들의 투자금을 처리한다 /

To counter this purchasing pattern, /
이런 구매 패턴을 대항하기 위해서 /

many companies now offer all of these services / under one roof.
많은 회사들은 현재 이 모든 서비스를 제공한다 / 한곳에서 /

For example, / Regions Financial Corporation offers /
예를 들면 / Regions Financial Corporation은 제공한다 /

retail and commercial banking, trust, mortgage, and insurance products /
소매 및 상업 은행업, 신탁, 담보 대출, 그리고 보험 상품을 /

to customers / in a network of more than 1,500

---

offices.
고객들에게 / 1,500개가 넘는 지사의 네트워크에서

The company tries to more fully serve /
그 회사는 (~를) 더 완벽히 만족시키려고 노력하며 /

the financial needs of its current customers, /
그것의 현재 고객들의 금융적 요구를 /

thereby acquiring a larger share of each customer's financial business.
그것에 의해 각 고객의 금융 거래에서 더 큰 점유율을 획득한다

By creating these types of relationships, /
이런 유형의 관계를 형성함으로써 /

customers have little incentive / to seek out competitive firms /
고객들은 동기를 거의 갖지 않는다 / 경쟁 회사를 찾을 /

to fulfill their financial services needs.
자신들의 금융 서비스 요구를 충족시키기 위해

고객과의 관계를 구축하기 위한 가장 생산적인 전략 중 하나는 회사의 시장 점유율보다 그것의 고객 점유율을 높이는 것이다. 이러한 전략은 대신에 기존 고객들의 요구를 더 완벽히 충족시키는 것에 집중하기 위해 신규 고객들을 ① 확보해서 거래를 늘린다는 오래된 인식을 버리는 것을 포함한다. 금융 서비스들이 이것의 좋은 예시이다. 대부분의 소비자들은 ② 다른 회사들로부터 금융 서비스를 구입한다. 그들은 한 기관과 은행 거래를 하고, 또 다른 기관으로부터 보험을 구매하며 다른 곳에서 자신의 투자금을 처리한다. 이런 구매 패턴을 ③ 확고하게 하기(→ 대항하기) 위해서 많은 회사들은 현재 이 모든 서비스를 한곳에서 제공한다. 예를 들면, Regions Financial Corporation은 1,500개가 넘는 지사의 네트워크에서 고객들에게 소매 및 상업 은행업, 신탁, 담보 대출, 그리고 보험 상품을 제공한다. 그 회사는 그것의 ④ 현재 고객들의 금융적 요구를 더 완벽히 만족시키려고 노력하며, 그것에 의해 각 고객의 금융거래에서 더 큰 점유율을 획득한다. 이런 유형의 관계를 형성함으로써 고객들은 자신들의 금융 서비스 요구를 충족시키기 위해 경쟁 회사를 찾을 동기를 ⑤ 거의 갖지 않는다.

문제풀이

소비자들이 각기 다른 기관에서 은행 거래를 하고 보험을 구매하고 투자금을 처리하는 패턴에 대항하기 위해 많은 회사들이 이 모든 서비스를 한곳에서 제공하고 있다는 것이 자연스러우므로, ③ 'solidify(확고하게 하다)'를 'counter(대항하다)'와 같은 단어로 바꿔 써야 한다.

👑 구조 다시보기

도입	고객과의 관계 구축에 있어 가장 생산적인 전략은 고객 점유율을 높이는 것임.
부연	기존 고객들의 요구를 더 완벽히 충족시키는 것에 집중하기 위한 것임.
예시	각기 다른 곳에서 다른 금융 상품을 처리하는 것에 대항하여 모든 서비스를 한곳에서 제공함.
사례	Regions Financial Corporation은 1,500개가 넘는 지사의 네트워크에서 고객들에게 다양한 상품을 제공하여 각 고객의 금융 거래에서 더 큰 점유율을 획득함.

《 어휘·어구 》

productive 생산적인
strategy 전략
involve 수반하다
acquire 얻다
transaction 거래
financial 금융의
institution 기관
insurance 보험
handle 처리하다, 다루다
investment 투자, 투자금
solidify 확고하게 하다
corporation 기업, 법인
retail 소매(小賣)
commercial 상업의, 상업적인
mortgage 대출, 융자
incentive 동기, 장려책
fulfill 다하다, 이행하다

---

12. ⑤   전쟁의 역사

직독/직해

Archaeologists and historians have found /
고고학자들과 역사학자들은 발견해 왔다 /

quite a bit of evidence of group-on-group conflict / during the last 10,000 years.
집단과 집단 간 갈등의 증거를 꽤 많이 / 지난 10,000년 동안

The conflicts took many forms / and occurred in many different places, /
그 갈등은 많은 형태를 취했다 / 그리고 많은 서로 다른 장소에서 발생했다 /

but scholars have noted common features / in the behavior of combatants, /
하지만 학자들은 공통적인 특징들에 주목해 왔다 / 전투원들의 행동에서 /

and we still observe them in people today.
그리고 우리는 오늘날 여전히 사람들 안에서 그것들을 관찰한다

The observations gave support to / the apemen competing in the savanna stories /
그 관찰들은 뒷받침해 주었다 / 사바나 역사에서 원인(猿人)들이 경쟁하는 것을 /

and the idea that it might be in the "nature" of humans / to fight for territory /
그리고 인간의 '본성'에 있을지도 모른다는 생각을 / 영토를 위해 싸우고 /

and hate those who are different.
그리고 서로 다른 사람들을 증오하는 것이

They suggested /
그것들은 시사했다 /

that warlike behavior might be somehow programmed into our genes /
전투적인 행동이 어떻게든 우리의 유전자에 프로그램화 될 수도 있다는 것을 /

and generated automatically / by our human brain.
그리고 자동으로 생성될 수도 있다는 것을 / 우리 인간의 뇌에 의해

If this were the case, /
이것이 사실이라면 /

the peaceful coexistence of different human groups / would be impossible.
서로 다른 인간 집단의 평화로운 공존은 / 불가능할 것이다

A deeper view of history / gives peacekeepers and diplomats more reason to hope.
역사에 대한 더 깊은 관점은 / 평화 유지군들과 외교관들에게 기대할 더 많은 이유를 준다

Far from being part of our ancient biology, /
우리 고대 생물학의 한 부분이기는커녕 /

going to war / seems to have begun rather recently / in our evolutionary history.
전쟁을 하는 것은 / 보다 최근에 시작된 것으로 보인다 / 우리 진화의 역사에서

The archaeological evidence suggests / that warfare was rare /
고고학적 증거는 시사한다 / 전쟁이 드물었다는 것을 /

before about 8,000 years ago.
약 8,000년 전에는

고고학자들과 역사학자들은 지난 10,000년 동안 집단과 집단 간 갈등의 증거를 꽤 많이 발견해 왔다. 그 갈등은 많은 형태를 취했고 많은 서로 다른 장소에서 발생했지만, 학자들은 전투원들의 행동에서 공통적인 특징들에 ① 주목해 왔고, 우리는 오늘날 여전히 사람들 안에서 그것들을 관찰한다. 그 관찰들은 사바나 역사에서 원인(猿人)들이 경쟁하는 것과, 영토를 위해 싸우고 서로 다른 사람들을 증오하는 것이 인간의 '본성'에 있을지도 모른다는 생각을 ② 뒷받침해 주었다. 그것들(관찰들)은 전투적인 행동이 어떻게든 우리의 유전자에 프로그램화되어 우리 인간의 뇌에 의해 ③ 자동으로 생성될 수도 있다는 것을 시사했다. 이것이 사실이라면, 서로 다른 인간 집단의 평화로운 공존은 ④ 불가능할 것이다. 역사에 대한 더 깊은 관점은 평화 유지군들과 외교관들에게 기대할 더 많은 이유를 준다. 전쟁을 하는 것은 우리 고대 생물학의 한 부분이기는커녕, 우리 진화의 역사에서 보다 최근에 시작된 것으로 보인다. 고고학적 증거는 약 8,000년 전에는 전쟁이 ⑤ 흔했다(→ 드물었다)는 것을 시사한다.

문제풀이

전쟁을 하는 것이 고대 생물학의 한 부분이 아니라 우리 진화의 역사에서 보다 최근에 시작된 것으로 보인다고 했으므로, 고고학적 증거는 약 8,000년 이전에는 전쟁이 드물었다고 하는 것이 자연스럽다. 따라서 ⑤ 'common(흔한)'을 'rare(드문)'과 같은 낱말로 고쳐 써야 한다.

《 어휘·어구 》

archaeologist 고고학자
conflict 충돌, 갈등
scholar 학자
feature 특징
territory 영토
generate 발생시키다, 만들어 내다
coexistence 공존
diplomat 외교관
far from ~이기는[하기는]커녕
biology 생물학
warfare 전쟁, 전투

03. 보어의 이해

A 출제 POINT
본문 014쪽

1. singer
2. sweet
3. hidden
4. drinking
5. cleaned
6. to stay
7. whether

1 [해석]▶ Bill은 매우 유명한 가수였다.
[해설]▶ 명사는 주격보어 역할을 할 수 있다.

2 [해석]▶ 책상 위의 라일락 꽃 냄새가 향기롭다.
[해설]▶ 2형식 문장으로서 동사 smell이 보어를 가져오는 경우 부사가 아닌 형용사 형태를 취해야 한다.

3 [해석]▶ 나는 그녀가 영원히 그 비밀을 숨겨둘 것으로 확신한다.
[해설]▶ keep 동사의 목적어(the secret)와 목적격보어 (hidden)의 관계가 수동 관계일 때는 목적격보어를 과거분사로 써야 한다.

4 [해석]▶ 우리는 사람들이 초콜릿을 곁들인 커피를 마시는 것을 보았다.
[해설]▶ 지각동사 다음에 목적어와 목적격보어의 관계가 능동인 경우 목적격보어는 동사원형 또는 진행형을 사용한다.

5 [해석]▶ 그는 상자를 정돈했다.
[해설]▶ 사역동사 get 다음에 목적어와 목적격보어가 능동 관계인 경우 to부정사를 사용하고, 수동 관계인 경우 과거분사를 사용한다.

6 [해석]▶ 오늘날 많은 국가들이 비자 없이 외국인이 머무르는 것을 허락하지 않는다.
[해설]▶ 「allow+목적어+목적격보어」 구조로서, 동사 allow는 목적격보어를 가져오는 경우, to부정사 형태를 취한다.

7 [해석]▶ 요점은 이것이 사실인지 아닌지 하는 점이다.
[해설]▶ 주격보어는 절이 나올 수 있는데 괄호 이하에서 or not이 있으므로 whether가 적절하다.

B 체크 POINT
본문 014쪽

1. connected
2. bad
3. thirsty
4. flashing
5. improve
6. to get
7. that

1 [해석]▶ 종종 많은 사람들이 사회안전망과 연결되었다고 느끼지 않는다.
[해설]▶ 2형식 동사 뒤에 형용사(과거분사)가 나와야 한다.

2 [해석]▶ 이 우유는 상한 맛이 난다.
[해설]▶ 2형식 동사 smell 뒤에 형용사가 나와야 한다.

3 [해석]▶ 콜라 한 캔이 나를 한층 더 목마르게 했다.
[해설]▶ 2형식이나 5형식 문장에서 보어는 부사가 아닌 형용사가 나온다.

4 [해석]▶ 나는 아름다운 미소가 그녀의 얼굴에 스치는 것을 보았다.

[해설]▶ 지각동사 watch는 5형식을 이끈다. 이 경우, 목적어와 목적격보어가 능동 관계인 경우 동사원형이나 현재분사를 사용한다.

5 [해석]▶ 문법책은 우리가 영어 문법에 대한 이해를 향상시키는 것을 돕는다.
[해설]▶ 준사역동사(help)의 목적어와 목적격보어가 능동 관계인 경우 목적격보어는 동사원형이나 to부정사가 나온다.

6 [해석]▶ 최신 기술은 언제든지 우리가 인터넷에 접근하는 것을 가능하게 했다.
[해설]▶ allow 동사는 목적격보어로 to부정사가 나온다.

7 [해석]▶ 그 잔치에서 가장 불쾌한 부분은 음식이 충분하지 않다는 것이다.
[해설]▶ '~하는 것'으로 what, that 둘 다 가능하지만 괄호 이하의 문장이 완전하므로 접속사 that이 필요하다.

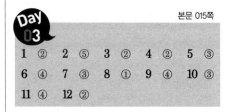
본문 015쪽

1 ②	2 ⑤	3 ②	4 ②	5 ③
6 ④	7 ③	8 ①	9 ④	10 ③
11 ④	12 ②			

1. ②
국가 통제주의와 자본주의에서의 독점 문제

직독 직해

The actual problems with monopolies / are caused by statism, / not capitalism.
독점의 실제 문제들은 / 국가 통제주의에 의해 발생된다 / 자본주의가 아니라

Under a statist social system, / taxes, subsidies, tariffs, and regulations /
국가 통제주의 사회 체제하에서 / 세금, 보조금, 관세와 규제가 /

often serve to protect existing large players / in the marketplace.
흔히 기존의 대기업들을 보호하는 역할을 한다 / 시장에서

Those players often use crony tactics / to retain or expand the protections:
그런 기업들은 정실 전략을 흔히 사용한다 / (~와 같은) 보호책들을 유지하거나 확대하기 위해 /

a new tariff preventing foreign competition, /
외국과의 경쟁을 막는 새로운 관세 /

a subsidy making it harder / for new players to compete with them, /
더 어렵게 만드는 보조금 / 신규 기업들이 그들과 경쟁하는 것을 /

or a regulatory measure / that a large company has the resources / to comply with.
혹은 규제 조치와 같은 / 대기업이 자산을 가지고 있어 / 준수할 수 있는

Under a capitalist social system, / on the other hand, /
자본주의 사회 체제하에서는 / 반면에 /

the government has no say / in how dominant a company may become / in its industry /
정부는 발언권이 없다 / 기업이 얼마나 우위를 점하게 될지 / 그것의 산업에서 /

or how companies take over and merge / with one another.
혹은 어떻게 기업들이 인수하고 합병하는지에 관해 / 서로

Furthermore, a capitalist society doesn't have /
뿐만 아니라 / 자본주의 사회는 가지고 있지 않다 /

rights-violating taxes, tariffs, subsidies, / or regulations favoring anybody /
권리를 침해하는 세금, 관세, 보조금, / 또는 누군가에게 유리한 규제를 /

nor does it have antitrust laws.
그것은 독점 금지법도 가지고 있지 않다

Under capitalism, / dominance can only be achieved /
자본주의하에서 / 우위는 오직 얻어질 수 있다 /

by becoming really good at / what you're doing.
정말 잘하게 됨으로써 / 당신이 하고 있는 것을

Column 1

정말 능숙해짐으로써 　　　　／ 여러분이 하고 있는 것에

And to maintain dominance, /
그리고 우위를 유지하기 위해서 /

you have to continue to stay ahead of the competition, /
여러분은 계속해서 경쟁자를 앞서 있어야 하고 /

which sees your dominance and profits /
이는 여러분의 우위와 이익을 여긴다 /

as a sign that there is money / to be made by others as well.
또한 돈이 있다는 신호로 (여긴다)　／ 다른 사람들이 벌 수 있는

독점의 실제 문제들은 자본주의가 아니라 국가 통제주의에 의해 발생된다. 국가 통제주의 사회 체제하에서 세금, 보조금, 관세와 규제가 흔히 시장에서 기존의 대기업들을 보호하는 역할을 한다. 그런 기업들은 외국과의 경쟁을 막는 새로운 관세, 신규 기업들이 그들과 경쟁하는 것을 더 어렵게 만드는 보조금, 혹은 대기업이 자산을 가지고 있어 준수할 수 있는 규제 조치와 같은 보호책들을 유지하거나 확대하기 위해 정실 전략을 흔히 사용한다. 반면에 자본주의 사회 체제하에서는 정부가 기업이 그것의 산업에서 얼마나 우위를 점하게 될지, 혹은 어떻게 기업들이 서로 인수하고 합병하는지에 관해 발언권이 없다. 뿐만 아니라 자본주의 사회는 권리를 침해하는 세금, 관세, 보조금 또는 누군가에게 유리한 규제를 가지고 있지 않고 그것은 독점 금지법도 가지고 있지 않다. 자본주의하에서 우위는 여러분이 하고 있는 것에 정말 능숙해짐으로써 오직 얻어질 수 있다. 그리고 우위를 유지하기 위해서 여러분은 계속해서 경쟁자를 앞서 있어야 하고, 이는 여러분의 우위와 이익을 또한 다른 사람들이 벌 수 있는 돈이 있다는 신호로 여긴다.

문제풀이

① [to부정사]
앞에 가목적어 it이 나왔으므로, 진목적어로 쓰인 to부정사 to compete가 온 것은 적절하다.

② [형용사 vs. 부사]
의문사 how 다음에는 become의 보어 역할을 하는 형용사가 와야 하므로, dominantly를 dominant로 고쳐야 한다.

③ [현재분사 vs. 과거분사]
regulations를 수식하는 분사가 와야 하는데 '유리한'이라는 능동의 의미이므로, 현재분사 favoring이 온 것은 적절하다.

④ [관계대명사 what]
뒤에 목적어가 빠진 불완전한 절이 왔고 앞에 선행사가 없으므로, 선행사를 포함한 관계대명사 what이 온 것은 적절하다.

⑤ [접속사 that]
뒤에 모든 문장 성분을 갖춘 완전한 절이 왔고 앞의 명사 a sign과 동격인 명사절을 이끄는 접속사가 와야 하므로, that이 온 것은 적절하다.

○ **이렇게 풀자** 어법상 틀린 부분을 찾는 문제는 밑줄이 있는 부분의 형태와 문맥을 보고 어법에 맞게 쓰였는지 확인해야 한다.
① to부정사에 밑줄이 그어진 경우, 문장에서 어떤 역할을 하는지 파악해야 한다.
② 부사에 밑줄이 있는 경우, 형용사가 와야 하는 자리가 아닌지 확인해야 한다. 부사는 동사의 앞이나 뒤에서 동사를 수식하거나 문장의 앞뒤에서 문장 전체를 수식할 수 있으며, 또한 형용사나 다른 부사를 수식할 수 있다. 형용사는 명사를 수식하거나 문장의 보어로 쓰일 수 있다.
③ 분사가 명사를 수식할 경우, 수동의 의미일 경우 과거분사가 오고 능동의 의미일 경우 현재분사가 온다.
④ 관계대명사 what 뒤에는 주어나 목적어가 빠진 불완전한 문장이 와야 하고 앞에 선행사가 없어야 하므로, what에 밑줄이 있는 경우 뒤에 온 문장이 성분을 모두 갖추고 있는지와 앞에 명사가 있는지 확인해야 한다.
⑤ that은 주어, 목적어, 보어 역할을 하는 명사절을 이끄는 접속사로 쓰일 수 있고, 동격의 명사절을 이끌기도 한다. that에 밑줄이 그어져 있을 경우, 명사절을 이끄는 접속사로 쓰인 것이 아닌지 판단하려면 뒤에 모든 문장 성분을 갖춘 완전한 절이 왔는지를 확인해야 한다.

《 어휘·어구 》

monopoly 독점

Column 2

capitalism 자본주의
subsidy 보조금, 장려금
tariff 관세
regulation 규제
tactic 전략, 전술
retain 유지하다
expand 확대되다
regulatory 규제력을 지닌
comply 따르다
dominantly 지배적으로, 우세하게
take over 인수하다
merge 합병하다
violate 위반하다, 침해하다
dominance 우위
achieve 성취하다, 얻다
maintain 유지하다
profit 이익

---

2. ⑤ 　　　　　　뉴스에 대한 선택적 노출

직독/직해

The idea / 생각이

that people selectively expose themselves to news content /
사람들이 선택적으로 뉴스 콘텐츠에 자신을 노출시킨다는 /

has been around for a long time, /
오랫동안 있어 왔다 /

but it is even more important today /
그러나 그것은 오늘날 훨씬 더 중요하다 /

with the fragmentation of audiences and the proliferation of choices.
구독자의 분열과 선택의 급증으로

Selective exposure is a psychological concept /
선택적 노출은 심리학적 개념이다 /

that says people seek out information /
사람들이 정보를 찾으려 한다고 말하는 /

that conforms to their existing belief systems /
자신의 기존 신념 체계에 부합하는 /

and avoid information 그리고 정보를 피하는 /

that challenges those beliefs.
그러한 신념에 도전하는

In the past / 과거에는 /

when there were few sources of news, /
뉴스의 공급처가 얼마 없었던 /

people could either expose themselves to mainstream news /
사람들이 주류 뉴스에 자신을 노출시키거나 /

— where they would likely see beliefs expressed counter to their own /
그들 자신의 신념과 상반되게 표현된 신념을 보게 될 수도 있는 /

— or they could avoid news altogether.
또는 뉴스를 전적으로 피할 수 있었다

Now with so many types of news constantly available /
이제 아주 많은 종류의 뉴스들이 끊임없이 이용 가능해지면서 /

to a full range of niche audiences, /
매우 다양한 틈새 구독자들에게

people can easily find a source of news /
사람들은 뉴스의 공급처를 쉽게 찾을 수 있다 /

that consistently confirms their own personal set of beliefs.
자신의 개인적 신념들을 지속적으로 확인해주는

This leads to the possibility of creating many different small groups of people /
이것은 많은 다양한 사람들의 소집단을 만들 수 있는 가능성으로 이어진다 /

with each strongly believing /
각자가 강하게 믿는 /

they are correct and everyone else is wrong /
자신들이 옳고 다른 모든 사람들이 틀리다고 /

about how the world works.
세상이 어떻게 돌아가는지에 대해

Column 3

사람들이 선택적으로 뉴스 콘텐츠에 자신을 노출시킨다는 생각이 오랫동안 있어 왔지만, 구독자의 분열과 선택의 급증으로 그것은 오늘날 훨씬 더 중요하다. 선택적 노출은 사람들이 자신의 기존 신념 체계에 부합하는 정보를 찾으려 하고 그러한 신념에 도전하는 정보를 피한다는 심리학적 개념이다. 뉴스의 공급처가 얼마 없었던 과거에는, 사람들이 그들 자신의 신념과 상반되게 표현된 신념을 보게 될 수도 있는 주류 뉴스에 자신을 노출시키거나 뉴스를 전적으로 피할 수 있었다. 아주 많은 종류의 뉴스들이 매우 다양한 틈새 구독자들에게 끊임없이 이용 가능해지면서 사람들은 자신의 개인적 신념들을 지속적으로 확인해주는 뉴스의 공급처를 쉽게 찾을 수 있다. 이것은 각자가 세상이 어떻게 돌아가는지에 대해 자신들이 옳고 다른 모든 사람들이 틀리다고 강하게 믿는 사람들의 많은 다양한 소집단을 만들 수 있는 가능성으로 이어진다.

문제풀이

① [형용사 vs 부사]
selectively는 동사 expose를 수식하는 부사로 올바르게 사용되었다.

② [병렬구조]
avoid는 문맥상 people을 주어로 갖는 앞의 동사 seek과 병렬을 이룬 것이므로 올바르게 사용되었다.

③ [과거분사]
expressed는 앞의 명사 beliefs를 수식하는 과거분사이고 beliefs와 의미상 수동의 관계이므로 과거분사를 사용한 것은 올바른 용법이다. counter는 '반대로'의 뜻을 갖는 부사이다.

④ [관계대명사]
that은 'a source of news'를 선행사로 하고 동사 confirms의 주어 역할을 하는 주격 관계대명사로 올바르게 사용되었다.

⑤ [정동사 vs 준동사]
전치사 with 뒤에는 정동사가 올 수 없다. 'with + 목적어+분사'의 구문이 되어야 한다. 따라서 정동사 believes를 현재분사 believing으로 고쳐야 한다.

《 어휘·어구 》

selectively 선택적으로
expose oneself to ~에 자신을 노출하다
seek out (노력해서) ~을 찾아내다
conform to ~에 부합하다
mainstream 주류의
counter to ~에 반대로
altogether 전부
constantly 지속적으로
a full range of 폭넓은, 다양한
consistently 지속적으로
confirm 확정하다, 확인하다

---

3. ② 　　거울 뉴런이라 불리는 특별한 신경 세포
　　　　　그룹에 의해 공감이 가능해진다.

직독/직해

Empathy is made possible / 공감은 가능해진다. /
by a special group of nerve cells /
특별한 신경세포 그룹에 의해 /
called mirror neurons. 거울 뉴런이라 불리는
These special cells /
이러한 특별한 세포들은 /
enable us to "mirror" emotions.
우리가 감정을 '반영'할 수 있도록 해준다.
Mirror neurons were first discovered /
거울 뉴런은 처음 발견되었는데. /
by Italian scientists who, / 이탈리아 과학자들에 의해
while looking at the activity of individual nerve cells /
그들은 개별 신경 세포의 활동을 보면서, /
inside the brains of monkeys, / noticed /
원숭이 뇌 속의　　　　　　／ 알아차렸다. /
that neurons in the same area of the brain /
뇌의 똑같은 부분의 뉴런이 /

were activated / 활성화된다는 것을/

whether the animals were performing a particular movement /
그 동물들이 특정한 행동을 하든지

or simply observing / 또는 단지 관찰하든지 간에 /

another monkey perform the same action.
다른 원숭이가 똑같은 행동을 하는 것을

It appeared / 그것은 보였다 /

as though the cells in the observer's brain /
마치 관찰자의 뇌 세포들이

"mirrored" the activity in the performer's brain.
행위자의 뇌의 행동을 '반영'하는 것처럼

A similar phenomenon takes place /
비슷한 현상이 발생한다.

when we watch someone experiencing an emotion /
우리가 어떤 사람이 감정을 겪는 것을 보고 /

and feel the same emotion in response.
그에 반응해서 똑같은 감정을 느낄 때

The same neural systems / get activated /
똑같은 신경 조직이 / 활성화된다.

in a part of the insula, /
뇌도의 한 영역과

which is part of the mirror neuron system,
그것은 거울 뉴런 조직의 한 부분인 /

and in the emotional brain areas / associated with the observed emotion.
감정의 뇌 영역에서 / 관찰된 감정과 관련이 있는

공감은 거울 뉴런이라 불리는 특별한 신경세포 그룹에 의해 가능해진다. 이러한 특별한 세포들은 우리가 감정을 "반영"할 수 있도록 해준다. 거울 뉴런은 이탈리아 과학자들에 의해 처음 발견되었는데, 그들은 원숭이 뇌 속의 개별 신경 세포의 활동을 보면서, 그 동물들이 특정한 행동을 하든지 또는 단지 다른 원숭이가 똑같은 행동을 하는 것을 관찰하든지 간에 뇌의 똑같은 부분의 뉴런이 활성화된다는 것을 알아차렸다. 그것은 마치 관찰자의 뇌세포들이 행위자의 뇌의 행동을"반영"하는 것처럼 보였다. 우리가 어떤 사람이 감정을 겪는 것을 보고 그에 반응해서 똑같은 감정을 느낄 때 비슷한 현상이 발생한다. 똑같은 신경 조직이 거울 뉴런 조직의 한 부분인 뇌도의 한 영역과 관찰된 감정과 관련이 있는 감정 뇌 영역에서 활성화된다.

문제풀이

(A) who 이하의 관계절에서 동사가 와야 하는 위치이므로 noticed가 어법상 적절하다. (B) 지각동사 watch의 목적보어로 능동의 의미를 지닌 현재분사 experiencing이 적절하다. (C) 주격관계대명사인 which가 와야 어법상 적절하다. 따라서 어법에 맞는 표현으로 가장 적절한 것은 ②이다.

어휘·어구

empathy 공감
nerve 신경
emotion 감정
activate 활성화시키다
discover 발견하다
particular 특별한
perform 실행하다
insula 뇌도

4. ② 고속도로 소음 민원 해결책으로 나무를 심자 사람들의 불평이 감소함

직독/직해

We do not hear with our eyes, /
눈으로 소리를 듣는 것은 아니지만, /

but sometimes it almost seems as if we do.
가끔은 마치 거의 그러는 것처럼 보인다.

An environment-agency official /
어느 환경청 공무원이 /

tells a surprising incident about some people
사람들에 관한 놀라운 사건을 이야기해 준다. /

who lived in an apartment building /
아파트에 살았던 /

close to a busy state highway.
번잡한 주(州)고속도로 근처의

The families were made miserable by the noise, /
그 가족들은 소음 때문에 괴로워서 /

and they complained to the city government.
시청에 항의를 했다.

City officials went to the state capital /
시 공무원들은 주의회에 갔다. /

again and again to ask / 여러 차례 ~을 요구하기 위해 /

that something be done / 어떤 조치를 취해 줄 것을 /

about quieting the highway noise.
고속도로의 소음을 줄이는 일에 관해

They were put off repeatedly. /
그들은 계속 발뺌을 당했다. /

At last / the city officials had an idea.
마침내 / 시 공무원들은 좋은 수를 생각해냈다.

They planted a single row of trees /
그들은 한 줄로 나무를 심었다. /

in front of the apartment house.
아파트 앞에

The trees made hardly any difference /
그 나무들이 거의 영향을 주지는 못했지만, /

in the amount of noise, /
소음의 양에는 /

but they did block the view of the highway.
고속도로의 모습이 보이지 않게 했다. /

After that, / there were very few complaints /
그 이후로, / 불평이 거의 나오지 않았다. /

from the people in the building.
건물에 사는 사람들에게서

눈으로 소리를 듣는 것은 아니지만, 가끔은 마치 거의 그러는 것처럼 보인다. 어느 환경청 공무원이 번잡한 주(州)고속도로 근처의 아파트에 살았던 사람들에 관한 놀라운 사건을 이야기해 준다. 그 가족들은 소음때문에 괴로워서 시청에 항의를 했다. 시 공무원들은 고속도로의 소음을 줄이는 일에 관해 어떤 조치를 취해 줄 것을 요구하기 위하여 여러 차례 주의회에 갔다. 그들은 계속 발뺌을 당했다. 마침내 시 공무원들은 좋은 수를 생각해냈다. 그들은 아파트 앞에 한 줄로 나무를 심었다. 그 나무들이 소음의 양에는 거의 영향을 주지는 못했지만, 고속도로의 모습이 보이지 않게 했다. 그 이후로, 건물에 사는 사람들에게서 불평이 거의 나오지 않았다.

문제풀이

②의 miserably는 능동문이라면 목적격보어의 역할을 하므로 miserable이 올바른 표현이다. 따라서 어법상 틀린 것은 ②이다.

어휘·어구

almost 거의
environment-agency 환경청
incident 사건
complain 불평하다, 항의하다
put off (핑계를 대어 사람, 요구 등을) 피하다, 발뺌하다
difference 차이

5. ③ 우리는 현재보다 과거나 미래에 사로잡혀 살아간다

직독/직해

We anticipate the future /
우리는 미래를 고대한다. /

as if we found it too slow in coming /
마치 미래가 너무 느리게 오고 있다고 생각해서 /

and we were trying to hurry it up.
그것을 서둘러 오게 하려고 하는 것이다.

So imprudent are we / 우리는 너무나 경솔해서 /

that we wander about in times / that are not ours
시간 속에서 방황하고 / 우리의 것이 아닌

and do not think of the one / that belongs to us.
생각하지 않는다. / 우리에게 속한 것에 대해

We try to support the present with the future /
우리는 미래를 가지고 현재를 지탱하려고 하며,

and think of arranging things / we cannot control,
조정하려고 생각한다. / 우리가 통제할 수 없는 것들을

for a time we have no certainty of reaching.
우리가 도달할 확실성이 전혀 없는 시간을 위해

Examine your thoughts, / 당신의 생각을 점검해보면, /

and you will find them wholly occupied
당신은 그것들이 완전히 ~에 사로잡혀 있다는 것을 알게 될 것이다.

with the past or the future. /
과거나 미래에

We almost never think of the present, /
우리는 현재에 대해서는 거의 전혀 생각을 하지 않으며,

and if we do so, / 만약 그렇게 한다 해도 /

it is only to shed light on our plans for the future.
그것은 단지 미래를 위한 우리의 계획을 비추기 위해서일 뿐이다.

The past and the present are our means; /
과거와 현재는 우리의 수단이고,

only the future is our end.
단지 미래만이 우리의 목적이다.

우리는 마치 미래가 너무 느리게 오고 있다고 생각해서 그것을 서둘러 오게 하려고 하는 것처럼 미래를 고대한다. 우리는 너무나 경솔해서 우리의 것이 아닌 시간 속에서 방황하고 우리에게 속한 것에 대해 생각하지 않는다. 우리는 미래를 가지고 현재를 지탱하려고 하며, 우리가 도달할 확실성이 전혀 없는 시간을 위해 우리가 통제할 수 없는 것들을 조정하려고 생각한다. 당신의 생각을 점검해보면, 당신은 그것들이 완전히 과거나 미래에 사로잡혀 있다는 것을 알게 될 것이다. 우리는 현재에 대해서는 거의 전혀 생각을 하지 않으며, 만약 그렇게 한다 해도 그것은 단지 미래를 위한 우리의 계획을 비추기 위해서일 뿐이다. 과거와 현재는 우리의 수단이고, 단지 미래만이 우리의 목적이다.

문제풀이

(A) 형용사 앞에 올 수 있는 것은 부사인 so이며, such는 「such+관사+형용사+명사」의 어순으로 많이 사용된다.
(B) 동사 try와 병렬 구조를 이루면서 주어인 We에 연결되는 think가 적절하다. 참고로, think가 to support와 연결되어도 문제가 없다.
(C) 「find+목적어+목적격보어」의 구문으로 목적어인 them이 occupy의 대상이므로 수동의 의미를 지니는 과거분사 occupied가 적절하다.

어휘·어구

anticipate 기대하다
imprudent 경솔한
wander 방황하다
arrange 조정하다
control 통제하다
occupy 차지하다
means 수단
end 목적

6. ④ 경작하는 땅을 갈아엎는 경우의 문제점

직독/직해

Farmers plow more and more fields /
농부들은 점점 더 많은 농경지를 경작한다. /

to produce more food /
더 많은 식량을 생산하기 위하여

for the increasing population.
늘어나는 인구를 위해 필요한

This increases pressure / on our soil resources.
이것으로 인해 압박이 증가하게 된다. / 우리의 토양 자원에 가하는

Farmers plow soil / to improve it for crops.
농부들은 땅을 갈아엎는다. /농작물이 자라기 좋게 하기 위해

They turn and loosen the soil, /
그들은 토양을 뒤엎고 느슨하게 만들어서, /

leaving it in the best condition for farming.
농사짓기에 가장 좋은 조건으로 만든다.

However, / this process / removes /
그렇지만 / 이러한 과정은 / 제거한다 /

the important plant cover /
중요한 역할을 하는 땅 표면의 식물들을

that holds soil particles in place, /
토양의 미세입자들을 붙잡아 두는 /

making soil defenseless / to wind and water erosion.

왼쪽 컬럼

그래서 토양을 무방비 상태가 되게 한다. / 바람이나 물에 의한 침식에 대해
Sometimes, / the wind blows soil /
때로, / 바람이 흙을 날려 버리기도 한다. /
from a plowed field. 갈아엎어 놓은 경작지에서
Soil erosion in many places occurs /
많은 곳에서 토양의 침식이 일어난다. /
at a much faster rate / 훨씬 더 빠른 속도로 /
than the natural processes of weathering can replace it.
자연적인 풍화 작용에 의해 대체되는 속도보다

농부들은 늘어나는 인구를 위해 필요한 더 많은 식량을 생산하기 위하여 점점 더 많은 농경지를 경작한다. 이것으로 인해 우리의 토양 자원에 가하는 압박이 증가하게 된다. 농부들은 농작물이 자라기 좋게 하기 위해 땅을 갈아엎는다. 그들은 토양을 뒤엎고 느슨하게 만들어서, 농사짓기에 가장 좋은 조건으로 만든다. 그렇지만 이러한 과정으로 인해 토양의 미세 입자들을 붙잡아 두는 중요한 역할을 하는 땅 표면의 식물이 없어지게 되어, 토양은 바람이나 물에 의한 침식에 대해 무방비 상태가 된다. 때로 바람이 갈아엎어 놓은 경작지에서 흙을 날려 버리기도 한다. 많은 곳에서 자연적인 풍화 작용에 의해 대체되는 속도보다 훨씬 더 빠른 속도로 토양의 침식이 일어난다.

문제풀이

① to부정사의 부사적 용법(목적)이다.
② it은 바로 앞 부분의 soil을 가리킨다.
③ 부사절 for they leave ~ 문장을 분사구문으로 바꾼 문장이다.
④ defenselessly → defenseless로 고쳐야 한다. 「make+목적어+목적격보어」 구문이다. 목적격보어에 부사가 오지 않고 형용사가 와야 한다.
⑤ much는 비교급 faster를 수식하는 강조어로 사용될 수 있다.

《 어휘 · 어구 》

plow 경작하다
field 농경지
population 인구
soil resources 토양 자원
crops 농작물
turn 갈아엎다
loosen 느슨하게 하다
remove 제거하다
particle 미세입자
defenseless 무기력한
wind 바람
water erosion 물침식

7. ③   부모를 닮은 배우자를 원하는 이유

직독 / 직해

The latest studies indicate /
최근 연구에 따르면 보여준다. /
that what people really want/
사람들이 정말로 원하는 것은 /
is a mate / that has qualities like their parents.
배우자이다 / 그들의 부모와 같은 특징을 지닌
Women are after a man who is like their father /
여성들은 아버지와 닮은 남성을 추구하고
and men want to be able to see their own mother
남성들은 자신의 어머니를 볼 수 있기를 원한다.
in the woman of their dreams.
그들의 이상적인 여성에서
Cognitive psychologist David Perrett studies /
인지심리학자인 David Perrett은 연구했다. /
what makes faces attractive.
무엇이 얼굴을 매력적으로 만드는지를
He has developed a computerized morphing system /
그는 컴퓨터 영상정보처리 시스템을 개발했다.
that can endlessly adjust faces / to suit his needs.
얼굴을 계속해서 변화시킬 수 있는 / 자신의 욕구에 맞도록

가운데 컬럼

Perrett suggests / Perrett에 의하면 /
that we find our own faces charming
우리들은 우리 자신의 얼굴을 매력적이라고 생각한다.
because they remind us of the faces /
왜냐하면 그것은 우리에게 그 얼굴을 상기시켜 주기 때문이다 /
we looked at constantly /
우리는가 계속해서 본 /
in our early childhood years — Mom and Dad.
우리가 어렸을 때부터 / – 엄마와 아빠라는

최근 연구에 따르면 사람들은 정말로 그들의 부모와 같은 특징을 지닌 배우자를 원한다고 한다. 여성들은 아버지와 닮은 남성을 추구하고 남성은 이상적인 여성에서 자신의 어머니를 볼 수 있기를 원한다. 인지심리학자인 David Perrett은 무엇이 얼굴을 매력적으로 만드는지를 연구했다. 그는 자신의 욕구에 맞도록 얼굴을 계속해서 변화시킬 수 있는 컴퓨터 영상정보처리 시스템을 개발했다. Perrett에 의하면 우리 자신의 얼굴이 우리가 어렸을 때 계속해서 본 엄마와 아빠의 얼굴을 상기시켜 주기 때문에 우리는 우리 자신의 얼굴을 매력적이라고 생각한다.

문제풀이

① what people really want가 문장의 주어 역할을 하고 있다.
② be after는 '~을 추구하다'는 의미이다.
③ 목적격보어의 역할을 하므로 attractively를 형용사인 attractive로 고쳐야 한다.
④ find가 5형식 동사로서 「find+목적어(our own faces)+목적격보어(charming)」로 사용되었다.
⑤ remind A of B 구문으로서 'A에게 B가 생각나게 하다'는 의미이다.

《 어휘 · 어구 》

mate 배우자
quality 특징
cognitive 인지의
psychologist 심리학자
attractive 매력적인
computerized morphing system 컴퓨터 영상정보처리 시스템
adjust 조정하다
suit (~에게) 좋다
charming 매력적인
constantly 끊임없이

8. ①   필자의 어머니에 대한 기억

직독 / 직해

Mom was an extraordinarily clean person.
어머니는 유별나게 청결한 분이셨다.
After feeding my brother and me breakfast, /
어머니는 나와 동생에게 아침 식사를 주고서는
she would scrub, mop, and dust everything
모든 물건들을 문지르고, 닦고, 먼지를 털어 내곤 했다.
As we grew older, / Mom made sure /
우리가 나이를 먹자, / 어머니는 강조하셨다. /
we did our part / 우리의 역할을 하라고 /
by keeping our rooms neat.
우리 방을 깨끗이 하는 것으로
Outside, / she would tend a small flower garden, /
바깥에서 / 어머니는 작은 정원을 손질하시곤 했는데, /
which was the envy of the neighborhood.
이웃들은 그 정원을 부러워했다.
With Mom, everything she touched / turned to gold.
어머니의 손이 닿는 모든 것은 / 황금으로 변했다.
She didn't believe in doing anything halfway.
어머니는 어느 것이든 대충한다는 생각을 하지 않았다.
She often told us / that we always had to do our best /
어머니는 종종 우리에게 말씀하시곤 했다. / 최선을 다해야 한다고 /
in whatever we did. 우리가 하는 모든 것에

어머니는 유별나게 청결한 분이셨다. 어머니는 나와 동생에게 아침 식사

오른쪽 컬럼

를 주고서는 모든 물건들을 문지르고, 닦고, 먼지를 털어 내곤 했다. 우리가 나이를 먹자, 어머니는 우리 방을 깨끗이 하는 것으로 우리의 역할을 하라고 강조하셨다. 어머니는 바깥에 작은 정원을 손질하곤 했는데, 이웃들은 그 정원을 부러워했다. 어머니의 손이 닿는 모든 것들은 황금으로 변했다. 어머니는 어느 것이든 대충하는 생각을 하지 않았다. 어머니는 종종 우리에게 우리가 하는 모든 것들에 최선을 다해야 한다고 말씀하시곤 했다.

문제풀이

(A) A, B, and C의 병렬 구조를 이루고 있으므로, C에는 동사가 와야 한다.
(B) 「keep+목적어+목적격보어(형용사)」는 목적어가 ~한 상태로 유지되도록 하다는 의미이다.
(C) 주어인 everything [that] she touched의 동사가 필요하므로, turned가 필요하다.

《 어휘 · 어구 》

extraordinarily 유별나게
scrub 문지르다
mop 닦다
dust 먼지를 털다
tend 돌보다
halfway 중도에, 불완전하게

9. ④   기술의 발달과 그 결과 예측

직독 / 직해

Just as there's a tendency to glorify technological progress, /
기술의 발달을 미화하는 경향이 있는 것과 마찬가지로 /
there's a countertendency to expect the worst of every new tool or machine.
모든 새로운 도구나 기계에서 최악의 것을 예상하는 반대 경향도 있다.
In Plato's *Phaedrus*, / Socrates bemoaned the development of writing.
플라톤의 *Phaedrus*에서 / 소크라테스는 글쓰기의 발전을 한탄했다.
He feared / that, as people came to rely on the written word /
그는 우려했다 / 사람들이 글로 쓰인 말에 의존하게 됨에 따라
as a substitute for the knowledge / they used to carry inside their heads, /
지식에 대한 대체물로서 / 그들이 머릿속에 지니고 다니던 /
they would, / in the words of one of the dialogue's characters, /
그들은 / 대화의 등장인물 중 한 사람의 말처럼 /
"cease to exercise their memory and become forgetful."
기억력을 발휘하는 것을 멈추고 잘 잊어버리게 될 것이라고
And because they would be able to "receive a quantity of information /
그리고 그들은 많은 양의 정보를 받을 수 있을 것이기 때문에 /
without proper instruction," / they would "be thought very knowledgeable /
적절한 가르침 없이 / 그들은 매우 박식하다고 생각될 것이라고 /
when they are for the most part quite ignorant."
그들이 대체로 상당히 무지할 때도
They would be "filled with the conceit of wisdom / instead of real wisdom."
그들은 지혜의 자만심으로 가득 차 있게 될 것이라고 / 진정한 지혜 대신
Socrates wasn't wrong / — the new technology did often have the effects /
소크라테스가 틀리지는 않았다 / 새로운 기술은 자주 결과를 실제로 가져왔다 /
he feared / — but he was shortsighted.
그가 두려워했던 / 그러나 그는 근시안적이었다.
He couldn't foresee the many ways /
그는 많은 방법을 예견할 수 없었다 /
that writing and reading would serve to spread information, /
쓰기와 읽기가 정보를 전파하는데 도움이 될 /
spark fresh ideas, and expand human knowledge / (if not wisdom).

신선한 생각을 촉발하며, 인간의 지식을 확장하는 데 / (지혜는 아닐지라도)

기술의 발달을 미화하는 경향이 있는 것과 마찬가지로, 모든 새로운 도구나 기계에서 최악의 것을 예상하는 반대 경향도 있다. 플라톤의 *Phaedrus*에서, 소크라테스는 글쓰기의 ① 발전을 한탄했다. 그는 사람들이 머릿속에 지니고 다니던 지식에 대한 ② 대체물로서, 글로 쓰인 말에 의존하게 됨에 따라, 대화의 등장인물 중 한 사람의 말처럼 그들은 '기억력을 발휘하는 것을 멈추고 잘 잊어버리게 될 것'이라고 우려했다. 그리고 그들은 '적절한 가르침 없이 많은 양의 정보를 ③ 받을 수 있을 것이기 때문에, '대체로 상당히 무지할 때도 매우 박식하다고 여겨질 것'이었다. 그들은 '진정한 지혜 대신 지혜의 자만심으로 가득 차 있게' 될 것이었다. 소크라테스가 ④ 맞지는(→ 틀리지는) 않아, 새로운 기술은 자주 그가 두려워했던 결과를 실제로 가져왔지만, 그는 근시안적이었다. 그는 쓰기와 읽기가 정보를 전파하고, 신선한 생각을 촉발하며, (지혜는 아닐지라도) 인간의 지식을 확장하는 데 도움이 될 많은 방법을 ⑤ 예견할 수 없었다.

문제풀이

사람들이 글로 쓰인 말에 의존하게 됨에 따라, 사람들은 잘 잊어버리게 될 것이고, 적절한 가르침 없이 많은 양의 정보를 획득할 수 있어서 상당히 무지할 때도 매우 박식하다고 여겨질 것이라고 하는 소크라테스의 의견이 언급된 후에 새로운 기술은 자주 그가 두려워했던 결과를 실제로 가져왔다고 했으므로 ④의 'right(맞는)'을 'wrong(틀린)'으로 바꾸어 '소크라테스가 틀리지는 않았다.'가 되어야 한다.

《 어휘·어구 》

tendency 경향
glorify 미화하다
progress 발달, 진보
countertendency 반대 경향
substitute 대체물
character 등장인물
cease 멈추다
a quantity of 많은
instruction 가르침, 훈련
knowledgeable 박식한
for the most part 대체로
ignorant 무지한
shortsighted 근시안적인
foresee 예견하다
serve 도움이 되다
spark 촉발하다
expand 확장하다

---

10. ③   유기농법의 단점

직독 직해

It has been suggested /
시사되어왔다 /

that "organic" methods, defined as those /
방식으로 정의되는 '유기농'법은 /

in which only natural products can be used as inputs, /
천연 제품들만 투입물로 사용되는 /

would be less damaging to the biosphere.
생물권에 해를 덜 끼친다고 /

Large-scale adoption of "organic" farming methods, /
'유기농' 경작 방식의 대규모 채택은 /

however, / 하지만 /

would reduce yields and increase production costs /
생산량을 줄이고 생산비를 증가시키게 된다 /

for many major crops.
많은 주요 작물의

Inorganic nitrogen supplies are essential /
무기질 질소 공급은 필수적인데 /

for maintaining moderate to high levels /
중상 수준으로 유지하는 데 /

of productivity for many of the non-leguminous crop species, /

many 비(非)콩과 작물 종의 생산성을 /

because organic supplies of nitrogenous materials /
왜냐하면 그것은 질소성 물질의 유기적 공급이 /

often are either limited or more expensive /
자주 제한적이거나 더 비싸기 때문이다 /

than inorganic nitrogen fertilizers.
무기 질소 비료보다

In addition, / there are constraints /
게다가 / 제약이 있다 /

to the extensive use of either manure or legumes /
거름이나 콩과 식물의 광범위한 사용에는 /

as "green manure" crops.
'친환경적인 거름' 작물로

In many cases, / weed control can be very difficult /
많은 경우에 / 잡초 방제가 매우 어려울 수 있다 /

or require much hand labor /
또는 많은 손일이 필요할 수 있는데 /

if chemicals cannot be used, /
화학 물질이 사용될 수 없으면 /

and fewer people are willing to do this work /
그리고 이 작업을 기꺼이 하려는 사람이 더 적을 것이다 /

as societies become wealthier.
사회가 부유해짐에 따라

Some methods used in "organic" farming, /
'유기농' 경작에서 사용되는 몇 가지 방식들은 /

however, / 하지만 /

such as the sensible use of crop rotations /
돌려짓기의 합리적인 사용과 같은 /

and specific combinations of cropping and livestock enterprises, /
그리고 경작과 가축 경영의 특정한 조합(과 같은) /

can make important contributions /
중요한 기여를 할 수 있다 /

to the sustainability of rural ecosystems.
농촌 생태계의 지속 가능성에

천연 제품들만 투입물로 사용되는 방식으로 정의되는 '유기농'법은 생물권에 해를 덜 끼친다고 시사되어왔다. 하지만 '유기농' 경작 방식의 대규모 채택은 많은 주요 작물의 생산량을 ① 줄이고 생산비를 증가시키게 된다. 무기질 질소 공급은 많은 비(非)콩과 작물 종의 생산성을 중상 수준으로 유지하는 데 ② 필수적인데, 왜냐하면 그것은 질소성 물질의 유기적 공급이 무기 질소 비료보다 자주 제한적이거나 더 비싸기 때문이다. 게다가, '친환경적인 거름' 작물로 거름이나 콩과 식물의 광범위한 사용에 ③ 이익(→ 제약)이 있다. 많은 경우에 화학 물질이 사용될 수 없으면 잡초 방제가 매우 어렵거나 많은 손일이 필요할 수 있는데, 사회가 부유해짐에 따라 이 작업을 기꺼이 하려는 사람이 ④ 더 적을 것이다. 하지만 돌려짓기의 합리적인 사용과 경작과 가축 경영의 특정한 조합과 같은 '유기농' 경작에서 사용되는 몇 가지 방식들은 농촌 생태계의 지속 가능성에 중요한 ⑤ 기여를 할 수 있다.

문제풀이

화학 물질을 사용하지 않으면 잡초 방제가 어렵고 손일이 많이 필요한데 그것을 하려는 사람이 더 적다고 했으므로, 거름이나 콩과 식물의 광범위한 사용의 제약이 있다고 하는 것이 자연스럽다. 따라서 ③ benefits(이점)를 constraints(제약)와 같은 낱말로 고쳐야 한다.

구조 다시보기

장점	유기농법은 생물권에 해를 덜 끼침
단점	유기농법의 채택은 주요 작물의 생산량을 줄이고 생산비를 증가시킴
근거 1	유기농법에 사용되는 질소성 물질의 유기적 공급이 제한적이거나 더 비쌈
근거 2	화학 물질을 사용하지 않으면 잡초 방제가 어렵고 손일이 많이 필요해서 광범위한 사용에 제약이 있음
반론	몇 가지 유기농법은 농촌 생태계의 지속 가능성에 중요한 기여를 함

《 어휘·어구 》

define 정의하다
input 투입(물)
biosphere 생물권

---

adoption 채택
yield 산출량, 생산량
inorganic 무기물의
maintain 유지하다
moderate 중간의
non-leguminous 비(非)콩과의
extensive 광범위한
be willing to do 기꺼이 ~하다
sensible 합리적인
crop rotation 돌려짓기
combination 조합
livestock 가축
enterprise 기업, 경영
contribution 기여, 이바지
sustainability 지속 가능성
ecosystem 생태계

---

11. ④   다른 사람의 행동에 반응하는 행동 패턴

직독 직해

How people behave / often depends /
사람들이 어떻게 행동하느냐는 / 흔히 달려 있다 /

on what others do.
다른 사람들이 하는 것에

If other car drivers or subway users leave for work at 8 a.m., /
만약 다른 운전자나 지하철 이용자들이 오전 8시에 출근한다면 /

it may be to my advantage to leave at 6 a.m., /
오전 6시에 출발하는 것이 나에게 유리할 것이다 /

even if that is really too early from my point of view.
비록 내 관점에서는 그것이 정말로 너무 이르더라도

In equilibrium, / flows stabilize /
균형 상태에서는 / 흐름이 안정된다 /

so that each person makes the best tradeoff /
그래서 각자 최상의 균형을 이룬다 /

between their ideal schedule and the congestion /
자신들의 이상적인 일정과 혼잡 사이에서 /

they will suffer on their commute.
자신들이 출퇴근 시 겪게 될

In making such choices, /
그러한 선택을 함에 있어 /

agents seek to differentiate their behavior /
행위자는 자신의 행동을 차별화하려고 한다 /

from that of others.
다른 행위자의 행동과

On other occasions, /
다른 경우에는 /

agents have a problem with coordination.
행위자가 조정에 문제를 겪기도 한다

They would like to choose to behave the same way as others.
그들은 다른 사람들과 똑같이 행동하는 것을 선택하려고 한다

For example, / 예를 들어 /

if most of my fellow citizens did not pay their parking tickets, /
만약 나의 동료 시민 대부분이 주차 위반 벌금을 내지 않는다면 /

there would be (unfortunately) strong pressure /
(유감스럽게도) 강한 압력이 있을 것이다 /

for an amnesty for such offenders, /
그런 위반자들을 사면해야 한다는 /

which would decrease my incentive /
이는 나의 동기를 또한 감소시킬 것이다 /

to pay my parking tickets too.
주차 위반 벌금을 내야 하는

There may be multiple equilibria, /
다양한 균형 상태가 존재할 수도 있다 /

so that two otherwise identical societies may adopt different behavioral patterns.
그래서 그렇지 않으면 똑같을 두 사회가 서로 다른 행동 패턴을 취할 수도 있다.

사람들이 어떻게 행동하느냐는 흔히 다른 사람들이 하는 것에 달려 있다. 만약 다른 운전자나 지하철 이용자들이 오전 8시에 출근한다면, 비록 내 관점에서는 그것이 정말로 너무 이르더라도, 오전 6시에 출발하는 것이 나에게 ① 유리할 것이다. 균형 상태에서는 (교통의) 흐름이 ② 안정되어 각자 자신들의 이상적인 일정과 자신들이 출퇴근 시 겪게 될 혼잡 사이에서 최상의 균형을 이룬다. 그러한 선택을 함에 있어 행위자는 다른 행위자의 행동과 자신의 행동을 ③ 차별화하려고 한다. 다른 경우에는 행위자가 조정에 문제를 겪기도 한다. 그들은 다른 사람들과 똑같이 행동하는 것을 선택하려고 한다. 예를 들어, 만약 나의 동료 시민들 대부분이 주차 위반 벌금을 내지 않는다면, (유감스럽게도) 그런 위반자들을 사면해야 한다는 강한 압력이 있을 것이고, 이는 주차 위반 벌금을 내야 하는 나의 동기를 또한 ④ 증가시킬(→ 감소시킬) 것이다. 다양한 균형 상태가 존재할 수도 있으며, 그렇지 않다면 똑같은 두 사회가 서로 다른 행동 패턴을 ⑤ 취할 수도 있다.

문제풀이

만약 다른 사람들이 오전 8시에 출근한다면, 교통 혼잡을 피하기 위해 오전 6시에 출근하는 것이 나에게 유리하기 때문에 다른 사람과 다르게 행동하고, 만약 나의 동료 시민들 대부분이 주차 위반 벌금을 내지 않는다면, 다른 사람들과 똑같이 나 역시 주차 위반 벌금을 내려고 하지 않을 것이라는 예시를 통해 사람들의 행동은 다른 사람들의 행동에 달려있다는 것이 글의 주된 내용이다. 따라서 나의 동료 시민들 대부분이 주차 위반 벌금을 내지 않는다면, 이는 주차 위반 벌금을 내야 하는 나의 동기를 증가시키는 것이 아니라 감소시킬 것이므로 ④ 'increase(증가시키다)'를 'decrease(감소시키다)'로 바꿔써야 한다.

구조 다시보기

주제	사람들의 행동은 다른 사람의 행동에 달려있음
예시 1	교통 혼잡을 피하기 위해 다른 사람들 보다 일찍 출발하는 것이 유리하기 때문에 다른 사람과 다르게 행동함
예시 2	다른 사람이 주차 위반 요금을 내지 않으면 나도 역시 주차 위반 요금을 내지 않음
마무리	다양한 균형 상태가 존재할 수 있으며, 그렇지 않다면 똑같은 두 사회가 다른 행동 패턴을 취할 수 있음

어휘·어구

point of view 관점
stabilize 안정되다
trade-off 균형, (타협을 위한) 거래
congestion 혼잡
commute 통근, 출퇴근
agent 행위자
differentiate A from B A를 B와 차별화하다
coordination 동등하게 맞춤, 조정
offender 위반자
incentive 동기
identical 똑같은

12. ② 생활 방식과 관련된 소비자 인식

직독 직해

It has become a commonplace / that audiences are conceived of /
흔한 일이 되었다 / 관객이 생각된다는 것은 /
in terms of their lifestyles.
그들의 생활 방식의 관점에서
Once more, / it would be naive to argue / that as members of society /
다시 한번 / 주장하는 것은 순진한 일일 것이다 / 사회 구성원으로서 /
we simply have lifestyles / which the market identifies and slots into.
우리는 생활 방식을 가지고 있을 뿐이라고 / 단순히 시장이 파악해 끼워 넣는
The market / (as all our cultural assumptions about consumption) /
시장은 / (소비에 관한 우리의 모든 문화적 가정으로서) /
has been around for so long /
매우 오랫동안 주위에 있어 왔기 때문에 /
that we are born into lifestyles / which it has already shaped.
우리는 생활 방식 속으로 태어난다 / 그것(시장)이 이미 형성해 놓은
We grow up into a set of assumptions / about what living is, what shopping is.
우리는 일련의 가정 속으로 성장해 들어간다 / 삶이란 무엇이며, 쇼핑이란 무엇인가에 대한
And the market continues to work on the idea of lifestyle /
그리고 시장은 생활 방식이라는 관념을 만들어 가는 일을 계속한다 /
through an apparently everlasting succession of campaigns.
겉으로 보기에 끊임없는 캠페인의 연속을 통해
It is constructing and reconstructing lifestyles all the time.
그것은 언제나 생활 방식을 구축하고 재구성하고 있다
The main thing that lifestyle is about / is the consumers' conception /
생활 방식과 관련된 중요한 것은 / 소비자의 인식이다 /
of their place in society, their social relations, their persona /
사회에서의 자신의 위치, 사회적 관계, 페르소나에 대한 /
— it has nothing to do with material needs as such.
즉 그것은 보통 말하는 물질적인 필요 자체와는 아무 관계가 없다
The possession of SUVs or 4×4 vehicles /
SUV(스포츠 실용차), 즉 사륜구동 차량을 소유하는 것은 /
is about how the owners wish to be seen by others.
그 소유자가 다른 사람들에게 어떻게 보이기를 원하는지와 관련이 있다
Few of these owners could support an argument /
이러한 소유자들 중 주장을 뒷받침할 수 있는 사람은 거의 없을 것이다 /
that the vehicle was necessary to their work /
그 차량이 자기 일에 필요하다는 /
or the material well-being of their family.
혹은 자기 가족의 물질적인 안녕에 (필요하다는)

관객은 그들의 생활 방식의 관점에서 생각된다는 것은 흔한 일이 되었다. 다시 한번, 사회 구성원으로서 우리는 단순히 시장이 ① 파악해 끼워 넣는 생활 방식을 가지고 있을 뿐이라고 주장하는 것은 순진한 일일 것이다. (소비에 관한 우리의 모든 문화적 가정으로서) 시장은 매우 오랫동안 주위에 있어 왔기 때문에, 우리는 그것이 이미 형성해 놓은 생활 방식 속으로 태어난다. 우리는 삶이란 무엇이며, 쇼핑이란 무엇인가에 대한 일련의 가정 속으로 성장해 들어간다. 그리고 시장은 겉으로 보기에 끊임없는 캠페인의 연속을 통해 생활 방식이라는 관념을 만들어 가는 일을 ② 그만둔다(→ 계속한다). 그것은 언제나 생활 방식을 구축하고 재구성하고 있다. 생활 방식과 관련된 중요한 것은 사회에서의 자신의 위치, 사회적 관계, 페르소나에 대한 소비자의 ③ 인식으로, 그것은 보통 말하는 물질적인 필요 자체와는 아무 관계가 없다. SUV(스포츠 실용차), 즉 사륜구동 차량을 ④ 소유하는 것은 그 소유자가 다른 사람들에게 어떻게 보이기를 원하는지와 관련이 있다. 이러한 소유자들 중 그 차량이 자기 일이나 자기 가족의 물질적인 안녕에 자동차가 ⑤ 필요하다는 주장을 뒷받침할 수 있는 사람은 거의 없을 것이다.

문제풀이

시장은 매우 오랫동안 주위에 있어 왔기 때문에 우리는 시장이 이미 형성해 놓은 생활 방식 속으로 태어나고, 시장은 언제나 생활 방식을 구축하고 재구성하고 있다고 하였으므로, 시장은 생활 방식이라는 관념을 만들어 가는 일을 그만둔다가 아니라 계속한다고 해야 문맥상 적절하다. 따라서 ② 'ceases(그만두다)'를 'continues(계속하다)' 등의 말로 고쳐야 한다.

어휘·어구

commonplace 흔한 일, 평범한 일
conceive 생각하다
naive 순진한
identify 확인하다
slot ~을 끼워 넣다
assumption 가정
persona 페르소나, (다른 사람들 눈에 비치는, 특히 그의

실제 성격과는 다른, 한 개인의) 모습
have nothing to do with ~와 관계가 없다

04. 수의 일치

• 정답 및 해설 •

A 출제 POINT
본문 020쪽

1. are	2. are	3. contain
4. have	5. was	6. think
7. that		

1 [해석]▶ 한 유명한 교수와 한 음악가가 그 문제를 토론하고 있다.
[해설]▶ 수 일치의 기본 원칙은 복수주어는 복수동사를 사용한다.

2 [해석]▶ 불쾌한 주제와 상황들을 무시함으로써 갈등을 피하는 가정들은 그것으로 인해 더 강해지는 것이 아니라 더 약해진다.
[해설]▶ 관계사절(that~)로 주어, 동사가 멀리 떨어져 있는 경우 주어를 잘 찾아 동사의 수를 일치시켜야 한다. 주어는 families로 복수주어이므로 복수동사가 나와야 한다.

3 [해석]▶ 아이들은 폭력이 담겨 있는 TV 프로그램을 봐서는 안 된다.
[해설]▶ 관계대명사절 안의 동사는 선행사의 수에 일치시킨다. 선행사가 복수주어(TV programs)이면 복수동사 (contain)를 사용해야 한다.

4 [해석]▶ 아름다운 잔디, 초목, 아름다운 연못이 있는 곳이 바로 골프장이다.
[해설]▶ It... that ~ 강조 구문에서 주어가 강조되면, that 바로 뒤의 동사는 강조된 주어에 맞게 수를 일치시킨다. 강조된 주어가 복수주어 golf courses이므로 복수동사 have가 나와야 한다.

5 [해석]▶ 그녀가 죽고 난 후에야, 나는 그녀의 고마움을 알 수 있었다.
[해설]▶ 도치 구문(only after her death)은 뒤에 나오는 주어(I)에 맞게 수를 일치시킨다.

6 [해석]▶ 그녀의 친구 중 일부는 그녀가 스마트워치 때문에 일하고 저축하는 것은 어리석은 일이라고 생각한다. 하지만 나는 그들의 생각에 동의하지 않는다.
[해설]▶ some of ~이 주어로 쓰인 경우, 동사는 of 뒤에 나오는 명사(구)의 수에 일치시킨다.

7 [해석]▶ 토끼의 꼬리는 고양이의 꼬리보다 더 짧다.
[해설]▶ 토끼의 꼬리(the tail)과 고양이의 꼬리를 비교하고 있으므로, 고양이의 꼬리를 나타내는 대명사는 단수로 표현해야 한다.

B 체크 POINT
본문 020쪽

1. is	2. is	3. have
4. is	5. does	6. are
7. it		

1 [해석]▶ 한 유명한 교수 겸 음악가가 전화로 통화를 하고 있다.
[해설]▶ 관사를 한 번만 사용했으므로 동일 인물을 나타낸다. 단수주어는 단수동사를 사용해야 한다.

2 [해석]▶ 신체에 보석을 치장하는 관습은 고대부터 그랬다.
[해설]▶ 분사구(decorating~)가 주어 the custom을 수식하고 있다. 주어가 단어주어(the custom)이므로, 단수동사를 사용해야 한다.

3 [해석]▶ 의사들이 지난 3개월 동안 그 약을 복용한 암환자들을 접촉하고 있다.
[해설]▶ 관계대명사절 안의 동사는 선행사의 수에 일치시킨다. 선행사가 복수명사 patients이므로 복수동사가 나와야 한다.

4 [해석]▶ 우리집 근처에는 지하철역이 없다.
[해설]▶ There be ~ 구문에서 주어는 be동사 뒤에 나온 어구이다. 주어가 단수명사 subway station이므로 단수동사를 써야 한다.

5 [해석]▶ Sam은 좀처럼 사람들에 대해 험담하지 않는다.
[해설]▶ 부정어(seldom)가 문장 가장 앞에 나와 주어와 동사가 도치된 문장이다. 주어가 Sam이므로 단수동사 does가 나와야 한다.

6 [해석]▶ 선반의 대부분이 비워있다.
[해설]▶ most of ~이 주어로 쓰인 경우, 동사는 of 뒤에 나오는 명사(구)의 수에 일치시킨다.

7 [해석]▶ 명사를 대신하는 대명사는 그 명사의 수와 일치해야 한다.
[해설]▶ 갈등을 공개적으로 표출하는 것은 가정의 문제를 처리하고 그것을 접근 가능한 범위 안에 두는 훌륭한 방법이다.
[해설]▶ 괄호의 대명사가 지칭한 것은 family conflict이므로 단수 대명사가 필요하다.

Day 04
본문 021쪽

1 ②	2 ⑤	3 ④	4 ⑤	5 ③
6 ④	7 ③	8 ③	9 ④	10 ⑤
11 ④	12 ⑤			

1. ②
문화 환경에 따라 다른 대처 방식

직독/직해

People from more individualistic cultural contexts /
더 개인주의적인 문화 환경의 출신자들은 /

tend to be motivated / 동기를 지니는 경향이 있다 /

to maintain self-focused agency or control /
자신에게 초점을 맞춘 주체성이나 통제력을 유지하려는 /

as these serve / as the basis of one's self-worth.
이러한 것들이 역할을 하기 때문이다 / 자아 존중감의 토대의

With this form of agency comes the belief /
이런 형태의 주체성의 결과로 믿음이 생겨나고 /

that individual successes depend primarily /
개인의 성공이 주로 달려 있다는 /

on one's own abilities and actions, /
자신의 능력과 행동에 /

and thus, / whether by influencing the environment /
따라서 / 환경에 영향을 미침에 의해서든 /

or trying to accept one's circumstances, /
또는 자신의 상황을 받아들이려고 노력함에 의해서든 /

the use of control / ultimately centers on the individual.
통제력의 사용은 / 궁극적으로 개인에게 집중된다

The independent self may be more driven /
독립적 자아는 더 많이 유도될지도 모른다 /

to cope / by appealing to a sense of agency or control.
대처하도록 / 주체 의식이나 통제 의식에 호소함으로써

However, people from more interdependent
cultural contexts /
하지만 더 상호의존적인 문화 환경의 출신자들은 /

tend to be less focused / 덜 집중하는 경향이 있다 /

on issues of individual success and agency /
개인의 성공과 주체성의 문제에 /

and more motivated / towards group goals and harmony.
그리고 더 많은 동기를 가지는 (경향이 있다) / 집단의 목표와 화합 쪽으로

Research has shown / that East Asians prefer to receive, /
연구는 보여주었다 / 동아시아인들은 받는 것을 선호한다는 것을 /

but not seek, / more social support /
추구하지는 않되 / 더 많은 사회적인 지원을 /

rather than seek personal control / in certain cases.
개인적인 통제를 추구하기보다는 / 어떤 경우에

Therefore, people / 따라서 사람들은 /

who hold a more interdependent self-construal /
더 상호의존적인 자기 구성을 지닌 /

may prefer to cope / in a way /
대처하는 것을 선호할 수 있다 / 방식으로 /

that promotes harmony / in relationships.
화합을 증진하는 / 관계 속에서

더 개인주의적인 문화 환경의 출신인 사람들은 자신에게 초점을 맞춘 주체성이나 통제력을 유지하려는 동기를 지니는 경향이 있는데, 이는 이러한 것들이 자아 존중감의 토대의 역할을 하기 때문이다. 이런 형태의 주체성의 결과로 개인의 성공이 주로 자신의 능력과 행동에 달려 있다는 믿음이 생겨나고, 따라서 환경에 영향을 미침에 의해서든, 자신의 상황을 받아들이려고 노력함에 의해서든, 통제력의 사용은 궁극적으로 개인에게 집중된다. 독립적 자아는 주체 의식이나 통제 의식에 호소함으로써 대처하도록 더 많이 유도될 수도 있다. 하지만 더 상호의존적인 문화 환경의 출신자들은 개인의 성공과 주체성의 문제에 덜 집중하고, 집단의 목표와 화합 쪽으로 더 많은 동기를 가지는 경향이 있다. 연구는 동아시아인들은 어떤 경우에 개인적인 통제를 추구하기보다는, 오히려 더 많은 사회적인 지원을, 추구하지는 않되, 받는 것을 선호한다는 것을 보여주었다. 따라서 더 상호의존적인 자기 구성을 지닌 사람들은 관계 속에서 화합을 증진하는 방식으로 대처하는 것을 선호할 수 있다.

문제풀이

① [접속사 as]
'~이기 때문에'라는 의미로 이유를 나타내는 부사절을 이끄는 접속사가 와야 한다. 따라서 접속사 as가 온 것은 적절하다.

② [정동사 vs 준동사]
the belief와 동격인 that절에서 주어인 individual successes에 이어 동사가 와야 하므로, depending을 depend로 고쳐 써야 한다.

③ [수동태]
주어인 The individual self가 '유도되는' 수동적 대상이므로, 수동태가 되도록 과거분사인 driven이 온 것은 적절하다.

④ [접속사 that]
has shown의 목적어 역할을 하는 명사절을 이끄는 접속사가 와야 하므로, 접속사 that이 온 것은 적절하다.

⑤ [관계대명사]
may prefer가 문장의 동사이고 who 뒤에 이어지는 절이 주어인 people을 수식하고 있으므로, 주격 관계대명사 who가 온 것은 적절하다.

❖ **이렇게 풀자** ① 부사절을 이끄는 접속사에 밑줄이 그어져 있는 경우, 이어진 두 문장의 관계를 고려하여 의미에 맞게 쓰였는지 확인해야 한다.
② 밑줄이 그어진 부분이 문장에서 동사가 쓰일 자리인지 준동사가 쓰일 자리인지를 파악해야 한다.
③ be동사 뒤의 과거분사에 밑줄이 있는 경우, 주어와의 관계를 파악하여 수동태로 쓰이는 것이 적절한지 살펴야 한다.
④ that 뒤에 문장 성분을 모두 갖춘 완전한 절이 왔다면 that은 명사절을 이끄는 접속사로 쓰인 것이다.
⑤ 문장에서 관계대명사가 필요한 경우인지를 확인한 후, 선행사의 종류 및 격에 따라 적절하게 쓰였는지 살펴봐야 한다.

《 어휘 · 어구 》

individualistic 개인주의적인
context 맥락, 환경
serve as ~의 역할을 하다
self-worth 자부심, 자아 존중감
agency 주체성, 주도성
primarily 주로
ultimately 결국, 궁극적으로
cope 대처하다
appeal to ~에 호소하다
interdependent 상호의존적인
promote 증진하다

---

2. ⑤ 애완동물의 애정이 사람들에게 미치는 영향

사람들이 진짜 역경, 즉 질병, 실직, 혹은 나이로 인한 장애에 직면할 때, 애완동물에게서 받는 애정은 새로운 의미를 띤다. 애완동물의 지속적인 애정은 고난을 견디는 사람들의 핵심적인 본질이 손상되지 않았다고 그들을 안심시켜 주기 때문에 매우 중요해진다. 그래서 애완동물은 우울증이 있거나 만성적인 질병이 있는 환자들의 치료에 중요하다. 게다가, 애완동물은 보호 시설에 있는 노인들에게 매우 유익하게 이용된다. 그러한 시설에서 직원들은 모든 환자가 건강이 쇠약해지고 있을 때 낙관주의를 유지하기가 어렵다. 방문하는 자녀들은 자신들의 부모님이나 조부모님이 예전에 어떠했는지를 기억하고 그들의 무능함에 의기소침해질 수밖에 없다. 그러나 동물은 정신적 능력에 대해 기대를 하지 않는다. 그것들은 젊음을 숭배하지 않는다. 그것들은 노인들이 예전에 어떠했는지에 대한 기억을 전혀 갖고 있지 않아서, 그들이(노인들이) 마치 어린이들인 것처럼 그들을 반긴다. 강아지를 안고 있는 노인은 완전히 정확하게 어린 시절의 순간을 다시 체험할 수 있다. 그의 기쁨과 그 동물의 반응은 똑같다.

문제풀이

① '사람들'의 의미를 나타내는 대명사로 those가 오는 것은 적절하다.
② 뒤에 나오는 명사인 patients를 수식하는 분사로 patients가 depress 되는 대상이므로 과거분사인 depressed가 오는 것은 적절하다.
③ pets가 use라는 동작을 받는 대상이므로 수동태를 만드는 과거분사인 used가 오는 것은 적절하다.
④ remember의 목적어 역할을 하는 명사절을 이끄는 의문사 what이 오는 것이 적절하다. what은 절 안에서 보어로 쓰였다.
⑤ 주어 the aged는 〈the+형용사〉로 복수 보통명사로 취급하기 때문에, 단수 동사 was가 아닌 복수 동사 were가 오는 것이 적절하다. 따라서 정답은 ⑤이다.

《 구문 및 어휘 》

*8행 In such institutions it is difficult for the staff [to retain optimism] {when all the patients are declining in health}.
(1) 「부사구(In such ~)+주절(it is difficult ~)+부사절(when all ~) 구조의 문장이다.
(2) it은 가주어이고, to retain optimism이 진주어이다. for the staff는 의미상 주어이다.
*14행 They have no memories about [what the aged once were] and greet them {as if they were children}.
(1) have와 greet는 문장의 동사로 병렬 연결되어 있다.
(2) what 이하는 전치사 about의 목적어로 쓰인 명사절로 「의문사+주어+동사」의 간접의문문 어순이다.

---

③ 「as if+가정법 과거」는 '마치 ~인 것처럼'이라고 해석하며, '실제로 그렇지 않지만 그런 척하다'라는 의미를 포함하고 있다.

《 어휘 · 어구 》

adversity 역경
disability 장애
affection 애정
crucially 결정적으로
hardship 어려움, 고난
reassure 안심시키다
chronically 만성적으로
to advantage 유익하게, 돋보이게
institutionalize 보호 시설에 보내다
retain 유지하다
optimism 낙관주의
incapacity 무능함, 무능력
worship 숭배하다
relive 다시 체험하다

---

3. ④ 초기 황무지의 훼손은 방문 규모에 따라 훼손의 정도 심하나 이미 정착된 야영지는 활동 제한으로 방문 규모의 영향을 덜 받는다

직독/직해

In most wilderness, / 황무지 대부분에서 /
the majority of groups visiting the area are small — /
그 지역을 방문하는 무리는 대부분 규모가 작다
usually between two and four people.
보통 2명에서 4명 사이로
But large groups do visit wilderness, /
그러나 규모가 큰 무리도 황무지를 실제로 방문하는데, /
and their potential to disturb campsites /
그들이 야영장을 훼손할 잠재적 가능성은 /
differs from that of small groups.
규모가 작은 무리의 그것과는 다르다.
Although the effect of party size on campsites /
무리의 크기가 야영지에 미치는 영향이 /
has never been formally studied, /
공식적으로 연구된 적은 전혀 없지만,
it makes sense / that a large group can cause impacts /
~점은 일리가 있다. / 큰 무리가 충격을 가할 수 있다는 /
on an undisturbed site
훼손되지 않은 지역에
more rapidly than a small group.
작은 무리보다 더 빠르게
For example, / along the New River in West Virginia, /
예를 들면, / West Virginia주의 New River 강가에서 /
the area of vegetation loss / on sites used /
초목이 손실된 지역은 / 사용된 장소에서 /
by large commercial rafting companies/
규모가 큰 상업적 래프팅 회사에 의해
was more than four times larger /
네 배 이상 넓었다. /
than the area on sites used /
사용된 장소의(초목이 손실된) 지역보다 /
by small groups of fishermen.
작은 규모의 어부들에 의해
At well-established campsites, / however, /
이미 정착된 야영지에서는 / 그러나 /
a big group need not be a problem,
규모가 큰 무리가 문제가 되지는 않는다.
as long as activities are confined /
활동이 제한되는 한, /
within the boundaries of the existing site.
현재 사용되는 장소의 경계 안쪽으로

황무지 대부분에서 그 지역을 방문하는 무리는 대부분 보통 2명에서 4명 사이로 규모가 작다. 그러나 규모가 큰 무리도 황무지를 실제로 방문하는데, 그들이 야영장을 훼손할 잠재적 가능성은 규모가 작은 무리의 그것과는 다르다. 무리의 크기가 야영지에 미치는 영향이 공식적으로 연구된 적

은 전혀 없지만, 큰 무리가 작은 무리보다 훼손되지 않은 지역에 더 빠르게 충격을 가할 수 있다는 점은 일리가 있다. 예를 들면, West Virginia 주의New River 강가에서 규모가 큰 상업적 래프팅 회사에 의해 사용된 장소에 초목이 손실된 지역은 작은 규모의 어부들에 의해 사용된 장소의(초목이 손실된) 지역보다 네 배 이상 넓었다. 그러나 이미 정착된 야영지에서는 현재 사용되는 장소의 경계 안쪽으로 활동이 제한되는 한, 규모가 큰 무리가 문제가 되지는 않는다.

문제풀이

For example, along the New River in West Virginia, the area of vegetation loss on sites used by large commercial rafting companies were more than four times larger than the area on sites used by small groups of fishermen. 에서 ④ were의 주어가 the area이므로 수의 일치에 따라 동사 were를 was로 써야 한다.

《 어휘 · 어구 》

majority 다수
disturb 훼손하다
commercial 상업의

---

4. ⑤ 생산성 측정의 어려움

직독/직해

I remember / one of the smartest I.T. executives /
나는 기억한다 / 가장 똑똑한 IT 중역 중 한 사람을 /
for whom I ever worked /
내가 전에 그 밑에서 일했던
strongly resisting the movement /
움직임에 강하게 반대했던 /
to measure programmer productivity /
프로그래머의 생산성을 측정하려는
that was popular at the time.
그 당시에 널리 퍼져 있었던
He was fond of saying / 그는 ~라고 말하는 것을 좋아했다.
that the biggest problem / 가장 큰 문제점은 /
with managing computer programmers /
컴퓨터 프로그래머를 관리하는 데 있어 /
is that you can never tell / 결코 알 수 없다는 것이라고 /
whether they are working / 그들이 일을 하고 있는지를 /
by looking at them. 겉으로 보아서는
Picture two programmers / working side by side.
두 명의 프로그래머를 상상해 보라. / 나란히 앉아 일하고 있는
One is leaning back in his chair /
한 명은 뒤로 기대어 의자에 앉아 있다. /
with his eyes closed /and his feet on the desk.
눈을 감고 / 책상 위에 발을 올린 채로
The other is working hard, /
다른 한 명은 열심히 일하고 있다. /
typing code into his computer.
컴퓨터에 코드를 타이핑해서 넣으며
The one with his feet up could be thinking, /
다리를 올리고 있는 사람은 생각하고 있을 수 있고
and the other one / may be too busy typing /
다른 한 명은 / 타이핑하는데 너무 바빠서 /
to give it enough thought.
그 일에 대해 충분한 생각을 하지 못할 수 있다.
In the end, / the busy typist could well produce /
결국, / 바쁘게 타이핑하는 사람은 만들어 낼 수 있지만,
ten times as many lines of code / as the thinker, /
열 배나 더 많은 줄의 코드를 / 생각하는 사람보다
which contain / twice as many new problems /
이것은 포함하고 있을 수 있다. / 두 배나 더 많은 새로운 문제를 /
as the thinker's.
생각하는 사람의 것보다
Unfortunately, / 불행하게도, /
most of the productivity measurement schemes /
생산성 측정 시책의 대부분은
I have encountered / 내가 접했던

measure effort or apparent activity.
노력이나 겉으로 보이는 활동을 측정한다.

They would reward him /
그것(생산성 측정 시책)은 그에게는 상을 주고 /

and punish his thoughtful neighbor.
깊이 생각하는 그의 동료에게는 벌을 주게 된다.

내가 전에 그 밑에서 일했던 가장 똑똑한 IT 중역 중 한 사람이 그 당시에 널리 퍼져 있었던 프로그래머의 생산성을 측정하려는 움직임에 강하게 반대했던 것을 나는 기억한다. 그는 컴퓨터 프로그래머를 관리하는 데 있어 가장 큰 문제점은 겉으로 보아서는 그들이 일을 하고 있는지를 결코 알 수 없다는 것이라고 말하는 것을 좋아했다. 나란히 앉아 일하고 있는 두 명의 프로그래머를 상상해 보라. 한 명은 눈을 감고 책상 위에 발을 올린 채로 뒤로 기대어 의자에 앉아 있다. 다른 한 명은 컴퓨터에 코드를 타이핑하며 넣으며 열심히 일하고 있다. 다리를 올리고 있는 사람은 생각하고 있을 수 있고, 다른 한 명은 타이핑하는데 너무 바빠서 그 일에 대해 충분한 생각을 하지 못할 수 있다. 결국, 바쁘게 타이핑하는 사람은 생각하는 사람보다 열 배나 더 많은 줄의 코드를 만들어 낼 수 있지만, 이것은 생각하는 사람의 것보다 두 배나 더 많은 새로운 문제를 포함하고 있을 수 있다. 불행하게도, 내가 접했던 생산성 측정 시책의 대부분은 노력이나 겉으로 보이는 활동을 측정한다. 그것(생산성 측정 시책)은 그에게는 상을 주고 깊이 생각하는 그의 동료에게는 벌을 주게 된다.

문제풀이

⑤에서 I have encountered는 관계사 구문으로 앞의 schemes를 수식하는 수식어구이다. 여기서 문장의 주어는 most of the productivity measurement schemes로 복수이므로 동사는 복수동사 measure가 나와야 한다. 참고로, 변형 전의 교육청 문제는 준동사 measuring을 measure로 고치는 문제였다.

《 어휘·어구 》

executive 중역
work for ~을 위해 일하다
measure 측정하다
productivity 생산성
be fond of ~을 좋아하다
picture ~을 상상하다
side by side 나란히
lean 기대다
code (컴퓨터) 코드
scheme 시책, 계획, 안
apparent 겉으로 보이는, 분명한
thoughtful 깊이 생각하는

---

5. ③ 상품 구매와 자아 정체성의 관계

직독/직해

No matter what we are shopping for, /
우리가 어떤 상품을 구매하던 간에,

it is not primarily a brand we are choosing, /
우리가 선택하는 것은 근본적으로 상표가 아니라 /

but a culture, / or rather the people /
문화이거나 / 오히려 사람들이다. /

associated with that culture.
그 문화와 관련된

Whether you wear torn jeans /
당신이 찢어진 청바지를 입던 /

or like to recite poetry, / by doing so /
시를 암송하기를 좋아하던, / 그렇게 함으로써 /

you make a statement / 당신은 말해준다. /
of belonging to a group of people.
한 집단의 사람들에 속해 있다는 것을

Who we believe we are /
우리가 믿는 우리가 누구인지는/

is a result of the choices we make /
우리가 만드는 선택들의 결과이며, /

about who we want to be like, /
우리가 비슷해지기를 원하는 사람에 대하여 /

and we subsequently demonstrate /
그 결과 우리는 나타낸다. /

---

this desired likeness to others /
다른 사람들과 비슷해지려는 이런 욕망을 /

in various and often subtle ways.
우리는 그 결과 다양하고 종종 미묘한 방법으로

Artificial as this process is, /
비록 이런 과정이 인위적이지만, /

this is what becomes our 'identity,' /
이것은 우리의 '정체성'이 되는 것이다.

an identity grounded on all the superficial differences /
즉 모든 피상적인 차이에 기초를 둔 정체성

we distinguish between ourselves and others.
우리가 우리 자신과 다른 사람들을 식별하는

This, / after all, / is what we are shopping for: /
이것이, / 요컨대, / 우리가 상품을 구매하는 목적이며,

self-identity, knowledge of who we are.
자아 정체성, 즉 우리가 누구인지에 대하여 아는 것이다.

우리가 어떤 상품을 구매하던 간에, 우리가 선택하는 것은 근본적으로 상표가 아니라 문화이거나 오히려 그 문화와 관련된 사람들이다. 당신이 찢어진 청바지를 입던, 시를 암송하기를 좋아하던, 그렇게 함으로써, 당신은 한 집단의 사람들에 속해 있다는 것을 말해준다. 우리가 믿는 우리가 누구인지는 우리가 비슷해지기를 원하는 사람에 대하여 우리가 만드는 선택들의 결과이며, 우리는 그 결과 다양하고 종종 미묘한 방법으로 다른 사람들과 비슷해지려는 이런 욕망을 나타낸다. 비록 이런 과정이 인위적이지만, 이것은 우리의 '정체성', 즉 우리가 우리 자신과 다른 사람들을 식별하는 모든 피상적인 차이에 기초를 둔 정체성이 되는 것이다. 요컨대, 이것이 우리가 상품을 구매하는 목적이며, 자아 정체성, 즉 우리가 누구인지에 대하여 아는 것이다.

문제풀이

(A) Whether A or B (A를 하든, B를 하든)의 구조가 사용되었으며, 뒤에 완전한 문장이 이어지므로 Whatever는 사용할 수 없다.
(B) 절(Who we believe we are)은 단수 취급을 하므로 단수동사(is)를 가져온다.
(C) an identity는 타동사 ground의 목적어에 해당하므로 과거분사 grounded를 사용해야 한다. 'an identity (which is) grounded on ~'로「관계대명사+be」가 생략되었다.

《 어휘·어구 》

primarily 본래, 근본적으로
recite 암송하다
subsequently 결과로서, 그 후
demonstrate 증명하다, 논증하다
subtle 미묘한
artificial 인위적인
identity 동일함, 정체성
superficial 피상적인
distinguish 구별하다, 식별하다

---

6. ④ 유기물의 조직 수준

직독/직해

Although life is different from nonlife, /
비록 생물과 무생물이 다르지만, /

it is not completely different.
이것이 완전히 다르지는 않다.

Living things exist in a nonliving universe /
살아있는 것들은 생명이 없는 우주에 존재하며 /

and depend on it in many ways.
여러 가지 면에서 이 우주에 의존한다.

Plants absorb energy from sunlight, /
식물은 태양으로부터 에너지를 흡수하고 /

and bats find shelter in caves.
박쥐는 동굴에서 서식지를 찾는다.

Indeed, living things are made of the same tiny particles /
사실 생명체는 동일한 작은 소립자로 구성되어 있다.

---

that make up nonliving things.
무생물체를 구성하는 것과

What makes organisms different /
유기체와 구분되게 만드는 것은 /

from the materials that compose them /
이 유기물을 구성하는 물질들을

is their level of organization.
이 유기물의 조직 수준이다.

Living things exhibit / not just one /
생명체는 보여준다. / 단지 하나가 아닌 /

but many layers of biological organization.
많은 층위의 생물학적 조직을

This tendency toward order /
위계를 지향하는 이러한 경향성은 /

is sometimes modeled / in a pyramid of life.
종종 모델이 되어 있다. / 생명의 피라미드에

비록 생물과 무생물이 다르지만, 이것이 완전히 다르지는 않다. 살아있는 것들은 생명이 없는 우주에 존재하여 여러 가지 면에서 이 우주에 의존한다. 식물은 태양으로부터 에너지를 흡수하고 박쥐는 동굴에서 서식지를 찾는다. 사실 생명체는 무생물체를 구성하는 것과 동일한 작은 소립자로 구성되어 있다. 유기물과 이 유기물을 구성하는 물질들을 구분되게 만드는 것은 이 유기물의 조직 수준이다. 생명체는 단지 하나가 아닌 많은 층위의 생물학적 조직을 보여준다. 위계를 지향하는 이러한 경향성은 종종 생명의 피라미드에 모델이 되어 있다.

문제풀이

① 부사 completely가 형용사 different를 수식하고 있다.
② it은 바로 앞의 단수명사 a nonliving universe를 가리킨다.
③ that은 주격 관계대명사로 사용되었다.
④ are를 is로 고쳐야 한다. 문장의 주어가 단수 형태인 관계대명사 What절이므로 is가 적절하다.
⑤ 동작의 주체가 아니라 대상이 되어서 수동태 is sometimes modeled로 사용되었다.

《 어휘·어구 》

life 생물
nonlife 무생물
plant 식물
absorb 흡수하다
sunlight 태양
bat 박쥐
shelter 서식지
cave 동굴
organism 유기체
compose 구성하다
organization 조직
exhibit 보여주다
biological 생물학적인
tiny 작은

---

7. ③ 문화적으로 훈련된 시간에 근거한 식습관

직독/직해

Most of us have been culturally conditioned /
우리들 대부분은 문화적으로 훈련되어 왔다 /

to eat at least three meals a day, /
적어도 하루에 세 끼를 먹도록 /

typically breakfast, lunch, and dinner.
보통 아침, 점심, 그리고 저녁

Thus, a day doesn't quite seem complete /
그렇기 때문에, 하루가 완전히 끝나는 것처럼 보이지 않는다 /

unless you've had all three of these, / at a minimum.
여러분이 이 모든 세 끼를 먹지 않으면 / 최소한

Our approach to eating / is similar to a to-do list: /
먹는 것에 대한 우리의 접근법은 / 해야 할 목록과 비슷하다 /

you have got to have breakfast, you have got to have lunch, /
여러분은 아침을 먹어야 하고, 점심을 먹어야 하며 /

and you have got to have dinner.
그리고 저녁을 먹어야 한다.

And you have got to do it / 그리고 그것을 해야 하는데 /

more or less at the culturally prescribed times: /
거의 문화적으로 규정된 시간에 /

Breakfasts are for morning, lunches are for midday, /
아침 식사는 아침에, 점심 식사는 한낮에 /

and dinners, or suppers, are to be saved until later
in the day.
그리고 저녁 식사 혹은 만찬은 그날의 늦게까지 남겨두어야 한다

This time-based three-meals-a-day paradigm /
이 시간에 기초한 하루 세끼의 패러다임은 /

overlooks the basic fact / 기본적인 사실을 간과한다 /

that our energy demands vary on a day-to-day basis /
우리의 에너지 수요는 매일 변화한다는 /

and that no two days are the same.
그리고 어떤 두 날도 똑같지 않다

As a result, / we eat when we don't feel like eating /
그 결과   / 우리는 먹고 싶지 않을 때 먹는다 /

and don't eat when we feel like eating — /
그리고 먹고 싶을 때 먹지 않는다 /

not because of the chaotic ebb and flow of the food
supply, / 왜냐하면 음식 공급의 혼란스러운 변화 때문이 아니라 /

but because our eating follows a mind schedule /
우리의 식사가 마음의 일정을 따르기 때문이다 /

rather than a body schedule. 신체 일정보다는

It's no wonder / 놀라운 일이 아니다 /

that this time-based eating results in mindless
overeating.
이러한 시간에 근거한 식습관이 아무 생각이 없는 과식을 초래하는 것은 /

우리들 대부분은 적어도 하루에 세 끼, 보통 아침, 점심, 그리고 저녁을 먹도록 문화적으로 훈련되어 왔다. 그렇기 때문에, 여러분이 최소한 이 모든 세 끼를 먹지 않으면 하루가 완전히 끝나는 것처럼 보이지 않다. 먹는 것에 대한 우리의 접근법은 해야 할 목록과 비슷한데, 여러분은 아침을 먹어야 하고, 점심을 먹어야 하며, 저녁을 먹어야 한다. 그 것을 거의 문화적으로 규정된 시간에 해야 하는데, 아침 식사는 아침에, 점심 식사는 한낮에, 그리고 저녁 식사 혹은 만찬은 그날의 늦게까지 남겨두어야 한다. 이 시간에 기초한 하루 세끼의 패러다임은 우리의 에너지 수요는 매일 변화하며 어떤 두 날도 똑같지 않다는 기본적인 사실을 간과한다. 그 결과, 우리는 먹고 싶지 않을 때 먹고, 먹고 싶을 때 먹지 않는데, 왜냐하면 음식 공급의 혼란스러운 변화 때문이 아니라, 우리의 식사가 신체 일정보다는 마음의 일정을 따르기 때문이다. 이러한 시간에 근거한 식습관이 아무 생각이 없는 과식을 초래하는 것은 놀라운 일이 아니다.

문제풀이

① [주격 보어]
동사 seem의 보어로 형용사 complete가 온 것은 적절하다.

② [과거분사]
'규정된, 미리 정해진'이라는 수동의 의미로 명사 times를 수식하는 과거분사가 와야 하므로, prescribed가 온 것은 적절하다.

③ [정동사 vs 준동사]
This time-based three-meals-a-day paradigm이 문장의 주어이고, the basic fact가 목적어이며 이어지는 두 개의 that절은 목적어인 the basic fact의 내용을 설명하고 있는 동격의 명사절로 문장의 동사가 없다. 따라서 overlooking을 동사 overlooks로 고쳐 써야 한다.

④ [전치사 vs 접속사]
뒤에 the chaotic ebb and flow of the food supply의 명사구가 왔으므로, 전치사구 because of가 온 것은 적절하다.

⑤ [가주어 – 진주어 구문]
It은 가주어이고 that 이하가 진주어인데, 진주어인 명사절을 이끌고 있으므로, 접속사가 와야 한다. 따라서 that이 온 것은 적절하다.

➋ 이렇게 풀자 어법상 틀린 부분을 찾는 문제는 밑줄이 있는 부분의 형태와 문맥을 보고 어법에 맞게 쓰였는지 확인해야 한다.
① 동사 seem 보어로 형용사를 취한다.

---

② 분사가 명사를 수식할 경우, 수동의 의미일 경우 과거분사가 오고 능동의 의미일 경우 현재분사가 온다.
③ 밑줄이 그어진 부분이 문장에서 어떤 성분으로 쓰였는지 문장의 구조를 파악해야 한다.
④ because of 다음에는 명사(구)가 오고, because 다음에는 주어와 동사를 갖춘 절이 와야 한다.
⑤ it 다음에 that절이 오면 가주어(it) – 진주어(that절) 구문이 아닌지 살펴본다. 접속사 that 뒤에는 주어, 동사, 목적어나 보어 등을 갖춘 의미상 완전한 문장이 와야 한다.

《 어휘 · 어구 》

condition 훈련시키다
at least 적어도, 최소한
typically 보통, 전형적으로
more or less 거의, 약
prescribed 미리 정해진, 규정된
midday 정오, 한낮
chaotic 혼란스러운
ebb and flow (정도, 수, 양의 주기적이고 반복적인) 변화

---

8. ③   영장류의 의사소통 체계

직독/직해

When the natural communication systems of primates
are examined, / 영장류의 자연적인 의사소통 체계를 살펴볼 때 /

no straightforward increase in complexity /
복잡성의 직접적인 증가는 없다 /

from monkeys to apes to humans is observed.
원숭이에서 유인원, 그리고 인간까지

Many researchers characterize /
많은 연구자는 특징이라고 기술한다 /

great ape communication systems /
유인원의 의사소통 체계가 /

as more limited in range than those of monkeys.
원숭이의 그것보다 범위가 더 제한적인 것으로

For example, monkeys, / but not other apes, /
예를 들면, 원숭이들은   / 다른 유인원들과 달리 /

have functionally referential alarm calls, /
지칭적 기능이 있는 경고성 울음 소리를 지니고 있다 /

although whether monkey calls /
비록 원숭이들이 내는 소리가 /

are truly referential like human language /
인간의 언어처럼 정말로 지칭적인지는 /

remains contested. 논쟁의 여지가 있지만

This particular ape-monkey difference /
유인원과 원숭이의 이런 특정한 차이는 /

makes biological sense. 생물학적으로 이치에 맞다

Great apes are larger and stronger than monkeys, /
유인원은 원숭이보다 더 크고 더 강하며 /

and hence are less vulnerable to predation.
그래서 포식에 덜 취약하다

Apes almost certainly didn't evolve referential alarm
calls /
유인원은 지칭적 경고성의 울음 소리를 발달시키지 않았음이 거의 확실하다 /

because they had comparatively little to be alarmed
about. 경고받을 일이 비교적 거의 없었기 때문에

Indeed, / there is little that is learned at all /
실제로   / 학습되는 것이 거의 없다 /

in the vocal communication of nonhuman apes.
비인간 유인원의 음성 의사소통에서는

Apes do possess gestures / to initiate play, /
유인원은 몸짓을 정말 갖고 있다   / 놀이를 시작하기 위해서 /

for instance, / 예를 들어 /

or when infants signal / they wish to be carried /
혹은 새끼들이 신호를 보내는 경우에 / 업히고 싶다는 /

— many of these gestures have learned elements.
이런 몸짓 중 많은 것에는 학습된 요소가 있다

However, / 하지만 /

apes seemingly do not use their gestures referentially, /
유인원은 외견상으로 자신들의 몸짓을 지칭적으로 사용하지 않는다 /

---

nor do their gestures exhibit /
몸짓이 보여 주지도 않는 것 같다 /

any symbolic or conventionalized features.
어떤 상징적이거나 관례화된 특징들을

영장류의 자연적인 의사소통 체계를 살펴볼 때, 원숭이에서 유인원, 그리고 인간까지 복잡성의 직접적인 증가는 없다. 많은 연구자는 유인원의 의사소통 체계가 원숭이의 그것보다 범위가 더 제한적인 것이 특징이라고 기술한다. 예를 들면, 비록 원숭이들이 내는 소리가 인간의 언어처럼 정말로 지칭적인지는 논쟁의 여지가 있지만, 다른 유인원들과 달리 원숭이들은 지칭적 기능이 있는 경고성 울음소리를 지니고 있다. 유인원과 원숭이의 이런 특정한 차이는 생물학적으로 이치에 맞다. 유인원은 원숭이보다 더 크고 더 강하며, 그래서 포식에 덜 취약하다. 유인원은 경고받을 일이 비교적 거의 없었기 때문에 지칭적 경고성의 울음소리를 발달시키지 않았음이 거의 확실하다. 실제로, 비인간 유인원의 음성 의사소통에서는 학습되는 것이 거의 없다. 예를 들어, 유인원은 놀이를 시작하기 위해서나 새끼들이 업히고 싶다는 신호를 보내는 경우에 몸짓을 정말 갖고 있는데, 이런 몸짓 중 많은 것에는 학습된 요소가 있다. 하지만, 유인원은 외견상으로 자신들의 몸짓을 지칭적으로 사용하지 않고 몸짓이 어떤 상징적이거나 관례화된 특징들을 보여 주지도 않는 것 같다.

문제풀이

① [주어와 동사의 수 일치]
문장의 주어는 no straightforward increase이고, in complexity from monkeys to apes to humans는 increase를 수식하는 전치사구이다. 문장의 주어가 단수이므로 단수동사 is는 적절하게 쓰였다.

② [대명사의 수 일치]
those는 앞에 있는 복수명사 communication systems를 대신하는 대명사이므로 적절하게 쓰였다.

③ [정동사 vs 준동사]
접속사 although가 이끄는 양보의 부사절에서 whether monkey calls are truly referential like human language가 주어이고 이에 대응하는 동사가 필요하므로, to remain을 remains로 고쳐야 한다.

④ [관계대명사]
that 뒤에 불완전한 문장이 왔고, 선행사인 little을 수식하는 주격 관계대명사가 필요하므로 that은 적절하게 쓰였다.

⑤ [도치 구문]
부정어 nor가 앞에 위치하면서 문장에 도치가 일어나야 한다. 주어는 their gestures이고 동사는 exhibit이라는 일반동사이므로 nor 뒤에 do가 쓰인 것은 적절하다.

《 어휘 · 어구 》

primate 영장류
straightforward 직접의, 솔직한
complexity 복잡성
characterize ~의 특성을 묘사하다
referential 지칭적인, 지시하는
contested 이론이 있는, 경쟁의
biological 생물학의
vulnerable 연약한, 취약한
predation (동물의) 포식
comparatively 비교적, 꽤
initiate 시작하다
symbolic 상징의
conventionalize ~의 관례에 따르게 하다

---

9. ④   운송의 특징

직독/직해

In economic systems / 경제 시스템에서 /

what takes place in one sector has impacts on
another; /
한 부문에서 일어나는 일이 다른 부문에 영향을 주며 /

demand for a good or service in one sector /

[Column 1]

한 부문에서의 재화나 서비스에 대한 수요는 /
is derived from another.
다른 부문에서 비롯되게 된다

For instance, / a consumer buying a good in a store /
예를 들면 / 가게에서 제품을 구매하는 소비자는 /

will likely trigger the replacement of this product, /
아마 이 제품의 대체를 유발할 것이다 /

which will generate demands for activities /
이것은 활동에 대한 수요를 만들어낼 것이다 /

such as manufacturing, resource extraction and, of course, transport.
제조, 자원추출, 그리고 물론 운송과 같은

What is different about transport /
운송이 다른 점은 /

is that it cannot exist alone /
그것이 혼자서는 존재할 수 없다는 것이다 /

and a movement cannot be stored.
그리고 이동은 저장될 수 없다 (것이다)

An unsold product can remain /
팔리지 않은 제품은 남아 있을 수 있다 /

on the shelf of a store /
가게 진열대에 /

until bought / (often with discount incentives), /
구매될 때까지 / (흔히 할인 인센티브로) /

but an unsold seat on a flight or unused cargo capacity in the same flight /
항공편의 팔리지 않은 좌석이나 동일 항공편의 미사용 화물 적재 용량은 /

remains unsold /
팔리지 않은 상태로 남게 된다 /

and cannot be brought back /
그리고 되돌릴 수 없다 /

as additional capacity later.
이후에 추가 수용 용량으로

In this case / 이 경우에 /

an opportunity has been seized, /
기회가 포착되었다 /

since the amount of transport being offered /
제공되는 운송량이 /

has exceeded the demand for it.
그것에 대한 수요를 초과하였기 때문에

The derived demand of transportation /
파생된 운송 수요는 /

is often very difficult /
종종 매우 어려워서 /

to reconcile with an equivalent supply, /
상응하는 공급과 조화를 이루기가 /

and actually transport companies would prefer /
그리고 실제로 운송 회사들은 선호할 것이다 /

to have some additional capacity /
얼마간의 추가 용량을 갖는 것을 /

to accommodate unforeseen demand /
예견되지 못한 수요를 수용할 수 있는 /

(often at much higher prices).
종종 훨씬 더 높은 가격으로

경제 시스템에서 한 부문에서 일어나는 일이 다른 부문에 영향을 주며, 한 부문에서의 재화나 서비스에 대한 수요는 다른 부문에서 비롯되게 된다. 예를 들면, 가게에서 제품을 구매하는 소비자는 아마 이 제품의 대체를 유발할 것이고, 이것은 제조, 자원추출, 그리고 물론 운송과 같은 활동에 대한 ① 수요를 만들어낼 것이다. 운송이 다른 점은 그것이 혼자서는 존재할 수 없고 이동은 ② 저장될 수 없다는 것이다. 팔리지 않은 제품은 (흔히 할인 인센티브로) 구매될 때까지 가게 진열대에 남아 있을 수 있지만, 항공편의 팔리지 않은 좌석이나 동일 항공편의 미사용 화물 적재 용량은 팔리지 않은 상태로 남게 되며 이후에 추가 수용 용량으로 되돌릴 수 없다. 이 경우에 제공되는 운송량이 그것에 대한 수요를 초과하였기 때문에 기회가 ④ 포착되었다(→ 상실되었다). 파생된 운송 수요는 종종 상응하는 공급과 조화를 이루기가 매우 어려워서, 실제로 운송 회사들은 (종종 훨씬 더 높은 가격으로) ⑤ 예견되지 못한 수요를 수용할 수 있는 얼마간의 추가 용량을 갖는 것을 선호할 것이다.

문제풀이

항공편의 팔리지 않은 좌석이나 미사용 화물 적재 용량은 제품과는 달리 팔리지 않을 경우 이후에 추가 수용 용량으로 되돌릴 수 없다고 했으므로, 운송량이 수요를 초과할 경우 그것을 이후에 사용할 수 있는 기회가 상실된 것이라고 해야 한다. 따라서 ④ 'seized(포착되었다)'는 'missed(상실되

[Column 2]

었다)'와 같은 낱말로 고쳐 써야 한다.

🌐 구조 다시보기

도입	경제 시스템에서는 한 부문이 다른 부문에 영향을 주고, 한 부문의 수요는 다른 부분에서 나옴
주제	운송의 다른 특징은 혼자 존재하지 않고 이동이 저장될 수 없음
부연	항공편의 좌석이나 미사용 화물 용량은 팔리지 않으면 나중에 추가 수용 용량으로 되돌릴 수 없음
결과	운송 수요는 공급과 조화가 어려워서 운송 회사는 예측하지 못한 수요를 수용하도록 추가 용량을 갖는 걸 선호함

〈어휘·어구〉

take place 일어나다
derive from ~에서 비롯되다
trigger 촉발하다
replacement 보충, 대체
extraction 추출
cargo 화물 적재
capacity 용량
exceed 초과하다
equivalent 상응하는, 동등한
accommodate 수용하다

---

10. ⑤   산업화 이전의 화물 운송 수단

직독직해

Prior to the Industrial Revolution, /
산업 혁명 이전에 /

the quantity of freight transported between nations was negligible /
국가 간 운송된 화물의 양은 무시해도 될 정도였다 /

by contemporary standards.
현대의 기준으로 볼 때

For instance, / during the Middle Ages, /
예를 들어 / 중세 시대에는 /

the totality of French imports /
프랑스 수입품의 총량은 /

via the Saint-Gothard Passage /
Saint-Gothard Passage를 통한 /

would not fill a freight train.
화물 열차 하나를 채우지 못했을 것이다

The amount of freight transported by the Venetian fleet, /
베네치아 선단에 의해 운송된 화물의 양은 /

which dominated Mediterranean trade, /
지중해 무역을 지배했던 /

would not fill a modern container ship.
현대의 화물선 하나를 채우지 못했을 것이다

The volume, but not the speed, of trade improved under mercantilism, /
속도는 아니지만 무역의 양은 중상주의 하에서 증대되었다 /

notably for maritime transportation.
특히 해상 운송에서

In spite of all, / distribution capacities were very limited /
이 모든 것에도 불구하고 / 유통량은 매우 제한적이었다 /

and speeds slow. 그리고 속도는 느렸다

For example, / 예를 들어 /

a stagecoach going through the English countryside /
영국 시골 지역을 통과하는 역마차는 /

in the sixteenth century / 16세기에 /

had an average speed of 2 miles per hour; /
평균 시속 2마일이었다 /

moving one ton of cargo 30 miles inland /
1톤의 화물을 내륙으로 30마일 이동시키는 것은 /

in the United States / 미국에서 /

by the late eighteenth century /
18세기 후반 무렵

[Column 3]

was as costly as moving it across the Atlantic.
대서양을 횡단하여 그것을 이동시키는 것만큼 비용이 많이 들었다

The inland transportation system was thus very limited.
그러므로 내륙의 운송 체계는 매우 제한적이었다

By the late eighteenth century, /
18세기 후반 무렵 /

canal systems started to emerge in Europe.
운하 체계가 유럽에서 부상하기 시작했다

They permitted the large movements of bulk freight inland /
그것은 내륙으로 선적 화물의 대규모 이동을 가능케 했다 /

and expanded regional trade.
그리고 지역의 무역을 확장시켰다

Maritime and riverine transportation were consequently the dominant modes /
해상 및 강 운송은 결과적으로 지배적인 방식이었다 /

of the pre-industrial era.
산업화 이전 시대의

산업 혁명 이전에, 국가 간 운송된 화물의 양은 현대의 기준으로 볼 때 무시해도 될 정도였다. 예를 들어, 중세 시대에는 Saint-Gothard Passage를 통한 프랑스 수입품의 총량은 화물 열차 하나를 채우지 못했을 것이다. 지중해 무역을 지배했던 베네치아 선단에 의해 운송된 화물의 양은 ② 현대의 화물선 하나를 채우지 못했을 것이다. 속도는 아니지만, 특히 해상 운송에서, 무역의 양은 중상주의 하에서 증대되었다. 이 모든 것에도 불구하고, 유통량은 매우 제한적이었고 속도는 ③ 느렸다. 예를 들어, 16세기에 영국 시골 지역을 통과하는 역마차는 평균 시속 2마일이었다. 18세기 후반 무렵 미국에서 1톤의 화물을 내륙으로 30마일 이동시키는 것은 대서양을 횡단하여 그것을 이동시키는 것만큼 비용이 많이 들었다. 그러므로 내륙의 운송 체계는 매우 ④ 제한적이었다. 18세기 후반 무렵 운하 체계가 유럽에서 부상하기 시작했다. 그것은 내륙으로 선적 화물의 대규모 이동을 가능케 했고 지역의 무역을 확장시켰다. 해상 및 강 운송은 결과적으로 산업화 이전 시대의 ⑤ 구식의(→ 지배적인) 방식이었다.

문제풀이

산업화 이전에 국가 간 운송의 화물의 양은 현대의 기준으로 볼 때 매우 미약하였고, 속도도 매우 느렸고, 특히 내륙의 운송 체계는 매우 제한적이어서, 주로 바다나 운하, 강 등을 이용하여 화물을 운송하였다는 내용의 글이므로 해상 및 강 운송은 산업화 이전 시대의 구식의 방식이 아니라 지배적인 방식이라고 해야 한다. 따라서 ⑤ 'outdated(구식의)'를 'dominant(지배적인)'로 고쳐야 한다.

✪ 이렇게 풀자 어휘 문제는 밑줄 친 어휘 주변을 살펴보는 것도 중요하지만, 밑줄 친 낱말과 전체 주제와의 관계를 확인하는 것이 중요하다. 이 글 전체의 주제는 산업화 이전의 운송 체계가 매우 열악하여, 그 양도 보잘 것 없었고, 속도도 매우 느렸으며, 내륙 운송 체계가 매우 제한적이어서 해상이나 운하 등을 사용하는 것이 지역의 무역을 확장시켰다는 내용의 글이라는 것을 인식하고 각 밑줄 친 낱말의 쓰임을 확인할 필요가 있다.

〈어휘·어구〉

prior to ~에 앞서
freight 화물
negligible 무시할만한
contemporary 현대의
totality 전체
dominate 지배하다
maritime 해상의
distribution capacity 유통량
stagecoach 역마차
cargo 화물
inland 내륙에서, 내륙의
costly 값비싼
canal 운하
emerge 등장하다
bulk 대량의
riverine 강의
pre-industrial 산업화 이전의

11. ④ 스포츠의 정서적 격렬함

직독/직해

Sport can trigger an emotional response /
스포츠는 정서적 반응을 촉발할 수 있다 /

in its consumers / 그것의 소비자에게 /

of the kind rarely brought forth by other products.
다른 제품이 좀처럼 생산하지 않는 종류의

Imagine bank customers buying memorabilia /
은행 고객이 기념품을 산다 상상해 보라 /

to show loyalty to their bank, /
그들 은행에 대한 충성심을 보여주기 위해서 /

or consumers identifying so strongly /
또는 고객이 매우 강한 동질감을 가져서 /

with their car insurance company /
그들 자동차 보험 회사에 대해 /

that they get a tattoo with its logo.
회사 로고로 문신을 한다 (상상해 보라)

We know / that some sport followers are so passionate /
우리는 안다 / 일부 스포츠팬들이 매우 열정적이어서 /

about players, teams and the sport itself /
선수, 팀, 그리고 스포츠 자체에 /

that their interest borders on obsession.
그들의 관심이 집착에 아주 가깝다는 것을

This addiction provides the emotional glue /
이러한 중독은 정서적 접착제를 제공한다 /

that binds fans to teams, / 팬을 팀과 묶어주는 /

and maintains loyalty / 그리고 충성심을 유지하게 한다 /

even in the face of on-field failure.
심지어 구장에서 일어나는 실패에도

While most managers can only dream of having customers /
대부분의 운영자는 오직 고객을 가지기를 꿈꾸지만 /

that are as passionate about their products /
그들 제품에 열정적인 /

as sport fans, / 스포츠팬만큼 /

the emotion triggered by sport /
스포츠로 인해 촉발되는 감정은 /

can also have a negative impact.
또한 부정적인 영향을 끼칠 수 있다

Sport's emotional intensity can mean /
스포츠의 정서적 격렬함은 의미할 수 있다 /

that organisations have strong attachments to the past /
과거에 조직이 강한 애착을 가지고 있다는 것을 /

through nostalgia and club tradition.
향수와 클럽 전통을 통해

As a result, / they may increase /
그 결과 / 그것은 증가시킬 수도 있다 /

efficiency, productivity /
효율성, 생산성 /

and the need to respond quickly /
그리고 신속하게 대응해야 할 필요성을 /

to changing market conditions.
변화하는 시장 상황에

For example, / 예를 들면 /

a proposal to change club colours /
클럽 색을 바꾸자는 제안은 /

in order to project a more attractive image /
더 매력적인 이미지를 투사하기 위해 /

may be defeated / 무산될지도 모른다 /

because it breaks a link with tradition.
그것이 전통과의 관계를 끊기 때문에

스포츠는 그것의 소비자에게 다른 제품이 좀처럼 생산하지 않는 종류의 정서적 반응을 촉발할 수 있다. 은행 고객이 기념품을 사거나, 고객이 그들 자동차 보험 회사에 대해 매우 강한 ① 동질감을 가져서 회사 로고로 문신을 한다고 상상해 보라. 우리는 일부 스포츠팬들이 선수, 팀, 그리고 그 스포츠 자체에 매우 ② 열정적이어서 그들의 관심이 집착에 아주 가깝다는 것을 안다. 이러한 중독은 팬을 팀과 묶어주는 정서적 접착제를 제공하고, 심지어 구장에서 일어나는 ③ 실패에도 충성심을 유지하게 한다. 대부분의 운영자는 스포츠팬만큼 그들 제품에 열정적인 고객을 가지기를 오직 꿈꾸지만, 스포츠로 인해 촉발된 감정은 또한 부정적인 영향을 끼칠 수 있다. 스포츠의 정서적 격렬함은 조직이 향수와 클럽 전통을 통해 과거에 강한 애착을 가지고 있다는 것을 의미할 수 있다. 그 결과, 그것은 효율성, 생산성 그리고

변화하는 시장 상황에 신속하게 대응해야 할 필요성을 ④ 증가시킬(→ 무시할) 수도 있다. 예를 들면, 더 매력적인 이미지를 투사하기 위해 클럽 색을 바꾸자는 제안은 그것이 전통과의 관계를 끊기 때문에 ⑤ 무산될지도 모른다.

문제풀이

스포츠의 정서적 격렬함은 조직이 과거에 강한 애착을 가지는 것을 의미할 수 있다고 했고 더 매력적인 이미지를 위해 클럽 색을 바꾸자는 제안이 전통과의 관계를 끊기 때문에 무산될 수도 있다고 한 예를 보아, 조직이 효율성, 생산성 그리고 변화하는 시장 상황에 신속하게 대응할 필요성을 무시할 수 있다고 하는 것이 자연스럽다. 따라서 ④ 'increase(증가시키다)'를 'ignore(무시하다)'와 같은 낱말로 고쳐 써야 한다.

《 어휘·어구 》

trigger 촉발시키다
emotional 정서적인
consumer 고객
bring forth ~을 생산하다[낳다]
loyalty 충성(심)
identify with ~와 동질감을 갖다
insurance company 보험 회사
tattoo 문신
follower 팬, 열심히 따르는 사람
border on ~에 아주 가깝다
addiction 중독
glue 접착제
maintain 유지하다
passionate 열정적인, 열렬한
intensity 강렬함, 강도
attachment 애착(물)
nostalgia 향수
efficiency 효율
project 투사하다
attractive 매력적인
break a link with ~과의 관계를 끊다

12. ⑤ 경쟁보다는 독점이 우월함

직독/직해

Traditionally, / the state has developed competition policy, /
전통적으로 / 국가는 경쟁 정책을 발전시켜 왔다 /

driven by the idea / that monopolies are bad and competition is good.
관념에 따라 / 독점은 나쁘고 경쟁은 좋다는

Today's top technology companies already find themselves /
오늘날 최고의 기술 기업들은 이미 자신들을 발견한다 /

clashing with the authorities / tasked with putting this policy into practice — /
(정부) 당국과 충돌하고 있는 / 이 정책을 실행하는 과업을 부여받은 /

because all of them aspire to monopoly power.
왜냐하면 그들 모두가 독점권을 열망하기 때문이다

This ambition is not unique to the world of technology.
이 야망은 기술의 세계에만 있는 것이 아니다

Look through the literature on management and strategy, /
경영과 전략에 관한 문헌을 살펴보라 /

and you will find plenty of ideas for achieving economic supremacy, /
그러면 여러분은 경제적 우위를 달성하기 위한 많은 견해들을 찾을 것이다 /

packaged in the disarmingly benign-sounding language of business writing.
상대방을 무장 해제시키듯 상냥하게 들리는 비즈니스 글쓰기 언어로 제시된

Take Michael Porter, / Michael Porter를 예로 들어 보자 /

the definitive business strategy guru of the last few decades, /
지난 수십 년간 최고의 비즈니스 전략 권위자인 /

whose 1980s books *Competitive Strategy* and *Competitive Advantage* /
그의 1980년 대 저서 'Competitive Strategy'와 'Competitive Advantage'가 /

were on the shelves of all discerning corporate leaders.
안목 있는 모든 기업 대표들의 책꽂이에 꽂혀 있었다

Those books guided readers / toward nothing less than economic domination: /
그 책들은 독자들을 인도했다 / 그야말로 경제적 지배로 /

first, / find markets ripe for monopolizing (or create new ones); /
첫째 / 독점하기에 적합한 시장을 찾아라 (또는 새로운 시장을) /

second, / dominate and exclude others / from these chosen markets.
둘째 / 다른 사람들을 지배하고 배제하라는 것이다 / 이 선택된 시장에서

Today, / the same advice is given even more forthrightly.
오늘날 / 동일한 조언이 훨씬 더 솔직하게 주어진다

"Competition is for losers," wrote Peter Thiel, the entrepreneur, /
기업가인 Peter Thiel은 '경쟁은 패자를 위한 것'이라고 저술했다 /

in the *Wall Street Journal*. 'Wall Street Journal'에

"If you want to create and capture lasting value, / look to build a monopoly."
여러분이 지속적인 가치를 창출하고 점유하고 싶다면 / 독점을 구축하기 위해 노력하라

전통적으로, 독점은 나쁘고 경쟁은 좋다는 관념에 따라, 국가는 경쟁 정책을 발전시켜 왔다. 오늘날 이 정책을 실행하는 과업을 부여받은 (정부) 당국과 자신들이 충돌하는 것을 이미 발견한다. 왜냐하면 그들 모두가 독점권을 ① 열망하기 때문이다. 이 야망은 기술의 세계에만 있는 것이 아니다. 경영과 전략에 관한 문헌을 살펴보면, 여러분은 상대방을 무장 해제시키듯 상냥하게 들리는 비즈니스 글쓰기 언어로 제시된, 경제적 우위를 ② 달성하기 위한 많은 견해들을 찾을 것이다. 지난 수십 년간 최고의 비즈니스 전략 권위자이자, 그의 1980년 대 저서 'Competitive Strategy'와 'Competitive Advantage'가 안목 있는 모든 기업 대표들의 책꽂이에 꽂혀 있던, Michael Porter를 예로 들어 보자. 그 책들은 독자들을 그야말로 경제적 ③ 지배로 인도했는데, 첫째, 독점하기에 적합한 시장을 찾고 (또는 새로운 시장을 만들고), 둘째, 이 선택된 시장에서 다른 사람들을 지배하고 배제하라는 것이다. 오늘날, 동일한 조언이 훨씬 더 ④ 솔직하게 주어진다. 기업가인 Peter Thiel은, 'Wall Street Journal'에 '경쟁은 패자를 위한 것'이라고 저술했다. "여러분이 지속적인 가치를 창출하고 점유하고 싶다면, ⑤ 협력(→ 독점)을 구축하기 위해 노력하라."

문제풀이

독점은 나쁘다고 생각한 전통적인 관념과는 달리 오늘날의 기업들은 독점권을 열망하고 있으며, 여러 문헌에서 경제적 우위를 달성하기 위한 많은 조언들을 찾을 수 있다고 했기 때문에 지속적인 가치를 창출하고 점유하기 위해서는 협력이 아니라 독점을 구축하라고 해야 문맥상 자연스러우므로, ⑤ 'cooperation(협력)'을 'monopoly(독점)' 등의 어휘로 고쳐야 한다.

◎ 이렇게 풀자 국가와 기업의 상반되는 가치관을 확인하고, 기업의 입장에서 쓰인 문헌들의 내용의 공통점을 살펴보면, 문맥상 쓰임이 적절하지 않은 것을 찾을 수 있다. 국가는 독점보다는 경쟁을 장려하지만, 기업은 독점권을 추구하고 있다는 내용으로, 'aspire to monopoly power(독점권을 열망하다)', 'achieving economic supremacy(경제적 우위를 달성하는 것)', 'economic domination(경제적 지배)' 등을 통해서 기업가인 Peter Thiel은 협력이 아니라 독점을 구축하라고 저술하였을 거라는 것을 알 수 있다.

《 어휘·어구 》

competition 경쟁
monopoly 독점
clash with ~와 충돌하다
disarmingly 상대방을 무장 해제시키듯
nothing less than 그야말로

O5. 동사의 시제

본문 026쪽

A 출제 POINT

1. causes
2. shows
3. met
4. gone
5. had lost
6. will have been
7. broke out

1 [해석]▶ Newton은 중력 때문에 물체가 낙하한다고 믿었다.
[해설]▶ 과학적 사실과 진리는 시제일치를 받지 않고, 항상 현재시제를 사용한다.

2 [해석]▶ Sam은 Sally가 파티에 나타난다면 기쁠 것이다.
[해설]▶ 조건과 시간을 나타내는 부사절은 미래 의미를 현재시제로 나타낸다.

3 [해석]▶ 그는 그녀를 지난주에 만났는데, 첫눈에 사랑하게 되었다.
[해설]▶ 과거를 뚜렷하게 나타내는 부사(구)[ago, yesterday, last week ~]가 있는 문장은 현재완료가 아닌, 과거시제로 나타내야 한다.

4 [해석]▶ Sally는 런던에 가고 없다. 그녀는 지금 여기 없다.
[해설]▶ have gone to는 '~에 가고 여기 없다'는 의미이고, has been to는 '~에 다녀왔다'는 의미이다.

5 [해석]▶ Sally는 집에 왔을 때, 자신의 집 열쇠를 잃어버린 것을 알았다.
[해설]▶ 과거 이전의 일에 대해 말할 때는 과거완료형을 사용한다.

6 [해석]▶ 이번 주 일요일까지 베키와 나는 함께한 지 100일이 되었다.
[해설]▶ 미래의 특정 시점까지 계속을 나타내고 싶을 때는 미래완료형이 사용된다.

7 [해석]▶ 나는 프랑스 혁명이 1789년에 발생한 것으로 배웠다.
[해설]▶ 역사적 사실은 시제일치에 따르지 않고 항상 과거시제로 사용한다.

B 체크 POINT

본문 026쪽

1. freezes
2. gets
3. started
4. hasn't shown
5. hadn't
6. leaves
7. moves

1 [해석]▶ 물은 100도에 끓고, 0도에 언다.
[해설]▶ 과학적 사실은 현재시제를 사용한다.

2 [해석]▶ Sally가 집에 도착할 무렵에는 그녀의 아버지가 파리를 향해 떠났을 것이다.
[해설]▶ 시간과 조건 부사절은 미래 의미를 현재시제로 나타낸다.

3 [해석]▶ 영화는 5분 전부터 시작하였다.
[해설]▶ 과거를 뚜렷하게 나타내는 부사(ago)가 있는 문장

은 현재완료가 아닌 과거시제로 나타내야 한다.

4 [해석]▶ 그는 30분 전에 도착하기로 되어 있는데, 아직도 도착하지 않았다.
[해설]▶ 과거의 행위나 상태가 현재에 미치는 경우 현재완료형을 사용한다.

5 [해석]▶ 그들은 예약을 하지 않아서 테이블을 구하지 못했다.
[해설]▶ 과거 이전에 일어난 일은 과거완료형으로 나타낸다.

6 [해석]▶ 그 비행기는 오늘밤 9시에 파리로 떠난다.
[해설]▶ 일정상 확실한 미래는 현재형이나 현재진행형으로 미래를 나타낼 수 있다.

7 [해석]▶ 갈릴레오는 지구가 태양 주위를 돈다고 믿었다.
[해설]▶ 불변의 진리나 과학적 사실은 시제 일치가 적용되지 않고 현재시제로 사용한다.

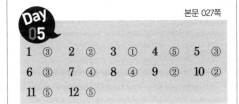
Day 05

본문 027쪽

1 ③	2 ②	3 ①	4 ⑤	5 ③
6 ③	7 ④	8 ④	9 ②	10 ②
11 ⑤	12 ⑤			

1. ③ 이산화탄소와 관련된 진실

직독 / 직해

Not many years ago, / schoolchildren were taught /
몇 년 전에 / 학교 아이들은 ~이라고 배웠다./
that carbon dioxide is the naturally occurring lifeblood of plants, /
이산화탄소가 식물에게 있어서 자연스럽게 발생하는 생명의 원천이라고
just as oxygen is ours.
산소가 우리에게 꼭 그런 것처럼
Today, / children are more likely to /
오늘날 / 아이들은 ~하기가 더 쉽다. /
think of carbon dioxide as a poison.
이산화탄소를 독소라고 생각하기가
That's because / 왜냐하면 ~때문이다 /
the amount of carbon dioxide in the atmosphere /
대기 중의 이산화탄소의 양이
has increased substantially /
크게 상승했기 때문이다. /
over the past one hundred years, /
지난 백년간에 걸쳐서 /
from about 280 parts per million to 380.
입자 백만 개당 약 280개에서 380개로
But what people don't know /
그러나 사람들이 모르고 있는 것은 /
is that the carbon dioxide level /
이산화탄소 수치가
some 80 million years ago— /
약 팔천만 년 전에 /
back when our mammalian ancestors were evolving —/
우리 포유류 조상이 진화하고 있던
was at least 1,000 parts per million.
적어도 입자 백만 개당 천 개였다는 것이다.
In fact, / that is the concentration of carbon dioxide /
사실 / 그 수치는 이산화탄소의 농도인데 /
you regularly breathe / if you work /
여러분이 정기적으로 내뿜는 / 여러분이 일하는 경우에 /
in a new energye-efficient office building, /
에너지 효율이 높은 사무실 건물에서

for that is the level established /
그것은 설정된 수준이다 /
by the engineering group / that sets standards /
기술자 집단에 의해 / 규준을 설정하는 /
for heating and ventilation systems.
난방과 환기 시스템을 위한
So not only is carbon dioxide plainly not poisonous, /
그러므로 이산화탄소는 명백히 독성을 가지고 있지 않을 뿐만 아니라
but changes in carbon dioxide levels /
이산화탄소 수치의 변화가 /
don't necessarily mirror human activity.
꼭 인간 활동을 반영하는 것은 아니다.
Nor has atmospheric carbon dioxide necessarily been the trigger
역사적으로 대기의 이산화탄소가 반드시 ~도 아니다
for global warming historically.
지구온난화의 원인이었던 것도

몇 년 전에 학교 아이들은 산소가 우리에게 꼭 그런 것처럼 이산화탄소가 식물에게 자연스럽게 발생하는 생명의 원천이라고 배웠다. 오늘날 아이들은 이산화탄소를 독소라고 생각하기가 더 쉽다. 왜냐하면 대기 중의 이산화탄소의 양이 지난 백년간에 걸쳐서 입자 백만 개당 약 280개에서 380개로 크게 상승했기 때문이다. 그러나 사람들이 모르고 있는 것은 우리 포유류 조상들이 진화하고 있던 약 팔천만 년 전에 이산화탄소 수치가 적어도 입자 백만 개당 천 개였다는 것이다. 사실, 그 수치는 여러분이 에너지 효율이 높은 사무실 건물에서 일하는 경우에 여러분이 정기적으로 내뿜는 이산화탄소의 농도인데, 그것은 난방과 환기 시스템을 위한 규준을 설정하는 기술자 집단에 의해 설정된 수준이다. 그러므로 이산화탄소는 명백히 독성을 가지고 있지 않을 뿐만 아니라 이산화탄소 수치의 변화가 꼭 인간 활동을 반영하는 것은 아니다. 역사적으로 대기의 이산화탄소가 반드시 지구온난화의 원인이었던 것도 아니다.

문제풀이

① 부사 naturally가 바로 뒤의 현재분사 occurring을 수식하고 있다.
② 지난 백년간의 변화를 말하고 있어서 현재완료형을 사용하였다.
③ that절 이하의 문장에서 명백한 과거를 나타내는 ago를 보면 동사는 to be가 아니라 was가 와야 한다.
④ that이 앞 부분 that is ~ office building을 가리키는 지시대명사로 사용되었다.
⑤ 부정어 not only가 앞에 나와 주어 동사가 도치된 문장이다. 주어가 carbon dioxide로서 단수 명사이므로 단수동사 is를 사용하였다.

어휘 · 어구

lifeblood 생명선, 생명의 원천
poison 독
atmosphere 대기
increase 증가하다
concentration 농도
ventilation 환기

2. ② 온라인 신문 읽기와 온라인 신문 광고비의 증가

직독 / 직해

In many countries, / amongst younger people, /
많은 나라에서 / 더 젊은 사람들 사이에서 /
the habit of reading newspapers /
신문을 읽는 습관이 /
has been on the decline / and some of the dollars /
감소해 오고 있으며, / 돈의 일부가 /
previously spent on newspaper advertising /
전에 신문 광고에 쓰였던 /
have migrated to the Internet.
인터넷으로 이동해 오고 있다.
Of course, / 물론, /
some of this decline in newspaper reading /
신문 읽기가 이처럼 감소하는 까닭의 일부는 /

[Column 1]

has been due to the fact / that we are doing /
사실 때문이다 / 우리들이 하고 있다는

more of our newspaper reading online.
신문 읽기를 온라인으로 더 많이 하고 있다는

We can read the news of the day, / or the latest/
우리는 하루 중의 뉴스를 읽을 수 있다 / 또는 최신 내용 /

on business, entertainment / or whatever news /
사업, 연예에 관한 / 또는 어떤 뉴스든지 /

on the websites /of the New York Times, / the Guardian/
웹사이트에서 / 〈New York Times〉, 〈Guardian〉이나

or almost any other major newspaper in the world
혹은 세상의 거의 모든 주요 신문의

Increasingly, / 점점 더. /

we can access these stories wirelessly /
우리는 이런 기사들을 무선으로 이용할 수 있다. /

by mobile devices as well as our computers.
컴퓨터는 물론 모바일 기기로

Advertising dollars / have simply been following /
광고비는 / 단순히 따라가고 있다.

the migration trail / across to these new technologies.
이동하는 코스를 / 이러한 새로운 기술로

많은 나라에서 더 젊은 사람들 사이에서 신문을 읽는 습관이 감소해 오고 있고 이와, 전에 신문 광고에 쓰였던 돈의 일부가 인터넷으로 이동해 오고 있다. 물론, 신문 읽기가 이처럼 감소하는 까닭의 일부는 우리들이 신문 읽기를 온라인으로 더 많이 하고 있다는 사실 때문이다. 우리는 〈New York Times〉, 〈Guardian〉 혹은 세상의 거의 모든 주요 신문의 웹사이트에서 하루 중의 뉴스나 사업, 연예 또는 어떤 뉴스든지 그에 관한 최신 내용을 읽을 수 있다. 점점 더, 우리는 컴퓨터는 물론 모바일 기기로 이런 기사들을 무선으로 이용할 수 있다. 광고비는 이러한 새로운 기술로 이동하는 코스를 단순히 따라가고 있다.

문제풀이

(A) 과거분사 spent가 뒤에서 some of the dollars를 수식하고 있다.
(B) '어떤 뉴스든지'라는 의미이므로 whatever가 적절하다. whatever가 바로 뒤에 오는 명사를 수식할 때 복합관계형용사라고 한다.
(C) '따라가고 있다'는 능동의 의미가 되어야 하므로 현재완료진행형이 되기 위해 현재분사 following이 적절하다. 또한 following이 바로 뒤에 목적어를 가져오고 있다.

어휘·어구

newspaper 신문
decline 감소하다
migrate 이동하다
access 이용하다, 접근하다
migration 이동
trail 루트[코스]

---

3. ①   브로콜리 저장 방법과 요리법

직독/직해

If properly stored, / 적절히 저장되면 /

broccoli will stay fresh for up to four days.
브로콜리는 4일까지 신선한 상태로 있을 것이다.

The best way / to store fresh bunches /
가장 좋은 방법은 / 신선한 송이들을 저장하는 /

is to refrigerate them / in an open plastic bag /
그것을 냉장하는 것인데. / 묶지 않은 비닐봉지에 담아 /

in the vegetable compartment, /
채소 칸에 /

which will give them the right balance of humidity and air, /
그것은 그것들에게 습도와 공기의 적절한 균형을 주고 /

and help preserve the vitamin C content.
비타민 C 성분을 보존하도록 도와준다.

Don't wash the broccoli / before storing it /
브로콜리를 물로 씻지 말라. / 저장하기 전에

[Column 2]

since moisture on its surface/ encourages the growth of mold. /
표면의 수분은 / 곰팡이의 성장을 촉진하므로

However, / like most vegetables, /
하지만 / 대부분의 채소들처럼 /

it is at its best condition /
그것은 최상의 상태에 있다. /

when used within a day or two /
1~2일 내에 사용될 때 /

after the purchase. 구입 후

Preparing broccoli is extremely easy,/
브로콜리를 준비하는 것은 매우 쉬워서 /

so all you have to do / is boil it in water /
당신이 해야 할 일이라고는 / 물에 삶는 것뿐이다 /

just until it is tender, three to five minutes.
그것이 부드러워질 때까지 3분에서 5분 동안

적절히 저장되면 브로콜리는 4일까지 신선한 상태로 있을 것이다. 신선한 송이들을 저장하는 가장 좋은 방법은 묶지 않은 비닐봉지에 담아 채소 칸에 냉장하는 것인데, 그것은 그것들에게 습도와 공기의 적절한 균형을 주고 비타민 C 성분을 보존하도록 도와준다. 표면의 수분은 곰팡이의 성장을 촉진하므로 저장하기 전에 브로콜리를 물로 씻지 말라. 하지만 대부분의 채소들처럼 그것은 구입 후 1~2일 내에 사용될 때 최상의 상태에 있다. 브로콜리를 준비하는 것은 매우 쉬워서 당신이 해야 할 일이라고는 그것이 부드러워질 때까지 3분에서 5분 동안 그것을 물에 삶는 것뿐이다.

문제풀이

(A) 주어가 way이므로 단수동사를 사용해야 한다.
(B) since 이하의 절에서 주어 moisture on its surface의 동사가 필요하므로 encourages가 맞다.
(C) 시간 부사절에서 미래적 의미를 표현할 때, 미래시제 대신 현재시제를 사용한다.

어휘·어구

store 저장하다
broccoli 브로콜리
bunch 송이
refrigerate 냉장 보관하다
humidity 습도
content 성분
moisture 수분
mold 곰팡이
purchase 구입
extremely 매우

---

4. ⑤   화장실 문이 고장나서 겪은 일

직독/직해

One day last summer / when I was in the bathroom, /
지난 여름 어느 날 / 화장실에 있는데.

the lock on the door jammed.
화장실 문이 고장이 나서 열리지 않았다.

I couln't get it unlocked / however hard I tried.
문을 열 수가 없었다. / 아무리 열심히 애를 써 봐도

I thoughted about my predicament.
내가 처한 곤경에 대해 생각해 보았다.

I didn't think the neighbors could hear me /
이웃 사람들이 들을 수 있을 것 같지 않았다. /

if I shouted. 소리를 지른다 해도

Then I remembered the small window /
그 때 작은 창문이 생각났다. /

on the back wall. 뒤쪽 벽에 있는

The basin near the window /
창문 근처에 있는 세면대가 /

provided an easy step up.
쉽게 올라갈 수 있는 발판을 제공해 주었다.

After climbing out the window, /
창문 밖으로 기어나간 후에 /

[Column 3]

I hung from the window sill /
창턱에 매달려 있다가 /

for a few seconds / 몇 초간 /

and then easily dropped to the ground.
쉽게 땅으로 뛰어 내렸다.

Later my mother came home /
나중에 어머니가 돌아오셔서 /

and asked me what I had been been doing.
뭘 하고 있었는지 물어보셨다.

Laughing, I responded, /
나는 웃으면서 대답했다 . /

"Oh, just hanging around."
"네. 그냥 돌아다녔어요."하고 대답했다.

지난 여름 어느 날 화장실에 있는데, 화장실 문이 고장이 나서 열리지 않았다. 아무리 열심히 애를 써 봐도 문을 열 수가 없었다. 내가 처한 곤경에 대해 생각해 보았다. 소리를 지른다 해도 이웃 사람들이 들을 수 있을 것 같지 않았다. 그 때 뒤쪽 벽에 있는 작은 창문이 생각났다. 창문 근처에 있는 세면대가 쉽게 올라갈 수 있는 발판을 제공해 주었다. 창문 밖으로 기어나간 후에 창턱에 몇 초간 매달려 있다가 쉽게 땅으로 뛰어 내렸다. 나중에 어머니가 돌아오셔서 뭘 하고 있었는지 물어보셨다. 나는 웃으면서 "네, 그냥 돌아다녔어요."하고 대답했다. (hang around는 원래 "할 일 없이 돌아다니다"라는 뜻이지만, 여기서는 "(창턱에) 매달려 있다"라는 의미까지도 포함하고 있다.)

문제풀이

(A) 복합관계부사 however가 바로 뒤에 형용사나 부사(hard)를 가져와 '아무리 ~할지라도'라는 양보의 의미를 가질 수 있다.
(B) near가 전치사로 사용될 경우, '가까운'의 의미이다. nearly는 부사로 '거의'의 의미이다.
(C) 엄마가 필자가 무엇을 했는지 묻는 시점은 과거인데, 필자가 한 일은 과거 이전이므로 '과거완료진행'으로 나타내야 한다.

어휘·어구

lock 고정하는 장치, 자물쇠
jam 고장나다
predicament 곤경
basin 세면대
step 발판사다리
hang around 돌아다니다, 매달리다

---

5. ③   주도권에 대한 우리의 근본적인 천성

직독/직해

Our basic nature is to act, / and not to be acted upon.
우리의 근본적인 천성은 (적극적으로) 행동하는 것이지 / 행동을 유발하는 바탕이 되는 것은 아니다.

Not only does this enable us to choose our response /
이는 우리로 하여금 우리의 반응을 선택할 수 있게 해줄뿐 아니라 /

to particular circumstances, /
특정 상황에 대한 /

but this encourages us to create circumstances.
우리로 하여금 상황을 창조하도록 장려하기도 한다.

Taking the initiative / 주도권을 잡는다는 것은 /

means recognizing our responsibility /
우리의 책무를 인식하고 있다는 것을 의미한다./

to make things happen. 뭔가를 이루어내야 하는

Over the years, / 수년간에 걸쳐서 /

I have frequently counseled people /
나는 수시로 조언을 해 주었다. /

who wanted better jobs / to show more initiative.
더 나은 직장을 원하는 사람들에게 / 더 많은 주도권을 잡기 위해

The response is usually agreement.
조언에 대한 반응은 대체로 수긍하는 것이다.

Most people can see / 대부분의 사람들은 확인할 수 있다. /

how powerfully such an approach /
그러한 접근 방식이 얼마나 강력하게

would affect their opportunities /
영향을 미치는지 /

for employment or advancement.
고용과 승진 기회에

우리의 근본적인 천성은 (적극적으로) 행동하는 것이지 행동을 유발하는 바탕이 되는 것은 아니다. 이는 우리로 하여금 특정 상황에 대한 우리의 반응을 선택할 수 있게 해 줄뿐 아니라 우리로 하여금 상황을 창조하도록 장려하기도 한다. 주도권을 잡는다는 것은 뭔가를 이루어내야 하는 우리의 책무를 인식하고 있다는 것을 의미한다. 수년간에 걸쳐서 나는 더 많은 주도권을 잡기 위해 더 나은 직장을 원하는 사람들에게 수시로 조언을 해 주었다. 조언에 대한 반응은 대체로 수긍하는 것이다. 대부분의 사람들은 그러한 접근 방식이 고용과 승진 기회에 얼마나 강력하게 영향을 미치는지 확인할 수 있다.

문제풀이

(A) 「encourage+목적어+to부정사」 구문이다. encourage는 to부정사를 목적격보어로 취하므로 (to) create가 적절하다.
(B)에는 지난 수년간(Over the years)에 계속 해 왔던 일을 언급하고 있으므로 현재완료형으로 나타내야 한다. 그러므로 have가 적절하다. counsel 뒤에 목적어(people)가 제시되어 있으므로 수동을 나타내는 be동사 am은 적절하지 않다.
(C) 부사 powerfully를 수식하고 있으므로 정도를 나타내는 의문사 how가 적절하다.

《 어휘 · 어구 》

act upon -에 따라 행동하다
circumstance 상황
initiative 주도권, 솔선하는 정신
recognize 알아보다, 인식하다
make things happen 뭔가를 이루다
counsel 조언하다, 협의하다

6. ③   Jimmy Cater Work Project 2001

직독/직해

Former U.S. President Jimmy Carter, /
미국의 전직 대통령이었던 Jimmy Carter는 /
who promotes Habitat or Humanity, /
인류를 위한 주거지를 장려하고 있는데, /
has toured various countries since 1994.
1994년 이후로 여러 나라들을 둘러보았다.
In the summer of 2001, / he visited Asan, Korea, /
2001년 여름, / 그는 한국의 아산에 방문하였다.
to participate in a house-building project.
집짓기 공사에 참여하려고
It was part of Habitat for Humanity International's campaign /
그것은 인류를 위한 주거지 국제 운동의 일부였다.
to build houses for homeless people.
집이 없는 사람들에게 집을 지어 주려는
He worked along with volunteers for the program, /
그는 이 행사를 위하여 자원봉사자들과 함께 일했는데, /
which is named after him— /
그것은 그의 이름을 따서 이름 붙여졌다 /
the Jimmy Carter Work Project 2001.
Jimmy Carter Work Project 2001이라고

미국의 전직 대통령이었던 Jimmy Carter는 인류를 위한 주거지를 장려하고 있다. 1994년 이후로 여러 나라들을 둘러보았다. 2001년 여름에, 그는 한국의 아산에, 집짓기 공사에 참여하였다. 그것은 집이 없는 사람들에게 집을 지어 주려는 인류를 위한 주거지 국제 운동의 일부였다. 그는 이 행사를 위하여 자원봉사자들과 함께 일했는데, 그의 이름을 따서 Jimmy Carter Work Project 2001이라고 이름 붙여졌다.

문제풀이

① who가 관계대명사의 계속적 용법으로 사용되었다. 선행사는 Former U.S. President Jimmy Carter이다.
② 「since+년도」는 '~이래로' 의미이다. 이 경우

보통 현재완료형(has toured)이 나온다.
③ '2001년 여름'이라는 명백한 과거의 일이므로, 현재완료(has visited)를 사용할 수 없고 과거(visited) 시제를 사용해야 한다.
④ to부정사의 부사적 용법(목적)으로 사용되었다.
⑤ name after는 '누구의 이름을 따서 붙이다'는 의미이다. program이 주체가 아니라 대상이므로 수동태(be named after ~)로 사용되었다.

《 어휘 · 어구 》

former 전직의
president 대통령
humanity 인간애, 인류
various 다양한
homeless 집이 없는
volunteer 자원봉사자

7. ④   횡단보도에서 일어난 교통 사고

직독/직해

One day / a truck hit a pedestrian / on the street.
어느 날 / 트럭이 보행자를 치었다. / 거리에서
The driver argued /
운전자는 말한다.
that the careless pedestrian was to blame /
부주의한 보행자가 책임져야 한다고
for the accident. 그 사고에 대해
It was difficult to determine exactly /
정확하게 판단하기 어렵다.
where the accident had taken place.
사고가 일어난 장소를
Many witnesses insisted /
많은 목격자들은 주장했다.
that the accident had taken place /
사고가 일어났다고
on the crosswalk. 횡단보도에서
So, / the driver was held responsible /
그래서 / 운전자가 책임을 져야 한다고 여겨졌다.
for the accident. 그 사고에 대해

어느 날 트럭이 거리에서 보행자를 치었다. 운전자는 부주의한 보행자가 그 사고에 대해 책임져야 한다고 말한다. 사고가 일어난 장소를 정확하게 판단하기 어렵다. 많은 목격자들은 사고가 횡단보도에서 일어났다고 주장했다. 그래서 운전자가 그 사고에 대해 책임을 져야 한다고 여겨졌다.

문제풀이

① hit의 3단 변화는 hit-hit-hit으로 여기서는 과거시제로 사용되었다.
② argued가 that 이하를 목적절로 취하고 있다. was to blame(책임져야 한다, 비난받아야 한다)은 to부정사의 「be+to부정사」 용법으로 '의무'에 해당한다.
③ It-to 가주어, 진주어 구문이다. determine이 where 이하의 목적절을 가져오고 있다. 주절의 시제는 과거시제이고, where 이하는 과거 이전의 내용이므로 대과거 시제가 나왔다.
④ 주장, 제안, 요구, 명령 등을 나타내는 동사 뒤에 '~해야 한다'는 내용이 나오면 「(should +) 동사원형」을 쓴다. 이를 가정법 현재 구문이라고 한다. '아직 사실이 아닌 것 혹은 실현되지 않은 것'을 나타낸다. 그러나 insist, suggest 동사 뒤의 목적절(that절)의 내용이 실제로 발생한 일을 나타낼 때는 직설법을 사용해야 한다. should take place를 had taken place로 고쳐야 한다.
⑤ was held는 수동태 구문으로 맞게 쓰였다.

《 어휘 · 어구 》

pedestrian 보행자
argue 논쟁하다
careless 부주의한
determine 판단하다
exactly 정확하게
crosswalk 횡단보도
responsible 책임 있는

8. ④   자기계발의 세계

직독/직해

We should not be too surprised /
우리는 너무 놀라서는 안 된다 /
when we discover / 우리가 알았을 때 /
that self-help techniques and well-meaning advice /
자기계발 기술과 선의의 조언이 /
don't necessarily deliver the changes / they promise.
변화를 반드시 제공되지는 않는다는 것을 / 그들이 약속하는
The bottom line is / 요컨대 /
that often the techniques don't work simply /
그 기술들은 종종 효과가 없는데 /
because there is no reason / why they should.
이유가 없기 때문이다 / 그것들이 그래야 할
There is precious little quality control /
품질 관리가 거의 없는데 /
in the world of self-help, / 자기계발의 세계에는 /
where conviction is all too often a willing stand-in /
그곳에서는 확신이 너무나 자주 기꺼이 대역으로 등장한다 /
for reasonable proof. 합리적인 증거의
The biologist Thomas Huxley once stated /
생물학자 Thomas Huxley는 말했다 /
that "The deepest sin against the human mind is /
"인간 정신에 반하는 가장 큰 죄는 /
to believe things / without evidence."
무언가를 믿는 것이다"라고 / 증거 없이
If he is right, / 만약 그가 옳다면 /
the self-help section of the bookstore / is truly sinful.
서점의 자기계발서 부문은 / 정말 죄가 많은 것이다
We may roll our eyes /
우리는 눈을 굴리며 의심해 볼지도 모르는데 /
at the medical practices / of times gone by, /
의학적인 관행들에 대해 / 지나간 시대의 /
when drilling holes in people's heads / was seen /
그 시절에는 사람들의 머리에 구멍을 내는 것이 / 간주되었다 /
as the best way / of letting out the demons.
가장 좋은 방법으로 / 악령을 내쫓는
But while contemporary remedies /
하지만 현대 의학의 치료법은 /
for the mental and emotional ills / of our age /
정신 질환과 정서 질환에 대한 / 우리 시대의 /
may be less dramatic, / 그보다 덜 극적인 반면, /
many of our own psychological cures and theories /
우리 자신이 가진 많은 심리학적 치료법과 이론은 /
boast scarcely more scientific validity.
자랑할 만한 더 많은 과학적인 타당성을 거의 갖고 있지 않다

우리는 자기계발 기술과 선의의 조언이 그것들이 약속하는 변화를 반드시 제공되지 않는다는 것을 알았을 때 너무 놀라서는 안 된다. 요컨대 그 기술들은 종종 효과가 없는데 그 이유는 그것들이 그래야 할(효과가 있어야 할) 이유가 없기 때문이다. 자기계발의 세계에는 품질 관리가 거의 없는데, 그곳에서는 확신이 너무나 자주 기꺼이 합리적인 증거의 대역으로 등장한다. 생물학자 Thomas Huxley는 "인간 정신에 반하는 가장 큰 죄는 증거 없이 무언가를 믿는 것이다"라고 말했다. 만약 그가 옳다면, 서점의 자기계발서 부문은 정말 죄가 많은 것이다. 우리는 지난 시대의 의학적인 관행에 대해 눈을 굴리며 의심해 볼지도 모르는데, 그 시절에는 사람들의 머리에 구멍을 내는 것이 악령을 내쫓는 가장 좋은 방법으로 간주되었다. 하지만 우리 시대의 정신 질환과 정서 질환에 대한 현대 의학의 치료법은 그보다 덜 극적인 반면, 우리 자신이 가진 많은 심리학적 치료법과 이론은 자랑할 만한 더 많은 과학적인 타당성을 거의 갖고 있지 않을 수도 있다.

문제풀이

① discover의 목적어이며 뒤에 이어지는 절이 주어(self-help techniques and well-meaning advice), 동사(don't ~ deliver)와 목적어(the changes)를 모두 갖추고 있으므로, 명사절을 이끄는 접속사 that이 온 것은 적절하다.
② 바로 앞에 언급된 복수 명사 the techniques를 가리키는 대명사이므로, they는 적절하다.
③ the world of self-help를 부연 설명하는 관계절을 이끄는 관계사로, where 뒤에 문장의 필수요소를 모두 갖춘 절이 왔으므로 관계부사 where가 온 것은 적절하다.
④ **drilling holes in people's heads가 when 절의 주어로, 뒤에는 동사가 와야 한다. 역사적인 과거의 사실을 나타내고 있으므로, to be를 과거동사인 was로 고쳐 써야 한다.**
⑤ 문맥상 형용사인 more scientific을 수식하므로, 부사 scarcely는 적절하다

《 어휘·어구 》

self-help 자립, 자조
well-meaning 선의의
deliver 전하다, 전달하다
the bottom line is that 요컨대 ~이다
precious little 극히 적은
quality control 품질 관리
conviction 확신
willing 기꺼이 하는, 자발적인
reasonable 합리적인, 타당한
evidence 증거
sinful 죄 많은
roll one's eyes 눈을 굴리다
practice 관행, 관례
go by 지나가다
demon 악령, 악마
contemporary 현대의, 동시대의
remedy 치료(법)
dramatic 극적인
validity 타당성

---

9. ② 직물로 만든 옷의 이점

직독/직해

It's likely / that for a very long time /
일 것 같다 / 오랜 시간 동안 /
people managed to survive /
사람들은 간신히 살아남았다 /
with draped animal pelts /
걸쳐진 짐승의 가죽으로 /
and then began roughly sewing these together.
그리고 나서 이것들을 대충 꿰매어 잇기 시작했다
Ultimately, / though, /
결국에는 / 그러나 /
the advantages of using woven fabric for clothing /
옷으로 직물을 사용하는 것의 이점이 /
would have become obvious.
명백해졌을 것이다
A fur pelt offers adequate thermal protection /
털가죽은 충분한 열 보호를 제공한다 /
if someone is sitting still, /
누군가가 가만히 앉아 있다면 /
but once on the move or in strong winds, /
그러나 일단 이동하거나 강한 바람을 맞으면 /
this is less true, / 이것이 덜 그러하다 /
because pelts aren't shaped close to the body.
왜냐하면 가죽은 몸에 밀착하도록 모양이 잡히지 않기 때문이다

The more air gets between the body and the clothing, /
더 많은 공기가 몸과 옷 사이에 들어올수록 /
the less effective it is /
그것은 덜 효과적이다 /
at trapping an insulating layer of air close to the skin.
공기의 단열층을 피부와 가까이에 있도록 가둬 두는 데
In fact, / 실제로는 /
the insulating properties of clothing decrease very much /
옷의 단열 속성은 매우 많이 줄어든다 /
when walking quickly.
빠르게 걸을 때
Clothing also needs to be breathable, /
옷은 또한 통기성이 있어야 한다 /
because damp clothes are bad /
축축한 옷이 나쁘기 때문이다 /
at keeping the wearer warm /
사람을 따뜻하게 유지해 주는데 /
and become very heavy.
그리고 매우 무거워진다
Woven fabrics are more breathable than fur /
직물은 털보다 더욱 통기가 잘된다 /
and, when specifically tailored to the body, /
그리고 특히나 몸에 맞게 만들어질 때 /
make excellent internal layers, /
우수한 내부의 층을 만든다 /
preventing cold air from getting direct access /
차가운 공기가 직접 닿는 것을 막아 주면서 /
to the skin's surface. 피부의 표면에
Thus the ability to create woven clothing /
따라서 직물 옷을 만드는 능력은 /
would have offered material advantages /
중요한 이점을 제공했을 것이다 /
to our early ancestors /
우리의 선조들에게 /
once they had left Africa for cooler areas.
그들이 아프리카에서 더 추운 지역으로 떠났을 때

매우 오랜 시간 동안 사람들은 걸쳐진 짐승의 가죽으로 간신히 살아남았고 그리고 나서 이것들을 대충 꿰매어 잇기 시작했을 것 같다. 그러나 결국에는 옷으로 직물을 사용하는 것의 ① 이점이 명백해졌을 것이다. 털가죽은 누군가가 가만히 앉아 있다면 ② 불충분한(→ 우수한) 열 보호를 제공하지만, 일단 이동하거나 강한 바람을 맞으면 이것이 덜 그러한데 왜냐하면 가죽은 몸에 밀착하도록 모양이 잡히지 않기 때문이다. 더 많은 공기가 몸과 옷 사이에 들어올수록 그것은 공기의 단열층을 피부와 가까이에 있도록 가둬 두는 데 덜 효과적이다. 실제로는 빠르게 걸을 때 옷의 단열 속성은 매우 많이 ③ 줄어든다. 옷은 또한 통기성이 있어야 하는데 이는 축축한 옷이 착용한 사람을 따뜻하게 유지해 주지 못하고 매우 무거워지기 때문이다. 직물은 털보다 더욱 통기가 잘되고 특히나 몸에 맞게 만들어질 때 우수한 내부의 층을 만들어 내며, 차가운 공기가 피부의 표면에 직접 닿는 것을 ④ 막아 준다. 따라서 직물 옷을 만드는 능력은 우리의 선조들에게 그들이 아프리카에서 ⑤ 더 추운 지역으로 떠났을 때 중요한 이점을 제공했을 것이다.

문제풀이

가죽으로 만든 옷보다 직물로 만든 옷이 여러 가지 장점이 있다는 내용의 글이다. 'but once on the move or in strong winds, this is less true, because pelts aren't shaped close to the body. (일단 이동하거나 강한 바람을 맞으면 이것이 덜 그러한데 왜냐하면 가죽은 몸에 밀착하도록 모양이 잡히지 않기 때문이다.)'에서 '덜 그러하다'는 열 보호를 제공하지 못한다는 의미이므로, but 앞의 내용은 사람들이 가만히 앉아 있으면 열 보호가 잘 된다는 것이 되어야 할 것이다. 따라서 ② 'inadequate(불충분한)'을 'adequate(충분한)' 등의 표현으로 고쳐야 한다.

《 어휘·어구 》

pelt 가죽
roughly 대충
sew 꿰메다, 바느질하다
ultimately 궁극적으로
woven fabric 직물

---

inadequate 불충분한
insulating layer 단열층
property 속성, 특성
breathable 통기성이 있는
internal 내부의
ancestor 조상, 선조

---

10. ② 과학적으로 설명될 수 없는 것을 배척하는 서양 과학 패러다임

직독/직해

Those who limit themselves /
스스로를 제한한 사람들은 /
to Western scientific research /
서양의 과학 연구에 /
have virtually ignored anything /
실질적으로 무엇이든 무시한다 /
that cannot be perceived / by the five senses /
감지할 수 없는 / 오감으로 /
and repeatedly measured or quantified.
그리고 반복적으로 측정하거나 정량화할 수 없는
Research is dismissed /
연구는 일축된다 /
as superstitious and invalid /
미신적이고 무효한 것으로 /
if it cannot be scientifically explained /
만일 그것이 과학적으로 설명될 수 없다면 /
by cause and effect. 원인과 결과에 의해
Many continue to cling /
많은 사람이 계속 집착한다 /
with an almost religious passion /
거의 종교적 열정을 가지고 /
to this cultural paradigm /
이 문화적 패러다임을 /
about the power of science / — more specifically, /
과학의 힘에 대한 / 더 구체적으로 /
the power that science gives them.
과학이 그들에게 주는 힘에 대한
By dismissing non-Western scientific paradigms /
비서양의 과학적 패러다임을 일축함으로 /
as inferior at best / 기껏해야 열등하고 /
and inaccurate at worst, /
그리고 최악의 경우 부정확하다고 /
the most rigid members of the conventional medical research community /
종래의 서양 의학 연구 단체의 가장 완고한 구성원들은 /
try to counter the threat /
위협에 반격하려 한다 /
that alternative therapies and research pose /
대체 의학 요법과 연구가 제기하는 /
to their work, their well-being, and their worldviews.
자신들의 연구, 자신들의 행복, 그리고 자신들의 세계관에
And yet, / biomedical research cannot explain /
그럼에도 불구하고 / 생물 의학 연구는 설명할 수 없다 /
many of the phenomena /
현상 중에 많은 것을 /
that concern alternative practitioners /
대체 의학 시술자들과 관련된 /
regarding caring-healing processes.
돌봄 치료 과정과 관련하여
When therapies such as acupuncture or homeopathy are observed /
침술이나 동종 요법 같은 치료법이 관찰될 때 /
to result in a physiological or clinical response /
생리적 또는 임상적 반응을 초래하는 것이 /
that cannot be explained /
설명될 수 없는 /
by the biomedical model, /
생물 의학적 모델에 의해 /
many have tried to deny the results /
많은 사람이 그 결과를 부정하려 애써 왔다 /
rather than modify the scientific model.
과학적인 모델을 수정하기보다는

서양의 과학 연구에 국한된 사람들은 오감으로 감지할 수 없고 반복적으로 측정하거나 정량화할 수 없는 것은 무엇이든 거의 ① 무시해 왔다. 연구는, 원인과 결과에 의해 과학적으로 설명할 수 없으면, 미신적이고 무효한 것으로 일축된다. 많은 사람이 과학의 힘, 더 구체적으로 과학이 그들에게 주는 힘에 대한 이 문화적 패러다임을 거의 종교적 열정을 가지고 계속 ② 반대한다(→ 집착한다). 비서양의 과학적 패러다임을 기꺼이 해야 열등하고 최악의 경우 부정확하다고 일축함으로써, 종래의 서양 의학 연구 단체의 가장 완고한 구성원들은 대체 의학 요법과 연구가 자신들의 연구, 자신들의 행복, 그리고 자신들의 세계관에 가하는 위협에 ③ 반격하려 한다. 그럼에도 불구하고, 생물 의학 연구는 돌봄 치료 과정과 ④ 관련하여 대체 의학 시술자들과 관련된 현상 중 많은 것에 대해 설명할 수 없다. 침술이나 동종 요법 같은 치료법이 생물 의학적 모델에 의해 설명될 수 없는 생리적 또는 임상적 반응을 초래할 때 관찰될 때, 많은 사람이 과학적인 모델을 수정하기보다는 그 결과를 ⑤ 부정하려 애써 왔다.

문제풀이

② 문장의 주어인 Many는 과학의 힘을 신봉하는 사람들이므로 'object(반대하다)'를 'cling(집착하다)'과 같은 낱말로 바꿔야 한다.

❖ 이렇게 풀자 문맥상 낱말의 쓰임이 적절하지 않은 것을 고르는 문제는 글의 논리적 흐름을 파악해서 그 흐름에 어긋나는 어휘를 찾아야 한다. 이 글은 서양의 과학 연구에 국한된 사람들이 측정 및 설명이 되지 않는 것을 무시하며 이를 미신적이고 무효한 것으로 일축한다고 언급하고 있다. 글이 논리적 흐름으로 보아 'Many continue to object to this cultural paradigm'에서 this cultural paradigm은 과학을 맹신하는 경향을 뜻하므로 이런 문화적 패러다임을 반대하는 것이 아니라 집착한다는 내용이 되어야 한다. 따라서 object to(~을 반대하다)가 아니라, '집착하다, 고수하다'의 뜻을 지닌 'cling to' 또는 'adhere to' 등으로 바꿔야 한다.

《 어휘 · 어구 》

virtually 거의, 사실상
perceive 감지하다
measure 측정하다, 재다
quantify 정량화하다
dismiss 일축하다, 묵살하다
superstitious 미신적인
invalid 무효한, 효력 없는
religious 종교적인
paradigm 패러다임
inaccurate 부정확한
rigid 완고한, 엄격한
conventional medicine 종래의 (서양) 의학
counter 반격하다, 반박하다
alternative 대체 의학의, 대체의
pose 가하다, 제기하다
biomedical 생물 의학의
phenomenon 현상 (pl. phenomena)
practitioner 시술자, (전문직 종사자, 특히) 의사
physiological 생리적인
modify 수정하다

---

11. ⑤   빛의 속도 측정에서 편승 효과의 발생

직독 직해

How the bandwagon effect occurs / is demonstrated /
편승 효과가 어떻게 발생하는지 / 보여진다 /
by the history of measurements of the speed of light.
빛의 속도 측정의 역사로
Because this speed is the basis of the theory of relativity, /
이 빛의 속도는 상대성 이론의 기초여서 /
it's one of the most frequently and carefully measured quantities /
그것은 가장 자주 면밀하게 측정된 물리량 중 하나이다 /
in science. 과학에서
As far as we know, / 우리가 아는 한 /
the speed hasn't changed over time.
빛의 속도는 시간이 지나면서 이제껏 아무런 변함이 없었다

However, from 1870 to 1900, /
하지만 1870년부터 1900년까지 /
all the experiments found speeds /
모든 실험에서 속도가 발견되었다 /
that were too high. 너무 높은
Then, from 1900 to 1950, / the opposite happened /
그다음에, 1900년부터 1950년까지 / 그 반대 현상이 일어나 /
— all the experiments found speeds /
모든 실험에서 속도가 발견되었다 /
that were too low! 너무 낮은
This kind of error, / 이 형태의 오류를 /
where results are always on one side of the real value, /
결과가 항상 실제 값의 어느 한쪽에 있는 /
is called "bias." '편향'이라고 부른다
It probably happened / because over time, /
그것은 아마 일어났을 것이다 / 왜냐하면 시간이 흐르면서 /
experimenters subconsciously adjusted their results /
실험자들이 잠재의식적으로 결과를 조정했기 때문에 /
to match what they expected to find.
자신들이 발견할 것이라 예상한 것과 일치하도록
If a result fit what they expected, / they kept it.
만약 결과가 그들이 예상한 것과 일치하면 / 그들은 그것을 유지했다
If a result didn't fit, / they threw it out.
만약 결과가 일치하지 않으면 / 그들은 그것을 버렸다
They weren't being intentionally dishonest, /
그들은 의도적으로 부정직한 것은 아니었고 /
just influenced by the conventional wisdom.
단지 일반 통념에 의한 영향을 받았을 뿐이었다
The pattern only changed /
그 패턴은 바뀌었다 /
when someone had the courage /
누군가가 용기를 가졌을 때가 되어서야 /
to report what was actually measured /
실제로 측정된 것을 보고할 /
instead of what was expected.
예상된 것 대신에

편승 효과가 어떻게 발생하는지는 빛의 속도 측정의 역사로 보여진다. 이 빛의 속도는 상대성 이론의 기초여서, 과학에서 가장 자주 면밀하게 측정된 ① 물리량 중 하나이다. 우리가 아는 한, 빛의 속도는 시간이 지나면서 이제껏 아무런 변함이 없었다. 하지만 1870년부터 1900년까지 모든 실험에서 너무 높은 속도가 발견되었다. 그다음에, 1900년부터 1950년까지 그 ② 반대 현상이 일어나, 모든 실험에서 너무 낮은 속도가 발견되었다! 결과가 항상 실제 값의 어느 한쪽에 있는 이 형태의 오류를 '편향'이라고 부른다. 그것은 아마 시간이 흐르면서 실험자들이 자신들이 발견할 것이라 예상한 것과 일치하도록 잠재의식적으로 결과를 조정했기 때문에 일어났을 것이다. 만약 결과가 그들이 예상한 것과 ③ 일치하면, 그들은 그것을 유지했다. 만약 결과가 일치하지 않으면, 그들은 그것을 버렸다. 그들은 의도적으로 부정직한 것은 아니었고, 단지 일반 통념에 의한 ④ 영향을 받았을 뿐이었다. 그 패턴은 누군가가 예상한 것 대신에 실제로 측정된 것을 보고할 용기가 ⑤ 부족했을(→ 가졌을) 때가 되어서야 바뀌었다.

문제풀이

빛의 속도는 시간이 흘러도 일정하지만 실험자가 자신의 예상과 일치하도록 일반 통념에 의한 영향을 받아 조정해서 시대별로 빠르거나 느리게 측정되는 편향이 발생했다고 했으므로, 패턴이 바뀐 것은 누군가가 예상된 것이 아니라 실제로 측정된 것을 보고할 용기가 있을 때 일어났을 것이다. 따라서 ⑤ 'lacked(부족했다)'를 'had(가졌다)'와 같은 낱말로 바꿔 써야 한다.

👀 구조 다시보기

도입	어떻게 편승 효과가 발생하는가?
예시	빛의 속도가 시대별로 빠르거나 느리게 측정되는 편향이 발생함
원인	실험자가 자신의 예상과 일치하도록 잠재 의식적으로 결과를 조정해서 일어난 것으로 예상됨
해결	예상이 아닌 실제 측정된 것을 보고할 수 있을 때에야 패턴 바뀜

《 어휘 · 어구 》

---

demonstrate 증거를 들어가며 보여주다, 입증하다
measurement 측정
theory of relativity 상대성 이론
as far as ~하는 한
subconsciously 잠재의식적으로
adjust 조정하다
throw out ~을 거부하다
intentionally 고의로, 의도적으로
conventional wisdom 일반 통념, 속된 지혜
courage 용기

---

12. ⑤   단일 행동 편향

직독 직해

A potential explanation for negative spillover / is single action bias.
부정적인 여파에 대한 한 가지 가능성 있는 설명은 / 단일 행동 편향이다
Single action bias shows / that some people, /
단일 행동 편향은 보여 준다 / 일부 사람이 /
in situations of uncertainty and risk, /
불확실성과 위험이 있는 상황에서 /
tend to simplify / their decision-making /
단순화하는 경향이 있다는 것을 / 자신의 의사 결정을 /
and focus on a single action.
그리고 단일 행동에 집중하는 (경향이 있다는 것을)
Thus, / consumers responding to a threat, /
따라서 / 위협에 반응하는 소비자는 /
such as potential environmental damage or negative social impact, /
잠재적 환경 훼손이나 부정적인 사회적 영향과 같은 /
are likely to focus on a single action, /
단일 행동에 집중할 가능성이 높다 /
irrespective of whether the action taken is the most effective option— /
취해지는 행동이 가장 효과적인 선택인지에 관계없이 /
or would benefit from further actions being taken.
혹은 더 추가적 행동이 취해지는 것이 이익이 있을 것인지에 (관계 없이)
The failure to engage in further or other actions /
더 추가적 행동이나 다른 행동을 하지 않게 되는 상황이 /
is likely to occur /
벌어질 가능성이 크다 /
as a result of the success of the first action.
첫 번째 행동의 성공 결과로 인해
As the first action is removing the cognitive dissonance or worry experienced, /
첫 번째 행동이 경험된 인지 부조화나 걱정을 제거하고 있기 때문에 /
following actions are no longer needed / to restore cognitive balance.
후속 행동이 더 이상 필요하지 않다 / 인지 균형을 회복하기 위해
In other words, / individuals following single action bias may feel /
다시 말해서 / 단일 행동 편향을 따르는 개개인은 느낄 수도 있다 /
as if they are doing enough, / and are thus doing without other actions /
자기가 충분히 하고 있다고 / 그리고 따라서 다른 행동을 하지 않고도 잘 해 내고 있다고 /
that would be beneficial.
이로울 수 있을
For example, / individuals may switch to energy efficient light bulbs /
예를 들어 / 개개인은 에너지 효율이 좋은 전구로 바꿀지도 모른다 /
in their home, / and feel that this single action is sufficient.
자신의 집에서 / 그리고 이 한 번의 행동으로 충분하다고 생각할 수도 있다.

부정적인 여파에 대한 한 가지 가능성 있는 설명은 단일 행동 편향이다. 단일 행동 편향은 불확실성과 위험이 있는 상황에서, 일부 사람이 자신의 의사 결정을 ① 단순화하고 단일 행동에 집중하는 경향이 있음을 보여 준다. 따라서, 잠재적 환경 훼손이나 부정적인 사회적 영향과 같은 위협에 반응하는 소비자는, 취해지는 행동이 가장 ② 효과적인 선택인지에 관계없이, 혹은 더 추가적 행동이 취해지는 것이 이익이 있을 것인지에 관계없이, 단일 행동에 집중할 가능성이 높다. 첫 번째 행동의 ③ 성공 결과로 인해 더 추가적 행동이나 다른 행동을 하지 않게 되는 상황이 벌어질 가능성이 크다. 첫 번째 행동이 경험된 인지 부조화나 걱정을 제거하고 있기 때문에,

---

인지 균형을 ④ 회복하기 위해 후속 행동이 더 이상 필요하지 않다. 다시 말해서, 단일 행동 편향을 따르는 개인은 자기가 충분히 하고 있으며, 따라서 이로울 수 있을 다른 행동을 하지 않고도 잘 해내고 있다고 느낄 수도 있다. 예를 들어, 개인은 자신의 집에서 에너지 효율이 좋은 전구로 바꾸고, 이 한 번의 행동으로 ⑤ 불충분하다고(→ 충분하다고) 생각할 수도 있다.

문제풀이

단일 행동 편향에 따르면 취해지는 행동이 가장 효과적인 선택인지, 혹은 더 추가적 행동이 취해지는 것이 이익이 있을 것인지에 관계없이 단일 행동에 집중할 가능성이 높고, 따라서 첫 번째 행동이 성공하게 되면 더 추가적인 행동이나 다른 행동을 하지 않게 된다는 것이 글의 주된 내용이다. 따라서 에너지 효율이 좋은 전구로 바꾸는 것과 같은 한 가지 행동을 한 후에 그것으로 충분하다고 생각하게 될 것이므로 ⑤ 'insufficient(불충분한)'을 'sufficient(충분한)'으로 바꿔 써야 한다.

❂ **이렇게 풀자** 문맥상 낱말의 쓰임이 적절하지 않은 어휘를 고르는 문제는 전체 글의 주제를 정확히 파악한 후에 각 밑줄 친 단어의 뜻이 주제와 어울리는지를 확인해야 한다. 'The failure to engage in further or other actions is likely to occur as a result of the success of the first action.(첫 번째 행동의 성공 결과로 인해 더 추가적 행동이나 다른 행동을 하지 않게 되는 상황이 벌어질 가능성이 크다.)'에 글의 주제가 잘 드러나 있다.

☝ 구조 다시보기

도입	단일 행동 편향에 따르면 사람들이 의사결정을 단순화하고 하나의 행동에 집중한다고 함
부연	소비자들은 추가적인 행동이 더 이익이 될 모르는 상황에서도 하나의 행동에 집중하는 경향이 있음
주제	첫 번째 행동이 성공하게 되면 더 추가적 행동이나 다른 행동을 하지 않게 되는 상황이 벌어질 가능성이 큼
상술	단일 행동 편향을 따르는 개인은 추가적인 행동을 하지 않고도 잘 해내고 있다고 느낌

〈 어휘·어구 〉

simplify 단순화하다
potential 가능성이 있는
bias 편향, 편견
impact 영향
irrespective of ~에 관계없이
beneficial 유익한
efficient 효율적인
insufficient 불충분한

---

06. 조동사

A 출제 POINT
본문 032쪽

1. will be able to   2. tell
3. should have paid   4. take
5. point   6. not wake   7. might

1 [해석]▶ 너는 너의 숙제를 할 수 있을 것이다.
[해설]▶ 조동사는 두 개를 나란히 쓸 수 없다.

2 [해석]▶ 너는 그의 파티에 갈 수 없다고 그에게 말해두는 것이 좋겠다.
[해설]▶ 「had better+동사원형」은 '~하는 편이 낫다'는 의미이다.

3 [해석]▶ 나는 그에게 관심을 갖지 못한 것을 후회했다. 다르게 말하면, 나는 그를 더 잘 돌봤어야 했는데 그렇지 못했다.
[해설]▶ should have p.p.는 '~했어야 했는데'라는 의미로 과거의 하지 못한 일에 대한 유감이나 후회를 나타낸다.

4 [해석]▶ 그녀는 나에게 일을 떠나 휴식을 취할 것을 제안했다.
[해설]▶ 제안(suggest) 동사 다음의 that절에는 「should+동사원형」 또는 동사원형을 쓴다.

5 [해석]▶ 나는 우리가 현실에 계속해서 직면해야 한다는 것을 지적하지 않을 수 없다.
[해설]▶ 「cannot but+동사원형」은 '~하지 않을 수 없다(=~해야만 한다)'는 의미가 있다.

6 [해석]▶ 당신이 들어올 때 Billy를 깨우지 않는 것이 좋을 거예요.
[해설]▶ had better를 부정할 때는 바로 뒤에 not을 쓴다.

7 [해석]▶ 그는 내게 그날 저녁 나를 만나러 와도 되는지를 물었다.
[해설]▶ 조동사 may는 주절이 과거인 경우, 시제 일치의 규칙에 따라 종속절에 might를 써야 한다.

B 체크 POINT
본문 032쪽

1. do   2. smoke
3. needn't have cooked   4. should be
5. ride   6. not go   7. might

1 [해석]▶ 그 일은 잘 되어 갈 것이다.
[해설]▶ 조동사 뒤에는 동사원형이 나온다.

2 [해석]▶ 그는 파이프 담배를 피곤했다. 지금은 전자담배를 핀다.
[해설]▶ 「used to+동사원형」은 '(과거에는) ~했는데 (지금은) 그렇지 않다'는 의미가 있다.

3 [해석]▶ 그녀는 그렇게 많이 음식을 만들 필요가 없었다. 그러나 그녀는 음식을 많이 만들었다.

[해설]▶ needn't have p.p.는 '~할 필요가 없는데 ~했다'는 의미이다. don't need to부정사는 '~할 필요가 없다. (그래서 ~ 하지 않았다)'는 의미이다. 이 표현이 들어가면 문맥이 어색하다.

4 [해석]▶ 그는 회의가 연기되어야 한다고 제안했다.
[해설]▶ 제안(suggest) 명령, 요구, 주장을 나타내는 동사에 이어지는 that절에서는 「주어+(should)+동사원형」으로 쓴다.

5 [해석]▶ 나는 그 버스를 다시 타고 갈 바에, 차라리 5마일을 걸어서 학교에 가겠다.
[해설]▶ would rather A than B는 'B할 바에야 차라리 A할 것이다'는 의미로 A, B 자리에는 동사원형이 나와야 한다.

6 [해석]▶ 너는 건강이 매우 안 좋아 보여. 오늘은 일하러 가지 않는 것이 좋겠다.
[해설]▶ 「had better+동사원형」은 '~하는 편이 낫다'는 의미로 부정을 하려면 had better 바로 뒤에 not을 붙인다.

7 [해석]▶ Tom은 그녀가 내년이면 29살이 될 거라고 말했다.
[해설]▶ 조동사 may는 주절이 과거인 경우, 시제 일치의 규칙에 따라 종속절에 might를 써야 한다.

Day 06
본문 033쪽

1 ③	2 ⑤	3 ②	4 ④	5 ⑤
6 ②	7 ⑤	8 ③	9 ③	10 ④
11 ④	12 ④			

1. ③
먼저, 창조적인 일을 하고, 그 다음에 대응적인 일을 하라

직독 / 직해

The single most important change /
가장 중요한 단 한 가지 변화는 /
you can make in your working habits /
여러분이 일하는 습관에서 이뤄낼 수 있는 /
is to switch / to creative work first, /
전환하는 것이다. / 창조적인 일을 먼저 하고 /
reactive work second.
대응적인 일은 그 다음에 하는 쪽으로
This means / 이것은 의미한다. /
blocking off a large chunk of time every day/
매일 많은 시간을 차단한다는 것을
for creative work on your own priorities, /
여러분 자신의 우선순위에 따라 창조적인 작업을 위해 /
with the phone and e-mail off.
전화기와 이메일을 끈 채,
I used to be a frustrated writer.
나는 좌절감을 느끼는 작가였다.
Making this switch / 이렇게 전환하자 /
turned me into a productive writer.
나는 생산적인 작가로 변신했다.
Yet there wasn't a single day / when I sat down /
하지만 단 하루도 없었다. / 내가 앉을 때마다 /
to write an article, blog post, or book chapter /
기사나 블로그 게시글 혹은 책의 한 챕터를 쓰려고
without a string of people waiting /
일련의 사람들이 기다리지 않은 날이 /
for me to get back to them.
내가 그들에게 답장을 주기를
It wasn't easy, / and it still isn't, /
그것은 쉽지 않았고, / 아직도 쉽지 않다. /
particularly when I get phone messages /
특히 전화 메시지를 받을 때는

Column 1

beginning "I sent you an e-mail two hours ago...!"
"2시간 전에" 이메일을 보냈어요...!"라고 시작하는

By definition, / this approach goes against the grain /
당연히, / 이러한 접근 방식은 ~에 맞지 않다 /

of others' expectations /
다른 사람들의 기대와 /

and the pressures they put on you.
그들이 여러분에게 가하는 압박에

It takes willpower to switch off the world, even for an hour.
단 한 시간 동안이라도 세상에 대한 스위치를 끄는 데는 의지가 필요하다.

It feels uncomfortable, / 그것은 불편한 느낌이 들고 /
and sometimes people get upset.
때로 사람들이 기분 상하기도 한다.

But it's better to disappoint a few people /
그러나 몇 사람을 실망하게 하는 것이 낫다 /

over small things, / than to abandon your dreams /
사소한 것에 대해 / 자신의 꿈을 포기하는 것보다 /

for an empty inbox.
빈 수신함을 위해(수신함을 늘 비어 있게 하려고)

Otherwise, / you're sacrificing your potential /
그렇게 하지 않으면, / 자신의 잠재력을 희생하고 있다 /

for the illusion of professionalism.
여러분은 전문성이라는 환상을 위해

여러분이 일하는 습관에서 이뤄낼 수 있는 가장 중요한 단 한 가지 변화는 창조적인 일을 먼저 하고 대응적인 일은 그 다음에 하는 쪽으로 전환하는 것이다. 이것은 전화기와 이메일을 끈 채, 여러분 자신의 우선순위에 따라 창조적인 작업을 위해 매일 많은 시간을 차단한다는 것을 의미한다. 나는 좌절감을 느끼는 작가였다. 이렇게 전환하자 나는 생산적인 작가로 변신했다. 하지만 내가 기사나 블로그 게시글 혹은 책의 한 챕터를 쓰려고 앉을 때마다 일련의 사람들이 내가 그들에게 답장을 주기를 기다리지 않은 날이 단 하루도 없었다. 그것은 쉽지 않았고, 특히 "2시간 전에" 이메일을 보냈어요...!"라고 시작하는 전화 메시지를 받을 때는 아직도 쉽지 않다. 당연히, 이러한 접근 방식은 다른 사람들의 기대와 그들이 여러분에게 가하는 압박에 맞지 않는다. 단 한 시간 동안이라도 세상에 대한 스위치를 끄는 데는 의지가 필요하다. 그것은 불편한 느낌이 들고, 때로 사람들이 기분 상하기도 한다. 그러나 빈 수신함을 위해(수신함을 늘 비어 있게 하려고) 자신의 꿈을 포기하는 것보다, 사소한 것에 대해 몇 사람 을 실망하게 하는 것이 낫다. 그렇게 하지 않으면, 여러분은 전문성이라는 환상을 위해 자신의 잠재력을 희생하고 있다.

문제풀이

① The single most important change (that) you can make in your working habits ~ 문장은 동사 make의 목적어 역할을 하는 관계대명사 목적격(that)이 생략되어 있다. 주어는 change이므로 단수동사 is가 왔다.
② mean은 동명사를 목적어로 가져올 수 있다.
③ **being → be**로 고쳐야 한다. 「used to+동사원형」은 '하곤 했다, 과거에는 그랬는데 지금은 더 이상 그렇지 않다'는 의미가 있다.
④ 2형식 동사 feel 다음에 형용사(uncomfortable)인 보어가 왔다.
⑤ But it's better A(to disappoint) ~ than B(to abandon)은 'B하는 것보다 A하는 것이 더 낫다'는 의미로 병렬 구조를 이루고 있다.

《 어휘·어구 》

switch to ~로 전환하다
reactive 대응적인
block off ~을 차단하다
chunk 많은 양, 덩어리
article 기사, 글
blog post 블로그 게시글
a string of 일련의
by definition 당연히, 분명히
go against the grain of ~에 맞지 않다, ~에 거스르다
sacrifice 희생하다

| 2.⑤ | 부모는 자녀를 바로 잡아줄 수 있는 사회의 심판관과 같다 |

Column 2

직독/직해

More often than not, / 종종 /
modern parents are paralyzed by the fear /
현대 부모들은 ~라는 두려움에 의해 마비된다 /

that they will no longer be liked /
그들이 더는 자신의 자녀 마음에 들지 않는다거나 /

or even loved by their children /
심지어 사랑받지 못할 것이라는 /

if they scold them for any reason.
만약 그들이 자녀를 어떤 이유로든 꾸짖는다면

They want their children's friendship above all, /
그들은 무엇보다도 자신의 자녀의 우정을 원하고 /

and are willing to sacrifice respect to get it.
그것을 얻기 위해 존경을 기꺼이 희생한다.

This is not good. 이것은 좋지 않다.

A child will have many friends, /
자녀는 친구는 많이 가질 것이나 /

but only two parents — / 부모는 둘 뿐이다. /

if that —/ and parents are more, not less, than friends.
그렇다면 / 부모는 친구 이하가 아니라 이상이다.

Friends have very limited authority / to correct.
친구들은 매우 제한된 권한을 가진다. / 바로잡아 줄 수 있는

Every parent therefore / needs to learn / to tolerate
모든 부모가 그러므로 / 배울 필요가 / 견뎌내는 것을

the momentary anger / or even hatred /
순간적인 분노나 / 증오까지도 /

directed toward them by their children,
자녀들에 의해 자신을 향하는

after necessary corrective action has been taken, /
필요한 바로잡는 행동이 취해진 후 /

as the capacity of children /
자녀의 능력이 /

to perceive or care about long-term consequences
장기적인 결과를 인지하거나 신경 쓰는

is very limited. 매우 제한적이기 때문에

Parents are the judges of society.
부모는 사회의 심판관이다.

They teach children / how to behave /
그들은 자녀에게 가르친다. / 행동하는 법을 /

so that other people / will be able to interact /
다른 사람들이 / 상호 작용할 수 있도록 /

meaningfully and productively / with them.
의미 있게 그리고 생산적으로 / 자녀와

종종 현대 부모들은 만약 그들이 자녀를 어떤 이유로든 꾸짖는다면 더는 자신의 자녀 마음에 들지 않는다거나 심지어 사랑받지 못할 것이라는 두려움에 의해 마비된다. 그들은 무엇보다도 자신의 자녀의 우정을 원하고 그것을 얻기 위해 존경을 기꺼이 희생한다. 이것은 좋지 않다. 자녀는 친구는 많이 가질 것이나 부모는 둘 뿐이다. 그렇다면 부모는 친구 이하가 아니라 이상이다. 친구들은 바로잡아 줄 수 있는 매우 제한된 권한을 가진다. 그러므로 장기적인 결과를 인지하거나 신경 쓰는 자녀의 능력이 매우 제한적이기 때문에. 필요한 바로잡는 행동이 취해진 후 모든 부모가 자신을 향하는 자녀의 순간적인 분노나 증오까지도 견뎌내는 것을 배울 필요가 있다. 부모는 사회의 심판관이다. 그들은 다른 사람들이 의미 있게 그리고 생산적으로 자녀와 상호 작용할 수 있도록 행동하는 법을 자녀에게 가르친다.

문제풀이

① will no longer [be liked] or even [loved] by~ 구문은 「will+be+p.p.」 형태의 조동사 수동태 구문으로서 병렬 구조를 이루고 있다.
② This가 앞 문장 전체를 가리키는 지시대명사로 사용되었다.
③ to correct는 앞 명사 authority를 수식하는 to 부정사의 형용사적 용법으로 사용되었다.
④ hated (which is) directed toward them~ 구문에서 「관계대명사+be동사」가 생략되어 있다.
⑤ 조동사는 두 개가 함께 나오지 못한다. will can을 will be able to로 고쳐야 한다.

《 어휘·어구 》

paralyze 마비되다
fear 두려움

Column 3

scold 꾸짖다
friendship 우정
sacrifice 희생하다
respect 존경
authority 권위
correct 바로잡다
tolerate 견뎌내다
momentary 순간적인
hatred 증오
interact 상호 작용하다
meaningfully 의미 있게

| 3.② | 직장과 가정에서의 균형 잡힌 삶의 비법 |

직독/직해

Jeffrey A. Rodgers, a vice president of a big company, /
한 대기업의 부사장인 Jeffrey A. Rodgers는 /

was once taught the simple idea /
예전에 간단한 아이디어를 배웠다. /

of pausing to refresh.
원기 회복을 위해 잠시 멈추는

It began when Jeff realized /
그것은 Jeff가 깨달았을 때 시작되었다. /

that as he drove home from work each evening /
매일 저녁 직장에서 집으로 차를 몰고 가던 중 /

his mind was still focused on work-related projects.
자신의 마음이 아직도 업무 관련 프로젝트에 집중되어 있다는 것을

We all know this feeling.
우리는 모두 이 기분을 안다.

We may have left the office physically, /
우리는 육체적으로는 사무실을 떠났을지 모르지만, /

but we are very much still there mentally,
정신적으로는 매우 많이 아직 그곳에 있는데,

as our minds get caught / in the endless loop /
왜냐하면 우리의 마음이 사로잡혀 있기 때문이다. / 끝없는 루프에 /

of replaying the events of today /
오늘의 사건들을 재생하고 /

and worrying about all the things
모든 일에 대해 걱정하는

we need to get done the following day.
이튿날 처리해야 할 필요가 있는

So now, / as he gets to the door of his house, /
그래서 지금, / 집 문 앞에 이르러, /

he applies / what he calls "the pause that refreshes."
그는 적용한다. / 자칭 '원기를 회복하게 하는 멈춤'을

He stops for just a moment.
그는 아주 잠깐 멈춘다.

He closes his eyes.
그는 눈을 감는다.

He breathes in and out once: / deeply and slowly.
그는 한 번, 숨을 들이쉬고 내쉰다. / 깊게 그리고 천천히

As he exhales, / he lets the work issues fall away.
숨을 내쉬면서 / 그는 일과 관련된 문제를 서서히 사라지게 한다.

This allows him to walk /
이렇게 하고 나면 그는 걸어갈 수 있게 된다. /

through the front door to his family /
현관문을 통해 그의 가족에게 /

with more singleness of purpose.
한 가지 목표에 더 몰두하면서

It supports / the sentiment attributed to Lao Tzu:
그것은 뒷받침한다. / 노자가 말한 것으로 여겨지는 다음과 같은 정서를

"In work, do what you enjoy. /
"직장에서는 당신이 즐기는 것을 하라. /

In family life, be completely present."
가정생활에서는 온전히 참여하라."

한 대기업의 부사장인 Jeffrey A. Rodgers는 예전에 원기 회복을 위해 잠시 멈추는 간단한 아이디어를 배웠다. 그것은 Jeff가 매일 저녁 직장에서 집으로 차를 몰고 가던 중 자신의 마음이 아직도 업무 관련 프로젝트에 집중되어 있다는 것을 깨달았을 때 시작되었다. 우리는 모두 이 기분을 안다. 우리는 육체적으로는 사무실을 떠났을지 모르지만, 정신적으로는 매우 많이 아직 그곳에 있는데, 왜냐하면 우리의 마음이 오늘의 사건

들을 재생하고 이튿날 처리해야 할 필요가 있는 모든 일에 대해 걱정하는 끝없는 루프에 사로잡혀 있기 때문이다. 그래서 지금, 집 문 앞에 이르러, 그는 자칭 '원기를 회복하게 하는 멈춤'을 적용한다. 그는 아주 잠깐 멈춘다. 그는 눈을 감는다. 그는 한 번, 깊게 그리고 천천히 숨을 들이쉬고 내쉰다. 숨을 내쉬면서 그는 일과 관련된 문제를 서서히 사라지게 한다. 이렇게 하고 나면 그는 한 가지 목표에 몰두하면서 현관문을 통해 그의 가족에게 걸어갈 수 있게 된다. 그것은 노자가 말한 것으로 여겨지는 다음과 같은 정서를 뒷받침한다. "직장에서는 당신이 즐기는 것을 하라. 가정생활에서는 온전히 참여하라."

문제풀이

① 부사 still(여전히)은 be동사, 조동사 뒤에 위치하며, 일반동사 앞에 위치한다. still이 형용사로 사용되면 '고요한'의 의미이다.
② 문맥상 과거에 떠났다고 생각했는데, 현재도 여전히 그곳에 있는 것처럼 느낀다는 것으로, may had left를 may have left(떠났을지 모른다)로 고쳐야 한다. 조동사의 기본 원칙은 조동사 바로 뒤에 동사원형이 나온다. 또한 조동사는 완료형과 결합하여 과거의 추측이나 과거의 일에 대한 유감, 비난 등을 나타낸다.
③ in the endless loop of (동명사) and (동명사) 구조로 병렬 구조를 이루고 있다.
④ 「사역동사 let+목적어(the work issues)+목적격보어(fall)」 구조로서 사역동사 뒤에 목적어와 목적격보어가 능동 관계인 경우 목적격보어는 동사원형을 취한다.
⑤ 「allow+목적어+to부정사(to walk)」 구문으로서 allow 동사는 목적격보어로 to부정사를 취한다.

《 어휘·어구 》

pause 멈추다
refresh 원기를 회복하다
mentally 정신적으로
get caught in ~에 사로잡히다
apply 적용하다
exhale (숨을) 내쉬다
singleness of purpose 한 가지 목적에 몰두함
sentiment 감정, 정서

---

4. ④ 　아이의 분리 불안에 대한 조언

직독 직해

Sonya asked for my advice /
Sonya는 나의 조언을 요청했다. /
about her five-year-old child's separation anxiety.
자신의 5살 아이의 분리 불안에 관해
"Anna wants to be with me at all times," she said.
"Anna는 항상 저와 함께 있고 싶어 해요"라고 그녀가 말했다.
In Anna's case, / there was an early attempt/
Anna의 사례에서 　/ 이른 시도가 있었다. /
to leave her / at a nice, small preschool /
그녀를 맡기려는 / 괜찮은 작은 유치원에 /
for half days. 반나절씩
She seemed to enjoy the school, /
그녀는 그 유치원을 좋아하는 것 같았지만. /
but was having a hard time /
힘들어하는 시기를 겪고 있었다. /
departing from her mother in the morning.
아침에 그녀의 엄마와 떨어져야 하는 것을
"She was fearful and clingy / and, over time, /
"그녀는 두려워하고 꼭 붙어 있으려고 해요. / 그리고 시간이 지나면서
she started to be more whiny at home and less happy," /
그녀는 집에서 더 투덜대고 덜 행복해하기 시작했어요" /
her mother said. 라고 그녀의 엄마가 말했다.
I suggested / that she stop taking her to preschool.
나는 제안했다. / 그녀가 그녀를 유치원에 데리고 가는 것을 그만두라고

The result was immediate and dramatic: /
그 결과는 즉각적이고 극적이었다. /
"I got my child back," Sonya said.
"우리 아이가 돌아왔어요."라고 Sonya가 말했다.
"She is happy again and self-engaged, /
"그녀는 다시 행복해하고 활발해졌지만,
but she is still unable to be away from me."
그녀는 여전히 내게서 못 떨어져요."
Anna will regain / her trust and confidence. /
Anna는 회복할 것이다. / 그녀의 신뢰와 자신감을 /
She needs time in which there is no reminder /
그녀는 생각나지 않는 시간이 필요한 것이다. /
of her experience of separation / from her mother.
그녀의 분리의 경험이 / 그녀의 엄마로부터

Sonya는 자신의 5살 아이의 분리 불안에 관해 조언을 요청했다. "Anna는 항상 저와 함께 있고 싶어 해요"라고 그녀가 말했다. Anna의 사례에서 괜찮은 작은 유치원에 반나절씩 그녀를 맡기려는 이른 시도가 있었다. 그녀는 그 유치원을 좋아하는 것 같았지만, 아침에 그녀의 엄마와 떨어져야 하는 것을 힘들어하는 시기를 겪고 있었다. "그녀는 두려워하고 꼭 붙어 있으려고 해요. 그리고 시간이 지나면서 그녀는 집에서 더 투덜대고 덜 행복해하기 시작했어요"라고 그녀의 엄마가 말했다. 나는 그녀가 그녀를 유치원에 데리고 가는 것을 그만두라고 제안했다. 그 결과는 즉각적이고 극적이었다. "우리 아이가 돌아왔어요. 그녀는 다시 행복해하고 활발해졌지만, 그녀는 여전히 내게서 못 떨어져요."라고 Sonya가 말했다. Anna는 그녀의 신뢰와 자신감을 회복할 것이다. 그녀는 그녀의 엄마로부터 그녀의 분리의 경험이 생각나지 않는 시간이 필요한 것이다.

문제풀이

① to부정사의 형용사적 용법으로 사용되었다.
② 「have a hard time (in)+동명사」 구조로서 '~하는 데 힘들어 하다'는 의미이다.
③ 형용사 clingy가 be동사 뒤에 나와 보어 역할을 하고 있다.
④ **I suggested that she stops taking her to preschool.** : suggest that 구문에서 suggest가 '당위', '제안'의 의미를 가질 때는 that절의 동사가 동사원형(stop)을 취한다.
⑤ 선행사가 time이므로 「전치사(in)+관계대명사(which)」는 관계부사 when으로 바꿀 수 있다.

《 어휘·어구 》

separation 분리
anxiety 불안
attempt 시도
clingy 꼭 붙어있는
depart from ~와 떨어지다

---

5. ⑤ 　Mark Alenderfer의 네팔 지역 인간 유골 탐사

직독 직해

Archaeologist Mark Aldenderfer set out last year/
고고학자 Mark Aldenderfer는 지난해에 탐사하려고 떠났다.
to explore remote cliffside caves /
외진 절벽 사면에 있는 동굴을 탐사하려고 /
in Nepal's Mustang district, /
네팔 Mustang 지역에 있는 /
aiming to find human remains /
인간의 유골을 찾기 위해, /
near an ancient settlement /
고대 정착지 근처에서 /
high in the Himalayas. 히말라야에 높이 자리 잡은
Almost at once, / 거의 즉시, /
he came face-to-face with what he was seeking:
그는 자신이 찾고 있는 것에 맞닥뜨렸다:
Sticking out from the rock, /
바위에서 툭 튀어나온 채, /
a skull was looking at him right /
해골 하나가 그를 똑바로 바라보고 있었다.

---

as he was looking at it. 그가 그것을 볼 때
The skull, / dating back perhaps 2,500 years, /
그 해골은 / 아마도 2,500년까지 거슬러 올라가는 /
was among many human bones /
많은 사람 뼈 사이에 있었다. /
piled inside several burial caves.
몇몇 매장 굴의 내부에 쌓아있는
Aldenderfer and his team hope /
Aldenderfer와 그의 팀은 기대하고 있는데 /
that DNA analysis will pinpoint /
DNA 분석이 정확히 찾아줄 것으로 /
the origins of this isolated region's inhabitants,
이 고립된 지역 거주자들의 기원을
who may have migrated /
그들은 이주해 왔을지도 모른다 /
from the Tibetan Plateau or southern points.
티베트 고원이나 남쪽 지역에서

고고학자 Mark Aldenderfer는 지난해에 히말라야에 높이 자리 잡은 고대 정착지 근처에서 인간의 유골을 찾기 위해, 네팔 Mustang 지역에 있는 외진 절벽 사면에 있는 동굴을 탐사하려고 떠났다. 거의 즉시, 그는 자신이 찾고 있는 것에 맞닥뜨렸다: 바위에서 툭 튀어나온 채, 해골 하나가 그가 그것을 볼 때 그를 똑바로 바라보고 있었다. 아마도 2,500년까지 거슬러 올라가는 그 해골은 몇몇 매장 굴의 내부에 쌓여있는 많은 사람 뼈 사이에 있었다. Aldenderfer와 그의 팀은 DNA 분석이 이 고립된 지역 거주자들의 기원을 정확히 찾아줄 것으로 기대하고 있는데, 그들은 티베트 고원이나 남쪽 지역에서 이주해 왔을지도 모른다.

문제풀이

① high in the Himalayas는 '히말라야에 높이 자리 잡은'의 의미이다. high가 부사로서 '높이, 높게'의 의미로 사용되었다.
② 관계사 what이 전치사 with의 목적절을 이끌고 있다.
③ 문맥상 접속사 as가 시간 접속사(~할 때)로 사용되고 있다.
④ many human bones (which were) piled~에서 「관계대명사+be동사」가 생략된 문장이다. '쌓여 있는 많은 사람의 뼈'라는 의미로 과거분사 piled가 바로 앞의 명사 human bones를 수식하고 있다.
⑤ migrate는 have migrated로 고쳐 써야 한다. 조동사는 완료형과 결합하여 과거의 추측이나 과거의 일에 대한 유감, 비난 등을 나타낸다. 거주자들(inhabitants)이 이주해 왔을지도 모른다는 과거 추측을 나타내므로 may migrate는 may have migrated가 되어야 한다.

《 어휘·어구 》

archaeologist 고고학자
explore 탐사하다
remote 외딴
district 지역
remains 유골, 유해
face to face 맞닥뜨리다
isolate 격리하다, 고립시키다
inhabitant 주민, 거주자
burial 매장
migrate 이주하다
plateau 고원

---

6. ② 　배심원 선정 과정 및 하는 일

직독 직해

There are several events that take place /
일어나는 몇 가지 일이 있다. /
while jury selection is proceeding.
배심원 선정이 진행되는 동안에

First, / everyone who has been summoned to appear /
우선 / 보이도록 소집된 모든 사람들은 /

at jury duty / must arrive by nine o'clock in the morning /
배심원의 임무를 위해 / 오전 9시까지 도착해 /

and assemble in the jury room. /
배심원 실에 모여야 한다.

A few minutes later, / 몇 분 후에, /

the court clerk usually shows a movie
법원의 서기는 보통 어떤 동영상을 보여준다.

outlining / what is going to happen /
요약해서 / 어떤 일이 진행되는지를 /

throughout the day / 하루 종일

as the jury is chosen for a particular trial.
특정 재판을 위해 배심원을 선정할 때

At around ten o'clock, / twenty people are chosen /
10시쯤에, / 20명의 사람들이 선정된다. /

from the jurors in attendance /
참석한 배심원단에서 /

and are taken to a courtroom /
그리고 그들은 법정으로 이동한다. /

where a judge describes /
그곳에서 판사는 설명해 준다. /

how the process is going to work.
재판 과정이 진행되는 절차를

About thirty minutes later, / ten people are called /
약 30분 후에 / 열 명의 사람들이 부름을 받는다 /

to sit in the jury box / to be questioned /
배심원석에 앉아 / 질문을 받게 된다 /

by the lawyers in the case.
사건에 대해 변호사들(lawyers)로부터

배심원 선정이 진행되는 동안에 일어나는 몇 가지 일이 있다. 우선 배심원의 임무를 위해 소집된 모든 사람들은 오전 9시까지 도착해 배심원 실에 모여야 한다. 몇 분 후에, 보통 법원의 서기는 어떤 동영상을 보여주는데, 이것은 배심원을 선정할 때 하루 종일 어떤 일이 진행되는지를 요약해서 보여준다. 10시쯤에, 참석한 배심원단에서 20명의 사람들이 선정된다. 그리고 그들은 판사가 재판 과정이 진행되는 절차를 설명해 주는 법정으로 이동한다. 약 30분 후에 열 명의 사람들이 배심원석에 앉아서 그 사건에 대해 변호사들(lawyers)로부터 질문을 받게 된다.

문제풀이

(A)의 뒷부분은 '도착해야 한다'는 의미로 쓰였으므로 arrive가 와야 한다. must have p.p.는 '~였음에 틀림 없다'는 과거의 추측을 나타낸다.
(B)의 경우, what 뒤에 목적어를 취하고 있으므로 능동의 의미를 지닌 outlining을 써야 한다. 일반적으로 과거분사와 현재분사를 구별하는 문제는 수동의 의미와 능동의 의미로 구분하기도 하지만, 현재분사 뒤에는 목적어가 나오는 특징이 있다.
(C)는 판사가 '어떻게 그 과정이 진행되는지' 설명한다는 의미이므로 부사 'how(어떻게)'를 쓴다.

〖 어휘·어구 〗

selection 선정
proceed 진행되다
jury 배심원단
assemble 모이다
court clerk 법원 서기
trial 재판
juror 배심원
in attendance 참석한
judge 판사
lawyer 변호사

---

7. ⑤ 학교 교육은 지식만을 제공하지 않고 창의력도 훈련시켜야 한다.

직독 / 직해

It is often believed /
종종 사람들은 믿는다. /

---

that the function of school is to produce knowledgeable people.
학교의 기능이 지식 있는 사람들을 양성하는 것이라고

If schools only provide knowledge, however, /
그러나 만약 학교가 단지 지식만을 제공한다면 /

they may destroy creativity, /
학교는 창의력을 파괴하여, /

producing ordinary people.
그저 평범한 사람들을 양성할 수도 있다.

We often hear stories of ordinary people /
우리는 종종 평범한 사람들에 대한 이야기를 듣는다. /

who, if education had focused on creativity, /
만약 교육이 창의력에만 초점을 맞추었다면, /

could have become great artists or scientists.
위대한 예술가나 과학자가 될 수도 있었던

Those victims of education /
교육의 희생자들은 /

should have received training /
훈련을 받았어야 했다. /

to develop creative talents /
창의적인 재능을 개발하기 위한 /

while in school. / It really is a pity that they did not.
학교에 다니는 동안 / 그들이 그렇지 않았던 것은 정말 유감이다.

종종 사람들은 학교의 기능이 지식 있는 사람들을 양성하는 것이라고 믿고 있다. 그러나 만약 학교가 단지 지식만을 제공한다면 학교는 창의력을 파괴하여, 그저 평범한 사람들을 양성할 수도 있다. 우리는 종종 만약 교육이 창의력에만 초점을 맞추었다면, 위대한 예술가나 과학자가 될 수도 있었던 평범한 사람들에 대한 이야기를 듣는다. 교육의 희생자들은 학교에 다니는 동안 창의적인 재능을 개발하기 위한 훈련을 받았어야만 했다. 그들이 그렇지 않았던 것은 정말 유감이다.

문제풀이

① to부정사의 명사적 용법으로서 보어 역할을 하고 있다.
② 부사 only는 수식하는 말 바로 앞에 위치한다. 즉 only가 동사 provide를 수식하고 있다.
③ and they may produce~를 분사구문으로 바꾼 문장으로 연속동작을 나타낸다.
④ 타동사 hear가 목적어 stories of ordinary people을 가져오고 있다.
⑤ 문맥상 교육의 희생자들이 (과거에) 창의력 개발 훈련을 받았어야만 했다는 내용이 되어야 한다. 그러므로 과거에 하지 못한 일에 대한 유감의 표현인 「should have+p.p.」를 사용해야 한다. **should receive를 should have received로 고쳐 써야 한다.**

〖 어휘·어구 〗

knowledgeable 지식 있는, 아는 것 많은
focus on ~에 초점을 맞추다, 집중하다
victim 희생자

---

8. ③ 무리한 운동의 결과

나는 Disneyland 리조트에서 휴가를 보내고 있었는데, 그곳에는 내가 전에 사용해 본 적이 없었던 몇 가지 최신 근력 운동 장비를 갖춘 멋진 피트니스 센터가 있었다. 나는 엉덩이가 근육을 키우는 헬스 기구에 매료되어, 그것을 써 봐야만 했다. 그러나 나는 너무 무거운 추로 시작했고, 너무 빨리했다. 그 후로 이틀 동안 나는 절뚝거렸다. 더 안전한 접근 방식은 더 낮은 무게의 추로 시작하고, 더 적은 횟수로 반복하고, 더 짧은 시간 동안 더 천천히 동작하는 것이었을 것이다. 나는 이틀간 다시 와서 내 운동의 강도를 늘려갈 수도 있었을 것이다. 나는 전에 해본 적이 없었던 방식으로 내 엉덩이가 근육을 사용 (또는 남용)했고 아픈 대가를 치렀다. 만약 당신이 근력을 키우는 프로그램을 막 시작하고 있다면, 염두에 둘 말은 '사려 깊은,' '느린.' 그리고 '점진적인'이다. 너무 많이 너무 빨리하면 더 오래

된 근육들이 더 쉽게 다친다. 부적절하게 들어 올리다가 근육을 찢거나 다치면 치료하는 데 보통 적어도 6주가 걸리는데, 그것은 상당한 차질이다. 부상의 위험을 감수할 가치는 없다.

문제풀이

① the Disneyland Resort를 부연 설명하는 계속적 용법의 관계대명사로 which가 알맞게 쓰였다.
② 주어인 I가 헬스 기구에 매료되었다는 의미이므로 수동태가 되는 것이 어법에 맞다.
③ **앞에 있는 could have come과 접속사 and로 병렬 연결되어야 하므로, increase를 완료형인 increased로 고쳐야 어법에 맞다.**
④ 부사 easily는 동사인 injured를 수식하므로 어법에 맞게 쓰였다.
⑤ '~하는 데 시간이 걸리다'라는 의미의 「it takes+ 시간+to부정사」 구문이 알맞게 쓰였다.

〖 구문 및 어휘 〗

*6행 A safer approach **would have been** to start with a lower weight, do fewer repetitions, and do slower movements for a shorter time.

(1) 「would have+p.p.」는 '~였을 것이다'라는 의미로, 단순한 유감이나 후회의 의미를 나타낸다.
(2) to start와 (to) do가 접속사 and로 병렬 연결되었다.

*8행 I could have come back in two days and increased the intensity of my workout.

(1) 「could have+p.p.」는 '~했었을 수도 있었을 텐데'라는 의미로, could have come과 (could have) increased가 접속사 and로 병렬 연결되었다.

*13행 If you lift improperly and tear or injure a muscle, **it** usually **takes** at least six weeks **to heal,** which is quite a setback.

(1) 「it takes+시간+to부정사」는 '~하는 데 시간이 걸리다'라는 의미이다.
(2) which는 앞 문장 전체를 선행사로 하는 계속적 용법의 관계대명사이다.

state-of-the-art 최신의
strength-training 근력 운동
equipment 장비, 용품
fascinate 매료되다
limp 절뚝거리다
repetition 반복
intensity 강도
workout 운동
improperly 그릇되게, 적절하지 않게
setback 차질, 좌절

---

9. ③ 집단주의자 집단과 개인주의자 집단의 특징

직독 / 직해

In collectivist groups, / 집단주의자 집단에서는 /
there is considerable emphasis /
많이 강조한다 /

on relationships, the maintenance of harmony, and "sticking with" the group.
관계, 조화의 유지와 그 집단 '안에 머무는 것'을

Members of collectivist groups are socialized /
집단주의자 집단의 구성원은 사회화되어 있다 /

to avoid conflict, / to empathize with others, /
갈등을 피하도록 / 다른 사람들과 공감하도록 /

Column 1

and to avoid drawing attention to themselves.
그리고 스스로에게 관심을 끄는 것을 피하도록 /

In contrast, / 대조적으로 /

members of individualist cultures tend to define themselves /
개인주의 문화의 구성원은 자신들을 규정짓는 경향이 있다 /

in terms of their independence from groups and autonomy /
집단으로부터의 독립과 자율의 관점에서 /

and are socialized / 그리고 사회화되어 있다 /

to value individual freedoms and individual expressions.
개인의 자유와 개인의 표현을 가치 있게 여기도록

In individualist cultures, / 개인주의자 문화에서는 /

standing out and being different is often seen /
눈에 띄는 것과 다른 것이 종종 여겨진다 /

as a sign of courage. 용기의 표시로

Implicit in the characterization of collectivist and individualist groups is /
집단주의자 집단과 개인주의자 집단의 특성 묘사에 내포한다 /

the assumption that deviance will be downgraded more /
일탈이 더 평가 절하될 것이라는 가정은 /

in groups that prescribe collectivism /
집단주의를 규정하는 집단에서 /

than in groups that prescribe individualism.
개인주의를 규정하는 집단에서보다

Indeed, empirical research shows /
실로, 경험적 연구는 보여준다 /

that individualist group norms broaden the latitude /
개인주의 집단 규범이 허용 범위를 넓힌다는 것을 /

of acceptable group member behavior and non-normative characteristics.
용인할 수 있는 집단 구성원의 행동과 비규범적인 특징의

집단주의자 집단에서는, 관계, 조화의 유지와 그 집단 '안에 머무는 것'을 많이 강조한다. 집단주의자 집단의 구성원은 갈등을 피하고, 다른 사람들과 ① 공감하며, 스스로에게 관심을 끄는 것을 피하도록 사회화되어 있다. 대조적으로, 개인주의 문화의 구성원은 집단으로부터의 독립과 자율의 관점에서 자신들을 규정짓는 경향이 있으며 개인의 자유와 개인의 표현을 ② 가치 있게 여기도록 사회화되어 있다. 개인주의자 문화에서는, 눈에 띄는 것과 다른 것이 종종 ③ 약점(→ 용기)의 표시로 여겨진다. 개인주의를 규정하는 집단에서보다 집단주의를 규정하는 집단에서 일탈이 더 평가 절하될 것이라는 가정은 개인주의자 집단과 개인주의자 집단의 특성 묘사에 내포한다. 실로, 경험적 연구는 개인주의 집단 규범이 ⑤ 용인할 수 있는 집단 구성원의 행동과 비규범적인 특징의 허용 범위를 넓힌다는 것을 보여준다.

문제풀이

개인주의 문화에서는 독립과 자율의 관점에서 스스로를 규정짓는 경향이 있고 개인의 자유와 표현을 중요하게 여기도록 사회화되어 있다고 했으므로, 튀는 것과 다른 것은 긍정적으로 여겨질 것이다. 따라서 ③ 'weakness(약점)'를 'courage(용기)'와 같은 긍정적인 낱말로 고쳐 써야 한다.

《 어휘·어구 》

collectivist 집단주의자
considerable 상당한, 많은
emphasis 강조
maintenance 유지
harmony 조화
stick with ~의 곁에 머물다
conflict 충돌
individualist 개인주의자
in terms of ~ 면에서는, ~에 관해서는
autonomy 자율
stand out 눈에 띄다
implicit 내포된
assumption 가정
downgrade 격하시키다
prescribe 규정하다
empirical 경험에 의거한, 실증적인
latitude 허용 범위, 위도
non-normative 비규범적인

Column 2

10. ④ 　　　반동 효과의 원인

직독 직해

If I say to you, / 'Don't think of a white bear', /
내가 여러분에게 말하면 / 백곰을 생각하지 마시오 /

you will find it difficult / not to think of a white bear.
여러분은 어려운 것을 알게 될 것이다 / 백곰을 생각하지 않는 것이

In this way, / 이러한 방식으로 /

'thought suppression can actually increase the thoughts /
사고의 억제는 실제로 생각을 증가시킬 수 있다 /

one wishes to suppress / instead of calming them'.
억누르고 싶은 / 그것들을 가라앉히는 대신에

One common example of this is /
이것의 한 가지 흔한 예는 ~이다 /

that people on a diet / who try not to think about food /
다이어트를 하고 있는 사람들이 / 음식에 대해 생각하지 않으려고 애쓰는 /

often begin to think much more about food.
종종 음식에 대해 훨씬 더 많이 생각하기 시작한다는 것이다

This process is therefore also known /
따라서 이 과정은 또한 알려져 있다 /

as the *rebound effect*. '반동 효과'라고

The ironic effect seems to be caused /
그 역설적인 결과는 생기는 것 같다 /

by the interplay of two related cognitive processes.
관련된 두 가지 인지 과정의 상호작용에 의해

This dual-process system involves, / first, /
이 이중 처리 체계는 포함하는데 / 우선 /

an intentional operating process, /
의도적인 운영 과정을 /

which consciously attempts to locate thoughts /
그것은 생각을 의식적으로 찾아내려고 한다 /

unrelated to the suppressed ones.
억제된 생각과 관련 없는

Second, and simultaneously, / 둘째로, 그리고 동시에, /

an unconscious monitoring process tests /
무의식적인 감시 과정은 검사한다 /

whether the operating system is functioning effectively.
운영 체계가 효과적으로 기능하고 있는지

If the monitoring system encounters thoughts /
만약 감시 체계가 생각과 마주친다면 /

inconsistent with the intended ones, /
의도된 생각과 일치하지 않는 /

it prompts the intentional operating process /
그것은 의도적인 운영 과정을 자극한다 /

to ensure that these are replaced by inappropriate thoughts.
반드시 이러한 생각이 부적절한 생각에 의해 대체되도록 한다

However, it is argued, /
하지만 주장되는 바로는 /

the intentional operating system can fail /
의도적인 운영 체계는 작동을 멈출 수 있다 /

due to increased cognitive load /
인지 부하의 증가 때문에 /

caused by fatigue, stress and emotional factors, /
피로, 스트레스, 정서적 요인에 의해 생긴 /

and so the monitoring process filters the inappropriate thoughts /
따라서 감시 과정이 부적절한 생각을 걸러서 스며들게 해 /

into consciousness, / making them highly accessible.
의식으로 / 그것의 접근성을 높이게 만든다는 것이다

내가 여러분에게 '백곰을 생각하지 마시오.'라고 말하면, 여러분은 백곰을 생각하지 않는 것이 어렵다는 것을 알게 될 것이다. 이러한 방식으로, '사고의 억제는 억누르고 싶은 생각을 가라앉히는 대신에 실제로는 그것을 증가시킬 수 있다.' 이것의 한 가지 흔한 예는 음식에 대해 생각하지 않으려고 애쓰는 다이어트를 하고 있는 사람들이 종종 음식에 대해 훨씬 ① 더 많이 생각하기 시작한다는 것이다. 따라서 이 과정은 또한 '반동 효과'라고 알려져 있다. 그 ② 역설적인 결과는 관련된 두 가지 인지 과정의 상호작용에 의해 생기는 것 같다. 우선, 이 이중 처리 체계는 의도적인 운영 과정을 포함하는데, 그것은 억제된 생각과 ③ 관련 없는 생각을 의식적으로 찾아내려고 한다. 둘째로, 그리고 동시에, 무의식적인 감시 과정은 운영 체계가 효과적으로 기능하고 있는지 검사한다. 만약 감시 체계가 의도된 생각과 일치하지 않는 생각과 마주친다면, 그것은 의도적인 운영 과정을 자극하여 반드시 이러한 생각이 ④ 부적절한(→ 적절한) 생각에 의해 대체되도록 한다. 하지만 주장되는 바로는, 의도적인 운영 체계는 피로, 스트레스, 정서적 요인에 의해 생긴 인지 부하의 증가 때문에 작동을 멈

Column 3

출 수 있고, 따라서 감시 과정이 부적절한 생각을 걸러서 의식으로 스며들게 해, 그것의 ⑤ 접근성을 높이게 만든다는 것이다.

문제풀이

억제된 생각과 관련 없는 생각을 의식적으로 찾아내려 하는 의도적인 운영 과정이 작동을 멈추게 될 경우, 무의식적인 감시 과정에 의해 걸러진 부적절한 생각이 의도적인 운영 과정에 의해 적절한 생각으로 대체되지 못하고 의식 속에 나타나게 된다고 해야 한다. 따라서 ④ 'inappropriate(부적절한)'를 'appropriate(적절한)'와 같은 낱말로 바꿔 써야 한다.

《 어휘·어구 》

suppression 억제, 억압
calm 진정시키다
rebound effect (심리학) 반동 효과
interplay 상호 작용
cognitive 인지의, 인식의
intentional 의도적인
consciously 의식적으로
simultaneously 동시에
monitor 감시하다
function 기능하다
effectively 효과적으로
encounter 마주치다
inconsistent 일치하지 않는
prompt 자극하다
ensure 반드시 ~하게 하다
replace 대체하다
load 부하, 부담
fatigue 피로
filter 거르다, 스며들게 하다
inappropriate 부적절한
accessible 접근하기 쉬운

11. ④ 　　　인구 과잉과 기근의 원인

직독 직해

At a time / 시기에 /

when concerns about overpopulation and famine were reaching their highest peak, /
인구 과잉과 기근에 대한 우려가 최고조에 달하고 있었던 /

Garrett Hardin did not blame these problems /
Garrett Hardin은 이런 문제를 탓으로 돌리지 않았다 /

on human ignorance / 인간의 무지 (탓으로) /

— a failure to take note of /
주목하지 못한 것과 같은 /

dwindling per capita food supplies, / for example.
감소하는 1인당 식량 공급 / 예를 들어

Instead, / his explanation focused on the discrepancy /
대신에 / 그의 설명은 불일치에 초점을 두었다 /

between the interests of individual households /
개별 가구의 이익 /

and those of society as a whole.
사회 전체의 이익 사이의

To understand excessive reproduction /
과도한 번식을 이해하기 위해 /

as a tragedy of the commons, / 공유지의 비극으로 /

bear in mind / that a typical household stands to gain /
유념하라 / 전형적인 가정은 이익을 얻을 것이라는 점에 /

from bringing another child into the world /
또 다른 아이를 세상에 낳음으로써 /

— in terms of the net contributions /
순기여도 측면에서 /

he or she makes to household earnings, /
아이가 가정의 수익에 가져오는 /

for example. 예를 들어

But while parents can be counted on to assess /
그러나 부모들에게 평가하도록 의존할 수 있는 반면에 /

how the well-being of their household is affected /
그들 가정의 행복이 어떻게 영향을 받는지를 /

by additional offspring, / 추가된 자식에 의해 /

they neglect other impacts of population growth, /
그들은 인구 증가의 다른 영향을 간과한다 /

such as diminished per capita food supplies for other people. 다른 사람들의 1인당 식량 공급 감소와 같은

In other words, / 다시 말해 /

the costs of reproduction are largely shared, /
번식에 드는 비용은 대체로 공유된다 /

rather than being shouldered entirely /
전적으로 떠맡겨지는 것이 아니라 /

by individual households. 개별 가구에

As a result, / reproduction is excessive.
그 결과   / 지나친 번식이 일어난다

인구 과잉과 기근에 대한 우려가 최고조에 달하고 있었던 시기에 Garrett Hardin은 이런 문제들을, 예를 들어 감소하는 1인당 식량 공급을 주목하지 못한 것과 같은 인간의 ① 무지 탓으로 돌리지 않았다. 대신에, 그의 설명은 개별 가구의 ② 이익과 사회 전체의 이익 사이의 불일치에 초점을 두었다. 과도한 번식을 공유지의 비극으로 이해하기 위해, 예를 들어 아이가 ③ 가정의 수익에 가져오는 순기여도 측면에서, 전형적인 가정은 또 다른 아이를 세상에 낳음으로써 이익을 얻을 것이라는 점에 유념하라. 그러나 그들 가정의 행복이 추가된 자식에 의해 어떻게 영향을 받는지를 부모들에게 평가하도록 의존할 수 있는 반면에, 그들은 다른 사람들의 1인당 식량 공급 감소와 같은 인구 증가의 다른 영향을 ④ 과대평가한다(→ 간과한다). 다시 말해, 번식에 드는 비용은 개별 가구에 전적으로 떠맡겨지는 것이 아니라 대체로 ⑤ 공유된다. 그 결과, 지나친 번식이 일어난다.

문제풀이

종속절에 쓰인 접속사 while로 보아 주절의 내용은 종속절과는 반대되는 내용이 나와야 함을 알 수 있다. 가정의 행복이 추가된 자식에 의해 어떻게 영향을 받는지를 부모들에게 평가하도록 '의존할 수' 있는 반면에, '평가하겠지만' 인구 증가의 다른 영향을 '간과한다'라는 내용이 되어야 문맥상 자연스럽다. 또한 바로 뒤 문장에서 번식에 드는 비용은 개별 가구에 전적으로 떠맡겨지는 것이 아니라 공유되어 그 결과 지나친 번식이 일어난다는 내용이 제시된 것으로 보아 ④ 'overvalue(과대평가하다)'를 'neglect(간과하다)'와 같은 낱말로 바꿔야 한다.

어휘·어구

concern 우려, 염려
overpopulation 인구 과잉
famine 기근
blame 탓하다, 비난하다
ignorance 무지
take note of ~을 주목하다
per capita 1인당
explanation 설명
discrepancy 차이, 불일치
household 가정의
excessive 과도한, 지나친
reproduction 생식, 번식
tragedy 비극
common 공유지
bear ~ in mind ~을 유념하다
in terms of ~의 관점에서
net contribution 순기여도
assess 평가하다
additional 추가의
offspring 자식
overvalue 과대평가하다
shoulder 짊어지다
entirely 전적으로, 완전히

---

12. ④ 자동화된 사회와 노동 시장의 관계

직독 직해

History suggests / that change happens in much more dialectical ways /
역사는 보여 준다 / 변화가 훨씬 더 변증법적인 방식으로 일어난다는 것을 /

than futurology usually recognizes.
미래학이 일반적으로 인정하는 것보다

Changes bring out other changes.
변화는 다른 변화를 끌어낸다

Trends generate countertrends.
유행은 역유행을 생성한다

New concentrations of power prompt coalitions and campaigns /
권력의 새로운 집중은 연합과 운동을 유발한다 /

to weaken them.
그것을 약화시키는

As a result, / simple linear forecasts /
그 결과   / 단순한 선형적 예측은 /

in which technologies just wipe out jobs /
기술이 그저 일자리를 말살한다는 /

are misleading.
오해를 불러일으킨다

This is partly a matter of economics.
이것은 부분적으로는 경제적 문제이다

To the extent / that robots or smart tools do replace existing jobs, /
정도로   / 로봇이나 스마트 기구가 기존의 일자리를 대체하는 /

relative price effects will kick in.
상대적 가격의 효과가 나타나기 시작할 것이다

Those sectors / where productivity dramatically increases /
그런 부문은 / 생산성이 극적으로 향상되는 /

will see price reductions, / and spending will shift over to other fields /
가격 삭감을 겪게 될 것이다 / 그리고 지출은 다른 분야로 이동할 것이다 /

that are harder to automate, /
자동화하기 더 어려운 /

such as personal coaches, tour guides, teachers, care workers, and craft workers.
개인 코치, 관광 가이드, 교사, 간병인, 그리고 공예가 같은

Their relative price will probably rise.
그것들의 상대적인 가격은 아마도 상승할 것이다

Labor markets have proven to be dynamic /
노동 시장은 역동적인 것으로 입증되어왔다 /

over the last two centuries, /
지난 2세기 동안 /

coping with massive destruction of jobs and equally massive creation, too.
일자리의 대규모 파괴와 또한 그에 상응하는 대규모 창출에 대처하면서

There is no obvious reason /
명확한 이유는 없다 /

why a much more automated society would necessarily have fewer jobs.
훨씬 더 자동화된 사회가 필연적으로 더 적은 일자리를 가지게 될 것이라는

역사는 변화가 미래학이 일반적으로 인정하는 것보다 훨씬 더 변증법적인 방식으로 일어난다는 것을 보여 준다. 변화는 다른 변화를 끌어낸다, 유행은 역유행을 생성한다. 권력의 새로운 집중은 그것을 ① 약화시키는 연합과 운동을 유발한다. 그 결과, 기술이 그저 일자리를 말살한다는 단순한 선형적 예측은 ② 오해를 불러일으킨다. 이것은 부분적으로는 경제적 문제이다. 로봇이나 스마트 기구가 기존의 일자리를 대체하는 정도로, 상대적 가격의 효과가 나타나기 시작할 것이다. 생산성이 극적으로 향상되는 그런 부문은 가격 삭감을 겪게 될 것이고, 지출은 개인 코치, 관광 가이드, 교사, 간병인, 그리고 공예가 같은, 자동화하기 ③ 더 어려운 다른 분야로 이동할 것이다. 그것들의 상대적인 가격은 아마도 ④ 하락(→상승)할 것이다. 일자리의 대규모 파괴와 또한 그에 상응하는 대규모 창출에 대처하면서, 노동 시장은 지난 2세기 동안 역동적인 것으로 입증되어왔다. 훨씬 더 자동화된 사회가 필연적으로 ⑤ 더 적은 일자리를 가지게 될 것이라는 명확한 이유는 없다.

문제풀이

자동화로 인해 생산성이 향상되는 부문에서는 공급이 늘어나서 가격 삭감이 생길 것이고, 그 대신 지출은 자동화하기 어려운 부문으로 이동하여 그 부문의 수요가 늘어나기 때문에 해당 부문의 공급

자들의 상대적인 가격은 하락하지 않고 상승할 것이므로, ④ 'fall(하락)'을 'rise(상승)' 등의 어휘로 고쳐야 한다.

어휘·어구

bring out ~을 드러나게 하다
countertrend 역유행, 반대의 경향
coalition 연합
linear 선형적인
cope with ~에 대처하다

07. 수동태

A 출제 POINT

1. has been cleared　2. was put up with
3. was given　4. to be left
5. to sing　6. is said
7. suddenly disappeared

1 [해석]▶ 그 지역은 지뢰가 제거되었다.
[해설]▶ 현재완료수동태는 have been p.p 형태를 취한다.

2 [해석]▶ 그녀는 고통을 참았다.
[해설]▶ 동사구는 하나의 동사로 취급해 수동태를 만든다.

3 [해석]▶ 그는 말할 기회를 얻었다.
[해설]▶ 4형식 문장에서 간접목적어가 주어로 나온 수동태 문장인데 yesterday가 있으므로 was given으로 표현해야 한다.

4 [해석]▶ 소녀는 밤에 혼자 남기는 것을 무서워했다.
[해설]▶ to부정사의 수동태는 to be p.p로 표현한다. 동명사 수동태로 나타내려면 be afraid of [being left]와 같이 of가 있어야 한다.

5 [해석]▶ 우리 아들이 한밤중에 혼자 노래했다.
[해설]▶ 지각동사는 수동태로 바꾸면 목적격보어가 to부정사 구조로 바뀐다.

6 [해석]▶ 사람들은 그녀가 신뢰할만한 사람이라고 말한다.
[해설]▶ say동사가 that절을 목적어로 갖는 경우, 수동태로 바꾸면 It is said that ~ 구조로 바뀐다.

7 [해석]▶ Sally가 갑자기 어둠속으로 사라졌다.
[해설]▶ 자동사(appear)는 수동태로 쓸 수 없다.

B 체크 POINT

1. has been collected　2. was called off
3. for　4. being dumped
5. to move　6. is thought　7. resemble

1 [해석]▶ 데이터는 수집되고 처리되어진 이후에만 유용할 수 있다.
[해설]▶ 현재완료 수동태는 has been p.p. 형태를 취한다.

2 [해석]▶ 그 야구 경기는 폭우로 인해 취소되었다.
[해설]▶ 동사구의 수동태 문장이다. be called off는 '~이 취소되다'는 의미이다.

3 [해석]▶ 그 야구 방망이는 아빠가 내게 사주셨다.
[해설]▶ buy동사가 들어간 4형식 문장을 3형식 문장으로 바꾸면 전치사 for가 간접목적어 앞에 붙는데, 수동태에서도 동일하게 적용된다.

4 [해석]▶ Sam은 차인 것을 어떻게 극복해야 할지 모른다.
[해설]▶ get over는 동명사를 목적어로 취하므로, get over

뒤에 동명사 수동태를 가져온다.

5 [해석]▶ 시냇물과 달리 빙하는 움직이는 것을 볼 수 없다.
[해설]▶ 지각동사의 목적격보어가 동사원형인 경우, 수동태로 바꾸면 「to+동사원형」이 된다.

6 [해석]▶ 유로화의 도입이 생활비의 상승을 초래했다고 생각한다.
[해설]▶ think동사가 that절을 목적어로 갖는 경우, 수동태로 바꾸면 It is thought that ~ 구조로 바뀐다.

7 [해석]▶ 너는 너의 엄마를 많이 닮았다.
[해설]▶ 타동사 resemble은 수동태로 바꿀 수 없다.

Day 07

1	④	2	④	3	③	4	①	5	②
6	①	7	④	8	④	9	③	10	③
11	④	12	④						

1. ④　지도자가 될 수 있게 해 주는 특성

직독 직해

The idea / 생각은 /
that leaders *inherently* possess certain physical, intellectual, or personality traits /
지도자는 특정한 신체적, 지적, 혹은 성격적 특성을 '선천적으로' 가지고 있다는 /
that distinguish them from nonleaders / was the foundational belief /
그들을 지도자가 아닌 사람과 구별해 주는 / 기초적인 믿음이었다 /
of the trait-based approach to leadership.
리더십에 대한 특성 기반 접근법의
This approach dominated leadership research /
이 접근법은 리더십 연구를 지배했다 /
from the late 1800s until the mid-1940s /
1800년대 후반부터 1940년대 중반까지 /
and has experienced a resurgence of interest in the last couple of decades.
그리고 지난 몇십 년 동안 관심이 되살아나는 것을 경험했다
Early trait theorists believed / that some individuals are born with the traits /
초기 특성 이론가들은 믿었다 / 어떤 사람들은 특성을 가지고 태어난다고 /
that allow them to become great leaders /
위대한 지도자가 될 수 있게 해 주는
Thus, / early research in this area often presented the widely stated argument /
따라서 / 이 분야의 초기 연구는 널리 언급되는 주장을 자주 제시하였다 /
that "leaders are born, not made."
'지도자는 만들어지는 것이 아니라 태어나는 것'이라는
Also, / some of the earliest leadership studies were grounded in /
또한 / 초기 리더십 연구 중 일부는 ~에 기반을 두었다 /
what was referred to as the "great man" theory /
'위인' 이론이라 불리는 것(에) /
because researchers at the time focused on identifying traits of highly visible leaders in history /
이는 그 당시 연구자들이 역사에서 매우 눈에 띄는 지도자들의 특징을 확인하는 데 초점을 맞췄기 때문이다 /
who were typically male and associated with the aristocracy or political or military leadership.
일반적으로 남성이면서 귀족이거나 정치나 군대의 리더십과 관련이 있는
In more recent history, / numerous authors have acknowledged /
더 최근의 역사에서 / 수많은 저자들은 인정했다 /
that there are many enduring qualities, / whether

---

innate or learned, /
많은 지속되는 자질이 있다는 것을 / 타고난 것이든 학습된 것이든 /
that contribute to leadership potential.
리더십 잠재력에 기여하는
These traits include such things as *drive, self-confidence, cognitive ability, conscientiousness, determination, intelligence,* and *integrity*.
이러한 특성에는 '추진력', '자신감', '인지 능력', '성실성', '결단력', '지능', 그리고 '청렴'과 같은 것이 포함된다

지도자는 그들을 지도자가 아닌 사람과 구별해 주는 특정한 신체적, 지적, 혹은 성격적 특성을 '선천적으로' 가지고 있다는 생각은 리더십에 대한 특성 기반 접근법의 기초적인 믿음이었다. 이 접근법은 1800년대 후반부터 1940년대 중반까지 리더십 연구를 지배했으며 지난 몇십 년 동안 관심이 되살아나는 것을 경험했다. 초기 특성 이론가들은, 어떤 사람들은 위대한 지도자가 될 수 있게 해 주는 특성을 가지고 태어난다고 믿었다. 따라서 이 분야의 초기 연구는 '지도자는 만들어지는 것이 아니라 태어나는 것'이라는 널리 언급되는 주장을 자주 제시하였다. 또한, 초기 리더십 연구 중 일부는 '위인' 이론이라 불리는 것에 기반을 두었는데, 이는 그 당시 연구자들이, 일반적으로 남성이면서 귀족이거나 정치나 군대의 리더십과 관련이 있는 역사에서 매우 눈에 띄는 지도자들의 특징을 확인하는 데 초점을 맞췄기 때문이다. 더 최근의 역사에서, 수많은 저자들은, 타고난 것이든 학습된 것이든, 리더십 잠재력에 기여하는 많은 지속되는 자질이 있다는 것을 인정했다. 이러한 특성에는 '추진력', '자신감', '인지 능력', '성실성', '결단력', '지능', 그리고 '청렴'과 같은 것이 포함된다.

문제풀이

① [주어·동사의 수일치]
동격절 'that leaders ~ nonleaders'의 수식을 받는 단수명사 the idea가 문장의 주어이므로 단수동사 was를 쓴 것을 올바른 용법이다.
② [대명사]
them의 앞의 복수명사 some individuals를 지칭하는 복수 대명사로 올바르게 사용되었다.
③ [동격절 접속사 that]
동격절 접속사 that은 '명사+that+완전한 문장'의 구조를 갖게 되는데, 이 문장에서는 명사 argument와 동격을 이루고, 그 뒤 문장 'leaders are born, not made'가 완전한 문장으로 올바르게 사용되었다.
④ [능동태 vs. 수동태]
'refer to A as B'는 'A를 B로 칭하다'의 뜻으로 'some of the earliest leadership studies were grounded in what referred to as the "great mean" theory'에서 referred to의 목적어가 보이지 않고 의미상으로도 '초기 리더십 연구 중 일부는 '위인' 이론이라 불리는 것에 기반을 두었다'가 되어 능동의 의미인 '불렀다'가 아니라 '불리었다'인 수동의 의미가 되어야 하므로 'referred'를 수동형인 'was referred'로 고쳐야 한다.
⑤ [부사절 접속사 whether]
whether는 명사절과 부사절을 이끌 수 있는 접속사로 종종 'whether A or B'의 형태를 취할 수 있고, 특히 부사절에서는 앞의 주어와 일치하는 주어와 be동사를 생략할 수 있다. 이 문장에서는 'whether (they are) innate or learned'에서 they are가 생략된 형태로 올바르게 사용되었다.

어휘 · 어구

inherently 선천적으로
intellectual 지적인
personality 성격
trait 특성
distinguish A from B A와 B를 구별하다
approach 접근(법)
dominate 지배하다
argument 주장
be grounded in ~에 기반[기초]을 두다
be referred to as ~이라고 불리다
visible 명백한
be associated with ~와 관련 있다

---

numerous 수많은
endure 지속하다
contribute to ~의 원인이 되다
potential 잠재력
cognitive 인지 능력
determination 결단력
intelligence 지능
integrity 청렴, 고결

2. ④   생물학적 단서로 유추할 수 없는 동물의 특성

어떤 동물이 어떤 유형의 행동을 하도록 선천적으로 타고난 다면, 생물학적 단서가 있을 가능성이 있다. 물고기가 지느 러미와 강력한 꼬리를 지닌 유선형이면서 매끄러운 몸을 갖고 있는 것은 우연이 아니다. 그들의 몸은 물에서 빠르게 움직이는 데 있어 구조적으로 적합하다. 마찬가지로, 여러분이 죽은 새나 모기를 발견한다면, 그것의 날개를 보고 비행이 그것이 보통 사용하는 이동 방식이라는 것을 추측할 수 있다. 그러나, 우리는 지나치게 낙관적이어서는 안 된다. 생물학적 단서는 필수적인 것이 아니다. 그것들이 발견되는 정도는 동물마다, 그리고 행동마다 다르다. 예를 들어, 새들이 둥지를 짓는 것을 그것들의 몸에서 추측하는 것은 불가능하고, 때때로 동물들은 유령거미가 엄청 긴 다리를 가지고 있지만 매우 짧은 가닥으로 거미집을 짓는 것과 같이 그것들의 신체적 형태에서 예상될 수 있는 것과 정반대의 방식으로 행동한다. 관찰을 하는 인간에게는 거미집 주위를 돌며 움직일 때 그것들의 다리는 매우 큰 방해물처럼 보인다.

문제풀이

① 「There+be동사 ~(~가 있다)」 구문에서 There는 유도부사이고, be동사 뒤에 진짜 주어가 나온다. 동사의 수는 주어인 biological clues에 일치시켜야 하므로 are가 적절하다.
② are의 보어로 형용사 smooth가 오는 것이 적절하다. streamlined와 smooth는 are의 보어로 and로 연결되어 병렬 관계이다.
③ a dead bird or mosquito를 받는 소유격 대명사로 its가 오는 것이 적절하다.
④ 주절의 주어는 The extent이고 동사는 varies이며 to which ~ finding은 주어(The extent)를 수식하는 관계대명사절이다. 관계대명사절의 주어인 they는 biological clues를 가리키며, 생물학적 단서가 발견하는 것이 아니라 발견되는 것이므로 현재분사 finding이 아닌 과거분사 found가 와야 한다.
⑤ what은 선행사를 포함한 관계대명사로 관계사절에서 주어 역할을 하는 관계대명사가 필요하므로 적절하다.

구문 및 어휘

*2행 It is no accident [**that** fish have bodies (**which** are streamlined and smooth), (**with** fins and a powerful tail)].
(1) It은 가주어이고, that 이하는 진주어이다.
(2) which 이하는 선행사 bodies를 수식하는 관계대명사절이다.
(3) with는 '~을 가진, ~이 달린'이라는 의미로 쓰인 전치사이다.

innately 선천적으로
biological 생물학의
streamlined 유선형의
fin 지느러미
structurally 구조상, 구조적으로
mosquito 모기
transport 이동

---

over-optimistic 지나치게 낙관적인
extent 정도
tremendously 엄청나게
weave 짜다, 엮다
thread 실
observer 보는 사람, 관찰자
hindrance 방해물

3. ③   스포츠에서 과정에 집중하는 이유

요즘에는 프로 스포츠에서 선수와 코치가 과정에 대하여 말하는 것을 듣는 것이 특이한 일이 아니다. 그들은 과정에 집중하고 과정을 따르는 것에 대하여 말한다. 그들은 골 넣기, 터치다운, 홈런, 점수, 혹은 명중시키는 것에 대해서는 좀처럼 말하지 않는다. 이는 전적으로 과정에 관한 것이다. 그러면 그들은 이것으로 무엇을 말하려는 것인가? 그들이 과정에 집중한다고 말하는 의미는 그들은 자신이 바라는 결과를 달성하기 위하여 할 필요가 있는 행동에 집중한다는 것이다. 그들은 결과 자체에 집중하지 않는다. 여기에서의 논리는 요구되는 단계들을 여러분이 따라간다면, 결과는 알아서 나올 거라는 것이다. 이것이 프로 스포츠인과 아마추어 스포츠인 간의 큰 차이 중 하나이다. 아마추어들은 보통 결과에 집중하고 거의 자동으로 결과로 이어질 모든 것들을 행하는 것에 대해서는 잊어버린다.

문제풀이

③이 있는 문장에서 that절의 의미상의 목적어는 the actions이고 take와의 관계가 능동이므로 be taken이 아닌 take로 쓰는 것이 올바르다.

구문 및 어휘

*4행 **Rarely** <u>do they talk</u> about scoring a goal, a touchdown, a home run, a point, or achieving a good shot.
(1) Rarely는 '거의 ~하지 않는'이라는 의미의 부정어로 문두에 나왔으므로, 뒤에 주어와 동사가 도치되어 「조동사(do)+주어(they)+동사원형(talk)」이 왔다.
(2) 전치사 about의 목적어로 동명사와 명사가 콤마(,)와 접속사 or로 연결되었다.

*6행 [**What** they mean by focusing on the process] is **that** they focus on the actions [they need to take] in order to achieve their desired result.
(1) [What ~ process]가 주어로 이때 What은 선행사를 포함한 관계대명사로 '~한 것'으로 해석하며 동사는 is이다. 동사 뒤의 that은 보어의 역할을 하는 명사절을 이끄는 접속사이다.
(2) [they need to take]는 the actions를 수식하는 관계대명사절로 목적격 관계대명사 that이 생략되었다.

reasoning 논리, 추론
lead to ~로 이어지다

4. ①   부서 간의 정보 교류가 회사에 도움을 준다.

직독/직해

Researchers studied two mobile phone companies /
연구원이 두 개의 휴대 전화 회사를 연구했다. /
trying to solve a technological problem.
기술적인 문제를 해결하려고 애쓰는
One company developed what it called a 'technology shelf,' /

한 회사는 '기술 선반'이라고 부르는 것을 개발했는데,
created by a small group of engineers, /
그것은 소집단의 기술자들에 의해 만들어졌고,
on which were placed possible technical solutions /
그 위에는 가능한 기술적인 해결책들이 올려져 있었다.
that other teams might use in the future. /
장차 다른 팀이 사용할 수도 있는
It also created an open-ended conversation /
그 회사는 또한 제한 없는 대화를 만들었다. /
among its engineers / 기술자들 간의
in which salespeople and designers were often included.
판매원들과 디자이너들이 자주 포함되어 있는
The boundaries among business units /
사업 단위 간의 경계는
were deliberately ambiguous
일부러 불명확하게 했는데,
because more than technical information was needed /
왜냐하면 기술적인 정보 이상의 것이 필요했기 때문이다.
to get a feeling for the problem.
문제에 대한 감을 얻기 위해서는
However, / the other company proceeded /
하지만, 다른 회사는 일을 진행했다.
with more seeming clarity and discipline,
겉으로 보기에는 보다 명료하게 그리고 질서 있게
dividing the problem into its parts.
문제를 각 부문으로 나누면서
Different departments protected their territory.
서로 다른 부서들은 각자의 영역을 보호했다.
Individuals and teams, competing with each other, /
개인과 팀들은 서로 경쟁하며,
stopped sharing information.
정보 공유를 중지했다.
The two companies did eventually solve the technological problem, /
그 두 회사는 결국 기술적인 문제를 해결했지만,
but the latter company had more difficulty than the former.
후자의 회사가 전자의 회사보다 어려움이 더 많았다.

- -

연구원들이 기술적인 문제를 해결하려고 애쓰는 두 개의 휴대 전화 회사를 연구했다. 한 회사는 "기술 선반"이라고 부르는 것을 개발했는데, 그것은 소집단의 기술자들에 의해 만들어졌고, 그 위에는 장차 다른 팀이 사용할 수도 있는 가능한 기술적인 해결책들이 올려져 있었다. 그 회사는 또한 판매원들과 디자이너들이 자주 포함되어 있는 기술자들 간의 제한 없는 대화를 만들었다. 사업 단위 간의 경계는 일부러 불명확하게 했는데, 왜냐하면 문제에 대한 감을 얻기 위해서는 기술적인 정보 이상의 것이 필요했기 때문이다. 하지만, 다른 회사는 문제를 각 부문으로 나누면서 겉으로 보기에는 보다 명료하게 그리고 질서 있게 일을 진행했다. 서로 다른 부서들은 각자의 영역을 보호했다. 개인과 팀들은 서로 경쟁하며, 정보 공유를 중지했다. 그 두 회사는 결국 기술적인 문제를 해결했지만, 후자의 회사가 전자의 회사보다 어려움이 더 많았다.

문제풀이

①이 들어 있는 부분에서 문장의 주어는 복수형인 **possible technical solutions**이므로, 단수동사 **was**를 복수동사 **were**로 고쳐야 한다. 이때 동사는 **were placed**로 수동태이다.
② its는 문맥상 단수명사 one company를 가리키므로 3인칭 단수 소유격을 사용하였다.
③ to부정사의 부사적 용법(목적)으로 사용되었다.
④ as it(= the other company) divided ~ 라는 부사절을 분사구문으로 바꾼 것이다. 부사절을 분사구문으로 바꿀 경우, 접속사를 제거하고, 부사절의 주어와 주절의 주어가 동일한 경우, 부사절의 주어를 제거하고, 동사의 시제가 동일할 경우 단순 분사구문(동사원형+-ing)을 사용한다.
⑤ 동사(solve)를 강조하고자 할 때 조동사 do/does/did를 사용할 수 있다.

어휘 / 어구

open-ended 제약[제한]을 두지 않은
conversation 대화

column 1

boundary 경계
deliberately 의도적으로
ambiguous 분명치 않은, 불명료한
clarity 명확, 명료
discipline 기강, 질서, 규율
territory 영역, 영토

---

5. ② 빙하의 특징과 분포

직독/직해

The bodies of flowing ice / we call glaciers /
움직이고 있는 얼음 덩어리는 / 우리가 빙하라고 부르는

are the most spectacular of natural features.
자연의 볼거리들 중에서 가장 장관을 이룬다.

They result from densely packed snow.
그것은 조밀하게 뭉쳐진 눈에서 생겨난다.

Unlike a stream, / a glacier cannot be seen to move.
시내와 달리 / 빙하는 움직이는 것을 볼 수 없다.

Accurate measurements, / however, /
정확하게 측정해 보면 / 하지만 /

show that it is flowing.
그것이 흐르고 있다는 것을 알 수 있다.

Erosion of bedrock by glaciers /
빙하에 의한 기반암의 침식과 /

and deposits of the eroded materials /
침식된 물질의 퇴적물은 /

are characteristic and easily recognizable.
특징을 가지고 있어 쉽게 알아 볼 수 있다.

Their distribution enables us to infer /
그것들의 분포는 추론할 수 있게 해준다. /

that in the recent past / 오래되지 않은 과거에 /

glaciers have been far more extensive
빙하가 훨씬 더 광범위하게 퍼져있다는 것을 /

than they are today. 오늘날보다

At the same time, / 동시에, /

this evidence has raised the problem/
이런 증거는 문제를 제기했다./

of the cause of the 'ice ages.'
빙하 시대'의 원인에 대해

우리가 빙하라고 부르는 움직이고 있는 얼음 덩어리는 자연의 볼거리들 중에서 가장 장관을 이룬다. 그것은 조밀하게 뭉쳐진 눈에서 생겨난다. 시내와 달리 빙하는 움직이는 것을 볼 수 없다. 하지만, 정확하게 측정해 보면 그것이 흐르고 있다는 것을 알 수 있다. 빙하에 의한 기반암의 침식과 침식된 물질의 퇴적물은 쉽게 알아 볼 수 있다. 그것들의 분포는 오래되지 않은 과거에 빙하가 오늘날보다 훨씬 더 광범위하게 퍼져있다는 것을 추론할 수 있게 해준다. 동시에, 이런 증거는 '빙하 시대'의 원인에 대해 문제를 제기했다.

문제풀이

① 문장의 주어는 the bodies로 복수주어에는 복수동사(are)를 사용한다. 수 일치의 기본 원칙은 단수주어는 단수동사, 복수동사는 복수동사를 사용한다.
②가 포함된 문장인 능동태는 Unlike a stream, we cannot see a glacier move를 수동태로 바꾼 문장인데, 지각동사의 목적격보어인 원형부정사 move는 수동태가 되면 to부정사로 바뀐다. Unlike a stream, a glacier cannot be seen to move.가 되어야 한다. 현대미국영어에서는 to move 대신 현재분사인 moving을 사용할 수도 있다.
③ 부사 easily가 형용사 recognizable을 수식하고 있다. 부사는 다른 부사, 형용사, 동사를 수식할 수 있다.
④ A has been 비교급 than B 구문으로 비교급 비교 문장이다. far는 비교급을 강조할 때 사용할 수 있다.
⑤ 타동사 raise는 문맥상 '(문제를) ~제기하다'의 의미로 사용되었으며, raise-raised-raised로 3

column 2

단 변화를 한다. 비슷한 단어 rise(일어나다)는 자동사로서 rise-rose-risen으로 3단 변화를 한다.

어휘 · 어구

glacier 빙하
spectacular 장관의, 구경거리가 되는
feature 특징, 볼만한 것
densely 밀집하게
measurement 측정
erosion 침식
deposit 퇴적물
recognizable 알아볼 수 있는
distribution 분포
infer 추론하다
extensive 광범위한
evidence 증거

---

6. ① 고대 이집트인의 고양이 숭배 사상

직독/직해

Cats were at their highest position /
고양이는 가장 높은 위치에 있었다. /

of domesticated life / in ancient Egypt.
집에서 기르는 동물 중 / 고대 이집트에서

There were more cats living in Egypt /
이집트에는 많은 고양이가 있었다. /

during the time of the pharaohs /
파라오 시대 동안

than in any other place in the world.
다른 어느 지역보다

This high concentration of cats /
고양이가 이렇게 많았던 것은 /

was probably due to the laws /
아마도 법률이 있어서 그런 것 같다. /

protecting the animal.
고양이를 보호하는

Cats were associated with /
고양이는 연관되어 있어서 /

the moon goddess, Bast, /
달의 신 Bast와 /

so the Egyptians worshiped them / as holy animals.
이집트인이 고양이를 숭배를 했다. / 신성한 동물로

If anyone was caught killing a cat, /
누구라도 고양이를 죽이다가 잡히면 /

the person could be put to death.
그 사람은 사형에 처해질 수 있었다.

Families in Egypt also mourned the death of a cat /
또한, 이집트 사람들은 고양이의 죽음을 애도했고

and had the body of the dead cat wrapped in cloth /
죽은 고양이를 천으로 싸서 묻었다 /

before it was finally laid to rest.
마침내 평안히 영면하도록 안치되기 전에

고대 이집트에서 고양이는 집에서 기르는 동물 중 가장 높은 위치에 있었다. 파라오 시대 동안 이집트에는 다른 어느 지역보다 많은 고양이가 있었다. 아마도 고양이를 보호하는 법률이 있어서 고양이가 이렇게 많았던 것 같다. 고양이는 달의 신 Bast와 연관되어 있어서 이집트인이 신성한 동물로 숭배를 했다. 누구라도 고양이를 죽이다가 잡히면 그 사람은 사형에 처해질 수 있었다. 또한, 이집트 사람들은 고양이의 죽음을 애도했고 마침내 평안히 영면하도록 안치되기 전에 죽은 고양이를 천으로 싸서 묻었다.

문제풀이

(A) There were more cats (which were) living in Egpyt~ 문장에서 「관계대명사+be동사」가 생략된 문장이다. '살고 있는'의 능동 의미이므로 현재분사형이 필요하다.
(B) 주어가 cats가 아니라 concentration임에 유

column 3

의해야 한다. 단수주어에는 단수동사를 사용한다. (C) it은 고양이를 가리키며, 땅에 묻히는 동작의 주체가 아니라 대상이 되므로 수동태로 나타낸 것이다. 그러므로 괄호에는 타동사의 과거분사가 필요하다. 타동사 lay(~을 놓다, 두다)의 3단 변화는 lay-laid-laid이다. 자동사 lie(누워있다, 눕다)의 3단 변화는 lie-lay-lain이다.

어휘 · 어구

domesticate (동물 따위를) 길들이다
ancient 고대의
pharaoh (이집트) 파라오, 왕
concentration 집중
protect 보호하다
be associated with ~과 연관되다
goddess 여신
mourn 애도하다
wrap (천으로) 싸다

---

7. ② 텔레비전 카메라가 비칠 때 사람들이 보여주는 행동

직독/직해

People act strangely / 사람들은 이상하게 행동한다. /

when a television camera comes their way.
텔레비전 카메라가 자신들을 비출 때

Some people engage in an activity /
어떤 사람들은 행동을 취한다. /

known as the cover-up.
은폐라고 알려진

They will be calmly watching /
그들은 차분히 지켜본다. /

a sports game or a televised event /
스포츠 경기나 텔레비전으로 중계되고 있는 행사를

when they realize the camera is focused on them.
카메라가 자신에게 집중되고 있다는 사실을 인식할 때

Then / there are those who practice their funny faces /
그리고 / 우스꽝스러운 얼굴 표정을 짓는 사람들이 있다. /

on the public. 일반 대중을 향해서

They take advantage of the television time /
그들은 텔레비전에 자신의 모습이 나가는 시간을 이용하여 /

to show off their talents,/
자신들의 재능을 보여주려고 하며 /

hoping to get that big chance /
그런 절호의 기회를 갖게 되기를 바란다. /

that will carry them to stardom.
그들을 스타덤에 오르게 해줄 수 있는

Finally, / there are those who pretend /
끝으로, / ~하는 척하는 사람들이 있다 /

they are not reacting for the camera.
카메라를 향해 아무런 반응을 보이지 않는.

They wipe an expression from their faces /
그들은 아무런 얼굴 표정도 짓지 않고 /

and appear to be interested in something else.
다른 일에 관심이 있는 것처럼 보인다.

Yet if the camera stays on them long enough, /
하지만 카메라가 그들을 꽤 오랜 시간 동안 계속 비추면 /

they will slyly check to see /
슬쩍 확인을 할 것이다. /

if they are still being watched.
자신들의 모습이 여전히 비춰지고 있는지 그렇지 않은지

텔레비전 카메라가 자신들을 비출 때 사람들은 이상하게 행동한다. 어떤 사람들은 은폐라고 알려진 행동을 취한다. 그들은 카메라가 자신에게 집중되고 있다는 사실을 인식할 때 스포츠 경기나 텔레비전으로 중계되고 있는 행사를 차분히 지켜본다. 그리고 일반 대중을 향해서 우스꽝스러운 얼굴 표정을 짓는 사람들이 있다. 그들은 텔레비전에 자신의 모습이 나가는 시간을 이용하여 자신들의 재능을 보여주려고 하며 그들을 스타덤에 오르게 해줄 수 있는 그런 절호의 기회를 갖게 되기를 바란다. 끝으로, 카메라를 향해 아무런 반응을 보이지 않는 척하는 사람들이 있다. 그들은 아무런 얼굴 표정도 짓지 않고 다른 일에 관심이 있는 것처럼 보인

다. 하지만 카메라가 그들을 꽤 오랜 시간 동안 계속 비추면 자신들의 모습이 여전히 비춰지고 있는지 그렇지 않은지 슬쩍 확인을 한다.

문제풀이

(A) 문맥상 '~할 때'의 의미가 필요하다. 또한 괄호 뒤에는 완전한 문장이 나오고 있으므로 관계부사가 적절하다. 그래서 관계부사 when이 적절하다.

(B) 괄호에 들어갈 인칭대명사는 They take advantage of ~의 They와 동일인물이며, 타동사 carry의 목적격이 필요하므로 인칭대명사 they의 목적격 them이 필요하다.

(C) 현재진행형을 넣어야 할지, 현재진행형의 수동태를 넣어야 할지 선택하는 문제이다. 그들이 비춰지고 있는 대상이므로 being watched가 적절하다.

《 어휘 · 어구 》

engage ~에 참여하다
cover-up 은폐
be focused on ~에 집중하다
show off ~을 자랑하다
pretend ~인 척하다
wipe ~을 지우다
slyly 슬쩍

---

8. ④   진실을 오도하는 사진 촬영법

직독 직해

Accurate and honest reportage with the camera has always been problematic.
카메라로 하는 정확하고 정직한 보도는 항상 문제가 되어 왔다

The saying that "a photograph never lies" / has been proven false many times.
'사진은 절대 거짓말을 하지 않는다'라는 말은 / 사실이 아니라는 것이 여러 번 증명되어 왔다

Photographers and picture editors have used lots of techniques /
사진작가들과 사진 편집자들은 여러 기술을 사용해 왔다 /

to mislead the viewer of a photograph.
사진을 보는 사람들을 오도하기 위해

Taking a subject out of context / by careful framing or cropping, / for example, /
피사체를 배경에서 빼내는 것은 / 세심한 사진 구성이나 다듬기로 / 예를 들어 /

is a simple way of giving the wrong impression of a person or event.
사람이나 사건에 대해 잘못된 인상을 주는 간단한 방법이다

Choice of lighting or camera angle, or the capture of a fleeting expression /
조명이나 카메라 앵글의 선택, 혹은 순간적인 표현을 담는 것은 /

are other ways of influencing viewers' responses /
사진을 보는 사람들의 반응에 영향을 주는 또 다른 방법이다 /

away from a truthful description of the situation.
상황에 대한 진실된 묘사에서 벗어나

Photographers have posed their subjects / to give misleading impressions.
사진작가들은 자신의 피사체를 배치해 왔다 / 오도하는 인상을 주기 위해

Even from the early days of photography, /
심지어 사진술의 초창기부터 /

some enterprising propagandists have found /
몇몇 진취적인 선전가들은 알아냈다 /

that outright manipulation of the photographs /
노골적인 사진 조작이 /

by cutting and pasting, rephotographing, retouching, or multiple printing techniques /
잘라내고 붙이기, 재촬영, 수정, 혹은 다양한 인화 기술에 의한 /

could present a completely false view of reality.
완전히 위조된 현실을 보여줄 수 있다는 것을

Digital image editing makes this manipulation process not only easier /
디지털 이미지 편집은 이런 조작 과정을 더 쉽게 만들 뿐만 아니라 /

but virtually undetectable in published photographs.
출판된 사진에서 거의 감지할 수 없게 만든다.

카메라로 하는 정확하고 정직한 보도는 항상 문제가 되어 왔다. '사진은 절대 거짓말을 하지 않는다'라는 말은 사실이 아니라는 것이 여러 번 증명되어 왔다. 사진작가들과 사진 편집자들은 사진을 보는 사람들을 오도하기 위해 여러 기술을 사용해 왔다. 예를 들어, 세심한 사진 구성이나 다듬기로 피사체를 배경에서 빼내는 것은 사람이나 사건에 대해 잘못된 인상을 주는 간단한 방법이다. 조명이나 카메라 앵글의 선택, 혹은 순간적인 표현을 담는 것은 상황에 대한 진실한 묘사에서 벗어나 사진을 보는 사람들의 반응에 영향을 미치는 또 다른 방법이다. 사진작가들은 오도하는 인상을 주기 위해 자신의 피사체를 배치해 왔다. 심지어 사진술의 초창기부터, 몇몇 진취적인 선전가들은 잘라내고 붙이기, 재촬영, 수정, 혹은 다양한 인화 기술에 의한 노골적인 사진 조작이 완전히 위조된 현실을 보여줄 수 있다는 것을 알아냈다. 디지털 이미지 편집은 이런 조작 과정을 더 쉽게 만들 뿐만 아니라 출판된 사진에서 거의 감지할 수 없게 만든다.

문제풀이

① [동격 접속사 that]
that은 The saying과 동격 관계인 명사절을 이끄는 접속사로 올바르게 사용되었다.

② [동명사]
Taking은 문장의 주어로 쓰인 동명사로 올바르게 사용되었다.

③ [to부정사의 부사적 용법]
to give는 '주기 위해서'의 뜻으로 목적의 의미인 to부정사구를 이끌고 있으므로 올바르게 사용되었다.

④ [수동태]
'a completely false view of reality'가 동사 'present'의 대상(목적어)이고 'outright manipulation of the photographs'가 동사 present의 주체이므로, 수동형인 'be presented'를 능동형인 'present'로 고쳐야 한다.

⑤ [목적보어로 쓰인 형용사]
undetectable은 easier와 함께 목적어 'this manipulation process'를 설명하는 목적보어로 쓰인 형용사로 올바르게 사용되었다.

《 어휘 · 어구 》

accurate 정확한
reportage 보도
mislead 오도하다
subject 피사체
fleeting 순간적인
enterprising 진취적인
outright 노골적인
manipulation 조작
virtually 거의, 사실상

---

9. ③   음악을 인식하고 기억하는 과정

직독 직해

Chunking is vital / for cognition of music.
덩어리로 나누는 것은 필수적이다 / 음악의 인식에서

If we had to encode it / in our brains / note by note, /
만약 우리가 그것을 부호화해야 한다면 / 우리의 뇌에서 / 한 음 한 음 /

we'd struggle / to make sense of anything more complex /
우리는 노력하게 될 것이다 / 더 복잡한 것은 어느 것이나 이해하기 위해 /

than the simplest children's songs.
가장 간단한 동요보다

Of course, most accomplished musicians /
물론, 대부분의 기량이 뛰어난 음악가들은 /

can play compositions / 작품을 연주할 수 있다 /

containing many thousands of notes /
수천 개의 음을 포함하는 /

entirely from memory, / 완전히 기억으로 /

without a note out of place. 한 음도 틀리지 않고

But this seemingly awesome accomplishment of recall /
하지만 겉보기에는 굉장한 것 같은 이런 기억의 성취는 /

i is made possible /
가능하게 되는 것이다 /

by remembering the musical *process*, /
음악적인 '과정'을 기억함으로써 /

not the individual notes / as such.
개별적인 음을 기억하는 것이 아닌 / 보통 말하는 그런

If you ask a pianist / to start a Mozart sonata /
만약 여러분이 피아니스트에게 요청하면 / 모차르트 소나타를 시작해 달라고 /

from bar forty-one, / 41번 마디부터 /

she'll probably have to mentally replay the music /
그녀는 아마도 그 음악을 머릿속으로 재생해야 할 것이다 /

from the start / until reaching that bar — /
처음부터 / 그 마디까지 /

the score is not simply laid out / in her mind, /
그 악보는 그저 펼쳐져 있는 것이 아니다 / 그녀의 머릿속에 /

to be read / from any random point.
읽히도록 / 어떤 임의의 지점부터

It's rather like describing / how you drive to work: /
그것은 흡사 설명하는 것과 같다 / 여러분이 운전해서 직장에 가는 방법을 /

you don't simply recite the names of roads /
여러분은 길의 이름을 열거하는 것이 아니라 /

as an abstract list, / 추상적인 목록으로 /

but have to construct your route /
여러분의 경로를 구성해야 한다 /

by mentally retracing it.
마음속에 그것을 되짚어감으로써

When musicians make a mistake / during rehearsal, /
음악가들이 실수할 때 / 리허설 중에 /

they wind back / to the start of a musical phrase /
그들은 되돌아간다 / 한 악구의 시작으로 /

('let's take it from the second verse') / before restarting.
2절부터 다시 하죠 / 다시 시작하기 전에

덩어리로 나누는 것은 음악의 인식에서 필수적이다. 만약 우리가 그것을 한 음 한 음 우리의 뇌에 부호화해야 한다면 우리는 가장 간단한 동요보다 더 복잡한 것은 어느 것이나 이해하기 위해 ① 노력하게 될 것이다. 물론, 대부분의 기량이 뛰어난 음악가들은 한 음도 틀리지 않고 수천 개의 음을 포함하는 작품을 완전히 ② 기억으로 연주할 수 있다. 하지만 겉보기에는 굉장한 것 같은 이런 기억의 성취는 보통 말하는 그런 개별적인 음을 기억하는 것이 아닌 음악적인 '과정'을 기억함으로써 ③ 일어날 것 같지 않게 되는(→ 가능해지는) 것이다. 만약 여러분이 피아니스트에게 모차르트 소나타를 41번 마디부터 시작해 달라고 요청하면, 그녀는 아마도 그 음악을 처음부터 ④ 머릿속으로 재생해서 그 마디까지 와야 할 것이다. 그 악보는 어떤 임의의 지점부터 읽히도록 그저 그녀의 머릿속에 펼쳐져 있는 것이 아니다. 그것은 흡사 여러분이 운전해서 직장에 가는 방법을 설명하는 것과 같다. 여러분은 추상적인 목록으로 길의 이름을 열거하는 것이 아니고 마음속에서 그것을 되짚어감으로써 여러분의 경로를 구성해야 한다. 음악가들이 리허설 중에 실수할 때, 그들은 다시 시작하기 전에 한 악구의 ⑤ 시작으로 되돌아간다('2절부터 다시 하죠').

문제풀이

개별 음이 아닌 덩어리로 나누어 과정을 인식하는 방식으로 음악을 기억한다는 내용의 글이므로, 수천 개의 음을 포함하는 작품을 한 음도 틀리지 않고 완전히 기억으로 연주할 수 있는 것은 한 음 한 음 개별적으로 기억하는 것이 아니라 음악적인 과정을 기억해서 가능해진다고 해야 한다. 따라서 ③ 'improbable(일어날 것 같지 않은)'을 'possible(가능한)'과 같은 낱말로 바꿔 써야 한다.

《 어휘 · 어구 》

vital 필수적인
cognition 인식
encode 부호화하다
note 음, 음표
struggle 고투하다, 고심하다
make sense of ~을 이해하다
accomplished 기량이 뛰어난
composition 작품
out of place 맞지 않는, 부적절한
seemingly 겉보기에는
awesome 굉장한

recall 기억
as such 보통 말하는 그런
score 악보, 작품
random 임의의, 무작위의
recite 열거하다
abstract 추상적인
retrace 되짚어가다
phrase 악구
verse (노래의) 절

10. ③ 동물들의 싸움 놀이의 의미

직독/직해

Play can be costly / 놀이는 대가를 치를 수 있다 /
because it takes energy and time /
에너지와 시간을 빼앗기 때문에 /
which could be spent foraging.
먹이를 찾아다니는 데 쓰일 수 있는
While playing, / the young animal may be at great risk.
노는 동안 / 어린 동물은 큰 위험에 처할 수도 있다
For example, / 86 percent of young Southern fur seals /
예를 들어 / 어린 남방 물개들 중 86%는 /
eaten by sea lions / were play-swimming with others /
바다사자들에게 잡아먹힌 / 다른 물개들과 물놀이를 하고 있었다 /
when they were caught. 그들이 잡힐 당시
Against these costs / 이런 대가의 반대로 /
many functions have been proposed for play, /
놀이에 있어 많은 기능들이 제기되어 왔다 /
including practice for adult behaviours /
다 자란 동물의 연습을 포함하여 /
such as hunting or fighting, / 사냥이나 싸움과 같은 /
and for developing motor and social interaction skills.
행동 및 운동과 사교 기술을 발달시키기 위한
However, for these theories, / 하지만 이런 이론들에 대해 /
there is little experimental evidence in animals.
동물들에 있어 실험적 증거는 거의 없다
For example, / detailed studies /
예를 들면 / 세부 연구들은 /
which tracked juvenile play and adult behaviour of
meerkats / 미어캣의 성장기 놀이와 다 자랐을 때의 행동을 추적한 /
couldn't prove / 증명할 수 없었다 /
that play-fighting influenced fighting ability as an adult.
싸움 놀이가 다 자랐을 때의 싸우는 능력에 영향을 미쳤다는 것을
Therefore, / 따라서 /
the persistence of play across so many animal species /
아주 많은 동물 종들에 걸친 놀이의 지속은 /
remains a mystery. 미스터리로 남아 있다
The answers are likely to involve /
해답은 포함할 가능성이 크다 /
diverse and multiple factors, / 다양한 다수의 요인들을 /
which may be quite different in different species, /
여러 종들에게 있어 꽤 다를지도 모른다 /
as might what we call *play* itself.
우리가 '놀이'라고 일컫는 것 자체가 그러하듯 .

놀이는 먹이를 찾아다니는 데 쓰일 수 있는 에너지와 시간을 빼앗기 때문
에 대가를 치를 수 있다. 노는 동안 어린 동물은 큰 (A) 위험에 처할 수도
있다. 예를 들어, 바다사자들에게 잡아먹힌 어린 남방 물개들 중 86%는
그들이 잡힐 당시 다른 물개들과 물놀이를 하고 있었다. 이런 대가와는
반대로, 사냥이나 싸움과 같은 다 자란 동물의 행동 및 운동과 사교 기술
을 발달시키기 위한 연습을 포함하여, 놀이에 있어 많은 기능들이 제기되
어 왔다. 하지만 이런 이론들에 대해 동물들에 있어 실험적 증거는 (B)
거의 없다. 예를 들면, 미어캣의 성장기 놀이와 다 자랐을 때의 행동을 추
적한 세부 연구들은 싸움 놀이가 다 자랐을 때의 싸우는 능력에 영향을
미쳤다는 것을 증명할 수 없었다. 따라서 아주 많은 동물 종들에 걸친 놀
이의 지속은 미스터리로 (C) 남아 있다. 해답은 다양한 다수의 요인들을
포함할 가능성이 큰데, 우리가 '놀이'라고 일컫는 것 자체가 그러하듯 여
러 종들에게 있어 꽤 다를지도 모른다.

① 편안 – 거의 없다 – 남아 있다   ② 편안 – 많다 – 해결하다
③ **위험 – 거의 없다 – 남아 있다**   ④ 위험 – 많다 – 남아 있다
⑤ 위험 – 거의 없다 – 해결하다

문제풀이

(A) 많은 어린 남방 물개들이 물놀이를 하고 있다
가 바다사자들에게 잡아먹혔다는 사례를 통해 어
린 동물은 노는 동안 '위험'에 처할 수 있다는 것을
유추할 수 있다. 따라서 'risk(위험)'가 적절하다.
(B) 놀이가 가지는 많은 기능들이 제기되어 왔지
만, 그러한 이론들에 대해서는 실험적인 증거가
없다는 것이 문맥상 적절하다. 따라서 'little(거의
없다)'이 적절하다.
(C) 이론들에 대해 동물들에 있어 실험적 증거가
없고, 싸움 놀이가 다 자랐을 때의 싸우는 능력에
영향을 미쳤다는 것을 증명할 수 없다는 내용으로
보아, 놀이의 지속은 동물 종들에게 있어 미스터
리로 남아 있다는 것을 알 수 있다. 또한 바로 뒤
문장에서 해답은 다양한 다수의 요인을 포함할 가
능성이 크다는 것으로 보아 연구가 불명확하다는
것을 알 수 있다. 따라서 'remains(남아 있다)'가
적절하다.

〈 어휘·어구 〉

costly 많은 비용이 드는, 대가가 큰
motor 운동의
social interaction 사교 기술
experimental 실험적인
persistence 지속
diverse 다양한
multiple 많은, 다양한
remain (~의 상태로) 남아 있다
resolve 풀다, 해결하다

11. ④ 임의 오차와 계통 오차

직독/직해

Random errors may be detected /
임의 오차는 발견될 수 있다 /
by repeating the measurements. 측정을 반복함으로써
Furthermore, / by taking more and more readings, /
그뿐만 아니라 / 더욱더 많은 측정값을 구함으로써 /
we obtain from the arithmetic mean /
우리는 산술 평균으로부터 얻는다 /
a value which approaches more and more closely /
더욱더 가까운 값을 /
to the true value. 참값에
Neither of these points / is true for a systematic error.
이 두 사실 중 어떤 것도 / 계통 오차에는 적용되지 않는다
Repeated measurements with the same apparatus /
동일한 도구를 가지고 반복적으로 측정해도 /
neither reveal nor do they eliminate a systematic error.
계통 오차를 드러내거나 제거하지도 않는다
For this reason / 이런 이유로 /
systematic errors are potentially more dangerous /
계통 오차는 잠재적으로 더 위험하다 /
than random errors. 임의 오차보다
If large random errors are present / in an experiment, /
만약 큰 임의 오차가 존재하면 / 어떤 실험에서 /
they will manifest themselves in a large value /
그것은 큰 값으로 드러날 것이다 /
of the final quoted error. 최종적으로 매겨진 오차의
Thus everyone is aware of the imprecision of the result, /
따라서 모두가 결과의 부정확함을 알게 되는데 /
and no harm is done / 어떤 해도 가해지지 않는다 /
— except possibly to the ego of the experimenter /
어쩌면 실험자의 자존심에 (가해질 수 있는 해) 말고는 /
when no one takes notice of his or her results.
아무도 실험자의 결과에 주목하지 않을 때
However, / 하지만 /
the concealed presence of a systematic error /
계통 오차의 숨겨진 존재는 /

may lead to an apparently reliable result, /
언뜻 믿을만한 결과로 이어질 수 있는데 /
given with a small estimated error, /
추정된 오차가 작다면 /
which is in fact seriously wrong.
이것은 실제로 심각하게 잘못된 것이다

임의 오차는 측정을 ① 반복함으로써 발견될 수 있다. 그뿐만 아니라, 더
욱더 많은 측정값을 구함으로써 우리는 참값에 더욱더 가까운 값을 산술
평균으로부터 얻는다. 이 두 사실 중 어떤 것도 계통 오차에는 적용되지
않는다. 동일한 도구를 가지고 반복적으로 측정해도 계통 오차를 ② 드러
내거나 제거하지도 않는다. 이런 이유로 계통 오차는 임의 오차보다 잠재
적으로 더 ③ 위험하다. 만약 어떤 실험에 큰 임의 오차가 존재하면, 그
것은 최종적으로 매겨진 오차의 큰 값으로 드러날 것이다. 따라서 모두가
결과의 부정확함을 ④ 모르게(→ 알게) 되는데, 아무도 실험자의 결과에
주목하지 않을 때는 어쩌면 실험자의 자존심에 (가해질 수 있는 해) 말고
는 어떤 해도 가해지지 않는다. 하지만 계통 오차의 숨겨진 존재는, 추정
된 오차가 작다면, 언뜻 ⑤ 믿을만한 결과로 이어질 수 있는데, 이것은 실
제로 심각하게 잘못된 것이다.

문제풀이

한 실험에서 큰 임의의 오차가 존재하면 최종적으
로 오차의 값이 큰 것으로 드러나기 때문에 모두가
결과의 부정확함을 알게 될 것이므로, ④ 'unware'
는 문맥상 적절하지 않다.

〈 어휘·어구 〉

random error 임의 오차, 무작위 오차
detect 발견하다
measurement 측정
reading 측정값
obtain 얻다
systematic error 계통 오차
eliminate 제거하다
manifest 드러내다
quote (값을) 매기다, 견적을 내다
imprecision 부정확함
ego 자존심, 자아
conceal 숨기다
take notice of ~을 주목하다, ~을 알아차리다
presence 존재
apparently 분명히, 명백히
reliable 신뢰도가 높은

12. ④ 비만이 빠르게 뇌를 수축시키는 이유

직독/직해

Why should obesity cause our brains to shrink /
왜 비만은 뇌를 수축시킬 수밖에 없는가 /
even more quickly / with age /
훨씬 더 빠르게 / 나이를 먹으면서 /
than they would otherwise?
다른 경우에 그러한 것보다
Damage to blood vessels in the brain /
뇌혈관의 손상이 /
associated with diabetes and pre-diabetic
conditions /
당뇨와 당뇨 전 단계의 질환으로 인한 /
could play a role.
하나의 역할을 할 수 있다
Reduced blood flow can directly cause tissue
damage /
감소한 혈류는 세포 손상을 직접적으로 유발할 수 있다 /
to the brain, /
뇌에 /
and it also slows down the clearance of neurotoxic
substances /
그리고 그것은 신경 독성의 물질의 제거 또한 늦춘다 /
that are produced / 생성되는 /
during the development of Alzheimer's disease.
알츠하이머병의 발병 동안

In addition, /
게다가 /

obese individuals are likely to be less physically active
비만한 사람들은 신체적으로 덜 활동적일 가능성이 있다 /

than non-obese individuals.
덜 비만한 사람들보다

Physical activity, which enhances cardiovascular health, /
심혈관의 건강을 향상하는 신체 활동은 /

is well known to decrease /
줄이는 것으로 잘 알려져 있다 /

the risk for developing dementia.
치매 발병의 위험을

So, / elderly obese individuals compound their risk /
그러므로 / 노령의 비만인들은 위험을 악화시킨다 /

for developing dementia / 치매 발병의 /

via the combined effects / 복합적인 영향으로 /

of vascular damage from diabetes-related conditions /
당뇨와 관련된 질환으로부터 발생하는 혈관 손상의 /

and the poor maintenance of cerebrovascular health /
그리고 좋지 않은 뇌혈관 건강 관리의 /

due to inactivity. 비활동으로 인한

This all sounds pretty depressing; / what's worse, /
이것은 모두 상당히 우울하게 들리며 / 설상가상으로 /

there is ultimately no way / 방법은 결국 없다 /

to avoid the cumulative effects of brain aging.
뇌의 노화의 축적되는 영향을 피할

However, / 그러나 /

at least diet and exercise provide a fairly straightforward path /
최소한 식단과 운동은 상당히 간단한 길을 제공한다 /

toward maintaining the health of not only the body but the brain /
신체뿐 아니라 뇌의 건강 유지를 위한 /

over the life span. 일생에 걸쳐

나이를 먹으면서 왜 비만은 다른 경우에 그러한 것보다 훨씬 더 빠르게 뇌를 수축시킬 수밖에 없는가? 당뇨와 당뇨 전 단계의 질환으로 인한 뇌혈관의 손상이 하나의 역할을 ① 할 수 있다. 감소한 혈류는 뇌에 세포 손상을 직접적으로 유발할 수 있을 뿐만 아니라, 알츠하이머병의 발병 동안 생성되는 신경 독성의 물질의 제거 또한 늦춘다. 게다가, 비만한 사람들은 덜 비만한 사람들보다 신체적으로 덜 ② 활동적일 가능성이 있다. 심혈관의 건강을 ③ 향상하는 신체 활동은, 치매 발병의 위험을 줄이는 것으로 잘 알려져 있다. 그러므로, 노령의 비만인들은 당뇨와 관련된 질환으로부터 발생하는 혈관 손상과 비활동으로 인한 좋지 않은 뇌혈관 건강 관리의 복합적인 영향으로 치매 발병 위험을 ④ 줄인다(→ 악화시킨다). 이것은 모두 상당히 우울하게 들리며, 설상가상으로, 뇌의 노화의 축적되는 영향을 피할 방법은 결국 없다. 그러나, 최소한 식단과 운동은 일생에 걸쳐 신체뿐 아니라 뇌의 건강 ⑤ 유지를 위한 상당히 간단한 길을 제공한다.

문제풀이

당뇨와 당뇨 전 단계의 질환으로 인한 뇌혈관의 손상이 뇌를 축소시킨다고 했고 심혈관 건강을 향상하는 신체 활동은 치매 발병 위험을 줄인다고 했다. 따라서 노령의 비만인은 당뇨 관련 질환에서 발생하는 뇌혈관 손상과 비활동으로 인한 나쁜 뇌혈관 관리의 영향으로 치매 발병 위험이 악화된다고 하는 것이 문맥상 적절하므로, ④ 'reduce(줄이다)'를 'compound(악화시키다)'와 같은 낱말로 고쳐 써야 한다.

🐛 구조 다시보기

문제 제기	나이가 들면서 왜 비만이 빠르게 뇌를 수축시키는가?
답변	당뇨 관련 질환으로 인한 뇌혈관의 손상이 원인이 될 수 있음
부연	감소한 혈류가 뇌 세포 손상을 직접적으로 유발하고 알츠하이머병의 발병 동안 생성되는 신경 독성 물질의 제거를 늦춤
추가	비만한 사람들은 신체적으로 덜 활동적인 가능성이 있는데 심혈관 건강을 향상하는 신체 활동이 치매 발병 위험을 줄임

결론	최소한 식단과 운동은 일생에 걸쳐 신체와 뇌 건강 유지 방법임

《 어휘·어구 》

obesity 비만
shrink 수축시키다, 줄어들게 하다
blood vessel 혈관
diabetes 당뇨병
pre-diabetic 당뇨 전 단계의
play a role 역할을 하다
tissue 조직
neurotoxic 신경 독성의
substance 물질
obese 비만인, 살찐
enhance 높이다
dementia 치매
ultimately 결국, 궁극적으로
cumulative 누적되는
cardiovascular 심혈관의
maintain 유지하다

08. 가정법

A 출제 POINT
본문 044쪽

1. had 2. had had 3. had taken
4. weren't 5. had had
6. Had she known 7. return

1 [해석]▶ 내가 약간의 돈을 가지고 있다면 그에게 그것을 빌려줄 텐데.
[해설]▶ 가정법 과거는 현재 사실과 반대되는 것을 가정한다. 형태는 「If+주어+과거동사 ~, 주어+조동사 과거형+동사원형~」이다.

2 [해석]▶ 그가 농구공이 있었더라면 그는 게임을 시작했을 텐데.
[해설]▶ 가정법 과거완료는 과거의 사실과 반대되는 것을 가정한다. 형태는 「If+주어+had+과거분사 ~, 주어+조동사 과거형+have+과거분사~」이다.

3 [해석]▶ 그때 그녀가 나의 충고를 들었더라면 그녀는 아직 살아있을 텐데.
[해설]▶ 혼합가정법은 과거의 일이 현재에 영향을 미칠 때 사용한다. 형태는 「If+주어+had+과거분사 ~, 주어+조동사 과거형+동사원형~」이다.

4 [해석]▶ 그가 지금 여기에 없으면 좋으련만.
[해설]▶ 「I wish+가정법 과거」는 이루기 어려운 소망을 나타내며, 주절과 종속절이 나타내는 시제가 동일할 때 쓰인다.

5 [해석]▶ 그는 나쁜 소식을 들은 것처럼 보였다.
[해설]▶ 「as if+가정법과거완료」는 '마치 ~이었던 것처럼'이라는 의미이다. as if+가정법 과거완료는 주절보다 종속절의 시제가 앞선 경우에 사용한다.

6 [해석]▶ 만약 그것이 위험한 것을 알았다라면 그 산을 오르러 가지 않았을 텐데.
[해설]▶ 가정법 「If+주어+동사~」에서 If가 생략되면, 「동사+주어」로 문장이 도치된다.

7 [해석]▶ 그는 그녀에게 자기한테 빌려간 책을 돌려줄 것을 요구했다.
[해설]▶ 요구(demand)를 나타내는 동사에 이어지는 that절에서는 「주어+(should)+동사원형」을 쓴다.

B 체크 POINT
본문 044쪽

1. snowed 2. have prepared 3. be
4. hadn't quit 5. were 6. Had
7. settled

1 [해석]▶ 네 결혼식 날 눈이 오면 어떻게 할 거니?
[해설]▶ 가정법 과거 형태는 「If+주어+과거동사 ~, 주어+조동사 과거형+동사원형~」이다.

2 [해석]▶ 당신이 오는 것을 알았더라면, 저녁을 준비했을 텐데.
[해설]▶ 가정법 과거완료 형태는 「If+주어+had+과거분사

~, 주어+조동사 과거형+have+과거분사~,이다.

3 [해석]▶ 당시에 네가 나의 충고를 따랐더라면, 지금은 행복했을 텐데.
[해설]▶ 혼합가정법은 과거의 일이 현재에 영향을 미칠 때 사용된다. 형태는 「If+주어+had+과거분사 ~, 주어+조동사 과거형+동사원형~」이다.

4 [해석]▶ 작년에 학교를 그만 두지 않았으면 좋았을 텐데.
[해설]▶ 「I wish+가정법 과거완료」는 이루기 어려운 소망을 나타내며 주절보다 종속절의 시제가 앞선 경우에 사용한다.

5 [해석]▶ Sally는 여왕처럼 행동한다. 사실 그녀는 여왕이 아니다.
[해설]▶ 「as if+가정법과거」는 '마치 ~인 것처럼'이라는 의미이다. 「as if+가정법 과거」는 주절과 종속절이 나타내는 시제가 동일할 때 쓰인다.

6 [해석]▶ Sam이 그녀에게 안전벨트를 차라고 말하지 않았더라면, 그녀는 더 심하게 다쳤을 텐데.
[해설]▶ 가정법 「If+주어+동사~」에서 If가 생략되면, 「동사+주어」로 문장이 도치된다.

7 [해석]▶ 당신은 부인과의 불화를 해소할 때입니다.
[해설]▶ It's time that ~ 뒤에는 가정법 과거 표현이 사용된다. 의미는 '~할 때이다'는 의미이다.

Day 08 본문 045쪽

1 ④	2 ⑤	3 ③	4 ④	5 ⑤
6 ②	7 ③	8 ④	9 ④	10 ⑤
11 ⑤	12 ⑤			

1. ④ Natalie가 경험한 첫 온라인 상담

직독/직해

As Natalie was logging in /
Natalie는 접속하면서, /
to her first online counseling session, /
자신의 첫 온라인 상담 시간에
she wondered, / 그녀는 의문을 가졌다. /
"How can I open my heart to the counselor /
"내가 상담사에게 어떻게 나의 마음을 열 수 있을까?"라는
through a computer screen?"
컴퓨터 화면을 통해
Since the counseling center was a long drive away, /
상담 센터가 차로 오래 가야 하는 곳에 있었기 때문에, /
she knew that this would save her a lot of time.
그녀는 이것이 자신에게 많은 시간을 절약해 줄 것임을 알고 있었다.
Natalie just wasn't sure /
다만 Natalie는 확신할 수 없었다. /
if it would be as helpful / as meeting her counselor in person.
그것이 도움이 될지 / 상담사를 직접 만나는 것만큼
Once the session began, / however, / her concerns went away.
일단 (상담) 시간이 시작되자, / 하지만 / 그녀의 걱정은 사라졌다.
She actually started thinking / that it was much more convenient than expected.
그녀는 생각하기 시작했다. / 실제로 그것이 예상했던 것보다 훨씬 더 편리하다고
She felt / as if the counselor was in the room with

her.
그녀는 느꼈다. /마치 상담사가 자기와 함께 같은 방 안에 있는 것처럼
As the session closed, / she told him with a smile, /
(상담) 시간이 끝났을 때, 그녀는 미소를 지으며 그에게 말했다.
"I'll definitely see you online again!"
"온라인에서 꼭 다시 만나요!"

Natalie는 자신의 첫 온라인 상담 시간에 접속하면서, "내가 컴퓨터 화면을 통해 상담사에게 어떻게 나의 마음을 열 수 있을까?"라는 의문을 가졌다. 상담 센터가 차로 오래 가야 하는 곳에 있었기 때문에, 그녀는 이것이 자신에게 많은 시간을 절약해 줄 것임을 알고 있었다. 다만 Natalie는 그것이 상담사를 직접 만나는 것만큼 도움이 될 지 확신할 수 없었다. 하지만 일단 (상담) 시간이 시작되자, 그녀의 걱정은 사라졌다. 그녀는 실제로 그것이 예상했던 것보다 훨씬 더 편리하다고 생각하기 시작했다. 그녀 는 마치 상담사가 자기와 함께 같은 방 안에 있는 것처럼 느꼈다. (상담) 시간이 끝났을 때, 그녀는 미소를 지으며 그에게 말했다. "온라인에서 꼭 다시 만나요!"

문제풀이

① 접속사 that 이하가 타동사 knew의 목적어 역할을 하고 있다. 접속사 that은 뒤에 완전한 문장이 나온다.
② wasn't sure 이하에 '~인지 아닌지'라는 불확실한 내용을 전달할 때는 접속사 if 또는 whether를 사용한다.
③ 접속사 once는 '일단 ~하자'라는 의미가 있다.
④ **is → were로 고쳐야 한다. 본동사가 과거시제(told)로 본동사와 같은 시제의 반대 사실을 나타내려면 'as if +가정법 과거」로 나타내야 한다.**
⑤ 접속사 as는 '시간 접속사'로 '~했을 때'의 의미로 사용되었다.

《 어휘 · 어구 》
log in to ~에 접속하다[로그인하다]
session 시간, 기간
counselor 상담사
save 절약하다
in person 직접, 몸소
concern 걱정, 우려
convenient 편리한
definitely 꼭, 분명히

2. ⑤ 긴장된 시험 성적 발표

직독/직해

I was waiting outside / 나는 밖에서 기다리고 있었다. /
when the exam grades were posted on the bulletin board.
게시판에 시험 성적이 게시될 때.
I was perspiring. / My heart started beating fast.
나는 땀이 나고 있었다. / 내 심장은 빠르게 뛰기 시작했다.
What if I failed? 내가 불합격하면 어떻게 하지?
A swarm of students rushed forward /
한 무리의 학생들이 앞으로 급히 달려갔다. /
to see the exam results. 시험 결과를 보려고
Fortunately, / 다행히도, /
I was tall enough to see over their heads.
나는 그들의 머리 너머로 볼 수 있을 만큼 충분히 키가 컸다.
The minute I saw the results, /
시험 결과를 보자마자 /
all my anxiety disappeared.
나의 모든 걱정은 사라졌다.
I walked quickly back to my dormitory /
나는 다시 기숙사로 빨리 걸어가서 /
and phoned my father. 아버지께 전화를 했다.
"Dad," I mumbled in a haze.
"아빠," 나는 흐려진 눈으로 우물거리며 말했다.
"You won't believe this, / but I passed the exams."
"이 말이 믿기지 않으시겠지만 / 제가 시험에 합격했어요."
My father was speechless. /

아버지는 말씀을 하지 못하셨다.
Finally he said, / "Son, that is good news.
마침내 아버지께서 ~라고 말씀하셨다. / "아들아, '정말' 좋은 소식이구나.
I frankly never thought you'd do it."
솔직히 네가 해낼 거라고 생각하지 못했단다."라고
I was overjoyed / as if I were walking on the cloud.
나는 너무나 기뻤다. / 구름 위를 걷고 있는 것처럼

게시판에 시험 성적이 게시될 때 나는 밖에서 기다리고 있었다 나는 땀이 나고 있었다 내 심장은 빠르게 뛰기 시작했다 내가 불합격하면 어떻게 하지 한 무리의 학생들이 시험 결과를 보려고 앞으로 급히 달려갔다 다행히도 나는 그들의 머리 너머로 볼 수 있을 만큼 충분히 키가 컸다 시험 결과를 보자마자 나의 모든 걱정은 사라졌다 나는 다시 기숙사로 빨리 걸어가서 아버지께 전화를 했다. "아빠," 나는 흐려진 눈으로 우물거리며 말했다. "이 말이 믿기지 않으시겠지만, 제가 시험에 합격했어요." 아버지는 말씀을 하지 못하셨다. 마침내 아버지께서 "아들아, 정말 좋은 소식이구나. 솔직히 네가 해낼 거라고 생각하지 못했단다."라고 말씀하셨다. 나는 구름 위를 걷고 있는 것처럼 너무나 기뻤다.

문제풀이

① the exam grades가 동작의 대상이므로 수동태로 나타나야 한다.
② swarm은 '(같은 방향으로 급히 이동 중인) 군중'을 나타낸다. a swarm of는 '한 무리의' 의미로서 바로 뒤의 셀 수 있는 명사 students를 꾸미고 있다.
③ 「형용사/부사+enough to부정사」는 '…할 정도로 충분히 ~하게'의 의미이다. enough가 형용사나 부사를 수식할 때는 형용사나 부사 뒤에 위치한다.
④ 「동사+등위접속사(and) +동사」 구조의 병렬 구조를 이루고 있다.
⑤ 「as if+가정법과거[과거완료]」는 '마치 ~인(이었던)것처럼'이라는 의미이다. 「as if+가정법 과거」는 주절과 종속절이 나타내는 시제가 동일할 때 쓰인다. had been walking을 were walking으로 고쳐야 한다.

《 어휘 · 어구 》
reconstruct 재구성하다
conception 개념
student centered 학생 중심의
be involved in ~에 참여하다
interpret 해석하다
analogy 유추, 비유
make sense 이치에 맞다
generate 만들어 내다
fit in with ~에 잘 들어맞다, 적합하다

3. ③ F. Yates의 대학 시절 스포츠 일화

직독/직해

There is a story about /
F. Yates, a prominent UK statistician.
~에 대한 이야기가 있다. /
영국의 저명한 통계학자, F. Yates
During his student years at St. John's College, Cambridge, /
Cambridge의 St. John's College에 다니던 학생 시절에,
Yates had been keen on a form of sport.
Yates는 스포츠의 한 형태에 매우 관심이 많았다.
It consisted of / climbing about the roofs and towers
그것은 ~으로 구성되었다. / 지붕과 탑들을 올라 다니는 것으로
of the college buildings / at night.
대학 건물들의 / 밤에
In particular, / the chapel of St. John's College
특히, / St. John's College 예배당에는
has a massive neo-Gothic tower /
거대한 신고딕 양식의 탑이 있는데, /

adorned with statues of saints,
성인들의 동상으로 장식된

and to Yates it appeared obvious /
Yates에게는 분명해 보였다.

that it would be more decorous/
더 품위 있어 보일 것이

if these saints were properly attired / in surplices.
이 성인들에게 적절하게 입혀 주면 / 흰 가운을

One night he climbed up / and did the job; /
어느 날 밤 그는 기어올라서 그 일을 했으며,

next morning / 다음날 아침 /

the result was generally much admired.
그 결과는 대체로 많은 칭찬을 받았다.

But the College authorities were unappreciative /
하지만 대학 당국자들은 인정해 주지 않았으며

and began to consider means of divesting /
벗기는 방안에 대해 고려하기 시작했다.

the saints of their newly acquired garments.
그 성인들에게서 새롭게 획득한 그들의 의복을

This was not easy, / 이것은 쉽지 않았다. /

since they were well out of reach of any ordinary ladder.
그것들은 일반 사다리로는 도무지 닿을 수 없는 곳에 있었기 때문에,

An attempt to lift the surplices off / from above, /
흰 가운을 들어 올리려는 시도가 / 위에서

using ropes with hooks attached, was unsuccessful.
갈고리가 달린 밧줄을 사용하여 / 성공하지 못했다.

No progress was being made /
아무런 진전도 이루어지지 않았으며

and eventually Yates came forward /
결국 Yates가 나서서

and volunteered / to climb up / in the daylight /
지원했다 / 기어올라 / 대낮에

and bring them down.
그것을 갖고 내려오겠다고

This he did to the admiration /
그는 이 일을 하여 감탄하게 했다. /

of the crowd that assembled.
모인 군중을

영국의 저명한 통계학자, F. Yates에 대한 이야기가 있다. Cambridge의 St. John's College에 다니던 학생 시절에, Yates는 스포츠의 한 형태에 매우 관심이 많았다. 그것은 밤에 대학 건물들의 지붕과 탑들을 올라 다니는 것으로 구성되었다. 특히, St. John's College 예배당에는 성인들의 동상으로 장식된 거대한 신고딕 양식의 탑이 있는데, Yates에게는 이 성인들에게 적절하게 흰 가운을 입혀 주면 더 품위 있어 보일 것이 분명해 보였다. 어느 날 밤 그는 기어올라서 그 일을 했으며, 다음날 아침 그 결과는 대체로 많은 칭찬을 받았다. 하지만 대학 당국자들은 인정해 주지 않았으며 그 성인들에게서, 새롭게 획득한 그들의 의복을 벗기는 방안에 대해 고려하기 시작했다. 그것들은 일반 사다리로는 도무지 닿을 수 없는 곳에 있었기 때문에, 이것은 쉽지 않았다. 갈고리가 달린 밧줄을 사용하여 위에서 흰 가운을 들어 올리려는 시도는 성공하지 못했다. 아무런 진전도 이루어지지 않았으며 결국 Yates가 나서서 대낮에 기어올라 그것들을 갖고 내려오겠다고 자원했다. 그는 이 일을 하여 모인 군중을 감탄하게 했다.

문제풀이

① consist of는 '~으로 구성되다'의 의미로 전치사 뒤에 동명사형이 나온다.
② 현재 사실은 현재시제를 사용한다.
③ **현재 사실의 반대를 나타내는 가정법 과거 문장이다. 형태는 「If+주어+과거동사 ~ 주어+조동사 과거형+동사원형~」의 형태를 갖는다. will을 would로 고쳐야 한다.**
④ 「with+목적어(hooks)+목적격보어」의 분사구문이다. '갈고리가 달려 있는' 것이므로 목적격보어를 과거분사로 나타내야 한다.
⑤ was being made는 과거진행형의 수동태 구문이다.

《 어휘 · 어구 》

prominent 저명한
statistician 통계학자
keen 매우 관심이 많은, 열중하는

---

consist of ~로 구성되다
chapel 예배당
massive 거대한
neoGothic 신고딕 양식의
adorn 장식하다, 꾸미다
statue 동상, 조각상
saint 성인
attire (옷을) 차려 입다
admire 칭찬하다, 감탄하다
authorities 당국자, 관계자
unappreciative 인정하지 않는
garment 의복
attempt 시도
hook 갈고리
progress 진전, 진척, 발전
eventually 결국
assemble 모이다, 조립하다

---

4. ④ | Conan Doyle과 소설가 Meredith에 관련된 일화

직독 직해

Sir Arthur Conan Doyle, /
Arthur Conan Doyle경은 /

the creator of Sherlock Holmes, /
Sherlock Holmes를 탄생시켰는데

had a great sense of delicacy /
대단히 섬세한 감각을 지녔다.

where other persons' feelings were concerned.
다른 사람들의 감정이 관련된 경우에 관한 한

He once paid a visit to George Meredith, the novelist, /
그는 한 번은 소설가 George Meredith를 방문했던 적이 있다.

when Meredith was old and weak.
그 때 Meredith는 늙고 허약했다

Meredith suffered from an unusual disease /
Meredith는 희귀한 질병을 앓고 있었다. /

that caused him to fall occasionally.
그것은 그로 하여금 이따금씩 쓰러지게 했다.

The two men were walking up a path /
그 두 남자는 길을 걷고 있던 중

toward Meredith's summerhouse, /
Meredith의 여름 별장을 향해 /

Conan Doyle in the lead, /
Conan Doyle이 앞장 선 채, /

when Conan Doyle heard the old novelist fall / behind him.
Conan Doyle은 그 나이든 소설가가 쓰러지는 소리를 들었다. / 그 뒤에서

He judged by the sound / that the fall was a mere slip /
그는 그 소리를 듣고 판단했다. / 넘어진 것이 단순히 미끄러진 것이어서

and could not have hurt Meredith.
Meredith가 다치지 않았을 거라고 판단했다.

Therefore, / he did not turn /
따라서 / 그는 뒤돌아보지도 않고 /

and he strode on / as if he had heard nothing.
계속 성큼성큼 걸어갔다. / 아무 소리도 듣지 못한 것처럼

"He was a fiercely proud old man," /
"그는 몹시 자존심이 강한 노인이었지요." /

Conan Doyle later explained,
Conan Doyle은 나중에 해명했다.

"and my instincts told me /
"나는 본능적으로 생각했어요 /

that his humiliation in being helped up /
그가 부축 받아 일어난다는 굴욕감이 /

would be far greater than any relief /
어떠한 구조보다 훨씬 더 강하리라고 " /

I could give him." 내가 그에게 제공할 수 있었던

Sherlock Holmes를 탄생시킨 Arthur Conan Doyle경은 다른 사람들의 감정이 관련된 경우에 대단히 섬세한 감각을 지녔다. 그가 늙고 허

약했던 소설가 George Meredith를 방문했던 적이 있다. Meredith는 이따금씩 쓰러지는 희귀한 질병을 앓고 있었다. Conan Doyle이 앞장 선 채, 그 두 남자는 Meredith의 여름 별장을 향해 길을 걷고 있던 중 Conan Doyle은 그 나이든 소설가가 뒤에서 쓰러지는 소리를 들었다. 그는 그 소리를 듣고 넘어진 것이 단순히 미끄러진 것이어서 Meredith가 다치지 않았을 거라고 판단했다. 따라서 그는 아무 소리도 듣지 못한 것처럼 뒤돌아보지도 않고 계속 성큼성큼 걸어갔다. "그는 몹시 자존심이 강한 노인이어서 나는 본능적으로 그가 부축 받아 일어난다는 굴욕감이 내가 그에게 제공할 수 있었던 어떠한 구조보다 훨씬 더 강하리라고 생각했어요."라고 Conan Doyle은 나중에 해명했다.

문제풀이

① 선행사가 a great sense of delicacy이며 관계부사 where 이하의 문장이 완전하다.
② 「cause+목적어+to부정사」는 '목적어가 ~하도록 원인을 제공하다, 야기시키다'는 의미이다.
③ that은 동사 judged의 목적절을 이끄는 접속사로 that 이하의 문장이 완전한 문장 구조를 갖추고 있다.
④ **「as if+가정법 과거완료」는 과거 사실의 반대 의미를 가지고 있다. heard를 had heard로 고쳐야 한다.**
⑤ far는 비교급(greater)을 강조하는 역할을 한다.

《 어휘 · 어구 》

delicacy 섬세함, 정교함
occasionally 이따금씩
summerhouse 여름 별장
stride 큰 걸음으로 걷다
instinct 본능
humiliation 굴욕, 수치
relief 구제, 구조

---

5. ⑤ | 인도양의 쓰나미 경보 시스템의 필요성

직독 직해

One of the most painful signs /
가장 쓰라린 표시들 중에 하나는 /

of the lack of readiness for the tsunami /
쓰나미에 대한 대비 부족의 /

in the Indian Ocean in 2004 /
2004년 인도양에서의 /

was the enthusiasm of children, /
아이들의 열광이었다.

who rushed excitedly down to the beach /
바닷가로 신나게 뛰어나간 /

to gather fish / 물고기를 잡으러 /

during the initial retreat of water.
처음 물이 빠졌을 때

Those ill-fated children / had no idea /
그 불운한 아이들은 / 몰랐다. /

what the sea's strange retreat meant.
바다의 이상한 퇴각이 무엇을 의미하는지

No one knew / 그 누구도 알지 못하였다. /

because nothing like that had happened /
그와 같은 일이 일어난 적이 없었으므로

in living memory / 생의 기억 속에 /

except for the 1883 tsunami disaster /
쓰나미 재난을 제외하고는 /

in the Indian Ocean. 1883년 인도양에서의

After the 19th century disaster, /
그 19세기의 재난 이후,

experts called for a tsunami warning system /
전문가들은 쓰나미 경보 시스템을 요구하였다. /

in the Indian Ocean. / 인도양에서의

similar to the successful one /
성공적인 쓰나미 경보 시스템과 유사한 /

now operating in the Pacific.
태평양에서 현재 작동되고 있는

If such a system had been up and running in the Indian Ocean, /
만일 이러한 시스템이 인도양에서 발효 되었더라면.

many of the thousands of lives
수천 명의 생명은

lost in places relatively distant /
from the center of the earthquake
비교적 먼 지역에서 잃은 /
진원으로부터

might have been saved.
구할 수도 있었을 것이다.

2004년 인도양에서 쓰나미에 대한 대비 부족의 가장 쓰라린 표시들 중에 하나는 처음 물이 빠졌을 때 물고기를 잡으러 바닷가로 신나게 뛰어나간 아이들의 열광이었다. 그 불운한 아이들은 바다의 이상한 퇴각이 무엇을 의미하는지 몰랐다. 1883년 인도양에서의 쓰나미 재난을 제외하고는 생의 기억 속에 그와 같은 일이 일어난 적이 없었으므로 그 누구도 알지 못하였다. 그 19세기의 재난 이후, 전문가들은 태평양에서 현재 작동되고 있는 성공적인 쓰나미 경보 시스템과 유사한 인도양에서의 쓰나미 경보 시스템을 요구하였다. 만일 이러한 시스템이 인도양에서 발효가 되었더라면, 진원으로부터 비교적 먼 지역에서 잃은 수천 명의 생명은 구할 수도 있었을 것이다.

문제풀이

① one of the 최상급 구문으로서 주어가 one이므로 단수동사 was가 나왔다.
② 관계대명사 what은 선행사를 포함하고 있으며, 관계절 안에서 타동사 meant의 목적어 역할을 하고 있다.
③ 주절의 knew보다 과거 이전의 사실을 나타내야 하므로 과거완료 시제(had happened)를 썼다.
④ ~the successful one (which is) now operating~에서 「관계대명사+be동사」가 생략된 문장이다.
⑤ 그러한 시스템(such a system)이 인도양에서 발효되었더라면 인명을 많이 구했을 거라는 가정법 과거완료 문장이다. 가정법 과거완료 형태는 「If+주어+had+과거분사~, 주어+조동사 과거형+have+과거분사~」이다. 그러므로 were를 had been으로 고쳐야 한다.

〈어휘·어구〉

tsunami 해일
enthusiasm 열광
rush 돌진하다
initial 최초의
retreat 뒤로 빠짐, 퇴각
call for 요구하다
operate 작동하다
relatively 비교적
earthquake 지진
might have been ~였을지도 모른다
ill-fated 불운한
except for ~를 제외하고

6.② 유사(流砂)의 특징과 빠지는 경우 생존법

직독/직해

Is quicksand for real? 유사(流砂)는 정말로 있는가?
Yes, / but it's not as deadly as it is / in the movies.
그렇다. / 그러나 유사는 그리 치명적인 것은 아니다. / 영화에서 보는 것만큼
Quicksand forms / 유사는 형성된다.
when sand gets mixed with too much water /
모래가 너무나 많은 물과 섞여서
and becomes loosened and soupy.
모래 성분이 분해되고 죽처럼 걸쭉해질 때
It may look like normal sand, /
겉으로 보면 일반적인 모래처럼 보일지 모르지만, /
but if you were to step on it, /
한걸음 디디면 /

---

the pressure from your foot /
발의 압력이
would cause the sand to act more like a liquid, /
모래를 좀 더 액체처럼 움직이게 해서 /
and you'd sink right in.
사람은 바로 가라앉는다.
Pressure from underground sources of water /
지하 수원에서 나오는 압력은 /
would separate and suspend the granular particles, /
모래 알갱이 입자를 분리하고 둥둥 뜨게 만들어서 /
reducing the friction between them.
모래 입자 간의 마찰력을 감소시킨다.
In quicksand, / the more you struggle, /
유사에서는 / 빠져 나오려고 애를 쓰면 쓸수록 /
the deeper you'll sink.
더욱 밑으로 가라앉는다.
But if you remain still, / you'll start to float.
그러나 가만히 있으면 / 위로 떠오르기 시작할 것이다.
So if you ever do fall into quicksand, /
그러므로 혹시나 여러분이 유사 속에 빠지기라도 한다면 /
remember to stay calm, /
침착하게 있어야 할 것을 기억하고, /
and don't move / until you've stopped sinking.
움직이지 말라. / 몸이 가라앉는 것이 멈출 때까지

유사(流砂)는 정말로 있는가? 그렇다. 그러나 유사는 영화에서 보는 것만큼 그리 치명적인 것은 아니다. 유사는 모래가 너무나 많은 물과 섞여서 모래 성분이 분해되고 죽처럼 걸쭉해질 때 형성된다. 겉으로 보면 일반적인 모래처럼 보일지 모르지만, 한걸음 디디면 발의 압력이 모래를 좀 더 액체처럼 움직이게 해서 사람은 바로 가라앉는다. 지하 수원에서 나오는 압력은 모래 알갱이 입자를 분리하고 둥둥 뜨게 만들어서 모래 입자 간의 마찰력을 감소시킨다. 유사 속에서는 빠져 나오려고 애를 쓰면 쓸수록 더욱 밑으로 가라앉는다. 그러나 가만히 있으면 위로 떠오르기 시작할 것이다. 그러므로 혹시나 여러분이 유사 속에 빠지기라도 한다면 침착하게 있어야 할 것을 기억하고, 몸이 가라앉는 것이 멈출 때까지 움직이지 말라.

문제풀이

① ~ when sand gets(동사) ~ and becomes(동사)~가 병렬 구조를 이루고 있다.
② **would have caused를 would cause로 고쳐야** 한다. 가정법 과거 문장은 현재 사실의 반대를 나타내며 형태는 「if+주어+과거동사···, 주어+조동사 과거형+동사원형~」이다.
③ 분사구문의 주어인 pressure가 동사 reduce의 주체이므로 능동의 의미인 reducing이 나와 있다.
④ 「the 비교급 ···, the 비교급 ~」문장이다.
⑤ 「stop+동명사」는 '~을 멈추다'는 의미이다. '몸이 가라앉은 것이 멈출 때까지 움직이지 마라'는 것이므로 문맥상 '~을 멈추다'는 동명사가 나와야 한다.

〈어휘·어구〉

quicksand 유사(流砂)
deadly 치명적인
soupy 걸쭉한
suspend 매달다, 부양시키다
crawl 기다

7.③ 클라우스의 구조 활동과 한 건의 익사 사고

직독/직해

After two hours surfing, /
두 시간 동안 파도타기를 한 뒤 /
Clauss was taking off his wet suit /
물에 젖은 수영복을 벗고 있던 클라우스에게
when a boy ran up, pointing to water.
한 소년이 달려와서 물 쪽을 보라고 가리켰다.
"Two kids are in trouble," he said.
"두 아이가 위험에 처해 있어요." 소년이 말했다.

Clauss saw a pair of swimmers /
클라우스는 두 아이를 보았다.
splashing and waving their arms.
물을 첨벙대면서 손을 흔들고 있는
Grabbing his board, / he ran into the waves.
서핑 보드를 잡고, / 그는 파도 속으로 뛰어들었다.
As he paddled furiously, /
맹렬하게 노를 저으며,
Clauss managed to reach one of the two /
클라우스는 두 아이 중 한 명에 가까스로 다가가서 /
and pick him up on his surfboard.
그의 서핑 보드 위에 들어 올려놓았다.
He dived into the chilly water seven times, /
그는 일곱 번이나 차가운 물속으로 뛰어들어 /
looking for the other boy 나머지 한 아이를 찾았지만
but had no luck. 운이 따르지 않았다.
A policeman, / who was on the beach, / said /
한 경찰관이 / 해변에 있었던 / 말했다.
that if Clauss hadn't reacted so quickly and decisively, /
만약 클라우스가 그렇게 빠르고 단호하게 반응하지 않았더라면 /
there would have been two drownings /
두 건의 익사 사고가 있었을 것이라고 /
instead of one. 한 건이 아닌

두 시간 동안 파도타기를 한 뒤 물에 젖은 수영복을 벗고 있던 클라우스에게 한 소년이 달려와서 물 쪽을 보라고 가리켰다. "두 아이가 위험에 처해 있어요." 소년이 말했다. 클라우스는 물을 첨벙대면서 손을 흔들고 있는 두 아이를 보았다. 서핑 보드를 잡고, 그는 파도 속으로 뛰어들었다. 맹렬하게 노를 저으며, 클라우스는 두 아이 중 한 명에 가까스로 다가가서 그의 서핑 보드 위에 들어 올려놓았다. 그는 일곱 번이나 차가운 물속으로 뛰어들어 나머지 한 아이를 찾았지만 운이 따르지 않았다. 해변에 있었던 한 경찰관은 만약 클라우스가 그렇게 빠르고 단호하게 반응하지 않았더라면 한 건이 아닌 두 건의 익사 사고가 있었을 것이라고 말했다.

문제풀이

(A) As he grabbed his board, he ran into the waves.라는 문장을 분사구문으로 바꾼 문장이다. 부사절을 분사구문을 바꿀 때는 먼저, 접속사를 없애고, 부사절과 주절의 주어가 같으면 부사절의 주어를 제거한다. 한편, 부사절의 동사(grabbed)와 주절의 동사(ran)가 같은 과거시제이므로 「동사원형+-ing」형의 단순 분사구문(Grabbing)으로 바꾼다.
(B) 두 명의 인물을 지시대명사로 표현하려면, 한 명을 one, 다른 한 명을 the other로 표현한다.
(C) 가정법 과거완료는 과거 사실의 반대를 가리키며 형태는 「If+주어+had+과거분사 ~ 주어+조동사 과거형+have+과거분사~」로 표현한다.

〈어휘·어구〉

take off (옷, 신발 등을) 벗다
run up 달려오다
point to ~를 가리키다
In trouble 위험에 처한, 곤경에 처한
a pair of 두 명의, 두 개의
splash (물 등을) 튀기다
wave (손 등을) 흔들다
grab (~을) 잡다
run into ~속으로 뛰어들다
wave 파도
paddle 노 젓다
furiously 맹렬하게, 사납게
manage to-v 가까스로 ~하다
pick up 들어 올리다, 집어 올리다
dive into ~속으로 뛰어들다, 다이빙하다
chilly 차가운, 추운
look for ~를 찾다
react 반응하다
decisively 단호히
drowning 익사 사고
instead of ~대신에

---

8. ④   부와 명성은 행복의 보장이 아님

부와 명성은 행복을 보장한다고 여겨진다. "내가 만약 백만 달러를 가지고 있기만 하면, 일생동안 정말 행복할 텐데." "내가 만약 유명하다면, 다른 것은 필요하지 않을 텐데." 여러분에게 이 말을 하는 누구에게든, 한 사람의 이름만 대기만 하면 된다. 바로 엘비스 프레슬리다. 그는 평생 쓸 돈보다 더 많은 돈을 갖고 있었고, 그의 명성은 사후 여러 해 동안 계속되고 있다. 그러나 그는 비참하게 너무 일찍 자살했다. 명성과 부에 잘못된 점이 있다고 말하는 것은 아니다. 나는 가난한 것보다는 부자인 것을 선호할 것이다. 그리고 나는 무명인 것보다는 유명한 것이 더 낫다. 잘못된 것은 이런 속성들이 행복의 보장이라고 믿는 것이다. 목표를 세우고 무언가를 향해 노력하는 것은 잘못된 것이 아니지만, 여러분의 행복이 그것을 획득하는지의 여부에 좌우되도록 하는 것은 잘못된 것이다.

문제풀이

① 현재 사실에 대한 반대를 나타내므로, 「if+주어+동사의 과거형 ~, 주어+would+동사원형」 형태인 가정법 과거가 쓰였다.
② 'more ~ than'의 비교급 구문이 쓰였다.
③ 동사 prefer의 목적어로 to부정사가 쓰였다.
④ that 절의 주어인 these things에 이어지는 동사가 있어야 하므로, being을 are로 바꿔야 한다.
⑤ 전치사 on의 목적어 자리에 whether가 이끄는 명사절이 쓰였다.

《 구문 및 어휘 》

*3행 **If I could** be famous, **I'd** never **want** anything else.
⑴ 현재 사실에 대한 반대를 나타내는 가정법 과거구문으로, 「if+주어+동사의 과거형 ~, 주어+would+동사원형」 형태가 왔다.

*10행 [What is wrong] is [to believe {that these things are guarantees to happiness}].
⑴ [What is wrong]은 선행사를 포함하는 관계대명사 what이 이끄는 절로, 문장의 주어이다.
⑵ [to believe ~ happiness]는 동사 is의 보어 역할을 한다.
⑶ {that these things are guarantees to happiness}는 believe의 목적어 역할을 하는 명사절이다.

*11행 It is not wrong [to set a goal or to work toward something], but it is wrong [to let your happiness depend on whether you can acquire it].
⑴ It은 가주어, to set a goal or to work toward something이 진주어이다.
⑵ it은 가주어, to let 이하가 진주어이다.
⑶ whether는 '~인지 아닌지'라는 의미로 명사절을 이끄는 접속사이다.

guarantee 보장
prematurely 너무 이르게

9. ④   잘못된 선택의 오류

직독/직해

Suppose we know that Paula suffers from a severe
Paula가 극심한 공포증을 겪는다는 것을 우리가 안다고 가정하자
phobia.
If we reason that Paula is afraid either of snakes
Paula가 뱀이나 거미 둘 중 하나를 두려워한다고 추론한다면 /

or spiders, /
and then establish that she is not afraid of snakes, /
그리고 나서 그녀가 뱀을 두려워하지 않음을 규명한다면 /
we will conclude that Paula is afraid of spiders.
우리는 Paula가 거미를 두려워한다고 결론지을 것이다
However, our conclusion is reasonable /
그러나 우리의 결론은 타당하다 /
only if Paula's fear really does concern either
Paula의 두려움이 실제로 뱀이나 거미와 관계가 있는 경우에만 /
snakes or spiders.
If we know only that Paula has a phobia, /
Paula가 공포증이 있다는 것만 안다면 /
then the fact that she's not afraid of snakes is
그녀가 뱀을 두려워하지 않는다는 사실은 전적으로 양립한다 /
entirely consistent /
with her being afraid of heights, water, dogs or the
그녀가 높은 곳, 물, 개, 또는 숫자 13을 두려워 한다는 것과
number thirteen.
More generally, / 더 일반적으로는 /
when we are presented with a list of alternative
우리에게 어떤 현상에 대한 일련의 대안적 설명이 제공될 때 /
explanations for some phenomenon, /
and are then persuaded that all but one of those
그런 다음 그 설명들 중 하나를 제외하고 모든 것이 부적절함을 확신한다면 /
explanations are unsatisfactory, /
we should pause to reflect.
우리는 멈춰서 심사숙고해야 한다
Before conceding that the remaining explanation is
남아 있는 그 설명이 옳은 것이라는 것을 인정하기 전에 /
the correct one, /
consider whether other plausible options are
타당해 보이는 다른 선택 사항들이 무시되거나 간과되고 있는지를 고려해 보라
being ignored or overlooked.
The fallacy of false choice misleads /
잘못된 선택의 오류는 오도한다 /
when we're insufficiently attentive to an important
우리가 숨어 있는 중요한 가정에 불충분하게 주의를 기울이면 /
hidden assumption, /
that the choices which have been made explicit /
명백한 것으로 밝혀진 선택 사항들이 /
exhaust the sensible alternatives.
합리적인 대안을 고갈시키도록

Paula가 극심한 공포증을 겪는다는 것을 우리가 안다고 가정해 보자. Paula가 뱀이나 거미 둘 중 하나를 두려워한다고 추론한 다음, 그녀가 뱀을 두려워하지 않는다는 것을 ① 규명한다면, 우리는 Paula가 거미를 두려워할 것이다. 그러나 우리의 결론은 실제로 Paula의 두려움이 뱀이나 거미 둘 중 하나와 관계가 있는 경우에만 타당하다. 만약 우리가 Paula가 공포증이 있다는 것만 알고 있다면, 그녀가 뱀을 두려워하지 않는다는 사실은 그녀가 높은 곳, 물, 개, 또는 숫자 13을 두려워한다는 것과 전적으로 ② 양립한다. 더 일반적으로는 우리에게 어떤 현상에 대한 일련의 대안적 설명이 제공되고, 그런 다음 그 설명들 중 하나를 제외하고 모든 것이 ③ 적절하지 않다는 것을 확신한다면, 우리는 멈춰서 심사숙고해야 한다. 남아 있는 그 설명이 옳은 것이라는 것을 ④ 부정하기(→ 인정하기) 전에, 타당해 보이는 다른 선택 사항들이 무시되거나 간과되고 있는지를 고려해 보라. 잘못된 선택의 오류는, 우리가 숨어 있는 중요한 가정에 불충분하게 주의를 기울이면, 명백한 것으로 밝혀진 선택 사항들이 ⑤ 합리적인 대안을 고갈시키도록 오도한다.

문제풀이

어떤 현상에 대한 여러 가지 대안적 설명들 중에서 다른 모든 설명이 적절하지 않을 경우, 남은 하나의 설명이 옳다고 인정하기 전에 간과된 다른 타당한 설명이 있는지 고려해보라는 흐름이 되어야 자연스럽다. 따라서 ④ 'denying(부정하다)'은 'conceding(인정하다)'과 같은 말로 바꿔야 한다.

《 어휘·어구 》

phobia 공포증
establish 규명하다, 밝히다
concern 관계가 있다
consistent 양립하는
reflect 심사숙고하다
overlook 간과하다
mislead 오도하다, 잘못된 길로 이끌다

---

assumption 가정
explicit 명백한
exhaust 고갈시키다

10. ⑤   농담에 대한 반응

직독/직해

Discovering how people are affected by jokes is
사람들이 어떻게 농담에 영향을 받는지 알아내는 것은 대체로 어렵다
often difficult.
People mask their reactions / because of politeness
사람들은 자신의 반응을 숨긴다 / 공손함이나 동일 집단의 압력 때문에
or peer pressure.
Moreover, people are sometimes unaware /
게다가 사람들은 때때로 인식하지 못한다 /
of how they, themselves, are affected.
그들이 어떻게 영향을 받는지 자신마저도
Denial, for example, may conceal from people /
예를 들어, 부정은 사람들로부터 숨길 수 있다 /
how deeply wounded they are by certain jokes.
사람들이 어떤 농담에 의해 얼마나 깊이 상처받는지를
Jokes can also be termites or time bombs, /
농담은 또한 흰개미나 시한폭탄일 수도 있다 /
lingering unnoticed in a person's subconscious, /
사람의 잠재의식 속에 눈에 띄지 않고 남아 /
gnawing on his or her self-esteem or exploding it at
그 사람의 자존감을 갉아먹거나 나중에 그것을 폭발시키는
a later time.
But even if one could accurately determine how
하지만 사람들이 어떻게 영향을 받는지 정확히 파악할 수 있다고 해도 /
people are affected, /
this would not be an accurate measure of hatefulness.
이것이 혐오에 대한 정확한 척도가 되지는 못할 것이다
People are often simply wrong /
사람들은 대체로 그냥 잘못 알고 있다 /
about whether a joke is acceptable or hateful.
농담이 용인될 수 있는지 혹은 혐오스러운지에 대해
For example, / 예를 들어
people notoriously find terribly hateful jokes about themselves or their sex, nationalities, professions, etc. unproblematic /
사람들은 자기 자신이나 자신의 성별, 국적, 직업 등에 대한 매우 혐오스러운 농담이 문제가 되지 않는다고 느끼는 것으로 악명 높다 /
until their consciousness becomes raised.
그들의 의식이 높아지기 전까지
And the raising of consciousness /
그리고 그 의식을 높이는 것은 /
is often followed by a period of hypersensitivity /
종종 과민증의 시기를 수반한다 /
where people are hurt or offended even by tasteful,
품위 있고 재치 있는 농담에도 사람들이 상처를 받거나 기분이 상하는
tactful jokes.

사람들이 어떻게 농담에 영향을 받는지를 알아내는 것은 대체로 어렵다. 사람들은 공손함이나 동일 집단의 압력 때문에 자신의 반응을 ① 숨긴다. 게다가 사람들은 때때로 그들이 어떻게 영향을 받는지 자신마저도 ② 인식하지 못한다. 예를 들어, 부정은 사람들이 어떤 농담에 의해 얼마나 깊이 상처받는지를 스스로 숨길 수 있다. 농담은 또한 사람의 잠재의식 속에 눈에 띄지 않고 남아, 그 사람의 자존감을 갉아먹거나 나중에 그것을 ③ 폭발시키는 흰개미나 시한폭탄일 수도 있다. 하지만 사람들이 어떻게 영향을 받는지 정확히 파악할 수 있다고 해도, 이것이 혐오에 대한 ④ 정확한 척도가 되지는 못할 것이다. 사람들은 대체로 농담이 용인될 수 있는지 혹은 혐오스러운지에 대해 그냥 잘못 알고 있다. 예를 들어, 사람들은 그들의 의식이 높아지기 전까지 자기 자신이나 자신의 성별, 국적, 직업 등에 대한 매우 혐오스러운 농담이 ⑤ 문제가 된다고(→ 문제가 되지 않는다고) 느끼는 것으로 악명 높다. 그리고 의식이 높아진 뒤에는 심지어 품위 있고 재치 있는 농담에도 사람들이 상처를 받거나 기분이 상하는 과민증의 시기가 흔히 뒤따른다.

문제풀이

⑤는 사람들이 농담이 용인될 수 있는지 혐오스러운지에 대해 잘못 알고 있는 경우의 한 예로서, 사람들이 의식이 높아지기 전까지는 매우 혐오스러운 농담이 ⑤ 문제가 되지 않는다고 느낀다는 흐름이

되어야 하므로, ⑤ 'probelematic(문제가 되는)'은 'unprobelematic(문제가 되지 않는)'과 같은 말로 바꿔야 한다.

《 어휘·어구 》

unaware ~을 알지 못하는
conceal 숨기다
linger 좀처럼 없어지지 않다
subconscious 잠재의식
self-esteem 자존감
notoriously 악명 높게
consciousness 의식
hypersensitivity 과민증
offend 불쾌하게 하다
tasteful 고상한
tactful 재치 있는

---

11. ⑤   진화에 영향을 미치는 생태적 환경 변화

직독/직해

One misconception that often appears /
자주 나타나는 한 가지 오해는 /

in the writings of physical scientists /
물리 과학자들의 글에서 /

who are looking at biology from the outside /
외부로부터 생물학을 보고 있는 /

is that the environment appears to them /
환경이 그들에게는 보인다는 것이다 /

to be a static entity, / 정적인 독립체로 /

which cannot contribute new bits of information /
새로운 정보를 제공할 수 없는 /

as evolution progresses. 진화가 진행됨에 따라

This, however, is by no means the case.
그러나 이것은 결코 사실이 아니다

Far from being static, / the environment is constantly
정적이기는커녕 / 환경은 끊임없이 변하고 있다

changing / and offering new challenges /
/ 그리고 새로운 도전을 제공하고 /

to evolving populations. 진화하는 개체군에

For higher organisms, / 고등 생물의 경우 /

the most significant changes in the environment /
환경의 가장 중요한 변화는 /

are those / 변화이다 /

produced by the contemporaneous evolution of
다른 생물의 동시대 진화에 의해 생성된

other organisms.

The evolution of a horse's hoof from a five-toed foot /
발가락이 다섯 개 달린 발로부터 말발굽으로의 진화는 /

has enabled the horse / to gallop rapidly over open
말을 ~할 수 있게 해 주었다 / 탁 트인 평야를 빠르게 질주할

plains.

But such galloping is of no advantage / to a horse /
그러나 그러한 질주는 이득이 되지 않는다 / 말에게 /

unless it is being chased by a predator.
그것이 포식자에 의해 쫓기지 않는 한

The horse's efficient mechanism for running /
달리기를 위한 말의 효율적인 기제는 /

would never have evolved / except for the fact /
절대 진화하지 않았을 것이다 / 사실이 없었다면 /

that meat-eating predators were at the same time
육식을 하는 포식자가 동시에 발전시키고 있었다는

evolving / more efficient methods of attack.
/ 더 효율적인 공격 방법을

Consequently, laws based upon ecological
결과적으로, 생태적 관계에 기초한 법칙은

relationships / among different kinds of organisms /
/ 서로 다른 종류의 생물 간의 /

are essential for understanding evolution and the
진화와 생물의 다양성을 이해하는 데 필수적이다

diversity of life / to which it has given rise.
/ 그것이 발생시킨

외부로부터 생물학을 보고 있는 물리 과학자들의 글에서 자주 나타나는 한 가지 오해는 환경이 그들에게는 진화가 진행됨에 따라 새로운 정보를 제공할 수 없는 정적인 독립체로 보인다는 것이다. 그러나 이것은 결코 사실이 아니다. 정적이기는커녕 오히려 환경은 끊임없이 변하고 있으며 진화하는 개체군에 새로운 ① 도전을 제공하고 있다. 고등 생물의 경우, 환경의 가장 중요한 변화는 다른 생물의 동시대 진화에 의해 생성된 변화이다. 발가락이 다섯 개 달린 발로부터 말발굽으로의 진화는 말을 탁 트인 평야를 빠르게 질주 ② 할 수 있게 해주었다. 그러나 그러한 질주는 포식자에 의해 쫓기지 않는 한 말에게 ③ 이득이 되지 않는다. 달리기를 위한 말의 효율적인 기제는 육식을 하는 포식자가 동시에 더 효율적인 ④ 공격 방법을 발전시키고 있었다는 사실이 없었다면 절대 진화하지 않았을 것이다. 결과적으로, 서로 다른 종류의 생물 간의 생태적 관계에 기초한 법칙은 진화와 그것이 발생시킨 생물의 다양성을 이해하는 데 ⑤ 선택적(→ 필수적)이다.

문제풀이

포식자가 효율적인 공격 방법을 발달시킴에 따라 말도 발가락이 다섯 개 달린 발에서 말발굽으로 진화하였다는 예를 들면서 환경은 계속 변화하면서 개체군에 새로운 도전을 제공하기 때문에 생물은 그 도전에 맞춰 진화한다고 했다. 따라서 서로 다른 종류의 생물 간의 생태적 관계에 기초한 법칙은 진화와 그것이 발생시킨 생물의 다양성을 이해하는 데 반드시 필요하다고 해야 하므로, ⑤ 'optional(선택적인)'은 'essential(필수적인)'로 고쳐야 한다.

《 어휘·어구 》

misconception 오해
static 정적인
entity 독립체
by no means 결코 ~이 아닌
far from ~이기는커녕 오히려
evolve 진화하다, 발전시키다
population 개체(군), 인구
contemporaneous 동시대의
plain 평야
of no advantage 이득이 되지 않는
chase 쫓다
mechanism 기제
ecological 생태적인, 생태학의
diversity 다양성
give rise to ~을 발생시키다, ~을 낳다

---

12. ⑤   기자가 갖추어야 할 소양

직독/직해

Many people believe /
많은 사람이 믿는다 /

that journalists should be impartial.
기자는 공정해야 한다고

At its most extreme, / this view proposes /
가장 극단적으로 볼 때 / 이러한 견해는 제안한다 /

that journalists should not have any personal political
views,
기자들이 어떤 개인적인 정치적 견해를 가져서는 안된다고

that they should be aloof from society /
그들은 사회에서 떨어져 있어야 한다고 /

and act as pure observers.
그리고 순수한 관찰자 역할을 해야 한다고

However, / 하지만 /

journalists do need to be concerned about the society /
기자는 사회에 대해 실제로 관심을 가질 필요가 있다 /

on which they are reporting and commenting.
그들이 보도하고 있고 논평하고 있는

If they are not concerned about it and not involved
in it, /
만일 그들이 사회에 관심을 가지지 않고 그것에 참여하지 않는다면 /

then they will probably be very poor journalists.
그러면 그들은 아마도 매우 실력 없는 기자가 될 것이다

Journalism is about people.
저널리즘은 사람에 관한 것이다

Journalists should be gregarious /
기자는 사교적이어야 한다 /

and interested in the people and the issues /
그리고 사람과 쟁점에 관심을 가져야 한다 /

on which they are reporting.
자신이 보도하고 있는

This means / that many reporters have political ideals /
이것은 의미한다 / 많은 기자가 정치적 이상을 가지고 있다는 것을 /

and are politically active.
그리고 정치적으로 활동적이라는 것을

Furthermore, / although some journalists find /
더군다나 / 일부 기자들이 느끼지만 /

their hours of work militate against joining various
clubs and societies, /
자신들의 근무 시간이 다양한 클럽과 사회 집단에 참여하는 것을 방해한다고 /

most journalists are involved in such groups and have
other outside interests.
대부분의 기자들은 그런 단체에 참여하고 다른 외부의 관심사를 가지고 있다

Because of this, / journalists, /
이로 인해 / 기자들은 /

more than many professional groups, /
많은 전문 집단보다 더 많이 /

enjoy each other's company.
서로 함께 있는 것을 즐긴다

많은 사람이 기자는 공정해야 한다고 믿는다. 가장 극단적으로 볼 때, 이러한 견해는 기자들이 어떤 개인적인 정치적 견해를 가져서는 안 되며, 그들은 사회에서 떨어져서 순수한 ① 관찰자 역할을 해야 한다고 제안한다. 그러나, 기자는 자신이 보도하고 있고 논평하고 있는 사회에 대해 실제로 관심을 가질 필요가 있다. 그들이 사회에 관심을 가지지 않고 그것에 참여하지 않는다면, 그들은 아마도 매우 ② 실력 없는 기자가 될 것이다. 저널리즘은 사람에 관한 것이다. 기자는 사교적이어야 하고 자신이 보도하고 있는 사람과 쟁점에 관심을 가져야 한다. 이것은 많은 기자들이 정치적 이상을 가지고 있으며 정치적으로 ③ 활동적이라는 것을 의미한다. 더군다나, 일부 기자들이 자신의 근무 시간이 다양한 클럽과 사회 집단에 참여하는 것을 방해한다고 느끼지만, 대부분의 기자들은 그런 단체에 참여하고 다른 ④ 외부의 관심사를 가지고 있다. 이로 인해, 많은 전문 집단보다 더 많이, 기자들은 서로 함께 있는 것을 ⑤ 싫어한다(→ 즐긴다).

문제풀이

많은 사람이 기자들은 공정해야 한다고 생각하지만, 자신이 취재하는 사람과 사회의 쟁점에 관심을 가지고 있어야만 하는 직업 특성상, 기자는 정치적 이상을 가지고 있으며 여러 단체에 참여하고 활동적일 수밖에 없다는 문맥이므로, ⑤의 'dislike(싫어하다)'를 'enjoy(즐기다)' 등의 어휘로 고쳐야 한다.

◉ 이렇게 풀자   적절한 어휘를 물어보는 문제는 글의 논리적 흐름 파악이 뒷받침되어야 한다. 글 전체 중심 내용을 파악한 후 각 밑줄 친 단어가 문맥과 자연스럽게 연결되는지 확인해야 한다. 이 글은 기자들이 사회에 관심을 갖고 참여해야 하고, 따라서 기자들은 다양한 클럽과 사회 집단에 참여하고 이를 즐긴다는 내용이므로 그와 상반되는 어휘를 찾으면 된다. 기자들이 서로 함께 있는 것을 싫어한다는 것은 글의 내용과 상반되므로 ④의 dislike가 문맥상 적절하지 않다는 것을 유추할 수 있다.

👄 구조 다시보기

일반적 견해	많은 사람들은 기자가 사회에서 떨어져서 순수한 관찰자 역할을 해야 한다고 믿음
비판(주제)	기자들은 사회에 관심을 갖고 참여해야 함
부연	대부분의 기자들은 사회 집단에 참여하고 서로 함께 있는 것을 즐김

《 어휘·어구 》

impartial 공정한
be concerned about ~에 관심을 가지다
be involved in ~에 연루되다, 관계되다
company 동행, 함께 있음

---

09. 부정사

A 출제 POINT
본문 050쪽

1. to emigrate 2. to pay 3. to get
4. to cooperate 5. to find
6. to carry 7. not to waste

1 [해석]▶ 그의 야망은 미국으로 이민 가는 것이다.
[해설]▶ to부정사가 문장 속에서 보어 역할을 하고 있다.

2 [해석]▶ 사람들은 새로운 세금을 지불하는 것을 거절할 것이다.
[해설]▶ refuse 동사는 to부정사를 목적어로 취한다.

3 [해석]▶ 이번 주 토요일에 있을 파티에 음식을 가져오는 것을 잊지 마.
[해설]▶ 미래에 대한 일을 말하고 있으므로 「forget+to부정사」를 사용해야 한다. 의미는 '~할 것을 잊다'는 의미이다.

4 [해석]▶ 협조하는 것을 그녀가 거부해 당혹스러웠다.
[해설]▶ to부정사는 형용사처럼 문장 속에서 명사(refusal)를 수식할 수 있다.

5 [해석]▶ Peter는 집에 와서 자기의 집이 불이 난 것을 발견했다.
[해설]▶ '~에 와서 ~한 결과를 발견한 것이므로', to부정사의 부사적 용법 중에서 결과를 나타낸다.

6 [해석]▶ 그 상자는 내가 나를 수 있을 정도로 가볍다.
[해설]▶ A enough to B는 'B할 만큼 충분히 A하다'는 의미이다. carry의 목적어인 The case가 문장 앞에 간 것이므로 carry 뒤에 it을 또 쓰면 안 된다.

7 [해석]▶ 꿈을 실현하기 위해, 그들은 돈을 낭비하지 않기로 결심했다.
[해설]▶ to부정사의 부정은 not을 to부정사 앞에 쓴다.

B 체크 POINT
본문 050쪽

1. to report 2. to take 3. swimming
4. to modernize 5. To see
6. too fat 7. of

1 [해석]▶ 내 직업은 알리는 것이지 논평하거나 판단하는 것이 아니다.
[해설]▶ to부정사가 주어의 직업을 설명하는 주격보어 역할을 하고 있다.

2 [해석]▶ CEO의 연설 후에 15분간 휴식을 갖기로 했다.
[해설]▶ decide는 to부정사를 목적어로 취한다.

3 [해석]▶ 어렸을 때 이 강에서 수영한 것이 기억난다.
[해설]▶ 「remember+동명사」는 '(과거) ~했던 것을 기억하다'는 의미이다.

4 [해석]▶ 그 회사는 현대화를 하지 못한 것이 쇠퇴의 원인이 되었다.
[해설]▶ to부정사가 형용사처럼 문장 속에서 명사(The

company's failure)를 수식하고 있다.

5 [해석]▶ 그녀가 걸어가는 것을 보면, 그녀가 맹인인 것을 알지 못할 것이다.
[해설]▶ to부정사는 문장 속에서 '~한다면(조건)'의 의미를 가질 수도 있다.

6 [해석]▶ 그 호랑이는 너무 살이 쪄서 나무를 올라갈 수 없다.
[해설]▶ too... to ~는 '너무 … 해서 ~할 수 없다'는 의미이다.

7 [해석]▶ 그렇게 불쌍한 아이들을 도와주다니 참 친절했구나.
[해설]▶ to부정사는 의미상의 주어를 쓸 수 있다. 의미상의 주어는 「for+목적격」으로 쓰며, kind, brave 등의 형용사 뒤에는 「of+목적격」을 의미상의 주어로 쓴다.

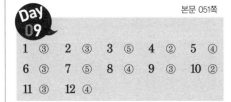
본문 051쪽

1 ③	2 ③	3 ⑤	4 ②	5 ④
6 ③	7 ⑤	8 ④	9 ③	10 ②
11 ③	12 ④			

1. ③ 국가는 오직 시장 실패를 고치거나 경쟁의 장을 평등하게 하기 위해서만 경제에 개입하는 것이 좋다.

직독 직해

The conventional view / of what the state should do /
통념적인 견해는 / 국가가 무엇을 해야 하는지에 대한
to foster innovation / is simple: /
혁신을 촉진하기 위해 / 간단한데
it just needs to get out of the way.
국가는 단지 방해가 안 되게 할 필요가 있다는 것이다.
At best, / governments merely facilitate /
기껏해야 / 정부는 단지 촉진할 뿐이고 /
the economic dynamism of the private sector;
민간 부문의 경제적 역동성을
at worst, / their lumbering, heavy-handed, and bureaucratic institutions /
최악의 경우에는 / 그들의 느릿느릿 움직이고, 위압적이며 관료적인 기관들이 /
actively inhibit it. 적극적으로 그것을 억제한다.
The fast moving, risk-loving, and pioneering private sector, /
빠르게 움직이고, 위험을 사랑하며, 선구적인 민간 부문이 /
by contrast, / 반면에 /
is what really drives the type of innovation /
혁신 유형을 실제로 추진하는 것이다.
that creates economic growth.
경제 성장을 창출하는
According to this view, /
이 견해에 따르면 /
the secret behind Silicon Valley /
실리콘 밸리의 비결은 /
lies in its entrepreneurs and venture capitalists.
기업가들과 벤처 투자가들에게 있다.
The state can intervene in the economy /
국가는 경제에 개입할 수 있지만, /
—but only to fix market failures /
오직 시장 실패를 바로 잡거나 /
or level the playing field.
경쟁의 장을 평등하게 하기 위해서만 그렇다.

It can regulate the private sector /
국가는 민간 부문을 규제할 수 있으며,
in order to account for the external costs /
외부 비용에 대해 책임지기 위해 /
companies may impose on the public, /
기업이 공공에 부과하는 /
such as pollution, / and it can invest in public goods, /
공해와 같이 / 그리고 국가는 공공재에 투자할 수 있다.
such as basic scientific research /
기초 과학 연구나 /
or the development of drugs /
의약품 개발과 같은 /
with little market potential.
시장 잠재력이 거의 없는
It should not, however, directly attempt /
그러나 국가는 직접 시도해서는 안 된다.
to create and shape markets.
시장을 만들고 형성하려고

혁신을 촉진하기 위해 국가가 무엇을 해야 하는지에 대한 통념적인 견해는 간단한데 국가는 단지 방해가 안 되게 할 필요가 있다는 것이다. 기껏해야 정부는 민간 부문의 경제적 역동성을 단지 촉진할 뿐이고, 최악의 경우에는 그들의 느릿느릿 움직이고, 위압적이며 관료적인 기관들이 적극적으로 그것을 억제한다. 반면에, 빠르게 움직이고, 위험을 사랑하며, 선구적인 민간 부문이 경제 성장을 창출하는 혁신 유형을 실제로 추진하는 것이다. 이 견해에 따르면 실리콘 밸리의 비결은 기업가들과 벤처 투자가들에게 있다. 국가는 경제에 개입할 수 있지만, 오직 시장 실패를 바로 잡거나 경쟁의 장을 평등하게 하기 위해서만 그렇다. 국가는 공해와 같이 기업이 공공에 부과하는 외부 비용에 대해 책임지기 위해 민간 부문을 규제할 수 있고, 기초 과학 연구나 시장 잠재력이 거의 없는 의약품 개발과 같은 공공재에 투자할 수 있다. 그러나 국가는 시장을 만들고 형성하려고 직접 시도해서는 안 된다.

문제풀이

① 문장의 주어는 conventional view이므로 단수 동사가 나와야 한다.
② 관계사 what이 이끄는 절이 문장에서 is의 보어 역할을 하고 있다. that creates economic growth는 선행사 the type of innovation을 수식하고 있다.
③ 밑줄 뒤에 목적어 market failures가 나오므로 부정사의 수동태가 아니라 능동태를 사용해야 한다. to be fixed를 to fix로 고쳐 써야 한다.
④ 인칭대명사 it은 the state를 가리킨다.
⑤ to create가 to부정사의 부사적 용법(목적)으로 사용되었다.

어휘·어구

conventional 통념적인
foster 촉진하다
innovation 혁신
facilitate 촉진하다
private sector 민간 부문
lumbering 느릿느릿 움직이는
heavy-handed 위압적인
bureaucratic 관료적인
inhibit 억제하다
economic growth 경제 성장
entrepreneur 기업가
venture capitalist 벤처 투자가
intervene 개입하다
market failure 시장 실패
level 평등하게 하다
account for 책임지다
external cost 외부 비용
impose 부과하다
market potential 시장 잠재력

2.③ 사업 현장에서 감사의 중요성

직독/직해

In business settings, / 사업 현장에서는 /
it's really easy to forget to take the time /
시간을 가져야 하는 것을 정말 잊기 쉽지만. /
to say Thank-You, / and yet, it's an essential part /
'감사'를 표현 / 그것은 필수적인 부분이다. /
of interaction with others.
다른 사람과의 교류에서
It's important to people /
사람들에게는 중요하다. /
that they feel valid, important, and respected.
그들이 소중하고, 중요하며, 존중되고 있다고 느끼는 것이
Just as saying sorry matters, /
미안하다고 말하는 것이 중요한 것과 똑같이 /
so does remembering to thank /
사람들에게 감사하는 것을 기억하는 것도 중요하다. /
those who help you move forward.
당신이 정진하도록 도와주는
And I think it's much nicer /
그리고 나는 훨씬 더 좋다고 생각한다. /
to send along a physical card/
실제의 카드를 보내는 것이 /
than an email. 이메일을 보내는 것보다
A personal note written by your own hand /
당신의 손으로 쓴 간단한 자필 편지는 /
matters far more than a few lines of typing /
몇 줄의 활자보다 훨씬 더 중요하다. /
into a window that's so easily available at your fingertips.
당신의 손가락 끝으로 화면에다 그토록 손쉽게 작성해 넣을 수 있는
One more thing: / if you're going to go this route,/
한 가지 더 덧붙이자면, / 만약 당신이 이 길로 갈 거면(이렇게 할 거면)
put in the extra few minutes /
별도의 몇 분을 더 들이고 /
to purchase a nice card / 좋은 카드를 구입하는 데 /
and use a pen that gives you a decent flow.
글씨를 깔끔하게 쓸 수 있는 펜을 사용하도록 하라.

사업 현장에서는 '감사'를 표현할 시간을 가져야 하는 것을 정말 잊기 쉽지만, 그것은 다른 사람과의 교류에서 필수적인 부분이다. 사람들에게는 그들이 소중하고, 중요하며, 존중되고 있다고 느끼는 것이 중요하다. 미안하다고 말하는 것이 중요한 것과 똑같이 당신이 정진하도록 도와주는 사람들에게 감사하는 것을 기억하는 것도 중요하다. 그리고 나는 이메일을 보내는 것보다 실제의 카드를 보내는 것이 훨씬 더 좋다고 생각한다. 당신의 손으로 쓴 간단한 자필 편지는 당신의 손가락 끝으로 화면에다 그토록 손쉽게 작성해 넣을 수 있는 몇 줄의 활자보다 훨씬 더 중요하다. 한 가지만 더 덧붙이자면, 만약 당신이 이 길로 갈 거면(이렇게 할 거면), 좋은 카드를 구입하는 데 별도의 몇 분을 더 들이고 글씨를 깔끔하게 쓸 수 있는 펜을 사용하도록 하라.

문제풀이

① 「forget+to부정사」는 '(~해야 하는 것)을 잊어 버리다'라는 의미이다.
② feel valid, important, and respected는 feel 다음에 형용사들이 병렬 구조를 이루고 있다.
③ it-to 가주어, 진주어 구문이다. 주어가 긴 경우, 가주어를 문장 앞으로 보내고, 진주어를 뒤로 보낸다. to부정사 바로 뒤에 목적어가 나오므로 to부정사의 수동태를 쓰지 않고, 능동태를 써야 한다.
④ far는 비교급을 강조하는 수식어로 사용되었다.
⑤ to purchase ~ and (to) use가 병렬 구조를 이루고 있다.

《 어휘 · 어구 》

essential 필수적인
interaction 상호 작용
valid 효과적인, 소중한
important 중요한
respected 존중받는
matter 중요하다

---

decent 호감이 가는
move forward 전진하다
personal note 자필 편지
fingertip 손가락 끝

3.⑤ Emma가 고음 연습 중 발생한 일

직독/직해

Emma was very fond of singing.
Emma는 노래 부르는 것을 매우 좋아했다.
She had a very good voice, / except /
그녀는 매우 좋은 목소리를 가지고 있었다 / 제외하면 말이다 /
that some of her high notes /
일부 고음에서
tended to sound like a gate /
문과 같은 소리가 나는 경향이 있다는 것만 /
which someone had forgotten to oil.
누군가 기름칠해야 할 것을 잊어버린
Emma was very conscious of this weakness /
Emma는 이 약점을 무척 의식해서, /
and took every opportunity she could find /
기회가 날 때마다 /
to practice these high notes.
이러한 고음을 연습했다.
As she lived in a small house, /
그녀는 작은 집에서 살았기 때문에 /
where she could not practice /
그곳에서는 연습할 수 없었다 /
without disturbing the rest of the family, /
다른 가족들을 방해하지 않고는
she usually practiced her high notes outside.
(그래서) 그녀는 보통은 밖에서 고음을 연습했다.
One afternoon, / a car passed her /
어느 날 오후 / 자동차 한 대가 지나갔다. /
while she was singing / some of her highest/
그녀가 노래하고 있을 때 / 가장 높고도 /
and most difficult notes.
어려운 음조 부분을
She saw / an anxious expression /
그녀는 보았다. / 걱정스러운 표정이 /
suddenly come over the driver's face.
운전자의 얼굴에 갑자기 떠오르는 것을 보았다.
He put his brakes on violently, / jumped out,/
그는 브레이크를 세게 밟더니, / 뛰어나와, /
and began to examine all his tires carefully.
모든 타이어를 주의 깊게 점검하기 시작했다.

Emma는 노래 부르는 것을 매우 좋아했다. 그녀는 매우 좋은 목소리를 가지고 있었다. 일부 고음에서 기름칠을 하지 않은 문과 같은 소리가 나는 경향이 있다는 것만 제외하면 말이다. Emma는 이 약점을 무척 의식해서, 기회가 날 때마다 이러한 고음을 연습했다. 그녀는 다른 가족들을 방해하지 않고 연습할 수 없는 작은 집에서 살았기 때문에 보통은 밖에서 고음을 연습했다. 어느 날 오후 그녀가 가장 높고 어려운 음조 부분을 노래하고 있을 때 자동차 한 대가 지나갔다. 그녀는 운전자의 얼굴에 갑자기 걱정스러운 표정이 떠오르는 것을 보았다. 그는 브레이크를 세게 밟더니, 뛰어나와, 모든 타이어를 주의 깊게 점검하기 시작했다.

문제풀이

(A) 「forget+to부정사」는 '미래의 해야 할 일을 잊다'는 의미이다. 문맥상 '해야 할 일을 잊은 것'이므로 forget 뒤에 to부정사가 나와야 한다.
(B) 선행사가 in a small house이며, 빈칸 뒤에 완전한 문장이 나왔으므로 관계부사 where가 적절하다. 선행사를 보충 설명하는 관계부사 where의 계속적 용법이다.
(C) 「지각동사+목적어+목적격보어」 구조로서, 지각동사의 목적어와 목적격보어가 능동 관계인 경우 목적격보어가 to부정사가 나오지 않고, 동사원형이 와야 한다.

《 어휘 · 어구 》

voice 목소리
high notes 고음
tend (…하는) 경향이 있다
oil 기름칠하다
weakness 약점
disturb 방해하다

4.② 헌법상 투표권의 의미

직독/직해

I was shocked by the news /
소식에 나는 충격을 받았다. /
that people with mental disorders /
정신질환이 있는 사람들이 /
can be kept from voting.
투표를 하지 못하게 될 수도 있다는
Our constitutional right to vote / does not require/
헌법상 우리의 투표권이 / 강요하는 것은 아니다. /
that any one of us should make a rational choice.
누구에게도 이성적인 선택을 하도록
We can vote for a candidate /
우리는 어떤 후보에게 투표를 할 수도 있고, /
because he or she seems most qualified, /
가장 적임자로 보여서 /
or simply because we like his or her appearance.
또는 단순히 외모가 마음에 들어서 투표할 수도 있다.
In addition, / the mentally ill are faced with /
게다가 / 정신질환자들은 직면해 있는데. /
a unique set of challenges, /
고유의 어려움에 /
and their interests will not be adequately represented /
정신 질환자들의 이익을 적절히 대변되지 못할 것이다. /
if they cannot vote.
그들로 하여금 투표를 할 수 없게 하면
To exclude those from voting /
투표에서 배제하는 것은
who are already socially isolated /
이미 사회적으로 소외된 사람들을 /
destroys our democracy, /
우리의 민주주의를 파괴한다. /
as it creates a caste system.
사회 계급 제도를 만들어 내어

정신질환이 있는 사람들이 투표를 하지 못하게 될 수도 있다는 소식에 나는 충격을 받았다. 헌법상 우리의 투표권이 누구에게도 이성적인 선택을 하도록 강요하는 것은 아니다. 우리는 가장 적임자로 보여서 어떤 후보에게 투표를 할 수도 있고, 또는 단순히 외모가 마음에 들어서 투표할 수도 있다. 게다가 정신질환자들은 고유의 어려움에 직면해 있는데, 그들로 하여금 투표를 할 수 없게 하면 정신 질환자들의 이익을 적절히 대변되지 못할 것이다. 이미 사회적으로 소외된 사람들을 투표에서 배제하는 것은 사회 계급 제도를 만들어 내어 우리의 민주주의를 파괴한다.

문제풀이

(A) keep A from -ing는 'A가 ~하도록 하지 못하게 하다'는 의미이다. They can keep people with mental disorders from voting. 문장을 수동태로 바꾸면 목적어에 해당하는 People with mental disorders가 수동태의 주어로 가고, 동사 부분은 「can be+p.p.(kept) from」 ~으로 변한다.
(B) the mentally ill은 「the+형용사」로서 복수보통명사를 가리킨다. 그러므로 소유격은 복수형 their로 나타내야 한다.
(C) To exclude ~ isolated가 to부정사구의 주어 역할을 하고 있다. to부정사구가 주어 역할을 할 때, 단수동사를 취한다.

《 어휘 · 어구 》

constitutional 헌법상의

rational 이성적인
candidate 후보자
qualified 적임의
appearance 외모
mentally ill 정신적으로 병든
adequately 적절히
exclude 배제하다
democracy 민주주의
caste (사회)계급, 카스트

---

5. ④ — 바쁜 대학 생활 중에도 휴식 시간을 확보해라

직독 / 직해

College life is busy. 대학 생활은 바쁘다.
There are too many demands / on your schedule.
고려해야 할 것들이 너무나 많다. / 일정을 계획할 때
Activities, friends, and pastimes /
활동, 친구, 그리고 오락 등은 /
may cause some difficulties /
약간의 어려움을 야기할 수 있다.
in your performing the real job at hand.
코앞에 닥친 실질적인 일을 수행하는데
When you are feeling overwhelmed /
여러분이 압도당하는 느낌이 들 때. /
by presentations, paper deadlines, or tests, /
발표, 보고서 마감 시간, 혹은 시험에 의해 /
you will probably spend all your time studying /
아마도 공부하는데 모든 시간을 사용할 것이다. /
to deal with these pressures.
급한 일들을 처리하기 위해
However, / this lack of time for relaxation /
하지만, / 이러한 휴식을 위한 시간의 부족은 /
makes it more difficult / 어렵게 만들 것이다. /
to get the most out of your studies.
공부에서 가장 많은 것을 얻는 것을
Promise yourself / 자신에게 약속을 하라. /
that no matter how much work you have, /
아무리 할 일이 많더라도 /
you will always relax during one full evening.
항상 하루 저녁은 온전히 쉬도록
You will work better / 일을 더 잘하게 될 것이다. /
if you take time off for relaxation.
휴식을 위해서 시간을 낸다면

대학 생활은 바쁘다. 일정을 계획할 때 고려해야 할 것들이 너무나 많다. 활동, 친구, 그리고 오락 등은 코앞에 닥친 실질적인 일을 수행하는데 약간의 어려움을 야기할 수 있다. 발표, 보고서 마감 시간, 혹은 시험에 의해 압도당하는 느낌이 들 때, 아마도 긴급한 일들을 처리하기 위해 공부하는데 모든 시간을 사용할 것이다. 하지만, 이러한 휴식을 위한 시간의 부족은 공부에서 가장 많은 것을 얻는 것을 어렵게 만들 것이다. 아무리 할 일이 많더라도 항상 하루 저녁은 온전히 쉬도록 자신에게 약속을 하라. 휴식을 위해서 시간을 낸다면 일을 더 잘하게 될 것이다.

문제풀이

① 「some difficulties in+의미상의 주어(your)+동명사(performing)」 구문이다.
② are feeling 뒤에 보어가 수동의 의미를 가지고 있는 과거분사(overwhelmed)가 나왔다.
③ to deal이 to부정사의 부사적 용법(목적)으로 쓰였다.
④ **get을 to get으로 고쳐야 한다.** 가목적어, 진목적어 구문으로, 가목적어 **it**이 가리키는 진목적어가 문장의 뒷부분에 와야 하므로 **get을 to get으로** 고쳐야 한다.
⑤ 명령문으로 주어(You)가 생략되어 있다. 주어와 목적어가 같은 사람이므로, 재귀대명사 yourself를 쓴 것이다.

《 어휘·어구 》

demand 요구사항
pastime 오락, 기분전환
perform 수행하다
at hand 바로 가까이에
overwhelm 압도하다
presentation 발표
pressure 압박
relaxation 휴식

---

6. ③ — 파리의 지하철 메트로

직독 / 직해

On most subway trains, / 대부분의 지하철 전동차에서 /
the doors open automatically / at each station.
문들은 자동으로 열린다. / 각각의 정거장에서
But when you are on the Mtro, the subway in Paris, /
그러나 파리의 지하철인 메트로를 타면 /
things are different. 사정이 다르다.
I watched a man on the Mtro /
나는 메트로를 탄 한 남자를 지켜보았다. /
try to get off the train and fail.
전동차에서 내리려다가 실패하는 것을
When the train came to his station, /
전동차가 그가 내릴 정거장으로 들어 왔을 때 /
he got up and stood patiently in front of the door, /
그는 자리에서 일어나 문 앞에 끈기 있게 서있었다. /
waiting for it to open. 문이 열리기를 기다리며
It never opened. 그런 일은 일어나지 않았다.
The train simply started up again /
전동차는 그저 다시 떠났고 /
and went on to the next station.
다음 정거장으로 계속 갔다.
In the Mtro, / 메트로에서는 /
you have to open the doors yourself /
승객 스스로 문을 열어야 한다. /
by pushing a button, depressing a lever or sliding them.
단추를 누르거나 레버를 내리누르거나 문을 옆으로 밀어서

대부분의 지하철 전동차에서 문들은 각각의 정거장에서 자동으로 열린다. 그러나 파리의 지하철인 메트로를 타면 사정이 다르다. 나는 메트로를 탄 남자가 전동차에서 내리려다가 실패하는 것을 지켜보았다. 전동차가 그가 내릴 정거장으로 들어 왔을 때 그는 자리에서 일어나 문 앞에 끈기 있게 서있었다(문이 열리지 않았다). 전동차는 그저 다시 떠났고 다음 정거장으로 계속 갔다. 메트로에서는 단추를 누르거나 레버를 내리누르거나 문을 옆으로 밀어서 승객 스스로 문을 열어야 한다.

문제풀이

(A) watch가 지각동사이므로 (A)에는 동사원형인 try가 맞다. 「지각동사+목적어+목적격보어」 구문은 목적어와 목적격보어가 능동 관계인 경우 동사원형이나 진행형을 쓴다. '한 남자가 내리려고 한 것'이므로 능동 관계이나.
(B) as he waited for it(= the door) to open~라는 문장을 분사구문으로 바꾼 것이다. (B)에는 to open이 맞다.
(C)는 A, B or C로 병렬 구조를 이루고 있다. 내용상 pushing a button, depressing a lever와 병렬 구조를 이루어야 하기 때문에 (C)에는 sliding이 맞다.

《 어휘·어구 》

métro 파리의 지하철
depress 내리누르다
lever 지레, 레버
slide 미끄러지듯 움직이다

---

7. ⑤ — Gordon의 음악 학습 이론

직독 / 직해

The primary goal of Gordon's Music Learning Theory /
Gordon의 음악 학습 이론의 주요 목표는 /
is to treat music education / in a manner /
음악 교육을 다루는 것이다 / 방식으로 /
similar to language learning right from birth.
태어나는 순간부터 언어 학습과 유사한
Through consistent exposure to and reinforcement of musical concepts,
음악적 개념에 대한 일관성 있는 노출과 강화를 통해 /
the teacher assists the child / through stages of musical development /
교사는 아이를 돕는다 / 음악적 발달 단계를 거치는 내내 /
that will provide him with the basic knowledge / to study music at school.
기초 지식을 아이에게 제공할 / 학교에서 음악을 공부하기 위한
Gordon believes / that as the child matures /
Gordon은 믿는다 / 아이가 성장함에 따라 /
he or she will learn to appreciate and participate / in the making of music,
그 또는 그녀가 음악을 감상하는 것을 배우고 참여하게 될 것이며 / 음악을 만드는 데 /
thus bringing more meaning to life.
따라서 삶에 더 많은 의미를 가져다줄 것이라고
Once the educator has an understanding of early childhood characteristics and development, /
일단 교사가 유아기의 특성과 발달에 대해 이해하게 되면 /
the next step / is to observe the child / and develop lesson plans /
그다음 단계는 / 아이를 관찰하는 것이다 / 그리고 수업 계획을 개발하는 것이다 /
based upon the learning style and personal interests of the child.
아이의 학습 스타일과 개인적인 관심사를 바탕으로
The most important tool in teaching this age group / is engagement through play, /
이 연령대를 가르치는 데 있어서 가장 중요한 도구는 / 놀이를 통한 참여이다 /
and with the child's own enthusiasm, motivation, and willingness to participate, /
그리고 아이 자신의 열정, 동기 부여, 그리고 기꺼이 참여하려는 마음이 있으면 /
the role of the educator / is simply to free the potential / for self-development.
교사의 역할은 / 잠재력을 자유롭게 해주는 것이다 / 단순히 자기 계발을 위한

Gordon의 음악 학습 이론의 주요 목표는 태어나는 순간부터 음악 교육을 언어 학습과 유사한 방식으로 다루는 것이다. 음악적 개념에 대한 일관성 있는 노출과 강화를 통해, 교사는 학교에서 음악을 공부하기 위한 기초 지식을 아이에게 제공할 음악적 발달 단계를 거치는 내내 아이를 돕는다. Gordon은 아이가 성장함에 따라 그 또는 그녀가 음악을 감상하는 것을 배우고 음악을 만드는 데 참여하게 되며 따라서 삶에 더 많은 의미를 가져다줄 것이라고 믿는다. 일단 교사가 유아기의 특성과 발달에 대해 이해하게 되면, 그다음 단계는 아이를 관찰하고 아이의 학습 스타일과 개인적인 관심사를 바탕으로 수업 계획을 개발하는 것이다. 이 연령대를 가르치는 데 있어서 가장 중요한 도구는 놀이를 통한 참여이며, 아이 자신의 열정, 동기 부여, 그리고 기꺼이 참여하려는 마음이 있으면, 교사의 역할은 단순히 자기 계발을 위한 잠재력을 자유롭게 해주는 것이다.

문제풀이

① [형용사]
앞의 명사 a manner를 수식하는 형용사구를 이끌고 있으므로, 형용사 similar가 온 것은 적절하다.
② [관계대명사]
뒤에 주어가 빠진 불완전한 문장이 왔고 선행사 stages of musical development를 수식하고 있으므로, 주격 관계대명사 that이 온 것은 적절하다.
③ [분사구문]
결과의 의미를 나타내는 분사구문으로 생략된 주어 it이 행위의 주체로 '가져다줄'이라는 능동의 의미이므로, 현재분사 bringing이 온 것은 적절하다.
④ [병렬구조]
주격보어 역할을 하는 to부정사구를 이끄는 to observe와 등위접속사 and로 연결되어 병렬구조

를 이루고 있으므로, to부정사에서 to를 생략한 형태인 develop가 온 것은 적절하다.

⑤ [to부정사]

willingness를 수식하는 형용사적 용법의 to부정사가 와야 하므로, **participate**를 to participate로 고쳐야 한다.

○ **이렇게 풀자** 어법상 틀린 부분을 찾는 문제는 밑줄이 있는 부분의 형태와 문맥을 보고 어법에 맞게 쓰였는지 확인해야 한다.

① 형용사구는 앞의 명사를 수식할 수 있다.
② 문장에서 관계대명사가 필요한 경우인지를 확인한 후, 선행사의 종류 및 격에 따라 적절하게 쓰였는지 살펴봐야 한다.
③ 분사구문에서 의미상 주어와의 관계가 능동일 때 현재분사가 와야 하고, 수동일 때 과거분사가 와야 한다.
④ 등위접속사 뒤에 위치한 동사에 밑줄이 있는 경우는 병렬구조가 아닌지 확인한다.
⑤ 동사에 밑줄이 있는 경우 문장 내에서 그 동사의 쓰임을 생각해 본다. to부정사나 동명사, 분사가 와야 하는 자리가 아닌지 확인해 본다.

《 **어휘·어구** 》

primary 주요한
consistent 일관성 있는
exposure 노출
reinforcement 강화
musical 음악의, 음악적인
concept 개념
assist 돕다, 도움이 되다
mature (충분히) 발달하다, 성숙해지다
appreciate 감상하다
participate 참가하다
educator 교육자
childhood 어린 시절
characteristic 특성
observe 관찰하다
engagement 관계함, 참여
enthusiasm 열광, 열정
motivation 동기
willingness 기꺼이 하는 마음

8.④   저에너지 전기 장치로의 전환

유럽연합 전역에서 저에너지 전구로의 전환은 1년에 2천만 톤 정도의 탄소 배출량을 줄이는 잠재력을 가지고 있다. 그러므로 2009년 유럽연합이 100와트 반투명 백열전구의 제조와 수입을 금지했던 것은 놀라운 것이 아니다. 훨씬 더 에너지 효율적으로 될 수 있게 하는 다른 종류의 많은 전기 기구가 있어서, 비슷한 미래의 결단력은 불가피하다. 오늘 나는 합해서 고작 41와트를 소비하는 저에너지 개인용 컴퓨터와 모니터로 이 말들을 치고 있다. 그에 반해서, 1년 전이었다면 나는 약 220와트를 소비한 아주 전형적인 데스크톱 하드웨어로 이 말들을 치고 있었을 것이다. 우리 모두에게 에너지 사용을 줄일 수 있는 아주 상당한 기회가 실제로 존재한다. 그것들이 또한 주는 비용절감을 고려하면, 우리 중 다수는 저에너지 전기 장치를 살 가능성이 있다.

문제풀이

① A switch가 주어이므로 단수동사 has가 온 것은 적절하다. to low-energy bulbs across the European Union은 A switch를 수식하는 전치사구이다.

② that 앞에 주어가 It이고, 다음에 주어나 목적어가 빠지지 않은 완전한 절이 왔다. 따라서 앞의 It이 가주

어이고 that이 이끄는 절은 진주어절이므로 접속사 that이 온 것은 적절하다.

③ many other kinds of electrical appliance를 수식하는 형용사 capable이 온 것은 적절하다.

④ 뒤에 술어 동사 do exist가 있으므로 동사가 쓰일 수 없다. 따라서 reduce를 앞의 Very significant opportunities를 수식하는 to부정사인 to reduce로 고쳐 써야 한다.

⑤ given은 '~을 고려하면, ~이 주어지면'의 의미의 전치사이다.

따라서 정답은 ④이다.

《 **구문 및 어휘** 》

*9행 I would have been typing them on <u>very typical desktop hardware</u> [**that** consumed around 220 watts].

① that consumed ~ 220 watts는 선행사 very typical desktop hardware를 수식하는 관계대명사절이다.

switch 전환
potential 가능성, 잠재력
emission 배출(량)
ban 금하다
import 수입품, 수입
appliance 기구, 적용(물)
energy efficient 에너지 효율적인
initiative 결단력, 주도성
inevitable 불가피한
consume 소모하다
typical 전형적인; 보통의, 일반적인
significant 상당한, 중요한
cost savings 비용[원가]절감

9.③   사후 과잉 확신 편향

직독/직해

One factor contributing to students' difficulty /
학생들의 어려움에 기여하는 한 요인은 /
in making accurate judgments of their own
자신의 지식에 대해 정확한 판단을 내리는 것에서
knowledge / is hindsight bias: /
/ 사후 과잉 확신 편향이다 /
the tendency to assume / once something happens /
가정하는 경향 / 일단 어떤 일이 발생하면 /
that one knew all along that it was going to happen.
그것이 일어날 것이라는 것을 처음부터 알고 있었다고
When students receive feedback / suggesting that
학생들이 피드백을 받을 때 / 그들의 지식이 불완전함을 시사하는 /
their knowledge is incomplete, /
/
such as getting an exam item incorrect, /
가령 시험 문항을 틀린 것과 같이 /
they may respond by telling themselves /
그들은 스스로에게 얘기함으로써 반응할 수도 있다 /
that they actually did know the information.
실제로는 그 정보를 정말 알고 있었다고
Although they do not have a strong grasp of the
그들은 내용을 완전히 파악하지 못하고 있음에도 불구하고
material, / they feel as if they do /
/ 그들은 완전히 파악하고 있는 것처럼 느낀다 /
because they recognize something about the item content.
그 문항의 내용에 대해 무언가를 인식하고 있기 때문에
Looking back, / once they know the answer, / the
되돌아보면 / 일단 그들이 정답을 알면 / 해답은 명확히 보인다
solution seems obvious.

This feeling of familiarity / 이러한 친숙함의 느낌은 /
can lead students to have an exaggerated sense /
학생들이 과장된 인식을 갖게 할 수 있다 /
of what they know. 자기가 알고 있는 것에 대하여
Hindsight bias therefore reinforces the feeling /
따라서 사후 과잉 확신 편향은 느낌을 강화한다 /
that their failure was due to the nature of the
assessment / 실패가 평가의 속성 때문이라는 /
rather than the nature of their knowledge — /
그들이 가진 지식의 속성 때문이라기보다 /
which makes it more difficult for them to learn
이것은 그들이 피드백으로부터 배우는 것을 더 어렵게 만든다
from feedback.

학생들이 자신의 지식에 대해 정확한 판단을 내리는 것을 어려워하는 것의 원인이 되는 하나의 요인은 사후 과잉 확신 편향, 즉 어떤 일이 일어났을 때 사람들이 그것이 일어날 것이라는 것을 처음부터 알고 있었다고 가정하는 경향이다. 학생들이 가령 시험 문항을 틀린 것과 같이 자신의 지식이 불완전함을 시사하는 피드백을 받을 때, 그들은 실제로 그 정보를 정말 알고 있었다고 스스로에게 얘기함으로써 (피드백에) 반응할 수도 있다. 그들은 내용을 완전히 파악하지 못하고 있음에도 불구하고 그 문항의 내용에 대해 무언가를 인식하고 있기 때문에 (그 내용을) 완전히 파악하고 있는 것처럼 느낀다. 되돌아보면 일단 그들이 정답을 알면 해답은 명확해 보인다. 이러한 (B) 친숙함의 느낌은 학생들이 자기가 알고 있는 것에 대하여 과장된 인식을 갖게 할 수 있다. 따라서 사후 과잉 확신 편향은 실패가 그들이 가진 지식의 속성 때문이라기보다 평가의 속성 때문이라는 느낌을 (C) 강화한다. 그리고 이것은 그들이 피드백으로부터 배우는 것을 더 어렵게 만든다.

문제풀이

(A) 그들의 지식이 불완전함을 시사하는 피드백을 받는 상황의 예이므로 'incorrect(틀린)'가 오는 것이 적절하다. right는 '옳은'이라는 의미이다.

(B) 틀린 답을 고른 후에 그들이 정답을 알고 나면 해답은 명확해 보이는 느낌이므로 'familarity(친숙함)'가 오는 것이 적절하다. novelty는 '선선함'이라는 의미이다.

(C) 사후 과잉 확신 편향은 실패가 그들이 가진 지식 때문이 아니라 평가의 속성 때문이라는 느낌을 강화한다는 의미가 되어야 하므로 'reinforce(강화하다)'가 오는 것이 적절하다. diminish는 '줄이다'라는 의미이다.

○ **이렇게 풀자** 글의 큰 흐름을 따라 읽으면서 쌍으로 제시된 어휘 주변의 문맥을 살펴야 한다. 네모 안에는 주로 반의어가 제시되는데 이 문제에서는 incorrect/right, familarity/novelty, diminish/reinforce로 출제되었다. 평소 어휘 학습을 할 때 반의어를 함께 익히는 것이 도움이 될 것이다.

구조 다시보기

도입	사후 과잉 확신 편향 때문에 자신의 지식에 대해 정확한 판단이 어려움
예시	· 지식이 부족하다는 피드백을 받을 경우 그 정보를 알고 있었다고 생각함 · 그 이유는 일단 답을 알고 나서 보면 해결책이 명백한 것처럼 보임
결론	사후 과잉 확신 편향은 피드백으로부터 배우는 것을 방해함

《 **어휘·어구** 》

contribute to ~의 원인이 되다
hindsight bias 사후 과잉 확신 편향
tendency 경향
assume 가정하다
all along 내내, 처음부터
grasp 이해, 파악
recognize 인식하다
obvious 명확한
exaggerated 과장된
assessment 평가

10. ② 타인에게서 받는 불신의 영향

직독/직해

Sometimes the awareness that one is distrusted /
때때로 누군가가 불신을 받는다는 인식은 /

can provide the necessary incentive /
필요한 동기를 제공할 수 있다 /

for self-reflection. 자기 성찰에

An employee who realizes /
깨달은 직원은 /

she isn't being trusted by her co-workers /
자신이 자신의 동료들로부터 신뢰를 받지 못하고 있다는 것을 /

with shared responsibilities at work might, /
직장에서의 공유하는 책임을 가진 /

upon reflection, / identify areas /
성찰하자마자 / 영역을 확인할 수 있을 것이다 /

where she has consistently let others down /
자신이 다른 사람들을 지속적으로 실망시키던 /

or failed to follow through on previous commitments.
또는 이전의 책무를 끝내지 못했던

Others' distrust of her might then forbid /
그러면 그녀에 대한 다른 사람들의 불신은 금지할 수도 있을 것이다 /

her to perform her share of the duties /
그녀가 자신의 몫의 의무를 수행하도록 /

in a way that makes her more worthy of their trust.
자신이 그들의 신뢰를 받을 만한 가치가 더 있도록 만드는 방식으로

But distrust of one who is sincere in her efforts /
그러나 노력을 진실되게 하는 사람에 대한 불신은 /

to be a trustworthy and dependable person /
믿음직하고 신뢰할 수 있는 사람이 되기 위해 /

can be disorienting /
방향감각에 혼란을 가져올 수 있다 /

and might cause her to doubt her own perceptions /
그리고 그녀가 자신의 인식을 의심하게 하게 할 수 있다 /

and to distrust herself. 그리고 자신을 불신하게 할 (수도 있다)

Consider, for instance, a teenager /
예를 들어, 10대 청소년을 생각해 보라 /

whose parents are suspicious and distrustful /
부모가 의심하고 불신하는 /

when she goes out at night; / 그녀가 밤에 외출할 때 /

even if she has been forthright about her plans /
비록 그녀가 자신의 계획에 대해 솔직하더라도 /

and is not breaking any agreed-upon rules, /
그리고 합의된 어떤 규칙도 어기고 있지 않더라도 /

her identity as a respectable moral subject /
훌륭한 도덕적인 주체로서의 그녀의 정체성은 /

is undermined by a pervasive parental attitude /
널리 스며있는 부모의 태도에 의해 훼손된다 /

that expects deceit and betrayal. 기만과 배신을 예상하는

때때로 누군가가 불신을 받는다는 인식은 자기 성찰에 필요한 동기를 제공할 수 있다. 자신이 직장에서의 공유하는 책임을 가진 동료들로부터 신뢰를 받지 못하고 있다는 것을 ① 깨달은 직원은, 성찰하자마자 자신이 다른 사람들을 지속적으로 실망시키거나 이전의 책무를 끝내지 못했던 영역을 확인할 수 있을 것이다. 그러면 그녀에 대한 다른 사람들의 불신은 자신이 그들의 신뢰를 받을 만한 가치가 더 있도록 만드는 방식으로 자신의 몫의 의무를 수행하도록 ② 금지할 수도 있을 것이다. 그러나 믿음직하고 신뢰할 수 있는 사람이 되기 위한 노력을 ③ 진실되게 하는 사람에 대한 불신은 방향감각에 혼란을 가져올 수 있고 그 자신의 인식을 의심하게 하고 자신을 불신하게 할 수도 있다. 예를 들어, 밤에 외출할 때 부모가 ④ 의심하고 불신하는 10대 청소년을 생각해 보라, 비록 그녀가 자신의 계획에 대해 솔직하고 합의된 어떤 규칙도 ⑤ 어기고 있지 않더라도, 훌륭한 도덕적인 주체로서의 그녀의 정체성은 기만과 배신을 예상하는 널리 스며있는 부모의 태도에 의해 훼손된다.

문제풀이

불신을 받는다는 인식이 자기 성찰에 필요한 동기를 제공한다는 것의 사례이므로, 동료에게서 신뢰를 받지 못한 직원은 성찰을 통해 그동안 자신이 실망시키거나 이전의 책무를 끝내지 못했던 영역을 확인하고 자신을 신뢰받을 만한 가치가 있는 존재로 만들기 위해 자신이 맡은 의무를 수행하고자 한다고 해야 문맥상 자연스럽다. 따라서 ② 'forbid(금지하다)'는 'encourage(고무하다, 격려하다)'로 바꿔야 한다.

🌱 구조 다시보기

주제 1	불신을 받는다는 인식이 자기 성찰에 필요한 동기를 제공함
예시	직장 동료들이 자신을 못 믿을 때, 자신을 성찰하고 자신의 의무를 수행하게 할 수 있음
주제 2	성실히 노력하는 사람에 대한 불신은 자기 불신을 일으킬 수 있음
예시	솔직하고 성실한 10대 청소년에 대한 부모의 불신이 훌륭한 도덕적 주체로서의 정체성을 훼손할 수 있음

《 어휘·어구 》

awareness 인식
distrust 불신하다
incentive 동기
self-reflection 자기성찰
identify 확인하다
consistently 지속적으로
let down ~을 실망시키다
follow through ~을 끝내다
previous 이전의
commitment 책무
trustworthy 믿음직스러운
dependable 신뢰할 수 있는
disorient 혼란스럽게 하다
perception 인식
suspicious 의심하는
distrustful 불신하는
agreed-upon 합의된
respectable 훌륭한
moral 도덕적인
subject 주체
undermine 훼손하다
parental 부모의
deceit 기만
betrayal 배신

---

11. ③ 건축에서 단순함에 대한 선호의 한계

직독/직해

The conscious preference for apparent simplicity /
분명한 단순함에 대한 의식적 선호는 /

in the early-twentieth-century modernist movement /
20세기 초반 근대주의 운동에서의 /

in prose and poetry / was echoed /
산문과 시에서 / 반영되었다 /

in what is known as the International Style of architecture. 건축의 국제 양식으로 알려진 것에

The new literature avoided / 이 새로운 문학은 피했다 /

old-fashioned words, elaborate images, grammatical
오래된 낱말, 정교한 비유, 문법적 도치를

inversions, / and sometimes even meter and rhyme.
/ 그리고 때때로 운율과 각운조차

In the same way, / 같은 방식으로 /

one of the basic principles of early modernist
architecture / 초기 근대주의 건축의 기본 원칙 중 하나는 /

was that every part of a building must be functional, /
건물의 모든 부분이 기능적이어야 한다는 것이다 /

without any unnecessary or fancy additions.
어떠한 불필요하거나 복잡한 추가물이 없이

Most International Style architecture aggressively banned / 대부분의 국제 양식 건축은 공격적으로 금했다 /

moldings and sometimes even window and door frames. 몰딩과 때때로 창과 문의 틀조차

Like the prose of Hemingway or Samuel Beckett, /
Hemingway나 Samuel Beckett의 산문처럼 /

it proclaimed, and sometimes proved, /
그것은 선언했고 가끔 증명했다 /

that less was more. 더 적은 것이 더 낫다는 것을

But some modern architects, unfortunately, /
하지만 일부 근대 건축가들은 불행히도 /

designed buildings / 건물을 설계했다 /

that looked simple and elegant / 단순하고 우아해 보이는 /

but didn't in fact function very well: /
하지만 사실은 잘 기능하지 않았던 /

their flat roofs leaked in wet climates /
그것들의 평평한 지붕은 비가 많은 기후 지역에서 물이 샜다 /

and their metal railings and window frames rusted.
그리고 그것들의 금속 난간과 창틀은 녹이 슬었다

Absolute simplicity, in most cases, /
대부분의 경우에서 절대적 단순함은 /

remained an ideal rather than a reality, /
현실이라기보다 이상으로 남았다 /

and in the early twentieth century /
그리고 20세기 초반에 /

complex architectural decorations continued to be
복잡한 건축 장식이 계속해서 사용되었다

used / in many private and public buildings.
/ 많은 민간 그리고 공공건물에서

산문과 시에서 20세기 초반 근대주의 운동에서의 분명한 단순함에 대한 의식적 선호는 건축의 국제양식으로 알려진 것에 반영되었다. 이 새로운 문학은 오래된 낱말, 정교한 비유, 문법적 도치, 그리고 때때로 운율과 각운조차 (A) 피했다. 같은 방식으로, 초기 근대주의 건축의 기본 원칙 중 하나는 건물의 모든 부분이 어떠한 불필요하거나 복잡한 추가물이 없이 (B) 기능적이어야 한다는 것이다. 대부분의 국제양식 건축은 몰딩과 때때로 창과 문의 틀조차 공격적으로 금했다. Hemingway나 Samuel Beckett의 산문처럼, 그것은 더 적은 것이 더 낫다는 것을 선언했고 가끔 증명했다. 하지만 일부 근대 건축가들은 불행히도 단순하고 우아해 보이지만 사실은 잘 기능하지 않았던 건물을 설계했다. 그것들의 평평한 지붕은 비가 많은 지역에서 물이 샜고 그것들의 금속 난간과 창틀은 녹이 슬었다. 대부분의 경우에서 절대적 (C) 단순함은 현실이라기보다 이상으로 남았고 20세기 초반에 복잡한 건축 장식이 많은 민간 그리고 공공건물에서 계속해서 사용되었다.

문제풀이

(A) 근대주의 운동에서는 산문과 시에서 분명한 단순함을 선호했다고 했으므로, 문학에서 오래된 낱말, 정교한 비유, 문법적 도치, 운율과 각운과 같은 글을 복잡하게 만드는 요소들을 피했을 것이다. 따라서 'avoided(피했다)'가 오는 것이 적절하다. embrace는 '받아들이다'라는 의미이다.

(B) 단순함을 선호한 것이 건축의 국제 양식에도 반영되었다고 했으며 건축의 모든 부분에 불필요하거나 복잡한 추가물이 없었다고 했으므로, 문맥상 건축의 모든 부분은 기능적이어야 했다고 해야 한다. 따라서 'functional(기능적인)'이 오는 것이 적절하다. decorative는 '장식이 된'이라는 의미이다.

(C) 단순함의 선호에도 불구하고 복잡한 건축 장식이 많은 건물에 계속 사용되었다고 했으므로, 문맥상 단순함은 현실보다는 이상이었다고 하는 것이 자연스럽다. 따라서 'simplicity(단순함)'가 오는 것이 적절하다. complexity는 '복잡함'이라는 의미이다.

따라서 정답은 ③이다.

《 어휘·어구 》

conscious 의식하는
apparent 분명한
prose 산문
elaborate 정교한
meter 운율
rhyme 각운
fancy 복잡한
principle 원리, 원칙
aggressively 공격적으로
ban 금하다
proclaim 선언하다
elegant 우아한, 멋지어
flat 평평한

leak 새다
rust 녹슬다
absolute 절대적인
decoration 장식

12. ④ 동시에 두 가지 과업을 수행하는 것의 어려움

직독/직해

A joint team of researchers from Tokyo University and Oxford University /
도쿄 대학교와 옥스퍼드 대학교 공동 연구팀은 /

conducted a study / 연구를 수행했다 /

on how well people can simultaneously perform two tasks.
사람들이 동시에 두 가지 과제를 얼마나 잘 수행할 수 있는지에 관한

They found / that doing two things at once /
그들은 발견했다 / 한 번에 두 가지 일을 하는 것이 /

often led to dual-task interference, / with the result /
흔히 이중 과업 간섭을 낳는다는 것을   / 결과와 함께 /

that both the tasks were poorly performed.
두 과제 모두 형편없이 수행되는

Researchers looked at single-neuron activity /
연구자들은 단일 신경 활동을 관찰했다 /

in monkeys' lateral prefrontal cortexes /
원숭이의 측면 전전두엽 피질의 /

while the animals performed tasks /
그 동물들이 과제를 수행하는 동안 /

that required both spatial attention and memory.
공간 주의력과 기억력 양쪽을 요하는

The monkeys were stimulated visually, /
원숭이들이 시각적으로 자극을 받았다 /

and then were distracted /
그리고 나서 산만하게 만들었다 /

with another task / 다른 과제로 /

while processing the visual information.
시각 정보를 처리하는 동안

The study showed / that the strain of doing multiple tasks /
그 연구는 보여 줬다   / 여러 과제를 수행하는 긴장이 /

weakened the brain's ability / to hold on to information /
뇌의 능력을 약화시킨다 것을   / 정보를 계속 보유하는 /

related to the tasks. 그 과제들과 관련된

Due to dual-task interference, / researchers said, /
이중 과업 간섭 때문에   / 연구자들은 말했다 /

it is virtually impossible /
사실상 불가능하다고 /

to carry out two tasks at once / with any proficiency.
동시에 두 과제를 수행하는 것은   / 능숙하게

도쿄 대학교와 옥스퍼드 대학교 공동 연구팀은 사람들이 ① 동시에 두 가지 과제를 얼마나 잘 수행할 수 있는지에 관한 연구를 수행했다. 그들은 한 번에 두 가지 일을 하는 것이 흔히 이중 과업 간섭을 낳아, 두 과제 모두 ② 형편없이 수행되는 결과를 갖는다는 것을 발견했다. 원숭이들이 공간 주의력과 기억력 양쪽을 요하는 과제를 수행하는 동안 연구자들은 원숭이의 측면 전전두엽 피질의 단일 신경 활동을 관찰했다. 원숭이들을 시각적으로 ③ 자극한 다음, 시각 정보를 처리하는 동안 다른 과제로 산만하게 해 보았다. 그 연구는 여러 과제를 수행하는 긴장이 그 과제들과 관련된 정보를 계속 보유하는 뇌의 능력을 ④ 향상시킨다(→ 약화시킨다)는 것을 보여 줬다. 이중 과업 간섭 때문에, 동시에 두 과제를 능숙하게 수행하는 것은 사실상 ⑤ 불가능하다고 연구자들은 말했다.

문제풀이

동시에 두 가지 과업을 수행하는 경우 이중 과업 간섭을 낳아, 두 과제 모두 형편없이 수행되는 결과를 갖는다는 내용의 글이고, 실제 원숭이들에게 동시에 여러 과제를 수행하게 하는 실험에서 한 과제를 수행하는 동안 다른 과제로 산만하게 했더니 동시에 두 가지 일을 수행하는 것이 과제 수행에 부정적인 영향을 준다는 것을 알 수 있었다는 내용이므로, ④ 'enhanced(향상시킨다)'를 'weakened(약화시킨다)' 등의 어휘로 고쳐야 한다.

《 어휘 · 어구 》

simultaneously 동시에
dual-task interference 이중 과업 간섭
lateral 측면(의)
spatial 공간의
distract (마음, 주의)를 산란하게 하다
strain 긴장
virtually 사실상
proficiency 숙달, 능숙

10. 동명사

A 출제 POINT
본문 056쪽

1. Setting
2. having done
3. learning
4. having been
5. her
6. being
7. dancing

1 [해석]▶ 목표를 세우고 포기하지 않는 것은 네가 인생에서 많은 일들을 성취하는 데 도움을 준다.
[해설]▶ 한 문장에서 동사가 두 개 나오면 안 된다. 그러므로 주어 역할을 하는 동명사구로 해야 한다.

2 [해석]▶ Sam은 그러한 어리석은 짓을 했다고 후회한다.
[해설]▶ regret는 동명사를 목적어로 취하며, 완료형 동명사(having done)는 문장의 술어동사의 시제(regrets)보다 한 시제 앞선 내용을 나타낼 때 사용한다. 「regret+동명사」는 '~한 것을 후회하다'는 의미이다.

3 [해석]▶ 이번 여름, 내 아들은 스쿠버 다이빙하는 법을 배우기를 매우 기대한다.
[해설]▶ look forward to(~을 기대하다)에서 to는 전치사이므로, 뒤에는 동명사가 나와야 한다.

4 [해석]▶ Sam은 그녀가 가수였다고 확신한다.
[해설]▶ 주절의 시제(is)는 현재이고, that 이하의 종속절의 시제(was)는 과거이므로 완료형 동명사로 나타내야 한다.

5 [해석]▶ 그는 그녀가 결백하다고 주장한다.
[해설]▶ 동명사의 의미상의 주어가 사람일 때는 소유격과 목적격을 모두 사용할 수 있다. her는 소유격이고 hers는 소유대명사이다. 소유대명사는 「소유격+명사」의 의미를 가지고 있다.

6 [해석]▶ 그 소년은 자신이 아이처럼 취급받는 것을 좋아하지 않는다.
[해설]▶ 소년이 아이처럼 취급받는 동작의 대상이므로 수동태로 나타내야 하는데, 주절의 시제가 현재(doesn't)이고, 종속절의 시제가 현재(is treated)이므로 단순 수동형 동명사를 사용해야 한다.

7 [해석]▶ 나는 지금 Sally와 춤을 추고 싶다.
[해설]▶ 동명사의 관용 표현 feel like -ing는 '~하고 싶다'는 의미이다.

B 체크 POINT
본문 056쪽

1. Understanding
2. fishing
3. succeeding
4. being
5. cars
6. being treated
7. crying

1 [해석]▶ 왜 역사적인 사건이 발생하는지 이해하는 것이 중요하다.
[해설]▶ 한 문장에서 동사가 두 개 나오면 안 된다. 또한 동명사는 문장에서 주어 역할을 할 수 있다.

2 [해석]▶ 나의 (직장) 상사는 주말 동안 낚시하는 것을 즐겼다.
[해설]▶ 동사 enjoy는 동명사를 목적어로 가질 수 있다.

3 [해석]▶ 인생의 성공의 열쇠 중 하나는 균형 감각을 가지고 사는 것이다.
[해설]▶ keys to ~는 '~에 대한 열쇠'라는 의미로 to는 전치사이므로 뒤에 동명사가 나온다.

4 [해석]▶ 그녀는 늦어서 미안함을 느낀다.
[해설]▶ 단순동명사는 주절의 시제와 that 이하의 종속절의 시제가 동일할 때 사용한다.

5 [해석]▶ 그 남자는 이곳에 차가 주차되는 것에 반대했다.
[해설]▶ 사물(car)을 동명사의 의미상의 주어로 사용할 때는 소유격으로 고치지 않고, 그대로 쓴다.

6 [해석]▶ Sally는 불공평하게 대접받는 것에 참지 못한다.
[해설]▶ Sally가 불공평하게 대접하는 주체가 아니라 대상이므로 동명사의 수동태로 나타내야 한다.

7 [해석]▶ 엎질러진 우유를 보고 울어봤자 소용없다.
[해설]▶ 동명사의 관용표현인 It's no use[good] -ing는 '~해도 소용없다'는 의미이다.

Day 10
본문 057쪽

1	⑤	2	④	3	①	4	④	5	①
6	②	7	⑤	8	⑤	9	⑤	10	⑤
11	⑤	12	③						

1. ⑤ 다양한 글쓰기가 잠드는 것에 미치는 영향

직독/직해

Baylor University researchers investigated /
Baylor 대학 연구자들은 조사하였다 /
whether different types of writing could ease people
다양한 유형의 글쓰기가 사람들을 편하게 하여 잠들게 해 줄 수 있는지를
into sleep.
To find out, / 알아보기 위해 /
they had 57 young adults spend five minutes before
그들은 57명의 젊은 성인들에게 잠자리에 들기 전에 5분 동안 쓰게 했다
bed writing / either a to-do list for the days ahead /
/ 앞으로 며칠 동안 해야 할 일들의 목록이나 /
or a list of tasks / they'd finished over the past few
일들의 목록 중 하나를 / 그들이 지난 며칠 동안 끝마친
days.
The results confirm / 그 결과는 확인해 준다 /
that not all pre-sleep writing is created equally.
모든 잠들기 전 글쓰기가 동일하게 만들어지지는 않는다는 것을
Those who made to-do lists before bed /
잠자리에 들기 전에 해야 할 일들의 목록을 만드는 사람들은 /
were able to fall asleep nine minutes faster /
9분 더 빨리 잠들 수 있었다 /
than those who wrote about past events.
지난 일들에 관해 쓰는 사람들보다
The quality of the lists mattered, too; /
목록의 질 또한 중요했는데 /
the more tasks and the more specific the to-do lists
과업이 더 많을수록 그리고 해야 할 일들의 목록이 더 구체적일수록
were, / the faster the writers fell asleep.
/ 글을 쓴 사람들은 더 빨리 잠들었다
The study authors figure / 그 연구의 저자들은 생각한다 /
that writing down future tasks unloads the thoughts /
미래의 과업을 적는 것은 생각들을 내려놓게 해서 /

so you can stop turning them over in your mind.
여러분은 그것들을 곰곰이 생각하는 것을 멈출 수 있다고
You're telling your brain / that the task will get done /
여러분은 여러분의 뇌에게 말하고 있다 / 그 과업이 처리될 것이지만 /
— just not right now. 단지 지금 당장은 아니라고

Baylor 대학 연구자들은 다양한 유형의 글쓰기가 사람들을 편하게 하여 잠들게 해 줄 수 있는지를 조사하였다. 알아보기 위해, 그들은 57명의 젊은 성인들에게 잠자리에 들기 전에 앞으로 며칠 동안 해야 할 일들의 목록과 지난 며칠 동안 끝마친 일들의 목록 중 하나를 5분 동안 쓰게 했다. 그 결과는 모든 잠들기 전 글쓰기가 동일하게 만들어지지는 않는다는 것을 확인해 준다. 잠자리에 들기 전에 해야 할 일들의 목록을 만드는 사람들은 지난 일들에 관해 쓰는 사람들보다 9분 더 빨리 잠들 수 있었다. 목록의 질 또한 중요했는데, 과업이 더 많을수록 그리고 해야 할 일들의 목록이 더 구체적일수록, 글을 쓴 사람들은 더 빨리 잠들었다. 그 연구의 저자들은 미래의 과업을 적는 것은 생각들을 내려놓게 해서, 여러분은 그것들을 곰곰이 생각하는 것을 멈출 수 있다고 생각한다. 여러분은 그 과업이 처리될 것이지만 단지 지금 당장은 아니라고 여러분의 뇌에게 말하고 있다.

문제풀이

① 문장의 동사 investigated의 목적어가 필요하고, 문맥상 '~인지 아닌지'라는 의미를 나타내야 하므로 접속사 whether는 적절하게 쓰였다.
② '~하는 데 시간을 쓰다'라는 의미의 「spend+시간+v-ing」 구문이 쓰였으므로, writing은 적절하게 쓰였다.
③ 문장의 주어는 Those이므로 복수동사인 were는 적절하게 쓰였다. who made to-do lists before bed는 Those를 수식하는 주격 관계대명사절이다.
④ '~하면 할수록 더 …하다'라는 의미의 「the+비교급, the+비교급」 구문이 쓰였고, 할 일들의 목록이 더 '구체적인'이라는 의미가 되어야 하므로 형용사인 specific은 적절하게 쓰였다.
⑤ that절 안의 주어는 **writing down future tasks**이고, 동사가 없으므로 단수동사인 **unloads**로 고쳐야 한다. 동명사 주어는 단수 취급한다.

어휘 · 어구

investigate 조사하다
ease 편안하게 만들다
to-do list 해야 할 일 목록
confirm 확인해 주다
pre-sleep 잠들기 전
matter 중요하다
specific 구체적인, 상세한
figure 결론짓다, 생각하다, 이해하다
unload 짐을 내려놓다, 부담을 덜다
turn ~ over in one's mind ~을 곰곰이 생각하다

2. ④ 완벽주의자가 만족스러운 삶을 사는 방법

가끔 완벽주의자들은 무엇을 하든지 결코 만족스럽지 않은 것처럼 보이기 때문에 그들이 괴롭다는 것을 알게 된다. 내가 "그것이 누구에게 만족스럽지 않은가?"라고 묻는다면, 그들이 항상 답을 아는 것은 아니다. 그것에 대해 생각을 한 후에 보통 그들은 자신들에게 만족스럽지 못하고, 자신들의 삶 속의 다른 중요한 사람들에게 만족스럽지 못하다는 결론을 내린다. 이것이 중요한 점인데, 왜냐하면 그것은 당신이 충족시키려고 애쓰고 있는 기준이 실제로는 당신 자신의 것이 아닐 수도 있다는 것을 암시하기 때문이다. 대신에 당신이 자신을 위해 세운 기준이 부모나 사장, 혹은 배우자와 같은 당신의 삶에서 어떤 중요한 사람의 기준일 수 있다. 다른 사람의 기대를 추구하며 당신의 삶을 사는 것은 힘든 삶의 방식이다. 당신이 세운 기준이 자신의 것이 아니라면, 당신의 개인적인 기대를 스스로 정하고 자기실현을 당신의 목표로 삼아야 할 때일 수도 있다.

문제풀이

(A) because가 이끄는 부사절 안에서 it never seems good enough가 주절이므로, 그 앞에 있는 부분은 부사절이어야 한다. 따라서 '무엇을 ~하더라도'라는 의미로 부사절을 이끄는 복합 관계대명사인 whatever가 적절하다. (B) 선행사인 the standard가 의미상 동사 meet의 목적어가 되어야 하므로 능동형인 meet가 적절하다. (C) 동사 is의 주어가 되어야 하므로 주어 역할을 할 수 있는 동명사 Living이 적절하다. 따라서 정답은 ④이다.

구문 및 어휘

*6행 This is a key point, because it suggests [that the standard {you may be struggling to meet} may not actually be your own].

(1) 「주절(This is ~)+부사절(because ~)」 구조의 문장이다.

(2) that ~ your own은 suggests의 목적어로 쓰인 명사절이다. that절의 주어는 the standard이고, 동사는 may not ~ be이다.

(3) you may be struggling to meet은 선행사 the standard를 수식하는 관계대명사절로, 앞에 목적격 관계대명사 that[which]이 생략되어 있다.

*13행 If the standards [you set] were not yours, it may be time to define your personal expectations for yourself and make selffulfillment your goal.

(1) 「부사절(if the standards ~)+주절(it may be ~)」 구조의 문장이다.

(2) you set은 선행사 the standards를 수식하는 관계대명사절로, 앞에 목적격 관계대명사 that[which]이 생략되어 있다.

(3) 「it is time+to부정사」는 '~할 시간이다'라는 의미이다. to define과 (to) make는 병렬 연결되어 있다.

perfectionist 완벽주의자
standard 기준
struggle 고투하다, 몸부림치다
spouse 배우자
pursuit 추구
define 정의하다
self-fulfillment 자기 충족

3. ①   끊임없는 학습의 중요성

Leonardo da Vinci는 지금껏 살았던 사람 가운데 가장 박식하고 다재다능한 사람 중 한 명이었다. 잠자리 날개부터 지구의 탄생에 이르기까지 전 우주는 그의 호기심 많은 지성의 놀이였다. 그러나 Leonardo는 신비하거나 타고난 통찰과 발명의 어떤 재능을 가지고 있었는가, 아니면 그의 탁월함이 학습되고 획득된 것인가? 분명 그는 비범한 정신과 다른 사람들이 보지 못하는 것을 보는 예리한 능력을 가지고 있었다. 하지만 6천 쪽의 자세한 메모와 그림은 부지런하고 호기심 많은 학생 즉, 부지런히 지식을 추구하는 가운데, 끊임없이 탐구하고, 의문을 제기하고, 시험하는 끊임없는 학습에 대한 분명한 증거를 보여준다. 여러분의 지성을 넓히는 것은 창의적으로 되는 것에 필수적이다. 그러므로 학습 기회에 정기적으로 투자하는 것은 여러분이 자신에게 줄 수 있는 가장 멋진 선물 가운데 하나이다.

문제풀이

(A)에는 주어 universe와 수 일치를 이루는 was가 적

절하고, (B)에는 선행사가 없으므로 선행사를 포함한 관계대명사 what이 알맞고, (C)에는 문장의 주어 역할을 할 수 있는 동명사 investing이 와야 하므로 ①이 정답이다.

구문 및 어휘

*6행 Certainly he had an unusual mind and an uncanny ability [to see what others didn't see].

(1) [to see what others didn't see]는 명사 ability를 수식하는 to부정사의 형용사적 용법이며, 이때 what은 the thing which[that]으로 쓸 수 있다.

*8행 But the six thousand pages [of detailed notes and drawings] present clear evidence of a diligent, curious student – a perpetual learner in laborious pursuit of wisdom [who was constantly exploring, questioning, and testing].

(1) 문장의 주어는 the six thousand pages이며 [of detailed ~ drawings]는 주어를 수식하는 전치사구이고, 동사는 present이다. 대시(–) 뒤에 제시된 명사구가 evidence의 내용을 나타낸다.

(2) [who was constantly exploring, questioning, and testing]은 a perpetual learner에 대한 부연 설명을 하는 관계절로 who는 주격 관계대명사이다.

well-rounded 다재다능한
dragonfly 잠자리
innate 타고난, 선천적인
uncanny 예리한
perpetual 끊임없이 계속되는
laborious 부지런한
pursuit 추구
constantly 끊임없이
vital 필수적인

4. ④   이삿짐 회사의 서비스를 이용해야 하는 이유

직독 직해

You may think / 당신은 생각할지 모른다. /
that moving a short distance is so easy/
가까운 거리를 이사하는 것은 너무나 쉬워서
that you can do it in no time / with little effort.
금방 해치울 수 있다고   / 거의 힘들이지 않고도
You may decide to use your own car /
당신은 당신 자신의 자동차를 사용하기로 결정할 수도 있다.
because you think that you don't need /
당신은 필요하지 않다고 생각하기 때문에
the services of a moving company.
이삿짐 회사의 서비스를
Well, you might be wrong.
그런데 당신의 생각은 틀릴 수도 있다.
You are under the false impression /
당신은 ~라는 잘못된 생각을 갖고 있다.
that you do not have as many items to pack/
이삿짐을 꾸릴 물건들이 많지 않다는 /
as you really do. 실제로 존재하는 만큼
You find out too late / 당신은 사실을 뒤늦게 깨닫는다. /
that your car cannot carry as much /
그다지 많이 실어 나르지 못한다는
as you thought it could. 당신의 차가 생각했던 것보다
So, it takes you far more trips / to your new home /
그래서 훨씬 더 여러 번 짐을 실어 운반해야 한다. /새로 이사 갈 집으로 /
than you thought it would. 당신이 생각했던 것보다
There is also the possibility of damaging your stuff, /
또한 물건을 훼손할 가능성도 있는데,
some of it valuable. 물건들 중에는 귀중한 것도 일부 있다.

All these things considered, / it might be better /
이러한 모든 것들을 고려해 본다면,   / 더 좋을 지도 모른다.
to ask for the services of a moving company.
이삿짐 회사에 부탁하는 것이

가까운 거리를 이사하는 것은 너무나 쉬워서 거의 힘들이지 않고도 금방 해치울 수 있다고 생각할지 모른다. 당신은 이삿짐 회사의 서비스를 필요로 하지 않는다고 생각하기 때문에 당신 자신의 자동차를 사용하기로 결정할 수도 있다. 그런데 당신의 생각은 틀릴 수도 있다. 당신은 이삿짐을 꾸릴 물건들이 실제로 존재하는 것만큼 많지 않다는 잘못된 생각을 갖고 있다. 당신은 당신의 차가 생각했던 것보다 그다지 많이 실어 나르지 못한다는 사실을 뒤늦게 깨닫는다. 그래서 생각했던 것보다 훨씬 더 여러 번 새로 이사 갈 집으로 짐을 실어 운반해야 한다. 또한 물건을 훼손할 가능성도 있는데, 물건들 중에는 귀중한 것도 일부 있다. 이러한 모든 것들을 고려해 본다면, 이삿짐 회사에 부탁하는 것이 더 좋을 지도 모른다.

문제풀이

① 셀 수 없는 명사(effort)를 수식할 때는 little, much를 사용한다.
② 반복된 표현(have)을 피하기 위해 대동사 do를 사용하였다.
③ 부사 too가 형용사(late) 앞에 위치하여 형용사를 수식하고 있다.
④ **damage**는 전치사 **of**의 목적어 역할을 하면서 **your stuff**를 목적어로 취할 수 있는 동명사 **damaging**으로 고쳐 써야 한다. 전치사 뒤에는 동명사가 나온다.
⑤ When all these things are considered, ~ 문장을 분사구문으로 바꾼 문장이다.
먼저 부사절 접속사 when을 없애고 부사절의 주어와 주절의 주어가 달라 부사절의 주어를 그대로 둔다. 부사절과 주절의 시제가 같아 「동사원형+ing」형인 단순분사구문으로 바꾼다. 그런데 수동 분사구문(being considered)에서 being은 생략 가능하므로 considered만 남았다.

어휘·어구

impression 인상
pack 꾸리다, 싸다
possibility 가능성
stuff 물건

5. ①   나의 첫 교사 생활

내게는 가르쳐야 할 20명의 시골 소녀들이 있었는데, 그들 중 몇 명은 너무나 강한 시골 사투리를 가지고 있어서 그들과의 거의 의사소통을 할 수가 없었다. 단지 3명 만이 읽을 수 있었고 쓸 수 있는 사람은 전혀 없었으며, 그래서 첫날이 끝날 무렵 에 나는 앞에 놓여있는 힘든 일을 생각하면서 아주 마음이 울적했다. 그러나 나는 내가 다행히도 어떤 일거리를 가졌으며, 매우 가난하기는 하지만 영국에서 가장 좋은 가정 출신의 아이들만큼 착하고 영리할 수도 있는 이런 소녀들을 가르치는데 틀림없이 익숙해질 거라고 스스로에게 상기시켰다.

문제풀이

(A) such a 명사 – that … (너무나 ~해서 …하다)'의 구문이므로 접속사 that이 적절하다.
(B) '마음이 울적하다'는 feel depressed로 표현한다. depressing은 '울적하게 하는'의 의미이므로 적절하지 않다.
(C) get used to –ing (~에 익숙해지다)의 표현이며, 필자가 가르치는 데 익숙해진다는 문맥이므로 능동형 teaching이 적절하다.

어휘·어구

accent 사투리, 강세
remind 상기시키다
fortunate 운이 좋은

6. ② 사자 Simba의 죽음

직독/직해

At the zoo, / Simba the lion was very sick.
그 동물원에서 / '심바'라는 사자가 매우 아팠었다.

The animal doctor came / 수의사가 와서 /
and tried giving him some red meat /
그에게 붉은 고기를 좀 주려고 했다. /
full of medicine. 약이 가득 들어 있는

Poor Simba did not even raise his head.
가엾은 심바는 머리조차 들지 못했다.

Finally, Simba stopped breathing.
마침내 심바는 숨을 거두었다.

The doctor said, / with tears in his eyes,
그 의사는 말했다. / 눈에 눈물이 가득한 채

"I regret to tell you / that Simba is dead."
"말씀드리게 되어서 유감입니다. / 심바가 죽었다는 것을"

The little children were very shocked to hear it.
어린아이들은 그 소식을 듣고 매우 충격을 받았다.

"I feel like / I've lost an old friend.
"저는 느낌이 듭니다. / 오랜 친구 하나를 잃었다는

I can remember reporting Simba's birth," said a reporter.
제가 심바의 탄생을 보도했던 것이 기억납니다."라고 한 기자가 말했다.

그 동물원에서 '심바'라는 사자가 매우 아팠었다. 수의사가 와서 그에게 약이 가득 들어 있는 붉은 고기를 좀 주려고 했다. 가엾은 심바는 머리조차 들지 못했다. 마침내 심바는 숨을 거두었다. 그 의사는 눈에 눈물이 가득하여 "심바가 죽었다는 것을 말씀드리게 되어서 유감입니다."라고 말했다. 어린아이들은 그 소식을 듣고 매우 충격을 받았다. "저는 오랜 친구 하나를 잃었다는 느낌이 듭니다. 제가 심바의 탄생을 보도했던 것이 기억납니다."라고 한 기자가 말했다.

문제풀이

① some read meat (which is) full of medicine에서 「관계대명사+be동사」가 생략된 구문이다. full of ~는 '~으로 가득 찬'의 의미이다.
② 문맥상 '숨을 멈추다'는 의미이므로 stopped to breathe를 stopped breathing으로 고쳐야 한다. 「stop+동명사」는 '~을 멈추다'는 의미이다.
③ 「with+목적어(tears)+전치사구(in his eyes)」는 분사구문으로서 '눈에 눈물이 가득한 채'라는 의미이다.
④ 동작의 주체는 능동태로, 동작의 대상은 수동태로 나타낸다. 소식을 듣고 아이들은 충격을 받은 것이므로 수동태(were very shocked)로 나타내었다.
⑤ 「remember+동명사」는 '(과거의 일) ~을 기억하다'는 구문이다.

어휘·어구

sick 아픈
meat (육류) 고기
breathe 숨을 쉬다
regret 애석하게 생각하다
reporter 기자

7. ⑤ 의식적인 경험

직독/직해

What exactly are the conscious experiences /
정확히 의식적인 경험이란 무엇인가 /
that constitute the flow of the mind?
마음의 흐름을 구성하는
Every subjective experience has two fundamental
모든 주관적인 경험은 두 개의 기본적인 특징이 있는데
characteristics: / sensation and desire.
/ 그것은 감각과 욕망이다
Robots and computers have no consciousness /
로봇과 컴퓨터는 의식을 가지고 있지 않다 /
because despite their countless abilities /
그들의 셀 수 없이 많은 능력에도 불구하고 /
they feel nothing and crave nothing.
그들이 아무것도 느끼지 않고 갈망하지 않기 때문에
A robot may have an energy sensor / that signals
로봇에는 에너지 센서가 있을 수 있다 / 중앙 처리 장치에 신호를 보내는 /
to its central processing unit /
when the battery is about to run out.
배터리가 막 방전되려고 할 때
The robot may then move toward an electrical socket, /
로봇은 그런 다음 전기 콘센트로 이동해서 /
plug itself in / and recharge its battery.
스스로 전원을 연결하고 / 배터리를 충전할 수 있다
However, / throughout this process the robot doesn't
하지만 / 이 과정을 통해 로봇은 어떤 것도 경험하지 않는다
experience anything.
In contrast, / a human being depleted of energy /
반대로 / 에너지가 고갈되는 인간은 /
feels hunger and craves / 배고픔과 갈망을 느낀다 /
to stop this unpleasant sensation.
이 불쾌한 감각을 멈추기 위해
That's why we say / that humans are conscious
그래서 우리가 말하는 이유이다 / 인간은 의식적인 존재이고
beings / and robots aren't, /
/ 로봇은 그렇지 않다고 /
and why it is a crime to make people work /
사람들을 일하게 하는 것이 범죄인 반면 /
until they collapse from hunger and exhaustion, /
배고픔과 탈진으로 쓰러질 때까지 /
whereas making robots work / until their batteries
로봇을 일하게 하는 것에는 / 그것의 배터리가 다 닳을 때까지
run out / carries no moral opprobrium.
/ 어떤 도덕적인 맹비난도 없다

정확히 마음의 흐름을 구성하는 의식적인 경험이란 무엇인가? 모든 주관적인 경험은 두 개의 기본적인 특징이 있는데, 그것은 감각과 욕망이다. 로봇과 컴퓨터는 그들의 셀 수 없이 많은 능력에도 불구하고 아무것도 느끼지 않고 갈망하지 않기 때문에 의식을 가지고 있지 않다. 로봇에는 배터리가 막 방전되려고 할 때 중앙 처리 장치에 신호를 보내는 에너지 센서가 있을 수 있다. 로봇은 그런 다음 전기 콘센트로 이동해서, 스스로 전원을 연결하고 배터리를 충전할 수 있다. 하지만, 이 과정을 통해 로봇은 어떤 것도 경험하지 않는다. 반대로, 에너지가 고갈되는 인간은 이 불쾌한 감각을 멈추기 위해 배고픔과 갈망을 느낀다. 그래서 우리는 인간은 의식적인 존재이고 로봇은 그렇지 않다고 말하는 이유이며, 사람들을 배고픔과 탈진으로 쓰러질 때까지 일하게 하는 것이 범죄인 반면, 그것의 배터리가 다 닳을 때까지 로봇을 일하게 하는 것에는 어떤 도덕적인 맹비난도 없다.

문제풀이

① 뒤에 명사구인 their countless abilities가 왔으므로, 전치사 despite는 적절하게 쓰였다.
② 「be about to+동사원형」은 '막 ~하려던 참이다'라는 의미로, about 다음에 to부정사가 오므로, to run은 적절하게 쓰였다.
③ plug라는 동사의 목적어 역할을 해야 하고 행위를 하는 주체와 대상이 모두 The robot이므로, 재귀대명사 itself는 적절하게 쓰였다.
④ depleted of energy는 문장의 주어인 a human being을 수식하는 과거분사로 쓰였다. 문장의 동사는 feels이다.
⑤ whereas가 이끄는 부사절에서 주어는 making robots work until their batteries run out이고, 동사가 필요하므로 carrying은 carries로 고쳐야 한다. 동명사구 주어는 단수 취급한다.

이렇게 풀자_ 어법상 틀린 부분을 찾는 문제는 밑줄이 있는 부분의 형태와 문맥을 보고 어법에 맞게 쓰였는지 확인해야 한다. ①은 전치사의 쓰임을, ②는 「be about to+동사원형」의 의미와 쓰임을, ③은 재귀대명사의 역할을, ④는 과거분사의 역할을, ⑤는 주어와 동사로 이루어진 문장의 구조를 알아야 한다.

어휘·어구

conscious 의식의, 의식적인
constitute 구성하다
subjective 주관적인
fundamental 근본적인, 필수적인
crave 갈망하다; 갈망
socket 콘센트
recharge 재충전하다
deplete of ~을 고갈시키다
collapse 쓰러지다
exhaustion 탈진, 기진맥진

8. ⑤ 빅 데이터의 잠재력과 위험

직독/직해

Although technology can't be blamed for the passion for growth, /
성장에 대한 열망을 기술 탓으로 돌릴 수는 없지만 /
it is a great enabler.
그것은 굉장한 동력이다
We are only just beginning to realize the potential of big data: /
우리는 빅데이터의 잠재력을 깨닫기 시작하고 있을 뿐이다 /
its capacity to deliver highly customized content and products /
즉 고도로 주문 제작된 내용과 제품을 전달할 수 있는 그것의 능력을 /
and to predict human behavior.
그리고 인간의 행동을 예측할 수 있는
The vast accumulation of personal data /
개인 데이터의 막대한 축적은 /
by Google, Amazon, Apple, and national governments /
구글, 아마존, 애플, 그리고 정부에 의한 /
promises everything /
모든 것을 약속한다 /
from automated, personalized health care to preventative law enforcement.
자동화되고 개인화된 건강 관리로부터 예방적 법 집행까지
But with these tantalizing powers /
그러나 이러한 흥미를 부추기는 힘과 함께 /
come, necessarily, big risks.
필연적으로 위기가 온다
Just as Apple computers used to be safer from viruses /
애플 컴퓨터가 바이러스로부터 더 안전했듯 /
because there were relatively fewer of them /
그 수가 상대적으로 적었기 때문에 /
— which made them not worth attacking /
그것은 그것들을 공격할 가치가 없도록 만들어서 /
— so the vast accumulation of personal data makes it an irresistible target /
개인 데이터의 막대한 축적은 그것이 거부할 수 없는 표적이 되도록 만든다 /
for hackers and malware.
해커와 악성 소프트웨어의
Governments and regulators worry about the personal information /
정부와 규제 기관은 개인 정보에 대해 걱정한다 /
stored and exploited by Google, /
구글에 의해 서장되고 활용되는 /
but it is precisely the scale of the accumulation of this information /
하지만 바로 이러한 정보 축적의 규모이다 /
that makes Google's servers such tempting targets.
구글 서버가 그토록 유혹적인 목표가 되게 만드는 것은

성장에 대한 열망을 기술 탓으로 돌릴 수는 없지만, 그것은 굉장한 동력이다. 우리는 빅데이터의 잠재력, 즉 고도로 주문 제작된 내용과 제품을 전달할 수 있고 인간의 행동을 예측할 수 있는 그것의 능력을 깨닫기 시작하고 있을 뿐이다. 구글, 아마존, 애플, 그리고 정부에 의한 개인 데이터의 막대한 축적은 자동화되고 개인화된 건강 관리로부터 예방적 법 집행까지 모든 것을 약속한다. 그러나 이러한 흥미를 부추기는 힘과 함께, 필연적으로 위기가 온다. 애플 컴퓨터의 수가 상대적으로 적었기 때문에, 즉 그것들이 공격할 가치가 없도록 만들었기 때문에, 바이러스로부터 더 안전했듯, 개인 데이터의 막대한 축적은 그것이 해커와 악성 소프트웨어의 거부할 수 없는 표적이 되도록 만든다. 정부와 규제 기관은 구글에 의해 저장되고 활용되는 개인 정보에 대해 걱정하지만, 이러한 정보 축적의 규모가 바로 구글 서버가 그토록 유혹적인 목표가 되게 만드는 것이다.

문제풀이

① [분사]
customized는 content and products를 수식하는 분사로 '내용과 제품이 주문 제작된' 수동의 의미이므로 과거분사를 쓴 것은 올바른 용법이다.

② [동사의 수]
promises는 단수 명사 The vast accumulation을 주어로 받는 동사이므로 단수 동사 promises는 적절하게 사용되었다.

③ [도치 구문]
전치사구 'with these tantalizing powers'가 문두에 위치하여 '주어, 동사'가 도치된 문장이다. 주어가 복수 명사 'big risks'이므로 복수 동사 'come'은 적절하게 사용되었다.

④ [목적어를 취하는 형용사 worth]
worth는 목적어를 취하는 형용사이므로 목적어로 쓰인 동명사 'attacking'은 올바른 용법이다.

⑤ ['it be ~ that' 강조구문]
but 뒤에 이어지는 절은 'it be ~ that' 강조구문으로 'precisely the scale of the accumulation of this information'이 강조되고 있는 구조이므로, what을 it으로 고쳐야 한다.

《 어휘 · 어구 》

potential 잠재력
customize 주문 제작하다
preventative law enforcement 예방적 법 집행
irresistible 거부할 수 없는
exploit 활용하다

---

9. ⑤ 창의성은 집단적인 구성체에서 나온다

직독 / 직해

Most people are confident /
대부분의 사람은 확신한다 /
that creativity is an individual possession, / not a collective phenomenon.
창의성은 개인적인 소유라고 / 집단적인 현상이 아니라
Despite some notable collaborations / in the arts
몇몇 주목할 만한 합작품에도 불구하고 / 예술과 과학에서
and sciences, / the most impressive acts of creative
그리고 / 창의적인 사고의 가장 인상적인 활동들은
thought / — from Archimedes to Jane Austen /
/ Archimedes부터 Jane Austen까지 /
— appear to have been the products of individuals /
개인들의 산물이었던 것으로 보인다 /
(and often isolated and eccentric individuals /
(그리고 보통 고립되고 기이한 개인들 /
who reject commonly held beliefs).
일반적으로 받아들여지는 생각을 거부하는)
I think / that this perception is something of an illusion, /
나는 생각한다 / 이런 인식이 상당한 착각인 것 같다 /
however. 하지만
It cannot be denied / that the primary source of
부정할 수가 없다 / 참신함의 원천이 있다는 것을
novelty lies / in the recombination of information /
/ 정보를 재조합하는 데에 /
within the individual brain. 개인의 뇌 속에 있는
But I suspect / that as individuals, /
하지만 나는 생각한다 / 개인으로서 /
we would and could accomplish little /
우리는 거의 성취하지도 성취할 수 없을 것이라고 /
in the way of creative thinking outside the context
슈퍼 브레인의 맥락을 벗어나 창의적인 사고방식으로는
of the super-brain, /
the integration of individual brains. 개인 지능의 집대성인
The heads of Archimedes, Jane Austen, /
Archimedes, Jane Austen의 머리는 /

---

and all the other original thinkers /
그리고 모든 다른 독창적인 사상가(의 머리는) /
who stretch back into the Middle Stone Age in Africa /
중석기 시대 아프리카로 거슬러 올라가는 /
were filled with the thoughts of others / from early
다른 사람들의 생각으로 꽉 차 있었다 / 아주 어린 시절부터 계속해서 /
childhood onward, /
including the ideas of those long dead or unknown.
오래전에 죽었거나 알려지지 않은 사람들의 생각을 포함한
How could they have created /
그들이 어떻게 창조할 수 있었겠는가 /
without the collective constructions of mathematics,
수학, 언어, 그리고 예술의 집단적인 구성체가 없었다면
language, and art?

대부분의 사람은 창의성은 개인적인 소유이지, 집단적인 현상이 아니라고 확신한다. 예술과 과학에서 몇몇 주목할 만한 ① 합작품에도 불구하고, Archimedes부터 Jane Austen까지 창의적인 사고의 가장 인상적인 활동들은 개인들(그리고 보통 일반적으로 받아들여지는 생각을 거부하는, 고립되고 기이한 개인들)의 산물이었던 것으로 보인다. 하지만 나는 이런 인식이 상당한 ② 착각인 것 같다. ③ 참신함의 원천이 개인의 뇌 속에 있는 정보를 재조합하는 데에 있다는 것을 부정할 수가 없다. 하지만 개인으로서 우리는 개인 지능의 집대성인 슈퍼 브레인의 맥락을 ④ 벗어나 창의적인 사고방식으로는 거의 성취하지도 성취할 수 없을 것이라고 나는 생각한다. Archimedes, Jane Austen, 그리고 중석기 시대 아프리카로 거슬러 올라가는 모든 다른 독창적인 사상가의 머리는 아주 어린 시절부터 계속해서, 오래전에 죽었거나 알려지지 않은 사람들의 생각을 포함한 다른 사람들의 생각으로 ⑤ 단절되어(→ 꽉 차) 있었다. 수학, 언어, 그리고 예술의 집단적인 구성체가 없었다면 그들이 어떻게 창조할 수 있었겠는가?

문제풀이

창의성은 집단적인 현상이 아닌 개인적인 소유라는 인식은 상당한 착각으로, 개인으로서 우리는 개인 지능의 집대성인 슈퍼 브레인의 맥락을 벗어나 창의적인 사고방식으로는 거의 성취하지도 성취할 수도 없을 것이라고 하면서, 수학, 언어, 예술의 집단적인 구성체가 없었다면 창조가 없었을 것이라는 내용으로 보아, ⑤ 'disconnected(단절된)'를 'filled(가득 찬)' 등으로 바꿔야 한다.

❂ 이렇게 풀자_ 창의성은 개인적인 소유임을 확신한다는 첫 문장을 상당한 착각으로 생각한다고 필자는 반박을 하고 있고, Archimedes, Jane Austen, 다른 독창적인 사상가의 머리는 아주 어린 시절부터 계속해서 다른 사람들의 생각으로 꽉 차 있어서 창조를 할 수 있었다는 내용을 반박의 근거로 제시하는 글이다.

♛ 구조 다시보기

통념	창의성은 집단적 현상이 아니라 개인의 소유이다.
반론	창의성은 개인의 소유라는 주장은 상당한 착각이다.
근거	Archimedes, Jane Austen, 다른 독창적인 사상가의 머리는 다른 사람들의 생각으로 꽉 차 있어서 창조를 할 수 있었다.

《 어휘 · 어구 》

possession 소유한 것, 소유물, 소유
collective 집단의, 집합적인
phenomenon 현상
notable 주목할 만한, 눈에 띄는
collaboration 합작품, 합작, 협력
impressive 인상적인, 인상 깊은
isolated 고립된, 외딴
perception 인식
illusion 착각
novelty 참신함
recombination 재조합
accomplish 성취하다
context 맥락
integration 집대성, 통합, 합병
onward 계속해서, 쭉
construction 구성체

---

10. ⑤ 배를 이용한 사냥의 이점

직독 / 직해

Europe's first *Homo sapiens* lived primarily on
유럽 최초의 '호모 사피엔스'는 주로 큰 사냥감을 먹고 살았다
large game, / particularly reindeer.
/ 특히 순록
Even under ideal circumstances, / 심지어 이상적인 상황에서도 /
hunting these fast animals with spear or bow and
이 빠른 동물들을 창이나 활, 그리고 화살을 가지고 사냥하는 것은
arrow / is an uncertain task.
/ 불확실한 일이다
The reindeer, however, / had a weakness that
하지만 순록에게는 / 인류가 인정사정없이 활용할 약점이 있었는데
mankind would mercilessly exploit: /
it swam poorly. 순록은 수영이 서툴다는 것이었다
While afloat, / it is uniquely vulnerable, /
물에 떠 있는 동안, / 그것은 유례없이 공격받기 쉽다 /
moving slowly with its antlers held high /
가지진 뿔을 높이 들고 천천히 움직이기 때문에 /
as it struggles to keep its nose above water.
순록은 코를 물 위로 내놓으려고 애쓰면서
At some point, / a Stone Age genius realized /
어느 시점에 / 한 석기 시대의 천재가 깨달았다 /
the enormous hunting advantage he would gain /
자신이 얻을 엄청난 사냥의 이점을 /
by being able to glide over the water's surface, /
수면 위를 미끄러지듯이 움직일 수 있음으로써 /
and built the first boat. 그리고 최초의 배를 만들었다
Once the easily overtaken and killed prey had been
일단 쉽게 따라잡아 도살한 먹잇감을 배 위로 힘들여 끌어 당기면
hauled aboard, / getting its body back to the tribal camp /
/ 사체를 부족이 머무는 곳에 가지고 가는 것 /
would have been far easier / by boat than on land.
훨씬 더 쉬웠을 것이다 / 육지에서보다 배로
It would not have taken long /
시간이 오래 걸리지 않았을 것이다 /
for mankind to apply this advantage to other goods.
인류가 이런 장점을 다른 물품에 적용하는 데

유럽 최초의 '호모 사피엔스'는 주로 큰 사냥감, 특히 순록을 먹고 살았다. 심지어 이상적인 상황에서도, 이 빠른 동물들을 창이나 활, 그리고 화살을 가지고 사냥하는 것은 불확실한 일이다. 하지만 순록에게는 인류가 인정사정없이 활용할 약점이 있었는데, 그것은 순록이 수영이 서툴다는 것이었다. 물에 떠 있는 동안, 순록은 코를 물 위로 내놓으려고 애쓰면서 가지진 뿔을 높이 들고 천천히 움직이기 때문에, 유례없이 공격받기 쉽다. 어느 시점에, 한 석기 시대의 천재가 수면 위를 미끄러지듯이 움직일 수 있음으로써 자신이 얻을 엄청난 사냥의 이점을 깨닫고 최초의 배를 만들었다. 일단 힘들게(→ 쉽게) 따라잡아 도살한 먹잇감을 배 위로 힘들여 끌어 당기면, 사체를 부족이 머무는 곳에 가지고 가는 것은 육지에서보다 배로 훨씬 더 쉬웠을 것이다. 인류가 이런 장점을 다른 물품에 적용하는 데 시간이 오래 걸리지 않았을 것이다.

문제풀이

순록은 수영이 서툴고 물에 떠 있는 동안은 가지진 뿔 때문에 천천히 움직여서 공격받기 쉽다는 내용이므로, ⑤ 'laboriously(힘들게)'를 'easily(쉽게)'로 고쳐야 한다.

❂ 이렇게 풀자_ 먼저 글의 주제와 흐름을 파악한 뒤, 밑줄 친 어휘가 포함된 문장 전후 문맥을 파악해서 적절하게 쓰였는지를 판단하면 된다. 수영이 서툰 순록을 사냥할 때 배를 이용해서 사냥감을 따라잡는 것은 상대적으로 쉬웠을 것이므로, ⑤ 'laboriously'가 문맥상 쓰임이 어색함을 알 수 있다.

《 어휘 · 어구 》

primarily 주로
game 사냥감
reindeer 순록
circumstance 환경
mercilessly 인정사정없이, 무자비하게
uniquely 유례없이
antler 가지진 뿔

---

enormous 막대한, 거대한
glide 미끄러지다
overtake 따라잡다
prey 먹잇감

---

11. ⑤ 국가 안보를 위해 관세가 필요하다는 주장의 타당성

직독/직해

Sometimes / 때때로 /
it is argued / that tariffs are a means /
주장된다 / 관세는 수단이라고 /
of preventing a nation from becoming too dependent /
한 국가가 너무 많이 의존하는 것을 막기 위한 /
on foreign suppliers of goods /
상품의 외국 공급자들에게 /
vital to national security. 국가 안보에 필수적인
That is, / 즉 /
by making foreign goods more expensive, /
외국 상품을 더 비싸게 만듦으로써 /
we can protect domestic suppliers.
우리는 국내 공급자들을 보호할 수 있다
However, / 하지만 /
if oil is vital / to operating planes and tanks, /
만약 석유가 필수적이라면 / 비행기나 탱크를 작동하는 데 /
losing foreign supplies of oil / during wartime /
외국의 석유 공급을 잃는 것은 / 전시에 /
could cripple a nation's defenses.
한 민족의 방어수단들을 무능하게 할 수 있다
The national security argument /
국가 안보(를 위해 관세가 필요하다는) 주장 /
is usually not valid. 대개 타당하지 않다
If a nation's own resources / are depletable, /
만약 한 나라 자체의 자원이 / 고갈될 수 있다면 /
tariff-imposed reliance / on domestic supplies /
관세를 부과하여 의존하는 것은 / 국내 공급에 /
will hasten depletion / of domestic reserves, /
고갈을 촉진시킬 것이고 / 국내 비축량의 /
making the country even more dependent /
그 나라가 훨씬 더 많이 의존하게 만들 것이다 /
on imports / in the future.
수입품에 / 장차
If we impose a high tariff / on foreign oil /
만약 우리가 높은 관세를 부과한다면 / 외국 석유에 /
to protect domestic producers, /
국내 생산자들을 보호하기 위해 /
we will increase / domestic output of oil /
우리는 증가시킬 것이다 / 석유의 국내 생산량을 /
in the short run.
단기적으로
In the process, / however, /
그 과정에서 / 그러나
we will deplete the stockpile / of available reserves.
우리는 비축량을 고갈시킬 것이다 / 가용 자원 매장량의
Thus, / 그러므로 /
the defense argument / is of questionable validity.
(국가 안보를 위해 관세가 필요하다는) 주장은 / 타당성이 의심스럽다
From a defense standpoint, / 그 관점에서 볼 때 /
it makes more sense / 더 이치에 맞다 /
to use foreign oil / in peacetime /
외국 석유를 사용하고 / 평화 시에는 /
and perhaps / stockpile "insurance" supplies /
어쩌면 / '보험' 공급을 비축하는 것이 /
so that larger domestic supplies /
더 많은 국내 공급이 /
would be available / during wartime.
이용 가능하도록 / 전시에

때때로 관세는 한 국가가 국가 안보에 필수적인 상품의 외국 공급자들에게 너무 많이 의존하는 것을 막기 위한 수단이라고 주장한다. 즉, 외국 상품을 더 ① 비싸게 만듦으로써, 우리는 국내 공급자들을 보호할 수 있다. 하지만, 만약 석유가 비행기나 탱크를 작동하는 데 필수적이라면, 전시에 외국의 석유 공급을 잃는 것은 한 민족의 방어수단들을 무능하게 할 수 있다. 국가 안보(를 위해 관세가 필요하다는) 주장은 대개 타당하지 않다. 만

약 한 나라 자체의 자원이 고갈될 수 있다면, 관세를 부과하여 국내 공급에 의존하는 것은 국내 비축량의 고갈을 ② 촉진시킬 것이고, 그 나라가 장차 수입품에 훨씬 더 많이 의존하게 만들 것이다. 만약 우리가 국내 생산자들을 보호하기 위해 외국 석유에 높은 관세를 부과한다면, 우리는 단기적으로 석유의 국내 생산량을 ③ 증가시킬 것이다. 그러나, 그 과정에서 우리는 가용 자원 매장량의 비축량을 고갈시킬 것이다. 그러므로, (국가 안보를 위해 관세가 필요하다는) 주장은 타당성이 ④ 의심스럽다. 그 관점에서 볼 때, 평화 시에는 외국 석유를 사용하고 어쩌면 전시에 더 많은 국내 공급품이 ⑤ 이용 가능하지 않도록(→ 이용 가능하도록) '보험' 공급을 비축하는 것이 더 이치에 맞다.

문제풀이

국가 안보를 위해 관세가 필요하다는 주장이 타당하지 않다는(the defense argument is of questionable validity) 내용의 글이다. 국가 안보의 관점에서 볼 때 평화 시에 외국 석유를 사용하고 국내 공급을 비축해두어야 전시에 더 많은 국내 공급이 이용 가능할 것이라는 맥락이 되어야 한다. 따라서 밑줄 친 ⑤를 포함한 문장은 '그 관점에서 볼 때, 평화 시에는 외국 석유를 사용하고 어쩌면 전시에 더 많은 국내 공급품이 이용 가능하도록 '보험' 공급을 비축하는 것이 더 이치에 맞다'라는 문맥이 적절하므로, ⑤ unavailable(이용 가능하지 않은)을 available(이용 가능한) 정도로 고쳐 써야 한다.

《 어휘·어구 》

tariff 관세
dependent 의존하는
supplier 공급자
vital 필수적인
security 안보, 보안
domestic 국내의
operate 작동하다
cripple 해치다, 무능하게 하다
valid 타당한
resources 자원
depletable 고갈될 수 있는
tariff-imposed 관세가 부과되는
depletion 고갈
reserves (석탄, 석유, 천연가스 등의) 비축[매장]량
import 수입(품)
impose 부과하다
output 생산량, 산출량
in the short run 단기적으로
stockpile 비축[축적]량; 비축하다
available 이용 가능한
questionable 의심스러운, 미심쩍은
validity 타당성
standpoint 관점
in peacetime 평화 시에

---

12. ③ 환경친화적인 글쓰기의 근원

직독/직해

At the root of environmental writing /
환경친화적인 글쓰기의 근원에는 /
is a desire to change current thinking /
현재의 생각을 변화시키려는 바람이 있다 /
so that people see themselves /
사람들이 자신들을 볼 수 있도록 /
as a part of the environment / 환경의 일부로 /
and not as masters / 주인으로서가 아니라 /
who have a right to exploit resources.
자원을 이용할 권리를 지닌
This is not a romantic ideal but a practical idea /
이것은 낭만적인 이상이 아니라 현실적인 생각이다 /
that stems from the politics of equitable distribution.
공정한 분배의 정치적 사상에서 비롯된

In fact, / such ideas have a traditional base in India.
실제로 / 그런 생각들은 인도에 전통적인 기반을 두고 있다
Here are a few examples.
여기에 몇 가지 사례들이 있다
This anecdote comes from someone /
이 일화는 사람에게서 비롯된다 /
who was researching traditional agricultural practices.
전통적인 농업 관습을 연구하고 있었던
During a conversation with a farmer /
한 농부와의 대화 동안 /
in which they were discussing / 그들이 토론하던 /
the ownership of land and produce, / the farmer said /
토지와 농산물의 소유권에 관해 / 그 농부는 말을 했다 /
something that can only be described as greatly liberal.
대단히 후하다고 밖에 표현될 수 없는
He said / that owning land did not mean /
그는 말했다 / 토지를 소유하는 것이 의미하는 것은 아니라고 /
he had a sole right / to everything on it.
그 사람이 독점권을 가졌다는 것을 / 그 토지의 모든 것에 대한
Of his right over his crops, / he said, /
자신의 농작물에 대한 권리 중 / 그는 말했다 /
"50 percent is for me, / 25 percent is for you /
50%는 나를 위한 것이다 / 25%는 여러분을 위한 것이다 /
(that is, / whoever in the community needed it) /
즉 / 공동체에서 그것을 필요로 하는 누구든 /
and 25 percent is for the birds."
그리고 25%는 새들을 위한 것이다
This belief and practice of mutual benefit and survival /
상호 이익과 생존에 대한 이런 신념과 실천은 /
stemmed from man's dependence /
인간의 의존에서 비롯되었다 /
on the natural world. 자연 세계에 대한
His acknowledgement of it /
그것에 대한 그의 인정은 /
made him assimilate with, /
그를 (환경과) 동화하게 만들었다 /
rather than try and dominate, the environment.
환경을 지배하려고 하기보다는

환경친화적인 글쓰기의 근원에는 사람들이 자신들을 자원을 ① 이용할 권리를 지닌 주인으로서가 아니라 환경의 일부로 볼 수 있도록 현재의 생각을 변화시키려는 바람이 있다. 이것은 낭만적인 이상이 아니라 ② 공정한 분배의 정치적 사상에서 비롯된 현실적인 생각이다. 실제로, 그런 생각들은 인도에 전통적인 기반을 두고 있다. 여기에 몇 가지 사례들이 있다. 이 일화는 전통적인 농업 관습을 연구하고 있던 사람에게서 비롯된다. 그들이 토지와 농산물의 소유권에 관해 토론하던 한 농부와의 대화 동안, 그 농부는 대단히 ③ 탐욕적이라고(→ 후하다고)밖에 표현될 수 없는 말을 했다. 그는 토지를 소유하는 것이 그 토지의 모든 것에 대한 독점권을 그 사람이 가졌다는 것을 의미하는 것은 아니라고 말했다. 그는 자신의 농작물에 대한 권리 중 '50%는 나를 위한 것이고, 25%는 여러분(즉, 공동체에서 그것을 필요로 하는 누구든)을 위한 것이며 25%는 새들을 위한 것'이라고 말했다. ④ 상호 이익과 생존에 대한 이런 신념과 실천은 자연 세계에 대한 인간의 의존에서 비롯되었다. 그것에 대한 그의 인정은 그가 환경을 지배하려고 하기 보다는 환경과 ⑤ 동화하게 만들었다.

문제풀이

토지를 소유하는 것은 토지의 모든 것에 대한 독점권을 그 사람이 가진 게 아니라, 50%는 본인이, 25%는 공동체에서 그것을 필요로 하는 사람이, 25%는 새들을 위한 것이라는 농부의 말을 통해 농부는 대단히 후하다는 내용이 되어야 문맥상 자연스럽다. 따라서 ③ 'greedy(탐욕스러운)'를 'liberal(후한)' 등으로 고쳐야 한다.

《 어휘·어구 》

exploit 이용하다, 활용하다
equitable 공정한
distribution 분배
anecdote 일화
mutual 상호의
acknowledgement 인정
assimilate 동화하다
dominate 지배하다

---

11. 분사, 분사구문

A 출제 POINT
본문 062쪽

1. published
2. interested
3. clawing
4. Having
5. Having found
6. closed
7. barking

1 [해석]▶ 올해 초 발행된 조사에 따르면, 10명 중 7명의 부모가 결코 자신의 자녀가 장난감 총으로 노는 것을 허락하지 않을 거라고 답했다.
[해설]▶ 발행된 조사이므로 수동의 의미를 가지고 있는 과거분사(published)가 명사(survey)를 수식해야 한다.

2 [해석]▶ 그는 흥미로운 작가이고, 나는 그가 쓰는 주제에 대해 흥미가 많다.
[해설]▶ be interested in는 '~에 흥미를 느끼다'의 의미이다. 내가 흥미를 주는 것이 아니라, 흥미를 느끼는 것이므로 수동 의미를 가지고 있는 과거분사로 표현해야 한다.

3 [해석]▶ Sam은 무언가가 그의 등위로 기어가는 것을 느꼈다.
[해설]▶ 목적어(something)와 목적격보어(clawing)가 능동 관계이면 목적격보어를 현재분사를 쓴다.

4 [해석]▶ 할 일이 없어서, 일찍 잠자리에 들었다.
[해설]▶ As I had nothing to do~와 같은 부사절을, 접속사를 제거하고, 주절의 주어와 같기 때문에 부사절의 주어를 제거하고, 시제가 동일해 [동사원형+-ing]형의 단순형 분사구문으로 바꾼 문장이다.

5 [해석]▶ 호텔을 잡은 후, 그들은 저녁 먹을 곳을 찾았다.
[해설]▶ After they had found ~ 문장을 분사구문으로 고친 것이다. 주절의 시제보다 부사절의 시제가 앞설 때, 완료 분사구문을 사용한다. 이 문장의 경우 주절의 시제는 과거, 부사절의 시제는 과거완료이다.

6 [해석]▶ 나는 눈을 감고서도 그것을 할 수 있다.
[해설]▶ 「with+목적어+분사」 구문은 '눈이 감긴 채'와 같이 목적어(my eyes)와 분사(closed)의 관계가 수동의 관계일 때는 분사를 과거분사를 쓴다.

7 [해석]▶ 개가 짖어서, 그는 도망쳤다.
[해설]▶ 분사구문의 주어(the dog)가 주절의 주어(he)가 다른 경우, 분사구문의 주어를 분사 앞에 명시해 주어야 한다.

B 체크 POINT
본문 062쪽

1. falling
2. bored
3. waiting
4. Situated
5. Having seen
6. following
7. Not knowing

1 [해석]▶ 나는 떨어지는 빗소리를 좋아한다.
[해설]▶ '떨어지는 빗소리'이므로 능동의 의미를 가지고 있는 현재분사로 표현한다.

---

2 [해석]▶ Sam의 일은 따분하다. 그래서 그는 지루해 한다.
[해설]▶ Sam이 지루함을 느끼게 되었으므로 수동의 의미를 가지고 있는 과거분사로 표현한다.

3 [해석]▶ 당신을 기다리게 해서 미안합니다.
[해설]▶ 목적어(you)와 목적격보어(waiting)가 능동 관계이므로 목적격보어를 현재분사로 표현한다. 목적어(you)가 기다리고 있는 중이므로 현재분사로 표현한다.

4 [해석]▶ 1300 미터 고도 지점에 위치해 있어, 그 도시는 일년내내 따뜻한 기후를 누린다.
[해설]▶ As the city is situated at ~의 부사절을 분사구문으로 바꾸면 (Being) Situated at ~이 된다.

5 [해석]▶ 사고를 보고난 후, 그녀는 차를 멈췄다.
[해설]▶ After she had seen an accident,~ 라는 부사절을 분사구문으로 바꾼 문장이다. 부사절은 과거완료, 주절은 과거이므로 완료분사구문으로 바꾸어야 한다.

6 [해석]▶ 그는 매일 개를 따르게 한 채 조깅을 한다.
[해설]▶ 「with+목적어+분사」 표현은 목적어와 분사의 관계가 능동이면 현재분사를 쓴다. 현재분사 following이 뒤에 목적어(him)를 가져오고 있다.

7 [해석]▶ 길을 몰랐기 때문에, 그들은 곧 길을 잃어 버렸다.
[해설]▶ 분사구문을 부정할 때는 부정어를 분사 바로 앞에 배치한다.

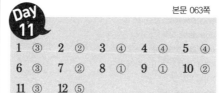

본문 063쪽

1 ③	2 ②	3 ④	4 ④	5 ④
6 ③	7 ②	8 ①	9 ①	10 ②
11 ③	12 ⑤			

1. ③
스파이더 차트

직독/직해

The spider chart, / also called a radar chart, / is a form of line graph.
스파이더 차트는 / 방사형 차트라고도 불리는 / 선 그래프의 한 형태이다

It helps the researcher to represent their data / in a chart
그것은 연구자가 그들의 데이터를 설명하도록 도와준다 / 차트로 /

that shows the relative size of a response / on one scale /
응답의 상대적 크기를 보여주는 / 하나의 척도에서 /

for interrelated variables.
상호 연관된 변수에 대해

Like the bar chart, / the data needs to have one scale /
막대그래프와 마찬가지로 / 데이터는 하나의 척도를 가져야 한다 /

which is common to all variables.
모든 변수에 공통인

The spider chart is drawn / with the variables spanning the chart, /
스파이더 차트는 그려지며 / 변수들이 차트에 걸치면서 /

creating a spider web.
거미줄을 만든다.

An example of this is seen / in a research study /
이것의 예는 보여진다 / 조사 연구에서 /

looking at self-reported confidence in year 7 students /
7학년 학생들의 스스로 보고된 자신감을 살펴본 /

across a range of subjects / taught in their first term in secondary school.
다양한 과목에 걸쳐 / 중등학교에서 첫 학기에 가르쳐진

The researcher takes the responses from a sample group /
연구자는 표본 집단으로부터 응답값들을 가져온다 /

and calculates the mean to plot on the spider chart.
그리고 스파이더 차트에 나타낼 평균치를 계산한다

The spider chart allows the researcher /
스파이더 차트는 연구자에게 허락한다 /

to easily compare and contrast the confidence level /
자신감 정도를 쉽게 비교하고 대조할 수 있도록

in different subjects for the sample group.
표본 집단의 여러 다른 과목에서의

The chart, / like the pie chart, / can then be broken down /
이 차트는 / 파이 차트와 마찬가지로 / 세분화될 수 있다 /

for different groups of students / within the study /
다른 학생 집단으로 / 연구 내의 /

to elicit further analysis of findings.
연구 결과의 추가 분석을 도출하기 위해

방사형 차트라고도 불리는 스파이더 차트는 선 그래프의 한 형태이다. 그것은 연구자가 상호 연관된 변수에 대해 하나의 척도에서 응답의 상대적 크기를 보여주는 차트로 그들의 데이터를 설명하도록 도와준다. 막대그래프와 마찬가지로 데이터는 모든 변수에 공통인 하나의 척도를 가져야 한다. 이것의 예는 중등학교에서 첫 학기에 가르쳐진 다양한 과목에 걸쳐 7학년 학생들의 스스로 보고된 자신감을 조사한 연구에서 보여진다. 연구자는 표본 집단으로부터 응답값들을 가져와 스파이더 차트에 나타낼 평균치를 계산한다. 스파이더 차트는 연구자가 표본 집단의 여러 다른 과목에서의 자신감 정도를 쉽게 비교하고 대조할 수 있도록 한다. 이후, 파이 차트와 마찬가지로, 이 차트는 연구 결과의 추가 분석을 도출하기 위해 연구 내의 다른 학생 집단으로 세분화될 수 있다.

문제풀이

① **[관계대명사 that]**
that은 a chart를 선행사로 하고, 동사 shows의 주어 역할을 하는 주격관계대명사로 올바르게 사용되었다.

② **[분사구문]**
전체 문장의 동사가 'is drawn'이고 접속사가 없으므로 creating은 결과를 나타내는 분사구문으로 올바르게 사용되었다.

③ **[정동사 VS 준동사]**
정동사 'is seen'과 'have taught'가 접속사나 관계사 없이 연결될 수 없다. 따라서 have taught는 앞의 명사 'a range of subjects'를 수식하는 분사가 되어야 한다. '가르쳐진'의 뜻을 지닌 수동의 의미가 되어야 하므로 'have taught'를 과거분사 taught로 고쳐야 한다.

④ **[병렬구문]**
'calculates'는 등위접속사 'and'에 의해서 앞의 동사 'takes'와 병렬을 이룬 동사로 올바르게 사용되었다.

⑤ **[to부정사]**
'to elicit'는 '도출하기 위해'의 뜻으로 목적의 의미인 to부정사구를 이끌고 있으므로 올바르게 사용되었다.

○ 이렇게 풀자 어법 문제에서는 '정동사의 개수 -1=접속사[관계사]'의 원칙을 적용하게 되면 쉽게 해결되는 문제가 많다. ①의 that은 관계대명사로 두 개의 정동사 helps와 shows를 연결하고 있고, ②의 creating은 준동사로 정동사 'is drawn'이 하나 있고 접속사나 관계사가 없으니 올바르게 사용되었다. ③의 have taught는 정동사의 형태로 이미 정동사 is seen이 있고, 접속사나 관계사가 없으므로 틀린 표현이다. ④의 calculates는 정동사 takes가 있고 접속사 and가 있으므로 올바른 표현이며, ⑤의 to elicit는 준동사로 정동사 can be broken이 있고 접속사나 관계사가 보이지 않으므로 올바르게 사용되었다.

《 어휘·어구 》

relative 상대적
response 응답
variable 변수
common 공통의
draw 그리다
span 걸치다
confidence 자신감
a range of 다양한
subject 과목
secondary 중등 교육의
calculate 계산하다
plot 나타내다, 표시하다
contrast 대조
elicit 알아내다
analysis 분석
finding 결과

2. ② 스포츠 분야에서의 찬가

직독/직해

According to its dictionary definition, /
사전적 정의에 따르면 /

an anthem is both a song of loyalty, /
찬가(讚歌)는 충성의 노래이다 /

often to a country, /
흔히 국가에 대한 /

and a piece of 'sacred music', /
그리고 한 곡의 '성스러운 음악'이다 /

definitions that are both applicable in sporting contexts.
이 정의는 둘 다 스포츠 상황에서도 적용이 가능하다

This genre is dominated, / although not exclusively, /
이 장르는 두드러지게 나타난다 / 독점적이지는 않을지라도 /

by football / and has produced a number of examples /
축구에 의해서 / 그리고 많은 사례를 만들어 냈다 /

where popular songs become synonymous with the club /
인기 있는 노래들이 구단과 밀접한 연관을 갖게 되는 /

and are enthusiastically adopted / by the fans.
그리고 열광적으로 받아들여지는 / 팬들에 의해

More than this /
이에 더하여 /

they are often spontaneous expressions of loyalty and identity /
그것들은 흔히 충성과 정체성의 자발적인 표현이다 /

and, according to Desmond Morris, /
그리고 Desmond Morris에 따르면 /

have 'reached the level of something approaching a local art form'.
지역 예술 형태에 근접하는 어떤 것의 수준에 도달했다

A strong element of the appeal of such sports songs /
그런 스포츠 노래들의 강력한 매력 요소는 /

is that they feature 'memorable and easily sung choruses /
그것들이 외우기 쉽고 부르기 쉬운 합창을 특징으로 한다는 것이다 /

in which fans can participate'.
팬들이 참여할 수 있는

This is a vital part of the team's performance /
이것은 팀의 수행에 아주 중요한 부분이다 /

as it makes the fans' presence more tangible.
그것이 팬들의 존재를 더 확실하게 느낄 수 있게 하기 때문에

This form of popular culture can be said /
이러한 형태의 대중문화는 말할 수 있다 /

to display pleasure and emotional excess /
즐거움과 감정적 과잉을 보여 준다고 /

in contrast to the dominant culture /
지배적인 문화와는 대조적으로 /

which tends to maintain 'respectable aesthetic distance and control'.
품위 있는 미적 거리와 통제를 유지하는 경향이 있는

사전적 정의에 따르면, 찬가(讚歌)는, 흔히 국가에 대한, 충성의 노래이자 한 곡의 '성스러운 음악'인데, 이 두 가지 정의는 모두 스포츠 상황에서도

적용이 가능하다. 이 장르는 독점적이지는 않을지라도 축구에서 가장 두드러지게 나타나며, 인기 있는 노래들이 구단과 밀접한 연관을 갖게 되고 팬들에 의해 열광적으로 받아들여지는 많은 사례를 만들어 냈다. 이에 더하여 그것들은 흔히 충성과 정체성의 자발적인 표현이며, Desmond Morris에 따르면, '지역 예술 형태에 근접하는 어떤 것의 수준에 도달했다'. 그런 스포츠 노래들의 강력한 매력 요소는 그것들이 '팬들이 참여할 수 있는 외우기 쉽고 부르기 쉬운 합창'을 특징으로 한다는 것이다. 이것은 팬들의 존재를 더 확실하게 느낄 수 있게 하기 때문에 팀의 (경기) 수행에 아주 중요한 부분이다. 이러한 형태의 대중문화는 '품위 있는 미적 거리와 통제'를 유지하는 경향이 있는 지배적인 문화와는 대조적으로, 즐거움과 감정적 과잉을 보여 준다고 말할 수 있다.

문제풀이

① [관계부사 where]
선행사가 a number of examples이고, 뒤 문장이 2형식의 완전한 문장이므로 관계부사 where는 올바르게 사용되었다.

② [분사]
문장의 정동사 have reached가 있으므로 approached는 something을 수식하는 분사이고, 뒤에 목적어 'a local art form'이 있어 '지역 예술 형태에 접근하는'의 능동의 의미이므로, approached를 approaching으로 바꿔야 한다.

③ [주어 동사의 수일치]
주어가 단수 명사인 a strong element이므로 단수 동사 is를 쓴 것은 올바른 용법이다.

④ [접속사 as]
as는 이유를 나타내는 부사절을 이끄는 접속사로 올바르게 사용되었다.

⑤ [to부정사]
'be said' 뒤의 to부정사는 'They say that S+V' → 'It is said that S+V' → 'S be said to부정사'구문이다. 'to display' 이하는 'S be said to부정사'구문으로 적절하게 사용되었다.

《 어휘 · 어구 》

definition 정의
anthem 찬가
loyalty 충성
sacred 신성한
dominate 지배하다
exclusively 배타적으로, 독점적으로
enthusiastically 열정적으로
spontaneous 자발적인
feature 특징으로 하다
vital 중대한

3. ④ 다양한 형태를 가진 전통적인 거래

직독/직해

The formats and frequencies of traditional trade /
전통적인 거래의 형식과 빈도는 /

encompass a spectrum.
전 범위를 망라한다

At the simplest level / are the occasional trips /
가장 단순한 단계에서 / 이따금 하는 왕래가 있다 /

made by individual !Kung and Dani /
!Kung족과 Dani족 일원에 의해서 행해지는 /

to visit their individual trading partners /
그들 각자의 거래 상대를 방문하기 위해 /

in other bands or villages.
다른 무리나 마을에 있는

Suggestive of our open-air markets and flea markets /
우리의 노천 시장과 벼룩시장을 연상시켰다 /

were the occasional markets /
이따금 서는 시장은 /

at which Sio villagers living on the coast of northeast New Guinea /
뉴기니 북동쪽 해안에 사는 Sio 마을 사람들이 /

met New Guineans from inland villages.
내륙 마을에서 온 뉴기니 사람들을 만나는

---

and the Sio villager / sitting opposite / responded /
그리고 Sio 마을 사람은 / 맞은 편에 앉은 / 응수했다 /

by offering a number of pots and coconuts /
몇 개의 단지와 코코넛을 내놓음으로써 /

judged equivalent in value / to the bag of food.
가치가 같다고 판단되는 / 그 망태기에 든 음식과

Trobriand Island canoe traders conducted similar markets /
Trobriand 섬의 카누 상인들은 비슷한 시장을 운영했다 /

on the islands /
섬에서 /

that they visited, /
그들이 방문한 /

exchanging utilitarian goods (food, pots, and bowls) /
실용품(음식, 단지, 그릇)을 교환하면서 /

by barter, /
물물 교환으로 /

at the same time /
동시에 /

as they and their individual trade partners gave each other /
그들과 그들의 개별 거래 상대들은 서로에게 주었다 /

reciprocated gifts of luxury items (shell necklaces and armbands).
사치품(조개목걸이와 팔찌)을 답례품으로

전통적인 거래의 형식과 빈도는 전 범위를 망라한다. 가장 단순한 단계에서 !Kung족과 Dani족 일원이 다른 무리나 마을에 있는 그들 각자의 거래 상대를 방문하기 위해 이따금 하는 왕래가 있다. 뉴기니 북동쪽 해안에 사는 Sio 마을 사람들이 내륙 마을에서 온 뉴기니 사람들을 만나는 이따금 서는 시장은 우리의 노천 시장과 벼룩시장을 연상시켰다. 각각의 편에서 서로 수십 명에 이르는 사람들이 줄을 서서 마주 보고 줄지어 섰었다. 한 내륙인이 10에서 35파운드 사이의 타로토란과 고구마가 든 망태기를 앞으로 내밀면, 맞은편에 앉은 Sio 마을 사람은 그 망태기에 든 음식과 가치가 같다고 판단되는 몇 개의 단지와 코코넛을 내놓아 응수했다. Trobriand 섬의 카누 상인들은 자신들이 방문하는 섬에서 비슷한 시장을 운영하며, 물물교환으로 실용품(음식, 단지, 그릇)을 교환했고, 동시에 그들과 그들의 개별 거래 상대들은 서로에게 사치품(조개목걸이와 팔찌)을 답례품으로 주었다.

문제풀이

① [주어와 동사의 수일치]
주어가 복수명사인 trips이므로 복수동사인 are를 쓴 것은 적절하다.

② [형용사 보어의 도치]
be동사의 보어인 형용사 suggestive가 도치된 문장으로 올바르게 사용되었다.

③ [자동사 sit vs 타동사 seat]
sat은 자동사 sit의 과거형으로 타동사 seat와 구별할 수 있어야 한다. 이 문장에서는 주어가 up to a few dozen people이고 목적어가 보이지 않으므로 자동사 sat을 사용한 것은 올바른 용법이다.

④ [현재분사 vs 과거분사]
a number of pots and coconuts는 judge의 대상이므로, 현재분사 judging을 과거분사 judged로 바꿔야 한다.

⑤ [관계대명사 that]
선행사가 islands이고 타동사 visited의 목적어 역할을 하므로, 관계대명사 that은 올바르게 사용되었다.

《 어휘 · 어구 》

frequency 빈도(수)
encompass 망라하다, 포함하다
spectrum 범위, 영역
band 무리
suggestive 연상시키는
flea market 벼룩시장
inland 내륙의
in rows 줄지어
net bag 망태기
equivalent 같은, 동등한
conduct 운영하다, 관리하다
utilitarian 실용적인
barter 물물교환

4. ④ 초기 인류의 자연 세계와 인간 사회의 관계

직독/직해

Speculations about the meaning and purpose of
선사 시대 예술의 의미와 목적에 대한 고찰은 /

prehistoric art /

rely heavily on analogies / drawn with modern-day
유사점에 많이 의존한다 / 현대의 수렵 채집 사회와의 사이에서 끌어낸

hunter-gatherer societies.

Such primitive societies, / 그런 원시 사회는 /

as Steven Mithen emphasizes in *The Prehistory of*
Steven Mithen이 'The Prehistory of the Modern Mind'에서 강조하듯이 /

the Modern Mind, /

tend to view man and beast, animal and plant,
organic and inorganic spheres, /
인간과 짐승, 동물과 식물, 생물체의 영역과 무생물체의 영역을 여기는 경향
이 있다 /

as participants in an integrated, animated totality.
통합적이고 살아 있는 총체에 대한 참여자로

The dual expressions of this tendency /
이런 경향이 표현된 두 가지가 /

are *anthropomorphism* (the practice of regarding
'의인화'(동물을 인간으로 간주하는 관행)

animals as humans)
동물을 인간으로

and *totemism* (the practice of regarding humans
그리고 '토테미즘'(인간을 동물로 간주하는 관행)인데

as animals), /

both of which spread through the visual art and
이 두 가지는 원시 문화의 시각 예술과 신학에 널리 퍼져 있다

the mythology of primitive cultures.

Thus the natural world is conceptualized / in terms
따라서 자연의 세계는 개념화 된다 / 인간의 사회적 관계 측면에서

of human social relations.

When considered in this light, /
이런 측면에서 고려될 때 /

the visual preoccupation of early humans with the
초기 인류가 인간 이외의 생명체들에 대하여 시각적으로 집착한 것은 /

nonhuman creatures

inhabiting their world / becomes profoundly
자신들의 세계에 살고 있는 / 깊은 의미를 띠게 된다

meaningful.

Among hunter-gatherers, / 수렵 채집인들에게 /

animals are not only good to eat, they are also
동물은 먹기 좋은 대상일 뿐만 아니라, '생각해 보기에도 좋은' 대상이다 /

good to think about, /

as Claude Lévi-Strauss has observed.
Claude Lévi-Strauss가 말했듯이

In the practice of totemism, / he has suggested, /
토템 신앙의 풍습에서 / 그는 말했다 /

an unlettered humanity "broods upon itself and its
문맹의 인류는 "자연 속에서 자신과 자신의 위치에 대해 숙고한다."라고

place in nature."

선사 시대 예술의 의미와 목적에 대한 고찰은 현대의 수렵 채집 사회
와의 사이에서 끌어낸 유사점에 많은 것을 의존한다. Steven Mithen이
'The Prehistory of the Modern Mind'에서 강조하듯이, 그런 원시
사회는 인간과 짐승, 동물과 식물, 생물체의 영역과 무생물체의 영역을
통합적이고 살아 있는 총체에 대한 참여자로 여기는 경향이 있다. 이런
경향이 표현된 두 가지가 '의인화'(동물을 인간으로 간주하는 관행)와 '토
테미즘'(인간을 동물로 간주하는 관행)인데, 이 두 가지는 원시 문화의 시
각 예술과 신화에 널리 퍼져 있다. 따라서 자연의 세계는 인간의 사회적
관계 측면에서 개념화 된다. 이런 측면에서 고려될 때, 초기 인류가 자신
들의 세계에 살고 있는 인간 이외의 생명체들에 대하여 시각적으로 집착
한 것은 깊은 의미를 띠게 된다. 인류학자인 Claude Lévi-Strauss가
말했듯이 수렵 채집인들에게 동물은 먹기 좋은 대상일 뿐만 아니라, '생
각해 보기에도 좋은' 대상이다. 토템 신앙의 풍습에서 문맹의 인류는 "자
연 속에서의 자신과 자신의 위치에 대해 곰이 생각한다."라고 그는 말
했다.

문제풀이

④가 속한 문장의 술어동사는 **becomes**이며, 밑줄
친 부분은 앞의 명사구 **the nonhuman creatures**
를 수식하는 분사구가 되어야 하는데 뒤에 목적어
인 **their world**가 있으므로 능동의 의미를 나타내
는 현재분사 **inhabiting**이 되어야 한다. 따라서
inhabited를 **inhabiting**으로 고쳐야 한다.
① Speculations가 문장의 주어이므로 술어동사

로서 복수형 동사 rely가 온 것은 적절하다.
② '~가 …하듯이'라는 의미의 접속사로서 as의
쓰임이 적절하다.
③ 콤마(,) 다음에 이어지는 관계대명사 which는
앞의 절의 내용 전체를 선행사로 받는 계속용법으
로서 쓰임이 적절하다.
⑤ 문장의 주어가 an unlettered humanity이므로
이에 대한 재귀대명사 itself의 쓰임이 적절하다.

◆ **이렇게 풀자**_ 어법상 틀린 부분을 찾는 문제는 밑줄
이 있는 부분의 형태와 문맥을 보고 어법에 맞게 쓰였는
지 확인해야 한다. ① 주어와 동사의 수일치를, ② 접속사
as의 쓰임을, ③ 계속용법의 관계대명사 which의 쓰임을,
④ 현재분사구의 쓰임을, ⑤ 재귀대명사의 쓰임을 알아야
한다.

《 어휘·어구 》

draw an analogy with ~과의 유사점을 끌어내다
hunter-gatherer society 수렵 채집 사회
primitive 원시의, 원시 시대의
integrated 통합된
animated 살아 있는, 생기 있는
mythology 신화
conceptualize 개념화하다
preoccupation 집착, 열중
inhabit ~에 거주하다
observe (의견·소견 등을) 말하다, 관찰하다, 준수하다
unlettered 문맹의, 무지의

---

5. ④   인터넷 발달에 따른 문제점

직독/직해

The Internet allows information to flow /
인터넷은 정보가 흐르도록 해 준다 /

more freely than ever before.
이전의 그 어느 때보다도 더 자유롭게

We can communicate and share ideas /
우리는 의사소통을 하고 아이디어를 나눌 수 있다 /

in unprecedented ways. 전례 없는 방식으로

These developments are revolutionizing our
이러한 발달은 우리의 자기표현을 혁신하고 있다

self-expression / and enhancing our freedom.
/ 그리고 우리의 자유를 향상시키고 있다

But there's a problem. 그러나 문제가 있다

We're heading toward a world /
우리는 세상으로 향하고 있다 /

where an extensive trail of information fragments
about us / 우리에 관한 광범위한 단편적 정보 조각의 흔적이 /

will be forever preserved on the Internet, /
인터넷에 영원히 보존될 /

displayed instantly in a search result.
검색 결과에서 즉각 보이게 될

We will be forced to live / 우리는 살 수밖에 없을 것이다 /

with a detailed record beginning with childhood /
어렸을 때부터 시작하는 세부적인 기록을 가지고 /

that will stay with us for life / wherever we go, /
평생 우리와 함께할 / 우리가 어디에 가든 /

searchable and accessible from anywhere in the
world. 전 세계 어느 곳에서도 검색할 수 있고 접근할 수 있는

This data can often be of dubious reliability; /
이러한 정보는 자주 신뢰성이 의심스러울 수 있다 /

it can be false; / 그것은 틀릴 수 있다 /

or it can be true but deeply humiliating.
또는 그것은 사실이지만 매우 창피하게 할 수도 있다

It may be increasingly difficult /
점점 더 어려워질지도 모른다 /

to have a fresh start or a second chance.
새 출발을 하거나 두 번째 기회를 얻는 것

We might find it harder / to engage in self-
우리는 더 어렵다는 것을 알게 될 수도 있다 / 자기 탐구를 하기가

---

exploration / if every false step and foolish act /
/ 만일 모든 실수와 어리석은 행동이 /

is preserved forever / in a permanent record.
영원히 보존된다면 / 영구적인 기록으로

인터넷은 정보가 이전의 그 어느 때보다도 더 자유롭게 흐르도록 해 준
다. 우리는 전례 없는 방식으로 의사소통을 하고 아이디어를 나눌 수 있
다. 이러한 발달은 우리의 자기표현을 혁신하고 우리의 자유를 향상시키
고 있다. 그러나 문제가 있다. 우리는 우리에 관한 광범위한 단편적 정보
조각의 흔적이 인터넷에 영원히 보존되어 검색 결과에서 즉각 보이게 될
세상으로 향하고 있다. 우리는 전 세계 어느 곳에서도 검색할 수 있고 접
근할 수 있는, 우리가 어디에 가든 평생 우리와 함께할, 어렸을 때부터 시
작하는 세부적인 기록을 가지고 살 수밖에 없을 것이다. 이러한 정보는
자주 신뢰성이 의심스러울 수 있거나, 틀릴 수 있거나, 또는 사실이지만
매우 창피하게 할 수도 있다. 새 출발을 하거나 두 번째 기회를 얻는 것
이 점점 더 어려워질지도 모른다. 만일 모든 실수와 어리석은 행동이 영
구적인 기록으로 영원히 보존된다면, 우리는 자기 탐구를 하기가 더 어렵
다는 것을 알게 될지도 모른다.

문제풀이

① 밑줄 친 freely는 동사 flow를 수식하는 부사
로 적절하게 쓰였다.
② 선행사가 a world이고 뒤에 완전한 절이 왔으므
로, 장소의 관계부사 where가 온 것은 적절하다.
③ 앞에 있는 a detailed record를 수식하는 분사
가 와야 하는 데, 어렸을 때부터 '시작하는' 세부적
인 기록이라는 능동의 의미이므로 현재분사
recording이 온 것은 적절하다.
④ humiliate의 동작 주체는 it(This data)인데 it
은 창피한 감정을 느끼는 것이 아니라 유발하는
것이므로, humiliated는 현재분사 humiliating로
바꿔 써야 한다.
⑤ 「가목적어 it-to부정사」 구문으로 뒤에 진목적
어 to engage in self-exploration가 왔다. 따라
서 가목적어 it이 온 것은 적절하다.

◆ **이렇게 풀자**_ 어법상 틀린 부분을 찾는 문제는 밑줄
이 있는 부분의 형태와 문맥을 보고 어법에 맞게 쓰였는
지 확인해야 한다. ① 부사의 역할을, ② 관계부사의 쓰임
을, ③ 현재분사의 쓰임을, ④ 과거분사와 현재분사의 쓰
임을, ⑤ 「가목적어 it-to부정사」 구문을 알아야 한다.

《 어휘·어구 》

unprecedented 전례 없는
revolutionize 혁신을 일으키다
enhance 높이다, 향상시키다
extensive 아주 넓은, 대규모의
fragment 조각, 파편
preserve 지키다, 보존하다
instantly 즉각, 즉시
searchable 검색이 가능한
accessible 접근 가능한
reliability 신뢰성
humiliate 굴욕감을 주다, 창피하게 하다
permanent 영구적인

---

6. ③   물개 어류의 먹이

직독/직해

It had long been something of a mystery /
오랫동안 다소 불가사의한 것이었다. /

where, and on what, / 어디에서 그리고 무엇을 /

the northern fur seals of the eastern Pacific
동태평양 북부의 모피 물개들이

feed / during the winter, / 먹고 사는지 / 겨울 동안 /

which they spend off the coast of North America /
북아메리카의 연안에서 보내는 /

from California to Alaska.
캘리포니아에서 알래스카까지

There is no evidence / that they are feeding /
증거는 없다. / 그것들이 먹고 살고 있다는 /

to any great extent / on sardines, mackerel, /
얼마큼이나 많이 / 정어리, 고등어 /

or other commercially important fishes.
또는 다른 상업적으로 중요한 어류를

Presumably four million seals could not compete /
추측컨대, 4백만 마리의 물개들이 다툴 수 없을 것이다.

with commercial fishermen / for the same species /
상업을 목적으로 하는 어부들과 / 같은 종을 놓고 /

without the fact being known. 알려진 사실이 없지만

But there is some evidence / 그러나 약간의 증거는 있고 /

on the diet of the fur seals, / 모피 물개들의 먹이에 관한

and it is highly significant. 그것은 대단히 의미심장하다.

Their stomachs have yielded / 그들의 위에서 나왔다 /

the bones of a species of fish / 한 종의 물고기 뼈가

that has never been seen alive.
살아있는 채로는 절대 본 적이 없는

Indeed, / not even its remains have been found /
사실 / 그것의 잔존물조차 발견된 적이 없었다. /

anywhere / except in the stomachs of seals.
어느 곳에서도 / 물개들의 위속을 제외하고

Ichthyologists say / 어류학자들은 말한다. /

that this 'seal fish' belongs to a group /
이 '물개 어류'가 한 집단에 속한다고

that typically inhabits very deep water,
보통 아주 깊은 물에서 서식하는 (한 집단에)

off the edge of the continental shelf.
대륙붕 가장자리에서 떨어진

동태평양 북부의 모피 물개들이 캘리포니아에서 알래스카까지 북아메리카의 연안에서 보내는 겨울 동안 그리고 무엇을 먹고 사는지는 오랫동안 다소 불가사의한 것이었다. 그것들이 얼마큼이나 많이 정어리, 고등어 또는 다른 상업적으로 중요한 어류를 먹고 살고 있다는 증거는 없다. 추측컨대, 알려진 사실이 없지만 4백만 마리의 물개들이 같은 종을 놓고 상업을 목적으로 하는 어부들과 다툴 수 없을 것이다. 그러나 모피 물개들의 먹이에 관한 약간의 증거는 있고 그것은 대단히 의미심장하다. 그들의 위에서 살아있는 채로는 절대 본 적이 없는 한 종의 물고기 뼈가 나왔다 사실 물개들의 위속을 제외하고 어느 곳에서도 그것의 잔존물조차 발견된 적이 없었다. 어류학자들은 이 '물개 어류'가 대륙붕 가장자리에서 떨어진 아주 깊은 물에서 보통 서식하는 한 집단에 속한다고 말한다.

문제풀이

(A) spend의 목적어인 the winter를 선행사로 취하는 관계사가 필요하다. 따라서 관계대명사인 which가 적절하다.
(B) 전치사 without의 목적어로 명사나 명사구가 와야 한다. 따라서 현재분사 being을 사용하여 being known이라는 분사구가 the fact를 수식하게 만들어야 한다.
(C) 주어의 핵심은 remains로 복수명사이므로 have와 수를 일치시키는 것이 맞다.

어휘·어구

to any great extent 얼마큼이나 많이
sardine 정어리
mackerel 고등어
presumably 추측컨대
compete 경쟁하다
significant 의미심장한, 중대한
yield 산출하다
remains 잔존물, 잔해, 유적
inhabit ~에 살다, 거주하다, 서식하다
continental shelf 대륙붕

7.② 휴대 전화를 물에 빠뜨렸을 때 조치법

직독/직해

Dropping your cell phone in water /
휴대 전화를 물에 빠뜨리는 것은 /

means you have to replace it, /
그것을 교체해야 한다는 것을 의미하지만,

but sometimes if you're fast enough, /
때로 어지간히 신속하기만 하다면, /

you might be able to save the phone!
전화기를 살릴 수도 있을 것이다.

If you want to suck the liquid /
물을 빨아내고자 한다면, /

out of the inner parts of the phone, /
전화기 속 부품에서

try using a vacuum cleaner.
진공청소기를 이용해 보라.

Remove all residual moisture / by drawing it away, /
모든 남아있는 습기를 제거하라 / 습기를 끌어내어 /

with a vacuum cleaner held / over the affected areas
진공청소기를 든 채로 / 물에 젖은 부분 위로

for up to twenty minutes. 이십 분 정도

This way / you can completely dry out your phone /
이리하여 / 전화기를 완전히 건조 시켜 /

and get it working in thirty minutes.
삼십 분 이내에 작동시킬 수 있다.

However, / 하지만 /

unless the exposure to water was extremely short, /
(전화기가) 물에 노출된 시간이 매우 짧은 경우가 아니라면.

it's not recommended to attempt /
시도하는 것은 바람직하지 않다. /

to turn your phone on this soon.
이렇게 빨리 전화기를 켜려고

Be careful not to hold the vacuum /
진공청소기를 대지 않도록 주의하라.

too close to the phone, / 전화기에 너무 가까이

as a vacuum can create static electricity.
진공청소기는 정전기를 유발할 수 있으므로

It is even worse for the phone.
그것은 전화기에 훨씬 더 좋지 않다.

The best way, / of course, /
물론 최선의 방법은 / 물론 /

is to bring your phone / 전화기를 가져가는 것이다. /

to the customer service center
고객 서비스 센터에

as soon as possible. 가능한 한 빨리

휴대 전화를 물에 빠뜨리는 것은 그것을 교체해야 한다는 것을 의미하지만, 때로 어지간히 신속하기만 하다면, 전화기를 살릴 수도 있을 것이다. 전화기 속 부품에서 물을 빨아내고자 한다면, 진공청소기를 이용해 보라. 이십 분 정도 물에 젖은 부분 위로 진공청소기를 든 채로 모든 남아있는 습기를 끌어내어 제거하라. 이리하여 전화기를 완전히 건조 시켜 삼십 분 이내에 작동시킬 수 있다. 하지만 (전화기가) 물에 노출된 시간이 매우 짧은 경우가 아니라면, 이렇게 빨리 전화기를 켜려고 시도하는 것은 바람직하지 않다. 진공청소기는 정전기를 유발할 수 있으므로 전화기에 너무 가까이 진공청소기를 대지 않도록 주의하라. 그것은 전화기에 훨씬 더 좋지 않다. 물론 최선의 방법은 전화기를 가능한 한 빨리 고객 서비스 센터에 가져가는 것이다.

문제풀이

②는 「with+목적어+분사구문」이다. 진공청소기가 들려지는 수동의 의미가 되어야 하므로 holding을 held로 바꿔 써야 한다.

어휘·어구

replace 대체하다, 교체하다
suck 빨다, 빨아들이다
liquid 액체

8.① 네팔의 수도, 카트만두 시

직독/직해

Situated at an elevation of 1,350m, the city of Kathmandu, /
해발 1,350미터에 위치한 카트만두 시는

which looks out on the sparkling Himalayas, /
반짝거리는 히말라야 산맥이 내다보이는데

enjoys a warm climate year-round /
연중 내내 기후가 온화하여

that makes living here pleasant.
살기 편한 곳이다.

Kathmandu sits almost in the middle of a basin, /
카트만두는 분지의 거의 한복판에 위치하고 있고, /

forming a square about 5km north-south and 5km east-west.
남북 5㎞, 동서 5㎞의 정사각형을 이루고 있다.

It was the site of the ancient kingdom of Nepal.
그 곳은 고대 네팔왕국이 있었던 곳이다.

It is now the capital of Nepal and, as such, /
지금은 네팔의 수도로서 /

the center of its government, economy, and culture.
네팔의 정치, 경제, 문화의 중심지이다.

해발 1,350미터에 위치하여 반짝거리는 히말라야 산맥이 내다보이는 카트만두 시는 연중 내내 기후가 온화하여 살기 편한 곳이다. 카트만두는 분지의 거의 한복판에 위치하고 있고, 남북 5㎞, 동서 5㎞의 정사각형을 이루고 있다. 그 곳은 고대 네팔왕국이 있었던 곳이다. 지금은 네팔의 수도로서 네팔의 정치, 경제, 문화의 중심지이다.

문제풀이

(A) Being이 생략된 분사구문이다. 원래 문장은 As it was situated at ~라는 부사절인데, 이것을 분사구문으로 바꾸면 (Being) Situated at~이 된다. 그런데 수동형 분사구문에서 (Being)은 생략 가능하므로 괄호에는 Situated가 된다. be situated in/on/at ~는 '~에 위치하다'의 의미이다.
(B)에는 makes의 목적어가 되고 목적보어 pleasant가 뒤에 온 구조이므로 동명사 living이 필요하다. to live를 사용하려면 어순을 makes it pleasant to live here로 바꾸어야 한다.
(C) 전치사 of 뒤에는 「소유격+명사」의 구조가 나와야 한다. 소유격 its는 '네팔'을 가리키고 있다.

어휘·어구

situate 위치시키다, (어떤 위치에) 두다
elevation 고도

9.① 독성 물질의 대안

직독/직해

For every toxic substance, process, or product
오늘날 사용 중인 모든 독성 물질, 공정, 혹은 제품에는

in use today, / there is a safer alternative — /
/ 더 안전한 대안이 있다 /

either already in existence, or waiting to be discovered / 이미 존재하거나 발견되기를 기다리고 있다 /

through the application of human intellect,
인간의 지력, 창의력, 그리고 노력의 적용을 통해

ingenuity, and effort.

In almost every case, / 거의 모든 경우에 /

the safer alternative is available /
더 안전한 대안은 이용할 수 있다 /

at a comparable cost. 비슷한 비용으로

Industry may reject these facts /
업계는 이러한 사실을 거부할 지도 모른다 /

and complain about the high cost of acting, /
그리고 높은 실행 비용에 대해 격렬하게 비난할 (지도 모른다) /

but history sets the record straight.
하지만 역사가 그런 내용을 바로잡는다

The chemical industry denied /
화학업계에서는 부인했다 /

that there were practical alternatives /
실용적인 대안이 있다는 것을

to ozone-depleting chemicals, /
오존을 고갈시키는 화학 물질에 대한 /

predicting not only economic disaster but
경제적인 재앙뿐만 아니라 수많은 사망자도 예측하면서

numerous deaths /

because food and vaccines would spoil /
식품과 백신이 상할 것이기 때문에 /

without refrigeration. 냉장을 하지 않으면
They were wrong. 그들은 틀렸다

The motor vehicle industry initially denied /
자동차업계에서는 처음에 부인했다 /

that cars caused air pollution, / then claimed /
자동차가 대기 오염을 유발한다는 것을 / 그다음에는 주장했다 /

that no technology existed / to reduce pollution
어떤 기술도 존재하지 않는다고 / 자동차로부터의 오염을 줄이는

from vehicles, / and later argued /
/ 그리고 나중에 주장했다 /

that installing devices to reduce air pollution /
대기 오염을 줄이는 장치를 설치하는 것이 /

would make cars extremely expensive.
자동차가 엄청나게 비싸지게 할 것이라고

They were wrong every time. 그들은 매번 틀렸다
The pesticide industry argues /
살충제업계에서는 주장한다 /

that synthetic pesticides are absolutely necessary /
합성 살충제가 절대적으로 필요하다고 /

to grow food. 식량을 재배하기 위해
Thousands of organic farmers are proving them
wrong. 수많은 유기농 농부들은 그들이 틀렸음을 입증하고 있다

오늘날 사용 중인 모든 독성 물질, 공정, 혹은 제품에는 더 안전한 대안이 있는데, 그것은 이미 존재하거나 인간의 지력, 창의력, 그리고 노력의 적용을 통해 발견되기를 기다리고 있다. 거의 모든 경우에, 더 안전한 대안은 (현재와) 비슷한 비용으로 (A) 이용할 수 있다. 업계는 이러한 사실을 거부하고 높은 실행 비용에 대해 격렬하게 비난할지도 모르지만, 역사는 그런 내용을 바로잡는다. 화학업계에서는 냉장을 하지 않으면 식품과 백신이 상할 것이기 때문에 경제적인 재앙뿐만 아니라 수많은 사망자도 (B) 예측하면서 오존을 고갈시키는 화학 물질에 대한 실용적인 대안이 있다는 것을 부인했다. 그들은 틀렸다. 자동차업계에서는 처음에 자동차가 대기 오염을 유발한다는 것을 부인하였고, 그다음에는 자동차로부터의 오염을 줄이는 어떤 기술도 존재하지 않는다고 주장했으며, 나중에는 대기 오염을 줄이는 장치를 설치하면 자동차가 엄청나게 비쌀 것이라고 주장했다. 그들은 매번 틀렸다. 살충제업계에서는 합성 살충제가 식량을 재배하기 위해 절대적으로 (C) 필요하다고 주장한다. 수많은 유기농 농부들은 그들이 틀렸음을 입증하고 있다.

문제풀이

(A) 업계가 높은 실행 비용이 있을 것이라고 비난할지도 모른다고 한 것으로 보아, (A)에는 available이 들어가서 더 안전한 대안은 비슷한 비용으로 이용할 수 있는데 업계가 이를 거부한다는 흐름이 되는 것이 적절하다. unavailable은 '이용할 수 없는'이라는 의미이다.

(B) 화학업계는 식품과 백신을 냉장 하지 않으면, 많은 사망자가 나올 것이라 예측해서 오존을 고갈시키는 화학 물질의 대안이 없다 주장했다고 하는 것이 문맥상 적절하므로, 'predicting(예측하면서)'이 와야 한다. prevent는 '막다, 방지하다'라는 의미이다.

(C) 수많은 유기농 농부들이 살충제업계의 주장이 틀렸음을 입증하고 있다고 했으므로, 살충제업계는 합성 살충제가 식량 재배를 위해 꼭 필요하다고 주장했다는 문맥이 되는 것이 적절하다. 따라서 'necessary(필요한)'가 와야한다. unnecessary는 '불필요한'이라는 의미이다.

따라서 정답은 ①이다.

어휘 · 어구

toxic 유독성의
alternative 대안
application 적용
ingenuity 창의력
comparable 비슷한

---

set straight ~의 생각[실수]을 바로잡아 주다
ozone-depleting 오존을 고갈시키는
spoil 상하다, 못 쓰게 만들다
refrigeration 냉장
install 설치하다
pesticide 살충제
synthetic 합성한
absolutely 전적으로, 틀림없이

---

10. ② 언어에서 문법의 발달

직독 직해

According to Derek Bickerton, /
Derek Bickerton에 따르면 /

human ancestors and relatives such as the
Neanderthals, / 네안데르탈인과 같은 인간의 조상들과 친척들은 /

may have had a relatively large lexicon of words, /
상대적으로 큰 어휘 목록을 가지고 있었을지도 모른다 /

each of which related to a mental concept /
각 단어는 정신적인 개념과 관련이 있었다 /

such as 'meat', 'fire', 'hunt' and so forth.
'고기', '불', '사냥' 등과 같은

They were able to string such words together /
그들은 그런 단어들을 결합시킬 수 있었다 /

but could do so / only in a nearly arbitrary fashion.
하지만 그렇게 할 수 있었다 / 거의 임의적인 방식으로만

Bickerton recognizes / Bickerton은 안다 /

that this could result in some ambiguity.
이것이 약간의 애매모호함을 발생시킬 수 있다는 것을

For instance, / would 'man killed bear' have meant /
예를 들어 / 'man killed bear'는 의미했을까 /

that a man has killed a bear / 사람이 곰을 죽였다는 것을 /

or that a bear has killed a man?
혹은 곰이 사람을 죽였다는 것을

Ray Jackendoff, a cognitive scientist, suggests /
인지과학자인 Ray Jackendoff는 제안한다 /

that simple rules such as 'agent-first' /
'행위자 먼저'와 같은 단순한 규칙이 /

(that is, the man killed the bear) /
(즉, 사람이 곰을 죽였다) /

might have reduced the potential ambiguity.
잠재적인 애매모호함을 줄였을 수도 있다고

Nevertheless, the number and complexity of /
그런데도, 가능한 발화의 수와 복잡성은 /

potential utterances /

would have been severely limited.
매우 한정적이었을 것이다

The transformation of such proto-language into
language / 그러한 원시 언어에서 언어로의 변형은 /

required the evolution of grammar— /
문법의 발달을 요구했다 /

rules that define the order / 순서를 정하는 규칙 /

in which a finite number of words can be strung
together / 유한한 수의 단어들이 결합될 수 있는 /

to create an infinite number of utterances, /
무한한 수의 발화를 만들기 위해 /

each with a specific meaning. 각각 특정한 의미를 지닌

Derek Bickerton에 따르면, 네안데르탈인과 같은 인간의 조상들과 친척들은 상대적으로 큰 어휘 목록을 가지고 있었을지도 모르고, 각 단어는 '고기', '불', '사냥' 등과 같은 정신적인 개념과 관련이 있었다. 그들은 그런 단어들을 결합시킬 수 있었지만 거의 (A) 임의적인 방식으로만 그렇게 할 수 있었다. Bickerton은 이것이 약간의 애매모호함을 발생시킬 수 있다는 것을 안다. 예를 들어, 'man killed bear'는 사람이 곰을 죽였다는 것을 의미했을까, 혹은 곰이 사람을 죽였다는 것을 의미했을까? 인지과학자인 Ray Jackendoff는 '행위자 먼저'(즉, 사람이 곰을 죽였다)와 같은 단순한 규칙이 잠재적인 애매모호함을 (B) 줄였을 수도 있다고 제안한다. 그런데도, 가능한 발화의 수와 복잡성은 매우 한정적이었을 것이다. 그러한 원시 언어에서 언어로의 변형은 유한한 수의 단어들이 각각 특정한 의미를 지닌 무한한 수의 발화를 만들기 위해 연결될 수 있는 순서를 정하는 규칙인 문법의 (C) 발달을 요구했다.

문제풀이

(A) 단어들을 연결하는 방식이 애매모호함을 발생

시킬 수 있었다고 했으므로, 임의적인 방식으로 그렇게 했다고 하는 것이 문맥상 알맞다. 따라서 'arbitrary(임의적인)'가 오는 것이 적절하다. consistent는 '일관된'이라는 의미이다.

(B) 행위자를 먼저 쓰게 하는 단순한 규칙은 잠재적인 애매모호함을 줄였을 것이므로, 'reduced(줄였다)'가 오는 것이 적절하다. increase는 '증가시키다'라는 의미이다.

(C) 규칙이 없던 원시 언어에서 진짜 언어로 변화될 때 유한한 수의 단어들을 가지고 다른 의미를 지닌 무한한 발화를 만들어 내려면 단어의 연결 순서를 규정하는 규칙적인 문법의 발달을 요구했을 것이다. 따라서 'evolution(발달)'이 오는 것이 적절하다. destruction은 '파괴'라는 의미이다.
따라서 정답은 ②이다.

○ **이렇게 풀자**_ 먼저 글의 주제와 흐름을 파악한 뒤, 네모 안의 어휘가 포함된 문장 전후 문맥을 파악해서 적절하게 쓰인 것을 고르면 된다. 'Bickerton recognizes that this could result in some ambiguity.(Bickerton은 이것이 약간의 애매모호함을 발생시킬 수 있다는 것을 안다.)'를 통해 (A)에 들어갈 말을, 'simple rules such as 'agent-first' (that is, the man killed the bear)'('행위자 먼저'(즉, 사람이 곰을 죽였다)와 같은 단순한 규칙)'을 통해 (B)에 들어갈 말을, 'rule that define the order in which a finite number of words can be strung together to create an infinite number of utterances, each with a specific meaning(각각 특정한 의미를 지닌 무한한 수의 발화를 만들기 위해 연결될 수 있는 순서를 정하는 규칙인)'을 통해 (C)에 들어갈 말을 유추해 낼 수 있다.

어휘 · 어구

and so forth ~ 등등
string together 연결하다, 결합시키다
ambiguity 애매모호함
cognitive 인식의, 인지의
agent 행위자
utterance 발화, 말
severely 심하게
transformation 변화
define 정의하다, 규정하다
finite 유한한, 한정된

---

11. ③ 사회에서 협동과 신뢰의 중요성

직독 직해

Cooperation and trust are important /
협동과 신뢰는 중요하다 /

in every sphere of society. 사회의 모든 분야에서
We often underestimate the role of trust /
우리는 종종 신뢰가 맡은 역할을 과소평가한다 /

in making our economy work /
우리의 경제가 작동하게 하는 데 /

or the importance of the social contract /
또는 사회적인 계약의 중요성을 /

that binds us together. 우리를 하나로 묶는
If every business contract had to be enforced /
만일 모든 사업상의 계약이 시행되어야 한다면 /

by one party's taking the other to court, /
한 쪽이 다른 쪽을 법정에 데려가는 것으로 /

our economy, and not just our politics, /
우리의 정치뿐만 아니라, 우리의 경제는 /

would be in gridlock. 정체 상태가 될 것이다
The legal system enforces certain aspects of "good
사법 체제는 '좋은 행동'의 특정한 측면을 시행하게 한다

behavior," / but most good behavior is mandatory.
/ 하지만 대부분의 좋은 행동은 의무적이다
Our system couldn't function otherwise.
우리의 체제는 다른 방식으로는 작동할 수 없다

If we littered / every time we could get away with it, /
만약 우리가 쓰레기를 버린다면 / 우리가 그것을 모면할 수 있을 때마다 /
our streets would be dirty, / 우리의 거리는 더러울 것이고 /
or we would have to spend an excessive amount /
혹은 우리는 지나친 금액을 써야 할 것이다 /
on policing / to keep them clean.
단속하는 데 / 그것들을 깨끗하게 유지하기 위해
If individuals cheated on every contract — /
만일 개인들이 모든 계약에서 부정행위를 한다면 /
so long as they could get away with it — /
그들이 그것을 모면할 수 있는 한 /
life would be unpleasant / 인생은 불쾌할 것이다 /
and economic dealings would be unmanageable.
그리고 경제적인 거래 관계는 다루기 어려울 것이다

협동과 신뢰는 사회의 모든 분야에서 중요하다. 우리는 경제가 작동하게 하는 데 신뢰가 맡은 역할이나 혹은 우리를 하나로 묶는 사회적인 계약의 중요성을 종종 ① 과소평가한다. 만일 모든 사업상의 계약이 한 쪽이 다른 쪽을 법정에 데려가는 것으로 ② 시행되어야 한다면, 우리의 정치뿐만 아니라, 우리의 경제는 정체 상태가 될 것이다. 사법 체제는 '좋은 행동'의 특정한 측면을 시행하게 하지만, 대부분의 좋은 행동은 ③ 의무적이다. 우리의 체제는 다른 방식으로는 작동할 수 없다. 우리가 모면할 수 있을 때마다 쓰레기를 버린다면, 우리의 거리는 더러울 것이고, 혹은 우리는 거리를 깨끗하게 유지하기 위해 ④ 단속하는 데 지나친 금액을 써야 할 것이다. 만일 개인들이 모면할 수 있는 한 모든 계약에서 ⑤ 부정행위를 한다면, 인생은 불쾌할 것이고 경제적인 거래 관계는 다루기 어려울 것이다.

문제풀이

사회에서 협동과 신뢰는 중요한데, 모든 사업상의 계약이 법정에 가는 것으로 시행되어야 하면 정치와 경제는 정체 상태가 될 것이라고 한 것과 모면할 수 있을 때마다 쓰레기를 버리면 더러워지고 단속하는 데 많은 금액을 써야 하고 모면할 수 있는 한 모든 계약에서 부정행위를 하면 불쾌하고 경제적인 거래를 다루기가 어려울 것이라고 한 예를 통해 좋은 행동이 자발적으로 이루어지지 않으면 사회적 비용이 과하게 지출될 것임을 알 수 있다. 따라서 문맥상 대부분의 좋은 행동은 자발적이라고 해야 하므로, ③ 'mandatory(의무적인)'를 'voluntary(자발적인)'로 고쳐야 한다.

⊙ 이렇게 풀자_ 'If every business contract had to be enforced by one party's taking the other to court, our economy, and not just our politics, would be in gridlock.(만일 모든 사업상의 계약이 한 쪽이 다른 쪽을 법정에 데려가는 것으로 시행되어야 한다면, 우리의 정치뿐만 아니라, 우리의 경제는 정체 상태가 될 것이다.)'과 'If we littered every time we could get away with it, our streets would be dirty, or we would have to spend an excessive amount on policing to keep them clean.(우리가 모면할 수 있을 때마다 쓰레기를 버린다면, 우리의 거리는 더러울 것이고, 혹은 우리는 거리를 깨끗하게 유지하기 위해 단속하는 데 지나친 금액을 써야 할 것이다.)'과 'If individuals cheated on every contract — so long as they could get away with it — life would be unpleasant and economic dealings would be unmanageable.(만일 개인들이 모면할 수 있는 한 모든 계약에서 부정행위를 한다면, 인생은 불쾌할 것이고 경제적인 거래 관계는 다루기 어려울 것이다.)'의 두 가지 예를 통해 좋은 행동의 자발성의 중요성을 이해하면 ③ 'mandatory'이 적절하지 않다는 것을 알 수 있다.

《 어휘·어구 》

sphere 영역, 범위, 분야
underestimate 과소평가하다
contract 계약, 계약서
bind 묶다, 결속시키다
enforce 집행하다, 시행하다
court 법정
legal 법률과 관련된
aspect 측면
mandatory 의무적인
litter 쓰레기를 버리다

---

get away with 처벌을 모면하다
excessive 지나친, 과도한
police 단속하다
cheat 속이다, 사기 치다
dealings (거래) 관계
unmanageable 다루기 어려운

---

12. ⑤   창의적인 아이디어가 어떻게 사람들에게 오는가

직독 직해

Wherever we find creativity, / we almost always find /
창의성이 발견되는 곳이면 어디든지 / 우리는 거의 항상 발견한다 /
it was the result of a person /
그것이 사람의 결과라는 것을 /
who willingly went to work on a real problem.
실제적인 문제를 기꺼이 해결하고자 했던
Thomas Edison once remarked /
한번은 Thomas Edison이 말한 적이 있다 /
that "Everything comes to him who hustles."
"모든 것은 힘차게 해내는 사람에게 온다."
Work. 일하라
Don't worry. 걱정하지 말라
That was Edison's advice.
그것이 Edison의 충고였다
And he proved its usefulness / by his own example.
그리고 그는 그것의 유용성을 입증했다 / 자신이 직접 본보기를 보임으로써
But despite Edison's experience /
하지만 Edison의 경험에도 불구하고 /
and that of countless others /
그리고 수많은 다른 사람들의 경험에도 불구하고 /
who continue to make breakthroughs, /
계속해서 획기적인 진전을 이루는 /
there remains considerable mystery /
상당한 의문이 남아 있다 /
about how creative ideas actually come to people.
창의적인 아이디어가 실제로 사람들에게 어떻게 다가오는지에 관해서는
When we read the words of people /
우리가 사람들의 말을 읽을 때 /
like Giacomo Puccini, /
Giacomo Puccini 같은 /
that great operatic composer, / who once remarked, /
그 위대한 오페라 작곡가 / 언젠가 말했던 /
"The music of this opera *Madame Butterfly* /
"이 오페라 'Madame Butterfly'의 음악은 /
was dictated to me by God; /
신에 의해 내게 내려진 지시였습니다 /
I was merely instrumental / in putting it on paper /
단지 나는 도구로 쓰였을 뿐입니다 / 그것을 종이에 써서 /
and communicating it to the public," /
그리고 그것을 대중에게 전달하는 데 있어서" /
what are we to think?
우리는 무슨 생각을 하게 될까
Obviously, / he and others feel /
분명 / 그와 (그와 비슷한 부류의) 다른 사람들은 느낀다 /
as though they are merely the instrument /
마치 자신이 도구에 불과하다고 /
through which creative energies are flowing.
창의적인 에너지가 흐르고 있는
While it might have felt this way to Puccini, /
Puccini에게는 이렇게 느껴졌을지 모르지만 /
it is also evident / 또한 분명하다 /
that Puccini underestimated his own abilities.
Puccini가 자신의 재능을 과소평가했다는 것은

창의성이 발견되는 곳이면 어디든지, 우리는 그것이 실제적인 문제를 기꺼이 해결하고자 했던 사람의 결과라는 것을 거의 항상 발견한다. 한번은 Thomas Edison이 "모든 것은 힘차게 해내는 사람에게 온다."라고 말한 적이 있다. 일하라. 걱정하지 말라. 그것이 Edison의 충고였다. 그리고 그는 자신이 직접 본보기를 보임으로써 그것의 ① 유용성을 입증했다. 하지만 Edison의 경험과 계속해서 획기적인 진전을 이루는 수많은 다른 사람들의 경험에도 불구하고, 창의적인 아이디어가 실제로 사람들에게 어떻게 다가오는지에 관해서는 상당한 ② 의문이 남아 있다. "이 오페라

'Madame Butterfly'의 음악은 신에 의해 내게 내려진 ③ 지시였습니다. 단지 나는 그것을 종이에 써서 대중에게 전달하는 데 있어서 도구로 쓰였을 뿐입니다"라고 언젠가 말했던 그 위대한 오페라 작곡가 Giacomo Puccini 같은 사람들의 말을 읽을 때, 우리는 무슨 생각을 하게 될까? 분명, 그와 (그와 비슷한 부류의) 다른 사람들은 마치 자신이 창의적인 에너지가 흐르고 있는 ④ 도구에 불과하다고 느낀다. Puccini에게는 이렇게 느껴졌을지 모르지만, Puccini가 자신의 재능을 ⑤ 과대평가했다(→ 과소평가했다)는 것 또한 분명하다.

문제풀이

창의적인 아이디어가 실제로 사람들에게 어떻게 다가오는지에 관해 Thomas Edison은 그것은 문제를 해결하는 데 열심히 노력한 사람의 결과라고 했고, Giacomo Puccini는 자신의 창의적인 재능을 신의 지시를 받고 전달한 것에 불과하다고 한 것으로 보아, Puccini는 자신의 재능을 과소평가했다는 문맥이 되어야 자연스럽다. 따라서 ⑤ 'overestimated (과대평가했다)'는 'underestimated(과소평가했다)'로 고쳐야 한다.

《 어휘·어구 》

breakthrough 획기적인 진전, 돌파구
instrumental 수단[도구]이 되는
overestimate 과대평가하다

12. 준동사

A 출제 POINT
본문 068쪽

1. to have left
2. Having already seen
3. be
4. lying
5. spending
6. His
7. his not

1 [해석]▶ 그가 나라를 떠났다고 사람들은 믿는다.
[해설]▶ 주절의 시제(is)보다 종속절의 시제(left)가 앞서 있으므로, 완료형 부정사가 필요하다.

2 [해석]▶ 그녀는 그 영화를 두 번 봐서, 극장에 가기를 원하지 않았다.
[해설]▶ 주절의 시제(didn't want: 과거)보다 종속절의 시제(had seen: 과거완료)가 앞설 때는 완료분사구문을 쓴다.

3 [해석]▶ Sally는 방해를 받고 싶지 않아 전화를 차단했다.
[해설]▶ Sally가 전화 때문에 방해를 받는 것이므로 부정사의 수동태(to be p.p.)가 필요하다.

4 [해석]▶ 나는 그녀가 바닥에 누워 있는 것을 발견했다.
[해설]▶ 그녀가 바닥에 누워 있는 관계, 즉 목적어(her)와 목적격보어(lying)가 능동 관계이므로 현재분사가 필요하다.

5 [해석]▶ 도시의 사람들과 얼마간의 시간을 보낸 후, 그는 문제들 중 하나가 도시계획과의 업무 수행이라는 것을 알아냈다.
[해설]▶ After he spent some time~라는 부사절을 분사구문으로 바꾼 문장이다. 그가 시간을 보낸 능동 관계이므로 현재분사로 나타내야 한다.

6 [해석]▶ 내가 집에 갑자기 돌아온 것을 그가 알고 있는 것이 이상하다.
[해설]▶ 동명사가 문장의 주어로 문두에 나올 때는 소유격을 쓴다.

7 [해석]▶ 나는 그가 눈치 채지 못한 것이 놀랍다.
[해설]▶ 동명사의 부정은 의미상의 주어 바로 뒤에 not을 쓴다.

B 체크 POINT
본문 068쪽

1. having wasted
2. Having completed
3. being spoken to
4. taken
5. frustrated
6. of
7. Not wanting

1 [해석]▶ 당신의 시간을 낭비한 것에 대해 유감입니다.
[해설]▶ 주절의 주어는 현재시제이고, 종속절의 시제는 과거시제이다. 술어 동사의 시제보다 앞선 경우, 완료형 동명사를 사용한다.

2 [해석]▶ 그녀는 일을 마친 후, 휴가를 떠났다.
[해설]▶ 부사절의 시제가 주절의 시제보다 앞선 경우, 완료분사구문을 사용한다.

3 [해석]▶ Sam은 누군가 말을 걸지 않으면 말을 전혀 하지 않는다.

[해설]▶ 전치사 without 뒤에 동명사형이 나와야 하며, Sam이 말을 거는 주체가 아니라 대상이므로 동명사 수동태 「being+p.p.」형태로 나타내야 한다.

4 [해석]▶ 나는 Mark가 경찰에 끌려가는 것을 봤다.
[해설]▶ 지각동사 뒤에 목적어와 목적격보어가 수동 관계인 경우, 과거분사를 사용해야 한다.

5 [해석]▶ 그의 서툰 연기에 실망한 연극 연출가가 그를 향해 소리를 질렀다.
[해설]▶ 분사구문이 주절의 주어와 수동 관계이면 과거분사를 써야 한다. 연극 연출가가 그의 서툰 연기로 실망한 것이므로 수동의 의미를 드러내도록 과거분사를 써야 한다.

6 [해석]▶ 그가 휴대폰을 버스에 놓고 내린 것은 부주의한 일이었다.
[해설]▶ 부정사의 의미상의 주어는 「for+목적격」으로 나타내지만, 성품 형용사(careless)가 바로 앞에 나온 경우, 「of+목적격」으로 나타낸다.

7 [해석]▶ 대화를 중단시키고 싶지 않아서, 그는 조용히 서 있었다.
[해설]▶ to부정사 부정은 to부정사 바로 앞에 not을 쓴다.

Day 12
본문 069쪽

1 ①	2 ⑤	3 ⑤	4 ①	5 ④
6 ③	7 ③	8 ④	9 ③	10 ④
11 ②	12 ②			

1. ① 교역의 중요성

직독 직해

It is difficult to exaggerate / 아무리 강조해도 지나치지 않다 /
the importance of trade / in our modern world.
교역의 중요성은 / 우리가 사는 현대 사회에서
The Founders, having read Adam Smith's *Wealth of*
Adam Smith의 '국부론'을 읽은 미국의 창시자들은
Nations, / recognized this early on.
/ 일찍이 이것을 인식했다
By including the commerce clause /
그들은 통상 조항을 포함시킴으로써 /
in the U.S. Constitution (Article 1, Section 8), /
미국 헌법(1조, 8항)에 /
they helped set the stage / 그들은 장을 마련하는 것을 도왔다 /
for the development of a highly prosperous free
아주 번창한 자유 무역 지대 발전을 위한
trade zone / within the United States.
/ 미국 내에서
Trade makes it possible / for most of us /
교역은 가능하게 만든다 / 우리 대부분이 /
to consume a bundle of goods /
많은 제품을 소비하는 것을 /
far beyond what we would be able to produce for
ourselves. 우리 스스로 생산할 수 있는 것을 훨씬 뛰어넘는
Can you imagine the difficulty /
여러분은 어려움을 상상할 수 있는가 /
involved in producing your own housing, clothing,
and food, / 스스로 자신의 의식주를 생산하는 것과 관련된 /
to say nothing of computers, television sets, /
컴퓨터, 텔레비전은 말할 필요도 없이 /
dishwashers, automobiles, and cell phones?
식기세척기, 자동차, 그리고 휴대 전화기
People who have these things / do so largely /
이런 것을 가진 사람들은 / 주로 그렇게 한다 /

because their economics are organized /
그들의 경제 조건이 짜여 있기 때문에 /
in such a way / 그런 방식으로 /
that individuals can cooperate, specialize, and
trade. 개인이 협력하고, 전문화하며, 교역할 수 있는
Countries that impose obstacles to exchange — /
교환하는 것에 장애물을 부과하는 나라는 /
either domestic or international — /
국내에서든 국제적으로든 /
reduce the ability of their citizens /
자국의 시민들의 능력을 줄인다 /
to achieve more prosperous lives.
더 유복한 생활을 이룰 수 있는

우리가 사는 현대 사회에서 교역의 중요성은 아무리 강조해도 지나치지 않다. Adam Smith의 '국부론'을 읽은 미국의 창시자들은 일찍이 이것을 인식했다. 그들은 미국 헌법(1조, 8항)에 통상 조항을 포함시킴으로써, 미국 내에 아주 번창한 자유 무역 지대 발전을 마련하는 것을 도왔다. 교역은 우리 스스로 생산할 수 있는 것을 훨씬 뛰어넘는 많은 제품을 우리 대부분이 소비하는 것을 가능하게 만든다. 컴퓨터, 텔레비전, 식기세척기, 자동차, 그리고 휴대 전화기는 말할 필요도 없이, 스스로 자신의 의식주를 생산하는 것과 어려움을 상상할 수 있는가? 이런 것을 가진 사람들은 주로 그들의 경제 조건이 개인이 협력하고, 전문화하며, 교역할 수 있는 그런 방식으로 짜여 있기 때문에 그렇게 가지고 있는 것이다. 국내에서든 국제적으로든, 교환하는 것에 장애물을 부과하는 나라는 자국의 시민들이 더 유복한 생활을 이룰 수 있는 능력을 줄인다.

문제풀이

① The Founders를 부연 설명하는 분사구문을 이끌고 있는데 주절의 시제보다 앞서 일어난 일을 나타내므로 완료형이 와야 한다. 또한 밑줄 뒤에 목적어가 나오므로 능동태를 써야 한다. 그래서 수동태 단순형 분사구문인 being read를 능동태 완료형 분사구문인 having read로 고치는 것이 적절하다.
② 동사 makes의 목적격보어로는 형용사가 와야 하므로, possible이 온 것은 적절하다.
③ involved가 the difficulty를 수식하고 있는데 문맥상 '관련된'이라는 수동의 의미로 과거분사 involved가 온 것은 적절하다.
④ a way의 내용을 보충 설명하는 문장 성분을 모두 갖춘 완전한 문장의 동격절이 왔으므로, 접속사 that이 온 것은 적절하다.
⑤ reduce가 주어인 Countries에 이어지는 동사의 역할을 하고 있는 맞는 문장이다. that impose obstacles to exchange — either domestic or international —는 Countries를 수식하는 관계대명사절이다.

어휘·어구

exaggerate 과장하다
commerce clause 통상 조항
Constitution 헌법
set the stage for ~을 준비하다
prosperous 번영한, 번창한
consume 소비하다
to say nothing of ~은 말할 필요도 없이
specialize 전문화하다
impose 부과하다, 지우다
obstacle 장애, 장애물
domestic 국내의

2. ⑤ Double Dutch

직독 직해

Double Dutch is a style of jumping rope /
Double Dutch는 줄넘기의 한 방법이다
in which there are two participants /
그 줄넘기에는 참가자 두 명이 있습니다 /

turning two ropes /
두 개의 줄을 돌리는 /

while either one or two participants /
한 명 또는 두 명의 참가자가 /

jump through the ropes. 그 줄을 통과해 뛰어넘는 동안
Double Dutch is a dynamic form of jumping rope /
Double Dutch는 역동적인 형태의 줄넘기이다. /

that kids really love. 아이들이 매우 좋아하는
In addition to its being a beneficial cardiovascular exercise, /
유익한 심장혈관 운동인 것에 덧붙여,

Double Dutch also improves /
Double Dutch는 향상시킨다 /

coordination and quickness.
조정 능력과 민첩성도

Furthermore, / 게다가 /

because it requires three to four participants /
그것은 필요로 하기 때문에 서너 명의 참가자가 /

working closely together,
함께 긴밀하게 움직이는 것을

it is also great for developing cooperative skills among children.
아이들 간의 협력 기술을 개발하는 데도 좋다.

At the most advanced levels, /
최상급 수준에서 /

Double Dutch is also being done /
Double Dutch는 행해지고 있다 /

as an extreme competition sport /
격렬한 경연 운동으로도 /

where groups of kids are doing high-energy dancing routines /
아이들 무리가 강렬한 에너지의 정해진 춤 동작을 하는 /

that are truly amazing. 매우 놀라운.

Double Dutch는 한두 명의 참가자가 그 줄을 통과해 뛰어넘는 동안, 참가자 두 명이 두 개의 줄을 돌리는 줄넘기의 한 방법이다. Double Dutch는 아이들이 매우 좋아하는 역동적인 형태의 줄넘기이다. 유익한 심장혈관 운동인 것에 덧붙여, Double Dutch는 조정 능력과 민첩성도 향상시킨다. 게다가 그것은 서너 명의 참가자가 함께 긴밀하게 움직이는 것을 필요로 하기 때문에, 아이들 간의 협력 기술을 개발하는 데도 좋다. 최상급 수준에서 Double Dutch는 아이들 무리가 매우 놀라운, 강렬한 에너지의 정해진 춤 동작을 하는 격렬한 경연 운동으로도 행해지고 있다.

문제풀이

(A)에서는 전치사의 목적어 기능을 하는 동명사가, (B)에서는 목적어를 수반하는 동명사가, (C)에서는 완전한 문장 구조와 결합되는 관계부사가 오는 것이 적합하다. 따라서 어법에 맞는 표현으로 가장 적절한 것은 ⑤이다.

《 어휘·어구 》

jumping rope 줄넘기
participant 참가자
dynamic 역동적인
beneficial 유익한
cardiovascular 심혈관의
improve 개선하다, 향상시키다
coordination 조정
routine 정해진 동작

---

3. ⑤ 현지 조사는 문화 인류의 특징이다

직독/직해

Fieldwork is the hallmark / of cultural anthropology.
현지 조사는 특징이다. / 문화 인류학의

It is the way we explore and learn /
그것은 우리가 탐구하고 배우는 방식이다. /

about the vast detailed intricacy of
많이 세분화되고 복잡한

human culture and individual behavior.
인류 문화와 개인적인 행동에 대해

And it is, importantly, /
그리고 중요하게도, /

the way in which most cultural anthropologists /
방법이다. / 대부분의 문화 인류학자들이 ~하는

earn and maintain their professional standing.
그들의 전문적인 입장을 획득하고 유지하는

Some of the early personal accounts /
초기의 개인적인 설명의 일부는 /

of anthropologists in the field /
현장에서 작업하던 인류학자들의

make fieldwork sound exciting, adventuresome,
현지 조사가 흥미롭고 모험적이고 들리도록 만들었다.

certainly exotic, sometimes easy.
확실히 색다르고 때때로 쉬운 것처럼

Malinowski, the classic anthropological fieldworker, /
대표적인 인류학 현지 조사자인 Malinowski는

describes the early stages of fieldwork /
현지 조사의 초기 단계를 ~라고 묘사했다.

as 'a strange, sometimes unpleasant, /
'낯설고 때로는 불쾌하고, /

sometimes intensely interesting adventure /
때로는 매우 흥미로운 모험'으로 /

which soon adopts quite a natural course.'
그런데 그것은 곧 자연스러운 과정으로 채택하는 (단계라고).

He goes on to describe / 그는 계속해서 묘사했다 /

his daily routine of strolling / through the village
산책하는 그의 일상을 / 마을 전체를

observing the intimate details of family life,
개인적인 가정생활의 세부 사항을 관찰하면서

and as he tells it, / 그가 말하는 대로 /

such observations seem possible and accessible.
그러한 관찰은 가능하고 (누구나) 접근하기 쉬운 것처럼 보인다.

현지 조사는 문화 인류학의 특징이다. 그것은 많이 세분화되고 복잡한 인류 문화와 개인적인 행동에 대해 우리가 탐구하고 배우는 방식이다. 그리고 중요하게도, 대부분의 문화 인류학자들이 그들의 전문적인 입장을 획득하고 유지하는 방법이다. 현장에서 작업하던 인류학자들의 초기의 개인적인 설명의 일부는 현지 조사가 흥미롭고 모험적이고 확실히 색다르고 때때로 쉬운 것처럼 들리도록 했다. 대표적인 인류학 현지 조사자인 Malinowski는 현지 조사의 초기 단계를 '곧 자연스러운 과정으로 채택되는 낯설고 때로는 불쾌하고, 때로는 매우 흥미로운 모험'으로 묘사했다. 그는 계속해서 개인적인 가정생활의 세부 사항을 관찰하면서 마을 전체를 산책하는 그의 일상을 묘사했는데, 그가 말하는 대로 그러한 관찰은 가능하고 (누구나) 접근하기 쉬운 것처럼 보인다.

문제풀이

① detailed는 뒤에 오는 명사 intricacy를 수식하는 형용사이다.
② in which 이하는 관계대명사절로 앞의 the way를 수식한다.
③ 사역동사 make의 목적격 보어 자리이므로, 동사원형인 sound가 와야 한다.
④ 주격 관계대명사절의 동사의 수는 앞에 있는 선행사와 일치한다. 선행사가 단수인 adventure이므로 단수동사인 adopts가 알맞다.
⑤ the intimate details of family life라는 목적어가 있으므로 현재분사인 observing이 알맞다.

《 어휘·어구 》

fieldwork 현지 조사
anthropology 인류학
intricacy 얽히고설킴, 복잡
standing 입장
account 묘사, 설명
adventuresome 모험적인
intensely 매우, 강렬하게
stroll 산책하다
intimate 사사로운, 은밀한

---

4. ① 듣는 사람의 기준에 따른 평가 결과

직독/직해

When induced to give spoken or written witness /
말이나 글로 증언하도록 유도하면 /

to something they doubt, /
그들이 확신하지 못하는 일에 대해

people will often feel bad about their deceit.
사람들은 그들의 속임수에 대해 종종 언짢게 느낄 것이다.

Nevertheless, / they begin to believe /
그럼에도 불구하고 / 그들은 믿기 시작한다 /

what they are saying.
그들이 말하고 있는 것을

When there is no compelling external explanation for one's words, /
그 말에 대해 납득할 만한 외적인 설명이 없다면

saying becomes believing.
말하는 것이 믿는 것이 된다.

Tory Higgins and his colleagues /
Tory Higgins와 그의 동료들은 /

had university students read /
대학생들에게 읽게 하고 나서

a personality description of someone /
어떤 사람에 대한 성격 묘사를 /

and then summarize it for someone else/
다른 어떤 사람에게 그것을 요약하게 하였다.

who was believed either to like or to dislike this person.
이 사람을 좋아하거나 싫어한다고 믿어지는

The students wrote a more positive description /
학생들은 더 긍정적으로 묘사했다 /

when the recipient liked the person.
듣는 사람이 그 사람을 좋아했을 때

Having said positive things, /
긍정적인 것을 말하고 나자,

they liked the person more themselves.
그들 스스로 또한 그 사람을 더욱 좋아하게 되었다.

Asked to recall what they had read, /
그들이 읽었던 것을 상기해 보라는 요청을 받자,

they remembered the description /
그들은 성격 기술을 기억했다.

as being more positive than it was.
원래보다 더 긍정적인 것으로

In short, / it seems that /
요약하자면 / ~인 것 같다 /

we are prone to adjust our messages to our listeners, /
우리는 듣는 사람들에게 우리의 메시지를 맞추고,

and, having done so, / 그리고 그렇게 함으로써 /

to believe the altered message.
변경된 메시지를 쉽게 믿는 것 같다.

그들이 확신하지 못하는 일에 대해 말이나 글로 증언하도록 유도하면 사람들은 그들의 속임수에 대해 종종 언짢게 느낄 것이다. 그럼에도 불구하고 그들은 그들이 말하고 있는 것을 믿기 시작한다. 그 말에 대해 납득할 만한 외적인 설명이 없다면 말하는 것이 믿는 것이 된다. Tory Higgins와 그의 동료들은 대학생들에게 어떤 사람에 대한 성격 묘사를 읽게 하고 나서 이 사람을 좋아하거나 싫어한다고 믿어지는 다른 어떤 사람에게 그것을 요약하게 하였다. 학생들은 듣는 사람이 그 사람을 좋아했을 때 더 긍정적으로 묘사했다. 긍정적인 것을 말하고 나자, 그들 스스로 또한 그 사람은 더욱 좋아하게 되었다. 그들이 읽었던 것을 싱기해 보라는 요청을 받자, 그들은 성격 기술을 원래보다 더 긍정적인 것으로 기억했다. 요약하자면 우리는 듣는 사람들에게 우리의 메시지를 맞추고, 그리고 그렇게 함으로써 변경된 메시지를 쉽게 믿는 것 같다.

문제풀이

(A) 주절의 동사 believe의 목적어가 되면서 동시에 관계사절의 say의 목적어가 되어야 하므로, 선행사를 포함하는 관계대명사 what이 알맞다.
(B) 사역동사 had의 목적보어로 쓰인 read와 병렬 구조를 이루어야 하므로, summarize가 알맞다.
(C) When they were asked to recall ~을 분사구문으로 나타낸 것으로, Asked 앞에 Being이 생략된 형태이다. 따라서 Asked가 알맞다.

《 어휘 · 어구 》

induce 권유하다
give witness 증언하다
deceit 속임수, 기만
compelling 설득력 있는, 납득할 만한
external 외부의, 외적인
personality 개성, 성격
summarize 요약하다
recipient 받는 사람, 수용자
recall 상기하다
in short 요컨대
adjust 맞추다, 조정하다
altered 변경된, 바뀐

---

5. ④ 예술에 파묻혀 지낸 북송조의 휘종

직독 / 직해

In China / 중국에서는 /
it has never been rare for emperors to paint, /
황제가 그림을 그리는 것이 흔한 일이었으나, /
but Huizong took it so seriously /
Huizong은 이것을 너무 진지하게 받아들여 /
that the entire Northern Song Dynasty /
북송조 전체가 /
is thought to have fallen / 붕괴했다고 여겨진다. /
because of it. 이로 인해
He was from a long line of artistic emperors, /
그는 여러 대에 걸쳐 예술을 애호하는 황제 가문의 출신으로, /
who added to the Imperial collections /
이 황제들은 황제의 소장품을 늘렸으며, /
and held discussions about painting, calligraphy, and art collecting.
그림, 서예, 예술품 수집에 대해 이야기를 (자주) 나누었다.
Collecting was easy for Huizong / ―
Huizong에게는 예술품 수집이 쉬운 일이었다. /
if he wanted a painting, / 그가 그림을 원하면 /
the owner would have to hand it over.
그림의 주인은 그것을 넘겨주어야만 했다.
When he inherited the throne, at age nineteen, /
그가 19세의 나이에 왕좌를 계승했을 때, /
it was expected / 다들 예상하였다 /
that he would continue his ancestors' royal patronage.
그가 당연히 자기 조상들처럼 (예술에 대한) 후원을 계속할거라고
This he did, / 실제로 그는 그렇게 하였다. /
but spent so much of the next twenty-five years involved in art /
그러나 그는 그 후(즉위) 25년 동안 너무나 많은 시간을 예술에 파묻혀 지내 /
that he ignored his official duties.
공식적인 의무를 소홀히 했다.

중국에서는 황제가 그림을 그리는 것이 흔한 일이었으나, Huizong은 이 것을 너무 진지하게 받아들여 북송조 전체가 이로 인해 붕괴했다고 여겨 진다. 그는 여러 대에 걸쳐 예술을 애호하는 황제 가문의 출신으로, 이 황 제들은 황제의 소장품을 늘렸으며, 그림, 서예, 예술품 수집에 대해 이야 기를 (자주) 나누었다. Huizong에게는 예술품 수집이 쉬운 일이었다. 그 가 그림을 원하면 그림의 주인은 그것을 넘겨주어야만 했다. 그가 19세 의 나이에 왕좌를 계승했을 때, 그가 당연히 자기 조상들처럼 (예술에 대 한) 후원을 계속할거라고 다들 예상하였고, 실제로 그는 그렇게 하였다. 그렇지만 그는 그 후 (즉위) 25년 동안 너무나 많은 시간을 예술에 파묻 혀 지내 공식적인 의무를 소홀히 했다.

문제풀이

(A)에서는 생각된 시점(현재)보다 북송조가 멸망 한 시점이 이전의 일(과거)이므로, 완료 부정사를 써야 한다.
(B)에서는 진주어인 that절 이하를 가리키는 가주 어 it이 쓰여야 한다.
(C)에서는 involve가 '열중시키다'라는 의미의 타 동사로 Huizong 스스로 예술에 몰입되어 있었으

므로 수동을 의미하는 과거분사가 필요하다.

《 어휘 · 어구 》

collections 소장품
calligraphy 서예
hand over 넘기다
patronage 후원

---

6. ③ 컴퓨터 인식 능력과 한계

직독 / 직해

When we enter a room, / 우리가 방에 들어갈 때, /
we immediately recognize / 우리는 즉각적으로 인식한다. /
the floor, chairs, furniture, tables, and so forth.
바닥, 의자, 가구, 탁자, 기타 등등을
But when a robot scans a room, /
그러나 로봇이 어떤 방을 훑어볼 때 /
it sees nothing but a vast collection of straight and curved lines, /
단지 직선과 곡선의 방대한 집합체로만 보며, /
which it converts to pixels. /
그리고 난 후, 로봇은 그것을 화소로 전환한다. /
It takes an enormous amount of computing time /
방대한 양의 계산 시간이 필요하다 /
to make sense out of this jumble of lines.
이런 뒤죽박죽 섞인 선들을 이해하기 위해서는
A computer sees only a collection /
컴퓨터는 한 집합체로만 보게 된다. /
of circles, ovals, spirals, straight lines, curly lines, corners, and so on.
원, 타원, 나선형, 직선, 곡선, 모퉁이 그리고 기타 등등의 (한 집합체로만)
Spending an enormous amount of computing time, /
상당한 계산 시간을 보내고 난 후에 /
a robot might finally recognize the object as a table.
로봇은 마침내 그 물체를 탁자로 인식하게 될 것이다.
But if you rotate the image, /
그러나 만약 당신이 그 이미지를 회전시키면, /
the computer has to start all over again.
컴퓨터는 모든 것을 다시 시작해야 한다.
In other words, / robots can see, /
다시 말해서 / 로봇은 볼 수 있고
and in fact they can see much better than humans,
사실 인간보다 훨씬 잘 볼 수 있지만
but they don't understand / what they are seeing.
이해하는 것은 아니다. / 자신이 보고 있는 것을

우리가 방에 들어갈 때, 즉각적으로 바닥, 의자, 가구, 탁자, 기타 등등을 인식한다. 그러나 로봇은 어떤 방을 훑어볼 때 단지 직선과 곡선의 방대 한 집합체로만 보며, 그리고 난 후, 로봇은 그것을 화소로 전환한다. 이런 뒤죽박죽 섞인 선들을 이해하기 위해서는 방대한 양의 계산 시간이 필요 하다. 컴퓨터는 원, 타원, 나선형, 직선, 곡선, 모퉁이 그리고 기타 등등의 한 집합체로만 보게 된다. 상당한 계산 시간을 보내고 난 후에 로봇은 마 침내 그 물체를 탁자로 인식하게 될 것이다. 그러나 만약 당신이 그 이미 지를 회전시키면, 컴퓨터는 모든 것을 다시 시작해야 한다. 다시 말해서 로봇은 볼 수 있고 사실 인간보다 훨씬 잘 볼 수 있지만 자신이 보고 있 는 것을 이해하는 것은 아니다.

문제풀이

(A)에서는 계속적 용법의 관계대명사 which를 써 야 한다. 선행사는 a vast collection of straight and curved lines이다. which는 타동사 converts의 목적어 역할을 하고 있다.
(B)에서는 분사구문의 능동형 분사 Spending을 써야 한다. 뒤에 목적어 an enormous amount of computing time이 나오고 있다.
(C)에서는 비교급을 수식하는 부사 much를 써야 한다.

《 어휘 · 어구 》

recognize 인식하다

---

scan 훑어보다
nothing but 단지
straight 직선의
curved 곡선의
convert 전환하다
pixel 화소
jumble 혼잡, 뒤범벅
oval 타원형의
spiral 나선형의
straight line 직선
curved line 곡선
corner 모퉁이

---

7. ③ 수학자가 되려면 분필과 토론할 클럽이 필요하다

직독 / 직해

To be a mathematician /
수학자가 되기 위해서 /
you don't need an expensive laboratory.
비싼 실험실이 필요하지는 않다.
The typical equipment of a mathematician /
수학자의 전형적인 장비는 /
is a blackboard and chalk.
흑판과 분필이다.
It is better to do mathematics on a blackboard /
흑판 위에서 수학을 하는 것이 더 낫다. /
than on a piece of paper
종이 위보다
because chalk is easier to erase, /
분필은 보다 쉽게 지울 수 있고 /
and mathematical research is often filled with mistakes.
수학적인 연구는 흔히 실수로 가득 차 있기 때문에
One more thing you need to do /
한 가지 더 해야 한다면 /
is to join a club devoted to mathematics.
수학에 전념하는 클럽에 가입하는 것이다.
Not many mathematicians can work alone; /
혼자서 작업하는 수학자는 많지 않다. /
they need to talk about / what they are doing.
그들은 토론할 필요가 있다. / 그들이 하고 있는 것에 대해
If you want to be a mathematician, /
수학자가 되기를 원한다면 /
you had better expose your new ideas /
새로운 생각을 노출시키는 편이 낫다. /
to the criticism of others.
다른 사람들의 비판에
It is so easy to include hidden assumptions /
숨어 있는 가정을 포함하고 있기가 너무도 쉽다. /
that you do not see / but that are obvious to others.
당신이 보지 못하지만, / 다른 사람들에겐 명백한

수학자가 되기 위해서 비싼 실험실이 필요하지는 않다. 수학자의 전형적 인 장비는 흑판과 분필이다. 분필은 보다 쉽게 지울 수 있고 수학적인 연 구는 흔히 실수로 가득 차 있기 때문에 종이 위보다 흑판 위에서 수학을 하는 것이 더 낫다. 한 가지 더 해야 한다면 수학에 전념하는 클럽에 가입 하는 것이다. 혼자서 작업하는 수학자는 많지 않다. 그들은 그들이 하고 있는 것에 대해 토론할 필요가 있다. 수학자가 되기를 원한다면 새로운 생각을 다른 사람들의 비판에 노출시키는 편이 낫다. 당신이 보지 못하지 만, 다른 사람들에겐 명백한 숨어 있는 가정을 포함하고 있기가 너무도 쉽다.

문제풀이

① 주어가 The typical equipment이므로 단수동 사 is가 필요하다.
② 앞에 비교급 better가 나왔으므로 than이 필요 하다.
③ ~ to join a club (which is) devoted to mathematics 문장은 「관계대명사+be동사」가 생략 된 구문이다. ③이 포함된 문장에는 이미 동사(is) 가 있고, 접속사가 하나도 없으므로 더 이상의 동

사(devotes)가 나올 수 없다. devotes를 devoted로 고쳐 써야 한다.
④ 「had better+동사원형」 구문으로 '~하는 편이 낫다'는 의미가 있다.
⑤ that은 hidden assumptions를 선행사로 사용된 관계대명사 목적격이다. ~ but that are obvious to others에 쓰인 that도 역시 hidden assumptions를 선행사로 받는다.

《 어휘·어구 》
laboratory 실험실
equipment 장비
expose 노출시키다
criticism 비판
assumption 가정, 가설

8.④   Mike와 Amy의 희망 사항

직독/직해

In order to make their dream come true, /
Mike와 Amy는 그들의 꿈을 실현시키기 위해서 /
Mike and Amy decided not to waste money. /
돈을 낭비하지 않기로 결정했다. /
By living temporarily with Mike's parents /
그들은 Mike의 부모님과 일시적으로 살기로 하고 /
and drastically cutting their leisure expenses, /
여가 활동비도 철저하게 줄이고 /
they hoped to save enough money /
그들은 충분한 돈을 저축하길 희망한다. /
to buy a modest house in two years.
2년 안에 적당한 집을 사기 위한 /

Mike와 Amy는 그들의 꿈을 실현시키기 위해서 돈을 낭비하지 않기로 결정했다. 그들은 Mike의 부모님과 일시적으로 살기로 하고 여가 활동비도 철저하게 줄이고 2년 안에 적당한 집을 사기 위한 그들은 충분한 돈을 저축하길 희망한다.

문제풀이

(A) 「make(사역동사)+목적어(their dream)+목적격보어(come true)」 구문이다. 사역동사는 목적어와 목적격보어가 능동 관계인 경우, 목적격보어를 동사원형을 사용한다.
(B) decide는 to부정사를 목적어로 가져오며, to부정사를 부정하는 경우 to부정사 바로 앞에 부정어(not)를 배치하면 된다.
(C) By living ~ and (by) drastically cutting~이 병렬 구조를 이루고 있다. drastically cut을 drastically cutting으로 고쳐야 한다.
(D) hope는 to부정사를 목적어로 가져오며, enough money는 to save의 목적어이다. enough가 명사를 수식하는 경우 주로 앞에서 수식하지만, 뒤에서 수식하는 경우도 있다.

《 어휘·어구 》
dream 꿈
come true 실현하다
waste 낭비하다
temporarily 일시적으로
leisure expenses 여가 활동비
modest 적당한

9.③   사실과 일치하지 않는 가설

직독/직해

Hypothesis is a tool / 가설은 도구이다
which can cause trouble / 문제를 일으킬 수 있는 /
if not used properly. 적절하게 사용되지 않으면
We must be ready / to abandon or modify our
우리는 준비가 되어 있어야 한다 / 우리의 가설을 폐기하거나 수정할 /
hypothesis /
as soon as it is shown / to be inconsistent with the
가설이 드러나자마자 / 사실들과 일치하지 않는다고
facts.
This is not as easy as it sounds. 이것은 말처럼 쉽지는 않다
When delighted / by the way /
즐거울 때 / 방식에 의해 /
one's beautiful idea offers promise of further
훌륭한 아이디어가 더 나아간 발전에 대한 가능성을 제공하는 /
advances, /
it is tempting / to overlook an observation /
솔깃한 일이다 / 관찰을 간과하거나 /
that does not fit into the pattern woven, /
그 짜인 패턴에 들어맞지 않는 /
or to try to explain it away.
그것을 변명하며 넘어가려는 것은
It is not at all rare / for investigators /
전혀 드문 일이 아니며 / 연구자들이 /
to adhere to their broken hypotheses, /
자신의 무너진 가설에 집착하는 것은 /
turning a blind eye to contrary evidence, /
반대되는 증거에 눈을 감으면서 /
and not altogether unknown / for them /
전혀 알려지지 않은 것은 아니다 / 그들이 /
to deliberately suppress contrary results.
반대되는 결과를 의도적으로 감추는 것이
If the experimental results or observations /
만약 실험의 결과나 관찰들이 /
are definitely opposed to the hypothesis /
확실하게 가설에 반대되거나 /
or if they necessitate / 그것들이 필요로 한다면 /
overly complicated or improbable subsidiary
지나치게 복잡하거나 있을 법하지 않은 부차적인 가설들을 /
hypotheses /
to accommodate them, / 그것들을 수용하기 위해 /
one has to discard the idea / with as few regrets as
그 아이디어를 폐기해야 한다 / 가능한 한 후회 없이
possible.
It is easier / to drop the old hypothesis /
더 쉽다 / 이전 가설을 버리기가 /
if one can find a new one / to replace it.
새로운 것을 찾을 수 있다면 / 그것을 대체할
The feeling of disappointment too will then vanish.
그러면 실망감도 사라질 것이다

가설은 적절하게 사용되지 않으면 문제를 일으킬 수 있는 도구이다. 우리는 가설이 사실들과 (A) 일치하지 않는다고 드러나자마자 우리의 가설을 폐기하거나 수정할 준비가 되어 있어야 한다. 이것은 말처럼 쉽지는 않다. 훌륭한 아이디어가 더 나아간 발전에 대한 가능성을 제공하는 방식에 의해 즐거울 때, 그 짜인 패턴에 들어맞지 않는 관찰을 간과하거나, 그것을 변명하며 넘어가려는 일이다. 연구자들이 반대되는 증거에 눈을 감으면서 자신의 무너진 가설에 집착하는 것은 전혀 드문 일이 아니며, 그들이 반대되는 결과를 (B) 의도적으로 감추는 것이 전혀 알려지지 않은 것은 아니다. 만약 실험의 결과나 관찰들이 확실하게 가설에 반대되거나 그것들을 수용하기 위해 지나치게 복잡하거나 있을 법하지 않은 부차적인 가설들을 필요로 한다면, 가능한 한 후회 없이 그 아이디어를 (C) 폐기해야 한다. 이전 가설을 대체할 새로운 것을 찾을 수 있다면 그것을 버리기가 더 쉽다. 그러면 실망감도 사라질 것이다.

문제풀이

(A) 'We must be ready to abandon or modify our hypothesis'에서 가설을 폐기하거나 수정할 준비가 되어 있어야 한다고 했다. 폐기하거나 수정해야 할 가설은 사실과 일치하지 않는 가설일 것이므로, 'inconsistent(일치하지 않는)'가 적절하다. consistent는 '일치하는'의 의미이다.
(B) 'It is not at all rare for investigators to adhere to their broken hypotheses, turning a blind eye to contrary evidence'에서 연구자들은 반대되는 증거에 눈을 감으면서 자신의 무너

진 가설에 집착한다고 했다. 따라서 연구자들은 가설과 반대되는 결과를 의도적으로 감추게 될 것이므로, 'deliberately(의도적으로)'가 적절하다. unintentionally는 '고의가 아니게, 무심코'의 의미이다.
(C) 'If the experimental results or observations are definitely opposed to the hypothesis or if they necessitate overly complicated or improbable subsidiary hypotheses to accommodate them'에서 실험의 결과나 관찰들이 가설에 반대되거나 그것들을 수용하기 위해 지나치게 복잡하거나 있을 법하지 않은 부차적인 가설들을 필요로 하는 경우를 가정하고 있다. 또 'It is easier to drop the old hypothesis if one can find a new one to replace it.'에서 이전 가설을 대체할 새로운 것을 찾을 수 있다면 더 버리기 쉽다고 했으므로, 아이디어를 폐기해야 한다는 내용이 되어야 함을 알 수 있다. 따라서 'discard(폐기하다)'가 적절하다. defend는 '방어하다'의 의미이다.

❶ 이렇게 풀자 _ 먼저 글의 주제와 전체적인 흐름을 파악한 후 각 네모 안의 낱말이 포함된 문장 전후 맥락을 살펴본다. 특히, 네모 안에서 적절한 낱말을 찾는 문제의 경우, 이 문제와 같이 주로 반의어(consistent/inconsistent, deliberately/unintentionally, defend/discard)가 제시되는 경우가 많으니 평소 어휘를 공부할 때 반의어까지 같이 암기해 두도록 한다.

《 어휘·어구 》
hypothesis 가설
properly 적절하게, 제대로
abandon 버리다, 폐기하다
modify 수정하다
advance 발전, 진전
tempting 솔깃한, 구미가 당기는
overlook 간과하다, 못 보고 넘어가다
observation 관찰
fit into ~에 꼭 들어맞다, ~에 어울리다
weave 짜다(weave - wove - woven)
explain away ~을 잘 해명하여 빠져나가다
investigator 연구자, 조사자
adhere to ~에 집착하다, ~을 고수하다
turn a blind eye to ~을 못 본 체하다
contrary (~와) 반대되는, 다른
suppress 숨기다, 감추다, 억압하다
experimental result 실험 결과
opposed to ~에 반대하는
necessitate ~을 필요하게 만들다, 필요로 하다
overly 지나치게, 몹시
complicated 복잡한
improbable 있을[일어날] 성싶지 않은, 정말 같지 않은
accommodate 수용하다
drop 그만두다, 중단하다
replace 대체하다, 교체하다
vanish 사라지다

10.④   세상에 대한 우리의 의존성

직독/직해

The repairman is called / 수리공을 부른다 /
in when the smooth operation of our world has
우리의 세상이 원활하게 돌아가지 않을 때 /
been disrupted, /
and at such moments / 그리고 그런 순간에 /
our dependence on things normally taken for
우리가 대개 당연하게 여겼던 것들에 대한 우리의 의존성이 /

granted / (for example, a toilet that flushes) /
(예를 들어, 물이 내려가는 변기에 대한) /

is brought to vivid awareness.
분명히 인식된다.

For this very reason, / the repairman's presence /
바로 이런 이유로 / 수리공의 존재가 /

may make the narcissist uncomfortable.
자아도취자를 불편하게 만들 수 있다

The problem isn't so much / 그렇게 문제가 되지 않는다 /
that he is dirty or the job is messy.
그가 더럽다거나 작업이 지저분한 것은

Rather, / he seems to pose a challenge / to our
오히려 / 그는 도전하는 것 같다 / 우리의

self-understanding / that is somehow fundamental.
자기 인식에 / 어쨌거나 뿌리 깊은

We're not as free and independent /
우리는 자유롭고 독립적이지 않다 /

as we thought. 우리가 생각했던 것만큼

Street-level work / that disrupts the infrastructure
거리 수준의 작업이 / 사회 기반 시설에 지장을 주는 /

(the sewer system below or the electrical grid
above) / (하부에 위치한 하수도 체계나 상부에 위치한 전력망)

brings our *shared* dependence into view.
우리의 *공유하는* 의존을 보이게 한다

People may inhabit very different worlds /
사람들은 매우 다른 세상에서 살 수 있다 /

even in the same city, / according to their wealth
or poverty.
심지어 같은 도시에서도 / 자신의 부나 가난에 따라

Yet we all live in the same physical reality, /
하지만 우리는 모두 같은 물리적 현실 속에 산다 /

ultimately, / and owe a common debt to the world.
궁극적으로 / 그리고 세상에 공통의 빚을 지고 있다

우리의 세상이 ① 원활하게 돌아가지 않을 때 수리공을 부르며, 그런 순간에 우리가 대개 당연하게 여겼던 것들(예를 들어, 물이 내려가는 변기)에 대한 우리의 의존성을 분명히 인식하게 된다. 바로 이런 이유로, 수리공의 ② 존재가 자아도취자를 불편하게 만들 수 있다. 그가 더럽다거나 작업이 지저분한 것은 그렇게 문제가 되지 않는다. 오히려, 그는 어쨌거나 뿌리 깊은 우리의 자기 인식에 ③ 도전하는 것 같다. 우리가 생각했던 것만큼 우리는 자유롭고 독립적이지 않다. 사회 기반 시설(하부에 위치한 하수도 체계나 상부에 위치한 전력망)에 지장을 주는 거리 수준의 작업은 우리의 '공유하는' ④ 고립(→의존)을 보이게 한다. 사람들은 심지어 같은 도시에서도 자신의 부나 가난에 따라 매우 다른 세상에서 살 수 있다. 하지만 우리는 모두 궁극적으로 같은 물리적 현실 속에 살며, 세상에 ⑤ 공통의 빚을 지고 있다.

문제풀이

세상에 대한 우리의 의존성에 관한 내용의 글로, 수리공에 대한 의존 및 사회 기반 시설에 지장을 주는 거리 작업의 예를 들며 'We're not as free and independent as we thought.(우리가 생각했던 것만큼 우리는 자유롭고 독립적이지 않다.)'고 이야기하고 있다. 따라서 ④의 'isolation(고립)'을 'dependence(의존)'로 바꿔야 문맥의 흐름이 자연스럽다.

🔑 **이렇게 풀자** _ 밑줄 친 어휘가 문맥상 적절하지 않은 것을 찾는 문제의 경우, 먼저 글의 주제와 흐름을 파악한 뒤, 밑줄 친 어휘가 포함된 문장 전후 문맥을 파악해서 적절하게 쓰였는지를 판단해야 한다. 이 글은, 수리공에 대한 예를 통해 세상에 대한 우리의 의존성에 관해 설명하고 있다.

《 어휘·어구 》

operation 활동
disrupt 방해하다, 지장을 주다
dependence 의존성
normally 보통
take ~ for granted ~을 당연히 여기다
vivid 분명한, 생생한
awareness 인식

---

presence 있음, 존재
messy 지저분한
fundamental 뿌리 깊은, 근본이 되는
infrastructure 사회 기반 시설
sewer system 하수도 체계
isolation 고립
inhabit (특정 지역에) 살다
physical 물리적인
ultimately 궁극적으로
owe a debt 빚을 지다

---

11. ② 시간적 문제로 인해 고고학에서 이윤과 지식을 모두 추구하는 것은 불가능하다

일부 저명한 언론인은 보물 사냥꾼이 과거에 대해 많은 것을 드러낼 수 있는 가치 있는 역사적 유물을 축적해왔기 때문에 고고학자가 보물 사냥꾼과 함께 작업해야 한다고 말한다. 그러나 도굴꾼 또한 가치 있는 역사적 유물을 가지고 있긴 하지만, 고고학자는 도굴꾼과 협력하도록 요구받지는 않는다. 이윤 추구와 지식 탐구는 ① 시간이라는 요인 때문에 고고학에서 공존할 수 없다. 상당히 믿기 어렵겠지만, 보물 탐사 기업에 의해 고용된 한 고고학자는 난파선의 유물이 판매되기 전에 그것들을 연구할 수 있도록 고고학자들에게 6개월이 주어지기만 하면, 어떠한 역사적 지식도 ② 발견되지(→ 사라지지) 않는다고 말했다! 그와는 반대로, 해양고고 연구소(INA)의 고고학자들과 보조원들은 자신들이 발굴한 서기 11세기 난파선의 모든 발굴물의 ③ 목록을 만들 수 있기까지 10여 년의 기간 내내 보존이 필요했다. 그런 다음 그러한 발굴물을 해석하기 위해서 그들은 러시아어, 불가리아어, 그리고 루마니아어를 ④ 배워야만 했는데, 그렇게 하지 않았다면 그들은 유적지의 실체를 결코 알지 못했을 것이다. '상업적인 고고학자'가 발굴물을 팔기 전에 10여 년 정도의 기간을 ⑤ 기다릴 수 있었겠는가?

문제풀이

보물 탐사선 기업에 의해 고용된 고고학자가 난파선의 유물이 판매되기 전에 그것들을 연구할 수 있도록 6개월이 주어지기만 하면 연구를 끝낼 수 있어서 어떠한 역사적 지식도 사라지지 않는다고 말했다는 의미가 되어야 문맥이 자연스러우므로, ② 'found(발견되다)'를 'lost(사라지다)'로 고쳐야 한다.

《 구문 및 어휘 》

*1행 Some prominent journalists say [that archaeologists should work with treasure hunters because treasure hunters have accumulated valuable historical artifacts {that can reveal much about the past}].

⑴ that archaeologists ~ the past는 동사 say의 목적어로 쓰인 명사절이다. say의 목적어절은 「주절(archaeologists should ~)+부사절(because treasure ~)」 구조이다.

⑵ that can reveal ~ the past는 선행사 valuable historical artifacts를 수식하는 관계대명사절이다.

*11행 On the contrary, archaeologists and assistants [from the INA (Institute of Nautical Archaeology)] needed more than a decade of year-round conservation before they could even catalog all the finds from an eleventh-century AD wreck [they had excavated].

⑴ 「주절(archaeologists ~)+부사절(before they ~)」 구조의 문장이다.

⑵ 주절의 주어는 archaeologists and assistants이고

---

needed가 동사이다. from the INA는 archaeologists and assistants를 수식하는 전치사구이다.

⑶ they had excavated는 선행사 an eleventh-century AD wreck을 수식하는 관계대명사절로 앞에 목적격 관계대명사 that[which]이 생략되어 있다.

journalist 언론인, 기자
archaeologist 고고학자
accumulate 축적하다
valuable 소중한, 귀중한
artifact (인공) 유물
reveal 드러내다, 밝히다.
tomb robber 도굴꾼
quest 탐구, 탐색
coexist 공존하다
incredibly 믿기 힘들게도
shipwreck 난파시키다
nautical 해상의, 선박의
year-round 연중 계속되는
conservation 보존
catalog ~의 목록을 만들다
find 발견물
wreck 난파선
interpret 해석하다
true nature 실체

---

12. ② 지역사회 지원 농업 사업

직독/직해

Community supported agriculture (CSA) projects /
지역사회 지원 농업(CSA) 사업은 /

are developing direct links /
직접적인 연계를 발전시키고 있다 /

between groups of member-consumers (often urban) /
회원인 소비자 집단과 (흔히 도시에 있는) /

and their CSA farms. 그들의 지역사회 지원 농업 농장 간의
Restaurant agriculture describes /
음식점 농업은 기술한다 /

a system of production and marketing /
생산 및 마케팅 체계를 /

in which farmers target their products directly to
restaurants.
농업인이 직접 음식점을 대상으로 자신의 제품을 생산하는

New grower-controlled marketing cooperatives are
emerging /
재배자가 통제하는 새로운 마케팅 협동조합들이 등장하고 있다 /

to more effectively tap regional markets.
더 효과적으로 지역 시장을 공략하기 위해

Marketing and trading clubs /
마케팅 및 트레이딩 클럽은 /

are groups of farmers / 농업인들의 집단이다 /
who share marketing information /
마케팅 정보를 공유하는 /

and may withdraw in commodity futures contracts.
그리고 상품의 선물 계약에서 투자할 수도 있는

Agricultural districts organized around particular
commodities /
특정 상품을 중심으로 조직된 농업 지구는 /

(such as wine) / (포도주와 같은) /
have served to stabilize farms and farmland /
농장과 농지를 안정시키는 역할을 해왔다 /

in many areas of the United States.
미국의 많은 지역에서

Community kitchens provide /
공동 주방은 제공한다 /

the infrastructure and technical expertise /
토대와 기술적 전문 지식을 /

necessary to launch new food-based enterprises.

식품에 기반한 새로운 사업을 출범시키는 데 필요한
What all of these efforts have in common /
이런 모든 노력이 가진 공통점은

is their potential / 잠재력이다 /

to nurture local economic development /
지역의 경제 발전을 육성할 수 있는 /

and maintain diversity and quality in products /
그리고 제품의 다양성과 품질을 유지할 수 있는 /

as well as to provide forums /
장을 제공할 뿐만 아니라 /

in which producers and consumers can come together /
생산자와 소비자가 함께 모일 수 있는 /

to solidify bonds of community.
지역사회의 유대를 공고히 할 수 있는

지역사회 지원 농업(CSA) 사업은 (흔히 도시에 있는) 회원인 소비자 집단과 그들의 지역사회 지원 농업 농장 간의 직접적인 연계를 발전시키고 있다. 음식점 농업은 농업인이 ① 직접 음식점을 대상으로 자신의 제품을 생산하는 생산 및 마케팅 체계를 기술한다. 보다 효과적으로 지역 시장을 공략하기 위해 재배자가 통제하는 새로운 마케팅 협동조합이 등장하고 있다. 마케팅 및 트레이딩 클럽은 마케팅 정보를 공유하고 상품의 선물 계약이나 ② 철회할(→ 투자할) 수도 있는 농업인들의 집단이다. (포도주와 같은) 특정 상품을 중심으로 조직된 농업 지구는 미국의 많은 지역에서 농장과 농지를 ③ 안정시키는 역할을 해왔다. 공동 주방은 식품에 기반한 새로운 사업을 출범시키는 데 ④ 필요한 토대와 기술적 전문 지식을 제공한다. 이런 모든 노력이 가진 공통점은 생산자와 소비자가 함께 모여 지역사회의 유대를 ⑤ 공고히 할 수 있는 장을 제공할 뿐만 아니라 지역의 경제 발전을 육성하고 제품의 다양성과 품질을 유지할 수 있는 잠재력이다.

문제풀이

지역사회 지원 농업 사업을 통해 농업인과 소비자의 직접적인 연계를 발전시키고 있고 재배자가 통제하는 새로운 마케팅 협동조합들이 등장하고 있다고 한 것으로 보아, 마케팅 및 트레이딩 클럽을 통해 마케팅 정보를 공유하고 선물 계약이 가능해졌다는 흐름이 되어야 자연스러우므로, ② 'withdraw(철회하다)'를 'invest(투자하다)'와 같은 낱말로 바꿔야 한다.

《 어휘 · 어구 》

agriculture 농업
cooperative 협동조합; 협력하는
emerge 나오다, 생겨나다
withdraw 철수하다, 물러나다
commodity 상품
district 지구, 구역
stabilize 안정시키다
infrastructure 토대, 사회 기반 시설
expertise 전문 지식
launch 착수하다
enterprise 기업, 대규모 사업
potential 잠재력, 가능성
nurture 육성하다, 양성하다
maintain 유지하다
diversity 다양성
solidify 굳히다, 확고히 하다
bond 유대

---

13. 접속사, 전치사

A 출제 POINT
본문 074쪽

1. as   2. study   3. nor
4. whether   5. unless   6. when
7. whatever

1 [해석]▶ 수요가 늘어남에 따라, 가격도 오른다.
[해설]▶ 「according to」는 뒤에 구가 나오고, 「according as」는 뒤에 절이 나온다.

2 [해석]▶ 나는 그 대학에 입학해 Kim 박사님 지도하에 공부하기를 원한다.
[해설]▶ 「주어+동사+ to go~ and (to) study~」 문장 구조이다. 등위접속사(and)가 to부정사와 to부정사를 병렬 구조로 연결하고 있다.

3 [해석]▶ 어떻게 너도 Sam도 나의 파티에 오지 않을 수 있니?
[해설]▶ 상관접속사 neither A nor B는 'A도 B도 아닌'의 의미이다.

4 [해석]▶ 그녀는 여권을 가져가야 할지 말아야 할지 몰랐다.
[해설]▶ 불확실한 내용(didn't know)을 말하고자 할 때 접속사는 whether[if]를 사용한다. whether는 or not과 함께 사용한다.

5 [해석]▶ 만약 당신이 그것을 봉인하지 않는다면, 우체국 직원은 우편을 받아주지 않을 것이다.
[해설]▶ 접속사 unless(~하지 않으면)는 if ~ not의 의미가 있다.

6 [해석]▶ 그는 집에 오자마자, 불평하기 시작했다.
[해설]▶ 「hardly(scarcely) 과거완료 when(before) 과거시제」 구문은 '~하자마자 …하다'는 의미이다.

7 [해석]▶ 무슨 일이 나더라도, 나는 너를 지지하겠다.
[해설]▶ 「의문사+ever」는 양보의 부사절을 이끌 수 있으며, whatever happens는 '무슨 일이 일어나더라도'의 의미이다.

B 체크 POINT
본문 074쪽

1. due to   2. making   3. but
4. Whether   5. Because   6. than
7. Wherever

1 [해석]▶ 폭설 때문에 모든 야외 활동은 취소되었다.
[해설]▶ due to는 '~ 때문에'의 의미를 가지고 있으며 뒤에 구(heavy snow)를 가져온다. because는 뒤에 절이 나온다.

2 [해석]▶ 그는 학교에서 어학 실력을 향상하고 친구를 사귀는 데 집중했다.
[해설]▶ concentrate on+[동명사+접속사(and)+동명사]가 병렬 구조를 이룬 문장이다.

3 [해석]▶ 그들의 영광은 성취에 있지 않고, 희생에 있다.
[해설]▶ not A but B는 'A가 아니라 B'다는 의미이다.

---

4 [해석]▶ 그녀가 올지 안 올지는 확실하지 않다.
[해설]▶ 불확실한 내용을 전달할 때는 접속사 whether를 사용한다.

5 [해석]▶ 모든 것들은 서로 연관되어 있기 때문에, 한 지역의 변화는 다른 지역에 영향을 줄지도 모른다.
[해설]▶ Because 뒤에는 주어, 동사로 이루어진 절이 나오고, Because of 뒤에는 구가 나온다.

6 [해석]▶ 세차를 끝마치자마자 비가 내리기 시작했다.
[해설]▶ no sooner... than ~ 구문은 '…하자마자 ~하다'는 의미이다.

7 [해석]▶ 그녀가 어디를 가더라도, 나는 바로 여기서 그녀를 기다리겠다.
[해설]▶ 「wherever+주어+동사」는 '(주어가) 어디로 ~하더라도'라는 양보의 의미이다.

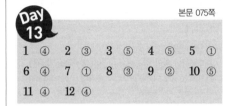
본문 075쪽

1 ④	2 ③	3 ⑤	4 ⑤	5 ①
6 ④	7 ①	8 ③	9 ②	10 ⑤
11 ④	12 ④			

1. ④
세포 주기

직독/직해

Like whole individuals, / cells have a life span.
모든 개체처럼, / 세포도 수명을 가진다

During their life cycle (cell cycle), /
그것의 생애 주기(세포 주기) 동안에 /

cell size, shape, and metabolic activities /
세포의 크기, 모양, 물질대사 활동이 /

can change dramatically.
극적으로 바뀔 수 있다

A cell is "born" as a twin /
세포는 쌍둥이로 태어난다 /

when its mother cell divides, /
모세포가 나눠질 때 /

producing two daughter cells.
두 개의 딸세포를 생성하면서

Each daughter cell is smaller than the mother cell, /
각각의 딸세포는 모세포보다 더 작다 /

and except for unusual cases, / each grows /
그리고 특이한 경우를 제외하고는 / 각각 자란다 /

until it becomes as large as the mother cell was.
모세포의 크기만큼 커질 때까지

During this time, / 이 기간 동안에 /

the cell absorbs water, sugars, amino acids, and other nutrients /
세포는 물, 당, 아미노산, 그리고 다른 영양소들을 흡수한다 /

and assembles them / into new, living protoplasm.
그리고 그것들을 만든다 / 새로운 살아있는 원형질로

After the cell has grown to the proper size, /
세포가 적절한 크기로 자란 후 /

its metabolism shifts / 그것의 물질대사가 변화한다 /

as it either prepares to divide or matures and differentiates into a specialized cell.
그것은 분열할 준비를 하거나 성숙하여 특화된 세포로 분화하면서

Both growth and development require /
성장과 발달 둘 다 요구한다 /

a complex and dynamic set of interactions /
일련의 복잡하고 역동적인 상호 작용을 /

involving all cell parts.
모든 세포 부분을 포함하는

That cell metabolism and structure should be complex /
세포의 물질대사와 구조가 복잡해야 하는 것은 /

would not be surprising, / 놀라운 것이 아니다 /

but actually, they are rather simple and logical.
하지만 실제로 그것들은 아주 간단하고 논리적이다

Even the most complex cell has only a small number of parts, /
가장 복잡한 세포조차도 그저 소수의 부분만을 가지고 있는데 /

each responsible for a distinct, well-defined aspect of cell life.
각각은 세포 생명의 뚜렷하고, 명확한 측면을 맡고 있다

모든 개체처럼, 세포도 수명을 가진다. 그것의 생애 주기(세포 주기) 동안에, 세포의 크기, 모양, 물질대사 활동이 극적으로 바뀔 수 있다. 세포는 모세포가 두 개의 딸세포를 생성하면서 나눠질 때, 쌍둥이로 태어난다. 각각의 딸세포는 모세포보다 더 작고, 특이한 경우를 제외하고는 각각 모세포의 크기만큼 커질 때까지 자란다. 이 기간 동안에 세포는 물, 당, 아미노산, 그리고 다른 영양소들을 흡수하는 새로운 살아있는 원형질로 만든다. 세포가 적절한 크기로 자란 후, 그것은 분열될 준비를 하거나 성숙하여 특화된 세포로 분화하면서 그것의 물질대사가 변화한다. 성장과 발달 둘 다 모든 세포 부분을 포함하는 일련의 복잡하고 역동적인 상호 작용을 요구한다. 세포의 물질대사와 구조가 복잡해야 하는 것은 놀라운 것이 아니겠지만, 실제로 그것들은 아주 간단하고 논리적이다. 가장 복잡한 세포조차도 그저 소수의 부분만을 가지고 있는데, 각각은 세포 생명의 뚜렷하고, 명확한 측면을 맡고 있다.

문제풀이

① **[분사구문]**
분사구문이 와야 하는데, '두 개의 딸세포를 생성하면서'라는 능동의 의미이므로, 현재분사 producing이 온 것은 적절하다.

② **[대동사]**
'컸다(was large)'는 의미의 모세포의 과거 사이즈를 지칭하는 대동사가 와야 하므로, was가 온 것은 적절하다. grows나 becomes를 받아 대동사 did를 사용하는 것은 의미상 적절하지 않다.

③ **[병렬 구조]**
부사절의 동사가 「either A or B(A나 B 둘 중 하나」 구문으로 연결되어 있다. 이때 A와 B는 병렬 구조이고 B에서 두 동사가 and로 연결되어 있으므로 마찬가지로 3인칭 단수형인 differentiates가 온 것은 적절하다.

④ **[접속사 that]**
뒤에 모든 문장 성분을 갖춘 완전한 문장이 왔으므로, what은 적절하지 않다. 주어로 쓰인 명사절을 이끄는 접속사가 와야 하므로, what을 접속사 that으로 바꿔야 한다.

⑤ **[분사구문]**
분사구문 each being responsible …에서 being이 생략되어 responsible이 온 것은 적절하다.

○ 이렇게 풀자 어법상 틀린 부분을 찾는 문제는 밑줄이 있는 부분의 형태와 문맥을 보고 어법에 맞게 쓰였는지 확인해야 한다.
① 분사구문에서 의미상 주어와의 관계가 능동일 때 현재분사가 와야 하고, 수동일 때 과거분사가 와야 한다.
② be동사 뒤에 보어나 전치사구가 없다면 대동사일 가능성이 높다. 대동사는 be동사를 받으면 be동사를 시제와 인칭에 맞게 쓰고 일반동사를 받으면 do를 시제와 인칭에 맞게 써야 한다.
③ 「either A or B」 구문에서 A와 B의 문법적 형태가 같아야 한다.
④ what 뒤에는 주어나 목적어가 빠진 불완전한 문장이 와야 하므로, 뒤에 온 문장이 성분을 모두 갖추고 있는지 확인해야 한다.
⑤ 분사구문에서 being은 생략될 수 있다.

《 어휘·어구 》

individual 개인, 개체
life span 수명
dramatically 극적으로
absorb 흡수하다

---

amino acid 아미노산
assemble 조립하다
nutrient 영양소
proper 적절한
metabolism 물질대사
mature 성숙하다
differentiate 분화하다
logical 논리적인
distinct 뚜렷한
well-defined 명확한

---

2. ③ 의사소통이 작동하는 방식

직독/직해

Accepting whatever others are communicating /
타인이 전달하고 있는 것이 무엇이든 그것을 받아들이는 것은 /

only pays off / ~만 성공한다 /

if their interests correspond to ours /
그들의 이익이 우리의 것과 일치할 때에 /

— think cells in a body, bees in a beehive.
체내의 세포, 벌집 속의 벌을 생각해 보라

As far as communication between humans is concerned, /
인간들 사이의 의사소통에 관한 한 /

such commonality of interests is rarely achieved; /
이익의 그러한 공통성은 좀처럼 이루어지지 않는데 /

even a pregnant mother has reasons /
심지어 임신한 어머니도 이유가 있다 /

to mistrust the chemical signals /
화학적 신호를 믿지 않을 /

sent by her fetus. 태아가 보내는

Fortunately, / 다행히도 /

there are ways of making communication work /
의사소통이 작동하도록 할 수 있는 방법이 있다 /

even in the most adversarial of relationships.
가장 적대적인 관계에서도

A prey can convince a predator / not to chase it.
먹잇감은 포식자를 설득할 수 있다 / 자신을 뒤쫓지 말도록

But for such communication to occur, /
하지만 그러한 의사소통이 일어나기 위해서는 /

there must be strong guarantees /
강력한 보장이 있어야 한다 /

that those who receive the signal /
신호를 받는 자가 /

will be better off believing it.
그것을 믿는 것이 더 좋을 것이라는

The messages have to be kept, / on the whole, /
메시지는 유지되어야만 한다 / 전체적으로 /

honest. 정직한 상태로

In the case of humans, / 인간의 경우에는 /

honesty is maintained by a set of cognitive mechanisms /
정직함은 일련의 인지 기제에 의해 유지된다 /

that evaluate communicated information.
전달된 정보를 평가하는

These mechanisms allow us /
이런 기제는 우리가 ~하게 해 준다 /

to accept most beneficial messages — to be open /
가장 유익한 메시지를 받아들이게(개방적이면서) /

— while rejecting most harmful messages — to be vigilant.
반면에 가장 해로운 메시지를 거부할(경계할) 수 있게 (해 준다)

타인이 전달하고 있는 것이 무엇이든 그것을 받아들이는 것은 그들의 이익이 우리의 것과 일치할 때에만 성공하는데, 체내의 세포, 벌집 속의 벌을 생각해 보라. 인간들 사이의 의사소통에 관한 한, 이익의 그러한 공통성은 좀처럼 이루어지지 않는데, 심지어 임신한 어머니도 태아가 보내는 화학적 신호를 믿지 않을 이유가 있다. 다행히도, 가장 적대적인 관계에서도 의사소통이 작동하도록 할 수 있는 방법이 있다. 먹잇감은 포식자에게 자신을 뒤쫓지 말도록 설득할 수 있다. 하지만 그러한 의사소통이 일어나기 위해서는, 신호를 받는 자가 그것을 믿는 것이 더 좋을 것이라는 강력한 보장이 있어야 한다. 메시지는 전체적으로 정직한 상태로 유지되어야만 한다. 인간의 경우에는 정직함은 전달된 정보를 평가하는 일련의

인지 기제에 의해 유지된다. 이런 기제는 우리가 가장 유익한 메시지를 받아들이며(개방적이면서), 반면에 가장 해로운 메시지를 거부할(경계할) 수 있게 해 준다.

문제풀이

① **[주어–동사 수일치]**
commonality가 주어이고 of interests는 주어 commonality를 수식하는 전치사구이다. 따라서 단수 주어에 맞춰 is가 온 것은 적절하다.

② **[대명사]**
앞에 나온 A prey를 가리키면서 chase의 목적어로 쓰인 대명사가 와야 하므로, it이 온 것은 적절하다.

③ **[동격의 접속사 that]**
뒤에 모든 문장 성분을 갖춘 완전한 문장이 왔고 **strong guarantees**와 동격인 명사절을 이끄는 접속사가 와야 하므로, **which**를 접속사 **that**으로 바꾸어야 한다.

④ **[목적격보어]**
수동태로 전환되기 이전에 동사 keep의 목적격보어로 형용사가 와야 하므로, honest가 온 것은 적절하다.

⑤ **[과거분사]**
'전달된'이라는 수동의 의미로 명사 information을 수식하는 과거분사가 와야 하므로, communicated가 온 것은 적절하다.

○ 이렇게 풀자 어법상 틀린 부분을 찾는 문제는 밑줄이 있는 부분의 형태와 문맥을 보고 어법에 맞게 쓰였는지 확인해야 한다.
① 동사에 밑줄이 있는 경우, 주어와 동사의 수일치를 묻는 문제인 경우가 많다. 특히 관계대명사절 및 전치사구와 같은 수식어구 또는 삽입절이 주어와 동사 사이에 위치해 있는 경우, 주어가 무엇인지를 분명히 파악해야 동사가 알맞게 쓰였는지 알 수 있다.
② 대명사가 쓰인 경우, 앞 문장이나 절에서 가리키는 명사를 찾아서 수가 일치하는지, 문법에 맞는 격이 사용되었는지 확인한다.
③ that은 주어, 목적어, 보어 역할을 하는 명사절을 이끄는 접속사로 쓰일 수 있고, 또한 동격의 명사절을 이끌기도 한다. that에 밑줄이 그어져 있을 경우, 명사절을 이끄는 접속사로 쓰인 것이 아닌지 판단하려면 뒤에 모든 문장 성분을 갖춘 완전한 절이 왔는지를 확인하면 된다.
④ 동사의 종류에 따라 목적격 보어로 to부정사가 오기도 하고 동사원형이 오기도 한다. 앞에 나온 동사를 잘 파악하여 어법에 맞는지 판단해야 한다.
⑤ 분사가 명사를 수식할 경우, 수동의 의미일 경우 과거분사가 오고 능동의 의미일 경우 현재분사가 온다.

《 어휘·어구 》

pay off 성공하다
correspond to ~과 일치하다, ~에 상응하다
beehive 벌집
as far as ~하는 한
commonality 공통성
pregnant 임신한
chemical 화학의, 화학적인
convince 설득하다
prey 먹잇감
predator 포식자
chase 쫓다
guarantee 보장
maintain 유지하다
cognitive 인지의
mechanism 기제
evaluate 평가하다
beneficial 이로운

3. ⑤   자기를 실험하는 것의 장점과 단점

직독/직해

Regulations covering scientific experiments on human subjects /
인간 피험자들에 관한 과학 실험을 다루는 규제는 /

are strict. 엄격하다

Subjects must give their informed, written consent, /
피험자는 충분한 설명에 입각한 서면 동의를 해야 한다 /

and experimenters must submit their proposed experiments /
그리고 실험자는 자신들의 계획된 실험을 제출해야 한다 /

to thorough examination / by overseeing bodies.
철저한 정밀 조사를 받아야 한다   감독 기관에 의한

Scientists who experiment on themselves /
자기 자신을 실험하는 과학자들은 /

can, functionally if not legally, / avoid the restrictions /
법률상으로는 아니지만 직무상으로는   규제를 피할 수 있다 /

associated with experimenting on other people.
다른 사람들을 실험하는 것과 관련된

They can also sidestep most of the ethical issues involved: /
그들은 또한 관련된 윤리적인 문제도 대부분 피할 수 있는데 /

nobody, presumably, is more aware of an experiment's potential hazards /
그것의 잠재적인 위험을 더 잘 알고 있는 사람은 짐작건대 없을 것이기 때문이다 /

than the scientist who devised it.
실험을 고안한 과학자보다

Nonetheless, / 그렇기는 하지만 /

experimenting on oneself remains deeply problematic.
자신을 실험하는 것은 여전히 문제가 많다

One obvious drawback is the danger involved; /
한 가지 분명한 문제점은 (실험에) 수반되는 위험인데 /

knowing that it exists /
그것이 존재한다는 것을 아는 것이 /

does nothing to reduce it.
그것을 줄이기 위해 어떤 일을 하는 것은 아니다

A less obvious drawback /
이보다 덜 분명한 문제점은 /

is the limited range of data /
제한된 범위의 데이터이다 /

that the experiment can generate.
실험이 만들어낼 수 있는

Human anatomy and physiology vary, /
인체의 해부학적 구조와 생리적 현상은 각기 다르며 /

in small but significant ways, /
사소하지만 의미 있는 방식으로 /

according to gender, age, lifestyle, and other factors.
성별, 나이, 생활 방식과 기타 요인에 따라

Experimental results derived from a single subject are, /
단 한 명의 피험자로부터 얻어진 실험 결과는 /

therefore, / 그러므로 /

of limited value; / there is no way to know /
가치가 제한적이며 / 알 방법이 없다 /

whether the subject's responses are typical or atypical /
그 피험자의 반응이 대표하는 것인지 아니면 이례적인 것인지 /

of the response of humans as a group.
집단으로서의 인간 반응을

인간 피험자들에 관한 과학 실험을 다루는 규제는 엄격하다. 피험자는 충분한 설명에 입각한 서면 동의를 해야 하고, 실험자는 자신들의 계획된 실험을 제출해 감독 기관에 의한 철저한 정밀 조사를 받아야 한다. 자기 자신을 실험하는 과학자들은, 법률상으로는 아니지만, 직무상으로는 다른 사람들을 실험하는 것과 관련된 규제를 피할 수 있다. 그들은 또한 관련된 윤리적인 문제도 대부분 피할 수 있는데, 실험을 고안한 과학자보다 그것의 잠재적인 위험을 더 잘 알고 있는 사람은 짐작건대 없을 것이기 때문이다. 그렇기는 하지만, 자신을 실험하는 것은 여전히 문제가 많다. 한 가지 분명한 문제점은 (실험에) 수반되는 위험인데, 위험이 존재한다는 것을 아는 것이 위험을 줄이기 위해 어떤 일을 하는 것은 아니다. 이보다 덜 분명한 문제점은 실험이 만들어낼 수 있는 제한된 범위의 데이터이다. 인체의 해부학적 구조와 생리적 현상은 성별, 나이, 생활 방식과 기타 요인에 따라 사소하지만, 의미 있는 방식으로 각기 다르다. 그러므로, 단 한 명의 피험자로부터 얻어진 실험 결과는 가치가 제한적이며, 그 피험자의 반응이 집단으로서의 인간 반응을 대표하는 것인지 아니면 이례적인 것인지 알 방법이 없다.

문제풀이

① [과거분사]
'관련된'이라는 수동의 의미로 명사 the restrictions를 수식하는 과거분사가 와야 하므로, associated가 온 것은 적절하다.

② [대명사]
앞의 명사 an experiment를 가리키면서 동사 devised의 목적어로 사용되었으므로, 대명사 it이 온 것은 적절하다.

③ [부사]
형용사 problematic을 수식하는 부사로, deeply가 온 것은 적절하다.

④ [주어와 동사의 수일치]
주어가 Knowing that it exists로 동명사구이므로, 단수동사가 와야 한다. 따라서 does가 온 것은 적절하다.

⑤ [관계대명사 what]
밑줄 친 what이 이끄는 절이 모든 문장 성분을 갖춘 완전한 문장이므로, 관계대명사 what이 들어가는 것은 적절하지 않다. 문맥상 '~인지 아닌지'의 의미이므로, 접속사 **whether**로 고쳐 써야 한다.

◐ 이렇게 풀자 ① 분사가 명사를 수식할 경우, 수동의 의미일 경우 과거분사가 오고 능동의 의미일 경우 현재분사가 온다.
② 대명사가 쓰인 경우, 앞 문장이나 절에서 가리키는 명사를 찾아서 대명사의 수가 일치하는지, 문법에 맞는 대명사의 격이 사용되었는지 확인한다.
③ 부사는 동사의 앞이나 뒤에서 동사를 수식하거나 문장의 앞뒤에서 문장 전체를 수식할 수 있으며, 또한 형용사나 다른 부사를 수식할 수 있다.
④ 동사에 밑줄이 있는 경우, 주어와 동사의 수일치를 묻는 문제인 경우가 많다. 주어가 동명사구인 경우 단수동사가 와야 한다.
⑤ 관계대명사 what 뒤에는 주어나 목적어가 빠져 있는 불완전한 문장이 온다. 특히 관계대명사 what은 선행사를 포함하고 있으므로 문장에 선행사가 없어야 하며, 관계대명사절에서 주어나 목적어, 보어로 사용되어야 한다.

《 어휘·어구 》

regulation 규제
subject 대상, 피험자
strict 엄격한
submit 제출하다
proposed 제안된
rigorous 철저한, 엄격한
oversee 감독하다
functionally 기능적으로, 직무상으로
legally 법률적으로, 합법적으로
restriction 규제, 제한
associated with ~와 관련된
sidestep 피하다
ethical 윤리적인
presumably 짐작건대, 아마
potential 잠재적인
hazard 위험
devise 고안하다, 생각해 내다
drawback 문제점, 결점
derive from ~에서 얻다
typical 전형적인
atypical 이례적인

4. ⑤   기아의 가치

직독/직해

Not all organisms are able to find sufficient food to survive, /
모든 유기체가 생존에 충분한 먹이를 구할 수 있는 것은 아니다 /

so starvation is a kind of disvalue often found in nature.
그래서 기아는 자연에서 흔히 발견되는 일종의 반(反)가치이다

It also is part of the process of selection /
그것은 또한 선택 과정의 일부이기도 하다 /

by which biological evolution functions.
(그것에 의해) 생물학적 진화가 기능하게 되는

Starvation helps filter out those less fit to survive, /
기아는 살아남기에 덜 적합한 것들을 걸러 내는 데 도움을 준다 /

those less resourceful in finding food /
먹이를 찾는 것에 수완이 모자란 /

for themselves and their young.
자신과 자신의 새끼들을 위한

In some circumstances, / 몇몇 상황에서 /

it may pave the way / for genetic variants /
그것은 길을 열어 줄지도 모른다 / 유전적 변형체가 /

to take hold in the population of a species /
종의 개체군을 장악하도록 /

and eventually allow the emergence of a new
그리고 결국에는 새로운 종이 출현하도록 해 줄지도 (모른다) /

species / in place of the old one.
/ 이전의 종을 대신하여

Thus starvation is a disvalue /
따라서 기아는 반가치이다 /

that can help make possible the good of greater diversity.
더 큰 다양성이라는 선(善)이 가능하도록 도울 수 있는

Starvation can be of practical or instrumental value, /
기아는 유용한, 즉 도구적 가치를 지닐 수 있다 /

even as it is an intrinsic disvalue.
/ 내재적 반가치인 동시에

That some organisms must starve in nature /
몇몇 유기체들이 자연에서 기아를 겪어야 한다는 것은 /

is deeply regrettable and sad.
매우 유감스럽고 슬픈 것이다

The statement remains implacably true, /
그 말은 여전히 확고히 진실이다 /

even though starvation also may sometimes
기아가 때로 목적에 공헌할 수도 있기는 하지만 /

subserve ends / that are good.
/ 좋은

모든 유기체가 생존에 충분한 먹이를 구할 수 있는 것은 아니어서, 기아는 자연에서 흔히 발견되는 일종의 반(反)가치이다. 그것은 또한 생물학적 진화가 기능하게 되는 선택 과정의 일부이기도 하다. 기아는 살아남기에 덜 적합한 것들, 즉 자신과 자신의 새끼들을 위한 먹이를 찾는 것에 수완이 모자란 것들을 걸러 내는 데 도움을 준다. 몇몇 상황에서 기아는 유전적 변형체가 종의 개체군을 장악하도록 길을 열어 주고 결국에는 이전의 종을 대신하여 새로운 종이 출현하도록 해 줄지도 모른다. 따라서 기아는 더 큰 다양성이라는 선(善)이 가능하도록 도울 수 있는 반가치이다. 기아는 내재적 반가치인 동시에 유용한, 즉 도구적 가치를 지닐 수 있다. 몇몇 유기체들이 자연에서 기아를 겪어야 한다는 것은 매우 유감스럽고 슬픈 것이다. 기아가 때로 좋은 목적에 공헌할 수도 있기는 하지만, 그 말은 여전히 확고히 진실이다.

문제풀이

① by which 이하는 선행사 the process of selection을 수식하는 관계대명사절이므로 관계대명사 which가 오는 것은 맞고, '선택의 과정에 의해 기능한다(functions by the process of selection)'라는 뜻으로 쓰여서 의미상으로도 전치사 by가 온 것은 적절하다.
② those less resourceful을 가리키는 대명사가 와야 하는데, 동일한 대상을 가리키므로 재귀대명사 themselves가 온 것은 적절하다.
③ 앞의 명사 the way를 수식하는 형용사적 용법의 to부정사로 to take가 온 것은 적절하다.
④ 동사 make의 목적어(the good of greater diversity)가 길어서 목적어와 목적보어(possible)가 도치된 형태로, 목적보어로 형용사 possible이 온 것은 적절하다.
⑤ 밑줄 친 what 뒤의 절 some ~ starve in nature는 동사 is의 주어 역할을 하는 명사절로, 완전한

문장이므로 관계대명사 what이 아니라 명사절을 이끄는 접속사 that이 와야 한다.

❖ **이렇게 풀자**_ 어법상 틀린 부분을 찾는 문제는 밑줄이 있는 부분의 형태와 문맥을 보고 어법에 맞게 쓰였는지 확인해야 한다. ① 「전치사+관계대명사」의 역할을, ② 재귀대명사의 쓰임을, ③ to부정사의 역할을, ④ 목적보어의 형태를, ⑤ 접속사 that과 관계대명사 what의 쓰임을 알아야 한다.

《 어휘 · 어구 》

organism 유기체
sufficient 충분한
starvation 기아
disvalue 부정적 가치, 반(反)가치
biological 생물학의
evolution 진화, 발전
filter out ~을 걸러 내다
resourceful 지략 있는, 수완이 좋은
pave the way 길을 열어 주다
genetic 유전의
variant 변종, 이형
take hold 장악하다
in place of ~을 대신하여
practical 현실적인, 실제적인
intrinsic 내재적인
regrettable 유감스러운
statement 진술, 말

---

5. ①   의뢰인의 정보 비밀 보장

법적 조언을 구하는 사람들은, 그들의 권리나 의무를 변호사와 논의할 때, 후자(변호사)가 받은 정보를 제삼자에게 누설하지 않을 것을 보장받아야 한다. 이런 비밀 유지 의무가 준수될 경우에만, 사람들은 자유롭게 변호사와 상담하고, 변호사가 의뢰인의 변호를 준비하는 데 필요한 정보를 제공할 것이다. (의뢰인이) 공개하는 정보의 종류와 관계없이, 의뢰인은 그것(정보)이 당국에 의해서나 어떤 다른 당사자에 의해 법정에서 자신에게 불리하게 사용되지 않을 것을 확신해야 한다. 그것은 일반적으로 법률 제도가 제대로 기능하기 위한 조건으로, 따라서 공익에 맞는 것으로 여겨진다. 변호사의 비밀 유지 특권은 통상 증거법보다 훨씬 이상의 것으로, 특정 소송의 사실에 한정되어 적용된다. 그것은 법의 집행이 전체적으로 기초를 두고 있는 기본 조건이다.

문제풀이

① which 뒤에 주어(the latter)와 동사(will not disclose), 목적어(the information provided)가 있는 완전한 절이 이어지고 있고, 문장에서 assured의 목적어 역할을 해야 하므로, 관계대명사 which는 접속사 that으로 고쳐야 한다.
② 부사 Only가 강조를 위해 문두로 나가면서 주어와 동사가 도치된 형태인 will people feel free to consult가 쓰였다.
③ 정보가 '공개되는' 것이므로 수동의 의미를 지닌 과거분사 disclosed는 어법상 적절하게 쓰였다.
④ 비교급 앞에 쓰여 비교급을 수식하여 '훨씬'이라는 의미를 갖는 much는 어법상 적절하게 쓰였다.
⑤ on which가 이끄는 관계대명사절에서, 주어인 the administration of justice에 맞는 동사로 rests는 적절하게 쓰였다.

《 구문 및 어휘 》

*1행 **People** [seeking legal advice] **should be assured**, [when discussing their rights or obli-gations with a lawyer], [that the latter will not disclose to third parties the information provided].
⑴ [seeking legal advice]는 문장의 주어인 People을 수식하는 현재분사구이고, 동사는 should be assured 이다.
⑵ [when discussing their rights or obligations with a lawyer]는 시간의 의미를 나타내는 접속사 when이 이끄는 부사절로, when과 discussing 사이에 주어와 be동사인 they are가 생략되었다.
⑶ [that the latter will not disclose to third parties the information provided]는 assured의 목적어 역할을 하는 명사절이다.
⑷ the latter는 a lawyer를 가리킨다.

*4행 **Only** if this duty of confidentiality is respected **will people feel free to consult** lawyers and provide the information [required for the lawyer to prepare the client's defense].
⑴ 부사 Only가 강조를 위해 문두로 나가면서 주어와 동사가 도치된 형태인 will people feel free to consult 가 쓰였다.
⑵ 「feel free to부정사」는 '마음껏 ~하다'라는 의미를 나타내는 표현으로, feel free to consult와 (feel free to) provide가 접속사 and로 병렬 연결되었다.
⑶ [required for the lawyer to prepare the client's defense]는 the information을 수식하는 과거분사구이다.

assure 보장하다
obligation 의무
disclose 밝히다, 드러내다
defense 변호
regardless of ~에 상관없이
authority 당국
legal professional privilege 변호사의 비밀 유지 특권
fundamental 기본적인
the administration of justice 법의 집행

---

6. ④   자동차가 더 안전해 지고 있는 이유

직독 직해

Do you think / the new or used vehicle /
당신은 생각하는가? / 신차, 혹은 중고차가 /
you are purchasing / is safe?
구매하려고 하는 / 안전하다고
Since the introduction of automotive crash-testing, /
자동차 충돌 시험이 도입된 이후로, /
the number of people killed and injured by motor vehicles
차량 사고로 사망하거나 부상당하는 사람들의 수가
has decreased in many countries.
많은 나라에서 감소해 왔다.
Obviously, / it would be ideal / to have no car crashes.
분명, / 이상적이다 / 차량 충돌이 발생하지 않는 것
However, / car crashes are a reality /
하지만 / 충돌사고는 현실이며 /
and you want the best possible chance of survival.
당신은 생존할 가능성이 최대한 높기를 바란다.
How are cars becoming safer?
자동차들은 어떻게 점점 더 안전해지고 있는가?
One of the reasons / cars have been getting safer /
이유 중 하나는 / 자동차가 더 안전해지고 있는 /
is that we can conduct / 우리가 실시할 수 있다는 것이다. /
a well-established crash test / with test dummies.
안정된 충돌 시험을 / 시험 인형으로
The dummy's job is / to simulate a human being /
충돌 시험 인형의 임무는 / 인간의 역할을 대신하는 것이다.
during a crash, / collecting data /
충돌 도중 / 데이터를 수집하면서 /
that would not be possible to collect from a human occupant.
인간으로부터는 수집할 수 없는
So far, / they have provided invaluable data on /
지금까지 / 그들은 귀중한 자료를 제공해 왔고
how human bodies react in crashes /
충돌에서 인간의 신체가 어떻게 반응하는지에 대한
and have contributed greatly /
큰 공헌을 해왔다. /
to improved vehicle design.
개선된 차량 설계에

당신이 구매하려고 하는 신차, 혹은 중고차가 안전하다고 생각하는가? 자동차 충돌 시험이 도입된 이후로, 차량 사고로 사망하거나 부상당하는 사람들의 수가 많은 나라에서 감소해 왔다. 분명, 차량 충돌이 발생하지 않는 것이 이상적이다. 하지만 충돌사고는 현실이고 당신은 생존할 가능성이 최대한 높기를 바란다. 자동차들은 어떻게 점점 더 안전해지고 있는가? 자동차가 더 안전해지고 있는 이유 중 하나는 우리가 충돌 시험 인형으로 안정된 시험을 실시할 수 있다는 것이다. 충돌 시험 인형의 임무는 충돌 도중 인간으로부터는 수집할 수 없는 데이터를 수집하면서 인간의 역할을 대신하는 것이다. 그들은 지금까지 충돌에서 인간의 신체가 어떻게 반응하는지에 대한 귀중한 자료를 제공해 왔고, 개선된 차량 설계에 큰 공헌을 해왔다.

문제풀이

while은 접속사이므로 명사인 a crash 앞에는 전치사 during이 적절하다. 따라서 어법에 맞지 않는 것은 ④이다.

《 어휘 · 어구 》

purchase 구매하다
crash 충돌; 추락
injure 부상당하다
decrease 감소하다
well-established 안정된, 정착된
simulate 모방하다
provide 제공하다

---

7. ①   불의 형태를 정의하기는 어렵다

직독 직해

It is difficult / to determine the shape of fire.
어렵다. / 불의 형태를 결정하는 것은
There is a simplified design, /
단순화된 디자인이 있다. /
adopted for use in posters and signs.
포스터와 표지에 사용하기 위해 채택된
It resembles / 그것은 닮았다. /
three upright tongues or a lotus flower.
세 개의 똑바로 선 혀나 연꽃을
The design is a typical symbol of fire.
그 디자인은 불의 전형적인 상징이다.
However, / the shape of fire is hard to define.
그러나 / 불의 형태를 정의 내리기는 어렵다.
In reality, / fire comes in many forms /
실제로 / 불은 많은 형태로 나타난다. /
like candle flame, charcoal fire, and torch light.
초의 불꽃, 숯불, 횃불과 같은
The various nature of the shape of fire is evident /
불의 형태의 다양한 속성은 명백히 나타나 있다. /
in many words / Koreans use /
많은 단어에 / 한국 사람들이 사용하는 /
to describe fire and its shape and movements.
불과 그것의 형태와 움직임을 묘사하기 위해서
For instance, / iggle-iggle is an adverb /
예를 들면 / '이글이글'은 부사이지만 /
that describes a fire burning, /
불이 타는 것을 묘사하는 /

불이 타는 모습을 묘사하는
but it focuses on the heat / 열기에 초점을 둔다. /
rather than the shape of the flame,
불꽃의 형태보다는
while hwal-hwal or hweol-hweol brings to mind flames that soar, /
반면에 '활활' 또는 '휠휠'은 치솟는 불꽃을 연상시킨다.
as if to rise to the heavens **마치 하늘로 올라가는 것처럼**

불의 형태를 결정하는 것은 어렵다. 포스터와 표지에 사용하기 위해 채택된 단순화된 디자인이 있다. 그것은 세 개의 똑바로 선 혀나 연꽃을 닮았다. 그 디자인은 불의 전형적인 상징이다. 그러나 불의 형태를 정의 내리기는 어렵다. 실제로 불은 초의 불꽃, 숯불, 횃불과 같은 많은 형태로 나타난다. 불의 형태의 다양한 속성은 한국 사람들이 불과 그것의 형태와 움직임을 묘사하기 위해 사용하는 많은 단어에 명백히 나타나 있다. 예를 들면 '이글이글'은 불이 타는 모습을 묘사하는 부사이지만 불꽃의 형태보다는 열기에 초점을 둔다. 반면에 '활활' 또는 '휠휠'은 마치 하늘로 올라가는 것처럼 치솟는 불꽃을 연상시킨다.

문제풀이

(A)에는 design과 adopt의 관계가 수동이므로 과거분사 adopted가 맞다. (B)에는 목적어를 수반하는 전치사 like가 맞다. alike는 형용사이다. (C)에는 '반면에'의 의미를 나타내며 부사절을 이끄는 접속사 while이 적합하다. 따라서 어법에 맞는 것은 ①이다.

《 어휘 · 어구 》
difficult 어려운
simplified 단순화된
resemble ~을 닮다
charcoal 숯
bring to mind 연상시키다
describe 묘사하다

8.③ 예술의 역할과 소통적 특성

직독/직해

Unquestionably, / 의심할 여지없이, /
the arts play a significant role in any society.
어떤 사회에서나 예술은 중요한 역할을 한다.
They can be used / 그것은 사용될 수 있다. /
to commemorate events or individuals.
사건이나 사람을 기념하기 위해서
Or they often teach moral lessons or values /
혹은 그것은 종종 도덕적인 교훈이나 가치를 가르쳐 주기도 하고 /
considered important in a society /
사회에서 중요하다고 여겨지는 /
and are also used to send political messages /
정치적 메시지를 전달하거나 이용되기도 한다. /
or draw attention to social issues.
사회적 문제에 대한 관심을 불러일으키기 위해서
Yet / the question is posed /
하지만 / 문제가 대두된다. /
whether the arts should reflect society's standards /
예술이 사회의 기준을 반영해야 하는지 /
or question them.
아니면 그에 대한 의문을 제기해야 하는지에 대한
Art and artists are also severely criticized /
예술과 예술가는 또한 신랄한 비난을 받는다. /
for being elitist, / 엘리트주의라는 /
for not making art / 예술을 만들어내지 않는다는 /
that would appeal to ordinary people.
즉 일반 대중의 마음을 끄는
It is because of their communicative properties /
바로 예술의 소통적 특성 때문이다. /
that intense debates continue /
뜨거운 논쟁이 계속되는 이유는 /
over the true role of the arts in today's world.
오늘날의 세계에서 예술의 올바른 역할에 대한

의심할 여지없이, 어떤 사회에서나 예술은 중요한 역할을 한다. 그것은 사건이나 사람을 기념하기 위해서 사용될 수 있다. 혹은 그것은 종종 사회에서 중요하다고 여겨지는 도덕적인 교훈이나 가치를 가르쳐 주기도 하고 정치적 메시지를 전달하거나 사회적 문제에 대한 관심을 불러일으키기 위해서 이용되기도 한다. 하지만 예술이 사회의 기준을 반영해야 하는지 아니면 그에 대한 의문을 제기해야 하는지에 대한 문제가 대두된다. 예술과 예술가는 또한 엘리트주의라는, 즉 일반 대중의 마음을 끄는 예술을 만들어내지 않는다는 신랄한 비난을 받는다. 오늘날의 세계에서 예술의 올바른 역할에 대한 뜨거운 논쟁이 계속되는 이유는 바로 예술의 소통적 특성 때문이다.

문제풀이

(A) morel lessons or values (where are) considered important ~ 문장으로 「관계대명사+be동사」가 생략되었다.
(B) 괄호 뒷부분의 문장이 완전하며, '~해야 하는지 아니면 ~하는지에 대한'의 의미이므로 접속사 whether가 필요하다.
(C) It is ~ that 강조 구문으로서 because of their communicative properties를 강조하고 있다. because는 뒤에 절이 나오고, because of는 뒤에 구가 나오는데, their communicative properties라는 명사구가 나왔으므로 because of를 사용해야 한다.

《 어휘 · 어구 》
significant 중요한
commemorte 기념하다
moral lessons 도덕적 교훈
vlaues 가치
criticize 비난하다
appeal (to) 흥미를 일으키다
communicative 소통적인
property 특성

9.② 독자 참여를 위해 작가가 행하는 방법

언론과는 완전히 다른 문학에서, 가장 유능한 작가들은 절대 이야기의 기본 뼈대가 자신들의 독자를 설득하기에 (A) 충분할 수 있다고 생각하지 않을 것이다. 그들은 폭행이나 홍수, 혹은 절도가 독자를 적절히 감동하게 하거나 격분하게 할 어느 정도의 내재적 흥미를 그 자체에 반드시 지니고 있다고 생각하지 않을 것이다. 이런 작가들은 아무리 충격적이라 할지라도, 어떤 사건도 (B) 참여를 전혀 보장할 수 없다는 것을 알고 있다. 이 후자의 목적(독자의 참여)을 위해서, 그들은 자기들의 독특한 기술을 숙련하면서 더 열심히 작업해야 하는데, 그것은 언어에 주의를 기울이고 속도와 구성을 엄격하게 통제하는 것을 의미한다. 어떤 상황에서는, 창의적인 작가들이 심지어 엄격한 정확성을 (C) 희생하는 선택을 할 수도 있는데, 그렇게 함으로써 범죄 행위를 감행하고 있다고 느끼기보다는 오히려, 그 대신에 정확성보다 훨씬 더 높은 목표를 위해서 때때로 변조가 행해져야 할 필요가 있을지도 모른다고 이해할 것이다.

문제풀이

(A) 언론과는 달리, 유능한 작가들은 이야기의 기본 뼈대가 독자들을 설득하기에 충분하다고 생각하지 않는다는 내용이 문맥상 자연스러우므로, (A)에는 'enough(충분한)'가 적절하다.
(B) 폭행, 홍수, 절도와 같이 아무리 충격적인 사건이라도 그 자체에 내재적 흥미를 반드시 지니고 있다고 생각하지 않기 때문에, 그것들로는 독자들의 참여를 보장할 수 없다는 것을 알 수 있으므로, (B)에는 'involvement(참여)'가 적절하다.
(C) 창의적인 작가들은 정확성보다 훨씬 더 높은 목표를 위해 때때로 변조가 행해져야 할 필요를 느낄 수도

있다는 것은 엄격한 정확성을 희생하는 것이므로, (C)에는 'sacrifice(희생하다)'가 적절하다.

《 구문 및 어휘 》

*3행 They will not suppose [that an attack or a flood or a theft must in and of itself carry **some intrinsic degree of interest** {which will cause the reader to be appropriately moved or outraged}].
⑴ that이 이끄는 절은 suppose의 목적어 역할을 하는 명사절이다.
⑵ in and of itself는 '그거 자체는'이라는 의미를 나타내는 표현이다.
⑶ {which will cause the reader to be appropriately moved or outraged}는 some intrinsic degree of interest를 수식하는 주격 관계대명사절이다.
⑷ 「cause A to부정사」는 'A가 ~하게 하다[원인이 되다]'라는 의미를 나타내는 표현이다.

*11행 In certain situations, creative writers may even choose to sacrifice strict accuracy, and **rather than** feel [that they are thereby carrying out a criminal act], they will instead understand [that falsifications may occasionally need to be committed in the service of a goal higher still than accuracy].
⑴ rather than은 '~보다는[대신에]'라는 의미를 나타내는 표현이다.
⑵ [that they are thereby carrying out a criminal act]는 feel의 목적어 역할을 하는 명사절이다.
⑶ [that falsifications may occasionally need to be committed in the service of a goal higher still than accuracy]는 understand의 목적어 역할을 하는 명사절이다.

distinct from ~와는 완전히 다른
win over 설득하다
audience 청중, 독자
intrinsic 내재한
be outraged 분노하다
guarantee 보장하다
distinctive 독특한
keep a tight rein 엄격하게 통제하다
strict accuracy 완전한 정확성
falsification 위조, 변조
occasionally 가끔, 때때로

10.⑤ 영화에서의 연기가 부자연스럽다고 느끼지 않는 이유

왜 영화의 '순전한' 연기가 결국 실제 현실에서 표현이 다소 불분명한 사람들에 익숙한 관객들에게 부자연스러워 보이지 않을까? 이러한 문제들에 대한 대부분 사람들의 인식은 그다지 날카롭지 않다. 그들은 실제 삶이나 영화에서 다른 사람들의 이목구비의 움직임을 자세히 관찰하는 습관을 지니고 있지 않다. 그들은 자신들이 보는 것의 의미를 이해하는 것으로 (A) 만족한다. 따라서 그들은 흔히 너무 자연스러운 그 어떤 것보다 영화배우들의 과장된 표현을 더 쉽게 받아들인다. 그리고 예술 애호가들에 관한 한, 그들은 영화에서 자연의 모방이 아닌 예술을 찾는다. 그들은 (B) 예술적 표현이 항상 묘사되는 사물을 설명하고, 다듬고, 명확하게 만들고 있는 것을 안다. 현실에서는 불완전하게 인식되고, 그저 암시되기만 하며, 다른 것들과 뒤엉킨 것들이 예술 작품에서는 완전하고, 온전하며 무관한 문제들로부터 (C) 자유로운 것처럼 보인다. 영화의 연기도 그러

하다.

문제풀이

(A) 관객들은 그들이 보는 것의 의미를 이해하는 것으로 만족해하기 때문에 영화 속 배우들의 과장된 연기를 부자연스럽게 받아들이지 않는다는 의미가 되어야 하므로, 'satisfied(만족한)'가 와야 한다. disappointed는 '실망한'이라는 의미이다.

(B) 예술 애호가들은 영화를 자연의 모방이 아닌 예술로 보기 때문에 묘사된 사물을 설명하고 다듬어 명확하게 하는 것은 영화와 같은 예술적 표현임을 안다는 의미가 되어야 하므로, 'artistic(예술의)'이 와야 한다. real은 '실제의'라는 의미이다.

(C) 현실에서 다른 것들과 뒤엉켜 불완전하게 인식되는 것들이 예술 작품 속에서는 무관한 문제들로부터 자유로워지고 완전하게 보인다는 의미가 되어야 하므로, 'free(자유로운)'가 적절하다. inseparable은 '분리할 수 없는'이라는 의미이다. 따라서 정답은 ⑤이다.

《구문 및 어휘》

*1행 Why does the "pure" acting of the movies not seem unnatural to the audience, [who, after all, are accustomed in real life to people {whose expression is more or less indistinct}]?

⑴ who ~ indistinct는 선행사 the audience에 대해 부연 설명해 주는 계속적 용법의 관계대명사절이다.

⑵ whose ~ indistinct는 선행사 people을 수식하는 관계대명사절이다.

*10행 And as far as lovers of art are concerned, they do not look at the movies for imitations of nature but for art.

⑴「부사절(as far as ~)+주절(they do not ~)」구조의 문장이다.

⑵ as far as ~ be concerned는 '~에 관한 한'이라는 의미이다.

⑶「not A but B」는 'A가 아닌 B'라는 의미이다.

indistinct 불분명한
closely 면밀히
feature 이목구비, 생김새
grasp 이해하다, 파악하다
take in ~를 받아들이다
overemphasized 과장된, 지나치게 강조된
as far as ~ be concerned ~에 관한 한
imitation 모방
representation 묘사, 표현
refine 순화하다, 다듬다
depict 묘사하다
irrelevant 무관한, 상관없는

11.④ | 먹이가 되는 동물이 먹이를 찾을 때 무리를 형성하는 이유

먹이가 되는 동물들이 먹이를 찾는 무리를 형성하는 이유가 있는데, 그것은 증가된 경계이다. 붉은발도요 한 마리가 먹이를 먹을 때 선택에 직면한다. 그것은 ① 포식자가 다가오는 것을 감시하며 자신의 모든 시간을 경계하는 데 보낼 수 있을 것이다. 만약 그렇게 한다면 그것은 갑자기 잡힐 가능성을 확실하게 상당히 줄이겠지만 또한 ② 굶어 죽게 될 것이다. 새 한 마리가 포식자를 살피면서 자신의 머리를 공중에 두는 동시에 먹이를 찾으며 자신의 머리를 아래로 둘 수는 없다. 실제로는 물론 하나의 개체는 자신이 처했다고 알게 되는 상황에 맞춰 그 두 가지 행동의 균

형을 맞추며, 무리의 한 구성원으로서 그것은 그 균형을 ③ 먹이를 먹는 쪽으로 옮길 수 있다. 새들의 무리가 더 크면 클수록 새 한 마리가 ④ 휴식(→경계)에 바치는 시간은 더 적어진다. 이것은 그 무리의 많은 일련의 눈의 ⑤ 존재가 항상 망을 볼 수 있는 누군가가 있다는 것을 실질적으로 의미하기 때문에 가능하다.

문제풀이

① 붉은발도요가 다가오는 것을 경계해야 할 대상은 포식자이므로 'predators(포식자)'는 적절하게 쓰였다.

② 자신의 모든 시간을 경계하는데 보낸다면 포식자에게 잡힐 가능성은 줄어들지만 먹이를 찾지 못해 굶어 죽게 될 것이므로 'starve(굶어 죽다)'가 온 것은 적절하다.

③ 한 개체는 자신이 처한 상황에 균형을 맞추는 데 무리에 속해 있으면 다른 개체들이 망을 봐 줄 수 있어서 균형을 먹이를 먹는 쪽으로 옮길 수 있을 것이므로 'feeding(먹이를 먹는)'이 온 것은 적절하다.

④ 새의 무리가 크면 클수록 망을 보는 새들이 많이 있어서 경계를 덜 해도 되기 때문에 휴식이 아니라 경계에 바치는 시간이 줄어들 것이다. 따라서 'relaxation(휴식)'이 온 것은 적절하지 않다.

⑤ 망을 볼 수 있는 누군가가 있다는 것은 눈의 존재가 많은 것이므로 'presence(존재)'가 온 것은 적절하다. 따라서 정답은 ④이다.

《구문 및 어휘》

*1행 There is a reason [that prey animals form foraging groups], and that is increased vigilance.

⑴ 'There is ~'와 'that is ~' 두 개의 절이 and에 의해 연결되어 있다.

⑵ that prey ~ groups는 선행사 a reason을 수식하는 관계부사절로 that 대신에 관계부사 why가 올 수 있다.

⑶ that is increase의 that은 the reason을 받는 지시대명사이다.

*3행 It could spend all of its time being vigilant, looking out for approaching predators.

⑴「주절(It could ~)+분사구문(looking out ~)」구조의 문장이다.

⑵「spend+시간+-ing」는 '~하는 데 (얼마의 시간)을 보내다'라는 의미이다.

⑶ looking out ~ predators는 '~하면서'라는 의미의 부대상황을 나타내는 분사구문이다.

*12행 The bigger the flock of birds, the less time an individual bird devotes to relaxation.

⑴「the+비교급, the+비교급」은 '~하면 할수록 더 …하다'라는 의미이다.

prey 먹이, 먹잇감
form 형성하다
forage 먹이를 찾다
individual 각각의, 개인의
redshank 붉은발도요
be faced with ~에 직면하다
vigilant 바짝 경계하는
look out 망보다
approach 다가가다, 다가오다
predator 포식자, 포식 동물
significantly 상당히
reduce 줄이다, 축소하다
starve 굶주리다, 굶어 죽다
scan 살피다, 훑어보다

---

in accordance with ~에 따라서
shift 옮기다, 이동하다
flock 떼, 무리
devote 바치다, 기울이다
effectively 효과적으로, 실질적으로

12.④ | 단 하나의 어떤 행동으로 그 사람의 행동을 예측하는 것의 부정확성

직독/직해

The finding / that as a general rule /
연구 결과는 / 일반적으로

global attitudes are poor predictors of specific behaviors /
전반적인 태도가 특정 행동에 대한 좋지 못한 예측 변수라는 /

should come as no surprise.
전혀 놀랄만한 일이 아니다

For global attitudes / to predict a particular behavior, /
전반적인 태도가 / 특정 행동을 예측하기 위해서는 /

the behavior in question / 문제 되는 행동이 /

must exhibit the latent attitudinal disposition — /
잠재적 태도적 성향을 나타내야 하는데 /

it must reflect the global attitude of interest.
그것은 이해관계의 전반적인 태도를 나타내야 한다

However, it is unreasonable /
그러나, 합리적이지 않다 /

to expect any single behavior /
단 하나의 어떤 행동을 예측하는 것은 /

to be representative of a broad attitudinal domain.
광범위한 태도 영역을 대표할 것이라고

Consider, for example, the relation /
예를 들어, 관계를 생각해 보자 /

between global attitudes toward African Americans /
아프리카계 미국인에 대한 전반적인 태도와 /

and willingness to have one's picture taken /
사진을 찍으려는 의지 사이의 /

with a black individual of the opposite sex /
반대되는 성(性)의 흑인 사람과 /

for a variety of purposes. 다양한 목적 때문에

Although refusal to pose for a picture with a black person / 흑인과 사진을 찍기 위해 포즈를 취하기를 거부하는 것은 /

may well be an indication of prejudice, /
아마도 편견을 나타내는 것일 수도 있지만 /

this behavior can also be influenced /
이 행동은 또한 영향을 받을 수도 있다 /

by a variety of other factors /
다양한 다른 요인들에 의해 /

that have nothing to do with prejudice.
편견과 전혀 관계가 없는

In fact, any single behavior in relation to African Americans /
사실, 아프리카계 미국인과 관련된 어떤 하나의 행동도 /

is likely to be multiply determined /
복합적으로 결정되어질 수 있다 /

and hence be a poor indicator of the underlying disposition; /
따라서 근본적인 성향에 대한 좋지 못한 지표일 수 있다 /

that is, the tendency to discriminate.
즉 차별하는 성향(에 대한)

- - - - - - - - - - - - - - - -

일반적으로 전반적인 태도가 특정 행동에 대한 좋지 못한 예측 변수라는 연구 결과는 전혀 놀랄만한 일이 아니다. 전반적인 태도가 특정 행동을 ① 예측하기 위해서는, 문제 되는 행동이 잠재적 태도적 성향을 나타내야 하는데, 그 것은 이해관계의 전반적인 태도를 나타내야 한다. 그러나, 단 하나의 어떤 행동이 광범위한 태도 영역을 ② 대표할 것이라고 예측하는 것은 합리적이지 않다. 예를 들어, 아프리카계 미국인에 대한 전반적인 태도와, 다양한 목적 때문에 반대되는 성(性)의 흑인 사람과 사진을 찍으려는 의지 사이의 ③ 관계를 생각해 보자. 흑인과 사진을 찍기 위해 포즈를 취하기를 거부하는 것은 아마도 편견을 나타내는 것일 수도 있지만, 이 행동은 또한 편견과 ④ 관계가 있는(→ 전혀 관계가 없는) 다양한 다른 요인에 의해 영향을 받을 수도 있다. 사실, 아프리카계 미국인과 관련된 어떤 하나의 행동도 복합적으로 결정되어질 수 있으며, 따라서 근본적인 성향, 즉 차별하는 성향에 대한 ⑤ 좋지 못한 지표일 수 있다.

문제풀이

단 하나의 어떤 행동으로 그 사람의 전반적인 태

도를 예측하는 것은 합리적이지 않다고 하면서 그에 대한 예가 이어지고 있으므로, 아프리카계 미국인과 사진을 찍기를 거부하는 것은 편견이겠지만 그런 행동은 편견과 전혀 관계가 없는 다양한 다른 요인에 의해 영향을 받을 수도 있다고 하는 것이 문맥상 적절하다. 따라서 ④ 'something'을 'nothing' 등의 낱말로 고쳐 써야 한다.

《 어휘 · 어구 》

attitude 태도
predictor 예측 변수
come as no surprise 놀라운 일이 아니다
exhibit 나타내다, 보이다
attitudinal 태도의, 사고방식의
disposition 기질, 성향
unreasonable 불합리한
representative 대표하는
indication 암시, 조짐
prejudice 편견
factor 요소
in relation to ~에 관하여
underlying 근본적인, 근원적인
discriminate 차별하다

---

14. 관계대명사

A 출제 POINT
본문 080쪽

1. that
2. What
3. who
4. that
5. as
6. than
7. Whoever

1 [해석]▶ 그는 내가 믿을 수 있는 유일한 분입니다.
[해설]▶ 선행사가 the only가 나오면 관계대명사는 that을 사용한다. 문장에서 that은 목적격으로 사용되었다.

2 [해석]▶ 인생에서 가장 중요한 것은 사랑이다.
[해설]▶ what은 선행사를 포함하고, what ~ in life가 주어부를 이루고, what절 안에서 what은 주어 역할을 하고 있다.

3 [해석]▶ 그녀는 그것을 친구와 상의했는데, 그녀의 친구는 변호사이다.
[해설]▶ 선행사는 her friend이고, 관계사 who가 선행사를 설명하는 계속적 용법으로 사용되었다.

4 [해석]▶ 나와 얘기했던 숙녀는 우리 이모야.
[해설]▶ 선행사가 사람(the lady)이고, 관계대명사는 전치사 with의 목적격 역할을 하고 있다. 이런 경우, 목적격 관계대명사 whom이나 that이 필요하다.

5 [해석]▶ 이것은 내가 잃어버린 시계와 같은 종류의 시계다.
[해설]▶ 선행사가 the same이 나온 경우, 유사 관계대명사 as를 쓴다.

6 [해석]▶ 그는 필요한 것보다 더 많은 돈을 가지고 있다.
[해설]▶ 선행사 앞에 비교급이 올 때, 유사관계대명사 than을 쓴다.

7 [해석]▶ 이 법을 어긴 사람은 누구든지 처벌을 받을 것이다. (Anyone who breaks this low~)
[해설]▶ 문맥상 이 법을 어긴 사람은 누구든지의 의미이므로 주어 역할을 하는 복합관계대명사 'whoever'가 필요하다.

B 체크 POINT
본문 080쪽

1. that
2. what
3. which
4. was
5. as
6. more
7. whichever

1 [해석]▶ 카페인을 포함한 소다는 몸에서 수분을 빼앗는다.
[해설]▶ 선행사가 사물(sodas)이고, 관계사 바로 뒤에 동사 have가 있으므로, 선행사가 사물인 주격관계대명사가 필요하다.

2 [해석]▶ 당신은 보지 않은 것을 믿을 수 있나요?
[해설]▶ 관계사절 앞에 선행사가 없고, 타동사 see의 목적어 역할을 하는 관계대명사가 필요하므로 선행사를 포함하고 있는 관계사 what이 필요하다.

3 [해석]▶ Sally는 빙판에서 넘어졌는데, 그것은 모두를 웃게 만들었다.
[해설]▶ 관계대명사 which가 선행사인 바로 앞 문장 전체를 설명하는 계속적 관계대명사 용법으로 사용되었다.

---

4 [해석]▶ 안내원으로 일하고 있던 그 남자는 새로운 직업을 찾는 중이었다.
[해설]▶ 관계대명사절의 동사는 선행사(the man)와 수를 일치시킨다. 선행사가 단수명사이므로 단수동사를 써야 한다.

5 [해석]▶ 너를 도와줄 그런 친구를 선택해.
[해설]▶ 선행사가 such~인 경우, 유사관계대명사 as를 사용한다. as는 동사 will help의 주어 역할을 하고 있다.

6 [해석]▶ 그녀는 내가 가진 것보다 더 많은 책을 가지고 있다.
[해설]▶ 선행사 앞에 비교급이 올 때 유사관계대명사 than을 쓴다.

7 [해석]▶ 네 마음에 드는 것은 어느 것이든지 가져도 된다.
[해설]▶ 복합관계대명사 whichever는 선행사를 포함하고 있으며 '~하는 것은 어느 것이든지'의 의미로 타동사 like의 목적어 역할을 하고 있다.

Day 14
본문 081쪽

1 ③	2 ④	3 ③	4 ③	5 ②
6 ⑤	7 ⑤	8 ④	9 ⑤	10 ③
11 ②	12 ③			

1. ③
생태계들의 구성과 범위

직독 직해

Ecosystems differ / in composition and extent.
생태계들은 다르다 / 구성과 범위가

They can be defined / as ranging /
그것들은 정의될 수 있다 / 범위에 이르는 것으로 /

from the communities and interactions of organisms / in your mouth /
유기체들의 군집과 상호 작용으로부터 / 여러분의 입속에 있는 /

or those in the canopy of a rain forest /
또는 열대 우림의 덮개 안에 있는 그것들에서부터 /

to all those in Earth's oceans.
지구의 바다에 있는 모든 그것들까지의

The processes governing them / differ in complexity and speed.
그것들을 지배하는 과정들은 / 복잡성과 속도의 면에서 다르다

There are systems that turn over in minutes, /
몇 분 안에 뒤바뀌는 시스템도 있다 /

and there are others / whose rhythmic time extends to hundreds of years.
그리고 다른 시스템도 있다 / 규칙적으로 순환하는 시간이 수백 년까지 이르는

Some ecosystems are extensive ('biomes', such as the African savanna); /
어떤 생태계는 광범위하고(아프리카 사바나 같은 '생물군계') /

some cover regions (river basins); /
어떤 생태계는 지역에 걸쳐 있으며(강의 유역) /

many involve clusters of villages (micro-watersheds); /
많은 생태계가 마을 군집을 포함하고(작은 분수령들) /

others are confined to the level of a single village (the village pond).
다른 생태계들은 단 하나의 마을 차원으로 국한된다(마을 연못)

In each example / there is an element of indivisibility.
각각의 사례에는 / 불가분성이라는 요소가 있다

Divide an ecosystem into parts / by creating barriers, /
어떤 생태계를 부분들로 나누면 / 장벽을 만들어 /

and the sum of the productivity of the parts /
그리고 그 부분들의 생산성의 합은 /

will typically be found to be lower / than the
productivity of the whole, /
더 낮다는 것이 밝혀질 것이다 / 일반적으로 전체의 생산성보다 /
other things being equal.
다른 것이 동일하다면
The mobility of biological populations / is a reason.
생물학적 개체군의 이동성이 / 하나의 이유이다
Safe passages, / for example, / enable migratory
species to survive.
안전한 통행은 / 예를 들면 / 이동하는 생물 종들을 생존하게 한다

생태계들은 구성과 범위가 다르다. 그것들은 여러分의 입속에 있는 유기
체들의 군집과 상호작용 또는 열대 우림의 덮개(최상부) 안에 있는 그것
들에서부터 지구의 바다에 있는 모든 그것들까지의 범위에 이르는 것으
로 정의될 수 있다. 그것들을 지배하는 과정들은 복잡성과 속도의 면에서
다르다. 몇 분 안에 뒤바뀌는 다른 시스템도 있고, 규칙적으로 순환하는
시간이 수백 년까지 이르는 시스템도 있다. 어떤 생태계는 광범위하고(아
프리카 사바나 같은 '생물군계'), 어떤 생태계는 지역들에 걸쳐 있으며(강
의 유역), 많은 생태계가 마을 군집을 포함하고(작은 분수령들), 다른 생
태계들은 단 하나의 마을 차원으로 국한된다(마을 연못). 각각의 사례에
는 불가분성이라는 요소가 있다. 어떤 생태계를 장벽을 만들어 부분들로
나누면, 그 부분들의 생산성의 합은 일반적으로, 다른 것이 동일하다면,
전체의 생산성보다 더 낮다는 것이 밝혀질 것이다. 생물학적 개체군의 이
동성이 하나의 이유이다. 예를 들면, 안전한 통행은 이동하는 생물 종들
을 생존하게 한다.

문제풀이

① **[지시대명사]**
앞에 있는 the communities and interactions of
organisms를 지칭하는 지시대명사가 와야 하므
로, those가 온 것은 적절하다.
② **[분사]**
The processes를 수식하는 분사가 와야 하는데
'지배하는'이라는 능동의 의미이므로, 현재분사
governing이 온 것은 적절하다.
③ **[관계대명사]**
선행사인 **others**를 수식하는 관계대명사절을 이
끌면서 뒤에 있는 **rhythmic time**을 수식할 수 있
는 소유격 관계대명사가 와야 하는 자리이다. 따라
서 **which**를 **whose**로 고쳐야 한다.
④ **[분사구문]**
분사구문이 와야 하는데, 의미상의 주어가 other
things로 '동일하다면'이라는 능동의 의미이므로,
현재분사 being이 온 것은 적절하다.
⑤ **[목적격보어]**
enable은 to부정사를 목적격보어로 취하는 동사이
므로, to survive가 온 것은 적절하다.

❍ 이렇게 풀자 어법상 틀린 부분을 찾는 문제는 밑줄
이 있는 부분의 형태와 문맥을 보고 어법에 맞게 쓰였는
지 확인해야 한다.
① 지시대명사가 쓰인 경우, 앞 문장이나 절에서 가리키는
명사를 찾아서 수가 일치하는지 확인해야 한다.
② 분사가 명사를 수식할 경우, 수동의 의미일 경우 과거
분사가 오고 능동의 의미일 경우 현재분사가 온다.
③ 문장에서 관계대명사가 필요한 경우인지를 확인한 후,
선행사의 종류 및 격에 따라 적절하게 쓰였는지 살펴봐야
한다.
④ 분사구문에서 의미상 주어와의 관계가 능동일 때 현재
분사가 와야 하고, 수동일 때 과거분사가 와야 한다.
⑤ 동사의 종류에 따라 목적격보어로 to부정사가 오기도
하고 동사원형이 오기도 한다. 앞에 나온 동사를 파악
하여 어법에 맞는지 판단해야 한다.

《 어휘·어구 》

ecosystem 생태계
composition 구성
extent 범위
range from A to B A에서 B까지의 범위에 이르다
community 군집
organism 유기체
turn over 바뀌다
rhythmic 규칙적으로 순환하는

---

extend 연장되다
extensive 광범위한
biome (숲·사막 같은 특정 환경 내의) 생물 군계
river basin (강의) 유역
cluster 군집, 무리
watershed 분수령
confine 제한하다
indivisibility 불가분성
barrier 장벽
productivity 생산성
mobility 이동성
migratory 이동하는, 이주하는

---

2. ④ 　　　　다른 사람을 뒷공론하는 이유

직독/직해

To begin with a psychological reason, /
심리적인 이유부터 시작하자면 /
the knowledge of another's personal affairs /
다른 사람의 개인적인 일에 대해 아는 것은 /
can tempt the possessor of this information /
이 정보를 가진 사람을 부추길 수 있는데 /
to repeat it as gossip / 그것을 뒷공론으로 반복하도록 /
because as unrevealed information /
왜냐하면 숨겨진 정보로서는 /
it remains socially inactive.
그것이 사회적으로 비활동적인 상태로 남기 때문이다
Only when the information is repeated /
그 정보가 반복될 때만 /
can its possessor turn the fact /
그 정보를 소유한 사람은 사실을 바꿀 수 있다 /
that he knows something / into something socially
자신이 무언가를 알고 있다는 / 사회적으로 가치 있는 것으로
valuable /
like social recognition, prestige, and notoriety.
사회적 인지, 명성 그리고 악명과 같은
As long as he keeps his information to himself, /
자신이 가진 정보를 남에게 말하지 않는 한 /
he may feel superior to those / who do not know it.
그는 사람들보다 우월하다고 느낄 수도 있다 / 그것을 알지 못하는
But knowing and not telling / does not give him that
그러나 알면서 말하지 않는 것은 / 그 기분을 그에게 주지 못한다
feeling / of "superiority /
/ 우월감이라는 /
that, so to say, latently contained in the secret, /
말하자면, 그 비밀 속에 잠재적으로 들어 있다가 /
fully actualizes itself only at the moment of
disclosure." 폭로의 순간에만 완전히 실현되는
This is the main motive for gossiping /
이것이 뒷공론을 하는 주요 동기이다 /
about well-known figures and superiors.
잘 알려진 인물과 우월한 사람에 대해
The gossip producer assumes /
뒷공론을 만들어 내는 사람은 생각한다 /
that some of the "fame" of the subject of gossip, /
그 뒷공론 대상의 '명성' 일부가 /
as whose "friend" he presents himself, / will rub
그가 자신이 그의 '친구'라고 소개하는 / 자신에게 옮겨질 것이라고
off on him.

심리적인 이유부터 시작하자면, 다른 사람의 개인적인 일에 대해 아는 것
은 이 정보를 가진 사람이 그것을 뒷공론으로 반복하도록 부추길 수 있는
데, 왜냐하면 숨겨진 정보로서는 그것이 사회적으로 비활동적인 상태로
남기 때문이다. 그 정보가 반복될 때만 그 정보를 소유한 사람은 자신이
무언가를 알고 있다는 사실을 사회적 인지, 명성 그리고 악명과 같은 사
회적으로 가치 있는 것으로 바꿀 수 있다. 자신이 가진 정보를 남에게 말
하지 않는 한, 그는 그것을 알지 못하는 사람들보다 우월하다고 느낄 수
도 있다. 그러나 알면서 말하지 않는 것은 '말하자면, 그 비밀 속에 잠재
적으로 들어 있다가, 폭로의 순간에만 완전히 실현되는 우월감'이라는 그
기분을 그에게 주지 못한다. 이것이 잘 알려진 인물과 우월한 사람에 대
해 뒷공론을 하는 주요 동기이다. 뒷공론을 만들어 내는 사람은 자신이
그의 '친구'라고 소개하는 뒷공론 대상의 '명성' 일부가 자신에게 옮겨
질 것이라고 생각한다.

문제풀이

① 동사 tempt는 「tempt+목적어+to부정사」 형태
로 쓰이며 '~가 …하도록 부추기다'의 의미이다.
따라서 목적격보어로 to부정사 to repeat가 온 것
은 적절하다.
② 부사절(Only when the information is
repeated)이 문두로 나와 주어와 동사가 도치된
문장으로 「조동사+주어+동사원형」의 어순이 되어
야 한다. 따라서 동사원형 turn이 온 것은 적절하다.
③ 「keep ~ to oneself」는 '~을 남에게 말하지 않
다'의 의미로, 주어 he와 전치사 to의 목적어가 동
일한 인물이므로, 재귀대명사 himself가 온 것은
적절하다.
④ **that feeling of superiority**를 선행사로 하는 주
격 관계대명사 **that**이 이끄는 관계사절 내에 동사가
와야 하는 자리이므로, **actualizing**을 **actualizes**로
고쳐야 한다. **so to say**와 **latently contained in
the secret**은 삽입된 구이다.
⑤ 앞의 the subject of gossip을 받고 뒤의 명사
friend를 수식하는 소유격 대명사 역할을 하면서
동시에 절을 이어주는 접속사 역할을 해야 하므
로, 소유격 관계대명사 whose가 온 것은 적절하다.
따라서 정답은 ④이다.

❍ 이렇게 풀자 어법상 틀린 부분을 찾는 문제는 밑줄
이 있는 부분의 형태와 문맥을 보고 어법에 맞게 쓰였는
지 확인해야 한다.
① 동사의 종류에 따라 목적격보어로 to부정사, 명사,
동사원형 등이 올 수 있다.
② 도치된 문장에서는 무엇이 주어이고 동사인지 파악해
서 주어에 맞춰 수일치를 해야 한다. 단, 도치되어 주어 앞
에 조동사가 있는 경우 주어 다음에 동사원형이 와야 한다.
③ 재귀대명사에 밑줄이 있는 경우 주어가 하는 동작의
대상이 주어 자신인지 확인해야 한다.
④ 밑줄이 그어진 부분이 문장에서 무엇으로 쓰이는지를
파악해야 한다.
⑤ 선행사의 종류 및 격에 따라 적절한 관계대명사가 쓰
였는지 살펴봐야 한다.

《 어휘·어구 》

psychological 심리적인
tempt 부추기다, 유혹하다
possessor 소유자
unrevealed 숨겨진, 밝혀지지 않은
inactive 비활동적인, 활동하지 않는
superior 우월한; 우월한 사람
so to say 말하자면
actualize 실현하다
disclosure 폭로, 발각, 드러남
motive 동기, 이유
figure 인물
fame 명성
subject 대상
present A as B A를 B로 소개하다
rub off on ~로 옮겨지다, ~에 영향을 주다

---

3. ③ 　　　　의학 치료에 있어서 선택의 어려움

직독/직해

When it comes to medical treatment, /
의학 치료에 관한 한 /
patients see choice as both a blessing and a
burden. 환자들은 선택을 축복이자 부담으로 여긴다
And the burden falls primarily on women, /
그리고 그 부담은 주로 여성들에게 주어지는데 /
who are typically the guardians /
그들은 보통 건강 수호자이다 /

---

not only of their own health, / 자신의 건강뿐만 아니라 /
but that of their husbands and children.
남편과 아이들의 건강도
"It is an overwhelming task / 매우 힘든 일이다 /
for women, and consumers in general, /
여성들이 그리고 보통 소비자들이 /
to be able to sort through the information /
정보를 자세히 살펴볼 수 있는 것은 /
they find / and make decisions," /
그들이 찾은 / 그리고 결정할 (수 있는 것은) /
says Amy Allina, program director of the National
National Women's Health Network의 프로그램 책임자인 Amy Allina는 말한다
Women's Health Network.
And what makes it overwhelming is /
그리고 그것을 굉장히 힘든 것으로 만드는 것은 ~이다 /
not only that the decision is ours, /
그 결정이 우리 자신의 것이라는 것뿐만 아니라 /
but that the number of sources of information /
정보 원천의 수가 /
from which we are to make the decisions /
우리가 결정을 내리는 데 근거가 되는 /
has exploded. 폭발적으로 늘고 있다는 것이다
It's not just a matter of /
그것은 그저 ~의 문제가 아니다 /
listening to your doctor lay out the options /
여러분의 의사가 선택 사항들을 제시하는 것을 듣는 /
and making a choice. 그리고 선택을 하는
We now have encyclopedic lay-people's guides to
지금 우리에게는 박식한 비전문가의 건강에 대한 안내가 있다 /
health, /
"better health" magazines, and the Internet.
'더 나은 건강' 잡지들과 인터넷
So now the prospect of medical decisions has
become / 그래서 이제 의학적 결정의 가능성은 ~가 되었다 /
everyone's worst nightmare of a term paper
모든 사람에게 기말보고서 과제와 같은 최악의 악몽이 /
assignment, /
with stakes infinitely higher than a grade in a
course. 한 강좌에서의 성적보다 걸려있는 것이 훨씬 더 많다

의학 치료에 관한 한 환자들은 선택을 축복이자 부담으로 여긴다. 그리고 그 부담은 주로 여성들에게 주어지는데, 그들은 보통 자신의 건강뿐만 아니라 남편과 아이들의 건강 수호자이다. "여성들이 그리고 보통 소비자들이, 그들이 찾은 정보를 자세히 살펴보고 결정할 수 있는 것은 매우 힘든 일이다."라고 National Women's Health Network의 프로그램 책임자인 Amy Allina는 말한다. 그리고 그것을 굉장히 힘든 것으로 만드는 것은 그 결정이 우리 자신의 것이라는 것뿐만 아니라, 우리가 결정을 내리는 데 근거가 되는 정보 원천의 수가 폭발적으로 늘고 있다는 것이다. 그것은 그저 여러분의 의사가 선택 사항들을 제시하는 것을 듣고 선택을 하는 문제가 아니다. 지금 우리에게는 박식한 비전문가의 건강에 대한 안내, '더 나은 건강' 잡지들과 인터넷이 있다. 그래서 이제 의학적 결정의 가능성은 모든 사람에게 기말보고서 과제와 같은 최악의 악몽이 되었는데, 한 강좌에서의 성적보다 걸려있는 것이 훨씬 더 많다.

문제풀이

① typically는 '보통, 전형적으로'라는 의미의 부사로 적절히 사용되었다.
② 앞에 있는 it은 가주어이고 to be 이하가 진주어로 쓰인 문장으로, to be는 적절히 사용되었다.
③ which 이하는 선행사 information을 수식하는 관계대명사절인데, '정보로부터'라는 뜻으로 쓰여서 의미상 전치사 from이 관계대명사 앞에 와야 한다. 따라서 which를 from which로 고쳐 써야 한다.
④ 등위접속사 and에 의해 전치사 of의 목적어로 쓰인 동명사 listening과 연결되어 병렬 구조를 이루고 있으므로, 마찬가지로 동명사 making이 온 것은 적절하다.
⑤ 주어는 the prospect이고, of medical decisions는 주어를 수식하는 전치사구이다. 따라서 단수 주어인 the prospect에 맞춰 단수동사 has가 온 것은 적절하다.
따라서 정답은 ③이다.

💡 **이렇게 풀자** _ 어법상 틀린 부분을 찾는 문제는 밑줄이 있는 부분의 형태와 문맥을 보고 어법에 맞게 쓰였는지 확인해야 한다. ①은 부사의 역할을, ②는 가주어-진주어 파악을, ③은 전치사+관계대명사의 쓰임을, ④는 병렬 관계 파악을, ⑤는 주어와 동사의 일치를 알아야 한다.

〈어휘·어구〉

blessing 축복
burden 부담
primarily 주로
guardian 수호자
overwhelming 매우 힘든, 견디기 어려운
in general 보통, 대개
sort through ~을 자세히 살펴보다
explode 폭발적으로 ~이 되다
lay out 제시하다
encyclopedic 박식한, 해박한
stake (내기 등에) 건 것, 건 돈
infinitely 대단히, 엄청

----

4. ③ 빠꾸기 벌의 번식 방법

대부분의 벌은 꽃을 방문하고 꽃가루를 모으면서 하루를 보내지만, 어떤 벌은 다른 벌의 힘든 노동을 이용한다. 도둑질하는 이런 벌은 이상한 눈치를 못 챈 (숙주라 알려진) '보통' 벌의 집으로 슬그머니 들어가, 숙주 벌이 자기 자신의 새끼를 위해 모으고 있는 꽃가루 덩어리 근처에 알을 낳고, 그러고 나서 슬그머니 다시 나온다. 그 도둑의 알이 부화하면, 그것은 숙주의 새끼를 죽이고 나서 자신의 희생자를 위해 마련한 꽃가루를 먹는다. 가끔 탁란 동물로 불리는 이 벌은 빠꾸기 벌이라고 불리기도 하는데, 다른 새의 둥지에 알을 낳고 그 새가 그것을 기르도록 두는 빠꾸기와 유사하기 때문이다. 그들은 더 전문적으로는 cleptoparasite라 불린다. 'clepto'는 그리스어로 '도둑'을 의미하여, 'cleptoparasite'라는 용어는 구체적으로 먹이를 훔침으로써 다른 것에 의지해 살아가는 생물을 가리킨다. 이 경우 그 cleptoparasite는 숙주가 애써 얻은 꽃가루 비축물을 먹고 산다.

문제풀이

① unsuspecting은 normal bee를 수식하는 분사인데 normal bee가 이상한 눈치를 채지 못하는 행위의 주체로 능동의 관계이다. 따라서 현재분사인 unsuspecting이 온 것은 적절하다.
② 뒤의 명사 victim을 수식하는 소유격이며, 문맥상 숙주의 둥지에서 부화한 도둑의 새끼벌을 가리키므로 단수 형태인 its가 온 것은 적절하다.
③ 계속적 용법의 주격 관계대명사 which의 선행사는 cuckoo birds이고, 앞의 **lay and egg in the nest of another bird** 동사구와 병렬 구조를 이루는 동사가 와야 한다. 따라서 단수 동사 **leaves**를 복수 동사 **leave**로 고쳐야 한다.
④ 동사 are called를 수식하는 부사가 와야 하므로, technically가 온 것은 적절하다.
⑤ that 뒤의 문장은 주어가 빠진 불완전 문장으로 an organism을 선행사로 한 주격 관계대명사가 와야 한다. 따라서 관계대명사 that이 온 것은 적절하다.
정답은 ③이다.

〈구문 및 어휘〉

*1행 Though most bees fill their days **visiting** flowers and **collecting** pollen, some bees take advantage of the hard work of others.
(1) 「부사절(Though most ~)+주절(some bees ~)」

구조의 문장이다.
(2) visiting과 collecting은 '~하면서'라는 의미이며 주어의 동작이나 상태를 보충 설명해 주는 현재분사로 and에 의해 병렬 연결되어 있다.

*3행 These thieving bees **sneak** into the nest of an unsuspecting "normal" bee (known as the host), **lay** an egg near the pollen mass [**being** gathered by the host bee for her own offspring], and then **sneak** back out.
(1) sneak (into), lay, sneak (back out)은 문장의 동사로 and에 의해 병렬 연결되어 있다.
(2) being gathered ~ own offspring은 the pollen mass를 수식하는 현재분사구이다.

pollen 꽃가루
take advantage of ~을 이용하다
thieve 도둑질하다
sneak 슬그머니 움직이다
nest (곤충의) 집, 보금자리
unsuspecting 의심하지 않는, 이상한 눈치를 못 챈
host (기생 동물의) 숙주
offspring 자식, 새끼
hatch 부화하다
refer (~을 …이라고) 부르다
cuckoo 빠꾸기
technically 전문적으로, 엄밀히 따지면
organism 생물, 유기체
live off ~에 의지해 살아가다
feed on ~을 먹고살다[먹다]
hard-earned 애써서 얻은
store 비축물

----

5. ② 내 삶의 두 번째 중요한 사건 — 독서

직독/직해

The most useful thing / 가장 유용한 것은 /
I brought out of my childhood /
나의 어린 시절로부터 가져온 /
was confidence in reading.
독서에서의 자신감이었다.
Not long ago, / 얼마 전에, /
I went on a weekend self-exploratory workshop, /
나는 주말의 자아 탐구 연수에 갔다.
in the hope of getting a clue about how to live.
어떻게 살아야 할지에 대한 단서를 얻으려는 희망에서
One of the exercises we were given /
우리에게 주어진 과제들 중 하나는 /
was to make a list / 목록을 작성하는 것이었다.
of the ten most important events of our lives.
우리의 삶에서 가장 중요한 10가지 사건들
Number one was: "I was born," / and you could put /
제일 처음 목록은 '나는 태어났다'였고, / 사람들은 적을 수 있었다. /
whatever you liked after that.
그 다음에 그들이 좋아하는 것은 무엇이나
Without even thinking about it, /
그것에 대해 생각도 해보지 않고 /
my hand wrote at number two: /
나의 손은 두 번째 항목을 적고 있었는데 /
"I learned to read."
그것은 '나는 읽는 것을 배웠다'였다.
"I was born and learned to read" /
'나는 태어나서 읽는 것을 배웠다'가 /
wouldn't be a sequence /
순서는 아닐 것인데 /
that occurs to many people, / I imagine.
많은 사람들에게 떠오르는 / 나는 생각했다.

But I knew what I meant to say.
그러나 나는 내가 말하고자 하는 것을 알고 있었다.

Being born was something done to me, /
태어난다는 것은 나에게 일어난 어떤 일이었지만, /

but my own life began / when I first made out /
내 자신의 삶은 시작되었다. /

the meaning of a sentence.
내가 처음 문장의 의미를 이해했을 때

나의 어린 시절로부터 가져온 가장 유용한 것은 독서에서의 자신감이 었다. 얼마 전에, 나는 어떻게 살아야 할지에 대한 단서를 얻으려는 희망에서 주말의 자아 탐구 연수에 갔다. 우리에게 주어진 과제들 중 하나는 우리의 삶에서 가장 중요한 10가지 사건들의 목록을 작성하는 것이었다. 제일 처음 목록은 '나는 태어났다'였고, 사람들은 그 다음에 그들이 좋아하는 것은 무엇이나 적을 수 있었다. 그것에 대해 생각도 해보지 않고 나의 손은 두 번째 항목을 적고 있었는데 그것은 '나는 읽는 것을 배웠다'였다. '나는 태어나서 읽는 것을 배웠다'가 많은 사람들에게 떠오르는 순서는 아닐 것이라고 나는 생각했다. 그러나 나는 내가 말하고자 하는 것을 알고 있었다. 태어난다는 것은 나에게 일어난 어떤 일이었지만, 내 자신의 삶은 내가 처음 문장의 의미를 이해했을 때 시작되었다.

⟨ 문제풀이 ⟩

(A) 주어가 One이므로 단수동사 was가 적절하다.
(B) 동사 put의 목적어가 될 수 있는 명사절을 이끄는 whatever(~하는 것은 무엇이나)가 적절하다. however는 부사절을 이끈다.
(C) something (which is) done to me ~ 문장에서 which is가 생략된 문장이다. 수식을 받는 something이 동사 do의 대상이므로 수동의 의미를 지닌 과거분사 done이 적절하다.

⟨ 어휘·어구 ⟩

confidence 자신감
self-exploratory 자아 탐구의
workshop 연수
sequence 순서
occur to ~에게 떠오르다
make out 이해하다

---

6. ⑤ 사람의 기억력

[직독 / 직해]

In general, / 일반적으로 /

one's memories of any period necessarily weaken /
어떤 시기에 대한 사람의 기억력은 필수적으로 약해진다. /

as one moves away from it.
그것으로부터 멀어짐에 따라

One is constantly learning new facts, /
사람들은 계속해서 새로운 사실을 배우며, /

and old ones have to drop out /
옛날 것은 떨어져 나가야만 한다. /

to make way for them.
새로운 것들에 자리를 양보하기 위해

At twenty, / I could have written /
20살 때, / 나는 글로 옮길 수도 있었을 것이다. /

the history of my school days /
내 학창 시절의 역사를 /

with an accuracy /
정확성으로 /

which would be quite impossible now.
지금은 전혀 불가능할 정확성으로

But it can also happen /
그러나 또한 일어날 수도 있다. /

that one's memories grow much sharper /
사람의 기억력은 훨씬 더 날카로워지는 일이 /

even after a long passage of time.
긴 시간이 경과한 후에도

This is because / 이것은 ~때문이다 /

one is looking at the past with fresh eyes /
새로운 눈으로 과거를 보고 /

and can isolate / and, as it were, / notice facts

사실들을 분리시키고, / 말하자면 / 그 사실들에 주목할 수 있기 (때문이다.)

which previously existed undifferentiated /
이전에는 구별되지 않은 채로 존재했던 /

among a mass of others.
수많은 다른 것들 사이에서

There are things / which in a sense I remembered, /
일들이 있다. / 어떤 의미에서 내가 기억했지만 /

but which did not strike me as strange or interesting /
나에게 이상하거나 흥미롭게 다가오지 않았던

until quite recently. 아주 최근까지

일반적으로 어떤 시기에 대한 사람의 기억력은 그것으로부터 멀어짐에 따라 필수적으로 약해진다. 사람은 계속해서 새로운 사실을 배우며, 옛날 것은 새로운 것들에 자리를 양보하기 위해 떨어져 나가야만 한다. 20살 때, 나는 지금은 전혀 불가능할 정확성으로 내 학창 시절의 역사를 글로 옮길 수도 있었을 것이다. 그러나 사람의 기억력은 긴 시간이 경과한 후에도 훨씬 더 날카로워지는 일이 또한 일어날 수도 있다. 이것은 새로운 눈으로 과거를 보고 이전에는 수많은 다른 것들 사이에서 구별되지 않은 채로 존재했던 사실들을 분리시키고, 말하자면 그 사실들에 주목할 수 있기 때문이다. 어떤 의미에서 내가 기억했지만 아주 최근까지 나에게 이상하거나 흥미롭게 다가오지 않았던 일들이 있다.

⟨ 문제풀이 ⟩

① 접속사 as가 '~함에 따라'는 비례의 의미를 가지고 있다.
② to부정사의 부사적 용법(목적)으로 사용되었다.
③ much는 비교급 강조어로 사용될 수 있다.
④ This is because ~ 구문은 '이것은 ~ 때문이다'는 의미를 가지고 있다.
⑤ **what**은 앞에 선행사인 **things**가 있으므로 **which**로 바꾸어야 한다. 이 **which**는 **remembered**의 목적어 역할을 하고 있다. 선행사 **things**를 수식하는 관계대명사 절이 두 개 연결되고 있는 구조이다.

⟨ 어휘·어구 ⟩

weaken 약해지다
make way for ~에 자리를 양보하다
accuracy 정확성
passage 경과
isolate 분리시키다
undifferentiated 분화되지 않은
recently 최근에

---

7. ⑤ 슈베르트의 인생 목적

[직독 / 직해]

Schubert spent his whole life / in poverty.
슈베르트는 인생을 보냈다 / 가난 속에서

But he had one noble purpose / in life.
그러나 그는 한 가지 고상한 목적을 가지고 있었다. / 인생에

That was to write down the beautiful musical thoughts /
그것은 아름다운 음악적 사고를 써 내려가는 것이었다 /

which seemed to flow from his brain /
그의 두뇌로부터 흘러나오는 듯한 /

in an endless rush of melody.
끊임없이 흘러나오는 멜로디로

As one of the most productive composers, /
가장 생산적인 작곡가 중의 한 명으로서 /

Schubert wrote music as freely /
슈베르트는 자유롭게 음악을 썼다. /

as one would write a friendly letter.
다정한 편지를 쓰는 사람만큼이나

He just produced what was in him, /
그는 그 자신 안에 있는 것을 썼고 /

and brought us a rich treasure of music.
우리에게 풍요로운 음악의 보물을 가져다주었다.

슈베르트는 인생을 가난 속에서 보냈다. 그러나 그는 인생에 한 가지 고상한 목적을 가지고 있었다. 그것을 끊임없이 흘러나오는 멜로디로 그의 두뇌로부터 흘러나오는 듯한 아름다운 음악적 사고를 써 내려가는 것이었다. 가장 생산적인 작곡가 중의 한 명으로서 슈베르트는 다정한 편지를 쓰는 사람만큼이나 자유롭게 음악을 썼다. 그는 그 자신 안에 있는 것을 썼고 우리에게 풍요로운 음악의 보물을 가져다 주었다.

⟨ 문제풀이 ⟩

⑤ 관계대명사 which는 선행사가 필요하다. 그러나 선행사가 빠져 있으므로 선행사를 포함하고 있는 관계대명사 what이 와야 한다.

⟨ 어휘·어구 ⟩

poverty 빈곤, 가난
noble 숭고한, 고결한
write down 기록하다
rush 돌진, 쇄도
productive 생산적인, 다작의
composer 작곡가, 작가
freely 자유로이, 마음대로
friendly 친한, 정다운
treasure 보물, 보배

---

8. ④ 운명이 정해진 길을 따라갈 것

[직독 / 직해]

No good can ever come /
어떤 좋은 것도 나올 수 없다 /

from deviating from the path /
그 길에서 벗어나는 것으로부터는 /

that you were destined to follow.
여러분이 따르도록 운명 지어진

Most often you deviate /
가장 빈번하게 여러분은 일탈한다 /

because of the temptation of money, /
돈의 유혹 때문에 /

of more immediate prospects of prosperity.
더 즉각적인 성공의 가능성의 (유혹 때문에)

Because this does not comply with something deep within you, /
이것이 여러분 내부의 깊은 곳에 있는 어떤 것과 일치하지 않기 때문에 /

your interest will lag / 여러분의 관심은 줄어들 것이다 /

and eventually the money will not come so easily.
그리고 결국 그 돈은 그렇게 쉽게 오지 않을 것이다

You will search for other easy sources of money, /
여러분은 돈의 다른 출처를 찾을 것이다 /

moving further and further away from your path.
여러분의 길에서 점점 더 멀리 이동하면서

Not seeing clearly ahead of you, /
여러분의 앞을 명확하게 보지 못하면 /

you will end up in a dead-end career.
여러분은 결국 경력의 막다른 골목에 빠질 것이다

Even if your material needs are met, /
비록 여러분의 물질적 욕구가 충족된다고 해도 /

you will feel an emptiness inside /
여러분은 내부의 공허함을 느낄 것이다 /

that you will need to fill / 여러분이 채울 필요가 있는 /

with any kind of belief system or diversions.
어떤 종류의 믿음 체계 혹은 주의를 딴 데로 돌리는 것으로

There is no compromise here, /
여기에는 어떤 타협도 없다 /

no way of escaping the dynamic.
역동성을 벗어날 방법도 없다

You will recognize / how far you have deviated /
여러분은 깨닫게 될 것이다 / 얼마나 멀리 벗어났는지를 /

by the depth of your pain and frustration.
여러분의 고통과 좌절의 깊이에 의해

You must listen to the message of this frustration and pain, / 여러분은 좌절과 고통의 메시지를 들어야 한다 /

and let it guide you /

[고3 영어 어법·어휘]

그리고 그것이 여러분을 인도하도록 해야 한다 /

as clearly as Fuller's voice guided him.
Fuller의 목소리가 그를 인도한 것처럼 분명하게

여러분이 따르도록 운명 지어진 길에서 벗어나는 것으로부터는 어떠한 좋은 것도 나올 수 없다. 여러분은 돈, 즉 더 즉각적인 성공의 가능성의 유혹 때문에 가장 빈번하게 일탈을 한다. 이것은 여러분 내부의 깊은 곳에 있는 어떤 것과 일치하지 않기 때문에, 여러분의 관심은 줄어들 것이고 결국 그 돈은 그렇게 쉽게 오지 않을 것이다. 여러분의 길에서 점점 더 멀리 이동하면서, 여러분은 쉽게 돈을 벌 다른 출처를 찾을 것이다. 여러분의 앞을 명확하게 보지 못하면, 여러분은 결국 경력의 막다른 골목에 빠지게 된다. 비록 여러분의 물질적 욕구가 충족된다고 해도, 여러분은 여러분이 어떤 종류의 믿음 체계 혹은 주의를 딴 데로 돌리게 하는 것으로 채워야 할 필요가 있는 내부의 공허함을 느낄 것이다. 여기에는 타협도 없고, 역동을 벗어날 방법도 없다. 여러분은 자신의 고통과 좌절의 깊이에 의해 얼마나 멀리 벗어났는지를 깨닫게 될 것이다. 여러분은 이 좌절과 고통의 메시지를 들어야 하며, 그것이 Fuller의 목소리가 그를 인도한 것처럼 분명하게 여러분을 인도하도록 해야 한다.

문제풀이

① [접속사 vs 전치사]
because of는 전치사구로 그 뒤에 명사구가 와야 한다. 따라 because of는 적절하다
② [부정대명사의 수식]
대명사 something을 수식하는 형용사이므로, deep은 적절하다.
③ [분사구문]
문두에 절이 있고 이후에 접속사가 없는 것으로 보아 and you will move를 분사구문 형태로 만든 것이므로, moving은 적절하다.
④ [관계대명사 vs 관계부사]
앞의 an emptiness를 지칭하면서 동시에 뒤에 있는 fill의 목적어의 역할을 하므로, 관계부사 where를 관계대명사 that으로 고쳐야 한다.
⑤ [대명사의 수일치]
단수 명사 the message를 대신하는 대명사이므로, it은 적절하다.

○ 이렇게 풀자 어법상 틀린 부분을 찾는 문제는 밑줄이 있는 부분의 형태와 문맥을 보고 어법에 맞게 쓰였는지 확인해야 한다.
① 전치사구 because of에 밑줄이 있는 경우, 그 뒤에 명사구가 왔는지 살펴보아야 한다. 뒤에 주어 동사를 갖춘 문장이 왔다면 because가 쓰여야 한다.
② 형용사와 부사를 구별하는 문제이다. deep은 형용사로 명사나 대명사를 수식하고, deeply는 부사이므로 형용사, 부사, 동사 등을 수식한다. 이 문장에서는 대명사 something을 수식하고 있으므로 형용사 deep은 적절하게 쓰인 것이다.
③ -ing 형태에 밑줄이 그어져 있을 경우에는 분사나 동명사의 용법을 떠올려야 한다. 이 문장에서는 절이 줄어든 형태인 분사구문으로 올바르게 사용된 것이다. 분사구문의 경우에는 분사구문의 시제도 염두에 두어야 한다. 즉 완료분사구문이 쓰여야 할 자리에 단순 분사구문이 쓰이지는 않았는지도 확인할 필요가 있다. 이 문장에서는 앞의 절의 시제와 일치하므로 단순 분사구문으로 쓰인 것은 올바르다.
④ 관계대명사와 관계부사의 구별을 묻는 문제이다. 관계부사는 뒤에 주어 동사를 갖춘 완전한 문장이 따라오며, 관계대명사는 그 뒤에 주어, 목적어, 보어 중 하나가 부족한 문장이 나온다. 이 문장에서는 주어가 보이지 않으므로 관계부사 where를 관계대명사 that으로 바꿔야 한다.
⑤ 대명사에 밑줄이 있는 경우에는 대명사가 가리키는 것이 무엇인지 파악하고, 그 선행사와 수가 일치하는지 확인해야 한다. 이 문장에서는 단수명사 the message를 가리키는 것이므로 단수 대명사 it은 적절하게 사용된 것이다.

《 어휘 · 어구 》

deviate 일탈하다, 벗어나다
destined ~할 운명인
temptation 유혹
immediate 즉각적인, 당면한

---

prospect 가능성, 전망
prosperity 성공, 번성
comply with ~에 순응하다, ~을 지키다
lag 줄어들다, 약해지다
eventually 결국, 궁극적으로
end up in 결국 ~로 끝나다
diversion 전환, 주의를 딴 데로 돌리게 하는 것
compromise 타협하다, 절충하다
recognize 인정하다, 인식하다
frustration 좌절

---

9. ⑤   정신 능력 훈련(MST)의 필요성

일부 코치들은 정신 능력 훈련(MST)이 고도로 숙련된 선수들의 기량을 완벽하게 하는 데에만 도움이 될 수 있다는 잘못된 믿음을 갖고 있다. 그 결과, 그들은 자신이 엘리트 선수를 지도하고 있지 않으므로 정신 능력 훈련이 덜 중요하다고 (A) 합리화하면서 정신 능력 훈련을 피한다. 높은 경쟁 수준에서 정신 능력이 점점 더 중요해지고 있다는 것은 사실이다. 선수들이 경쟁의 사다리를 올라갈수록 신체 능력의 측면에서는 더 비슷해진다. 사실상 높은 경쟁 수준에서는 모든 선수가 성공할 수 있는 신체 능력을 갖추고 있다. 결과적으로 (B) 정신적 요인에서의 어떠한 작은 차이라 하더라도 경기력의 결과를 결정하는 데 엄청난 역할을 할 수 있다. 그러나 우리는 개인의 성장과 경기력이, 정신 능력 훈련을 받지 않는 선수에서보다는 정신 능력 훈련을 받는 어리고 성장 중인 선수에게서 더 빠르게 진보할 것이라고 예상할 수 있다. 사실상, 정신 능력 훈련을 도입하기 위한 최적의 시간은, 선수들이 처음 운동을 시작할 때일지도 모른다. 선수 생활의 (C) 초기에 정신 능력 훈련을 도입하는 것은, 그들이 잠재 능력의 최고치까지 발달하도록 돕는 토대를 세울 수도 있다.

문제풀이

(A) 일부 코치들은 정신 능력 훈련이 고도로 숙련된 선수들에게만 도움이 된다고 잘못 알고 있다고 했으므로, 자신이 엘리트 선수를 지도하고 있지 않기 때문에 정신 능력 훈련이 덜 중요하다고 합리화한다는 의미가 되어야 한다. 따라서 'rationalizing(합리화하다)'이 적절하다. deny는 '부정하다'라는 의미이다.
(B) 선수들의 경쟁 수준이 높아질수록 신체 능력의 측면에서는 더 비슷해지고 사실상 경기력의 결과를 결정하는 것은 정신적 요인이라는 의미가 되어야 한다. 따라서 'mental(정신적인)'이 적절하다. physical은 '신체적인'이라는 의미이다.
(C) 정신 능력 훈련을 도입하기 위한 최적의 시간은 선수들이 운동을 처음 시작할 때일지도 모른다고 했으므로, 선수 생활의 초기에 훈련을 도입하는 것이 잠재 능력을 발달하도록 돕는다는 의미가 되어야 한다. 따라서, 'early(초기에)'가 적절하다. later는 '나중에'라는 의미이다. 따라서 정답은 ⑤이다.

《 구문 및 어휘 》

*3행 As a result, they shy away from MST, [**rationalizing** {that because they are not coaching elite athletes, mental skills training is less important}].
⑴「주절(they shy ~)+분사구문(rationalizing ~)」구조의 문장이다.
⑵ rationalizing ~ less important는 '~하면서'라는 의미의 부대상황을 나타내는 분사구문이다.
⑶ that because ~ less important는 rationalizing의 목적어로 쓰인 명사절이다. that절은 「부사절(because

---

they ~)+주절(mental skills ~)」 구조이다.
*6행 It is true [**that** mental skills become increasingly important at high levels of competition].
⑴ It은 가주어이고, that mental skills ~ of competition이 진주어이다.
*12행 However, we can anticipate [**that** personal growth and performance will progress faster in young, **developing** athletes {**who** are given mental skills training} than in athletes {not exposed to MST}].
⑴ that personal growth ~ to MST는 동사 anticipate의 목적어로 쓰인 명사절이다.
⑵ developing은 '성장 중인'이라는 의미로 뒤의 명사 athletes를 수식하는 현재분사이다.
⑶ who are given ~ training은 선행사 young, developing athletes를 수식하는 관계대명사절이다.
⑷ not exposed to MST는 athletes를 수식하는 과거분사구로 앞에 who[that] are가 생략되어 있다.
*15행 In fact, the optimal time [for introducing MST] may be [**when** athletes are first beginning their sport].
⑴ the optimal time이 문장의 주어이고, may be가 동사이다. for introducing MST는 the optimal time을 수식하는 전치사구이다.
⑵ when athletes ~ their sport는 관계부사절로 앞에 선행사 the time이 생략되어 있다.
*17행 [**Introducing** MST early in athletes' careers] **may lay** the foundation [**that** will help them develop to their full potential].
⑴ 동명사구 Introducing MST ~ careers가 문장의 주어이고 may lay가 동사이다.
⑵ that will ~ potential은 선행사 the foundation을 수식하는 관계대명사절이다.
⑶「help+목적어+동사원형」은 '~가 …하는 것을 돕다'라는 의미이다.

《 어휘 · 어구 》

erroneously 잘못되게, 틀리게
performance 기량
highly 고도로
skilled 숙련된
competitor 경쟁자
shy away from ~을 피하다
increasingly 점점 더
competition 경쟁
ladder 사다리
in terms of ~의 면에서, ~에 관해서는
consequently 결과적으로
play a role in ~에 역할을 하다
determine 결정하다
outcome 결과
anticipate 예상하다
expose ~ to … ~이 …을 받게[경험하게] 하다
lay the foundation 기초를 놓다, 토대를 세우다
potential 잠재 능력

---

10. ③   제삼자를 이용하여 친구 되기

당신은 친구가 되고 싶은 한 사람을 칭찬하기 위해 제삼자

를 이용해서 여전히 당신의 칭찬 대상이 자신에 대해 좋은 감정을 느끼고, 나아가 당신에 대해서 좋은 감정을 느끼게 한 것으로 '인정'받을 수 있다. 당신이 다른 사람들, 특히 당신이 그들로부터 무언가를 원할지도 모른다고 의심하는 누군가를 (A) 직접 칭찬할 때, 그들은 당신이 아첨을 통해 고의로 그들에게 영향을 미치려고 노력하고 있다고 의심하기 때문에 당신의 노력을 무시하는 경향이 있다. 제삼자의 칭찬은 이런 의심을 (B) 없앤다. 제삼자의 칭찬을 만들어내기 위해서 당신은 당신과 당신의 관심 대상인 사람을 모두 알고 있는 공통의 친구나 아는 사람을 찾을 필요가 있을 것이다. 더욱이 당신은 자신이 선택한 제삼자가 당신의 칭찬을 그것이 의도된 그 사람에게 전달해 줄 거라는 것을 어느 정도 확신해야 한다. 이 정보의 (C) 전달이 성공하면 당신이 당신의 관심 대상인 사람을 다음에 만났을 때 그 사람은 긍정적인 관점에서 당신을 보게 될 것이다.

문제풀이

(A) 아첨을 통해 그들에게 영향을 미치려고 노력하고 있다고 의심받을 수 있는 상황은 직접 칭찬할 때이므로 제삼자를 이용해 칭찬을 하라고 했다. 따라서 'directly(직접)'가 적절하다. indirectly는 '간접'이라는 의미이다.
(B) 친구가 되고 싶다면 제삼자를 이용해서 칭찬하는 것이 좋다는 내용이므로, 제삼자의 칭찬은 아첨을 통해 고의로 영향을 미친다는 의심을 '없앤다'는 문맥이 되는 것이 의미상 자연스러우므로 'eliminates(없애다)'가 적절하다. encourage는 '고무하다'라는 의미이다.
(C)는 앞 문장에서 자신이 선택한 제삼자가 칭찬을 의도된 그 사람에게 전달해 준다면 그 사람이 자신을 긍정적인 관점에서 보게 된다고 했으므로, 'transmission(전달)'이 적절하다. clarification은 '설명'이라는 의미이다. 따라서 정답은 ③이다.

구문 및 어휘

*1행 You can use a third party **to compliment** a person [you want to befriend] and still get the "credit" for **making the target of your compliment feel** good about themselves and, by extension, **feel** good about you.
(1) use와 get은 can에 이어지는 동사로 and에 의해 병렬 연결되어 있다.
(2) to compliment ~ befriend는 목적을 나타내는 부사적 용법의 to부정사구이다.
(3) you want to befriend는 선행사 a person을 수식하는 관계대명사절로, 앞에 목적격 관계대명사 who(m)[that]가 생략되어 있다.
(4) 「make(사역동사)+목적어+동사원형」은 '~를 …하게 하다'라는 의미이다. 두 개의 feel은 and에 의해 병렬 연결되어 있다.
*4행 When you directly compliment other people, particularly anybody [who suspects {you might want something from them}], they tend to discount your efforts because they suspect [you are intentionally trying to influence them through flattery].
(1) 「부사절(When you ~)+주절(they tend ~)」 구조의 문장이다. 주절은 「주절(they tend ~)+부사절(because they ~)」 구조이다.
(2) who ~ from them은 선행사 anybody를 수식하는 관계대명사절이다.
(3) you might ~ from them은 동사 suspects의 목적어로 쓰인 명사절로 앞에 접속사 that이 생략되어 있다.
(4) you are ~ flattery은 동사 suspect의 목적어로 쓰

인 명사절로 앞에 접속사 that이 생략되어 있다.
*12행 **Further**, you should **be** relatively **certain** [**that** the third-party individual {you choose} will be likely to pass along your compliment to the person {for whom it was intended}].
(1) further는 '게다가'라는 의미로 쓰였다.
(2) 「be certain that+주어+동사」는 '~하는 것을 확신하다'라는 의미이다.
(3) that절의 주어는 the third-party individual이고, will be likely to pass가 동사이다.
(4) you choose는 선행사 the third-party individual을 수식하는 관계대명사절로, 앞에 that[who(m)]이 생략되어 있다.
(5) for whom ~ intended는 선행사 the person을 수식하는 관계대명사절이다.

third-party 제삼자
befriend 친구가 되어 주다
compliment 칭찬하다; 칭찬
by extension 더 나아가
particularly 특히, 특별히
suspect 의심하다
discount 치부하다, 무시하다
intentionally 고의로
flattery 아첨
skepticism 의심
mutual 공동의, 공통의
acquaintance 아는 사람
positive 긍정적인
perspective 관점

11. ②   음악의 고전적인 특징

작곡가들이 형식과 디자인을 자유롭게 실험하기 시작했던 20세기까지, 고전 음악은 화음은 말할 것도 없이, 구조와 관련 있는 기본적인 규칙들을 계속해서 따랐다. 여전히 위대한 작곡가들은 규칙을 따르지 않고, 규칙이 그들을 따르게 하는 (A) 개성을 발휘할 여지는 있었지만, 디자인 이면에는 항상 기본적인 비율과 논리가 있었다. 더 최근에는 많은 규칙이 급진적인 개념에 의해 (B) 뒤집어진 이후에도, 대개 작곡가들은 여전히 전체적이고 통일적인 구조를 생산해내는 방식으로 자신들의 생각을 구성했다. 그것이, 두 명의 20세기 모더니즘 작곡가를 예로 들어, Arnold Schönberg나 Karlheinz Stockhausen에 의해 작곡된 무조의 매우 복잡한 작품들이 그럼에도 불구하고 (C) 접근 할 수 있는 하나의 이유이다. 그 소리는 아주 이상할 수도 있지만, 그 결과는 여전히 구성의 측면에서 확실히 고전적이다.

문제풀이

(A) 위대한 작곡가들이 규칙을 따르지 않고 규칙들이 그들을 따르도록 했다는 것은 개성을 발휘할 여지가 있었다는 것이므로, 'individuality(개성)'가 적절하다. conformity는 '복종, 순응'의 의미이다.
(B) 더 최근에 급진적인 개념에 의해서 규칙들이 뒤집혔을 것이므로, 'overturn(뒤집히다)'이 적절하다. maintain은 '유지하다'라는 의미이다.
(C) 소리는 이상할 수 있지만 결과물은 구성적 측면에서 확실하게 고전적이었다고 했으므로, 복잡한 작품들에도 접근이 가능하다. 따라서 'approachable(접근할 수 있는)'이 적절하다. inaccessible는 '접근할 수 없는'이라는 의미이다. 따라서 정답은 ②이다.

구문 및 어휘

*1행 Until the twentieth century, [**when** composers began experimenting freely with form and design], classical music continued to follow basic rules [**relating** to structure, **not to mention** harmony].
(1) when ~ and design은 선행사 the twentieth century에 대해 부연 설명해 주는 계속적 용법의 관계부사절이다.
(2) relating to ~ harmony는 basic rules를 수식하는 현재분사구이다.
(3) not to mention은 '~는 말할 것도 없이'라는 의미이다.
*7행 Even after many of the rules were overturned by radical concepts in more recent times, composers, **more often than not**, still organized their thoughts in ways [**that** produced an overall, unifying structure].
(1) 「부사절(Even after ~)+주절(composers ~)」 구조의 문장이다.
(2) more often than not은 '대개'라는 의미이다.
(3) that ~ unifying structure는 선행사 ways를 수식하는 관계대명사절이다.

composer 작곡가
experiment with ~을 실험하다
relate to ~와 관련되다
structure 구조
not to mention ~은 말할 것도 없이
harmony 화음, 조화
fundamental 기본적인
proportion 비율, 비, 균형
logic 논리
radical 급진적인
more often than not 대개
overall 전반적인
unifying 통일적인
incredibly 매우, 엄청나게
to name 예를 들면
nonetheless 그럼에도 불구하고
decidedly 확실히
in terms of ~의 측면에서

12. ③   포식자와 먹잇감의 끝나지 않는 싸움

직독/직해

When a bat is scanning its environment, /
박쥐는 환경을 살필 때 /
it emits about ten to twenty clicks every second.
매 초마다 10~20번의 혀 차는 소리를 낸다
But when it picks up an echo / returned from a target, /
그러나 그것이 울림소리를 듣게 될 때 / 표적에서 되돌아온 /
it increases that rate / 그것은 그 속도를 증가시킨다
to as many as two hundred clicks a second /
초당 2백 번까지나 많게 /
in order to aim at the position and identity of its prey. 먹잇감의 위치와 정체를 겨냥하기 위해
Some species of moth, / 나방의 어떤 종들은 /
upon hearing a bat's clicks, /
박쥐의 혀 차는 소리를 듣자마자 /
will instantly fold their wings / 즉시 날개를 접는다 /
and drop straight down / to avoid getting caught.
그리고 곧장 하강을 한다 / 잡히는 것을 피하기 위해
Bats, / in turn, /
박쥐는 / 결과적으로 /
have evolved ways of reducing their clicks /

혀 차는 소리를 줄이는 방법을 발전시켰다 /

to take in a wide area / 넓은 지역을 포함하기 위해 /

in which even a plummeting bug will be tracked.
심지어 곤두박질치는 벌레도 추적할

Some moths have counter-adapted /
어떤 나방들은 역으로 적응을 한다 /

and evolved long extensions /
그리고 연장된 긴 부분을 진화시켰다 /

to the backs of their wings / that twirl in flight /
날개의 뒷부분으로   / 날 때 빙빙 도는 /

to attract bats' attention. 박쥐의 관심을 끌기 위해

The extensions are disposable to the moth, /
연장된 부분은 나방에게 일회용이다 /

so if a bat targets / 그래서 박쥐가 목표로 삼는다면 /

and succeeds at biting them, /
그리고 그것들을 무는데 성공한다면 /

the moth will simply break away and escape.
나방은 쉽게 끊어버리고 달아날 것이다

It is a neverending battle / 이것은 결코 끝나지 않는 싸움이다 /
between predator and prey / 포식자와 먹잇감 사이의 /

— one in which bats will surely adapt once again /
그 싸움에서 박쥐들은 분명 다시 한번 적응할 것이다 /

to refine their already outstanding ability to echolocate.
이미 뛰어난 초음파를 통해 위치를 탐지하는 능력을 개선하기 위해

박쥐는 환경을 살필 때, 매 초마다 10~20번의 혀 차는 소리를 낸다. 그러나 그것이 표적에서 되돌아온 울림소리를 듣게 될 때, 그것은 먹잇감의 위치와 정체를 겨냥하기 위해 그 속도를 초당 2백 번까지나 많게 ① 증가시킨다. 박쥐의 혀 차는 소리를 듣자마자, 나방의 어떤 종들은 잡히는 것을 ② 피하기 위해 즉시 날개를 접고 곧장 하강을 한다. 결과적으로, 박쥐들은 곤두박질치는 벌레도 추적할 넓은 지역을 포함하기 위해 혀 차는 소리를 ③ 줄이는(→ 늘리는) 방법을 발전시켰다. 어떤 나방들은 역으로 적응을 해서 박쥐의 관심을 끌기 위해 날 때 빙빙 도는 날개의 뒷부분으로 연장된 긴 부분을 진화시켰다. 연장된 부분은 나방에게 일회용이어서, 박쥐가 그것을 의식하고 무는 데 성공한다면, 나방은 (연장된 부분이) 쉽게 끊어져 버리면서 달아날 것이다. 이것은 포식자와 먹잇감 사이의 결코 끝나지 않는 싸움으로, 그 싸움에서 박쥐들은 이미 뛰어난 초음파를 통해 위치를 탐지하는 능력을 ⑤ 개선하기 위해 분명 다시 한번 적응할 것이다.

문제풀이

이 글은 먹이를 찾기 위해 혀 차는 소리를 사용하는 박쥐와, 박쥐에게 잡히는 것을 피하기 위해 날개를 접고 하강을 하거나, 날개의 뒷부분으로 연장된 부분을 진화시키는 나방의 특징, 그리고 또한 그것에 적응하기 위해 혀 차는 소리를 늘리는 박쥐의 특징에 관하여 언급하고 있다. 나방이 잡히는 것을 피하기 위해 하강을 할 때, 이를 추적할 넓은 지역을 포함하기 위해 혀차는 소리를 늘릴 것임을 알 수 있으므로 ③ 'reducing(줄이는)'을 'increasing(늘리는)' 등의 어휘로 고쳐야 한다.

《 어휘 · 어구 》

emit (빛 · 열 · 가스 · 소리 등을) 내다[내뿜다]

click 혀 차는 소리

pick up ~을 듣다[보게 되다]

aim at ~을 겨냥하다, 노리다

identity 정체성

prey 먹이

moth 나방

upon -ing ~하자마자

in turn 결국, 결과적으로

evolve 진화하다

extension 확장

twirl 빙빙 돌다

disposable 일회용의

break away 달아나다

predator 포식자

outstanding 뛰어난

---

15. 관계부사

A 출제 POINT
본문 086쪽

1. there   2. when   3. the way
4. where   5. from   6. that
7. whenever

1 [해석]▶ 결혼 후 아파트 한 채를 샀는데, 그곳에서 이후 10년간 살았다.
[해설]▶ 관계부사(where)는 「접속사(and)+부사(there)」의 역할을 한다.

2 [해석]▶ 네가 진정한 사랑을 찾을 시간이 올 것이다.
[해설]▶ 선행사가 시간(a time) 표현이 나오고 괄호 이하 부분이 완전한 문장이 나왔으므로 관계부사 when이 필요하다.

3 [해석]▶ 나는 그가 나를 보는 방식이 마음에 들지 않는다.
[해설]▶ 관계부사 how는 선행사(the way)와 함께 쓰지 않고 둘 중 하나만 써야 한다.

4 [해석]▶ 그들은 마침내 산 정상에 도달했는데, 그들은 그곳에서 주변에 구름을 제외하고 아무 것도 볼 수가 없었다.
[해설]▶ 선행사가 the mountaintop인 관계부사 where의 계속적 용법이다.

5 [해석]▶ 그것은 처방전에 있는 약을 받을 수 있는 자동 판매기이다.
[해설]▶ 관계부사는 「전치사+관계대명사」로 바꾸어 쓸 수 있다. That's a vending machine where(= from which) you can get prescriptions drugs.

6 [해석]▶ 그들은 결정을 내려야 할 시간에 이르렀다.
[해설]▶ 관계부사 when 대신 that을 사용할 수 있다.

7 [해석]▶ 네가 필요할 때는 언제든지 전화해.
[해설]▶ 복합관계부사 whenever는 '~할 때는 언제나(= at any time when)'의 의미를 가지고 있다.

B 체크 POINT
본문 086쪽

1. there   2. why   3. the way
4. when   5. at   6. that
7. Wherever

1 [해석]▶ 우리는 마침내 지리산 정상에 도착했지만, 그곳에서 구름을 제외하고 아무 것도 볼 수 없었다.
[해설]▶ 관계부사는 접속사(but)+부사(there)로 바꿀 수 있다.

2 [해석]▶ 나는 Sally가 나의 초대를 왜 거절했는지 그 이유를 모른다.
[해설]▶ 이유를 나타내는 선행사(the reason)가 나오고 괄호 이하의 문장은 완전하므로 관계부사 why가 필요하다.

3 [해석]▶ 나는 그녀가 나를 바라보는 방식이 맘에 든다.
[해설]▶ 선행사 the way나 관계부사 how는 '~하는 방식'의 의미를 가지고 있다. 주어진 문장은 I like the way.와 She looks at me in the way.라는 두 문장을 앞 문장의 the way를 선행사로 만들고, 뒷 문장의 in the way를 in which

---

로 바꾼 문장이다.

4 [해석]▶ 내가 좋아하는 달은 2월인데, 그 달에 우리는 발렌타인데이를 기념한다.
[해설]▶ 선행사 the Fruary를 설명하는 관계부사 when의 계속적 용법이다.

5 [해석]▶ 이곳은 그녀가 스마트폰을 잃은 장소이다.
[해설]▶ 관계부사는 「전치사+관계대명사」로 바꾸어 쓸 수 있다. 주어진 문장은 This is the place where(= at which) she lost her smartphone.에서 관계부사 where를 「전치사+관계대명사」로 바꾼 문장이다.

6 [해석]▶ 이것이 철새들이 길을 찾아가는 방법이다.
[해설]▶ 선행사가 the way(방식)는 관계부사 how와 함께 쓸 수 없다. 관계부사 how 대신 that을 쓸 수 있다.

7 [해석]▶ 네가 어디에 있든지 내가 너와 함께 있을게.
[해설]▶ 복합관계부사 wherever는 '~하는 곳은 어디나(= at any place where)의 의미가 있다.

Day 15
본문 087쪽

1	①	2	③	3	②	4	③	5	④
6	①	7	②	8	⑤	9	④	10	⑤
11	②	12	④

1. ①
탁월함에 중점을 두는 건설적인 피드백의 필요성

직독 직해

Competitive activities can be /
경쟁을 하는 활동은 ~일 수 있다 /

more than just performance showcases /
단지 수행 기량을 보여주는 공개 행사 그 이상 /

where the best is recognized /
최고는 인정받는 /

and the rest are overlooked.
그리고 나머지는 무시되는

The provision of timely, constructive feedback /
때맞춘 건설적인 피드백을 제공하는 것은 /

to participants / on performance /
참가자에게 / 수행 기량에 대한 /

is an asset / 자산이다 /

that some competitions and contests offer.
일부 대회와 경연이 제공하는

In a sense, / all competitions give feedback.
어떤 의미에서는 / 모든 대회가 피드백을 제공한다

For many, / this is restricted to information /
많은 경우에 / 이것은 정보에 한정된다 /

about whether the participant is an award- or prizewinner.
참가자가 상을 받는지에 관한

The provision of that type of feedback /
그러한 유형의 피드백을 제공하는 것은 /

can be interpreted / 해석될 수 있다 /

as shifting the emphasis to demonstrating superior performance /
강조점을 우월한 수행 기량을 보여주는 것으로 이동하는 것으로 /

but not necessarily excellence.
반드시 탁월함은 아닌

The best competitions promote excellence, /
최고의 대회는 탁월함을 증진한다 /

not just winning or "beating" others.
단순히 승리하는 것이나 다른 사람을 "패배시키는 것"만이 아닌

The emphasis on superiority / is what we typically see /
우월성에 대한 강조 / 우리가 일반적으로 간주하는 것이다 /

as fostering a detrimental effect of competition.
유해한 경쟁 효과를 조장하는 것으로

Performance feedback requires /
수행 기량에 대한 피드백은 요구한다 /

that the program go beyond the "win, place, or show"
level of feedback.
프로그램이 '이기거나, 입상하거나, 혹은 보여주는' 수준의 피드백을 넘어설 것을

Information about performance / can be very helpful, /
수행 기량에 관한 정보는 / 아주 도움이 될 수 있다 /

not only to the participant / who does not win or place /
참가자뿐만 아니라 / 못 이기거나 입상하지 못하는 /

but also to those who do.
이기거나 입상하는 참가자에게도

경쟁을 하는 활동은 최고는 인정받고 나머지는 무시되는, 단지 수행 기량을 보여주는 공개 행사 그 이상일 수 있다. 참가자에게 수행 기량에 대한 때맞춘 건설적인 피드백을 제공하는 것은 일부 대회와 경연이 제공하는 자산이다. 어떤 의미에서는 모든 대회가 피드백을 제공한다. 많은 경우에, 이것은 참가자가 상을 받는지에 관한 정보에 한정된다. 그러한 유형의 피드백을 제공하는 것은 반드시 탁월함은 아닌, 우월한 수행 기량을 보여주는 것으로 강조점을 이동하는 것으로 해석될 수 있다. 최고의 대회는 단순히 승리하는 것이나 다른 사람을 '패배시키는 것'만이 아닌 탁월함을 증진한다. 우월성에 대한 강조는 우리가 일반적으로 유해한 경쟁 효과로 간주하는 것을 조장하는 것으로 간주하는 것이다. 수행 기량에 대한 피드백은 프로그램이 '이기거나, 입상하거나, 혹은 보여주는' 수준의 피드백을 넘어설 것을 요구한다. 수행 기량에 관한 정보는 못 이기거나 입상하지 못하는 참가자뿐만 아니라 이기거나 입상하는 참가자에게도 아주 도움이 될 수 있다.

문제풀이

① [관계대명사]
which 뒤에 이어진 the best is recognized와 the rest are overlooked는 둘 다 주어가 있고 동사는 수동태로 쓰여 완전한 절이므로, 관계대명사 which가 올 수는 없다. 선행사가 performance showcases이므로, which를 관계부사 where로 고쳐 써야 한다.

② [주어-동사 수일치]
주어는 The provision이고 of timely, constructive feedback to participants on performance는 The provision을 수식하는 전치사구이므로, 단수 주어에 맞춰 단수동사 is가 오는 것이 적절하다.

③ [부사]
not necessarily는 '반드시 ~은 아닌'이라는 의미의 부분 부정인데, not necessarily와 excellence 사이에 demonstrating이 생략된 것으로 볼 수 있으므로, demonstrating을 수식하는 부사 necessarily는 어법상 적절하다.

④ [동명사]
'A를 B로 간주하다'라는 뜻의 'see A as B'에서 전치사 as의 목적어가 와야 하므로, 동명사 fostering이 온 것은 적절하다.

⑤ [대동사]
앞의 win or place의 반복을 피하기 위한 대동사가 와야 하므로, 일반동사를 받는 대동사 do가 온 것은 적절하다.

> ○ 이렇게 풀자 어법상 틀린 부분을 찾는 문제는 밑줄이 있는 부분의 형태와 문맥을 보고 어법에 맞게 쓰였는지 확인해야 한다.
> ① 관계대명사에 밑줄이 있는 경우, 선행사의 종류에 맞게 사용되었는지 살펴야 한다. 또한 관계대명사 뒤에는 주어나 목적어가 빠진 불완전한 절이 오고, 관계부사의 경우 뒤에 완전한 절이 온다는 것을 기억하면서 관계부사가 와야 하는 것은 아닌지 살펴야 한다.
> ② 동사에 밑줄이 그어진 경우, 주어와 동사의 수일치를 묻는 문제인 경우가 많다. 따라서 주어를 분명히 파악하는 것이 중요하다.
> ③ 부사는 동사의 앞이나 뒤에서 동사를 수식하거나 문장의 앞뒤에서 문장 전체를 수식할 수 있으며, 또한 형용사나 다른 부사를 수식할 수 있다.
> ④ 전치사의 목적어로는 동명사가 와야 한다.
> ⑤ 동사 do의 목적어가 없다면 대동사일 가능성이 높다. 대동사는 일반동사를 받으면 do를 쓰고 be동사를 받으면 be동사를 쓴다.

〈 어휘·어구 〉

competitive 경쟁을 하는
showcase 공개 행사, 진열장
overlook 무시하다, 간과하다
provision 제공, 공급
timely 시기적절한, 때맞춘
constructive 건설적인
asset 자산, 재산
restrict 한정하다
interpret 해석하다, 이해하다
emphasis 강조(점), 주안점
demonstrate 보여주다, 입증하다
promote 장려하다, 증진하다
beat 패배시키다, 이기다

---

2. ③ 직장에서 최고의 날을 만드는 동료 의식

직독 직해

When asked, / 질문을 받을 때 /
"What was one of your best days at work?" /
"직장에서 최고의 날 중 하나는 언제였습니까?"라는

very few of us recount the time /
우리 중 그 때를 이야기하는 사람은 극히 드물다 /

everything went smoothly /
모든 것이 순조롭게 진행되는 /

and the big project / we were working on /
그리고 큰 프로젝트가 / 우리가 공들이고 있던 /

came in on time and under budget.
제 때에 그리고 예산 범위 내에서 이루어진

Considering how we work so hard /
우리가 얼마나 정말 열심히 일하는지를 고려하면 /

to make things go well, / 일이 잘 되게 하려고 /

that example should count /
그 사례는 간주되어야 한다 /

as a pretty good day at work.
직장에서 꽤 좋은 날로

But strangely, / the days everything goes smoothly /
그러나 이상하게도 / 모든 것이 순조롭게 진행되는 날은 /

and as planned / 그리고 계획대로 (진행되는) /

are not the ones / we remember with fondness.
날들이 아니다 / 우리가 애정을 가지고 기억하는

For most of us, / we have warmer feelings /
우리 대부분에 있어 / 우리는 더 따뜻한 감정을 가지고 있다 /

for the projects / 프로젝트에 대해 /

we worked on / where everything seemed to go wrong.
우리가 공들였던 / 모든 것이 잘못되어 가는 것처럼 보였던

We remember / 우리는 기억한다 /

how the group stayed at work until 3 a.m., /
어떻게 그 집단이 새벽 3시까지 일했는지 /

ate cold pizza / 식어버린 피자를 먹었는지 /

and barely made the deadline.
그리고 마감 시간을 가까스로 맞췄는지

Those are the experiences / we remember /
그것들은 경험들이다 / 우리가 기억하는 /

as some of our best days at work.
우리가 직장에서 가장 좋았던 날 중 일부로

It was not because of the hardship, / per se, /
그것은 고난 때문이 아니다 / 그 자체로 /

but because the hardship was shared.
고난을 함께했기 때문이었다

It is not the work / we remember with fondness, /
일이 아니다 / 우리가 애정을 가지고 기억하는 것은 /

but the fellowship, / 동료 의식이다 /

how the group came together / to get things done.
그 집단이 하나로 합쳤던 방식이다 / 일을 해내려고

"직장에서 최고의 날 중 하나는 언제였습니까?"라는 질문을 받으면, 모든 것이 순조롭게 진행되고, 우리가 공들이고 있었던 큰 프로젝트가 제 때에 그리고 예산 범위 내에서 이루어진 때를 얘기하는 사람은 우리 중 극히 드물다. 우리가 일이 잘 되게 하려고 얼마나 정말 열심히 일하는지를 고려하면, 그 사례는 직장에서 꽤 좋은 날로 간주되어야 한다. 그러나

이상하게도 모든 것이 순조롭게 그리고 계획대로 진행되는 날은 우리가 애정을 가지고 기억하는 날이 아니다. 우리 대부분에 있어, 모든 것이 잘못되어 가는 것처럼 보였던 우리가 공들였던 프로젝트에 대해 우리는 더 따뜻한 감정을 가지고 있다. 우리는 그 집단이 새벽 3시까지 일하면서 식어버린 피자를 먹고 마감 시간을 가까스로 맞췄던 것을 기억한다. 그것들은 우리가 직장에서 가장 좋았던 날 중 일부로 기억하는 경험들이다. 그것은 고난, 그 자체 때문이 아니라 고난을 함께했기 때문이었다. 우리가 애정을 가지고 기억하는 것은 일이 아니라 동료 의식, 즉 일을 해내려고 그 집단이 하나로 합쳤던 방식이다.

문제풀이

① [전치사]
'Considering'은 '~을 고려하면'의 의미를 지닌 전치사로, 명사절인 'how we work~'를 목적어로 취하고 있으므로 적절하다.

② [주어와 동사의 수일치]
문장의 주어는 the days이고 'everything goes smoothly and as planned'는 the days를 수식하는 관계사절이므로 복수동사 are는 적절하다.

③ [관계대명사 vs 관계부사]
which가 포함된 문장에서 'we worked on'과 'which everything seemed to go wrong'은 모두 the projects 수식하는 관계사절인데, 'everything seemed to go wrong'은 문장의 성분을 모두 갖춘 2형식의 완전한 절로 주어와 목적어 역할을 해야 하는 관계대명사 which는 사용할 수 없으므로, 관계부사 where로 고쳐야 한다.

④ [병렬 구조]
made는 앞의 stayed, ate와 병렬 구조를 이루고 있는 동사로 어법상 적절하다.

⑤ [to부정사]
to get은 '~하기 위해'라는 목적의 의미를 나타내는 to부정사로 어법상 적절하다.

〈 어휘·어구 〉

recount (자기가 경험한 것에 대해) 이야기하다
work on ~에 공들이다
barely 가까스로, 간신히
make the deadline 마감 시간에 맞추다
fellowship 동료 의식, 동료애

---

3. ② 빠른 음악과 빠른 운전 속도와의 상관관계

직독 직해

Given that music appears to enhance physical and mental skills, /
음악이 신체적, 정신적 기술을 향상시키는 듯하다는 점을 감안할 때 /

are there circumstances /
상황이 있는가? /

where music is damaging to performance?
음악이 작업 수행에 해로운

One domain / 한 영역 중 하나는 /

where this is of considerable significance /
이것이 상당히 중요한 의미를 갖는 /

is music's potentially damaging effects /
음악이 ~에 잠재적으로 미칠 수 있는 손상이다. /

on the ability to drive safely.
안전 운전 능력에

Evidence suggests / 제시하는 증거가 있는데, /

an association between loud, fast music and reckless driving,
시끄럽고 빠른 음악과 난폭한 운전 사이의 연관성을

but how might music's ability to influence /
어떻게 음악의 영향력이 /

driving in this way / 이런 방식으로 운전하는데 대한 /

be explained? 설명될 수 있을까?

One possibility is / that drivers adjust to /
한 가지 가능성은 ~이다 / 운전자가 적응한다는 것 /

temporal regularities in music, /
음악에 있어서 박자의 규칙성에 /

and that their speed is influenced accordingly.
그리고 그들의 속도가 그에 따라 영향을 받는다는 것(이다)

In other words, / 다시 말해, /

just as faster music causes people to eat faster, /
보다 빠른 음악이 사람들에게 더 빨리 음식을 먹도록 하는 것과 마찬가지로

so it causes people to drive at faster speeds, /
보다 빠른 음악은 사람들로 하여금 더 빠른 속도로 운전하게 한다는 것이다.

as they engage mentally and physically /
정신적, 신체적으로 맞물리면서

with ongoing repeated structures in the music.
계속 반복되는 음악 구조에

음악이 신체적, 정신적 기술을 향상시키는 듯하다는 점을 감안할 때, 음악이 작업 수행에 해로운 상황이 있는가? 이것이 상당히 중요한 의미를 갖는 한 영역 중 하나는 음악이 안전 운전 능력에 미칠 수 있는 손상이다. 시끄럽고 빠른 음악과 난폭한 운전 사이의 연관성을 제시하는 증거가 있는데, 이런 방식으로 운전하는데 음악의 음향력이 어떻게 설명될 수 있을까? 한 가지 가능성은 운전자가 음악에 있어서 박자의 규칙성에 적응한다는 것, 그리고 그들의 속도가 그에 따라 영향을 받는다는 것이다. 다시 말해, 보다 빠른 음악이 사람들로 하여금 더 빨리 음식을 먹도록 하는 것과 꼭 마찬가지로 보다 빠른 음악은 사람들로 하여금 계속 반복되는 음악 구조에 정신적, 신체적으로 맞물리면서 더 빠른 속도로 운전하게 한다는 것이다.

문제풀이

① damaging은 '해로운'이라는 뜻의 형용사로 주어의 상태를 설명하는 보어이다.
② 뒤에 오는 문장이 기본 요소를 모두 갖춘 완전한 문장이므로 관계대명사 which를 관계부사 where로 고쳐 써야 한다.
③ 의문사 how가 이끄는 의문문의 주어는 music's ability ~ this way이고 동사는 might be explained이다. 주어가 동작의 대상이므로 수동태로 나타내었다. 또한 의문문이므로 might가 주어 앞으로 도치되었다.
④ 접속사 that이 이끄는 that their speed ~ accordingly와 앞에 있는 that drivers ~ music이 서로 병렬 구조를 이루어 is의보어로 사용되었다.
⑤에서 'just as ~, so …'구조가 사용되었다.

어휘·어구

enhance 향상시키다
domain 분야
association 연관성
reckless 난폭한, 무모한

4. ③   후발 예술, 혼합 예술로 불리는 영화의 특징

직독/직해

We take it for granted / 우리는 당연시한다. /
that film directors are in the game of recycling.
영화감독들이 재활용 게임을 하고 있다는 것을

Adapting novels / 소설을 가색하는 것은 /
is one of the most respectable of movie projects, /
가장 훌륭한 영화 프로젝트들 중 하나인 반면,
while a book that calls itself the novelization of a film /
영화를 소설화했다고 하는 책은
is considered barbarous.   상스럽게 여겨진다.
Being a hybrid art as well as a late one, /
후발 예술이면서 동시에 혼합 예술이기도 한
film has always been in a dialogue /
영화는 항상 대화를 해왔다. /
with other narrative genres.
다른 서사 장르와
Movies were first seen /
영화는 초기에 ~로 보였다 /
as an exceptionally potent kind of illusionist theatre,
특별히 유력한 일종의 미술 공연장으로

---

the rectangle of the screen /
직사각형 모양의 화면이 /
corresponding to the proscenium of a stage, /
앞무대와 유사하게 보이면서,
of which appear actors.   배우가 출연하는
Starting in the early silent period, /
초창기 무성 영화기를 시발점으로 /
plays were regularly "turned into" films.
연극은 자주 영화로 '전환'되었다.
But filming plays did not encourage /
하지만 연극을 영화화하는 것은 조장하지 못했다.
the evolution of what truly was distinctive about a movie:
영화의 진정한 독특함의 발전을
the intervention of the camera /
즉 카메라의 개입 /
— its mobility of vision.
다시 말해 그것의 시각적 기동성의 (발전을)
As a source of plot, character, and dialogue, /
줄거리, 등장인물, 대화의 공급원으로서
the novel seemed more suitable.
소설이 (연극보다 영화에) 더 적합해 보였다.
Many early successes of cinema /
영화의 초기 성공작의 다수가 /
were adaptations of popular novels.
유명 소설을 각색한 것이었다.

우리는 영화감독들이 재활용 게임을 하고 있다는 것을 당연시한다. 소설을 각색하는 것은 가장 훌륭한 영화 프로젝트들 중 하나인 반면, 영화를 소설화했다고 하는 책은 상스럽게 여겨진다. 후발 예술이면서 동시에 혼합 예술이기도 한 영화는 다른 서사 장르와 항상 대화를 해왔다. 직사각형 모양의 화면이 앞무대와 유사하게 보이면서, 초기 영화는 특별히 유력한 일종의 미술 공연장으로 보였다. 초창기 무성 영화기를 시발점으로 연극은 자주 영화로 '전환'되었다. 하지만 연극을 영화화하는 것은 영화의 진정한 독특함, 즉 카메라의 개입, 다시 말해 그것의 시각적 기동성의 발전을 조장하지 못했다. 줄거리, 등장인물, 대화의 공급원으로서 소설이 (연극보다 영화에) 더 적합해 보였다. 영화의 초기 성공작의 다수가 유명 소설을 각색한 것이었다.

문제풀이

① 동명사 주어는 단수동사를 취한다.
② 형용사 other가 복수명사 genres를 수식하고 있다.
③ the proscenium of a stage를 선행사로 하는 「전치사+관계대명사」의 형태가 되어야 하므로, which를 on which로 고쳐 써야 한다. 뒤 문장을 분석하면 actors appear on the stage이므로 전치사 'on'이 필요하다.
④ filming plays가 동명사 주어 역할을 하고 있다.
⑤ 형용사 비교급 more suitable이 동사 seemed의 보어 역할을 하고 있다.

어휘·어구

adapt 각색[개작]하다, 적용하다
respectable 존경할 만한
novelization 소설화
barbarous 상스러운, 야만적인
hybrid 혼합, 삽종
potent 유력한, 강한
correspond to ~와 일치하다
distinctive 독특한
intervention 개입
mobility 기동력, 유동성

5. ④   해류를 따라 이동하던 장난감의 회귀

직독/직해

On January 10, 1992, /
1992년 1월 10일, /
a ship traveling through rough seas /
거친 바다를 항해하던 배 한 척이 /

---

lost 12 cargo containers, /
12개의 화물 컨테이너를 잃었는데, /
one of which held 28,800 floating bath toys
그 중 하나는 28,800개의 물에 뜨는 욕실 장난감을 담고 있었다.
Brightly colored ducks, frogs, and turtles /
밝은 색의 오리, 개구리, 그리고 거북이 모양의 장난감들은 /
were set adrift / in the middle of the Pacific Ocean.
표류하게 되었다 / 태평양 한가운데에
After seven months, / 7개월 후에 /
the first toys made landfall on beaches
해변 육지에 첫 번째 장난감들이 도달했다.
near Sitka, Alaska, / 알래스카의 Sitka 근처에 /
3,540 kilometers from where they were lost.
잃어버린 장소에서 3,540킬로미터 떨어진
Other toys floated north and west /
다른 장난감들은 북쪽과 서쪽으로 떠다녔다. /
along the Alaskan coast /
알래스카 해안을 따라 /
and across the Bering Sea.
그리고 베링 해를 가로질러
Some toy animals / stayed at sea even longer.
어떤 장난감들은 / 바다에 훨씬 더 오래 있었다.
They floated completely /
그것들은 완전히 떠다녔고, /
along the North Pacific currents, /
북태평양 해류를 따라
ending up back in Sitka. 결국에는 Sitka로 되돌아갔다.

1992년 1월 10일, 거친 바다를 항해하던 배 한 척이 12개의 화물 컨테이너를 잃었는데, 그 중 하나는 28,800개의 물에 뜨는 욕실 장난감을 담고 있었다. 밝은 색의 오리, 개구리, 그리고 거북이 모양의 장난감들은 태평양 한가운데에 표류하게 되었다. 7개월 후에 잃어버린 장소에서 3,540킬로미터 떨어진 알래스카의 Sitka 근처 해변 육지에 첫 번째 장난감들이 도달했다. 다른 장난감들은 알래스카 해안을 따라 그리고 베링 해를 가로질러 북쪽과 서쪽으로 떠다녔다. 어떤 장난감들은 바다에 훨씬 더 오래 있었다. 그것들은 완전히 북태평양 해류를 따라 떠다녔고, 결국에는 Sitka로 되돌아갔다.

문제풀이

(A) '거친 바다를 통해 항해하던 배 한 척'이라는 뜻으로, '항해하던'이 능동의 의미로 a ship을 수식하므로 현재분사 traveling이 와야 한다.
(B) '잃어버린 곳'이라는 뜻이므로 장소를 나타내는 관계부사 where가 와야 한다.
(C) '훨씬'이라는 뜻으로 비교급 longer를 강조하려면 even이 적절하다.

어휘·어구

adrift 표류하는
landfall 육지 도착, 육지 접근
completely 완전히
current 해류, 조류

6. ①   감사의 유익

직독/직해

Energize your life / 삶에 활력을 더하라. /
by starting each day with gratitude.
매일 감사하는 마음으로 시작함으로써
When you wake up, / before you do anything else, /
일어나면   / 다른 일을 하기 전에 잠깐 멈춰서, /
stop and count your blessings.
당신이 받은 축복을 세어보라.
Then find something special about each day /
그런 다음 그날 하루의 특별한 것을 찾아라. /
for which you can be thankful.
당신이 감사할 수 있는
It's a great way / 아주 좋은 방법이며, /
to get each day started on a positive note, /
긍정적인 마음가짐으로 하루를 시작하는 것은

and it can make a major difference /
이것은 큰 차이를 만들어 낼 수 있다. /

throughout the day. 그날 내내

Actively practicing gratitude on a regular basis /
규칙적으로 감사함을 적극적으로 행하는 것은 /

will keep you in touch / 계속해서 접할 수 있도록 해준다 /

with the very best of your possibilities.
당신이 지닌 최상의 가능성을

It will enable you / to see opportunities /
그것은 당신으로 하여금 해줄 것이다 / 기회를 인식하고, /

and utilize resources / 당신의 재원(능력)을 활용할 수 있게

which may otherwise have remained hidden.
규칙적으로 감사함을 실행하지 않았더라면 묻혔을지도 모를 (재원)

So in a very real sense / it will add value /
그러므로, 진정한 의미에 있어. / 이것은 가치를 더해줄 것이다. /

to each moment of the day. 하루하루의 매 순간에

There are many good things in your life, /
당신의 삶에는 좋은 것들이 많이 있다. /

waiting for you to fully appreciate and enjoy.
당신이 그것을 (찾아) 누리기를 기다리고 있다.

When you do this, / 당신이 그렇게 할 때 /

those positive things will grow even stronger
이런 긍정적인 것들은 훨씬 더 강해질 것이다.

매일 감사하는 마음으로 시작함으로써 삶에 활력을 더하라. 일어나면 다른 일을 하기 전에 잠깐 멈춰서, 당신이 받은 축복을 세어보라. 그런 다음 당신이 감사할 수 있는 그날 특별한 것을 찾아라. 긍정적인 마음가짐으로 하루를 시작하는 것은 아주 좋은 방법이며, 이것은 그날 내내 큰 차이를 만들어 낼 수 있다. 규칙적으로 감사함을 적극적으로 행하는 것은 당신이 지닌 최상의 가능성을 계속해서 접할 수 있도록 해준다. 그것은 당신으로 하여금 기회를 인식하고, 규칙적으로 감사함을 실행하지 않았더라면 묻혔을 지도 모를 당신의 재원(능력)을 활용할 수 있게 해줄 것이다. 그러므로 진정한 의미에 있어, 이것은 하루하루의 매 순간에 가치를 더해줄 것이다. 당신의 삶에는 좋은 것들이 많이 있다. 당신이 그것을 (찾아) 누리기를 기다리고 있다. 당신이 그렇게 할 때 이런 긍정적인 것들은 훨씬 더 강해질 것이다.

문제풀이

①은 원래 thankful for (something special)이므로, 전치사 for가 필요하다. 그 위치는 thankful 다음 혹은 관계대명사 앞으로 옮겨간다면 for which가 되어야 한다. 참고로, 관계사 that 앞에는 전치사를 쓸 수 없다. 한편, 접속사 역할을 하는 in that(~라는 점에서)이라는 표현도 익혀두면 좋다.

《 어휘 · 어구 》

energize 활력을 더하다
gratitude 감사
count 세다
blessing 축복
opportunity 기회
utilize 활용하다

---

7. ②   Alejandro Selkirk라고 불리는 섬

직독 직해

In the South Pacific Ocean, five hundred miles off
칠레 중부 해안에서 500마일 떨어진 남태평양에 /

the coast of central Chile, /
칠레 중부 해안에서 /

is a forbiddingly vertical volcanic island, seven
길이 7마일, 너비 4마일의 무섭게 정도로 수직인 화산섬이 있다

miles long and four miles wide.

It is populated by millions of seabirds and
수백만 마리의 바닷새와 수천 마리의 물개가 살고 있다

thousands of fur seals / but is devoid of people, /
/ 하지만 사람이 없다 /

except in the warmer months, when a handful of
몇몇 어부들이 바다가재를 잡으러 오는 따뜻한 여러 달을 제외하고는

fishermen come out to catch lobsters.

To reach the island, / which is officially called
섬에 도달하기 위해 / 공식적으로 Alejandro Selkirk라고 불리는 /

Alejandro Selkirk, /

---

you fly from Santiago in an eight-seater /
당신은 Santiago에서 8인승 비행기를 타야 한다 /

that makes twice-weekly flights to an island a
동쪽으로 100마일 떨어진 섬으로 주 2회 비행하는

hundred miles to the east.

Then you have to travel in a small boat from the
그런 다음 보트를 타고 활주로에서 그 섬의 유일한 마을로 이동해야 한다 /

airstrip to the island's only village, /

wait for a ride on another boat that occasionally
때때로 12시간 항해를 하는 또 다른 보트의 탑승을 기다려야 한다 /

makes the twelve-hour voyage, /

and then, often, wait further, sometimes for days, /
그러고 나서, 가끔 며칠 씩, 종종 더 기다려야 한다 /

for weather conducive to landing on the rocky shore.
암석 해안에 상륙하기에 좋은 날씨를

In the 1960s, / Chilean tourism officials renamed
1960년대에 / 칠레 관광청 공무원들이 섬의 이름을 바꿨다 /

the island /

after Alexander Selkirk, the Scottish adventurer /
스코틀랜드 탐험가 Alexander Selkirk를 따라 /

whose tale of solitary life on the island /
그 섬에서의 그의 고독한 삶의 이야기가 /

was probably the basis for Daniel Defoe's novel
아마도 Daniel Defoe의 소설 Robinson Crusoe의 토대였을지 모르는 /

Robinson Crusoe, /

but the locals still use its original name, Masafuera.
하지만 현지인들은 여전히 원래 이름 Masafuera를 사용한다

칠레 중부 해안에서 500마일 떨어진 남태평양에 길이 7마일, 너비 4마일의 무섭게 정도로 수직인 화산섬이 있다. 수백만 마리의 바닷새와 수천 마리의 물개가 살지만, 몇몇 어부들이 바다가재를 잡으러 오는 따뜻한 여러 달을 제외하고는 사람들은 없다. 공식적으로 Alejandro Selkirk라고 불리는 이 섬에 도달하기 위해서, 당신은 주 2회 비행하는 8인승 비행기를 타고 Santiago에서 동쪽으로 100마일 떨어진 섬으로 날아와야 한다. 그런 다음 보트를 타고 활주로에서 그 섬의 유일한 마을로 이동하여, 때때로 12시간 항해를 하는 또 다른 보트의 탑승을 기다리고, 그리고 나서 암석 해안에 상륙하기에 좋은 날씨를 흔히 더 기다려야 하는데, 종종 수일 동안 기다려야 하기도 한다. 1960년대에, 칠레 관광청 공무원들이 그 섬에서의 고독한 삶의 이야기가 아마도 Daniel Defoe의 소설 Robinson Crusoe의 토대가 된 스코틀랜드 탐험가 Alexander Selkirk를 따라 섬의 이름을 바꿨지만, 현지인들은 여전히 원래 이름인 Masafuera를 사용한다.

문제풀이

② 두 개의 절을 이어주며, 여기서는 선행사 the warmer months를 수식하는 관계부사절을 이끄는 관계부사가 들어갈 자리이므로 then은 관계부사 when으로 고쳐야 한다.
① 전치사구가 문두로 나오면서 주어(a forbiddingly vertical volcanic island)와 동사(is)가 도치된 문장이므로, is의 쓰임은 적절하다.
③ 선행사 an eight-seater에 이어지는 주격관계대명사 절의 동사이므로, makes는 쓰임이 적절하다.
④ conducive to는 '~에 도움이 되는'이라는 의미이다. 여기서 동명사 landing은 전치사 to의 목적어로서 쓰임이 적절하다.
⑤ 뒤에 완전한 절이 이어지고 the Scottish adventurer를 선행사로 하는 소유격 관계대명사로 쓰였으므로, whose는 적절하다.

❂ 이렇게 풀자_ 어법상 틀린 부분을 찾는 문제는 밑줄이 있는 부분의 형태와 문맥을 보고 어법에 맞게 쓰였는지 확인해야 한다. ① 도치를, ② 관계부사 when의 쓰임을, ③ 주격관계대명사 절에서의 수일치를, ④ 동명사의 쓰임을, ⑤ 소유격관계대명사의 쓰임을 알아야 한다.

《 어휘 · 어구 》

forbiddingly 기분 나쁘게, 무섭게
vertical 수직의
populate 살게 하다, 거주하게 하다
devoid of ~이 없는, 결여된
airstrip 활주로
voyage 항해
solitary 고독한, 외로운

---

local 그 고장 사람

8. ⑤   인류세

직독 직해

Researchers of the Earth's system have been focused, appropriately, /
지구 시스템 연구자들은 적절하게 집중해 왔다 /

on developing a better understanding /
더 잘 이해하는 데 /

of the vast and interconnected processes /
광대하고 상호 연관된 과정을 /

that create our environment, /
우리의 환경을 만들어 내는 /

and they have made a great deal of progress /
그리고 그들은 많은 진보를 했다 /

since the publication of *A Sand County Almanac*, /
'A Sand County Almanac'의 출간 이후에 /

a 1949 non-fiction book by Aldo Leopold.
Aldo Leopold가 쓴 1949년 논픽션 도서인

Although there are many problems left to solve, /
비록 해결하도록 남겨진 많은 문제가 있지만 /

knowledge about planetary life-support systems /
지구의 생명 유지 체계에 관한 지식은 /

has progressed far more rapidly /
훨씬 더 빠르게 발전했다 /

than society's willingness to use this knowledge.
이 지식을 사용하려는 사회의 의향보다

The biggest challenge facing humanity is /
인류가 직면하고 있는 가장 큰 문제는 ~이다 /

that our political, social, and economic systems are shortsighted.
우리의 정치적, 사회적, 그리고 경제적 체계가 근시안적이라는 것(이다)

Long-term planning typically considers years or decades, /
장기 설계는 보통 몇 년이나 몇십 년을 고려한다 /

but the global environmental processes /
하지만 지구의 환경적인 과정은 /

we are now influencing /
우리가 지금 영향을 미치고 있는 /

play out over centuries, millennia, or more.
수백 년, 수천 년, 혹은 그보다 더 많은 세월에 걸쳐 전개된다

We need to instill / a sense of geologic time /
우리는 서서히 불어넣을 필요가 있다 / 지질학적 시간 감각을 /

into our culture and our planning, /
우리의 문화와 우리의 설계에 /

to incorporate truly long-term thinking /
진정으로 장기적인 사고를 포함하기 위해서 /

into social and political decision making.
사회적이고 정치적인 의사 결정에

This is / what "thinking like a mountain" /
이것은 ~이다 / '산처럼 생각하기'가 /

should come to mean in the Anthropocene.
인류세에서 의미하게 되어야 하는 (것이다)

If we succeed in transforming our culture, /
만약 우리가 우리의 문화를 완전히 바꾸는 데 성공하면 /

residents of the later Anthropocene /
후대의 인류세 주민들은 /

will look back on the early twenty-first century /
21세기 초반을 돌아볼 것이다 /

as a time of human enlightenment, /
인류 계몽의 시기로 /

where people learned to truly think like mountains /
사람들이 진정으로 산처럼 생각할 수 있게 된 때를 /

by anticipating their long-lasting and complex effects on the world.
지구에 미치는 자신들의 오래 지속되는 복잡한 영향을 예견함으로써

지구 시스템 연구자들은 우리의 환경을 만들어 내는 광대하고 상호 연관된 과정을 더 잘 이해하는 데 적절하게 집중해 왔고, 그들은 Aldo Leopold가 쓴 1949년 논픽션 도서인 'A Sand County Almanac'의 출간 이후에 많은 진보를 했다. 비록 해결하도록 남겨진 많은 문제가 있지만, 지구의 생명 유지 체계에 관한 지식은 이 지식을 사용하려는 사회의 의향보다 훨씬 더 빠르게 발전했다. 인류가 직면하고 있는 가장 큰 문

Day 15 · 관계부사

제는 우리의 정치적, 사회적, 그리고 경제적 체계가 근시안적이라는 것이다. 장기 설계는 보통 몇 년이나 몇십 년을 고려하지만, 우리가 지금 영향을 미치고 있는 지구의 환경적인 과정은 수백 년, 수천 년, 혹은 그보다 더 많은 세월에 걸쳐 전개된다. 우리는 사회적이고 정치적인 의사 결정에 진정으로 장기적인 사고를 포함하기 위해서 우리의 문화와 우리의 설계에 지질학적 시간 감각을 서서히 불어넣을 필요가 있다. 이것이 '산처럼 생각하기'가 인류세에서 의미하게 되어야 하는 것이다. 만약 우리가 우리의 문화를 완전히 바꾸는 데 성공하면, 후대의 인류세 주민들은 21세기 초반인, 사람들이 지구에 미치는 자신의 오래 지속되는 복잡한 영향을 예견함으로써 진정으로 산처럼 생각할 수 있게 된 때를, 인류 계몽의 시기로 돌아볼 것이다.

문제풀이

① [현재완료 시제]
since 뒤에 과거 시제의 절이 이어지면 주절의 시제는 현재완료 시제가 와야 하므로, have made는 적절하게 쓰였다.

② [부사]
동사인 has progressed를 수식하므로 부사 rapidly는 적절하게 쓰였다.

③ [관계대명사절의 동사]
the global environmental processes를 선행사로 하는 관계대명사절에 동사가 필요하므로 are influencing은 적절하게 쓰였다.

④ [to부정사]
to incorporate는 '~하기 위하여'의 뜻을 갖는 to부정사의 부사적 용법(목적)으로 적절하게 쓰였다.

⑤ [관계부사]
which 뒤에 완전한 절이 왔고 a time of human enlightenment를 선행사로 취하므로 which를 관계부사 where로 고쳐야 한다.

어휘·어구

appropriately 적당하게
interconnected 상호 연결된
publication 출판, 발행
planetary 행성의
willingness 기꺼이 하는 마음
humanity 인류
shortsighted 근시안적인
play out 전개되다, 일어나다
geologic 지질학의
incorporate 포함하다
transform 완전히 바꿔 놓다
look back on ~을 뒤돌아보다
enlightenment 계몽
anticipate 예상하다, 기대하다

9.④ 홀로 일하는 교사의 한계

교사가 홀로 일할 때 그들은 오직 한 쌍의 눈, 즉 자기 자신의 눈으로만 세상을 보는 경향이 있다. 이런저런 과목이나 수업을 가르치는 데 있어서 더 성공적일 수 있는 누군가가 '같은 건물이나 같은 지역의 어딘가에 있을 수도 있다는 사실은, 문을 닫고 거의 혼자서 학교의 연간 행사 예정표를 처음부터 끝까지 실천해 나가는 교사는 (A) 이해하지 못한다. 일을 더 잘하거나 최소한 다르게 하는 이들을 벤치마킹하게 (B) 해 주는 과정이 부재한 상황에서, 교사들은 하나의 시각, 즉 자기 자신의 시각만을 갖게 된다. 나는 사회학 분야에 속한 다양한 과목을 가르쳤는데 똑같은 과목을 가르치는 나의 동료들이 어떻게 가르치는가에 관해 거의 아는 게 없었다. 의견이나 정보를 교환하고, 공동 평가를 계획하고, 자신이 잘했던 것을 공유하기 위해서 정기적으로 만난다는 생각을 우리는 (C) 절대 해보지 않았다. 오히려 우리는 사회 교과 연구실에서 시간이 부족한 것에 대해 불평하면서, 그리고 서로 비난하고 책임 전가를 하면서 많은 시간을 보냈다.

문제풀이

(A) 홀로 일하는 교사는 자기 자신의 눈으로만 세상을 보는 경향이 있다는 내용을 고려해 볼 때, 홀로 일하는 교사는 가르치는 일에 있어서 더 성공적일 수 있는 누군가가 주변에 있다는 사실을 이해할 수 없다는 의미가 되어야 하므로, lost(이해할 수 없는)가 적절하다. based는 '(~에) 기반을 둔'이라는 의미이다. (B) 교사가 자기 자신의 시각만을 갖고 일하게 되는 이유 중 하나는 다른 사람이 일하는 방식을 벤치마킹할 수 있게 해 주는 과정이 부재하기 때문이라는 의미가 되어야 하므로, allows(허락하다)가 적절하다. forbid는 '금지하다'라는 의미이다. (C) 필자는 사회학 과목을 가르쳤는데 똑같은 과목을 가르치는 동료들의 수업 방식에 관해 거의 아는 게 없었다고 했으므로, never(절대 ~ 않다)가 적절하다. mostly는 '주로, 일반적으로'라는 의미이다. 따라서 정답은 ④이다.

구문 및 어휘

*2행 The fact [that there might be someone somewhere in the same building or district {who may be more successful at teaching this or that subject or lesson}] is lost on teachers {who close the door and work their way through the school calendar virtually alone}}.

⑴ The fact와 [that ~ lesson]은 동격으로 that절의 내용이 The fact를 보충 설명해 주고 있다. The fact가 주어이고, is가 동사이다.

⑵ who may be 이하는 선행사 someone을 수식하는 관계대명사절이다.

⑶ who close ~ alone은 선행사 teachers를 수식하는 관계대명사절이다.

⑷ close와 work는 관계대명사절의 동사로 병렬 연결되어 있다.

*6행 In the absence of a process [that allows them to benchmark those {who do things better or at least differently}], teachers are left with that one perspective — their own.

⑴ that 이하는 선행사 a process를 수식하는 관계대명사절로 that은 주격이다.

⑵ 「allow+목적어+to부정사」는 '~가 …하도록 허락하다'라는 의미이다.

⑶ those who는 '~하는 사람들'이라고 해석하며, who ~ differently는 선행사 those를 수식하는 관계대명사절이다.

*12행 The idea of [meeting regularly to compare notes, plan common assessments, and share what we did well] never occurred to us.

⑴ The idea가 주어이고, (never) occurred가 동사이다.

⑵ The idea와 meeting 이하는 동격으로 meeting 이하의 내용이 The idea를 보충 설명해 주고 있다.

⑶ to compare, (to) plan, (to) share는 모두 목적을 나타내는 부사 용법의 to부정사로 병렬 연결되어 있다.

⑷ what은 선행사를 포함한 관계대명사로 the thing which[that]으로 바꿀 수 있다.

*14행 Rather, we spent much time in the social studies office complaining about a lack of time and playing the blame game.

⑴ 「spend+시간+-ing」는 '~하는데 (시간)을 보내다'라는 의미이다. complaining과 playing은 동명사로 병렬 연결되어 있다.

---

in isolation 홀로, 고립되어
district 지역, 구역
work one's way through ~을 처음부터 끝까지 다 하다
school calendar 학교의 연간 행사 예정표
in the absence of ~이 없는 상태에서
benchmark 벤치마킹하다
perspective 시각, 관점
social studies 사회학
peer 동료
compare notes 의견이나 정보를 교환하다
assessment 평가
blame game 비난 게임(어떤 실패 상황이나 부적절한 결과에 대해 단독 책임을 인정하지 않으려는 사람들이 서로 비난하고 책임을 전가하는 것)

10.⑤ 흔치 않은 질문으로 대화를 시작하라

대화하는 삶에 깊이와 신나는 일이 부족할 수 있는 한 가지 이유는 '잘 지내요?', '날씨가 어땠어요?', '무슨 일을 하세요?', '주말은 어땠어요?'와 같은 ① 상투적인 질문을 사용하여 대화를 쉽게 시작한다는 것이다. 그러한 질문들이 이 사회생활에서 중요한 윤활유가 될 수는 있지만, 그것은 자체로는 매력적이고 풍요로운 감정 이입의 대화를 대체로 ② 유발하지 못한다. 우리는 "좋아요."라거나 "알았어요."라고 대답하고 나서 복도를 걸어간다. 대화가 ③ 시작되는 방식은 대화가 어디로 가는지에 대한 주요 결정 요인일 수 있다. 그래서 대담한 첫 문장으로 대화를 시도해 볼 가치가 있다. "어떻게 지내세요?"라는 말로 동료에게 인사를 하는 대신, "오늘 아침에 무슨 생각을 하고 있었나요?" 또는 "주말에 당신에게 일어난 가장 놀라운 일은 무엇이었나요?"와 같은 약간 ④ 흔치 않은 질문을 하면서 다른 방향으로 대화를 시도해 보라. 당신은 당신 자신의 성격에 맞는 그런 질문을 생각해 내야 한다. 주요한 점은 당신의 대화가 활기를 띠고, 기억할 만하고, 공감의 발견 수단이 될 수 있도록 관행을 ⑤ 따르는(→깨는) 것이다.

문제풀이

① 'How are you?, ~ How was your weekend?'는 모두 상투적인 질문들이므로 'formulaic(상투적인)'이 오는 것은 적절하다. ② 상투적인 질문들은 'Fine'이나 'OK'와 같은 대답을 하게 하고 감정 이입의 대화를 유발하지는 못하기 때문에 'spark(유발하다)'가 오는 것은 적절하다. ③ 대화가 시작되는 방식이 대화의 흐름을 좌우하기 때문에 흔치 않은 질문을 하면서 다른 방향으로 대화를 시작하라고 했으므로, 'begins(시작하다)'가 오는 것은 적절하다. ④ 'What have you been thinking about this morning?' 등은 흔치 않은 질문이므로, unusual(흔치 않은)이 오는 것은 적절하다. ⑤ 흔치 않은 질문으로 대화를 의미 있게 하려면 관행(상투적인 질문)을 깨야 하므로, 'follow(따르다)'가 아닌 'break(깨다)'가 와야 한다. 따라서 정답은 ⑤이다.

구문 및 어휘

*8행 The way [a conversation begins] can be a major determinant of [where it goes].

⑴ The way가 문장의 주어이고, can be가 동사이다.

⑵ a conversation begins는 선행사 The way를 수식하는 관계부사절로 앞에 관계부사 how가 생략되어 있다. the way와 관계부사 how는 함께 쓸 수 없다.

⑶ where it goes는 전치사 of의 목적어로 쓰인 간접의문문으로 「의문사+주어+동사」의 어순이다.

*16행 The point is to follow conventions [so your conversations become energizing, memorable, and vehicles for empathic discovery].

(1) to follow는 보어로 쓰인 명사적 용법의 to부정사이다.

(2) 「so+(that)+주어+동사」는 '~할 수 있도록'이라는 의미이다. 여기서 so 다음에 that이 생략되어 있다.

dialogue 대화
engaging 호감이 가는, 매력적인
enriching 내용을 풍부하게 하는
empathic 감정 이입의
corridor 복도
determinant 결정 요인
adventurous 대담한
mildly 약간, 가볍게
come up with ~를 생각해내다
convention 관습, 관례
memorable 기억할 만한
vehicle 수단, 매개체

11. ②　　민주주의 체제

여러분이 서로의 흥미나 관심사에 대해 이웃과 이야기할 수 없다면 여러분은 민주주의 체제를 가질 수 없다. 민주주의에 꾸준한 관심이 있었던 Thomas Jefferson은 이와 유사한 결론에 이르렀다. 그는 기업에서든, 정치적 지도자들에게서든, 혹은 배타적인 정치 기관에서든, (A) 집중된 권력의 위험성을 이해하는 데 있어 선견지명이 있었다. 시민들의 직접적인 참여는 미국 혁명을 가능하게 만든 것이었고, 새로운 공화국에 활력과 미래에 대한 희망을 부여했던 것이었다. 그러한 참여가 없다면 그 공화국은 사라질 것이다. 결국, 그는 국가가 '(지방 의회 구성단위가 되는) 구'로 (B) 세분되어야 할 필요성을 인식했는데, 그것(구)은 그곳에 사는 모든 사람들이 정치적 과정에 직접 참여할 수 있을 정도로 작은 정치 단위였다. 수도에 있는 각 구의 대표자들은 이러한 방식으로 조직된 시민들에게 (C) 반응해야 할 것이다. 그런 다음 지역적으로 운영되는 활기찬 민주주의 체제는 공화국의 민주적 삶을 위한 활발한 기본적 단위를 제공할 것이다. 그러한 종류의 참여가 있으면, 공화국은 생존하고 번영할 것이다.

문제풀이

(A) 앞에는 서로의 흥미와 관심사를 이웃과 이야기하는 것이 민주주의 체제를 가능하게 한다는 내용이 나오며 (A) 뒤에는 공화국이 존속하려면 시민들의 직접적인 참여가 필요하다는 내용이 나온다. 따라서 민주주의 체제에서는 권력의 집중을 지양하고 분산을 지향함을 알 수 있으므로, (A)에는 concentrated(집중된)가 적절하다. limited는 '제한된'이라는 의미이다. 민주주의에 관심이 있었던 Thomas Jefferson은 정치적 과정에 모든 사람들이 직접 참여할 수 있도록 국가가 작은 단위로 세분될 필요성을 인식했을 것이므로, (B)에는 subdivided(세분되다)가 적절하다. blended는 '섞이다'라는 의미이다. 시민들의 직접 참여를 보장하는 민주주의 체제 내에서는 구의 대표자들이 시민들에게 반응해야 할 것으로 추론할 수 있으므로, (C)에는 responsive(반응하는)가 적절하다. resistant는 '저항하는'이라는 의미이다. 따라서 정답은 ②이다.

구문 및 어휘

*7행 Direct involvement (of citizens) was [what had made the American Revolution possible and

given the new republic vitality and hope for the future].

(1) Direct involvement가 주어이고, was가 동사이다. of citizens는 Direct involvement를 수식하는 전치사구이다.

(2) what은 선행사를 포함한 관계대명사이고 had made와 (had) given은 관계대명사절의 동사로 병렬관계이다.

*9행 [Without that involvement], the republic would die.

(1) Without이 이끄는 부사구가 가정법의 if절을 대신하고 있다. If it were not for that involvement로 바꿔 쓸 수 있다.

*17행 [With that kind of involvement], the republic might survive and prosper.

(1) With가 이끄는 부사구가 가정법의 if절을 대신하고 있으며, 여기서 With는 '~가 있다면'이라고 해석한다.

democracy 민주주의 체제, 민주주의
mutual 서로의, 상호적인
enduring 지속적인
corporation 기업
exclusionary 배타적인
institution 기관
involvement 참여, 관여
vitality 활력, 생기
ward (지방 의회 구성단위가 되는) 구
representative 대표
prosper 번영하다

12. ④　　개방표지 위약 효과

직독 직해

Research published in 2017 /
2017년에 발표된 연구는 /
on what's called "open-label placebos" /
소위 '개방표지 위약'이라고 불리는 것에 대하여 /
is especially fascinating, /
특히 흥미롭다 /
since it supports the power of the subconscious and suggestibility.
그것이 잠재의식과 암시 감응성의 힘을 뒷받침하기 때문이다
Unlike the traditional placebo study /
전통적인 위약 연구와는 달리 /
— where the patient doesn't know /
환자가 모르는 /
if he's getting the sugar pill or the drug — /
설탕 알약(위약)을 받는지 (진짜) 약을 받는지를 /
open-label placebo studies are those /
개방표지 위약 연구는 그런 것이다 /
in which patients are actually told,
연구 중 환자들이 실제로 말을 듣는 /
"Yes, you are definitely getting the sugar pill."
"네, 환자분은 분명 위약을 복용하고 계십니다."
The doctor delivers this /
의사는 이 말을 전달한다 /
with a positive suggestion, /
긍정적인 암시와 함께 /
telling the patient / 환자에게 말하면서 /
that although it is indeed a placebo, /
비록 그것이 정말로 위약이긴 하지만 /
it has been shown / 그것이 밝혀졌다고 /
to produce improvement through healing /
치유를 통해 상태가 호전되는 것이 /

that originates in the mind.
마음으로부터 비롯되는
We know / that's how placebos work, / don't we?
우리는 안다 / 위약이 그런 식으로 효과를 낸다는 것을 / 그렇지 않은가
A review of five studies showed /
5개의 연구에 관한 보고서는 보여주었다 /
that open-label placebos /
개방표지 위약이 /
— where patients knew /
환자들이 아는 /
they weren't getting any real drug — /
자신이 진짜 약을 전혀 받고 있지 않다는 것을 /
had a positive effect /
긍정적인 영향을 미쳤다는 것을 /
on depression, back pain, ADHD, and hay fever.
우울증, 허리 통증, 주의력 결핍 및 과잉 행동 장애, 그리고 꽃가루 알레르기에
The placebo effect extends / even to the pill color /
위약 효과는 확장된다 / 심지어 알약 색에 까지도 /
because our brains associate certain colors /
우리의 두뇌가 색을 연관시키기 때문에 /
with certain effects, /
특정한 효과와 /
thus making a pill more or less effective.
그래서 알약이 어느 정도 효과를 나타내도록 만든다

소위 '개방표지 위약'이라고 불리는 것에 대하여 2017년에 발표된 연구는 특히 흥미로운데, 그것이 잠재의식과 암시 감응성의 힘을 ① 뒷받침하기 때문이다. 환자가 설탕 알약(위약)을 받는지 (진짜) 약을 받는지를 모르는 전통적인 위약 연구와는 달리, 개방표지 위약 연구는 연구 중 환자들이 실제로 "네, 환자분은 분명 위약을 복용하고 계십니다."라는 ② 말을 듣는 연구이다. 의사는 이 말을 긍정적인 암시와 함께 전달하며, 그 환자에게 비록 그것이 정말로 위약이긴 하지만, 마음으로부터 비롯되는 ③ 치유를 통해 상태가 호전되는 것이 밝혀졌다고 말한다. 우리는 위약이 그런 식으로 효과를 낸다는 것을 안다. 그렇지 않은가? 5개의 연구에 관한 보고서는 환자들이 자신이 진짜 약을 전혀 받고 있지 않다는 것을 아는 개방표지 위약이 우울증, 허리 통증, 주의력 결핍 및 과잉 행동 장애, 그리고 꽃가루 알레르기에 ④ 부정적인(→ 긍정적인) 영향을 미쳤다는 것을 보여 주었다. 위약 효과는 심지어 알약 색에까지도 확장되는데 그 이유는 우리의 두뇌가 색을 특정한 효과와 연관시키고, 그래서 알약이 어느 정도 ⑤ 효과를 나타내도록 만들기 때문이다.

문제풀이

이글은 환자들이 위약을 투여받고 있다는 사실을 알고 있을 때조차도, 긍정적인 암시와 함께 복용할 경우에 마음으로부터 비롯되는 치유를 통해 상태가 호전된다는 내용의 글이다. 그러므로 개방표지 위약이 여러 가지 질병에 대해서 부정적인 영향을 미쳤다는 것은 글의 흐름으로 어색하다. 따라서 ④ 'negative(부정적인)'을 'positive(긍정적인)'으로 바꿔 써야 한다.

○ 이렇게 풀자 문맥상 낱말의 쓰임이 적절하지 않은 어휘를 고르는 문제는 전체 글의 주제를 정확히 파악한 후에 각 밑줄 친 단어의 뜻이 주제와 어울리는지를 확인해야 한다. 'although it is indeed a placebo, it has been shown to produce improvement through healing that originates in the mind(그것이 정말로 위약이긴 하지만, 마음으로부터 비롯되는 치유를 통해 상태가 호전되는 것이 밝혀졌다)'에 글의 주제가 잘 드러나 있다.

어휘 · 어구

what is called 소위, 이른바
placebo 위약
fascinating 대단히 흥미로운, 매력적인
subconscious 잠재 의식
definitely 분명히
originate 비롯되다, 유래하다
depression 우울증
ADHD 주의력 결핍 및 과잉 행동 장애(= Attention Deficit Hyperactivity Disorder)
hay fever 꽃가루 알레르기, 고초열
associate 연관시키다, 연상하다
more or less 다소

16. 병렬 구조

본문 092쪽

A 출제 POINT

1. swallows　　2. eating　　3. act
4. but　　　　5. is　　　　6. mine
7. that

1 [해석]▶ 그것은 번개 같이 재빠르게 턱을 벌려 경계를 하고 있지 않던 먹이를 붙잡아 머리부터 먼저 삼킨다.

[해설]▶ 등위접속사 and가 동사(seizes, swallows)를 병렬 구조로 연결하고 있다.

2 [해석]▶ 그녀는 이탈리아에 가서 매일 훌륭한 파스타를 요리를 먹고 싶어 한다.

[해설]▶ look forward to는 '~을 기대하다'의 의미로, 목적어로 동명사를 가져온다. 본문의 문장은 look forward to+[동명사] and [동명사]인 병렬 구조를 이루고 있다.

3 [해석]▶ 하지만 이제 디지털 시대의 도구들은 우리에게 정보를 쉽게 얻고, 공유하고, 새로운 방식으로 행동할 수 있는 방법을 제공한다.

[해설]▶ 등위접속사 and가 to부정사 to easily get, (to) share, and (to) act를 를 병렬 구조로 연결하고 있다.

4 [해석]▶ 몽골 제국은 통일된 국가가 아니라, 군사력에 의해 하나로 묶인 광대한 영토의 집합이었다.

[해설]▶ not A but B는 'A가 아니라 B'라는 의미이며, A와 B가 명사구가 나와 병렬 구조로 연결되어 있다.

5 [해석]▶ Jack뿐만 아니라 Mary도 나의 친한 친구이다.

[해설]▶ B as well as A는 'A뿐만 아니라 B'도 라는 의미이며 B에 동사의 수를 일치시킨다. B가 단수명사 Mary이므로 단수동사 is가 나와야 한다.

6 [해석]▶ 그의 아이디어는 내 아이디어보다 더 낫다.

[해설]▶ 비교 구문에서도 병렬 구조를 지켜야 한다. His idea와 mine(= my idea)를 비교하고 있으므로 mine이 나와야 한다.

7 [해석]▶ 도쿄의 인구는 서울의 인구보다 더 많다.

[해설]▶ 비교 구문이 병렬 구조를 이루는 경우, 명사의 반복(the population)을 피하기 위해 that을 쓴다.

B 체크 POINT

본문 092쪽

1. humorous　2. playing　　3. study
4. nor　　　　5. has　　　　6. hers
7. that

1 [해석]▶ Sally는 똑똑하고 아름다우며 재미있다.

[해설]▶ A(형용사), B(형용사), and C(형용사)가 병렬 구조를 이루고 있다.

2 [해석]▶ 어른들은 음식을 준비하고 아이들을 지키며, 배구 경기하느라 바빴다.

[해설]▶ busy+목적어+(in) A, B, and C의 병렬 구조이다. A, B처럼 C에도 동명사가 들어가야 한다.

3 [해석]▶ 그는 런던 대학에 들어가 이 박사님 밑에서 공

부하기를 희망한다.

[해설]▶ hopes to go ~ and (to) study의 병렬 구조이다.

4 [해석]▶ Peter나 그의 아내도 이사 가는 것에 대해 아무 말도 하지 않았다.

[해설]▶ Neither A nor B는 'A도 B도 둘 다 아닌'의 의미이다.

5 [해석]▶ 너와 네 누나 중 한 명은 여기에 남아야 한다.

[해설]▶ either A or B는 'B'에 동사의 수를 일치시킨다.

6 [해석]▶ 나의 스마트폰은 색상과 모양에서 그녀의 것과 비슷해.

[해설]▶ 비교 구문에서도 병렬 구조를 지켜야 한다. my smartphone과 hers(= her smartphone)를 비교하고 있다.

7 [해석]▶ 일본은 전자 제품의 생산이 증가했지만, 일본의 증가는 한국의 그것보다 더 작았다.

[해설]▶ 비교 구문이 병렬 구조를 이루는 경우, 명사의 반복(the increase)을 피하기 위해 that을 쓴다.

Day 16

본문 093쪽

1	⑤	2	④	3	③	4	④	5	②
6	⑤	7	③	8	②	9	②	10	⑤
11	③	12	⑤						

1. ⑤ 　규칙성과 예측 가능성을 위한 도구

직독/직해

Most historians of science /
대부분의 과학 역사가들은 /

point to the need for a reliable calendar /
믿을 만한 달력의 필요성을 지적한다 /

to regulate agricultural activity /
농업 활동을 규제하기 위한 /

as the motivation for learning /
배우고자 하는 동기로 /

about what we now call astronomy, /
우리가 현재 천문학이라 부르는 것에 관해 /

the study of stars and planets.
별과 행성에 대한 연구인

Early astronomy provided information /
초기 천문학은 정보를 제공했다 /

about when to plant crops /
언제 작물을 심어야 하는지에 관한 /

and gave humans their first formal method /
그리고 인간에게 그들 최초의 공식적인 방법을 제공했다 /

of recording the passage of time.
시간의 흐름을 기록하는

Stonehenge, the 4,000-year-old ring of stones in southern Britain, /
영국 남부에 있는 4,000년 된 고리 모양을 한 돌들인 스톤헨지는 /

is perhaps the best-known monument /
아마도 가장 잘 알려진 기념비일 것이다 /

to the discovery of regularity and predictability /
규칙성과 예측 가능성의 발견에 대한 /

in the world / we inhabit.
세계에서 / 우리가 살고 있는

The great markers of Stonehenge point /
스톤헨지의 큰 표식은 나타낸다 /

to the spots on the horizon /
지평선의 장소를 /

where the sun rises at the solstices and equinoxes /
지점(至點)과 분점(分點)에서 태양이 뜨는 /

— the dates we still use /
우리가 여전히 사용하는 날짜인 /

---

to mark the beginnings of the seasons.
계절의 시작을 표시하기 위해

The stones may even have been used /
그 돌들은 심지어 사용되었을 수도 있다 /

to predict eclipses. (해·달의) 식(蝕)을 예측하는 데
(해·달의) 식(蝕)을 예측하는 데

The existence of Stonehenge, /
스톤헨지의 존재는 /

built by people without writing, /
글이 없던 시절 사람들이 지은 /

bears silent testimony /
말 없이 증언해 준다 /

both to the regularity of nature and to the ability of the human mind /
자연의 규칙성과 인간의 정신적 능력 둘 다를 /

to see behind immediate appearances /
눈앞에 보이는 모습의 이면을 보는 /

and discover deeper meanings in events.
그리고 사건에서 더 깊은 의미를 발견할 수 있는

대부분의 과학 역사가들은 별과 행성에 관한 연구, 즉 우리가 현재 천문학이라 부르는 것에 대해 배우고자 하는 동기로 농업 활동을 규제하기 위한 믿을 만한 달력의 필요성을 지적한다. 초기 천문학은 언제 작물을 심어야 하는지에 관한 정보를 제공하고 인간에게 시간의 흐름을 기록하는 그들 최초의 공식적인 방법을 제공했다. 영국 남부에 있는 4,000년 된 고리 모양을 한 돌들인 스톤헨지는 아마도 우리가 살고 있는 세계에서 규칙성과 예측 가능성을 발견에 대한 가장 잘 알려진 기념비일 것이다. 스톤헨지의 큰 표식은 우리가 계절의 시작을 표시하기 위해 여전히 사용하는 날짜인 지점(至點)과 분점(分點)에서 태양이 뜨는 지평선의 장소를 나타낸다. 그 돌들은 심지어 (해·달의) 식(蝕)을 예측하는 데 사용되었을 수도 있다. 글이 없던 시절 사람들이 지은 스톤헨지의 존재는 자연의 규칙성과 눈앞에 보이는 모습의 이면을 보고 사건에서 더 깊은 의미를 발견한 인간의 정신적 능력 둘 다를 말 없이 증언해 준다.

문제풀이

① [대명사]
앞의 humans를 가리키면서 명사구 first formal method를 수식하는 소유격으로 사용되었으므로, 대명사 their가 온 것은 적절하다.

② [주어와 동사의 수 일치]
주어가 Stonehenge이므로, 단수동사가 와야 한다. 따라서 is가 온 것은 적절하다. the 4,000-year-old ring of stones in southern Britain은 Stonehenge를 부연 설명하는 동격어구이다.

③ [관계부사]
주어(the sun), 동사(rises), 부사구(at the solstices and equinoxes)를 모두 갖춘 완전한 절이 왔으므로, 선행사 the spots on the horizon을 수식하는 관계사절을 이끄는 관계부사 where가 온 것은 적절하다.

④ [수동태]
주어인 The stones가 사용되는 대상이므로, 수동태가 와야 한다. 따라서 may have been used가 온 것은 적절하다.

⑤ [병렬 구조]
상관접속사 'both A and B' 구문에서 to see와 병렬 구조를 to부정사가 B에 나와야 하므로, **discovers**를 discover로 고쳐야 한다.

○ **이렇게 풀자**　① 대명사가 쓰인 경우, 앞 문장이나 절에서 가리키는 명사를 찾아서 수가 일치하는지, 문법에 맞는 격이 사용되었는지 확인한다.
② 동사에 밑줄이 있는 경우, 주어와 동사의 수 일치를 묻는 문제인 경우가 많다. 따라서 주어를 분명히 파악하는 것이 중요하다.
③ 관계부사에 밑줄이 있는 경우, 뒤에 문장 성분을 모두 갖춘 완전한 문장이 왔는지 확인해야 한다.
④ 'be동사+p.p'에 밑줄이 있는 경우, 주어와의 관계를 파악하여 수동태로 쓰이는 것이 적절한지 살펴야 한다.
⑤ 'both A and B' 구문에서 A와 B는 문법적으로 대등한 관계여야 한다.

《 어휘·어구 》

point to　~을 지적하다. ~을 나타내다

---

reliable 믿을 만한
regulate 규제하다
agricultural 농업의
astronomy 천문학
passage 흐름
regularity 규칙성
predictability 예측 가능성
inhabit 살다
solstice 지점(至點)(태양이 적도로부터 북쪽 또는 남쪽으로 가장 치우쳤을 때)
equinox 분점(分點)(태양이 적도를 통과하는 점)
immediate 눈앞에 있는

2. ④ 최후통첩 게임

직독/직해

Humans are so averse to feeling / that they're
인간은 느끼는 것을 너무나도 싫어해서 / 그들이 속고 있다고 /

being cheated /

that they often respond / in ways that seemingly
그들은 종종 반응한다 / 겉보기에 거의 말이 되지 않는 방법으로

make little sense.

Behavioral economists / — the economists who
행동 경제학자들은 / — 실제로 연구하는 경제학자들인 /

actually study /

what people do / as opposed to the kind /
사람들이 하는 것을 / 부류와는 달리 /

who simply assume / the human mind works /
단순히 가정하는 / 인간의 정신이 작동한다고 /

like a calculator / — have shown again and again /
계산기처럼 / — 반복해서 보여주었다 /

that people reject unfair offers /
사람들이 불공정한 제안을 거부한다는 것을 /

even if it costs them money / to do so.
심지어 돈을 잃더라도 / 불공정한 제안을 거부하는 것으로

The typical experiment / uses a task /
대표적인 실험은 / 과업을 이용한다 /

called the ultimatum game. 최후통첩 게임이라 불리는

It's pretty straightforward. 그것은 꽤 간단하다

One person in a pair / is given some money /
두 사람 중 한 사람에게 / 약간의 돈을 준다 /

— say $10. – 가령 10달러 정도

She then has the opportunity / to offer some
그러고 나서 그녀는 기회를 가진다 / 그 돈의 일부를 제공할 /

amount of it /

to her partner. 상대방에게

The partner only has / two options.
상대방은 오직 갖고 있다 / 두 가지 선택을

He can take / what's offered / or refuse to take
그는 받을 수 있다 / 제공되는 것을 / 혹은 받는 것을 거절할 (수 있다)

anything.

There's no room / for negotiation; /
여지가 없다 / 협상의 /

that's why it's called / the ultimatum game.
그래서 그게 불리는 이유이다 / 최후통첩 게임이라

What typically happens? 일반적으로 무슨 일이 일어나는가

Many people offer an equal split / to the partner, /
많은 사람이 절반을 제안한다 / 상대방에게 /

leaving both individuals happy / and willing to trust /
그것은 두 사람 모두 행복하게 하고 / 기꺼이 신뢰할 수 있게 한다 /

each other in the future. 미래에 서로를

인간은 속고 있다고 느끼는 것을 너무나도 싫어해서 종종 겉보기에 거의 말이 되지 않는 방법으로 반응한다. 단순히 인간의 정신이 계산기처럼 작동한다고 가정하는 부류와는 달리 사람들이 하는 것을 실제로 연구하는 경제학자들인 행동 경제학자들은 심지어 사람들이 불공정한 제안을 거부함으로 인해 돈을 잃더라도 그것을 거부한다는 것을 반복해서 보여주었다. 대표적인 실험은 최후통첩 게임이라 불리는 과업을 이용한다. 꽤 간단하다. 두 사람 중 한 사람에게 가령 10달러 정도 약간의 돈을 준다. 그러고 나서 그녀는 상대방에게 그 돈의 일부를 제공할 기회를 가진다. 상대방은 두 가지 선택만 할 수 있다. 그는 제공되는 것을 받거나, 받는 것을 거절할 수 있다. 협상의 여지가 없다. 그래서 그게 최후통첩 게임

이라 불리는 이유이다. 일반적으로 무슨 일이 일어나는가? 많은 사람이 상대방에게 절반을 제안하며, 그것은 두 사람 모두 행복하게 하고 미래에 서로를 기꺼이 신뢰할 수 있게 한다.

문제풀이

① '너무 ~해서 …하다'라는 의미를 나타내는 구문인 「so+형용사/부사+that ~」 구문이 쓰였으므로, that은 적절하게 쓰였다.
② 뒤에 있는 do의 목적어 역할을 하면서 절 전체가 study의 목적어 역할을 할 수 있도록 명사절을 이끌어야 하므로, 관계대명사 what은 적절하게 쓰였다.
③ 진주어인 to do so를 받는 가주어이므로, it은 적절하게 쓰였다.
④ 문맥상 앞에 있는 동사 take와 병렬 구조를 이뤄야 하므로 refused를 refuse로 고쳐야 한다.
⑤ 상대방에게 절반을 제안하는 것이 두 사람 모두 행복하게 한다는 의미가 되어야 하므로, 능동의 의미를 갖는 leaving은 적절하게 쓰였다.

❸ 이렇게 풀자_ 어법상 틀린 부분을 찾는 문제는 밑줄이 있는 부분의 형태와 문맥을 보고 어법에 맞게 쓰였는지 확인해야 한다. ①은 「so+형용사/부사+that ~」 구문을, ②는 관계대명사 what의 역할을, ③은 진주어와 가주어의 쓰임을, ④는 병렬 구조를, ⑤는 분사구문의 역할을 알아야 한다.

《 어휘 · 어구 》

seemingly 겉보기에, 외견상으로
make sense 말이 되다, 타당하다
reject 거부하다, 거절하다
unfair 불공정한
typical 대표적인, 전형적인
straightforward 간단한, 복잡하지 않은
room 여지
negotiation 협상

3. ③ 유인과 무인 우주 임무의 비용과 성과 비교

직독/직해

While manned space missions /
유인 우주 임무는 /

are more costly than unmanned ones, /
무인 우주 임무보다 더 비용이 많이 들지만, /

they are more successful.
그것들은 더 성공적이다.

Robots and astronauts use /
로봇과 우주 비행사는 사용한다. /

much of the same equipment in space.
우주 공간에서 거의 똑같은 장비를

But a human is much more capable of /
하지만 인간은 훨씬 더 많은 능력을 지니고 있다. /

operating those instruments correctly /
그러한 도구들을 올바르게 조작하고

and placing them in appropriate and useful positions.
그것들을 적절하고 유용한 위치에 설치하는데 있어서

Rarely is a computer / 컴퓨터는 ~ 않다 /

more sensitive and accurate than a human /
인간보다 민감하지도 못하며 정확하지도

in managing the same geographical or environmental factors.
동일한 지역적인 혹은 환경적인 요소들을 관리하는 데 있어서

Robots are also not equipped with capabilities like humans /
로봇은 또한 인간처럼 능력이 갖추어져 있지 않으며,

to solve problems / as they arise, /
그것을 해결할 수 있는(능력이) / 문제가 발생할 때에 /

and they often collect data /
종종 자료들을 수집하기도 한다. /

that are unhelpful or irrelevant.
도움이 되지 못하거나 부적절한

무인 우주 임무보다 유인 우주 임무가 비용이 더 많이 들기는 하지만, 그것들은 더 성공적이다. 로봇과 우주 비행사는 우주 공간에서 거의 똑같은 장비를 사용한다. 하지만 인간은 그러한 도구를 올바르게 조작하고 그것들을 적절하고 유용한 위치에 설치하는데 있어서 훨씬 더 많은 능력을 지니고 있다. 컴퓨터는 동일한 지역적인 혹은 환경적인 요소들을 관리하는 데 있어서 인간보다 민감하지도 못하며 정확하지도 않다. 로봇은 또한 문제가 발생할 때에 그것을 해결할 수 있는 능력이 인간처럼 갖추어져 있지 않으며, 종종 도움이 되지 못하거나 부적절한 자료들을 수집하기도 한다.

문제풀이

접속사 and가 operating과 placing을 연결해 주는 구조가 되어야 어법상 옳다. 따라서 ③ 'to place'를 'placing'으로 바꾸어야 한다.

《 어휘 · 어구 》

manned 사람이 탑승한
astronaut 우주 비행사
operate 작동하다, 조작하다
appropriate 적절한
sensitive 민감한
geographical 지리적인
capability 능력
irrelevant 부적절한

4. ④ Francis Galton의 책 「여행의 기술」

직독/직해

If you ever feel ill / 속이 안 좋으면 /

when traveling in remote foreign parts, /
먼 외국을 여행하다가 /

just drop some gunpowder /
화약을 넣어 /

into a glass of warm, soapy water, and swallow it.
따뜻한 비눗물에 마셔 보라.

That was the advice of Francis Galton /
그것은 Francis Galton이 하는 충고다. /

in a book called The Art of Travel.
「여행의 기술」이라는 책에서

Bee stings? 벌에 쏘였다면?

Well, the tar scraped out of tobacco pipe /
담뱃대에서 긁어낸 타르를 /

and applied on the skin / relieves the pain.
피부에 바르면 / 통증이 줄어든다.

Galton's book proved a bestseller.
Galton의 책은 베스트셀러가 되었다.

It covered every situation, /
그 책은 모든 상황을 다루었다. /

from constructing boats, huts, and tents in a hurry
빠른 시간에 보트, 오두막, 텐트 등을 만드는 것부터

to catch fish without a line.
낚싯줄이 없이 고기를 잡는 것까지

It told readers / 그 책은 독자들에게 알려주었다. /

how to find firewood in a rainstorm /
폭풍우 가운데서 땔나무 찾는 법과

(under the roots of a tree) / (나무뿌리 아래쪽)

and where to put your clothes / when it's raining /
어디에 둘 것인지 / 비가 올 때

so that they don't get wet / 옷을 젖지 않게 /

(just take them off and sit on them).
(벗어서 깔고 앉으면 된다)는 것도

먼 외국을 여행하다가 속이 안 좋으면 따뜻한 비눗물에 화약을 넣어 마셔 보라. 그것은 「여행의 기술」이라는 책에서 Francis Galton이 하는 충고다. 벌에 쏘였다면? 담뱃대에서 긁어낸 타르를 피부에 바르면 통증이 줄어든다. Galton의 책은 빠른 시간에 보트, 오두막, 텐트 등을 만드는 것부터 낚싯줄이 없이 고기를 잡는 것까지 모든 상황을 다루었다. 그 책은 독자들에게 폭풍우 가운데서 땔나무 찾는 법(나무뿌리 아래쪽)과 비가 올 때 옷을 젖지 않게 어디에 둘 것인지(벗어서 깔고 앉으면 된다)도 알려주었다.

문제풀이

④ from A to B 구문에서 A, B가 동명사를 넣어 병렬 구조를 이루고 있다.
그러므로 to catch → to catching으로 고쳐야 한다.

《 어휘·어구 》

gunpowder 화약
sting (벌에) 쏘다
scrape 긁어내다
hut 오두막
firewood 땔나무

---

5. ② | 이런저런 생각하기

직독직해

Jerome Singer, a legendary cognitive psychologist, /
전설적인 인지 심리학자 Jerome Singer는 /
was the first scientist to suggest /
~(라고) 말한 첫 번째 과학자였다 /
that the mental state in which the mind is allowed
생각이 자유롭게 다른 데로 흘러갈 수 있게 허용되는 정신 상태가
to wander freely / is, in fact, our "default" state.
/ 사실은 우리의 '기본' 상태라고
Singer further argued in his 1966 book, *Daydreaming*, /
Singer는 나아가 1966년에 출간한 자신의 저서 《Daydreaming》에서 주장했다 /
that daydreaming, imagination, and fantasy /
백일몽과, 상상, 공상이 /
are essential elements of a healthy mental life.
건강한 정신생활에 필수적인 요소라고
These elements include / self-awareness, creative
이 요소들은 포함한다 / 자기 인식, 창의적인 숙고, 자전적 계획을 /
incubation, autobiographical planning, /
consideration of the meaning of events and
사건과 상호 작용의 의미에 대한 고찰과
interactions, / taking another person's perspective, /
/ 다른 사람의 관점을 취하는 것 /
reflecting on your own and others' emotions, /
자기 자신과 다른 사람의 감정에 대해 깊이 생각하는 것 /
and moral reasoning. 그리고 도덕적인 추론을
All of this leads / 이 모든 것이 이어진다 /
to what we think of as "aha!" moments.
우리가 '아하!'하고 깨닫는 순간이라 생각하는 것으로
The musician, bestseller writer, and neuroscientist
음악가이자, 베스트셀러 작가이며, 신경 과학자인 Daniel J. Levitin은 강조한다
Daniel J. Levitin emphasizes /
that insights are far more likely to come /
통찰이 올 가능성이 훨씬 더 많다는 것을 /
when you are in the mind-wandering mode /
여러분이 이런저런 생각을 하는 상태에 있을 때 /
than in the task-focused mode.
업무에 집중하는 상태에 있을 때보다
It is only when we let our minds wander /
바로 우리가 이런저런 생각을 할 때뿐이다 /
that we make unexpected connections /
우리가 예상 밖의 관계를 발견하는 것은 /
between things that we did not realize were
우리가 관계있을 것으로 생각하지 못했던 것들 사이에서
connected.
This can help you solve problems /
이것은 여러분이 문제를 해결하도록 도와줄 수 있다 /
that previously seemed to be unsolvable.
이전에 해결 불가한 것으로 보였던

- -

전설적인 인지 심리학자 Jerome Singer는 생각이 자유롭게 다른 데로 흘러갈 수 있게 허용되는 정신 상태가 사실은 우리의 '기본' 상태라고 말한 첫 번째 과학자였다. Singer는 나아가 1966년에 출간한 자신의 저서 《Daydreaming》에서 백일몽과, 상상, 공상이 건강한 정신생활에 필수적인 요소라고 주장했다. 이 요소들은 자기 인식, 창의적인 숙고, 자전적 계획, 사건과 상호 작용의 의미에 대한 고찰, 다른 사람의 관점을 취하는 것, 자기 자신과 다른 사람의 감정에 대해 깊이 생각하는 것, 그리고 도덕적인 추론을 포함한다. 이 모든 것이 우리가 '아하!'하고 깨닫는 순간이라 생각하는 것으로 이어진다. 음악가이자, 베스트셀러 작가이며, 신경 과학

자인 Daniel J. Levitin은 통찰이 업무에 집중하는 상태에 있을 때보다 이런저런 생각을 하는 상태에 있을 때 올 가능성이 훨씬 더 많다는 것을 강조한다. 우리가 관계있을 것으로 생각하지 못했던 것들 사이에서 예상 밖의 관계를 발견하는 것은 바로 우리가 이런저런 생각을 할 때문이다. 이것은 여러분이 이전에 해결 불가한 것으로 보였던 문제를 해결하도록 도와줄 수 있다.

문제풀이

① 동사 wander을 수식하는 부사가 와야 하는 자리이므로, freely가 온 것은 적절하다.
② These elements가 주어이고, include가 동사이며, self-awareness ~ moral reasoning이 and에 의해 병렬로 연결된 목적어로 쓰인 구조이다. 컴마(,)와 등위접속사 and에 의해 동사 include의 목적어로 쓰인 self-awareness, creative incubation, autobiographical planning, consideration of ~, reflecting on ~, 그리고 moral reasoning의 명사구와 병렬 구조를 이루어야 하므로, take를 동명사 taking으로 고쳐야 한다.
③ 전치사 to의 목적어 역할을 하면서, 선행사가 없으므로, 관계대명사 what이 온 것은 적절하다.
④ 주어가 The musician이고 bestselling writer, and neuroscientist Daniel J. Levitin은 The musician과 동격을 이루는 구이므로, 단수동사 emphasizes가 온 것은 적절하다.
⑤ 선행사 things가 주어로 수동의 의미가 되어야 하므로, 과거분사 connected가 온 것은 적절하다.

⚙ 이렇게 풀자 _ 어법상 틀린 부분을 찾는 문제는 밑줄이 있는 부분의 형태와 문맥을 보고 어법에 맞게 쓰였는지 확인해야 한다.
① 부사는 문장의 앞이나 뒤에서 문장 전체를 수식하거나 동사, 형용사, 다른 부사를 수식할 수 있다. 부사에 밑줄이 있는 경우는 보어처럼 부사가 아니라 형용사가 와야 하는 위치가 아닌지 잘 살피도록 한다.
② 컴마(,)나 등위접속사 뒤에 위치한 동사원형에 밑줄이 있는 경우는 병렬 구조가 아닌지 확인해 본다.
③ 관계대명사 what은 선행사를 포함하고 있으므로 문장에 선행사가 없어야 하고, 문장에서 주어나 목적어로 사용되어야 한다.
④ 동사에 밑줄이 그어진 경우, 주어, 동사의 수일치를 묻는 문제인 경우가 많다. 특히 관계사절 및 전치사구와 같은 수식어구 또는 삽입절이 주어와 동사 사이에 위치해 있는 경우, 주어가 무엇인지를 분명히 파악해야 동사가 알맞게 쓰였는지 알 수 있다.
⑤ 주어가 무엇인지를 정확히 파악하여 능동태가 와야 하는지 수동태가 와야 하는지를 판단해야 한다.

《 어휘·어구 》

legendary 전설적인
cognitive psychologist 인지 심리학자
mental 정신의
wander (마음, 생각이) 다른 데로 흐르다
self-awareness 자기 인식, 자각
autobiographical 자전적인, 자서전적인
reflect on ~에 대해 깊이 생각하다
moral 도덕적인
reasoning 추론, 추리
neuroscientist 신경 과학자
insight 통찰, 통찰력
previously 이전에, 사전에
unsolvable 풀 수 없는, 해결 불가능한

---

6. ⑤ | 사회적 관계에 대한 통찰을 제공하는 문학 소설

직독직해

Literary fiction provides / much insight into social
relations /

문학 소설은 제공한다 / 사회적 관계에 대한 많은 통찰을 /
in novels or short stories.
(장편) 소설이나 단편 소설에서
But it does not usually claim to offer /
하지만 그것은 보통 제공한다고 주장하지는 않는다 /
systematic interpretation of social phenomena.
사회 현상에 대한 체계적인 해석을
Its great power is / in the rich presentation of
particularity /
그것의 큰 힘은 ~에 있다 / 특수성을 풍부하게 보여 주는 데 /
in a way that evokes general interest.
일반적인 관심을 불러일으키는 방식으로
The telling of stories, / the evocation of mood,
character and circumstances /
이야기를 전달하는 것 / 즉 분위기와 등장인물, 그리고 상황을 환기시키는 것은 /
can present human individuality /
인간의 개성을 제시할 수 있다 /
as simultaneously a matter of unique and
universal experiences.
독특할 뿐만 아니라 동시에 보편적인 경험의 문제로
Fiction can offer to the reader a means / of
reflecting on the nature of the social world.
소설은 독자에게 수단을 제공할 수 있다 / 사회 세계의 본질을 심사숙고할
It does this / when it inspires the conviction /
그것(소설)은 이렇게 한다 / 확신을 불어넣을 때 /
that its ideas extend social experience /
그것의 아이디어가 사회적 경험을 확장한다는 /
— the experience or observation of the reader.
즉 독자의 경험이나 관찰을 (확장한다는)
Fiction contributes to sociological ideas / when it
creates in the reader the sense /
소설은 사회학적 아이디어에 기여한다 / 독자 안에 의식을 만들 때 /
that its stories, characterizations and evocations, /
그것의 이야기, 성격 묘사와 환기 /
or certain elements in them, / can be used to
interpret /
또는 그 안에 있는 특정 요소가 / 해석하는 데 사용될 수 있다는 /
aspects of social experience. 사회적 경험의 양상을
The reader may empathize with characters / or
imagine situations /
독자는 등장인물과 공감하거나 / 또는 상황을 상상할 수도 있다)
as if they were presented / as factual reports of
experience.
마치 그들(등장인물과 상황)이 제시되는 것처럼 / 경험에 관한 사실적인 보고로
Empathy and imagination supply / empirical
reference for fiction, /
공감과 상상은 제공한다 / 소설에 대한 경험적인 참조를 /
and give it its power to supply insight / into 'the
human condition' /
그리고 그것(소설)에 통찰을 제공하는 힘을 준다 / '인간의 조건'에 대한 /
in some sense. 어떤 의미에서는

- -

문학 소설은 (장편) 소설이나 단편 소설에서 사회적 관계에 대한 많은 통찰을 제공한다. 하지만 그것은 보통 사회 현상에 대한 체계적인 해석을 제공한다고 주장하지는 않는다. 그것의 큰 힘은 일반적인 관심을 불러일으키는 방식으로 특수성을 풍부하게 보여 주는 데 있다. 이야기를 전달하는 것, 즉 분위기와 등장인물, 그리고 상황을 환기시키는 것은 인간의 개성을 독특할 뿐만 아니라 동시에 보편적인 경험의 문제로 제시할 수 있다. 소설은 독자에게 사회 세계의 본질을 심사숙고할 수단을 제공할 수 있다. 소설은 그것의 아이디어가 사회적 경험, 즉 독자의 경험이나 관찰을 확장한다는 확신을 불어넣을 때 이렇게 한다. 소설은 그것의 이야기, 성격 묘사와 환기, 또는 그 안에 있는 특정 요소가 사회적 경험의 양상을 해석하는 데 사용될 수 있다는 의식을 독자 안에 만들 때 사회학적 아이디어에 기여한다. 독자는 마치 등장인물이나 상황이 경험에 관한 사실적인 보고로 제시되는 것처럼 등장인물과 공감하거나 상황을 상상할 수도 있다. 공감과 상상은 소설에 대한 경험적인 참조를 제공하고, 어떤 의미에서는 그것(소설)에 '인간의 조건'에 대한 통찰을 제공하는 힘을 준다.

문제풀이

① [관계대명사]
that 뒤에 불완전한 문장이 왔고, 앞에 있는 선행사 a way를 수식하는 주격 관계대명사절이므로 단수동사인 evokes는 적절하게 쓰였다.
② [simultaneously A and B]
'A이기도 하면서 동시에 B'라는 의미의 표현

『simultaneously A and B』가 쓰였으므로, simultaneously는 적절하다.

③ [접속사]

that 뒤에 완벽한 절이 왔고 의미상 the conviction과 동격이므로 명사절을 이끄는 접속사 that은 적절하게 쓰였다.

④ [to 부정사]

의미상 '목적'의 의미를 나타내고 있으므로, 부사적 용법의 to interpret는 적절하게 쓰였다.

⑤ [문장의 동사]

문장의 주어인 Empathy and imagination의 동사로 supply와 and로 병렬적으로 연결되어야 하므로 giving을 give로 고쳐야 한다.

《 어휘 · 어구 》

literary 문학의
insight 통찰력
relation 관계
systematic 체계적인
interpretation 해석
presentation 제시
particularity 특수성
evocation 환기(시킴)
mood 분위기
character 등장인물
circumstances 상황, 환경
individuality 개성
simultaneously 동시에
unique 독특한
universal 보편적인
fiction 소설
reflect 숙고하다
conviction 확신
extend 확장하다
observation 관찰
contribute to ~에 기여하다
sociological 사회학의
characterization 성격 묘사
empathize 공감하다
imagination 상상
reference 참조

---

7. ③　　　　　　　　Albert Einstein

어린 시절 Albert Einstein은 1년을 목적 없이 빈둥거리며 보냈다. 여러분은 시간을 '허비하지' 않고는 아무것도 할 수 없다. 유감스럽게도 이것은 십 대의 부모들이 자주 잊는 것이다. 그는 Pavia에 있었다. 그는 가족에게 갔고 독일 고등학교의 고됨을 견딜 수 없어서 독일에서의 공부를 포기했다. 20세기가 시작되고 있었고 이탈리아에서는 산업혁명이 시작되고 있었다. Albert는 Kant의 서적을 읽고 그곳에 등록하거나 시험에 관해 생각할 필요 없이 그저 즐거움을 위해 Pavia 대학에 이따금씩 강의를 들었다. 이렇게 해서 진지한 과학자가 자라난 것이다. 이후 그는 Zurich 대학에 등록했고 물리학 공부에 몰두했다. 몇 년 후인 1905년, 그는 세 편의 논문을 그 시대의 가장 명망 있는 과학 학회지인 'Annalen der Physik'(물리학 연보)에 보냈다. 이 논문 각각은 노벨상을 받을 가치가 있다.

문제풀이

① something을 수식하며 forget의 목적어가 되는 목적격 관계대명사이므로 적절하다.
② 주절의 원인이 되는 상황을 설명하는 분사구문이며 being이 생략된 형태이므로 적절하다.

---

③ being과 등위접속사 or로 연결되어 전치사 without과 이어지는 동명사구를 이루어야 하므로 had가 아니라 동명사인 having을 써야 한다.
④ immersed의 목적어와 주어가 같은 대상을 지칭하므로 목적어를 himself를 쓰는 것이 적절하다.
⑤ each of ~는 단수 취급하며, 현재까지 지속되는 평가이므로, 단수주어이며 현재시제에 맞추어 be동사를 is로 쓰는 것이 적절하다.

《 구문 및 어휘 》

*4행 He had joined his family, [**having** abandoned his studies in Germany], [**unable** to endure the rigors of his high school there].

(1) having abandoned his studies in Germany는 시간을 나타내는 분사구문으로, 학업을 포기한 후에 가족에게 갔다는 전후 관계를 생각해 보면 'after he had abandoned his studies in Germany'로 바꿔 쓸 수 있다.
(2) unable 이하도 분사구문으로서, 앞에 being이 생략되었다. 'because[as] he was unable'의 의미이다.

get[go] anywhere 성과를 거두다, 잘 되다
aimlessly 목적 없이
rigor 고됨, 혹독함
industrial revolution 산업혁명
occasional 가끔의
register 등록하다
immerse 몰두하게 하다, 담그다
article 글, 기사

---

8. ②　　　　　　　　훌륭한 영화의 줄거리

훌륭한 영화는 항상 줄거리의 주요한 요소들을 분명하게 제시하면서 시작한다. 극적인 갈등이 분명하지 않다면, 줄거리는 관객들에게 무의미하고 지루해 보이리라는 것을 감독은 알고 있다. 분명함은 영화 제작의 가장 중요한 원칙들 중 하나이다. 영화 각본가는 줄거리가 무엇에 관한 것인지에 대한 분명한 생각을 가지고 있어야 하고, 그렇지 않다면 그 결과로 만들어지는 영화는 혼란스러울 것이다. 주제를 분명하게 제시하는 것은 영화에서만큼이나 멀티미디어 체계에서도 중요하다. 사용자가 무엇이 진행되고 있는지를 처음부터 바로 이해하지 못한다면, 그 사람은 흥미를 잃을 수 있다. 비록 많은 멀티미디어 시스템들이 극적인 줄거리를 중심으로 하고 있지는 않지만, 그 시스템의 목적을 분명하게 말해 주어서 사용자가 어떤 정보를 찾기를 기대할 수 있는지, 그것이 어디에서 발견될 수 있는지, 그리고 그것이 어떻게 발견될 수 있는지를 분명히 해 줄 필요가 있다.

문제풀이

(A) 동사 knows의 목적어 역할을 하는 절이고, 그 절 안에 주어와 목적어 등 절 구성의 필수 요소가 모두 포함되어 있으므로 that이 와야 한다. (B) 주어인 the resulting movie에 관해 서술하고 있는데, the resulting movie의 역할이 confuse의 대상이 아니라 유발하는 요소이므로 능동의 의미를 나타내는 confusing이 적절하다. (C) 앞에서 a need를 수식하는 to부정사구(to state the purpose of the system clearly)와 and로 병렬 연결되었으므로 마찬가지로 to부정사구인 to make가 적절하다. 따라서 정답은 ②이다.

《 구문 및 어휘 》

*7행 {A clear presentation [of the subject matter]} is just **as** important in a multimedia system **as** in a

---

movie.

(1) A clear presentation이 문장의 주어이고, of the subject matter는 주어를 수식하는 전치사구이다. is는 동사이다.
(2)「as+원급+as」는 '~만큼 …한'의 의미이다.

*11행 [**Even though** many multimedia systems are not centered around a dramatic story line], there is a need **to state** the purpose of the system clearly and **to make** it clear [which information the user can expect to find], [where it can be found], and [how it can be found].

(1)「부사절(Even though~)+주절(there is a need~)」구조의 문장이다. even though는 '비록 ~일지라도'의 의미이다.
(2) to state와 to make는 a need를 수식하는 형용사적 용법의 to부정사이다.
(3) it은 가목적어이고, which information the user can expect to find, where it can be found와 how it can be found의 3개의 명사절이 it의 진목적어로 병렬 연결되었다.

element 요소, 성분
dramatic 극적인
conflict 충돌
clarity 분명함
principle 원칙
screen-writer 영화 각본가
clear-cut 분명한

---

9. ②　　　　　　　　E-prime 이론

E-prime 이론은 당신이 be동사를 사용하지 않고 영어를 쓰거나 말한다면, 사건을 더 정확하게 묘사할 수 있다고 주장한다. 예를 들면, "Johnny는 실패한 사람이다."라고 말할 때, 동사 is는 '실패'가 Johnny에 대한 당신의 관찰 안에 있다기 보다는 Johnny 안에 있다는 것을 암시한다. ('is', 'are'과 'am'과 같은 형태로) be동사는 (A) 영구성도 암시하는데, 그것은 실패가 Johnny 안에 있어서 그것은 항상 거기에 있을 것이다. 그것은 Johnny가 항상 실패한 사람일 것임을 암시한다. 더 (B) 정확한 말은 아마도 "Johnny는 자신의 지난 두 번의 수학 시험에서 실패했다." 일 것이다. 이 이론이 당신에 관해 생각하는 것에 적용되는 것으로 생각해 보라. 예를 들면, 당신이 "나는 사람들 앞에서 말을 잘하지 못한다." 또는 "나는 인기가 없다." 또는 "나는 게으르다."라고 말하면, 당신은 이러한 특성들이 당신 안에 있다는 것을 암시한다. 그러나 이것들은 단순히 정확하지 않을 수도 있고, 혹은 적어도 부분적으로 정확하다고 해도, 시간이 지남에 따라 바뀔 수도 있는 (C) 평가이다.

문제풀이

실패가 Johnny 안에 있어서 항상 거기에 있을 것이라고 했기 때문에 (A)에는 계속 그럴 것이라는 의미의 permanence(영구성)가 적절하다. 뒤에 나온 "Johnny failed his last two math exams." 는 앞의 be동사를 사용하여 말한 것보다 더 정확하게 말한 것이기 때문에 (B)에는 precise(정확한)가 오는 것이 적절하다. 앞에 나온 "I'm not good at public speaking", "I'm unpopular", "I'm lazy"는 자신에 대한 평가의 내용이므로 (C)에는 evaluations(평가)가 적절하다. 따라서 정답은 ②이다.

구문 및 어휘

*1행 The theory of E-prime argues [that (**if you wrote and spoke** English without the verb to be, you'd **describe** events more accurately)].

⑴that 이하는 argues의 목적어로 쓰인 명사절로 「If+주어+동사의 과거형 ~, 주어+would+동사원형 ~」은 '~라면 …일 텐데'의 의미인 가정법 과거가 사용되었다.

argue 주장하다
accurately 정확히
imply 암시하다
observation 관찰
implication 암시
statement 말, 진술
at least 적어도

---

10. ⑤   운동 기구와 운동 강도

2001년에 Wayne 주립대학교 연구자들은 한 집단의 대학생 지원자들에게 러닝머신, 고정 자전거, 스테퍼의 세 가지 운동 기구에서 각각 (A) 자신이 선택한 속도로 20분 동안 운동할 것을 요청했다. 심박 수, 산소 소모량, 그리고 인지된 운동 강도가 세 가지 운동 모두가 진행되는 내내 측정되었다. 연구자들은 실험 대상자들이 각 활동에서 무의식적으로 비교적 똑같은 생리학적인 강도를 목표로 함을 발견할 것으로 예상했다. 어쩌면 그들은 어떤 기계를 사용하고 있는지와 상관없이 (B) 무의식적으로 최대 심박 수의 65퍼센트로 운동할 것이었다. 혹은 어쩌면 그들은 세 가지 운동 모두에서 산소 소모 최대 속도의 70퍼센트라는 리듬에 본능적으로 자리 잡을 것이었다. 그러나 일어난 일은 그렇지 않았다. 사실 세 가지 종목에서 심박 수와 산소 소모량의 측정에서 (C) 일관성이 없었다. 대신, 실험 대상자들은 러닝머신, 자전거, 그리고 스테퍼에서 똑같은 수준의 인지된 운동 강도를 선택했던 것으로 밝혀졌다.

문제풀이

(A) 실험 대상자들은 세 가지 운동 기구에서 운동하면서 같은 수준의 인지된 운동 강도를 '선택했다'고 하였으므로, self-selected(자신이 선택한)가 적절하다. (B) unconsciously, instinctively와 같은 표현이 쓰인 것으로 보아, automatically(무의식적으로)가 적절하다. (C) 연구자들은 세 가지 운동 기구에서 운동하는 실험 대상자들의 심박 수나 산소 소모량이 사용 중인 운동 기구와 관계없이 동일할 것이라고 예상했으나 사실은 그렇지 않았다는 내용이고, 빈칸 앞에 부정어 no가 있으므로 빈칸에는 consistency(일관성)가 적절하다. 따라서 정답은 ⑤이다.

구문 및 어휘

*8행 Perhaps they would automatically exercise (**at 65 percent of their maximum heart rate**) regardless of [which machine they were using].

⑴at은 '(속도를) ~로'라는 의미로 쓰인 전치사이다.
⑵which 이하는 전치사 regardless of의 목적어로 쓰인 「의문사+주어+동사」 어순의 간접의문문이다.

stationary bike 고정 자전거
stair climber 스테퍼(계단 오르기 운동 기구)
measurement 측정
oxygen 산소
consumption 소모
perceived 인지된
unconsciously 무의식적으로
relative 상대적인

---

intensity 강도, 세기, 격렬함
automatically 무의식적으로, 자동적으로
regardless of ~에 관계없이
instinctively 본능적으로
settle into ~에 자리 잡다
discipline 종목

---

11. ③   위계질서와 권력 차이의 관계

권력 차이에 있어서, 당신의 문화나 배경이 더 위계질서가 있을수록 권력 차이가 더 커지는 경향이 있다. 왜냐하면 이는 위계질서가 있는 문화가 관리자와 직원들 사이에 차이를 (A) 강화시키기 때문이다. 만약 당신이 자신의 성향에 있어서 더 위계적인 경향이 있다면 당신은 권위 있는 위치에 있는 사람들을 더 높은 레벨에 두려는 경향이 있으며, 심지어는 그것을 차지하는 사람들과는 분리되어 그 지위나 위치에 대한 더 많은 존경이 있다. 만약 당신이 위계질서를 선호한다면 (B) 거리감이 좋은 것으로 생각된다. 관리자는 그의 직원들과 너무 가까운 것은 적절하지 않은 것이다. 그 결과는 존재하는 모든 권력의 차이가 이러한 차원의 렌즈를 통해 확대된다. 더 큰 권력 차이는 늘어난 오해와 충돌뿐만 아니라 줄어든 소통을 초래할 수 있고, 어쩌면 중요한 사업적, 직업적 관계를 형성하는 데 (C) 놓쳐버린 기회들로 이어진다.

문제풀이

(A) 문화나 배경이 더 위계질서가 있을수록 권력 차이가 커진다고 했으므로, 위계질서가 있는 문화가 직원들 사이에 차이를 강화시킨다(reinforce)는 흐름이 되는 것이 적절하다. (B) 뒤에서 관리자는 직원들과 너무 가까운 것은 적절하지 않다고 했으므로, 위계질서를 선호하면 거리(distance)를 두는 것을 좋게 생각할 것이다. (C) 줄어든 소통은 중요한 사업적, 직업적 관계를 형성하는 기회를 놓치게(missed) 할 것이다. 그러므로 정답은 ③이다.

구문 및 어휘

*1행 [With a power gap], the more hierarchical your culture or background, the greater the power gap is apt to be.

⑴「the+비교급 ~, the+비교급 …」는 '~하면 할수록 더 …하다'라는 의미이다. 「be apt to부정사는」는 '~하는 경향이 있다'라는 뜻이다.

*9행 It wouldn't be proper **for a manager** [**to be** too familiar with his employees].

⑴It은 가주어로 to be 이하가 진주어이다. for a manager는 to부정사의 의미상의 주어이다.

*11행 The effect is [that any power gap (that exists) is magnified through the lens of this dimension].

⑴that 이하는 문장에서 보어 역할을 하는 명사절이다.
⑵that exists는 선행사 any power gap을 수식하는 관계대명사절이다.

hierarchical 계급에 따른
be apt to ~하기 쉽다, ~하는 경향이 있다
orientation 성향
magnify 확대하다
dimension 크기

---

12. ⑤   고용 영역에서 유리해진 노인들

직독 / 직해

Today's ageing adults will be more advantaged /
오늘날 나이가 들어가는 성인들은 더 유리하게 될 것이다 /
in the employment domain / as they age.
고용 영역에서 / 나이가 들수록
Attitudes about older employees are becoming more favorable.
나이 든 직원에 대한 태도가 더 호의적으로 되어가고 있다
In addition, / 게다가 /
because of the post-baby boom declines in birth rates, /
베이비 붐 이후의 출산율 감소 때문에 /
the number of employable adults will decrease /
고용할 수 있는 성인들의 수가 감소할 것이다 /
relative to the number of new jobs.
새로운 일자리의 수와 관련된
Consequently, / 결과적으로 /
older workers will become more valued and sought after, /
나이 든 근로자들은 더 소중하게 여겨지고 더 찾아지게 될 것이다 /
and those who do not feel ready to retire /
그리고 은퇴할 준비가 되어 있지 않다고 느끼는 근로자들은 /
will be less likely to be compelled to do so.
그렇게 하도록 강요될 가능성이 적을 것이다
The standard retirement age is rising, /
표준 은퇴 나이는 증가하고 있다 /
based on observations / 관찰에 근거해서 /
that, in terms of health and life expectancy, /
건강과 기대 수명의 관점에서 /
age 70 today is roughly the equivalent of age 65 in the 1930s /
오늘날 70세의 나이는 1930년대의 65세와 거의 동등한 나이라는 /
when Social Security was established in the USA.
미국에서 사회 보장 제도가 수립된
Although most individuals /
비록 대부분의 개인들이 /
who have adequate (or better) financial resources /
충분한 (혹은 더 나은) 재원을 가진 /
will retire at the usual time / 평상시에 은퇴할지라도 /
or follow the trend toward early retirement, /
또는 조기 은퇴에 대한 유행을 따르게 된다 하더라도 /
physically healthy elders will be able to choose /
신체적으로 건강한 노인들은 선택할 수 있을 것이다 /
whether or not they will continue to work.
그들이 계속 일을 할 것인지 아닌지를

오늘날 나이가 들어가는 성인들은 나이가 들수록 고용 영역에서 더 유리해지게 될 것이다. 나이 든 직원에 대한 태도가 더 ① 호의적으로 되어가고 있다. 게다가, 베이비 붐 이후의 출산율 감소 때문에, 새로운 일자리의 수와 관련하여 고용할 수 있는 성인들의 수가 ② 감소할 것이다. 결과적으로, 나이 든 근로자들은 더 소중하게 여겨지고 더 찾아지게 될 것이며, 은퇴할 준비가 되어 있지 않다고 느끼는 근로자들은 은퇴하도록 강요당할 가능성이 ③ 적을 것이다. 건강과 기대 수명의 관점에서, 오늘날 70세의 나이는 미국에서 사회 보장 제도가 수립된 1930년대의 65세와 거의 동등한 나이라는 관찰에 근거할 때, 표준 은퇴 나이는 ④ 증가하고 있다. 비록 충분한 (혹은 더 나은) 재원을 가진 대부분의 개인들이 평상시에 은퇴하거나 조기 은퇴에 대한 유행을 ⑤ 뒤엎게(→ 따르게) 될지라도, 신체적으로 건강한 노인들은 그들이 계속 일을 할 것인지 아닌지를 선택할 수 있을 것이다.

문제풀이

이 글은 오늘날의 성인들은 나이가 들수록 고용 영역에서 더 유리해지게 된다는 내용의 글이다. 은퇴할 준비가 되어 있지 않다고 느끼는 근로자들은 은퇴하도록 강요받지 않을 것이고, 표준 은퇴 나이도 증가하고 있다고 언급하고 있으며, 은퇴할 여건이 된다 할지라도 계속 일을 할지를 선택할 수 있을 것이라 전망하고 있다. 따라서 '충분한 재원을 가지고 있어서 조기 은퇴에 대한 유행을 꺼리게 된다 할지라도'는 글의 맥락상 어울리지 않는다. 그러므로 ⑤의 'reverse(꺼리게)'를 'follow(따르게)'와 같은 말로 바꿔 써야 한다.

❖ 이렇게 풀자 상반접속사 'Although'가 이끄는 양보절은 주절의 내용과 반대되는 내용이 나와야 한다. 양보절의 내용이 'physically healthy elders will be able to

---

choose whether or not they will continue to work. (신체적으로 건강한 노인들은 일을 계속할 것인지 아닌지를 선택할 수 있다)'라고 언급한 주절의 내용과 상반된 내용이 맞는지를 확인해야 한다. 'reverse the trend toward early retirement(조기 은퇴에 대한 유행을 뒤엎다)'는 주절의 내용과 같은 내용이 되므로 문맥상 어울리지 않는다.

《 어휘·어구 》

ageing 나이가 들어가는
domain 영역
attitude 태도, 마음가짐
favorable 호의적인
decline 감소하다, 기울다
relative to ~와 관련된, ~에 대한
seek after ~을 청하다, 요구하다
compel A to do A가 ~하도록 강요하다, 강제하다
in terms of ~의 관점에서
roughly 거의, 대략
equivalent 동등한 것[사람], 등가물
adequate 충분한, 적당한
financial resources 재원, 재력

17. 대명사

A 출제 POINT
본문 098쪽

1. its 2. ourselves 3. hers
4. that 5. the other
6. what you like 7. it

1 [해석]▶ 성능이 좋은 회전 전등이 우리의 길을 쉽게 비추어 줄 것이고, 바닷속 모습을 진정한 색채 그대로 보여줄 것이다.
[해설]▶ '진정한 색채 그대로'는 바닷속(marine life)을 가리키므로 단수 소유격인 its로 써야 한다.

2 [해석]▶ 지난밤에 우리는 맘껏 즐겼다.
[해설]▶ 재귀대명사는 주어와 동일한 대상을 지칭하는 목적어에 사용한다. 주어가 복수 we이므로 ourselves로 써야 한다.

3 [해석]▶ 그것은 그의 책이니? 아니오. 그것은 그녀의 책입니다.
[해설]▶ '그녀의 책'은 「소유격+명사」인 her book 또는 「소유대명사」 hers로 표현해야 한다.

4 [해석]▶ 사람들은 2030년이면 중국 경제는 미국 경제의 2.5배에 달할 거라고 말한다.
[해설]▶ '중국의 경제'와 '미국의 경제'를 비교하고 있다. the economy of US에서 단수명사 the economy의 반복을 피하기 위해서 지시대명사 that을 써도 된다.

5 [해석]▶ 우리는 강아지가 두 마리 있는데, 하나는 흰색이고, 다른 하나는 검정색이다.
[해설]▶ one..., the other ~는 '(둘 중에서) 하나는 …, 다른 하나는 ~'의 의미이다.

6 [해석]▶ 네 직업에 대해서 무엇을 가장 좋아하는지 말해 줄 수 있나요?
[해설]▶ What do you like most about your job?이라는 직접의문문을 앞 문장의 일부로 보내면 「의문사+주어+동사」의 어순으로 변한다.

7 [해석]▶ 어떤 의미에서 순수 미술 작품은 대중적인 소비를 위해 복제할 수 있기 때문에 가치 있게 여겨진다.
[해설]▶ 구체적인 명사구 the find art object를 가리키므로 it을 사용한다.

B 체크 POINT
본문 098쪽

1. write them down 2. himself
3. yours 4. this 5. others
6. the others 7. some

1 [해석]▶ 아마도 목표에 집중하는 가장 효과적인 방법은 그것을 적는 것이다.
[해설]▶ 대명사가 목적어일 때, 「타동사+대명사+부사」의 어순으로 써야 한다.

2 [해석]▶ 나는 비서가 아닌 이사님 본인에게 이야기하고 싶습니다.

[해설]▶ 재귀대명사 강조 용법은 명사를 강조하기 위해 사용하고 생략 가능하다.

3 [해석]▶ 나는 내 연필을 가지고 있는데, 너는 네 것을 가지고 있니?
[해설]▶ 소유대명사(yours)는 「소유격(your)+명사(pencil)」를 대신하는 말이다.

4 [해석]▶ 내가 언급한 사진이 여기 이것이다.
[해설]▶ 지시대명사는 앞에 언급된 어구나 내용을 받는다. 가리키는 대상이 단수명사(the picture)이므로 지시대명사 this를 사용한다.

5 [해석]▶ 어떤 관광객들은 해변에 갔고, 다른 관광객들은 도시를 답사했다.
[해설]▶ some... others~는 '(막연한 다수 중) 일부는 …, 다른 일부는 ~'을 의미한다.

6 [해석]▶ 6권의 책이 있는데, 하나는 내 책이고, 나머지는 모두 남동생의 책이다.
[해설]▶ 한정된 6권 중에서 1권을 제외한 나머지 5권을 말하고 있으므로 the others로 표현해야 한다.

7 [해석]▶ 나에게 온 편지가 있나요? 예, 몇 개 왔어요.
[해설]▶ any letters가 막연한 대상으로 복수명사이므로, 이것을 복수 대명사로 표현하려면 some을 사용한다.

Day 17
본문 099쪽

1 ②	2 ②	3 ②	4 ②	5 ⑤
6 ③	7 ④	8 ③	9 ⑤	10 ③
11 ③	12 ④			

1. ②
패션의 역할

직독 직해

Trends constantly suggest new opportunities / for individuals / to restage themselves, /
유행은 새로운 기회를 계속해서 제시하고 / 사람들이 / 자신을 재조정할 /

representing occasions for change.
변화의 경우를 나타낸다

To understand / how trends can ultimately give individuals power and freedom, /
이해하기 위해서 / 유행이 궁극적으로 어떻게 개인에게 힘과 자유를 줄 수 있는지를 /

one must first discuss fashion's importance / as a basis for change.
먼저 패션의 중요성에 대해 논의해야 한다 / 변화를 위한 기본으로서의

The most common explanation offered by my informants /
나의 정보 제공자들이 제공한 가장 일반적인 설명은 /

as to why fashion is so appealing /
왜 패션이 그렇게도 매력적인가에 대해 /

is that it constitutes a kind of theatrical costumery.
그것이 일종의 연극적인 복장을 구성한다는 것이다

Clothes are part of how people present themselves to the world, /
옷은 사람들이 자신을 세상에 제시하는 방식의 일부이다 /

and fashion locates them in the present, /
그리고 패션은 그들을 현재에 위치시킨다 /

relative to what is happening in society / and to fashion's own history.
사회에서 일어나고 있는 일과 관련하여 / 그리고 패션 자체의 역사와 (관련하여)

As a form of expression, / fashion contains a host of ambiguities, /

[고3 영어 어법·어휘]

표현 형태로서 / 패션은 다수의 모호함을 담고 있어 /
enabling individuals to recreate the meanings /
개인이 의미를 다시 만들어낼 수 있게 한다 /

associated with specific pieces of clothing.
특정한 옷과 연관된

Fashion is among the simplest and cheapest methods of self-expression: /
패션은 자기표현의 가장 단순하고 값싼 방법 중의 하나로 /

clothes can be inexpensively purchased /
옷은 값싸게 구매할 수 있으며 /

while making it easy to convey /
쉽게 전달할 수 있다 /

notions of wealth, intellectual stature, relaxation or environmental consciousness, /
부, 지적 능력, 휴식 혹은 환경 의식에 대한 개념을 /

even if none of these is true.
비록 이것 중 어느 것도 사실이 아니라 해도

Fashion can also strengthen agency / in various ways, /
패션은 또한 행동력을 강화할 수 있다   / 다양한 방식으로 /

opening up space for action.
행동을 위한 공간을 열어주면서

유행은 사람들이 자신을 재조정할 새로운 기회를 계속해서 제시하고, 변화의 경우를 나타낸다. 유행이 궁극적으로 어떻게 개인에게 힘과 자유를 줄 수 있는지를 이해하기 위해서 먼저 변화를 위한 기본으로서의 패션의 중요성에 대해 논의해야 한다. 왜 패션이 그렇게도 매력적인지는 나의 정보 제공자들이 제공한 가장 일반적인 설명은 그것이 일종의 연극적인 복장을 구성한다는 것이다. 옷은 사람들이 자신을 세상에 제시하는 방식의 일부이고, 패션은 사회에서 일어나고 있는 일, 그리고 패션 자체의 역사와 관련하여 그들을 현재에 위치시킨다. 표현 형태로서 패션은 다수의 모호함을 담고 있어 개인이 특정한 옷과 연관된 의미를 다시 만들어낼 수 있게 한다. 패션은 자기표현의 가장 단순하고 값싼 방법 중의 하나로, 옷은 값싸게 구매할 수 있으며, 부, 지적 능력, 휴식 혹은 환경 의식에 대한 개념을, 비록 이것 중 어느 것도 사실이 아니라 해도, 쉽게 전달할 수 있다. 패션은 또한 행동을 위한 공간을 열어주면서 다양한 방식으로 행동력을 강화할 수 있다.

문제풀이

① [접속사 that]
뒤에 문장 성분을 모두 갖춘 완전한 문장이 왔으므로, 문장의 보어 역할을 하는 명사절을 이끄는 접속사 that이 온 것은 적절하다.

② [재귀대명사]
'사람들이 자신들을 세상에 제시하는'이라는 의미가 되어야 하는데 주어 people과 목적어가 가리키는 대상이 같으므로, them을 재귀대명사 themselves로 바꿔 써야 한다.

③ [과거분사]
'연관된'이라는 의미로 앞의 명사 the meanings를 수식하는 과거분사가 되어야 하므로, associated가 온 것은 적절하다.

④ [부사]
과거분사 purchased를 수식하므로 부사로 inexpensively가 온 것은 적절하다.

⑤ [분사구문]
분사구문이 와야 하는데, '행동을 위한 공간을 열어주면서'라는 능동의 의미이므로, 현재분사 opening이 온 것은 적절하다.

◐ 이렇게 풀자 어법상 틀린 부분을 찾는 문제는 밑줄이 있는 부분의 형태와 문맥을 보고 어법에 맞게 쓰였는지 확인해야 한다.
① that 뒤에 문장 성분을 모두 갖춘 완전한 절이 왔다면 that은 명사절을 이끄는 접속사로 쓰인 것이다.
② 주어와 목적어가 같은 사람을 가리킬 때 목적어로는 재귀대명사가 와야 한다.
③ 분사가 명사를 수식할 경우, 수동의 의미일 경우 과거분사가 오고 능동의 의미일 경우 현재분사가 온다.
④ 부사는 형용사(과거분사 / 현재분사)나 다른 부사를 수식할 수 있다. 또한 동사의 앞이나 뒤에서 동사를 수식하거나 문장의 앞뒤에서 문장 전체를 수식할 수 있다.
⑤ 분사구문에서 의미상 주어와의 관계가 능동일 때 현재분사가 와야 하고, 수동일 때 과거분사가 와야 한다.

《 어휘 · 어구 》

represent 나타내다, 표현하다
occasion 때, 경우
ultimately 궁극적으로, 결국
informant 정보 제공자
as to ~에 관해
appealing 매력적인
constitute 구성하다
costumery 복장
a host of 다수의
ambiguity 모호함
convey 전달하다
notion 개념
consciousness 의식
strengthen 강화하다

---

2. ②   증가하는 수면 부족

직독 / 직해

The old maxim "I'll sleep when I'm dead" /
'잠은 죽어서 자는 것이다'라는 옛 격언은 /

is unfortunate. 유감스럽다
Adopt this mind-set, / and you will be dead sooner /
이런 사고방식을 가져라   / 그러면 여러분은 더 빨리 죽게 될 것이고 /

and the quality of that life / will be worse.
그리고 그런 삶의 질은   / 더 나빠질 것이다

The elastic band of sleep deprivation / can stretch /
수면 부족이라는 고무 밴드는   / 늘어날 수 있다 /

only so far before it snaps.
오직 그것이 끊어지기 전까지만

Sadly, / human beings are in fact the only species /
애석하게도 / 인간은 사실상 유일한 종이다 /

that will deliberately deprive themselves of sleep /
의도적으로 잠을 스스로 자제하는 /

without legitimate gain. 합당한 이익 없이
Every component of wellness, /
건강의 모든 요소 /

and countless seams of societal fabric, /
그리고 수많은 사회 구조의 이음매는 /

are being eroded by our costly state of sleep neglect: /
손실이 큰 우리의 수면 무시 상태로 인해 약화되고 있다 /

human and financial alike. 인간적 그리고 재정적 측면 둘 다
So much so that the World Health Organization
이제 세계 보건 기구(WHO)에서 선포할 정도였다 /

(WHO) has now declared /
a sleep loss epidemic / 수면 부족 유행병을
throughout industrialized nations. 산업화된 국가 전역에
It is no coincidence / 우연히도
that countries where sleep time has declined /
수면 시간이 줄어든 국가들이 /

most dramatically / over the past century, /
가장 급격하게   / 지난 세기에 걸쳐 /

such as the US, the UK, Japan, and South Korea, /
미국, 영국, 일본, 한국과 같이 /

and several in Western Europe, /
그리고 몇몇 서유럽 국가들과 (같이) /

are also those suffering the greatest increase /
또한 가장 많은 증가를 겪고 있는 국가들이라는 것은 /

in rates of physical diseases and mental disorders.
신체 질환과 정신 질환 비율에 있어

'잠은 죽어서 자는 것이다'라는 옛 격언은 유감스럽다. 이런 사고방식을 가져라, 그러면 여러분은 더 빨리 죽게 될 것이고, 그런 삶의 질은 더 나빠질 것이다. 수면 부족이라는 고무 밴드는 오직 그것이 끊어지기 전까지만 늘어날 수 있다. 애석하게도, 인간은 사실상 합당한 이익 없이 의도적으로 잠을 스스로 자제하는 유일한 종이다. 건강의 모든 요소와 수많은 사회 구조의 이음매는 인간적, 재정적 측면 둘 다 손실이 큰 우리의 수면 무시 상태로 인해 약화되고 있다. 이제 세계 보건 기구(WHO)에서 산업화된 국가 전역에 수면 부족 유행병을 선포할 정도였다. 미국, 영국, 일본, 한국, 그리고 몇몇 서유럽 국가들과 같이, 지난 세기에 걸쳐 수면 시

간이 가장 급격하게 줄어든 국가들이 신체 질환과 정신 질환 비율에 있어 또한 가장 많은 증가를 겪고 있는 국가들이라는 것은 우연이 아니다.

문제풀이

(A) 「명령문, and …」는 '~해라, 그러면 …할 것이다'라는 의미를 나타내는 구문이므로, Adopt가 적절하다.
(B) 동사 deprive의 동작 주체와 대상이 같으므로 재귀대명사인 themselves를 써야 한다.
(C) 뒤에 오는 절이 문장의 요소를 모두 갖춘 완전한 형태이고, 앞에 나온 선행사가 장소를 나타내므로 관계부사 where를 써야 한다.

◐ 이렇게 풀자_ 어법상 틀린 부분을 찾는 문제는 밑줄이 있는 부분의 형태와 문맥을 보고 어법에 맞게 쓰였는지 확인해야 한다. (A)는 명령문 뒤에 접속사 or나 and가 왔을 경우 어떤 의미를 갖는지를 알아야 하고, (B)는 재귀대명사의 쓰임을 알아야 하며, (C)는 선행사에 따른 관계부사의 쓰임을 알아야 한다.

《 어휘 · 어구 》

maxim 격언, 금언
unfortunate 유감스러운, 불쾌한, 불행한
mind-set 사고방식
elastic 고무로 된, 탄력 있는
deprivation (필수적인 것의) 부족, 박탈
snap 툭 끊어지다[부러지다]
deliberately 의도적으로
deprive oneself of ~을 자제하다
legitimate 합당한
component (구성) 요소
wellness 건강
seam 이음매, 접합선
fabric (사회의) 구조, 직물
erode 약화시키다, 침식하다
neglect 무시
so much so that ~할 정도로
declare 선포하다
epidemic 유행병, 급속한 유행
coincidence 우연의 일치
mental disorder 정신 질환

---

3. ②   필기의 이점 — 집중력 유지와 기억에 도움을 준다

직독 / 직해

Note taking is one of the activities /
필기는 활동 중 하나이지만 /

by which students attempt to stay attentive, /
학생들이 집중력이 있는 상태를 유지하기 위해 시도하는 /

but it is also an aid to memory.
그것은 또한 기억을 돕는 방법이다.

"Working memory," / or "short term memory" /
'작동 기억' 또는 '단기 기억'은 /

is a term used to describe the fact /
사실을 설명하기 위해 사용되는 용어이다.

that one can hold / 우리가 기억할 수 있다는 /
only a given amount of material in mind at one time.
마음에 한 번에 단지 주어진 자료의 일정량만을

When a lecturer presents a succession of new concepts, /
강사가 연속적으로 새로운 개념을 제시하면, /

students' faces begin to show /
학생들의 얼굴에서 보이기 시작한다 /

signs of anguish and frustration;
고통과 좌절의 표시가

some write furiously in their notebooks, /
어떤 학생들은 노트에 열심히 필기를 하고, /

Column 1

while others give up writing in complete discouragement.
한편 어떤 학생들은 완전히 낙담해서 필기를 포기한다.

Note taking thus is dependent on one's ability /
따라서 필기는 개인의 능력에 따라 달라진다. /

to maintain attention, /
집중력을 유지할 수 있는, /

understand what is being said, /
강의되고 있는 내용을 이해하는 능력, /

and hold it in working memory /
작동 기억 속에 지니고 있는 능력 /

long enough to write it down.
(들은 내용을) 필기 할 때까지 충분히 오래

필기는 학생들이 집중력이 있는 상태를 유지하기 위해 시도하는 활동 중 하나이지만 그것은 또한 기억을 돕는 방법이다. '작동 기억' 또는 '단기 기억'은 우리가 한 번에 단지 주어진 자료의 일정량만을 기억할 수 있다는 사실을 설명하기 위해 사용되는 용어이다. 강사가 연속적으로 새로운 개념을 제시하면, 학생들의 얼굴에서 고통과 좌절의 표시가 보이기 시작한다. 어떤 학생들은 노트에 열심히 필기를 하고, 한편 어떤 학생들은 완전히 낙담해서 필기를 포기한다. 따라서 필기는 집중력을 유지할 수 있는 개인의 능력, 강의되고 있는 내용을 이해하는 능력, 들은 내용을 필기할 때까지 작동 기억 속에 충분히 오래 지니고 있는 능력에 따라 달라진다.

문제풀이

(A) 「사물(term)+(관계대명사+be동사)+과거분사(used)」 구문으로 「관계대명사+be동사」가 생략되어 있다.
(B) some과 대구를 이루며 동시에 give up의 주어인 others가 필요하다. some... others ~ 구문은 '일부는 …, 다른 일부는 ~ 하다'는 의미가 있다.
(C)에서는 구동사의 목적어가 대명사일 때는 대명사가 동사와 부사 사이에 위치한다. 참고로, 목적어가 명사일 때는 「동사+명사+부사」 또는 「동사+부사+명사」가 모두 가능하다.

어휘·어구

note taking 필기
attentive 집중하는
memory 기억
working memory 작동 기억
short-term memory 단기 기억
term 용어
succession 연속
anguish 고통
frustration 좌절
attention 집중력

4. ② 야생화 향기 가득한 낙원 같은 정원

직독 직해

The first thing I notice / upon entering this garden /
내가 처음 알아차린 것은 / 이 정원에 들어오자마자 /

is that the ankle-high grass is greener than /
발목 높이의 풀이 더 푸르다는 것이다. /

that on the other side of the fence.
울타리 반대편의 풀보다

Dozens of wildflowers of countless varieties /
무수히 다양한 품종의 야생화 수십 그루가 /

cover the ground to both sides of the path.
길 양편으로 땅을 덮고 있다.

Creeping plants cover the polished silver gate /
덩굴 식물들은 윤이 나는 은빛의 대문을 덮고 있고

and the sound of bubbling water comes from somewhere.
거품을 내며 흐르는 물소리가 어디에선가 들려온다.

The perfume of wildflowers fills the air /
야생화 향기는 공기 중에 가득하다. /

as the grass dances upon a gentle breeze.
풀은 산들바람에 춤을 추며

Column 2

A large basket of herbs rests /
풀이 들어 있는 큰 바구니가 놓여 있다. /

against the fence to the west.
서쪽 울타리에 기대어

Every time I walk in this garden, /
나는 이 정원으로 걸어들어 올 때마다 /

I think, "Now I know what it is like /
"이제야 알겠어."라고 생각한다. /

to live in paradise." "낙원에 사는 것이 어떤 것인지를"

이 정원에 들어오자마자 내가 처음 알아차린 것은 발목 높이의 풀이 울타리 반대편의 풀보다 더 푸르다는 것이다. 무수히 다양한 품종의 야생화 수십 그루가 길 양편으로 땅을 덮고 있다. 덩굴 식물들은 윤이 나는 은빛의 대문을 덮고 거품을 내며 흐르는 물소리가 어디에선가 들려온다. 야생화 향기는 공기 중에 가득하고 풀은 산들바람에 춤을 준다. 풀이 들어 있는 큰 바구니가 서쪽 울타리에 기대어 놓여 있다. 나는 이 정원으로 걸어들어 올 때마다 "낙원에 사는 것이 어떤 것인지를 이제야 알겠어."라고 생각한다.

문제풀이

(A) 단수명사 the grass를 대신하는 단수형의 지시대명사가 필요하므로 that이 적절하다. 참고로, those는 비교되는 대상이 복수일 때 사용한다. ex. The ears of a rabbit is longer than those of a cat.
(B) 복수형 명사 앞이므로 both가 적절하다. either는 '둘 중 하나'라는 선택의 의미로 뒤에 단수형 명사가 온다.
(C) 주어가 단수명사 The perfume이므로 동사는 단수동사 fills가 적절하다.

어휘·어구

ankle-high 발목 높이의
countless 수많은
variety 품종, 변종
polish 품위있게 하다, 윤이 나다
bubble 거품을 내며 흐르다
perfume 향기
breeze 산들바람

5. ⑤ 성공의 비결은 승리할 때까지 경기에 남는 것이다.

직독 직해

I wonder how many people give up /
얼마나 많은 사람들이 포기를 하는지 궁금하다. /

just when success is almost within reach.
성공이 거의 손에 닿을 수 있는 곳에 있을 때

They endure day after day, / 그들은 매일 인내하다가 /

and just when they're about to make it, /
막 성공하려고 할 때 /

decide they can't take any more.
더 이상 참고 견딜 수 없다고 결정을 내린다.

The difference between success and failure /
성공과 실패 사이의 차이점은 /

is not that great.
그렇게 대단하지 않다.

Successful people have simply learned /
성공한 사람들은 단순히 배웠던 것이다 /

the value of staying
계속 남아있는 것의 가치를

in the game until it is won.
경기에 승리할 때까지

Those who never make it /
결코 성공하지 못하는 사람들은 /

are the ones who quit too soon.
너무나 빨리 그만두는 사람들이다.

When things are darkest, /
사물이 가장 어두울 때 /

successful people refuse to give up

Column 3

성공하는 사람들은 포기하기를 거부한다.

because they know they're almost there.
자신들이 그곳에(성공에) 거의 다 왔다는 것을 알기 때문에

Things often seem at their worst /
최악의 상태인 것처럼 보이는 일이 종종 있다. /

just before they get better.
일들이 더 좋아지기 전에

The mountain is steepest at the summit, /
산은 정상에서 가장 가파르지만 /

but that's no reason to turn back.
그것이 되돌아갈 이유는 아니다.

성공이 거의 손에 닿을 수 있는 곳에 있을 때 얼마나 많은 사람들이 포기를 하는지 궁금하다. 그들은 매일 인내하다가 막 성공하려고 할 때 더 이상 참고 견딜 수 없다고 결정을 내린다. 성공과 실패 사이의 차이점은 그렇게 대단하지 않다. 성공한 사람들은 경기에 승리할 때까지 경기에 계속 남아있는 것의 가치를 배웠던 것이다. 결코 성공하지 못하는 사람들은 너무나 빨리 그만두는 사람들이다. 사물이 가장 어두울 때 성공하는 사람들은 자신들이 그곳에(성공에) 거의 다 왔다는 것을 알기 때문에 포기를 거부한다. 일들이 더 좋아지기 전에 최악의 상태인 것처럼 보이는 일이 종종 있다. 산은 정상에서 가장 가파르지만 그것이 되돌아갈 이유는 아니다.

문제풀이

① 「be about to+부정사」는 '막 ~를 하려 하다'의 의미이다.
② that이 형용사 great 앞에서 '그렇게'의 뜻을 갖는 지시부사로 쓰였다.
③ it가 the game을 받는 대명사이고 win it(= the game)이 수동태가 된 것이다. 그러므로 is won이 맞다.
④ Those who never make it의 주어는 it이 아니라 Those이므로 복수동사 are가 나왔다.
⑤ 문장의 주어는 복수(Things)이므로 ⑤는 their가 되어야 한다. its를 their로 고쳐 써야 한다. at one's worst는 '최악의 상태에'의 뜻이다.

어휘·어구

within reach 손이 닿는 곳에, 힘이 미치는 곳에
endure 인내하다, 참다
day after day 매일
make it 성공하다
steep 가파른
summit 정상, 꼭대기

6. ③ 면역과 김치의 관계

직독 직해

Recently, a severe disease hit Asian nations hard, /
최근에 심각한 질병이 아시아 국가에 퍼지면서 /

causing several hundred deaths.
수백 명이 사망하게 되었다.

Many people who live in this part of the world /
이 지역 국가에 사는 많은 사람들은 /

are likely to be worried again /
또다시 우려하고 있는 것 같다. /

with the beginning of the cold weather.
추운 날씨가 시작되면서

In spite of its their close location to these countries, /
한국은 이러한 국가들과 지리적으로 인접해 있으면서도

however, / Korea has remained /
그러나 / 한국은 상태를 유지하고 있다. /

free of the deadly disease.
이 치명적인 질병으로부터 면역된

Many people think / the secret is kimchi, /
많은 사람들은 생각한다. / 그 비결은 김치라고 /

a traditional Korean dish /
전통 한국 음식인 /

served with almost every meal.
거의 매 식사 때마다 먹는

최근에 심각한 질병이 아시아 국가에 퍼지면서 수백 명이 사망하게 되었다

다. 이 지역 국가에 사는 많은 사람들은 추운 날씨가 시작되면서, 또다시 우려하고 있는 것 같다. 그러나 한국은 이러한 국가들과 지리적으로 인접해 있으면서도 이 치명적인 질병으로부터 면역된 상태를 유지하고 있다. 많은 사람들은 한국인들이 거의 매 식사 때마다 먹는 전통 음식인 김치가 그 비결이라고 생각한다.

문제풀이

① , and it caused ~ 라는 문장을 분사구문으로 바꾼 문장이다.
② 문장의 주어는 world가 아니라 복수명사 people이므로 복수동사 are가 나왔다.
③ their → its로 고쳐 써야 한다. their는 문맥 속에서 한국을 가리키므로, 단수 it의 소유격인 its를 사용해야 한다. 국가가 지리적인 위치를 나타낼 때는 대명사 it의 소유격인 its를 사용하며, 정치적인 의미를 나타낼 때는 대명사 she의 소유격인 her를 쓴다.
④ 국가명 Korea는 단수명사이므로 동사가 나올 때는 단수동사를 쓴다.
⑤ 부사 almost가 형용사 every를 수식하고 있다. almost every meal은 '거의 모든 식사마다'의 의미이다.

《 어휘·어구 》

disease 질병
death 죽음, 사망
in spite of ~에도 불구하고
free of ~이 없는
deadly 치명적인
secret 비밀
traditional 전통적인
dish 음식

7.④ 실패 분석과 성공 가능성을 높이는 법

직독/직해

When you attempt to do something and fail, /
여러분이 어떤 일을 시도해보고 실패하면, /
you have to ask yourself /
여러분은 자문해야 한다. /
why you have failed to do what you intended.
왜 의도했던 일에 실패했을까 하고
Answering this question in a new, unexpected way /
이 질문에 대해 새롭고도 예상치 못했던 방법으로 답변하는 것은
is the essential creative act.
근본적으로 창조적인 활동이다.
It will improve your chances of succeeding next time. /
그렇게 하면, 다음번에는 여러분이 성공할 가능성이 높아진다.

여러분이 어떤 일을 시도해보고 실패하면, 여러분은 왜 의도했던 일에 실패했을까 하고 자문하게 된다. 이 질문에 대해 새롭고도 예상치 못했던 방법으로 답변하는 것은 근본적으로 창조적인 활동이다. 그렇게 하면, 다음번에는 여러분이 성공할 가능성이 높아진다.

문제풀이

(A) 주어와 목적어가 같을 경우에는 목적어로 재귀대명사를 써야 한다.
(B) 동사(is)의 주어가 와야 하므로 동명사를 써야 한다.
(C) 앞에 나온 the essential creative act를 가리키므로 단수 지시대명사를 써야 한다.

《 어휘·어구 》

attempt 시도하다
fail 실패하다
intend 의도하다

unexpected 예상치 못한
essential 필수적인, 근본적인
creative 창조적인
improve 높이다, 증진하다
chance 기회

8.③ '여가'라는 용어의 정의 변화

보다 더 최근 들어 여가가 사람들의 자유 시간에 관여되는 활동 형태이거나 혹은 오히려 어떤 의무나 강요로부터 자유로운 시간으로 개념화되고 있다. 따라서 보통 말하는 '여가'라는 용어는 이제 (해야 할 의무가 있는) 직장에서 보내지 않은 시간을 특징짓는 데 광범위하게 사용된다. 물론 여가가 아닌 것에 의해 여가를 정의할 때, 극히 추상적인 문제들은 대부분 미해결된 채로 남아있다. 예를 들어, 준비하고 직장으로 가고 직장에서 오는 도중에 소모된 시간과 같이 일과 관련된 시간을 어떻게 분류하는지에 대한 질문이 있다. 그리고 때때로 한 사람의 천직과 다른 사람의 취미 간의 차이점을 도출해내기에는 어려움이 있다. 사람들은 자기들의 취미 활동을 꽤 열심히 '하는' 것으로 알려져 있다. 정의에 대한 그러한 문제들이 아주 흔히 나타날지라도, 다행히도 근본적 개념의 분석에 영향을 끼치지는 않는다.

문제풀이

③ those는 문맥상 앞에 언급된 불가산명사인 time을 가리키는 것이어야 하므로, those가 아니라 that으로 고쳐야 한다.

《 구문 및 어휘 》

*1행 Leisure has more recently been conceptualized **either** as a form of activity [engaged in by people in their free time] or, preferably, as time free from any sense of obligation or compulsion.

(1) 「either A or B」 구문이 사용된 문장으로 as a form ~와 as time ~가 병렬 구조로 연결되어 있다.
(2) [engaged ~ free time]은 activity를 수식하는 관계대명사절이며 주격 관계대명사와 be동사가 생략되어 있다.

*7행 There is, for example, a question of **how to categorize** work-related time **such as that** [**consumed** in preparation for, and in transit to and from, the workplace].

(1) 「how to+동사원형」은 '~하는 방법'이라는 의미이고, such as는 '~와 같은'이라는 의미로 work-related time에 대한 구체적인 설명을 하기 위해 사용되었다.
(2) that은 time을 지칭하며 [consumed in ~ the workplace]는 that(time)을 수식하는 관계대명사절로 앞에 주격 관계대명사와 be동사가 생략되어 있다.

conceptualize 개념화하다
compulsion 강요, 필수
vocation 천직
underlying 근본적인

9.⑤ 능력과 주도력의 감각을 확립시키는 방법

취학 전 시기의 기본 과제는 능력과 주도력의 감각을 확립하는 것이다. 핵심 난제는 주도력과 죄책감 사이에 있다. 취학 전 아이들은 자신의 직접 ① 선택한 활동에 신체적으

로 그리고 심리적으로 참여할 준비가 되면서 많은 자기 활동을 주도하기 시작한다. 자신의 결정의 일부를 내릴 실질적인 자유가 허용되면 그들은 주도하고 완수하는 자신의 능력에 있어 자신감을 특징으로 하는 ② 긍정적인 성향을 발달시키게 된다. 그러나 만약 자신들의 선택이 조롱을 받는다면 그들은 죄책감을 겪고 ③ 적극적인 태도를 보이는 것에서 결국 손을 떼는 경향이 있다. 우리와 이야기를 나눈 중년 여성은 여전히 자신이 ④ 바보로 여겨지는 것에 매우 취약하다는 것을 안다. 그녀는 어린 시절 동안 가족 구성원이 어떤 일을 하는 그녀의 시도를 비웃었다는 것을 기억해 낸다. 그녀는 자신의 가족에게서 받은 어떤 메시지들을 받아들였고 이 메시지들은 그녀의 태도와 행동에 크게 영향을 미쳤다. 지금도 그녀는 자신의 머릿속에 이런 장면들을 생생하게 지니고 있고 이 메시지들은 그녀의 삶을 통제하는 것을 ⑤ 멈춘다(→ 계속한다).

문제풀이

중년이 되어서도 바보로 여겨지는 것에 취약한 한 여성이 어렸을 때 가족에게서 받은 부정적인 메시지가 그녀의 태도와 행동에 크게 영향을 미쳤고 그 장면들을 머릿속에 생생히 지니고 있다고 했으므로, 이 메시지들이 그녀의 삶을 통제하는 것을 멈추는 것이 아니라 계속 통제할 것이므로, ⑤ cease(멈추다)는 continue(계속하다)로 바꾸어 써야 맞다.

《 구문 및 어휘 》

*13행 One middle-aged woman [we talked with] still finds herself extremely vulnerable to **being seen** as foolish.

(1) we talked with는 선행사 One middle-aged woman을 수식하는 관계대명사절로 목적격 관계대명사 that이나 whom이 생략되었다.
(2) to는 전치사로 그 중년 여성이 '여겨지는 것'에 취약하다는 의미이므로 수동형 동명사 being seen이 왔다.

preschool 취학 전의
establish 확립하다
competence 능력
initiative 주도력
core 핵심적인
struggle 난제(難題)
guilt 죄책감
initiate 주도하다
engage in ~에 참여하다
pursuit 활동, 일
orientation 성향
characterize (~의) 특징이 되다
follow through 끝내다
ridicule 놀리다
ultimately 궁극적으로
withdraw from ~에서 손을 떼다
stance 태도, 입장
extremely 매우
vulnerable 취약한
recall 생각해 내다
attempt 시도, 노력
vividly 생생하게
cease 멈추다

10.③ Atitlán Giant Grebe 새가 생존에 어려움을 겪게 된 원인

Atitlán Giant Grebe는 훨씬 더 널리 퍼져 있었고 크기가 더 작은 Pied-billed Grebe에서 진화한 날지 못하는

큰 새였다. 1965년 무렵, Atitlán 호수에 80마리 정도만 이 남아 있었다. 한 가지 직접적인 원인은 알아내기 충분 히 쉬웠다. 현지인들이 맹렬한 속도로 갈대밭을 베고 있었 던 것이었다. 이러한 (A) 파괴는 빠르게 성장하는 매트 제 조 산업의 필요에 의해 행해졌다. 그러나 다른 문제점들이 있었다. 한 미국 항공사가 그 호수를 낚시꾼들을 위한 관 광지로 개발하는 데 몹시 관심을 보였다. 하지만, 이 생각 에는 큰 문제가 있었는데, 그 호수에는 어떠한 적절한 낚 시용 물고기도 (B) 없었다! 이러한 다소 분명한 결함을 보 완하기 위해 Large-mouthed Bass라고 불리는 특별히 선택된 물고기 종이 도입되었다. 그 도입된 개체는 즉각 그 호수에 살고 있던 게와 작은 물고기에게 관심을 돌렸 고, 그리하여 몇 마리밖에 남지 않은 Grebe와 먹이를 두 고 (C) 경쟁했다. 그것들이 가끔 얼룩무늬가 있는 Atitlán Giant Grebe의 새끼들을 게걸스럽게 먹어치웠 음에도 거의 의심의 여지가 없다.

문제풀이

(A)에는 현지인들이 맹렬한 속도로 갈대밭을 '베어 넘 어뜨리는 행위'를 대신하는 단어가 와야 하므로 '파괴 (destruction)'가 적절하다. (B) 낚시꾼들을 위한 관광 지로서 호수가 가지고 있는 결함을 보충하기 위해 Large -mouthed Bass를 도입했다고 언급하고 있으므로 그 호수에는 낚시용 물고기가 '없었다(lacked)'는 것을 알 수 있다. (C) 뒷문장에서 Bass가 Grebe의 새끼들을 먹어 치우기도 했다고 한 것으로 보아, 새로 도입된 Large-mouthed Bass가 먹이를 두고 Grebe와 '경쟁 하게(competing)' 되었다는 흐름이 적절하다.

《 구문 및 어휘 》

*1행 The Atitlán Giant Grebe was <u>a large,</u> <u>flightless bird</u> [**that** <u>had evolved</u> from the much more widespread and smaller Pied-billed Grebe].

⑴ [that had evolved ~ Pied-billed Grebe]는 a large, flightless bird를 수식하는 관계대명사절이며, 이때 that은 주격 관계대명사로 쓰였다.

⑵ 문장의 시제는 과거이고, 진화한 것은 더 이전부터 일어난 일이므로 과거완료 had evolved를 사용했다.

*14행 The introduced individuals immediately turned their attentions to <u>the crabs and small fish</u> [**that** lived in the lake], **thus competing** with the few remaining grebes for food.

⑴ [that lived in the lake]는 the crabs and small fish를 수식하는 주격 관계대명사절이다.

⑵ thus competing ~은 결과를 나타내는 분사구문으 로 의미를 명확히 하기 위해 접속사를 생략하지 않았다.

flightless 날지 못하는
evolve 진화하다
immediate 즉각적인, 직접적인
spot 알아내다, 분간하다
reed beds 갈대밭
accommodation 순응
intent 강한 관심을 보이는
compensate for ~을 보완하다
chick (새의) 새끼, 병아리

---

11. ③   디지털 혁명으로 바뀐 세계화

20세기 중반까지는 단지 소수의 이민자만이 죽기 전에 한 두 번 고국을 방문했을 뿐, 대부분은 자기가 태어난 땅으 로 다시는 돌아가지 못했다. 이러한 경향은 의사소통을 (A) 향상시킨 디지털 혁명과 더불어 세계화의 도래로 완전

히 바뀌었다. 결과적으로 이민은 과거의 모습과는 매우 다 른 경험이 되었다. 이민자 가족들이 전화와 텔레비전과 인 터넷을 통하여 그들의 옛 문화에 (B) 다시 연결될 수 있다 는 것은 주류 미국 사회 속으로의 통합에 대한 그들의 접 근 방식을 바꾸었다. 이것은 또한 어린이들에게 있어 사회 화에 대한 이민자 관행에도 크게 영향을 미쳤다. 출신 국 가와의 접촉은 이제 더 빈번해졌으며, 더 많은 이민자 가 족들이 고국에서 가져온 문화 양식을 (C) 유지하고 그들 의 자녀들도 그것을 유지하도록 영향을 주려고 시도하게 끔 영향 받게 되는 결과를 초래한다.

문제풀이

(A) 예전에는 이민자들이 자신이 태어난 땅에 다시는 돌아가지 못했지만 디지털 혁명과 세계화의 영향으로 바뀌었다고 했으므로 이러한 경향이 의사소통을 '향상 시켰다'고 볼 수 있다. (B) 따라서 그들이 이런 디지털 기기를 통해 자신들의 옛 문화와 '다시 연결되었다'고 볼 수 있다. (C) 이러한 발전으로 이민자들이 고국과 좀 더 자주 접촉한다고 했으므로 그들의 문화를 '유지 할' 수 있을 것임을 알 수 있다.

《 구문 및 어휘 》

*3행 This pattern **has** completely **changed** with the advent of globalization, **coupled with** <u>the digital revolution</u> [**that** has enhanced communication].

⑴ 주어인 This pattern은 앞 문장에서 언급한 이민자 들이 자신의 고국에 돌아가기 힘들었던 상황을 지칭하 며, 동사인 has changed는 현재완료 구문으로 '결과' 용법으로 쓰였다.

⑵ coupled with는 '~와 더불어'라는 의미로 앞의 with the advent ~와 연결되어 쓰였다.

⑶ [that ~ communication]은 the digital revolution 을 선행사로 수식하는 주격 관계대명사절이다.

*12행 Contacts [with the country of origin] <u>are</u> now more frequent, and <u>result</u> in more immigrant families being influenced **to maintain** cultural patterns from the homeland, and **to attempt** to influence their children to keep <u>them</u>.

⑴ 문장의 동사 are와 result가 접속사 and로 연결되어 있으며, [with the country of origin]은 Contacts를 수식하는 전치사구이다.

⑵ influenced와 연결된 to maintain과 to attempt가 접속사 and로 연결되어 있으며, 마지막 them은 cultural patterns를 지칭한다.

advent 도래, 출현
enhance 향상시키다, 높이다
hinder 방해[저해]하다
integration 통합

---

12. ④   중국의 농업 투자에 있어서 문제점

직독 / 직해

In the past several decades, / 지난 수십 년간 /
China achieved rapid economic growth /
중국은 급속한 경제 성장을 이루었다 /
with monetary, mercantile, and military policies.
통화, 상업, 그리고 군사 정책으로
It continued to push massive food and water development projects.
중국은 대규모 식량 및 물 개발 프로젝트를 계속해서 추진했다
On the other hand, in 2014, / 다른 한편, 2014년에 /
the desert area of China was nearly ten times the size of Japan. 중국의 사막 지역은 일본 크기의 거의 10배였다

In particular, for the last several decades, /
특히 지난 수십 년간 /
China's desert area expanded every year /
중국의 사막 지역은 매년 팽창했다 /
by more than two thousand square kilometers /
2천 평방킬로미터 넘게 /
on average. 평균
As a result, the ecological system is also collapsing /
이에 따라, 생태계 역시 붕괴되고 있다 /
in the wide area. 넓은 지역에서
The problem has prompted China /
그 문제는 중국을 자극했다 /
to develop vast farming areas in Africa /
아프리카에 광대한 농지를 개발하도록 /
and lease vast agricultural lands /
방대한 농지를 임차하도록 /
from Ukraine and other Eastern European countries /
그리고 우크라이나와 다른 동유럽 국가들로부터 /
to secure its growing domestic food needs.
증가하는 국내 식량 수요를 확보하기 위해
However, China's agricultural investment concentrates /
그러나, 중국의 농업 투자는 집중된다 /
in a few kinds of cereals and animals.
몇 가지 종류의 곡물과 동물에
It is unhelpful / to the ecological diversity /
그것은 도움이 되지 않는다 / 생태학적 다양성에 /
of the developed or leased areas. 개발되거나 임차한 지역의
If a serious drought or flood takes place /
심각한 가뭄이나 홍수가 발생하면 /
in those areas, / 그 지역에서 /
it will bring about social chaos, /
사회적 혼란을 불러올 것이나 /
not only there, but in China itself /
그곳뿐만 아니라, 중국 자체에도 /
because of the sudden food shortage.
급작스러운 식량 부족 때문에

지난 수십 년간, 중국은 통화, 상업, 그리고 군사 정책으로 급속한 경제 성장을 이루었다. 중국은 대규모 식량 및 물 개발 프로젝트를 ① 계속해 서 추진했다. 다른 한편, 2014년에 중국의 사막 지역은 일본 크기의 거 의 10배였다. 특히 지난 수십 년간, 중국의 사막 지역은 매년 평균 2천 평방킬로미터 넘게 ② 팽창했다. 이에 따라, 넓은 지역에서 생태계 역시 붕괴되고 있다. 그 문제는 중국이 증가하는 국내 식량 수요를 확보하기 위해, 아프리카에 광대한 농지를 개발하고 우크라이나와 다른 동유럽 국 가들로부터 방대한 농지를 임차하도록 ③ 자극했다. 그러나, 중국의 농업 투자는 몇 가지 종류의 곡물과 동물에 집중된다. 그것은 개발되거나 임차 한 지역의 생태학적 다양성에 ④ 도움이 된다(→ 도움이 되지 않는다). 그 지역에서 심각한 가뭄이나 홍수가 발생하면, 급작스러운 식량 ⑤ 부족 때 문에 그곳뿐만 아니라, 중국 자체도 사회적 혼란을 불러올 것이다.

문제풀이

중국이 아프리카와 우크라이나 그리고 다른 동유 럽 국가의 농지를 개발하거나 임차했는데, 그곳에 서의 농업 투자가 몇 가지 종류의 곡물과 동물에 집중된다고 했으므로, 해당 지역의 생태학적 다양 성에 도움이 되지 않았다고 해야 한다. 따라서 ④ 'helpful(도움이 되는)'을 'unhelpful(도움이 되지 않는)' 등과 같은 낱말로 고쳐 써야 한다.

🔧 구조 다시보기

도입	중국의 대규모 식량 및 물 개발 프로젝트 추진
원인	중국의 사막 지역 확대와 이에 따른 넓은 지역의 생 태계 붕괴
해결책	증가하는 식량 수요 확보를 위해 아프리카, 우크라 이나와 다른 동유럽 국가의 농지 개발 및 농지 임차
문제점	투자가 몇 가지 곡물과 동물에 집중되어 문제 발생

《 어휘·어구 》

monetary 통화의
massive 거대한, 엄청나게 큰
decade 십 년
expand 팽창하다

collapse 붕괴하다
prompt 즉각적인
lease 임차하다, 빌리다
Ukraine 우크라이나
agricultural 농업의
domestic 국내의
drought 가뭄
take place 일어나다, 벌어지다
shortage 부족

18. 형용사, 부사

A 출제 POINT
본문 104쪽

1. do　　2. alike　　3. completely
4. highly　5. Most　　6. turn it up
7. old enough

1 [해석]▶ 왜 노인들이 혼자 사나요?
[해설]▶ 「the+형용사(elderly)」는 복수 보통명사(elderly people)를 나타낸다.

2 [해석]▶ 그들은 가족이 아니지만, 닮아 보인다.
[해설]▶ 형용사 alike는 서술적 용법으로 사용된다. look alike는 '~처럼 보이다'는 뜻이다.

3 [해석]▶ 그는 자신의 시대의 편견에 전적으로 의존한다.
[해설]▶ 부사 completely가 바로 뒤에 위치한 형용사 dependent를 수식한다.

4 [해석]▶ 나는 새로운 곳에 있다는 기대감이 가득했으며 매우 기분이 좋았다.
[해설]▶ 부사 highly는 very(매우)의 의미가 있다.

5 [해석]▶ 많은 사람들이 사과를 좋아한다.
[해설]▶ most(대부분의)가 형용사로서 바로 뒤의 복수명사 people을 수식하고 있다.

6 [해석]▶ 나는 그녀에게 볼륨을 높이라고 하지 않고, 낮추라고 말했다.
[해설]▶ 동사와 부사가 결합된 동사구에서 목적어가 대명사일 경우에는 「동사+대명사+부사」의 어순이 되어야 한다.

7 [해석]▶ 그는 그 프로그램을 보기에는 너무 어리다.
[해설]▶ enough가 형용사, 부사를 수식하는 경우, 「형용사[부사]+enough+to부정사」 순서로 나온다.

B 체크 POINT
본문 104쪽

1. talk　　2. live　　3. usually go
4. high　　5. almost　6. put it off
7. ripe enough

1 [해석]▶ 영국 사람들은 날씨에 대해 많이 이야기한다.
[해설]▶ 「the+형용사(English)」가 복수 보통명사의 의미로 '영국 사람들'을 의미한다.

2 [해석]▶ 삼촌은 살아 있는 문어를 먹는 것을 좋아하십니다.
[해설]▶ live와 alive는 형용사로서 '살아 있는'의 의미이지만, 한정 용법으로 사용할 때는 live를 쓰고, be동사 뒤에 나와 서술 용법으로 사용할 때는 alive를 쓴다.

3 [해석]▶ 우리는 보통 저녁을 밖에서 먹는다.
[해설]▶ 빈도부사는 대개 일반동사 앞에 위치한다.

4 [해석]▶ 내 형의 연은 하늘 높이 올랐다.
[해설]▶ high는 형용사와 부사의 형태가 같다. 이 문장에서 high(높이)는 부사로서 동사 rose를 수식하고 있다.

5 [해석]▶ 그녀는 좀처럼 약속 시간을 어기는 법이 없다.
[해설]▶ almost(거의)는 부사로서 다른 부사 always를 수식하고 있다. almost always는 '거의 항상'의 의미이다.

6 [해석]▶ 지금 과학 숙제를 해라. 내일까지 미루지 마.
[해설]▶ 동사(put)와 부사(off)가 결합된 동사구에서 목적어가 대명사일 경우에는 「동사+대명사+부사」의 어순이 되어야 한다.

7 [해석]▶ 저 토마토들은 먹을 수 있을 만큼 충분히 익지 않았다.
[해설]▶ enough가 형용사, 부사를 수식하는 경우. 「형용사[부사]+enough+to부정사」 순서로 나온다.

Day 18
본문 105쪽

1	⑤	2	④	3	④	4	①	5	④
6	③	7	①	8	③	9	④	10	④
11	②	12	③						

1. ⑤　선형적 쓰기 체계인 수메르 쐐기 문자

직독 직해

The world's first complex writing form, Sumerian cuneiform, /
세계 최초의 복잡한 쓰기 형태인 수메르 쐐기 문자는 /

followed an evolutionary path, /
진화적 경로를 따라갔다 /

moving around 3500 BCE /
기원전 3500년경에 나아가며 /

from pictographic to ideographic representations, /
그림 문자에서 표의 문자적 표현으로 /

from the depiction of objects to that of abstract notions.
즉 사물의 묘사에서 추상적 개념의 그것(묘사)으로

Sumerian cuneiform was a linear writing system, /
수메르 쐐기 문자는 선형적 쓰기 체계였다 /

its symbols usually set in columns, /
그것의 기호가 세로 단에 놓이고 /

read from top to bottom and from left to right.
위에서 아래로 그리고 왼쪽에서 오른쪽으로 읽히는 /

This regimentation was a form of abstraction: /
이 조직화는 일종의 추상 개념이었다 /

the world is not a linear place, /
즉 세상이 선형적 공간이 아니라 /

and objects do not organize themselves horizontally or vertically /
그리고 사물은 수평적으로나 수직적으로 스스로를 구조화하지 않는다는 것이었다 /

in real life. 실제 삶에서

Early rock paintings, /
초기의 암각화들은 /

thought to have been created for ritual purposes, /
의례적 목적으로 만들어졌다고 여겨지는 /

were possibly shaped and organized /
아마도 형상화되고 구조화됐을 것이다 /

to follow the walls of the cave, or the desires of the painters, /
동굴의 벽이나 화가의 바람을 따르도록 /

who may have organized them symbolically, or artistically, or even randomly.
그들은 상징적으로, 예술적으로, 심지어는 무작위로 그것들을 구조화했을지도 모른다

Yet after cuneiform, / virtually every form of script /
하지만 쐐기 문자 이후에는 / 사실상 모든 형태의 문자는 /

that has emerged / 등장한 /

has been set out in rows /
줄로 나열되어 왔다 /

with a clear beginning and endpoint.
분명한 시작과 종료 지점이 있는

So uniform is this expectation, indeed, /
실제로 이러한 예상은 너무도 획일적이어서 /

that the odd exception is noteworthy, /
특이한 예외는 주목할 만하다 /

and generally established for a specific purpose.
그리고 일반적으로 특정한 목적을 위해 설정된다

세계 최초의 복잡한 쓰기 형태인 수메르 쐐기 문자는 기원전 3500년경에 그림 문자에서 표의 문자적 표현으로, 즉 사물의 묘사에서 추상적 개념의 그것(묘사)으로 나아가며 진화적 경로를 따라갔다. 수메르 쐐기 문자는 선형적 쓰기 체계였는데, 보통은 그것의 기호가 세로 단에 놓인 채로 위에서 아래로 그리고 왼쪽에서 오른쪽으로 읽혔다. 이 조직화는 일종의 추상 개념으로, 세상이 선형적 공간이 아니라 사물을 실제 삶에서 수평적으로나 수직적으로 스스로를 구조화하지 않는다는 것이었다. 의례적 목적으로 만들어졌다고 여겨지는 초기의 암각화들은 아마도 동굴의 벽이나 화가의 바람을 따르도록 형상화된 것이었고, 그들(화가)은 상징적으로, 예술적으로, 심지어는 무작위로 그것(암각화)들을 구조화했을지도 모른다. 하지만 쐐기 문자 이후에는 등장한 사실상 모든 형태의 문자는 분명한 시작과 종료 지점이 있는 줄로 나열되어 왔다. 실제로 이러한 예상은 너무나도 획일적이어서 특이한 예외는 주목할 만하며 일반적으로 특정한 목적을 위해 설정된다.

문제풀이

① [대명사의 수]
앞에 나온 명사를 반복해서 쓸 경우 단수명사를 받을 때는 that을, 복수명사를 받을 때는 those를 사용한다. 이 문장에서는 the depiction을 지칭하는 것이므로 that을 쓴 것은 어법상 적절하다.

② [독립분사구문]
주절의 주어와 분사구문의 주어가 다른 독립분사구문이다. 분사구문의 의미상의 주어인 'its symbols'가 놓는 주체가 아니라 놓여지는 대상이므로, 수동의 의미를 갖는 과거분사 set을 사용한 것은 어법상 적절하다.

③ [재귀대명사]
타동사의 목적어가 주어와 같을 경우에는 재귀대명사를 써야 한다. 이 문장에서는 주어 objects와 목적어가 같으므로, 재귀대명사 themselves를 쓴 것은 어법상 적절하다.

④ [to 부정사]
to follow는 동사를 수식하는 to부정사의 부사적 용법으로 사용되었다.

⑤ [형용사 vs 부사]
'so 형용사/부사 that' 구문에서 'so 형용사/부사' 부분이 강조되어 도치된 문장이다. 정치된 문장으로 써 보면 'this expectation is so uniformly that ~'이 되고, 여기서 uniformly는 be동사의 보어이므로 부사가 아니라 형용사를 써야 한다. 따라서 부사 uniformly를 형용사 uniform으로 바꿔야 한다.

《 어휘 · 어구 》

complex 복잡한
evolutionary 진화의
pictographic 상형 문자의
ideographic 표의 문자의
representation 표현
notion 개념, 관념, 생각
depiction 묘사
abstract 추상적인
linear 선형의
column 세로줄, 기둥
horizontally 수평으로
vertically 수직으로
ritual 의례의
symbolically 상징적으로
artistically 예술적으로
randomly 무작위로

---

virtually 사실상
script 문자
endpoint 종점
odd 이상한, 특이한
noteworthy 주목할 만한

2. ④ 심적 표상

직독/직해

Mental representation is the mental imagery /
심적 표상은 심상이다 /

of things that are not actually present to the senses.
감각에 실제로 존재하지 않는 것들에 대한

In general, / mental representations can help us learn.
일반적으로 / 심적 표상은 우리가 학습하는 데 도움을 줄 수 있다

Some of the best evidence for this /
이에 대한 최고의 증거 중 몇몇은 /

comes from the field of musical performance.
음악 연주 분야에서 온다

Several researchers have examined /
몇몇 연구자들은 조사해 왔다 /

what differentiates the best musicians from lesser ones, /
최고의 음악가들과 실력이 더 낮은 음악가들을 구분 짓는 것이 무엇인지를 /

and one of the major differences /
그리고 주요 차이점들 중 하나는 /

lies in the quality of the mental representations /
심적 표상의 질에 있다 /

the best ones create. 최고의 음악가들이 만드는

When practicing a new piece, / 새로운 작품을 연습할 때 /
advanced musicians have a very detailed mental representation /
상급 음악가들은 매우 상세한 심적 표상을 가지고 있다 /

of the music they use / to guide their practice /
그들이 사용하는 음악에 대한 / 자신의 연주를 이끌기 위해 /

and, ultimately, their performance of a piece.
그리고 궁극적으로 작품에 대한 자신의 연습

In particular, / they use their mental representations /
특히 / 그들은 심적 표상을 사용한다 /

to provide their own feedback /
자기 자신의 피드백을 제공하기 위해 /

so that they know how close they are /
그래서 자신이 얼마나 근접했는지를 안다 /

to getting the piece right / 그 작품을 제대로 이해하는 것에 /
and what they need to do differently to improve.
그리고 그들이 향상하기 위해 다르게 해야 하는 것이 무엇인지를

The beginners and intermediate students /
초급과 중급 학생들은 /

may have crude representations of the music /
음악에 대한 투박한 표상을 가질 수도 있다 /

that allow them to tell, / 그들이 알게 해주는 /
for instance, / when they hit a wrong note, /
예를 들어 / 자신이 언제 틀린 음을 쳤는지 /

but they must rely on feedback from their teachers /
하지만 그들은 자기 선생님의 피드백에 의존해야 한다 /

to identify / 알아내기 위해서는 /

the more subtle mistakes and weaknesses.
더 미묘한 실수와 약점을

심적 표상은 감각에 실제로 존재하지 않는 것들에 대한 심상이다. 일반적으로, 심적 표상은 우리가 학습하는 데 도움을 줄 수 있다. 이에 대한 최고의 증거 중 몇몇은 음악 연주 분야에서 온다. 몇몇 연구자들은 최고의 음악가들과 실력이 더 낮은 음악가들을 구분 짓는 것이 무엇인지를 조사해 왔으며, 주요 차이점들 중 하나는 최고의 음악가들이 만드는 심적 표상의 질에 있다. 새로운 작품을 연습할 때, 상급 음악가들은 작품에 대한 자신의 연습, 그리고 궁극적으로 자신의 연주를 이끌기 위해 사용하는 음악에 대한 매우 상세한 심적 표상을 가지고 있다. 특히, 그들은 자기 자신의 피드백을 제공하기 위해 심적 표상을 사용한다. 그래서 자신이 그 작품을 제대로 이해하는 것에 얼마나 근접했는지와 그들이 향상하기 위해 다르게 해야 하는 것이 무엇인지를 안다. 초급과 중급 학생들은 예를 들어 자신이 언제 틀린 음을 쳤는지 알게 해주는 음악에 대한 투박한 표상을 가질 수도 있지만, 더 미묘한 실수와 약점을 알아내기 위해서는 자기 선생님의 피드백에 의존해야 한다.

문제풀이

① [주어와 동사의 수일치]
〈some of the[one's] 단수명사〉에서 some은 단수명사의 일부이므로, 전체를 단수취급한다. 문장의 주어인 Some of the best evidence for this에서 evidence가 불가산명사로 단수명사이므로, 전체를 단수취급하여 단수동사 comes를 쓴 것은 적절하다.

② [관계대명사 what]
have examined의 목적어가 필요하고, what이 이끄는 절 뒤에 불완전한 문장이 왔으므로 선행사를 포함하는 관계대명사 what은 적절하게 쓰였다.

③ [분사구문]
접속사 When을 남겨둔 분사구문의 형태이다. advanced musicians가 연습을 하는 주체이므로 현재분사 practicing의 의미상 주어를 생략한 것은 적절하다.

④ [보어로 쓰이는 형용사]
are의 보어가 필요하고 보어 자리에는 형용사나 명사가 와야 하는데 문맥상 형용사가 필요하므로 close로 고쳐 써야 한다.

⑤ [관계대명사 that]
that 뒤에 불완전한 문장이 왔고, 앞에 crude representations of the music이라는 선행사가 있으므로 주격 관계대명사 that은 적절하게 쓰였다.

《 어휘 · 어구 》

mental representation 심적 표상
mental imagery 심상
evidence 증거
differentiate A from B A와 B를 구별하다, 구분 짓다
lesser 덜한
piece 작품
ultimately 궁극적으로, 결국
rely on ~에 의존하다
subtle 미묘한
weaknesses 약점

3. ④ 시간의 흐름

직독/직해

The present moment feels special.
현재 순간은 특별하게 느껴진다

It is real. 그것은 실재이다

However much you may remember the past /
여러분이 아무리 많이 과거를 기억하더라도 /

or anticipate the future, / you live in the present.
혹은 미래를 예상하더라도 / 여러분은 현재에 살고 있다

Of course, / 물론 /

the moment during which you read that sentence /
여러분이 그 문장을 읽었던 그 순간은 /

is no longer happening. 더 이상 일어나고 있지 않다

This one is. 이것은 일어나고 있다

In other words, it feels / as though time flows, /
다시 말해서, 느낌이 든다 / 시간은 흐르는 것 같은 /

in the sense / that the present is constantly updating itself.
의미에서 / 현재가 지속적으로 그 자체를 갱신하고 있다는

We have a deep intuition / 우리는 깊은 직관력을 지니고 있다 /
that the future is open / until it becomes present /
미래가 열려 있다는 / 그것이 현재가 될 때까지 /

and that the past is fixed. 그리고 과거는 고정되어 있다는

As time flows, / 시간이 흐르면서 /

this structure of fixed past, immediate present and
고정된 과거, 당면한 현재 그리고 열린 미래라는 이 구조가

open future / gets carried forward in time.
/ 시간 안에서 앞으로 흘러간다

Yet as natural as this way of thinking is, /
하지만 비록 이런 사고방식이 자연스럽더라도 /

you will not find it reflected in science.
여러분은 그것이 과학에 반영된 것은 발견하지 못할 것이다

The equations of physics do not tell us /
물리학의 방정식들은 우리에게 말해 주지 않는데 /

which events are occurring right now— /
어떤 일들이 바로 지금 발생하고 있는지 /

they are like a map / 그것들은 지도와 같다 /

without the "you are here" symbol.
'현재 위치' 표시가 없는

The present moment does not exist in them, /
현재 순간은 그것들 안에 존재하지 않는다 /

and therefore neither does the flow of time.
따라서 시간의 흐름도 그렇지 않다

현재 순간은 특별하게 느껴진다. 그것은 실재이다. 여러분이 아무리 많이 과거를 기억하거나 미래를 예상하더라도, 여러분은 현재에 살고 있다. 물론, 여러분이 그 문장을 읽었던 그 순간은 더 이상 일어나지 않고 있다. 이 순간은 일어나고 있다. 다시 말해서, 현재가 지속적으로 그 자체를 갱신하고 있다는 의미에서 시간은 흐르는 것 같은 느낌이 든다. 우리는 미래가 그것이 현재가 될 때까지 열려 있고 과거는 고정되어 있다는 깊은 직관력을 지니고 있다. 시간이 흐르면서, 고정된 과거, 당면한 현재 그리고 열린 미래라는 그 구조가 시간 안에서 앞으로 흘러간다. 하지만 비록 이런 사고방식이 자연스럽더라도, 여러분은 그것이 과학에 반영된 것은 발견하지 못할 것이다. 물리학의 방정식들은 어떤 일들이 바로 지금 발생하고 있는지 우리에게 말해 주지 않는데, 그것들은 '현재 위치' 표시가 없는 지도와 같다. 현재 순간은 그것들 안에 존재하지 않으며, 따라서 시간의 흐름도 그렇지 않다.

문제풀이

① during which 뒤에 모든 문장 성분을 갖춘 완전한 문장이 와서「전치사+관계대명사」가 온 것이 적절하고, during which 이하는 선행사 the moment를 수식하는 관계대명사절이므로 관계대명사 which가 온 것은 적절하며, '그 순간 동안(during the moment)'라는 의미로 쓰여서 의미상으로 전치사 during이 온 것도 적절하다.
② 가리키는 것이 주어인 the present이므로, 재귀대명사 itself가 온 것은 적절하다.
③ 등위접속사 and에 의해 a deep intuition과 동격인 that절과 연결되어 병렬 구조를 이루고 있으므로, 마찬가지로 동격의 절을 이끄는 접속사 that이 온 것은 적절하다.
④ '비록 ~이더라도'라는 의미의「(as)+원급+as+주어+동사」구문인데, 여기에서「as+원급+as」는 동사 is의 보어로 쓰였다. 따라서 부사 naturally를 형용사 natural로 고쳐야 한다.
⑤ neither가 앞으로 나오면서「동사+주어」로 도치된 문장인데 the flow of time이 주어로 목적어가 없으므로 does는 일반동사 does not exist를 받는 대동사로 쓰인 것이다. 문장의 시제가 현재이고 주어가 the flow of time으로 단수이기 때문에 does가 온 것은 적절하다.
따라서 정답은 ④이다.

❖ 이렇게 풀자 _ 어법상 틀린 부분을 찾는 문제는 밑줄이 있는 부분의 형태와 문맥을 보고 어법에 맞게 쓰였는지 확인해야 한다.
① 「전치사+관계대명사」에 밑줄이 있는 경우에는 뒤에 완전한 문장이 왔는지 확인해야 하며, 관계대명사가 선행사에 맞게 쓰였는지 문맥상 적절한 전치사가 온 것인지도 확인해야 한다.
② 재귀대명사에 밑줄이 있는 경우, 재귀대명사가 가리키는 것이 무엇인지 확인해야 한다. 주어를 받고 있으면 재귀대명사를 쓰는 것이 맞고, 다른 것을 받고 있으면 대명사가 와야 한다.
③ 등위 접속사 뒤에 that절이 온 경우 병렬 구조가 아닌지 확인해 본다.
④ 부사는 동사, 형용사, 다른 부사를 수식하거나 문장 전체를 수식하며, 형용사는 문장에서 보어로 쓰이거나 명사를 수식한다. 밑줄 친 단어가 문장에서 어떤 역할을 하는지 확인해야 한다.

---

⑤ do동사의 목적어가 없다면 대동사일 가능성이 높다. 대동사는 일반동사를 받으면 do를 be동사를 받으면 be동사를 쓰는데, 문장의 시제와 주어의 수에 맞게 바꿔 써야 한다.

〈 어휘 · 어구 〉

anticipate 예상하다
constantly 계속해서, 지속적으로
intuition 직관
immediate 당면한, 즉각적인
reflect 반영하다
equation 방정식
physics 물리학

---

4. ① 피드백을 구하고 경청하는 훈련의 필요성

직독/직해

People avoid feedback / 사람들은 피드백을 회피한다. /
because they hate being criticized.
비판 받는 것을 싫어하기 때문에

Psychologists have a lot of theories /
심리학자들은 많은 이론을 가지고 있다.

about why people are so sensitive to hearing /
사람들이 왜 듣는 것에 그렇게 민감한지에 대한 /

about their own imperfections.
자기 자신의 불완전함에 대해

One is that they associate feedback /
그 하나는 그들이 피드백을 연관 짓는다는 것이다 /

with the critical comments
비판적인 말과

received in their younger years /
어린 시절에 받은 /

from parents and teachers.
부모와 교사로부터

Whatever the cause of our discomfort is, /
우리의 불편함의 원인이 무엇이든지 간에

most of us have to train ourselves /
우리들 대부분은 자신을 훈련시켜야 한다. /

to seek feedback / 피드백을 구하도록

and listen carefully when we hear it.
그것을 들을 때 주의 깊게 경청하도록

Without that training, / 그러한 훈련 없이는 /

the very threat of critical feedback /
비판적인 피드백에 대한 바로 그 위협이 /

often leads us to practice /
종종 ~을 하도록 우리를 이끈다. /

destructive, maladaptive behaviors/
파괴적이고 부적응적인 행동(을)

that negatively affect / 부정적으로 영향을 미치는 /

not only our work / 우리의 일뿐만 아니라 /

but the overall health of our organizations.
우리가 속한 조직의 전체적인 건강에까지

사람들은 비판 받는 것을 싫어하기 때문에 피드백을 회피한다. 심리학자들은 사람들이 왜 자기 자신의 불완전함에 대해 듣는 것에 그렇게 민감한지에 대한 많은 이론을 가지고 있다. 그 하나는 그들이 피드백을 어린 시절에 부모와 교사로부터 받은 비판적인 말과 연관 짓는다는 것이다. 우리의 불편함의 원인이 무엇이든지 간에 우리들 대부분은 피드백을 구하고 그것을 들을 때 주의 깊게 경청하도록 자신을 훈련시켜야 한다. 그러한 훈련 없이는 종종 비판적인 피드백에 대한 바로 그 위협이 우리의 일뿐만 아니라 우리가 속한 조직의 전체적인 건강까지 부정적으로 영향을 미치는 파괴적이고 부적응적인 행동을 하도록 우리를 이끈다.

문제풀이

(A) be동사의 보어인 형용사 sensitive가 필요하다.
(B) 양보의 의미를 가지는 복합관계대명사 Whatever가 필요하다. 'Whatever the cause of' ~는 '~의 원인이 무엇이든지'의 의미이다.
(C) lead A to B는 'A가 B에 이르도록 이끌다'는 의미인데, 어법상 능동의 의미인 동사원형

---

practice가 적합하다. 괄호 바로 뒤에 practice의 목적어 destructive, maladaptive behaviors가 나오고 있다.

〈 어휘 · 어구 〉

avoid 피하다
feedback 피드백, 환류
criticize 비난하다
sensitive 민감함
imperfection 불완전함
associate A with B A와 B를 연계하다
critical 비판적인
cause 원인
discomfort 불편함
destructive 비판적인
maladaptive 부적응의
affect ~에 영향을 미치다

---

5. ④ 내가 만든 '타임머신' 게임과 게임의 효과

직독/직해

Almost every day / I play a game with myself /
거의 매일 / 나는 게임을 혼자서 한다.

that I call 'time machine.'
내가 '타임머신'이라고 부르는

I made it up / in response to my erroneous belief /
나는 그것을 만들었다. / 나의 잘못된 믿음에 대한 반응으로

that what I got angry about / was really important.
내가 화를 내고 있는 일이 / 대단히 중요한 일이라는

To play 'time machine' / all you have to do /
'타임머신'을 작동시키기 위해서 / 당신이 해야 하는 것의 전부는

is to imagine / 상상하는 것이다.

that whatever circumstance you are dealing with /
당신이 다루고 있는 어떠한 상황도

is not happening right now / but a year from now.
당장에 일어나지 않고 / 지금부터 일 년 후에 발생한다고

It might be an argument with your spouse, /
그것은 배우자와의 논쟁,

a mistake, or a lost opportunity, /
실수 또는 놓쳐버린 기회일 수도 있지만,

but it is highly likely / that a year from now /
가능성은 아주 높다. / 지금부터 1년 후에는

you are not going to care.
당신이 그것에 신경을 쓰지 않을

It will be one more irrelevant detail / in your life.
그것은 또 하나의 관련 없는 세세한 문제가 될 것이다. / 당신의 삶에서

While this simple game /
이러한 단순한 게임이 /

will not solve all your problems,
당신의 모든 문제를 해결하지 못할지라도,

it can give you an enormous amount /
그것은 당신에게 대단히 많이 줄 수 있다. /

of needed perspective. 필요한 관점을

I find myself laughing at things /
나는 나 자신이 웃어넘기고 있는 나 자신을 발견한다.

that I used to take far too seriously.
과거에 너무도 심각하게 받아들였던 일에 대해

거의 매일 나는 내가 '타임머신'이라고 부르는 게임을 혼자서 한다. 나는 내가 화를 내고 있는 일이 대단히 중요한 일이라는 나의 잘못된 믿음에 대한 반응으로 그것을 만들었다. '타임머신'을 작동시키기 위해서 당신이 해야 하는 것의 전부는 당신이 다루고 있는 어떠한 상황도 당장이 아니라 지금부터 일 년 후에 발생한다고 상상하는 것이다. 그것은 배우자와의 논쟁, 실수 또는 놓쳐버린 기회일 수도 있지만, 지금부터 1년 후에는 당신이 그것에 신경을 쓰지 않을 가능성은 아주 높다. 그것은 당신의 삶에서도 또 하나의 관련 없는 세세한 문제가 될 것이다. 이러한 단순한 게임이 당신의 모든 문제를 해결하지 못할지라도, 그것은 당신에게 필요한 관점을 대단히 많이 줄 수 있다. 나는 나 자신이 과거에 너무도 심각하게 받아들였던 일에 대해 웃어넘기고 있는 나 자신을 발견한다.

문제풀이

① 관계대명사 that은 call 동사의 목적어 역할을 하고 있다. call은 5형식 동사이다.
② to부정사의 명사적 용법(주어)으로 사용되었다.
③ but it is (highly) likely that ~은 '하지만 그것은 (매우) ~일 수 있다'의 의미로 형용사 likely가 부사 higly(매우)의 수식을 받으며 be동사의 보어로 사용되었다.
④ every는 단수명사 앞에 사용하고, 복수명사 앞에는 올 수 없다. 그러므로 every를 all로 바꿔야 한다.
⑤ 「used to+동사원형」 구문은 '~하곤 했다'의 의미이다.

어휘·어구

in response to ~에 응하여
erroneous 잘못된, 틀린
be worked up about ~에 화가 나다
circumstance 상황
spouse 배우자
irrelevant 관련 없는
perspective 관점, 시각

6. ③ 상품 판매 방식의 변천

직독 직해

If you need to buy food, /
만일 당신이 음식을 살 필요가 있다면 /
there is probably a shop / or a department store /
상점이나 백화점이 아마 있을 것이다.
close to your home / that sells just what you want.
당신의 집 근처에 / 당신이 원하는 것을 파는
But shopping has not always been so easy.
그러나 쇼핑이 항상 그렇게 쉬웠던 것은 아니었다.
Shops started / only with the introduction of money.
상점들은 시작되었다. / 단지 화폐가 도입되면서
In earlier times, / people traded /
초기 시절에는 / 사람들이 교환했다. /
crops or objects they had made /
작물이나 그들이 만든 물건들을
in exchange for the goods they needed.
그들이 필요로 하는 상품들과 교환으로
The first shops sold / 최초의 상점들은 팔았다. /
just a few products such as meat and bread.
단지 고기와 빵과 같은 소수의 상품들만
In 1850, / the first department store, /
1850년에 / 최초의 백화점이 /
a shop which sells many different items /
많은 다양한 품목들을 파는 상점인 /
under one roof, / opened in Paris.
한 지붕 아래서 / 파리에서 문을 열었다.
Self-service stores developed /
셀프 서비스 가게들은 발달했다. /
in the United States in the 1930s.
1930년대에 미국에서
They replaced the old methods /
그것들은 옛날 방식을 대체했다 /
of serving customers individually /
고객들에게 개별적으로 서비스하던 /
by selling prepackaged goods /
미리 포장되어 있는 상품들을 /
straight from the shelves.
선반에서 곧바로 판매함으로써

만일 당신이 음식을 살 필요가 있다면 당신의 집 근처에 당신이 원하는 것을 파는 상점이나 백화점이 아마 있을 것이다. 그러나 쇼핑이 항상 그렇게 쉬웠던 것은 아니었다. 상점들은 단지 화폐가 도입되면서 시작되었다. 초기 시절에는 사람들이 작물이나 그들이 만든 물건들을 그들이 필요

로 하는 상품들과 교환했다. 최초의 상점들은 단지 고기와 빵과 같은 소수의 상품들만 팔았다. 1850년에 한 지붕 아래서 많은 다양한 품목들을 파는 상점인 최초의 백화점이 파리에서 문을 열었다. 셀프 서비스 가게들은 1930년대에 미국에서 발달했다. 그것들은 미리 포장되어 있는 상품들을 선반에서 곧바로 판매함으로써 고객들에게 개별적으로 서비스하던 옛날 방식을 대체했다.

문제풀이

(A) 네모 앞에 선행사가 없으며 want의 목적어 역할을 하는 관계사가 필요하므로 관계대명사 what이 적절하다.
(B) 셀 수 있는 명사의 복수형을 수식하고 있으므로 a few가 적절하다.
(C) 바로 다음에 목적어가 이어지고 있으므로 능동형의 동명사인 selling이 적절하다.

어휘·어구

introduction 도입
trade 교환하다, 무역하다
item 물품, 항목
replace 대체하다
individually 개별적으로
prepackaged 미리 포장되어 있는

7. ① 사랑에 빠질 때 느끼는 감정

직독 직해

Falling in love / is like being wrapped /
사랑에 빠지는 것은 / 싸여 있는 것과 같다. /
in a magical cloud. 신비한 구름에
The air feels fresher, / the flowers smell sweeter, /
공기의 느낌이 더 신선해지고, / 꽃 냄새가 더 향긋해지고, /
food tastes more delicious, / 음식 맛이 더 좋아지며, /
and the stars shine more brilliantly in the night sky.
밤하늘의 별이 더 찬란하게 반짝이게 된다.
You feel light and happy /
당신은 경쾌하고 행복한 느낌을 갖게 된다. /
as though you are sailing through life.
마치 인생을 순항하듯이
Your problems and challenges /
당신의 고민과 난제들이 /
suddenly seem insignificant.
갑자기 대수롭지 않은 것으로 보이게 된다.
Your body feels alive, /
몸에 활력을 느끼면서 /
and you jump out of bed each morning /
아침마다 잠자리에서 힘차게 나오게 된다. /
with a smile on your face.
당신은 얼굴에 미소를 띤 채
You are in a state of supreme delight.
당신은 기쁨의 최고의 경지에 도달한다.

사랑에 빠지는 것은 신비한 구름에 싸여 있는 것과 같다. 공기의 느낌이 더 신선해지고, 꽃 냄새가 더 향긋해지고, 음식 맛이 더 좋아지며, 밤하늘의 별이 더 찬란하게 반짝이게 된다. 당신은 마치 인생을 순항하듯이 경쾌하고 행복한 느낌을 갖게 된다. 당신의 고민과 난제들이 갑자기 대수롭지 않은 것으로 보이게 된다. 몸에 활력을 느끼면서 당신은 아침마다 얼굴에 미소를 띤 채 잠자리에서 힘차게 나오게 된다. 당신은 기쁨의 최고의 경지에 도달한다.

문제풀이

① alike는 서술적 용법으로 사용되는 형용사로서 동명사를 목적어로 취하는 구조에 사용될 수 없다. 따라서 ①의 alike를 전치사 like로 고쳐 써야 한다.
② brilliantly는 부사로서 비교급은 more brilliantly이다. 문장에서 동사 shine을 수식하고 있다.
③ as if는 뒤에 가정법이 나올 수도 있고, 직설법

이 나올 수도 있다. as if 뒤에 가정법이 나온 경우는 사실과 반대되는 이야기를 할 때 사용한다. as if 뒤에 직설법이 나온 경우는 가능성과 아닐 가능성을 모두 열어 둘 때, 사용한다.
④ 동사 seem 뒤에 형용사 보어(insignificant)가 나왔다.
⑤ 「with+목적어(a smile)+전치사구(on your face)」는 '얼굴에 미소를 띤 채'의 의미로 분사구문이다.

어휘·어구

wrap ~을 감싸다, 포장하다
magical 신비한
brilliantly 찬란하게
sail 항해하다
insignificant 대수롭지 않은
alive 살아 있는
supreme 최고의
delight 기쁨

8. ③ 정보 획득과 행동 방법의 변천 역사

직독 직해

The jobs that most companies are doing with information today /
오늘날 회사들이 정보를 통해서 하는 일들은
would have been impossible several years ago.
몇 년 전에는 불가능했을 일이다.
At that time, / 그 당시에는 /
getting rich information was very expensive, /
풍부한 정보를 얻는 것은 매우 비쌌고, /
and the tools for analyzing it weren't even available /
그것을 분석하기 위한 도구들은 구할 수 없었다. /
until the early 1990s. 1990년대 초까지
But now the tools of the digital age give us a way /
그러나 이제 디지털 시대의 도구는 우리에게 방법을 제공한다.
to easily get, share, and act on information /
정보를 쉽게 얻고 공유하고 행동할 수 있는 /
in new ways. 새로운 방법으로

오늘날 회사들이 정보를 통해서 하는 일들은 몇 년 전에는 불가능했을 일들이다. 그 당시에는, 풍부한 정보를 얻는 것은 매우 비쌌고, 분석 도구들은 1990년대 초가 되어서야 구할 수 있었다. 그러나 이제 디지털 시대의 도구는 우리에게 새로운 방법으로 정보를 쉽게 얻고 공유하고 행동할 수 있는 방법을 제공한다.

문제풀이

(A) 「형용사 most+명사」는 '대부분의 ~'의 의미이다.
(B) 빈칸 바로 뒤에 목적어 it이 나오므로, 목적어를 가질 수 있는 동명사가 와야 한다.
(C) A, B, and C의 병렬 구조를 이루어야 하므로, 동사원형이 와야 한다.

어휘·어구

information 정보
rich 풍부한
expensive 비싼
analyze 분석하다
available 이용 가능한
tool 도구

9. ④ 변호사에 관한 두 나라의 견해 차이

캐나다인 손님을 접대한 후에, 한 이집트인 중역이 그에게 새로운 벤처 사업에서의 합작 제휴를 제의했다. 그 제의에 기뻐서, 캐나다인은 세부 사항을 마무리하기 위해 다음날 아침에 ① 각자의 변호사와 함께 다시 만날 것을 제안했다. 이집트인은 결코 나타나지 않았다. 놀라고 실망한 캐나다인이 무엇이 잘못된 것인지 이해하려고 했다. 이집트인은 시간 엄수 관념이 ② 없었는가? 그 이집트인이 수정 제안을 기대하고 있었는가? 카이로에서는 변호사를 구할 수 없었는가? 이들 설명 중 어떤 것도 올바른 것으로 판명되지 않았다. 오히려, 문제는 캐나다인과 이집트인이 변호사를 불러들이는 서로 다른 의미에 의해 ③ 야기되었다. 그 캐나다인은 변호사의 ④ 부재(→ 참석)을 협상의 성공적인 마무리를 용이하게 하는 것으로 여겼고, 그 이집트인은 그것을 캐나다인이 그의 구두 약속의 불신을 암시하는 것이라고 해석했다. 캐나다인은 흔히 ⑤ 합의를 끝내기 위해 변호사의 도움을 받는, 사사로움에 치우지지 않는 형식상의 절차를 이용한다. 이와 대조적으로 이집트인은 같은 목적을 완수하기 위해 거래 상대자 간의 개인적인 관계에 더 자주 의존한다.

문제풀이

캐나다인은 변호사가 '참석'한 상태에서 협상을 끝내는 것이 성공적인 마무리를 위해 도움이 된다고 생각했다는 내용이므로 ④ absence를 presence로 바꿔야 한다.

《구문 및 어휘》

*3행 The Canadian, [**delighted** with the offer], suggested [**that** they meet again the next morning with their respective lawyers to finalize the details].

(1) [delighted ~ offer]는 Canadian을 수식하는 과거분사구이다.

(2) that은 suggested의 목적절로 이때 that은 명사절을 이끄는 접속사로 쓰였으며, that절의 to finalize는 목적을 나타내는 부사적 용법의 to부정사이다.

*5행 The surprised and disappointed Canadian tried to understand [**what** had gone wrong]: Did Egyptians lack punctuality?

(1) surprised와 disappointed는 형용사의 역할을 하는 과거분사 형태이고, 접속사 and로 병렬 연결되어 주어 Canadian을 수식한다.

(2) [what ~ wrong]은 간접의문문으로 「의문사 주어(what)+동사(had gone)」의 형태로 썼다. had gone wrong은 과거완료 시제 구문으로 '(과거의 어느 시점 이전에) ~했었다'로 해석한다.

respective 각자의
finalize 마무리 짓다
punctuality 시간 엄수, 정확함
counter-offer 대응되는 제안, 수정 제안
facilitate 용이하게 하다
impersonal 개인적인 것이 개입되지 않은
bargain 거래하다

---

10. ④   우위 감정이 논거의 결론에 미치는 영향

논거에 대한 결론의 우위는 감정이 결부되는 곳에서 가장 두드러진다. 심리학자 Paul Slovic은 사람들이 좋아하는 것과 싫어하는 것이 세상에 대한 그들의 믿음을 결정한다는 이론을 제시했다. 여러분의 정치적 ① 선호는 여러분이 설득력이 있다고 생각하는 논거를 결정한다. 만일 여러분이 현재의 보건 정책을 좋아한다면 여러분은 그것의 이점이 상당히 많고 그것의 비용이 대안들의 비용보다 ② 더

관리할 만하다고 믿는다. 만약 여러분이 다른 나라에 대하여 강경론자의 태도를 취한다면, 여러분은 아마 그들이 비교적 약하고 여러분 나라의 뜻에 ③ 굴복하기 쉬울 거라고 생각할 것이다. 만일 여러분이 온건론자라면 아마 그들이 강하고 쉽게 설득되지 않을 거라고 생각할 것이다. 육류, 원자력, 문신 또는 오토바이와 같은 것들에 대한 여러분의 감정적인 태도는 그것들의 이점과 위험에 대한 여러분의 믿음을 ④ 따른다(→이끈다). 만약 여러분이 이것들 중 어떤 것이라도 ⑤ 싫어한다면 여러분은 아마 그것들의 위험은 높고 이점은 사소하다고 믿을 것이다.

문제풀이

사람들이 좋아하는 것과 싫어하는 것이 그들의 믿음을 결정한다는 주장을 제시한 후 예시를 들어 주장을 뒷받침하고 있다. 따라서 감정적인 태도가 여러분의 믿음을 '이끈다'는 내용이 되는 것이 글의 흐름에 적절하므로 ④ follows를 drives로 고쳐 쓰는 것이 올바르다.

《구문 및 어휘》

*2행 The psychologist Paul Slovic has proposed a theory **in which** people let their likes and dislikes determine their beliefs about the world.

(1) in which는 '접속사+관계대명사'로 이를 where로 쓸 수 있으며 which는 a theory를 가리킨다.

(2) let their ~ determine은 「let A B (A가 B 하게 하다)」 사역동사 구문으로 B에는 동사원형이 와야 한다. 이는 「allow A to B」 구문인 allow their ~ dislikes to determine ~와 바꿔 쓸 수 있다.

*15행 If you dislike any of these things, you probably believe [that its risks are high and its benefits negligible].

(1) 가정을 나타내는 If가 사용되었으며 주절에서 [that its risks ~ negligible]은 believe의 목적절이다. 이때 its는 any of these things를 가리킨다.

dominance 우위, 우세, 우월
compelling 설득력 있는, 강렬한
substantial (양 등이) 상당한
hawk (정치적, 군사적) 강경론자, 강경파
submit 굴복[항복]하다
negligible 사소한, 보잘 것 없는

---

11. ②   사막 메뚜기의 두 가지 서식 방식

사막 메뚜기는 식량원의 입수 가능성과 지역 메뚜기 개체군의 밀도에 따라 현저히 다른 두 가지 방식으로 산다. 그들이 원래 사는 사막의 서식지에서 보통 그렇듯 식량이 부족할 때는 메뚜기들이 위장을 위해 고안된 색채를 갖고 다이니며 (A) 혼자 살아간다. 드물긴 하지만 상당량의 비가 내리는 기간이 와서 초목이 크게 성장하게 되면, 모든 것이 변한다. 처음에는 그 메뚜기들이 그저 (B) 풍부한 식량 공급량을 맘껏 먹어치우면서 계속 혼자 산다. 그러나 그 여분의 초목이 죽어 없어지기 시작하면, 메뚜기들은 자신들이 (수가 많아져서) 서로 혼잡하게 있다는 것을 알게 된다. 갑자기, 밝은 색을 띠고 함께 있기를 갈망하는 새끼 메뚜기들이 태어난다. 서로를 피하고 위장과 활동을 하지 않음을 통해 포식자들로부터 몸을 숨기는 대신 이 메뚜기들은 떼를 짓고, 함께 먹으며, 순전히 숫자를 통해 포식자들을 (C) 압도한다.

문제풀이

(A) 이어지는 두 문장의 내용을 보면 비가 오면 상황이 변하는데 처음에는 원래의 생활 방식인 loners로

살아간다고 했으므로 (A)에는 혼자 살아간다는 의미가 되도록 solitary가 들어가야 한다. (B) 앞 문장의 내용을 보면 비가 와서 초목이 자랐다고 했으므로 (B)에는 풍부해졌다는 의미의 abundant가 적절하다. (C) 개체수가 급증한 이후에 모여 사는 방식으로 메뚜기가 생존 방식을 바꾼다는 내용이므로 (C)에는 포식자를 압도한다는 의미의 표현인 overwhelm이 와야 한다.

《구문 및 어휘》

*3행 When food is scarce, as it usually is in their native desert habitat, locusts are born with coloring [**designed** for camouflage and lead solitary lives].

(1) as it usually is ~에서 it은 상황을 가리키는 비인칭주어이며, is 뒤에는 scarce가 생략되었다.

(2) [designed for ~ lives]는 과거분사구로 앞에 being이 생략되었다. 원문은 coloring is designed for camouflage ~이며 이를 which is designed ~의 관계사절로 쓸 수도 있다.

locust 메뚜기
density 밀도
scarce 부족한
vegetation 초목, 식물
loner 혼자 있는 동물[사람]
feast off 맘껏 먹어치우다
predator 포식자
overestimate 과대평가하다

오H 많이 틀렸을까?

보기에 제시된 단어들은 그렇게 어렵지 않지만, 본문의 내용을 이해하지 못해 다소 어렵게 느낀 친구들도 있었을 거야. 사실 (A)를 앞 문장만 보고는 풀 수 없었어. But 뒤의 상황에서 처음에는 계속 혼자 산다고 하였으므로, 처음 나온 사막 메뚜기에 관한 이야기는 '혼자서' 살아간다는 내용임을 알 수 있어. (B)에서는 혼자 산다고 생각하니까 음식 공급이 충분하지 않다(insufficient)고 짐작했을 수도 있지만, 초목이 크게 성장한다고 했으므로 풍부한(abundant)이 정답이야. 이렇게 But과 같은 역접의 접속사가 자주 쓰이면 같은 내용끼리 표시를 해가면서 읽는 것도 도움이 될 수 있어.

---

12. ③   아기들의 선천적 능력

직독/직해

Psychologists used to assume /
심리학자들은 가정하곤 했다 /

that infant minds were blank slates.
유아의 정신은 빈 서판이라고

But when developmental psychologists invented ways /
하지만 발달 심리학자들이 방법을 고안해 냈을 때 /

to look into infant minds, /
유아의 정신을 들여다 볼 /

they found a great deal of writing already on that slate.
그들은 그 서판(유아의 정신)에 이미 많은 기록이 있음을 발견했다

The trick was to see / what surprises babies.
그 비결은 보는 것이었다   / 무엇이 아기들을 놀라게 하는지

Infants as young as two months old will look longer at an event /
두달 밖에 안된 유아들은 한 사건을 더 오래 지켜볼 것이다 /

that surprises them / 그들을 놀라게 하는

than at an event they were expecting.
그들이 기대하고 있던 사건보다는

If everything is a buzzing confusion, /
만일 모든 것이 소란스러운 혼란이라면 /

then everything should be equally surprising.
그러면 모든 것들이 똑같이 놀라울 것이다

But if the infant's mind comes already wired /
그러나 유아의 정신이 이미 갖춰져 있다면 /

to interpret events in certain ways, /
특정한 방식으로 사건들을 해석하도록 /

then infants can be surprised /
그러면 유아들은 놀랄 수 있다 /

when the world violates their expectations.
세상이 그들의 기대를 위반할 때

Psychologists discovered / that infants are born /
심리학자들은 발견했다 / 유아들이 태어난다고 /

with some knowledge of physics and mechanics, /
물리학과 역학에 대한 약간의 지식을 지니고 /

and they get startled / 그리고 그들은 놀라게 된다 /

when shown scenes / 보여지는 장면들이 /

that should be physically impossible /
물리학적으로 불가능 할 것같은 /

such as a toy car / 장난감 자동차와 같은 /

seeming to pass through a solid object.
딱딱한 물체를 관통하는 것처럼 보이는

Psychologists know this / 심리학자들은 이것을 안다 /

because infants stare longer at impossible scenes /
왜냐하면 유아들이 불가능한 장면들을 더 오래 응시하기 때문에 /

than at similar but less magical scenes.
유사하지만 덜 마술적인 장면보다

Babies seem to have the innate ability /
아기들은 타고난 능력을 갖고 있는 것 같다 /

to process events in their physical world.
그들의 물리적 세계의 사건을 처리하는

심리학자들은 유아의 정신이 ① 빈 서판이라고 가정했었다. 하지만 발달 심리학자들이 유아의 정신을 들여다볼 방법을 고안해 냈을 때, 그들은 그 서판(유아의 정신)에 이미 많은 기록이 있음을 발견했다. (심리학자들이 사용한) 비결은 무엇이 아기를 놀라게 하는지 보는 것이었다. 두 달밖에 안된 유아들은 그들이 기대하고 있던 사건보다는 그들을 놀라게 만드는 사건을 ② 오래 지켜볼 것이다. 모든 것이 소란스러운 혼란이라면, 모든 것이 똑같이 놀라울 것이다. 하지만 유아의 정신이 특정한 방식으로 사건을 해석하도록 이미 갖춰져 있다면, 유아들은 세상이 그들의 기대를 ③ 충족(→ 위반)할 때 놀랄 수 있다. 심리학자들은 유아들이 물리학과 역학에 대한 약간의 지식을 가지고 태어나고, 딱딱한 물체를 관통하는 것처럼 보이는 장난감 자동차와 같은 물리적으로 불가능한 장면을 보면 ④ 깜짝 놀란다는 것을 발견했다. 심리학자들은 이것을 알고 있는데 왜냐하면 유아들이 유사하되 덜 마술적인 장면보다 불가능한 장면들을 더 오래 응시하기 때문이다. 아기들은 물리적 세계의 사건을 처리하는 ⑤ 타고난 능력을 갖고 있는 것 같다.

문제풀이

아기들이 태어날 때 아무것도 모르는 백지 상태로 태어나는 것이 아니라 어느 정도의 지식과 정보 처리 능력을 가지고 태어나고, 이 지식과 정보 처리 능력을 넘어서는 대상을 만나게 되면 놀라게 되고 그 대상을 더 오래 응시한다는 것이 글의 주된 내용이다. 따라서 아이들이 놀라는 것은 기대를 충족시키는 것이 아니라 위반할 때이므로 ③ 'meets(충족하다)'를 'violates(위반하다)'로 바꿔 써야 한다.

구조 다시보기

일반적 견해	유아의 정신이 빈 서판이라고 가정
비판 (주제문)	유아의 정신에 이미 많은 기록이 있다
예시 1	유아들은 그들을 놀라게 하는 것을 더 오래 지켜본다
예시 2	유아들은 물리적으로 불가능한 장면을 보고 놀란다
주제 재진술	유아들은 물리적 사건을 처리하는 타고난 능력을 갖고 있다.

《 어휘·어구 》

psychologist 심리학자
blank slate 빈 서판, 백지 상태
trick 비결, 요령
buzzing 윙윙거리는, 소란스러운
confusion 혼란, 혼동

---

wired 갖춰진, 연결된
interpret 해석하다, 이해하다
startle 깜짝 놀라게 하다
physics 물리학
mechanics 역학, 기계학
innate 타고난, 선천적인
process 처리하다, 가공하다, 과정, 절차

---

19. 비교 구문

A 출제 POINT
본문 110쪽

1. diligent   2. much   3. the taller
4. novelists   5. best   6. than
7. less

1 [해석]▶ Sam은 그의 형만큼 부지런하다.
[해설]▶ 원급 비교는「as+형용사/부사+as」의 형태이며, be 동사의 보어 역할을 하므로 형용사를 써야 한다.

2 [해석]▶ Sally는 그녀의 친구들보다 더 현명하다.
[해설]▶ 비교급을 강조하는 경우 비교급 앞에 much, even, still, far, a lot 등을 쓴다.

3 [해석]▶ Peter는 2명 중에서 더 키가 크다.
[해설]▶ 비교급은 정관사 the를 붙이지 않지만, of the two가 나오면 비교급에 정관사 the를 붙인다.

4 [해석]▶ 그는 한국에서 가장 훌륭한 소설가 중의 한 명이다.
[해설]▶ 「one of the 최상급+ 복수명사」는 '가장 ~중의 하나'라는 의미이다.

5 [해석]▶ 네가 그녀를 제일 잘 아니까 네가 그녀에게 물어봐야 해.
[해설]▶ 최상급은 정관사 the를 붙이지만, 부사의 최상급은 정관사 the를 붙이지 않는다. best가 동사 know를 수식하고 있다.

6 [해석]▶ 어떤 것도 건강보다 더 소중하지는 않다.
[해설]▶ 부정주어 ~ 비교급 than은 '어떤 ~도 …보다 ~하지 않다'는 의미이다.

7 [해석]▶ 어린이는 적어도 하루에 8시간은 자야 한다.
[해설]▶ not less than은 '적어도'의 의미이다.

B 체크 POINT
본문 110쪽

1. as   2. prettier   3. the longer
4. boy   5. deepest   6. than
7. more

1 [해석]▶ Sally는 그녀의 언니만큼 아름답지는 않다.
[해설]▶ not as ~as…는 '…만큼 ~하지 않다'의 의미이다.

2 [해석]▶ Sarah는 Jane보다 더 예쁘다.
[해설]▶ 비교급 비교는 「비교급+than」의 형태를 취한다. than 앞에 비교급이 나와야 한다.

3 [해석]▶ 두 개의 펜 중에서 이것이 더 길다.
[해설]▶ of the two가 나오면 비교급에 정관사 the를 붙인다.

4 [해석]▶ Jack은 그의 반에서 가장 용감한 소년이다.
[해설]▶ 「as ~ as any+단수명사」(다른 어떤 …못지 않게 ~한)는 최상급의 의미를 가지고 있다.

5 [해석]▶ 이 호수는 이 지점이 가장 깊다.
[해설]▶ 동일 대상 내에서 최상급 비교는 정관사 the를 붙이지 않는다.

6 [해석]▶ 내게 있어서, 낚시만큼 재미있는 것은 없다.
[해설]▶ 부정주어~ 비교급 than은 '어떤 ~도 …보다 ~하지 않다'는 의미이다.

7 [해석]▶ Tom은 기껏해야 평범한 영업사원이다.
[해설]▶ not more than은 '단지, 기껏해야'의 의미이다.

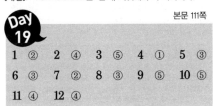

본문 111쪽

1 ②	2 ④	3 ⑤	4 ①	5 ③
6 ③	7 ②	8 ③	9 ⑤	10 ⑤
11 ④	12 ④			

1. ② 고대 그리스 음악의 소리

직독 / 직해

We don't know / what ancient Greek music sounded like, /
우리는 모른다 / 고대 그리스 음악이 어떤 소리를 냈는지 /

because there are no examples of it / in written or notated form, /
그것의 사례가 없기 때문에 / 기록되거나 악보에 적힌 형태로 되어 있는 /

nor has it survived in oral tradition.
그리고 그것은 구전으로도 살아남지 못했다

Much of it was probably improvised anyway, /
어쨌든 그것의 대부분은 아마도 즉흥적으로 연주되었을 것이다 /

within certain rules and conventions.
특정 규칙과 관례 내에서

So we are forced largely to guess at its basis /
그래서 우리는 주로 그것의 토대를 추측할 수밖에 없다 /

from the accounts of writers / such as Plato and Aristotle, /
작가들의 설명으로부터 / 플라톤과 아리스토텔레스와 같은 /

who were generally more concerned with writing about music /
그들은 음악에 대해 글을 쓰는 것에 대체로 더 관심이 있었다 /

as a philosophical and ethical exercise /
철학적이고 윤리적인 실천으로서의 /

than with providing a technical primer on its practice.
실제에 대한 기술적인 입문서를 제공하는 것보다

It seems Greek music was predominantly a vocal form, /
그리스 음악은 대개 성악 형식이었던 것으로 보인다 /

consisting of sung verse accompanied by instruments /
악기의 반주에 의해 노래되는 운문으로 구성된 /

such as the lyre or the plucked kithara (the root of 'guitar').
수금(竪琴)이나 통기는 키타라('기타'의 뿌리)와 같은

In fact, / Plato considered music / in which the lyre and flute played alone /
사실 / 플라톤은 음악을 여겼다 / 수금(竪琴)과 피리만 연주되는 /

and not as the accompaniment of dance or song /
춤이나 노래의 반주로서가 아닌 /

to be 'exceedingly coarse and tasteless'.
'매우 조잡하고 무미건조하다'고

The melodies seem to have had a very limited pitch range, /
그 선율은 매우 제한된 음역을 가지고 있었던 것으로 보인다 /

since the instruments generally span only an octave, /
왜냐하면 그 악기들은 일반적으로 단지 한 옥타브에만 걸쳐 있기 때문이다 /

from one E (as we'd now define it) to the next.
한 E에서 (우리가 그것을 현재 정의하는 대로) 다음 E까지

우리는 고대 그리스 음악이 어떤 소리를 냈는지 알지 못하는데, 그 이유는 그것이 기록되거나 악보에 적힌 형태로 되어 있는 사례가 없고, 구전으로도 살아남지 못했기 때문이다. 어쨌든 그것의 대부분은 아마도 특정 규칙과 관례 내에서 즉흥적으로 연주되었을 것이다. 그래서 우리는 주로 플라톤과 아리스토텔레스와 같은 작가들의 설명으로부터 그것의 토대를 추측할 수밖에 없는데, 그들은 실제에 대한 기술적인 입문서를 제공하는 것보다 철학적이고 윤리적인 실천으로서의 음악에 대해 글을 쓰는 것에 대체로 더 관심이 있었다. 그리스 음악은 대개 성악 형식이었고, 수금(竪琴)이나 통기는 키타라('기타'의 뿌리)와 같은 악기의 반주에 의해 노래되는 운문으로 구성된 것으로 보인다. 사실, 플라톤은 춤이나 노래의 반주로서가 아닌 수금(竪琴)과 피리만 연주되는 음악을 '매우 조잡하고 무미건조하다'고 여겼다. 그 선율은 매우 제한된 음역을 가지고 있었던 것으로 보이는데, 왜냐하면 그 악기들은 일반적으로 (우리가 그것을 현재 정의하는 대로)한 E에서 다음 E까지 단지 한 옥타브에만 걸쳐 있기 때문이다.

문제풀이

① [도치구문]
부정의 의미를 지닌 접속사 nor 다음에는 주어 동사가 도치되어야 하므로 올바르게 쓰였다.
② [비교구문]
as는 앞의 '~로서'의 의미를 지닌 자격을 나타내는 전치사 as와 연결된 것이 아니라 그 앞의 more와 연결된 비교 구문이므로 **as**를 **than**으로 바꿔야 한다.
③ [분사구문]
consisting of는 완전한 문장에 연결된 분사구문이고, consist는 자동사이므로 현재분사를 쓴 것은 올바른 용법이다.
④ [목적보어로 쓰인 to부정사]
consider는 '동사+목적어+to부정사'의 구조를 갖는 5형식 동사이므로 'to be'는 consider의 목적보어로 쓰인 to부정사로 올바르게 쓰였다.
⑤ [형용사 vs 부사]
generally는 동사 span을 수식하는 부사로 올바르게 쓰였다.

어휘·어구

notate 악보에 적다
oral tradition 구전(口傳)
improvise 즉흥 연주를 하다
convention 관례, 관행, 약속
account 설명
be concerned with ~에 관심이 있다
philosophical 철학의
ethical 윤리적인
primer 입문서
predominantly 대개
consist of ~으로 구성되다
verse 운문
accompany 반주해 주다
instrument 악기
pluck (현악기를) 통기다, 뽑다
accompaniment 반주
exceedingly 매우
tasteless 무미건조한, 멋없는
melody 선율
limited 제한된
pitch range 음역
span 걸치다

2. ④ 손발의 피부 각질층은 물을 흡수하면 팽창과 주름 생성 효과를 일으킨다

직독 / 직해

Why does the skin on the extremities wrinkle after a bath?
왜 목욕 후 손발의 피부가 주름질까?

And why only the extremities?
그리고 왜 손발만일까?

Despite its appearance, /
그것의 겉모양에도 불구하고, /

your skin isn't shrinking / after your bath.
여러분의 피부는 오그라들고 있는 것이 아니다. / 여러분이 목욕한 후

Actually, / it is expanding. /
사실, / 그것은 팽창하고 있는 것이다. /

The skin on the fingers, palms, toes, and soles wrinkles /
손가락, 손바닥, 발가락, 그리고 발바닥의 피부는 주름이 진다./

only after it is soaked with water.
물에 흠뻑 적셔진 후에야

The stratum corneum / 피부 각질층은 /
—the thick, dead, rough layer of the skin /
두껍고, 무감각하고, 거친 피부층인 /

that protects us from the environment /
환경으로부터 우리를 보호하고

and that makes the skin on our hands and feet /
우리의 손과 발의 피부를 /

tougher and thicker / 더 억세고 더 두껍게 만드는/
than that on our stomachs or faces /
복부나 얼굴의 그것(피부)보다

— expands / when it soaks up water.
팽창한다. / 그것이 물을 흡수할 때

This expansion causes the wrinkling effect.
이 팽창은 주름 생성 효과를 일으킨다.

So why doesn't the skin on other parts of the body /
그러면 왜 몸의 다른 부분의 피부 또한 /

also wrinkle / when soaked?
주름지지 않을까? / 물에 흠뻑 적셔졌을 때

Actually, it does, / but there is more room /
사실, 그것은 그렇게 되지만 / 더 많은 공간이 있다. /

for the moisture to be absorbed /
수분이 흡수될 /

in these less densely packed areas /
이 덜 빽빽하게 채워진 부위에는 /

before it shows. 그것이 나타나기 전에
One doctor we contacted said / that soldiers /
우리가 접촉한 한 의사는 / 군인들은 /

whose feet are submerged in wet boots
그들의 발이 물에 흠뻑 젖은 장화에 잠겨 있는

for a long period / will exhibit wrinkling /
오랫동안 / 주름지는 것을 보일 것이라고 말했다. /

all over the covered area.
그 덮여 있는 부위 전체에서

왜 목욕 후 손발의 피부가 주름질까? 그리고 왜 손발만일까? 그것의 겉모양에도 불구하고, 여러분의 피부는 여러분이 목욕한 후 오그라들고 있는 것이 아니다. 사실, 그것은 팽창하고 있는 것이다. 손가락, 손바닥, 발가락, 그리고 발바닥의 피부는 물에 흠뻑 적셔진 후에야 주름이 진다. 환경으로부터 우리를 보호하고 우리의 손과 발의 피부를 복부나 얼굴의 그것(피부)보다 더 억세고 더 두껍게 만드는 두껍고, 무감각하고, 거친 피부층인 피부 각질층은 그것이 물을 흡수할 때 팽창한다. 이 팽창은 주름 생성 효과를 일으킨다. 그러면 왜 몸의 다른 부분의 피부 또한 물에 흠뻑 적셔졌을 때 주름지지 않을까? 사실, 그것은 그렇게 되지만, 이 덜 빽빽하게 채워진 부위에는 그것이 나타나기 전에 수분이 흡수될 더 많은 공간이 있다. 우리가 접촉한 한 의사는 물에 흠뻑 젖은 장화에 발이 오랫동안 잠겨 있는 군인들은 그 덮여 있는 부위 전체에서 주름지는 것을 보일 것이라고 말했다.

문제풀이

① despite는 전치사로서 '~에도 불구하고'의 의미가 있다. 뒤에 명사(구) its appearance를 가져왔다. 비슷한 의미의 접속사 though는 뒤에 절을 가져온다.
② 문장의 주어는 the skin이며 on the fingers ~ soles는 전치사구로서 주어 the skin을 수식하고 있다. 단수주어는 단수동사를 취하므로 wrinkles는 맞는 문장이다.
③ tougher and thicker는 「비교급 and 비교급」으로서 '점점 더 ~하다'의 의미이다.
④ **less dense를 less densely로 고쳐야 한다.** densely가 뒤에 나오는 형용사 packed를 수식하고 있기 때문이다.
⑤ 소유격 관계대명사 whose 뒤에 명사(feet)가 나온 문장으로 whose ~ period가 선행사 soldiers를 수식하고 있다.

어휘·어구

extremities 손발

shrink 오그라들다
finger 손가락
palm 손바닥
toe 발가락
sole 발바닥
wrinkle 주름지다
stratum corneum 각질층
expand 팽창하다
soak 흠뻑 젖다
moisture 수분
submerge (물에) 잠그다

---

3. ⑤ | 농업 혁신이 식량 생산량을 늘리면서도 자연 훼손을 억제했다

직독/직해

The immense improvement in the yield of farming /
농업 생산량의 엄청난 향상은, /

during the twentieth century, / 20세기 동안

as a result of innovations / (~에서의) 혁신의 결과인

in mechanization, fertilizer, new varieties,
pesticides and genetic engineering,
기계화, 비료, 신품종, 살충제, 유전 공학에서의

has banished famine from the face of the planet
almost entirely, /
지구상에서 기근을 거의 완전히 몰아냈고, /

and drastically reduced malnutrition, /
영양실조를 대폭 줄였다. /

even while the human population has continued to
expand.
심지어 인구가 계속 팽창하는 동안에도,

Few predicted this, / yet many are concerned /
이를 예상한 사람은 거의 없었지만, 많은 사람들은 우려한다. /

that this improvement has come /
이러한 향상이 이루어졌다고 /

at the expense of nature.
자연을 훼손하면서

In fact / 실제로는 /

the evidence is strong that the opposite is the case.
그 반대가 사실이라는 증거가 강력하다.

Innovation in food production /
식량 생산의 혁신은 /

has spared land and forest
땅과 숲을 대규모로 절약해왔다.

from the plough, the cow and the axe /
쟁기, 소 그리고 도끼로부터 /

on a grand scale 대규모로

by increasing the productivity of the land /
땅의 생산성을 높임으로써 /

we do farm. 우리가 실제로 경작하는

It turns out / 그것은 드러났다 /

that this 'land sparing' has been much better /
이 '토지 절약'이 훨씬 더 나은 것으로 /

for biodiversity / 생물 다양성에 /

than land sharing would have been—/
토지 공유가 그랬을 것보다

by which is meant / growing crops at low yields /
이것(토지 공유)은 의미한다. / 낮은 생산량으로 농작물을 재배하는 것을

in the hope / that abundant wildlife lives in fields /
바라면서 / 풍부한 야생 동물이 밭에 살기를 /

alongside crops. 농작물과 함께

기계화, 비료, 신품종, 살충제, 유전 공학에서의 혁신의 결과인 20세기 농업 생산량의 엄청난 향상은, 심지어 인구가 계속 팽창하는 동안에도, 지구상에서 기근을 거의 완전히 몰아냈고, 영양실조를 대폭 줄였다. 이를 예상한 사람은 거의 없었지만, 많은 사람들은 이러한 향상이 자연을 훼손하면서 이루어졌다고 우려한다. 실제로는 그 반대가 사실이라는 증거가 강력하다. 쟁기, 소 그리고 도끼로부터 땅과 숲을 대규모로 절약해왔다. 이 '토지 절약'이 토지 공유가 그랬을 것보다 생물 다양성에 훨씬 더 나은 것으로 드러나는데, 이것(토지 공유)은 풍부한 야생 동물이 농작물과 함께 밭에 살기를 바라면서 낮은 생산량으로 농작물을 재배하는 것을 의미한다.

문제풀이

① 주어가 the immense improvement이며, 20세기의 농업 생산량 향상이 현재도 영향을 미치고 있으므로 현재완료 has banished로 쓴 것이 적절하다.
② 부사 almost(거의)가 다른 부사 entirely를 수식하고 있다. almost entirely는 '거의 완전히'의 의미이다.
③ 대명사 many가 복수동사와 함께 쓰여 '많은 사람들'의 의미를 가지고 있다.
④ 전치사 by 뒤에 동명사(구)가 나온다.
⑤ **very**를 **much**로 고쳐 써야 한다. 원급 강조어는 **very**, 비교급 강조어는 **much, far, still, a lot** 등을 사용한다.

〔어휘·어구〕

innovations 혁신
mechanization 기계화
fertilizer 비료
pesticide 살충제
genetic engineering 유전 공학
banish 몰아내다
famine 기근
expand 팽창하다
plough 쟁기
axe 도끼
wild lifee 야생 동물

---

4. ① | 거짓말할 때 나타나는 통상적인 행동 패턴의 변화

직독/직해

You have to pay close attention to someone's
normal pattern /
당신은 그의 통상적인 패턴에 주의를 면밀히 기울여야 한다. /

in order to notice a deviation from it /
그의 통상적인 패턴에서 벗어나는 것을 알아채기 위해 /

when he or she lies.
누군가가 거짓말을 할 때.

Sometimes the variation is / as subtle as a pause.
때로는 그 변화는 / 아무 일도 없는 것처럼 감지하기 힘들다.

Other times / it is obvious and abrupt.
어떤 때는 / 그것은 명백하고 갑작스럽다.

I recently saw a news interview /
나는 최근에 뉴스 인터뷰를 봤는데 /

with an acquaintance /
아는 사람과의

who I was certain was going to lie /
거짓말을 할 거라고 내가 확신한, /

about a few particularly sensitive issues, /
몇 가지 특별히 민감한 화젯거리에 대해 /

and lie she did.
그녀는 거짓말을 했다.

During most of her interview /
인터뷰하는 동안 대부분 /

she was calm and direct,
그녀는 차분하고 솔직했지만

but when she started lying, /
거짓말을 하기 시작할 때, /

her manner changed dramatically
그녀의 태도는 극적으로 변했다.

she threw her head back, / laughed in 'disbelief,'
그녀는 머리를 뒤로 젖히고, / '불신'의 웃음을 짓고,

and shook her head back and forth.
머리를 앞뒤로 흔들었다.

It is true / 사실이지만, /

that the questions dealt with very personal issues, /
그 질문들이 매우 사적인 화젯거리를 다룬 것은 /

but I have found / that in general, /

나는 알았다. / 일반적으로 /

no matter how touchy the question, /
질문이 아무리 다루기 힘든 것이라 할지라도

if a person is telling the truth /
누군가가 진실을 말하고 있다면,

his or her manner will not change /
그의 태도가 변하지는 않을 것이라는 점을 /

significantly or abruptly.
상당히 또는 갑작스럽게

누군가가 거짓말을 할 때, 그의 통상적인 패턴에서 벗어나는 것을 알아채기 위해 당신은 그의 통상적인 패턴에 주의를 면밀히 기울여야 한다. 때때로 그 변화는 아무 일도 없는 것처럼 감지하기 힘들다. 어떤 때는 그것은 명백하고 갑작스럽다. 나는 최근에 몇 가지 특별히 민감한 화젯거리에 대해 거짓말을 할 거라고 내가 확신한, 아는 사람과의 뉴스 인터뷰를 봤는데 그녀는 거짓말을 했다. 인터뷰하는 동안 대부분 그녀는 차분하고 솔직했지만 거짓말을 하기 시작할 때, 그녀의 태도는 극적으로 변했다. 그녀는 머리를 뒤로 젖히고, '불신'의 웃음을 짓고, 머리를 앞뒤로 흔들었다. 그 질문이 매우 사적인 화젯거리를 다룬 것은 사실이지만, 일반적으로 질문이 아무리 다루기 힘든 것이라 할지라도 누군가가 진실을 말하고 있다면, 그의 태도가 상당히 또는 갑작스럽게 변하지는 않을 것이라는 점을 나는 알았다.

문제풀이

(A) 동사 is의 보어로 형용사 subtle이 와야한다. as subtle as ~는 '~처럼 감지하기 힘든'의 의미이다.
(B) 관계대명사절 안에서 I was certain이 삽입절로 쓰여 동사 was going to의 주어가 없으므로, 주격 관계대명사가 필요하다.
(C) that절 안에서 the questions를 주어로 하는 동사가 와야 하므로 deal의 과거형인 dealt가 적절하다.

〔어휘·어구〕

deviation 벗어남
variation 변화
subtle 미묘한, 감지하기 힘든
pause 휴지(休止)
abrupt 갑작스러운
acquaintance 아는 사람

---

5. ③ | 초음파 화상 진단에 사용되는 음파의 주파수

직독/직해

Ultrasound, / an imaging technique, /
초음파는, / 화상 진단 기술인데 /

produces an image / by bouncing sound waves off /
이미지를 만들어낸다 / 음파가 부딪혀 되돌아오게 함으로써 /

an object inside the body.
신체 내부의 기관에

A picture is then made / 그러면 사진이 만들어진다. /

using the reflected sound waves.
반사된 음파를 이용함으로써

The frequency of sound waves /
음파의 주파수는 /

used in ultrasound imaging/
초음파 화상 진단에 사용되는 /

ranges above human hearing.
사람이 들을 수 있는 범위 이상이다.

The choice of frequency depends on /
주파수의 선택은 ~ 에 달려있다. /

how deep into the body /
몸 안으로 얼마나 깊이 /

the sound waves are needed to penetrate.
음파가 들어가야 할 필요가 있을지

Lower frequencies allow doctors to see structures /
더 낮은 주파수는 의사가 구조를 볼 수 있게 해준다 /

deeper inside the body. 몸속 더 깊은 곳의

The lower the frequency, however, /
주파수가 낮을수록, / 그러나

---

the less clear the image will become.
이미지는 덜 선명해진다.

Doctors use ultrasound /
의사는 초음파를 이용한다. /

to visualize the size and structure of internal organs.
내부 장기의 크기와 구조를 시각화하기 위해

초음파는 화상 진단 기술인데 음파가 신체 내부의 기관에 부딪혀 되돌아 오게 함으로써 이미지를 만들어낸다. 그러면 반사된 음파를 이용하여 사진이 만들어진다. 초음파 화상 진단에 사용되는 음파의 주파수는 사람들이 들을 수 있는 범위 이상이다. 주파수의 선택은 음파가 몸 안으로 얼마나 깊이 들어 가야 할 필요가 있을지에 달려있다. 더 낮은 주파수는 의사가 몸속 더 깊은 곳의 구조를 볼 수 있게 해준다. 그러나 주파수가 낮을수록, 이미지는 덜 선명해진다. 의사는 내부 장기의 크기와 구조를 시 화하기 위해 초음파를 이용한다

문제풀이

(A) 전치사 by가 있으므로 전치사 by의 목적어 역할을 하는 동명사 bouncing이 옳다.
(B) 문장의 주어가 Frequency이므로, 동사인 ranges가 옳다.
(C) become의 보어가 와야 하므로, 형용사 clear 가 옳다. 'the lower... the less~'는 '더 낮을수록 덜 ~하다'는 의미이다.

어휘·어구

ultrasound 초음파
technique 기술
bounce 반사시키다
reflect 반사시키다
frequency 주파수, 빈도
depend on ~에 의존하다
penetrate 관통하다, 꿰뚫다
visualize 시각화하다
organ (신체의) 기관

6.③ 수면 부족은 면역 체계에 큰 영향을 미친다

직독/직해

Sleep deprivation has a great influence on the immune system.
수면 부족은 면역 체계에 큰 영향을 미친다.

Consider what happens in public schools in December /
12월에 공립학교에서 어떤 일이 일어나는지 생각해 보라. /

just before the winter break.
겨울방학이 시작되기 직전인

Kids get sick. 아이들이 아프다.

Teachers get sick. 교사들이 아프다.

Parents get sick. 학부모들도 아프다.

We tend to think there are just a lot of viruses going around.
우리는 그저 바이러스가 많이 떠돌아다닌다고 생각하는 경향이 있다.

In reality, the main reason for these minor but unpleasant illnesses is /
사실, 경미하지만 반갑지 않은 이런 질병들의 주요 원인은 /

that we are exhausted. 피로 때문이다.

Students and teachers are all sleep-deprived from the constant stress of the first semester, /
학생들과 교사들은 모두 첫 학기의 계속되는 스트레스로 인해 잠이 부족한 상태이고, /

and it begins to catch up with us.
그것은 우리에게 나쁜 영향을 미치기 시작한다.

Our immune systems are not functioning as effective as they do /
면역 체계는 효과적으로 기능하지 못하고 /

when we are well rested, / 우리가 휴식을 잘 취했을 때만큼 /

and we get sick. 우리는 아프게 된다.

What do most of us do when the winter break comes? /
겨울 방학이 오면 우리 대부분은 무엇을 하는가? /

We try to get caught up on sleep.

가운데 열

잠을 만회하기 위해 애쓴다

수면 부족은 면역 체계에 큰 영향을 미친다. 겨울방학이 시작되기 직전인 12월에 공립학교에서 어떤 일이 일어나는지 생각해 보라. 아이들이 아프다. 교사들이 아프다. 학부모들도 아프다. 우리는 그저 바이러스가 많이 떠돌아다닌다고 생각하는 경향이 있다. 사실, 경미하지만 반갑지 않은 이런 질병들의 주요 원인은 피로 때문이다. 학생들과 교사들은 모두 첫 학기의 계속되는 스트레스로 인해 잠이 부족한 상태이고, 그것은 우리에게 나쁜 영향을 미치기 시작한다. 면역 체계는 우리가 휴식을 잘 취했을 때만큼 효과적으로 기능하지 못하고 우리는 아프게 된다. 겨울 방학이 오면 우리 대부분은 무엇을 하는가? 잠을 만회하기 위해 애쓴다

문제풀이

(A)에는 virus와 go의 관계가 능동이며, virus를 꾸며 주는 역할을 하는 going와야 한다. (B)에는 주어가 the main reason이므로 단수동사 is가 와야 한다. (C)에는 동사 are not functioning을 수식하므로 부사 effectively가 와야 한다. 'as effectively as~'는 '~만큼 효과적으로'의 의미이다. 따라서 어법에 맞는 표현으로 가장 적절한 것은 ③이다.

어휘·어구

sleep deprivation 수면 결핍[부족]
influence 영향
immune system 면역 체계
reason 원인, 이유
exhausted 지친, 기진맥진한
constant 계속되는

7.② 출생 순서와 성인기 삶의 성취와의 관계

직독/직해

Many social scientists have believed for some time /
많은 사회과학자들은 한동안 믿어 왔다. /

that birth order directly affects /
출생 순서가 직접적으로 영향을 미친다고 /

both personality and achievement in adult life.
성격과 성인기의 삶의 성취에

In fact, / people have been using birth order /
사실, / 사람들은 출생 순서를 사용해 왔다. /

to account for personality factors /
성격 요인을 설명하기 위해 /

such as an aggressive behavior or a passive temperament.
공격적인 행동과 수동적인 기질과 같은

One might say, / 사람들은 ~라고 말할 수도 있다. /

"Oh, I'm the eldest of three sisters, /
"아, 나는 세 자매 중에 맏이라서 /

so I can't help that I'm so overbearing," /
내가 거만하게 행동하는 것을 피할 수 없어." /

or "I'm not very successful in business, /
또는 "나는 사업에 그다지 성공적이지 못해." /

because I'm the youngest child and thus less aggressive /
막내라서 덜 적극적이어서 (라고) /

than my older brothers and sisters."
형이나 누나들보다

Recent studies, / however, /
최근의 연구들은, / 그러나, /

have proved this belief to be false.
이러한 믿음이 잘못된 것이라는 것을 입증하였다.

In other words, / 다시 말해, /

birth order may define your role within a family, /
출생 순서가 가족 내에서 역할을 규정지을 수는 있지만, /

but as you mature into adulthood, /
우리가 어른으로 성장해가며 /

accepting other social roles, /
다른 사회적 역할들을 받아들일 때, /

birth order becomes insignificant.
출생 순서는 덜 중요하게 된다.

많은 사회과학자들은 한동안 출생 순서가 성격과 성인기의 삶의 성취에 직접적으로 영향을 미친다고 믿어 왔다. 사실, 사람들은 공격적인 행동과 수동적인 기질과 같은 성격 요인을 설명하기 위해 출생 순서를 사용해 왔다. 사람들은 "아, 나는 세 자매 중에 맏이라서 내가 거만하게 행동하는 것을 피할 수 없어." 또는 "나는 막내라서 형이나 누나들보다 덜 적극적이어서 사업에 그다지 성공적이지 못해."라고 말할 수도 있다. 그러나 최근의 연구들은 이러한 믿음이 잘못된 것이라는 것을 입증하였다. 다시 말해, 출생 순서가 가족 내에서 역할을 규정지을 수는 있지만, 우리가 어른으로 성장해가며 다른 사회적 역할들을 받아들일 때, 출생 순서는 덜 중요하게 된다.

문제풀이

(A) have believed의 목적어가 되는 절을 이끌 수 있는 접속사 that이 적절하다.
(B) ~ and thus I am less aggressive의 문맥이므로 be동사의 보어 역할을 할 수 있는 형용사 aggressive가 적절하다.
(C) as you accept other social roles (당신이 다른 사회적인 역할을 받아들이면서)를 분사구문으로 바꾼 형태이므로 accepting이 적절하다.

어휘·어구

birth order 출생 순서
account for ~을 설명하다
aggressive 적극적인, 공격적인
temperament 기질
overbearing 거만한
define 정의하다
mature 성숙하다
insignificant 중요하지 않은

8.③ 목표에 집중하는 가장 효과적인 방법은 먼저 목표를 적는 것이다

직독/직해

Possibly the most effective way /
아마도 가장 효과적인 방법은 /

to focus on your goals / 당신이 정한 여러 목표에 집중하는 /

is to write them down. 그것들을 적어두는 것이다.

Although this may sound like an obvious first step, /
이것이 당연한 첫 단계라고 들릴지 모르지만 /

it is a step that many people ignore.
많은 사람들이 무시하는 단계이다.

As a result, / their goals often remain unfocused, /
그 결과 / 그들의 목표는 흔히 흐지부지되어 /

and therefore unrealized.
결국 실현되지 못하게 된다.

Go to a fairly quiet place /
아주 조용한 곳으로 가라. /

where you are not likely to be disturbed.
당신이 방해를 받지 않을 만한

Make a list of every goal you have.
당신이 정한 모든 목표를 목록으로 만들어라.

Include goals / 목표를 포함시켜라. /

about finances, relationships, and your career.
자금, 인간관계, 그리고 경력에 관한

Be as specific as possible.
될 수 있는 한 구체적으로 작성하라.

아마도 당신이 정한 여러 목표에 집중하는 가장 효과적인 방법은 그것들을 적어두는 것이다. 이것이 당연한 첫 단계라고 들릴지 모르지만 많은 사람들이 무시하는 단계이다. 그 결과 그들의 목표는 흔히 흐지부지되어 결국 실현되지 못하게 된다. 당신이 방해를 받지 않을 만한 아주 조용한 곳으로 가라. 당신이 정한 모든 목표를 목록으로 만들어라. 자금, 인간관계, 그리고 경력에 관한 목표를 포함시켜라. 될 수 있는 한 구체적으로 작성하라.

문제풀이

(A)에는 write down이「동사 + 부사」의 동사구이므로 대명사 목적어인 them은 그 사이에 위치해

야 한다. 즉 「동사+대명사+부사」의 구조를 갖는다. 명사가 올 때는 「동사+명사+부사」 또는 「동사+부사+명사」가 나와도 된다.

(B)에는 disturb가 '방해하다'의 의미를 지니고 의미상 주어가 you이므로 문맥상 '방해를 받지 않을' 의미로 나타내야 한다. 그러므로 수동형인 be disturbed가 필요하다. 부정사의 수동태는 to be+p.p. 형태를 가지고 있다.
(C)에는 Be의 보어가 될 수 있는 말이 와야 하므로 형용사 specific이 적절하다.

《 어휘 · 어구 》

effective 효과적인
obvious 명백한
ignore 무시하다
unfocused 집중되지 않는, 흐지부지한
unrealized 실현되지 않는
disturb 방해하다
specific 구체적인

---

9. ⑤ 　어두운 옷이 더운 날씨에 갖는 유리함

우리는 모두 학교에서 하얀색은 햇빛을 반사하고 검은색은 그것을 흡수해서, 당신의 옷이 ①엷은 색일수록, 당신은 더 시원할 것이라고 듣는다. 그러나 그것은 그다지 간단하지가 않다. 많은 더운 나라에서 현지인은 흔히 ②어두운 색을 입는다. 예를 들어, 중국의 농부들과 남부 유럽의 노부인들은 전통적으로 검은색을 입고, 사하라의 유목민인 투아레그족은 남색을 선호한다. 이런 옷들은 동시에 두 가지의 열처리 과정이 일어나고 있기 때문에 ③효과적이다. 열은 태양에서 아래쪽으로 내려오고 있지만, 그것은 또한 몸에서 바깥쪽으로 나가고도 있다. 엷은 색의 옷들이 태양열을 더 잘 ④반사하지만, 어두운 색의 옷들은 몸의 열을 더 잘 방출한다. 더운 기후에서 태어난 어느 누구도 선뜻 직사광에 서 있으려 하지 않는다는 것을 고려해 볼 때, 어두운 색의 옷은 그늘에 있을 때 당신을 더 시원하게 해주기 때문에 ⑤단점(→ 유리함)을 가진다.

문제풀이

마지막 문장에서 어두운 색의 옷들은 몸의 열을 더 잘 방출하므로 그늘에 있을 때 더 시원하게 해준다고 언급하고 있다. 그것은 단점이 아닌 유리함(edge)을 가진다는 의미이므로 ⑤가 적절하지 않은 표현이다.

《 구문 및 어휘 》

＊1행 We're all told at school [that white reflects sunlight and black absorbs it], so **the paler** your clothes are, **the cooler** you'll be.
(1) [that white ~ it]은 동사 told의 목적절이며 이때 it은 sunlight을 가리킨다.
(2) The paler ~, the cooler …는 「the 비교급+주어+동사, the 비교급+주어+동사」 형태로 '더 ~할수록 더 …하다'의 의미이다. 이는 As your clothes are paler, you'll be cooler.와 같은 의미이다.
＊12행 [Given that no one born in a hot climate willingly stands in direct sunlight], the dark clothing has the edge because it keeps you cooler when you're in the shade.
(1) [Given that no one ~ sunlight]는 조건을 설명하는 분사구문으로, As no one born in ~이나 Considering that no one born ~으로 쓸 수 있다.

---

(2) it은 the dark clothing을 가리킨다.

absorb 흡수하다
local 현지인
peasant 농부
nomadic 유목의
reflect 반사하다; 비추다
radiate 방출하다

---

10. ⑤ 　성격 특성과 행동 사이의 상관 관계

흔히 활동적인 사람은 부끄럼이 많은 사람보다 친구를 더 쉽게 사귈 수 있고 성실한 사람은 성실하지 않은 사람보다 마감 기한을 맞추는 경우가 더 많을 것이라고 여겨진다. 하지만 Walter Mischel은 성격 특성과 행동 사이의 전형적인 상관관계가 그리 크지 않다는 것을 발견했다. 이 소식은 정말 충격적이었는데, 그것은 본질적으로 성격 심리학자들이 측정하고 있던 특성이라는 것이 행동을 예측하는 데 있어서 점성술의 별자리보다 단지 약간 나을 뿐이라고 말했기 때문이었다. Mischel은 그 문제점을 지적해냈을 뿐 아니라 그 이유를 진단했다. 그는 성격 심리학자들이 사람들의 성격과는 무관하게 사회적 상황이 사람들의 행동을 결정하는 정도를 과소평가했다고 주장했다. 예를 들어, 어떤 사람이 마감 기한을 맞출 것인지 예측하기 위해서는 성실성 측정에서 그 사람이 받은 점수보다 (그 사람이 처한) 상황에 대해 무언가를 아는 것이 더 유용할 수 있다. 상황적 영향이라는 것은 매우 강력해서 때로 개인의 성격 차이를 압도할 수 있다.

문제풀이

첫 문장은 성격 특성과 행동이 연관이 있을 것으로 여겨진다는 의미이며, (A)가 포함된 문장은 첫 문장에 역접의 접속사 however로 연결되었으므로 반대의 의미일 것으로 추측할 수 있다. (A)뒤 문장의 내용 또한 성격 심리학자들이 측정하는 특성이 행동을 예측하는데 있어 점성술의 별자리보다 약간 나을 뿐이라는 내용이므로, (A)에 modest가 들어가서, 성격 특성과 행동 사이의 전형적인 상관관계가 그리 크지 않다는 것을 발견했다는 의미가 되는 것이 적절하다. (B)에는 Mischel이 이유를 진단했다는 문장 뒤이므로 사회적 상황이 사람들의 행동을 결정하는 정도를 과소평가했다(underestimated)는 흐름이 되는 것이 적절하다. (C)는 앞 문장을 뒷받침하는 예시를 요약 정리한 문장이므로, 상황적 영향이 매우 강력해서 개인의 성격 차이를 '압도(overwhelming)'한다는 흐름이 되는 것이 알맞다. 따라서 정답은 ⑤이다.

typical 전형적인
correlation 상관관계
trait 특성
apparent 분명한
modest 지나치지 않은, 적당한
essentially 본질적으로
measure 측정하다; 측정
diagnose 진단하다
overestimate 과대평가하다
underestimate 과소평가하다
independently of ~와 관계없이
overwhelm 압도하다

---

11. ④ 　고고학 현장에서 발굴된 더 얇은 껍질을 가진 씨앗의 의미

사람들이 저장된 씨앗 종자를 의도적으로 심기 시작했을 때 그들은 또한 자신들의 식물을 보호하기 시작했다. 이것은 이들 식용 식물이 더 이상

자연환경 속에서 살아남아야 할 필요성이 없어지면서 그것들이 경험한 진화적 압력을 변화시켰다. 대신에, 사람들은 그것들을 위한 새로운 환경을 창조했고, 자연이 이전에 선택한 것과는 다른 특징들을 선택했다. 고고학적 현장에서 발굴된 씨앗들은 농부들이 더 큰 씨앗 그리고 더 얇은 껍질을 선택했다는 것을 명백히 보여준다. 두꺼운 껍질은 흔히 씨앗이 자연환경에서 생존하는 데 필수적인데 (그것은) 많은 야생식물의 씨앗이 겨울이 끝나고 비가 오기 시작할 때까지 여러 달을 휴면 상태로 남아 있어야 하기 때문이다. 하지만 인간의 관리하에서 두꺼운 씨앗 껍질은 불필요한데, (그것은) 농부들이 수분과 포식자로부터 씨앗을 보호하여 저장하는 책임을 피하기(→ 넘겨받기) 때문이다. 사실, 더 얇은 껍질을 가진 씨앗은 그 것이 먹거나 가루로 가공하기가 더 수월하고 파종되었을 때 묘목이 더 빠르게 발아하기 때문에 선호되었다.

문제풀이

밑줄 친 ④의 문장 내용은 인간의 관리하에서 두꺼운 씨앗 껍질은 불필요한데, 그것은 농부들이 수분과 포식자로부터 씨앗을 보호하여 저장하는 책임을 넘겨받기 때문이다. 따라서 ④의 evade(피하다)를 take over(넘겨 받다)로 고쳐 써야한다.

《 어휘 · 어구 》

seed stock (심기 위해 보관된) 종자
deliberately 의도적으로, 일부러
recovered 발굴된, 되찾은
archaeological 고고학의
dormant 휴지기의
set in 시작되다
seedling 묘목, 모종
sprout 발아하다, 발육하다

---

12. ④ 　지속 가능한 소비의 방향

직독/직해

A general and seemingly applicable assumption is /
일반적이며 적절해 보이는 가정은 ~이다 /
that consumers and producers maximize the benefit /
소비자와 생산자가 이익을 최대화한다는 것 /
related to the opportunity / accessible in their
기회와 관련된 　　　　　　／ 자신들의 특정 상황에서 이용할 수 있는
particular circumstance.
특정한 상황에서
The desire to reach an optimal outcome / for a
최적의 결과에 도달하려는 욕구는 　　　　　／ 주어진 시점 동안
given point in time / is subjective and specific /
　　　　　　　　　　／ 주관적이며 다른데 /
to how these economic agents view the concept of
이러한 경제적인 주체들이 최대화라는 개념을 어떻게 보느냐에 따라
maximization, /
which in turn is likely to be highly correlated with
이는 결국 문화적 가치와 매우 밀접하게 서로 관련되어 있을 가능성이 있다
cultural values.
For example, in indigenous societies there is
evidence / 예를 들어, 토착민 사회에서는 증거가 있다 /
that a balance between present and future periods /
현재와 미래 시간 사이의 균형이 /
along with that of the environmental system, /
환경 시스템의 균형과 더불어 /
as a whole, / 총체적으로 /
was included in decision-making and optimization.
의사 결정과 최적화에 포함되었다는
In present consumerism-fostered economies, /
소비주의에 의해 조성되는 오늘날의 경제 체제에서 /
the cultural values are less likely or unlikely /
문화적 가치가 ~(할) 가능성은 더 적거나 없을 것이다 /
to incorporate environmental and social justice
환경적, 사회적 정의라는 변수를 사전에 적극적으로 포함할
parameters proactively.
The focus of observable and marketed consumption /
관찰 가능한, 시장을 통한 소비의 초점은 /
is immediate gratification. 즉각적인 만족에 있다
However, as consumer awareness of both the impact
하지만, 소비의 영향과 소비의 힘 양쪽 모두에 대한 소비자 인식이 /

of consumption and the power of consumption /
to modify and catalyze economic outcomes /
경제적 결과를 바꾸고 촉진하는 /
increases / there is growing evidence /
증가함에 따라 / 증거가 늘어나고 있다 /
of a shifting cultural paradigm to one of sustainability.
지속 가능성의 패러다임으로 변화하는 문화적 패러다임의

일반적이며 적절해 보이는 가정은, 소비자와 생산자가 자신들의 특정 상황에서 ① 이용할 수 있는 기회와 관련된 이익을 최대화한다는 것이다. 주어진 시점 동안 최적의 결과에 도달하려는 욕구는 주관적이며 이러한 ② 경제적인 주체들이 최대화라는 개념을 어떻게 보느냐에 따라 다른데, 이는 결국 문화적 가치와 매우 밀접하게 서로 관련되어 있을 가능성이 있다. 예를 들어, 토착민 사회에서는 총체적으로 환경 시스템의 균형과 더불어 현재와 미래 시간 사이의 균형이 의사 결정과 최적화에 ③ 포함되었다는 증거가 있다. 소비주의에 의해 조성되는 오늘날의 경제 체제에서, 문화적 가치가 환경적, 사회적 정의라는 변수를 사전에 적극적으로 ④ 무시할(→ 포함할) 가능성은 더 적거나 없을 것이다. 관찰 가능한, 시장을 통한 소비의 만족에 있다. 하지만, 경제적 결과를 바꾸고 촉진하는 소비의 영향과 소비의 힘 양쪽 모두에 대한 소비자 인식이 ⑤ 증가에 따라 지속 가능성의 패러다임으로 변화하는 문화적 패러다임의 증거가 늘어나고 있다.

문제풀이

관찰 가능한, 시장을 통한 소비의 초점은 즉각적인 만족에 있다고 했으므로, 소비주의에 의해 조성되는 오늘날의 경제 체제에서 문화적 가치가 환경적, 사회적 정의의 변수를 사전에 적극적으로 포함할 가능성은 적거나 없다고 해야 한다. 따라서 ④ 'disregard(무시하다)'는 'incorporate(포함하다)'와 같은 낱말로 고쳐야 한다.

⊙ **이렇게 풀자** _ 먼저 글의 주제와 흐름을 파악한 뒤, 밑줄 친 어휘가 포함된 문장 전후 문맥을 파악해서 적절하게 쓰였는지를 판단하면 된다. 'The focus of observable and marketed consumption is immediate gratification. (관찰 가능한, 시장을 통한 소비의 초점은 즉각적인 만족에 있다.)'을 통해 즉각적인 만족이 환경적 사회적 정의라는 변수를 생각할 시간이 없다는 것을 의미한다는 것을 알면 ④ disregard가 적절하지 않다는 것을 알 수 있다.

⚘ 구조 다시보기

도입	소비자와 생산자는 이익을 최대화하려 하고 이익 최대화의 개념은 문화적 가치의 영향을 받음
예시	토착민 사회는 현재와 미래의 균형, 환경과 인간의 균형을 중요하게 보지만, 현대는 즉각적인 만족을 중요시함
역접	최근 소비자의 인식이 개선되면서 지속 가능성의 패러다임으로 소비 방향이 변화하고 있음

◀ 어휘 · 어구 ▶

seemingly 겉보기에
applicable 적절한
assumption 가정
maximize 최대화하다
accessible 이용할 수 있는
optimal 최적의
outcome 결과
subjective 주관적인
agent 주체, 행위자
correlate (밀접한) 연관성이 있다
indigenous 토착의, 원산의
optimization 최적화
consumerism 소비주의
foster 조성하다, 육성하다
incorporate 포함하다
proactively 사전에 적극적으로
observable 관찰 가능한
gratification 만족
awareness 인식
modify 바꾸다
shifting 변화하는, 이동하는
sustainability 지속 가능성

---

20. 특수 구문

A 출제 POINT 본문 116쪽

1. could they   2. does Sam
3. comes the writer   4. who
5. do   6. Not every 7. do

1 [해석]▶ 그들은 앞을 전혀 볼 수 없었을 뿐만 아니라 지치고 병이 들어서 더 이상 걸을 수가 없었다.
[해설]▶ 부정어구(not only)가 문장 앞에 오면 「주어+(조)동사」가 도치된다.

2 [해석]▶ 단지 그의 가족에 대한 사랑 때문에 Sam은 그 렇게 힘든 일을 했다.
[해설]▶ Only가 포함된 어구가 문장 앞에 오면 「주어+(조)동사」가 도치된다.

3 [해석]▶ 이곳에 그 작가가 와!
[해설]▶ 장소와 방향을 나타내는 부사(here)가 문장 앞에 오면 주어와 동사가 도치된다.

4 [해석]▶ 우리가 가야할 길을 닦은 사람들은 끊임없는 시행착오를 거쳤던 바로 그러한 탐험가들이다.
[해설]▶ It ~ that 강조 구문으로서 those explores가 강조되고 있다. 강조되는 어구가 사람을 가리키므로 that 대신 who를 사용할 수 있다.

5 [해석]▶ 롤링의 책이 초자연적 생명체를 담고 있는 것은 사실이다.
[해설]▶ 조동사 do를 사용하여 동사를 강조할 수 있다. 주어가 복수이므로 do를 써야 한다.

6 [해석]▶ 인터넷에 있는 모든 뉴스가 다 진실인 것은 아니다.
[해설]▶ 전체를 나타내는 어구가 not과 함께 쓰이면 부분 부정의 의미를 나타낸다. not every는 '전부 ~인 것은 아니다'의 의미이다.

7 [해석]▶ 나의 단짝, Sally는 나보다 더 피아노를 잘 친다.
[해설]▶ 일반동사로 시작하는 어구가 반복되면 대동사 do를 사용하여 생략한다. play를 반복 사용하지 않기 위해 대동사를 사용할 수 있는데, 주어가 I이므로, do를 써야 한다.

B 체크 POINT 본문 116쪽

1. had she   2. can rest
3. are the poor   4. which
5. the very 6. Not everyone 7. did

1 [해석]▶ 그녀가 가자마자 그는 그녀를 욕하기 시작했다.
[해설]▶ 부정어구(hardly)가 문두에 나오면 「주어+(조)동사」가 도치된다.

2 [해석]▶ 열심히 일한 후에만 진정으로 휴식을 즐길 수 있다.
[해설]▶ Only가 포함된 어구가 문장 앞에 오면 「주어+(조)동사」가 도치된다. 이 문장에서 rest는 '휴식'이라는 말로 주어 역할을 하고 있다.

---

3 [해석]▶ 마음이 가난한 사람은 복이 있다.
[해설]▶ 보어가 문장의 앞에 오면, 주어와 be동사가 도치된다.

4 [해석]▶ 우리가 매우 불쾌하다고 생각한 것은 바로 그녀가 한 말이 아니었다.
[해설]▶ It ~ that 강조 구문으로서, 강조 대상이 사물(not her remarks)이면 that 대신 which를 사용할 수 있다.

5 [해석]▶ 그녀는 며칠 전 나를 도와주었던 바로 그 여인이다.
[해설]▶ 명사를 강조하고 싶은 때는 the very를 사용하여 명사를 강조할 수 있다.

6 [해석]▶ 당신이 나를 싫어해도 괜찮아요, 모든 사람이 좋은 취향을 가진 건 아니니까요.
[해설]▶ not everyone은 '모두 다 ~인 것은 아니다'라는 부분 부정의 의미이다.

7 [해석]▶ 그녀는 파티에서 즐거운 시간을 보내리라고 기대하지 않았지만, 실제로는 좋은 시간을 보냈다.
[해설]▶ ~ but she actually had a good time이라는 문장에서 had a good time을 반복하지 않기 위해 대동사 did를 사용하였다.

Day 20 본문 117쪽

1 ②	2 ③	3 ⑤	4 ⑤	5 ①
6 ⑤	7 ⑤	8 ②	9 ⑤	10 ②
11 ③	12 ④			

1. ② 이집트 예술의 기념비성이라는 특성

직독/직해

"Monumental" is a word that comes very close /
'기념비적'은 매우 근접한 단어이다 /
to expressing the basic characteristic of Egyptian art. 이집트 예술의 기본적인 특징을 나타내는데
Never before and never since / has the quality of
그 전에도 그 이후에도 결코 / 기념비성이라는 특성은 달성된 적이 없었다 /
monumentality been achieved /
as fully as it was in Egypt. 이집트에서 그랬던 것처럼 완전히
The reason for this / is not the external size and
이에 대한 이유는 / 그들 작품의 외적 크기와 거대함이 아니다 /
massiveness of their works, /
although the Egyptians admittedly achieved some
비록 이집트인들이 몇 가지 놀라운 것들을 달성했다는 것이 인정되지만
amazing things / in this respect.
/ 이 점에서
Many modern structures exceed those of Egypt /
많은 현대의 구조물은 이집트의 그것들을 능가한다 /
in terms of purely physical size.
순전히 물리적인 크기 면에서
But massiveness has nothing to do with monumentality.
하지만 거대함은 기념비성과는 아무런 관련이 없다
An Egyptian sculpture no bigger than a person's hand / 겨우 사람 손 크기 만한 이집트 조각품이 /
is more monumental than that gigantic pile of stones / 그 거대한 돌무더기보다도 더욱 기념비적이다 /
that constitutes the war memorial in Leipzig for instance. 예를 들어 Leipzig의 전쟁 기념비를 구성하는
Monumentality is not a matter of external weight, /
기념비성은 외적 무게의 문제가 아니다 /
but of "inner weight." '내적 무게'의 문제이다
This inner weight is the quality / 이 내적 무게는 특성인데 /
which Egyptian art possesses / 이집트 예술이 지닌 /
to such a degree that everything in it /
그 안에 있는 모든 것이 ~정도의

seems to be made of primeval stone, /
원시 시대의 돌로 만들어진 것처럼 보일 (정도의)

like a mountain range, / 마치 산맥처럼 /

even if it is only a few inches across or carved in wood. 비록 그것이 폭이 몇 인치에 불과하거나 나무에 새겨져 있을지라도

'기념비적'은 이집트 예술의 기본적인 특징을 나타내는데 매우 근접한 단어이다. 그 전에도 그 이후에도, 기념비성이라는 특성은 이집트에서 그랬던 것처럼 완전히 달성된 적은 결코 없었다. 이에 대한 이유는, 비록 이집트인들이 이 점에 있어 몇 가지 놀라운 것들을 달성했다는 것이 인정되지만, 그들 작품의 외적 크기와 거대함이 아니다. 많은 현대의 구조물은 순전히 물리적인 크기 면에서 이집트의 그것들을 능가한다. 하지만 거대함은 기념비성과는 아무런 관련이 없다. 예를 들어, 겨우 사람 손 크기 만한 이집트 조각상이 Leipzig의 전쟁 기념비를 구성하는 그 거대한 돌무더기보다 더욱 기념비적이다. 기념비성은 외적 무게의 문제가 아닌 '내적 무게'의 문제이다. 이 내적 무게는 이집트 예술이 지닌 특성인데, 이집트 예술은 비록 그 안에 있는 모든 작품이 폭이 몇 인치에 불과하거나 나무에 새겨져 있을지라도, 마치 산맥처럼 원시 시대의 돌로 만들어진 것처럼 보일 정도의 특성을 지니고 있다.

문제풀이

① 전치사 to 뒤에는 명사 상당어구가 와야 하므로 동명사인 expressing은 적절하게 쓰였다.
② it은 the quality of monumentality를 가리키고, 문맥상 그것이 '달성되었다'는 의미가 되어야 한다. 따라서 was achieved를 대신하는 대동사 was가 와야 한다.
③ 앞에 나온 복수명사 structures를 대신하는 those는 어법에 맞게 쓰였다.
④ 선행사인 that gigantic pile of stones를 수식하고 관계사절 내에서 주어 역할을 해야 하므로, 주격 관계대명사 that은 적절하게 쓰였다.
⑤ even if it is에 이어지는 표현이고, 문맥상 나무에 '새겨진다'라는 의미가 되어야 하므로 과거분사인 carved는 어법에 맞게 쓰였다.

❖ 이렇게 풀자 어법상 틀린 부분을 찾는 문제는 밑줄이 있는 부분의 형태와 문맥을 보고 어법에 맞게 쓰였는지 확인해야 한다. ①은 전치사 뒤에 오는 동명사의 쓰임을, ②는 대동사의 쓰임을, ③은 지시대명사의 역할을, ④는 주격 관계대명사의 역할을, ⑤는 과거분사의 쓰임을 알아야 한다.

《 어휘 · 어구 》

monumental 기념비적인
characteristic 특성, 특징
external 외부의
massiveness 거대함
admittedly 인정하건대
exceed 넘다, 능가하다
purely 순전히, 전적으로
have nothing to do with ~와 아무 관련 없다
monumentality 기념비성
constitute 구성하다
war memorial 전쟁 기념비
mountain range 산맥
across 폭으로, 지름으로

---

2. ③ 인간이 체지방을 걱정하는 것은 최근의 짧은 시기에서 시작됐다

직독 / 직해

With all the passion for being slim, /
날씬해지고 싶은 모든 열정으로, /

it is no wonder /
~은 놀랄 일이 아니다. /

that many people view /
많은 사람들이 여기는 것은 /

any amount of visible fat /
눈에 띄는 지방이 얼마만큼 이든 간에 /

on the body / as something to get rid of.
자신의 몸에 있는 / 그것을 없애야 하는 것으로

However, / the human body has evolved over time /
그러나 / 인간의 몸은 시간이 흐르면서 진화해왔다. /

in environments of food scarcity; /
식량이 부족한 환경에서 /

hence, / the ability to store fat efficiently /
따라서 / 지방을 효율적으로 저장하는 능력은 /

is a valuable physiological function /
소중한 생리학적인 기능이다. /

that served our ancestors well for thousands of years.
우리 조상에게 수천 년 동안 많은 도움을 준

Only in the last few decades, /
겨우 지난 몇 십 년 동안에서야 비로소, /

in the primarily industrially developed economies, /
주요 산업 선진 경제국에서 /

has food become so plentiful / and easy to obtain
식량이 매우 풍부해지고 / 구하기 쉬워져서 /

as to cause fat-related health problems.
지방 관련 건강 문제를 야기하게 되었다.

People no longer have to spend /
사람들은 더 이상 소비할 필요가 없다. /

most of their time and energy /
대부분의 시간과 에너지를 /

gathering berries and seeds /
열매와 씨앗을 모으고,

and hoping / that a hunting party will return with meat.
바라면서 / 사냥 나간 무리가 고기를 가지고 돌아오기를

All we have to do nowadays is drive /
요즘 우리는 운전하여 가기만 하면 된다, /

to the supermarket or the fast-food restaurant, /
슈퍼마켓이나 패스트푸드 식당으로 /

where for very low cost / 거기서 아주 적은 비용으로 /

we can obtain nearly all of our daily calories.
하루 열량의 거의 전부를 얻을 수 있다.

인간이 체지방을 걱정하는 것은 최근의 짧은 시기에서 시작됐다. 날씬해지고 싶은 모든 열정으로, 많은 사람들이 자신의 몸에 있는 눈에 띄는 지방이 얼마만큼 이든 간에 그것을 없애야 하는 것으로 여기는 것은 놀랄 일이 아니다. 그러나 인간의 몸은 식량이 부족한 환경에서 시간이 흐르면서 진화해왔다. 따라서 지방을 효율적으로 저장하는 능력은 우리 조상에게 수천 년 동안 많은 도움을 준 소중한 생리학적인 기능이다. 겨우 지난 몇 십 년 동안에서야 비로소, 주요 산업 선진 경제국에서 식량이 매우 풍부해지고 구하기 쉬워져서 지방 관련 건강 문제를 야기하게 되었다. 사람들은 더 이상 대부분의 시간과 에너지를 열매와 씨앗을 모으고, 사냥 나간 무리가 고기를 가지고 돌아오기를 바라면서 소비할 필요가 없다. 요즘 우리는 슈퍼마켓이나 패스트푸드 식당으로 운전하여 가기만 하면 되고, 거기서 아주 적은 비용으로 하루 열량의 거의 전부를 얻을 수 있다.

문제풀이

① wonder의 목적어로 쓰인 명사절을 이끄는 접속사 that은 적절하다. wonder가 동사로 '궁금하다'로 쓰인 것이 아니기에 whether가 될 수는 없다.
② to store가 명사(the ability)를 수식하는 형용사적 용법으로 사용되고 있으므로 to부정사를 수식하려면 부사 efficiently가 나오는 것이 적절하다.
③ only가 전치구와 함께 문두로 나오면서 도치가 된 것으로 food가 주어이므로 ③의 have를 has로 고쳐 써야 한다.
④ 「spend + 시간/돈 + -ing (동명사)」 구문이다. '시간(돈)을 ~하는 데 쓰다'는 의미이다.
⑤ the supermarket or the fast-food restaurant를 선행사로 갖는 관계부사 where가 계속적 용법으로 쓰였다.

《 어휘 · 어구 》

get rid of 제거하다
evolve 진화하다
environment 환경
scarcity 부족, 결핍
physiological 생리(학)의
function 기능
obtain 얻다

---

3. ⑤ 대중 앞에서 말할 때는 언어적 유창함이 비언어적 유창함과 어울려야 한다

직독 / 직해

Most amateur speakers do not understand /
대부분의 아마추어 연사들은 이해하지 못한다. /

that when they are on stage /
그들이 무대에 있을 때 /

they are actors and actresses.
자신들이 배우 노릇을 해야 한다는 것을

Most do have some idea /
대부분의 연사들은 생각은 갖고 있지만, /

that they should speak with more power on stage /
무대에서 더 강력하게 말해야 한다는 /

than they do on a one-to-one basis,
일대일로 말할 때보다 /

but they do not realize /
하지만 그들은 깨닫지 못한다. /

that their verbal eloquence must be matched /
언어적 유창함이 어울려야 한다는 것은 /

with a nonverbal eloquence.
비언어적 유창함과

If you move your hand two inches /
손을 2인치 움직인다면, /

to emphasize a point /
어떤 부분을 강조하기 위해 /

when speaking to one person, /
한 사람에게 말할 때 /

you may have to move it / as much as two feet
손을 움직여야 할지도 모른다. / 2피트만큼이나 /

in front of a large audience.
많은 청중 앞에서 말할 때는

The general rule is, /
일반적인 규칙은 /

the bigger the audience, / the bigger the motion.
청중의 규모가 크면 클수록 / 동작이 더욱 더 커진다는 점이다.

This is so difficult for people, /
이것이 사람들에게 너무 어렵다. /

especially businesspeople /
특히 사업가들에게 /

whose general style is that of understatement, /
그들의 일반적인 스타일은 말을 적게 하는 스타일이어서 /

that they should take an acting course /
그들은 연기 수업을 받아야 한다 /

before they take a speech course.
연설 수업을 받기 전에

대부분의 아마추어 연사들은 무대에 있을 때 자신들이 배우 노릇을 해야 한다는 것을 이해하지 못한 다. 대부분의 연사들은 일대일로 말할 때보다 무대에서 더 강력하게 말해야 한다는 생각은 갖고 있지만, 언어적 유창함이 비언어적 유창함과 어울려야 한다는 것은 깨닫지 못한다. 한 사람에게 말할 때 어떤 부분을 강조하기 위해 손을 2인치 움직인다면, 많은 청중 앞에서 말할 때는 손을 2피트만큼이나 움직여야 할지도 모른다. 일반적인 규칙은 청중의 규모가 크면 클수록 동작이 더욱 더 커진다는 점이다. 이것이 사람들, 특히 말을 적게 하는 것이 일반적인 스타일인 사업가들에게는 너무 어려워서, 그들은 연설 수업을 받기 전에 연기 수업을 받아야 한다.

문제풀이

(A) 같은 동사의 반복을 피하기 위해 일반동사 speak를 대신하여 대동사 do를 사용하여야 한다.
(B) 부사절 when (you are) speking to~ 문장에서 「주어+be 동사」가 생략되어 있으므로 when 뒤에는 speaking을 써야 한다.
(C) 'so ~ that' 구문이 되어야 하므로 that이 옳다.

《 어휘 · 어구 》

verbal 말의, 언어적인
nonverbal 비언어적인
eloquence 화술, 설득력
emphasize 강조하다
understatement 삼가서 말을 함

---

4. ⑤   'jack-of-all-trades(만물박사)' 표현의 유래

직독/직해

The phrase, 'jack-of-all-trades' /
'jack-of-all-trades(만물박사)'라는 말은 /

is a shortened version / 축약된 형태이다.

of 'jack of all trades and master of none.'
'jack of all trades and master of none(모든 일을 다 잘하지만 정말 잘하는 것은 없는 사람)'이

It refers to those / who claim to be proficient /
그것은 사람들을 가리킨다. / 능숙하다고 주장하지만. /

at countless tasks,/ 수많은 업무에 /

but cannot perform a single one of them well.
그것들 중 한 가지도 잘 수행하지 못하는

The phrase was first used in England/
이 말은 영국에서 처음 사용되었다.

at the start of the Industrial Revolution.
산업혁명이 시작될 때에

A large number of efficiency experts /
많은 수의 효율성 전문가들이 /

set up shop in London, / 런던에 사무소를 차렸다.

advertising themselves / as knowledgeable /
자신들을 광고하면서 / 잘 알고 있다고 /

about every type of new manufacturing process,/
모든 유형의 새로운 제조 과정,

trade, and business. 무역, 사업에 대해

For a substantial fee, / 상당한 액수의 비용을 받고, /

they would impart their knowledge /
그들은 자신의 지식을 알려주곤 했다. /

to their clients. 고객들에게

But it soon became evident /
하지만 얼마 안 가서 사실이 분명해졌다.

that their knowledge was limited /
그들의 지식은 제한되어 있으며 /

and of no practical value.
현실적으로 아무런 가치가 없다는 (사실이)

Doubtful industrialists started calling /
의심을 품게 된 생산업자들은 부르기 시작했다 /

these self-appointed experts /
이러한 자칭 전문가라고 주장하는 사람들을

'jacks of all trades and masters of none.'
'jacks of all trades and masters of none'이라고

These experts are still with us, /
이러한 전문가들은 아직도 우리 주변에 있으며, /

and as a result so is the phrase.
그 결과 이 말 또한 우리 곁에 있다.

'jack-of-all-trades(만물박사)'라는 말은 'jack of all trades and master of none(모든 일을 다 잘하지만 정말 잘하는 것은 없는 사람)'이 축약된 형태이다. 그것은 수많은 업무에 능숙하다고 주장하지만, 그것들 중 한 가지도 잘 수행하지 못하는 사람들을 가리킨다. 이 말은 산업혁명이 시작될 때에 영국에서 처음 사용되었다. 많은 수의 효율성 전문가들이 모든 유형의 새로운 제조 과정, 무역, 사업에 대해 잘 알고 있다고 자신들을 광고하면서 런던에 사무소를 차렸다. 상당한 액수의 비용을 받고, 그들은 자신의 지식을 고객들에게 알려주곤 했다. 하지만 얼마 안 가서 그들의 지식은 제한되어 있으며 현실적으로 아무런 가치가 없다는 사실이 분명해졌다. 의심을 품게 된 생산업자들은 이러한 자칭 전문가라고 주장하는 사람들을 'jacks of all trades and masters of none'이라고 부르기 시작했다. 이러한 전문가들은 아직도 우리 주변에 있으며, 그 결과 이 말 또한 우리 곁에 있다.

문제풀이

① shortened는 형용사로서 '축약된'의 의미이다.
② 관계대명사절 안의 동사는 선행사와 수를 일치시킨다. 선행사가 those이므로 복수동사가 필요하다.
③ as they advertised ~ 문장을 분사구문으로 바꾼 문장이다.
④ 형용사 evident(명백한)는 became 동사의 보어로 사용되었다.
⑤ **앞에 be동사가 쓰였으므로 대동사 does를 is로 고쳐 써야 한다.** 「so+동사+주어」는 '~도 또한 그렇다'는 의미이다.

《 어휘·어구 》

jack-of-all-trades 만물박사
proficient 능숙한, 숙달된
knowledgeable 식견이 있는
substantial 실질적인, 내용이 풍부한
self-appointed 자칭의, 혼자 생각의

---

5. ①   내 인생의 첫 자동차 경주 관람

직독/직해

I was five years old / 내가 다섯 살 때였다.

when my father introduced me to motor sports.
나의 아빠가 나에게 자동차 경주에 대해 소개한 것은

Dad thought it was a normal family outing /
아빠는 정상적인 가족 외출이라고 생각했다.

to go to a car racing event.
자동차 경주 대회에 가는 것이

It was his way of spending some quality time /
그것은 좋은 시간을 보내는 아빠의 방식이었다.

with his wife and kids.
아내와 아이들과 함께

Little did he know / 그는 결코 알지 못했다. /

that he was fueling his son with a passion /
그가 아들에게 열정을 불어 넣고 있다는 사실을

that would last for lifetime.
평생토록 계속될

I still remember that awesome feeling /
나는 최고의 감정을 여전히 기억한다. /

I had on / that day in May
내가 느꼈던 / 5월의 그날

when my little feet carried me up the stairs
나의 작은 발이 나를 계단으로 이끌었던

into the grandstands at the car racing stadium.
자동차 대회 경기장에 있는 특별관람석으로 이르는

나의 아빠가 나에게 자동차 경주에 대해 소개한 것은 내가 다섯 살 때였다. 아빠는 자동차 경주대회에 가는 것이 정상적인 가족 외출이라고 생각했다. 그것은 아내와 아이들과 함께 좋은 시간을 보내는 아빠의 방식이었다. 그는 아들에게 평생토록 계속될 열정을 불어 넣고 있다는 사실을 결코 알지 못했다. 나는 나의 작은 발이 나를 자동차 대회 경기장에 있는 특별관람석으로 이르는 계단으로 이끌었던 5월의 그날 내가 느꼈던 최고의 감정을 여전히 기억한다.

문제풀이

(A) It~to 가주어, 진주어 구문이다. 문장 뒤에 나오는 진주어 to go to a car~를 대신할 수 있는 가주어 it이 문장 앞에 필요하다.
(B) He little knew that ~ 에서 부정의 의미를 지닌 부사인 little을 강조하기 위해 문장의 앞부분으로 옮긴 도치 구문이다. He few knew that ~ 이라고 쓰지 못하므로 little이 적절하다.
(C) 바로 다음에 오는 목적어 me를 취할 수 있는 타동사 carried 가 적절하다. my little feet가 carry의 주체이므로 수동태가 필요한 곳이 아니다.

《 어휘·어구 》

outgoing 외출
passion 열정
awesome 근사한, 멋진
grandstand 특별관람석

---

6. ⑤   빅 데이터의 잠재력과 위험

직독/직해

Although technology can't be blamed for the passion for growth, /
성장에 대한 열망을 기술 탓으로 돌릴 수는 없지만 /

---

it is a great enabler.
그것은 굉장한 동력이다

We are only just beginning to realize the potential of big data: /
우리는 빅데이터의 잠재력을 깨닫기 시작하고 있을 뿐이다 /

its capacity to deliver highly customized content and products /
즉 고도로 주문 제작된 내용과 제품을 전달할 수 있는 그것의 능력을 /

and to predict human behavior.
그리고 인간의 행동을 예측할 수 있는

The vast accumulation of personal data /
개인 데이터의 막대한 축적은 /

by Google, Amazon, Apple, and national governments /
구글, 아마존, 애플, 그리고 정부에 의한 /

promises everything /
모든 것을 약속한다 /

from automated, personalized health care to preventative law enforcement.
자동화되고 개인화된 건강 관리로부터 예방적 법 집행까지

But with these tantalizing powers /
그러나 이러한 흥미를 부추기는 힘과 함께 /

come, necessarily, big risks.
필연적으로 위기가 온다.

Just as Apple computers used to be safer from viruses /
애플 컴퓨터가 바이러스로부터 더 안전했듯 /

because there were relatively fewer of them /
그 수가 상대적으로 적었기 때문에 /

— which made them not worth attacking /
그것은 그것들을 공격할 가치가 없도록 만들어서 /

— so the vast accumulation of personal data makes it an irresistible target /
개인 데이터의 막대한 축적은 그것이 거부할 수 없는 표적이 되도록 만든다 /

for hackers and malware.
해커와 악성 소프트웨어의

Governments and regulators worry about the personal information /
정부와 규제 기관은 개인 정보에 대해 걱정한다 /

stored and exploited by Google, /
구글에 의해 저장되고 활용되는 /

but it is precisely the scale of the accumulation of this information /
하지만 바로 이러한 정보 축적의 규모이다 /

that makes Google's servers such tempting targets.
구글 서버가 그토록 유혹적인 목표가 되게 만드는 것은

성장에 대한 열망을 기술 탓으로 돌릴 수는 없지만, 그것은 굉장한 동력이다. 우리는 빅데이터의 잠재력, 즉 고도로 주문 제작된 내용과 제품을 전달할 수 있고 인간의 행동을 예측할 수 있는 그것의 능력을 깨닫기 시작하고 있을 뿐이다. 구글, 아마존, 애플, 그리고 정부에 의한 개인 데이터의 막대한 축적은 자동화되고 개인화된 건강 관리로부터 예방적 법 집행까지 모든 것을 약속한다. 그러나 이러한 흥미를 부추기는 힘과 함께, 필연적으로 위기가 온다. 애플 컴퓨터의 수가 상대적으로 적었기 때문에, 즉 그것들을 공격할 가치가 없도록 바이러스로부터 더 안전했듯, 개인 데이터의 막대한 축적은 그것이 해커와 악성 소프트웨어의 거부할 수 없는 표적이 되도록 만든다. 정부와 규제 기관은 구글에 의해 저장되고 활용되는 개인 정보에 대해 걱정하지만, 이러한 정보 축적의 규모가 바로 구글 서버가 그토록 유혹적인 목표가 되게 만드는 것이다.

문제풀이

① [분사]
customized는 content and products를 수식하는 분사로 '내용과 제품이 주문 제작된' 수동의 의미이므로 과거분사를 쓴 것은 올바른 용법이다.
② [동사의 수]
promises는 단수 명사 The vast accumulation을 주어로 받는 동사이므로 단수 동사 promises는 적절하게 사용되었다.
③ [도치 구문]
전치사구 'with these tantalizing powers'가 문두에 위치하여 '주어, 동사'가 도치된 문장이다. 주어가 복수 명사 'big risks'이므로 복수 동사 'come'은 적절하게 사용되었다.
④ [목적어를 취하는 형용사 worth]
worth는 목적어를 취하는 형용사이므로 목적어로 쓰인 동명사 'attacking'은 올바른 용법이다.

---

⑤ ['it ~ that' 강조구문]

but 뒤에 이어지는 절은 'it be ~ that' 강조구문으로 'precisely the scale of the accumulation of this information'이 강조되고 있는 구조이므로, what을 it으로 고쳐야 한다.

《 어휘 · 어구 》

potential 잠재력
customize 주문 제작하다
preventative law enforcement 예방적 법 집행
irresistible 거부할 수 없는
exploit 활용하다

---

7. ⑤ 인간이 음악적이게 된 이유

직독/직해

Charles Darwin, / the 19th century naturalist and
Charles Darwin은 / 19세기 동식물 연구가이자 진화 생물학의 아버지인 /
father of evolutionary biology, /
was one of the first to try to explain /
(~를) 설명하려고 처음으로 시도한 사람들 중 한 사람이었다 /
why humans became musical.
인간이 왜 음악적이게 되었는지를
In his 1871 book on evolutionary theory, /
진화론에 관한 그의 1871년 저서인 /
The Descent of Man, and Selection in Relation to
'인간의 유래 및 성에 관한 선택'에서 /
Sex, / he proposed it was analogous to bird song, /
그는 그것이 새의 지저귐과 비슷했다고 제시했다 /
in that it helped males attract mates /
그것이 수컷이 짝을 유혹하는 데 도움을 준다는 점에서 /
and warn off rivals.
그리고 경쟁자에게 가까이 오지 말라고 경고하는 데
The idea has now largely fallen out of fashion,
하지만 그 생각은 이제 대부분 유행이 지났다 /
though, /
because singing is not an exclusively male pastime: /
노래하는 것이 수컷만을 위한 취미 활동은 아니기 때문이다 /
in almost three-quarters of songbirds, for instance, /
예를 들어, 지저귀는 새의 거의 4분의 3의 경우에 /
females sing, too. 암컷 역시 지저귄다
More recently Thomas Geissmann /
좀 더 최근에 Thomas Geissmann은 /
at the University of Zurich in Switzerland, /
스위스에 있는 Zurich 대학의 /
came up with another interesting theory.
또 다른 흥미로운 이론을 제안했다
In a book published in the year 2000, /
2000년에 출판된 책에서 /
he pointed out that the four other singing primates /
그는 노래하는 4개의 다른 영장류들은 (~한다고) 지적했다 /
[some lemurs, tarsiers, titi monkeys and gibbons] /
(일부 여우원숭이, 안경원숭이, 티티원숭이, 그리고 긴팔원숭이)
all form monogamous breeding pairs /
모두 일부일처를 통해 새끼를 기르는 쌍을 이룬다(고) /
— as do many humans, / 많은 인간들이 그러는 것처럼 /
and amongst birds duetting /
그리고 새 가운데 이중창을 하는 새는 /
mainly occurs in monogamous species.
일부일처제를 이루는 종에서 주로 발견된다(고)
Perhaps, Geissmann suggested, /
어쩌면, Geissmann이 보여 주었듯이 /
singing is somehow related to the evolution of
노래하는 것이 어떻게든 일부일처제의 발전과 관련이 있다 /
monogamy /
— although exactly how or why is still unclear.
~이기는 하지만, 정확한 방식이나 이유는 여전히 불분명하다

19세기 동식물 연구가이자 진화 생물학의 아버지인 Charles Darwin은 인간이 왜 음악적이게 되었는지를 설명하려고 처음으로 시도한 사람들

중 한 사람이었다. 진화론에 관한 그의 1871년 저서 '인간의 유래 및 성에 관한 선택'에서, 그는 그것이 수컷이 짝을 유혹하고 경쟁자에게 가까이 오지 말라고 경고하는 데 도움을 준다는 점에서, 새의 지저귐과 비슷했다고 제시했다. 하지만 그 생각은 이제 대부분 유행이 지났는데, 노래하는 것이 수컷만을 위한 취미 활동은 아니기 때문이다. 예를 들어, 지저귀는 새의 거의 4분의 3의 경우에, 암컷 역시 지저귄다. 좀 더 최근에 스위스에 있는 Zurich 대학의 Thomas Geissmann은 또 다른 흥미로운 이론을 제안했다. 2000년에 출판된 책에서, 그는 노래하는 4개의 다른 영장류들(일부 여우원숭이, 안경원숭이, 티티원숭이, 그리고 긴팔원숭이)은, 많은 인간들이 그러는 것처럼, 모두 일부일처를 통해 새끼를 기르는 쌍을 이루고, 새들 가운데 이중창을 하는 새는 일부일처제를 이루는 종에서 주로 발견된다고 지적했다. Geissmann이 보여 주었듯이, 어쩌면 노래하는 것이 어떻게든 일부일처제의 발전과 관련이 있기는 하지만, 정확한 방식이나 이유는 여전히 불분명하다.

문제풀이

① the first를 수식하는 to부정사로, to try는 적절하다.
②「in that ~」은 '~라는 점에서'라는 뜻의 이유를 나타내는 부사절을 이끄는 표현으로, that의 쓰임은 적절하다.
③ 뒷부분에 암컷 역시 지저귄다는 내용이 이어지는 것으로 보아 형용사 male을 수식하는 부사로 exclusively는 적절하다.
④ 뒤에 나오는 단수 명사 theory를 수식하는 형용사로 another는 적절하다.
⑤ 문맥상 앞에 있는 that절의 동사 form을 대신하는 대동사가 와야 하므로 **are를 do로 고쳐 써야 한다.** 따라서 정답은 ⑤이다.

《 어휘 · 어구 》

naturalist 동식물 연구가
evolutionary biology 진화 생물학
propose 제안하다, 제의하다
analogous to ~와 비슷한
warn off ~에게 가까이 오지 말라고 경고하다
exclusively 오로지, 오직 ~뿐
pastime 취미 활동, 여가 활동
primate 영장류
lemur 여우원숭이
tarsier 안경원숭이
gibbon 긴팔원숭이
monogamy 일부일처제

---

8. ② 통제감이 신경 과학에 미치는 영향

신경 과학은 우리가 통제하고 있는 경험을 더 많이 할수록, 우리의 고차원적 뇌가 더 잘 기능한다는 것을 보여 주었다. 우리가 실질적인 뇌의 둔화와 봉착할 때는 바로 우리가 통제할 수 없는 것들에 의해 영향을 받고, 차이를 만들어 낼 어떤 것도 통제하고 있다는 감각을 되찾을 수 없을 때이다. 여러분은 왜 삶에서 선택권이 거의 없다고 느끼는 사람들이 더 많이 포기하는 경향이 있고, 부정적인 소용돌이에 빠지는지를 알 수 있다. 그러나 만약 그들이 통제감을 되찾을 수 있다면, 아주 좋은 일들이 일어난다. 이것이 바로 지도자가 '만사를 자기 뜻대로 하려는 사람'이 되어야 하는 이유인데, 그것은 단지 우리가 보통 생각하는 방식으로서는 아니다. 만사를 자기 뜻대로 하려는 사람의 일반적인 의미는 모든 것을 통제하려고 하고, 주위의 모든 사람을 미치게 만드는 사람이다. 내가 여기서 의미하는 바는 자신의 사람들이 결과에 직접 영향을 끼치는 그들 자신의 활동을 추진할 수 있도록, 그들 자신에 대한 통제력을 회복하도록 돕는 것에 집중하게 집중하는 지도자이다.

문제풀이

①「the+비교급 ~, the+비교급 …」은 '~하면 할수록, 더욱 더 …하다'라는 의미를 나타낸다.
② **what** 바로 뒤의 문장에서 주어, 동사, 목적어가 모

두 있는 완벽한 절이 왔으므로, 선행사를 포함한 관계대명사 what은 올 수가 없다. 「It ~ that …」 강조구문에 의해 부사절인 when we are affected by ~ make a difference가 강조되고 있는 구문이므로, what은 that으로 고쳐야 한다.
③ why는 관계부사로 앞에 선행사 the reason이 생략되었다.
④ drives는 주격 관계대명사 who가 이끄는 관계대명사절의 동사로, and에 의해 tries와 병렬 연결되었다.
⑤ 전치사 of의 목적어 역할을 하면서, 앞에 나온 his or her people을 가리켜야 하므로, 재귀대명사 themselves는 어법상 적절하게 쓰였다.

《 구문 및 어휘 》

*2행 It is [when we are affected by things outside of our control — and cannot regain a sense of being in control of **anything** {that will make a difference}] — **that** we hit a real brain slowdown.
(1)「It ~ that …」 강조구문으로 부사절인 [when we are affected by ~ make a difference]를 It과 that 사이에 두어 강조했다.
(2) when이 이끄는 부사절에서 동사로 are affected와 cannot regain이 접속사 and로 병렬 연결되었다.
(3) {that will make a difference}는 anything을 수식하는 주격 관계대명사절이다.
*5행 You can see [why people {who feel like they have little choice in life} are more **apt to give up** and **go** into negative spirals}].
(1) [why people who feel like they have little choice ~ go into negative spirals]는 see의 목적어 역할을 하는 의문사절이다.
(2) {who feel like they have little choice in life}는 why가 이끄는 의문사절 안에서 주어인 people을 수식하는 주격 관계대명사절이고, 동사로 are apt to give up과 go가 접속사 and로 병렬 연결되었다.
(3)「be apt to부정사」는 '~하기 쉽다'라는 의미를 나타내는 표현이다.
*12행 [What I mean here] is a leader [who obsessively focuses on helping his or her people get back in control of themselves, **to drive** their own activities {that directly affect outcomes}].
(1) [What I mean here]는 선행사를 포함하는 관계대명사 What이 이끄는 관계사절로, 문장에서 주어 역할을 하고, 동사는 is이다.
(2) who가 이끄는 절은 a leader를 수식하는 주격 관계대명사절이다.
(3) 준사역동사 help의 목적격보어로 동사원형인 get이 쓰였다.
(4) to drive는 to부정사로 목적을 나타내는 부사적 용법으로 쓰였다.
(5) {that directly affect outcomes}는 their own activities를 수식하는 주격 관계대명사절이다.

neuroscience 신경 과학
slowdown 둔화
be apt to ~하기 쉽다
spiral 소용돌이
control freak 만사를 자기 뜻대로 하려는 사람
obsessively 집요하게

9. ⑤ 측정 능력을 판단 능력과 결합하는 유일한 감각 기관인 귀

눈은 표면에서 보지만, 귀는 표면 아래로 침투하는 경향이 있다. Joachim-Ernst Berendt는 자신의 책에서 귀는 측정 능력을 판단 능력과 결합하는 유일한 감각 기관이라고 지적하고 있다. 서로 다른 색깔은 우리가 분간할 수 있지만, 여러 다른 소리에 정확한 '숫자'를 부여할 수 있다. 우리 눈은 우리가 이런 종류의 정확성을 가지고 지각하도록 해주지는 않는다. 음악에 소질이 없는 사람이라도 한 옥타브를 인지할 수 있고, 아마도 일단 배우게 되면 음정의 특성, 다시 말해서, 도 혹은 반음 높은 바를 인지할 수 있다. Berendt는 시각적 착각은 많지만 '청각적 착각', 즉 어떤 것이 사실은 그것이 아닌 어떤 것처럼 들리는 일은 거의 없다는 것을 지적한다. 귀는 거짓말을 하지 않는다. 청각은 보이지 않는 근원적인 사물의 질서와 우리를 놀라울 정도로 연결시켜 준다. 귀를 통해서 우리는 우리 주변에 있는 모든 것의 근저에 있는 진동에 접근하게 된다. 상대방의 음성의 어조와 음악적 음향을 감지하는 것은 그 사람에 대해, 그 사람의 삶에 대한 태도나 의향에 대해 엄청난 양의 정보를 우리에게 준다.

문제풀이

(A) ⟨fuse ~ with …⟩는 '~을 …와 결합[융합]하다'라는 의미이고, ⟨replace A with B⟩는 'A를 B로 대체하다'라는 의미이다. 뒤에 이어지는 청각의 예가 측정 능력과 판단 능력을 결합하는 내용이므로 문맥에 맞는 낱말로 적절한 것은 fuses이다.

(B) diversity는 '다양성'을 의미하고, precision은 '정확성'을 의미한다. 이어지는 내용에서 '청각적 착각'은 거의없다고 했으므로 문맥에 맞는 낱말로 적절한 것은 precision이다.

(C) underlie는 '~의 근저에 있다, ~의 기반이되다'라는 의미이고, undermine은 '~을 훼손[손상]하다'라는 의미이다. 우리 주변에 있는 모든 것의 근저에 있는 진동이라고 해야 글의 흐름이 자연스러우므로 문맥에 맞는 낱말로 적절한 것은 underlies이다.

《 어휘 · 어구 》

penetrate 침투하다, 스며들다
measure 측정하다
discern 분간하다, 차이를 식별하다
unmusical 음악에 소질이 없는
tone 음정, 음색
illusion 착각, 환각
optical 시각의
stance 태도, 자세

10. ② 개구리 왕자 이야기

"개구리 왕자" 이야기에서 공주는 그녀가 좋아하는 공을 연못에서 잃어버린다. 그러나 개구리가 나타나서, 그녀의 식탁에서 밥을 먹고, 그녀의 컵에서 물을 마시고, 그녀의 침대에서 잠을 자도록 허락해 준다면, 그녀에게 공을 되찾아 주겠다고 약속한다. 공주는 그녀의 공을 절실하게 다시 찾고 싶어서, 그에게 동의한다. 그러나 그 다음 날 개구리가 그녀의 문에 나타났을 때, 그녀는 진실해야 하고 약속을 이행해야 한다는 생각에 혐오감이 든다. 그러나 왕인 그녀의 아버지가 그녀에게 선택권을 주지 않아서 그녀는 그녀의 약속을 수행할 수밖에 없다. 약속이 수행되었을 때 그 개구리는 사라지고, 그 자리는 멋진 왕자가 차지하게 되고, 공주는 그와 사랑에 빠진다. 비록 그녀의 아버지의 고집에 의한 것이었지만, 그녀가 진실되고 약속을 지킨 것에 감사해서, 그 왕자는 공주와 결혼해서 그 후로 행복하게 산다.

문제풀이

(A)에는 공을 찾고 싶은 마음이므로 Desperate이 적절하다.
(B)에는 자신에게는 선택권이 없으므로 어쩔 수 없이 할 수밖에 없는 상황이므로 compelled가 적절하다.
(C)에는 자신의 의지가 아닌 아버지의 고집이라는 내용이 문맥상 적절하므로 insistence가 적절하다.

《 어휘 · 어구 》

---

ball 공
pond 연못
promise 약속하다
retrieve 되찾다
desperate 필사적인
unwilling 꺼리는
prospect 예상
fulfill 완수하다
indifference 무관심
insistence 고집

11. ③ 좋은 사회적 관계를 유지하는 것은 죄책감에 대한 수용 능력에 달려 있다

연구자들은 사회적으로 좋은 관계를 유지하는 것이 두 가지 상호보완적인 과정, 즉 타인의 요구에 민감한 것과 위반 행위가 정말로 생기면 보상이나 배상이 가능하도록 자극을 받는 것에 달려 있다는 점을 언급해왔다. 요약하면, 좋은 사회적 관계를 유지하는 것은 죄책감에 대한 수용 능력에 달려 있다. Martin L. Hoffman은, 타인에게 해를 입히면 생기는 죄책감에 초점을 맞춰 왔는데, 그는 이러한 죄책감에 대해 동기가 유발되는 기반은 고통의 공감이라고 시사한다. 고통의 공감은 자신들의 행동이 다른 사람에게 손해나 고통을 일으켰음을 부인할(→깨달을) 때 생긴다. 죄책감으로 인해 자극을 받을 때, 사람들은 자신의 행동에 대해 보상을 하려는 경향이 있다. 보상하는 것은 손상된 사회적 관계를 회복하고 집단의 화합을 복원하는 역할을 한다.

문제풀이

Martin L. Hoffman은 죄책감에 대해 동기 유발 기반은 (타인의) 고통의 공감이라고 시사했다. 그런데 고통의 공감은 자신의 행동이 다른 사람에게 손해나 고통을 일으켰음을 깨달을 때 생긴다. 따라서 문맥상 낱말의 쓰임이 적절하지 않은 것은 ③번이다.

《 어휘 · 어구 》

researcher 연구자
complementary 상호보완적인, 보충하는
sensitive 민감한, 예민한
make amends 보상하다
compensation 배상, 변상
capacity 수용 능력
guilt 죄책감, 죄의식
empathetic 공감할 수 있는, 감정 이입의
distress 고민, 고통

12. ④ 비대중화된 사회에서의 합의의 붕괴

직독 직해

The rise of diversity means / 다양성의 부상은 의미한다 /
that, although our political systems are theoretically
우리의 정치 체계가 이론적으로 다수결 원칙에 기초를 두고 있지만 /
founded on majority rule, /
it may be impossible to form a majority /
다수를 형성하는 것이 불가능할지도 모른다는 것을 /
even on issues crucial to survival.
생존에 중요한 문제들에 대해서조차
In turn, / this collapse of consensus means /
결국 / 이런 합의의 붕괴는 의미한다 /
that more and more governments are minority
점점 더 많은 정부가 소수의 정부라는 것을
governments, / based on shifting and uncertain coalitions.
/ 변하기 쉽고 불안정한 연합에 바탕을 둔
The missing majority / makes a mockery of standard
사라지는 다수는 / 일반적인 민주주의의 수사적 표현을 조롱거리로 만든다
democratic rhetoric.
It forces us to question /
그것은 우리에게 질문을 하지 않을 수 없게 한다 /
whether, under the convergence of speed and
속도와 다양성의 수렴 하에

---

diversity, / any constituency can ever be "represented."
/ 과연 어떤 유권자가 '대표될' 수 있는지
In a mass industrial society, / 대중 산업 사회에서 /
when people and their needs were fairly uniform
사람들과 그들의 욕구가 상당히 동일하고 기본적인 것이었을 때
and basic, / consensus was an attainable goal.
/ 합의가 달성 가능한 목표였다
In a demassified society, / we not only lack national
비대중화된 사회에서 / 우리는 국가적인 목표가 거의 없을 뿐만 아니라
purpose, / we also lack regional, statewide, or
/ 지역의, 주 전체의, 또는 도시 전체의 목표도 거의 없다
citywide purpose.
The diversity in any congressional district or
어떤 의회 지역구 또는 의회 선거구에서 다양성이 /
parliamentary constituency, /
whether in France, Japan or Sweden, / is so great /
프랑스에서든 일본이나 스웨덴에서든 / 너무나도 커서 /
that its "representative" cannot legitimately claim /
그것의 '대표자'는 정당하게 주장할 수 없다 /
to speak for a consensus. 대다수의 의견을 대변한다고
He or she cannot represent the general will /
대표자는 일반적인 의사를 대표할 수 없다 /
for the simple reason that there is none.
그런 것이 없다는 간단한 이유 때문에
What, then, happens / 그렇다고 한다면, 무슨 일이 일어나는 것인가 /
to the very notion of "representative democracy"?
'대의 민주주의'라는 바로 그 개념에

다양성의 부상은 우리의 정치 체계가 이론적으로 다수결 원칙에 기초를 두고 있지만, 생존에 중요한 문제들에 대해서조차 다수를 형성하는 것이 불가능할지도 모른다는 것을 의미한다. 결국, 이런 합의의 붕괴는 점점 더 많은 정부가, 변하기 쉽고 불안정한 연합에 바탕을 둔 소수의 정부라는 것을 의미한다. 사라지는 다수는 일반적인 민주주의의 수사적 표현을 조롱거리로 만든다. 그것은 우리에게 속도와 다양성의 수렴 하에, 과연 어떤 유권자가 '대표될' 수 있는지 질문을 하지 않을 수 없게 한다. 대중 산업 사회에서, 사람들과 그들의 욕구는 상당히 동일하고 기본적인 것이었을 때, 합의가 달성 가능한 목표였다. 비대중화된 사회에서, 우리는 국가적인 목표가 거의 없을 뿐만 아니라, 지역의, 주 전체의, 또는 도시 전체의 목표도 거의 없다. 프랑스에서든 일본이나 스웨덴에서든, 어떤 의회 지역구 또는 의회 선거구에서 다양성이 너무나도 희귀해서(→ 커서) 그것의 '대표자'가 대다수의 의견을 대변한다고 정당하게 주장할 수 없다. 대표자는 그런 것이 없다는 간단한 이유 때문에 일반적인 의사를 대표할 수 없다. 그렇다고 한다면, '대의 민주주의'라는 바로 그 개념에 무슨 일이 일어나는 것인가?

문제풀이

대중 산업 사회에서는 사람들의 욕구가 상당히 동일하고 기본적인 것이어서 합의에 이르는 것이 가능했지만, 비대중화된 사회에서는 전체의 목표가 거의 없어서 합의라는 것이 불가능하고 어떤 대표라도 자신이 대다수의 의사를 대변한다고 주장할 수 없다고 했다. 이것은 다양성이 너무 희귀해서(rare)가 아니라 너무 다양해서 일 것이므로, ④ 'rare'는 문맥상 적절하지 않다.

《 어휘 · 어구 》

diversity 다양성
theoretically 이론적으로
majority 다수
crucial 중요한, 결정적인
consensus 합의
minority 소수
rhetoric 수사적 표현
convergence 수렴, 집중
demassify 비(非)대중화하다, 비획일화하다
congressional 의회의
district 지구, 지역
parliamentary 의회의
speak for ~을 대변하다

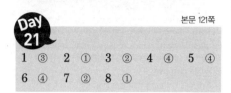

미니 고난도 Test 1회

본문 121쪽

Day 21

| 1 ③ | 2 ① | 3 ② | 4 ④ | 5 ④ |
| 6 ④ | 7 ② | 8 ① | | |

---

1. ③   수학 지도에서 고려해야 할 점

직독/직해

Mathematical practices and discourses should be situated /
수학 연습과 담화는 위치되어야 한다 /

within cultural contexts, student interests, and real-life situations /
문화적 맥락, 학생 관심사, 그리고 실생활 상황 안에 /

where all students develop positive identities /
모든 학생이 긍정적인 정체성을 발달시키는 /

as mathematics learners.
수학 학습자로서

Instruction in mathematics skills / in isolation /
수학 기술을 지도하는 것은 / 고립적으로 /

and devoid of student understandings and identities /
그리고 학생들의 이해와 정체성이 결여된 채 /

renders them helpless /
그들이 무력하게 만든다 /

to benefit from explicit instruction.
명시적 지도로 이익을 얻는 데

Thus, we agree / 그러므로 우리는 동의한다 /

that explicit instruction benefits students /
명시적 지도가 학생들에게 유익하다는 것에는 /

but propose / 하지만 제안한다 /

that incorporating culturally relevant pedagogy /
문화적으로 적절한 교수법을 포함하는 것이 /

and consideration of nonacademic factors /
그리고 비학습 영역에 대한 고려를 (포함하는 것이) /

that promote learning and mastery /
학습 및 숙달을 촉진하는 /

must enhance explicit instruction /
명시적 지도를 필연적으로 강화한다고 /

in mathematics instruction.
수학 지도에서

Furthermore, teachers play a critical role /
게다가 교사는 중요한 역할을 한다 /

in developing environments /
환경을 개발하는 데 /

that encourage student identities, agency, and independence /
학생의 정체성, 주체성, 그리고 독립심을 장려하는 /

through discourses and practices in the classroom.
교실에서의 담화와 연습을 통해

Students who are actively engaged /
적극적으로 참여하는 학생들은 /

in a contextualized learning process /
맥락화된 학습 과정에 /

are in control of the learning process /
학습 과정을 통제하고 있다 /

and are able to make connections /
그리고 연계를 맺을 수 있다 /

with past learning experiences /
과거 학습 경험과 /

to foster deeper and more meaningful learning.
그래서 더 깊고 더 의미 있는 학습을 촉진한다

수학 연습과 담화는 모든 학생이 수학 학습자로서 긍정적인 정체성을 발달시키는 문화적 맥락, 학생 관심사, 그리고 실생활 상황 안에 위치되어

야 한다. 수학 기술을 고립적으로 그리고 학생들의 이해와 정체성이 결여된 채 지도하는 것은 그들이 명시적 지도로 이익을 얻는 데 무력하게 만든다. 그러므로 우리는 명시적 지도가 학생들에게 유익하다는 것에는 동의하지만, 문화적으로 적절한 교수법과 학습 및 숙달을 촉진하는 비학습 영역에 대한 고려를 포함하는 것이 수학 지도에서 명시적 지도를 필연적으로 강화한다고 제안한다. 게다가 교사는 교실에서의 담화와 연습을 통해 학생의 정체성, 주체성, 그리고 독립심을 장려하는 환경을 개발하는 데 중요한 역할을 한다. 맥락화된 학습 과정에 적극적으로 참여하는 학생들은 학습 과정을 통제하고 있고, 과거 학습 경험과 연계를 맺을 수 있어서 더 깊고 더 의미 있는 학습을 촉진한다.

문제풀이

① [관계부사]
뒤에 주어(all students)와 목적어(positive identities)를 모두 갖춘 완전한 절이 왔으므로, 관계부사 where이 온 것이 적절하다.

② [목적격보어]
render의 목적격보어로는 형용사가 와야 하므로, helpless가 온 것이 적절하다.

③ [정동사 vs 준동사]
앞의 that은 선행사 nonacademic factors를 수식하는 주격 관계대명사로 뒤에 동사가 나와야 한다. 따라서 promoting를 promote로 고쳐 써야 한다.

④ [관계대명사]
뒤에 이어지는 절에서 주어 역할을 하며 선행사 environments를 수식하고 있으므로, 주격 관계대명사 that이 온 것은 적절하다.

⑤ [to부정사]
결과를 나타내는 부사적 용법 to부정사가 오는 것이 적절하므로, to foster가 온 것이 적절하다.

○ 이렇게 풀자 어법상 틀린 부분을 찾는 문제는 밑줄이 있는 부분의 형태와 문맥을 보고 어법에 맞게 쓰였는지 확인해야 한다.
① 관계부사에 밑줄이 있는 경우, 뒤에 문장 성분을 모두 갖춘 완전한 문장이 왔는지 확인해야 한다.
② 동사의 종류에 따라 목적격보어로 to부정사가 오기도 하고 동사원형이 오기도 한다. 앞에 나온 동사를 잘 파악하여 어법에 맞는지 판단해야 한다.
③ 밑줄이 그어진 부분이 문장에서 동사의 역할을 하는지, 아니면 형용사나 부사의 역할을 하는지 파악해야 한다.
④ 문장에서 관계대명사가 필요한 경우인지를 확인한 후, 선행사의 종류 및 격에 따라 적절하게 쓰였는지 살펴봐야 한다.
⑤ to부정사에 밑줄이 그어진 경우, 문장에서 명사, 형용사, 또는 부사의 역할을 하는지 파악한다.

어휘·어구

discourse 담화
context 맥락
identity 정체성
instruction 지도, 지시
isolation 고립
devoid of ~이 결여된
explicit 명시적
incorporate 포함하다
relevant 적절한, 관련 있는
factor 요소
promote 촉진하다
enhance 높이다, 향상시키다
critical 중요한
engage in ~에 참여하다
contextualize 맥락과 관련짓다
foster 촉진하다

---

2. ①   야구와 시간의 관계

전통 사회에서의 삶과 마찬가지로, 그러나 다른 팀 스포츠

와는 다르게, 야구는 시계에 의해 좌우되지 않는다. 미식 축구 경기는 정확히 60분 경기로 구성되고, 농구 경기는 40분이나 48분의 경기로 구성되지만, 야구에는 경기를 끝내야 하는 정해진 시간의 길이가 없다. 따라서 측정한 시간, 마감 기한, 일정, 시간 단위로 지급되는 임금과 같은 규율이 있기 이전의 세상과 마찬가지로 경기 속도가 여유롭고 느긋하다. 야구는 사람들이 "저는 시간이 많지 않아요."라고 말하지 않았던 그러한 종류의 세상에 속한다. 야구 경기는 '정말로' 온종일 경기가 진행된다. 그러나 그것이 그 경기가 영원히 계속될 수 있다는 것을 의미하는 것은 아니다. 전통적인 삶과 마찬가지로 야구는 자연의 리듬, 구체적으로 말하면 지구의 자전에 따라 진행된다. 그것(야구)의 첫 반세기 동안 경기가 밤에는 진행되지 않았는데, 그것은 야구 경기가 전통적인 근무일처럼 해가 질 때 끝났다는 것을 의미했다.

문제풀이

(A)는 be동사의 보어 자리이고, (A)와 병렬 구조를 이루고 있는 leisurely 역시 부사가 아닌 형용사이기 때문에 unhurried가 오는 것이 적절하다.
(B) 다음에 완전한 문장이 왔으므로, 관계부사의 역할을 하는 in which가 오는 것이 적절하다.
(C) that절의 주어인 baseball game 뒤에 동사가 와야 하므로 ended가 오는 것이 적절하다. like the traditional은 삽입된 전치사구이다. 따라서 정답은 ① 이다.

구문 및 어휘

*2행 A football game is comprised of exactly sixty minutes of play, **a basketball game forty or forty-eight minutes**, but baseball has no set length of time [**within which** the game must be completed].

⑴ be comprised of는 '~로 이루어져 있다'의 의미이다.
⑵ a basketball game과 forty or forty-eight minutes 사이에 is comprised of가 생략되어 있다.
⑶ within which는 선행사 time을 수식하는 관계대명사절이다. 관계대명사가 관계사절 안에서 전치사의 목적어로 쓰이는 경우, 전치사는 관계대명사 앞 또는 관계사절의 동사 뒤에 올 수 있다.

govern 좌우하다, 지배하다
be comprised of ~로 구성되다
leisurely 여유로운
unhurried 서두르지 않는, 느긋한
discipline 규율
belong to ~에 속하다
proceed 진행하다
according to ~에 따르면
specifically 구체적으로 말하면
rotation 자전, 회전

---

3. ②   식량 불안정의 원인

직독/직해

Food insecurity can be generated by dynamics / that may appear overall positive.
식량 불안정은 역학에 의해 발생할 수 있다 / 전반적으로 긍정적으로 보일 수도 있는

In many cities, / gentrification, /
많은 도시에서 / '고급 주택화'는 /

the process / through which whole neighborhoods are revitalized /
과정인 / 이웃 전체가 활성화되는 /

through the influx of higher-income inhabitants, /
고소득 주민들의 유입을 통해 /

has undesirable collateral effects.
바람직하지 않은 부차적 영향을 미친다.

The arrival of new dwellers / in previously low-income neighborhoods /
새로운 거주자의 도착은 / 이전에는 저소득이던 지역에 /

often pushes real estate, rent, services, and food costs up.
부동산, 임대료, 서비스, 그리고 음식 비용을 흔히 상승시킨다

Small farm-to-table restaurants, gourmet cafes, and natural food stores /
농장에서 식탁까지의 소규모 식당, 미식가 카페, 그리고 자연식품 가게들이 /

open to meet the needs and preferences of the newcomers.
새로 온 사람들의 요구와 선호를 충족시키기 위해 문을 연다

The markets / that cities had built in previous decades /
시장은   / 도시들이 지난 수십 년간 건설했던 /

to provide food for local dwellers of all walks of life /
각계각층의 지역 거주민들에게 음식을 제공하기 위해 /

are turned into glamorous food halls, leisure places /
화려한 식품 판매점, 여가 공간으로 변모한다 /

for affluent consumers and tourists.
부유한 소비자와 관광객을 위한

Abandoned factories /
버려진 공장 /

and whole neighborhoods previously dedicated to industrial activities
그리고 이전에 산업 활동에 전념했던 모든 지역이 /

become hubs /
중심지가 된다 /

for food innovation, creative manufacturing, and intriguing new restaurants.
음식 혁신, 창의적 제조, 그리고 흥미를 자아내는 새로운 식당의

However, / prices inevitably increase, /
그러나   / 가격은 불가피하게 오른다 /

making finding affordable food difficult.
저렴한 음식을 찾는 것이 어렵게 만들면서

The changes often end up forcing /
그 변화는 강요하는 것으로 끝나게 된다 /

the poorest segments of the preexisting communities /
기존 지역 사회의 가장 빈곤한 부문들로 하여금 /

to move to more affordable destinations.
더 저렴한 곳으로 이동하도록

식량 불안정은 전반적으로 긍정적으로 보일 수도 있는 역학에 의해 발생할 수 있다. 많은 도시에서, 고소득 주민들의 유입을 통해 이웃 전체가 활성화되는 과정인 '고급 주택화'는 바람직하지 않은 부차적 영향을 미친다. 이전에는 저소득이던 지역에 새로운 거주자들이 도착하면서 부동산, 임대료, 서비스, 그리고 음식 비용을 흔히 상승시킨다. 농장에서 식탁까지의 소규모 식당, 미식가 카페, 그리고 자연식품 가게들이 새로 온 사람들의 요구와 선호를 충족시키기 위해 문을 연다. 도시들이 지난 수십 년간 각계각층의 지역 거주민들에게 음식을 제공하기 위해 건설했던 시장은 화려한 식품 판매점, 부유한 소비자와 관광객을 위한 여가 공간으로 변모한다. 버려진 공장과 이전에 산업 활동에 전념했던 모든 지역이 음식 혁신, 창의적 제조, 그리고 흥미를 자아내는 새로운 식당의 중심지가 된다. 그러나 가격은 불가피하게 오르고, 저렴한 음식을 찾는 것이 어려워진다. 그 변화는 흔히 기존 지역 사회의 가장 빈곤한 부문들로 하여금 더 저렴한 곳으로 이동하도록 강요하는 것으로 끝나게 된다.

문제풀이

① [전치사 + 관계대명사]
관계대명사절인 'through which whole neighborhoods are revitalized~'에서 '전치사+관계대명사' 뒤의 문장이 'S+be+p.p'의 완전한 구조를 취하고 있으므로 'through which'는 올바르게 사용되었다. 선행사 'the process'를 대입하여 해석하면 '그 과정을 통해서 전체 이웃이 활성화되었다'가 된다.

② [주어 동사의 수 일치]
전치사구 of new dwellers in previously low-income neighborhoods의 수식을 받는 주어 부분의 핵심어는 단수 명사 arrival이므로, push는 단수 동사 pushes로 고쳐야 한다.

③ [수동태]

관계절 that ~ life의 수식을 받는 주어의 핵심어는 markets인데 그것이 turn의 행위를 당하는 대상이므로, 과거분사 turned는 적절하다.

④ [동명사]
결과의 의미를 나타내는 분사구문에서 동명사구 finding affordable food가 making의 목적어 역할을 하는 구조이므로, finding은 적절하다.

⑤ [목적보어로 쓰인 to부정사]
force는 5형식 동사로 'force+목+to부정사'를 취하므로 to move는 force의 목적보어로 쓰인 to부정사구로 적절하게 쓰였다.

《 어휘·어구 》

insecurity 불안정
revitalize 활성화하다
influx 유입, 흘러듦
real estate 부동산
farm-to-table 농장에서 식탁까지의(농장 직거래 운동으로 농장에서 재배한 유기농 농산물을 식탁에 올리는 운동)
all walks of life 사회 각계각층, 온갖 계층의 사람들
glamorous 화려한, 매력이 넘치는
affluent 부유한
intriguing 흥미를 자아내는
affordable 저렴한, (가격 등이) 알맞은

---

4. ④   물체를 바라보는 그리스인과 중국인의 다른 시각

그리스인들의 두드러진 물체와 그것의 속성에 대한 집중은 인과 관계의 근본적인 성질의 이해에 대한 실패로 이어졌다. 아리스토텔레스는 돌이 공중에서 떨어지는 이유는 돌이 '중력'이라는 성질을 갖고 있기 때문이라고 설명했다. 그러나 물론 물에 던져진 나무 조각은 가라앉는 대신 떠오른다. 아리스토텔레스는 이러한 현상을 나무가 '가벼움'이라는 성질을 갖고 있기 때문이라고 설명했다! 두 경우 모두, 그 물체 바깥의 어떤 힘이 관련되어 있을지도 모른다는 가능성에는 주의를 기울이지 않고, 오로지 그 물체에만 초점을 두고 있다. 그러나 중국인은 세계를 끊임없이 상호 작용하는 물질들로 이루어진 것으로 보았고, 따라서 그것을 이해하려 하는 그들의 시도는 그들로 하여금 전체적인 '장(場)', 다시 말해 전체 맥락이나 환경의 복잡성에 중점을 두도록 만들었다. 사건은 항상 힘이 작용하는 장에서 생겨난다는 개념은 중국인에게 전적으로 직관적이었을 것이다.

문제풀이

④ 등위접속사 so에 의해 두 개의 절이 연결되어 있는데, so 뒤의 절에서 their attempts to understand it이 주어이고 이에 이어지는 동사가 필요하므로, causing은 caused로 고쳐야 한다.

《 구문 및 어휘 》

*14행 The notion [**that** events always occur in a field of forces] would have been completely intuitive to the Chinese.

① [that ~ forces]는 주어인 The notion을 동격으로 설명하는 절로 이때 that은 접속사이다. would have been은 「would+have p.p.」 형태로 '~이었을 것이다'의 의미이다.

attribute 속성, 자질, 특질
fundamental 근본적인, 본질적인
causality 인과 관계, 상관성
property 성질, 속성

---

gravity 중력
oriented toward ~에 중점을 둔, ~을 지향하는
complexity 복잡성
notion 개념, 관념
intuitive 직관적인

---

5. ④   판단할 때, 단순한 공식의 중요성

직독/직해

There is evidence / 증거가 있다 /
that even very simple algorithms can outperform expert judgement /
심지어 매우 간단한 알고리즘도 전문가의 판단을 능가할 수 있다는 /
on simple prediction problems. 단순한 예측 문제에 대한
For example, / algorithms have proved more accurate than humans /
예를 들면   / 알고리즘이 인간보다 더 정확하다는 것이 증명했다 /
in predicting / whether a prisoner released on parole /
예측하는데   / 가석방으로 풀려난 죄수가 /
will go on to commit another crime, /
계속 다른 범죄를 저지를 것인지 /
or in predicting / whether a potential candidate will perform well /
또는 예측하는 데 / 잠재적인 지원자가 일을 잘할 것인지를 /
in a job in future. 장차 직장에서
In over 100 studies across many different domains, / half of all cases show /
많은 다른 영역에 걸친 100개가 넘는 연구에서 / 모든 경우의 절반은 보여 준다 /
simple formulas make better significant predictions / than human experts, /
단순한 공식이 중요한 예측을 더 잘한다는 것을 / 인간 전문가보다 /
and the remainder (except a very small handful), /
그리고 그 나머지(아주 적은 소수를 제외하고)는 /
show a tie between the two.
둘 사이의 무승부를 보여 준다
When there are a lot of different factors involved /
관련된 많은 다른 요인이 있을 때 /
and a situation is very uncertain, / simple formulas can win out /
그리고 상황이 매우 불확실할 때 / 단순한 공식이 승리할 수 있다 /
by focusing on the most important factors / and being consistent, /
가장 중요한 요소에 초점을 맞춤으로써 / 그리고 일관성을 유지함으로써 /
while human judgement is too easily influenced /
반면에 인간의 판단은 너무 쉽게 영향을 받는다 /
by particularly salient and perhaps irrelevant considerations.
특히 두드러지고 아마도 무관한 고려 사항에 의해
A similar idea is supported by further evidence /
유사한 아이디어가 추가적인 증거에 의해 뒷받침되고 있다 /
that 'checklists' can improve the quality of expert decisions / in a range of domains
'체크리스트'가 전문가의 판단의 질을 향상할 수 있다는 (증거에 의해) / 다양한 영역에서 /
by ensuring that important steps or considerations aren't missed /
중요한 단계나 고려 사항을 놓치지 않도록 함으로써 /
when people are feeling overloaded.
사람들이 일이 너무 많다고 느낄 때
For example, / treating patients in intensive care /
예를 들면   / 집중 치료 중인 환자를 치료하는 것은 /
can require hundreds of small actions per day, /
하루에 수백 가지의 작은 조치를 필요로 할 수 있다 /
and one small error could cost a life.
그런데 작은 실수 하나가 목숨을 잃게 할 수 있다
Using checklists / to ensure that no crucial steps are missed /
체크리스트를 사용하는 것은 / 어떤 중요한 단계도 놓치지 않기 위해 /
has proved to be remarkably effective / in a range of medical contexts, /
놀라울 정도로 효과적이라는 것이 증명되었다 / 다양한 의료 맥락에서 /

현저하게 효과적이라는 것이 입증되었다 / 다양한 의학적 상황에서 /
from preventing live infections to reducing pneumonia.
당면한 감염을 예방하는 것에서부터 폐렴을 줄이는 것에 이르기까지
- -

심지어 매우 간단한 알고리즘도 단순한 예측 문제에 대한 전문가의 판단을 능가할 수 있다는 증거가 있다. 예를 들면, 가석방으로 풀려난 죄수가 계속 다른 범죄를 저지를 것인지 예측하거나, 잠재적인 지원자가 장차 직장에서 일을 잘할 것인지를 예측하는 데 알고리즘이 인간보다 더 (a) 정확하다는 것이 증명했다. 많은 다른 영역에 걸친 100개가 넘는 연구에서, 모든 경우의 절반은 단순한 공식이 인간 전문가보다 중요한 예측을 (b) 더 잘하고, 그 나머지(아주 적은 소수를 제외하고는)는 둘 사이의 무승부를 보여준다. 관련된 많은 다른 요인이 있고 상황이 매우 불확실할 때, 가장 중요한 요소에 초점을 맞추고 일관성을 유지함으로써 단순한 공식이 승리할 수 있는 반면, 인간의 판단은 특히 두드러지고 아마도 (c) 무관한 고려 사항에 의해 너무 쉽게 영향을 받는다. 사람들이 (d) 편안하다고 (→ 일이 너무 많다고) 느낄 때 중요한 조치나 고려 사항을 놓치지 않도록 함으로써 '체크리스트'가 다양한 영역에서 전문가의 판단의 질을 향상할 수 있다는 추가적인 증거가 유사한 아이디어를 뒷받침한다. 예를 들면, 집중 치료 중인 환자를 치료하는 것은 하루에 수백 가지의 작은 조치를 필요로 할 수 있는데, 작은 실수 하나는 목숨을 잃게 할 수 있다. 어떤 중요한 단계도 놓치지 않게 체크리스트를 사용하는 것은 당면한 감염을 예방하는 것에서부터 폐렴을 줄이는 것에 이르기까지 다양한 의학적 상황에서 현저하게 (e) 효과적이라는 것이 입증되었다.

〖 어휘·어구 〗

outperform 능가하다, 더 나은 결과를 내다
accurate 정확한
commit (범죄를) 저지르다, 범하다
potential 잠재적인
candidate 후보, 지원자
domain 영역
remainder 나머지
handful 몇 안 되는 수
consistent 일관성이 있는
irrelevant 무관한
intensive care 집중 치료
cost 희생시키다, 잃게 하다
crucial 중요한
remarkably 현저하게, 뚜렷하게
live 당면한, 생생한
infection 감염
formula 공식
prioritise 우선순위를 매기다

👒 구조 다시보기

증거 1	의사 결정할 때 간단한 공식의 힘 1: 매우 간단한 알고리즘조차도 단순한 예측 문제에 대한 전문가의 판단을 능가할 수 있음
예시	가석방된 죄수가 다른 범죄를 저지를 것인지 예측하는 문제와 잠재적 지원자가 장차 직장에서 일을 잘할 것인지 예측하는 문제에서 알고리즘이 인간보다 더 정확하다는 것이 입증됨
증거 2	의사 결정할 때 간단한 공식의 힘 2: 다양한 영역의 100개가 넘는 사례 연구에서, 모든 사례의 절반은 단순한 공식이 인간 전문가보다 예측을 더 잘했고, 나머지는 무승부를 보여줌
주제	관련된 여러 요인이 있을 때 중요한 요소에 초점을 맞추고 일관성을 유지하는 간단한 공식은 무관한 고려 사항에 쉽게 영향을 받는 인간의 판단을 이길 수 있음
증거 3	의사 결정할 때 간단한 공식의 힘 3: 체크리스트를 마련해서 이용하면 다양한 영역에서 전문가의 결정의 질을 향상할 수 있음
예시	많은 조치가 필요한 집중 치료 중인 환자를 치료할 때 중요한 단계를 놓치지 않게 체크리스트를 사용하는 것이 효과적임

정답률 62%

5. ④

〖 문제풀이 〗

집중 치료를 받는 환자에게 하루에 수백 가지의 작

은 조치가 필요한 상황에서 어떤 중요한 것도 놓치지 않기 위해 체크리스트가 필요하다고 했는데, 이는 사람들이 처리할 일이 많을 때 중요한 조치를 놓치지 않도록 체크리스트를 만든다는 의미이다. 따라서 (d) 'relaxed(편안한)'를 'overloaded(일이 너무 많은)'와 같은 낱말로 바꾸어야 한다.

6. ④ | 접영의 탄생 배경

1920년대까지는 경쟁을 벌이는 수영 영법에는 자유형, 배영, 그리고 평영 이 세 가지밖에 없었고, 각 영법에는 그것이 어떻게 행해져야 하는가를 서술하는 구체적인 규칙들이 있었다. 평영의 규칙은 두 팔이 물 밑에서 함께 당겨져야 하고, 그런 다음 동시에 다음번 팔 젓기를 시작하기 위해서 당기는 자세의 출발로 돌아와야 한다고 진술했다. 대부분의 사람들은 이런 팔의 복귀를 물 밑 복귀를 뜻하는 것으로 이해했다. 그러나 1920년대 누군가가 그 규칙에 도전하여 이런 팔의 복귀를 물 밖 복귀를 뜻하는 것으로 재해석했다. 이런 새로운 평영이 약 15퍼센트나 더 느렸기(→ 더 빨랐기) 때문에, 전통적인 평영을 이용하는 사람들은 효과적으로 경쟁을 할 수 없었다. 그 문제를 해결하기 위해서 어떤 조치가 행해져야만 했다. 마침내, 현재 '접영'으로 알려진 이 새 영법은 네 번째 수영 영법으로 인정을 받게 되었고, 1956년에 올림픽 종목이 되었다.

〖 문제풀이 〗

새로운 평영이 약 15퍼센트나 '더 빨랐기' 때문에 전통적인 평영 영법을 하는 사람들이 효과적으로 경쟁을 할 수 없었던 것이므로, ④의 slower를 faster로 바꾸는 것이 문맥상 적절하다.

〖 어휘·어구 〗

competitive 경쟁을 벌이는, 경쟁의
stroke (수영의) 영법, 팔 젓기
freestyle 자유형
backstroke 배영
breaststroke 평영
conventional 전통적인
butterfly 접영

7. ② | 걱정은 지적 능력을 약화시킨다

걱정은 모든 종류의 정신적인 활동에 해로운 영향을 준다. 그것은 어떤 면에서 실패로 돌아간 유용한 반응 — 예상된 위협에 대한 지나치게 열성적인 정신적 준비이다. 그러나 그러한 정신적인 예행연습이 주의력을 빼앗아 다른 곳에 집중하려는 온갖 시도를 방해하는 진부한 일상에 사로잡힐 때, 그것은 파멸적인 인지적 정지 상태가 된다. 걱정은 지적 능력을 약화시킨다. 예를 들어 항공교통관제사와 같이 복잡하고 지적으로 힘들고 압박이 심한 업무에서는 만성적으로 많은 걱정을 하는 것은 그 사람이 결국 훈련이나 실전에서 실패할 것임을 거의 정확히 예언한다. 항공 교통관제사 훈련을 받는 1,790명의 학생에 대한 연구에서 밝혀진 바와 같이, 걱정이 많은 사람들은 지능검사에서 더 우수한 성적으로 받았을 때조차도 통과하지 못할 가능성이 높다. 걱정은 또한 모든 종류의 학업을 방해한다. 36,000명 넘게 대상으로 한 126가지의 다른 연구는 걱정에 빠지기 쉬운 사람일수록 학업 성취도가 더 부진하다는 것을 발견했다.

〖 문제풀이 〗

(A)에는 걱정에 사로잡히는 것은 정신적인 활동에 방해가 된다고 했으므로, disastrous(파멸을 초래하는)가 적절하다. constructive는 '건설적인'이라는 의미이다.
(B)에는 걱정과 불안을 지닌 사람은 지능 지수가 더 높더라도 실패할 가능성이 많다는 내용이 자연스러우므로, superior(더 우수한)가 적절하다. inferior는 '더 열등한'이라는 의미이다.
(C)에는 걱정에 빠지기 쉬운 사람일수록 학업 성취도가 낮다는 내용이 자연스러우므로, prone(하기 쉬운)이 적절하다. resistant는 '저항하는, 저항력이 있는'이라는 의미이다.

〖 어휘·어구 〗

---

zealous 열광적인
cognitive 인식의
static 공전 상태, 정지 상태
stale 진부한, 상해가는
intrude on ~에 끼어들다, 방해하다
demanding 지나친 요구를 하는
air traffic controller 항공교통관제사
chronically 만성적으로
sabotage 고의로 방해하다

8. ① | 오래된 옷이 개인에게 주는 의미

우리 중에서 물질 중심적이지 않다고 주장하는 사람들조차도 특정한 옷에 대한 애착을 형성하지 않을 수 없게 된다. 옛날 노래에 나오는 구절처럼 옷은 소중한 추억과 가슴 아픈 기억을 모두 생각나게 할 수 있다. 닳아서 얇아진 드레스는 여러 해 동안 입지 않았더라도 벽장 뒤편에 걸려 있을 수 있는데, 그 이유는 그 옷에 남아 있는 옅은 소나무 향이 바로 어떤 사람의 열여섯 살 여름의 모든 잔존물이기 때문이다. 실용성이 떨어지는 흰색 스카프는 그것의 소유자에게 한때 우아함에 대한 기대였기 때문에 기증품 자루에 들어가는 마지막 순간에 빼내어질 수 있다. 그리고 찢어진 티셔츠는 한때 그 위에 쓰여진 록밴드 이름이 희미해진 지 오래된 후에도 걸레통에서 꺼내어질 수 있다. 화석이 고고학자들에게 시간을 나타내는 것과 같은 방식으로 옷은 우리에게 개인의 이력을 보여준다.

〖 문제풀이 〗

(A) 옷이 소중한 추억과 가슴 아픈 기억을 '생각나게 할 수 있다'라는 의미가 되어야 하므로, evoke(기억·감정을) 불러일으키다가 적절하다. erase는 '(마음에서) 없애다, 잊어버리다'라는 의미이다.
(B) '실용성이 떨어지는' 흰색 스카프가 그것을 소유한 사람에게 한때 우아함의 기대였다는 의미가 되어야 하므로, impractical(비실용적인, 비현실적인)이 적절하다. brand-new는 '아주 새로운, 신품'이라는 의미이다.
(C) 찢어진 티셔츠가 한때 그 위에 쓰여진 록밴드 이름이 희미해진 후에도 걸레통에서 '꺼내어질 수' 있다는 의미가 되어야 하므로, rescued가 적절하다. rescue는 '구하다, 탈환하다', forget은 '망각하다, 소홀히 하다'라는 의미이다.

〖 어휘·어구 〗

materialistic 유물주의적인
attachment 애착, 집착
promise 기대, 약속
document ~로 증명하다, (상세히) 보도하다
chart (도표로) 나타내다

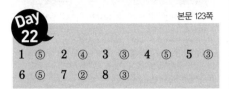

미니 고난도 Test 2회

Day 22
본문 123쪽

| 1 ⑤ | 2 ④ | 3 ③ | 4 ⑤ | 5 ③ |
| 6 ⑤ | 7 ② | 8 ③ | | |

---

1. ⑤ 　　아이들에게 통제권 주기

직독 / 직해

When children are young, / 아이들이 어릴 때 /

much of the work is demonstrating to them /
일의 많은 부분은 그들에게 보여 주는 것이다 /

that they do have control.
아이들이 통제권을 정말로 가지고 있음을

One wise friend of ours / 우리의 현명한 친구 한 명은 /

who was a parent educator for twenty years /
20년 동안 부모 교육자로 일했던 /

advises giving calendars to preschool-age children /
취학 전 연령의 아이들에게 달력을 주라고 조언하는데 /

and writing down all the important events /
그리고 중요한 모든 일을 적어 보라고 (조언하는데) /

in their life, / 그들의 생활에서 /

in part because it helps children understand /
이는 부분적으로 아이들이 이해하도록 도움을 주기 때문이다 /

the passage of time better, / 시간의 흐름을 더 잘 /

and how their days will unfold.
그리고 자신들의 하루하루가 어떻게 펼쳐질지

We can't overstate the importance of the calendar
tool / 달력이라는 도구의 중요성은 아무리 과장해도 지나치지 않다 /

in helping kids feel in control of their day.
아이들이 자신의 하루를 통제하고 있다고 느끼도록 돕는 데 있어

Have them cross off days of the week /
아이들이 그 요일들을 지우게 하라 /

as you come to them. 요일들에 다가가면서

Spend time going over the schedule for the day, /
그날의 일정을 검토하는 데 시간을 보내라 /

giving them choice in that schedule /
아이들에게 그 일정에 대한 선택권을 주면서 /

wherever possible. 가능한 경우마다

This communication expresses respect /
이런 의사소통은 존중을 보여 준다 /

— they see / that they are not just a tagalong /
그들은 알게 된다 / 자신들이 그저 붙어서 따라다니는 사람이 아니라는 것을 /

to your day and your plans, / and they understand
여러분의 하루와 여러분의 계획에 / 그들은 이해하게 된다 /

what is going to happen, when, and why.
어떤 일이 언제 그리고 왜 일어나게 될지

As they get older, / 그들은 나이가 더 들어감에 따라 /

children will then start to write /
아이들은 그다음에는 적기 시작할 것이며 /

in important things for themselves, /
스스로 중요한 일들을 /

which further helps them develop /
그것은 나아가 그들이 발달시키는 데 도움이 된다 /

their sense of control. 자신의 통제감을

아이들이 어릴 때, 일의 많은 부분은 아이들이 통제권을 정말로 가지고 있음을 그들에게 보여 주는 것이다. 20년 동안 부모 교육자로 일했던 우리의 현명한 친구 한 명은 취학 전 연령의 아이들에게 달력을 주고 그들의 생활에서 중요한 모든 일을 적어 보라고 조언하는데, 이는 부분적으로 아이들이 시간의 흐름을 더 잘 이해하도록, 그리고 자신들의 하루하루가 어떻게 펼쳐질지 이해하도록 도움을 주기 때문이다. 아이들이 자신의 하루를 통제하고 있다고 느끼도록 돕는 데 있어 달력이라는 도구의 중요성은 아무리 과장해도 지나치지 않다. 요일들에 다가가면서, 아이들이 그 요일들을 지우게 하라. 가능한 경우마다 그 일정에 대해 아이들에게 선택권을 주면서 그날의 일정을 검토하는 데 시간을 보내라. 이런 의사소통은 존중을 보여 주어, 아이들이 자신들이 그저 여러분의 하루와 여러분의 계획에 붙어서 따라다니는 사람이 아니라는 것을 알게 되고, 어떤 일이 언제 그리고 왜 일어나게 될지 이해하게 된다. 아이들은 나이가 더 들어감에 따라, 그다음에는 스스로 중요한 일들을 적기 시작할 것이며, 그것은 나아가 그들이 자신의 통제감을 발달시키는 데 도움이 된다.

문제풀이

① [강조동사 do]
동사인 have를 강조하기 위해 강조의 do가 쓰였다.

② [주어와 동사의 수 일치]
문장의 주어는 One wise friend이므로 단수동사인 advises는 적절하게 쓰였다. of ours who was a parent educator for twenty years는 주어인 One wise friend를 수식하는 전치사구이다.

③ [사역동사 have]
사역동사 have는 목적격보어로 동사원형이 와야 하므로 cross는 적절하게 쓰였다.

④ [주어, 동사의 생략]
'wherever it is possible'에서 관계부사절의 주어와 동사인 it is가 생략된 형태이다.

⑤ [관계대명사 which]
문맥상 두 개의 절을 연결해야 하므로 대명사 it은 적절하지 않다. 앞 문장을 선행사로 하는 관계대명사 which로 바꿔 써야 한다.

《 어휘 · 어구 》

demonstrate (실례를 통해) 보여 주다, 설명하다
preschool-age 취학 전 연령
passage 흐름, 경과, 추이
unfold 펼쳐지다, 전개되다
overstate 과장하다, 허풍을 떨다
cross off ~을 지우다
go over ~을 검토하다
tagalong 붙어서 따라다니는 사람
sense of control 통제감

---

2. ④ 　　문명 간의 접촉과 문명 내의 접촉

문명 간의 가장 극적이고 중요한 접촉은 한 문명의 사람들이 또 다른 문명의 사람들을 정복하고 제거했을 때였다. 이런 접촉은 보통 폭력적일 뿐만 아니라 짧았으며, 그것들은 가끔씩 발생했다. 서기 7세기에 시작하여, 비교적 지속적이고 때로는 격렬한 문명 간의 접촉이 이슬람과 서양 사이와 이슬람과 인도 사이에 일어났다. 하지만 대부분의 상업적, 문화적, 군사적 상호 작용은 문명 내에 있었다. 예를 들면, 인도와 중국이 가끔 다른 민족들을(몽족, 몽골족에게) 침략당하고 지배당했을 때, 두 문명 모두가 그들 자신의 문명 내에서도 '전쟁 중인 국가들'의 긴 시대가 있었다. 마찬가지로, 그리스인들은 페르시아인들이나 다른 그리스인이 아닌 사람들과 그랬던 것보다 자기들끼리 훨씬 더 자주 싸우고 무역을 했다.

문제풀이

① '~할 때'라는 의미의 관계부사인 when이 온 것은 적절하다. when 앞에 선행사 the time이 생략되어 있다.

② these contacts를 받는 대명사가 주어로 쓰였으므로 they가 온 것은 적절하다.

③ intercivilizational contacts를 수식하는 '지속된'이라는 의미의 형용사로 'sustained'가 온 것은 적절하다.

④ 주절의 주어는 both civilizations이고 뒤에 동사가 와야 하므로 having을 과거시제인 had로 고쳐야 한다.

⑤ traded를 받는 대동사로 과거시제인 일반동사를 대

신하므로 did가 온 것은 적절하다.
따라서 정답은 ④이다.

《 구문 및 어휘 》

*3행 These contacts normally were **not only** violent **but** brief, and they occurred only occasionally.

(1) 'These contacts ~'와 'they occurred ~' 두 개의 절이 and에 의해 연결되어 있다.

(2) 「not only A but (also) B」는 'A뿐만 아니라 B도'라는 의미이다.

dramatic 극적인
significant 중요한
contact 접촉
civilization 문명
conquer 정복하다, 이기다
eliminate 없애다, 제거하다
normally 보통
violent 폭력적인, 난폭한
brief 짧은, 잠시 동안의
occasionally 가끔
relatively 비교적
intense 극심한, 강렬한
commercial 상업의
military 군사의
interaction 상호 작용
invade 침략하다
subject 지배하에 두다
extensive 광범위한, 폭넓은
trade 거래하다, 무역하다

---

3. ③ 　　처방대로 약을 먹지 않는 환자들

직독 / 직해

If there is one problem in medicine /
만일 의학에 한 가지 문제가 있다면 /

that confounds doctors, insurers, and pharmaceutical companies alike, /
의사와 보험 회사, 제약 회사 모두를 당황시키는 /

it's noncompliance / 그것은 불복종이다 /

— the unfriendly term for patients' not following doctors' orders.
환자들이 의사의 지시를 따르지 않는 것에 대한 비우호적인 용어인

Most vexing are patients /
환자들이 가장 짜증나게 한다 /

who don't take their medications as prescribed, /
처방대로 약을 먹지 않는 /

which, / it turns out, /
그것은 / 판명된다 /

is pretty much most of us.
우리들 모두가 해당되는 것으로

Studies have shown / that about half of patients /
연구가 보여줘 왔다 / 환자의 약 절반이 /

who are prescribed medication /
약 처방받은 /

take their pills as directed.
처방대로 약을 복용한다

For drugs like statin, / which must be used for years, /
스타틴과 같은 약물의 경우 / 수년간 복용해야 하는 /

the rate is even worse, /
그 비율은 훨씬 좋지 않아서 /

drops to around 30 percent after a year.
1년 후에는 약 30퍼센트로 떨어진다

Since the effects of these drugs can be invisible, /
이 약의 효과가 눈에 보이지 않아서 /

the thinking goes, / 생각한 것처럼 /

---

patients don't detect any benefit from them.
환자들은 약에서 어떤 이점을 감지하지 못한다

Research has found / 연구가 발견해 왔다 /

that noncompliance adds $100 billion annually to US healthcare costs /
불복종은 미국의 의료 비용을 연간 천억 달러를 증가시킨다 /

and leads to 125,000 unnecessary deaths /
그리고 125,000명의 불필요한 죽음을 낳는다 /

from cardiovascular diseases alone every year.
매년 심혈관 질환 하나로 인한

And it can be blamed almost entirely on human error /
그리고 이것은 전적으로 인간적인 결함 탓으로 돌릴 수 있다 /

— people failing to do what they know they should.
즉 사람들은 해야 한다는 것을 알면서도 하지 않는다

의사와 보험 회사, 제약 회사 모두를 당황시키는 의학의 한 문제가 있다면, 이는 환자들이 의사의 지시를 따르지 않는 것에 대한 비우호적인 용어, 즉 불복종이다. 처방대로 약을 먹지 않는 환자들이 가장 짜증나게 하는데, 실상 거의 우리들 모두가 해당된다. 연구에 따르면, 약을 처방받은 환자의 약 절반이 처방대로 약을 복용한다. 수년간 복용해야 하는 스타틴과 같은 약물의 경우, 그 비율은 훨씬 좋지 않아서, 1년 후에는 약 30퍼센트로 떨어진다. 생각한 것처럼 이 약의 효과가 눈에 보이지 않아서, 환자들은 약에서 어떤 이점도 감지하지 못한다. 연구에 따르면 불복종은 미국의 의료 비용을 연간 천억 달러를 증가시키고, 심혈관 질환 하나로 인하여 매년 125,000명의 불필요한 죽음을 낳는다. 이는 전적으로 인간적인 결함 탓으로 돌릴 수 있는데, 사람들이 자신들이 해야할 것을 알면서도 하지 않는다는 것이다.

문제풀이

① [주어, 동사 수일치]
형용사 보어 vexing이 문두로 나와 주어, 동사가 도치된 구조이다. 주어가 복수명사 people이므로, 복수동사 are는 적절하다.

② [수동태, 주어와 동사의 수일치]
환자들이 약을 처방받는 것이므로, 수동태 are prescribed는 적절하다. 또한 'half of 복수명사'는 복수취급하므로 복수동사 are prescribed가 쓰인 것은 적절하다.

③ [분사구문]
바로 앞 문장인 the rate is even worse가 주어, 동사, 보어를 취한 완전한 절의 형태를 갖추고 있기 때문에 접속사 없이 두 번째 동사가 오는 것은 적절하지 않고, 밑줄 친 부분 이하는 분사구문이 되는 것이 적절하므로, **drops**는 분사구를 이끄는 **dropping**으로 고쳐야 한다.

④ [병렬 구조]
명사절인 that절 내에서 의미상 앞의 동사 adds와 병렬을 이루고 있으므로, leads는 적절하다.

⑤ [선행사를 포함하는 관계대명사 what]
do의 목적어 역할을 하는 명사절을 이끌면서, 그 명사절 내의 should 다음에 생략되어있는 do의 목적어 역할을 하는 선행사를 포함한 관계대명사 what은 적절하다.

《 어휘·어구 》

confound 당황시키다
insurer 보험 회사
pharmaceutical 제약의
noncompliance 불복종, 불순종
vexing 짜증나게 하는, 성가신
medication 약물, 의약품, 약물 치료
prescribe 처방하다
invisible 눈에 보이지 않는
detect 감지하다, 탐지하다
annually 해마다
entirely 전적으로

---

4. ⑤　　　초기의 백화점

1800년대 후반에 백화점이 다양한 고객들에게 의류와 가정용품을 제공하면서 '(한 상점에서 각종 상품을 다 살 수 있는) 원스톱 쇼핑'이라는 목적으로 나타났다. 1848년에 A. T. Stewart의 '백화점'이라는 아이디어는 뉴욕시에서 가동되었다. 이 상점은 2,000명을 고용해서 폭넓게 분류된 제조품을 팔았다. 하지만 그때도 오늘날처럼 그 도시는 미국의 여타 지역과 아주 달랐다. 그래서 수입 사치품을 거기서 사는 것은 가능했지만, 이 사치품이 멀리 떨어진 지역에는 도달할 수 있었던 것은 철도망이 건설되고 마케팅 전략이 개발되고서야 가능했다. 아주 초기의 몇몇 백화점에서는 새로운 사업 전략을 시행했다. 이러한 전략에는 여유롭게 둘러보는 것에 대한 장려와 '정찰제'가 포함되어 있었는데, 그 정찰제는 가격을 협상할 필요가 없어서 상품이 교환되거나 환불되는 것을 가능하게 했다.

문제풀이

① put ~ into operation은 '~을 가동시키다'라는 뜻인데, 주어인 A. T. Stewart's idea of a "department store"가 가동시키는 주체가 아니라 대상이므로 수동태가 오는 것은 적절하다.

② manufactured가 수식하는 명사 articles(물품들)는 제조되는 것이므로 과거분사인 manufactured가 오는 것은 적절하다.

③ 형용사 different를 부사 much가 수식하는 적절한 표현이다.

④ outlying은 '멀리 떨어진, 외딴'이라는 뜻의 형용사로 뒤의 명사 areas를 수식한다.

⑤ These tactics included ~ or refunded.가 한 문장이 되기 위해서는 the "one-price policy"를 선행사로 하는, 계속적 용법의 관계대명사가 와야 하므로 which로 고쳐야 한다. 따라서 정답은 ⑤이다.

《 구문 및 어휘 》

*1행 During the late 1800s, the department store emerged as a "one-stop shopping" destination, **offering** apparel and household goods to a diverse clientele.

(1) 「주절(the department ~)+분사구문(offering ~)」 구조의 문장이다.

(2) as는 '~로서'라는 의미의 전치사로 쓰였다.

(3) offering 이하는 부대상황을 나타내는 분사구문이다.

emerge 나오다, 드러나다
apparel 의류
diverse 다양한
clientele 고객
assortment 분류
article 물품
merchandise 상품
outlying 멀리 떨어진
implement 시행하다
tactic 전략, 전술
eliminate 없애다, 제거하다
negotiate 협상하다
leisurely 한가한, 여유로운
browse 둘러보다

---

5. ③　　　언어의 분류적 특성

직독 직해

Classifying things together into groups / is something /
사물들을 묶어서 그룹으로 분류하는 것은 / 일이다 /

we do all the time, / and it isn't hard / to see why.
우리가 늘 하는 / 그리고 어렵지 않다 / 그 이유를 이해하는 것은

Imagine trying to shop in a supermarket /
쇼핑하려고 한다고 상상해 보라 /

where the food was arranged / in random order /
배열된 슈퍼마켓에서 / 무작위로 /

on the shelves: / 음식이 진열대에 /

tomato soup next to the white bread / in one aisle, /
흰 빵 옆에 토마토 수프가 있고 / 한 통로에서는 /

chicken soup in the back next to the 60-watt light bulbs, /
치킨 수프는 뒤쪽에 있는 60와트 백열전구 옆에 있고 /

one brand of cream cheese in front and another /
한 크림치즈 브랜드는 앞쪽에, 또 다른 하나는 /

in aisle 8 near the cookies.
쿠키 근처의 8번 통로에 있다

The task of finding what you want /
여러분이 원하는 것을 찾는 일은 /

would be time-consuming and extremely difficult, /
시간이 많이 걸리고 매우 어려울 것이다 /

if not impossible.
불가능하지는 않아도

In the case of a supermarket, /
슈퍼마켓의 경우 /

someone had to design the system of classification.
누군가는 분류 체계를 설계해야 했다

But there is also a ready-made system of classification /
그러나 또한 기성의 분류 체계도 있다 /

embodied in our language.
우리 언어에 포함되어 있는

The word "dog," / for example, /
'개'라는 단어는 / 예를 들면 /

groups together a certain class of animals /
특정 부류의 동물들을 함께 분류한다 /

and distinguishes them from other animals.
그리고 다른 동물들과 구별한다

Such a grouping may seem too obvious /
그런 분류가 너무 명백하게 보일 수 있다 /

to be called a classification, /
분류라고 불리기에는 /

but this is only /
하지만 이것은 단지 ~이다 /

because you have already mastered the word.
여러분이 이미 그 단어를 숙달했기 때문

As a child learning to speak, /
말하기를 배우는 아이로서 /

you had to work hard /
여러분은 결심히 노력해야 했다 /

to learn the system of classification /
분류 체계를 배우려고 /

your parents were trying to teach you.
여러분은 부모님이 가르쳐주려 애썼던

Before you got the hang of it, /
여러분이 그것을 이해하기 전에 /

you probably made mistakes, /
여러분은 아마 실수를 했을 것이다 /

like calling the cat a dog.
고양이를 개라고 부르는 것과 같은

If you hadn't learned to speak, /
만일 여러분이 말하기를 배우지 않았다면 /

the whole world would seem like the unorganized supermarket; /
온 세상이 정돈되지 않은 슈퍼마켓처럼 보일 것이다 /

you would be in the position of an infant, /
여러분은 유아의 입장에 있을 것이다 /

for whom every object is new and unfamiliar.
모든 물건이 새롭고 낯선

In learning the principles of classification, / therefore, /
분류의 원칙을 배울 때 / 따라서 /

we'll be learning about the structure /
우리는 구조에 대해 배우고 있는 것이다 /

that lies at the core of our language.
언어의 핵심에 놓여 있는

사물들을 묶어서 그룹으로 분류하는 것은 우리가 늘 하는 일이며, 그 이유를 이해하는 것은 어렵지 않다. 음식이 진열대에 무작위로 배열된 슈퍼마켓에서 쇼핑하려고 한다고 상상해 보라. 한 통로에서는 흰 빵 옆에 토마토 수프가 있고, 치킨 수프는 뒤쪽에 있는 60와트 백열전구 옆에 있고,

한 크림치즈 브랜드는 앞쪽에, 또 다른 하나는 쿠키 근처의 8번 통로에 있다. 여러분이 원하는 것을 찾는 일은, 불가능하지는 않아도, (a) 시간이 많이 걸리고 매우 어려울 것이다.
슈퍼마켓의 경우, 누군가는 분류 체계를 (b) 설계해야 했다. 그러나 또한 우리 언어에 포함되어 있는 기성의 분류 체계도 있다. 예를 들면, '개'라는 단어는 특정 부류의 동물들을 함께 분류하여 다른 동물들과 구별한다. 분류라고 불리기에는 그런 분류가 너무 (c) 추상적이게(→ 명백하게) 보일 수 있지만, 이것은 단지 여러분이 이미 그 단어를 숙달했기 때문이다. 말하기를 배우는 아이로서, 여러분은 부모님이 가르쳐주려 애썼던 분류 체계를 (d) 배우려고 열심히 노력해야 한다. 그리고 그것을 이해하기 전에, 아마 고양이를 개라고 부르는 것과 같은 실수를 했을 것이다. 만일 여러분이 말하기를 배우지 않았다면, 온 세상이 (e) 정돈되지 않은 슈퍼마켓처럼 보일 것이다. 여러분은 모든 물건이 새롭고 낯선 유아의 입장에 있을 것이다. 따라서 분류의 원칙을 배울 때, 우리는 언어의 핵심에 놓여 있는 구조에 대해 배우고 있는 것이다.

《 어휘·어구 》

classify A into B A를 B로 분류하다
arrange 배열하다, 정리하다
random 무작위의, 임의로
aisle 통로
light bulb 백열 전구
time-consuming 시간이 많이 걸리는
classification 분류
ready-made 이미 만들어진
embody 포함하다, 담다
distinguish A from B A를 B로부터 구별하다
abstract 추상적인
get the hang of ~을 이해하다
unorganized 잘 정돈되지 않은
infant 유아
unfamiliar 낯선
principle 원칙, 원리
core 핵심
strategy 전략
inherent 내재된
categorization 범주화

정답률 61%
5. ③

문제풀이

뒤에서 분류를 이해하기 전에는 고양이를 개라고 부르는 것과 같은 실수를 했다고 했으므로, 단어를 숙달했다면 '개'라는 단어가 특정 부류의 동물들을 함께 분류하여 다른 동물과 구분하는 것이 명백하다고 하는 것이 적절하다. 따라서 (c) 'abstract(추상적인)'는 'obvious(명백한)'와 같은 낱말로 고쳐 써야 한다.

6. ⑤   현 순간의 즐거움을 고려한 카메라 사용

많은 사람들이 여행이나 휴가 중에 아니면 삶의 중요한 축하를 할 때 미래를 위해 그 경험을 보존해 두려고 수많은 사진을 찍는다. 그러나 사진사의 역할이 현 순간의 즐거움을 실제로 손상시킬 수 있다. 나는 첫 아이이자 외동아이의 탄생 사진을 찍는 데 진지하게 몰두하던 한 아버지를 안다. 사진들은 아름다웠지만 자기 아들의 삶에서 가장 중요한 첫 번째 순간을 놓쳤다는 생각이 들었다고 나중에 그는 탄식했다. 카메라 렌즈를 통해 바라보는 것은 그를 현장에서 분리되도록 만들어 버렸다. 그는 체험자가 아니라 단지 관찰자였다. 사물을 진심으로 바라보고 아름답고 의미 있는 것을 발견하는 것을 통해 진행되고 있는 경험을 무시하는(→ 증진시키는) 방법으로 카메라를 사용할 수 있도록 스스로 가르쳐라.

문제풀이

사진을 찍다 보면 현 순간의 즐거움을 누리지 못하고 관찰자가 되기 쉽다. 그래서 필자는 카메라를 사용할 때 현재 진행되고 있는 경험을 '증진시키는' 방법으로 사용하라고 조언하고 있다. 그러므로 밑줄 친 ⑤의 neglects를 enhances로 고쳐 써야 한다.

《 어휘·어구 》

celebration 축하, 기념
preserve 보존하다
detract from ~을 손상시키다
lament 슬퍼하다
detached 떨어진, 분리된
neglect 소홀히 하다, 무시하다
ongoing 진행하는

7. ②   노력으로 얻어진 우리 삶의 최고의 순간

우리가 대체로 믿고 있는 것과는 반대로, 우리 삶의 최고의 순간들은 수동적이고, 수용적이며, 긴장을 풀고 있는 시간들이 아니다. 물론 그러한 것들을 얻기 위해서 우리가 열심히 노력했다면 그러한 경험들도 즐길 수도 있긴 하지만 말이다. 최고의 순간들은 어렵고 가치 있는 어떤 것을 성취하기 위한 자발적인 노력 속에서 한 개인의 신체나 정신이 그 한계점에 이르게 될 때에 주로 생겨난다. 따라서 최적의 경험은 우리가 직접 발생하게 만드는 어떤 것이다. 어린아이에게 있어서 그것은 떨리는 손가락으로 그녀가 지금껏 만들었던 그 어느 것보다 더 높은 자신이 만든 탑 위에 마지막 블록을 놓는 것일 수 있고, 단거리 선수에게는 자신의 기록을 깨려고 애쓰는 것일 수 있으며, 바이올린 연주자에게 있어서는 복잡한 악절을 완벽하게 숙달하는 것일 수 있다. 각 사람에게 있어서 자신을 발전시킬 수 있는 수천 가지의 기회와 도전이 있다.

문제풀이

(A) 최고의 순간은 정적인 것이 아니라 그러한 순간을 즐길 수 있는 동적인 것이다. 만약 우리가 그것을 얻기 위해 열심히 노력한다면, 문맥상 그것을 '피하기 위해(avoid)'가 아니라 '얻기 위해(attain)'가 적절하다.
(B) minimal은 '최소의'라는 뜻이다. 자발적인 노력에 의해 '최적의(optimal)' 경험을 만든다고 하는 것이 자연스럽다.
(C) 어려운 것을 달성하기 위해 도전하는 것이므로, intricate(복잡한)을 쓰는 것이 자연스럽다. uncomplicated 는 '복잡하지 않은'이라는 뜻이다.

《 어휘·어구 》

contrary to ~와는 반대로
receptive 받아들이는
attain 달성하다
voluntary 자발적인
sprinter 단거리 선수
intricate 뒤얽힌, 복잡한
passage 악절
expand 넓히다, 확장시키다

8. ③   설문 조사 결과를 검토할 때 고려할 점

조사 설문에 대한 반응은 사건에 의해 영향을 받는데, 우리는 조사의 결과를 검토할 때 이것을 고려해야 한다. 예를 들어, 만약 항공기 추락 사고 후에 어떤 조사가 이루어진다면 항공사에 대한 명성은 손상될 것이다. 어느 컴퓨터 회사의 생산품 결함에 대한 주요 뉴스의 보도가 있은 직후 그 회사는 그 명성을 잃었다. 긍정적인 면을 보면, 한 음료 회사에 의해 이루어진 회사의 이미지에 대한 조사 결과 올림픽에서의 막대한 투자가 있은 직후에 일반인들의 매우 호의적인 태도가 나타났다. 결과적으로 조사 설문은 조사받는 집단이 뉴스에 나오거나 여론에 영향을 줄 수 있는 중대한 사건에 관계되지 않을 때 수행되어야 한다. 중립적인 상황에서 그 집단의 명성, 생산품, 또는 서비스에 관한 보다 타당성 있는 조사가 수행될 수 있다.

문제풀이

(A) 항공기 추락사고 후에 항공사에 대한 조사가 있으면 그 회사의 명성은 손상을 입을(damaged) 것이다. recover는 '회복하다'의 의미로 반대 의미를 갖는다.
(B) 음료 회사가 올림픽 때 집중 투자를 하면 일반인들은 그 회사에 대해 우호적인(favorable) 태도

를 보일 것이다. hostile은 favorable의 반의어로 '적대적인'의 의미이다.
(C) 중립적 상황에서 조사 설문이 이루어지면 타당성 있는(valid) 조사가 수행될 것이다. biased는 '편견이 있는'의 의미로 반대되는 내용의 어휘이다.

《 어휘·어구 》

reputation 평판, 명성
crash 추락
coverage 보도
defect 결함
beverage 음료
massive 막대한
investment 투자
consequently 결과적으로
organization 조직체, 집단
significant 중대한
neutral 중립적인
context 상황, 맥락

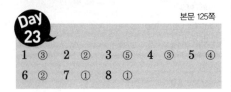

미니 고난도 Test 3회

본문 125쪽

Day 23

| 1 | ③ | 2 | ② | 3 | ⑤ | 4 | ③ | 5 | ④ |
| 6 | ② | 7 | ① | 8 | ① |

---

1. ③ 　　뇌의 에너지 사용

직독 / 직해

The modern adult human brain weighs only 1/50
현대 성인의 뇌는 무게가 전체 체중의 50분의 1에 불과하다 /

of the total body weight /

but uses up to 1/5 of the total energy needs.
하지만 총 에너지 필요량의 5분의 1까지 사용한다

The brain's running costs are about eight to ten
뇌의 유지 비용은 8배에서 10배 정도이다

times as high, / per unit mass, /
/ 단위 질량당 /

as those of the body's muscles. 신체 근육의 유지 비용의

And around 3/4 of that energy is expended on
neurons, / 그리고 그 에너지의 약 4분의 3은 뉴런에 사용된다

the specialized brain cells that communicate in
vast networks / 광대한 연결망에서 소통하는 분화된 뇌세포인 /

to generate our thoughts and behaviours.
우리의 생각과 행동을 만들어 내기 위해

An individual neuron sending a signal in the brain /
뇌에서 신호를 보내고 있는 개개의 뉴런은

uses as much energy as a leg muscle cell /
다리 근육 세포만큼의 에너지를 사용한다 /

running a marathon. 마라톤을 하고 있는

Of course, we use more energy overall when we
물론, 우리는 전반적으로는 달리고 있을 때 더 많은 에너지를 사용한다

are running, / but we are not always on the move, /
/ 하지만 우리가 항상 움직이고 있는 것은 아니다 /

whereas our brains never switch off.
반면 우리의 뇌는 절대 꺼지지 않는다

Even though the brain is metabolically greedy, /
비록 뇌가 신진대사 작용에서 탐욕스럽기는 해도 /

it still outclasses any desktop computer /
그것은 여전히 어떤 데스크톱 컴퓨터보다도 훨씬 낫다 /

both in terms of the calculations it can perform
and the efficiency at which it does this.
수행할 수 있는 계산과 이를 수행하는 효율 두 가지 면에서

We may have built computers /
우리가 컴퓨터를 만들었을지 모른다 /

that can beat our top Grand Master chess players, /
최고의 그랜드 마스터 체스 선수들을 이길 수 있는 /

but we are still far away from designing one /
하지만 컴퓨터를 설계하는 것과는 아직 거리가 멀다 /

that is capable of recognizing and picking up one
체스의 말 중 하나를 인식하고 그것을 집어들 수 있는 /

of the chess pieces /

as easily as a typical three-year-old child can.
일반적인 세 살배기 아이가 할 수 있는 것만큼 쉽게

현대 성인의 뇌는 무게가 전체 체중의 50분의 1에 불과하지만, 총 에너지 필요량의 최대 5분의 1까지 사용한다. 단위 질량당, 뇌의 유지 비용은 신체 근육의 유지 비용의 8배에서 10배 정도이다. 그리고 그 에너지의 약 4분의 3은 우리의 생각과 행동을 만들어 내기 위해 광대한 연결망에서 소통하는 분화된 뇌세포인 뉴런에 사용된다. 뇌에서 신호를 보내고 있는 개개의 뉴런은 마라톤을 하고 있는 다리 근육 세포만큼의 에너지를 사용한다. 물론, 전반적으로는 달리고 있을 때 더 많은 에너지를 사용하지만, 우리가 항상 움직이고 있는 것은 아닌 반면 우리의 뇌는 절대 꺼지지 않는다. 비록 뇌가 신진대사 작용에서 탐욕스럽기는 해도, 수행할 수 있는 계산과 이를 수행하는 효율 두 가지 면에서 그것은 여전히 어떤 데스크

톱 컴퓨터보다도 훨씬 낫다. 우리가 최고의 그랜드 마스터 체스 선수들을 이길 수 있는 컴퓨터를 만들었을지는 모르지만, 일반적인 세 살배기 아이가 할 수 있는 것만큼 쉽게 체스의 말 중 하나를 인식하고 그것을 집어들 수 있는 컴퓨터를 설계하는 것은 아직도 거리가 멀다.

문제풀이

③ 문장의 술어동사는 uses이며 문맥상 sends는 현재분사로 바꿔 앞의 명사구 An individual neuron을 수식하는 구조가 되어야 하므로 sending 으로 고쳐야 한다.

① 복수명사 costs를 대신해 쓴 대명사 those가 바르게 쓰였다.

② specialized는 과거분사로서 brain cells를 수식하고 있으며 the specialized brain cells는 앞의 명사 neurons와 동격을 이룬다.

④ '전치사+관계대명사'의 구조로서 완전한 절이 뒤따르고 있으며 이 '전치사+관계대명사 절'이 선행사 the efficiency를 바르게 수식하고 있다.

⑤ picking up을 수식하는 부사로서 easily는 바르게 쓰였다.

❍ **이렇게 풀자** _ 어법상 틀린 것을 찾는 문제에서는 밑줄이 있는 부분의 형태가 문맥상 어법에 맞게 쓰였는지 확인해야 한다. ① 대명사의 쓰임, ② 과거분사의 쓰임, ③ 현재분사의 쓰임, ④ '전치사+관계대명사'의 쓰임, ⑤ 동등비교 'as ~ as'의 구조 등을 알아야 한다.

어휘·어구

expend (돈·시간·에너지) 쏟다
vast 광대한
generate 만들어 내다
metabolically 신진대사로
greedy 탐욕스러운
outclass (경쟁 상대를) 압도하다
efficiency 효율
recognize 인식하다
typical 일반적인

---

2. ② 　　활성 산소는 노화의 강력한 동인이다

중요한 것은 바로 산소이다. 역설적이게도, 우리에게 생명을 주는 것이 결국 그것(생명)을 죽인다. 궁극적인 생명력은 우리가 들이쉬는 거의 모든 산소를 태우는, 미토콘드리아라고 불리는 아주 작은 에너지 세포 공장에 있다. 그러나 호흡에는 대가가 있다. 우리를 살아있게 하고 활동적이게 유지하는 산소 연소는 활성 산소라고 불리는 부산물을 내보낸다. 그것들(활성산소)은 지킬박사와 하이드 씨의 특징을 가지고 있다(서로 다른 이중적인 특징을 가지고 있다). 한편으로, 그것들은 우리의 생존 보장을 돕는다. 예를 들어, 감염원과 싸워 물리치기 위해 신체가 동원될 때, 그것(신체)은 침입자들을 매우 효율적으로 파괴하기 위해 한바탕 활성 산소를 생산한다. 다른 한편으로, 활성 산소는 통제할 수 없을 정도로 신체를 돌아다니면서 세포를 공격하고, 세포의 단백질을 부식시키고, 세포막을 뚫고 세포의 유전 암호를 변질시켜 마침내 그 세포는 제대로 기능을 하지 못하게 되고 때로는 포기하여 죽어버린다. 보호자인 동시에 보복자로 생명체의 일부가 되어 있는 이런 사나운 활성 산소는 노화의 강력한 동인이다.

문제풀이

② 문장에는 시제와 수, 그리고 인칭이 표시되는 동사가 있어야 한다. The combustion of oxygen ~ and active가 주어이므로 sending을 동사인 sends로 바꾸어야 한다.

① that은 tiny cellular factories of energy를 선행사로 취하고 관계절에서 주어 역할을 하는 주격 관계대명사이다.

③ to부정사인 to fight는 목적을 나타내어 동사 mobilizes를 수식한다.

④ 동사 move를 수식하므로 부사인 uncontrollably 를 사용하고 있다.

⑤ 의미상 주어인 These fierce radicals가 분사가 나타내는 동작의 대상이므로 과거분사 built를 사용하고 있다.

어휘·어구

combustion 연소
mobilize 동원되다
infectious agent 감염원(感染源, 전염병의 병원체)
burst 한바탕 터뜨림
uncontrollably 통제할 수 없게
pierce 뚫다
genetic code 유전 암호
dysfunctional 제대로 기능을 하지 않는
agent 동인(動因), 요인
purify 정화하다
avenger 보복자
antibiotic 항생제

---

3. ⑤ 　　국제 산업 규제의 어려움

직독 / 직해

There is one effective way of balancing /
비교 검토하는 한 가지 효율적인 방법이 있다 /

the popular demand for greater regulation /
더 큰 규제에 대한 대중의 요구와

against the compliance costs that regulation imposes,
규제가 부과하는 준수 비용을

and governments are likely to follow this.
그리고 정부는 이것을 따를 가능성이 높다

It is to subcontract regulation to independent, single-function bodies /
그것은 독립된, 단일 기능의 단체에 규제의 하청을 주는 것이다 /

which specialize in regulating a particular area.
특정한 영역의 규제를 전문으로 하는

All the evidence is that good regulation is an extremely subtle, flexible business.
모든 증거에 의하면 좋은 규제란 극도로 절묘하고, 유연한 일이다

It involves deals between the regulator and the regulated, /
그것은 규제 주체와 규제받는 사람들 사이의 거래를 수반한다 /

where cost and thoroughness are traded-off against each other.
그리고 거기에서는 비용과 철저함이 서로 거래된다

It involves regulatory bodies in different countries co-operating with each other,
그것은 서로 다른 국가들의 규제 단체가 서로 협력하는 것을 수반한다

for the greater the freedom of businesses to migrate, /
왜냐하면 사업체들이 이주할 자유가 더 클수록 /

the greater the need for worldwide regulation.
국제적인 규제의 필요성이 더 크기 때문이다

International banking provides perhaps the best example /
아마도 국제 은행업은 가장 좋은 사례를 제시한다 /

of how a worldwide regulatory system can be built, /
세계적인 규제 체계가 만들어질 수 있는 방식의 /

for the central banks of the main industrial countries operate /
왜냐하면 주요 산업 국가들의 중앙은행은 운영하기 때문이다 /

a series of mutual agreements / on bank capital requirements /
일련의 상호 협정을 　　　　/ 은행 필요자본량에 대한 /

which, in theory, should prevent any one country securing an unfair comparative advantage /
이론상, 어느 한 국가가 불공정한 비교 우위를 확보하는 것을 막을 /

or any bank escaping the net of international regulation.
또는 어느 은행도 국제 규제의 그물망을 피하는 것을 (막을)

However, / the fact that BCCI did slip through shows /
하지만 　　/ BCCI가 정말로 빠져나갔다는 사실은 보여준다 /

just how difficult it is / to regulate a wholly international industry.
정말 얼마나 어려운지를 　　/ 완전히 국제적인 산업을 규제하는 것이

더 큰 규제에 대한 대중의 요구와 규제가 부과하는 준수 비용을 비교 검토하는 한 가지 효율적인 방법이 있는데, 정부는 이것을 따를 가능성이 높다. 그것은 특정한 영역의 규제를 전문으로 하는 독립된, 단일 기능의 단체에 규제의 하청을 주는 것이다. 모든 증거에 의하면 좋은 규제란 극도로 절묘한 일이다. 그것은 규제 주체와 규제받는 사람들 사이의 거래를 수반하는데, 거기에서는 비용과 철저함이 서로 거래된다. 그것은 서로 다른 국가들의 규제 단체가 서로 협력하는 것을 수반하는데, 그 이유는 사업체들이 이주할 자유가 더 클수록, 국제적인 규제의 필요성이 더 크기 때문이다. 아마도 국제 은행업은 세계적인 규제 체계가 만들어질 수 있는 방식의 가장 좋은 사례를 제시하는데, 그 이유는 주요 산업 국가들의 중앙은행은, 이론상, 어느 한 국가가 불공정한 비교 우위를 확보하거나 어느 은행도 국제 규제의 그물망을 피하는 것을 막을, 은행 필요자본량에 대한 일련의 상호 협정을 운영하기 때문이다. 하지만, BCCI가 정말로 빠져나갔다는 사실은 완전히 국제적인 산업을 규제하는 것이 정말 얼마나 어려운지를 보여 준다.

문제풀이

① [주격 관계대명사 which]
'which'는 'independent, single-function bodies'를 선행사로 하고, 동사 'specialize'의 주어 역할하는 주격 관계대명사로 올바르게 사용되었다.

② [the+과거분사]
'the+형용사/현재분사/과거분사'는 '~한 사람들'의 의미를 지니는데, 이 때 능동의 의미일 경우에는 현재분사를, 수동의 의미일 때는 과거분사를 사용한다. 'the regulated'는 '규제받는 사람들'의 의미를 나타내어 'regulate'의 동작의 대상을 가리키므로 'regulated'는 올바르게 사용되었다.

③ [to부정사]
'to migrate'는 'the freedom of businesses'를 수식하는 to부정사의 형용사적 용법으로 올바르게 사용되었다. cf) 이 문장은 'the 비교급 S+V, the 비교급 S+V'구문에서 동사에 해당하는 'be동사'가 생략된 형태이다.

④ [명사절 접속사 how]
'how'는 전치사 of의 목적어로 쓰인 명사절을 유도하며, 명사절에서 '~한 방식'의 의미를 나타내는 접속사로 올바르게 사용되었다.

⑤ [정동사 vs. 준동사]
'that BCCI did slip through'는 'the fact'와 동격관계를 나타내는 명사절이고, 문장의 주어 'the fact'에 대응하는 술어 동사가 필요하다. 따라서 분사 'showing'을 정동사 'shows'로 고쳐야 한다.

《어휘·어구》

balance A against B A와 B를 비교 검토하다
compliance cost (규제의) 준수 비용
regulation 규제, 규정
subtle 미묘한, 절묘한
flexible 유연한, 잘 구부러지는
thoroughness 철저함
trade-off 거래하다
mutual 상호의
capital requirement 필요자본량, 자금 수요
slip through ~을 빠져나가다

---

4. ③   FoMO

FoMO에 시달리고 있는가? 만약 그렇다면 당신만 그런 것이 아니다. FoMO란 '(정보를) 놓치는 것에 대한 두려움'을 나타내는 말인데, 다른 사람의 생활에서 무슨 일이 일어나고 있는지 알지 못할까봐 불안한 마음을 설명하기 위해 만들어진 용어이다. 다른 사람의 활동을 놓치지 않고 따라가려는 욕망은 새로운 것이 아니지만, 소셜 미디어는 그것을 과도한 수준까지 올렸다. (정보를) 놓칠까봐 극심한 두려움을 가진 사람들은 운전 중에 메시지를 확인하고

보내고 수업 중에 이메일과 문자메시지를 확인할 가능성이 다른 사람보다 더 높다. 그러나 그것은 문제의 일부분에 불과하다. FoMO는 사람들의 직장에서의 효율성도 방해하고 있다. 효과적으로 의사소통을 하는 사람들은 소통하는 시간의 60 내지 70퍼센트 정도 시선 접촉을 하지만, 오늘날 많은 사람들은 그것보다 더 적게, 때로는 (소통하는) 시간의 30퍼센트 정도 밖에 안되게 시선 접촉을 한다. 시선 접촉이 줄어든 이유의 가장 큰 부분은 디지털 기기에 모든 주의를 기울이고 있기 때문이다.

문제풀이

(A) knowing의 목적절이 필요하므로 what을 써서 간접의문문이 되는 것이 어법에 알맞다. (B) 앞에 more likely (than others)와 함께 be likely to do 구문이 되는 것이 적절하므로 to check가 어법상 알맞다. (C) 문장의 동사가 필요하므로 is가 와야 한다.

《구문 및 어휘》

*1행 FoMO stands for "fear of missing out," **which** is a term coined to describe anxiety about not knowing [**what** is going on in others' lives].

(1) which는 계속적 용법을 나타내는 주격 관계대명사이며 이때 which는 FoMO를 가리킨다.

(2) to describe는 목적을 나타내는 부사적 용법의 to부정사이다.

(3) what이 이끄는 절은 knowing의 목적어 역할을 하며 knowing은 전치사 about의 목적어로 쓰인 동명사이다.

*5행 People [**who** have a high fear of missing out] are more likely [than others] to check and send messages [when driving] and to check [emails and text messages during class].

(1) 주절의 동사는 are이고, [who have ~ missing out]은 주어 People을 수식하는 관계대명사절이며 who는 주격 관계대명사이다.

(2) to check and (to) send와 to check는 접속사 and로 연결된 병렬관계이다.

(3) [when ~ driving]는 부사절로 앞의 to check and send messages를 수식한다.

coin 신조어를 만들다
keep up with 따라가다, 뒤떨어지지 않게 하다
kick ~ into overdrive ~을 과도한 수준으로 올리다
interfere with ~을 방해하다

오H 말이 틀렸을까?

문법 문제는 기본적인 문장 구조만 파악하면 쉽게 해결할 수 있어. 이번 문제도 (A)를 보면 know라는 동사 뒤에 오는 목적어가 시작하는 자리라는 것을 알 수 있어. 이때 목적어의 자리에 that이 온다면 접속사 that만 올 수 있는데 빈칸 뒤에는 완벽한 문장이 아니기 때문에 답이 될 수 없는 거지. 또 (C)를 보면 빈칸 앞부분이 긴 주어라는 것을 알 수 있어. 그래서 빈칸에 be가 온다면 빈칸 뒤에 그 전체 문장의 동사가 와야 하는데 없으니까 is가 답인 것을 알 수 있어. 마지막으로 (B)는 be likely to라는 숙어를 알고 있다면 쉽게 답을 찾을 수 있지.

---

5. ④   동물 행동의 복잡성

직독 직해

Our irresistible tendency to see things /
사물을 보는 우리의 억누를 수 없는 경향 /

---

in human terms / 인간의 관점에서 /
— that we are often mistaken /
우리가 종종 잘못 생각하는 것은 /
in attributing complex human motives and processing abilities to other species — /
다른 종들에게 복잡한 인간의 동기와 처리 능력이 있다고 /
does not mean / 의미하지는 않는다 /
that an animal's behavior is not, in fact, complex.
동물의 행동이 실제로 복잡하지 않다는 것을
Rather, it means / 오히려 그것은 의미한다 /
that the complexity of the animal's behavior /
동물 행동의 복잡성이 /
is not purely a product of its internal complexity.
순전히 그것의 내적 복잡성의 산물이 아니라는 것을
Herbert Simon's "parable of the ant" /
Herbert Simon의 '개미 우화'는 /
makes this point very clearly.
이러한 점을 매우 명확하게 해 준다
Imagine an ant walking along a beach, /
한 마리의 개미가 해변을 따라 걷고 있는 것을 상상하라 /
and visualize tracking the trajectory of the ant /
그리고 그 이동 경로를 추적하는 것을 머릿속에 그려보라 /
as it moves. 그것이 이동함에 따라
The trajectory would show a lot of twists and turns, /
그 이동 경로는 많이 구부러지고 방향이 바뀔 것이다 /
and would be very irregular and complicated.
그리고 매우 불규칙하고 복잡할 것이다
One could then suppose /
그렇다면 가정할 수 있을 것이다 /
that the ant had equally complicated internal navigational abilities, /
그 개미에게 똑같이 복잡한 내적인 항행 능력이 있다고 /
and work out / what these were likely to be /
그리고 알아낼 수 있을 것이다 / 이것이 무엇일 수 있는지를 /
by analyzing the trajectory /
그 이동 경로를 분석함으로써 /
to infer the rules and mechanisms /
규칙과 구조를 추론하기 위해 /
that could produce such a complex navigational path.
그런 복잡한 항행 경로를 만들어 낼 수 있는
The complexity of the trajectory, however, /
그러나 그 이동 경로의 복잡성은 /
"is really a complexity in the surface of the beach, /
실제로 해변 지면에서의 복잡성이지 /
not a complexity in the ant."
그 개미의 내적 복잡성이 아니다
In reality, / 사실 /
the ant may be using a set of very simple rules: /
그 개미는 일련의 매우 단순한 규칙들을 사용하고 있을 수도 있는데 /
it is the interaction of these rules with the environment /
바로 이 규칙들과 환경의 상호 작용이 /
that actually produces the complex trajectory, /
그 복잡한 이동 경로를 실제로 만들어 내는 것은 /
not the ant alone. 그 개미 혼자서는 아니다
Put more generally, /
좀 더 일반적으로 말하자면 /
the parable of the ant illustrates /
개미 우화는 보여준다 /
that there is no necessary correlation /
필연적인 상관관계가 없음을 /
between the complexity of an observed behavior and the complexity of the mechanism /
관찰된 행동의 복잡성과 구조의 복잡성 사이의 /
that produces it. 그것을 만들어 내는

인간의 관점에서 사물을 보는 우리의 억누를 수 없는 경향, 즉 다른 종들에게 복잡한 인간의 동기와 처리 능력이 있다고 우리가 종종 잘못 생각하는 것은 동물의 행동이 실제로 복잡하지 않다는 것을 의미하지는 않는다. 오히려 그것은 동물 행동의 복잡성이 순전히 그것의 내적 복잡성의 (a) 산물이 아니라는 것을 의미한다. Herbert Simon의 '개미 우화'는 이러한 점을 매우 명확하게 해 준다. 한 마리의 개미가 해변을 따라 걷고 있는 것을 상상하고, 그 개미가 이동함에 따라 그 이동 경로를 추적하는 것을 (b) 머릿속에 그려보라. 그 이동 경로는 많이 구부러지고 방향이 바뀌고, 매우 불규칙할 것이다. 그렇다면 그 개미에게 똑같이 복잡한 (c) 내적인 항행 능력이 있다고 가정하고, 그런 복잡한 항행 경로를 만들어 낼 수 있는 규칙과 구조를 추론하기 위해 그 이동 경로를 분석함

로써 이것이 무엇일 수 있는지를 알아낼 수 있을 것이다. 그러나 그 이동 경로의 복잡성은 '실제로 해변 지면에서의 복잡성이지 그 개미의 내적 복잡성이 아니다.' 사실 그 개미는 일련의 매우 (d) 복잡한(→ 단순한) 규칙들을 사용하고 있을 수도 있는데, 그 복잡한 이동 경로를 만들어 내는 것은 바로 이 규칙들과 환경의 상호 작용이지, 그 개미 혼자서는 아니다. 좀 더 일반적으로 말하자면, 개미 우화는 (e) 관찰된 행동의 복잡성과 그것을 만들어 내는 구조의 복잡성 사이의 필연적인 상관관계가 없음을 보여준다.

《 어휘·어구 》

irresistible 억누를 수 없는
tendency 경향
term 관점, 견지
attribute (성질 등이) 있다고 생각하다
purely 순전히, 전적으로
visualize 머릿속에 그리다
irregular 불규칙적인
complicated 복잡한
navigational 항행의, 항해의
analyze 분석하다
infer 추론하다
mechanism 구조
interaction 상호 작용
correlation 상관관계

정답률 74%

5. ④

【문제풀이】

개미의 이동 경로의 복잡성은 개미의 내적 복잡성이 아니며 동물의 단순한 행동 규칙이 환경과 상호 작용할 때 그것이 복잡한 이동 경로를 만들어 낼 수 있다고 했으므로, 그 규칙은 복잡한 내적 항행 능력을 반영하는 복잡한 규칙이 아니다. 따라서 (d) 'complex(복잡한)'를 'simple(단순한)'과 같은 낱말로 바꿔 써야 한다.

○ 이렇게 풀자 먼저 글의 주제와 흐름을 파악한 뒤 밑줄 친 어휘가 포함된 문장 전후 문맥을 파악해서 적절하게 쓰였는지를 판단하면 된다. 'The complexity of the trajectory, however, "is really a complexity in the surface of the beach, not a complexity in the ant."(그러나 그 이동 경로의 복잡성은 '실제로 해변 지면에서의 복잡성이지 그 개미의 내적 복잡성이 아니다.')'와 'it is the interaction of these rules with the environment that actually produces the complex trajectory, not the ant alone(그 복잡한 이동 경로를 실제로 만들어 내는 것은 바로 이 규칙들과 환경의 상호 작용이지, 그 개미 혼자서는 아니다)'를 통해 개미가 복잡하지 않은 규칙을 사용하고 있다는 것을 알면 (d) complex가 적절하지 않다는 것을 알 수 있다.

6. ② 텔레비전 방송의 첫 실험과 사람들이 새 기술 사용을 주저한 이유

텔레비전 방송의 첫 실험은 1930년대에 프랑스에서 시작되었지만, 프랑스인들은 그 새로운 기술을 사용하는데 느렸다. 이러한 주저함에는 몇 가지 이유가 있다. 라디오가 정부 자원의 대부분을 사용했고, 그래서 프랑스 정부는 텔레비전 방송을 위한 전국적인 네트워크를 개발하는 재정적인 부담을 기꺼이 떠맡으려고 하지 않았다. 텔레비전의 프로그램을 짜는 비용은 너무나 비쌌고, 그에 상응하게 프로그램의 산출량은 적었다. 최소한의 제공 편수와 결합된 빈약한 배급은 그 새로운 상품을 구매할 유인을 거의 제공하지 않았다. 더욱이, 텔레비전 수상기는, 수수한 생활수준으로 인해 특히 1930년대와 1940년대에 사치스런 상품의 취득할 수 없었던 일반 대중의 수입을 넘어서서 가격이 매겨져 있었다. 이데올로기적인 영향력도 또한 요인에 들어 있었는데, 특히 엘리트들은 텔레비전에 대해 회의적이었고 그것을 대중문화와 미국화의 전령으로 인식했다.

【문제풀이】

(A) 바로 앞에서 새로운 기술을 사용하는데 느렸다고 했으므로 hesitancy (주저함, 망설임)가 적절하다. consistency는 '일관성'을 의미한다.

(B) 프로그램 제공 편수가 적었고 그것이 제대로 배급되지 않았다는 문맥이므로 distribution (배급, 분포)이 적절하다. description은 '묘사'를 의미한다.

(C) 엘리트들이 텔레비전에 대해 부정적인 견해를 가지고 있었다는 문맥이므로 skeptical (회의적인)이 적절하다. optimistic은 '낙천적인'의 의미이다.

《 어휘·어구 》

employ 사용하다, 고용하다
absorb 사용하다, 흡수하다
majority 대부분
be reluctant to ~하기를 꺼리다
shoulder 떠맡다
financial 재정적인
burden 부담
output 산출(량)
correspondingly 상응하여, 일치하여
minimal 최소한의
incentive 유인, 동기
modest 수수한, 하찮은
acquisition 취득, 습득
luxury 사치스런
messenger 전령, 사자

7. ① 음악의 힘과 영향력

어느 정도로라도 음악에 반응하지 않는 사람은 거의 없다. 음악의 힘은 다양하며 사람들은 다르게 반응한다. 어떤 사람들에게 음악은 주로 거기에 맞추어 춤을 추거나 몸을 움직이는 본능적이고 신나는 소리이다. 다른 사람들은 음악의 메시지를 들으려 하거나, 음악의 형식과 구조에 지적으로 접근하여 그것의 형식적 패턴이나 독창성을 감상한다. 그러나 무엇보다도, 어떤 종류의 음악에 의해 감동받지 않는 사람은 거의 있을 수가 없다. 음악은 감정의 전 범위를 아우른다. 그것은 우리를 기쁘게 혹은 슬프게, 무기력하게 혹은 기운 넘치게 만들 수 있으며 어떤 음악은 정신이 그 밖의 모든 것을 잊을 때까지 정신을 압도할 수 있다. 그것은 무의식에 작용해서 분위기를 만들어 내거나 고양시켜 주며 깊은 기억들을 풀어낸다.

【문제풀이】

(A) 음악에 맞추어 춤을 추거나 몸을 움직이는 것은 본능적으로 소리에 반응하는 것이므로 '본능적인'이라는 뜻의 instinctive가 적절하다.

(B) 음악에 대해 지적인 접근을 한다고 했으므로, 음악을 감상한다는 말이 나와야 하므로 appreciating이 나오는 것이 적절하다.

(C) 다음 문장이 여러 가지 감정을 언급하고 있으므로 감정의 모든 범위를 망라한다는 말이 나와야 하므로 '망라하다'는 뜻의 covers가 나오는 것이 적절하다.

《 어휘·어구 》

diverse 다양한
instinctive 본능적인
inactive 활발하지 않은
intellectual 지적인
approach 접근, 연구
construction 구조, 구성
originality 독창성
cover 포함하다, 망라하다
overtake 압도하다
unlock 열다, 털어놓다

8. ① 다이아몬드의 산업적 유용성

비록 대부분의 사람들이 이것을 보석으로 인정하지만, 다이아몬드는 도구로서 우리의 일상생활에 가장 직접적으로 영향을 끼친다. 공업용 다이

아몬드는 너무나 중요해서 그것이 부족하면 금속 세공업의 붕괴를 초래할 것이며 대량생산이 허물어질 것이다. 공업용 다이아몬드는 으깨어지고 가루로 되어, 많은 연마, 광택 작업에 사용된다. 다이아몬드의 사용처의 범위는 치과의 드릴부터 바위 절단용 톱과 유리 절단기까지 이른다. 다이아몬드의 굉장한 경도는 다이아몬드를 우리에게 알려진 가장 중요한 공업용 물질 중 하나가 되게 한다.

【문제풀이】

(A) 다이아몬드의 산업적인 유용성을 언급한 문장으로 다이아몬드 부족이 가져올 문제를 말하고 있으므로 부족에 해당하는 'shortage'가 나와야 적절하다.

(B) 뒤에 나오는 from ~ to 의 내용이 다이아몬드 사용 범위를 나타내고 있으므로 ranges가 나와야 적절하다.

(C) 다이아몬드가 산업 용도로 쓰이는 것은 그것이 지닌 경도 때문이기 때문에 hardness가 정답이다.

《 어휘·어구 》

breakdown 붕괴, 몰락
metal-working 금속 세공술의
mass production 대량 생산
crush 분쇄하다
powder 가루로 하다
grinding 연마, 분쇄
range from A to B 범위가 A에서 B까지 걸쳐 있다

미니 고난도 Test 4회

Day 24
본문 127쪽

| 1 ④ | 2 ⑤ | 3 ③ | 4 ④ | 5 ④ |
| 6 ⑤ | 7 ④ | 8 ① | | |

1. ④ 근사치를 통한 양의 대략적인 이해

직독/직해

According to Pierre Pica, / Pierre Pica에 따르면 /
understanding quantities approximately /
양을 대략적으로 이해하는 것이 /
in terms of estimating ratios / 비율을 어림잡는 방식으로 /
is a universal human intuition.
보편적인 인간의 직관이다.
In fact, / 사실 /
humans / who do not have numbers /
사람들은 / 수를 가지고 있지 않은 /
have no choice but to see the world / in this way.
세상을 바라볼 수밖에 없다 / 이런 방식으로
By contrast, / 반면에 /
understanding quantities / in terms of exact
양을 이해하는 것은 / 정확한 수에 의해서 /
numbers /
is not a universal intuition; / 보편적인 직관이 아닌데 /
it is a product of culture. 즉 그것은 문화의 산물이다
The precedence of approximations and ratios /
근사치와 비율의 선행은 /
over exact numbers, / 정확한 수보다 /
Pica suggests, / Pica는 주장한다 /
is due to the fact / 사실 때문이라고 /
that ratios are much more important / for survival /
비율이 훨씬 더 중요하다는 / 생존에 /
in the wild / 야생에서의 /
than the ability / to count.
능력보다 / 수를 세는
Faced with a group of spear-wielding adversaries, /
창을 휘두르는 적들과 직면했을 때 /
we needed to know / instantly /
우리는 알아야만 했다 / 바로 /
whether there were more of them / than us.
그들이 더 많은지를 / 우리보다
When we saw two trees / we needed to know /
우리가 나무 두 그루를 보았을 때 / 알아야 했다 /
instantly / 즉시 /
which had more fruit / hanging from it.
어느 것이 과일을 더 많이 가졌는지를 / 그것에 매달린
In neither case / 어떤 경우에도 없었다 /
was it necessary / 필요는 /
to enumerate every enemy or every fruit /
모든 적은 모든 과일을 일일이 셀 /
individually. 하나씩
The crucial thing / 중요한 것은 /
was to be able to make quick estimates / of the
재빨리 어림잡을 수 있어야만 하는 것이었다 / 상대적인 양을
relative amounts.

Pierre Pica에 따르면, 비율을 어림잡는 방식으로 양을 대략적으로 이해하는 것이 보편적인 인간의 직관이다. 사실, 수를 가지고 있지 않은 사람들은 이런 방식으로 세상을 바라볼 수밖에 없다. 반면에, 정확한 수에 의해서 양을 이해하는 것은 보편적인 직관이 아닌데, 즉 그것은 문화의 산물이다. Pica는 정확한 수보다 근사치와 비율의 선행은 비율이 수를 세는 능력보다 야생에서의 생존에 훨씬 더 중요하다는 사실 때문이라고 주장한다. 창을 휘두르는 적들과 직면했을 때, 우리는 우리보다 그들이 더 많은지를 바로 알아야만 했다.

우리가 나무 두 그루를 보았을 때 어느 것이 그것에 매달린 과일을 더 많이 가졌는지를 즉시 알아야 했다. 어떤 경우에도 모든 적 혹은 모든 과일을 하나씩 일일이 셀 필요는 없었다. 중요한 것은 상대적인 양을 재빨리 어림잡을 수 있어야만 하는 것이었다.

문제풀이

① 「have no choice but to부정사」 구문으로, but 뒤에 to부정사가 와야 하므로, to see는 적절하다.
② Pica suggests는 삽입절이며, 문장의 주어는 The precedence (of approximations and ratios over exact numbers)이므로 단수동사인 is는 적절하다.
③ 분사구문으로, 원래 문장은 When we were faced with a group of spear-wielding adversaries, ~.이다. 이를 분사구문으로 전환한 Being faced with a group of spear-wielding adversaries,에서 Being이 생략되어 Faced with a group of spear-wielding adversaries, ~.의 형태가 된 것으로 Faced는 적절히 사용되었다.
④ that had more fruit hanging from it은 to know의 목적어에 해당하는데, 문맥상 '두 그루의 나무 중 어느 나무가 더 많은 과일을 가졌는지'라는 의미가 되어야 하므로, that을 의문사 which로 고쳐 써야 한다.
⑤ 부정의 의미를 지닌 In neither case를 강조하기 위해 문장 앞에 쓴 도치 구문이다. 원래는 it was necessary to enumerate ~.로 be동사 was의 보어로 쓰인 형용사 necessary는 적절하다.

🔑 **이렇게 풀자** _ ①은 「have no choice but to부정사」, ②는 '주어·동사의 수 일치', ③은 분사구문에서 '현재분사(능동)와 과거분사(수동)의 구별', ④는 '의문사와 관계대명사의 구별', ⑤는 '형용사의 쓰임(be동사의 보어)'을 알고 있는 지를 묻는 문제이다.

《 어휘·어구 》

in terms of ~의 면에서, ~에 관하여
estimate 어림잡다, 추정하다
ratio 비율, 비
intuition 직관, 직관력
have no choice but to do ~할 수밖에 없다
by contrast 그에 반해서, 그와 대조적으로
precedence 선행, 우선함, 앞섬
approximation 근사치
survival 생존
be faced with ~에 직면하다
spear-wielding 창을 쓰는[휘두르는]
adversary 상대방, 적수
instantly 즉각, 즉시
individually 개별적으로, 각각 따로
make an estimate 예측하다, 견적을 내다
relative 비교상의, 상대적인

2. ⑤ 뉴스에서 유명인을 다루는 방법 제안

미래의 이상적인 뉴스 서비스에서, 모든 유명인의 이야기는 그 자체가 교육의 한 부분이 될 것이다. 즉 그것은 어떻게 자신의 약간 더 좋은 버전이 될 수 있을지에 대해 존경받을 만한 사람으로부터 배우도록 초청하는 것이 될 것이다. 우리는 유명인을 '모방하는' 사람들이 가엾다고 생각하는 데 익숙하지만, 그 가장 높은 형태에서, 경외에 근거한 모방은 선한 삶에 필수적인 것이다. 존경하는 것을 거부하고, 훌륭한 다른 사람들이 하고 있는 것에 대해 관심을 가지지 않는 것은, 우리 스스로를 중요한 지식으로부터 차단하는 것이다. 뉴스의 역할은 유명인란을 지금처럼 흥미 있게 만드는 한편, 우리의 상상력을 자극할 특정하고 고결한 사람들의 심리적으로 풍요롭고 교육적인 초상을

우리들에게 제공하는 것을 확실하게 하는 것인데, 그 이유는 그들이 우리가 자신의 인격의 결함을 다루는 데 적절하게 도움을 주기 때문이다. 인기인에 대한 성숙한 형태의 뉴스는 그것을 통해 우리가 현재의 우리 자신보다 더 나아지는 법을 배우는 진지하고 존경받을 만한 매체가 되어야 한다.

문제풀이

① 형용사의 비교급인 better를 수식하는 부사 slightly는 적절히 사용되었다.
② 「be used to+명사구」는 '~에 익숙하다'라는 의미로 to 다음에 동명사가 와야 하므로 thinking은 적절히 사용되었다.
③ 전치사 in의 목적어인 명사절을 이끌며 distinguished의 주어 역할을 해야 하므로 관계대명사 what은 적절히 사용되었다.
④ it is exciting에서 is exciting을 받는 대동사가 와야 하므로 is는 적절히 사용되었다.
⑤ 뒤에 온 절이 완전한 형태를 갖추고 있으므로 관계대명사 which는 적절하지 않고, 관계부사 how나 「전치사+관계대명사」인 through which로 고쳐 써야 한다.
따라서 정답은 ⑤이다.

《 구문 및 어휘 》

*4행 We are used to thinking [**that** anyone {**who** 'copies' a celebrity} **is** sad], but in its highest form, imitation [**founded** on admiration] is integral to a good life].

⑴ 'We are used ~'와 'in the highest ~'의 두 개의 절이 but으로 연결되어 있다.
⑵ that anyone ~ is sad는 동명사 thinking의 목적어로 쓰인 명사절이다.
⑶ that절의 주어는 anyone이고, 동사는 is이다. who 'copies' a celebrity는 선행사 anyone을 수식하는 관계대명사절이다.
⑷ but 뒤의 절에서 imitation이 주어이고, is가 동사이다. founded on admiration은 imitation을 수식하는 과거분사구로 앞에 which[that] is가 생략되어 있다.

*8행 The job of the news is to make the celebrity section **no less exciting than** it is now, **while ensuring** [that it provides us with psychologically rich, educational portraits of certain noble-minded individuals {**who** will spark our imaginations} because they properly help us to address the flaws in our personalities].

⑴ 「주절(The job ~)+분사구문(while ensuring ~)」 구조의 글이다.
⑵ 「no less ... than」 ~은 '~만큼이나 ...한'이라는 의미이다.
⑶ while ensuring은 접속사를 생략하지 않은 분사구문이다. while은 '~하는 한 편'이라는 의미이다.
⑷ that it ~ our personalities는 ensuring의 목적어로 쓰인 명사절이다. that절은 「주절(it provides ~)+부사절(because they ~)」 구조이다.
⑸ 「provide A with B」는 'A에게 B를 제공하다'라는 의미이다.
⑹ who will ~ imaginations는 선행사 certain noble-minded individuals를 수식하는 관계대명사절이다.
⑺ 「help+목적어+to부정사」는 '~가 ...하도록 돕다'라는 의미이다.

ideal 이상적인
celebrity 유명 인사
education 교육
admirable 감탄스러운, 존경스러운
slightly 약간, 조금
admiration 감탄, 존경
integral 필수적인
refuse 거부하다
distinguish 구별하다, 구별 짓다
ensure 반드시 ~하게 하다
psychologically 심리적으로
portrait 초상
noble 고결한, 숭고한
individual 개인
spark 고무하다, 유발하다
properly 제대로, 적절히
flaw 결함
personality 성격, 인격
respectable 존경할 만한
medium 매체
currently 현재, 지금

---

3. ③   잉카 문화에서 음료를 흘리는 것의 의미

컵을 똑바로 쥐라는 엄마의 권고를 여러 해 동안 따른 뒤에, 우리는 잉카 문화에서는 음료를 흘리는 것이 완전히 용인된다는 것을 알게 된다. 사실은, 그렇게 하도록 기대된다. 잉카의 다산의 여신인 Pachamama를 숭배하면서, 원래는 후추 열매로 만들다가 지금은 옥수수로 만드는 음료인 chicha를 마시는 사람들은 첫 모금을 일부러 땅에 흘린다. 그것은 'challa'라고 부르는 건배 의식으로 많은 사람들이 매일 그 건배 의식을 행한다. 그리고 매년 Martes de Challa라고 부르는 특별한 축하 행사가 있는데, 그때 사람들은 음료를 버릴 뿐만 아니라 음식을 땅에 묻으며, 그들이 yatiri(전통 사제)인 경우에는 기니피그를 제물로 바친다. 그것은 Pachamama(대지의 어머니)에게 폐를 끼친 우리가 저지른 모든 일에 대해 그 여신에게 드리는 보잘것없는 사죄이다. yatiri는 요청하는 사람들을 위해 약초와 작은 설탕 정제를 상징물(집, 심장, 콘도르 등)과 함께 싸서 정기적으로 공물을 만드는데 그 위에 chicha를 끼얹은 후에 태운다.

문제풀이

③이 있는 문장에서 접속사 but 뒤에 주어 they, 동사 bury가 나오고 접속사 and로 연결되어 있으므로 ③ sacrificing을 주어 they에 이어지는 동사인 sacrifice로 고쳐야 한다. 콤마 사이의 if they're a yatiri (a traditional priest)는 조건을 나타내는 if절이 삽입된 것이므로 원래 주어와 동사에 영향을 주지 않는다.

《구문 및 어휘》

*1행 [After years of following our mother's advice to hold our cups up straight], we find that in the Incan culture, it's perfectly acceptable to spill your drink.

(1) 전치사 After가 이끄는 명사구 안에서 to부정사구인 to hold our cups up straight는 our mother's advice의 내용을 설명하는 형용사적 용법으로 쓰였다.
(2) that in the ~ drink는 주절의 동사 find의 목적어 역할을 하며, 가주어 it과 진주어 to spill이 사용되었다.

*3행 In reverence to Pachamama, the Incan

---

fertility goddess, drinkers of chicha, [a drink originally **made from** the berries of the pepper plant, now **made with** corn], purposely spill the first sip on the ground.

(1) the Incan fertility goddess는 앞의 Pachamama를 동격으로 수식하는 삽입구이며, [a drink originally ~ corn]은 앞에 나오는 chicha를 동격으로 수식하는 또 다른 삽입구이다.
(2) 두 번째 삽입구에서 made from ~ 과 made with corn은 앞에 나온 명사 a drink를 수식한다.

fertility 다산(多産)
chicha (중남미의) 발효한 옥수수로 만드는 맥주
sip 한 모금
priest 사제, 신부

---

4. ④   음악에서 아이들이 인식하는 감정

직독직해

To the extent / that cues to emotion in music are based /
경우라면 / 음악에서 감정의 단서가 기초하는 /
on cues to emotion in speech, /
말에서 감정의 단서에 /
we should expect children to recognize emotion in music early.
우리는 아이들이 음악에서 감정을 일찍 인식하기를 기대해야 한다
And they do.
그리고 그들은 그렇다
By age five, / children use tempo as a cue to emotion, /
다섯 살이 되면 / 아이들은 감정의 단서로 박자를 사용한다 /
with faster tempos conveying positive emotions, /
더 빠른 박자는 긍정적인 감정을 전달하고 /
and slower ones sounding more negative.
더 느린 박자는 더 부정적으로 들리게 된다
Tempo conveys emotion /
박자는 감정을 전달한다 /
in the same way in both speech and music.
말과 음악 모두에서 똑같은 방식으로 /
So do pitch and loudness; /
음의 높이와 소리의 강도도 마찬가지다 /
when asked to sing songs showing basic emotions, /
기본적인 감정을 드러내는 노래를 부르라는 요청을 받을 때 /
children use the cues of tempo, pitch, and loudness /
아이들은 박자, 음의 높이, 그리고 소리의 강도라는 단서를 사용한다 /
by the age of five.
다섯 살이 될 때까지
Mode (major and minor), / however, /
음계(장조와 단조)는 / 그러나 /
has no counterpart in speech, /
언어에서 상응하는 것이 없다 /
and though one small study in 1990 showed /
그리고 1990년의 한 소규모의 연구가 보여주었지만 /
that even three-year-olds heard major-minor /
as happy-sad, /
심지어 세 살짜리의 아이들도 장조-단조를 행복-슬픔으로 들었다는 것을 /
a more recent study found no sensitivity to mode until age six.
보다 최근의 연구는 여섯 살까지 음계에 대한 어떤 감성도 찾지 못했다
Sensitivity to the difference in emotional tone /
감정적 음색 사이의 차이에 대한 감성은 /
between major and minor modes /
장조 음계와 단조 음계 사이의 /
may thus emerge /
나타날 수 있다 /
only once children have been exposed to this contrast, /
오직 아이들이 이러한 대조에 노출된 적이 있을 때에만 /
suggesting that this is a learned association /
이는 이것이 학습된 연상이라는 것을 시사한다 /
rather than a natural one.
자연적인 연상이라기보다는

음악에서 감정의 단서가 말에서 감정의 단서에 기초하는 경우라면, 우리는 아이들이 음악에서 감정을 일찍 인식하기를 기대해야 한다. 그리고 그들은 그렇다. 다섯 살이 되면, 아이들은 감정의 단서로 박자를 사용하는데, 더 빠른 박자는 긍정적인 감정을 전달하고, 더 느린 박자는 더 부정적으로 들리게 된다. 박자는 말과 음악 모두에서 똑같은 방식으로 감정을 전달한다. 음의 높이와 소리의 강도도 마찬가지인데, 기본적인 감정을 드러내는 노래를 부르라는 요청을 받을 때, 아이들은 다섯 살이 될 때까지 박자, 음의 높이, 그리고 소리의 강도라는 단서를 사용한다. 그러나, 음계(장조와 단조)는 언어에 상응하는 것이 없으며, 1990년의 한 소규모의 연구가 심지어 세 살짜리의 아이들도 장조-단조를 행복-슬픔으로 들었다는 것을 보여 주었지만, 보다 최근의 연구는 여섯 살까지 음계에 대한 어떤 감성도 찾지 못했다. 따라서 장조 음계와 단조 음계 사이의 감정적 음색 사이의 차이에 대한 감성은 오직 아이들이 이러한 대조에 노출된 적이 있을 때에만 나타날 수도 있으며, 이는 이것이 자연적인 연상이라기보다는 학습된 연상이라는 것을 시사한다.

문제풀이

① [대동사]
앞에 있는 they는 children을 지칭하고 do는 대동사로 recognize emotion in music early를 대신하므로, do는 적절하다.
② [형용사 보어]
2형식 동사 sound의 보어로 쓰인 형용사이므로, negative는 적절하다.
③ [분사]
when 다음에 주절의 주어인 children을 가리키는 they와 be동사 are가 생략된 구조이므로, 수동태를 구성하는 ask의 과거분사 asked는 적절하다.
④ [정동사 vs 준동사]
and 다음에 though가 이끄는 부사절이 온 다음, 콤마 이하에서 주절이 이어지고 있는데 주어 a more recent study에 해당하는 동사가 없으므로, to find를 정동사 found로 고쳐야 한다.
⑤ [분사구문]
앞의 내용 전체를 부연 설명하는 분사구문을 이끌고 있으므로, suggesting은 적절하다.

《어휘·어구》

to the extent that ~일 경우에, ~인 한, ~할 정도까지
counterpart 상응하는 것
sensitivity 감성
contrast 대조
association 연상

---

5. ④   과학 학습에서 체험보다 중요한 사고

직독직해

For quite some time, science educators believed /
상당 기간 동안, 과학 교육자들은 믿었다 /
that "hands-on" activities were the answer to
'직접 해보는' 활동이 아이들이 이해하는 것에 대한 대답이라고
children's understanding /
through their participation in science-related activities. 과학 관련 활동에 참여하는 것을 통해
Many teachers believed / 많은 교사들은 믿었다 /
that students merely engaging in activities and
학생들이 단지 활동에 참여하고 사물을 조작하는 것만으로
manipulating objects /
would organize the information to be gained and
얻게 되는 정보와 이해하게 되는 지식을 체계화할 것이라고
the knowledge to be understood /
into concept comprehension. 개념 이해로
Educators began to notice /
교육자들은 깨닫기 시작했다 /
that the pendulum had swung too far to the
'직접 해보는' 탐구의 요소 쪽으로 추가 너무 많이 기울었다는 것을
"hands-on" component of inquiry /
as they realized / 깨달으면서 /

that the knowledge was not inherent in the
지식이 자료 자체에 내재되어 있는 것이 아니라 /

materials themselves, /

but in the thought and metacognition about what
students had done in the activity.
학생들이 그 활동에서 한 것에 대한 생각과 초(超)인지에 있다는 것을 깨달으면서

We now know that "hands-on" is a dangerous
이제 우리는 '직접 해보는'이 위험한 문구라는 것을 안다

phrase / when speaking about learning science.
/ 과학을 배우는 것에 대해 말 할 때

The missing ingredient is the "minds-on" part of
누락된 요소는 교육 경험의 '사고를 요구하는' 부분이다

the instructional experience.

Uncertainty about the knowledge intended in any
어떤 활동에서든 의도된 지식에 대한 불확실성은

activity / comes from each student's re-creation of
/ 각 학생의 개념 재창조에서 비롯된다 /

concepts — /

and discussing, thinking, arguing, listening, and
evaluating one's own preconceptions /
그리고 자신의 선입견에 대해 토론하고, 사고하고, 논쟁하고, 듣고, 평가하는
것을 통해서 /

after the activities, / 그 활동들 이후에 /

under the leadership of a thoughtful teacher, /
사려 깊은 선생님의 지도하에 /

can bring this about. 이것을 가져올 수 있다

After all, a food fight is a hands-on activity, /
결국, 음식물 던지기 장난은 직접 해보는 활동이다 /

but about all you would learn /
하지만 여러분이 배우게 되는 것은 /

was something about the aerodynamics of flying
으깬 감자를 날리는 공기 역학에 관한 것이었다

mashed potatoes!

Our view of what students need to build their
knowledge and theories /
지식과 이론을 구축하기 위해 학생들이 필요로 하는 것에 대한 우리의 견해는 /

about the natural world / 자연 세계에 대한 /

extends far beyond a "hands-on activity."
'직접 해보는 활동'을 훨씬 넘어서는 것이다

While it is important for students to use and
interact with materials in science class, /
과학 수업에서 학생들이 재료를 사용하고 상호 작용하는 것이 중요하기는 하지만 /

the learning comes from the sense-making of
students' "hands-on" experiences.
학습은 '직접 해보는' 학생들의 경험에 대해 의미를 부여하는 것으로부터 나온다

한동안, 과학 교육자들은 "직접 해 보는" 활동들이 아이들의 과학 관련 활동 참여를 통한 자신들의 이해에 대한 답변이었다고 믿었다. 많은 교사들은 단순히 활동과 물체를 (a) 다루는 일에 참여한 학생들이 언제 될 정보와 이해될 지식을 체계적으로 개념 이해를 하게 된다고 믿었다. 교육자들은 지식이 재료 자체에 (b) 내재된 것이 아니라 학생들이 활동에서 했던 것들에 대한 생각과 초인지에 내재해 있다는 것을 깨달으면서, "직접 해 보는" 요소 쪽으로 연구의 추가 너무 멀리 흔들렸다는 것을 간파하기 시작했다. 우리는 이제 과학을 배우는 것에 관해 말할 때 "직접 해 보는 것"이 위험한 말이라는 것을 알고 있다. (c) 빠져 있는 요소는 교육 경험의 "생각해 보는" 부분이다. 어떤 활동에서든 의도된 지식에 대한 (d) 불확실성은 각 학생의 개념에 대한 재창조에서 나오며, 활동 후에 사려 깊은 교사의 지도력 하에서, 토론하고, 생각해보고, 논쟁하고, 귀담아듣고, 자기 자신의 예상을 평가하는 것이 이를 불러일으킬 수 있다. 결국 음식 싸움은 직접 해 보는 활동이지만, 여러분이 배우게 되는 것이라곤 으깬 감자의 공기역학에 관한 것이었다! 학생들이 자연 세계에 대한 자신들의 지식과 이론을 수립하기 위해 필요한 것에 대한 우리의 견해는 "직접 해 보는 활동"을 훨씬 넘어서까지 (e) 확대된다. 학생들이 과학 수업에서 재료를 사용하고 재료와 상호작용하는 것이 중요하지만 학습은 학생들의 "직접 해 보는" 경험에 대한 감각으로부터 나온다.

《 어휘 · 어구 》

hands-on 직접 해보는
engage in ~에 참여하다
comprehension 이해
component 요소
inquiry 탐구, 연구
ingredient 요소, 성분
instructional 교육의
evaluate 평가하다

---

preconception 선입견
bring about ~을 유발하다
mash 으깨다

5. ④

문제풀이

활동 후 토론, 사고, 논쟁 등을 통한 개념에 대한 재창조를 통해 얻을 수 있는 것은 'Uncertainty(불확실성)'이 아니라 'Clarity(명료성)' 등의 단어가 되어야 한다.

6. ⑤   방패연의 과학적 원리

한국 연들의 형태는 그것들이 바람을 잘 이용하게 해주는 과학적인 원리에 기초를 두고 있다. 한 가지 특별한 한국의 연은 직사각형의 "방패연"인데, 그것은 중앙에 특이한 구멍을 가지고 있다. 이 구멍은 바람이 약한 날에는 바람을 모으고, 바람이 강하게 불 때는 그것이 통과해가도록 함으로써 바람의 속도에 상관없이 연을 빨리 날게 하도록 도와준다. 또한 중앙의 구멍은 연이 연을 날리는 사람의 통제에 빨리 반응하게 해준다. 이런 이유 때문에 방패연과 같은 한국의 연은 "연 싸움"에 능숙하다.

문제풀이

(A) particle은 '미립자'를, principle은 '원리, 원칙'을 뜻하기 때문에 principles가 적절하다.
(B) concentrate는 '집중하다'를, contaminate는 '오염시키다'를 의미하므로 concentrating이 적절하다.
(C) command는 '명령, 통제'를, comment는 '논평, 설명'을 뜻하므로 commands가 적절하다.

《 어휘 · 어구 》

shape 형태
rectangular 직사각형의
shield 방패
regardless of~ ~에 상관없이
respond to~ ~에 반응하다

7. ④   시장 변화에 적응하고 있는 장미꽃 업계

다른 모든 사업들과 마찬가지로 장미꽃 업계도 시장의 변화하는 상황에 적응해야 한다. 과거에는 꽃집이 재배자로부터 장미를 구입한 도매상에게서 장미를 사들이는 대부분 소규모이고 독립적인 업체였다. 밸런타인데이와 같은 특별한 날에는 높은 수요로 인해 12송이의 장미 값이 두 배 또는 그 이상으로 뛰었다. 오늘날에는 대형 슈퍼마켓 체인점, 곳곳에 산재한 직판 도매상, 그리고 직판 통신 판매자 등이 장미 공급업자에 포함되고 있다. 장미에 담긴 로맨스는 경제 현실에 의해 자리바꿈되었다.

문제풀이

(A)에는 전치사 to를 뒤에 두어 '-에 적응하다'라는 의미를 갖는 adapt가 적절하다.
(B)에는 장미 가격이 오르는 원인이 되는 것이어야 하므로 문맥상 demand(수요)가 적절하다.
(C)에는 realities를 수식할 수 있는 형용사 economic이 적절하다. adopt는 '받아들이다, 채용하다'라는 의미의 타동사이고, supply는 demand의 반의어로서 '공급'을 의미하고, economics는 명사로서 '경제학'을 의미한다.

《 어휘 · 어구 》

industry 산업
adapt to ~에 적응하다
florist 꽃장수
wholesaler 도매업자
purchase 구입하다
dozen 12개의

---

location 지역, 위치
replace 대체시키다, 대신하다.

8. ①   Sunshine 자선 단체 개선 위원회 가입을 요청 드림

Sunshine 자선 단체를 개선하기 위한 위원회를 만드는 것을 도와달라는 부탁을 받았습니다. 저희은 강력한 위원회를 만들려고 노력하고 있고 저는 당신이 그 단체에 가입하기를 요청하라는 부탁을 받았습니다. 저는 당신이 저희의 위원회의 목적에 관심을 가지실 것이라는 것을 알고 있습니다. 당신의 조언과 도움이 얼마나 귀중할지를 저희들은 모두 알고 있습니다. 첫 번째 모임은 다음 주 목요일 11시에 이곳에서 개최될 예정입니다. 저는 당신이 오셔서 위원회의 일원이 되시는 데에 동의하실 것을 기대합니다.

문제풀이

(A) assist는 '돕다'의 뜻이고 resist는 '저항하다'의 뜻이다. 자선 단체를 개선하기 위한 위원회를 만드는데 도와달라는 부탁을 받았다고 해야 글의 흐름에 맞으므로 (A)에는 assist가 맞다.
(B) objective는 '목표, 목적'의 뜻이고 objection은 '반대, 이의'의 뜻이다. 위원회의 목적에 관심을 갖는다고 해야지 위원회의 반대에 관심을 갖는다고 하면 글 전체의 흐름에 맞지 않으므로 (B)에는 objective가 맞다.
(C) sit는 '앉다'의 뜻을 갖는 자동사이고 seat은 '앉히다'의 뜻을 갖는 타동사이다. (C) 다음에 목적어가 없기 때문에 자동사 sit이 맞다. sit on the committee는 '위원회의 일원이 되다'는 뜻이다.

《 어휘 · 어구 》

assist 돕다, 원조하다
resist 저항하다
committee 위원회
charity 자선, 자선 단체
form 만들다, 형성하다
objective 목표, 목적
objection 반대, 이의
invaluable 값을 헤아릴 수 없는, 아주 귀중한
sit on the committee 위원회의 일원이 되다

- keep in touch 계속 연락하다
- call for ~을 요구하다, ~을 필요로 하다
- from time to time 때때로
- emerge from ~에서 나오다(나타나다)
- far into the night 밤늦도록
- at every turn 자주, 늘, 예외없이
- in person 직접, 몸소
- feed on (동물이) ~을 먹고 살다
- let go (of) (~을) 놓다, 석방하다
- by nature 나면서부터, 본래

- odds and ends 나머지, 잡동사니
- coincide with ~과 일치하다, 동시에 발생하다
- for good 영원히
- come up with 생산해내다, 떠올리다
- under one's breath 목소리를 낮추어, 소곤소곤, 처음으로
- in terms of ~면에서는
- run for ~에 입후보하다
- in vain 헛되이, 보람 없이
- refer to 언급하다, 참조(문의)하다
- of necessity 필연적으로, 당연히, 부득이

- go through 관통하다, 겪다, 거치다
- in demand 수요가 있는
- in any case 여하튼, 좌우간
- of itself 저절로
- hold back 억제하다
- for the first time 처음으로
- hang on (전화를 끊지 않고) 기다리다
- by no means 결코 ~아닌
- lay eggs 알을 낳다
- have an eye for 안목이 있다, 기호나 취향을 가지다

- on a diet 다이어트 중인
- after all 결국, ~에도 불구하고
- die of ~으로 죽다
- no more than 단지 ~밖에, 겨우
- scores of 수십의, 다수의
- make sense 뜻이 통하다, 이해가 되다
- run(take) a risk 위험을 무릅쓰다
- operate on ~에게 수술을 하다
- to one's taste 취미(기호·비위)에 맞아(맞도록)
- persist in ~을 고집하다

- take steps 조치를 취하다
- go so far as to do 심지어 ~하기까지 하다
- on the increase 증가 중인, 증가 일로의
- miss the point 요점을 놓치다
- hold good (계속) 유효하다
- deprive A of B A에게서 B를 빼앗다
- for one's age 나이에 비해
- starve to death 굶어 죽다
- but for ~이 없다면(없었다면)
- come to light 밝혀내다, 밝혀지다, 발견하다

- keep one's fingers crossed 행운을 빌다
- at present 현재는
- so far 지금까지, 어느 정도까지만
- in search of ~을 찾아서, ~을 추구하여
- on leave 휴가로, 휴가를 얻어
- at the mercy of ~의 처분(마음)대로, ~에 좌우되어
- in support of ~을 지지하여
- contend with ~와 경쟁하다, ~와 싸우다
- let alone ~을 커녕
- manage to do 용케(가까스로) ~하다

- under way (계획 등이) 진행 중인
- by far 〈비교급·최상급 강조〉 훨씬, 단연
- as a (general) rule 대체로, 일반적으로
- have no idea ~을 알지 못하다
- subscribe to ~을 구독하다
- have a talent for ~에 재능이 있다
- in other words 달리 말하면, 즉
- for the time being 당분간, 당장은, 일시적으로
- regardless of ~와 관계 없이, ~에도 불구하고
- command a fine view 전망이 좋다

- a great(good) deal of 많은, 대량의
- attach A to B A를 B에 붙이다(첨부하다)
- near by 바로 가까이에
- keep track of 추적하다
- not a few 꽤 많은 수(의)
- in time 이윽고
- hunt for(after) ~을 찾다(구하다)
- no fewer than ~만큼 많은, 최소한
- bring to an end 끝내다, 끝나다
- by means of ~에 의하여

□ **the other way round** 반대로, 거꾸로

□ **stand out** 두드러지다, 탁월(걸출)하다

□ **fall ill(sick)** 병이 나다

□ **be fed up with** ～에 진저리가 나다

□ **long for** ～을 갈망(열망)하다

□ **eat one's words** 앞서 한 말을 취소하다

□ **come of age** 성년에 이르다

□ **beware of** 주의(조심)하다

□ **in general** 대개(대체로), 일반적으로

□ **none other than** 다름 아닌 바로 ～인

□ **give way to** ～에 양보하다, ～에 굴복하다

□ **on end** 세로로, 똑바로; 계속

□ **apologize (to A) for B** (A에게) B에 대해 사과(변명)하다

□ **go into details** 상세하게 말하다(논하다)

□ **form the habit of ~ing** ～하는 습관을 들이다(붙이다)

□ **in a row** 연속하여

□ **give ~ a ride(lift)** ～을 차에 태워 주다

□ **be in charge of** ～을 떠맡다, 담당하다, 책임지다

□ **in turn** 차례차례, 결국

□ **single out** 선발하다, 지목하다

□ **carry out** 수행하다, 성취하다

□ **with all one's might** 전력을 다하여, 힘껏

□ **every inch** 완전히

□ **get along with** ～와 잘 지내다

□ **at first** 처음에는, 원래는

□ **lie on one's back** 반듯이(등을 대고) 눕다

□ **by degrees** 서서히, 조금씩, 점차로

□ **at odds with** ～와 의견이 일치하지 않는

□ **cope with** ～에 대처하다, 겨루다

□ **in consequence of** ～의 결과, ～때문에

□ **far from** 결코 ～아닌, ～하기는 커녕

□ **for a change** 뭔가 색다르게, 기분 전환으로

□ **dwell on(upon)** ～을 깊이 생각하다

□ **comply with** ～에 따르다(응하다)

□ **go dutch** (비용을) 각자 내다

□ **near at hand** 가까이에, 머지않아

□ **in part** 일부분, 부분적으로, 어느 정도

□ **for some reason or other** 무슨(어찌된) 이유에선지

□ **happen to do** 우연히(어쩌다가, 마침) ～하다

□ **go astray** 길을 잘못 들다, 길을 잃다

□ **contribute A to B** A를 B에 기부하다, B에 기여(공헌)하다

□ **figure out** 계산하다, 이해하다

□ **engage in** ～에 종사하다

□ **set ~ free** ～을 석방하다(자유롭게 하다)

□ **out of breath** 숨이 차서, 헐떡이며

□ **keep a diary** 일기를 쓰다

□ **cut off** 잘라내다, 중단(단절)하다

□ **for the present** 당분간, 지금은

□ **bring ~ to light** 밝히다, 폭로하다

□ **reflect on** ～을 반성(숙고)하다

□ **by way of** ～을 경유하여(지나서), ～의 수단(방법)으로

□ **in pursuit of** ～을 추구하여

□ **make progress (in)** 진보(전진 · 향상)하다

□ **under no circumstances** 결코 ～ 않다, 무슨 일이 있어도 ～ 않다

□ **work out** 운동하다, (일이) 잘 진행되다, 해결하다

□ **have one's own way** 제멋대로 하다

□ **in the light of** ～을 고려하여

□ **in honor of** ～에 경의를 표하여, ～을 기념하여

□ **on the face of it** 겉보기에는, 표면상

□ **hasten to do** 서둘러 ～하다

□ **just in case** 만일의 경우에

□ **upside down** 거꾸로, 뒤집어서, 뒤죽박죽, 엉망으로

□ **approve of** ～을 승인하다, ～을 찬성하다

□ **take place** 일어나다, 행해지다, 개최되다

□ **once (and) for all** 단 한 번만, 이번만

□ **indulge in** ～에 빠지다, ～을 마음껏 즐기다

□ **as well** ～ 역시, 게다가

□ **count for little(nothing)** 거의(전혀) 가치가 없다

□ **be to blame (for)** (～에 대해) 책임이 있다

□ **in a way** 어떤 관점(면)에서는

□ **at (the) bottom** 내심(속마음)은, 실은, 근본은

□ **at any rate** 여하튼, 적어도

□ **more or less** 다소간, 어느 정도, 대략

□ **close to** ～의 가까이에, 약, 대체로

□ **in effect** 사실상, 실제로는

□ **as yet** 지금까지는, 지금으로서는, 아직

□ **clear A of B** A에서 B를 (깨끗이) 없애다(치우다)

□ **in all** 전부, 모두 합쳐

□ **cure A of B** A에게서 B를 낫게 하다(치유하다)

□ **leave ~ behind** ～을 남기고 가다(오다)

□ **behave oneself** 처신(행동)하다, 예의 바르게 행동하다
□ **gaze at** ～을 응시하다
□ **refrain from** ～을 삼가다
□ **make one's way** 앞으로 나아가다
□ **as to** ～에 관하여
□ **serve as(for)** ～의 역할을 하다
□ **hang out with** 어울려 다니다
□ **in need of** ～을 필요로 하여
□ **hurt one's feelings** ～의 감정을 상하게 하다
□ **inform A of B** A에게 B를 알리다

□ **in return for** ～에 대한 답으로, 답례로
□ **quite a bit** 꽤 많은
□ **for the sake of** ～을 위하여
□ **confess A to B** A를 B에게 고백(자백)하다
□ **feel at home** 마음 편하다
□ **catch fire** 불이 붙다
□ **in view of** ～을 고려하여, ～에 비추어, ～때문에
□ **be all ears** 주의깊게 듣다
□ **decide on** ～으로 정하다
□ **get rid of** 처리하다, 없애다

□ **B as well as A** A뿐만 아니라 B도
□ **in all likelihood** 아마도, 십중팔구
□ **come to an end** 끝내다, 끝나다
□ **come by** 곁을 지나가다, 들르다
□ **at stake** 위험에 처한, 성패가 달려 있는
□ **break off** (갑자기) 그만두다
□ **by and large** 대체로, 일반적으로
□ **object to** ～에 반대하다
□ **as follows** 다음과 같이
□ **in fashion** 유행하고 있는

□ **rain cats and dogs** 비가 억수같이 내리다
□ **in response to** ～에 답하여, ～에 응하여
□ **make one's living** 생계비를 벌다
□ **look back on(upon)** ～을 회고(회상)하다
□ **take notice of** ～에 주의(주목)하다
□ **think over** ～을 숙고하다
□ **wait for** ～을 기다리다
□ **as far as** ～하는 한, ～에 까지
□ **by hand** (기계 아닌) 사람 손으로
□ **bring about** ～을 야기시키다, 가져오다

□ **get back** 돌아오다, 되찾다
□ **ascribe A to B** A를 B의 탓으로 돌리다
□ **look one in the face** ～의 얼굴을 똑바로 보다
□ **adjust A to B** A를 B에 적합시키다(맞추어 조절하다)
□ **look over** 조사하다; 눈감아주다
□ **in spite of** ～에도 불구하고
□ **in connection with** ～와 관련하여
□ **prior to** ～보다 앞선, 이전에
□ **out of place** 제자리에 놓여 있지 않은, 부적절한
□ **go wrong (with)** (일이) 잘못되다, 실패하다, 고장 나다

□ **lay(put) emphasis on** ～을 강조하다
□ **on an(the) average** 평균해서, 대체로
□ **high and low** 도처에, 모든 곳에
□ **bear fruit** 열매(결실)를 맺다
□ **for lack of** ～이 부족하여(모자라서)
□ **get a grip on** 이해하다
□ **by now** 지금쯤은 (이미)
□ **beyond one's power** ～의 능력 밖인, 힘에 부치는
□ **for nothing** 무료(공짜)로, 무익하게
□ **something of** 얼마간, 어느 정도(의)

□ **fill in for** ～을 대신하다
□ **at issue** 논쟁 중인, 고려 중인
□ **set a high value on** ～을 높이 평가하다
□ **fall behind** ～에 뒤지다, 낙오하다
□ **sooner or later** 조만간, 언젠가는, 결국
□ **get lost** 나가다, 사라지다
□ **come down with** (병에) 걸리다
□ **dawn on(upon)** 생각나다
□ **at intervals** 때때로(이따금), 사이를 두고
□ **keep company with** ～와 사귀다

□ **make room for** ～에 양보하다
□ **for the most part** 대부분은, 대개는, 대체로
□ **in consideration of** ～을 고려하여, ～의 답례(보수)로서
□ **just around the corner** 아주 가까이, 곧
□ **of one's own accord** 자발적으로, 저절로
□ **reach (out) for** ～을 잡으려고 (손이나 팔을) 뻗치다
□ **at all events** 아무튼, 무슨 일이 있더라도
□ **give in** 제출하다, 건네다
□ **in case** 만약 ～이면, ～인 경우에는
□ **be on board** 승선하다

□ **under construction** 건설 중인

□ **in the first place** 우선, 첫째로

□ **go on strike** 파업하다

□ **at heart** 속마음(내심)은, 마음 속은, 진심은

□ **as for** ～에 관해 말하자면, ～에 관한 한

□ **in proportion to** ～에 비례하여

□ **in question** 문제의, 논의가 되고 있는

□ **make use of** ～을 이용하다

□ **just like that** 그렇게, 그런 식으로

□ **a man of few words** 말수가 적은 사람

□ **hope for** ～을 바라다(기대하다)

□ **in detail** 상세히, 자세히

□ **with ease** 쉽게

□ **in place of** ～대신에

□ **by halves** 불완전하게, 어중간하게

□ **at random** 아무렇게나, 닥치는 대로

□ **allow for** ～을 참작(고려)하다

□ **have a good command of** ～을 잘 구사(사용)하다

□ **for all I know** 내가 아는 한, 아마도

□ **come into(in) sight** 보이게 되다, 눈에 들어오다

□ **all along** 처음부터 죽

□ **burst into laughter** 갑자기 웃음을 터뜨리다

□ **get to** ～에 도착하다, ～할 수 있게 되다

□ **call it a day** 하루 일을 마치다

□ **have (～) on** ～을 입고 있다, 계획(약속)이 있다

□ **all (the) year round** 연중, 일년 내내

□ **on duty** 근무 시간 중인, 당번인

□ **at short notice** 예고 없이, 촉박하게

□ **that is (to say)** 즉, 다시 말하면

□ **come into existence** 출현하다, 태어나다, 생겨나다

□ **take hold of** ～을 붙잡다

□ **fall on(upon)** ～에 해당하다

□ **quite the contrary** 그와는 정반대인

□ **play trick on** ～에게 장난을 치다

□ **by mistake** 잘못하여, 실수로

□ **all in all** 전반적(전체적)으로 보아, 대체로

□ **by trade** 직업상

□ **on time** 시간에 맞추어, 정시(정각)에

□ **enter into** 시작하다, 종사하다, 다루다

□ **interfere with** ～을 방해하다, 해치다

□ **tell on** ～을 고자질하다

□ **go too far** 지나치다

□ **have the guts** 용기가 있다

□ **make a fool of** ～을 웃음거리로 만들다, 바보 취급하다

□ **if anything** 어느 편인가 하면, 오히려

□ **call off** 취소하다

□ **fall back on(upon)** ～에 의지하다

□ **as a result of** ～의 결과로서, ～때문에

□ **on the spot** 즉시, 즉석에서, 현장에서

□ **if any** 만약 있다손치더라도, 만약 있다면

□ **glance at** ～을 힐끗(얼핏) 보다

□ **avail oneself of** ～을 이용하다

□ **in the long run** 결국

□ **keep an(one's) eye on** ～에서 눈을 떼지 않다, ～을 감시하다

□ **answer for** ～을 책임지다, ～을 보증하다

□ **go with** ～와 어울리다

□ **other than** ～ 외에, ～와 다른

□ **no longer** 이미 (더 이상) ～이 아닌

□ **for once** 이번에는, 이번만은

□ **in accordance with** ～에 따라서

□ **at will** 마음대로, 뜻대로

□ **beyond description** 말로 표현할 수 없을 정도인

□ **come up to** ～에 부응하다, 필적하다

□ **all the same** 그렇지만, 여전히, 차이가 없는, 중요하지 않은

□ **go by** 지나가다, 흐르다

□ **embark on** 착수(시작)하다, 진출하다

□ **pass out** 기절하다

□ **second to none** 누구(무엇)에도 뒤지지 않는

□ **carry on** 계속하다, 경영하다

□ **more often than not** 종종, 자주, 대체로

□ **compete with A (for B)** (B를 얻기 위해) A와 경쟁하다(다투다)

□ **hold one's tongue** 입 다물다, 침묵하다

□ **in(with) relation to** ～와 관련하여

□ **on sale** 할인 판매 중인, 염가로

□ **read between the lines** 행간(숨은 의미)을 알아내다

□ **have nothing to do with** ～와 관계가 없다

□ **have (an) influence on** ～에 영향을 미치다

□ **what is more** 게다가, 더욱이

□ **convince A of B** A에게 B를 확신시키다, 설득하다

□ **graduate from** ～을 졸업하다

시험 직전까지 꼭 챙겨 봐야 할 영어 오답 Note

틀린 문제를 붙이고 틀린 이유, 몰랐던 단어, 숙어와 문장을 정리하여 나만의 오답노트를 작성해보세요.
꾸준히 작성한 오답노트를 유형별로 분류해보면 자신이 자주 틀리는 유형이 무엇인지, 어떤 실수가 반복되는지 알 수 있어,
자신의 약점을 파악하고 고쳐나가는 데 큰 도움이 됩니다.

시험명	2021년 4월 경기 교육청	번호	29	유형	어법 문제

✓ 왜 틀렸나
- ☐ 단어 / 숙어가 어려움
- ☐ 문장의 해설이 복잡
- ☐ 글 내용을 이해하지 못함
- ☑ 문법 사항이 어려움
- ☐ 기타 (   )

2021년 4월 고3 경기교육청

29. 다음 글의 밑줄 친 부분 중, 어법상 틀린 것은? [3점]

The world's first complex writing form, Sumerian cuneiform, followed an evolutionary path, moving around 3500 BCE from pictographic to ideographic representations, from the depiction of objects to ① that of abstract notions. Sumerian cuneiform was a linear writing system, its symbols usually ② set in columns, read from top to bottom and from left to right. This regimentation was a form of abstraction: the world is not a linear place, and objects do not organize ③ themselves horizontally or vertically in real life. Early rock paintings, thought to have been created for ritual purposes, were possibly shaped and organized ④ to follow the walls of the cave, or the desires of the painters, who may have organized them symbolically, or artistically, or even randomly. Yet after cuneiform, virtually every form of script that has emerged has been set out in rows with a clear beginning and endpoint. So ⑤ uniformly is this expectation, indeed, that the odd exception is noteworthy, and generally established for a specific purpose.

* cuneiform: 쐐기 문자 ** regimentation: 조직화

◇ 정답 & 오답

＊정답

⑤ 'so 형용사/부사 that' 구문에서 'so 형용사/부사' 부분이 강조되어 도치된 문장이다. 여기서 uniformly는 be동사의 보어이다. 따라서
★ 부사 uniformly를 형용사 uniform으로 바꿔야 한다.

＊내가 고른 오답

③ 타동사의 목적어가 주어와 같을 경우에는 재귀대명사를 써야 한다.
★주어 objects와 목적어가 같으므로, 재귀대명사 themselves를 사용함.

☁ 해석이 안 되거나 어려웠던 문장

1) Sumerian cuneiform was a linear writing system, its symbols usually set in columns, read from top to bottom and from left to right. : 주절의 주어와 분사구문의 주어가 다른 독립분사 구문이다.

2) So uniformly is this expectation, indeed, that the odd exception is noteworthy, ~: 도치 문장으로서 정치된 문장으로 써 보면 'this expection is so uniformly that ~'이 된다.

🖋 몰랐던 단어 / 숙어 / 표현 정리
- ☐ pictographic 상형 문자의
- ☐ ideographic 표의 문자의
- ☐ abstract 추상적인
- ☐ linear 선형의
- ☐ from top to bottom 위에서 아래로
- ☐

---

1 틀린 문제를 복사해서 붙입니다.

2 왜 틀렸는지 체크합니다. 단어가 모자라서였는지, 해석이 안 되어서였는지, 아니면 내용을 이해하지 못해서였는지 생각해보고 틀린 이유를 중심으로 오답노트를 기록하세요.

3 정답을 확인한 뒤 내가 고른 오답은 무엇이고, 틀린 이유가 무엇이었는지 써보세요. 틀린 이유를 확실히 파악해야 같은 실수를 반복하지 않습니다.

4 해석이 안 돼서 건너뛰었거나 구조를 제대로 파악하지 못한 문장을 쓰고 해설편의 직독직해를 참고하여 분석해 보세요. 복습한 문장들이 차곡차곡 쌓여서 독해력의 바탕이 되어줄 것입니다.

5 몰랐던 단어, 숙어를 정리하고 복습하세요. 오답노트에 따로 정리해 둔 단어는 시험 직전에 다시 한 번 꼭 확인하세요.

뒷면에 있는 오답노트 양식을 가위로 잘라내 복사하거나, PDF 파일을 프린트하여 사용하세요.
골드교육 홈페이지(www.goldedu.co.kr)에서 오답노트의 PDF 파일을 무료로 다운받을 수 있습니다.